Capital and Ideology

CAPITAL
AND
IDEOLOGY

Thomas Piketty

Translated by Arthur Goldhammer

The Belknap Press of Harvard University Press

CAMBRIDGE, MASSACHUSETTS
LONDON, ENGLAND
2020

First published in French as *Capital et idéologie*
Copyright © Éditions du Seuil, 2019

First printing

Design by Dean Bornstein

Library of Congress Cataloging-in-Publication Data
Names: Piketty, Thomas, 1971– author. | Goldhammer, Arthur, translator.
Title: Capital and ideology / Thomas Piketty, translated by Arthur Goldhammer.
Other titles: Capital et idéologie. English
Description: Cambridge, Massachusetts : Harvard University Press, 2020. |
"First published in French as Capital et idéologie, Éditions du Seuil,
Paris, 2019"—Title page verso. | Includes bibliographical
references and index. |
Identifiers: LCCN 2019040839 (print) | LCCN 2019040840 (ebook) |
ISBN 9780674980822 (cloth) | ISBN 9780674245082 (epub) |
ISBN 9780674245099 (mobi) | ISBN 9780674245075 (pdf)
Subjects: LCSH: Equality. | Ideology—Economic aspects. | Socialism. |
Economics—Political aspects. | Social change. | Property.
Classification: LCC HM821 .P5513 2020 (print) | LCC HM821 (ebook) |
DDC 305—dc23
LC record available at https://lccn.loc.gov/2019040839
LC ebook record available at https://lccn.loc.gov/2019040840

Contents

Preface and Acknowledgments

This book is in large part a sequel to *Capital in the Twenty-First Century* (French edition, 2013; English, 2014), but it can be read independently. Like the previous work, it is the culmination of a collective effort in the sense that it would never have seen the light of day without the help and support of numerous friends and colleagues. I am of course solely responsible for the interpretations and analyses developed in the pages that follow, but by myself I would never have been able to assemble the historical sources on which this research rests.

I rely in particular on the data collected in the *World Inequality Database* (http://WID.world). This project represents the combined effort of more than a hundred researchers in more than eighty countries around the world. It is currently the largest database available for the historical study of income and wealth inequality both between and within countries. For the purposes of this book I have also collected numerous other sources and documents concerning periods, countries, and aspects of inequality not well covered by WID.world, including, for example, data on preindustrial and colonial societies; on inequalities of education, gender, race, religion, and status; and also on religious beliefs, political attitudes, and electoral behavior.

Only the principal references are cited in the text and footnotes. Readers interested in detailed information regarding the whole range of historical sources, bibliographic references, and methods used in this book are urged to consult the online technical appendix at http://piketty.pse.ens.fr/ideology.

Interested readers will also find in the online appendix many graphs and data series not included in the text due to space limitations. I sometimes refer to these sources in the footnotes.

The glossary at the end of this book contains definitions for several terms that may be unfamiliar to readers, which are marked with an asterisk in the text.

I am particularly grateful to Facundo Alvaredo, Lucas Chancel, Emmanuel Saez, and Gabriel Zucman, with whom I codirected the WID.world project and the World Inequality Lab at the Paris School of Economics and the University of California at Berkeley. Out of this joint venture came the recent *World Inequality Report 2018* (http://wir2018.wid.world), of which I make abundant use in this book. I also wish to thank the institutions that made this project possible, first and foremost the École des Hautes Études en Sciences Sociales (EHESS), where I have taught since 2000—one of the few institutions in the world where social scientists of all stripes can listen to and exchange ideas with one another. I also wish to thank the École Normale Supérieure and all the other institutions that joined forces in 2007 to create the Paris School of Economics, which I hope will contribute to the development of the economics of the twenty-first century, an economics that is at once political and historical, multipolar and multidisciplinary.

For their invaluable assistance I also wish to thank Lydia Assouad, Abhijit Banerjee, Adam Barbé, Charlotte Bartels, Erik Bengtsson, Asma Benhenda, Yonatan Berman, Nitin Bharti, Thomas Blanchet, Cécile Bonneau, Manon Bouju, Jérôme Bourdieu, Antoine Bozio, Cameron Campbell, Guillaume Carré, Guilhem Cassan, Amélie Chelly, Bijia Chen, Denis Cogneau, Léo Czajka, Anne-Laure Delatte, Mauricio De Rosa, Richard Dewever, Mark Dincecco, Esther Duflo, Luis Estevez-Bauluz, Ignacio Flores, Juliette Fournier, Bertrand Garbinti, Amory Gethin, Jonathan Goupille-Lebret, Yajna Govind, Julien Grenet, Jean-Yves Grenier, Malka Guillot, Pierre-Cyrille Hautcoeur, Stéphanie Hennette, Simon Henochsberg, Cheuk Ting Hung, Thanasak Jemmama, Francesca Jensenius, Fabian Kosse, Attila Lindner, Noam Maggor, Clara Martinez Toledano, Ewan McGaughey, Cyril Milhaud, Eric Monnet, Marc Morgan, Mathilde Munoz, Alix Myczkowski, Delphine Nougayrede, Filip Novokmet, Katharina Pistor, Gilles Postel-Vinay, Jean-Laurent Rosenthal, Nina Rousille, Guillaume Sacriste, Aurélie Sotura, Alessandro Stanziani, Blaise Truong-Loï, Antoine Vauchez, Sebastien Veg, Marlous van Waijenburg, Richard Von Glahn, Daniel Waldenström, Li Yang, Tom Zawisza, and Roxane Zighed as well as all my friends and colleagues at the Centre François-Simiand d'Histoire Économique et Sociale and the Centre de Recherches Historiques of the EHESS and the Paris School of Economics.

I also owe special thanks to Arthur Goldhammer. Every time I go through the pages of the English version of *Capital in the Twenty-First Century* or *Capital and Ideology,* I realize how fortunate I was to have Art as my translator. Without his help, I would never have been able to communicate with English-speaking readers with the same precision and elegance.

This book has also benefited from the numerous debates and discussions in which I have had the good fortune to participate since the publication of *Capital in the Twenty-First Century.* I spent much of 2014–2016 traveling around the world, meeting readers, researchers, dissenters, and citizens eager to join the debate. I participated in hundreds of discussions about my book and the questions it raised. From these many encounters I learned an immense amount, which has helped me to delve deeper into the historical dynamics of inequality.

Among the many shortcomings of my previous book, two deserve special mention. First, that work focused too exclusively on the historical experience of the wealthy countries of the world (in Western Europe, North America, and Japan). This was due in part to the difficulty of accessing historical sources adequate for the study of other countries and regions. It was nevertheless a choice that sharply restricted my focus and thinking. Second, the earlier book tended to treat the political and ideological changes associated with inequality and redistribution as a sort of black box. I did propose a number of hypotheses concerning, for example, changes in political ideas and attitudes in regard to inequality and private property as a result of the two world wars of the twentieth century, economic crises, and the communist challenge, but I never tackled head-on the question of how inegalitarian ideologies evolved. In this new work I attempt to do this much more explicitly by examining the question in a much broader temporal, spatial, and comparative perspective.

Thanks to the success of the earlier book and the support of numerous citizens, researchers, and journalists, I was able to gain access to tax records and other historical documents previously restricted by the governments of Brazil, India, South Africa, Tunisia, Lebanon, Ivory Coast, Korea, Taiwan, Poland, Hungary, and many other countries around the world. Access to similar records in China and Russia was unfortunately more limited, but we were nevertheless able to make some progress. With this information it was possible to break out of the largely Western framework of the previous book and develop a deeper analysis of the nature of inequality regimes* and their possible trajectories* and switch points. Importantly, these years of encounters, discussions, and reading gave me an opportunity to learn more about the political and ideological dynamics of inequality and thus to write a book that is, I believe, richer than the one it follows. The result is now in your hands, and you, the reader, are free to judge for yourself.

None of this would have been possible without my close family. Six years of happiness have passed since the publication of *Capital in the Twenty-First Century*. My three darling daughters have become young adults (or almost: just two more years, Hélène, and you will join the club with Déborah and Juliette!). Without their love and energy, life would not be the same. And Julia and I have not stopped traveling, meeting people, exchanging ideas, rereading and rewriting each other's work, and remaking the world. She alone knows how much both this book and its author owe to her. And the best is yet to come!

Introduction

Every human society must justify its inequalities: unless reasons for them are found, the whole political and social edifice stands in danger of collapse. Every epoch therefore develops a range of contradictory discourses and ideologies for the purpose of legitimizing the inequality that already exists or that people believe should exist. From these discourses emerge certain economic, social, and political rules, which people then use to make sense of the ambient social structure. Out of the clash of contradictory discourses—a clash that is at once economic, social, and political—comes a dominant narrative or narratives, which bolster the existing inequality regime.

In today's societies, these justificatory narratives comprise themes of property, entrepreneurship, and meritocracy: modern inequality is said to be just because it is the result of a freely chosen process in which everyone enjoys equal access to the market and to property and automatically benefits from the wealth accumulated by the wealthiest individuals, who are also the most enterprising, deserving, and useful. Hence modern inequality is said to be diametrically opposed to the kind of inequality found in premodern societies, which was based on rigid, arbitrary, and often despotic differences of status.

The problem is that this proprietarian* and meritocratic narrative, which first flourished in the nineteenth century after the collapse of the Old Regime and its society of orders* and which was radically revised for a global audience at the end of the twentieth century following the fall of Soviet communism and the triumph of hypercapitalism, is looking more and more fragile. From it a variety of contradictions have emerged—contradictions which take very different forms in Europe and the United States, in India and Brazil, in China and South Africa, in Venezuela and the Middle East. And yet today, two decades into the twenty-first century, the various trajectories* of these different countries are increasingly interconnected, their distinctive individual histories notwithstanding. Only by adopting a transnational perspective can we hope to understand the weaknesses of these narratives and begin to construct an alternative.

Indeed, socioeconomic inequality has increased in all regions of the world since the 1980s. In some cases it has become so extreme that it is difficult to

1

justify in terms of the general interest. Nearly everywhere a gaping chasm divides the official meritocratic discourse from the reality of access to education and wealth for society's least favored classes. The discourse of meritocracy and entrepreneurship often seems to serve primarily as a way for the winners in today's economy to justify any level of inequality whatsoever while peremptorily blaming the losers for lacking talent, virtue, and diligence. In previous inequality regimes, the poor were not blamed for their own poverty, or at any rate not to the same extent; earlier justificatory narratives stressed instead the functional complementarity of different social groups.

Modern inequality also exhibits a range of discriminatory practices based on status, race, and religion, practices pursued with a violence that the meritocratic fairy tale utterly fails to acknowledge. In these respects, modern society can be as brutal as the premodern societies from which it likes to distinguish itself. Consider, for example, the discrimination faced by the homeless, immigrants, and people of color. Think, too, of the many migrants who have drowned while trying to cross the Mediterranean. Without a credible new universalistic and egalitarian narrative, it is all too likely that the challenges of rising inequality, immigration, and climate change will precipitate a retreat into identitarian* nationalist politics based on fears of a "great replacement" of one population by another. We saw this in Europe in the first half of the twentieth century, and it seems to be happening again in various parts of the world in the first decades of the twenty-first century.

It was World War I that spelled the end of the so-called Belle Époque (1880–1914), which was *belle* only when compared with the explosion of violence that followed. In fact, it was *belle* primarily for those who owned property, especially if they were white males. If we do not radically transform the present economic system to make it less inegalitarian, more equitable, and more sustainable, xenophobic "populism" could well triumph at the ballot box and initiate changes that will destroy the global, hypercapitalist, digital economy that has dominated the world since 1990.

To avoid this danger, historical understanding remains our best tool. Every human society needs to justify its inequalities, and every justification contains its share of truth and exaggeration, boldness and cowardice, idealism and self-interest. For the purposes of this book, an inequality regime will be defined as a set of discourses and institutional arrangements intended to justify and structure the economic, social, and political inequalities of a given society. Every such regime has its weaknesses. In order to survive, it must permanently redefine itself, often by way of violent conflict but also by availing itself of shared experience and knowledge. The subject of this book is the history and evolution of inequality regimes. By bringing together historical data bearing on societies of many different types, societies which have not previously been subjected to this sort of comparison, I hope to shed light on ongoing transformations in a global and transnational perspective.

From this historical analysis one important conclusion emerges: what made economic development and human progress possible was the struggle for equality and education and not the sanctification of property, stability, or inequality. The hyper-inegalitarian narrative that took hold after 1980 was in part a product of history, most notably the failure of communism. But it was also the fruit of ignorance and of disciplinary division in the academy. The excesses of identity politics and fatalist resignation that plague us today are in large part consequences of that narrative's success. By turning to history from a multidisciplinary perspective, we can construct a more balanced narrative and sketch the outlines of a new participatory socialism for the twenty-first century. By this I mean a new universalistic egalitarian narrative, a new ideology of equality, social ownership, education, and knowledge and power sharing. This new narrative presents a more optimistic picture of human nature than did its predecessors—and not only more optimistic but also more precise and convincing because it is more firmly rooted in the lessons of global history. Of course, it is up to each of us to judge the merits of these tentative and provisional lessons, to rework them as necessary, and to carry them forward.

What Is an Ideology?

Before I explain how this book is organized, I want to discuss the principal sources on which I rely and how the present work relates to *Capital in the Twenty-First Century*. But first I need to say a few words about the notion of ideology as I use it in this study.

I use "ideology" in a positive and constructive sense to refer to a set of a priori plausible ideas and discourses describing how society should be structured. An ideology has social, economic, and political dimensions. It is an attempt to respond to a broad set of questions concerning the desirable or ideal organization of society. Given the complexity of the issues, it should be obvious that no ideology can ever command full and total assent: ideological conflict and disagreement are inherent in the very notion of ideology. Nevertheless, every society must attempt to answer questions about how it should be organized, usually on the basis of its own historical experience but sometimes also on the experiences of other societies. Individuals will usually also feel called on to form opinions of their own on these fundamental existential issues, however vague or unsatisfactory they may be.

What are these fundamental issues? One is the question of what the nature of the political regime should be. By "political regime" I mean the set of rules describing the boundaries of the community and its territory, the mechanisms of collective decision making, and the political rights of members. These rules govern forms of political participation and specify the respective roles of citizens and foreigners as well as the functions of executives and legislators, ministers and kings, parties and elections, empires and colonies.

Another fundamental issue has to do with the property regime, by which I mean the set of rules describing the different possible forms of ownership as well as the legal and practical procedures for regulating property relations between different social groups. Such rules may pertain to private or public property, real estate, financial assets, land or mineral resources, slaves or serfs, intellectual and other immaterial forms of property, and relations between landlords and tenants, nobles and peasants, masters and slaves, or shareholders and wage earners.

Every society, every inequality regime, is characterized by a set of more or less coherent and persistent answers to these questions about its political and property regimes. These two sets of answers are often closely related because they depend in large part on some theory of inequality between different social groups (whether real or imagined, legitimate or illegitimate). The answers generally imply a range of other intellectual and institutional commitments: for instance, commitments to an educational regime (that is, the rules governing institutions and organizations responsible for transmitting spiritual values, knowledge, and ideas, including families, churches, parents, and schools and universities) and a tax regime (that is, arrangements for providing states or regions; towns or empires; and social, religious, or other collective organizations with adequate resources). The answers to these questions can vary widely. People can agree about the political regime but not the property regime or about certain fiscal or educational arrangements but not others. Ideological conflict is almost always multidimensional, even if one axis takes priority for a time, giving the illusion of majoritarian consensus allowing broad collective mobilization and historical transformations of great magnitude.

Borders and Property

To simplify, we can say that every inequality regime, every inegalitarian ideology, rests on both a theory of borders and a theory of property.

The border question is of primary importance. Every society must explain who belongs to the human political community it comprises and who does not, what territory it governs under what institutions, and how it will organize its relations with other communities within the universal human community (which, depending on the ideology involved, may or may not be explicitly acknowledged). The border question and the political regime question are of course closely linked. The answer to the border question also has significant implications for social inequality, especially between citizens and noncitizens.

The property question must also be answered. What is a person allowed to own? Can one person own others? Can he or she own land, buildings, firms, natural resources, knowledge, financial assets, and public debt? What practical guidelines and laws should govern relations between owners of property and nonowners? How should ownership be transmitted across generations? Along with the educational and fiscal regime, the property regime determines the structure and evolution of social inequality.

In most premodern societies, the questions of the political regime and the property regime are intimately related. In other words, power over individuals and power over things are not independent. Here, "things" refers to possessed objects, which may be persons in the case of slavery. Furthermore, power over things may imply power over persons. This is obviously true in slave societies, where the two questions essentially merge into one: some individuals own others and therefore also rule over them.

The same is true, but in more subtle fashion, in what I call ternary or "trifunctional" societies (that is, societies divided into three functional classes—a clerical and religious class, a noble and warrior class, and a common and laboring class). In this historical form, which we find in most premodern civilizations, the two dominant classes are both ruling classes, in the senses of exercising the regalian powers of security and justice, and property-owning classes. For centuries, the "landlord" was also the "ruler" *(seigneur)* of the people who lived and worked on his land, just as much as he was the *seigneur* ("lord") of the land itself.

By contrast, ownership (or proprietarian) societies* of the sort that flourished in Europe in the nineteenth century drew a sharp distinction between the property question (with universal property rights theoretically open to all) and the power question (with the centralized state claiming a monopoly of regalian rights*). The political regime and the property regime were nevertheless closely related, in part because political rights were long restricted to property owners and in part because constitutional restrictions then and now severely limited the possibility for political majorities to modify the property regime by legal and peaceful means.

As we shall see, political and property regimes have remained inextricably intertwined from premodern* ternary* and slave societies to modern postcolonial and hypercapitalist ones, including, along the way, the communist and social-democratic societies that arose in reaction to the crises of inequality and identity that ownership society provoked.

To analyze these historical transformations I therefore rely on the notion of an "inequality regime"* which encompasses both the political regime and the property regime (as well as the educational and fiscal regimes) and clarifies the relation between them. To illustrate the persistent structural links between the political regime and the property regime in today's world, consider the absence of any democratic mechanism that would allow a majority of citizens of the European Union (and a fortiori citizens of the world) to adopt a common tax or a redistributive or developmental scheme. This is because each member state, no matter how small its population or what benefits it derives from commercial and financial integration, has the right to veto all forms of fiscal legislation.

More generally, inequality today is strongly influenced by the system of borders and national sovereignty, which determines the allocation of social and political rights. This has given rise to intractable multidimensional ideological conflicts over inequality, immigration, and national identity, conflicts that have made it very difficult to achieve majority coalitions capable of countering the rise of inequality. Specifically, ethno-religious and national cleavages often prevent people of different ethnic and national origins from coming together politically, thus strengthening the hand of the rich and contributing to the growth of inequality. The reason for this failure is the lack of an ideology capable of persuading disadvantaged social groups that what unites them is more important than what divides them. I will examine these issues in due course. Here I want simply to emphasize the fact that political and property regimes have been intimately related for a very long time. This durable structural relationship cannot be properly analyzed without adopting a long-run transnational historical perspective.

Taking Ideology Seriously

Inequality is neither economic nor technological; it is ideological and political. This is no doubt the most striking conclusion to emerge from the historical approach I take in this book. In other words, the market and competition, profits and wages, capital and debt, skilled and unskilled workers, natives and aliens, tax havens and competitiveness—none of these things exist as such. All are social and historical constructs, which depend entirely on the legal, fiscal, educational, and political systems that people choose to adopt and the conceptual definitions they choose to work with. These choices are shaped by each society's conception of social justice and economic fairness and by the relative political and ideological power of contending groups and discourses. Importantly, this relative power is not exclusively material; it is also intellectual and ideological. In other words, ideas and ideologies count in history. They enable us to imagine new worlds and different types of society. Many paths are possible.

This approach runs counter to the common conservative argument that inequality has a basis in "nature." It is hardly surprising that the elites of many societies, in all periods and climes, have sought to "naturalize" inequality. They argue that existing social disparities benefit not only the poor but also society as a whole and that any attempt to alter the existing order of things will cause great pain. History proves the opposite: inequality varies widely in time and space, in structure as well as magnitude. Changes have occurred rapidly in ways that contemporaries could not have imagined only a short while before they came about. Misfortune did sometimes follow. Broadly speaking, however, political processes, including revolutionary transformations, that led to a reduction of inequality proved to be immensely successful. From them came our most precious institutions—those that have made human progress a reality, including universal suffrage, free and compulsory public schools, universal health insurance, and progressive taxation. In all likelihood the future will be no different. The inequalities and institutions that exist today are not the only ones possible, whatever conservatives may say to the contrary. Change is permanent and inevitable.

Nevertheless, the approach taken in this book—based on ideologies, institutions, and the possibility of alternative pathways—also differs from approaches sometimes characterized as "Marxist," according to which the state of the economic forces and relations of production determines a society's ideological "superstructure" in an almost mechanical fashion. In contrast, I insist that the realm of ideas, the political-ideological sphere, is truly autonomous.

Given an economy and a set of productive forces in a certain state of development (supposing one can attach a definite meaning to those words, which is by no means certain), a range of possible ideological, political, and inequality regimes always exists. For instance, the theory that holds that a transition from "feudalism" to "capitalism" occurred as a more or less mechanical response to the Industrial Revolution cannot explain the complexity and multiplicity of the political and ideological pathways we actually observe in different countries and regions. In particular, it fails to explain the differences that exist between and within colonizing and colonized regions. Above all, it fails to impart lessons useful for understanding subsequent stages of history. When we look closely at what followed, we find that alternatives always existed—and always will. At every level of development, economic, social, and political systems can be structured in many different ways; property relations can be organized differently; different fiscal and educational regimes are possible; problems of public and private debt can be handled differently; numerous ways to manage relations between human communities exist; and so on. There are always several ways of organizing a society and its constitutive power and property relations. More specifically, today, in the twenty-first century, property relations can be organized in many ways. Clearly stating the alternatives may be more useful in transcending capitalism than simply threatening to destroy it without explaining what comes next.

The study of these different historical pathways, as well as of the many paths not taken, is the best antidote to both the conservatism of the elite and the alibis of would-be revolutionaries who argue that nothing can be done until the conditions for revolution are ripe. The problem with these alibis is that they indefinitely defer all thinking about the postrevolutionary future. What this usually means in practice is that all power is granted to a hypertrophied state, which may turn out to be just as dangerous as the quasi-sacred property relations that the revolution sought to overthrow. In the twentieth century such thinking did considerable human and political damage for which we are still paying the price. Today, the postcommunist societies of Russia, China, and to a certain extent Eastern Europe (despite their different historical trajectories) have become hypercapitalism's staunchest allies. This is a direct consequence of the disasters of Stalinism and Maoism and the consequent rejection of all egalitarian internationalist ambitions. So great was the communist disaster that it overshadowed even the damage done by the ideologies of slavery, colonialism, and racialism and obscured the strong ties between those ideologies and the ideologies of ownership and hypercapitalism—no mean feat.

In this book I take ideology very seriously. I try to reconstruct the internal coherence of different types of ideology, with special emphasis on six main categories which I will call proprietarian, social-democratic, communist, trifunctional,* slaveist *(esclavagiste),* and colonialist ideologies. I start with the hypothesis that every ideology, no matter how extreme it may seem in its defense of inequality, expresses a certain idea of social justice. There is always some plausible basis for this idea, some sincere and consistent foundation, from which it is possible to draw useful lessons. But we cannot do this unless we take a concrete rather than an abstract (which is to say, ahistorical and noninstitutional) approach to the study of political and ideological structures. We must look at concrete societies and specific historical periods and at specific institutions defined by specific forms of property and specific fiscal and educational regimes. These must be rigorously analyzed. We must not shrink from investigating legal systems, tax schedules, and educational resources—the conditions and rules under which societies function. Without these, institutions and ideologies are mere empty shells, incapable of effecting real social change or inspiring lasting allegiance.

I am of course well aware that the word "ideology" can be used pejoratively, sometimes with good reason. Dogmatic ideas divorced from facts are frequently characterized as ideological. Yet often it is those who claim to be purely pragmatic who are in fact most "ideological" (in the pejorative sense): their claim to be post-ideological barely conceals their disdain for evidence, historical ignorance, distorting biases, and class interests. This book will therefore lean heavily on "facts." I will discuss the history of inequality in several societies, partly because this was my original specialty and partly because I am convinced that unbiased examination of the available sources is the only way to make progress. In so doing I will compare societies which are very different from one another. Some are even said to be "exceptional" and therefore unsuitable for comparative study, but this is incorrect.

I am well placed to know, however, that the available sources are never sufficient to resolve every dispute. From "facts" alone we will never be able to deduce the ideal political regime or property regime or fiscal or educational regime. Why? Because "facts" are largely the products of institutions (such as censuses, surveys, tax records, and so on). Societies create social, fiscal, and legal categories to describe, measure, and transform themselves. Hence "facts" are themselves constructs. To appreciate them properly we must understand their context, which consists of complex, overlapping, self-interested interactions between the observational apparatus and the society under study. This of course does not mean that these cognitive constructs have nothing to teach us. It means, rather, that to learn from them, we must take this complexity and reflexivity into account.

Furthermore, the questions that interest us, which pertain to the nature of the ideal social, economic, and political organization, are far too complex to allow answers to emerge from a simple "objective" examination of the "facts," which inevitably reflect the limitations of past experiences and the incompleteness of our knowledge and of the deliberative processes to which we were exposed. Finally, it is entirely conceivable that the "ideal" regime (however we interpret the word "ideal") is not unique and depends on specific characteristics of each society.

Collective Learning and the Social Sciences

Nevertheless, my position is not one of indiscriminate relativism. It is too easy for the social scientist to avoid taking a stand. So I will eventually make my position clear, especially in the final part of the book, but in so doing I will attempt to explain how and why I reached my conclusions.

Social ideologies usually evolve in response to historical experience. For instance, the French Revolution stemmed in part from the injustices and frustrations of the Ancien Régime. The Revolution in turn brought about changes that permanently altered perceptions of the ideal inequality regime as various social groups judged the success or failure of revolutionary experiments with different forms of political organization, property regimes, and social, fiscal, and educational systems. What was learned from this experience inevitably influenced future political transformations and so on down the line. Each nation's political and ideological trajectory can be seen as a vast process of collective learning and historical experimentation. Conflict is inherent in the process because different social and political groups have not only different interests and aspirations but also different memories. Hence they interpret past events differently and draw from them different implications regarding the future. From such learning experiences, national consensus on certain points can nevertheless emerge, at least for a time.

Though partly rational, these collective learning processes nevertheless have their limits. Nations tend to have short memories (people often forget their own country's experiences after a few decades or else remember only scattered bits, seldom chosen at random). Worse than that, memory is usually strictly nationalistic. Perhaps that is putting it too strongly: every country occasionally learns from the experiences of other countries, whether indirectly or through direct contact (in the form of war, colonization, occupation, or treaty—forms of learning that may be neither welcome nor beneficial). For the most part, however, nations form their visions of the ideal political or property regime or just legal, fiscal, or educational system from their own experiences and are almost completely unaware of the experiences of other countries, particularly when they are geographically remote or thought to belong to a distinct civilization or religious or moral tradition or, again, when contact with the other has been violent (which can reinforce the sense of radical foreignness). More generally, collective learning experiences are often based on relatively crude or imprecise notions of the institutional arrangements that exist in other societies (or even within the same country or in neighboring countries). This is true not only in the political realm but also in regard to legal, fiscal, and educational institutions. The usefulness of the lessons derived from such collective learning experiences is therefore somewhat limited.

This limitation is not inevitable, however. Many factors can enhance the learning process: schools and books, immigration and intermarriage, parties and trade unions, travel and encounters, newspapers and other media, to name a few. The social sciences can also play a part. I am convinced that social scientists can contribute to the understanding of ongoing changes by carefully comparing the histories of countries with different cultural traditions, systematically exploiting all available resources, and studying the evolution of inequality and of political and ideological regimes in different parts of the world. Such a comparative, historical, transnational approach can help us to form a more accurate picture of what a better political, economic, and social organization might look like and especially what a better global society might look like, since the global community is the one political community to which we all belong. Of course, I do not claim that the conclusions I offer throughout the book are the only ones possible, but they are, in my view, the best conclusions we can draw from the sources I have explored. I will try to explain in detail which events and comparisons I found most persuasive in reaching these conclusions. I will not hide the uncertainties that remain. Obviously, however, these conclusions depend on the very limited state of our present knowledge. This book is but one small step in a vast process of collective learning. I am impatient to discover what the next steps in the human adventure will be.

I hasten to add, for the benefit of those who lament the rise of inequality and of identity politics as well as for those who think that I protest too much, that this book is in no way a book of lamentations. I am an optimist by nature, and my primary goal is to seek solutions to our common problems. Human beings have demonstrated an astonishing capacity to imagine new institutions and develop new forms of cooperation, to forge bonds among millions (or hundreds of millions or even billions) of people who have never met and will never meet and who might well choose to annihilate one another rather than live together in peace. This is admirable. What is more, societies can accomplish these feats even though we know little about what an ideal regime might look like and therefore about what rules are justifiable. Nevertheless, our ability to imagine new institutions has its limits. We therefore need the assistance of rational analysis. To say that inequality is ideological and political rather than economic or technological does not mean that it can be eliminated by a wave of some magic wand. It means, more modestly, that we must take seriously the ideological and institutional diversity of human society. We must beware of anyone who tries to naturalize inequality or deny the existence of alternative forms of social organization. It means, too, that we must carefully study in detail the institutional arrangements and legal, fiscal, and educational systems of other countries, for it is these details that determine whether cooperation succeeds or fails and whether equality increases or decreases. Good will is not enough without solid conceptual and institutional underpinnings. If I can communicate to you, the reader, a little of my educated amazement at the successes of the past and persuade you that knowledge of history and economics is too important to leave to historians and economists, then I will have achieved my goal.

The Sources Used in This Book: Inequalities and Ideologies

This book is based on historical sources of two kinds: first, sources that enable us to measure the evolution of inequality in a multidimensional historical and comparative perspective (including inequalities of income, wages, wealth, education, gender, age, profession, origin, religion, race, status, etc.) and second, sources that allow us to study changes in ideology, political beliefs, and representations of inequality and of the economic, social, and political institutions that shape them.

Regarding inequality, I rely in particular on the data collected in the *World Inequality Database* (WID.world). This project represents the combined effort of more than a hundred researchers in eighty countries around the world. It is currently the largest database available for the historical study of wealth and income inequality both within and between countries. The WID.world project grew out of work I did with Anthony Atkinson and Emmanuel Saez in the early 2000s, which sought to extend and generalize research begun in the 1950s and 1970s by Atkinson, Simon Kuznets, and Alan Harrison.[1] This project is based on systematic comparison of available sources, including national accounts data, survey data, and fiscal and estate data. With these data it is generally possible to go back as far as the late nineteenth and early twentieth centuries, when many countries established progressive income and estate taxes. From the same data we can also infer conclusions about the distribution of wealth (taxes invariably give rise to new sources of knowledge and not only to tax receipts and popular discontent). For some countries we can push the limits of our knowledge back as far as the late eighteenth or early nineteenth centuries. This is true, for instance, of France, where the Revolution established an early version of a unified system of property and estate records. By drawing on this research I was able to set the post-1980 rise of inequality in a long-term historical perspective. This spurred a global debate on inequality, as the interest aroused by the publication in 2013 of *Capital in the Twenty-First Century* illustrates. The *World Inequality Report 2018* continued this debate.[2] People want to participate in the democratic process and therefore demand a more democratic diffusion of economic knowledge, as the enthusiastic reception of the WID.world project shows. As people become better educated and informed, economic and financial issues can no longer be left to a small group of experts whose competence is, in any case, dubious. It is only natural for more and more citizens to want to form their own opinions and participate in public debate. The economy is at the heart of politics; responsibility for it cannot be delegated, any more than democracy itself can.

1. See the fundamental work of S. Kuznets, *Shares of Upper Income Groups in Income and Savings* (National Bureau of Economic Research [NBER], 1953) (based on US data from the period 1913–1948, drawn from income tax records and national accounts data, which Kuznets helped to create), and A. Atkinson and A. Harrison, *Distribution of Personal Wealth in Britain* (Cambridge University Press, 1978) (based on British estate records for the period 1923–1972). See also T. Piketty, *Top Incomes in France in the Twentieth Century,* trans. S. Ackerman (Belknap, 2018); A. Atkinson and T. Piketty, *Top Incomes over the 20th Century: A Contrast Between Continental-European and English-Speaking Countries* (Oxford University Press, 2007); *Top Incomes: A Global Perspective* (Oxford University Press, 2010); T. Piketty, *Capital in the Twenty-First Century,* trans. A. Goldhammer (Harvard University Press, 2014), pp. 16–20.

2. See F. Alvaredo et al., *World Inequality Report 2018* (Harvard University Press, 2018); also available online at https://wir2018.wid.world/.

The available data on inequality are unfortunately incomplete, largely because of the difficulty of gaining access to fiscal, administrative, and banking records in many countries. There is a general lack of transparency in economic and financial matters. With the help of hundreds of citizens, researchers, and journalists in many countries, I was able to gain access to previously closed sources in Brazil, India, South Africa, Tunisia, Lebanon, Ivory Coast, Korea, Taiwan, Poland, and Hungary and, to a lesser extent, China and Russia. One of many shortcomings of my previous book, *Capital in the Twenty-First Century*, included a too-exclusive focus on the historical experience of the wealthy countries of the world (that is, in Western Europe, North America, and Japan), partly because it was so difficult to access historical data for other countries and regions. The newly available data enabled me to go beyond the largely Western framework of my previous book and delve more deeply into the nature of inequality regimes and their possible trajectories. Despite this progress, numerous deficiencies remain in the data from rich countries as well as poor.

For the present book I also collected many other sources and documents dealing with periods, countries, or aspects of inequality not well covered by WID.world, including data about preindustrial and colonial societies as well as inequalities of status, profession, education, gender, race, and religion.

For the study of ideology I naturally relied on a wide range of sources. Some will be familiar to scholars: minutes of parliamentary debates, transcripts of speeches, and party platforms. I look at the writings of both theorists and political actors to see how inequalities were justified in different times and places. In the eleventh century, for example, bishops wrote in justification the trifunctional society, which consisted of three classes: clergy, warriors, and laborers. In the early 1980s Friedrich von Hayek published *Law, Legislation, and Liberty*, an influential neo-proprietarian and semi-dictatorial treatise. In between those dates, in the 1830s, John Calhoun, a Democratic senator from South Carolina and vice president of the United States, justified "slavery as a positive good." Xi Jinping's writings on China's neo-communist dream or op-eds published in the *Global Times* are no less revealing than Donald Trump's tweets or articles in praise of Anglo-American hypercapitalism in the *Wall Street Journal* or the *Financial Times*. All these ideologies must be taken seriously, not only because of their influence on the course of events but also because every ideology attempts (more or less successfully) to impose meaning on a complex social reality. Human beings will inevitably attempt to make sense of the societies they live in, no matter how unequal or unjust they may be. I start from the premise that there is always something to learn from such attempts. Studying them in historical perspective may yield lessons that can help guide our steps in the future.

I will also make use of literature, which is often one of our best sources when it comes to understanding how representations of inequality change. In *Capital in the Twenty-First Century* I drew on classic nineteenth-century novels by Honoré de Balzac and Jane Austen, which offer matchless insights into the ownership societies that flourished in France and England between 1790 and 1840. Both novelists possessed intimate knowledge of the property hierarchies of their time. They had deeper insight than others into the secret motives and hidden boundaries that existed in their day and understood how these affected people's hopes and fears and determined who met whom and how men and women plotted marital strategies. Writers analyzed the deep structure of inequality—how it was justified, how it impinged on the lives of individuals—and they did so with an evocative power that no political speech or social scientific treatise can rival.

Literature's unique ability to capture the relations of power and domination between social groups and to detect the way in which inequalities are experienced by individuals exists, as we shall see, in all societies. We will therefore draw heavily on literary works for invaluable insights into a wide variety of inequality regimes. In *Destiny and Desire,* the splendid fresco that Carlos Fuentes published in 2008 a few years before his death, we discover a revealing portrait of Mexican capitalism and endemic social violence. In *This Earth of Mankind,* published in 1980, Pramoedya Ananta Toer shows us how the inegalitarian Dutch colonial regime worked in Indonesia in the late nineteenth and early twentieth centuries; his book achieves a brutal truthfulness unmatched by any other source. In *Americanah* (2013), Chimamanda Ngozi Adichie offers us a proud, ironic view of the migratory routes her characters Ifemelu and Obinze follow from Nigeria to the United States and Europe, providing unique insight into one of the most important aspects of today's inequality regime.

To study ideologies and their transformations, I also make systematic and novel use of the postelection surveys that have been carried out since the end of World War II in most countries where elections are held. Despite their limitations, these surveys offer an incomparable view of the structure of political, ideological, and electoral conflict from the 1940s to the present, not only in most Western countries (including France, the United States, and the United Kingdom, to which I will devote special attention) but also in many other countries, including India, Brazil, and South Africa. One of the most important shortcomings of my previous book, apart from its focus on the rich countries, was its tendency to treat political and ideological changes associated with inequality and redistribution as a black box. I proposed a number of hypotheses concerning, for example, changing political attitudes toward inequality and private property owing to world war, economic crisis, and the communist challenge in the twentieth century, but I never really tackled head on the question of how inegalitarian ideologies evolve. In the present work I try to do this much more explicitly by situating the question in a broader temporal and spatial perspective. In doing so I make extensive use of postelection surveys and other relevant sources.

Human Progress, the Revival of Inequality, and Global Diversity

Now to the heart of the matter: human progress exists, but it is fragile. It is constantly threatened by inegalitarian and identitarian tendencies. To believe that human progress exists, it suffices to look at statistics for health and education worldwide over the past two centuries (Fig. I.1). Average life expectancy at birth rose from around 26 years in 1820 to 72 years in 2020. At the turn of the nineteenth century, around 20 percent of all newborns died in their first year, compared with 1 percent today. The life expectancy of children who reach the age of 1 has increased from roughly 32 years in 1820 to 73 today. We could focus on any number of other indicators: the probability of a newborn surviving until age 10, of an adult reaching age 60, or of a retiree enjoying five or ten years of good health. Using any of these indicators, the long-run improvement is impressive. It is of course possible to cite countries or periods in which life expectancy declined even in peacetime, as in the Soviet Union in the 1970s or the United States in the 2010s. This is generally not a good sign for the regimes in which it occurs. In the long run, however, there can be no doubt that things have improved everywhere in the world, notwithstanding the limitations of available demographic sources.[3]

---

3. Circa 1820, the life expectancy of a child who survived to the age of 1 was roughly 30 years in Africa and Asia and 41 in Western Europe, for a global average of about 32. In 2020 it was 56 in sub-Saharan Africa and more than 80 in the wealthiest countries of Europe and Asia, for a world average of about 73. Although these estimates are imperfect, the orders of magnitude are clear. All life expectancies are based on mortality by age in the year considered (the life expectancy of a person born in that year is therefore slightly higher). See the online appendix.

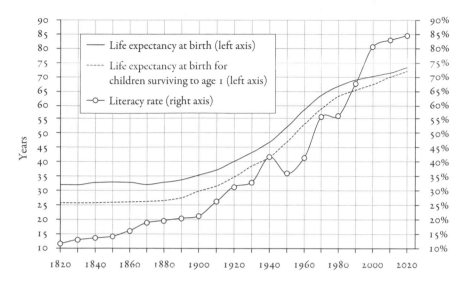

FIG. I.1. Health and education in the world, 1820–2020

Interpretation: Life expectancy at birth worldwide increased from an average of 26 years in 1820 to 72 years in 2020. Life expectancy at birth for those living to age 1 increased from 32 to 73 years (because infant mortality before age 1 decreased from roughly 20 percent in 1820 to less than 1 percent in 2020). The literacy rate of those 15 years and older worldwide rose from 12 to 85 percent. *Sources and series:* piketty. pse.ens.fr/ideology.

People are healthier today than ever before. They also have more access to education and culture. UNESCO defines literacy as the "ability to identify, understand, interpret, create, communicate and compute, using printed and written materials associated with varying contexts." Although no such definition existed at the turn of the nineteenth century, we can deduce from various surveys and census data that barely 10 percent of the world's population aged 15 and older could be classified as literate compared with more than 85 percent today. This finding is confirmed by more precise indices such as years of schooling, which has risen from barely one year two centuries ago to eight years today and to more than twelve years in the most advanced countries. In the age of Austen and Balzac, fewer than 10 percent of the world's population attended primary school; in the age of Adichie and Fuentes, more than half of all children in the wealthiest countries attend university. What had always been a class privilege is now available to the majority.

To gauge the magnitude of these changes, it is also important to note that the world's population is more than ten times larger today than it was in the

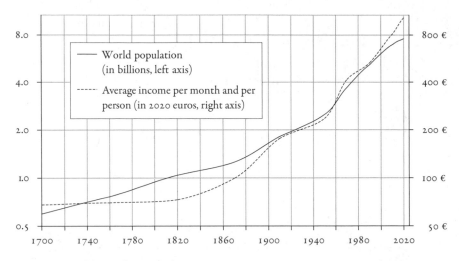

FIG. I.2. World population and income, 1700–2020

Interpretation: Global population and average national income increased more than tenfold between 1700 and 2020: population rose from 600 million in 1700 to more than 7 billion in 2020; income, expressed in terms of 2020 euros and purchasing power parity, increased from barely 80 euros per month per person in 1700 to roughly 1,000 euros per month per person in 2020. *Sources and series:* piketty.pse.ens.fr/ideology.

eighteenth century, and the average per capita income is ten times higher. From 600 million in 1700 the population of the world has grown to more than 7 billion today, while average income, insofar as it can be measured, has grown from a purchasing power of less than 100 (expressed in 2020 euros) a month in 1700 to roughly 1,000 today (Fig. I.2). This is a significant quantitative gain, although it should be noted that it corresponds to an annual growth rate of just 0.8 percent (extended over three centuries, which proves, if proof were needed, that earthly paradise can be achieved without a growth rate of 5 percent). Whether this increase in population and average monthly income represents "progress" as indubitable as that achieved in health and education is open to question, however.

It is difficult to interpret the meaning of these changes and their future implications. The growth of the world's population is due in part to the decline in infant mortality and the fact that growing numbers of parents lived long enough to care for their children to the brink of adulthood. If this rate of population growth continues for another three centuries, however, the population of the planet will grow to more than 70 billion, which seems neither desirable nor sustainable. The growth of average per capita income has meant a very substantial improvement in standards of living: three-quarters of the globe's inhabitants lived close to the subsistence threshold in the eighteenth century compared with less than a fifth today. People today enjoy unprecedented opportunities for travel and recreation and for meeting other people and achieving emancipation. Yet several issues bedevil the national accounts I rely on to describe the long-term trajectory of average income. Because national accounts deal with aggregates, they take no account of inequality and have been slow to incorporate data on sustainability, human capital, and natural capital. Because they try to sum up the economy in a single-figure, total national income, they are not very useful for studying long-run changes in such multidimensional variables as standards of living and purchasing power.[4]

While the progress made in the areas of health, education, and purchasing power has been real, it has masked vast inequalities and vulnerabilities. In 2018, the infant mortality rate was less than 0.1 percent in the wealthiest countries of Europe, North America, and Asia, but nearly 10 percent in the poorest African countries. Average per capita income rose to 1,000 euros per month, but it was barely 100–200 euros a month in the poorest countries and more than 3,000–4,000 a month in the wealthiest. In a few tiny tax havens, which are suspected (rightly) of robbing the rest of the planet, it is even higher, as is also the case in certain petro-monarchies whose wealth comes at the price of future global warming. There has been real progress, but we can always do better, so we would be foolish to rest on our laurels.

Although there can be no doubt about the progress made between the eighteenth century and now, there have also been phases of regression, during which inequality increased and civilization declined. The Euro-American Enlightenment and the Industrial Revolution coincided with extremely violent systems of property ownership, slavery, and colonialism, which attained historic proportions in the eighteenth, nineteenth, and twentieth centuries. Between 1914 and 1945 the European powers themselves succumbed to a phase of genocidal self-destruction. In the 1950s and 1960s the colonial powers were

---

4. National income is defined as gross domestic product (GDP) minus capital depreciation (which in practice amounts to 10–15 percent of GDP), plus net income from abroad (which can be positive or negative for a given country but sums to zero globally). See Piketty, *Capital in the Twenty-First Century,* chaps. 1–2. I will return several times to the social and political issues raised by national accounts and their various shortcomings, especially in regard to durable and equitable development. See esp. Chap. 13.

obliged to decolonize, while at the same time the United States finally granted civil rights to the descendants of slaves. Owing to the conflict between capitalism and communism, the world had long lived with fears of nuclear annihilation. With the collapse of the Soviet empire in 1989–1991, those fears dissipated. South African apartheid was abolished in 1991–1994. Yet soon thereafter, in the early 2000s, a new regressive phase began, as the climate warmed and xenophobic identity politics gained a foothold in many countries. All of this took place against a background of growing socioeconomic inequality after 1980–1990, propelled by a particularly radical form of neo-proprietarian ideology. It would make little sense to assert that everything that happened between the eighteenth century and today was somehow necessary to achieve the progress noted above. Other paths could have been followed; other inequality regimes could have been chosen. More just and egalitarian societies are always possible.

If there is a lesson to be learned from the past three centuries of world history, it is that human progress is not linear. It is wrong to assume that every change will always be for the best or that free competition between states and among economic actors will somehow miraculously lead to universal social harmony. Progress exists, but it is a struggle, and it depends above all on rational analysis of historical changes and all their consequences, positive as well as negative.

The Return of Inequality: Initial Bearings

Among the most worrisome structural changes facing us today is the revival of inequality nearly everywhere since the 1980s. It is hard to envision solutions to other major problems such as immigration and climate change if we cannot both reduce inequality and establish a standard of justice acceptable to a majority of the world's people.

Let us begin by looking at a simple indicator, the share of the top decile (that is, the top 10 percent) of the income distribution in various places since 1980. If perfect social equality existed, the top decile's share would be exactly 10 percent. If perfect inequality prevailed, it would be 100 percent. In reality it falls somewhere between these two extremes, but the exact figure varies widely in time and space. Over the past few decades we find that the top decile's share has risen almost everywhere. Take, for example, India, the United States, Russia, China, and Europe. The share of the top decile in each of these five regions stood at around 25–35 percent in 1980 but by 2018 had risen to between 35 and 55 percent (Fig. I.3). How much higher can it go? Could it rise to 55 or even

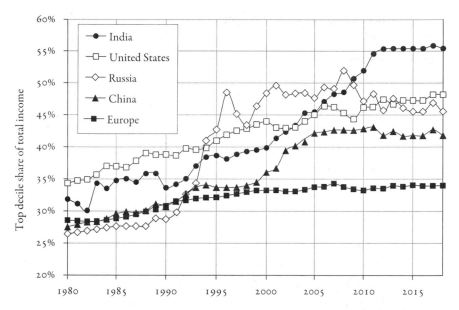

FIG. I.3. The rise of inequality around the world, 1980–2018

Interpretation: The share of the top decile (the 10 percent of highest earners) in total national income ranged from 26 to 34 percent in different parts of the world and from 34 to 56 percent in 2018. Inequality increased everywhere, but the size of the increase varied sharply from country to country at all levels of development. For example, it was greater in the United States than in Europe (enlarged European Union, 540 million inhabitants) and greater in India than in China. *Sources and series:* piketty.pse.ens.fr/ideology.

75 percent over the next few decades? Note, too, that there is considerable variation in the magnitude of the increase from region to region, even at comparable levels of development. The top decile's share has risen much more rapidly in the United States than in Europe and much more in India than in China.

When we look more closely at the data, we find that the increase in inequality has come at the expense of the bottom 50 percent of the distribution, whose share of total income stood at about 20–25 percent in 1980 in all five regions but had fallen to 15–20 percent in 2018 (and, indeed, as low as 10 percent in the United States, which is particularly worrisome).[5]

---

5. For the purposes of Fig. I.3 (and in the remainder of the book unless otherwise specified), Europe is defined as the European Union plus allied countries such as Switzerland and Norway, with a total population of 540 million, roughly 420 million of whom live in Western Europe, 120 million in Eastern Europe, and 520 million

If we take a longer view, we find that the five major regions of the world represented in Fig. I.3 enjoyed a relatively egalitarian phase between 1950 and 1980 before entering a phase of rising inequality since then. The egalitarian phase was marked by different political regimes in different regions: communist regimes in China and Russia and social-democratic regimes in Europe and to a certain extent in the United States and India. We will be looking much more closely at the differences among these various political regimes in what follows, but for now we can say that all favored some degree of socioeconomic equality (which does not mean that other forms of inequality can be ignored).

If we now expand our view to include other parts of the world, we see that inequalities were even greater elsewhere (Fig. I.4). For instance, the top decile claimed 54 percent of total income in sub-Saharan Africa (and as much as 65 percent in South Africa), 56 percent in Brazil, and 64 percent in the Middle East, which stands out as the world's most inegalitarian region in 2018 (almost on a par with South Africa). There, the bottom 50 percent of the distribution earns less than 10 percent of total income.[6] The causes of inequality vary widely from region to region. For instance, the historical legacy of racial and colonial discrimination and slavery weighs heavily in Brazil and South Africa as well as in the United States. In the Middle East more "modern" factors are at play: petroleum wealth and the financial assets into which it has been converted are concentrated in very few hands thanks to the workings of global markets and sophisticated legal systems. South Africa, Brazil, and the Middle East stand at the frontier of modern inequality, with top decile shares of 55–65 percent. Despite deficiencies in the available historical data, moreover, it appears that inequality in these regions has always been high: they never experienced a relatively egalitarian "social-democratic" phase (much less a communist one).

To sum up, inequality has increased in nearly every region of the world since 1980, except in those countries that have always been highly inegalitarian. In a sense, what is happening is that regions that enjoyed a phase of relative equality

---

in the European Union as such, including the United Kingdom. Russia, Ukraine, and Belarus are not included. If attention is focused on Western Europe alone, the difference from the United States is even more marked. See Fig. 12.9.

6. The estimates for the Middle East (and other regions) should be considered as lower bounds, given that income amassed in tax havens cannot be accurately accounted for. For alternative estimates, see Chap. 13. The Middle East is defined here as the region extending from Egypt to Iran and Turkey to the Arabian Peninsula, with a population of roughly 420 million.

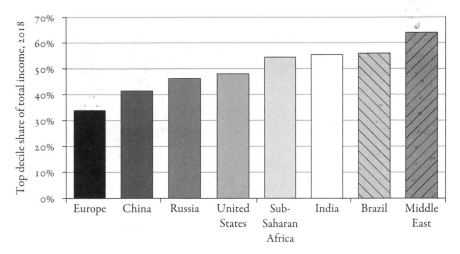

FIG. I.4. Inequality in different regions of the world in 2018

Interpretation: In 2018, the share of the top decile (the highest 10 percent of earners) in national income was 34 percent in Europe, 41 percent in China, 46 percent in Russia, 48 percent in the United States, 54 percent in sub-Saharan Africa, 55 percent in India, 56 percent in Brazil, and 64 percent in the Middle East. *Sources and series:* piketty.pse. ens.fr/ideology.

between 1950 and 1980 are moving back toward the inegalitarian frontier, albeit with large variations from country to country.

The Elephant Curve: A Sober Debate about Globalization

The revival of within-country inequality after 1980 is by now a well-established and widely recognized phenomenon. There is, however, no agreement on what to do about it. The key question is not the level of inequality but rather its origin and justification. For instance, it is perfectly possible to argue that the level of income inequality was kept artificially and excessively low under Russian and Chinese Communism before 1980. Hence there is nothing wrong with the growing income inequality observed since then; inequality has actually stimulated innovation and growth for the benefit of all, especially in China, where the poverty rate has decreased dramatically. But to what extent is this argument correct? Care is necessary in evaluating the data. Was it justifiable, for example, for Russian and Chinese oligarchs to capture so much natural wealth and so many formerly public enterprises in the period 2000–2020, especially when those oligarchs frequently failed to demonstrate much talent for innovation, except when it came to inventing legal and fiscal stratagems to secure the wealth they appropriated? To fully answer this question one cannot simply say that there was too little inequality prior to 1980.

A similar argument could be made about India, Europe, and the United States—namely, that equality had gone too far in the period 1950–1980 and had to be curtailed for the sake of the poor. Here, however, the problems are even greater than in the case of Russia or China. Even if this argument were partly correct, would it justify a priori any level of inequality whatsoever, without so much as a glance at the data? Growth rates in both Europe and the United States were higher, for example, in the egalitarian period (1950–1980) than in the subsequent phase of rising inequality. This casts doubt on the argument that greater inequality is always socially useful. After 1980, inequality increased more in the United States than in Europe, but this did not lead to a higher rate of growth, much less benefit the bottom 50 percent of the income distribution, whose standard of living stagnated in absolute terms and fell sharply compared to that of top earners. In other words, overall growth of national income decreased in the United States, as did the share of the bottom half. In India, inequality increased much more sharply after 1980 than in China, but India's growth rate was lower so that the bottom 50 percent was doubly penalized by both a lower growth rate and a decreased share of national income. Clearly, then, the argument that the income gap between high and low earners had been compressed too much in the period 1950–1980, thus calling for a corrective, has its shortcomings. Nevertheless, it should be taken seriously, up to a point, and we will do so in what follows.

One clear way of representing the distribution of global growth in the period 1980–2018 is to plot the cumulative income growth of each decile of the global income distribution. The result is sometimes referred to as "the elephant curve" (Fig. I.5).[7] This can be summarized as follows. The sixth to ninth deciles of global income (comprising people who belonged to neither the bottom 60 percent nor the top 10 percent of the income distribution or, in other words, the global middle class) did not benefit much at all from global economic growth in this period. By contrast, the groups above and below this global middle class benefited a great deal. Some relatively poor households (in the

---

7. The "elephant curve" was first formulated by C. Lakner and B. Milanovic in "Global Income Distribution: From the Fall of the Berlin Wall to the Great Recession," *World Bank Economic Review,* 2015. The estimates given here are from the *World Inequality Report 2018* and the WID.world database, which give a better picture of the top end of the distribution.

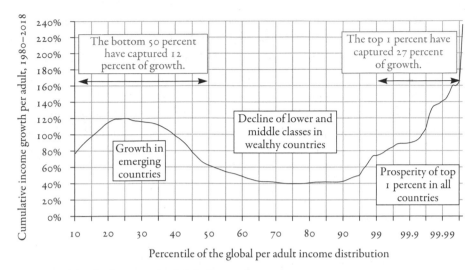

FIG. I.5. The elephant curve of global inequality, 1980–2018

Interpretation: The bottom 50 percent of the global income distribution saw substantial growth in purchasing power between 1980 and 2018 (60–120 percent). The top centile saw even stronger growth (80–240 percent). Intermediate categories grew less. In sum, inequality decreased between the bottom and middle of the income distribution and increased between the middle and the top. *Sources and series:* piketty.pse.ens.fr/ideology.

second, third, and fourth deciles of the world income distribution) did improve their position; some of the wealthiest households in the wealthiest countries gained even more (namely, those in the tip of the elephant's trunk, the ninety-ninth percentile or top 1 percent, and especially the top tenth and one-hundredth of a percent, whose incomes rose by several hundred percent). If the global income distribution were stable, this curve would be flat: each percentile would progress at the same rate as all the others. There would still be rich people and poor people as well as upward and downward mobility, but the average income of each percentile would increase at the same rate.[8] In other words, "a rising tide would lift all boats," to use an expression that became popular in the postwar era, when the tide did seem to be rising. The fact that the elephant curve is so far from flat illustrates the magnitude of the change we have been witnessing over the past three decades.

---

8. The elephant curve plots the growth of average income for a given percentile of the distribution between two dates. Of course, a given percentile group does not contain the same individuals at both dates, as a given individual may move to a different group or be born or die between the start and end dates.

The elephant curve is fundamental because it explains why globalization is so politically controversial: for some observers the most striking fact is that the remarkable growth of certain less developed countries has so dramatically reduced global poverty and inequality while others deplore the sharp increase of inequality at the top due to the excesses of global hypercapitalism. Both sides have a point: inequality between the bottom and middle of the global income distribution has decreased, while inequality between the middle and top has increased. Both aspects of the globalization story are real. The point is not to deny either part of the story but rather to figure out how to retain the good features of globalization while getting rid of the bad. Here we see the importance of choosing the right terminology and conceptual framework. If we tried to describe inequality using a single indicator, such as the Gini coefficient,* we could easily deceive ourselves. Because we would then lack the means to perceive complex, multidimensional changes, we might think that nothing had changed at all: with a single indicator, several disparate phenomena can cancel one another out. For that reason, I avoid relying on any single "synthetic" index. I will always be careful to distinguish the various deciles and percentiles of the relevant wealth and income distributions (and thus the social groups to which they correspond).[9]

Some critics object that the elephant curve focuses too much attention on the top 1 or 0.1 percent of the global population, where the gains have been highest. It is foolish, they say, to arouse envy of such a tiny group rather than rejoice in the manifest growth at the lower end of the distribution. In fact, recent research confirms the importance of looking at top incomes; indeed, it shows that the gains at the top are even larger than the original elephant curve suggested. Between 1980 and 2018, the top 1 percent captured 27 percent

---

9. The Gini coefficient was invented in the early twentieth century by the Italian economist and statistician Corrado Gini, who shared with his compatriot Vilfredo Pareto a relatively conservative view of inequality as a permanent feature of all economies. See Piketty, *Capital in the Twenty-First Century*, pp. 266–270. I will have more to say about the importance of statistical indices and the ambiguous role played in these debates by national and international statistical agencies (see Chap. 13). All Gini coefficients for distributions of wealth and income mentioned in this book are available in the online appendix. Simply stated: the Gini coefficient, which by definition always lies between zero (total equality) and one (total inequality), generally lies between 0.8 and 0.9 when the top decile's share is 80–90 percent, and falls to 0.1–0.2 when the top decile's share drops to 10–20 percent. We learn much more, however, from the shares captured by different groups (such as the bottom 50 percent, the top 10 percent, and so on), so I urge the reader to think in these terms, focusing on orders of magnitude rather than on Gini coefficients.

of global income growth, versus just 12 percent for the bottom 50 percent (Fig. I.5). In other words, the tip of the pachyderm's trunk may concern only a tiny segment of the population, but it has captured an elephant-sized portion of the world's growth—its share is twice as large as that of the 3.5 billion individuals at the bottom end.[10] In other words, a growth model only slightly less beneficial to those at the top would have permitted a much more rapid reduction in global poverty (and could still do so in the future).

Although this type of data can clarify the issues, it cannot end the debate. Everything depends on the causes of inequality and how it is justified. How much can the growth of top incomes be justified by the benefits the wealthy contribute to the rest of society? If one believes that greater inequality always and everywhere leads to higher income and better living standards for the poorest 50 percent, can one justify the 27 percent of world income growth captured by the top 1 percent—or perhaps even at higher percentages—why not 40 or 60 or even 80 percent? The cases mentioned earlier—the United States versus Europe and India versus China—suggest that this is not a very persuasive argument, however, because the countries where top earners gained the most are not those where the poor reaped the largest benefits. Analysis of these cases suggests that the share going to the top 1 percent could have been reduced to 10 or 20 percent, or perhaps even less, while still allowing significant improvement in the living standards of the bottom 50 percent. These issues are important enough to call for more detailed investigation. In any case, the data suggest that there is no reason to believe that there is just one way to organize the global economy. There is no reason to believe that the top 1 percent must capture precisely 27 percent of income growth (versus 12 percent for the bottom 50). What the global growth figures reveal is that the distribution of gains is just as important as overall growth. Hence there is ample room for debate about the political and institutional choices that affect distribution.

On the Justification of Extreme Inequality

The world's largest fortunes have grown since 1980 at even faster rates than the world's top incomes depicted in Fig. I.5. Great fortunes grew extremely rapidly in all parts of the world: among the leading beneficiaries were Russian oligarchs,

---

10. The scale adopted in Fig. I.5 overstates the size of the top 1 percent in terms of population but understates its share of total growth. See the *World Inequality Report 2018* (wir2018.wid.world).

Mexican magnates, Chinese billionaires, Indonesian financiers, Saudi investors, Indian industrialists, European rentiers, and wealthy Americans. In the period 1980–2018, large fortunes grew at rates three to four times the growth rate of the global economy. Such phenomenal growth cannot continue indefinitely, unless one is prepared to believe that nearly all global wealth is destined to end up in the hands of billionaires. Nevertheless, the gap between top fortunes and the rest continued to grow even in the decade after the financial crisis of 2008 at virtually the same rate as in the two previous decades, which suggests that we may not yet have seen the end of a massive change in the structure of the world's wealth.[11]

In the face of such spectacular change, many justifications of wealth inequality have been proposed, some of them quite surprising. In the West, for example, apologists like to divide the rich into two categories. On the one hand, there are Russian oligarchs, Middle Eastern oil sheiks, and billionaires of various nationalities, be they Chinese, Mexican, Guinean, Indian, or Indonesian. Critics question whether such people "deserve" their wealth, which they allegedly owe to close ties to the powers that be in their respective countries: for example, it is often insinuated that these fortunes originated with unfair appropriation natural resources or illegitimate licensing arrangements. The beneficiaries supposedly did little to stimulate economic growth. On the other hand, there are entrepreneurs, usually European or American, of whom Silicon Valley innovators serve as a paradigmatic example. Their contributions to global prosperity are widely praised. If they were properly rewarded for their efforts, some say, they would be even richer than they are. Society, their champions argue, owes them a moral debt, which it should perhaps repay in the form of tax breaks or political influence (which in some countries they may already have achieved on their own). Such hyper-meritocratic, Western-centric justifications of inequality demonstrate the irrepressible human need to make sense of social inequality, at times in ways that stretch credulity. This quasi-beatification of wealth often ignores inconvenient facts. Would Bill Gates and his fellow techno-billionaires have been able to build their businesses without the hundreds of billions of dollars of public money invested in basic research over many decades? Would the quasi-monopolies they have built by patenting public knowledge have reaped such enormous profits without the active support of legal and tax codes?

Most justifications of extreme wealth inequality are less grandiose, however. The need for stability and protection of property rights is often emphasized.

---

11. See Fig. 13.1.

In other words, defenders admit that inequality of wealth may not be entirely just or invariably useful, especially when it reaches the level observed in places like California. But, they argue, challenging the status quo might initiate a self-reinforcing process whose effect on the poorest members of society would ultimately be negative. This quasi-religious defense of property rights as the sine qua non of social and political stability was characteristic of the ownership societies that flourished in Europe and the United States in the nineteenth and early twentieth centuries. The need for stability also figured in justifications of trifunctional and slave societies. Lately, the stability argument has been augmented by the claim that states are less inefficient than private philanthropy—an old argument that has recently regained prominence. All of these justifications of inequality deserve a hearing, but they can be refuted by applying the lessons of history.

Learning from History: The Lessons of the Twentieth Century

To understand and learn from what has been happening in the world since 1980, we must adopt a long-term historical and comparative perspective. The current inequality regime, which I call neo-proprietarian, bears traces of all the regimes that preceded it. To study it properly, we must begin by examining how the trifunctional societies of the premodern era, which were based on a ternary structure (clergy, nobility, and third estate), evolved into the ownership societies of the eighteenth and nineteenth centuries and then how those societies collapsed in the twentieth century in the face of challenges from communism and social democracy, world war, and, finally, wars of national liberation, which put an end to centuries of colonial domination. All human societies need to make sense of their inequalities, and the justifications given in the past turn out, if studied carefully, to be no more incoherent than those of the present. By examining them all in their concrete historical contexts, paying close attention to the multiplicity of possible trajectories and forks in the road, we can shed light on the present inequality regime and begin to see how it might be transformed.

The collapse of ownership and colonialist society in the twentieth century plays an especially important role in this history. It radically transformed the structure and justification of inequality, leading directly to the present state of affairs. The countries of Western Europe—most notably France, the United Kingdom, and Germany, which had been more inegalitarian than the United States on the eve of World War I—became more egalitarian over

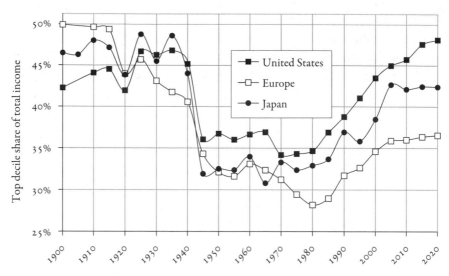

FIG. I.6. Inequality, 1900–2020: Europe, United States, and Japan

Interpretation: The top decile's share of total national income was about 50 percent in Western Europe in 1900–1910 before decreasing to roughly 30 percent in 1950–1980 and then rising again to more than 35 percent in 2010–2020. Inequality grew more strongly in the United States, where the top decile share approached 50 percent in 2010–2020, exceeding the level of 1900–1910. Japan was in an intermediate position. *Sources and series:* piketty.pse.ens.fr/ideology.

the course of the twentieth century, partly because the shocks of the period 1914–1945 resulted in a greater compression of inequalities there and partly because inequality increased more in the United States after 1980 (Fig. I.6).[12] In both Europe and the United States, the compression of inequality in the period 1914–1970 can be explained by legal, social, and fiscal changes hastened by two world wars, the Bolshevik Revolution of 1917, and the Great Depression of 1929. In an intellectual and political sense, however, those changes were already under way by the end of the nineteenth century, and it is reasonable to think that they would have occurred in one form or another even if those crises had not occurred. Historical change takes place when evolving ideas confront

12. For the purposes of Fig. I.6, Western Europe is defined as the average of the United Kingdom, France, Germany, and Sweden. See Figs. 10.1–10.3 for a separate analysis of long-term developments in the various countries of Europe. See also the online appendix, Fig. S0.6, for the corresponding annual series.

the logic of events: neither has much effect without the other. We will encounter this lesson numerous times in what follows, for example, when we analyze the events of the French Revolution or changes in the structure of inequality in India since the end of the colonial era.

Among the changes that contributed to the reduction of inequality in the twentieth century was the widespread emergence of a system of progressive taxation of both income and inherited wealth. The highest incomes and largest fortunes were taxed more heavily than smaller ones. In this the United States led the way: in the Gilded Age (1865–1900) and beyond, as industrial and financial wealth accumulated, Americans worried that their country might one day become as inegalitarian as the societies of the Old World, which they viewed as oligarchic and therefore at odds with the democratic spirit of the United States. The United Kingdom also turned to progressive taxation. Although the United Kingdom experienced much less destruction of wealth than either France or Germany between 1914 and 1945, it nevertheless chose (in calmer political circumstances than prevailed on the continent) to reject its highly inegalitarian past by imposing steeply progressive taxes on income and estates.

In the period 1932–1980, the top marginal income rate averaged 81 percent in the United States and 89 percent in the United Kingdom compared with "only" 58 percent in German and 60 percent in France (Fig. I.7). Note that these rates include only the income tax (and not other levies such as consumption taxes). In the United States they include only the federal income tax and not state income taxes (which can add 5–10 percent on top of the federal tax). Clearly, the fact that top marginal rates remained above 80 percent for nearly half a century did not destroy capitalism in the United States—quite the opposite.

As we will see, highly progressive taxation contributed strongly to the reduction of inequality in the twentieth century. We will also analyze in detail how progressive taxation was undone in the 1980s, especially in the United States and United Kingdom, and investigate what lessons can be drawn from this. The drastic reduction of top tax rates was the signature issue of the "conservative revolution" waged by the Republican Party under Ronald Reagan in the United States and the Conservative Party under Margaret Thatcher in Britain in the late 1970s and early 1980s. The ensuing political and ideological shift had a marked impact on taxes and inequality not only in the United States and United Kingdom but also around the world. Moreover, the turn to the right was never really challenged by the parties and governments that followed

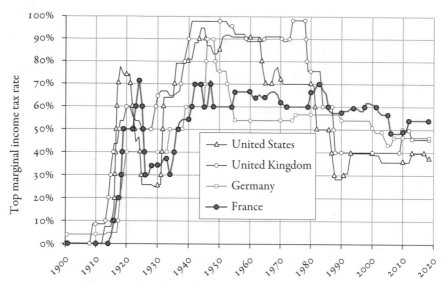

FIG. I.7. Top income tax rates, 1900–2020

Interpretation: The top marginal tax rate applied to the highest incomes averaged 23 percent in the United States from 1900 to 1932, 81 percent from 1932 to 1980, and 39 percent from 1980 to 2018. Over the same period, the top rates averaged 30, 89, and 46 percent in the United Kingdom; 18, 58, and 50 percent in Germany; and 23, 60, and 57 percent in France. The tax system was most progressive in the middle of the century, particularly in the United States and United Kingdom. *Sources and series:* piketty.pse.ens.fr/ideology.

Reagan and Thatcher. In the United States the top marginal federal income tax rate has fluctuated between 30 and 40 percent since the end of the 1980s. In the United Kingdom it has ranged from 40 to 45 percent, with a slight upward trend since the crisis of 2008. In both cases, the top rate between 1980 and 2018 has remained at roughly half that of the period 1932–1980 (40 percent compared with 80 percent; see Fig. I.7).

For champions of the fiscal turn, the spectacular decrease of progressivity was justified by the idea that top marginal rates had risen to unconscionable levels prior to 1980. Some argued that high top rates had sapped the entrepreneurial spirit of British and American innovators, allowing the United States and United Kingdom to be overtaken by West European and Japanese competitors (a prominent campaign issue in both countries in the 1970s and 1980s). In hindsight, these arguments cannot withstand scrutiny. The issue deserves a fresh look. Many other factors explain why Germany, France, Sweden, and

Japan caught up with the United States and United Kingdom in the period 1950–1980. Those countries had fallen seriously behind the leaders, especially the United States, and a growth spurt was all but inevitable. Growth was also spurred by institutional factors, including relatively ambitious (and egalitarian) social and educational policies adopted after World War II. These policies helped rivals catch up with the United States and surge ahead of the United Kingdom, where the educational system had been seriously neglected since the late nineteenth century. And once again, it should be stressed that productivity growth in the United States and United Kingdom was higher in the period 1950–1990 than in 1990–2020, thus casting serious doubt on the argument that reducing top marginal tax rates spurs economic growth.

In the end, it is fair to say that the move to a less progressive tax system in the 1980s played a large part in the unprecedented growth of inequality in the United States and United Kingdom between 1980 and 2018. The share of national income going to the bottom half of the income distribution collapsed, contributing perhaps to the feeling on the part of the middle and lower classes that they had been abandoned in addition to fueling the rise of xenophobia and identity politics in both countries. These developments came to a head in 2016, with the British vote to leave the European Union (Brexit) and the election of Donald Trump. With this recent history in mind, the time has come to rethink the wisdom of progressive taxation of both income and wealth, in rich countries as well as poor—the latter being the first to suffer from fiscal competition and lack of financial transparency. The free and unchecked circulation of capital without sharing of information between national tax authorities has been one of the primary means by which the conservative fiscal revolution of the 1980s has been protected and extended. It has adversely affected the process of state building and the development of just tax systems everywhere. Which raises another key question: Why have the social-democratic coalitions that emerged in the postwar era proved so unable to respond to these challenges? In particular, why have social democrats been so inept at constructing a progressive transnational tax system? Why have they not promoted the idea of social and temporary private ownership? If there were a sufficiently progressive tax on the largest holders of private property, such an idea would emerge naturally, because property owners would then be obliged to return a significant fraction of what they owned to the community every year. This political, intellectual, and ideological failure of social democracy must count among the reasons for the revival of inequality, reversing the historic trend toward ever greater equality.

On the Ideological Freeze and New Educational Inequalities

To understand what is happening, we will also need to look at political and ideological changes affecting other political and social institutions that have contributed to the reduction and regulation of inequality. I am thinking primarily of economic power sharing and employee involvement in business decision making and strategy setting. In the 1950s, several countries, including Germany and Sweden, were pioneers in this area, but until recently their innovations were not widely adopted or improved on. The reasons for this failure surely have to do with the specific histories of individual countries. Until the 1980s, for instance, the British Labour Party and French Socialists favored programs of nationalization, but after the fall of the Berlin Wall and the collapse of communism they abruptly gave up on redistribution altogether. Moreover, in no region has enough attention been paid to transcending private property in its present form.

Everyone is familiar with the effects of the Cold War on the system of international relations, but its consequences did not end there. In many ways the Cold War also created an ideological freeze, which discouraged new thinking about ways of transcending capitalism. The anticommunist euphoria that followed the fall of the Berlin Wall similarly discouraged fresh thinking right up to the Great Recession of 2008. Hence it is only recently that people have begun to think once again about imposing firmer social controls on capitalist economic forces.

This is particularly true when it comes to the crucial issue of investment in and access to education. The most striking fact about the increase of inequality in the United States is the collapse of the share of total national income going to the bottom 50 percent, which fell from about 20 percent in 1980 to a little more than 12 in 2018. Such a dramatic collapse from an already low level can only be explained by a multiplicity of factors. One such factor was the sharp decrease in the federal minimum wage (in real terms) since 1980. Another was significant inequality of access to education. It is striking to discover the degree to which access to a university education in the United States depends on parental income. It has been shown that the probability of access to higher education (including two-year junior college degrees) was just slightly above 20 percent for the 10 percent of young adults whose parents had the lowest income, increasing linearly to more than 90 percent for those whose parents had the highest income (Fig. I.8).[13] Furthermore, access to higher education does not mean the same thing for those at the top and bottom of the distribu-

---

13. This is based on the work of Raj Chetty and Emmanuel Saez. See the online appendix.

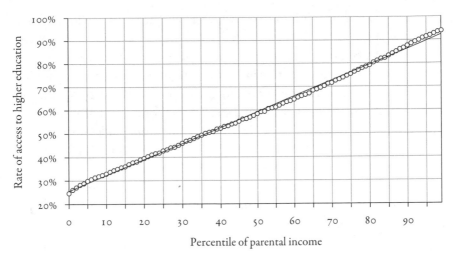

FIG. I.8. Parental income and university access, United States, 2014

Interpretation: In 2014, the rate of access to higher education (percentage of individuals age 19–21 enrolled in a college, university, or other institution of higher education) was barely 30 percent for children of the poorest 10 percent in the United States and 90 percent for the richest 10 percent. *Sources and series:* piketty.pse.ens.fr/ideology.

tion. The concentration of educational investment in elitist institutions is particularly extreme in the United States, where admissions procedures are opaque and public regulation is almost entirely lacking.

These results are striking because they illustrate the wide gap that separates official meritocratic pronouncements (which emphasize—theoretically and rhetorically, at any rate—equality of opportunity) from the realities facing the most disadvantaged students. Inequality of access to and financing of education is somewhat less extreme in Europe and Japan, and this may account for part of the extreme gap between top and bottom incomes in the United States. Nevertheless, educational inequality and absence of democratic transparency in this area are issues everywhere. And here again, as with rethinking private property, social democracy has failed.

The Return of Multiple Elites and the Difficulty of Forging an Egalitarian Coalition

In what follows we will try to understand the conditions under which egalitarian coalitions came to exist in the mid-twentieth century and why, after a period of success in reducing inequality, they ultimately stalled. We will also try to imagine the conditions under which new egalitarian coalitions might emerge today.

We must first be clear about one thing. The broadly social-democratic redistributive coalitions that arose in the mid-twentieth century were not just electoral or institutional or party coalitions but also intellectual and ideological. The battle was fought and won above all on the battleground of ideas. It was of course essential that those ideas found embodiment in political parties, whether explicitly social-democratic parties such as the Swedish SAP or the German SPD (which both occupied key positions in the 1920s)[14] or parties like Labour (which won an absolute majority in the United Kingdom in 1945) or the Democrats (who held the presidency in the United States from 1932 until 1952 under Roosevelt and then Truman). In France and elsewhere, moreover, one finds alliances of one kind or another between socialists and communists (who came to power in France, for example, in 1936 and 1945). Details aside, however, the fact remains that the real seizure of power was ideological and intellectual before it was political. In the period 1930–1980, even right-wing parties were influenced by ideas for reducing inequality and transforming legal, fiscal, and social systems. This transformation of politics depended not only on mobilizing (broadly) social-democratic coalitions but also on the involvement of civil society (including unions, activists, media, and intellectuals) and on a sweeping transformation of the dominant ideology, which throughout the long nineteenth century had been shaped by a quasi-religious theology of markets, inequality, and private property.

The most important factor in the emergence of this new coalition of ideas and new vision of the state's role was the discrediting of the system of private property and free markets. This began in the late nineteenth and early twentieth centuries owing to the enormous concentration of industrial wealth and the consequent sense of injustice; it picked up speed after World War I and the Great Depression. The existence of a communist countermodel in the Soviet Union also played a crucial role, not only by obliging reluctant conservatives to embrace an ambitious redistributive agenda but also by accelerating decol-

---

14. The SAP (Sveriges Socialdemokratiska Arbetareparti) first came to power in the early 1920s and ruled more or less continuously after 1932. The SPD (Sozialdemokratische Partei Deutschlands) was the party of Friedrich Ebert, the first president of the Weimar Republic. The party has usually been either in opposition or part of a governing coalition, especially during the long period of Christian Democratic domination between 1949 and 1966.

onization in Europe's empires and spurring the extension of civil rights in the United States.

When we look at the evolution of (broadly) social-democratic electorates after 1945, it is striking to see how similar developments were in Europe and the United States. In view of the very different histories of national party systems, it is by no means obvious why this should have been the case. Between 1950 and 1970, the Democratic Party's share of the vote in the United States was especially high among less educated voters with relatively low incomes and little if any wealth, whereas the Republican vote share was higher among the more highly educated with relatively high incomes and large fortunes. We find the same electoral structure in France, in almost identical proportions: between 1950 and 1970 the Socialist, Communist, and Radical parties attracted more votes among less educated, lower-income, and less wealthy voters and conversely for the parties of the center-right and right. This electoral structure began to change in the late 1960s and 1970s, and in the period 1980–2000 we find a noticeably different structure, once again almost identical in France and the United States: both the Democrats and the Socialist-Communist alliance began to attract voters who were better educated but not among the highest earners. This pattern did not last, however. In the US presidential election of 2016, not only the best educated but also the highest-income voters preferred the Democrats to the Republicans, thus completely reversing the social structure of the vote compared with the period 1950–1970 (Fig. I.9).

In other words, the decomposition of the left-right cleavage of the postwar era, on which the mid-twentieth-century reduction of inequality depended, has been a long time coming. To see it properly, we must view it in long-term historical perspective.

We find similar transformations (at least with respect to education levels) in the Labour vote in the United Kingdom and the social-democratic vote in various places in Europe.[15] Between 1950 and 1980 the (broadly) social-democratic vote corresponded to the workers' party; between 1990 and 2010 it mainly reflected the choice of the educated. Nevertheless, the wealthiest voters continued to be wary of social-democratic, workers, and socialist parties, including the Democratic Party in the United States (though to a dimin-

---

15. See Chaps. 14–16. One observes similar transformations by comparing not the top 10 percent and the bottom 90 percent (as we do in Fig. I.9) but rather the top 50 percent and the bottom 50 percent or, for that matter, any other division of the distribution of educational degrees, income, or wealth.

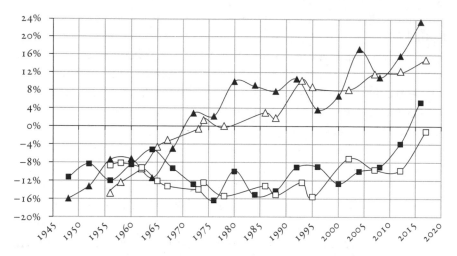

—▲— United States: difference between percentage of Democratic vote of the most highly educated 10 percent and the least educated 90 percent (after controls)

—△— France: difference between percentage of left-wing party vote of the most highly educated 10 percent and the least educated 90 percent (after controls)

—■— United States: difference between percentage of Democratic vote of the 10 percent with highest income and the 90 percent with lowest income (after controls)

—□— France: difference between percentage of left-wing party vote of the 10 percent with highest income and the 90 percent with lowest income (after controls)

FIG. I.9. Transformation of political and electoral conflict, 1945–2020: Emergence of a multiple-elites party system, or great reversal?

Interpretation: In the period 1950–1970 the vote for the Democratic Party in the United States and for the left-wing parties in France (Socialists, Communists, Radicals, Ecologists) was associated with less educated and lower-income voters; in the period 1980–2000, it became associated with more educated voters, and in the period 2010–2020 it has also become associated with higher-income voters, especially in the United States. *Sources and series:* piketty.pse.ens.fr/ideology.

ishing extent). The key point is that these different dimensions of social inequality (education, income, and wealth) have always been imperfectly correlated. In both periods one finds many people whose position in the educational hierarchy is higher than their position in the wealth hierarchy and vice versa.[16] What matters is the ability of a political party or coalition to integrate or differentiate the various dimensions of social inequality.

---

16. The correlation of education, income, and wealth does not appear to have changed substantially during the period under study. See Chap. 14.

Concretely, in the period 1950–1980 the various dimensions of social inequality were politically aligned. The people at the bottom of the social hierarchy on all three axes (education, income, and wealth) tended to vote for the same party or coalition. Standing at a lower position along several axes had a cumulative effect on a person's vote. Political conflict was therefore structured along class lines, in the sense that classes placed lower in the social hierarchy opposed classes placed higher, no matter what axis one chose to define their class (even though class identity is in practice highly complex and multidimensional, which is why forging majority coalitions is so complicated).

In the period 1980–2000, however, the various dimensions of social inequality ceased to line up with one another. The resulting division of the elite changed the structure of political conflict: one party or coalition attracts the votes of the more highly educated (the intellectual and cultural elite), while another draws the votes of the wealthiest and also (to some extent) of the highest income group (the commercial and financial elite). From this came many problems, including the fact that people without either an advanced degree, a large fortune, or a high income began to feel entirely left out, which may explain why voter turnout has collapsed in this group in recent decades in contrast to the period 1950–1970, when people in this group were as likely to vote as their better-off counterparts. If one wants to explain the rise of "populism" (a catch-all term frequently used by elites to discredit political movements they deem to be insufficiently under their control), it might not be a bad idea to begin by looking at the rise of "elitist" political parties. Note, too, that the modern multiple-elites regime bears a certain resemblance to the old trifunctional regime, in which the clerical elite and warrior elite counterbalanced each other, although the discourse of legitimation was obviously different in the distant past.

Rethinking Justice in Ownership, Education, and Immigration

We will attempt to delve in detail into the origins and implications of these changes in political cleavage structures and voting patterns after 1970. The story is complex, and one can analyze the relevant political changes as either a cause or a consequence of rising inequality. To deal with this in a totally satisfactory way would require drawing on a wider range of documents and research than I have been able to do in this book. On the one hand, one might argue that inequality increased because of the conservative revolution of the 1980s and the social and financial deregulation that followed, with a significant assist from the failure of social-democratic parties to devote sufficient thought to alternative ways of organizing the global economy and transcending the nation-state. As a result, the existing social-democratic parties and co-alitions gradually abandoned any real ambition to reduce inequality and redistribute wealth. Indeed, they themselves helped to promote greater fiscal competition and free movement of goods and capital in exchange for which they received nothing in the way of fiscal justice or greater social benefits. As a result, they forfeited the support of the least well-off voters and began to focus more and more on the better educated, the primary beneficiaries of globalization.

On the other hand, however, one might also argue that deep racial and ethno-religious divisions developed within the working class, first in the United States in the wake of the civil rights movement of the 1960s and later in Europe, as issues connected with immigration and postcolonialism gained prominence in the 1980s. Ultimately, these divisions led to the breakup of the egalitarian coalition that had prevailed from 1950 until 1980, as the white native-born working class succumbed to nativist xenophobia. In short, the first argument holds that the social-democratic parties abandoned the working class, while the second holds that it was the other way around.

Both arguments are partly correct, but if we compare many different national histories, we find that both can be subsumed in a more general argument, namely that the egalitarian social-democratic coalition of the postwar era proved incapable of revising and renewing its program and ideology. Instead of blaming either liberal globalization (which did not fall from the sky) or working-class racism (which is no more inevitable than elitist racism), we would do better to explore the ideological failures of the egalitarian coalition.

Prominent among those ideological failures was the inability to conceptualize or organize progressive taxation and redistribution at the transnational level. During the period of successful redistribution at the national level, social democrats largely avoided this issue. To date they have never really grappled with it even at the level of the European Union, much less globally. They also failed to grapple with the issue of ethnic diversity as it relates to redistribution—an issue that did not really arise prior to 1960, because people of different national, racial, or ethno-religious backgrounds seldom came into contact within national borders except in the context of colonial rule or conflict between states. Both ideological failures point to the same fundamental question: What defines the boundaries of the human community in terms of which collective life is organized, especially when it comes to reducing inequality and establishing norms of equality acceptable to a majority? As technological advances in transportation and communication bring formerly remote parts of the world into closer contact, the frame within which political action is imagined must be permanently rethought. The context of social justice must be explicitly global and transnational.

Furthermore, social democrats never really reconsidered the issue of just ownership after the collapse of communism. The postwar social-democratic compromise was built in haste, and issues such as progressive taxation, temporary ownership, circulation of ownership (for example, by means of a universal capital grant financed by a progressive tax on property and inheritances), power sharing in firms (via co-management or self-management), democratic budgeting, and public ownership were never explored as fully or systematically as they might have been.

When higher education ceased to be limited to a tiny elite, moreover, new issues of educational justice arose. Progressive educational policy was simple when it involved nothing more than allocating the resources necessary to ensure that all students would receive first primary and later secondary schooling. Expanding access to higher education then raised new problems. An ideology said to be based on equal opportunity quickly emerged, but its real purpose was to glorify the winners of the educational sweepstakes, with the result that educational resources were allocated in a particularly unequal and hypocritical fashion (Fig. I.8). The inability of social democrats to persuade the less well-off that they cared not only about elite institutions for their own children but also about schools for the rest helps to explain why social-democratic parties became parties of the educated elite. In view of the failure to develop a just and transparent set of educational policies, none of this is surprising.

In the final part of this book, I reflect on how we might use the lessons of history to achieve greater justice in ownership, education, and immigration. My conclusions should be taken for what they are: incomplete, tentative, and provisional. Together they point toward a form of participatory socialism and social federalism. One of the most important lessons of this book is the following: ideas and ideologies count in history, but unless they are set against the logic of events, with due attention to historical experimentation and concrete institutional practices (to say nothing of potentially violent crises), they are useless. One thing is certain: given the profound transformation of political cleavage structures and voting patterns since 1980, a new egalitarian coalition is unlikely to emerge in the absence of a radical redefinition of its intellectual, ideological and programmatic basis.

The Diversity of the World: The Indispensability of the Longue Durée

Before returning to these recent changes, this book begins with a lengthy detour in which I delve into the history of several different inequality regimes. Specifically, I look first at how premodern trifunctional societies were transformed into ownership societies and then at how contact with European ownership and colonialist societies influenced the development of non-European societies. I have already explained why this detour via the *longue durée* is necessary. It will allow us to explore the political and ideological diversity of inequality regimes that followed numerous different trajectories. Human beings have demonstrated great creativity in devising ways to justify and organize social inequality, and it would be wrong to view the resulting ideological and political constructs as mere veils intended only to conceal the perpetual domination of ruling elites. In fact, these constructs reflect struggles between contending social visions, each of which is to some extent sincere and plausible. From them we can therefore draw useful lessons. Large-scale social organization is never simple, and criticism of an existing regime is never enough to ensure that something better will replace it. The ideological constructs of the past must be taken seriously in part because they are not always more incoherent than those of the present and in part because our distance from them offers an opportunity for more objective analysis. We will also discover that many current debates have roots in the remote past: during the French Revolution, for example, people were already discussing progressive taxation and redistribution. We need to study this genealogy to gain a better understanding of how to deal with future conflicts.

Above all, a long detour through history is indispensable because the various regions of the world have only gradually come into contact with one another. For centuries most societies had little to do with foreigners. Trade in goods and ideas broke down barriers, and some states conquered others or established colonies on foreign soil. Only since the end of the Cold War and the era of decolonization have the various parts of the world become intimately intertwined, however, not only through financial and economic interactions but also to a greater degree through human and cultural exchange. Before 1960–1970, for example, many European countries had little contact with people from other continents or different religious backgrounds. The migrant flows of the postcolonial era changed this, and the effect on ideological and political conflict within Europe has been considerable. Other parts of the world such as India, the United States, Brazil, and South Africa have had longer experience with the mingling of populations that see themselves as radically different for religious, social, or religious reasons. To one degree or another they have dealt with the ensuing problems through compromise and intermarriage, yet hostility has in some cases proved to be persistent and difficult to overcome. Without studying such encounters and the inequality regimes that developed from them in historical perspective, we have no hope of imagining the next stages of this long shared history of interconnected human societies.

On the Complementarity of Natural Language and Mathematical Language

I next want to clarify a point about method. This book will rely primarily on natural language (about which there is nothing particularly natural). To a lesser degree I will also make use of the language of mathematics and statistics. For instance, I will frequently refer to deciles and percentiles when discussing inequality of income, wealth, or education. My intent is not to replace class warfare with war between the deciles. Social identities are always flexible and multidimensional. In each society various social groups use natural language to designate professions and occupations and identify the qualifications, expectations, and experiences associated with each. There is no substitute for natural language when it comes to expressing social identities or defining political ideologies. By the same token there is no substitute for natural language when it comes to doing research in social science or thinking about the just society. Those who believe that we will one day be able to rely on a mathematical formula, algorithm, or econometric model to determine the "socially optimal" level of inequality are destined to be disappointed. This will thankfully never happen. Only open, democratic deliberation, conducted in plain natural language (or rather in several natural languages—not a minor point), can promise the level of nuance and subtlety necessary to make choices of such magnitude.

Nevertheless, this book relies heavily on the language of mathematics, statistical series, graphs, and tables. These devices also play an important role in political deliberation and historical change. Once again, however, it bears repeating that the statistics, historical data, and other quantitative measures presented in this book are imperfect, provisional, tentative social constructs. I do not contend that "truth" is found only in numbers or certainty only in "facts." In my view, the primary purpose of statistics is to establish orders of magnitude and to compare different and perhaps remote periods, societies, and cultures as meaningfully as possible. Perfect comparison of societies remote in space and time is never possible. Despite the radical uniqueness of every society, however, it may not be unreasonable to attempt comparisons. It may make sense, for example, to compare the concentration of wealth in the United States in 2018 with that of France in 1914 or Britain in 1800.

To be sure, the conditions under which property rights were exercised were different in each case. The relevant legal, fiscal, and social systems differed in many ways, as did asset categories (land, buildings, financial assets, immaterial goods, and so on). Nevertheless, if one is aware of all these differences and never loses sight of the social and political conditions under which the source documents were constructed, comparison may still make sense. For instance, one can estimate the share of wealth held by the wealthiest 10 percent and the poorest 50 percent in each of these three societies. Historical statistics are also the best measure of our ignorance. Citing data always reveals the need for additional data, which usually cannot be found, and it is important to explain why it cannot. One can then be explicit about which comparisons are possible and which are not. In practice, some comparisons always make sense, even between societies that think of themselves as exceptional or as so radically different from others that learning from them is impossible. One of the main goals of social science research is to identify possible comparisons while excluding impossible ones.

Comparison is useful because it can extract lessons from different political experiences and historical paths, analyze the effects of different legal and fiscal systems, establish common norms of social and economic justice, and build institutions acceptable to the majority. Social scientists too often settle for saying that every statistic is a social construct. This is of course true, but it cannot be left at that, because to do so is to abandon key debates—on economic issues, for example—to others. It is fundamentally a conservative attitude or at any rate an attitude that betrays deep skepticism about the possibility of deriving lessons from imperfect historical sources.

Many historical processes of social and political emancipation have relied on statistical and mathematical constructs of one sort or another. For instance, it is difficult to organize a fair system of universal suffrage without the census data necessary to draw district boundaries in such a way as to ensure that each voter has identical weight. Mathematics can also help when it comes to defining rules for translating votes into decisions. Fiscal justice is impossible without tax schedules, which rely on well-defined rules instead of the discretionary judgments of the tax collector. Those rules are derived in turn from abstract theoretical concepts such as income and capital. These are difficult to define, but without them it is hard to get different social groups to negotiate the compromises needed to devise an acceptably fair fiscal system. In the future, people may come to realize that educational justice is impossible without similar concepts for measuring whether the public resources available to less favored groups are at least equivalent to those available to the favored (rather than markedly inferior, as is the case today in most countries). When used carefully and in moderation, the language of mathematics and statistics is an indispensable complement to natural language when it comes to combating intellectual nationalism and overcoming elite resistance.

Outline of the Book

The remainder of this book is divided into four parts comprising seventeen chapters. Part One, entitled "Inequality Regimes in History," consists of five chapters. Chapter 1 is a general introduction to what I call ternary (or trifunctional) societies, that is, societies comprising three functional groups (clergy, nobility, and third estate). Chapter 2 is devoted to European "societies of orders," based on an equilibrium between intellectual and warrior elites and on specific forms of ownership and power relations. Chapter 3 looks at the advent of ownership society, especially in the symbolic rupture of the French Revolution, which attempted to establish a radical division between property rights (theoretically open to all) and regalian rights (henceforth the monopoly of the state) but which came to grief over the issue of persistent inequality of wealth. Chapter 4 examines the development of a hyper-inegalitarian form of ownership society in nineteenth-century France (up to the eve of World War I). Chapter 5 studies European variants of the transition from trifunctional to proprietarian logics, focusing on the British and Swedish cases. This will illustrate the variety of possible trajectories as well as the importance of collective mobilizations and help us to understand the influence of political and ideological differences on the transformation of inequality regimes.

Part Two, entitled "Slave and Colonial Societies," consists of four chapters. Chapter 6 looks at slave society, the most extreme type of inequality regime. I focus particularly on the abolition of slavery in the nineteenth century and on the types of compensation offered to slaveowners. This will help us to appreciate the power of the quasi-sacred ownership regime that existed in this period, which has left its stamp on the world we live in today. Chapter 7 looks at the structure of inequality in postslavery colonial societies, which, though less extreme than the slave societies they supplanted, nevertheless also profoundly influenced the structure of today's inequality, both between and within countries. Chapters 8 and 9 examine the way in which non-European trifunctional societies were affected by contact with European colonial and proprietarian powers. I focus first on the case of India (where ancient status divisions proved unusually tenacious, partly because of their rigid codification by the British colonizers). I then take a broader Eurasian perspective, looking at China, Japan, and Iran.

Part Three, entitled "The Great Transformation of the Twentieth Century," has four chapters. Chapter 10 analyzes the collapse of ownership society in the wake of two world wars, the Great Depression, the communist challenge, and decolonization, combined with popular and ideological mobilizations (including the rise of trade unions and social democracy) that had been brewing since the late nineteenth century. The result was a type of society less unequal than the ownership society that preceded it. Chapter 11 looks at the achievements and limitations of postwar social democracy. Among social democracy's shortcomings were its failure to develop a more just idea of property, its inability to confront the challenge of inequality in higher education, and its lack of a theory of transnational redistribution. Chapter 12 considers the communist and postcommunist societies of Russia, China, and Eastern Europe, including the postcommunist contribution to the recent rise of inequality and turn to identity politics. Chapter 13 views the current global hypercapitalist inequality regime in historical perspective, with an emphasis on its inability to respond adequately to the two crises that are undermining it: the crisis of inequality and the environmental crisis.

Part Four, entitled "Rethinking the Dimensions of Political Conflict," consists of four chapters, in which I study the changing social structure of party electorates and political movements since the mid-twentieth century and speculate about changes yet to come. Chapter 14 looks at the historical conditions under which an egalitarian coalition first developed and later fell apart. In France the redistributive program of social democracy was convincing enough to draw support from working-class people of different backgrounds. Chapter 15 considers the disaggregation, gentrification, and "Brahminization" of postwar social democracy in the United States and United Kingdom and finds common structural causes in both countries. Chapter 16 extends the analysis to other Western democracies as well as to Eastern Europe, India, and Brazil. I also consider the emergence of a social-nativist trap in the first two decades of the twenty-first century. Today's identity politics is fueled, I argue, by the lack of a persuasive internationalist egalitarian platform—in other words, by the absence of a truly credible social federalism. Chapter 17 derives lessons from the historical experiences recounted in the previous chapters and envisions a participatory form of socialism for the present century. In particular, I consider a possible basis for a just property regime resting on two main pillars: first, authentic power sharing and voting rights within firms as steps beyond co-management and self-management and toward true social ownership, and second, a strongly progressive tax on property, the proceeds of which would finance capital grants to every young adult, thereby instituting a system of provisional ownership and permanent circulation of wealth. I also look into how educational and fiscal justice might be guaranteed by citizen oversight. Finally, I investigate what is necessary to ensure a just democracy and a just border system. The key issue here is how to reorganize the global economy along social federalist lines so as to allow the emergence of new forms of fiscal, social, and environmental solidarity, with the ultimate goal of substituting true global governance for the treaties that today mandate free movement of goods and capital.

Hurried readers might be tempted to turn directly to the final chapter and conclusion. Although I cannot stop them, I warn them that they may find it difficult to follow the argument without at least glancing at Parts One through Four. Others may feel that the material presented in Parts One and Two deals with such ancient history that they fail to grasp its relevance and therefore prefer to focus on Parts Three and Four. I have tried to begin each section and chapter with enough recapitulations and references to allow the book to be read in more than one way. Each reader is thus free to choose a path, even though the most logical sequence is to read the chapters in the order they are presented.

Only the principal sources and references are cited in the text and footnotes. Readers seeking more detailed information about the historical sources, bibliographic references, and methods used in this book are invited to consult the online technical appendix at http://piketty.pse.ens.fr/ideology.[17]

---

17. All statistical series, graphs, and tables in this book are also available online at http://piketty.pse.ens.fr/ideology.

INEQUALITY REGIMES
IN HISTORY

{ ONE }

Ternary Societies: Trifunctional Inequality

The purpose of Parts One and Two of this book is to set the history of inequality regimes in a long-term historical perspective. More specifically, we will look at the transition from the ternary and slave societies of the premodern era to the ownership and colonial societies of the nineteenth century. This was a complex process, which followed a number of different pathways. In Part One we look at European societies of orders and their transformation into ownership societies. Part Two will examine slave and colonial societies and at the way in which the evolution of trifunctional societies outside Europe was affected by contact with European powers. Part Three will analyze the twentieth-century crisis of ownership and colonial society precipitated by world war and the challenge of communism. In Part Four we will look at their regeneration and possible transformation in the postcolonial and neo-proprietarian world of the late twentieth and early twenty-first centuries.

The Trifunctional Logic: Clergy, Nobility, Third Estate

We begin our investigation by looking at what I call "ternary societies." The oldest and most common type of inequality regime, the ternary model has left a durable imprint on today's world. There is no way to study later political and ideological developments without first examining the ternary matrix that gave social inequality its initial shape and justification.

The simplest type of ternary society comprised three distinct social groups, each of which fulfilled an essential function of service to the community. These were the clergy, the nobility, and the third estate. The clergy was the religious and intellectual class. It was responsible for the spiritual leadership of the community, its values and education; it made sense of the community's history and future by providing necessary moral and intellectual norms and guideposts. The nobility was the military class. With its arms it provided security, protection, and stability, thus sparing the community the scourge of permanent chaos and uncontrolled violence. The third estate, the common people, did the work. Peasants, artisans, and merchants provided the food and clothing that allowed the entire community to thrive. Because each of these three groups fulfilled a specific function, ternary society can also be called trifunctional society. In practice, ternary societies were more complex and diverse. Each group could contain a number of subgroups, but the justification of this type of social organization generally referred to these three functions. In some cases, the formal political organization of society also invoked the same three functions.

The same general type of social organization could be found not only throughout Christian Europe down to the time of the French Revolution but also, in one form or another, in many non-European societies and in most religions, including Hinduism and both Shi'a and Sunni Islam. At one time anthropologists believed that the "tripartite" social systems found in Europe and India had a common Indo-European origin, traces of which could be seen in mythology and language.[1] More recent theories, still incomplete, suggest that tripartite social organization is actually far more general, thus casting doubt on the old idea of a single origin. The ternary pattern can be found in nearly all premodern societies throughout the world, including China and Japan. Many variants exist, however, and the differences between them are ultimately more interesting than the superficial similarities. Astonishment at what is taken to be intangible often reflects a certain political and social conservatism; historical reality is always various and changeable, full of unexpected possibilities and surprising and tenuous institutional experiments, unstable compromises, and abortive offshoots. To understand this reality and to anticipate future developments, we must analyze historical change as well as continuity. This is true not only for ternary societies but also for societies in general. It will therefore be useful to compare social dynamics observed over long periods in a variety of contexts, primarily in Europe and India but more generally in a comparative transnational perspective. This will be the task of this and subsequent chapters.

---

1. See esp. G. Dumézil, *Jupiter. Mars. Quirinus. Essai sur la conception indo-européenne de la société et les origines de Rome* (Gallimard, 1941); G. Dumézil, "Métiers et classes fonctionnelles chez divers peuples indo-européennes," *Annales. Économies, Sociétés, Civilisations,* 1958; G. Dumézil, *Mythe et épopée. L'idéologie des trois fonctions dans les épopées des peuples indo-européens* (Gallimard, 1968).

Ternary Societies and the Formation of the Modern State

Ternary societies differ from later historical forms in two important and closely related ways: first, the justification of inequality in terms of a trifunctional schema, and second, the fact that these premodern societies preceded the advent of the modern centralized states. In ternary societies political and economic powers were inextricably intertwined and initially exercised at the local level, often over a small territory, and in some cases with relatively loose ties to a more or less distant monarchical or imperial power. A few key institutions— village, rural community, castle, fortress, church, temple, monastery—defined the social order, which was highly decentralized, with limited coordination between different territories and centers of power. Rudimentary means of transportation meant that communication among dispersed power centers was difficult. Despite this decentralization of power, social relations of domination were nevertheless brutal, but the modalities and configurations were different from those found in modern centralized states.

In concrete terms, property rights and regalian functions in traditional ternary societies were inextricably intertwined with power relations at the local level. The two ruling classes—clergy and nobility—were of course propertied classes. They generally owned the majority (and sometimes nearly all) of the cultivatable land, which is the basis of economic and political power in all rural societies. In the case of the clergy, property was often held by ecclesiastical institutions (such as churches, temples, bishoprics, religious foundations, and monasteries), which existed in one form or another in Christian, Hindu, and Muslim regions. By contrast, noble property was generally held by individuals or, more commonly, associated with a noble lineage or title. Ownership was in some cases subject to entail or other restrictions intended to prevent dispersal of wealth and loss of rank.

In all cases the important point is that the property rights of clergy and nobility went hand in hand with essential regalian powers necessary for maintaining order and exercising military and police functions (which in theory were monopolized by the warrior nobility but could also be exercised on behalf of an ecclesiastical lord). Property rights also went hand in hand with judicial powers: justice was normally rendered in the name of the local lord, whether noble or religious. In medieval Europe and pre-colonial India, the masters of the land were also the masters of the people who worked the land, regardless of whether they were French seigneurs, English landlords, Spanish bishops, Indian Brahmins or Rajputs, or their equivalents elsewhere. They were endowed with both property rights and regalian rights of various and changing types.

Thus, in all premodern ternary societies, whether in Europe, India, or elsewhere, and regardless of the class (clerical or noble) to which the lord belonged, we find that power and property relations were very deeply intertwined at the local level. In their most extreme form this meant forced labor or serfdom, implying that the mobility of most if not all workers was strictly limited: workers were not free to leave one place to go work in another. In this sense they belonged to their noble or religious lord, even if the ownership relationship was of a different nature from the one we will study in the chapter devoted to slave societies.

Less extreme and potentially more benevolent forms of control also existed, and these could give rise to quasi-state formations at the local level, with the clergy and nobility sharing the leading roles in various ways. In addition to powers of police and justice, the most important forms of social control in traditional ternary societies included supervision and registration of births, deaths, and marriages. This was an essential function bearing on the perpetuation and regulation of the community; it was closely linked to religious ceremonies and rules pertaining to marriage and family life (especially in all things related to sexuality, paternal power, the role of women, and child-rearing). This function was generally the monopoly of the clerical class, and the relevant registers were kept in the churches or temples of the relevant religious authority.

The registration of transactions and contracts was another important function. It played a key role in the regulation of economic activity and property relations and could be exercised by either a noble or a religious lord, generally in association with the local judicial authority, which dealt with civil, commercial, and successoral* disputes. Other collective functions and services such as teaching and medical care (often rudimentary but sometimes more elaborate) also played important roles in traditional ternary societies; infrastructure such as mills, bridges, roads, and wells should also be mentioned. Note that the regalian powers exercised by the clergy and nobility were seen as the natural counterpart of the services those two orders rendered to the third—services having to do with security and spirituality and, more generally, with structuring the community. Everything fit together in trifunctional society: each group had its place in a structure of closely interrelated rights, duties, and powers at the local level.

To what extent did the rise of the modern centralized state spell the end of ternary societies? As we will see, the interactions between these two fundamental political-economic processes were too complex to be described in a mechanical, deterministic, or unidirectional fashion. In some cases, the trifunctional ideological scheme found durable support in the structures of the centralized state, redefining itself in such a way as to survive, for a time at any rate, in this new setting. Think, for instance, of the British House of Lords, a noble and clerical institution directly descended from medieval trifunctional society, which nevertheless played a central role in the government of the first global colonial empire through most of the nineteenth and into the twentieth century. Think, too, of Iran's Shi'ite clergy, which constitutionalized its role in the late-twentieth-century Islamic Republic with the creation of the Guardian Council and Assembly of Experts (an elected chamber reserved for clergy and charged with choosing the Supreme Leader). This historically unprecedented regime remains in place to this day.

The Delegitimation of Ternary Societies: Between Revolutions and Colonizations

Nevertheless, the advent of the modern state inevitably tends to undermine the trifunctional order and generally gives rise to rival ideological forms, such as the ideologies of ownership, colonialism, or communism. In the end these competitors usually replace or even eradicate the trifunctional scheme as the dominant ideology. Once the centralized state can guarantee the security of people and goods throughout a sizable territory by mobilizing its own administrative personnel (police, soldiers, and officials) without drawing on the old warrior nobility, the legitimacy of the nobility as the guarantor of order and security will obviously be greatly diminished. By the same token, once civil institutions, schools, and universities capable of educating individuals and producing new knowledge and wisdom come into being under the aegis of new networks of teachers, intellectuals, physicians, scientists, and philosophers without ties to the old clerical class, the legitimacy of the clergy as the spiritual guide of the community will also be seriously impaired.

The delegitimation of the old noble and clerical classes can be quite gradual, in some cases unfolding over several centuries. In many European countries (such as the United Kingdom and Sweden, to which I will return), the transformation of the society of orders into an ownership society took quite a long time, beginning in the sixteenth century (or even earlier) and ending only in the first two decades of the twentieth century. Furthermore, the process is still not complete, since traces of trifunctionalism persist to this day, if only in the monarchical institutions that still survive in several Western European states, preserving largely symbolic vestiges of noble and clerical power (the British House of Lords being one example).[2]

There have also been phases of rapid acceleration, when new ideologies and associated state structures worked together to transform, radically and deliberately, old ternary societies. We will be taking a closer look at one such case, the French Revolution, which is one of the most emblematic examples, as well as the best documented. Following the abolition of the "privileges" of the nobility and clergy on the night of August 4, 1789, revolutionary assemblies and their associated administrations and tribunals were obliged to define precisely what the word "privilege" meant. Within a very short period of time it became necessary to draw a clear line between what the revolutionary legislators regarded as the legitimate exercise of property rights (including situations in which those rights were exercised by a formerly "privileged" individual, who may have acquired and solidified them in dubious circumstances) and what they considered to be illegitimate appropriations of outmoded local regalian powers (henceforth reserved exclusively for the central state). Because property and regalian rights in practice were so inextricably intertwined, this was a difficult exercise. By studying this period we can gain a better understanding of how these rights and powers were interconnected in traditional ternary societies, especially European societies of orders.

We will also look closely at a very different but equally instructive historical episode involving British efforts to understand and transform the trifunctional structure they found when they colonized India. We will focus in particular on caste censuses conducted between 1871 and 1941. What happened there was in a sense the opposite of what happened in the French Revolution: in India, a foreign power sought to reconfigure a traditional ternary society and disrupt an ongoing native process of state building and social transformation. By comparing these two very different episodes (along with other transitions in which the post-ternary and postcolonial logics were combined, as in China,

---

2. In 2004, on the eve of its enlargement through incorporation of the formerly communist states of Eastern Europe (all of which became republics despite a few attempts to restore monarchy after the fall of communism), the European Union consisted of fifteen member states, seven of which were parliamentary monarchies (Belgium, Denmark, Spain, Luxembourg, the Netherlands, the United Kingdom, and Sweden) and eight of which were republics (Germany, Austria, Italy, Ireland, Finland, France, Greece, and Portugal).

Japan, and Iran), we will gain a better understanding of what trajectories were possible and what mechanisms were at work.

On Ternary Societies Today

Before proceeding further, however, I need to answer an obvious question: Apart from historical interest, why study ternary societies? Some readers might be tempted to think that these relics of the distant past are of little use for understanding the modern world. With their strict status differences, aren't these societies diametrically opposed to modern meritocratic and democratic societies, which claim to offer equal access to every occupation—that is, both social fluidity and intergenerational mobility? It would be a serious mistake, however, to ignore ternary society, for at least two reasons. First, the structure of inequality in premodern ternary societies is less radically different from the structure of inequality in modern societies than is sometimes imagined. Second and more importantly, the conditions under which trifunctional society came to an end varied widely by country, region, religious context, and colonial or postcolonial circumstances, and we see indelible traces of these differences in the contemporary world.

To begin with, although rigid status structures were the norm in trifunctional society, mobility between classes was never totally absent, as in modern societies. We will discover, for example, that the size and resources of the clerical, noble, and common classes varied widely in time and space, largely due to variations in the rules of membership and marital strategies adopted by the dominant groups, some of which were more open, others less so. Institutions also mattered, as did the relative power of different groups. By the eve of the French Revolution, the two dominant classes (clergy and nobility) accounted for just over 2 percent of the adult male population, compared with 5 percent two centuries earlier. They accounted for roughly 11 percent of the population of Spain in the eighteenth century and more than 10 percent for the two *varnas* corresponding to the clerical and warrior classes—Brahmins and Kshatriyas—in nineteenth-century India (the figure rises to 20 percent if we included the other high castes). These figures reflect very different human, economic, and political realities (Fig. I.1). In other words, the boundaries dividing the three classes of ternary society were not fixed; they were subject to continual negotiation and conflict, which could radically alter their location. Note, too, that in terms of the size of the two top classes, Spain resembles India more closely than France. This suggests, perhaps, that the radical contrasts that are sometimes

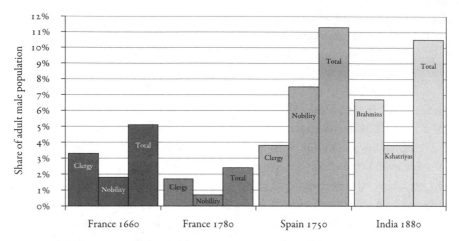

FIG. 1.1. The structure of ternary societies: Europe-India, 1660–1880

Interpretation: In 1660, the clergy accounted for 3.3 percent of the adult male population in France and the nobility for 1.8 percent, for a total of 5.1 percent for the two dominant classes of trifunctional society. In 1880, the Brahmins (the ancient priest class, as measured by the British colonial census) accounted for roughly 6.7 percent of the adult male population in India, and the Kshatriyas (ancient warrior class) for roughly 3.8 percent, for a total of 10.5 percent for the two dominant classes. *Sources and series:* piketty.pse.ens.fr/ideology.

said to exist between civilizations, cultures, and religions (when, for instance, Westerners remark on the oddity of India's caste system or take it to be a symbol of oriental despotism) are actually less important than the social, political, and institutional processes by which social structures are transformed.

We will also discover that estimates of the size of the three classes are themselves complex social and political constructs. They are often the result of attempts by emergent state authorities (absolute monarchies or colonial empires) to study the clergy and nobility or to conduct a census of the colonized population and its constituent subgroups. These efforts yield knowledge but are at the same time political acts in service of social domination. The categories used and the information generated tell us as much about the political intentions of the study's authors as about the structure of the society under study. This is not to say that there is nothing to be learned from such studies—quite the contrary. Provided one takes the time to contextualize and analyze the results, these studies are invaluable sources for understanding conflicts, changes, and ruptures taking place in societies that should not be seen as static or stagnant or more different from one another than they really are.

Ternary societies often generated a variety of theories concerning the real or imagined ethnic origins of dominant and dominated groups. In France, for example, the nobility was said to be of Frankish origin, the people Gallo-Roman; in England, the nobility was reputedly of Norman descent, the people Anglo-Saxon; and in India, nobles were said to be of Aryan origin, the commoners Dravidian. These theories were used sometimes to legitimize, at other times to delegitimize, the existing system of domination. One sees this as well in colonial societies, which liked nothing so much as to radically differentiate between colonizers and colonized. The latter were assigned an identity that set them apart from European modernity, which was characterized as dynamic and mobile. Nevertheless, the historical evidence suggests that classes mixed to such a degree that any supposed ethnic differences disappeared almost entirely within a few generations. Social mobility in ternary societies was probably less significant quantitatively than in today's societies, although it is hard to make precise comparisons. One can find any number of examples to the contrary, where new elites and nobilities arose in both India and Europe. Ternary ideology found ways to legitimate them after the fact—showing that it could be quite flexible. In any case, the difference was one of degree rather than principle and should be studied as such. In all trifunctional societies, including those in which clerical status was theoretically hereditary, one finds clerics who were born into either of the two other classes, commoners who were ennobled for their feats of arms or other talents and achievements, clerics who took up arms, and so on. Although social fluidity was not the norm, it was never entirely absent. Social identities and class divisions were matters of negotiation and dispute in ternary societies as in others.

On the Justification of Inequality in Ternary Societies

In general, it is wrong to think that ternary societies were intrinsically unjust, despotic, and arbitrary and therefore radically different from modern meritocratic societies, said to be harmonious and just. All societies have two essential needs—meaning and security. This is true in particular of less developed societies, where the territory is fragmented, communication difficult, instability chronic, and existence precarious. Pillage, mayhem, and disease are constant threats. If religious and military groups can provide credible responses to these needs by supplying institutions and ideologies adapted to their time and place, it should come as no surprise that trifunctional order emerges and is accepted as legitimate by the people. The clergy provides meaning by developing a narrative of the community's origins and future, while the military defines the scope of legitimate violence and provides security for people and goods. Why would anyone risk everything to attack powers that provide material and spiritual security without knowing what would replace them? So impenetrable are the mysteries of politics and of the ideal social organization, and so extreme the uncertainty about how to achieve the ideal in practice, that any government offering a tested model of stability based on a simple and intelligible division of these two major social functions is likely to succeed.

Success obviously does not require consensus as to the exact distribution of power and resources among the three groups. The trifunctional schema is not an idealist rational discourse proposing a clearly defined theory of justice open to deliberation. It is authoritarian, hierarchical, and violently inegalitarian. It allows religious and military elites to assert their dominance, often in shameless, brutal, and excessive fashion. In ternary societies it is not uncommon for clergy and nobility to press their advantage and overestimate their coercive power; this can lead to rebellion and ultimately to their transformation or overthrow. My point is simply that the trifunctional justification of inequality that one finds in ternary societies—namely, the idea that each of the three social groups fulfills a specific function and that this tripartite division of labor benefits the entire community—must enjoy a minimum degree of plausibility if the system is to endure. In ternary or any other kind of society, an inequality regime can persist only through a complex combination of coercion and consent. Pure coercion is not enough: the social model championed by the dominant groups must elicit from the population (or a significant portion of it) a minimum level of adhesion. Political leadership always requires some level of moral and intellectual leadership, which depends in turn on a credible theory of the public good or general interest.[3] This is probably the most important thing that trifunctional societies share with the societies that came after them.

What distinguishes ternary societies is the specific way they justify inequality: each social group fulfills a function the other groups cannot do

---

3. The same comment has often been applied to systems of global domination: the dominant power, whether European in the nineteenth century or American in the twentieth, has always needed a credible narrative to explain why the Pax Britannica or Pax Americana served the general interest. This is not to say that the narrative has to be entirely convincing. But this way of looking at things can help us to understand how the existing system of domination can ultimately be replaced. See esp. I. Wallerstein, *The Modern World System* (Academic Press, 1974–1988), and G. Arrighi, *The Long Twentieth Century: Money, Power and the Origins of Our Time* (Verso, 1994).

without; each performs a vital service, just as the various parts of the human body do. The bodily metaphor frequently appears in theoretical treatises on trifunctional society: for instance, in the *Manusmriti,* a north Indian legal and political text dating from the second century BCE, more than a millennium before the first Christian texts dealing with the ternary schema appeared in medieval Europe. The metaphor assigns each group a place in a coherent whole: the dominated group is usually compared to the feet or legs, while dominant groups correspond to the head and arms. These analogies may not be very flattering to the dominated, but at least they are recognized as performing a useful function in service of the community.

This mode of justification deserves to be studied for what it is. It is especially important to pay attention to the conditions under which it was transformed and supplanted and to compare it with modern justifications of inequality, which sometimes resemble it in certain ways even if the functions have evolved and equality of access to various occupations is now proclaimed as a cardinal principle (while avoiding the question of whether equal access is real or theoretical). The political regimes that succeeded ternary society have made it their business to denigrate it, as is only natural. Think, for example, of the way the nineteenth-century French bourgeoisie criticized the nobility of the Ancien Régime or of the way British colonizers spoke of Indian Brahmins. Those discourses sought to justify other systems of inequality and domination, systems that did not always treat the dominated groups any better. These too call for further investigation.

Divided Elites, United People?

Why begin our inquiry with the study of ternary societies in their many variants and manifold transformations? The answer is simple: however different ternary societies may be from modern ones, the historical trajectories and transitions that led to their disappearance have left an indelible stamp on the world we live in. We will discover, in particular, that the main differences among ternary societies derived from the nature of their dominant political and religious ideologies, especially in regard to two key issues: the division of the elites, which elites themselves more or less embraced, and the real or imagined unity of the people.

The first issue involved the hierarchy and complementarity of the two dominant groups, the clergy and nobility. In most European societies of orders, including Ancien Régime France, the first order was officially the clergy, and the nobility had to settle for second place in the protocol of processions. But who really exercised supreme power in ternary societies, and how was the co-existence of the spiritual power of the clergy and the temporal power of the nobility organized? The question is by no means banal. Different answers were given in different times and places.

This first issue was closely associated with another, namely, how the celibacy or non-celibacy of priests affected the reproduction of the clergy as a distinct social group. In Hinduism the clergy could reproduce itself and therefore constituted a true hereditary class: the Brahmins, clerical intellectuals who in practice often occupied a politically and economically dominant position vis-à-vis the Kshatriyas, or warrior nobility. This we will need to understand. The clergy could also reproduce itself in Islam, both Shi'ite and Sunni; the Shi'ite clergy was a true hereditary class, organized and powerful, with many clerics heading local quasi-states and a few ruling the central state itself. Clerics could also reproduce in Judaism and most other religions. The one notable exception was Christianity (at least in its modern Roman Catholic version), where the clergy needed to constantly replenish its ranks by drawing on the two other groups (in practice, the high clergy drew from the nobility and the low clergy from the third estate). For this reason, Europe is a very special case in the long history of ternary societies and of inequality regimes in general, which may help to explain certain aspects of the subsequent European trajectory, especially its economic-financial ideology and juridical organization. In Part Four we will also see that competition between different types of elites (clerical or warrior) and different discourses of legitimacy can shed light on the conflict between intellectual and business elites that one finds in modern political systems, even if the nature of that competition today is very different from that of the trifunctional era.

A second issue has to do with whether, on the one hand, all statuses within the class of workers are more or less the same, or, on the other hand, different forms of servile labor (serfdom, slavery) persist. The importance ascribed to occupational identities and corporations in the process of central state formation and traditional religious ideology is also crucial. In theory, ternary society is based on the idea that all workers belong to the same class and share the same status and rank. In practice, things are often much more complex. In India, for example, there are persistent inequalities between groups stemming from the lower castes (Dalits or untouchables) and those stemming from middle castes (ex-Shudras, former proletarian or servile laborers, less discriminated against than the Dalits), a distinction that still influences social and political conflict in India today. In Europe, the unification of worker statuses and the gradual extinction of serfdom took nearly a millennium, beginning around the year 1000 and continuing until the end of the nineteenth century in the eastern part of the continent. Traces of this process survive today in the form of certain discriminatory attitudes, the Roma being a case in point. Most importantly, Euro-American proprietarian modernity went hand in hand with unprecedented expansion of slavery and colonialism, which has given rise to persistent racial inequality in the United States and inequality between native and postcolonial immigrant populations in Europe; the modalities are different but nevertheless comparable.

To recapitulate: inequalities linked to different statuses and ethno-religious origins, whether real or perceived, continue to play a key role in modern inequality. The meritocratic fantasy that one often hears is not the whole story—far from it. To understand this key dimension of modern inequality, it is best to begin by studying traditional ternary societies and their variants. The goal is to understand how those societies were gradually transformed, starting in the eighteenth century, into a complex mix of ownership societies (in which status and ethno-religious differences are theoretically effaced but differences of income and wealth can attain unbelievable levels) and slave, colonial, or postcolonial societies (in which status and ethno-religious differences play a central role, potentially in conjunction with significant income and wealth inequalities). More generally, the study of the diversity of post-ternary trajectories is essential for understanding the role of religious institutions and ideologies in structuring modern societies, especially by way of their influence on the educational system and, more broadly, on the regulation and representation of social inequalities.

Ternary Societies and State Formation: Europe, India, China, Iran

This book will not provide a complete history of ternary society, in part because to do so would take many volumes and in part because the primary sources that would be needed are not yet available and in some respects never will be, precisely because ternary societies were by nature extremely decentralized and left few records. The purpose of this and subsequent chapters is more modest: namely, to map out what such a comparative global history might look like, focusing on those aspects most important for the analysis of the subsequent development of modern inequality regimes.

In the remainder of Part One, I will take a more detailed look at the case of France and other European countries. The French case is emblematic because the Revolution of 1789 marked a particularly clear rupture with the Ancien Régime, which can be taken as a paradigmatic example of ternary society, while the bourgeois society that flourished in France in the nineteenth century can be taken as the archetype of the ownership society, the major historical form that succeeded ternary society in a number of countries. The expression "third estate" comes from France and clearly conveys the idea of a society divided into three classes. By studying the French trajectory and comparing it with other European and non-European trajectories, we can also learn a great deal about the respective roles of revolutionary processes and longer-term trends (having to do with state formation and the evolution of socioeconomic structures) in the transformation of ternary societies. The British and Swedish cases offer a particularly useful counterpoint: both countries remain monarchies to this day, and the transformation from ternary to successor society was more gradual there than in France. We will discover, however, that moments of rupture played just as crucial a role in those countries as in France, and that their two trajectories also illustrate the multiplicity and diversity of possible switch points* within the same overall pattern of evolution.

In Part Two I will analyze non-European variants of ternary (and sometimes quaternary) societies. I am particularly interested in how their evolution was affected by the slave and colonial systems of domination established by European powers. I focus especially on India, where the stigmata of the old ternary divisions remain exceptionally salient, despite the desire of successive governments to eliminate them after India achieved its independence in 1947. India is the ideal place to observe the results of the violent encounter between a premodern ternary civilization, the oldest in the world, and British colonialism—an encounter that had a tremendous impact on state formation and social transformation in the Indian subcontinent. Furthermore, comparing India with China and Japan will suggest several hypotheses concerning possible postternary trajectories. Finally, I will touch on the case of Iran, where the establishment of the Islamic Republic in 1979 offers a striking example of late constitutionalization and persistent clerical power. With these lessons in mind, we can then move on to Part Three, where I analyze the collapse of ownership society in the wake of twentieth-century crises, as well as its possible regeneration in the neo-proprietarian and postcolonial world of the late twentieth and early twenty-first centuries.

TWO

European Societies of Orders: Power and Property

In this chapter we will begin the study of ternary societies and their transformation by looking at European societies of orders, especially France. The goal will be to gain a better understanding of the nature of power and property relations among the three classes that constituted these tripartite societies. We will first examine how the trifunctional order was generally justified in the Middle Ages. What we will find is that ternary inequality discourse promoted a specific idea of political and social equilibrium between two a priori plausible forms of legitimacy: that of the intellectual and religious elite on the one hand and of the warrior and military elite on the other. Both were seen as indispensable to the perpetuation of the social order and of society as such.

Then we will study how the size and resources of the noble and ecclesiastical classes evolved in the Ancien Régime, and how trifunctional ideology was embodied in sophisticated modes of property relations and economic regulation. In particular, we will look at the role of the Catholic Church as a property-owning organization and author of economic, financial, familial, and educational norms. These lessons will prove useful in subsequent chapters, when we come to study the conditions under which ternary societies were transformed into ownership societies.

Societies of Orders: A Balance of Powers?

Many medieval European texts, the earliest of which date back to the year 1000, describe and theorize the division of society into three orders. For example, in the late tenth and early eleventh centuries, Archbishop Wolfsan of York (in northern England) and Bishop Adalbéron of Laon (in northern France) explained that Christian society was divided into three groups: *oratores* (those who pray, that is, the clergy), *bellatores* (those who fight, the nobility), and *laboratores* (those who work, usually by tilling the soil—the third estate).

To properly understand the alternative discourses these authors were challenging, one needs to be aware of Christian society's need in this period for stability and, especially, its fear of rebellion. The primary goal was to justify existing social hierarchies so that the *laboratores* would accept their lot and understand that, as good Christians here below, they were obliged to respect the ternary order and therefore the authority of the clergy and nobility. Many sources allude to the harshness of the life of toil, but this harshness was deemed necessary for the survival of the other two orders and of society itself. The sources also contain vivid descriptions of the corporal punishments meted out to rebels. Take, for instance, the monk Guillaume de Jumièges's mid-eleventh-century account of a revolt that broke out in Normandy: "Without waiting for orders, Count Raoul immediately took all the peasants into custody, had their hands and feet cut off, and returned them, powerless, to their families. From then on their relatives refrained from such acts, and the fear of enduring an even worse fate gave them still greater pause. . . . The peasants, educated by the experience, abandoned their assemblies and hastily returned to their plows."[1]

Peasants were not the only audience; the ternary discourse was also addressed to elites. Bishop Adalbéron of Laon sought to persuade kings and nobles to govern wisely and prudently, which meant heeding the counsel of clerics (that is, members of the secular or regular clergy, who in addition to their strictly religious functions also served princes in numerous other essential capacities as men of letters, scribes, ambassadors, accountants, physicians, and so on).[2] In one of his texts, Adalbéron described a strange procession in which the world was stood on its head: peasants wearing crowns led the way, followed by king, warriors, monks, and bishops walking naked behind a plow. The point was to show what might happen if the king were to allow his warriors free rein,

---

1. Text translated and quoted in M. Arnoux, *Le temps des laboureurs* (Albin Michel, 2012), p. 116.
2. The secular clergy—those who lived "in the world" among the laity, to whom they administered or assisted in administering the sacraments—included priests, curates, canons, vicars, and so on. The regular clergy lived according to a "rule" in a religious community or monastic order (including monasteries, abbeys, convents, priories, and so on). Members of the regular clergy might or might not be ordained priests (ordination was required to administer the sacraments). Unless otherwise specified, I use the terms "clergy" and "clerics" in the broadest possible sense, including both the secular and regular clergy.

thereby upsetting the equilibrium of the three orders on which social stability depended.[3]

Interestingly, Adalbéron also explicitly addressed members of his own order, the clergy, and in particular Cluniac monks, who were tempted in the early eleventh century to take up arms and assert their military might against lay warriors. Stopping clerics from bearing arms was a recurrent theme in medieval texts; members of the monastic orders were particularly rambunctious. In short, ternary discourse was more complex and subtle than it might seem: it sought both to pacify the elites and to unify the people. The goal was not simply to persuade the dominated class to accept its lot; it was also to persuade the elites to accept their division into two distinct groups, the clerical and intellectual class on one side and the warrior and noble class on the other, with each group sticking strictly to its assigned role. Warriors were enjoined to behave like good Christians and heed the wise counsel of the clerics, who in turn were admonished not to take themselves for warriors. The aim was a balance of power, with the prerogatives of each group self-limited; in practice this could not be taken for granted.

Recent historiography has stressed the importance of the trifunctional ideology in the slow process of unifying all workers in a single status. To provide a theory of the society of orders meant more than simply justifying the authority of the first two orders over the third. The theory also affirmed the equal dignity of all workers belonging to the third order, which made it necessary to challenge slavery and serfdom, at least up to a point. For the historian Mathieu Arnoux, the trifunctional schema thus began the process of ending forced labor and uniting all workers in a single order, which in turn paved the way for the impressive demographic growth of the period 1000–1350. The laborers who tilled the soil and cleared the land worked harder and became more productive, Arnoux argues, when they were at last honored and celebrated as free laborers rather than despised as an inferior and partly servile class.[4] From literary and ecclesiastical texts we know that slavery was still quite prevalent in Western Europe in the year 1000. At the end of the eleventh century, slaves and

---

3. See G. Duby, *The Three Orders: Feudal Society Imagined,* trans. A. Goldhammer (University of Chicago Press, 1980); and J. Le Goff, "Les trois fonctions indo-européennes, l'historien et l'Europe féodale," *Annales: Économies, sociétés, civilisations,* 1979, p. 1199.

4. M. Arnoux, *Le temps des laboureurs. Travail, ordre social et croissance en Europe (11e–14e siècle)* (Albin Michel, 2012).

serfs still accounted for a significant part of the population of England and France.[5] By 1350, however, only a residue of slavery remained in Western Europe, and serfdom seems to have virtually disappeared, at least in its harshest forms.[6] Between 1000 and 1350, as the discourse celebrating the three orders spread, there gradually emerged a clearer recognition of the legal personhood of workers, including civil and personal rights as well as the right to own property and move about.

For Arnoux, the promotion of free labor was thus well under way before the Great Plague of 1347–1352 and the demographic slowdown of 1350–1450. This chronological point is important, because scarcity of labor after the Great Plague is often cited as the reason why serfdom ended in Western Europe (and sometimes, notwithstanding the inconsistency, to explain its persistence in the east as well).[7] Arnoux instead emphasizes political and ideological factors, especially the trifunctional schema. He also points to specific institutions that encouraged productive cooperation (such as fallowing, tithes, markets, and mills). Cooperation was made possible by new alliances among the three classes of ternary society, alliances that involved workers (the true silent artisans of this labor revolution), ecclesiastical organizations (the tithe paid to the clergy financed communal grain storage, the first schools, and assistance to the needy),

---

5. The servile population (slaves and serfs combined) represented 10–25 percent of the population of English counties in 1086 according to the *Domesday Book,* an inventory of English property established at the end of the reign of William the Conqueror. See Arnoux, *Le temps des laboureurs,* pp. 67–68. See also S. Victor, *Les Fils de Canaan. L'esclavage au Moyen-Age* (Vendemiaire, 2019).

6. In practice, there was a continuum of forms of labor ranging from slavery and serfdom to free labor; precise numbers are therefore impossible. I will return to the question of definitions in Chapter 6, which is devoted to slave society.

7. See, for example, R. Brenner, "Agrarian class structure and economic development in pre-industrial Europe," *Past and Present,* 1976; T. Aston and C. Philpin, *The Brenner Debate* (Cambridge University Press, 1985). In 1959 the Polish historian Marian Malowist suggested that the apparent intensification of serfdom in the east (especially in the Baltic countries) after the Great Plague could be explained by an increase in grain exports to the west. For an overview of this debate, see M. Cerman, *Villagers and Lords in Eastern Europe 1300–1800* (Palgrave, 2012). See also T. Raster, *Serfs and the Market: Second Serfdom and the East-West Goods Exchange, 1579–1857* (Paris School of Economics, 2019). Recent work has also shown that serfdom intensified in Western Europe in the fourteenth century, for example, on estates belonging to the abbey of Saint-Claude (a large ecclesiastical seigneurie in the Jura). See V. Carriol, *Les serfs de Saint-Claude. Etude sur la condition servile au Moyen-âge* (Presses Universitaires de Rennes, 2009).

and lords (who played a part in the development and regulation of water mills and the expansion of agriculture). Crises notwithstanding, these mutually reinforcing processes may have contributed to a significant increase of agricultural output and population in Western Europe in the period 1000–1500. Progress in this period left an indelible imprint on the landscape, as forests were cut down to make way for new plantings. All of this coincided with the gradual end of servile labor.[8]

Trifunctional Order, the Promotion of Free Labor, and the Fate of Europe

Other medieval historians had already underscored the historic role of trifunctional ideology in the unification of worker statuses. For instance, Jacques Le Goff has argued that if the trifunctional schema was no longer convincing in the eighteenth century, it was because it had fallen victim to its own success. From 1000 to 1789 the theory of the three orders promoted the value of labor. With its historical task accomplished, the ternary ideology could disappear to make room for more ambitious egalitarian ideologies.[9] Arnoux takes this argument even further. He sees the trifunctional ideology and the European labor unification process as the main reasons why Latin Christendom, which in 1000 had seemed to be under attack on all sides (by the Vikings, Saracens, and Hungarians) and weaker than other political-religious entities (such as the Byzantine Empire and the Muslim Arab world), had by 1450–1500 revived to the point where it stood on the brink of world conquest, with a large, young, and dynamic population and an agriculture productive enough to

---

8. Available estimates suggest that the population of Western Europe more than doubled between 1000 and 1500, from around 20 million to nearly 50 million. The population of what is today's France rose from 6 million to 15 million; of today's United Kingdom from 2 million to 4.5 million; of today's Germany from 4 million to 12 million; and of today's Italy from 5 million to 11 million. This marked a sharp break with the previous centuries: the population of Western Europe appears to have all but stagnated from the year 0 to 1000 at around 20 million. Most of the increase between 1000 and 1500 seems to have occurred between 1000 and 1350. The Great Plague of 1347–1352 reduced the population by about a third, and it took nearly a century (1350–1450) to overcome that loss and return to a clear upward trend in the period 1450–1500. See the online appendix.

9. Le Goff, "Les trois fonctions indo-européennes, l'historien et l'Europe féodale."

sustain both the early stages of urbanization and the military and maritime adventures to come.[10]

Unfortunately, the quality of the available data is not sufficient to resolve the issue, and some of these hypotheses may well be based on a rather too rosy vision of the mutually beneficial cooperation that the ternary ideology supposedly made possible in medieval Europe. Many other factors contributed to the specificity of the European trajectory. Nevertheless, the cited works deserve full credit for insisting on the complexity of the issues surrounding the trifunctional schema and for clarifying the variety of political and ideological positions with which it was associated over its lengthy history.

Take, for example, Abbé Sieyès, a member of the clergy who was nevertheless elected as a representative of the third estate in the Estates General and who became well known for the pamphlet he published in January 1789, which began with these famous words: "What is the Third Estate? Everything. What has it been in the political order to date? Nothing. What does it want? To become something." After an introductory blast denouncing the wrongs of the French nobility, which he compared "to the castes of the Greater Indies and ancient Egypt" (although Sieyès does not elaborate on the comparison, he clearly did not intend it as a compliment), he set forth his principal demand: that the three orders which King Louis XVI had just convoked to a meeting in Versailles in April 1789 be allowed to sit together, with as many votes for the third estate as for the two other orders combined (in other words, the third estate would get 50 percent of the votes). This was a revolutionary demand, since the normal practice was for each of the three orders to meet and vote separately, which guaranteed that the privileged orders would have two votes against one for the third estate in case of disagreement. For Sieyès it was unacceptable for the privileged orders to enjoy a guaranteed majority, given that according to his estimates, the third estate represented 98–99 percent of the total population of France. Note, however, that he was willing to settle, for the time being, at any rate, for just 50 percent of the votes. Ultimately, in the heat of events, it was at his behest that the representatives of the third estate proposed in June 1789 that the two other orders join them to form a "National Assembly." A few representatives of the clergy and nobility accepted this proposition, and it was this assembly, consisting primarily of representatives of the third estate, that seized control of the Revolution and voted on the night of August 4, 1789, to abolish the "privileges" of the other two orders.

---

10. Arnoux, *Le temps des laboureurs*, pp. 9–13.

A few months later, however, Sieyès expressed deep disagreement with the way this historic vote had been applied in practice. In particular, he protested the nationalization of clerical property and the abolition of the ecclesiastical tithe *(dîme)*. In Ancien Régime France, the tithe was a tax on agricultural production and animals, whose rate varied according to the crop and local custom; generally it amounted to 8–10 percent of the value of the harvest and was usually paid in kind. The tithe applied to all land, including in theory noble land (unlike the *taille*, a royal tax from which nobles were exempt), and its proceeds went directly to ecclesiastical organizations, with complex rules governing the precise allocation to parishes, bishoprics, and monasteries. The origins of the tithe were very old: it gradually supplanted voluntary contributions that Christians used to make to the Church as far back as the early Middle Ages. With support from the Carolingian monarchy, these voluntary contributions were transformed in the eighth century into a legally obligatory tax. Subsequent dynasties reaffirmed support for the tax, thus sealing the compact between church and crown and cementing a firm alliance between clergy and nobility.[11] Along with the income generated by church property, the tithe was the main source of financing for ecclesiastical institutions and clerical emoluments. It was above all the tithe that transformed the Church into a de facto state with the means to regulate social relations and fulfill leadership functions that were at once spiritual, social, educational, and moral.

For Sieyès (with whom Arnoux tends to agree on this point), the abolition of the tithe would not only prevent the Church from fulfilling its role but also transfer tens of millions of *livres tournois** to wealthy private landowners (both bourgeois and noble). One might object that the educational and social benefits procured by French Catholic institutions in the eighteenth century seem quite modest in comparison with those that would later be provided by state and local institutions. One might also note that the tithe financed the lifestyle of bishops, curates, and monks, whose first concern may not have been the welfare of the poor. Indeed, the tithe often weighed heavily on the standard of

---

11. In 585 the Council of Macon declared that anyone who refused to voluntarily pay the church a portion of the fruits of the earth was a "thief and robber of God's property." The church had recommended such voluntary payments from its earliest days, but its recommendation was not always heeded. Not until the Capitularies of Pepin the Short and Charlemagne in 765 and 779 did the council's decision receive royal sanction, giving the tithe the force of law. For a classic history of the tithe, see H. Marion, *La dîme ecclésiastique en France au 18ᵉ siècle et sa suppression* (Cadoret, 1913).

living of society's humblest members and not just wealthy landowners. The tithe provided no mechanism for extracting larger contributions from the rich: it was a proportional tax, not a progressive one, and at no time did the clergy propose that it should be any other way.[12]

The point here is not to settle this debate, however, nor is it to rehash the controversy between Abbé Sieyès (who would have preferred protecting the clergy and demanding more of the nobility) and the anticlerical Marquis de Mirabeau (who distinguished himself with speeches demanding the end of the tithe and the nationalization of church property but was a good deal less aggressive when it came to expropriating the nobility). It is rather to illustrate the complexity of the relations of exchange and domination that exist in ternary society—a complexity that at different times gave rise to contradictory yet plausible discourses. Sieyès clearly believed that it was possible and desirable to put an end to the most exorbitant privileges of both dominant orders while maintaining an important social role (and therefore appropriate financial support) for the Catholic Church, particularly in education. In many modern societies debate continues about the role of different religious and educational institutions and how to finance them, even in countries like France, which have opted for supposed republican and secular regimes, as well as in countries that preserve aspects of monarchy or grant official recognition to certain religions, such as the United Kingdom and Germany. I will say more about this later. At this stage, note simply that these debates have ancient roots, stemming from the trifunctional organization of social inequality.

The Size and Resources of the Clergy and Nobility: The Case of France

Unfortunately, very little is known about the long-term evolution of the size and resources of the clergy, nobility, and other social groups in ternary societies. There are deep reasons for this: at their inception ternary societies consisted of a web of powers that derived their political and economic legitimacy

---

12. Furthermore, the wars of religion of the sixteenth and seventeenth centuries were in many ways social and fiscal struggles sparked by refusal to pay the tithe to Catholic institutions. The royal government took advantage of public fatigue with the disturbances to shore up its own power. See Noiriel, *Une histoire populaire de la France* (Agone, 2018), pp. 62–99.

from their local roots. This localist logic ran directly counter to the logic of the centralized modern state, part of whose mission is to collect data and impose uniformity on its component parts. Ternary societies did not define clear social, political, and economic categories that could be applied in a standard way across a broad swath of territory. They did not conduct administrative surveys or systematic censuses. Or, rather, when they did do so, and categories and group boundaries began to emerge, it usually meant that centralized state formation was already well advanced and that ternary society was nearing its end or close to a fundamental transformation or radical reformulation. Traditional ternary societies lived in the shadows. By the time the lights came on, they were already no longer fully themselves.

In this respect the case of the French monarchy is particularly interesting because the three orders were early on granted official political recognition by the centralized state. From 1302 on, the so-called Estates General of the Kingdom, which included representatives of the clergy, nobility, and third estate, were convoked from time to time to consider issues of particular importance to the entire country; generally these were fiscal, judicial, or religious in nature. Institutionally, the Estates General were themselves an emblematic incarnation of trifunctional ideology, or perhaps better, a provisional and ultimately fruitless attempt to provide a formal trifunctional underpinning for the emerging centralized monarchical state, ternary society having functioned perfectly well at the local level for centuries without the slightest role for the Estates General. In practice, the estates were a fragile institution, which met quite irregularly and lacked a firm legal foundation. In 1789, the convocation of the Estates General was in fact a last resort, a desperate attempt to revamp the fiscal system to deal with a financial and moral crisis that would ultimately prove fatal to the Ancien Régime. The most recent convocation of the estates prior to that had taken place in 1614.

One problem was that there was no centralized electoral list or standard procedure for choosing the representatives of the three orders. Everything was left to local customs and laws. In practice, it was mainly the urban bourgeoisie and the wealthiest commoners who chose the representatives of the third estate. There were also recurrent conflicts about the definition of nobility, especially between the old *noblesse d'épée* (the warrior elite of "nobles of the sword") and the new *noblesse de robe* (consisting of jurists and magistrates of the courts known as *Parlements,* the "nobles of pen and ink"). The former always sought to relegate the latter to the third estate, usually successfully, as only a small minority of *"hauts robins"* (senior justices) were generally recognized as full members of the noble group.[13]

When the Estates General were convoked in 1614, moreover, separate elections were organized within the third estate to choose, on the one hand, representatives of the *noblesse de robe* and, on the other hand, representatives of the rest of the third estate (bourgeois, merchants, and so on), so that in some respects one could say that there were four orders rather than three. The jurist Charles Loyseau, who in 1610 wrote an influential *Traité sur les ordres et les seigneuries* (Treatise on Orders and Seigneuries), came close to urging that the nobility of pen and ink, the administrative and legal backbone of the emerging monarchical state, should become the true first order of the realm in place of the clergy (even going so far as to note that, among the Gauls, the Druids were the first magistrates). He never quite took the final step, however, because that would have required a radical redefinition of the whole political and religious order. Still, Loyseau was quite harshly critical of the nobility of the sword, which he accused of having taken advantage of weak monarchs in centuries past to transform privileges stemming from past military service—privileges that Loyseau believed should have been limited and temporary—into permanent, exorbitant, and hereditary rights. In this, Loyseau showed himself to be an unbending advocate of the centralized state, sapping the very underpinnings of the trifunctional order and laying the groundwork for 1789. There was also sharp conflict between the nobles of the sword and royal officeholders, who were accused of having taken advantage of the crown's need for cash to appropriate for themselves certain privileges and public revenues, and in some cases,

---

13. The function of the provincial parlements under the Ancien Régime was primarily to approve and register royal edicts and ensure their compatibility with local law and custom. Beyond technicalities, this allowed the parlements in practice to set conditions, demand amendments, and thus politically counterbalance the powers of the King's Council (and of the great feudal lords who sat on it). Of course, the king could always reclaim any jurisdictional or legislative powers he granted to the parlements by holding what was called a *"lit de justice"* to require a parlement to register any edict. He could not, however, avail himself of this theoretical power too often without running the risk of undermining the equilibrium of the system. In many provinces the parlements also served as courts of appeal for the local seigneurial courts, with much variation from region to region in both the juridical and fiscal domains. For a classic study, see R. Mousnier, *The Institutions of France under the Absolute Monarchy,* trans. A. Goldhammer (University of Chicago Press, 1984). On justice in the Ancien Régime, see also J. P. Royer, *Histoire de la justice en France* (Presses Universitaires de France, 1995).

even noble titles by availing themselves of their financial resources, usually deemed to have derived from sordid mercantile activities beneath the dignity of the nobility.[14]

Accordingly, there are no centralized voter lists that one might use to gauge the size of the different classes: all the procedures for choosing representatives of the three orders took place at the local level, with much variation from region to region. The only surviving records are quite disparate and rely on classifications that varied with time and place. Bear in mind, too, that the first real French census did not take place until the nineteenth century. It seems obvious that without census data there can be no real social or demographic understanding. How can a state function without such information (for example, to determine how much funding should be allocated to different towns or what number of seats should be ascribed to each voting district)? But collecting such information requires, beyond a desire to know, measure, and administer, organizational capacity and suitable means of transportation. These requirements were not always met; everything depended on specific political and ideological processes.

Under the Ancien Régime, one sometimes counted the number of "hearths" (that is, family groups living under one roof) but never individuals, and this was done only in certain provinces and never with standardized definitions of orders, occupations, statuses, or classes. The first truly national census was not conducted until 1801, and even that was little more than a rudimentary headcount. Not until 1851 do we find the first census lists of named individuals with information about the age, sex, and occupation of each. As the modern census evolved, population statistics and socio-professional classifications constantly improved.

Under the Ancien Régime, there was much debate about the population of each order, especially in the eighteenth century, but no official estimates

---

14. Royal offices usually involved administrative and regalian functions (tax collection, financial oversight, registration of official acts and documents, licensing associated with the growth of markets and trace, and so on). Some of these positions were newly created while others had previously been held by nobles before being put up for sale by the monarch in the sixteenth and seventeenth centuries, largely to compensate for falling fiscal revenues. On these conflicts, see R. Blaufarb, *The Great Demarcation. The French Revolution and the Invention of Modern Property* (Oxford University Press, 2016), pp. 22–23, about which I will have more to say in the next chapter. See also Le Goff, "Les trois fonctions indo-européennes, l'historien et l'Europe féodale."

existed. It took ingenuity to extrapolate from local data about the number of parishes, nobles, and hearths to national estimates. As Sieyès himself noted in his famous pamphlet: "With respect to population, the third order is known to be immensely larger than the first two. Like everyone else, I have no idea what the true ratio is, but like everyone else I will allow myself to make my own calculation." What followed was a relatively low estimate of the size of the nobility, based on a very rough calculation of the number of noble families in Brittany multiplied by a very low estimate of the size of each family. Sieyès's method betrayed his desire to call attention to the small size of the nobility compared with its scandalously exaggerated political influence.

Broadly speaking, while the sources more or less agree on the number of noble families (in the sense of lineages), things are much more complicated when it comes to estimating the total number of individuals. The first uncertainty has to do with the average number of individuals associated with each "hearth" or household (which requires hypotheses about the number of children, surviving spouses, and intergenerational cohabitations). The second, even knottier problem is the number of distinct hearths and family groups to assign to each noble lineage (and the uncertainty is compounded by the fact that it is not always obvious whether a younger branch should still be counted as nobility).

For the seventeenth century and later, one can turn to the vast surveys of the nobility and clergy conducted in the 1660s under Louis XIV and his minister Jean-Baptiste Colbert as well as to data stemming from the *capitation,* a tax established in 1695 to which the nobility was subject (unlike the *taille*). Marshal Vauban, well known for the celebrated fortifications he built in the four corners of France as well as for his efforts to estimate the country's landed wealth and for his projects of tax reform, drew up a plan for future censuses in 1710, but it was never acted on. For the fourteenth, fifteenth, and sixteenth centuries, a number of historians have made use of locally compiled lists of nobles available for combat if required (the so-called *ban* and *arrière-ban*). Despite the serious shortcomings of these sources, they are good enough to estimate orders of magnitude and trends, especially for the period from the middle of the seventeenth century to the end of the eighteenth.

The farther back in time one goes, the more one finds that nobility was above all a matter of recognition by one's peers at the local level, hence the less sense it makes to think in terms of national estimates. In the Middle Ages, a noble was anyone "who lives nobly," that is, with sword in hand, without being obliged to engage in degrading (meaning commercial) activities to maintain his status. In theory, a merchant who purchased a noble fief could not be considered a noble and was deleted from the lists of taxpayers subject to the *taille* until several generations had passed—that is, until his son and grandson succeeded in showing that they, too, lived nobly, sword in hand, "without engaging in commerce." In practice, everything depended on being recognized by other noble families living in the same area, especially when it came to marriage: would nobles of ancient local lineages agree to allow their children to marry the newcomers (a central issue to which we will return when we look at high castes in India).

The Shrinking Nobility and Clergy in the Late Ancien Régime

Despite these many uncertainties, it will be useful to look at the information we have about the evolution of the noble and clerical populations in France under the Ancien Régime. The estimates we will analyze were established by combining work done on the *capitation* data, the *ban* and *arrière-ban* lists, and the surveys of nobility and clergy from the period 1660–1670. They are good mainly for deriving orders of magnitude as well as for making a few tentative geographical and historical comparisons. Two points appear to be well established. First, the clerical and noble populations in France in the final centuries of the monarchy were relatively small. According to the best available estimates, the two privileged orders represented 3–4 percent of the total population from the late fourteenth to the late seventeenth centuries: roughly 1.5 percent for the clergy and 2 percent for the nobility.[15]

Second, the numbers begin to decrease significantly starting in the final third of the seventeenth century under Louis XIV, continuing throughout the eighteenth century under Louis XV and XVI. Overall, the size of the first two orders as a percentage of the total population seems to have decreased by more than half between 1660 and 1780. On the eve of the French Revolution it stood at about 1.5 percent of the population: roughly 0.7 percent for the clergy and 0.8 percent for the nobility (Fig. 2.1).

Several points call for clarification. First, although uncertainties about levels remain, the trend is relatively clear. On the one hand, it is impossible to

---

15. It is possible that these populations were larger in earlier periods, particularly that of the nobility in the Carolingian era (eighth to tenth centuries) and the Crusades (eleventh to thirteenth centuries), when it may have been as high as 5–10 percent of the population (to judge by the example of other European countries; see Chap. 5). No source provides precise quantitative data, however.

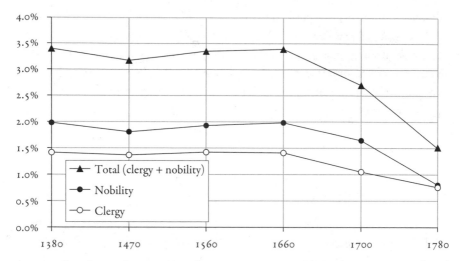

FIG. 2.1. Population shares in French ternary society, 1380–1780 (as percentage of total population)

Interpretation: In 1780, the nobility and clergy accounted respectively for 0.8 and 0.7 percent of the total French population, or 1.5 percent for the first two orders and 98.5 percent for the third estate; in 1660, the nobility and clergy accounted respectively for 2.0 and 1.4 percent of the total population, or 3.4 percent for the first two orders and 96.6 percent for the third estate. These proportions remained fairly stable from 1380 to 1660, followed by a sharp drop from 1660 to 1780. *Sources and series:* piketty.pse.ens.fr/ideology.

be certain that nobles accounted for exactly 0.8 percent of the population of France on the eve of the Revolution. Depending on what sources and methods one uses, one can obtain significantly lower or higher estimates.[16] On the other hand, for a given source and method of estimation, we consistently note a very sharp decrease in the size of the first two orders and especially in the nobility in the final century of the Ancien Régime.[17] By contrast, no clear tendency is apparent for earlier centuries.[18]

16. Here I have chosen a middle-of-the-road estimate of the size of the nobility in the 1780s: roughly 0.8 percent of the total population, whereas the lowest estimates are about 0.4 percent and the highest around 1.2 percent.

17. The trends indicated here were estimated from the work of M. Nassiet and P. Contamine, who rely on data from the *capitation* (for the late seventeenth and eighteenth centuries) and the *ban* and *arrière-ban* (for the fourteenth to sixteenth centuries). For bibliographic and methodological details, see the online appendix.

18. Do not be misled, however, by the apparent stability of the size of the nobility and clergy as a percentage of the total population between the fourteenth and late sev-

How should we interpret the relatively small size and shrinking proportion of the first two orders in the final century of the French monarchy? Before looking at the context of these changes, I should note that the population of France increased significantly during this period, from a little over 11 million in 1380 to nearly 22 million in 1700 and around 28 million in 1780, according to available estimates. By comparison, the population of England was less than 8 million in 1780; the United Kingdom of Great Britain and Ireland, around 13 million; and the newly independent United States of America, barely 3 million (including slaves). Once again, do not be misled by the precision of the numbers. Nevertheless, the orders of magnitude are clear. In the seventeenth and eighteenth centuries the Kingdom of France was by far the most populous country in the West, which no doubt explains the international importance of the French language in the era of the Enlightenment as well as the considerable influence of the French Revolution on neighboring countries and on European history. If the most powerful monarchy in Europe could collapse, did this not signify that the whole trifunctional world order was also on the verge of going under? What is more, France's demographic exuberance was no doubt partly responsible for setting off the Revolution: all signs are that strong demographic growth contributed to wage stagnation in agriculture and skyrocketing ground rents in the final decades before the explosion of 1789. Although this rising inequality was not the only cause of the French Revolution, it clearly exacerbated the unpopularity of the nobility and political regime.[19]

The sharp increase of population also means that the relative stability of the size of the clergy and nobility as a proportion of the population from the fourteenth through the seventeenth centuries actually masks a significant increase in the number of clerics and nobles, who in absolute terms were never as numerous as in the 1660s. From that point on, however, the absolute size of the first two orders decreased, slightly at first, then more sharply between 1700 and 1780, especially for the nobility, whose population seems to have decreased more than 30 percent over the course of the eighteenth century. In a context

---

enteenth centuries. It reflects the fact that the available sources do not allow us to detect any robust trend over this long period, whether upward or downward. It is nevertheless perfectly possible that more accurate sources would show significant variations over these three centuries.

19. On the fall in agricultural wages (relative to prices and rents), see the classic study by E. Labrousse, *Esquisse du mouvement des prix et des revenus en France au 18ᵉ siècle* (Librairie Dalloz, 1933).

TABLE 2.1

Clergy and nobility in France, 1380–1780 (as percent of total population)

	1380	1470	1560	1660	1700	1780
Clergy	1.4	1.3	1.4	1.4	1.1	0.7
Nobility	2.0	1.8	1.9	2.0	1.6	0.8
Total clergy + nobility	3.4	3.1	3.3	3.4	2.7	1.5
Third estate	96.6	96.9	96.7	96.6	97.3	98.5
Total population (millions)	11	14	17	19	22	28
Clergy (thousands)	160	190	240	260	230	200
Nobility (thousands)	220	250	320	360	340	210

Interpretation: In 1780 the clergy and nobility accounted respectively for about 0.7 and 0.8 percent of the total population, or about 1.5 percent for the first two orders (roughly 410,000 out of 28 million people).

Sources and series: piketty.pse.ens.fr/ideology.

of rapid demographic growth, the nobility's share of the population fell by more than half in less than a century (Table 2.1).

As for the clergy, it is useful to express its share as a percentage of the adult male population. In the Catholic Church, priests are not allowed to have wives or children, which systematically decreases the size of the clergy compared with countries and religions where priests have families equivalent in size (or in some cases slightly larger than) the families of other classes—for example, the Protestant and Orthodox clergy, the Shi'ite clergy in Iran, and the Brahmins in India, which we will study in subsequent chapters. In comparing different civilizations, therefore, it might make sense to consider each social group's size as a share of the adult male population (there are good reasons for both choices, and they offer complementary perspectives useful for comparing different social structures).

In the French case, surveys conducted in the 1660s put the clerical population at about 260,000, 100,000 of whom were secular clergy (bishops, curates, canons, deacons, and vicars, hence all men) and 160,000 regular clergy (members of religious orders living under monastic rules). The latter group consisted of two roughly equal parts: 80,000 monks and 80,000 nuns. Men thus represented about 70 percent of the clergy (180,000 out of 260,000). Using this estimate, in the seventeenth century the male clergy represented 3.3 percent of the adult male population, or one adult male in thirty, which is a lot. In the eighteenth century this fell to a little below 2 percent, which still accounts for nearly one adult male in fifty (Table 2.2). Compare this with France today,

TABLE 2.2

Clergy and nobility in France, 1380–1780 (as percent of total adult male population)

	1380	1470	1560	1660	1700	1780
Clergy	3.3	3.2	3.3	3.3	2.5	1.7
Nobility	1.8	1.6	1.8	1.8	1.5	0.7
Total clergy + nobility	5.1	4.8	5.1	5.1	4.0	2.4
Third estate	94.9	95.2	94.9	94.9	96.0	97.6
Adult male population (millions)	3.4	4.2	5.1	5.6	6.5	8.3
Clergy (thousands)	110	130	160	180	160	140
Nobility (thousands)	60	60	90	100	90	60

Interpretation: In 1780, the clergy and nobility accounted respectively for 1.7 and 0.7 percent of the adult male population, for a total of 2.4 percent (about 200,000 adult males out of 8.3 million).

Sources and series: piketty.pse.ens.fr/ideology.

where one adult male in a thousand is a member of the clergy (all religions combined). Over the past three centuries, the religious class has completely disappeared.[20] Of course, there is still an intellectual class in France as in all other Western societies (where holders of doctoral degrees now account for nearly 2 percent of the electorate, one voter in every fifty, compared with less than one per 1,000 a century ago), and it even plays an important role in shaping political conflict and the inequality regime, but in very different ways from those observed in the trifunctional era.[21]

If we combine the first two orders, we find that between the fourteenth and the late seventeenth centuries, the clergy and nobility together represented about 5 percent of the adult male population (compared with 3.5 percent of

---

20. If we include all members of the Catholic clergy (regular and secular) as well as all individuals classified as exercising religious functions (in any religion) in the French censuses for 1990, 1999, and 2014, in each case we find fewer than 20,000 (out of a total population of 65 million in 2014, or barely 0.03 percent), compared with 260,000 for the Catholic clergy alone in 1660 (out of a total population of 19 million, or nearly 1.5 percent). The religious class as a proportion of the population has thus shrunk today to less than a fiftieth of what it was at the end of the seventeenth century.

21. On the evolution of educational levels in various countries and the role of educational cleavages in structuring modern political conflict, see Parts Three and Four.

the total population); this fell to a little above 2 percent on the eve of the Revolution (compared with 1.5 percent of the total population; Tables 2.1 and 2.2).[22]

How to Explain the Decline in the Number of Nobles?

Why did the relative size of the clergy and even more of the nobility decline in France during the last century of the Ancien Régime? To be candid, the available sources do not allow a perfectly precise and convincing answer to this question. There is no shortage of possible explanations, however. One is that the decline was a consequence of a long-term process linked to the formation of the centralized state and the gradual delegitimation of clerical and noble functions. Political and ideological factors specific to each era also played a part, and we will find analogous phenomena in other European countries, especially the United Kingdom and Sweden, but with interesting variations in chronology and modality. In France, it is likely that the sharp decline that began in the middle of the seventeenth century was at least partly a consequence of a deliberate policy pursued by an absolute monarchy in a phase of rapid growth and increasing self-confidence. Indeed, the purpose of the surveys of the nobility and clergy conducted in the 1660s under Louis XIV and Colbert was precisely to allow the emerging central state to take the measure of the privileged orders and in some ways to exert control over them. Once the state knew who was who and how many people there were in each category, it could redraw the boundaries between classes and negotiate the prerogatives of both clergy and nobility. The crown also sought to tighten the rules defining nobility: for instance, a royal declaration of 1664 demanded "authentic proof" of any claim to nobility predating 1560, arousing considerable controversy over what kind of proof could count as "authentic."[23]

In the late seventeenth and early eighteenth centuries, moreover, the French monarchy multiplied its efforts to limit the size of the nobility. Its motives were both political (to show that the emerging centralized state had no need of a

---

22. Both methods give virtually the same result for the nobility, because the average size of a noble family was similar to that of a common family (to a first approximation). For the clergy, the share is a little more than twice as great as a percentage of the adult male population compared with the total population. See Tables 2.1 and 2.2 and, in the online appendix, Fig. S2.1.

23. See esp. Mousnier, *The Institutions of France under the Absolute Monarchy,* and *Les hiérarchies sociales de 1450 à nos jours* (Presses universitaires de France, 1969), pp. 61–69.

bloated, idle nobility) and budgetary, since reducing the number of nobles also reduced the number of people exempt from taxation. The *capitation,* created in 1695, did finally require the nobility to contribute to the finances of the state, but nobles as a class remained exempt from many royal taxes, especially the *taille,* until 1789. The only way to increase royal revenue was therefore to tighten the definition of nobility. This goal was never fully achieved, since the monarchy had only limited influence on the local institutions and administrative procedures that determined noble status and therefore exemption from taxation. In any case, it could not and would not run the risk of alienating the nobility, so the question was never really resolved before the Revolution. Nevertheless, the fact remains that the process of paring back the nobility, as difficult as it was, had been set in motion long before.

At the same time, the monarchy hesitantly sought to diminish the distance between the old warrior nobility and the new commercial and financial elite, in part by selling charges and offices (sometimes accompanied by titles of nobility) to people with financial resources and in part by allowing nobles to engage in new activities without derogation. In 1627, for example, the king decreed that maritime commerce would no longer stain the honor of a gentleman; in 1767, this dispensation was extended to banking and manufacturing.[24] This gradual process of unification and monetization of the elites, which would culminate in the nineteenth century with the introduction of property qualifications for voting, was already well under way in the seventeenth and eighteenth centuries, even as the size of the traditional noble class began to decrease.

It is nevertheless difficult to attribute all of the decrease in size of the nobility to the deliberate action of the centralized state and the people who controlled it. In view of the sharp decline that occurred between 1660 and 1780, it seems likely that other factors (beginning with the strategies of nobles themselves) played an important if not preponderant role. Many scholars have shown, for example, that the noble class began to take a more and more "Malthusian" attitude to reproduction in the eighteenth century: not only did couples have fewer children, but celibacy also increased among daughters and younger sons. In France and elsewhere in Europe, primogeniture also became more common in this period, so that most family property was passed on to just the eldest son, as had long been the case among the English nobility. In France and elsewhere on the continent, inheritance practices had always been

---

24. See J. Lukowski, *The European Nobility in the 18th Century* (Palgrave, 2003), pp. 84–90.

more varied.[25] Along with growing celibacy among younger sons and concentration of estates on the eldest went an increasing interest in high clerical posts: in the eighteenth century more than 95 percent of bishops came from the nobility, compared with 63 percent at the start of the seventeenth century and 78 percent at the end.[26]

It is also tempting to analyze these changes as a (witting or unwitting) *offensive* choice, not to say an assertion of power by noble families on the English model. Once the centralized state guaranteed that property rights would be broadly respected, it ceased to be necessary for noble heads of household to fortify themselves with large numbers of sons prepared to take up arms to defend their fief and rank; hence they may have decided to avoid repeated subdivision and fragmentation of their estates and to concentrate power instead in a shrinking elite. A bloated elite ceases to be an elite. Yet such Malthusian family strategies can also be interpreted as a *defensive* choice, intended to prevent a loss of status. In a time of rapid demographic growth, economic expansion, and diversification of the elite (as nobles and clerics were joined by *robins,* merchants, financiers, and other bourgeois), it may have seemed that limiting the number of progeny and bequeathing estates to eldest sons was the only way for the nobility to maintain its relative rank vis-à-vis the newcomers.

The available sources are insufficient to allow us to assign precise weights to these various factors, interpretations, and motives. It is nevertheless striking to see that conflicts over protocol, rank, and precedence did not disappear toward the end of the Ancien Régime; on the contrary, they seem to have intensified.[27] In a period marked by the growing centralization of the modern state and by changes to an inegalitarian, hierarchical regime that threatened the status of many individuals, it would be wrong to think that by the grace of universal monetary equivalence, economic rationality, and the desire to concentrate property in the fewest possible number of hands, all elites came together in a single, universal communion. On the occasion of a royal entry into Paris in 1660, the usual disputes between nobles of the sword and robe were compounded by numerous conflicts within the Grande Chancellerie (an institution that played a dual role as ministry of justice and central administration of the monarchy). For instance, the *gardes des rôles,* or keepers of the rolls,

---

25. Lukowski, *The European Nobility in the 18th Century,* pp. 118–120.
26. See the online appendix.
27. On these issues see the enlightening book by F. Cosandey, *Le rang. Préséances et hiérarchies dans la France d'Ancien Régime* (Gallimard, 2016).

who maintained various fiscal and administrative registers and lists, demanded rank and costumes equivalent to those of the *maîtres des comptes* and *grands audienciers* and above those of the *huissiers,* whom they deemed inferior.

In this period people began codifying not only the order of processions but also the size of the cloaks and hats that different ranks were allowed to wear, as well as the stools they were permitted to sit on during ceremonies, the color of their shoes, and so on. Conflicts over dress, protocol, processions, and ranks also colored relations between members of different guilds and corporations. In the eighteenth century these delicate questions demanded close attention: one had to deal, for example, with where princes and princesses of the royal blood (as well as royal bastards, for whom kings had recently won recognition, though not without a fight) stood relative to the high nobility (especially dukes and peers). Memoirists of course regularly lamented the disappearance of the old protocol of the battlefield—the feudal warrior order symbolized by the banquet in the *Song of Roland,* in which twelve peers flanked the king and no one challenged the hierarchical rules governing the order of access to meats and other dishes. In any case, these disputes over court rank under the absolute monarchy remind us that the society of orders was still alive and well at the end of the Ancien Régime. Its characteristically complex symbolic hierarchies had by no means dissolved into a one-dimensional ranking based on money and property. Only after the Revolution were social hierarchies radically transformed.

The Nobility: A Propertied Class Between the Revolution and the Restoration

If we want to understand how the clergy and nobility maintained their dominance over the rest of Ancien Régime society, it is obviously not enough to look simply at the relative size of the classes. We must also analyze the inextricably symbolic, patrimonial, and political resources at the disposal of the two privileged orders. As noted, the clergy and nobility represented only a few percent of the population, and that share decreased in the century prior to the Revolution. One key fact remains, however: no matter how sweeping the transformations under way, the two dominant classes continued to hold a significant share of France's material wealth and economic power on the eve of the Revolution of 1789.

Although the sources are imperfect, the orders of magnitude are relatively clear, at least regarding property in land. By 1780 the nobility and clergy represented roughly 1.5 percent of the total population but owned nearly half the land: 40–45 percent according to available estimates, with 25–30 percent belonging to the nobility and 15 percent to the clergy and with considerable variation from province to province (in some regions the clergy owned barely 5 percent, in others more than 20 percent). The two privileged orders' share of land ownership rises to 55–60 percent if one capitalizes the revenue from the tithe, which was not property, strictly speaking, but procured similar advantages, since it allowed the Church to claim in perpetuity a substantial share of the country's agricultural output. The share of the privileged orders would be higher still if one counted income from judicial and other seigneurial and regalian rights linked to property rights; I have not tried to do this here.

The Revolution would radically upset this equilibrium, particularly regarding the clergy. Ecclesiastical ownership was reduced to virtually nothing after church properties were confiscated and the tithe was eliminated. For comparison, the nobility's land holdings were cut approximately in half, and some of the losses were later restored, so that the break was less dramatic than in the case of the clergy. In the Nord *département,* for example, the share of land held by the two privileged orders decreased from 42 percent in 1788 (22 percent for the nobility, 20 percent for the clergy) to a little less than 12 percent in 1802 (11 percent for the nobility, less than 1 percent for the clergy). Available estimates for other *départements* confirm these orders of magnitude.[28]

All in all, we can say that the nobility owned from a quarter to a third of France's land on the eve of the Revolution and that its share decreased to between a tenth and fifth in the early decades of the nineteenth century—which is still a lot. Note, moreover, that these estimates understate the nobility's share of the largest fortunes, which was much greater than its share of total wealth—despite the drop from a very high share at the end of the Ancien Régime to a still quite significant share during the Restoration.

Inheritance records allow us to estimate that nobles accounted for roughly 50 percent of the largest 0.1 percent of Parisian bequests on the eve of the Revolution, falling to 25–30 percent between 1800 and 1810 and then rising again to 40–45 percent between 1830 and 1850 under the so-called *monarchie censitaire,* which imposed a property qualification *(le cens)* on voting. Then, during the second half of the nineteenth century, it gradually fell to roughly 10 percent in the period 1900–1910 (Fig. 2.2).

---

28. See the online appendix.

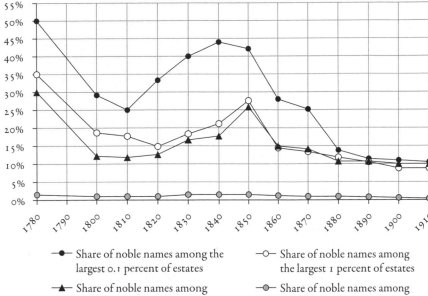

Share of noble names among the largest 0.1 percent of estates

Share of noble names among the largest 1 percent of estates

Share of noble names among all estates

Share of noble names among total deceased

FIG. 2.2. Share of nobility in Paris inheritances, 1780–1910

Interpretation: The share of noble names among the largest 0.1 percent of inheritances fell from 50 percent to 25 percent between 1780 and 1810 before climbing to about 40–45 percent during the censitary* monarchies (1815–1848), then falling to 10 percent in the late nineteenth and early twentieth centuries. By comparison, noble names accounted for fewer than 2 percent of all deaths in the period 1780–1910. *Sources and series:* piketty.pse.ens.fr/ideology.

This evolution calls for comment on several points. First, these results show that a very small group (noble names accounted for barely 1–2 percent of the Paris population throughout the period 1780–1910) accounted for a considerable share of the largest fortunes and therefore of economic and financial power. These estimates are based on the digitization of several hundred thousand inheritance records from the Paris archives, work I did in collaboration with Gilles Postel-Vinay and Jean-Laurent Rosenthal. This source is not without shortcomings: in particular, we were obliged to use family names to classify the deceased as nobles, a method with many drawbacks whose results must be viewed as approximate.[29] Nevertheless, the observed trends are quite clear, both

---

29. It is nevertheless hard to imagine a better method, since there was no longer any legal definition of nobility in France after the abolition of privileges in 1789 (if one

for the rise between 1810 and 1850 and the fall between 1850 and 1910. Note, moreover, that the data come from a system of inheritance records established by the Revolution—a system that was surprisingly comprehensive for its time and that has no equivalent in other countries, since it concerns all forms of property (land, buildings, professional tools, financial assets, and so on), regardless of value or status of the owner (noble or common). This system remained in place throughout the nineteenth century and down to the present, with very low tax rates from the Revolution to World War I (1–2 percent on direct bequests from parents to children). There is no comparable source anywhere else in the world for analyzing the long-term history of property, and we will come back to it when we study the evolution of the concentration of wealth in the ownership society that developed in France over the course of the nineteenth century and into the early decades of the twentieth. At this stage, note simply that it allows us to quantify the evolution of the nobility's share of large fortunes.[30]

Finally, the graphs in Fig. 2.2 show the importance of political and ideological (as well as military and geopolitical) factors in the transformation of ternary societies. To be sure, the size of the nobility was already shrinking in the eighteenth century, and this can be explained as the result of a slow socioeconomic process of elite renewal and state formation (combined with the Malthusian strategies that nobles adopted in response). Similarly, the decrease in the nobility's share of the largest fortunes between 1850 and 1910 was partly a consequence of socioeconomic factors, especially the growth of industrial and financial sectors in which the old noble elite often took a back seat to the new bourgeois and commercial elites. Nevertheless, a purely socioeconomic approach would have a hard time explaining the abrupt decline of the noble share between 1780 and 1810, followed by a sharp increase through 1850. The fall was a result of redistribution achieved under the Revolution (although the extent of this should not be exaggerated, as we will see in the next chapter when

---

excepts both the tiny group of Peers of France that existed from 1815 to 1848 and the so-called *noblesse d'empire*). Indeed, the legal definition of nobility was also quite ambiguous before 1789.

30. The inheritance records in the Archives de l'Enregistrement are well preserved from 1800 onward. The estimate given for 1780 is based on available data concerning the decrease in the share of noble property from 1789 to 1800. We also had access to Paris inheritance records through 1960, which allowed us to determine that the decrease in the share of noble names continued after 1900 (noble names figured in fewer than 5 percent of the largest 0.1 percent of estates in the 1950s). See the online appendix.

we study the new property regime put in place by revolutionary lawmakers) and, above all, of the temporary exile of part of the nobility. By contrast, the rise can be explained by the return of the nobility at the time of the Restoration (1814–1815), largely thanks to the defeat of Napoleon's armies by a coalition of European monarchies, together with the favors the nobility enjoyed in the period 1815–1848.

Think, for example, of the famous "émigré billion," a symbolic measure debated in the early years of the Restoration and ultimately adopted in 1825, the purpose of which was to compensate former émigré nobles for land and rent lost during the Revolution; the large sums needed, amounting to nearly 15 percent of national income, were financed entirely by taxpayers and public borrowing. The governments of Louis XVIII and Charles X (both brothers of Louis XVI, guillotined in 1793), led by Joseph, comte de Villèle, also imposed on Haiti a penalty of 150 million francs (more than three years of the country's national income at the time) to compensate former slaveowners, many of whom were aristocrats, for the property they lost when Haiti became independent.[31] Broadly speaking, the entire judicial system and state bureaucracy took a clear pro-noble stance between 1815 and 1848, especially regarding the many lawsuits stemming from the redistribution of property during the Revolution. The political chronology shows that the transformation of the trifunctional society into an ownership society was not a smooth process in France or, for that matter, anywhere else in Europe. The rupture of 1789, as significant as it was, did not preclude any number of subsequent trajectories.

The Christian Church as a Property-Owning Organization

Return now to the question of the share of property owned by the clerical class and ecclesiastical organizations in ternary societies. The available sources suggest that the Catholic Church owned about 15 percent of French land in the 1780s. If we add the capitalized value of the tithe, the Church's share rises to about 25 percent.

Available estimates for other European countries suggest comparable orders of magnitude. To be sure, there are many uncertainties in these estimates, first because the very idea of property rights took on a specific meaning in trifunctional society (which included judicial and regalian rights not taken

---

31. I will have more to say about the magnitude of these property transfers, especially the Haitian indemnity paid to former slaveowners, in Chapter 6.

into account here) and, second, because of deficiencies in the sources themselves.

For Spain, however, we have the famous Cadastre of the Ansedana, compiled in the 1750s, from which we learn that the Church owned 24 percent of the agricultural land.[32] One should add to this the Spanish equivalent of the French tithe, but this is not easy to do. From the time of the Reconquista, relations between the Spanish Crown and the Catholic Church were complicated; a constantly renegotiated share of the Church's revenues was regularly transferred to royal coffers. The initial justification for these transfers was that they were necessary to finance the "reconquest" of Spain from the Muslim infidels in the period 718–1492. Subsequently, payments continued in a variety of forms.[33] The negotiations that took place in Spain between royal and ecclesiastical authorities show the extent to which questions of property in ternary societies were intimately related to broader political questions, beginning with the key question of the legitimacy of different elites and their respective contributions—martial and religious—to the community.

We know little about property other than agricultural land. The latter accounted for most—half to two-thirds—of all property (including land, buildings, tools, and financial assets, net of debt) in France, Spain, and the United Kingdom in the eighteenth century. But other property should not be neglected, especially residences, warehouses and factories, and financial assets. Very little is known about the Church's share of these other types of property. For instance, recent work has shown that the Spanish Church's share of mortgage lending (that is, lending that used land and buildings as collateral) was considerable, ranging from 45 percent in the seventeenth century to 70 percent by the mid-eighteenth century. By combining data from several sources, one can estimate that the Church held 30 percent or more of all property in Spain in 1750.[34]

---

32. More precisely, the Church owned 15 percent of the agricultural surface area, but thanks to the high quality of its lands, it captured 24 percent of agricultural revenue (which is a better index of the Church's share). See the online appendix.

33. The Church generally transferred a tenth to a quarter of its revenues to the Crown, but at times the figure rose to as much as a half. See S. Perrone, *Charles V and the Castillian Assembly of the Clergy: Negotiations for the Ecclesiastical Subsidy* (Brill, 2008).

34. On mortgage lending in Spain, see C. Milhaud, *Sacré Crédit! The Rise and Fall of Ecclesiastical Credit in Early Modern Spain,* doctoral thesis, EHESS, 2018, pp. 17–19.

Uncertainties notwithstanding, the key point here is that the Church owned a very large share of all property in European ternary societies, typically around 25–35 percent. We find similar orders of magnitude for ecclesiastical institutions in very different contexts: for example, the Ethiopian Church owned about 30 percent of Ethiopian land in 1700.[35] This is a very large amount: when an organization owns a quarter to a third of all there is to own in a country, its power to structure and control that society is enormous, especially through its remuneration of large numbers of clerics and its provision of services of many kinds, including in the areas of education and health.

Of course, enormous influence is not the same thing as hegemony, such as one finds in the communist bloc during the Soviet era. Although this is an extreme case, the comparison is nevertheless useful. As we will see, under communism the state owned nearly everything there was to own, typically 70–90 percent. As trifunctional ideology makes clear, the Christian Church was an important actor in a pluralist political system but not a hegemonic actor. Still, the Church was the largest property owner in all Christian monarchies: no individual noble owned as much, not even the king. This gave it a capacity for action often greater than that of the state itself.

For the sake of comparison, it may be useful to note that nonprofit organizations today own a much smaller share of all property: 1 percent in France, 3 percent in Japan, and not quite 6 percent in the United States, where the foundation sector is especially large (Fig. 2.3). Note that these estimates, based on official national accounts, include all nonprofit institutions, counting not only property owned by religious organizations (of all faiths) but also that owned by nonreligious nonprofit foundations and institutions, including universities, museums, hospitals, and charitable organizations. In some cases the figures may include foundations that theoretically operate in the public interest but in practice serve mainly the interests of a single family, which for one reason or another has donated part of its wealth to the foundation, sometimes for tax purposes, other times for internal family reasons. The officials responsible for compiling national accounts data are not always sure how to classify such institutions. In theory, assets held by "family trusts" and other foundations serving private individuals should be included in the household sector and not counted as nonprofit institutions, but the dividing line is not always clear, any more than it is easy to know whether ecclesiastical property in the Ancien Régime served

---

35. See N. Guebreyesus, *Les transferts fonciers dans un domaine ecclésiastique à Gondär (Ethiopie) au 18e siècle* (doctoral thesis, EHESS, 2017), pp. 264–265.

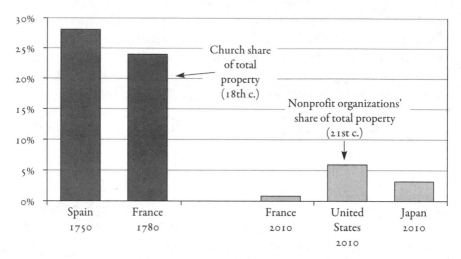

FIG. 2.3. The Church as property-owning organization, 1750–1780

Interpretation: In the period 1750–1780 the Church owned 25–30 percent of all property in Spain and nearly 25 percent in France (including land, buildings, financial assets, etc., as well as the capitalized value of the tithe). By comparison, in 2010, all nonprofit organizations (including religious organizations of all faiths, universities, museums, foundations, etc.) held less than 1 percent of all property in France, 6 percent in the United States, and 3 percent in Japan. *Sources and series:* piketty.pse.ens.fr/ideology.

the interests of the clergy or the mass of the faithful. National accounts (and in particular the attempts to estimate national capital and income that originated in the late seventeenth and early eighteenth century in the United Kingdom and France and that still play a significant part in contemporary debate) are social and historical constructs that reflect the priorities of an era and of their inventors. They are seldom much concerned with issues of inequality or natural capital; I will have more to say about this later.

In any case, the important point is that even when one includes such disparate entities, one ends up with today's nonprofits owning a relatively small share of all property, between 1 and 6 percent. This shows how powerful the Church was in Ancien Régime Europe, when it owned 20–35 percent of all property. However uncertain the data and no matter how the sources were constructed, the differences in order of magnitude are clear.

The specificity of this structure of ownership, which is fundamentally different from the structure of ownership in the other types of society we will study, is one of the defining characteristics of trifunctional society. In trifunctional societies, the two legitimate dominant classes, the clergy and the nobility, each playing a distinct organizational role, control significant shares of all goods and resources (roughly a quarter to a third of all property for each group, or half to two-thirds for both combined, and even more in some countries, such as the United Kingdom). With such vast resources they are able to fulfill their dominant social and political roles. Like all inegalitarian ideologies, the ternary ideology finds embodiment in a regime that is at once a political regime and an ownership regime, and this determines its specific human, social, and material form.

Note, too, that the roughly 30 percent of all property that the Church owned in the Ancien Régime is similar to the share of national capital that the Chinese government, which is controlled in practice by the Chinese Communist Party (CCP), owns today.[36] Clearly the CCP and the Catholic Church of the Ancien Régime are organizations of very different types whose legitimacy derives from very different sources. Yet both are associated with ambitious projects of economic development and social control, which would be inconceivable without a solid basis of substantial wealth.

The Wealthy Church versus Wealthy Families and Inheritance Practices

Interestingly, the Church began accumulating property very early in the history of Christianity. As church ownership increased, Christian doctrine evolved to deal with questions of property, family inheritance, and economic rights. This paralleled the development of trifunctional ideology and the unification of labor statuses.

At the very beginning of the Christian era, Jesus taught his disciples that it was "easier for a camel to go through the eye of a needle than for a rich man to enter the kingdom of God." But once wealthy Roman families embraced the new faith and began to take over bishoprics and other important positions in the Church in the fourth and fifth centuries, Christian doctrine was obliged to confront the question of wealth and make pragmatic accommodations. Society had become almost entirely Christian, something that had been unthinkable only a short time earlier, and the Church had begun to accumulate vast wealth, so it quickly became necessary to think about what forms of ownership were just and what kind of economy might be compatible with the new faith.

---

36. See Chap. 12.

To simplify, wealth could be accepted as a positive feature of Christian society provided that two conditions were met. First, a portion of the goods accumulated by the faithful would have to be passed on to the Church, which would thereby acquire the means to carry out its mission of shaping the political, religious, and educational structure of society. Second, certain economic and financial rules would have to be respected. The role of ecclesiastical wealth was different from that of private wealth, and its legitimacy rested on different grounds. Historians of late Antiquity such as Peter Brown have studied the transformation of Christian doctrine concerning wealth in the fourth and fifth centuries, a transformation that coincided with a series of spectacular donations to the Church by wealthy individuals.[37]

Some anthropologists have gone so far as to argue that the only distinctive feature of European family structures as compared with family structures elsewhere in the vast expanses of Eurasia was the specificity of the Catholic Church's position on wealth, especially its firm desire to acquire and hold property. According to Jack Goody, this is what led ecclesiastical authorities to develop a series of norms aimed at maximizing gifts to the Church (notably by stigmatizing remarriage of widows and adoptions, thereby reversing Roman rules, which encouraged remarriage and adoption in order to promote circulation of wealth). More generally, the Church sought to limit the ability of family groups to concentrate control over property (for instance, by forbidding marriages between cousins, albeit with limited success, since cousin marriage has always been a convenient matrimonial and patrimonial strategy for wealthy families in all civilizations—yet another sign of the radicalism of the Catholic Church's political project). In each instance the goal was to consolidate the position of the Church vis-à-vis family dynasties whose wealth and political influence it saw as a challenge to its authority.

Whatever the exact roles of these new rules may have been, the church's patrimonial strategy proved immensely successful. For more than a millennium, from the fifth or sixth century to the eighteenth or nineteenth century, the church owned a significant share of all property, and especially land, throughout Western Christendom—typically a quarter to a third, thanks to gifts from the faithful (and not just widows, reputed to be particularly generous) and sound

---

37. See esp. P. Brown, *Through the Eye of a Needle: Wealth, the Fall of Rome, and the Making of Christianity in the West, 350–550 AD* (Princeton University Press, 2013).

economic and legal management.[38] With this wealth it was able to sustain a large clerical class during this entire period and also, in theory if not in practice, to finance various social services, such as schools and hospitals.

Recent research also shows that the church's role as a property-owning organization would not have been possible without the development in the Middle Ages of a specific body of law dealing with economic and financial matters. These laws dealt with very concrete issues of estate management, usury (whether open or disguised), innovative debt instruments, and restoration of church property lost as a result of deceptive contracts (which the clergy often blamed on Jews and infidels, who were said to lack respect for Christian property). Giacomo Todeschini has studied the evolution of Christian doctrine from the eleventh to the fifteenth century in very great detail. Throughout this period trade was intensifying and more complex forms of ownership were emerging as new land was cleared, Christian kingdoms expanded, and populations and cities grew. Todeschini analyzes the role of Christian scholars in developing new economic, financial, and legal concepts, which he believes formed the basis of modern capitalism.[39] These legal concepts helped to protect church property from both temporal powers and private parties; new institutions emerged to provide adequate legal protections. Todeschini also touches on the development of new methods of financial accounting, which made it possible when necessary to circumvent the supposed ban on usury.

Ecclesiastical Property—The Basis of Economic Law and Capitalism?

In fact, contrary to what is sometimes argued, the problem for medieval Christian doctrine was clearly not that capital yields revenue without labor: this basic reality was the very essence of ecclesiastical property, which allowed priests to pray and attend to social needs without being obliged to till the soil. Indeed, this was the essence of property in general. The problem, to which the Church

---

38. According to some sources, the process of wealth accumulation moved quite rapidly. In Gaul, for instance, the Church is said to have acquired around a third of all arable land between the fifth and eighth centuries. See J. Goody, *The European Family* (Blackwell, 2000), p. 36.

39. G. Todeschini, *Les Marchands et le Temple. La société chrétienne et le cercle vertueux de la richesse du Moyen-Âge à l'Epoque moderne* (Albin Michel, 2017).

adopted an increasingly pragmatic approach, was rather to regulate acceptable forms of investment and ownership and to establish adequate social and political controls to ensure that capital would serve the social and political purposes set forth in Christian doctrine. Specifically, the fact that land yielded rent to its owner (or a tithe to the Church on lands it did not own directly) never really posed a moral or conceptual problem. The real issue was what kinds of investments in property other than land should be authorized; more specifically, the difficulty lay with commercial and financial investments and what kinds of remuneration were acceptable.

One sees this doctrinal flexibility in a text written by Pope Innocent IV, himself a canon lawyer, in the thirteenth century. In it he explained that the problem was not usury as such; if usury yielded too much interest with too much certainty, however, the wealthy might be induced "by avidity for profit, or to guarantee the security of their money," to invest "in usury rather than in less secure businesses." The pontiff went on to cite as examples of "less secure businesses" investments "in livestock and agricultural implements," goods that "the poor do not own" yet which are indispensable for increasing true wealth. He concluded his discussion by saying that the rate of interest should not exceed a certain limit.[40] A central banker determined to stimulate investment in the real economy today might well offer a similar justification for reducing the discount rate to nearly zero (despite limited prospects of success, but that is another discussion).

The same period witnessed the development of new financial technologies in defiance of old rules: for instance, the sale of rents and various forms of debt-financed purchases, which were no longer considered usurious as long as Christian doctrine identified them as useful for putting property to better use. Todeschini also emphasizes the growing influence of arguments justifying the expropriation of Jews and other infidels. These texts pointed to such people's "inability to understand the meaning and proper use of wealth" (as well as the threat that this posed to Church property) at a time when Christians were beginning to avail themselves of new forms of credit (and more specifically, in the late fifteenth century and throughout the sixteenth century, new forms of public debt). Other authors point out that the Anglo-Saxon "trust," a form of ownership that allowed for the beneficial owner of a property to be someone other than its manager (the trustee), thereby offering better protection of assets, originated with modes of ownership developed as early as the thirteenth

---

40. Todeschini, *Les Marchands et le Temple,* p. 96.

century by Franciscan monks, who could not or would not be seen as direct owners.[41]

Ultimately, the underlying thesis is that modern property law (in its emancipatory as well as its inegalitarian and exclusionary aspects) does not date from 1688, when both noble and bourgeois English property owners sought to protect themselves from the king, or from 1789, when the French Revolution sought to distinguish between legitimate ownership of rights over goods and illegitimate ownership of rights over persons. It originated instead with Christian doctrine, which sought over many centuries to secure the property rights of the Church as both a religious and a property-owning organization.

Indeed, the Church's efforts to conceptualize and formalize economic and financial laws were especially necessary in ternary Christian societies because the clerical class existed not as a hereditary class but only as an abstract perpetual organization (somewhat like modern foundations, capitalist corporations, and state administrations). In Hinduism and Islam there was certainly no shortage of temples and pious foundations, but these were controlled by powerful hereditary clerical classes. Power over ecclesiastical property thus depended more on personal and family networks than in Christian society, so that there was less need to codify and formalize economic and financial relationships. Some authors suggest that the tightening of celibacy rules after the Gregorian reforms of the eleventh century (prior to which concubinage was still common and tolerated among the Western Catholic clergy) was a way to avoid a turn toward more dynastic and hereditary practice and to reinforce the role of the Church as an ownership organization.[42]

I do not mean to imply that the fate of Europe depended entirely on the celibacy of priests, Christian sexual morality, and the power of the Church as a property-owning organization. Subsequent processes and switch points reveal various other specificities of the European trajectory, and no doubt these were far more decisive. In particular, competition among European states led to military and financial innovations that had a direct impact on colonial conquests, capitalist and industrial development, and the structure of modern inequality both within and between countries. I will have much more to say about this in what follows.

---

41. K. Pistor, *The Code of Capital: How the Law Creates Wealth and Inequality* (Princeton University Press, 2019), pp. 49–50.

42. J. Goody, *The European Family* (Blackwell, 2000), p. 39.

The key point I want to stress here is simply that the many variants of trifunctional society have also left traces in modern societies that merit our full attention. Specifically, trifunctional society developed sophisticated political and ideological constructs whose purpose was to define the conditions of a just inequality, consistent with a certain idea of the general interest, along with the institutions needed to bring those conditions about. To do this in any society requires resolving a series of practical questions bearing on the organization of property relations, family relations, and access to education. Ternary societies are no exception. They developed a range of imaginative responses to the relevant practical questions—responses based on the general trifunctional schema. Those responses had their flaws and for the most part have not withstood the test of time. Yet their history is replete with lessons for what came after them.

THREE

The Invention of Ownership Societies

In the previous chapter we looked at some general characteristics of ternary (or trifunctional) societies, especially European societies of orders. The purpose of this chapter is to analyze how those trifunctional societies were gradually transformed into ownership societies in the eighteenth and nineteenth centuries, at a pace and via pathways that varied from country to country. In Part Two we will look at non-European ternary societies (especially India and China) and examine how their encounter with European proprietarian and colonial powers influenced the conditions under which states emerged and premodern trifunctional structures were transformed, which also yielded a variety of specific trajectories. Before we do that, however, we need to pursue the analysis of European trajectories a bit further.

In this chapter I will take a more detailed look at the French Revolution of 1789, which marked an emblematic rupture between the Ancien Régime society of orders and the bourgeois ownership society that flourished in France in the nineteenth century. In the space of a few years revolutionary lawmakers attempted a complete overhaul of all power and property relations. Analyzing what they did will give us a better grasp on the magnitude of the task and the contradictions they encountered. We will also discover how complex and ambiguous political and legal processes collided with the issue of inequality and concentration of wealth. Ultimately, the French Revolution gave rise to an extremely inegalitarian proprietarian society, which lasted from 1800 to 1914; this will be the subject of the next chapter. Comparison with other European countries, especially the United Kingdom and Sweden, will then afford us insight into the respective roles of revolutionary processes versus long-term trends (associated with state formation and the evolution of socioeconomic structures) in the transformation of ternary societies into ownership societies. We will see that many trajectories and forks in the road are possible.

The "Great Demarcation" of 1789 and the Invention of Modern Property

To gain a better understanding of the "Great Demarcation"* of 1789 separating trifunctional societies from the ownership societies that succeeded them, let us begin by looking at what was probably the most decisive moment in this transition. On the night of August 4, 1789, the French National Assembly voted to abolish the privileges of the clergy and nobility. In the months, weeks, and years that followed, the challenge was to define exactly what the word "privilege" meant and thus to establish the dividing line between prerogatives that should simply be abolished and those that were legitimate and therefore worthy of perpetuation or compensation, perhaps requiring reformulation in a new political and legal language.

The theory of power and property to which revolutionary lawmakers adhered was in principle fairly clear. Its purpose was to draw a sharp distinction between, on the one hand, the regalian powers (of security, justice, and legitimate violence) henceforth to be monopolized by the centralized state and, on the other hand, property rights, which only individuals could claim. The latter were to be full, complete, and inviolable, as well as guaranteed by the state, whose primary if not sole mission should be to protect them. In practice, however, establishing the rights of property proved to be a far more complex undertaking than this simple theory would suggest. This was because regalian powers and property rights were so intimately intertwined at the local level that it was extremely difficult to define consistent norms of justice acceptable to all the relevant actors, particularly when it came to the initial allocation of property rights. Once this initial allocation was firmly established, people knew (or thought they knew) how to proceed. But it proved very difficult to decide which existing claims deserved to be preserved as new property rights and which should simply be suppressed.

Recent work, especially that of Rafe Blaufarb, has shown that in order to understand these debates, one needs to distinguish several periods.[1] In the first phase (1789–1790), the committee of the National Assembly in charge of these

---

1. See the illuminating book by R. Blaufarb, *The Great Demarcation: The French Revolution and the Invention of Modern Property* (Oxford University Press, 2016), which makes pioneering use of parlement, administrative, and court records from the revolutionary period (along with many seventeenth- and eighteenth-century legal and political treatises). I borrow the term Great Demarcation from the title of this work.

delicate issues adopted what it termed a "historical" approach. The idea was to examine the origins of each right in order to determine its legitimacy and in particular whether it was of a "contractual" nature (in which case it should be maintained) or a "noncontractual" nature (in which case it should be abolished). For instance, a right linked to the unwarranted exercise of seigneurial power (hence "feudal") or derived from the illegitimate appropriation of some aspect of public authority should be deemed "noncontractual" and therefore abolished without compensation. Fiscal privileges were the most obvious example of this: the nobility and clergy were exempt from the payment of certain taxes. Jurisdictional powers were also deemed noncontractual. The right to dispense justice within a specified territory (sometimes known as *seigneurie publique*) was therefore withdrawn from lords and transferred to the centralized state without compensation. The immediate consequence of this was disruption of the lower levels of the judicial system (which to a large extent relied on seigneurial courts). The idea that the state should exercise a monopoly of the judicial function became firmly fixed in people's minds.

The ecclesiastical tithe was also abolished, and church property was nationalized, again without compensation, which provoked vigorous debate since many people (among them Abbé Sieyès, as noted in the previous chapter) feared that the religious, educational, and hospital services previously provided by the Church would suffer. But proponents of abolishing the tithe and nationalizing clerical property insisted that public sovereignty could not be divided and that it was therefore intolerable for the Church to remain the permanent beneficiary of a state-enforced tax, which would have left it in the position of a quasi-state organization. For good measure, crown property was included along with Church property under the head of *biens nationaux* to be sold at auction. The general philosophy was that the state—one and indivisible—would finance itself in the future through annual taxes duly approved by representatives of the citizenry, whereas the exploitation of perpetual property would henceforth be left to private individuals.[2]

Beyond these few relatively clear cases (fiscal privileges, public seigneuries, tithe, and Church property), it proved very difficult to agree on other "privileges" to be eliminated without compensation. In particular, most seigneurial dues—that is, payments in cash or kind by peasants to nobles—were in fact

---

2. The conceptual break with the old order stands out even more clearly when one realizes that in the budgets of the monarchy, revenue stemming from royal estates was counted as "ordinary revenue," whereas tax revenue was classified as "extraordinary."

maintained, at least initially. Take the paradigmatic case of a peasant who farmed a plot of land in exchange for which he paid rent to a landlord: the general principle was that such rent was legitimate. The landlord-tenant relationship had the appearance of a legitimate "contractual" relationship as revolutionary legislators understood it; hence the former seigneurial dues should be continued in the form of rent. The lord could continue to collect rents—this was called *seigneurie privée*—but could no longer dispense justice *(seigneurie publique)*. All legislative effort went to distinguishing these two components of the seigneurial relationship so as to set the new, modern concept of ownership apart from the old feudal system.

Corvées, Banalités, Loyers: *From Feudalism to Proprietarianism*

As early as 1789–1790, however, an exception was made for the *corvée,* that is, the peasant's obligation to provide the landlord with a certain number of days of unpaid labor. Traditionally, peasants had been required to work one or two days a week and sometimes even more on the lord's land. Also excepted were *banalités,* or seigneurial monopolies on various local services, such as mills, bridges, presses, ovens, and so on. Both were in principle to be abolished without compensation. *Corvées* in particular smacked too much of serfdom and the old seigneurial order. This had supposedly disappeared centuries earlier, but the terminology (if not the reality) persisted in the French countryside. Maintaining these privileges openly and without limitation would have been interpreted as an unacceptable betrayal of the revolutionary spirit and the meaning of the Night of August 4.

In practice, however, the committees and tribunals charged with applying the directives of the National Assembly found in many cases that the *corvée* had a contractual basis. It was seen as a kind of rent *(loyer);* the difference between a rent paid in cash or kind and a labor service was often more a matter of words than anything else. Accordingly, such services were to be maintained or else explicitly transformed into rent paid in cash or kind: for instance, a *corvée* of one day a week could be converted into a rent equal to a fifth or sixth or the harvest. Or it could be redeemed (that is, wiped out by a cash payment from the peasant to the lord), a solution many legislators regarded as a compromise. Many were afraid that straightforward elimination of the *corvée* without redemption or compensation of any kind might undermine the very concept of rent, if not of property in general.

Most poor peasants could not afford to redeem *corvées* or other seigneurial dues, however, especially since the assembly and its committees set a high price on redemption. The value of land was fixed at the equivalent of twenty years of rent for payments in cash and twenty-five years for payments in kind, which reflected the fact that the average yield of agricultural land at the time amounted to 4–5 percent of the local land price. This was completely out of reach for most peasants. Where the *corvée* was particularly onerous (say, several days a week of unpaid labor), the price of redemption might be high enough to leave the peasant in a situation of perpetual debt close to serfdom or slavery. In practice, redemption of seigneurial rights and national properties was limited to a small minority of noble or non-noble buyers with sufficient cash reserves; most peasants were excluded.

In some cases, *banalités* were also maintained, especially where it was difficult to provide a public service in any form other than a monopoly; for instance, when conditions were such that constructing a mill would have been particularly costly so that building several mills would have had a detrimental effect on their economic viability. Such natural monopolies were acknowledged to be justified, and so it was only right, legislators reasoned, that the profits should go to the person who built and owned the facility, which usually meant the local lord, unless he had sold out to some newcomer. These were difficult issues to resolve in practice. Again, they illustrate the inextricable mingling of property rights with quasi-public services in trifunctional society. The problem here was the same as with the tithe—its champions argued that it financed schools, dispensaries, and granaries for the poor. In practice, *banalités* were not preserved as often as *corvées,* yet they still provoked violent opposition from the peasantry when they were.

Broadly speaking, the "historical" approach taken in 1789–1790 faced one major obstacle: how to establish the "contractual" origin of any particular right. Provided one went far enough, perhaps several centuries, back in time, it was obvious to everyone that violence played a part in the acquisition of most seigneurial rights, which stemmed from conquest and serfdom. If one followed this logic to the end, it was clear that the very idea of a contractual origin of property rights was pure fiction. For revolutionary legislators, most of whom were bourgeois property owners or at any rate people less destitute than the masses, the goal was more modest: namely, to strike a reasonable compromise that would reestablish society on a stable foundation without undermining property rights in general. They feared that any other approach would lead straight to chaos, to say nothing of threatening their own property rights.

The historical approach was therefore in reality quite conservative. In practice, it allowed most seigneurial rights to continue with little change as long as enough time had passed to give them the appearance of settled acquisitions. The logical was "historical," not in the sense that legislators sought to discover the real historic origins of any particular right but rather in the sense that any property right (or similar relationship) that had existed for a long enough time was regarded as prima facie legitimate.

This approach was often summed up by the famous adage *"nulle terre sans seigneur,"* no land without a lord. In other words, without incontestable proof to the contrary, and apart from a few explicitly inventoried cases, the basic principle was that payments in cash or kind received by the lord had a legitimate contractual origin and therefore remained enforceable, even if the terms of the contract now had to be rephrased in a new language.

In some provinces, especially in the south of France, however, a quite different legal tradition prevailed: its principle was "no lord without title." In other words, without written evidence of title, ownership could not be established, and no payment was justified. In that region, where written law predominated, the assembly's directives were not well received. In any case, most property titles, even when they did exist, were to be treated with caution since many had been established by the lords themselves or else by courts they controlled. As a result, peasants in many areas attacked lords in their castles in 1789, seeking to burn any titles they could find, which only added to the confusion.

The situation veered out of control as tensions with foreign governments increased, and the Revolution took a harsher turn. The National Assembly became the Constituent Assembly and adopted a new constitution, turning France into a constitutional monarchy with a property qualification for voting. In June 1791 Louis XVI attempted to flee and was arrested at Varennes in eastern France. The king was accused (not without reason) of seeking to join exiled nobles and plotting with foreign monarchies to crush the Revolution militarily. As war clouds gathered, an insurrection in August 1792 ended with the king's arrest; five months later, in January 1793, he was guillotined. A new assembly known as the National Convention was put in place and charged with drafting a republican constitution based on universal suffrage; this was adopted but did not go into effect before the convention itself was toppled in 1795. Meanwhile, French forces won a decisive victory at Valmy in September 1792, marking the triumph of the republican idea and the symbolic defeat of the trifunctional order. Although France's armies were deprived of their natural leaders, who had fled abroad, they triumphed over the combined forces of monarchy led by nobles from across Europe. Here was living proof that the people in arms could do without the old noble warrior class. Goethe, who witnessed the battle from a nearby hilltop, was in no doubt about the meaning of the event: "In this place on this date begins a new era in world history."

Meanwhile, enforcement of the privilege-abolishing law of August 4, 1789, took a more radical turn. From 1792 on it became increasingly common to reverse the burden of proof by demanding that lords prove the contractual basis of their claims to property rights. In July 1793 the convention issued a decree that took this one step further, adopting what was called a "linguistic" approach: all seigneurial rights and ground rents were to be abolished immediately, without compensation, if the terminology designating them was directly linked to the old feudal order.

This decree applied not only to *corvées* and *banalités* but also to many similar obligations, such as *cens* and *lods*. The *cens* was a form of rent paid to a lord and at one point was linked to a tie of vassalage (that is, political and military subordination). The *lod* was even more interesting, partly because it was so common (in many provinces it was the primary mode of payment to landlords) and partly because it so perfectly illustrated the intimate connection between former regalian rights (which the revolutionaries considered illegitimate) and modern property rights (which they deemed legitimate).

Lods *and the Superposition of Perpetual Rights under the Ancien Régime*

Under the Ancien Régime, the *lod* was a seigneurial *droit de mutation*: a peasant who had acquired the right to use a plot of land in perpetuity (sometimes known as *seigneurie utile*) and who wished to sell that right to another person had to purchase a "right of mutation" (the *lod*) from the lord who had *seigneurie directe* over the property. The term *seigneurie directe* could itself be decomposed into two parts, private and public. The private part covered rights to the land while the public part referred to the judicial rights that went along with ownership. In practice, the *lod* could represent a significant sum, which varied from a twelfth to half of the amount of the sale (or two to ten years of rent).[3] The origin of this payment was generally linked to the lord's judicial power over the region in question: because the lord rendered justice, recorded transactions,

---

3. Recall that the price of land was generally fixed at about twenty years of rent; in other words, the annual rent on a property was about 5 percent of its value.

guaranteed the security of persons and property, and settled disputes, he was entitled to payment of the *lod* when usage rights of a property were transferred from one person to another.

The *lod* might or might not be accompanied by other payments that were sometimes annual, sometimes paid at fixed intervals (the term *lod* often referred to a package of obligations and payments rather than a single sum). Because the *lod* originated with the lord's judicial powers, one might have expected it to be abolished without compensation, like the tithe and the *seigneurie publique*. In practice, however, usage of the *lod* had expanded well beyond its original purpose; revolutionary legislators (or at any rate the most conservative and least bold among them) therefore feared that eliminating it without compensation might undermine the entire proprietarian social order, plunging the country into chaos.

Broadly speaking, one of the characteristics of property relations in the Ancien Régime (and, more generally, in many premodern ternary societies) was the superposition of different types of perpetual rights over the same piece of land (or other property). For instance, one person might enjoy the right to perpetual use of a plot of land (including the right to sell to other individuals), while another might enjoy the right to receive a perpetual payment on a regular basis (such as an annual rent in cash or kind, possibly dependent on the size of the harvest), and yet another might benefit from a right exercised when a transaction took place (a *lod*). Still another individual might hold a monopoly on the oven or mill needed to prepare the product of the land for market (a *banalité*), and another might be entitled to payment of part of a harvest on the occasion of a religious holiday or other ceremony. And so on.

These individual "owners" might be lords, peasants, bishoprics, religious or military orders, monasteries, corporations, or bourgeois. The French Revolution put an end to the superposition of rights and declared that the only perpetual right belonged to the owner of the property; all other rights were necessarily temporary (such as a lease or fixed-term rental contract), with the exception of the state's perpetual right to collect taxes and promulgate new rules.[4] Instead of superposing perpetual rights subject to the rights and duties

---

4. The question of the term of a lease gave rise to complex debates. Revolutionary legislators rejected the idea of perpetual leases (because this would have recreated superpositions of perpetual rights of the feudal type). But some deputies (like Sieyès, always quick to defend the small farmer against the lords, whom he accused of robbing the clergy), pointed out that extending the term of leases might be the

of the two privileged orders as under the Ancien Régime, the Revolution sought to restructure society around two primary actors: the private property owner and the centralized state.

In the case of the *lod,* the solution adopted by the Revolution was to create a public cadastre, the central and emblematic institution of the new ownership society, of which this was the foundational act. Henceforth, the centralized state would maintain a vast register listing all legitimate owners of fields and forests, houses and other buildings, warehouses and factories, and goods and property of every imaginable description. This register would have branches at the local and regional level: prefects and subprefects carefully established maps of *départements* and *communes,* which took the place of a complex patchwork of overlapping territories and jurisdictions that constituted the Ancien Régime.

It was therefore quite natural for revolutionary assemblies to transfer the *lod* to the state in the context of the new fiscal system established in 1790–1791. The *droits de mutations* (sales taxes on property transfers) created at that time took the form of a fairly heavy proportional tax on sales of land and buildings. Payment of the tax allowed the new owner to register his property (and if need be establish his title to it); the proceeds went to the government (apart from a small additional component paid to the notary charged with drawing up the necessary documents). These *droits de mutation* still exist in France to this day, in virtually the same form as when they were created; they amount to roughly two years of rent, which is not insignificant.[5] During debates in the period 1789–1790, there was never any doubt that the *lod* would become a tax paid to the state (and cease to be a seigneurial right) nor that maintaining the cadastre and protecting property rights would become a state responsibility: this was the very foundation of the new proprietarian political regime. The question was what would be done about the existing *lods.* Should they be abolished

---

best way to improve the social standing of peasants who lacked the cash necessary to buy a property; a perpetual lease was in some ways like a perpetual loan. Experiments with agrarian reform in the nineteenth and twentieth centuries in several countries relied (de facto) on a combination of lease term extension and rent reduction; in some cases this amounted to a straightforward transfer of ownership to the user of the land for a very modest price or even free of charge. If reimbursement was too costly, however, it could amount to a perpetual trap.

5. In 2019, the *droits de mutation* amounted to 5–6 percent of the sale value (including both local and state shares, and depending on the *département*). If notary fees are included, this rises to 7–8 percent (or roughly two or more years of rent).

without compensation for the existing beneficiaries, or should they be treated as legitimate property rights, which would then be translated into the new judicial vocabulary? Or—a third possibility—should they be eliminated, but with compensation?

In 1789–1790, the assembly opted for full compensation of the *lods*. A schedule of payments was even established: a peasant (or other holder of usage rights for a plot of land or other property who was by no means always the actual tiller of the soil) could redeem the *lod* for a sum ranging from one-third to five-sixths of the most recent sale, depending on the rate of the *lod* to be redeemed; this was a fairly high price.[6] If the potential buyer could not come up with the sum required, the *lod* could be replaced by an equivalent rent: for example, a half-rent if the *lod* was fixed at half the value of the property (all this in addition to the state *droit de mutation*). Thus the assembly envisioned that an authentic former feudal right would become a modern property right, just as former *corvées*, linked to serfdom, were transformed into rents.

In 1793, the convention decided to reject this logic: *lods* were to be abolished without compensation, so that users of the land would become full owners without being forced to pay out of pocket in the form of a redemption fee or rent. More than any other measure, this reflected the convention's ambition to redistribute wealth. But this approach was relatively short-lived (1793–1794). Under the French Directory (1795–1799) and even more under the French Consulate and First French Empire (1799–1814), the country's new leaders reinstated the property qualifications and other more conservative dispositions of the early stages of the Revolution.[7] They nevertheless ran into trouble when it came to canceling transfers of ownership (through straightforward abolition of the *lods*) decided in 1793–1794, as the concerned peasants and other beneficiaries were not about to give up their new rights without a fight. Broadly

---

6. The *lod* itself generally ranged from one-twelfth to one-half of the property value. The schedule for the redemption of *lods* thus explicitly took account of the fact that higher sales taxes led to less frequent sales. See Blaufarb, *The Great Demarcation*, p. 73.

7. There were very interesting debates when Italian, Dutch, and German territories were departmentalized in 1810–1814. This led to an extremely conservative application of revolutionary proprietarian jurisprudence in these territories, where the Napoleonic authorities had no desire to create new classes of smallholders. Instead, they preferred to reclaim old feudal rights on behalf of the imperial state and use them to bolster new elites of their choosing. See Blaufarb, *The Great Demarcation*, pp. 111–117.

speaking, the many legal twists and turns of the revolutionary years gave rise to a spate of lawsuits, which would occupy the courts through much of the nineteenth century, especially when property was sold or passed on to heirs.

Can Property Be Placed on a New Footing Without Measuring Its Extent?

Among the difficulties that the convention faced in 1793–1794, the most problematic was the fact that the term *lod* appeared very frequently in land contracts during the Ancien Régime. Many contracts between parties who had no noble or "feudal" antecedents used the word to designate the payment to be made in exchange for the right to use the land, even when it took the form of a quasi-rent (usually paid quarterly or annually) rather than a sum paid only when usage rights changed hands. In many cases the word *lod* thus became a synonym for ground rent *(rente foncière)* or rent in general *(loyer)*, regardless of its exact form.

With the "linguistic" approach, one could therefore find oneself outright expropriating a non-noble (and not necessarily wealthy) landowner who had simply rented land acquired a few years before the Revolution but who had had the unfortunate idea of using the word *lod* or *cens* in the rental contract. However, an authentic aristocrat could go on placidly collecting significant seigneurial dues acquired by violent means in the feudal era as long as the vocabulary used in his dealings with the peasants used the words *rente* or *loyer* instead of *lod* or *cens*. In the face of such glaring injustices, revolutionary committees and tribunals were often forced to backtrack so that no one knew any longer what new principles were being followed.

In hindsight, of course, it is possible to imagine other possible solutions that would have avoided the pitfalls of both the "historical" and "linguistic" approaches. Was it really possible to define the conditions of just ownership without taking inequality of ownership into account—that is, without taking into account the value of each property and the extent of the patrimonial holdings in question? In other words, to establish the property regime on a new footing acceptable to the majority, would it not have made more sense to treat small holdings (such as plots suitable for a family farm) differently from very large holdings (such as estates large enough to support hundreds or thousands of family farms), regardless of the vocabulary used to designate the remuneration in each case (*lods, rentes, loyers,* and so on)? It is not always a good idea to search for origins when seeking patrimonial justice. And even if it is sometimes inevitable, it is probably best to think about the size and social significance of the fortunes involved. The task is not simple, but is there any other way to go about it?

In fact, the revolutionary assemblies did provide a stage on which many debates about progressive taxation of income and wealth played out, especially in connection with various projects to establish a *droit national d'hérédité* (national inheritance tax), the rate of which varied with the size of the bequest. For instance, in a bill proposed in the fall of 1792 by Sieur Lacoste, an administrator in the Registry of National Estates, the smallest bequests were to be taxed at less than 5 percent, whereas the rate on the largest was to be more than 65 percent (even for direct line bequests—that is, from parents to children).[8] Ambitious progressive tax proposals had also been put forward in the decades prior to the Revolution, such as the one published in 1767 by Louis Graslin, a tax collector and city planner in Nantes, who envisioned a tax gradually rising from 5 percent on the lowest incomes to 75 percent on the highest (Table 3.1).[9] To be sure, the highest rates proposed in these pamphlets applied only to extremely high incomes (more than a thousand times the average income of the day). But such extreme disparities did exist in late-eighteenth-century French society, and if these tax schedules had been applied within the framework of the law and parliamentary procedure, those inequalities could have been cor-

---

8. See *Du droit national d'hérédité ou moyen de supprimer la contribution foncière,* 1792, Collection Portiez de l'Oise, pièce n°22, La Bibliothèque de l'Assemblée Nationale, Paris, France. According to this proposal, the tax on direct-line bequests exceeding 3 million *livres tournois* was to amount to two shares (that is, 67 percent where there was one heir, 50 percent where there were two, 40 percent where there were three, etc.). A fortune of 3 million livres was roughly 1,500 times the average wealth per adult at the time (which was around 2,000 livres). For direct-line bequests of 50,000 livres (or twenty-five times the average wealth), the tax was to be one-half share (or 33 percent with one heir, 20 percent with two heirs, 14 percent with three heirs, etc.). For fortunes below 2,000 livres (roughly the average), the tax was set at two-tenths of a share (or 17 percent with one heir, 9 percent with two, 6 percent with three). The rates for other bequests (outside the direct line) were higher still. Many similar brochures have been preserved in the archives, attesting to the vigor of contemporary debate.

9. L. Graslin, *Essai analytique sur la richesse et l'impôt* (1767), pp. 292–293. Graslin proposed an effective rate of 5 percent on annual incomes of 150 *livres tournois* (roughly half the average adult income at the time), 15 percent on incomes of 6,000 livres (twenty times the average), 50 percent on 60,000 livres (200 times the average), and 75 percent on 400,000 livres (more than 1,300 times the average).

TABLE 3.1

Progressive tax proposals in eighteenth-century France

Graslin: Progressive income tax (*Essai analytique sur la richesse et l'impôt,* 1767)		Lacoste: Progressive inheritance tax (*Du droit national d'hérédité,* 1792)	
Multiple of average income	Effective tax rate	Multiple of average estate	Effective tax rate
0.5	5%	0.3	6%
20	15%	8	14%
200	50%	500	40%
1300	75%	1500	67%

Interpretation: In the progressive income tax proposed by Graslin in 1767, the effective tax rate rose gradually from 5 percent on an annual income of 150 *livres tournois* (roughly half the average income of the time) to 75 percent on an income of 400,000 livres (roughly 1,300 times the average). Lacoste's proposed progressive inheritance tax exhibits similar progressivity.

Sources: piketty.pse.ens.fr/ideology.

rected. The proposed tax schedules envisioned substantial rates on the order of 20–30 percent (which was quite high, especially for an inheritance tax) for levels of wealth and income on the order of ten to twenty times the average, well below the levels associated with the high nobility and *haute bourgeoisie* of the era. This shows that the authors had fairly ambitious ideas of social reform and redistribution, ideas that could not be limited to a tiny minority of the super-privileged if they were to have any real effect.

Yet no tangible progressive tax was ultimately adopted during the Revolution. True, there were a few brief experiments with progressive local taxes in 1793–1794, when the convention dispatched missions to a number of *départements.* Emergency financial measures of a progressive character were put in place to finance the war, most notably the forced loan of 1793 (which reached a level of 25 percent for incomes of 3,000 *livres tournois,* roughly ten times the average income at the time, and 70 percent for incomes of 15,000, or fifty times the average, while incomes less than a third of the average were exempted).[10]

---

10. On local experiments and emergency measures in the period 1793–1794, see J.-P. Gross, "Progressive Taxation and Social Justice in 18th Century France," *Past and Present,* 1993. For a more detailed analysis, see J.-P. Gross, *Egalitarisme jacobin et droits de l'homme (1793–1794)* (Arcanteres, 2000). Various systems of "maximal succession"

Nevertheless, the central fact remains that the new tax system established by the Revolution in 1790–1791 consisted mainly of strictly proportional taxes with the same moderate rate applied to all levels of income and wealth, no matter how minuscule or gigantic. Note, too, that no agrarian reform or other broad program of wealth redistribution as ambitious as Lacoste or Graslin's tax proposals was ever explicitly formulated.

As we will see, the legal and fiscal system adopted during the Revolution encouraged the accumulation of large fortunes, which goes a long way toward explaining the growing concentration of wealth in France in the nineteenth century. Not until the crises of the early twentieth century did there emerge a steeply progressive system of taxation of income and wealth in France or anywhere else. The same is true of explicitly redistributive agrarian reform programs, comparable to those that emerged in very different contexts in the late nineteenth and early twentieth centuries. No such program was ever attempted in France during the revolutionary period.

Even during the most ambitiously redistributive phase of the Revolution, 1793–1794, debate focused mainly on the issue of *corvées* and *banalités, lods,* and redemption of rights. Legislators tried first a "historical" and later a "linguistic" approach to the abolition of privileges. This gave rise to complex and passionate debate, but the question of inequality in the size of individual patrimonial holdings was never really approached in an explicit and coherent way. Things might have gone differently but didn't, and it is interesting to try to understand why.

Knowledge, Power, and Emancipation: The Transformation of Ternary Societies

To recapitulate, the French Revolution can be seen as an experiment with accelerated transformation of a premodern ternary society. A fundamental feature of this experiment was the "Great Demarcation" project, which created a dividing line between old and new forms of power and property. The goal of the Great Demarcation was to create a strict separation between regalian functions (henceforth the monopoly of the centralized state) and property rights

---

and "national succession" (open to all) were also debated in 1793–1794 but never applied. On this subject, see F. Brunel, "La politique sociale de l'an II: un 'collectivisme individualiste?'" in S. Roza and P. Crétois, eds., *Le républicanisme social: Une exception française?* (Publications de la Sorbonne, 2014), pp. 107–128.

(henceforth to be granted solely to private individuals), whereas trifunctional society was based on an inextricable imbrication of both. The Great Demarcation was in some ways a success in that it contributed to a durable transformation of French society and, to some extent, neighboring societies as well. It was also the first attempt to create a social and political order founded on equal rights for everyone, independent of social origin. All this took place, moreover, in what was by contemporary standards a very large country that for centuries had been organized around enormous status and geographic inequalities. Still, this ambitious Great Demarcation ran into many problems: for all its limitations and injustices, trifunctional society had its own coherence, and the reorganization proposed by the new proprietarian regime contained numerous contradictions. The social role of the Church was eliminated without creating a social state to replace it; the definition of private property was tightened without expanding access to it; and so on.

On the key question of inequality of ownership, moreover, the failure of the French Revolution is clear. One does see a renewal of elites over the course of the nineteenth century (continuing a process that was already under way in earlier centuries, although we lack the tools to measure its extent in different periods), but the fact is that patrimonial holdings remained extremely concentrated between 1789 and 1914 (with a sharp increase in the late nineteenth and early twentieth centuries, as we will see in Chapter 4)—and in the end the Revolution had little effect in this regard. Why this partial failure? It was not only because the issues were novel and complex but also because political time accelerated: although certain ideas were ripe for application, there was no time to put them to the test in concrete experiments. Events—rather than knowledge patiently accumulated—dictated their law to revolutionary legislators and France's new leaders.

Furthermore, the experience of the French Revolution illustrates a more general lesson that we will encounter again and again: historical change stems from the interaction between, on the one hand, the short-term logic of political events and, on the other hand, the long-term logic of political ideologies. Evolving ideas are nothing unless they lead to institutional experiments and practical demonstrations; ideas must find their application in the heat of events, in social struggles, insurrections, and crises. Conversely, political actors caught up in fast-moving events often have no choice but to draw on a repertoire of political and economic ideologies elaborated in the past. At times they may be able to invent new tools on the spur of the moment, but to do so takes time and a capacity for experimentation that are generally lacking.

In the case of the French Revolution, it is interesting to note that debates about the legitimate or illegitimate origins of seigneurial rights had to some extent already taken place in previous centuries. The problem was that those debates often hinged on general historical considerations and offered no truly operational solutions to the concrete questions that would arise in the heat of action. As far back as the late sixteenth and early seventeenth centuries, jurists such as Charles Dumoulin, Jean Bodin, and Charles Loyseau had criticized the way lords—some of whom owed their titles to very early waves of invasion (especially by Franks, Huns, and Normans between the fifth and eleventh centuries)—had taken advantage of the weakness of princes to acquire excessive rights. On the other hand, champions of the seigneurial view, such as Henri de Boulainvilliers and Montesquieu in the eighteenth century, insisted that while the Franks had certainly profited from their initial position of strength, they had subsequently acquired new legitimacy by protecting populations over the course of many centuries, notably against the Normans and Hungarians. The problem was that such discussions of military history, as revealing as they may be about the legitimation of the nobility as a warrior class in the eighteenth century, were not of much use in establishing the conditions for a just refoundation of property rights.

Those earlier debates dealt essentially with the respective roles of the centralized state and local elites. Both Boulainvilliers and Montesquieu defended the idea of preserving *seigneuries publiques* and the sale of charges and offices (a practice that was also abolished during the Revolution, usually with financial compensation to existing officeholders); it was important, they reasoned, to maintain the separation of powers and provide a check on the power of the king. Montesquieu's *De l'esprit des lois (The Spirit of the Laws)*, published in 1748, became an essential reference on the question of separation of powers. Commentators often forget to mention, however, that for Montesquieu, who had himself inherited the highly lucrative position of president of the Parlement of Bordeaux, it was not enough to separate the executive, legislative, and judiciary branches of government. It was also necessary to preserve local seigneurial courts and the "venality" (that is, vendibility and heritability) of charges and offices in the provincial parlements in order to limit the power of the central state and prevent the monarch from becoming a despot like the sultan of Turkey (note in passing that negative comments on the Orient come quite as naturally to the pen of Sieyès, who denounced noble privileges, as to that of Montesquieu, who defended them). The Revolution rejected the view of authors like Boulainvilliers and Montesquieu: the power to render justice was transferred from the old seigneurial class to the centralized state, and the venality of offices was ended.[11]

In retrospect, it is easy to criticize the conservative positions taken by the champions of seigneurial jurisdictional privileges and the venality of judicial and administrative functions. With the advantage of more than two centuries of hindsight, it seems obvious—as it may already have seemed to the most clairvoyant observers in the eighteenth century—that justice can be rendered in a more satisfactory and impartial way in the framework of a universal public service organized by the central state than in seigneurial courts or a system based on the venality of charges and offices. More generally, it seems fairly clear today that a properly organized state is in a better position to guarantee fundamental rights and individual liberties than a trifunctional system based on the power of local elites and the privileges of noble and clerical classes. French peasants were certainly freer in the nineteenth and twentieth centuries than in the eighteenth century, if only because they were no longer subject to arbitrary seigneurial justice.

It is nevertheless important to emphasize that the question of confidence in the centralized state, which underlies these fundamental debates, is a highly complex one, which had no obvious answer until concrete experiments had been conducted with the new state powers. Confidence in the state's ability to render justice fairly and impartially throughout a vast territory, to guarantee security, collect taxes, and provide police, educational, and medical services more justly and efficiently than the old privileged orders was not something that could be decreed from an academic chair. It had to be demonstrated in practice. At bottom, Montesquieu's fears of a potentially despotic state (which led to his defense of local seigneurial courts) are not very different from the suspicions of various forms of supranational state power that one sees today.

For instance, many defenders of interstate competition ignore the fact that some states establish opaque laws that allow them to function as tax or regulatory havens (of particular benefit to the wealthy), justifying their position by pointing to the risk to individual freedom that would result from overcentralization of information and judicial authority under the aegis of a single state.

---

11. See Blaufarb, *The Great Demarcation,* pp. 36–40. In *Considérations sur la noblesse* (1815), Louis de Bonald would also attempt to give new legitimacy to the nobility as a class of magistrates as well as warriors. See B. Karsenti, *D'une philosophie à l'autre. Les sciences sociales et la politique des modernes* (Gallimard, 2013), pp. 82–87.

Such arguments are of course often covertly self-serving (as in Montesquieu's case). Nevertheless, their (at least partial) plausibility makes them that much more politically effective, and only successful historical experimentation can lead to a radical shift in the political and ideological balance of power with issues of this type.

The Revolution, the Centralized State, and Learning about Justice

To sum up, the central question that the French Revolution resolved was that of regalian powers and the centralized state; it did not have an answer when it came to the just distribution of property. Its primary objective was to transfer regalian powers from local noble and clerical elites to the central state, not to organize a broad redistribution of wealth. However, it quickly became apparent that it was not easy to separate the two objectives so neatly. Indeed, the revolutionaries' claim to have abolished all "privileges" on the Night of August 4 opened up a range of possible interpretations and alternatives.

In fact, it is not difficult to imagine one or more series of events that might have produced a more egalitarian result from the abolition of privileges. It is too easy to conclude that "minds were not yet ready" for progressive taxes or land redistribution in the late eighteenth or early nineteenth century and that such innovations "necessarily" had to await the crises of the early twentieth century. It is often tempting in retrospect to lean toward deterministic readings of history and in this case to conclude that the thoroughly bourgeois French Revolution could not have led to anything but a proprietarian regime and an ownership society without any real attempt to reduce inequality. Although it is true that the invention of a new definition of property guaranteed by the centralized state was a complex undertaking, which many revolutionary legislators saw as the central if not sole purpose of the Revolution, it would be reductive to view the complex debates of the time as concerned only with this one approach. When one looks at how events unfolded and at what proposals were made by various participants, it becomes apparent that the idea of abolishing privileges could be interpreted in many different ways and could have led to many different legislative proposals. Had largely contingent circumstances been different, events might have taken many alternative paths, even though the course actually followed was already quite sinuous (as the "historical" and "linguistic" approaches suggest).

Beyond conflicts of interest, which should never be neglected, there were also intellectual conflicts. No one, then or now, has ready-made totally convincing solutions that would at once define "privileges," explain how to eliminate them, and say how property should be regulated and inequality curbed in the society to come. During the Revolution, everyone could point to past experiences and ideas, and the whole community was involved in a vast and conflictual process of social learning. Everyone felt that *corvées, banalités,* and *lods* belonged to the past, yet many feared that eliminating them without compensation would undermine the whole system of rents and unequal ownership. Because no one could say where such a process would end, there was a temptation to maintain old rights in one form or another. While quite conservative, this position was comprehensible, yet it became the object of violent attacks by those who did not share it. Conflict and uncertainty are inevitable in events such as these.

Recent work has also shown that very vigorous debate on these issues, including inequality and property, agitated Europeans during the Enlightenment, contrary to the consensus view put forward by some scholars. Jonathan Israel distinguishes between a "radical" Enlightenment (represented by Diderot, Condorcet, Holbach, and Paine) and a "moderate" Enlightenment (represented by Voltaire, Montesquieu, Turgot, and Smith). The radicals generally supported the idea of a single assembly instead of separate chambers for each order as well as an end to the privileges of nobility and clergy and some form of redistribution of property. More generally, they favored greater equality of classes, sexes, and races. The "moderates" (who might equally well be characterized as "conservatives") were suspicious of single assemblies and radical abolition of property rights, whether of landlords or slaveowners; they also had greater faith in natural, gradual progress. Outside of France, one of the most celebrated moderates was Adam Smith, the originator of the "invisible hand" of the market. According to the moderates, the principal virtue of the market was precisely that it made for human progress without violent upheaval or disruption of venerable political institutions.[12]

When one looks more closely at the positions of both groups on inequality and property, however, the differences are not always so clear. Many of the "radicals" also tended to rely on "natural forces." Take, for example, this typical optimistic passage from the "radical" Condorcet's *Esquisse d'un tableau historique des progress de l'esprit humain* (1794): "It is easy to prove that fortunes tend naturally toward equality, and their excessive disproportion either cannot

---

12. J. Israel, *A Revolution of the Mind: Radical Enlightenment and the Intellectual Origins of Modern Democracy* (Princeton University Press, 2010).

exist or must promptly cease if civil laws do not establish artificial means of perpetuating and combining them, and if freedom of commerce and industry eliminate the advantages that any prohibitive law or fiscal right gives to acquired wealth."[13] In other words, it is enough to eliminate privileges and charges and to establish equal access to different occupations and to property rights for existing inequalities to disappear at once. The fact that on the eve of World War I, more than a century after the abolition of "privileges," the concentration of wealth in France was even higher than it was at the time of the Revolution, unfortunately proves that this optimistic view was wrong. To be sure, Condorcet did propose a form of progressive taxation in 1792, but it was a relatively modest measure (with a maximum rate of less than 5 percent on the highest incomes). Condorcet's proposal was much more limited than those of less celebrated writers such as Lacoste and Graslin, who interestingly enough were practitioners in the areas of taxation and public administration rather than philosophers or academics; this did not prevent them from contributing bold and imaginative suggestions—quite the opposite.[14] The most subversive actors were not always the ones identified by scholars.

In any case, specific reform proposals did exist, and some of them came from the most emblematic representatives of the Enlightenment. The Revolution might well have taken a different course, particularly if military and political tensions had not run so high in the period 1792–1795, thus allowing revolutionary legislators a little more time to experiment with concrete measures to redistribute wealth and reduce inequality. Think, too, of the pamphlet Thomas Paine addressed to French legislators in 1795, *Agrarian Justice*. He proposed a 10 percent tax on inheritances, the proceeds of which would go to finance an ambitious universal income—an idea that was far ahead of its

---

13. M. de Condorcet, *Esquisse d'un tableau historique des progrès de l'esprit humain* (1794), p. 380.

14. In his *Mémoire sur la fixation de l'impôt,* Condorcet proposed that any new tax on personal furniture (the ancestor of today's *taxe d'habitation,* or residential tax) should include a progressive rate on the rental value of the principal residence, with a maximum of 50 percent. Since rents decreased with income (contemporary estimates suggest that the poorest tenants paid more than 20 percent of their income in rent, compared with less than 10 percent for the wealthiest), Condorcet's proposal was meant primarily to correct the structural regressivity of this tax (unfortunately, it was not adopted). On Condorcet's fiscal proposals, see also J.-P. Gross, "Progressive Taxation and Social Justice in 18th Century France," pp. 109–110.

time.[15] The 10 percent rate was admittedly quite moderate compared with the highly progressive tax schedules discussed and then enacted in the twentieth century; what is more, Paine's proposal was for a quasi-proportional tax, whereas many more progressive proposals had been debated in previous years. It was nevertheless more substantial than the modest 1 percent tax that was finally adopted for direct line bequests under the tax system that was introduced during the French Revolution and that persisted throughout the nineteenth century.[16]

The rapidity with which things changed after World War I, when progressive taxes on income and inheritances were introduced in Europe and the United States, suggests that things could have been different. The rapid change of mentalities is even more telling: a tax schedule that had once seemed totally inconceivable was deemed acceptable by nearly everyone only a few years later. Had it been possible to experiment in a calm, serious way, even for just a few years, with concrete measures of the sort advocated by Condorcet and Paine in the 1790s (insofar as it is possible to experiment with institutions of this kind) under the aegis of a duly elected legislature, the course of events might have been different. It was by no means inevitable that the conservative and Napoleonic reaction would consolidate its position so quickly, with the return first of property qualifications for voting and then of émigré nobles and slavery, during which Napoleon created a new imperial nobility. The point here is not to rewrite history but simply to stress the importance of the logic of events and of concrete historical experimentation in moments of political and ideological flux around issues of property and inequality. Rather than read history deterministically, it is more interesting to look at past events as

---

15. Born in England, Paine was a fervent proponent of American independence and later of the Revolution in France, where he settled in the 1790s. On the differences between Paine and Condorcet and the more innovative nature of Paine's proposals, see Y. Bosc, "Républicanisme et protection sociale: l'opposition Paine-Condorcet," in Roza and Crétois, eds., *Le républicanisme social*, pp. 129–146.

16. Note, moreover, that in *The Rights of Man* (1792) Paine proposed a tax rate of 80–90 percent on the highest incomes, starting at around 20,000 pounds sterling per year (roughly a thousand times the average British income at the time), a rate comparable to that proposed by Graslin in 1767. On Paine's proposals, see also H. Phelps Brown, *Egalitarianism and the Generation of Inequality* (Oxford University Press, 1998), pp. 139–142.

crossroads of ideas, forks in the road where history might have taken a different course.[17]

Proprietarian Ideology: Between Emancipation and Sacralization

More generally, the French Revolution illustrates a tension that we will encounter again and again in what follows. On the one hand, proprietarian ideology has an emancipatory dimension, which is real and should never be forgotten. On the other hand, it tends to bestow quasi-sacred status on existing property rights, regardless of origin or extent. This is just as real, and the inegalitarian and authoritarian consequences can be considerable.

Fundamentally, proprietarian ideology rests not only on a promise of social and political stability but also on an idea of individual emancipation through property rights, which are supposedly open to anyone—or at least any adult male, because nineteenth- and early twentieth-century ownership societies were resolutely patriarchal, bringing to bear all the force and inevitability of a modern centralized legal system. In theory, property rights are enforced without regard to social or family origin under the equitable protection of the state. Compared with trifunctional societies, which were based on relatively rigid status disparities between clergy, nobility, and third estate and on a promise of functional complementarity, equilibrium, and cross-class alliances, ownership society saw itself as based on equal rights. In ownership societies the "privileges" of the clergy and nobility no longer existed (or were at least considerably curtailed). Everyone was entitled to secure enjoyment of his property—safe from arbitrary encroachment by king, lord, or bishop—under the protection of stable, predictable rules in a state of laws, not men. Everyone therefore had an incentive to derive the maximum fruits from his property,

---

17. During the Cold War, the historiography of the Revolution was unfortunately divided between Marxist approaches (based on the highly disputable hypotheses that the Russian Revolution of 1917 was a natural sequel to the events of 1793–1794 in France) and anti-Marxist ones (based on the (equally debatable) principle that any ambitious attempt at social redistribution necessarily leads to terror and Soviet-like totalitarianism). See the online appendix for the main references (Albert Soboul versus François Furet). This often caricatural instrumentalization of the French Revolution for the purposes of twentieth-century ideological combat explains why more refined political-ideological approaches such as Rafe Blaufarb's on the redefinition of the property regime were slow to develop.

using whatever knowledge and talent he had at his disposal. Such clever use of every person's abilities was supposed to lead naturally to general prosperity and social harmony.

This promise of equality and harmony found unambiguous expression in solemn declarations issuing from the "Atlantic revolutions" of the late eighteenth century. The Declaration of Independence that was adopted in Philadelphia, Pennsylvania, on July 4, 1776, begins with a ringing affirmation: "We hold these truths to be self-evident, that all men are created equal, that they are endowed by their Creator with certain unalienable Rights, that among these are Life, Liberty and the pursuit of Happiness." The reality was more complex, however. Thomas Jefferson, the author of the declaration, owned some 200 slaves in Virginia but forgot to mention their existence or the fact that they would obviously continue to be somewhat less equal than their owners. Yet for the white settlers of the United States, the Declaration of Independence was an affirmation of equality and liberty in defiance of the arbitrary power of the king of England and the privileges of the House of Lords and House of Commons. Those assemblies of the privileged were exhorted to leave the settlers alone, to refrain from taxing them unfairly, and to stop interfering in their pursuit of happiness and conduct of affairs, including their management of their own property and inequalities.

We find the same radicality and comparable ambiguity in a different inegalitarian context with the Declaration of the Rights of Man and the Citizen, adopted by the National Assembly in August 1789 shortly after the vote to abolish privileges. Article 1 begins with a promise of absolute equality, marking a clear break with the old society of orders: "Men are born and remain free and equal in rights." The remainder of the article raises the possibility of a just inequality, on which it nevertheless places conditions: "Social distinctions can only be based on common utility." Article 2 clarifies things by according the right to property the status of an imprescriptible natural right: "The purpose of any political association is to preserve the natural and imprescriptible rights of Man. Those rights are liberty, property, security, and resistance to oppression." In the end, the text can be interpreted in contradictory ways, and in practice it was. For instance, Article 1 can be given a relatively redistributive reading: "social distinctions"—that is, inequalities broadly construed—are acceptable only if they are of common utility and serve the general interest, which might mean that they have to serve the interests of the poorest members of society. This article could therefore be mobilized to call for redistribution of property in some form and thus to help the poor gain access to wealth. But

Article 2 could be read in a much more restrictive sense, since it implies that property rights acquired in the past are "natural and imprescriptible" and therefore difficult to challenge. In fact, this article was used in revolutionary debates to justify great caution when it came to the redistribution of property. More generally, references to property rights in various declarations of rights and constitutions were often used in the nineteenth and twentieth centuries to impose drastic legal limits on any possibility of a peaceful, legal redefinition of the property regime, and this continues to be the case today.

Indeed, once the abolition of privileges is proclaimed, many possible ways forward exist within the proprietarian schema, as we saw in the case of the French Revolution, with all its hesitations and ambiguities. For instance, one might argue that the best way to encourage equal access to property is to levy a steeply progressive tax on income and estates, and specific proposals along these lines were indeed formulated in the eighteenth century. More generally, one can make use of the emancipatory aspects of private property institutions (to allow room for the expression of various individual aspirations—something twentieth-century communist societies tragically chose to forget) while regulating and instrumentalizing those aspirations within the social state. One can also make use of redistributive institutions such as progressive taxes or pass laws to democratize access to knowledge, power, and wealth (as social-democratic societies tried to do in the twentieth century, even if their efforts were insufficient and incomplete; we will come back to this). Or, finally, one can rely on absolute protection of private property to resolve nearly all problems, which in some cases can lead to a quasi-sacralization of property and deep suspicion of any attempt to call it into question.

Critical proprietarianism (for simplicity, of the social-democratic type, which depends on mixed private, public, and social ownership) attempts to instrumentalize private property on behalf of higher objectives; exacerbated proprietarianism sacralizes it and transforms it into a systematic solution. Beyond these two general pathways there exists an infinite variety of imaginable solutions and trajectories. Importantly, still other paths remain to be invented. Throughout the nineteenth century and until World War I, exacerbated proprietarianism held sway with its quasi-sacralization of private property, not only in France but also throughout Europe. On the basis of the historical experience we have now acquired, it seems to me that this form of proprietarianism must be rejected. But it is important to understand the reasons why this ideological schema was successful, especially in nineteenth-century European ownership societies.

On the Justification of Inequality in Ownership Societies

Ultimately, the argument put forward by proprietarian ideology, implicitly in declarations of rights and constitutions and much more explicitly in the political debates around property that took place during the French Revolution and throughout the nineteenth century, can be summarized as follows. If one begins to question property rights acquired in the past, and the inequality that derives from them, in the name of a respectable but always imperfectly defined and contested conception of social justice about which consensus will never be achieved, doesn't one run the risk of not knowing where this dangerous process will end? Political instability and permanent chaos may then ensue, ultimately to the detriment of people of modest means. It is therefore wrong to run this risk, argue intransigent proprietarians; redistribution is a Pandora's box, which should never be opened. One runs into this type of argument repeatedly in the French Revolution; it explains many ambiguities and hesitations, in particular the hesitation about whether to adopt a "historical" or "linguistic" approach to existing rights and their retranscription as new property rights. If one questioned *corvées* and *lods,* wasn't there a risk of undermining *loyers* and indeed the whole system of property rights in general? These arguments recur in the ownership societies of the nineteenth and early twentieth centuries, and we will also find that they continue to play a fundamental role in contemporary political debate, particularly since the powerful revival of neo-proprietarian discourse in the late twentieth century.

The sacralization of private property is basically a natural response to fear of the void. The trifunctional schema had established a balance of power between warriors and clerics that was based on a large dose of religious transcendence (which was indispensable for bestowing legitimacy on the sage counsel of the clergy). Once this was abandoned, new ways of ensuring social stability had to be found. Absolute respect for property rights acquired in the past offered a new form of transcendence, which made it possible to avoid widespread chaos and fill the void left by the end of trifunctional ideology. The sacralization of property was in some ways a response to the end of religion as an explicit political ideology.

On the basis of historical experience, and of the rational knowledge that has been constructed out of that experience, I believe it is possible to do better. While the sacralization response was natural and comprehensible, it was also somewhat lazy and nihilistic as well as short on optimism regarding human nature. This book will try to convince the reader that one can draw on the lessons of history to develop more satisfactory norms of social justice and equality, of economic regulation and redistribution of wealth, rather than using simple sacralization of existing property rights. Those norms must of course evolve over time and be open to permanent deliberation, yet they will still represent an improvement over the convenient option of settling for what already exists and taking as natural the inequalities produced by the "market." Indeed, it was on such a pragmatic, empirical, and historical basis that the social-democratic societies of the twentieth century developed. For all their shortcomings, they showed that the extreme inequality of wealth that existed in the nineteenth century was by no means indispensable for maintaining stability and prosperity—far from it. We can build today's innovative ideologies and political movements on this same basis.

The great weakness of proprietarian ideology was that property rights stemming from the past often raised serious problems of legitimacy. We saw this in the French Revolution, which simply transformed *corvées* into rents, and we will often encounter it again. For example, when slavery was abolished in French and British colonies, it was decided that slaveowners would have to be compensated, but not slaves. Another case in point concerns the postcommunist privatization of public property and private pillaging of natural resources. More generally, the problem is that—notwithstanding the possible violent or illegitimate origins of initial appropriations—significant, durable, and largely arbitrary inequalities of wealth tend to reconstitute themselves in today's modern hypercapitalist societies, just as they did in premodern societies.

In any case, it is not easy to construct norms of justice acceptable to the majority. We cannot really tackle this complex question until we have completed our study and examined all available historical experiences, especially the crucial experiences of the twentieth century with respect to progressive taxation and, more generally, redistribution of wealth. These constitute not only material historical evidence that extreme inequality is by no means inevitable but also concrete operational knowledge of what minimal level of inequality one can hope to achieve. To be sure, the proprietarian argument concerning the need for institutional stability deserves to be taken seriously and carefully evaluated. So does the meritocratic argument, which played a less central role in the proprietarian ideology of the nineteenth century than in the neo-proprietarian ideology that has held sway since the late twentieth century. There will be much more to say about these various political and ideological twists and turns.

Broadly speaking, hard-core proprietarian ideology should be analyzed for what it is: a sophisticated discourse, which is potentially convincing in certain respects, because private property, when correctly redefined within proper limits, is one of the institutions that enable the aspirations and subjectivities of different individuals to find expression and interact constructively. But it is also an inegalitarian ideology, which in its harshest, most extreme form seeks simply to justify a specific form of social domination, often in excessive and caricatural fashion. Indeed, it is a very useful ideology for people and countries that find themselves at the top of the heap. The wealthiest individuals can use it to justify their position vis-à-vis the poorest: they deserve what they have, they say, because of their talent and effort, and in any case inequality contributes to social stability, which supposedly benefits everyone. The wealthiest countries can also justify their domination over the poorest on the grounds that their laws and institutions are superior. The problem is that the arguments and facts advanced in support of these positions are not always convincing. Before we analyze this history and the crises to which it led, however, we need to study how ownership societies evolved in France and elsewhere in Europe following their ambiguous beginnings in the French Revolution.

FOUR

Ownership Societies: The Case of France

In the previous chapter we looked at the French Revolution as a moment of emblematic rupture in the history of inegalitarian regimes. Within the space of a few years, revolutionary lawmakers tried to redefine the relations of power and property they inherited from the trifunctional scheme and to introduce a strict separation between regalian powers (henceforth to be a monopoly of the state) and property rights (ostensibly open to all). We were able to gain a sense of the magnitude of the task and of the contradictions they encountered and specifically of the way complex political and legal processes and events ultimately collided with the question of inequality and redistribution of wealth. As a result, the new proprietarian language often enshrined rights that stemmed from old trifunctional relations of domination, such as *corvées* and *lods*.

We will now look at how the distribution of property evolved in nineteenth-century France. The French Revolution opened up several possible ways forward, but the one ultimately chosen led to the development of an extremely inegalitarian form of ownership regime that endured from 1800 to 1914. This outcome was strongly assisted by the fiscal system established by the Revolution, which persisted without much change until World War I for reasons we will try to understand. Comparison with the course followed by other European countries such as the United Kingdom and Sweden (Chapter 5) will help us to understand both the similarity and diversity of European ownership regimes in the nineteenth and early twentieth centuries.

The French Revolution and the Development of an Ownership Society

What can we say about the evolution of property ownership and concentration in the century following the French Revolution? For this we are able to call on an abundance of sources. For although the Revolution of 1789 did not succeed in establishing social justice here below, it did leave us an incomparable resource for the study of wealth: namely, inheritance archives, which recorded property of many kinds, using a system of classification which itself is a reflection of proprietarian ideology. Thanks to the digitization of hundreds of thousands of inheritance records from these incomparably rich archives, it has been possible to study in detail the evolving distribution of wealth of all kinds (land, buildings, tools and equipment, stocks, bonds, shares of partnerships, and other financial investments) from the time of the Revolution to the present. The results presented here are the product of a large joint research effort, which drew extensively on the Paris archives in particular. National tax records from different periods were also used, along with records from *département* archives from the beginning of the nineteenth century on.[1]

The most striking conclusion is this: the concentration of private property, which was already extremely high in 1800–1810, only slightly lower than on the eve of the Revolution, steadily increased throughout the nineteenth century and up to the eve of World War I. Concretely, looking at France as a whole, we find that the top centile of the wealth distribution (that is, the wealthiest 1 percent) owned roughly 45 percent of private property of all kinds in the period 1800–1810; by 1900–1910 this figure had risen to almost 55 percent. The case of Paris is especially noteworthy: there, the wealthiest 1 percent owned nearly 50 percent of all property in 1800–1810 and more than 65 percent on the eve of World War I (Fig. 4.1).

Indeed, wealth inequality rose even more rapidly in the Belle Époque (1880–1914). In the decades prior to World War I, there seemed to be no limit to the concentration of fortunes. Looking at these curves, one cannot help wondering how high the concentration of private property might have risen had the two world wars and the violent political cataclysms of the twentieth century not occurred. There is also good reason to wonder whether those cataclysms and wars were not themselves consequences, at least in part, of the extreme social tensions due to rising inequality. I will have more to say about this in Part Three.

Several points deserve emphasis. First, it is important to bear in mind that the concentration of wealth has always been extremely high in countries like France, not only in the nineteenth century but also in the twentieth and twenty-first centuries. Although the top centile share decreased considerably over the

---

1. The Paris work was conducted by G. Postel-Vinay and J.-L. Rosenthal. The *départemental* work was organized primarily by J. Bourdieu, L. Kesztenbaum, and A. Suwa-Eisenman. See esp. T. Piketty, G. Postel-Vinay, and J. L. Rosenthal, "Wealth Concentration in a Developing Economy: Paris and France, 1807–1994," *American Economic Review,* 2006. See online appendix for a full bibliography.

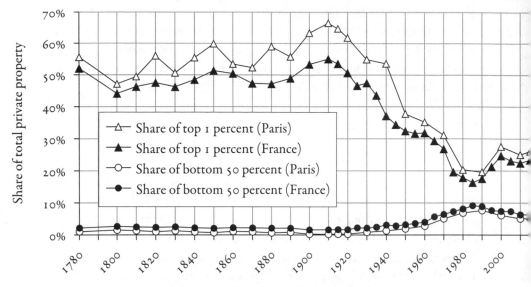

FIG. 4.1. The failure of the French Revolution: The rise of proprietarian inequality in nineteenth-century France

Interpretation: In Paris, the wealthiest 1 percent held roughly 67 percent of all private property in 1910, compared with 49 percent in 1810 and 55 percent in 1780. After a slight decrease during the French Revolution, the concentration of wealth increased in France (and even more in Paris) during the nineteenth century to the eve of World War I. Over the long run, inequality fell after the two world wars (1914–1945) but not after the French Revolution. *Sources and series:* piketty.pse.ens.fr/ideology.

course of the twentieth century (from 55–65 percent of total wealth in France and Paris on the eve of 1914 to 20–30 percent after 1980), the share owned by the poorest 50 percent has always been extremely low: roughly 2 percent in the nineteenth century and a little over 5 percent today (Fig. 4.1). Thus the poorest half of the population—a vast social group fifty times larger than the top centile, by definition—owned something on the order of one-thirtieth the wealth of the top 1 percent in the nineteenth century. This means that the average wealth of the top centile was roughly 1,500 times the average wealth of the bottom 50 percent. Similarly, the poorest half owned roughly one-fifth the wealth of the top centile in the late twentieth century, as it does today (which implies that the average wealth of a 1 percenter is "only" 250 times that of a person in the bottom half of the distribution). Note, moreover, that in both periods we find the same extreme inequality within each age cohort, from youngest to oldest.[2] These orders of magnitude are important, because they tell us that we should not overestimate the extent of the diffusion of ownership that has taken place over the past two centuries: the egalitarian ownership society— or even, more modestly, a society in which the poorest half of the population owns more than a token share of the wealth—has yet to be invented.

Reducing Inequality: The Invention of a "Patrimonial Middle Class"

When we look at the evolution of the distribution of wealth in France, it is striking to find that in the nineteenth century, the "upper classes" (that is, the wealthiest 10 percent) owned between 80 and 90 percent of the wealth, while today they own between 50 and 60 percent—still a significant share (Fig. 4.2). For comparison, the concentration of income, including both income from capital (which is as concentrated as ownership of capital, indeed slightly higher) and income from labor (which is significantly less unequally distributed), has always been less extreme: the top 10 percent of the income distribution claimed about 50 percent of total income in the nineteenth century, compared with 30–35 percent today (Fig. 4.3).

Nevertheless, it is a fact that wealth inequality has decreased over the long run. However, this profound transformation has not benefited the "lower classes" (the bottom 50 percent), whose share remains quite limited. The benefits have gone almost exclusively to what I have called the "patrimonial (or property-owning) middle class,"* by which I mean the 40 percent in the middle of the distribution, between the poorest 50 percent and the wealthiest 10 percent, whose share of total wealth was less than 15 percent in the nineteenth century and stands at about 40 percent today (Fig. 4.2). The emergence of this "middle class" of owners, who individually are not very rich but collectively over the course of the twentieth century acquired wealth greater than that owned by the top centile (with a concomitant decrease in the top centile's share), was a social, economic, and political transformation of fundamental importance. As we will see, it explains most of the reduction of wealth inequality over the long run in France and most other European countries. Furthermore,

---

2. See B. Garbinti, J. Goupille-Lebret, and T. Piketty, "Accounting for Wealth Inequality Dynamics: Methods and Estimates for France (1800–2014)," WID.world, 2017. In Part Three I will return to the current structure of wealth inequality. See esp. Chap. 11, Fig. 11.17.

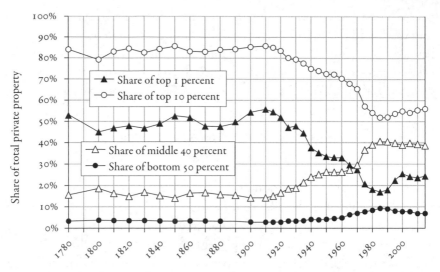

FIG. 4.2. The distribution of property in France, 1780–2015

Interpretation: The share of the wealthiest 10 percent of all private property (real estate, professional equipment, and financial assets, net of debt) varied from 80 to 90 percent in France between 1780 and 1910. Deconcentration of wealth began after World War I and ended in the early 1980s. The principal beneficiary was the "patrimonial middle class" (the 40 percent in the middle of the distribution), here defined as the group between the "lower class" (bottom 50 percent) and the "upper class" (wealthiest 10 percent). *Sources and series:* piketty.pse.ens.fr/ideology.

this deconcentration of ownership does not seem to have impaired innovation or economic growth—quite the opposite: the emergence of the "middle class" went hand in hand with greater social mobility, and growth since the middle of the twentieth century has been stronger than ever before, in particular stronger than it was before 1914. I will come back to this, but for now the key point to notice is that this deconcentration of wealth did not begin until after World War I. Until 1914, wealth inequality seemed to be growing without limit in France, and especially in Paris.

Paris, Capital of Inequality: From Literature to Inheritance Archives

The evolution that took place in Paris between 1800 and 1914 is particularly emblematic, because the capital was both the seat of the largest fortunes and

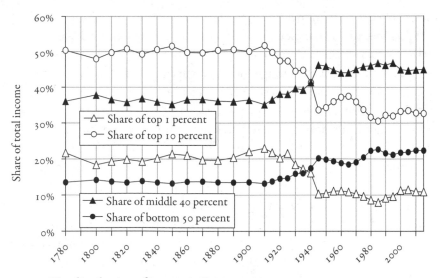

FIG. 4.3. The distribution of income in France, 1780–2015

Interpretation: The share of the top 10 percent of earners in total income from both capital (rent, dividends, interest, and profits) and labor (wages, nonwage income, pensions, and unemployment insurance) was about 50 percent in France from 1780 to 1910. Deconcentration began after World War I, with the "lower class" (bottom 50 percent) and "middle class" (middle 40 percent) as the main beneficiaries at the expense of the "upper class" (top 10 percent). *Sources and series:* piketty.pse.ens.fr/ideology.

the site of the most extreme inequalities. This reality stands out clearly in literature, especially the classic novels of the nineteenth century, as well as in the inheritance archives (Fig. 4.1).

At the end of the nineteenth century, about 5 percent of the population of France lived in Paris (2 million people out of a total population of about 40 million), but residents of the capital owned about 25 percent of the country's private wealth. Put differently, the average Parisian was five times wealthier than the average citizen of France. Paris was also the place where the gap between the poorest and the wealthiest citizens was the largest. In the nineteenth century, half of the people who died in France had no property to pass on. In Paris, the percentage who died propertyless varied from 69 to 74 percent over the period 1800–1914, with a slight upward trend. In practice, this group included people whose personal effects (furniture, clothing, dinnerware) had such little market value that the authorities saw no reason to record the amount. When meager belongings went entirely to cover the costs of burial or repay debts, heirs might choose to renounce the inheritance and file no declaration. Still, it is striking that among the estates recorded in the archives, we find many that are extremely small. The law required both the authorities and the heirs to register even very small estates, failing which the heirs' property rights might not be recognized. This could have serious consequences: specifically, the police could not be called if unregistered property was pilfered. If a person inherited a building or business or financial assets, it was essential to file an estate declaration.

Among the 70 percent of Parisians who died propertyless in the nineteenth century was Balzac's memorable fictional character Père Goriot, who, according to the novelist, died in 1821, abandoned by his daughters, Delphine and Anastasie, in the most abject poverty. His landlord, Madame Vauquer, dunned Rastignac for Goriot's unpaid room and board, and he also had to pay the cost of burial, which by itself exceeded the value of the old man's personal effects. Yet Goriot had amassed a fortune in the pasta and grain trade during the revolutionary and Napoleonic wars before spending it all to ensure that his two daughters would marry into good Parisian society. Unlike him, many who died with nothing had never owned anything and died as poor as they had lived. Strikingly, the percentage of Parisians who died with nothing to pass on to their heirs was just as high a century later in 1914, on the eve of the war, despite the considerable growth of France's wealth and industrial development since the era of Balzac and Père Goriot.[3]

At the other end of the scale, Belle Époque Paris was also the place where the greatest wealth was concentrated: the wealthiest 1 percent of decedents alone accounted for half the value of all bequests in the 1810s as well as almost two-thirds a century later.[4] The share of the wealthiest 10 percent was

---

3. Between 1800 and 1914, average wealth at death was multiplied by more than six in Paris (from 20,000 to roughly 130,000 francs, counting those who died with nothing) and by nearly five in all of France (from 5,000 to 25,000 francs). This increase was real, not just nominal, because the purchasing power of the franc did not very much in this period. See T. Piketty, G. Postel-Vinay, and J.-L. Rosenthal, "Wealth Concentration in a Developing Economy: Paris and France, 1807–1994." See also J. Bourdieu, G. Postel-Vinay, and A. Suwa-Eisenmann, "Pourquoi la richesse ne s'est-elle pas diffusée avec la croissance? Le degré zéro de l'inégalité en France et son évolution en France 1800–1940," *Histoire et mesure*, 2003.

4. The graphs in Figs. 4.1 and 4.2 reflect inequality of wealth among living adults at each date. We started with wealth at time of death and then reweighted each observation according to the number of living individuals in each age cohort, taking into account different mortality rates at different levels of wealth. In practice, this did not make much difference. Concentration of wealth among the living is barely

80–90 percent of the total in the period 1800–1914 and more than 90 percent in Paris, in both cases with an upward trend.

To sum up, nearly all property was concentrated in the top decile and most of it in the top centile, while the vast majority of the population owned nothing. For a more concrete sense of inequality in Paris at the time, note that, according to the cadastre, almost no one in Paris owned an individual apartment before World War I. In other words, one normally owned an entire building (or several buildings), or else one owned nothing and paid rent to a landlord.

It was this hyperconcentration of wealth that led the sinister Vautrin to explain to young Rastignac that he had best not count on the study of law if he wished to succeed in life. The only way to achieve a comfortable position was to lay hands on a fortune by whatever means were available. Vautrin's lecture, replete with comments on the income of lawyers, judges, and landlords, reflected more than just Balzac's obsession with money and wealth (he himself was heavily in debt after a series of bad investments and wrote constantly in the hope of climbing out of his hole). The evidence collected from the archives suggests that Balzac was painting a fairly accurate picture of the distribution of income and wealth in 1820 and, more broadly, in the period 1800–1914. Vautrin's lecture perfectly captured the ownership society—that is, a society in which access to comfort, high society, status, and political influence was almost entirely determined by the size of one's fortune.[5]

Portfolio Diversification and Forms of Property

It is important to note that this extreme concentration of wealth, which grew more extreme over the long nineteenth century, took place in a context of modernization and extensive transformation of the very forms in which wealth was held; economic and financial institutions were reshaped as portfolios became increasingly international. The very detailed inheritance records we have gathered show that Parisian fortunes had become increasingly diversified by the end of the period. In 1912, 35 percent of Parisians' wealth consisted of real estate (24 percent in Paris and 11 percent in the provinces); 62 percent financial assets; and barely 3 percent furniture, precious objects, and other personal effects (Table 4.1). The preponderance of financial assets reflects the growth

a few percentage points greater than inequality of wealth at death, and all temporal evolutions are more or less the same. See the online appendix.

5. On Vautrin's lesson, see T. Piketty, *Capital in the Twenty-First Century,* trans. A. Goldhammer (Harvard University Press, 2014), pp. 228–232.

TABLE 4.1

Composition of Parisian wealth in the period 1872–1912 (in percent)

	Real estate (buildings, houses, agricultural land, etc.)	Paris real estate	Provincial real estate	Financial assets (equity, bonds, etc.)	French equity (stocks)	Foreign equity (stocks)
Composition of total wealth						
1872	41	28	13	56	14	1
1912	35	24	11	62	13	7
Composition of the largest 1 percent of estates						
1872	43	30	13	55	15	1
1912	32	22	10	66	15	10
Composition of the next-largest 9 percent						
1872	42	27	15	56	13	1
1912	42	30	12	55	11	2
Composition of the next-largest 40 percent						
1872	27	1	26	62	12	1
1912	31	7	24	59	12	1

Interpretation: In 1912, real estate accounted for 35 percent of total Parisian wealth, financial assets for 62 percent (including 21 percent for foreign financial assets), and for furniture and precious objects, 3 percent. Of the largest 1 percent of fortunes, the share of financial assets rose to 66 percent (of which 25 percent were foreign).

Sources: piketty.pse.ens.fr/ideology.

of industry and the importance of the stock market, with investment not only in manufacturing (where textiles were on the brink of being overtaken by steel and coal at the end of the nineteenth century and then by chemistry and automobiles in the twentieth) but also in food processing, railroads, and banking—and it was the banking sector that was doing particularly well.

The 62 percent of wealth held in the form of financial assets was itself quite varied: 20 percent consisted of shares in firms (whether listed on the stock exchange or not), of which 13 percent was invested in French firms and 7 percent foreign firms; 19 percent consisted of private debt instruments (including notes, bonds, and other commercial paper; 14 percent French and 5 percent foreign);

French private bonds	Foreign private bonds	French government bonds	Foreign government bonds	Other financial assets (deposits, cash, etc.)	*Total foreign financial assets*	Furniture, precious objects, etc.
17	2	10	3	9	*6*	3
14	5	5	9	9	*21*	3
14	2	9	4	10	*7*	2
14	5	4	10	8	*25*	2
21	2	10	2	7	*5*	2
14	4	7	8	9	*14*	3
23	1	14	2	9	*4*	11
20	2	10	4	10	*7*	10

14 percent was public debt (that is, government bonds; 5 percent French and 9 percent foreign); and 9 percent consisted of other financial assets (deposits, cash, miscellaneous shares, and so on). This looks like the sort of well-diversified portfolio one might find in a modern finance textbook, except that this was reality as reflected in Paris inheritance records in the late nineteenth and early twentieth centuries. For each deceased person one can identify exactly which stocks and bonds were held in which firms and which sectors.

Two additional results are worth noting. First, the largest fortunes had an even larger share of financial assets than the others. In 1912, the top 1 percent of fortunes consisted of 66 percent financial assets, compared with 55 percent for the next 9 percent. Among the wealthiest 1 percent of Parisians, who alone owned more than two-thirds of all wealth in 1912, real estate accounted for barely 22 percent of their assets and provincial real estate just 10 percent, whereas stocks alone accounted for 25 percent, private-sector bonds for 19 percent, and public-sector bonds and other financial assets for 22 percent.[6] The preponderance of stocks, bonds, bank deposits, and other monetary assets over real estate reflects a profound reality: the ownership elite of the Belle Époque was primarily a financial, capitalist, and industrial elite.

Second, foreign financial investments grew enormously between 1872 and 1912. Their share of Parisian wealth rose from 6 to 21 percent. This evolution is particularly noticeable in the largest 1 percent of fortunes, where most international assets were held: the share of foreign investment among their assets rose from 7 percent in 1872 to 25 percent in 1912, compared with just 14 percent for the 90th–99th percentile of wealth and barely 5 percent for the 50th–90th percentile (Table 4.1). In other words, only the largest portfolios contained substantial shares of foreign assets; domestic assets accounted for a larger proportion of smaller fortunes.

The spectacular growth of foreign investment, whose share more than tripled in forty years, involved all types of instruments, including foreign public debt, whose share in the largest 1 percent of fortunes rose from 4 to 10 percent in the period 1872–1912. Of particular interest are the famous Russian loans, which expanded rapidly after the French Republic signed a military and economic treaty with the czarist empire in 1892. But many other foreign bonds also figured in French portfolios (especially those of European states and also Argentina, the Ottoman Empire, China, Morocco, and so on, sometimes in connection with colonial appropriation strategies). French investors earned solid returns on their foreign lending, often with government guarantees (which were thought to be golden prior to the shocks of World War I and the Russian revolution). The share of foreign private-sector stocks and bonds increased even more rapidly, from 3 to 15 percent of total assets in the richest 1 percent of portfolios between 1872 and 1912. There were investments in the Suez and Panama

---

6. Note that the percentage of Paris real estate is highest in the 90th–99th percentiles and drops in the 50th–90th percentiles. This is because the latter group was far too poor to own Paris real estate, and their real estate holdings consisted mainly of provincial (and especially rural) properties. Note, too, that I did not include debts in Table 4.1 (on average barely 2 percent of gross assets in 1872 and 5 percent in 1912). See the online appendix for complete results.

Canals; Russian, Argentine, and American railroads; Indochinese rubber; and countless other companies around the world.

The Belle Époque (1880–1914): A Proprietarian and Inegalitarian Modernity

These results are essential, because they show that the upward trend in the concentration of wealth in France and Paris over the long nineteenth century, and especially the Belle Époque (1880–1914), was a phenomenon of "modernity."

If we look at this period from a distance, through the distorting lens of the early twenty-first century—the age of the digital economy, of start-ups and boundless innovation—we might be tempted to view the hyper-inegalitarian society of the eve of World War I as the culmination of a bygone era, a static world of quiet estates of little relevance to today's supposedly more dynamic and meritocratic societies. Nothing could be further from the truth. In fact, the wealth of the Belle Époque had little in common with that of the Ancien Régime or even the era of Père Goriot, César Birotteau, or the Parisian bankers of the 1820s, whom Balzac describes so well (and who in any case had a dynamism of their own).

In reality, capital is never quiet and was not quiet in the eighteenth century, a time of rapid demographic, agricultural, and commercial development and large-scale renewal of elites. Balzac's world was not tranquil either—quite the opposite. If Goriot was able to make a fortune in pasta and grain, it was because he had no peer when it came to identifying the best wheat, perfecting production technologies, and setting up warehouses and distribution networks so that his merchandise could be delivered to the right place at the right time. While lying on his deathbed in 1821, he was still thinking up juicy strategies for investing in Odessa on the shores of the Black Sea. Whether property took the form of factories and warehouses in 1800 or heavy industry and high finance in 1900, the crucial fact is that it was always in perpetual motion even as it was becoming ever more concentrated.

César Birotteau, another Balzac character emblematic of the ownership society of his day, was a brilliant inventor of perfumes and cosmetics, which Balzac tells us were all the rage in Paris in 1818. The novelist had no way of knowing that nearly a century later, in 1907, another Parisian, the chemist Eugène Schueller, was about to perfect a very useful hair dye (initially named "L'Auréale," after a female hair style of the time that was reminiscent of an aureole). Schueller's line of products inevitably calls to mind that of Birotteau.

In any case, in 1936 Schueller founded a company known as L'Oréal, which in 2019 is still the world leader in cosmetics. Birotteau took a different route. His wife tried to persuade him to reinvest the profits from his perfume factory in placid country estates and solid government bonds, as Goriot did when he sold his business and set about marrying off his daughters. But Birotteau wouldn't hear of it: instead, he set out to triple his fortune by investing in real estate in the Madeleine district, which was just taking off in the 1820s. He ended up bankrupt, which reminds us that there is nothing particularly tranquil about investing in real estate. Other audacious promoters have been more successful, including Donald Trump, who after plastering his name on skyscrapers in New York and Chicago worked his way up to occupying the White House in 2016.

Between 1880 and 1914 the world was in perpetual flux. The automobile, the electric light, the trans-Atlantic steamship, the telegraph, and radio—all were invented in the space of a few decades. The economic and social consequences of those inventions were surely as important as those of Facebook, Amazon, and Uber. The point is crucial, because it shows that the hyper-inegalitarianism of the prewar era was not a consequence of a bygone era with little or no similarity to today's world. In fact, the Belle Époque resembles today's world in many ways, even if essential differences remain. It was also "modern" in its financial infrastructure and forms of ownership. Not until the very end of the twentieth century do we find levels of stock-market capitalization as high as those seen in Paris and London in 1914 (relative to national output or income). Foreign investments by French and British property owners of the day have never been equaled (again relative to a year of output or income, which is the least preposterous way of making this type of historical comparison). The Belle Époque, especially in Paris, embodies the modernity of the first great financial and commercial globalization the world had ever seen—a century before the globalization of the late twentieth century.

Yet this was also an intensely inegalitarian society, in which 70 percent of the population owned nothing at death and 1 percent of the deceased owned nearly 70 percent of all there was to own. The concentration of property was considerably greater in Paris in 1900–1914 than it was in 1810–1820, the era of Père Goriot and César Birotteau, and even more extreme than it was in the 1780s, on the eve of the Revolution. Recall that it is difficult to estimate accurately how wealth was distributed before 1789, partly because we do not have comparable inheritance records and partly because the very idea of property had changed (jurisdictional privileges disappeared and the distinction between regalian rights and property rights sharpened). By using available estimates of the redistribution carried out during the Revolution, we can, however, state that the share of property of all kinds held by the top centile on the eve of the Revolution was just slightly above that of 1800–1810 and considerably lower than in the Belle Époque (Fig. 4.1). In any case, in view of the extreme concentration of wealth observed in 1900–1914 when the top decile in Paris held more than 90 percent and the top centile nearly 70 percent, it is hard to imagine a higher level in the Ancien Régime, despite the limitations of the sources.

The fact that the concentration of wealth could rise so rapidly and to such a high level in the period 1880–1914, a century after the abolition of privileges in 1789, is an arresting result. It raises questions for the future and for the analysis of what took place from 1980 until today. It is a discovery that made a deep impression on me both as a researcher and as a citizen. My colleagues and I did not expect to find such a large and rapid increase when we began our work on the inheritance archives, particularly since many contemporaries did not describe Belle Époque society in these terms. Indeed, the political and economic elites of the Third Republic liked to describe France as a country of "small-holders," which the French Revolution had made profoundly egalitarian once and for all. The fiscal and jurisdictional privileges of the nobility and clergy had in fact been abolished by the Revolution and were never restored (not even during the Restoration of 1815, which continued to rely on the tax system it inherited from the Revolution, with the same rules for all). But that did not prevent the concentration of property and economic power from attaining a level at the beginning of the twentieth century even higher than under the Ancien Régime—not at all what a certain Enlightenment optimism had led people to expect. Think, for example, of the words of Condorcet, who asserted in 1794 that "fortunes tend naturally toward equality" once one eliminates "artificial means of perpetuating them" and establishes "freedom of commerce and industry." Between 1880 and 1914, even though numerous signs suggested that the forward march toward greater equality had long since been halted, republican elites largely continued to believe in progress.

The Tax System in France from 1880 to 1914: Tranquil Accumulation

How do we explain the inegalitarian turn in the period 1880–1914 and then the reduction of inequality over the course of the twentieth century? Now that another inegalitarian turn has taken place in the 1980s, what can history teach us about how to deal with it? We will be returning to these questions again and again, especially when we study the crisis of ownership society following the shocks of 1914–1945 and the challenges of communism and social democracy.

For now, I simply want to insist on the fact that the inegalitarian turn of 1800–1914 was greatly facilitated by the tax system established during the French Revolution. In broad outline this remained in use without major changes until 1901 and, to a great extent, until World War I. The system adopted in the 1790s rested on two main components: first, a system of *droits de mutation* (sales tax on property and duties on inheritance and gifts), and second, a set of four direct taxes, which came to be called *les quatre vieilles* (the four old ladies) on account of their exceptional longevity.

The *droits de mutation,* which belonged to the larger category of *droits d'enregistrement* (registration fees), were fees charged for recording property transfers, that is, changes in the identity of the owners of a property. They were established by the Constitution of Year VIII (1799). Revolutionary legislators took care to distinguish between *mutations à titre onéreux* (that is, transfers of property in exchange for cash or other consideration—in other words, sales) and *mutations à titre gratuit* (that is, transfers without payment, a category that included inheritances, called *mutations par décès,* as well as gifts *inter vivos*). The *droits de mutations à titre onéreux* replaced the seigneurial *lods* of the Ancien Régime and, as noted earlier, continue to be applied to real estate transactions to this day.

The tax on direct-line bequests—that is, between parents and children—was set at the very low rate of 1 percent in 1799. Furthermore, it was an entirely proportional tax: every inheritance was taxed at the same 1 percent rate, regardless of its size, and no portion was exempt. The proportional rate did vary with degree of kinship: the tax on nondirect heirs, such as brothers, sisters, cousins, and so on, as well as on bequests to nonrelatives, was slightly higher than on direct bequests; but it never varied with the size of the inheritance. The possibility of introducing a progressive rate schedule or a higher tax on direct bequests was debated many times, especially after the revolution of 1848 and then again in the 1870s after the advent of the Third Republic, but nothing was ever done.[7]

In 1872, an attempt was made to increase the tax on the largest bequests from parents to children to 1.5 percent. The reform was modest, but both the

---

7. On the evolution of inheritance tax law over the long nineteenth century, see T. Piketty, *Top Incomes in France in the Twentieth Century,* trans. S. Ackerman (Harvard University Press, 2018), pp. 301–304, 991–1012.

legislative committee and the entire assembly flatly rejected it, invoking the natural right of direct descendants: "When a son succeeds his father, it is not strictly speaking a transmission of property that takes place; it is merely continued enjoyment of the property," said the authors of the Code Civil (or Napoleonic Code). "If applied in an absolute sense, this doctrine would exclude any tax on direct bequests; at the very least it requires extreme moderation in setting the rate."[8] In this instance, a majority of deputies felt that a rate of 1 percent satisfied the requirement of "extreme moderation" but that a rate of 1.5 percent would have violated it. For many deputies, a hike in the rate risked unleashing a dangerous escalation in the demand for redistribution. If they were not careful, this might ultimately undermine private property and its natural transmission.

In hindsight, it is easy to make fun of this conservatism. Inheritance tax rates on the largest fortunes reached much higher levels in most Western countries in the twentieth century (at least 30–40 percent, and sometimes as high as 70–80 percent, for decades). This did not lead to social disintegration or undermine property rights, nor did it reduce economic dynamism and growth—quite the opposite. Certainly, these political positions reflected interests, but more than that they reflected a plausible proprietarian ideology or at any rate an ideology with a sufficiently powerful appearance of plausibility. The point that emerges clearly from these debates is the risk of escalation. At the time, for a majority of deputies the purpose of the inheritance tax was to record ownership and protect property rights; it was in no way intended to redistribute wealth or reduce inequality. Once one moved outside this framework and began to tax the largest direct bequests at substantial rates, there was a danger that the Pandora's box of progressive taxation would never be closed. Unduly progressive taxes would lead to political chaos that would ultimately harm the most modest members of society, if not society itself. That, at least, was one of the propositions by which fiscal conservatism was justified.

Note, too, that the establishment of *droits de mutation* in the 1790s went hand in hand with the development of an impressive cadastral system: a register in which all property and all changes of ownership could be listed. The scope of the task was immense, especially since the property law was supposed

---

8. See *Impressions parlementaires*, vol. 4, no. 482. On these debates see also A. Daumard, *Les fortunes françaises au 19ᵉ siècle. Enquête sur la répartition et la composition des capitaux privés d'après l'enregistrement des déclarations de successions* (Mouton, 1973), pp. 15–23.

to apply to everyone, independent of social origins, in a country of nearly 30 million people (by far the most populous in Europe) that covered a vast territory in a time when means of transport were limited. This ambitious project rested on a theory of power and property that was just as immense: it was hoped that state protection of property rights would lead to economic prosperity, social harmony, and equality for all. There was no reason to take the risk of spoiling everything by indulging egalitarian fantasies when the country had never been as prosperous and its power extended throughout the world.

Growing numbers of other political actors nevertheless favored other options, such as a voluntary system for limiting wealth inequality and enabling large numbers of people to acquire property. As early as the late eighteenth century, people like Graslin, Lacoste, and Paine were proposing specific and ambitious tax reforms. During the nineteenth century, new inequalities became visible as industry expanded in the 1830s, and these lent legitimacy to calls for redistribution. Yet it was no easy task to put together a majority coalition around issues of redistribution and progressive taxation. In the early decades of the Third Republic and universal suffrage, the main issues were the republican regime itself and the place of the Church in it. In addition, peasants and other rural dwellers, including some who were not very rich, were wary of the ultimate designs of socialists and urban proletarians, whom they suspected of wanting to do away with private property altogether. Indeed, their fears were not totally unfounded, and the wealthy did not shrink from stoking them to frighten the less well-off. Progressive taxation has never been and will never be as uncontroversial as some people believe. Even with universal suffrage, a majority coalition in favor of progressive taxation does not come magically into existence. Because political conflict is multidimensional and the issues are complex, coalitions cannot be assumed and must be built; the ability to do so depends on mobilizing shared historical and intellectual experience.

Not until 1901 was the sacrosanct principle of proportionality in taxation finally undone. The law of February 25, 1901, established a progressive tax on inheritances, the first progressive tax adopted in France. A progressive tax on income followed with the law of July 15, 1914. Both taxes occasioned lengthy parliamentary debates, and it was the French Senate—the more conservative of the two chambers, because rural areas and *notables* were overrepresented in it—that delayed adoption of the progressive inheritance tax, which the Chamber of Deputies had passed as early as 1895. Note in passing that it was not until the advent of the Fourth Republic in 1946 that the Senate lost its veto power, leaving the last word to deputies elected by direct universal suffrage, which made it possible to move forward in several areas of social and fiscal legislation.

The fact remains that the tax rates established by the law of 1901 were extremely modest: the rate on direct-line bequests was 1 percent in the majority of cases, as it had been under the proportional regime; it rose to a maximum of 2.5 percent on the portion of an estate above 1 million francs per heir (which applied to just 0.1 percent of all estates). The highest rate was raised to 5 percent in 1902 and then to 6.5 percent in 1910 to contribute to the financing of another law providing for "worker and peasant retirements" adopted that same year. Although it was not until after World War I that the rates applicable to the largest fortunes attained more substantial levels (several tens of percent) and "modern" fiscal progressivity was put in place, a decisive step was taken in 1901, and perhaps an even more decisive one in 1910, because the decision to establish an explicit relationship between a more progressive inheritance tax and paying for worker pensions expressed a clear desire to reduce social inequality generally.

To sum up, the inheritance tax had only a marginal effect on the accumulation and transmission of large fortunes in the period 1800–1914. The law of 1901 nevertheless marked an important change in fiscal philosophy regarding inheritances by introducing progressivity, whose effects began to be fully felt in the interwar years.

The "Quatre Vieilles," the Tax on Capital, and the Income Tax

Let us turn now to the progressive income tax introduced in 1914. Recall that the four direct taxes created by revolutionary legislators in 1790–1791 (the *quatre vieilles*) did not depend directly on the income of the taxpayer; this was their essential characteristic.[9] Bluntly rejecting the inquisitorial procedures associated with the Ancien Régime, revolutionary legislators, who probably also wished to spare the burgeoning bourgeoisie from paying too much in taxes, opted for what was called an "indicial" tax system because each tax was based

---

9. On the *quatre vieilles* and the transition to an income tax, see Piketty, *Top Incomes in France*, pp. 234–242. See also C. Allix and M. Lecerclé, *L'impôt sur le revenu (impôts cédulaires et impôt général). Traité théorique et pratique* (1926).

not on income but on "indices" intended to measure the capacity of each tax-payer to pay; income never had to be declared.[10]

For instance, the *contribution sur les portes et fenêtres,* or "doors and windows tax," was based on the number of doors and windows in the taxpayer's principal residence, an index of wealth that, from the taxpayer's point of view, had the great merit of allowing the tax collector to determine the amount due without entering the taxpayer's home, much less peering into his account books. The *contribution personnelle-mobilière* (corresponding to today's residential tax) was based on the rental value of each taxpayer's principal residence. Like the other direct taxes (apart from the doors and windows tax, which was finally eliminated in 1925), it became a local tax when the national income tax system was established in 1914–1917, and to this day it continues to finance local and regional governments.[11] The *contribution des patentes* (today's local business tax) was paid by artisans, merchants, and manufacturers, with different schedules for each profession based on the size of the enterprise and the equipment employed; it was not directly linked to actual profits, which did not have to be declared.

Finally, the *contribution foncière,* corresponding to today's land tax *(taxe foncière),* was levied on the owners of real estate, including homes and buildings as well as land, forests, and so on, based on the rental value (equivalent annual rental income) of the property, regardless of its use (whether personal, rental, or professional). The rental value, like that used in the calculation of the *con-*

---

10. The monarchy had attempted to introduce limited forms of fiscal progressivity in the eighteenth century, especially in the form of the *taille tarifée,* which distinguished several classes of taxpayer on the basis of the approximate level of their resources while maintaining exemptions for the nobility and the clergy in other parts of the tax system, which was hardly consistent. In some ways, the Revolution simplified things by imposing proportionality for everyone on an indicial basis and eliminating any direct reference to income. On the *taille tarifée,* see M. Touzery, *L'invention de l'impôt sur le revenu. La taille tarifée (1715–1789)* (CHEFF, 1994).

11. The *contribution personnelle-mobilière* was no doubt the most complex of the *quatre vieilles,* since it initially included not just the tax based on the rental value of the principal residence, which was its main component, but also a tax on servants, a tax equal to the value of three days of work, and a tax on horses, mules, etc. This was the tax that Condorcet proposed to reform in 1792 by introducing a schedule of progressive rates on rental values as a correction to the tax's inherent regressivity. The residential tax, the direct descendant of this tax, is to be gradually eliminated between 2017 and 2019, and it is not yet known what local tax will replace it.

tribution personnelle-mobilière, did not have to be declared by the taxpayer. It was set on the basis of surveys conducted every ten to fifteen years by the tax authorities, who catalogued the country's real estate, taking note of new construction, recent sales, and various other additions to the cadastre. Since there was virtually no inflation in the period 1815–1914 and prices evolved very slowly, it was felt that periodic adjustments were sufficient, especially since this spared taxpayers the trouble of filing declarations.

The land or real estate tax was by far the most important of the *quatre vieilles,* since it alone accounted for more than two-thirds of total receipts at the beginning of the nineteenth century and still for nearly half at the beginning of the twentieth century. It was in fact a tax on capital, except that only capital in the form of real estate was counted. Stocks, bonds, shares of partnerships, and other financial assets were excluded or, rather, were taxed only indirectly, to the extent that the associated businesses owned real estate, such as offices or warehouses, in which case they had to pay the corresponding *contribution foncière.* But in the case of industrial and financial firms whose principal assets were immaterial (such as patents, know-how, networks, reputation, organizational capacity, etc.) or in the form of foreign investments or other assets not covered by the real estate tax or other direct taxes (such as machinery and other equipment in theory subject to the *patente* but in practice taxed at well below their actual profitability), the capital in question was in actuality exempt from taxation or taxed at a very low rate. In the late eighteenth century such assets no doubt seemed relatively unimportant compared with real assets (such as houses, land, buildings, factories, and warehouses), but the fact is that they played an increasingly central role in the nineteenth and early twentieth centuries.

In any case, the important point is that the real estate tax, like the inheritance tax until 1901, was a strictly proportional tax on capital. In no way was the goal to redistribute property or reduce inequality; it was rather to tax property at a low and painless rate. In practice, the annual rate of taxation throughout the long nineteenth century was 3–4 percent of the rental value of the property, that is, less than 0.2 percent of the market value (since annual rents generally ran about 4–5 percent of a property's market value).[12]

---

12. In other words, a property valued at 1,000 francs produced a rent on the order of 50 francs per year (5 percent of 1,000 francs), which called for a payment of just 2 francs in taxes (4 percent of 50 francs), equivalent to a rate of 0.2 percent on the capital of 1,000 francs. See Piketty, *Top Incomes in France,* pp. 238–239.

It is important to note that a tax on capital that is strictly proportional and assessed at such a low rate serves the owners of capital well. Indeed, during the French Revolution and throughout the period 1800–1914, capitalists saw this as the ideal tax system. By paying barely 0.2 percent a year on the value of capital and an additional 1 percent when "son succeeded father," every capitalist obtained the right to enrich himself and accumulate ever more capital in peace, to derive the maximum profit from his property without having to declare the income or profits it generated, with the guarantee that any taxes due would not depend on the profits or rents actually realized. Because a low proportional tax on capital is not very intrusive and gives every advantage to the owners of capital, it has often been the preference of the wealthy. This was the case not only at the time of the French Revolution and throughout the nineteenth century but also throughout the twentieth century, and it continues to this day.[13] In contrast, a tax on capital in the form of a truly progressive tax on wealth tends to frighten property owners, as we will see when we study the debates that erupted in the course of the twentieth century.

The real estate tax, which taxed capital at a low rate, was also the institutional tool with which political power was placed in the hands of property owners in the era of censitary monarchy (1815–1848). "Censitary" means that there was a property qualification for voting, which one met by paying above a certain amount in tax. During the Restoration, the right to vote was reserved to men over the age of 30 who paid at least 300 francs in direct taxes (which in practice granted eligibility to vote to about 100,000 people, or roughly 1 percent of adult males). In practice, since the *contribution foncière* accounted for the bulk of the receipts from the *quatre vieilles,* this meant as a first approximation that only the wealthiest 1 percent of real estate owners enjoyed the right to vote. In other words, the fiscal rules favored tranquil accumulation of capital while at the same allowing those who benefited from that system to formulate the political rules that ensured they would continue to do so. It would be difficult to imagine a clearer illustration of the inegalitarian proprietarian regime: the ownership society that flourished in France from 1815 to 1848 explicitly and openly relied on a property regime together with a political regime which guaranteed that that property regime would continue. In Chapter 5

---

13. For example, it was in this spirit, and in the name of economic efficiency, that Maurice Allais proposed in the 1970s to eliminate the income tax and replace it with a low-rate tax on real capital, very similar in principle to the *contribution foncière.* See M. Allais, *L'impôt sur le capital et la réforme monétaire* (Hermann, 1977).

we will see similar mechanisms at work in other European countries (such as the United Kingdom and Sweden).

Universal Suffrage, New Knowledge, War

After the revolution of 1848, in the brief interval of universal suffrage under the Second Republic, and then again with the advent of the Third Republic and the return of universal suffrage in 1871, debate on progressive taxation and the income tax resumed.[14] In a context of rapid industrial and financial expansion, when it was plain to everyone that industrialists and bankers were reaping handsome profits while wages stagnated, plunging the new urban proletariat into misery, it seemed increasingly unthinkable that the new sources of wealth should not somehow be taxed. Although the idea of progressive taxation still frightened people, something had to be done. It was in this context that the law of June 28, 1872, was adopted, instituting a tax on income from securities *(valeurs mobilières)* known as the *impôt sur le revenu des valeurs mobilières,* or IRVM.

This tax was seen as a complement to the *quatre vieilles,* since it was levied on forms of income largely forgotten by the system of direct taxes established in 1790–1791. Indeed, for its time, the IRVM was a paragon of fiscal modernity, especially since its base was very large: it was levied not only on dividends from stocks and interest from bonds but also on "income of all kinds" that an owner of securities might receive in addition to any reimbursement of the capital invested, regardless of the precise legal category of the remuneration (including reserve distributions, bonuses, capital gains realized on the dissolution of a company, etc.). The data that emerged from the collection of the IRVM were also used to measure for the first time the rapid growth of this type of income between 1872 and 1914. What is more, the tax was collected at the source: in other words, it was paid directly by the issuer of the securities (banks, investment partnerships, insurance companies, and so on).

In terms of rates, however, the IRVM conformed to the pattern of the existing tax regime: the new tax was strictly proportional, with a single rate of 3 percent on income from all securities, from the tiny interest payments col-

---

14. The Second Republic (1848–1852) ended when the Second Empire was proclaimed by Louis-Napoléon Bonaparte, who had been elected president by universal suffrage in December 1848. His uncle Napoleon had ended the First Republic (1792–1804) when he, too, decided to have himself crowned as emperor.

lected by a person who had purchased a few small bonds for his retirement to the enormous dividends, amounting to hundreds of years of the average man's income, paid to wealthy stockholders with diversified portfolios. The rate was increased to 4 percent in 1890 and remained there until World War I. It would have been technically easy to raise rates quite a bit more and to make them progressive. But no government was prepared to assume the responsibility, so the IRVM ultimately had virtually no effect on the accumulation and perpetuation of large fortunes in the period 1872–1914.

Debate continued, and after many twists and turns the Chamber of Deputies in 1909 passed a law creating a general income tax (*impôt général sur le revenu,* or IGR). This was a progressive tax on all income (including wages, profits, rents, dividends, interest, and so on). In keeping with the bill filed in 1907 by the Radical Party's minister of finance Joseph Caillaux, the system also included a package of so-called *impôts cédulaires* (levied separately on each *cédule,* or type of income). This was aimed at a larger number of individuals than the IGR, which was designed to tap only a minority of wealthy individuals, who were to be taxed progressively so as to achieve some degree of redistribution.

Caillaux's bill was relatively modest, however: the rate on the highest incomes under the IGR was only 5 percent. Opponents nevertheless denounced it as an "infernal machine," which, once set in motion, could never be stopped. This was the same argument that had been invoked against the inheritance tax, but it was advanced with even greater vehemence because the requirement for individuals to declare their income was considered intolerably intrusive. The Senate, which was as hostile to the progressive income tax as it had been to the progressive inheritance tax, refused to vote on the bill and blocked application of the new system until 1914. Caillaux and other proponents of the income tax used all the arguments at their disposal. In particular, they pointed out to those of their adversaries who predicted that top rates would quickly rise to astronomical levels that the rates of the progressive inheritance tax had actually changed relatively little since 1901–1902.[15]

---

15. In the Chamber of Deputies on January 20, 1908, Caillaux put this argument clearly: "Since we have had a progressive tax on the books for six years with a change of rates, do not tell us that a progressive system must necessarily lead in a short period of time to higher rates." See J. Caillaux, *L'impôt sur le revenu* (Berger-Levrault, 1910), p. 115.

Among the factors that played an important role in the evolution of ideas, it is particularly interesting to note that the publication of statistics derived from inheritance tax declarations, which began shortly after the creation of the progressive inheritance tax on February 25, 1901, helped to undermine the idea of an "egalitarian" France, which was often invoked by adversaries of progressive taxation. In parliamentary debates in 1907–1908, proponents of the income tax frequently alluded to this new knowledge to show that France was not the country of "smallholders" that their adversaries liked to describe. Joseph Caillaux himself read to the deputies from these statistics, and after showing that the number and size of very large estates declared in France every year had attained astronomical levels, he concluded: "We have been led to believe and to say that France was a country of small fortunes, of capital fragmented and dispersed ad infinitum. The statistics that the new inheritance regime has provided us force us to back away from that idea. . . . Gentlemen, I cannot hide from you the fact that these figures have forced me to modify in my own mind some of the preconceived ideas to which I alluded earlier, and have led me to certain reflections. The fact is that a very small number of individuals hold most of the country's fortune."[16]

Here we see how a major institutional innovation—in this case the introduction of a progressive inheritance tax—can lead, beyond its direct effect on inequality, to the production of new knowledge and categories, which in turn influence evolving political ideas and ideologies. Caillaux did not go so far as to calculate the share of different deciles and centiles in the annual estate figures of the time; the raw numbers spoke eloquently enough that everyone could see that France bore no resemblance to the "country of smallholders" described by the adversaries of progressivity. These arguments were not without influence on the chamber, which decided to make the inheritance tax more progressive in 1910, but they proved insufficient to persuade the Senate to accept a progressive income tax.

It is hard to say how much longer the Senate would have continued to resist had World War I not broken out, but there is no doubt that the international tensions of 1913–1914 and especially the new financial burdens created by the law mandating three years of military service and the "imperatives of national defense" played a decisive role in eliminating the roadblock and probably a greater role than the good results achieved by the Radicals and Socialists in the May 1914 elections. The debate took many turns, the most spectacular

16. Caillaux, *L'impôt sur le revenu,* pp. 530–532.

of which was no doubt the Calmette affair.[17] In any case, the Senate agreed at the last minute to include the IGR passed by the Chamber of Deputies in 1909 in an emergency finance bill that was adopted on July 15, 1914, two weeks after the assassination of Archduke Ferdinand in Sarajevo and a little more than two weeks before the declaration of war. In exchange, the senators obtained a further reduction in the progressivity of the tax (the top rate was reduced from 5 to 2 percent).[18] This was the progressive income tax that was applied for the first time in France in 1915, in the midst of war, and that has continued to be applied ever since, not without numerous reforms and revisions. As with the inheritance tax, it was not until the interwar years that the top rates attained modern levels (several tens of percent).

To sum up, from the French Revolution to World War I, the French tax system offered ideal conditions for the accumulation and concentration of wealth, with tax rates on the highest incomes and largest fortunes that were never more than a few percent—hence purely symbolic, without real impact on the conditions of accumulation and transmission. Thanks to new political coalitions and deep changes in political thinking and ideologies, a new tax system began to be put in place before the war, most notably with the adoption of a progressive inheritance tax in 1901. The full effects of this new system were not felt until the interwar years, however, and even more under the new social, fiscal, and political pact that was achieved in 1945, at the end of World War II.

The Revolution, France, and Equality

Ever since the Revolution of 1789, France has presented itself to the world as the land of liberty, equality, and fraternity. The promise of equality at the heart

---

17. Named for the editor of *Le Figaro*, who was murdered in his office on March 16, 1914, by Joseph Caillaux's wife in the wake of the newspaper's unremitting attacks on her husband, climaxing with the publication on March 13, 1914, of a letter from Caillaux to his mistress. The letter, signed "Ton Jo," had been written in 1901, following the failure of the first Caillaux bill, of which Caillaux wrote that he had "crushed the income tax while appearing to defend it." This letter was supposed to show that the promoters of the income tax were only opportunists who were using the wretched bill solely to advance their political careers.

18. The law of July 15, 1914, instituting the IGR was completed by the law of July 31, 1917, which created the *impôts cédulaires* envisioned in the Caillaux reform. For details, see Piketty, *Top Incomes in France*, pp. 246–262.

of this great national narrative does have some tangible support, such as the abolition of the fiscal privileges of the nobility and clergy on the Night of August 4, 1789, as well as the attempt to establish a republican regime based on universal suffrage in 1792–1794, a bold undertaking for the time. All this took place in a country with a much larger population than other Western monarchies. Indeed, the constitution of a central government capable of ending seigneurial jurisdictional privileges and working toward greater equality was no mean achievement.

As for achieving real equality, however, the great promise of the Revolution went unfulfilled. The fact that the concentration of ownership steadily increased throughout the nineteenth century and into the twentieth, so that it stood higher on the eve of World War I than at the time of the Revolution, shows how wide the gap was between the promise of the Revolution and the reality. And when a progressive income tax was finally adopted on July 15, 1914, it was not to finance schools or public services but to pay for war with Germany.

It is particularly striking to note that France, the self-proclaimed land of equality, was actually one of the last of the wealthy countries to adopt a progressive income tax. Denmark did so in 1870, Japan in 1887, Prussia in 1891, Sweden in 1903, the United Kingdom in 1909, and the United States in 1913.[19] To be sure, it was only a few years before the war that this emblematic fiscal reform was adopted in the United States and United Kingdom, and in both cases it came only after epic political battles and major constitutional reforms. But at least these were peacetime reforms intended to finance civil expenditures and reduce inequality rather than responses to nationalist and military pressures as in France's case. No doubt the income tax would have been adopted in the absence of the war, to judge by the experience of other countries; or it might have come in response to other financial or military crises. Yet the fact remains that France was the last country in the list to adopt a progressive income tax.

It is also important to note that the reason why France lagged behind other countries and displayed such hypocrisy about equality had a great deal to do with its intellectual nationalism and historical self-satisfaction. From 1871 to 1914, the political and economic elites of the Third Republic used and abused the argument that the Revolution had made France an egalitarian country so

---

19. In the United Kingdom a separate proportional tax on each of several categories of income (interest, rent, profits, wages, etc.) was established in 1842, but it was not until 1909 that a progressive tax on total income was adopted.

that it had no need for confiscatory, inquisitorial taxes, unlike its aristocratic and authoritarian neighbors (starting with the United Kingdom and Germany, which were well advised to adopt progressive taxes in order to have a chance to come closer to the French egalitarian ideal). Unfortunately, this French egalitarian exceptionalism had no basis in fact. The inheritance archives show that nineteenth-century France was hugely inegalitarian and that concentration of wealth continued to increase right up to the eve of World War I. Joseph Caillaux invoked these very statistics in a debate in 1907–1908, but the prejudices and interests of senators were so strong that Senate approval proved impossible to obtain in the ideological and political climate of the time.

Third Republic elites did cite potentially relevant comparisons, such as the fact that land ownership was considerably more fragmented in France than in the United Kingdom (in part because the Revolution had redistributed land to a limited degree but mostly because land holdings were exceptionally concentrated on the other side of the English Channel). They also noted that the Code Civil (1804) had introduced the principle of equal partition of estates among siblings. Equipartition, which in practice applied only to brothers (because sisters, once married, forfeited most of their rights to their husbands under the highly patriarchal proprietarian regime in force in the nineteenth century) was attacked throughout the nineteenth century by counterrevolutionary and anti-egalitarian thinkers, who held it responsible for harmful fragmentation of parcels and above all for fathers' loss of authority over their sons, who could no longer be disinherited.[20] In fact, the legal, fiscal, and monetary regime in force until 1914 strongly favored extreme concentration of wealth, and this played a far more important role than the equipartition of estates among brothers instituted by the Revolution.

Reading about these episodes today, at some distance from the Belle Époque, one is struck by the hypocrisy of much of the French elite, including many economists, who did not hesitate to deny against all evidence that inequality posed

---

20. Under the "available quota" *(quotité disponible)* system instituted in 1804 and still in force today, parents could freely dispose of half their property if they had one child (the other half went automatically to the child, even if all relations had been broken off); this fell to one-third if they had two children (with equal division of the remaining two-thirds between the siblings); and one-quarter if they had three or more children (with equipartition of the remaining three-quarters). Denunciation of the supposedly harmful effects of this system was a major conservative and counterrevolutionary theme in the nineteenth century, especially in the work of Frédéric Le Play. This criticism largely disappeared in the twentieth century.

any problem whatsoever.[21] One can of course read this as a sign of panic that a harmful wave of redistribution might be unleashed. At the time, no one had any direct experience with large-scale progressive taxation, so it was not unreasonable to think that it might threaten the country's prosperity. Still, reading about these exaggerated warnings should put us on our guard against such wildly pessimistic counsel in the future.

As we will see, such short-sighted use of grand national narratives is unfortunately quite common in the history of inegalitarian regimes. In France, the myth of the country's egalitarian exceptionalism and moral superiority has often served to disguise self-interest and national failure, whether as an excuse for colonial rule in the nineteenth and early twentieth centuries or for the glaring inequalities in the French educational system today. We will find similar intellectual nationalism in the United States, where the ideology of American exceptionalism has often served as a cover for the country's inequalities and plutocratic excesses, especially in the period 1990–2020. It is equally plausible that a similar form of historical self-satisfaction will develop soon in China, if it hasn't done so already. Before turning to these matters, we need to continue our study of the transformation of European societies of orders into ownership societies to gain a better understanding of the many possible trajectories and switch points.

Capitalism: A Proprietarianism for the Industrial Age

Before continuing, I also want to clarify the connection between proprietarianism and capitalism as I see it for the purposes of this study. In this book I

---

21. Take Paul Leroy-Beaulieu, one of the most influential liberal economists of his time as well as an enthusiastic spokesman for colonization, and his famous *Essai sur la répartition des richesses et sur la tendance à une moindre inégalité des conditions*, published in 1881 and regularly reprinted for the next thirty years. Although all the available statistical sources suggested the opposite, he defended the idea that the tendency is for inequality to fall, even if he had to invent implausible arguments to do so. For instance, he noted with satisfaction that the number of indigents needing assistance grew by 40 percent in France between 1837 and 1860, even as the number of charity offices almost doubled. One had to be very optimistic indeed to deduce from these figures that the actual number of indigents had fallen (which he did without hesitation), but beyond that, even a decrease in the absolute number of poor in a growth context would obviously tell us nothing about the size or evolution of the gap between rich and poor. See Piketty, *Top Incomes in France*, pp. 522–531.

have chosen to stress the ideas of proprietarian ideology and the ownership society. I propose to think of capitalism as the particular form that proprietarianism assumed in the era of heavy industry and international financial investment, that is, primarily in the second half of the nineteenth and early twentieth
centuries. Generally speaking, whether we are talking about the capitalism of
the first industrial and financial globalization (in the Belle Époque, 1880–1914)
or the globalized digital hypercapitalism that began around 1990 and continues
to this day, capitalism can be seen as a historical movement that seeks constantly
to expand the limits of private property and asset accumulation beyond traditional forms of ownership and existing state boundaries. It is a movement that
depends on advances in transport and communication, which enable it to increase global trade, output, and accumulation. At a still more fundamental level,
it depends on the development of an increasingly sophisticated and globalized
legal system, which "codifies" different forms of material and immaterial property so as to protect ownership claims as long as possible while concealing its
activities from those who might wish to challenge those claims (starting with
people who own nothing) as well as from states and national courts.[22]

In this respect, capitalism is closely related to proprietarianism, which I define in this study as a political ideology whose fundamental purpose is to provide absolute protection to private property (conceived as a universal right,
open to everyone regardless of old status inequalities). The classic capitalism
of the Belle Époque is an outgrowth of the proprietarianism of the age of heavy
industry and international finance, just as today's hypercapitalism is an outgrowth of the era of the digital revolution and tax havens. In both cases, new
forms of holding and protecting property were put in place to protect and extend accumulated wealth. There is nevertheless a benefit to distinguishing between proprietarianism and capitalism, because the proprietarian ideology developed in the eighteenth century, well before heavy industry and international
finance. It emerged in societies that were still largely preindustrial as a way of
transcending the logic of trifunctionalism in a context of new possibilities offered by the formation of a centralized state with a new capacity to discharge
regalian functions and protect property rights in general.

As an ideology, proprietarianism might in theory be applied in primarily
rural communities with relatively strict and traditional forms of property
holding, in order to preserve them. In practice, the logic of accumulation tends

---

22. See Pistor, *The Code of Capital: How the Law Creates Wealth and Inequality* (Princeton
University Press, 2019).

to drive proprietarianism to extend the frontiers and forms of property to the maximum possible extent, unless other ideologies or institutions intervene to establish limits. In the case that concerns us here, the capitalism of the late nineteenth and early twentieth centuries coincided with a hardening of proprietarianism in the era of heavy industry that witnessed growing tensions between stockholders on the one hand and the new urban proletariat, concentrated in huge production units and united against capital, on the other.

This hardening was reflected, moreover, in the nineteenth-century novel's depiction of property relations. The ownership society of 1810–1830 that Balzac describes is a world in which property has become a universal equivalent, yielding reliable annual incomes and structuring the social order; yet direct confrontation with those who work to produce those incomes is largely absent. The Balzacian universe is profoundly proprietarian, as is that of Jane Austen, whose novels are set in England in the period 1790–1810. In both cases we are a long way from the world of heavy industry.

In contrast, when Émile Zola published *Germinal* in 1885, social tensions in the mining and industrial regions of northern France were at an all-time high. When the workers exhaust the meager funds they have collected to support their very bitter strike against the Compagnie des Mines, the grocer Maigrat refuses to extend credit. He ends up emasculated by the town's women, who, disgusted by the sexual favors this vile agent of capital has so long demanded of them and their daughters, are exhausted and out for blood after weeks of struggle. What is left of his body is publicly exposed and dragged through the streets. We are a long way from Balzac's Paris salons and Jane Austen's elegant balls. Proprietarianism has become capitalism; the end is near.

FIVE

Ownership Societies: European Trajectories

In the previous chapter we looked at the inegalitarian evolution of the owner-ship society that flourished in France in the century from the French Revolution of 1789 to the eve of World War I. Though illuminating and interesting, and to some extent influential on neighboring countries, the French case is nev-ertheless rather special in European and world history. If we stand back a bit and look at the variety of national trajectories on the European continent, we find considerable diversity in the processes by which trifunctional societies were transformed into ownership societies. We turn next to the study of these dif-ferent trajectories.

I will begin by presenting some general features of the European comparison before taking a more detailed look at two particularly significant cases: the United Kingdom and Sweden. The British case is distinguished by a very gradual transition from ternary to proprietarian logic, which in some respects might seem to be the exact opposite of the French case. We will see, however, that rup-tures also played an essential role in Britain, again illustrating the importance of crises and switch points in the social transformation process as well as the deep imbrication of property regimes and political regimes in the history of inequality. The Swedish case offers an astonishing example of early constitutionalization of a society with four orders, followed by an extreme proprietarian transition, with voting rights proportional to wealth. It illustrates to perfection the importance of mass mobilization and sociopolitical processes in the transformation of inequality regimes: once the most restrictive of ownership societies, Sweden became easily the most egalitarian of social democracies. Comparison of the French, British, and Swedish cases is all the more interesting because these three countries played key roles in the global history of inequality, first in the ternary and proprietarian eras and then in the age of colonialism and social democracy.

The Size of the Clergy and Nobility: European Diversity

One way to analyze the variety of European trajectories is to compare the size and resources of the clerical and noble classes in different countries. This approach has its limits, however, especially since the available sources are not ideal for comparison. We can, however, identify common patterns and major differences.

Begin with the size of the clergy. To a first approximation, we find fairly similar evolutions over the long run. Take, for instance, the cases of Spain, France, and the United Kingdom (Fig. 5.1). In all three countries we see that the size of the clergy as a percentage of the adult male population reached very high levels in the sixteenth and seventeenth centuries, on the order of 3–3.5 percent or one of every thirty adult males (and rose even higher, close to 5 percent, in Spain in 1700—that is, one adult male in twenty). The clergy's share then decreased steadily in all three countries, falling to around 0.5 percent (barely one of every 200 adult males) in the nineteenth and early twentieth centuries. These estimates are far from perfect, but the orders of magnitude are quite clear. Today the clerical class represents less than 0.1 percent of the population (less than one person in a thousand) in all three countries, all religions combined. We will also discover that religious practice has declined and that the portion of the population describing itself as "without religion" has increased significantly (to between a third and a half), in most European countries today.[1]

Although the long-term evolutions are fairly similar, notable in particular for the virtual disappearance of the religious class and collapse of religious practice, the precise chronologies differ markedly from country to country. We can therefore tell several different stories, each of which reflects the evolution of power relations in a specific society, as well as the political and ideological confrontations that took place between state and religious institutions and monarchical and ecclesiastical powers. In France, as noted in the previous chapter, the size of the clerical class was already decreasing rapidly in the final third of the seventeenth century and throughout the eighteenth, before being hit hard by revolutionary expropriations and continuing to decline in the nineteenth century.

In the United Kingdom the process began much earlier. There was a sharp drop in the percentage of clerics in the population as early as the sixteenth century, a consequence of Henry VIII's decision to dissolve the monasteries in the 1530s. There were political and theological reasons for this decision, having to do with the conflict between the British monarchy and the Pope, which eventually gave rise to Anglicanism. The Pope's refusal to sanction Henry VIII's

---

1. See Chaps. 14 and 15.

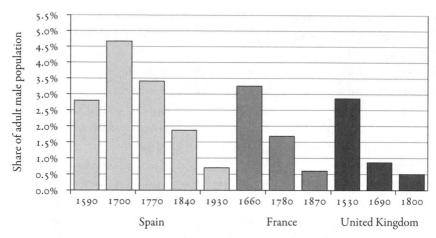

FIG. 5.1. The weight of the clergy in Europe, 1530–1930

Interpretation: The clergy represented 4.5 percent of the adult male population in Spain in 1700, less than 3.5 percent of the population in 1770, and less than 2 percent in 1840. We find a general falling trend, but the periodization varies with country: it falls later in Spain, earlier in the United Kingdom, and in the intermediate years in France. *Sources and series:* piketty.pse.ens.fr/ideology.

divorce and remarriage was only one of many bones of contention between the two powers, but it was nonetheless significant. The question was to what extent the monarchy and nobility were obliged, within the trifunctional order that held sway in European Christian societies, to submit to norms promulgated by the Pope and the clergy—norms that were at once moral, familial, spiritual, and political. There were also financial reasons for the break at a time of budgetary difficulty for the Crown: the dissolution and expropriation of the monasteries, followed by the gradual auctioning off of the monastic estates, brought significant and lasting new resources to the royal exchequer while undermining the financial and political independence of the clerical class.[2]

In any case, the dissolution of the monasteries, which came at a time when English monks alone accounted for about 2 percent of the male population, dealt an early and crippling blow to the ecclesiastical class in Britain in terms of both personnel and property, while strengthening the Crown and nobility, which bought up many monastic estates and thereby strengthened its hold on Britain's landed capital. According to available estimates, the size of the clergy

2. G. W. Bernard, "The Dissolution of Monasteries," *Journal of the Historical Association,* 2011.

had fallen to less than 1 percent of the adult male population by the end of the seventeenth century, at which point it still remained above 3 percent in France (Fig. 5.1). This early ecclesiastical decline in Britain went hand in hand with the development of a novel and extreme form of proprietarianism.

By contrast, the clerical decline came much later in Spain than in Britain or France. The Church, on which the monarchy and nobility had relied during the centuries of the *Reconquista,* even saw its numbers grow between 1590 and 1700. The Spanish clergy still represented 3 percent of the adult male population at the time of the French Revolution, and it was not until the nineteenth century that it began to shed both property and population share. Throughout the nineteenth century, *desamortizacion* laws gradually stripped the church of some of its possessions, both financial assets and land, through forced sales of ecclesiastical property for the benefit of the state, which was attempting to modernize itself and to strengthen civil and state institutions. The process continued in the early twentieth century, not without provoking violent opposition and creating strong social and political tensions. In 1911 and again in 1932, tax exemptions that encouraged private donations to religious institutions were challenged.[3] In 1931 the Second Spanish Republic met with great difficulty when it tried to seize the assets of the Jesuit order (which had just been dissolved in Spain). To escape earlier expropriations, many of those assets had been registered in the name of supporters of the church rather than religious institutions themselves.

Recall, too, that an ambitious agrarian reform launched in 1932–1933 played a crucial role in the series of events that led to the Spanish Civil War. The reform had nevertheless been conceived in a conciliatory spirit and with only moderate redistributive intent. Landowners were authorized to hold hundreds of acres per commune, with thresholds dependent on crop type. Substantial indemnities were provided, with a schedule that depended on both the size of the parcel and the income of the owner, except for the high nobility, the so-called *Grandes de España,* whose holdings above a certain threshold were to be expropriated without compensation in view of the special privileges they had enjoyed in the past. Agrarian reform became a rallying point for opponents of the republican government, however, partly because of the threat it posed

---

3. See online the Spanish estate data collected by M. Artola, See also the work of C. Milhaud on church property and that of M. Artola, L. Baulusz, and C. Martinez-Toledano on the evolution of property structure in Spain since the nineteenth century.

to what remained of the vast ecclesiastical and especially noble property that had not yet been redistributed and partly because of the fear it aroused among smaller landowners, who recalled the unauthorized occupation of land in 1932–1933 and worried about a potential reprise following the return to power of parties of the left in February 1936.[4] The measures adopted by the republicans in favor of secular schools and against religious ones also played an important role in mobilizing the Catholic camp. The coup d'état of August 1936, the Civil War, and the forty years of Franco dictatorship that followed attest to the violence of the transformation of trifunctional societies into ownership and later social-democratic societies; durable traces of these conflictual processes remain everywhere.

Warrior Nobilities, Owner Nobilities

Turning now to the size of the nobility in the various countries of Europe, we again find great diversity, even greater than in the case of the clergy. As we saw previously in the case of France, these spatial and temporal comparisons need to be done carefully because the nobility was usually defined at the local level and its nature varied widely in space and time. The sources are not good enough to allow detailed comparisons of the chronologies and trajectories of different countries.

However, the available sources are adequate to distinguish two extreme patterns: in some countries the nobility represented a fairly small portion of the population in the seventeenth and eighteenth centuries (generally between 1 and 2 percent, and sometimes less than 1 percent); in others, it was significantly larger (typically 5 to 8 percent of the population). There were no doubt many intermediate cases, but with the sources we currently have it is hard to be precise.

The first group of countries, in which the nobility was small, includes France, the United Kingdom, and Sweden (Fig. 5.2). In the case of the United Kingdom, the figures we have given (1.4 percent of the population in 1690 and 1.1 percent in 1800) correspond to a fairly broad definition of nobility, which includes the gentry. Had we included only the small fraction of the nobility that enjoyed political privileges, its share of the population would be much

---

4. For a classic study of this dramatic sequence of events, see E. Malefakis, *Agrarian Reform and Peasant Revolution in Spain. Origins of the Civil War* (Yale University Press, 1970).

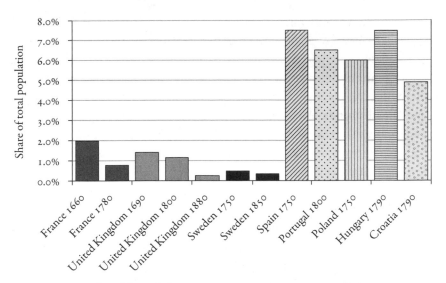

FIG. 5.2. The weight of the nobility in Europe, 1660–1880

Interpretation: The nobility represented less than 2 percent of the population in France, the United Kingdom, and Sweden in the seventeenth to nineteenth centuries (with a downward trend) and between 5 and 8 percent in Spain, Portugal, Poland, Hungary, and Croatia during the same time. *Sources and series:* piketty.pse.ens.fr/ideology.

smaller (less than 0.1 percent). In the case of Sweden, the figures indicated (0.5 percent of the population in 1750 and 0.3 percent in 1850) are taken from official censuses commissioned by the royal authorities to measure the size of the various orders and organize representative bodies. They therefore reflect reality as seen from the standpoint of the central government. I will come back to these two cases. For now, note simply that the first group includes countries where the process of centralized state formation was already extremely advanced in the seventeenth and eighteenth centuries.

The second group, which consists of countries with large noble classes (representing 5 to 8 percent of the population), includes Spain, Portugal, Poland, Hungary, and Croatia (Fig. 5.2). For the last two countries, the figures are fairly accurate thanks to censuses of the orders conducted in the late eighteenth century by the Austro-Hungarian Empire. The estimates for the other countries are less precise. Nevertheless, the orders of magnitude can be taken as significant. In particular, the gap between these countries and those in the first group is quite clear.

How should we interpret the fact that the noble class in some countries was five to ten times as large as in others? Clearly, such differences tell us that the human, economic, and political status of the nobility varied widely. When the noble class is very large, it follows that a significant number of nobles do not own large estates; in practice, many possessed little beyond their title, a certain prestige stemming from previous military service (recognition for which varied with period and country) and perhaps some status advantages. By contrast, a reduced aristocratic class, such as existed in the United Kingdom, Sweden, and France, meant that the nobility had succeeded in constituting itself as a small ownership elite, which held significant amounts of wealth and enjoyed considerable political and economic power.

To explain these important differences between countries, we need to look at the territorial, political, ideological, military, and fiscal history of each European state and at the compromises struck among contending social groups in different periods. For instance, in Spain and Portugal, during the centuries of the *Reconquista,* the procedures of ennoblement were closely related to the shifting border between Christian- and Muslim-held territory. In practice, the incorporation of new territory into the Christian kingdom often led to the ennoblement of entire villages, decreed by the king or in some cases by the villagers themselves, in exchange for their loyalty and future fiscal privileges. This quickly swelled the ranks of the Spanish nobility, in which huge inequalities separated the elite *grandes,* who commanded vast estates, from the mass of *hidalgos,* most of whom were rather poor. In the centuries that followed, the Spanish monarchy met with great difficulty when it came to collecting taxes from the latter; usually it was obliged instead to pay them meager pensions, the cost of which weighed on the royal treasury and impeded modernization of the state.

We find comparable processes and similar inequalities in the Polish, Hungarian, and Croatian nobilities. For instance, the Polish-Lithuanian monarchy expanded its territory and reincorporated lost fiefs in the fifteenth and sixteenth centuries.[5] In Portugal, as early as the thirteenth and fourteenth centuries while the *Reconquista* was still under way, so-called *Livros de Linhagens* proliferated; these were books in which the lesser nobility enumerated its many lineages and recounted its military exploits and acts of bravery so that subsequent generations and future monarchs would not forget them.[6] Documents of this

---

5. See, for example, M. Lukowski, *The European Nobility in the 18th Century* (Palgrave-Macmillan, 2003), pp. 12–19.

6. See A. Duggan, ed., *Nobles and Nobility in Medieval Europe* (Boydell Press, 2000), pp. 223–235.

type are particularly interesting, because they remind us how much the fate of these various nobilities depended not only on the strategies of states and monarchs but also on intellectual and political tools developed by nobles themselves—both lesser and greater—to take stock of their positions and defend their rights and privileges.

It would take many volumes to describe the rise and fall of all these various forms of nobility, and the task is far beyond the scope of this book and in any case exceeds my competence. Instead, I set myself a more modest goal: to add some further details to the British and Swedish cases, which are both well documented and particularly pertinent to the remainder of our inquiry.

The United Kingdom and Ternary-Proprietarian Gradualism

The case of the United Kingdom is obviously of great interest, in part because the British monarchy led the first global colonial and industrial empire from the nineteenth until the middle of the twentieth century and in part because it is in some ways an opposite to the French case. Whereas the French trajectory was marked by the caesura of the French Revolution and by numerous later ruptures and restorations—monarchical, imperial, authoritarian, and republican—over the course of the nineteenth and twentieth centuries, the British trajectory seems to have been one of strictly gradual change.

It would nevertheless be a mistake to think that it was solely by small touches that the social and political organization of the United Kingdom moved from the trifunctional schema first to a proprietarian logic and then later to the logic of Labour and neo-proprietarianism. The moments of rupture were of crucial importance; they bear emphasizing because they illustrate yet again the multiplicity of possible trajectories and switch points as well as the importance of crises and the sequencing of events in the history of inegalitarian regimes. Two points in particular should be singled out: first, the central role that the battle for progressive taxation played in the fall of the House of Lords, especially in the fateful crisis of 1909–1911; and second, the importance of the Irish question in undermining the dominant order in the period 1880–1920. The Irish question is important because it touched on three aspects of the inequality regime simultaneously: namely, its trifunctional, proprietarian, and quasi-colonial dimensions.

To begin, recall the general context. The British Parliament has ancient roots, dating back to the eleventh to thirteenth centuries. The King's Council, consisting of representatives of the high nobility and clergy, was gradually enlarged to include representatives of towns and counties. The division of Parliament into two houses, the House of Lords and the House of Commons, took place in the fourteenth century. These institutions reflect the trifunctional structure of society at that time. In particular, the House of Lords was composed of members of the two dominant classes, which initially carried equal weight: on one side were the lords spiritual: that is, the bishops, archbishops, abbots, and other representatives of the clerical and religious class; on the other, the lords temporal: dukes, marquesses, earls, and other representatives of the noble and warrior class. In medieval English texts expounding the theory of the three orders, such as that of Archbishop Wolfsan of York, one finds the same concern with equilibrium we noted in comparable French texts. Nobles were enjoined to heed the clergy's wise counsel of moderation, while clerics were urged in turn not to mistake themselves for warriors and abuse their power, lest the legitimacy of the trifunctional system be undermined.

This equilibrium was seriously upset for the first time in the sixteenth century. In the wake of political conflict with the papacy and Henry VIII's decision to dissolve the monasteries in the 1530s, the spiritual lords were sanctioned, and their political role diminished. Their presence in the House of Lords was reduced to a small minority, leaving the temporal lords in nearly total control. In the eighteenth and nineteenth centuries, the number of spiritual lords was limited to twenty-six bishops, whereas the temporal lords held 460 seats. In the fifteenth century, moreover, the high nobility successfully imposed the principle that nearly all noble seats should be occupied by hereditary peers, that is, dukes, marquesses, earls, viscounts, and barons, who transmitted their peerages from father to son, generally according to the rule of primogeniture.

As a result, this group enjoyed both permanence and preeminence, shielded from royal power, electoral politics, and rivalry within the nobility (the lower and middling ranks of the nobility played no part in the nomination of peers or perpetuation of peerages). To be sure, the king could in theory always create new lords, in principle without limit, and in case of grave crisis this power allowed him to exert full control over the kingdom's affairs. In practice, however, this right was always exercised with extreme caution, usually in very specific circumstances and under the control of Parliament, as in the aftermath of the acts of union with Scotland (1707) and Ireland (1800), which led to the nomination of new lords (twenty-eight peers and four bishops in the Irish case, along with a hundred new seats in the House of Commons). The balance of power was not altered.

Many works have shown how extreme the concentration of power and landed property was in the high English aristocracy as compared with other European nobilities. It has been estimated that in 1880, nearly 80 percent of the land in the United Kingdom was still owned by 7,000 noble families (less than 0.1 percent of the population), with more than half belonging to just 250 families (0.01 percent of the population), a tiny group that largely coincided with the hereditary peers who sat in the House of Lords.[7] By comparison, on the eve of the Revolution the French nobility owned roughly 25–30 percent of French land; recall, however, that the clergy in France had not yet been expropriated.

Note, too, that the House of Lords played a clearly dominant role in British bicameralism until the last third of the nineteenth century. In the eighteenth and nineteenth centuries, the majority of prime ministers and members of the government issued from the House of Lords, whether they were members of the Conservative (Tory) Party or the Whig Party (officially rebaptized as the Liberal Party in 1859). This tradition would endure until the end of the long mandate of Lord Salisbury, the third marquess of that name, who served as Tory prime minister from 1885 to 1892 and again from 1895 to 1901; subsequent heads of government would issue from the House of Commons.[8]

Furthermore, the vast majority of the House of Commons itself consisted of members of the nobility in the eighteenth and most of the nineteenth centuries until the 1860s. The Bill of Rights, adopted in the wake of the Glorious Revolution of 1688 and the removal of King James II, confirmed and guaranteed the rights of Parliament, especially regarding taxes and budgets. Yet this foundational text changed nothing in the structure of Parliament or its mode of election. On the contrary, it consolidated a parliamentary regime that was fundamentally aristocratic and oligarchic. Specifically, all laws had to be ap-

---

7. D. Cannadine, *The Decline and Fall of the British Aristocracy* (Yale University Press, 1990), p. 9, table 1.1.

8. Alec Douglas-Home, who served as Tory prime minister in 1963–1964, was, like Salisbury, a member of the House of Lords, but he resigned upon being named head of government; times had changed, and it seemed incongruous for the country to be led by a lord. Winston Churchill, Tory prime minister from 1940 to 1945 and 1951 to 1955, was born into an aristocratic family that included several members of the House of Lords, but he himself was elected to the Commons. He even spent a brief period as a Liberal in 1905 before returning to the Tories in 1924, which his adversaries took as proof of his opportunism and lack of loyalty to traditional aristocratic values.

proved in identical terms by both houses, effectively conferring veto power over all legislation, including fiscal and budgetary matters and anything to do with property rights, on the House of Lords (and thus on a few hundred hereditary peers). Furthermore, the members of the House of Commons were still elected by a minority of property owners. The rules that specified how much tax a person had to pay or how much property he had to own in order to vote were complex and varied from district to district; what is more, they were controlled by local elites. In practice, those rules favored landowners, whose influence was further increased by electoral districting that granted more seats to rural areas.

In the early 1860s, roughly 75 percent of the seats in the House of Commons were still occupied by members of the aristocracy, which accounted for less than 0.5 percent of the British population at the time.[9] On the benches of the House of Commons one found representatives of the three principal components of the British nobility: the peerage, other titled nobility, and the gentry (untitled nobility). The peerage was well represented, notably by younger sons of hereditary peers, who normally had no chance of sitting in the House of Lords and therefore chose to embark on political careers in the Commons, generally by standing for election in constituencies where the family held vast amounts of land. In the Commons one also found elder sons of peers awaiting their chance to move up to the House of Lords. For example, Salisbury sat in the House of Commons from 1853 until his father's death in 1868, at which time he took a seat in the House of Lords before becoming prime minister in 1885.

The Commons also included many members of the titled nobility, especially baronets and knights. This component of the British nobility played no direct political role and enjoyed no special legal or fiscal privileges, but their titles were nevertheless protected by the state, and members were recognized in the protocol of official processions and ceremonies, just behind the hereditary peers. This was a highly prestigious group, only slightly larger than the peerage, to which the monarch could grant access by letters patent following a procedure similar to that used for naming lords. The monarch could in theory nominate as many new nobles as he wished, but in practice moderation was the watchword, as it was with the peers. In the early 1880s there were some 856 baronets in Britain who ranked just below the 460 hereditary peers in the House of Lords, followed by several hundred knights. The title of baronet could also pave the way to a peerage, in case a line of peers was extinguished for want

---

9. D. Cannadine, *The Decline and Fall of the British Aristocracy*, pp. 11–16.

of offspring. Today the Lord Chancellor maintains the Official Roll of the Baronetage.[10]

Finally, a large number of gentry also sat in the House of Commons. The gentry is the untitled nobility, the largest group in the British aristocracy in the eighteenth and nineteenth centuries; it had no official existence of any kind, no titles recognized by the state, and no place in processions and ceremonies.

The British Aristocracy, a Proprietarian Nobility

Because the British aristocracy was divided into three groups (peers seated in the House of Lords, other titled nobility, and unofficial gentry), it is very difficult to estimate how its size evolved. The difficulties are somewhat different from those we encountered in the case of France. In the eighteenth century the entire French nobility had a legal existence, since all members enjoyed political privileges (such as the right to choose representatives of the noble order in the Estates General), fiscal privileges (such as exemption from certain taxes, like the *taille*), and jurisdictional privileges (in seigneurial courts). But nobility was defined at the local level in ways that have left disparate traces that are hard to compare across provinces so that there are important uncertainties about the total size of the group.[11] In this same period, the British nobility included on the one hand a tiny titled group (less than 0.1 percent of the population), which included the hereditary peerage, endowed with extensive political privileges (beginning with the right of veto exercised by the House of Lords over all legislation until 1911) and vast landed estates; and, on the other hand, the gentry, by far the more numerous group, since the size of the noble class as a whole is usually estimated to have been about 1 percent of the population in the eighteenth century and 0.5 percent at the end of the nineteenth (Fig. 5.2). But the gentry had no official legal existence.[12]

---

10. In 2019 some 962 baronets figured on this list, which includes the title created for Dennis Thatcher (husband of Margaret), which was passed on to his son in 2003.

11. See Chap. 3.

12. Available estimates put the size of the gentry at between 15,000 and 25,000 adult males in the eighteenth and nineteenth centuries. Their absolute number seems not to have changed very much (apart from a slight increase in the eighteenth century and slight decrease in the nineteenth century). As a portion of the population, however, the gentry was in rapid decline because the population as a whole was increasing from barely two million heads of family in England and Wales at the end of the eighteenth century to six million in the 1880s. The gentry thus declined

The gentry formed a class of prosperous property owners, larger than the tiny titled nobility but still quite small when compared to the bloated ranks of the lesser Spanish, Portuguese, or Polish nobility. Even though it enjoyed no explicit political or fiscal privileges, the gentry clearly benefited greatly from the prevailing political regime, which in many ways reflected a proprietarian rather than a trifunctional logic. The gentry, which included the offspring of younger sons of peers, baronets, and knights as well as descendants of the old Anglo-Saxon feudal warrior class, expanded by welcoming the newly wealthy through strategies of marriage and recognition. The rules that determined the right to vote in elections to the House of Commons were defined at the local level and generally favored landowners; this indirectly advantaged members of the gentry who maintained extensive holdings in land over newly rich town dwellers and merchants whose wealth stemmed exclusively from manufacturing, urban real estate, or finance.

The important point, however, is that the boundaries between different owner groups were relatively porous. No one knew for sure where the gentry ended: one belonged to the group only if other members of the local gentry recognized one's membership. In practice, many landed aristocratic fortunes were gradually reinvested in mercantile, colonial, or industrial activities in the eighteenth and nineteenth centuries so that many members of the gentry possessed diversified fortunes. Conversely, many merchants and other bourgeois without the slightest feudal or warrior background had the good taste to acquire substantial estates, adopt a suitable lifestyle, and marry appropriately to secure their entry into the gentry.[13] A marriage to an authentic scion of an ancient feudal warrior lineage or even to offspring of titled nobility of more recent vintage made it easier to gain recognition as a member of the gentry but was not indispensable. In many ways the social and political regime that pre-

---

from 1.1 percent of the population to 0.3 percent between 1800 and 1880. In any case, it was much larger than the titled nobility (with 1,000–1,500 titles, counting lords, baronets, and knights). The gentry itself consisted of some 3,000 to 5,000 esquires and 15,000 to 20,000 gentlemen. See the online appendix.

13. D. Cannadine, *The Decline and Fall of the British Aristocracy*. The political promotion of the new bourgeois and mercantile elites, which in the best of cases led to their integration into the gentry, began in the Middle Ages in cities and royal territories where the right to vote was easier to obtain than on noble or ecclesiastical lands. See, for example, C. Angelucci, S. Meraglia, and N. Voigtlaender, *How Merchant Towns Shaped Parliaments: From the Norman Conquest of England to the Great Reform Act* (NBER Working Paper 23606, 2017).

vailed in the United Kingdom in the eighteenth and much of the nineteenth century represented a gradual fusion of aristocratic and proprietarian logics.

The rules governing the right to vote were also defined by local elites. The first real attempt at electoral reform at the national level did not occur until 1832. In that year social agitation in favor of extending the franchise led, against considerable resistance, to Parliament's passage of the Reform Bill. Some members of the House of Commons saw a chance to improve their standing relative to the Lords. Only about 5 percent of adult males were eligible to vote in 1820: though a small minority, this was still a much larger group than the gentry. The Reform Bill of 1832 greatly increased this number, though those eligible to vote remained a small minority. They represented only 14 percent of the adult male population in 1840 with significant regional variations, as each constituency retained the right to define the exact rules of eligibility, therefore reflecting the strategies of local elites, especially the gentry. Further modification of the rules had to await the truly decisive reforms of 1867 and 1884. It bears emphasizing that the secret ballot was not introduced until 1872. Before that, each individual vote was announced publicly and recorded (researchers can still consult the voting records of elections prior to that date—a precious historical source). Hence it was not easy for voters to make political choices that went against the wishes of their landlords or employers. In practice, many seats went uncontested. The local member of Parliament (MP) was reelected in election after election and often in generation after generation. In 1860 the House of Commons was still profoundly aristocratic and oligarchic.

Ownership Societies in Classic Novels

The porosity of the boundaries between nobles and owners emerges with particular clarity in the literature of the time, most notably the novels of Jane Austen, whose characters illustrate to perfection the diversity of the British gentry as well as the proprietarian logic they shared in the period 1790–1810. All owned landed estates and fine homes, as is only to be expected, and the action moves from gala ball to gala ball and country house to country house. When we look more closely, however, we find that the wealth of Austen's gentry was quite diversified, including both foreign assets and the gilt-edged bonds that the British government issued in large numbers to finance its colonial and continental military expeditions. Foreign direct investment, especially in slaves and sugar, was also common. In *Mansfield Park,* Fanny's uncle, Sir Thomas, has to go to the Antilles for a year with his eldest son to tend to his plantations and business dealings. Austen is silent about the difficulties the two men might have been having with their slave plantations, then at their apogee in British and French colonies. But reading between the lines, one gathers that it was not easy to administer such investments from thousands of miles away. Sir Thomas is nevertheless a baronet and member of Parliament.

Jane Austen's protagonists are calmer and more rustic than Balzac's characters, who dream of pasta and perfume factories and bold mortgage schemes and real estate deals in 1820s Paris (although they, too, sometimes dream of earning handsome dividends on investments in slaves in the American South, as Vautrin does in his famous lecture to Rastignac).[14] Austen's characters attest to a world in which various forms of wealth have entered into communion. In practice, what counted was the size of one's fortune, not the mix or origins of the properties it contained. What determines the possibility that various characters will meet and potentially marry is above all the yield on their capital. The all-important question is whether one's annual income is 100 pounds sterling (barely three time the average income of the day), or 1,000 pounds (thirty times the average), or 4,000 pounds (more than a hundred times). The first case describes the not very enviable situation in which the three sisters Elinor, Marianne, and Margaret find themselves in *Sense and Sensibility;* it is almost impossible for them to marry. With 4,000 pounds of income, however, one is closer to the substantial position of their half-brother John Dashwood, who in the very opening pages of the novel seals the sisters' fate by refusing, in a chilling conversation with his wife Fanny, to share his wealth with the sisters. Between these two extremes lay a whole range of modes of living and socializing, possible encounters, and conceivable fates. Subtle differences divided one subgroup of society from the next, and Austen and Balzac describe these hidden boundaries and spell out their implications with unrivaled power. Both describe ownership societies characterized by very steep hierarchies, in which it seems quite difficult to live with a modicum of dignity and elegance unless one's income is at least twenty or thirty times the average.[15]

---

14. See T. Piketty, *Capital in the Twenty-First Century,* trans. A. Goldhammer (Harvard University Press, 2014), pp. 238–242.

15. The incomes of the various characters are given in terms of the ratio to the average national income per adult at the time. It is interesting to note that the amounts mentioned by Balzac are almost identical to those imagined by Austen, taking the exchange rate into account (between 1800 and 1914 the pound sterling was worth about 25 gold francs). See Piketty, *Capital in the Twenty-First Century,* pp. 411–416.

The nature of the property that yielded this income—whether land or financial assets, factories or colonial plantations, real estate or slaves—ultimately mattered very little, because all these social groups and forms of property were henceforth united by the grace of the universal monetary equivalent and, above all, by the fact that political, economic, and institutional developments (including monetary, legal, and fiscal systems, transport infrastructures, and more generally, the unification of national and international markets through the construction of the centralized state) made it increasingly possible to realize that equivalence in practice. The classic European novels of the early nineteenth century are one of the clearest signs of this golden age of ownership society, especially in its British and French variants.

What is striking is not the intimate knowledge that Austen and Balzac possess of the era's hierarchy of wealth and lifestyles, nor it is their perfect mastery of the various forms of ownership and relations of power and domination that characterized the societies they lived in. It is their ability not to make heroes of their characters, whom they neither condemn nor glorify. This enables them to convey both their complexity and humanity.

Generally speaking, ownership societies obeyed logics more complex and subtle than did trifunctional societies. In the trifunctional order, the ascription of roles and temperaments was perfectly clear. The grand narrative was one of interclass alliance: the religious, warrior, and laboring classes played distinct but complementary roles, which structured the society, gave it stability, and allowed it to perpetuate itself for the greater good of the entire community. The corresponding literature, from the *Song of Roland* to *Robin Hood,* is filled with heroism: noble attitudes, sacrifice, and Christian charity are paramount. The trifunctional schema proposes such clearly defined roles and functions that it has often served as an inspiration for film and science fiction.[16] No trace of such heroism remains in ownership society: in the novels of Austen and Balzac, there is no clear relation between the size of one's fortune and one's functional abilities or aptitudes. Some people own considerable wealth while others have modest incomes or work as servants. In fact, little is said about the latter, for

---

16. In *The Planet of the Apes,* the gorillas are the warriors, the orangutans are the priests, and the chimpanzees are the third estate (following the well-known ternary structure, soon to be complicated by the integration of humans, former slave drivers who now had become slaves). In *Star Wars* the Jedi are both wise and great warriors. The "force" that guides them embodies the fusion of the two elites of trifunctional society.

their lives are too dull. At no time, however, do the novelists suggest that they are in any way less deserving or less useful than their employers. Each person plays the role assigned by his or her capital on a scale that seems eternal and immutable. Everyone has a place in ownership society, in which the universal monetary equivalent allows for communication across vast communities and far-flung investments while guaranteeing social stability. Neither Austen nor Balzac needs to explain to readers that the annual income of capital is about 5 percent of its value or, conversely, that the value of capital is about twenty times its annual yield. Everyone knows that it takes capital on the order of 200,000 pounds to yield an annual income of 10,000 pounds, more or less independent of the nature of the property. For both nineteenth-century novelists and their readers, it was easy to move from one scale to the other, as if the two were perfectly synonymous—two parallel languages spoken by everyone. Capital no longer obeyed a logic of functional utility, as in ternary societies, but only a logic of equivalence among different forms of ownership, thus opening new possibilities of exchange and accumulation.

In the classic novels of the early nineteenth century, inequality of wealth was implicitly justified by its ability to bring remote worlds into contact and by the need for social stability. It is not the role of the novelist, Austen and Balzac seem to say, to imagine a different form of political and economic organization; their task is rather to show us the feelings of individuals and the space that remains for freedom, detachment, and irony, notwithstanding the deterministic laws of capital and the cynical ways of money. By contrast, meritocratic discourse plays no part in the justification of ownership society. Such discourse would come into its own only later, with the rise of industrial and financial capitalism in the Belle Époque and especially in the hypercapitalist era 1990–2020, which celebrates winners and denigrates losers more aggressively than any earlier regime; I will come back to this.

At times, one senses in the nineteenth-century novel the emergence of another possible justification of wealth inequality, namely, the fact that without it, there would be no possibility of a small social group with the means to be concerned with things other than its own subsistence. In other words, in a poor society, inequality may seem to be a condition of civilization. Austen describes in minute detail what life was like in her time: she explains how much it cost to eat, to buy clothing and furniture, and to move about. The reader discovers that if, in addition to these things, one also wants to buy books or musical instruments, one needs at least twenty to thirty times the average income, which is possible only if wealth and the income that derives from it is extremely concentrated. But once again, irony is never far from Austen's pen, and she, like Balzac, never fails to mock the pretensions of her characters and their supposedly irreducible needs.

Burke's Peerage: *From Baronets to Petro-Billionaires*

Another very interesting document (though a good deal less subtle than the novels of Austen and Balzac), from which we can glean a sense of how the logic of aristocracy mingled with that of ownership in the British gentry of the era, is *Burke's Peerage, Baronetage and Landed Gentry of the United Kingdom.*

A genealogist by profession, John Burke became famous early in the nineteenth century for his celebrated annual catalogs of the British nobility. His lists of names and lineages soon became the ultimate reference for the study of the British aristocracy of this era. His authoritative listing filled a need because there was no official compilation of members of the gentry, even though it was the largest subgroup of the nobility. The first *Burke's Peerage,* published in 1826, met with such resounding success that it was revised and reprinted throughout the century. Every Briton with a claim to gentry status wanted his name to appear in it and delighted in reading Burke's learned analyses of lineages and fortunes, marriages and estates, glorious remote ancestors and famous contemporary exploits. Some editions concentrated on peers and titled nobility, especially those baronets so illustrious that Burke openly lamented their lack of an official role in service to the realm. In other volumes Burke compiled lists of nobles without official title. The 1883 edition included no fewer than 4,250 families belonging to both the titled nobility and the gentry. Burke's catalogs were respected throughout the nineteenth century by members of the nobility and their allies but mocked by people irritated by the obsequiously reverential tone that Burke and his successors used to describe these remarkable families that had given so much to the country.[17]

One finds similar catalogs, royal almanacs, and *bottins mondains* in many other countries, starting with the *Livro de Linhagens* compiled in Portugal in the thirteenth and fourteenth centuries and continuing through the annual compilations of the nineteenth and twentieth centuries. Here, nobles and their allies could take stock, sing their own praises, and express their demands. Many such catalogs continued to exist long after the nobility had officially disappeared. For instance, if you believe the twenty-eighth edition of the *Annuaire*

---

17. Cannadine, *The Decline and Fall of the British Aristocracy,* pp. 15–16.

de la Noblesse de France, published in 1872, no fewer than 225 deputies (occupying one-third of all seats in the National Assembly) were authentic nobles; they had been elected in 1871 in elections which in hindsight are considered to have been the first of the Third Republic but which took place at a time when no one knew whether the new regime, born of French defeat at the hands of the Prussians, would choose to be a republic or opt for yet another restoration of the monarchy. A writer for the *Annuaire* expressed joy at "the nation's *cri du coeur,* its spontaneous enthusiasm": "Into what arms could it [the nation] throw itself with greater assurance and sympathy than those of the nobility, whose scions, worthy heirs of the bravery and virtues of their ancestors, so generously shed their blood at Reichschoffen and Sedan? Furthermore, while all the illustrious personages who rallied to the Empire have withdrawn from the battle, it is forty years since we have seen in the elected chamber so brilliant a gathering of illustrious aristocratic names."[18] Nevertheless, the proportion of noble deputies would fall to less than 10 percent in 1914 and less than 5 percent between the wars.[19] The *Annuaire* itself ceased publication in 1938.

As for *Burke's Peerage,* it continues to publish to this day. Having counted peers and baronets through the entire nineteenth century, later versions of the catalog include "the great families of Europe, America, Africa, and the Middle East." In the latest editions, one finds new classes of billionaires who made their money in oil or silicon, a strange mixture of crowned heads and wealthy owners of oil wells and mines and stocks and bonds, all described in the same admiring and reverential tones. The spirit is not far removed from the listings of billionaires published by magazines like *Forbes* in the United States since 1987 or *Challenges* in France since 1998. Often owned by illustrious multimillionaires themselves, these publications are generally filled with stereotypical glorifications of wealth well deserved and useful inequality.[20]

---

18. The *Annuaire* went on to enumerate among the noble deputies no fewer than nine princes and dukes, thirty-one marquises, forty-nine counts, nineteen viscounts, nineteen barons, and eighty "bearing only a noble *particule,*" adding: "We cannot fully guarantee the accuracy of this classification, although it is based as much as possible on authentic documents. Some deputies neglect or refuse to assume their titles, while others claim what are not even courtesy titles, to which they have no right." See *Annuaire de la noblesse de France* (1872), pp. 419–424.

19. See J. Bécarud, "Noblesse et représentation parlementaire: les députés nobles de 1871 à 1968," *Revue française de science politique,* 1973.

20. To some extent these classifications are also a response to legitimate demands for information about the top of the social hierarchy, which government statistics

Burke's Peerage in its original and later incarnations illustrates two key points. First, the British nobility in the nineteenth century was inextricably aristocratic and proprietarian. Second, beyond the British case and the transformation of inequality regimes, there are deep affinities among trifunctional, proprietarian, and neo-proprietarian justifications of inequality. The issue of inequality always arouses ideological conflict. Many discourses clash, some more subtle than others, and the weapons they use take many different forms, from novels to catalogs, from political programs to newspaper columns, from pamphlets to magazines. All of these sources provide useful information about the size of the various contending social groups as well as their respective resources and merits.

The House of Lords, Protector of the Proprietarian Order

We turn now to the fateful fall of the House of Lords and British proprietarianism. The two events are intimately related. Throughout the eighteenth and much of the nineteenth centuries, the House of Lords governed the country and played a central role in the hardening, protection, and increasingly ferocious sacralization of the right of property. Think of the famous Enclosure Acts, enacted and several times reinforced by Parliament, led by the Lords, most notably in 1773 and 1801. Their purpose was to put hedges around fields and put an end to right of poor peasants to use communal land for crops and pasturage.

Also important to mention was the famous Black Act of 1723, which stipulated the death penalty for anyone caught pilfering wood or poaching game on land they did not own. Humble folk had taken to blackening their faces and trying their luck by night, and landlords in the House of Lords and their allies in the House of Commons were determined to prevent this. Anyone who killed a deer, cut down a tree, poached fish from a breeding pond, pulled up plants, or abetted or incited such activity fell under the shadow of the act and could be sentenced to death by hanging without trial of any kind. Initially intended to expire after three years, the law was renewed and reinforced over the next century until these acts of rebellion ceased and the proprietarian order was restored.[21]

---

largely ignore. See Piketty, *Capital in the Twenty-First Century,* pp. 432–446.

21. See E. P. Thompson's classic book, *Whigs and Hunters. The Origin of the Black Act* (Allen Lane, 1975). Similar harsh measures to enforce property rights can be seen

Rather than view the House of Lords as a survival of the trifunctional order amid the ownership society that emerged in the eighteenth and nineteenth centuries, it is more accurate to see it as the protector of the new proprietarian order and the hyperconcentration of wealth. During the French Revolution, it was in the name of the proprietarian order (rather than the trifunctional order based on equilibrium between nobility and clergy, which would have been particularly out of place since the clergy had long since lost its status in England) that British elites spoke out against what was happening in Paris.

For example, Arthur Young, who was completing his absorbing account of his travels in France when the Revolution broke out, was convinced that the country was on its way to ruin when it was decided in 1789 that nobles and the third estate should sit together in the same assembly. For the traveling agronomist, there could be no doubt that peaceful, harmonious development was possible only in a political system like the English, which afforded a veto to the high nobility, that is, to great landlords—responsible, far-sighted men who worried about the future. For the British elites of that time, the fact that representatives of the third estate were elected under a property-qualified suffrage was not a sufficient guarantee, no doubt because they felt that some day the right to vote would be extended to broader, less responsible classes. The separate vote by orders and the right of veto granted to the high nobility through the House of Lords ensured that no ill-considered policy of redistribution could ever pass into law; because the country could not thus be plunged into chaos and property rights called into question, British prosperity and power remained in safe hands.

The Battle for Progressive Taxation and the Fall of the House of Lords

In fact, it was the extension of the right to elect members of the House of Commons, combined with the issue of progressive taxation, that ultimately led first to the fall of the House of Lords and then of ownership society in general.

---

elsewhere in Europe; for example, in Prussia in 1821, which made an impression on young Karl Marx. Raoul Peck's biographical film of Marx (*The Young Karl Marx,* 2017) opens with a scene of peasants collecting wood being attacked by a landlord's militia. The French Revolution ordered the opening of private land and forests to hunters, a measure that is still in place today and that is defended by the French Communist Party.

The movement to extend the suffrage intensified in the middle of the nineteenth century. Universal male suffrage was tried in France from 1848 to 1852 and again after 1871. In the United Kingdom it was not until the electoral reforms of 1867 and 1884 that voting rules were standardized throughout the kingdom, increasing the percentage of voters first to 30 percent and then 60 percent of the adult male population. Universal male suffrage was established in 1918, and the vote was finally extended to women in 1928. This final phase of reform also witnessed the first decisive successes of the Labour Party.[22] Before that, however, it was the reforms of 1867 and 1884, coupled with the abolition of public recording of the vote in 1872, that totally transformed the balance of power between the Commons and the House of Lords. After 1884, more than 60 percent of adult males were entitled to choose their own MPs by secret ballot, compared with just 10 percent before 1864 (and at that time of course subject to supervision by local elites). The extension of male suffrage in Britain was certainly slower than in France, which went directly from severely restricted censitary* suffrage to universal male suffrage (Fig. 5.3). Still, political competition in the United Kingdom was totally overhauled in the space of a few decades.[23]

More specifically, the first effect of these reforms was to induce the old Whig Party, renamed the Liberal Party in 1859, to take up the cause of the new voters and therefore to adopt a platform and ideology much more favorable to the middle and working class. The Reform Act of 1867 did much to ensure the victory of the Liberals in 1880, which paved the way for the Third Reform Act of 1884. This led directly to the loss of dozens of rural constituencies previously held by noble families, which in some cases had held seats without interrup-

---

22. N. Johnston, *The History of the Parliamentary Franchise* (House of Commons Research Paper, 2013). It is interesting to note that prior to the Reform Bill of 1832 (the first national legislation on the right to vote), no formal rule limited this right to men. It was merely a custom, and there may have been cases of female landlords who voted. The right to vote was partially extended to women over the age of 30 in 1918.

23. In addition, these forms went together with ambitious (and, for the time, quite innovative) measures to regulate candidate spending: the Corrupt Practices Prevention Act of 1854, which obliged candidates to declare their expenses, and the Corrupt and Illegal Practice Act of 1883, which drastically limited total expenditures. J. Cagé and E. Dewitte, "It Takes Money to Make MPs: New Evidence from 150 Years of British Campaign Spending" (Sciences Po, 2019).

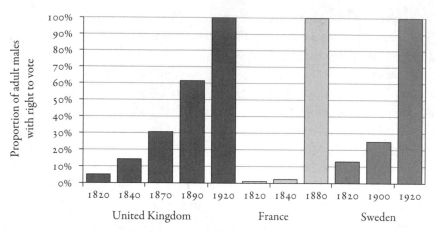

FIG. 5.3. Evolution of male suffrage in Europe, 1820–1920

Interpretation: The percentage of adult males with the right to vote (allowing for property qualifications) increased from 5 percent in 1820 to 30 percent in 1870 and 100 percent in 1920 in the United Kingdom, and from 1 percent in 1820 to 100 percent in 1880 in France. *Sources and series:* piketty.pse.ens.fr/ideology.

tion for centuries.[24] After 1880 the Liberals backed the Tories, who controlled the House of Lords, into their last redoubts and established their own legitimacy as a governing party. Having distinguished themselves in the fight to abolish the Corn Laws in 1846 and to reduce tariffs and other indirect taxes weighing on workers (while the Tories were suspected, rightly, of wanting to keep grain prices high to protect the profits of their estates), the Liberals began in the 1880s to formulate ever bolder social policies along with progressive taxes on income and estates.[25]

---

24. Cannadine, *The Decline and Fall of the British Aristocracy,* pp. 142–143.
25. The Corn Laws, which limited imports of grain and other agricultural products and protected domestic production, were repealed in 1846 under a Tory government led by Robert Peel, but the vote divided the party, so much so that supporters of Peel (including Gladstone) eventually quit the party and joined the Whigs, ultimately leading to the foundation of the Liberal Party in 1859. This mobilization of the Liberals in favor of workers and against the protectionist landed aristocracy had a lasting impact on attitudes toward free trade and competition in the United Kingdom, in contrast to France, where the landed aristocracy had largely disappeared and the defense of the small independent peasant producer played a fundamental role in structuring the political system, a role that continues to this day. On this, see D. Spector, *La gauche, la droite et le marché. Histoire d'une idée controversée (19ᵉ-21ᵉ siècles)* (Odile Jacob, 2017), pp. 43–52.

In the 1880s, Salisbury, the leader of the Tories, imprudently proposed a referendum theory: morally and politically, he argued, the Lords had the right and duty to oppose legislation adopted by the Commons if the majority of the House of Commons had not been elected explicitly on the basis of that specific law, clearly spelled out to the country prior to the election. At first, the Tories thought they had found the answer to the expanded suffrage: in 1894, the Lords vetoed the reforms that William Gladstone, the leader of the Liberals, proposed for Ireland on the grounds that the bill, which was moderately popular in England, had not been explicitly presented to the voters prior to passage. This allowed the Conservatives to win the elections of 1895 and return to power.

But Salisbury had been too confident of the superior ability of the Lords and the Tories to interpret the deep will of the people, and the imprudence of his strategy soon became apparent. Returned to power under Lloyd George, the Liberals won passage of their famous People's Budget in 1909, at the heart of which was an explosive cocktail: a progressive tax on total income (or "supertax," levied on top of the quasi-proportional taxes on separate categories of income that had been in force since 1842); an increase in "death duties" on the largest estates; and to top it all off, an increase in the land tax, which hit large landed estates particularly hard. With this package it was possible to finance a series of new social measures, especially worker pensions, at a time when Liberals feared that they would gradually be replaced by the Labour Party (which ultimately did happen); therefore they felt that they had to do something for the working class. The whole package was perfectly calibrated to win the approval of a majority of the House of Commons and above all of the new voters while confronting the Lords with an unacceptable provocation to the delight of Lloyd George, who never missed an opportunity to mock the idleness and uselessness of the aristocratic class. The Lords fell into the trap and vetoed the People's Budget, despite having voted in 1906–1907 for new labor laws granting additional rights to workers and unions. But by vetoing tax measures that affected them directly, they took the fatal risk of exposing their class bias to the light of day.

Lloyd George then doubled down by having the Commons pass a new law, this time of a constitutional nature, blocking the Lords from amending finance bills (which henceforth became the sole province of the Commons) and limiting their power to block other legislation to a period of no more than one year. Unsurprisingly, the Lords vetoed this suicidal measure, and new elections were held, leading to another victory for the Liberals. By virtue of the Salisbury doctrine, the Lords should then have resigned and agreed to accept the controversial legislation, which was now both fiscal and constitutional. But given the historic issues at stake, many Lords were prepared to reject their leader's commitment, which in any case was only informal. According to witnesses in a position to know, it seems that the king then threatened to create up to 500 new seats in the House of Lords (in keeping with a secret promise he supposedly made to Lloyd George before the election), and this played a decisive role. It is nevertheless very difficult to say what actually would have happened if the Lords had not finally resigned themselves to passing the new constitutional law in May 1911.[26] The fact remains that this was the precise moment when the House of Lords forfeited all real legislative power. Since 1911, it is the will of the majority as expressed at the ballot box and in the House of Commons that has force of law in the United Kingdom, and the House of Lords has been reduced to a purely consultative and largely ceremonial role. The political institution that had governed the United Kingdom for centuries and presided over the emergence of a global colonial and industrial empire had in fact ceased to exist as a decision-making body.

Other less far-reaching constitutional reforms followed: life peerages (as opposed to hereditary peerages) were introduced in 1959, and their number was significantly increased in 1999 so that the majority of members of the House of Lords today are people appointed for their competence or service to the kingdom who cannot pass their seats on to their descendants.[27] But it was indeed the crisis of 1910–1911 concerning the issue of progressive taxation and

---

26. Note that a royal threat to create new seats in the House of Lords to overturn the majority there had already played an important role in the adoption of the Reform Bill of 1832. But there, too, it is very difficult to know if the king would have made good on his threat if a compromise (less ambitious than the original form) had not been struck with the Lords. See D. Cannadine, *Victorious Century: The United Kingdom 1800–1906* (Viking, 2017), p. 159.

27. In 2019, the House of Lords comprised 792 members, including twenty-six lords spiritual (Anglican bishops), ninety-two hereditary lords temporal, and 674 lords temporal appointed for life (life peers). A reform to have 80 percent of members chosen by election was debated in 2010–2012 but ultimately abandoned (there was no agreement on how to define electoral rules distinct from those of the Commons but still justifiable). The Parliament Act of 1949 reduced to one year the period during which the Lord could block a nonbudgetary law (a period finally set at two years in 1911). This does not prevent the Lords from reminding the Commons of their existence from time to time, as during the Brexit debate of 2018–2019, though without lasting consequences.

the reduction of social inequality that proved to be the fateful moment when the Lords lost their power. In 1945, a little more than thirty years later, an absolute majority of Labour deputies came to power for the first time. They issued from a political movement whose purpose was to represent the working class, and the new Labour government they established would proceed to establish the National Health Service and implement an array of social and fiscal policies that radically transformed the structure of inequality in Britain, as we will see in what follows.

Ireland Between Trifunctional, Proprietarian, and Colonialist Ideology

Although progressive taxation and the reduction of social inequality were the central issues in the fall of the House of Lords in the period 1909–1911, it is also important to note the role of the Irish question (with its trifunctional, proprietarian, and quasi-colonial dimensions) in the broad challenge to inequality mounted in Britain between 1880 and 1920.

The Irish case was one of extreme inequality stemming from the combined effects of a range of political and ideological causes. In the eighteenth and nineteenth centuries, Ireland was much poorer than England: its agricultural and manufacturing output per capita was half as large. The gap in the standard of living was aggravated by the fact that most agricultural land in Ireland was held by very wealthy landlords residing in England, most of whom were members of the House of Lords. Although Ireland suffered from the same problem of extremely concentrated land ownership that we saw in England, the issue of absentee landlords, who collected their rents from their English manors, lent a particular coloration to the Irish question. In addition, 80 percent of the Irish population was Catholic, and the civil and political rights of Irish Catholics were severely limited. They were required to pay a tithe to the Church of Ireland (part of the Anglican Communion), to which they did not adhere, and they did not have the right to elect members of the Irish Parliament, which in any case had been subordinate to the Parliament at Westminster since 1494 and could make no decision without its approval. In short, Ireland was in the position of a British colony.

Nevertheless, the British Crown and Parliament, shaken by the American war for independence (1775–1783) and worried about French invasion (1796–1798), passed the Act of Union in 1800; this was not so much a union as a takeover of the Emerald Isle, at best a fool's bargain. The wealthiest Irish Catholics did obtain the right to vote with a property qualification, and Ireland gained the privilege of electing 100 representatives to the House of Commons. Representation was highly imbalanced, however: although there were, according to the 1801 census, more than five million Irish and barely nine million Britons, the latter were entitled to more than 500 seats, compared to merely 100 for the former. In exchange for Irish representation in the House of Commons in London, the Irish Parliament was abolished, clearly to spare the government in Westminster the need to deal with a Catholic majority in Ireland. In addition, Catholics still had to pay a tithe to the Anglican Church of Ireland, which would become the source of increasingly violent conflict.

The situation grew even more tense after the great Irish famine of 1845–1848, the most severe famine in nineteenth-century Europe: nearly one million died, and 1.5 million more would emigrate in the years that followed out of an initial population of around 8 million.[28] Abundant evidence shows that British elites were aware of the disaster and refused to take the necessary steps to prevent it, in some cases with the quasi-explicit Malthusian goal of reducing the number of poor and the number of rebels to boot. The Irish famine is often compared to the great famine in Bengal (1943–1944), in which some four million people died out of a population of fifty million. The comparison is not wholly unjustified, in the sense that while adequate food stores existed in both cases, authorities refused to arrange for immediate transfers to the distressed areas, in part on the grounds that prices should be allowed to rise in order to signal to sellers that the time had come to respond to market demand.[29]

These events unleashed the rage of the Irish against absentee British landlords, who, not content to collect their rents from afar, allowed the tragedy to unfold on the other side of the Irish Sea. More generally, in the period 1860–1870, a multifarious movement of protest against landlords began to grow, not only in Ireland but also in Scotland and Wales: tenants refused to pay rent and in many cases occupied the land, at times leading to violent clashes with police and landlord militias. Their top demand, especially in Ireland, was to be allowed to work their own land—in other words, to own property.

The Gladstone government then passed the Irish Land Act of 1870, which made it more difficult to evict tenants and provided government loans for tenants who wished to buy their plots, with compensation for those who were

---

28. Cannadine, *Victorious Century*, pp. 211–212.
29. See A. Sen. *Poverty and Famines: An Essay on Entitlement and Deprivation* (Oxford University Press, 1981).

driven from their land after making improvements (such as drainage or irrigation)—a common complaint of tenant farmers in all parts of the world. The legal system then in force was extremely favorable to landlords, however, so these measures had virtually no effect. Landlords had only to raise rents just enough to force the departure of any troublemaking tenants. No court or government of the time would have dreamed of interfering with the freedom of contract. To have done more would have risked inflaming relations between landless tenants and landlords not only in Ireland but also in England. It was feared that this might lead to similar demands in other sectors of the agricultural economy and to threats against property rights in general, endangering the owners of real estate and factories as well. If anyone who occupied a property or worked with capital in one form or another could now demand to become its owner on the grounds of having done so for a sufficient length of time, society might simply collapse. In the Irish land debate we hear the same argument that had been raised in the debates over *corvées* and *lods* during the French Revolution: namely, that any attempt to question the legitimacy of existing property rights threatened to open Pandora's box; no one could say where the ensuing crisis would end or whether society would emerge unscathed.

The situation in Ireland became increasingly violent as land occupations and rent strikes spread. Then, with the expansion of the right to vote for MPs in the 1880s, thinking began to change, and fear switched camps, as it were. As long as the Tories were in power in London, they remained pitiless in policing the agitators, adopting for instance the Crime Act of 1891, which gave the police additional powers beyond those already approved in 1881 to arrest "terrorists" and if necessary send them to prison. Meanwhile, everyone concerned— Tories, Liberals, and above all landlords themselves—began to realize that if Irish land was not quickly redistributed to poor Catholic farmers by legal and peaceful means, the situation might rapidly spiral out of control, leading ultimately to Irish independence and complete expropriation of absentee landlords.

This ultimately came to pass with the creation of the Irish Free State in 1922 and then the Republic of Ireland in 1937 following a series of violent clashes whose traces remain visible to this day. What is interesting for our purposes, however, is that the very real threat of Irish independence compelled the British political system in the period 1880–1920 to accept various agrarian reforms and land redistributions in Ireland, each of which struck a blow at the prevailing proprietarian ideology. Specifically, the government decided to allocate gradually increasing sums to help Irish farmers buy land. In the end, the government itself oversaw the redistribution of Irish lands but with substantial compensation for landlords paid out of the public exchequer. A law to achieve this, far more ambitious and better financed than that of 1870, was passed in 1891. It was followed by another Land Act in 1903, which allowed former tenants to purchase their land with seventy-year loans at a nominal rate of 3 percent (at the time, no one foresaw the inflationary episodes that lay ahead, which in practice reduced the cost of these purchases to virtually nothing); additional aid in the form of government subsidies of 12 percent of the land's value was also provided. To top it all off, another law was passed in 1923, obliging remaining landlords to sell their land to the new Irish government, which in turn sold it to tenants at low prices. But according to some estimates, nearly three-quarters of the land had already changed hands before the war, thanks in part to the laws of 1870, 1891, and 1903 and, above all, to the mobilization of Irish farmers themselves.[30]

The Irish experience is revealing in several ways. First, the quasi-colonial situation of Ireland and the enormous inequalities it created led to a more general questioning of the legitimacy of the whole system of private property and the persistent inequality that went with it. For instance, in response to accusations that land ownership had become hyperconcentrated not just in Ireland but throughout the United Kingdom, the Lords agreed to a series of land surveys in the 1870s, which showed that ownership was even more concentrated than even the most pessimistic previous estimates had suggested. These surveys played an important role in the evolution of thinking about inequality and redistribution because they showed that even if Britain was a leader in creating a modern industrial economy, it was a laggard in regard to inequality; what is more, these two realities were by no means contradictory—quite the opposite (rather like Belle Époque France). The Irish case is especially interesting because it points to problems of redistribution and agrarian reform that would arise in other postcolonial contexts, such as South Africa in the 1990s. Furthermore, the Irish experience illustrates the close connection between the question of frontiers and that of redistribution as well as between the political regime and the property regime. The interactions between systems of frontiers and structures of inequality—interactions shaped by questions of politics, wealth, and

---

30. Cannadine, *The Decline and Fall of the British Aristocracy*, pp. 104–105. Note, however, that but for future inflation and Irish independence, the cost of paying for redistributed land would have weighed heavily on the budgets of Irish farmers for a long time to come.

in some cases immigration—continue to play a key role to this day, not only in Britain and Europe but throughout the world.

Sweden and the Constitutionalization of a Society of Four Orders

We turn now to the case of Sweden, which offers a surprising and relatively little-known example of early constitutionalization of a society of four orders, followed by a novel transition to ownership society in the course of which the Kingdom of Sweden pursued proprietarian logic to a greater extent than either France or the United Kingdom: specifically, Sweden in the late nineteenth century adopted an audacious system of proportional representation based on the amount of property each voter owned (or the amount of tax paid).

The Swedish case is even more interesting because in the twentieth century the country became synonymous with social democracy. The social democrats of the SAP came to power in the early 1920s, when the party's historical leader, Hjamal Brenting, was elected prime minister. The party subsequently held power more or less permanently from 1932 to 2006, and this long period in government allowed it to develop a very sophisticated welfare and tax system, which in turn achieved one of the lowest levels of inequality ever observed anywhere. People therefore often think of Sweden as a country that has always been inherently egalitarian.[31] This is not true: until the early twentieth century Sweden was a profoundly inegalitarian country, in some respects more inegalitarian than countries elsewhere in Europe; or, rather, it was more sophisticated in organizing its inequality and more systematic in expressing its proprietarian ideology and shaping its institutional incarnation. Sweden was able to change its trajectory only thanks to unusually effective popular mobilization, specific political strategies, and distinctive social and fiscal institutions.

People sometimes imagine that each culture or civilization has some "essence" that makes it naturally egalitarian or inegalitarian. Hence Sweden and its social democrats are supposed to have been egalitarians from time immemorial, as if equality were somehow a Viking passion. By contrast, India with its caste system is supposed to have been eternally inegalitarian, no doubt on

---

31. For an illuminating analysis of the myth of Swedish exceptionalism, as constructed over the course of the twentieth century, see E. Bengtsonn, "The Swedish *Sonderweg* in Question: Democratization and Inequality in Comparative Perspective, c. 1750–1920," *Past and Present*, 2018.

account of some Aryan mystique. In fact, everything depends on the rules and institutions that each human society establishes, and things can change very quickly depending on the balance of political and ideological power among contending social groups as well as on the logic of events and on unstable historical trajectories, which can be understood only through detailed study. The Swedish case is the perfect antidote to the conservative identitarian arguments that crop up all too often in debates about equality and inequality. Sweden reminds us that equality is always a fragile sociopolitical construct, and nothing can be considered permanent: what was transformed in the past by institutions and the mobilization of political movements and ideologies can be transformed again by similar means, for better or for worse.

Let us begin by reviewing the history. From 1527 to 1865, the Swedish monarchy relied on a parliament, the Riksdag, which consisted of representatives of four orders or estates: the nobility, the clergy, the urban bourgeoisie, and the landowning peasantry. In contrast to trifunctional society, the organization was thus explicitly quaternary rather than ternary. Each of the four orders designated its representatives according to its own specific rules; in practice, only the wealthiest bourgeois and peasants, who paid the most in taxes, had the right to vote. In the Riksdag each order voted separately, as in the Estates General in Ancien Régime France. The rules established by the *Riksdagsordning* of 1617 specified that the king could cast the decisive vote if the orders were split in half.

Under the *Riksdagsordning* of 1810, however, the four orders were supposed to continue debating and voting until a three-to-one or four-to-zero majority emerged. In practice, the nobility played a clearly dominant role in this theoretically quaternary system. Its representatives outnumbered those of the other orders, which allowed it to dominate the committees where decisions were debated.[32] More importantly, members of the government were chosen by the king, who himself wielded important legislative and budgetary prerogatives, and in practice the principal ministers were generally nobles. The first nonnoble head of government did not take office until 1883. Looking at all Swedish governments from 1844 to 1905, we find that 56 percent of ministers were members of the nobility, which accounted for only 0.5 percent of the population.[33]

---

32. In 1809, for example, the Riksdag included 700 representatives of the nobility, forty-two of the clergy, seventy-two of the bourgeoisie, and 144 of the peasantry.

33. Bengtsonn, "The Swedish *Sonderweg* in Question," p. 20.

Unlike the United Kingdom and France, Sweden began conducting systematic censuses very early on. Relatively sophisticated population surveys began as early as 1750. This led to an administrative definition of the nobility based on certified genealogies tracing ancestry back to the feudal warrior elite or letters of ennoblement issued by the monarch. Neither France nor the United Kingdom had such an official definition of nobility, except for peers of France and the tiny titled nobility in Britain. From census records we see that the Swedish nobility was already relatively small in the mid-eighteenth century; it subsequently grew less rapidly than the total population: the noble class accounted for about 0.5 percent of the population in 1750, 0.4 percent in 1800, and not even 0.3 percent in the censuses of 1850 and 1900. These levels are not very different from those estimated for France and the United Kingdom (Fig. 5.2), except that in Sweden nobility was an official administrative and political category. In Sweden, therefore, we find an unusually close symbiosis between the formation of the centralized state and the redefinition of the trifunctional schema (here in its quaternary variant).

The quaternary Riksdag regime was replaced in 1865–1866 by a censitary parliament with two chambers: an upper house elected by a small minority of large property owners (barely 9,000 electors, less than 1 percent of the adult male population), and a lower house, also censitary but considerably more open in that roughly 20 percent of adult males were entitled to vote for its members.

Compared with other European countries that reformed their voting systems in the same period, Sweden remained quite restrictive: universal male suffrage was definitively restored in France in 1871, and the British reforms of 1867 and 1884 increased the percentage of adult males with the right to vote first to 30 percent and then to 60 percent. The suffrage was not expanded in Sweden until the reforms of 1909–1911, and it was not until 1919 that all property qualifications were eliminated for men; the vote was then extended to women in 1921. In 1900, when only a little more than 20 percent of adult males had the right to vote, Sweden was among the least advanced countries in Europe, particularly when compared with France and the United Kingdom (Fig. 5.3) and also compared with the other countries of northern Europe.[34]

---

34. The data depicted in Fig. 5.3 only take into account restrictions linked to property qualifications. The conclusion is the same if one takes into account the fact that not everyone who had the right to vote was actually registered and if one compares Sweden to other Nordic countries. See the online appendix.

One Man, One Hundred Votes: Hyper-Censitary Democracy in Sweden (1865–1911)

What was unique about the censitary system in effect in Sweden from 1865 to 1911 was that the number of votes each voter could cast depended on the size of that voter's tax payments, property, and income. The men sufficiently wealthy to vote in elections for the lower house were divided into forty-odd groups, and each group was assigned a different electoral weight. Specifically, each member of the least wealthy group could cast one vote, while each member of the wealthiest group could cast as many as fifty-four votes. The exact weight assigned to each voter was set by a formula (*fyrkar*) that took into account tax payments, wealth, and income.[35]

A similar system applied to municipal elections in Sweden in the period 1862–1909, with the additional wrinkle that corporations also had the right to vote in local elections, again casting a number of ballots that depended on their tax payments, property, and profits. No voter in an urban municipal election, whether a private individual or a corporation, could cast more than one hundred ballots. In rural towns, however, there was no such ceiling; indeed, in the municipal elections of 1871, there were fifty-four rural towns in Sweden where one voter cast more than 50 percent of the votes. Among these perfectly legitimate democratic dictators was the prime minister himself: in the 1880s Count Arvid Posse alone cast the majority of ballots in his home town, where his family owned a vast estate. A single voter cast more than 25 percent of the ballots in 414 Swedish towns.[36]

We can learn a great deal from this extreme Swedish distortion of the "one man, one vote" principle, which was tempered by the electoral reforms of 1911 and finally ended by the advent of universal suffrage in 1919–1921. First, it shows that inequality is not the product of some essential cultural predisposition: in the space of a few years Sweden moved from the most extreme hyperinegalitarian proprietarian system, which survived until 1909–1911, to a quintessential egalitarian social-democratic society once the SAP came to power in the 1920s and then ruled almost continuously from 1932 to 2006 (the only such case in Europe). Indeed, the second phase may have been a response to the excesses of the first, at least in part: in Sweden, the working and middle classes,

---

35. Bengtsonn, "The Swedish *Sonderweg* in Question," pp. 18–19.
36. E. Bengtsonn and T. Berger, "Democracy, Inequality, and Redistribution: Evidence from Swedish Municipalities, 1871–1904" (Lund University, 2017).

which were exceptionally well educated for the time, were exposed to an extreme form of proprietarianism, and this may have persuaded them that it was time to get rid of this hypocritical ideology and move on to something else, in this instance by adopting a radically different ideology. We will encounter numerous examples of sudden changes of direction in national political ideology; for instance, the rather chaotic shifts in attitudes toward progressive taxation and acceptable inequality in the United States and United Kingdom over the course of the twentieth century.

There is also reason to believe that the construction of the modern centralized state, which came particularly early in Sweden, naturally opened the way to a variety of possible trajectories. In other words, a given highly structured state organization can implement different kinds of political projects. The censuses that the Swedish state conducted of orders and classes and of taxes and wealth in the eighteenth century made it possible to assign different weights to each voter in the nineteenth century. Then, thanks to significant ideological transformations and social-democratic control of the state apparatus, the same state capacity could be put to use by the modern welfare state. In any event, the very rapid transformation that took place in Sweden demonstrates the importance of popular mobilization, political parties, and reformist programs in the transformation of inequality regimes. When conditions are right, these processes can lead to rapid radical transformation by legal parliamentary means, without violent upheaval.

Shareholder Society, Censitary Suffrage: What Limits to the Power of Money?

The Swedish experience also shows that proprietarian ideology is not monolithic. It always needs to fill some kind of political void or uncertainty. In some cases this can give rise to significant social coercion and domination of some groups over others. Proprietarian ideology rests on a simple idea, namely that the primary purpose of the social and political order is to protect private property rights for the sake of both individual emancipation and social stability. But this fundamental premise leaves the question of the political regime largely open. To be sure, it implies that it may be preferable to accord more political power to property owners, who (it is claimed) are more likely to take the long view and not sacrifice the country's future for the sake of satisfying immediate passions. But this says nothing about how far one ought to go in this direction or by what means.

In the British censitary system as well as in most other European countries and ownership societies, things were relatively simple. Citizens were divided into two groups: those who were sufficiently wealthy to be classified as active citizens and granted the right to vote for MPs and those who did not meet that criterion, who were expected to content themselves with being passive citizens without representation in Parliament. The absence of a secret ballot before 1872 allowed the wealthiest landlords and most powerful citizens to influence the votes of others, but they did so indirectly rather than explicitly—in contrast to Sweden, where the wealthiest voters could cast extra ballots, and some active citizens enjoyed more rights than others.

The censitary system in France in the period 1815–1848 was quite similar to the English system of the same era, and indeed much of the high French nobility had spent time in England between 1789 and 1815. The French parliament had a Chamber of Peers (composed primarily of hereditary peers chosen by the king among the high nobility, like the House of Lords), and a Chamber of Deputies, elected by censitary suffrage more restrictive than that applied to the House of Commons. French jurists introduced one innovation, however: there were two categories of active citizens in France. During the Restoration (1815–1830), the right to vote was granted to men above the age of 30 who paid more than 300 francs in direct taxes (the *quatre vieilles*), a group of about 100,000 men, or barely 1 percent of the adult male population. But in order to be elected a deputy, one had to be 40 or older and pay more than 1,000 francs in direct taxes, which limited eligibility to about 16,000 men or less than 0.2 percent of the adult male population. In 1820, a so-called "double vote" law was promulgated: this allowed the wealthiest quarter of those with the right to vote (a group corresponding roughly to those eligible to be elected deputies) to vote a second time for some members of the Chamber of Deputies. Following the revolution of 1830, the suffrage was slightly enlarged: under the July Monarchy (1830–1848), the number of voters increased to slightly more than 2 percent of the adult male population, and the number eligible to be elected rose to about 0.4 percent. But the principle of two categories of active citizens was maintained, though no attempt was made to push this logic further.[37] Prussia, which dominated the German Reich from 1871 to 1918, relied from 1848 until 1918 on a novel system with three classes of voters defined by

---

37. In the United Kingdom from the seventeenth century until 1950, the House of Commons included "university seats," which essentially allowed graduates of Oxford and Cambridge to vote twice in legislative elections (once in their home con-

the amount of tax they paid, with each group chosen so that its members, taken together, paid one-third of the total tax bill.[38]

The Swedish approach in the period 1865–1911 can be seen as a generalization of the censitary model: the wealthiest citizens could cast as many as 100 ballots in urban municipalities or, if they were rich enough, nearly all the votes in certain rural towns. Such a system is analogous to the voting system in a meeting of corporate stockholders, where votes are apportioned according to the number of shares each person owns. Interestingly, this analogy was drawn explicitly in some nineteenth-century ownership societies. For example, joint-stock companies in the United Kingdom gradually introduced systems with several classes of shareholders, so that the largest contributors of capital could exercise more votes, without going so far as to make the number of votes strictly proportional to the size of the investment because it was feared that this would concentrate too much power in the hands of a small number of shareholders and thus impair relations among partners and the quality of their deliberation. Typically, all stockholders holding a number of shares above a certain threshold were entitled to the same number of votes, thus establishing a ceiling on the maximum number of ballots any single individual could cast. One finds similar systems in the United States in the early nineteenth century: many companies granted fixed voting rights, sometimes in several tranches, so as to limit the power of the largest shareholders.[39] It was only in the second half of the nineteenth century that the "one share, one vote" model was accepted as a norm as a result of pressure from large shareholders. In the United Kingdom, the Company Law of 1906 enshrined in law the principle of proportionality between shares held and voting rights as the default mode of governance of British corporations.[40] It is interesting to note that these debates on shareholder voting

stituencies and again as graduates of their respective universities). This system was extended to other universities in 1918 before being definitively abolished in 1950.

38. More specifically, Prussian voters were divided into three classes, chosen so that, taken together, the members of each group paid a third of total tax receipts. Each class then elected a third of the grand electors, who in turn elected the deputies. The Nordic countries (Denmark, Norway, and Finland) used fairly standard censitary systems in the nineteenth century and did not seem to have been tempted by the Swedish example. See the online appendix.

39. See E. Hilt, "Shareholder Voting Rights in Early American Corporations," *Business History*, 2013.

40. The decisive step was taken in 1876, when the Court of Appeal held that company statutes could do away with any ceiling on voting rights and apply strict

(especially in colonial companies, such as the various India Companies and the Virginia Company) and voting rules for regional assemblies and parliaments were themselves preceded by complex and long-running debates about the rules of voting in ecclesiastical assemblies.[41]

These historical experiences are quite important for many contemporary debates about how best to limit the power of money and property. Of course, no one today is proposing that the right to vote should depend explicitly on wealth, as in the past. Nevertheless, recent years have witnessed the development of various doctrines and ideologies, most notably in the US Supreme Court, whose purpose is to eliminate ceilings on private contributions to political campaigns; this is tantamount to granting potentially unlimited electoral influence to the wealthiest individuals. The issue of limiting the power of wealth also comes up in relation to jurisdictional inequalities: for instance, certain disputes are now subject to private arbitration, which allows the wealthy to avoid judgment by the public court system. Access to higher education is also influenced by wealth: many American and international universities give special consideration to the children of wealthy donors, yet tellingly, these policies are rarely discussed in public. And so on. Later we will see that there have been important innovations in shareholder voting and corporate governance. Many countries, including Sweden and Germany, have curtailed shareholder rights and increased the power of workers and their representatives (who are entitled to a third to a half of the seats on corporate boards). These innovations are currently under active debate in many countries that initially resisted them (such as France, the United Kingdom, and the United States) and could well lead to further developments.[42]

More generally, I want once again to insist on the diversity and complexity of the political, ideological, and institutional trajectories that led, in the eighteenth and nineteenth centuries, from trifunctional societies to the triumph of ownership societies and then to the social-democratic, communist, and neo-proprietarian societies of the twentieth and early twenty-first centuries. Once the primacy of private property rights, presumably open to all, and the mono-

---

proportionality instead. On these very interesting debates, see E. McGaughey, *Participation in Corporate Governance* (PhD dissertation, Law Department, London School of Economics, 2014), pp. 105–115.

41. See O. Christin, *Vox Populi: Une histoire du vote avant le suffrage universel* (Seuil, 2014).

42. See esp. Chap. 11.

poly of the centralized state over regalian powers (justice, police, and legitimate violence) was established, numerous issues remained to be clarified, starting with the organization of state power.

Prior to the nineteenth century, some societies had gone quite a long way toward monetizing relations of power and public functions. In France, for example, the venality of charges and offices had become quite widespread in the seventeenth and eighteenth centuries: growing numbers of public offices and charges had been put up for sale, particularly in the areas of tax collection and justice. This was both a consequence of the financial needs of the absolute monarchy (and its inability to raise sufficient funds through taxation) and a reflection of proprietarian logic and incentives. A person prepared to hand over a significant amount of capital in return for a public office could not be all bad; in any event, he would bear the cost of his own errors and mismanagement and therefore have every incentive to act for the benefit of the community. Traces of this logic persist to this day. Candidates for some public jobs—police in Indonesia, for example, or the French tax officials known as *trésoriers payeurs généraux*—must put up large sums of money before taking office; in case of malfeasance these "surety bonds" are not returned.[43] The French Revolution put an end to most of these venal offices, with compensation to their owners: the sovereignty of the state could no longer be sold piecemeal, but that was no reason to mistreat those who had invested their money in offices before the Revolution.[44]

These debates show that proprietarian ideology can take more than one form, and some of those forms still have resonance today. No one today would think of selling government posts and offices (although the American practice of rewarding large political donors with important diplomatic posts is clearly a form of venality). Yet as public debt in the rich countries climbs to historic highs, in some cases exceeding the value of all public assets combined, one might argue that the public treasury and the functions of the state are once

---

43. Another relic of the venality of office is the sale of Paris taxi licenses, but here the logic is no doubt more financial than incentivizing. The licenses yielded large sums to the government when first put up for sale, and the cost of redeeming them now would be significant. This has largely blocked reform of a system that has been widely criticized, for good reason.

44. High military posts also required the posting of a kind of surety bond in the United Kingdom in the nineteenth century, but this practice was ended in 1871 to widen the social base of recruitment for such posts, apparently with limited effect. See Cannadine, *Victorious Century,* p. 350.

again subject to control by private creditors. This extends the range of what it is possible to own; the form of ownership is different from that of venal offices, but the effect in extending the reach of private wealth is similar if not greater, given the sophistication of today's legal and financial system. In the twenty-first century, as in the nineteenth, property relations are never simple: they depend on the legal, fiscal, and social system in which they are embedded. That is why it is impossible to study twenty-first-century neo-proprietarianism without first analyzing the various forms of nineteenth-century ownership society.

The Inegalitarian Tendencies of Nineteenth-Century Ownership Societies

What can we say about the evolution of the concentration of ownership in the United Kingdom and Sweden in the nineteenth and early twentieth centuries? How do the trajectories of those two countries compare with that of France? Although British and Swedish estate records are not as rich or comprehensive as those that the Revolution bequeathed to France, they are nevertheless largely sufficient to establish key orders of magnitude.

The most striking finding is that despite all the differences in the trajectories of these three countries, all exhibit a similarly high degree of concentration of ownership throughout the long nineteenth century. The key fact is that inequality increased during the Belle Époque (1880–1914); only after World War I and the violent political shocks of the period 1914–1945 do we see a significant decrease in the concentration of wealth. This conclusion holds for both the United Kingdom (Fig. 5.4) and Sweden (Fig. 5.5), as well as France[45] and all other countries for which we possess adequate historical documentation.[46]

---

45. See Fig. 4.2.
46. The British series presented here represents work by Atkinson, Harrison, and Lindert as well as more recent work by Alvaredo and Morelli. The Swedish series is based on work by Ohlsonn, Roine, and Waldenström as well as more recent work by Bengtsonn. Unfortunately, the tax records for many other countries go back only as far as World War I, so that it is often difficult to set the shocks due to the war in a longer historical perspective. Wherever the sources allow, however, we find that no clear tendency toward reduction of inequality is visible before the war: this is true of Germany, Denmark, Holland, the United States, and Japan. See the online appendix.

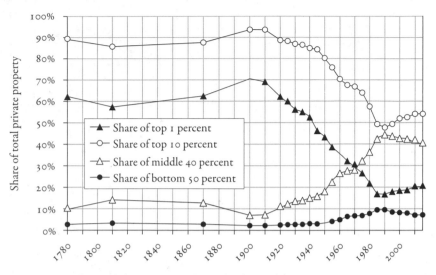

FIG. 5.4. Distribution of property in the United Kingdom, 1780–2015

Interpretation: The share of total private property (real estate, professional, and financial assets, net of debt) belonging to the wealthiest 10 percent was roughly 85–92 percent in the United Kingdom from 1780 to 1910. Deconcentration began after World War I and ended in the 1980s. The principal beneficiary was the "patrimonial middle class" (the middle 40 percent), here defined as the group between the "lower class" (bottom 50 percent) and the "upper class" (wealthiest 10 percent). *Sources and series:* piketty.pse. ens.fr/ideology.

Several points call for clarification. First, the fact that the compression of wealth inequality does not really begin until World War I obviously does not mean that it would not have occurred had there been no war. The inegalitarian tendencies of nineteenth-century ownership society, contradicting the emancipatory promises that had followed the downfall of the preceding ternary societies, were abetted by a specific legal and fiscal system. The growth of inequality strongly contributed to the emergence of socialist, communist, social-democratic, and Labourite movements of one kind or another in the second half of the nineteenth century. As we have seen, movements in favor of universal suffrage and progressive taxation began to yield tangible reforms in the late nineteenth and early twentieth centuries. True, the full effects of these reforms would not be felt until after 1914; in particular, top marginal tax rates did not reach modern levels before World War I—with rates in the tens of percent on the highest incomes and largest estates—in France, the United Kingdom, Sweden, or other Western countries. Nevertheless, there is good

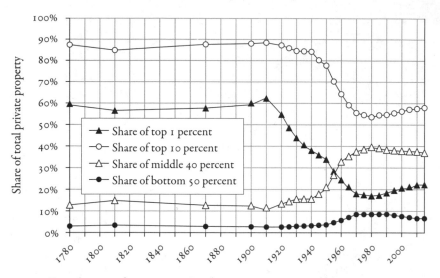

FIG. 5.5. Distribution of property in Sweden, 1780–2015

Interpretation: The share of total private property (real estate and professional and financial assets, net of debt) belonging to the wealthiest 10 percent was roughly 84–88 percent in Sweden from 1780 to 1910. Deconcentration began after World War I and ended in the 1980s. The principal beneficiary was the "patrimonial middle class" (the middle 40 percent), here defined as the group between the "lower class" (poorest 50 percent) and "upper class" (wealthiest 10 percent). *Sources and series:* piketty.pse.ens. fr/ideology.

reason to think that the powerful social and political tensions stemming from rising inequality contributed to the rise of nationalism and therefore the likelihood of war. In addition, it is quite easy to imagine other series of events that might have led to other crises—whether military, financial, social, or political—that could have had a similar triggering effect. We will return to this point when we examine the fall of ownership societies in the twentieth century.[47]

Second, it is important to note that significant differences existed among the three countries: concentration of wealth was exceptionally high in the United Kingdom, slightly lower in Sweden, and still lower in France. Specifically, the wealthiest 10 percent of Britons owned 92 percent of private wealth in the United Kingdom on the eve of World War I, compared with "only" 88 percent in Sweden and 85 percent in France. More significantly, the wealth-

47. See Chap. 10.

iest 1 percent owned 70 percent of the wealth in the United Kingdom, compared with roughly 60 percent in Sweden and 55 percent in France (but more than 65 percent in Paris).[48] The higher concentration in Britain can be explained by the exceptionally high concentration of wealth in land. But the fact is that at the beginning of the twentieth century, agricultural land no longer accounted for more than a small fraction of total private wealth (barely 5 percent in the United Kingdom and between 10 and 15 percent in Sweden and France).[49] The vast majority of wealth took the form of urban real estate, shares in financial and nonfinancial corporations, and foreign investments, and the legal and fiscal system that allowed this type of accumulation was to a first approximation just as favorable to the owners of capital in republican France as in the United Kingdom and Sweden, notwithstanding the contrary opinion of the Third Republic's elites.

The point here is not to blur the political and institutional differences among these countries, which were real. Nevertheless, in a comparative long-run perspective, the various ownership societies that flourished in Europe during the long nineteenth century shared many striking common features. Averaging over all countries in the period 1880–1914, we find that European ownership society was characterized by extreme inequality, with 85–90 percent of the wealth held by the wealthiest 10 percent, only 1–2 percent of the wealth held by the poorest 50 percent, and roughly 10–15 percent by the middle 40 percent (Fig. 5.6). Turning to the distribution of income, including both income from capital (which was as unequally distributed as wealth, if not slightly more so) and income from work (distinctly less unequally distributed), we find that income in the European ownership society of the Belle Époque was quite unevenly distributed but noticeably less so than wealth, with roughly 50–55 percent of the income going to the top 10 percent of earners, 10–15 percent to the bottom 50 percent, and roughly 35 percent to the middle 40 percent (Fig. 5.7). These figures will serve as useful guideposts, providing orders of magnitude we can compare with the other inequality regimes we will encounter in what follows.

---

48. See Fig. 4.1.

49. See online appendix and T. Piketty, *Le capital au XXIe siècle* (Seuil, 2013), Figs. 3.1–3.2.

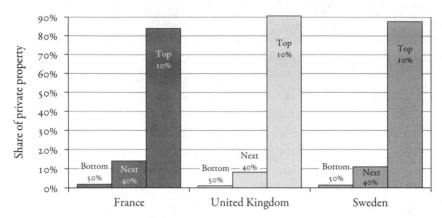

FIG. 5.6. Extreme wealth inequality: European ownership societies in the Belle Époque, 1880–1914

Interpretation: The top 10 percent share of total private property (real estate, land, professional and financial assets, net of debt) was on average 84 percent in France from 1880 to 1914 (compared with 14 percent for the middle 40 percent and 2 percent for the poorest 50 percent); in the United Kingdom the comparable figures were 91, 8, and 1 percent, and in Sweden 88, 11, and 1 percent. *Sources and series:* piketty.pse.ens.fr /ideology.

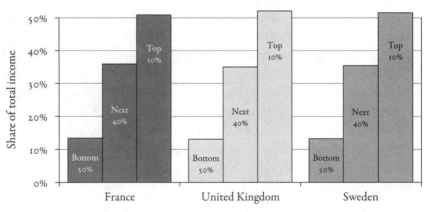

FIG. 5.7. Income inequality in European ownership societies in the Belle Époque, 1880–1914

Interpretation: The top 10 percent of earners claimed on average 51 percent of total income from capital and labor in France between 1880 and 1914 (compared with 36 percent for the middle 40 percent and 13 percent for the bottom 50 percent of the distribution; comparable figures for the United Kingdom were 55, 33, and 12, and for Sweden, 53, 34, and 13. *Sources and series:* piketty.pse.ens.fr/ideology.

The Three Challenges of Ownership Society

Let me sum up what we have learned about ownership societies and see where we stand in our inquiry. Compared with trifunctional societies, which depended on relatively rigid status disparities among clergy, nobility, and third estate and a promise of functional complementarity, balance of power, and cross-class alliances, ownership society rested on a promise of social stability coupled with individual emancipation through the right of property, supposedly open to all, independent of social and familial origin. In practice, however, in the first phase of its historical development as a dominant ideology (in the nineteenth and early twentieth centuries), proprietarian ideology encountered three major obstacles.

First, the internal challenge of inequality: the concentration of wealth rose to extreme heights in all European ownership societies in the nineteenth century, equal to or greater than the levels of inequality observed in the societies of orders that preceded them and in any case much higher than could be easily justified as serving the general interest. This happened, moreover, at a time when economic and industrial development required educational equality, not sacralization of property rights, which ultimately threatened to undermine social stability (an essential condition of economic development, which requires a minimum of equality, or at any rate the construction of a norm of inequality reasonable enough to command the approval of a majority). The challenge of inequality led to the emergence first of a counter-discourse and then of social-democratic and communist counter-regimes in the late nineteenth and first half of the twentieth centuries.

Second, the external challenge of colonialism: European prosperity, which stood out with increasing clarity when compared with the situation of other continents in the eighteenth and nineteenth centuries, depended more on its extractive capacity and military, colonial, and slave-based domination over the rest of the world than on its supposed moral, institutional, and proprietarian superiority. The West's *mission civilisatrice* was long justified on moral and institutional grounds, but its fragility became increasingly apparent to many of the colonizers and above all to the colonized, who mobilized to get rid of it. The counter-discourse of social-democratic and communist counter-regimes also fueled the denunciation of the colonial (and, to a lesser degree, patriarchal) dimension of the proprietarian order.

Finally, the nationalist and identitarian challenge: the European nation-states responsible for the protection of property rights and the promotion of economic and industrial development across vast swaths of territory themselves embarked on a phase of exacerbated competition and reinforced national identities and borders in the nineteenth century; this was followed by a self-destructive phase in the period 1914–1945. The first two challenges actually helped give rise to the third, to the extent that social tensions at home and colonial competition abroad contributed substantially to the rise of nationalism and the march toward war that would ultimately sweep away the nineteenth-century proprietarian order.

One of the main objectives of this book is to analyze how these three fragilities combined to produce an extremely intense crisis of ownership society in the twentieth century, as it confronted world war, social-democratic and communist challenges, and colonial independence movements. Today's world is a direct consequence of this crisis, yet its lessons are all too often forgotten, especially since the revival of neo-proprietarian ideology in the late twentieth and early twenty-first centuries following the communist debacle. Before we take up that question, however, it is time to look beyond Europe and to begin our analysis of colonial and slave societies. More generally, we want to look at how the transformation of trifunctional societies outside Europe was affected by the intervention of proprietarian colonial powers in their developmental processes.

SLAVE AND COLONIAL SOCIETIES

SIX

Slave Societies: Extreme Inequality

In Part One of this book we analyzed the transformation of ternary societies into ownership societies, focusing on European trajectories. In so doing, we overlooked not only the case of non-European trifunctional societies but also the fact that between 1500 and 1960 or so, European countries established systems of colonial domination throughout the world. These systems profoundly affected not only the development of Europe but also that of the entire globe. In Part Two, we will study slave and colonial societies and the way in which the transformation of non-European trifunctional societies (notably India, where ancient status distinctions remain unusually visible to this day) was altered by their encounter with proprietarian European colonial powers. These processes and trajectories are crucial for understanding the present structure of global inequality both within and between countries.

This chapter begins by looking at what is without a doubt the most extreme type of inequality regime: slave society. Slave societies existed long before European colonialism, and the history of how they grew, were justified, and disappeared raises fundamental questions for any general history of inequality regimes. In particular, we will discover that the ways in which slavery was abolished in the modern era—in the United Kingdom in 1833, France in 1848, the United States in 1865, and Brazil in 1888—as well as the various forms of financial compensation offered to slaveowners (but not to slaves) tell us a great deal about the quasi-sacralization of private property in the nineteenth century, out of which came the modern world we know today. In the United States, moreover, the question of slavery and racial inequality has had a lasting impact on both the structure of inequality and the political party system. In subsequent chapters we will study postslavery colonial societies in the context of what might be called the "second colonial era" (1850–1960), dwelling first on the case of Africa and then on India and other countries (notably China, Japan, and Iran) to see how their inegalitarian trajectories were altered by colonialism.

Societies with Slaves; Slave Societies

Slavery was present in the most ancient societies of which written traces survive, specifically in the Near East in the second and first millennia BCE, in Pharaonic Egypt and Mesopotamia. The Babylonian Code of Hammurabi, which dates from about 1750 BCE, details the rights of slaveowners. Theft of a slave was punishable by death, and a barber who cut the lock of hair by which slaves were identified at the time could have his hand cut off. In the Old Testament, which dates from the first millennium BCE, vanquished peoples were regularly enslaved by their conquerors, and parents sold their children into slavery when they could not pay their debts. Traces of slavery survive from well before the explicit emergence of the trifunctional schema, which sought to organize society around three classes (clergy, warriors, and workers, with a laboring class that was unified and free, at least in theory); this was formalized around the year 1000 in Europe and as early as the second century BCE in India. In practice, slave and trifunctional logics long coexisted in certain societies because the process of unifying the status of workers, which in theory implied not only the end of slavery but also the end of serfdom and other forms of forced labor, was a complex one that lasted for centuries in Europe, India, and other civilizations.[1]

It is useful to begin by recalling Moses Finley's distinction between, on the one hand, "societies with slaves," in which slaves existed but played a relatively minor role and represented only a small fraction of the population (usually only a few percent), and on the other hand, "slave societies," in which slaves occupied a central place in the structure of production and power and property relations and accounted for a significant share of the population (on the order of several dozen percent). Slaves were found in nearly all societies before the nineteenth century. These were "societies with slaves" in Finley's sense, generally with fairly small slave populations. For Finley, there were very few true slave societies: Athens and Rome in antiquity and then Brazil, the southern United States, and the West Indies in the eighteenth and nineteenth centuries. In these cases, slaves may have represented from 30 to 50 percent of the total population (or even more in the West Indies).[2]

Subsequent research has shown that slave societies, while relatively rare, were quite a bit more common than Finley imagined. In antiquity one finds

---

1. See Chap. 2 for the European case and Chap. 8 for India.
2. See M. Finley, *Ancient Slavery and Modern Ideology* (Penguin, 1980).

substantial concentrations of slaves throughout the Mediterranean and Near East, in Carthage and Israel as well as numerous Greek and Roman cities, with important variations depending on the political-ideological, economic, monetary, and commercial context.[3] Between the fifteenth and nineteenth centuries, we find many examples of non-Western slave societies, such as the Kingdom of the Kongo (comprising parts of Angola, Gabon, and present-day Congo), the Sokoto Caliphate (in the northern part of what is now Nigeria), and the Kingdom of Aceh (on the island of Sumatra in today's Indonesia), where slaves are estimated to have accounted for 20–50 percent of the population. The Sokoto Caliphate, considered the largest African state at the end of the nineteenth century (with a population of more than 6 million, of whom about 2 million were slaves), is a particularly important case, because slavery and other forms of forced labor continued there until it was incorporated into the British Empire at the beginning of the twentieth century.[4] There were very likely other slave societies that have yet to be discovered and still others that have not left sufficient traces to be studied in detail.[5] As for the African slave trade, it has been estimated that it involved some 20 million enslaved persons between 1500 and 1900 (two-thirds of whom were shipped across the Atlantic to the West Indies and the Americas and one-third across the Sahara to the Red Sea and Indian Ocean). The trade was organized both by states and by European, Arab, and African traders. Such numbers represent a significant demographic drain on sub-Saharan Africa, given the limited population of the continent in this period.[6]

The other limitation of Finley's classification is that in practice there exist many forms of slavery and forced labor. What we see in history is a continuum

---

3. See D. M. Lewis, *Greek Slave Systems in Their Eastern Mediterranean Context, c.800–146 BC* (Oxford University Press, 2018). See also J. Zurbach, "La formation des cités grecques. Statuts, classes et systèmes fonciers," *Annales. Histoire, sciences sociales,* 2013.

4. See P. Lovejoy and J. Hogendorn, *Slow Death for Slavery: The Course of Abolition in Northern Nigeria, 1897–1936* (Cambridge University Press, 1993); P. Lovejoy, *Jihad in West Africa During the Age of Revolutions* (Ohio University Press, 2016).

5. There are also many intermediate cases in which slaves represented a fraction of the population that was neither tiny nor dominant: for instance, from 10 to 15 percent in Portugal and Morocco in the late fifteenth and sixteenth centuries. See the online appendix (piketty.pse.ens.fr/ideology).

6. The population of sub-Saharan Africa has been estimated at 40 million in 1500 and 60 million in 1820. Many researchers have measured the extremely negative long-term effects on the regions that lost the most population. See the online appendix.

of labor statuses ranging from absolute servitude to complete "freedom," an infinite variety of situations defined by the actual rights of individuals, which are always a specific sociohistorical construct. In the most extreme "industrial" forms of slavery, such as we find in the Atlantic trade, slaves had virtually no rights. Pure labor power, they were treated as movable property (chattel slavery). Slaves then had no personal identity (not even an officially recognized name); no right to private life, family, or marriage; no property rights; and of course no mobility rights. Their mortality rate was extremely high (roughly one-fifth died in crossing the Atlantic and almost another fifth in the year that followed), and they were continually replaced by new slaves from Africa. Under the Black Code of 1685, promulgated by Louis XIV to regulate slavery in the French West Indies and in part to limit abuses there, slaves could own nothing; their meager personal effects belonged to their owners.

By contrast, under serfdom, serfs certainly had no mobility rights, since they were required to work the lord's land and could not leave to work elsewhere. But they did have a personal identity: some signed parish registers, and they generally enjoyed the right to marry (though in some cases this required approval by the lord) as well as in principle the right to own property, generally of small value (and again with the master's approval). In practice, however, the boundary between slavery and serfdom was never clear and could vary quite a bit depending on the context and the owner.[7] By a gradual process that began in the final decades of the eighteenth century and accelerated after the abolition of the Atlantic trade in 1807 (which took several more decades to take full effect), plantations in the West Indies, United States, and Brazil began to rely on the natural increase of the Negro population. In the United States, this second phase of slavery proved more profitable than the first, and the number of slaves increased from 1 million in 1800 to 4 million in 1860. In some cases, fear of slave revolts led to harsher treatment of slaves: for instance, Virginia, the Carolinas, and Louisiana adopted laws in the period 1820–1840 that mandated heavy sentences for anyone who taught a slave to read. Nevertheless, the mere fact that forms of private and family life developed in this period made the situation of slaves in the United States, West Indies, and Brazil quite different from that of slaves in the era of continual replenishment of the labor

---

7. The terms used to denote the various forms of forced labor have ambiguous origins. The words *esclave* and *slave* come from raids on Slavic populations in the fifth to eighth centuries, and the exploitation that followed was described as *servage* (serfdom).

force by new arrivals from overseas. It is by no means certain that the condition of serfs in medieval Europe was much better than that of slaves in the New World.

In the current state of research, it would appear that the 4 million slaves exploited in the southern United States on the eve of the Civil War (1861–1865) constituted the largest concentration of slaves that ever existed. Our knowledge of ancient slave societies is quite limited, however, as are the sources available for the study of slave systems other than the Euro-American trans-Atlantic systems of the eighteenth and nineteenth centuries. The most common estimates of ancient slavery suggest that about 1 million slaves (compared with a free population of about 1 million) worked in the region of Rome in the first century, and from 150,000 to 200,000 slaves worked in the region of Athens in the fifth century BCE (compared to 200,000 free citizens). These estimates do not cover all of Roman Italy or ancient Greece, however, and should be regarded as suggestive orders of magnitude and nothing more.[8]

More importantly, the meaning of servile status varied so widely that such purely quantitative comparisons make only limited sense. In the Sokoto Caliphate in the nineteenth century, some slaves held high positions in the bureaucracy and army.[9] In Egypt from the thirteenth to the sixteenth centuries, the Mamluks were freed slaves who rose to occupy high military posts and ultimately seized control of the state. Slave soldiers played an important role in the Ottoman Empire until the eighteenth or nineteenth centuries, as did female domestic and sex slaves.[10] In ancient Greece, some slaves (a small minority, to be sure) served as high public officials, often in positions calling for high skills such as the certification and archiving of judicial documents, verification of coinage, and inventorying of temple properties—tasks requiring expertise that it was deemed best to remove from the political arena and assign to

---

8. See, for example, Lewis, *Greek Slave Systems*, as well as W. Scheidel, "Human Mobility in Roman Italy: The Slave Population," *Journal of Roman Studies*, 2005.

9. See P. Lovejoy, *Jihad in West Africa*. Lovejoy also insists on the fact that the large slave populations in Sokoto in the nineteenth century (1.5–2 million at the end of the century, and nearly 4 million if one includes West Africa) should be compared with the rapid growth in the United States. In both cases, the growth of the slave population was fueled by the end of the Atlantic trade, which Sokoto's Muslim leaders pressured Britain to implement in the late eighteenth and early nineteenth centuries.

10. See M. Zilfi, *Women and Slavery in the Late Ottoman Empire* (Cambridge University Press, 2010).

individuals without civil rights and therefore no claim to higher office.[11] We find no trace of such subtle distinctions in Atlantic slavery. Slaves were assigned to work on plantations, and the virtually absolute separation of the black slave population from the white free population was unusually strict, unlike in most other slave societies.

The United Kingdom: The Abolition Compensation of 1833–1843

Our next task will be to review the various abolitions of Atlantic and Euro-American slavery in the nineteenth century. This will give us a better understanding of the various arguments advanced to justify or condemn slavery as well as the variety of possible postslavery trajectories. The UK case is particularly interesting because, like the British transition from trifunctional to proprietarian logic, it was extremely gradual.

Parliament passed the Slavery Abolition Act in 1833, and between then and 1843 it was gradually put into effect, with complete indemnification of slaveowners. No funds were appropriated to compensate slaves for the damages they or their ancestors had suffered, whether serious physical harm or mere loss of wages for centuries of unpaid labor. Indeed, slaves were never compensated, not under this abolition law or any other. To the contrary, as we will discover, former slaves, once emancipated, were obliged to sign relatively rigid and undercompensated long-term labor contracts, which left most of them in semi-forced labor for long periods after their official liberation. By contrast, in the British case slaveowners were entitled to full compensation for their loss of property.

Concretely, the British government agreed to pay slaveholders an indemnity roughly equal to the market value of their stock of slaves. Fairly sophisticated payment schedules were established in function of each slave's age, sex, and productivity so as to offer the fairest and most precise compensation possible. Some 20 million pounds sterling, or 5 percent of the UK's national income at the time, was paid to some 4,000 slaveowners. If the British government had decided in 2018 to spend a similar proportion of national income, it would have had to disburse 120 billion euros, or an average of 30 million euros for each of 4,000 slaveowners. Clearly, these were very wealthy people, many of whom owned hundreds of slaves and in some cases several thousand. The

---

11. See P. Isnard, *La démocratie contre les experts. L'esclavage public en Grèce ancienne* (Seuil, 2015). There were barely 2,000 such public slaves, however, out of a total of 200,000.

expenditure was financed by a corresponding increase of public debt, which was repaid by British taxpayers; in practice this meant mostly modest or average families, in view of the highly regressive tax system in force at the time (based primarily on indirect taxes on consumption and trade, like most tax systems before the twentieth century). To get an idea of orders of magnitude, note that total public spending on schools and other instruction (at all levels) was less than 0.5 percent of annual national income in the United Kingdom in the nineteenth century. Compensation to slaveowners thus amounted to more than ten years' worth of educational spending.[12] The comparison is all the more striking when one realizes that underinvestment in education is generally considered one of the major causes of Britain's decline in the twentieth century.[13]

It so happens that the parliamentary archives chronicling these decisions, which at the time seemed perfectly reasonable and justified (at least in the eyes of the minority of property-owning citizens who wielded political power), have recently been the subject of extensive study, which has culminated in the publication of two books and a comprehensive online database.[14] Among the descendants of the slaveholders who were generously indemnified in the 1830s was a cousin of former prime minister David Cameron. Some voices demanded that the state be reimbursed for the sums paid out—sums that formed the basis of many a family fortune still intact today, with slave assets having long since been replaced by real estate and financial holdings. Nothing came of those demands, however.

The Slavery Abolition Act of 1833 emancipated roughly 800,000 slaves, mostly (some 700,000 in all) in the British West Indies (Jamaica, Trinidad and Tobago, Barbados, the Bahamas, and British Guiana), together with a smaller number in the Cape Colony in South Africa and the island of Mauritius in the

---

12. See the online appendix for an analysis of the amounts at state. In terms of 2018 euros, the 120 billion paid in indemnities amounted to an average of 150,000 euros for each of 800,000 slaves, or a payment of about 30 million to an average slaveholder with 200 slaves. See below the discussion of the price of slaves (in terms of average income at the time) in the US context.

13. See Chap. 11.

14. See N. Draper, *The Price of Emancipation: Slave-Ownership, Compensation and British Society at the End of Slavery* (Cambridge University Press, 2010); C. Hall, N. Draper, K. McClelland, K. Donington, and R. Lang, *Legacies of British Slave-Ownership: Colonial Slavery and the Formation of Victorian Britain* (Cambridge University Press, 2014). The Legacies of British Slave-Ownership (LBS) database can be consulted at http://www.ucl.ac.uk/lbs/.

Indian Ocean. The population in these territories consisted mostly of slaves, but compared with the population of the United Kingdom in the 1830s (roughly 24 million), the number of emancipated slaves represented only about 3 percent of the total metropolitan population. Otherwise, without the large number of British taxpayers relative to the number of emancipated slaves, it would have been impossible to bear the high cost of completely indemnifying slaveholders. As we will see, things looked very different in the United States: the amount of the compensation that would have been required all but ruled out a financial solution.

On the Proprietarian Justification for Compensating Slaveholders

It is important to insist on the fact that the policy of indemnifying slaveowners seemed self-evidently reasonable to British elites at the time. If one confiscated slave property without compensation, why wouldn't one confiscate the property of those who had owned slaves in the past but exchanged them for other assets? Wouldn't all existing claims to property then be in danger? These are the same proprietarian arguments we encountered previously in other contexts, in connection for instance with *corvées* during the French Revolution and absentee landlords in Ireland in the late nineteenth and early twentieth centuries.[15]

Think, too, of the novels of Jane Austen I discussed in the previous chapter. In *Mansfield Park,* it so happens that Sir Thomas owns plantations in Antigua while Henry Crawford does not, but these facts have no particular moral connotation given the extent to which different kinds of assets and different forms of wealth (land, government bonds, buildings, financial investments, plantations, and so on) seem to be interchangeable, as long as they yield the expected annual income. By what right should Parliament be allowed to ruin one of these gentlemen and not the other? Indeed, it was not easy to see an "ideal" solution as long as one refused to question the logic of proprietarianism. Of course, it might have been deemed just to demand more of those who had enriched themselves through slaveownership, not only by depriving them of their "property" but also by compensating the slaves, for example, by transferring to them ownership of the parcels on which they had worked for so long without remuneration. But to finance the indemnity, it might also have been justifiable to tax *all* property owners on a sliding scale according to their wealth. This would

---

15. See Chaps. 3–5.

have made it possible to share the burden with the many people who had owned slaves in the past and, more generally, all who had enriched themselves by conducting business with slaveholders, for instance, by buying the cotton and sugar they produced, which played a central role in the economy of the day. But it was precisely this general questioning of property, which would have become almost inevitable once one raised the question of compensating slaves (or simply accepted noncompensation of slaveowners), that nineteenth-century elites wished to avoid.

The necessity of compensating slaveowners was obvious not only to the political and economic elites of the time but also to many thinkers and intellectuals. We come back to the distinction between the "radical" and "moderate" Enlightenment that we encountered in the discussion of the French Revolution.[16] Although some "radicals" such as Condorcet defended the idea of abolition without compensation,[17] most "liberals" and "moderates" considered compensation of owners to be a self-evident and uncontroversial preliminary to any discussion. Among them was Alexis de Tocqueville, who stood out in French debates on abolition in the 1840s for compensation proposals that he believed to be ingenious (and they were, for slaveowners, as we will see later). To be sure, moral arguments about equal human dignity did play a role in abolitionist debates. But as long as those arguments failed to provide a comprehensive vision of how society and the economy were organized and a precise plan describing how abolition would fit into the proprietarian order, they failed to elicit much support.

In the eighteenth and nineteenth centuries, numerous Christian abolitionists tried to explain that Christian doctrine itself demanded an immediate end to slavery and that it was the advent of Christianity that had made ending ancient slavery possible. Unfortunately, this argument was incorrect. Any number of bishoprics in Christian Europe owned slaves until at least the sixth or seventh century, and this hastened conversions and abetted Islam's penetration into Spain in the eighth century.[18] Not until the year 1000 did slavery end in Western Europe, and it took several more centuries for serfdom to disappear,

---

16. Chap. 3.

17. In *Réflexions sur l'esclavage des nègres* (1781), Condorcet even proposed that slave-masters pay compensation in the form of a pension to former slaves.

18. This negative experienced encouraged Christian kingdoms in northern Spain to reduce their dependence on slavery from the eighth or ninth century on. See R. Blackburn, *The Making of New World Slavery. From the Baroque to the Modern* (Verso, 1997), pp. 39–40.

while in Orthodox Russia it lingered until the end of the nineteenth century. In these debates, many historians and scholars of the antiquity, notably in the German school, opposed the arguments of Christian abolitionists on the ground that it was slavery that allowed the other classes of society to engage in the higher artistic and political pursuits that made ancient civilizations, especially Greece and Rome, great. To oppose slavery was therefore tantamount to opposing civilization and settling for egalitarian mediocrity. Some even sought to prove that slavery and civilization were intimately related by arguing that humanity had achieved its highest population level in antiquity, which was no truer than the assertions of the Christian abolitionists but at least seemed plausible, given the intellectual climate of the period: from the Renaissance to the nineteenth century, the Middle Ages were seen as dark ages.[19]

It is also interesting to note that debates on abolition, which were particularly spirited in the United Kingdom and France between 1750 and 1850, made free use of figures and statistics thought to reveal the comparative merits of servile and free labor.[20] Abolitionists such as Pierre Samuel Du Pont de Nemours (1771) and André-Daniel Laffon de Ladebat (whose calculations in 1788 were more sophisticated) estimated that free workers were so much more productive than slaves that planters should have been able to earn greater profits by emancipating their slaves and transporting to the West Indies some of the cheap labor that could be found in abundance in rural France and elsewhere in Europe. Slaveowners were not persuaded by these scientific calculations (which in fact were not very credible). Indeed, they estimated that servile labor was just as productive as free labor if not more so given the harshness of the work and the need for corporal punishment. Slaveowners in many countries also insisted that since free labor was more costly but no more productive than slave labor, switching would straightaway make it impossible to compete with rivals in other colonial empires. No one would buy their sugar, cotton, or tobacco, and the nation's output would plummet along with its greatness if somehow the anti-economic and antipatriotic fantasies of the abolitionists were put into practice.

In the end, there is no evidence that the end of the Atlantic slave trade in 1807 damaged the profitability of plantations. Those who had lived off the trade

---

19. See Finley, *Ancient Slavery and Modern Ideology,* chap. 1.
20. On these debates, see the impressive book by C. Oudin-Bastide and P. Steiner, *Calcul et Morale. Coûts de l'esclavage et valeur de l'émancipation (18ᵉ–19ᵉ siècles)* (Albin Michel, 2015).

did have to find other employment, but planters soon realized that it could be less costly to rely on the natural increase of the slave population. The decision to end the slave trade was in any case taken first by Britain, followed by the United States and France in 1808–1810, and then by other European powers at the Congress of Vienna in 1815, at a time when new breeding practices had already become widespread and proven their efficacy. If Britain's landowning and industrial elites agreed to support abolition in 1833, it was probably in part because they believed that at that moment wage labor would allow for economic growth just as profitable as slave labor (and of course it may have been tempting to take revenge against the Americans for their independent ways and economic backwardness)—provided, of course, that slaveowners were fully compensated for their losses, as in Britain, since it was highly unlikely that free labor's greater efficiency would have sufficed to compensate the slaveholders, notwithstanding the abolitionists' protests to the contrary. The abolition of slavery imposed a cost on slaveowners, and in the United Kingdom the public choice was for British taxpayers to bear that cost, thus illustrating both the political power of the slaveholders and the grip of proprietarian ideology.

France: The Double Abolition of 1794–1848

The abolition of slavery in the French colonies was unusual in that it took place in two stages. The first abolition was decided by the Convention in 1794 following a slave revolt in Saint-Domingue (Haiti), but slavery was subsequently reinstated under Napoleon. Ultimately, abolition was definitively adopted in 1848, following the fall of the monarchy and advent of the Second Republic. The French case reminds us of what was no doubt the primary reason for the abolition of slavery: not the magnanimity of Euro-American abolitionists or the pecuniary calculations of slaveowners but the rebellions staged by slaves themselves and the fear of further unrest. The crucial role of slave rebellion is obvious in the abolition of 1794, the first major abolition of modern times, which was a direct consequence of the fact that Haitian slaves had already freed themselves by force of arms and were preparing to declare their country's independence.

It is also quite clear in the case of the British Slavery Abolition Act of 1833, which came less than two years after the Christmas Rebellion of 1831 in Jamaica—a revolt whose bloody echoes in the British press made a deep impression on public opinion, reinforcing the abolitionist position in the debates of 1832–1833 and persuading slaveowners that it would be wiser to accept generous financial compensation than to take the risk that their plantations in Jamaica and Barbados might someday meet the same fate as those of Haiti. The Christmas Rebellion, which ended with mass executions, itself followed another uprising in British Guiana in 1815 and the Guadeloupe revolt of 1802, which ended with the execution or deportation of roughly 10,000 slaves, some 10 percent of the population—an event that led the French authorities to temporarily reinstate the slave trade in the 1810s in order to repopulate the island and get the sugar plantations going again.[21]

It is important to bear in mind that the largest concentration of slaves in the Euro-American world on the eve of the French Revolution was found in France's island colonies. In the 1780s, French plantations in the West Indies and Indian Ocean were home to 700,000 slaves (or 3 percent of the population of metropolitan France at the time, which was about 28 million), compared with 600,000 in British possessions and 500,000 on plantations in the southern United States (which had just won its independence from Britain). In the French West Indies, the major concentrations of slaves were found in Martinique, Guadeloupe, and above all Saint-Domingue, which alone was home to 450,000 slaves. Renamed Haiti (from an old Amerindian name) when independence was proclaimed in 1804, Saint-Domingue at the end of the eighteenth century was the jewel of French colonies, the most prosperous and profitable of all, thanks to its production of sugar, coffee, and cotton. Occupying the western part of the island of Hispaniola, where Columbus had landed in 1492, it had been a French colony since 1626; the eastern part of the island belonged to Spain (and later became the Dominican Republic), as did the large nearby island of Cuba (where slavery would continue until 1886).

In the Indian Ocean, the two French slave isles were Île-de-France (the larger of the two in the eighteenth century; it was occupied by the English in 1810 and became a British possession under the name Mauritius after the defeat of Napoleon in 1815) and the Île Bourbon, which was renamed Réunion during the Revolution and remained French in 1815. Plantations on those two islands housed nearly 100,000 slaves in the 1780s, compared with 600,000 in the French West Indies, 450,000 of them in Saint-Domingue alone.

---

21. On the strange period of on-again/off-again abolition in Guadeloupe prior to the official restoration of slavery in 1802, see F. Régent, *Esclavage, métissage et liberté. La Révolution française en Guadeloupe 1789–1802* (Grasset, 2004). On the context of abolition in Britain in 1833, see esp. the books of N. Draper and C. Hall (LBS) cited above in note 14.

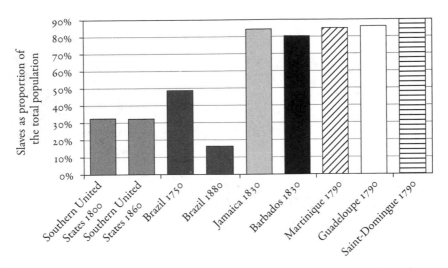

FIG. 6.1. Atlantic slave societies, eighteenth and nineteenth centuries

Interpretation: Slaves represented roughly a third of the population of the southern United States from 1800 to 1860. The slave share fell from nearly 50 percent to less than 20 percent between 1750 and 1880. It surpassed 80 percent in the British and French West Indies in the period 1780–1830 and rose as high as 90 percent in Saint-Domingue (Haiti) in 1790. *Sources and series:* piketty.pse.ens.fr/ideology.

Note, moreover, that these were veritable slave islands: slaves accounted for 90 percent of the population of Saint-Domingue in the late 1780s (or even 95 percent, if one counts metis, mulattos, and free men of color). We find comparable levels in the rest of the British and French West Indies in the period 1780–1830: 84 percent in Jamaica, 80 percent in Barbados, 85 percent in Martinique, and 86 percent in Guadeloupe. These were the most extreme levels ever observed in the history of Atlantic slave societies and, more generally, in the global history of slave societies (Fig. 6.1). For comparison, slaves represented 30 to 50 percent of the population of the southern United States and Brazil in the same period, and available sources suggest comparable proportions in ancient Athens and Rome. The British and French West Indies of the eighteenth and early nineteenth centuries are the best documented historical examples of societies in which nearly the entire population consisted of slaves.

It is quite obvious that when the proportion of slaves reaches 80 or 90 percent, the risk of rebellion is very high, no matter how fierce the repressive apparatus. The case of Haiti was particularly extreme in that the slave population grew at a very rapid rate and the number of slaves was significantly

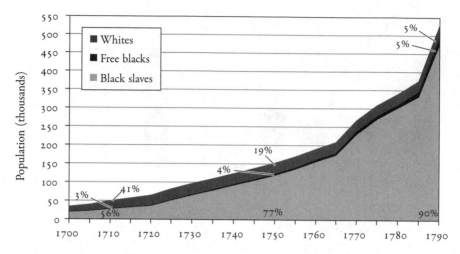

FIG. 6.2. A slave island in expansion: Saint-Domingue, 1700–1790

Interpretation: The total population of Saint-Domingue (Haiti) increased from barely 50,000 in 1700–1710 (of which 56 percent were slaves, 3 percent free people of color and mixed race, and 41 percent white) to more than 500,000 in 1790 (of which 90 percent were slaves, 5 percent free people of color and mixed race, and 5 percent white. *Sources and series:* piketty.pse.ens.fr/ideology.

greater than on the other islands. Around 1700, the total population of the island was about 30,000, more than half of whom were slaves. In the early 1750s, Haiti was home to 120,000 slaves (77 percent of the total population), 25,000 whites (19 percent), and 5,000 metis and free men of color (4 percent). At the end of the 1780s, the colony comprised more than 470,000 slaves (90 percent of the total population); 28,000 whites (5 percent); and 25,000 metis, mulattos, and free people of color (5 percent; Fig. 6.2).

On the eve of 1789, roughly 40,000 Africans were arriving every year in Port-au-Prince and Cap-Français to replace deceased slaves and replenish the slave supply, which was then growing at an extremely rapid rate. The system was in a phase of accelerated expansion when the French Revolution broke out. In 1789–1790 free blacks began demanding the right to vote and to participate in assemblies. This seemed logical in view of the grand proclamations about equal rights emanating from Paris, but their demands were rejected. The great slave uprising began in August 1791 after a meeting at Bois-Caïman in the Northern Plain; among the participants were thousands of *marrons,* or fugitive slaves, who for decades had used the mountain's islands as a refuge. Despite military reinforcements dispatched from France, the insurgents quickly gained the upper hand and seized control of the plantations while the planters fled the country. The commissioners sent from Paris had no choice but to declare the emancipation of all slaves in August 1793, a decision that the Convention extended to all the colonies in February 1794, setting the revolutionary government apart from previous regimes (even if the decision was in reality imposed by the revolts). Yet the decision barely had time to take effect before the slaveowners persuaded Napoleon to restore slavery in 1802 on all the slave islands except Haiti, which declared its independence in 1804. It was not until 1825 that Charles X recognized Haiti's independence and 1848 that abolition was extended to other territories, including Martinique, Guadeloupe, and Réunion.

Haiti: When Slave Property Becomes Public Debt

The Haitian case is emblematic, not only because it was the first abolition of the modern era following a victorious slave revolt and the first independence secured by a black population from a European power but also because the episode ended with a gigantic public debt that did much to undermine the development of Haiti over the next two centuries. If France finally agreed to recognize Haitian independence in 1825 and to end its threat to invade the island with French troops, it was only because Charles X extracted from the Haitian government a promise to pay 150 million gold francs to compensate slaveowners for the loss of their property. The government in Port-au-Prince really had no choice, given France's obvious military superiority, the embargo imposed by the French fleet pending a settlement, and the real risk of an occupation of the island.

It is important to measure the significance of that sum of 150 million gold francs, which was fixed in 1825. Following lengthy negotiations, the figure was based on the profitability of the plantations and the value of slaves prior to the Haitian revolution. It represented 2 percent of French national income at the time or the equivalent of 40 billion euros in today's money.[22] The amount is

---

22. Taking equivalent percentages of GDP or national income at different points in time seems to me the best way to compare sums over the course of history. It is tantamount to indexing amounts to nominal growth of the economy, which leads to results between indexing by price level and indexing by nominal average yield on invested capital (which is distinctly higher than nominal long-run growth). See the online appendix for a more detailed discussion of these issues.

therefore comparable to the sum paid to British slaveowners following the Slavery Abolition Act, taking account of the fact that the number of slaves "emancipated" in Haiti was half the number of British slaves freed in 1833. More significant, however, is the ratio of the debt to the resources at Haiti's disposal at the time. Recent research has shown that the sum of 150 million gold francs represented more than 300 percent of Haiti's national income in 1825—in other words, three years of production. The treaty also provided that the entire amount should be paid within five years to the Caisse des Dépôts et Consignation (a public banking institution created during the revolution and still in existence today), where it would be paid out to the despoiled slaveowners (which was done), while the Haitian government was required to refinance the loan from the Caisse with new loans from private French banks so as to spread the payments out over time (which was also done). It is crucial to recognize the magnitude of the sums involved. With refinancing at an annual interest of 5 percent, typical for the time—not even counting the juicy commissions that the bankers did not fail to add on in the course of numerous partial defaults and renegotiations over the subsequent decades—this meant that Haiti was obliged to repay the equivalent of 15 percent of its national product every year, indefinitely, simply to pay the interest on the debt without even beginning to pay down the principal.

Of course, former French slaveowners had no difficulty showing that the island had been far more profitable during the era of slavery. In fact, on the basis of estimates that it is possible to make today, roughly 70 percent of Saint-Domingue's output from 1750 to 1780 was realized as profit to French planters and slaveholders (who represented just over 5 percent of the island's population)—a particularly extreme and well-documented example of egregious colonial extraction.[23] Of course, it was difficult to require a theoretically sovereign country to continue to pay 15 percent of its output indefinitely to its former owners merely because it no longer wished to live in slavery. Meanwhile, the island's economy had suffered greatly from the aftermath of the revolution, the embargo, and the fact that much of its sugar production had been relocated to Cuba, which remained a slave society and where many planters had sought

---

23. See the online appendix and the estimates of S. Henochsberg, *Public Debt and Slavery: The Case of Haiti (1760–1815)* (Paris School of Economics, 2016). The equivalent of roughly 55 percent of domestic output (or, more precisely, value added) was exported for the benefit of the owners while 15 percent was consumed or accumulated locally by the planters.

refuge during the insurrection, in certain cases taking some of their slaves with them. Haiti's insertion into the regional economy was complicated, moreover, by the fact that the United States, worried by the Haitian precedent and little disposed to sympathy for slave rebellions, refused to recognize or deal with the country until 1864.

Though subject to multiple and often chaotic renegotiations, the Haitian debt was largely repaid. In particular, Haiti ran very significant trade surpluses throughout the nineteenth and into the early twentieth centuries. After the earthquake of 1842 and the subsequent fire in Port-au-Prince, France agreed to a moratorium on interest payments from 1843 to 1849. But the payments resumed thereafter, and recent research shows that French creditors managed to extract an average of 5 percent of Haiti's national income from 1849 to 1915, with substantial variation depending on the period and the political state of the country: the island's trade surplus often amounted to 10 percent of national income but sometimes fell to zero or slightly below, with an average of about 5 percent over this period. This is a significant average payment to sustain for such a long period of time. It was nevertheless less than the amount implied by the agreement of 1825, which led French banks to complain regularly that Haiti was a delinquent borrower. With the support of the French government, the banks ultimately decided to cede the rest of their loans to the United States, which occupied Haiti from 1915 to 1934 to restore order and protect American financial interests. The 1825 debt was not definitively repaid and officially wiped from the books until the early 1950s. For more than a century, from 1825 to 1950, the price that France insisted Haiti pay for its freedom had one main consequence: namely, that the island's economic and political development was subordinated to the question of the indemnity, which was sometimes violently denounced and at other times accepted with resignation, according to the ebb and flow of endless political and ideological cycles.[24]

This episode is fundamental. It illustrates how the logic of slavery and colonialism was related to the logic of proprietarianism. It also shows how deeply

---

24. These devastating cycles began as early as 1804, when power was seized by Jean-Jacques Dessalines, who put in place a hyperauthoritarian, monarchical, anti-white, isolationist regime following the surrender in 1803 of the French expeditionary force (whose mission was to exterminate all the insurgents) and the 1802 arrest of Toussaint Louverture (who vigorously defended a continuing white presence and the possible of peaceful partnership with the metropole and integration into the internal economy). The subsequent history of the island has been marked by similar cycles of denunciation and resignation.

ambivalent the French Revolution was regarding questions of inequality and property. At bottom, the slaves of Haiti took the Revolution's message of emancipation more seriously than anyone else, including the French, and it cost them dearly. These events also remind us of the close and persistent relation between slavery and debt. In antiquity, slavery for debt was quite common; we find traces of it in the Bible as well as on Mesopotamian and Egyptian steles, which depict endless cycles of debt accumulation and enslavement, sometimes punctuated by periods during which debts were canceled and slaves freed in order to restore social peace.[25] In English, the importance of the historical link between slavery and debt is illustrated by the term "bondage," which refers to the relations of dependency that characterize the servile or slave condition. From the thirteenth century on, "bond" also refers to the legal and financial ties between creditor and debtor as well as to the ties of dependency between landlord and peasant. The legal systems that took hold in the nineteenth century abolished slavery, and at the same time, they ended imprisonment for debt and, above all, intergenerational transmission of debt. There is, however, one form of debt that can still be transmitted across generations, allowing potentially unlimited financial burdens to weigh on progeny, who must pay for the sins of their parents: namely, public debt, like that which postslavery Haiti was obliged to repay from 1825 to 1950. We find many similar cases of colonial debt in the nineteenth and twentieth centuries, to say nothing of the growing public debt that many countries have incurred in recent decades.[26]

Abolition of 1848: Compensation, Disciplinary Workshops, and Indentured Workers

Let us turn now to the abolition of 1848. Following the passage of the British Slavery Abolition Act of 1833 and its implementation in the period 1833–1843, the abolition debate became ubiquitous in France. There were still 250,000

---

25. See, for example, D. Graeber, *Debt: The First 5000 Years* (Melville House, 2011), pp. 81–84. See also A. Testard, *L'esclave, la dette et le pouvoir* (Errance, 2001).
26. Think, for example, of the debts that Greece and other southern European countries owe to Germany, France, and other northern European countries, or of the recent debts that many African and Asian countries have incurred toward China, or of the Argentine debt to a consortium of international creditors. We will have more to say about the differences and similarities among these cases as well as the debt that France imposed on Germany with the Treaty of Versailles. See esp. Chaps. 10 and 12.

slaves in the French colonies, especially Martinique, Guadeloupe, and Réunion, whereas those of Jamaica and Mauritius had been set free, arousing fears of new revolts. Nevertheless, debate once again hit a snag over the question of compensation. For slaveowners and their supporters, it was inconceivable that they should be deprived of their property without a fair indemnity. But the idea that the full burden should be borne by public treasury, and therefore the taxpayers, who had already been called on to finance the "émigré billion" in 1825, did not seem quite right.[27] Shouldn't the slaves, who after all would be the primary beneficiaries of the measure, also pay? Alexandre Moreau de Jonnès, a dedicated abolitionist well known for his statistics on slaves and masters in the colonies, which he had compiled using census data and administrative surveys from the early seventeenth century on, proposed in 1842 that slaves should reimburse the entire amount of the indemnity by performing "special work projects" *(travaux spéciaux)* without pay for as long as necessary. He also insisted that this would be a way of teaching slaves the meaning of work.[28] Some commentators pointed out that this transitional reimbursement period might well last quite some time, which would be tantamount to not emancipating the slaves at all: it would merely transform the servile condition into a condition of perpetual debt, just as the former *corvées* had been transformed into debt during the Revolution.

Tocqueville thought he had found the perfect combination when he proposed in 1843 that half the indemnity be paid to slaveholders in the form of government annuities (hence by increasing the public debt, to be repaid by the

27. See Chap. 4. The "émigré billion," intended to compensate the nobility for rent and property lost between 1789 and 1815, affected a far larger number of noble landowners and represented roughly 15 percent of annual GDP in 1825; the 300 million francs envisaged for abolition represented about 2 percent of annual GDP in 1840.

28. "Emancipation should be gradual and partial, not simultaneous and en masse, because otherwise it might turn into a subversive revolution, as in Haiti. The masters of slaves must be compensated by an indemnity, which should be equivalent, insofar as possible, to the value of the property of which they have been deprived. This indemnity cannot be borne by the Metropole, because it constitutes a capital of 300 million francs, the mere interest on which would soon overload the public debt of France. . . . It is obvious that since sacrifices must be made to this end, the slaves, who will derive immense benefits from it, should naturally and necessarily make them. As they are being admitted to the class of citizens, it will be useful to instruct them, through salutary practice, that a common law holds that every man ameliorate his position by hard and intelligent labor." A. Moreau de Jonnès, *Recherches statistiques sur l'esclavage colonial et les moyens de le supprimer* (1842), pp. 252–253.

taxpayers) and the other half by the slaves themselves, who would work for the state for ten years at low wages, allowing the wage differential to be used to reimburse their former owners. In that way, he argued, the solution would be "fair to all participating parties," since the former slaveowners would, after ten years, be obliged to pay "the increased price of labor" due to emancipation.[29] Taxpayers, slaves, and slaveowners would thus all be made to pay their fair share. A parliamentary committee chaired by Victor de Broglie came up with a similar solution. No one involved in these debates—which admittedly took place in fora dominated by property owners (since just over 2 percent of adult males were eligible to vote for the Chamber of Deputies between 1830 and 1848, and they had to choose their representatives from among the 0.3 percent of wealthiest individuals)—seems to have given serious consideration to the idea that it was the slaves who ought to be indemnified for centuries of unpaid labor. This would have allowed them to become owners of a portion of the land on which they had worked as slaves, and they might then have been able to work for themselves, as Irish peasants did under the agrarian reforms of the late nineteenth and early twentieth centuries (admittedly with generous state compensation to the landlords, at least up to the time of independence).

In any case, the debate went nowhere until the mid-1840s because slaveowners rejected emancipation and threatened to stop it, with armed force if necessary. Only after the fall of the monarchy and the proclamation of the Second Republic in 1848 was Victor Schoelcher's committee able to secure passage of an abolition bill, which provided compensation for slaveholders somewhat less generous than the British act of 1833 under a cost-sharing arrangement ultimately similar to the one proposed by Tocqueville. Slaveowners received an indemnity calculated on a basis half as large as previously envisioned (which was nevertheless quite substantial).[30] In addition to indemnifying slaveholders, the abolition decrees promulgated on April 27, 1848, included articles "punishing vagabondage and begging while calling for disciplinary workshops in the colonies," the purpose of which was to ensure that planters would have an adequate supply of cheap labor. In other words, under the Schoelcher emancipation, not only were slaves not indemnified or offered access to landownership,

---

29. See Oudin-Bastide and Steiner, *Calcul et Morale,* pp. 122–123.

30. In the debates of the 1840s the proposed indemnity averaged around 1,300 francs per slave (leading to a total estimate of 300 million francs), whereas the reference value in the 1848 bill was 600 francs (or four to six years of waves for an equivalent free worker). See the online appendix.

but in addition, slaveowners were paid and a regime of semi-forced labor was established, which kept former slaves under the control of planters and allied state authorities. In Réunion, the prefect immediately explained how the new regime would work: former slaves would be required to sign long-term work contracts either as plantation workers or domestic employees or else be arrested for vagabondage and sent to the disciplinary workshops envisioned by the law promulgated in Paris.[31]

To understand the context of the time, it is important to note that laws of this type, in which the state de facto served employers and landlords by imposing strict discipline on labor and keeping wages as low as possible, were common everywhere; they simply caught a second wind in the colonies after the abolition of slavery. Specifically, since many emancipated slaves refused to work for their former masters, British and French authorities developed new systems that allowed workers to be shipped in from elsewhere. In the case of Réunion and Mauritius, the additional labor came from India, for example. The French called these imported laborers *engagés,* and the British, "indentured workers." *Engagement* meant that the Indian workers brought in to replace the slaves were required to reimburse the cost of transportation borne by their employers; this reimbursement extended over a lengthy period, say ten years, and was taken out of their wages. If their job performance was unsatisfactory or, worse, if they were accused of some disciplinary infraction, the reimbursement period could be extended for another ten years or more. Surviving court documents from Mauritius and Réunion show clearly that, since the courts were strongly biased in favor of employers, this system led to exploitation and injustice not identical to slavery but not far removed from it either. The sources also show how employers and courts in a sense negotiated the transformation of the labor discipline regime. Owners slowly agreed to abandon the methods of corporal punishment that had been in wide use under slavery, but only on condition that the authorities help them by imposing financial and legal sanctions that had the same effect.[32]

---

31. In 1843, Tocqueville proposed that former slaves be deprived of property rights for a long period of time, from ten to twenty years, to give them time to acquire a taste for work and effort; this lesson might be lost if they were to discover the comforts of property too quickly (and "unnaturally"). This proposal was ultimately omitted from the 1848 law, however. See Oudin-Bastide and Steiner, *Calcul et morale,* pp. 202–203. On the background of the 1848 decrees, see also N. Schmidt, *La France a-t-elle aboli l'esclavage? Guadeloupe, Martinique, Guyane 1830–1935* (Perrin, 2009).

32. See esp. A. Stanziani, "Beyond Colonialism: Servants, Wage Earners and Indentured Migrants in Rural France and on Reunion Island (c. 1750–1900)," *Labor*

It also bears emphasizing that this type of legal regime, which was very hard on workers (and on the poor generally), was also quite widespread in European labor markets. In 1885, Sweden still had a law on the books allowing anyone without either a job or sufficient property to live on to be arrested and sentenced to a term of forced labor.[33] We find similar laws throughout Europe, notably in the United Kingdom and France, but Swedish law was particularly harsh and remained in force for an unusually long time, which is consistent with what we have seen of Sweden's exacerbated proprietarianism in the late nineteenth century.[34] As it happens, this regime was about to be radically transformed in a number of European countries, including Sweden, in the late nineteenth and early twentieth centuries as unions were authorized, workers obtained the right to strike and engage in collective bargaining, and so on. In the colonies—and not just the former slave islands—the transition took longer: in Chapter 7 we will see that perfectly legal forms of *corvée* and forced labor persisted into the twentieth century in the French colonial empire, especially in the interwar years and virtually up to the time of decolonization.

Forced Labor, Proprietarian Sacralization, and the Question of Reparations

Several lessons emerge from these episodes. First, there are many gradations of labor between forced and free, and it is important to look closely at the *details* of the relevant legal system (the point being that they are not *merely* details). This is true in particular regarding immigrant workers today, whose right to

---

History, 2013; A. Stanziani, *Sailors, Slaves, and Immigrants: Bondage in the Indian Ocean World 1750–1914* (Palgrave Macmillan, 2014); and A. Stanziani, *Labor on the Fringes of Empire: Voice, Exit and the Law* (Palgrave, 2018). See also R. Allen, "Slaves, Convicts, Abolitionism and the Global Origins of the Post-Emancipation Indentured Labor System," *Slavery and Abolition,* 2014.

33. See E. Bengtsson, "The Swedish *Sonderweg* in Question: Democratization and Inequality in Comparative Perspective, c. 1750–11920," *Past and Present,* 2018, p. 10.

34. In the United Kingdom, the "Master and Servant Law" remained on the books until 1875. See S. Naidu and N. Yuchtman, "Coercive Contract Enforcement: Law and the Labor Market in 19th Century Industrial Britain," *American Economic Review,* 2013. In France, the *livret ouvrier* (work permit), which was toughened in 1854 and abolished in 1890, allowed former employers to warn future employers about troublesome workers and thus seriously harm the prospects of workers deemed to be troublesome. See R. Castel, *Les métamorphoses de la question sociale* (Fayard, 1995), pp. 414–415.

negotiate wages and working conditions is often quite limited, whether in the petro-monarchies of the Persian Gulf or in Europe and elsewhere in the world (particularly for undocumented workers). Indeed, labor law in general calls for close attention. Second, these debates attest to the power of the quasi-sacralized private property regime that dominated the nineteenth century. Had conflicts and events taken a different course, other decisions might have resulted. But those that were taken demonstrate the power of the proprietarian schema.

Schoelcher, who is remembered as a leading abolitionist, said he was embarrassed by the compensation paid to slaveholders but insisted that it was impossible to proceed in any other way once slavery was enshrined in a legal setting. The Romantic poet Lamartine, also an abolitionist, forcefully voiced the same argument in the Chamber of Deputies: it was absolutely necessary, he said, to grant "an indemnity to the colonists for the portion of their legally owned property in slaves, which is to be confiscated. We will never do anything else. Only revolutions confiscate without compensation. Legislators do not act that way: they change, they transform, but they never ruin. They always respect acquired rights, no matter what their origin."[35] No clearer statement of the case is imaginable: the refusal to distinguish among different types of acquired rights to property was the basis of the belief that slaveowners should be compensated (and not slaves). These episodes are fundamental. For one thing, they enable us to set in perspective the reemergence of certain forms of quasi-sacralization of property in the twenty-first century (regarding, in particular, integral repayment of public debt, no matter what its amount or duration, as well as the argument that the private wealth of billionaires is fully legitimate and sacrosanct, regardless of magnitude or origin). For another, they shed new light on the persistence of ethno-racial inequalities in the modern world, as well as the complex but unavoidable issue of reparations.

In 1904, when Haiti celebrated the hundredth anniversary of its independence, the government of the Third Republic refused to send an official delegation. French officials were in fact quite dissatisfied with the rate at which Haiti had been paying down its 1825 debt and felt that it was out of the question to indulge such a delinquent borrower, particularly at a time when the colonial empire, then in a phase of rapid expansion, frequently needed to be disciplined with coercive debt strategies. In 2004, when Haiti celebrated the bicentennial of its independence in a very different political context, the government of the Fifth Republic came to the same conclusion but for different reasons. The

---

35. See Chamber of Deputies, sessions of April 22, 1835, and May 25, 1836.

French president refused to attend the ceremony because it was feared (not without reason) that Haitian president Aristide would seize the opportunity to demand that France compensate Haiti for the odious debt that the small island republic had been obliged to repay for more than century (the value of which Aristide put at 20 billion in 2003 US dollars)—a demand that the French government had no intention of entertaining on any grounds whatsoever. In 2015, the French president, on a visit to Haiti in the wake of the 2010 earthquake and the lengthy reconstruction operations that followed, reiterated this position. To be sure, France owed Haiti a sort of "moral" debt, but it was out of the question even to consider any kind of financial or monetary reparations.

It is not my place to resolve this complex issue here or to say what exact form French compensation to Haiti ought to take (especially when there is nothing to prevent us from thinking about more ambitious forms of transnational justice or intergenerational reparations; I will come back to this later).[36] Nevertheless, I must point out the extreme weakness of the arguments raised by those who refused to reopen the Haitian case while defending other forms of reparation. In particular, the argument that all this is ancient history cannot withstand scrutiny. Haiti reimbursed its French and American creditors from 1825 to 1950, that is, until the middle of the twentieth century. But compensation is still being paid today for expropriations and injustices that took place in the first half of the twentieth century. Think, for example, of the confiscation of Jewish property by the Nazis and allied regimes (including the Vichy government in France) during World War II. It took far too long to establish lawful restoration procedures for these injustices, but eventually it was done, and repayment continues to this day. Think, too, of current reparations for expropriations by Communist regimes in Eastern Europe after World War II, or of the law passed in the United States in 1988 granting $20,000 to Japanese Americans interned during the war.[37] By refusing any discussion of the debt Haiti was forced to pay back to France because it no longer wished to be enslaved, even though the payments made from 1825 to 1950 are well documented and wholly uncontested, one inevitably runs the risk of giving the impression that some crimes are more deserving of punishment than others.

---

36. That is, forms of transnational justice based on equal rights, independent of place of birth, or distant origins. See Chap. 17.
37. The American indemnity was limited to persons still living in 1988 (roughly 60,000 of the 120,000 Japanese Americans interned between 1942 and 1946), for a cost of $1.2 billion.

Since the early 2000s, several French organizations have been calling for an exercise in national transparency regarding the compensation to former slave-owners paid by the Caisse des Dépôts in connection with the indemnity of 1825 as well as the compensation paid under the law of 1848.[38] Neither case has been examined in detail, unlike the British compensation of slaveowners (which admittedly was investigated only recently). It is possible that the relevant French archives are not as well preserved as Britain's parliamentary archives. That should not prevent a thorough examination of the issues, nor should it prevent France from paying substantial reparations to Haiti or, for that matter, from paying for appropriate educational materials and museum exhibits (there is no museum of slavery worthy of the name in France, not even in Bordeaux or Nantes, ports that owe their prosperity to the slave trade). The cost of the latter would be ridiculously small compared to the cost of reparations to Haiti, but the pedagogical benefit would be huge.

On May 10, 2001, the French National Assembly, acting at the behest of Christiane Taubira (a representative from French Guiana), passed a law "tending toward the recognition of the slave trade and slavery as a crime against humanity." But the government and majority at the time took care to excise Article 5, which set forth the principle of reparations and would have established a commission to look into the issues; it would never see the light of day.[39] Apart from the question of financial reparations to Haiti, another large-scale compensation also backed by Taubira seems difficult to avoid: the question of agrarian reform in Réunion, Martinique, Guadeloupe, and Guiana, the purpose of which would be to allow the descendants of former slaves to have access to parcels of land in places where most of the land and financial assets remain in the hands of the white population, often descended from the families of planters who benefited from the indemnities of 1848. In 2015, Taubira, by then minister of justice, sought unsuccessfully to remind the French president of the importance of the Haitian debt issue and of agrarian reform in France's overseas *départements*.

---

38. See esp. L. G. Tin, *Esclavage et réparations. Comment faire face aux crimes de l'histoire*, (Stock, 2013). The author is also president of the Conseil représentatif des associations noires (CRAN).

39. Article 5 read as follows: "A committee of qualified persons is charged with determine the damages suffered and examining the conditions of reparations due as a result of this crime. The competence and mission of this committee will be set by decree of the Council of State."

Yet to judge by the indemnification of Japanese Americans, which American leaders resisted for decades, or that of French Jews whose property was confiscated during the war and who had to wait until the early 2000s for a committee to be named to look into their grievances, it is quite possible that agitation around these outstanding slavery-related issues will someday succeed and lead to reparations that seem unthinkable today. On the other hand, the case of the Japanese Americans, who received compensation that continues to be denied to the descendants of former African American slaves and to the Mexican Americans who were deported in veritable anti-foreigner pogroms during the Depression (especially in California), reminds us that racial and cultural biases (along with the legal, financial, and political resources available to those seeking indemnities) sometimes play a role in determining who gets what.[40]

United States: Abolition by War, 1860–1865

We turn now to the case of the United States, which is particularly important for our study given the preeminent role that the United States, self-proclaimed leader of the "free" world since 1945, plays in the global interstate system. It is also the only case of abolition precipitated by a violent civil war, in a country where legal racial discrimination persisted until the 1960s and ethno-racial inequalities (or inequalities perceived and represented as ethno-racial) continue to play a structuring role today in the economy, society, and politics. The countries of Europe, which long regarded America's singular history with astonishment, continue to wonder how the Democratic Party, which was the party of slavery at the time of the Civil War (1860–1865), became the party of the New Deal in the 1930s, of civil rights in the 1960s, and finally of Barack Obama in the period 2008–2016, changing imperceptibly and without major discontinuity. Europeans would nevertheless do well to follow the US trajectory in detail because it is not totally unrelated to the structure of inequality, political conflict, and debates over immigration that has emerged in postcolonial

---

40. Estimates of the number of Mexican Americans expelled in the period 1929–1936 range from 1 to 1.5 million (of whom some 60 percent were born in the United States). Deportations were often organized with the support of local and federal authorities. Some recent estimates put the number of deported as high as 1.8 million (most of whom never returned). See A. Wagner, "America's Forgotten History of Illegal Deportations," *The Atlantic,* 2017.

European societies over the past several decades and whose long-term evolution raises many similar questions.

To begin, it is important to note that the system of slavery that existed in the United States in the second slave era (1800–1860) enjoyed an extremely prosperous existence. The number of slaves increased sharply from 1 million in 1800 to 4 million in 1860, or five times the number of slaves on the French and British slave islands at their peak. Although it is true that the slave trade persisted in clandestine fashion until 1820 or so, the fact remains that the dizzying growth in the number of slaves was achieved mainly through natural increase, thanks to a certain improvement in living conditions and the development among the enslaved of forms of private and family life unknown in the eighteenth century; in some cases, this went together with forms of religious education and expansion of literacy, a slow and subterranean process, which despite repressive southern laws to stop it helped arm black abolitionists for the struggle ahead. At the time, however, nothing augured the end of the system. The population of the southern states was 2.6 million in 1800: 1.7 million whites (66 percent) and 0.9 million blacks (34 percent). By 1860 the population had increased nearly fivefold to more than 12 million: 8 million whites (67 percent) and 4 million blacks (33 percent; Table 6.1). In other words, the system was experiencing rapid but relatively balanced growth, and nothing portended impending doom.

In some states, to be sure, the population was as much as 50–60 percent black, but nowhere did the black share of the population attain the levels seen in the West Indies (80–90 percent). Between the 1790s and the 1850s, land use in the United States became increasingly specialized. While the proportion of slaves remained constant in Virginia at around 40 percent throughout this period, in South Carolina it rose gradually from 42 percent in 1800 to 57–58 percent in the 1850s; it also rose in Georgia and North Carolina. In Mississippi and Alabama, newly admitted to the Union from 1817 to 1819, the proportion of slaves increased significantly between the 1820 census and that of 1860, rising to 55 percent in Mississippi, almost as high as in South Carolina. Meanwhile, states close to the Mason-Dixon line separating North from South saw their proportion of slaves stagnate, as in Kentucky (at around 20 percent), or sharply decline, as in Delaware (which went from 15 percent in 1790 to less than 5 in 1860). In New Jersey and New York, where slaves accounted for less than 5 percent of the population in the 1790 census, slavery was gradually abolished after 1804, and no slaves remained in official census figures after 1830 (Fig. 6.3).

TABLE 6.1

The structure of the slave and free population in the United States, 1800–1860

	Total (thousands)	Black slaves	Free blacks	Whites	Total (%)	Black slaves	Free blacks	Whites
Total United States, 1800	5,210	880	110	4,220	100%	17%	2%	81%
Northern states	2,630	40	80	2,510	100%	2%	3%	95%
Southern states	2,580	840	30	1,710	100%	33%	1%	66%
Total United States, 1860	31,180	3,950	490	26,740	100%	13%	2%	85%
Northern states	18,940	0	340	18,600	100%	0%	2%	98%
Southern states	12,240	3,950	150	8,140	100%	32%	1%	67%

Interpretation: The number of slaves in the United States quadrupled between 1800 and 1860 (from 880,000 to nearly 3.95 million) while the slave share of the population in the South remained fairly stable (at about one-third). The slave share of total population declined (owing to the even more rapid growth of the population in the North). *Note*: All slave states as of 1860 are classified as Southern: Alabama, Arkansas, North and South Carolina, Delaware, Florida, Georgia, Kentucky, Louisiana, Maryland, Mississippi, Missouri, Tennessee, Texas, and Virginia. *Sources and series*: piketty.pse.ens.fr/ideology.

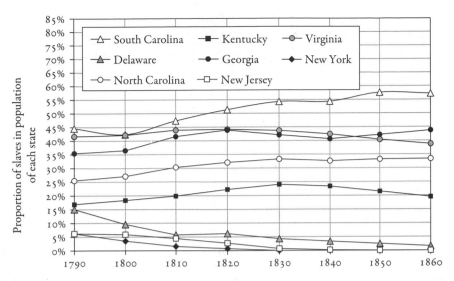

FIG. 6.3. Proportion of slaves in the United States, 1790–1860

Interpretation: The proportion of slaves in the population increased or remained at a high level in the principal slave states of the South between 1790 and 1860 (35–55 percent in 1850–1860 and as high as 57–58 percent in South Carolina), whereas slavery disappeared in the Northern states. *Sources and series:* piketty.pse.ens.fr/ideology.

It bears emphasizing that these figures are very well known in the US case because a census of both free and slave populations was conducted every ten years from 1790 on. The census was particularly important because, under the terms of the famous "Three-Fifths Compromise," the number of slaves played a key role in determining the number of seats assigned to each state in the House of Representatives and therefore the number of members of the Electoral College, which chooses the president: each slave counted for three-fifths of a free person. Beyond that, it is important to recall the importance of slaveownership in the birth of the Republic. Virginia was by far the most populous state (with a total population of 750,000, including slaves, in the first census of 1790, which was equal to the combined population of the two most populous northern states, Pennsylvania and Massachusetts). Virginia furnished the country with four of its first five presidents (Washington, Jefferson, Madison, and Monroe, all slaveowners), the only exception being John Adams of Massachusetts. Of the fifteen presidents who served prior to the election of the Republican Abraham Lincoln in 1860, no fewer than eleven were slaveowners.

The slave system in the southern United States was also of decisive importance for the production of cotton, without which the textile industry could not have developed in the North, and which was also crucial for industrial de-velopment in Britain and Europe. It is important to keep in mind the unpre-cedented scale of the Euro-American slave system in the period 1750–1860 (Fig. 6.4), which was truly the crucial period in Europe's rise to industrial dom-inance. Until the 1780s, the West Indies, and especially Saint-Domingue, had been the principal producer of cotton. After the collapse of Saint-Domingue's slave plantations in the 1790s, the torch was passed to the southern states of the United States, which achieved new heights in the number of slaves and cotton production capacity in the period 1800–1860: the slave population was multiplied by four and cotton output by ten, thanks to improved techniques and intensified production. In the 1850s, on the eve of the American Civil War, 75 percent of the cotton imported by European textile factories came from the southern United States. As Sven Beckert has recently shown, it was this "em-pire of cotton," intimately associated with slave plantations, that was the heart of the Industrial Revolution and more generally of the economic domination

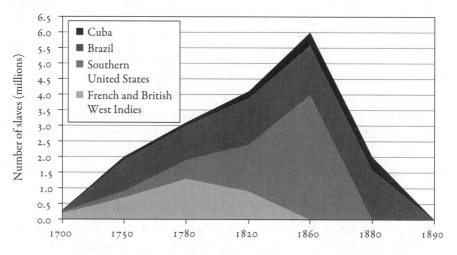

FIG. 6.4. The rise and fall of Euro-American slavery, 1700–1890

Interpretation: The total number of slaves on Euro-American plantations in the Atlantic region reached 6 million in 1860 (4 million of whom were in the southern United States, 1.6 million in Brazil, and 0.4 million in Cuba). Slavery in the French and British West Indies (to which I have added Mauritius, Réunion, and the Cape Colony) reached its zenith in 1780–1790 (1.3 million), then declined following the revolt in Saint-Domingue (Haiti) and the abolitions of 1833 and 1848. *Sources and series:* piketty.pse.ens.fr /ideology.

of Europe and the United States. In the eighteenth and early nineteenth centuries, the British and French were still uncertain what they might sell to the rest of the world, so much so that they were prepared to launch the Opium Wars of 1839–1842 and 1856–1860 to capture the China drug trade, but the transcontinental organization of the empire of cotton enabled them to establish their control over global textile production, radically increasing its scale and ultimately flooding the planet's textile markets during the second half of the nineteenth century.[41]

Meanwhile, the internal balance of political and ideological power in the United States also changed radically between 1800 and 1860. In 1800, the population of the United States was roughly 5.2 million, almost equally divided between the southern slave states (with a population of 2.6 million, including slaves) and the northern nonslave states (also with a population of 2.6 million). Many of the northern states had only recently abolished slavery following the lead of Massachusetts in 1783 (although strict racial discrimination continued there until the Civil War, especially in the schools, much as it would continue in the South until the 1960s). By 1860, the picture looked quite different: although the population of the South nearly quintupled (from 2.6 to more than 12 million), that of the North had grown sevenfold (from 2.5 to nearly 19 million). Thus nonslave states now represented more than 60 percent of the total population and more than two-thirds of the free population (Table 6.1). The North had also become considerably more diversified since it now consisted of two distinct parts with different economic bases and different political and ideological attitudes: on the one hand, the Northeast, which included the metropolises of New York and Boston and the industrial and financial fortunes of New England; and on the other hand, the Midwest, represented by both the small farmers of the new Western frontier states and the great meat and grain distribution networks that flourished around Chicago, the region from which Lincoln sprang. In other words, although the slave South with its cotton plantations was growing rapidly, it belonged to a political space that was growing even more rapidly, whose economic and political-ideological models were based on free labor. The West and frontier territories remembered their coming of age before being admitted to statehood themselves, under the "colonial" tutelage of the federal government and the original states: hard-won land was often confiscated by the central government for the benefit of powerful interests.

---

41. See S. Beckert, *Empire of Cotton. A Global History* (Knopf, 2014). In Chap. 9 I will return to the role of slavery and colonial rule in the Industrial Revolution.

Bear in mind, however, that the North initially had no intention of demanding immediate abolition of slavery in the South (much less racial equality). The central issue was the status of the new territories to the west. Lincoln and the Republicans wanted them to be free because that was the development model they knew, and they could see the West's full potential as part of an integrated continental and global economy. "The great interior region ... already has above 10,000,000 people, and will have 50,000,000 within fifty years if not prevented by any political folly or mistake," Lincoln declared to Congress in 1862, adding that this prosperity called for a united nation because this vast interior region "has no seacoast—touches no ocean anywhere. As part of one nation, its people now find, and may forever find, their way to Europe by New York, to South America and Africa by New Orleans, and to Asia by San Francisco; but separate our common country into two nations, as designed by the present rebellion, and every man of this great interior region is thereby cut off from some one or more of these outlets, not perhaps by a physical barrier, but by embarrassing and onerous trade regulations."[42] By contrast, southerners feared that if free states were allowed to develop in the West, the slave states would end up a minority in the United States, unable to defend their distinct way of life (a judgment that was not entirely wrong). Slaves began to flee in growing numbers, and even though the Fugitive Slave Act, passed by Congress in 1850, significantly reinforced previous laws, compelling authorities in the free states to assist slave hunters in tracking down their presumed property and providing stiff prison sentences for anyone convicted of aiding fugitive slaves, the southern states felt that they needed a solid political coalition to defend their economic model over the long run.[43]

Lincoln was elected in November 1860 on a promise to refuse to extend slavery to the new states of the West. In late 1860 and early 1861, he repeatedly stated that he asked for nothing more than unequivocal acceptance of the fact that the new states would be free, along with the beginning of an

---

42. Quoted in N. Barreyre, *L'or et la liberté* (Editions de l'EHESS, 2014), p. 27; published in English as *Gold and Freedom: The Political Economy of Reconstruction,* trans. A. Goldhammer (University of Virginia Press, 2015), p. 17.

43. The Fugitive Slave Act led to an increase of 15–30 percent in the price of slaves in the border states compared with states farther south, which suggests that the risk of flight was deemed to be serious by slave dealers. See C. Lennon, "Slave Escape, Prices and the Fugitive Act of 1850," *Journal of Law and Economics,* 2016. Kidnapping of free blacks in the North was common and inspired the film *Twelve Years a Slave,* dir. S. McQueen (Fox Searchlight, 2013).

extremely gradual process of emancipation in the South, with compensation for slaveholders—a process which, had it been accepted, might have prolonged slavery until 1880 or 1900, if not longer. But southerners, like the white minorities in South Africa and Algeria in the twentieth century, refused to give in to a majority they judged to be distant and alien to their world; they chose secession instead. South Carolina voted to secede from the Union in December 1860, and by February 1861 it had already been joined by six other states, forming the Confederate States of America. Lincoln still held out hope for dialogue, but in April 1861, shortly after the inauguration of the new president, the Confederates seized Fort Sumter in the harbor of Charleston, South Carolina, capturing the federal troops stationed there, which left Lincoln no choice but to go to war or accept the partition of the country.

Four years and more than 600,000 dead later (that is, more dead than in all other conflicts in which the United States has been involved, including the two world wars, Korea, Vietnam, and Iraq), the war was over: the Confederate armies surrendered in May 1865. In view of the damage done by the southern forces, compensating former slaveowners was unthinkable. To enlist black support for the Union armies, Lincoln persuaded Congress to pass the Thirteenth Amendment, emancipating the slaves, in April 1864 (without any compensation to either slaveholders or slaves); this was ratified by all the states, including the southern states occupied by the armies of the North, in December 1865. It was made clear that the amendment carried no implication concerning political, social, or economic rights for freed slaves. Early in 1865, Union military authorities had indeed hinted to emancipated slaves that they would receive "forty acres and a mule" when the war was over; had this program been adopted nationwide, it would have amounted to a large-scale agrarian redistribution. No law to compensate slaves was adopted by Congress, and the "forty acres and a mule" slogan became a symbol of Yankee deception and hypocrisy.[44]

On the Impossibility of Gradual Abolition and Compensation in the United States

Could gradual abolition with compensation of slaveowners, such as Lincoln proposed to the South in 1860–1861, have worked in the United States? Given the sums at stake, it seems unlikely without a very large (and highly improbable)

---

44. Indeed, the film director Spike Lee ironically chose it as the name of his production company: "Forty Acres and a Mule."

transfer of funds from the North to southern slaveholders, or else a very long transition period, extending to the very end of the nineteenth century or the early decades of the twentieth. Without the war or slave revolts (hard to imagine because the slave population was a smaller proportion of the population than in the West Indies),[45] the most probable outcome would have been continuation of the slave system. With powerful interests at stake and the slave regime prospering and expanding rapidly in 1860, the South was not ready to accept a peaceful end to slavery.

To gain a better idea of the sums involved, recall that the compensation paid by the British in 1833 cost taxpayers roughly 5 percent of GDP, which is a lot, even though the number of slaves was smaller (about 3 percent of the British population at the time) and British GDP per capita was extremely high for the era. Slaves were then very valuable assets, and the market price of a slave was generally about ten to twelve years of an equivalent free worker's wages. What does this work out today in today's terms? Assume a slave does work for which a free worker would be paid 30,000 euros (2,500 euros a month, or roughly the average wage in France and Western Europe today), and assume that this labor brings in at least that much revenue for the slave's employer. Then the selling price of that slave would be between 300,000 and 360,000 euros. It is easy to see that in a society where slaves represented virtually the entire work force, their market value could reach astronomical levels, potentially as high as seven or eight years of annual production (700–800 percent of national income).[46] Recall that France saddled Haiti with a debt equivalent to three years of Haitian national income in 1825 yet remained convinced that it was making sacrifices compared to what slaves in Saint-Domingue actually yielded in profit.

In the case of the American South, where slaves represented about a third of the population, there exist numerous sources that tell us how the price of slaves varied with age, sex, and productivity. Recent research has shown that

---

45. The proportion of slaves was as high as 75 percent in some counties, such as Nottoway County in Virginia, not far from Southampton County where Nat Turner led a rebellion in 1831, recently dramatized in *The Birth of a Nation,* dir. N. Parker (Fox Searchlight, 2016).

46. Assuming that wages account for 60–70 percent of GDP, which itself depends on many factors and in particular on the legal regime defining "free" labor. With an average yield on capital on the order of 5 percent, the price of slaves could in principle approach twenty years of wages, but allowing for risk and the cost of slave upkeep (food and clothing) explains why the apparent yield was closer to 8–10 percent. See the online appendix.

in 1860, the market value of slaves exceeded 250 percent of the annual income of the southern states and came close to 100 percent of the annual income of all the states.[47] If compensation had been paid, it would have been necessary to increase the public debt, and taxpayers would have been saddled with interest and principal payments for decades.

To sum up, in order to free the slaves without despoiling their owners, the country as a whole would have had to bear the financial burden. The former slaveowners would have become bondholders, to whom US taxpayers (including former slaves) would have owed a substantial debt. This is exactly what happened in the United Kingdom and France (with the special case of Haiti), except that in the United States the sums at stake were considerably larger given the scope of the slave system. Recall that annual public expenditure on education, at all levels of government, did not exceed 1 percent of national income in any country in the nineteenth century. A federal debt of 100 percent of national income would therefore have represented more than a century of investment in education, to say nothing of the fact that interest on that debt alone (roughly 5 percent of national income) would have consumed five times the amount of tax revenue spent on all primary schools, high schools, and colleges and universities in the country. Note, moreover, that the debt contracted during the Civil War—the first major federal debt in US history, stemming from the mobilization, upkeep, and arming of more than 2 million Union soldiers for five years—amounted to $2.3 billion in 1865, or roughly 30 percent of US national income, which at the time seemed a gigantic amount; repayment of that debt was the source of complex political conflicts in the decades to come. It would have taken three or four times the cost of the war itself to compensate former slaveowners at market prices. It is reasonable to think that the people involved were no fools: when Lincoln proposed abolition with compensation in 1860–1861, everyone knew that true compensation was impossible: one side or the other would have found the amounts unacceptable. The real question was therefore whether to put the problem off until later or to accept an immediate freeze on extension of slavery to the new states in the West. Southern slaveowners rejected the latter option.

---

47. In the South, the market value of all slaves exceeded the value of all other private property (land, buildings, and equipment). See T. Piketty, *Capital in the Twenty-First Century*, trans. A. Goldhammer (Harvard University Press, 2014), figs. 4.10–4.11 and the online appendix.

It is interesting, moreover, to note that both Jefferson and Madison tried to estimate the cost of compensation in the 1810s; both discovered that it would have been enormous (on the order of one year's national income at the time). Both also submitted proposals for coming up with such a sum. It could have been done, they argued, by selling a third to a half of all land in the public domain, particularly new land in the West.[48] This would have meant giving vast estates in the new territories to the former slaveholders, estates that would have replaced the small family farms of the settlers then moving into those territories, which would have provoked significant social and political tensions. Proposals of this sort were entertained from time to time between 1820 and 1860, but it was difficult to imagine circumstances under which a majority coalition prepared to run the risk could have been assembled at the federal level without radically altering the political system.

On the Proprietarian and Social Justification of Slavery

The abolition of slavery posed difficult ideological problems to nineteenth-century proprietarian societies, which feared that abolition without compensation of slaveowners would ultimately undermine the whole proprietarian order and system of private property. In the US case, this fear was aggravated by the magnitude of the compensation that would have been required; had it been attempted, it might have provoked other kinds of tension, so in the end it became difficult to see any way out of the country's predicament.

Beyond these proprietarian concerns, the conflict over slavery in the United States had very deep political and ideological underpinnings, which stemmed from quite distinct models of development and visions of the future. The southern rural slaveholder position was forcefully articulated by John Calhoun, who served as vice president of the United States from 1825 to 1832 in addition to stints as secretary of war, secretary of state, and long service as a senator from South Carolina, a post he held until his death in 1850. As leader of the slave power in the Senate, Calhoun repeatedly described "slavery as a positive good" rather than the "necessary evil" acknowledged by other defenders of the system, whom he deemed pusillanimous. Calhoun's principal argument rested

---

48. See W. Shade, *Democratizing the Old Dominion: Virginia and the Second Party System, 1824–1861* (University Press of Virginia, 1996), pp. 191–193. On the amounts involved, see the online appendix.

on the values of paternalism and solidarity that he saw as essential to the slave system. For instance, according to the Democratic senator, the ill and elderly were much better treated on southern plantations than in the urban industrial centers of the North, the United Kingdom, and Europe where workers who were no longer able to work were left to die in the streets or in wretched poorhouses.

According to Calhoun, that would never happen on a plantation, where the old and sick remained members of the community and were treated with dignity and respect until the day they died.[49] For Calhoun, plantation owners like himself embodied an ideal of agrarian republicanism and local community. By contrast, the industrialists and financiers of the North were hypocrites who pretended to worry about the fate of the slaves but whose real objective was to turn them into proletarians to be exploited like the rest, only to be discarded once they could no longer work. No doubt Calhoun's speeches failed to sway dedicated abolitionists, who were familiar with accounts of corporal punishment and mutilation inflicted on plantation slaves and had heard the tales of fugitive slaves like Frederick Douglass. But for many other Americans at the time, the idea that southern planters took at least as much interest in their slaves as northern capitalists did in their workers seemed plausible (and in some cases, no doubt, the claim was not totally false).

Calhoun's rural republican ideal had points in common with Thomas Jefferson's ideal of a democracy of yeoman farmers but with one essential difference: Jefferson saw slavery as an evil he did not know how to eliminate. "I tremble for my country when I reflect that God is just, and that his justice cannot sleep forever," worried the man who wrote the Declaration of Independence and who nevertheless could not imagine the possibility of a peaceful emancipation. "We have a wolf by the ears, and we can neither hold him, nor safely let him go. Justice is in one scale, and self-preservation in the other." For Jefferson, who was speaking at the time in the 1820 congressional debate about extending slavery to Missouri (which he supported, as he supported the right

---

49. "I may say with truth, that in few countries so much is left to the share of the laborer, and so little exacted from him, or where there is more kind attention paid to him in sickness or infirmities of age. Compare his condition with the tenants of the poor houses in the more civilized portions of Europe—look at the sick, and the old and infirm slave, on one hand, in the midst of his family and friends, under the kind superintending care of his master and mistress, and compare it with the forlorn and wretched condition of the pauper in the poorhouse." Speech delivered by John Calhoun on February 6, 1837, in the Senate.

of Missouri settlers to refuse to admit free blacks to the new state), emancipation could be envisioned only if it was accompanied not only by just compensation for the slaveowners but also by immediate expatriation of all former slaves.[50]

Such fears of inevitable vengeance by freed slaves, or merely of the impossibility of cohabitation, were widespread among slaveowners. This explains the creation of the American Colonization Society (ACS) in 1816. Its mission, ardently supported by Jefferson, Madison, Monroe, and many other slaveowners, was precisely to deport emancipated slaves to Africa. This was in a sense an extreme form of the segregation of blacks and whites practiced in the South from 1865 to 1965. If the two groups were to be separated, why not put an ocean between them? This project was a resounding failure. Between 1816 and 1867, the ACS relocated fewer than 13,000 emancipated African-Americans to Liberia, less than 0.5 percent of the total number of slaves (which was nevertheless enough to seriously perturb the subsequent development of Liberia, which has remained divided between "Americos" and natives to this day).[51] Whatever Jefferson may have thought, emancipation could only have taken place on American soil, and steps would have needed to be taken to ensure good relations between whites and blacks afterward, for instance, by seeing to it that former slaves and their children would have access to schools and political rights. Unfortunately, this was not the path that was chosen, no doubt because former slaveholders were convinced that peaceful cohabitation with their former slaves was impossible.

---

50. "The cessation of that kind of property, for so it is misnamed, is a bagatelle which would not cost me a second thought, if, in that way, a general emancipation and *expatriation* could be effected; and, gradually, and with due sacrifices, I think it might be. But as it is, we have a wolf by the ears, and we can neither hold him, nor safely let him go. Justice is in one scale, and self-preservation in the other." Thomas Jefferson to John Holmes from Monticello (April 22, 1820), *The Writings of Thomas Jefferson,* vol.15 (1903), pp. 248–250. See also B. Shaw, "A Wolf by the Ears: M. Finley's *Ancient Slavery and Modern Ideology* in Historical Context," in M. I. Moses, *Ancient Slavery and Modern Ideology,* ed. B. Shaw (Markus Weiner, 1998).

51. Note, too, that many slaveholders supported the ACS's idea of deporting free blacks, whose growing numbers and alleged propensity to foment revolts worried them—all while maintaining slavery. See Shade, *Democratizing the Old Dominion,* pp. 194–195. The Liberian constitution of 1846, adopted with guidance from the ACS, reserved political power and the right to vote for the Americos, who held the post of president exclusively until 1980.

"Reconstruction" and the Birth of Social Nativism in the United States

These debates about the justification of slavery must be taken seriously because they had a fundamental impact on what came later, not only in terms of persisting racial inequality and discrimination in the United States but also, more generally, regarding the specific structure of political, ideological, and electoral conflict in the United States since the nineteenth century. Foreign observers—and sometimes natives as well—are often astonished that the Democratic Party, which in 1860 defended slavery against Lincoln's Republican Party, often with arguments close to those of Calhoun and Jefferson (both eminent Democrats), subsequently became the party of Franklin D. Roosevelt and the New Deal and, in the 1960s, the party of John F. Kennedy, Lyndon B. Johnson, the Civil Rights Act, and the War on Poverty, before becoming the party of Bill Clinton and Barack Obama (1992–2000, 2008–2016). We will come back to this in Part Four, when we compare the evolution of socioeconomic structures and political cleavages in the United States and Europe in the twentieth and early twenty-first centuries, along with other large democratic countries such as India and Brazil. And we will see then that this peculiar political-ideological trajectory is in fact rich in instruction and implications for the entire world.

At this stage, note simply that it was by small adjustments and without major discontinuity that the Democratic Party ceased to be Jeffersonian and Calhounian to become Rooseveltian and Johnsonian (and ultimately Clintonian and Obamian). In particular, it was by denouncing what they perceived as the hypocrisy and selfishness of the Republican industrial and financial elites of the Northeast, rather as Calhoun had done in the 1830s, that the Democrats were able to regain power at the federal level in the 1870s and establish the basis of the coalition that would bring them success in the era of the New Deal. From 1820 to 1860, conflict at the ballot box usually pitted Democrats, who were especially well established in the South (as they were throughout the period 1790–1960), against the Whigs, who replaced the Federalists in the 1830s before themselves being replaced by the Republicans in the 1850s and who usually scored their best results in the Northeast. Until 1860, when the Republicans adopted a platform advocating the extension of "free labor" to the West (along with gradual abolition of slavery in the South), the two camps had carefully avoided confrontation over the slavery question, which had been temporarily closed with the Missouri Compromise of 1820 (under the terms of which

Missouri was admitted to the United States as a slave state at the same time as the free state of Maine). Constant tension remained, however, especially around the issue of fugitive slaves. In the South, candidates of both parties vied to defend slavery, with each camp accusing the other of tolerating northern abolitionists. In practice, within each southern state, the Democrats drew their main support from white voters in rural counties where plantations were dominant (so that it was difficult to imagine a future without slavery), while the Whigs drew the educated urban vote.[52]

During Reconstruction, which lasted from 1865 to 1880 or so, the Democrats were quite assiduous in denouncing the financial and industrial elites of the Northeast, who they claimed pulled the strings of the Republican Party for the sole purpose of defending their interests and increasing their profits.[53] They focused their accusations on one issue in particular: repayment of the war debt, in relation to the monetary system with its dual gold and silver standards (bimetallism). Briefly, Democrats alleged that Boston and New York bankers were concerned solely with collecting comfortable interest on the sums they

---

52. See Shade, *Democratizing the Old Dominion.* See also R. McCormick, *The Second Party System: Party Formation in the Jacksonian Era* (Norton, 1966). The "first party system" featured Democratic-Republicans (renamed Democrats in 1828) against the Federalists. After the presidential election of 1796, won by John Adams (a Boston Federalist), the Federalists suffered heavier and heavier losses and were replaced in the 1830s by the Whigs, named for the British liberal party of that name. This gave rise to the "second party system," Democrats versus Whigs. The third system began in 1860, when Lincoln's Republicans took on the Democrats. The principal point of stability in the period 1790–1960 is that the Democrats (and their predecessors, the Democratic-Republicans) always scored their best results in the South, while the Federalist-Whig-Republicans did best in the Northeast. A useful source for mapping presidential elections from 1792 to 2016 is the American Presidency Project. An analysis widely accepted by American political scientists is that the third-party system was transformed into a fourth in 1896–1900 with the arrival of the "populist" movement and demands for redistribution, and then a fifth in 1932 with the arrival of the Roosevelt coalition, and a sixth after 1960 and the civil rights movement. (Some see a seventh since the election of Donald Trump.) See, for example, S. Maisel and M. Brewer, *Parties and Elections in America* (Rowman, 2011). On the evolution of the US party system, see Chaps. 14 and 15.

53. On the structure of political conflict in Reconstruction, see N. Barreyre's excellent book, *L'or et la liberté. Une histoire spatiale des Etats-Unis après la guerre de sécession* (Éditions de l'EHESS, 2014); published in English as *Gold and Freedom: The Political Economy of Reconstruction,* trans. A. Goldhammer (University of Virginia Press, 2015).

had lent to pay for the war, whereas the country needed a loose money policy to expand credit to small farmers and manufacturers and finance modest pensions for veterans, even if it meant tolerating moderate inflation and privileging paper money (the so-called greenbacks) and silver dollars over the gold standard to which the bankers wanted to return immediately. The other major issue was the customs tariff: like the Federalists and Whigs before them, the Republicans wanted to impose high tariffs on imported textiles and manufactured goods from the United Kingdom and Europe to protect industry in the Northeast and ensure a flow of cash into the federal treasury (partly to repay the debt and partly to finance infrastructure they deemed useful for industrial development).[54] The Democrats, traditionally protective of states' rights and wary of expanding the federal government, had a field day denouncing the selfishness of New England elites, who they said were always eager to take money from people's pockets to feather their own nests, whereas the West and South needed free trade to expand the market for their agricultural produce.

The Democrats also took up the cause of new immigrants from Europe, mainly Irish and Italian, whom Protestant Republican elites viewed with a wary eye and sought to deny the right to vote by delaying the grant of American citizenship and imposing educational requirements on suffrage. It was partly for this reason, moreover, that northerners allowed southern whites to regain control of their states and deny former slaves the right to vote. At bottom, many Republicans believed that blacks were not ready for citizenship; hence they had no interest in fighting to give them the vote, especially since they wanted to go on denying that right to newly arrived immigrants in the Northeast (at a time when Democrats in New York and Boston were trying to naturalize Irish and Italian immigrants as fast as they could to swell the ranks of their supporters). The Fourteenth Amendment, adopted in 1868 to replace the three-fifths rule, provided that seats in the House of Representatives would henceforth be

---

54. On the ideas and strategies of Boston financial elites (called "Brahmins" in the political vocabulary of the time), see the illuminating book by N. Maggor, *Brahmin Capitalism: Frontiers of Wealth and Populism in America's First Gilded Age* (Harvard University Press, 2017). Some Bostonians tried to invest in southern plantations but soon realized that the "darkies" had no intention of working for nothing (and nursed the "chimerical" hope of owning their own land). Many then reoriented their priorities for investing capital accumulated in northeastern textiles by turning to the West (where they had to deal with pioneers also seeking to protect themselves by, for instance, writing public regulation of water and railroads into their state constitutions).

apportioned on the basis of population, but if the right of adult males to vote was "in any way abridged . . . the basis of representation . . . shall be reduced." This provision might have provided an efficient way to exert pressure on the southern states, but it was never enforced, because the states of the Northeast realized that they had a great deal to lose in view of their own interest in limiting the right to vote.[55] This was clearly an important fork in the road.

Finally, the Fifteenth Amendment, adopted in 1870, forbade (in theory) any racial discrimination regarding the right to vote, but its application was left entirely to the states. Segregationist Democrats were on the way to regaining control of the southern states in a climate of extreme violence marked by numerous lynchings and attacks on former slaves who attempted to assert their new rights and show themselves in public. At times the situation verged on insurrection, as in Louisiana in 1873, when there were two rival governors (one a Democrat, the other a Republican elected with black votes). In view of the determination and organization of the segregationists, who had always held power in the South, it would have taken a very strong will on the part of the North to impose racial equality, and that will simply did not exist. Most northerners blamed the war on a small minority of extremists among the large plantation owners and felt that it was time to leave the rest of the South in peace to manage its own affairs and deal with inequality as it saw fit. Once southerners regained control of their state governments, police, constitutions, and courts and, above all, once the last federal troops departed in 1877 (the date that marks the official end of Reconstruction), southern Democrats were free to put in place the segregationist regime that for nearly a century would allow them to deny blacks the right to vote and exclude them from white schools and public facilities.[56] A specially tailored labor law that made it possible to keep plantation wages low was also introduced,[57] and growing num-

---

55. See Barreyre, *L'or et la liberté*, pp. 175–176.

56. In the 1870s, many blacks had the right to vote (and voted massively Republican) in southern states; some of these (such as Louisiana and South Carolina) had up to 40 percent black representation in their legislatures. Then segregationist laws and rigged educational tests were introduced, decreasing black participation in southern elections from 61 percent to 2 percent between 1885 and 1908. See S. Levitsky and D. Ziblatt, *How Democracies Die* (Penguin, 2018), pp. 89–91.

57. It was illegal, for example, to offer plantation workers higher wages to lure them away from their jobs; violators faced high fines. See S. Naidu, "Recruitment Restrictions and Labor Markets: Evidence from Postbellum U.S. South," *Journal of Labor Economics,* 2010.

bers of blacks who had briefly nursed the hope of full freedom and of some day being able to work their own land began to consider the possibility of a "great migration" to the North.[58]

Such was the new Democratic platform: intransigent defense of segregation in the South, loose money and restructuring of the war debt, opposition to tariffs on manufactured goods, and support for white immigration in the North. More generally, Democrats opposed what they saw as the financial and industrial aristocracy of the Northeast, which had waged the Civil War and freed the slaves only to increase its profits and defend its interests. It was on this complex mix of issues that the Democrats won a majority in Congress in 1874 and won the presidential election of 1884 (having already won more votes, but not the presidency, in 1876, only a little more than ten years after the end of the Civil War). Alternation between parties is normal in a democracy, and these Democratic victories were in part a consequence of the voters' natural fatigue with the Republicans, who had also been tarnished by various financial scandals, as often happens to parties in power. Nevertheless, it is interesting to try to understand the coalition of ideas and aspirations that allowed this alternation to take place so soon after the war, as this coalition would exert great influence on what came later.

Succinctly put, the political ideology that the Democratic Party developed during Reconstruction partook of what one might call "social nativism," or, in this instance perhaps, "social racialism," because blacks were just as much natives of the United States as whites (and more so than the Irish and Italians), even if slaveowners would have been glad to deport them to Africa. One might also speak of "social differentialism" to denote political ideologies that promote a measure of social equality but only within a segment of the population— among whites, say, or people considered to be true "natives" of the territory in question (with the understanding that what is at stake has more to do with the supposed legitimacy of different groups with a claim to occupy the land than with their actual native status), as opposed to blacks or others considered to be outside the community (like non-European immigrants in Europe today). In this instance, the "social" dimension of social nativism was just as real as the "nativism": Democrats succeeded in convincing white voters from the lower

---

58. This process was very gradual. The proportion of African Americans living in the South decreased slowly from 92 percent in 1860 to 85 percent in 1920 before dropping rapidly to 68 percent in 1950 and 53 percent in 1970, where it then stabilized (with a slight upward tendency since 2000).

and middle classes that they were more apt to defend their interests and advance their prospects than the Republicans.

Later in this book we will see how this social-nativist Democratic coalition from the era of Reconstruction contributed to an ambitious program of inequality reduction in the United States, especially with the creation of federal income and estate taxes in the 1910s and the New Deal in the 1930s before finally jettisoning its nativism with the turn to civil rights in the 1960s. We will also study the common features and above all the profound differences between the trajectory of the Democratic Party in the United States in the period 1860–1960 and the development of social nativism in the early twenty-first century, especially in Europe and the United States (but now under the auspices of the Republican Party).[59]

Brazil: Imperial and Mixed-Race Abolition, 1888

We turn now to the case of Brazil. Although less studied than the British, French, and American cases, the abolition of slavery in Brazil in 1888 is also highly instructive. In contrast to the American South, where the number of slaves jumped from 1 million to 4 million between 1800 and 1860, Brazil did not experience spectacular growth of its slave population in the nineteenth century. The country was already home to 1.5 million slaves in 1800, and their number increased only slightly between then and abolition in 1888 (Fig. 6.4). Despite increasingly urgent complaints from the British, Brazilian slave traders continued to do business throughout much of the nineteenth century, at least until 1860, but on a steadily diminishing scale. The important point is that the trade did not allow for growth as rapid as that achieved through natural increase in the United States. Racial mixing and gradual emancipation were also much more widely practiced in Brazil, which helped limit growth of the slave population. In the 2010 Brazil census, 48 percent of the population declared itself to be "white," 43 percent "mixed race," 8 percent "black," and 1 percent "Asian" or "indigenous." In fact, the available research suggests that, however people may describe themselves, more than 90 percent of Brazilians today are of mixed origins, European African and/or European Amerindian, including many who describe themselves as "white." All signs are that racial mixing was already extremely advanced in Brazil by the end of the nineteenth century while

---

59. See Chaps. 10–11 and Chaps. 14–16.

it remains quite marginal to this day in the United States.[60] However, racial mixing does not prevent social distance, discrimination, or inequality (which remains exceptionally high in Brazil today).

The relative stability of the number of slaves (1–1.5 million) in a rapidly growing population in the period 1750–1850 is reflected in the decreasing proportion of slaves, which fell from 50 percent in 1750 to 15–20 percent in 1880—still a high number (Fig. 6.1). Note, too, that the proportion remained above 30 percent in some regions. Historically, the largest concentrations of slaves were found in the sugar plantations of the Nordeste, particularly around Bahia. During the eighteenth century some slaves were moved south (especially to Minas Gerais) following the development of gold and diamond mines, which were soon exhausted; more slaves were then moved south with the development of coffee plantations in the regions of Rio de Janeiro and São Paulo in the nineteenth century. In 1850, the population of Rio was 250,000, of whom 110,000 were slaves (44 percent), a slightly higher proportion than in Salvador de Bahia (33 percent).

In 1807–1808, when the court of Lisbon abandoned the Portuguese capital under threat from Napoleon's troops and moved to Rio de Janeiro, the population of Brazil was around 3 million (half of whom were slaves), roughly the same as the population of Portugal. An event unique in the annals of European colonialism then ensued: in 1822, the heir to the Portuguese throne— after renouncing his Portuguese title to the great consternation of his court— became emperor of Brazil under the name Pedro I, the first head of the newly independent state. The decades that followed were marked by numerous slave rebellions in a country that had already seen many autonomous communities founded by fugitive slaves, starting with the *quilombo dos Palmares* in the seventeenth century, a veritable black republic that survived in a mountainous region for more than a century before succumbing to troops dispatched to put an end to this subversive experiment.[61] A first law mandating emancipation of slaves at age 60 was passed in 1865 after lengthy debate. In 1867, Emperor Pedro II delivered a long speech in which he raised the issue of slavery, provoking an outcry in the Chamber of Deputies and the Senate, then dominated by wealthy property owners and elected by less than 1 percent of the population, with many slaveholders among them.

---

60. See the online appendix.

61. See, for example, B. Bennassar and R. Marin, *Histoire du Brésil* (Pluriel, 2014), pp. 102–108.

Faced with a new surge of slave revolts and threats of dissolution, Brazil's Parliament finally agreed in 1871 to pass a so-called free womb law declaring that children born to enslaved mothers would be emancipated, thus leading gradually to complete abolition. Owners of the mothers of the beneficiaries of this law, known as "ingenues," were obliged to raise them until the age of 6 in order to qualify for a state indemnity, paid in annual rents *(juros)* of 6 percent; alternatively, they could keep the young blacks until the age of 21, forcing them to work without pay, in exchange for a smaller indemnity. Meanwhile, debate on outright abolition continued. From 1880 on, the tension in the country was palpable, so much so that many travelers in the Rio and São Paolo provinces in 1883–1884 believed that revolution was imminent. In 1887 the army declared that it could no longer cope with slave revolts and would no longer arrest fugitive slaves. It was in this context that Parliament enacted general abolition in May 1888, shortly before the fall of the imperial regime in 1889, after it was abandoned by the landed aristocracy whose interests it had been unable to defend. The fall of the regime led to the adoption of the first republican constitution in 1891.[62]

Slavery was ended, but Brazil had not seen the end of the extreme inequality that flowed from it. The constitution of 1891 eliminated the wealth qualification for voting but took care to deny the vote to the illiterate, a provision extended by the constitutions of 1934 and 1946. This immediately excluded about 70 percent of the adult population from the polls in the 1890s; the excluded still represented more than 50 percent of the population in 1950 and roughly 20 percent in 1980. In practice, it was not only former slaves but the poor in general who were banished from political life for a century, from the 1890s to the 1980s. For comparison, India did not hesitate to introduce true universal suffrage in 1947 despite vast social and status differences inherited from the past and despite the country's poverty. Note, too, that if the European countries that extended the suffrage to all men in the late nineteenth and early twentieth centuries had made the right to vote conditional on literacy, a substantial proportion of citizens (particularly in rural districts and among the elderly) would have been excluded. In practice, moreover, literacy requirements often end up granting inordinate power to local officials in charge of registering voters. Similar requirements were used to prevent blacks from voting in the southern United States until the 1960s.

---

62. See Bennassar and Marin, *Histoire du Brésil,* pp. 369–370.

Beyond the slavery question and access to the vote and education, relations between workers and employers remained extremely harsh in Brazil throughout the twentieth century, particularly between landowners on the one hand and agricultural workers and landless peasants on the other. Abundant evidence attests to the extreme violence of social relations in the sugar-producing regions of the Nordeste, where landlords relied on police and state officials to quell strikes, restrain wages, and exploit agricultural labor without limit, especially after the military coup of 1964.[63] Not until the end of the military dictatorship in 1985 and the promulgation of the constitution of 1988 was the right to vote finally extended to everyone, regardless of education. The first election by universal suffrage took place in 1989. In Part Four I will return to the evolution of political conflict in Brazil during the first decades of universal suffrage.[64] At this stage, I will simply insist on a conclusion we have encountered before: namely, that it is impossible to understand the structure of inequality today without taking into account the heavy inegalitarian legacy of slavery and colonialism.

Russia: The Abolition of Serfdom with a Weak State, 1861

We turn finally to the abolition of serfdom in Russia, decided by Tsar Alexander II in 1861. Besides the fact that this major turning point in Russian and European history coincides exactly with the American Civil War, it is interesting to note that the debates surrounding it raised issues comparable with the issue of compensation to slaveowners but with specificities linked to the weakness of the Russian imperial state. Note, too, that the form of serfdom practiced in Russia in the eighteenth and nineteenth centuries was generally considered to be quite harsh. In particular, serfs were not allowed to leave their estates or have access to the courts. Until 1848, serfs were in theory not allowed to own land or buildings. Yet there was in practice quite a wide range of situations across the huge expanse of Russian territory. On the eve of abolition, it has been estimated that European Russia was home to more than 22 million

---

63. This is true especially for the Nordeste, especially in the Pernambuco region, whose democratically elected governor—a man who had tried to develop cooperatives, launch ambitious literacy programs, and enforce some minimal respect for work rules—was violently overthrown by putschists after the coup. See F. Juliao, *Cambao (le joug). La face cachée du Brésil* (Maspero, 1968); R. Linhart, *Le sucre et la faim. Enquête dans les régions sucrières du nord-est brésilien* (Editions de minuit, 1981).

64. See Chap. 16.

serfs, or nearly 40 percent of the population of Russia west of the Urals, dispersed over a vast landscape. Many worked on immense estates, some of which employed thousands of serfs. Rights and living conditions varied with the region and owner. In some cases, serfs rose to occupy positions in which they helped administer estates and were able to accumulate property.[65]

The emancipation of the serfs in 1861, triggered in part by Russia's defeat in the Crimean War (1853–1856), involved many different processes—making it impossible to analyze here. In particular, the abolition of serfdom was followed by agrarian reform, which ultimately gave rise to various forms of communal property, whose effects on agricultural growth have generally been deemed to be much less positive than emancipation itself.[66] One important aspect of the Russian Emancipation Act of 1861 was that it included a complex mechanism for indemnifying the owners of serfs for their loss of property, in some ways comparable to the compensation of slaveowners in the British, French, and Brazilian cases (1833, 1848, and 1888 respectively). The general principle was that, to gain access to communal lands, former serfs were required to pay reimbursements to the state and to their former owners for a period of forty-nine years. In principle, then, these payments would have continued until 1910. The terms of the law were renegotiated many times, however, and most of the payments ended in the 1880s.

Broadly speaking, it is important to note that the process was fairly chaotic and not carefully monitored by the central government, whose administrative and judicial capacity was limited. In particular, there was no imperial cadastre so that it was difficult to allocate or guarantee new land access rights. Tax collection, recruitment of soldiers, and the lower echelons of the court system were largely delegated to the nobility and local elites, as was often the case in trifunctional societies in which the formation of the central state had not progressed very far. Hence the ability of the imperial government to transform power relations in the Russian countryside was relatively limited. The mobility of peasants continued to be restricted, officially under community control, to be sure, but in practice all signs are that former serf owners continued to play a preponderant role.

---

65. See esp. T. Dennison, "Contract Enforcement in Russian Serf Society, 1750–1860," *Economic History Review,* 2013.

66. See A. Markevitch and E. Zhuravskaya, "The Economic Effects of the Abolition of Serfdom: Evidence from the Russian Empire," *American Economic Review,* 2018.

In the eyes of many historians, the emancipation acts of 1861 even led in many cases to reinforced landlord control over the peasantry, for nothing was really done to develop an independent justice system or professional imperial bureaucracy, which would have required a significant increase in the yield of the tax system.[67] The fragile fiscal and financial organization of the Russian central state also explains in part why the imperial government required former serfs to pay landlords for forty-nine years to secure their redemption, rather than envisioning a monetary indemnity financed by public debt and therefore by taxpayers, as in the United Kingdom and France for the abolition of slavery. A new wave of agrarian reforms was attempted in Russia in 1906, with limited effect. Finally, in April 1916, in the midst of World War I, the imperial government opted for a fiscal reform much more ambitious than anything previously attempted, including a progressive tax on total income rather similar to the one adopted in France in July 1914.[68]

Clearly, it was too late. The Bolshevik Revolution broke out in October 1917 before much headway had been made with this reform; it is impossible to know whether the imperial Russian state could have carried it out successfully. The failed experiment with abolition of serfdom in Russia reminds us of a crucial fact: the transformation of trifunctional and slave societies into ownership societies requires the formation of a centralized state capable of guaranteeing property rights; exercising a monopoly of legitimate violence; and establishing a relatively autonomous legal, fiscal, and justice system—otherwise local elites will continue to wield power and maintain subaltern classes in a state of dependence. In Russia, the transition was made directly to something new: a communist society of the soviet type.

---

67. See T. Dennison, "The Institutional Framework of Serfdom in Russia: The View from 1861," in S. Cavacioocchi, *Serfdom and Slavery in the European Economy, 11th–18th Centuries* (Firenze University Press, 2014). See also N. Moon, *The Abolition of Serfdom in Russia, 1762–1907* (Routledge, 2001).

68. See N. Platonova, "L'introduction de l'impôt sur le revenu en Russie impériale: la genèse et l'élaboration d'une réforme inachevée," *Revue historique de droit français et étranger,* 2015.

{ SEVEN }

Colonial Societies: Diversity and Domination

In the previous chapter we looked at slave societies and the manner of their disappearance, particularly in the Atlantic and Euro-American space. This allowed us to observe some surprising facets of the quasi-sacralized private property regime characteristic of the nineteenth century. We saw why it was necessary to indemnify slaveowners but not slaves when slavery was abolished. And we discovered that in Haiti, freed slaves were required to pay a heavy tribute to their former owners as the price of their freedom—a tribute that continued until the middle of the twentieth century. We also analyzed how the American Civil War and the end of slavery in the United States led to the development of a specific system of political parties and ideological cleavages, with important consequences for the subsequent evolution and current structure of inequality and political conflict not only in the United States but also in Europe and in other parts of the world.

We turn now to forms of domination and inequality that were less extreme than slavery but encompassed far vaster regions of the planet under the aegis of Europe's colonial empires, which survived until the 1960s, with far-reaching consequences for today's world. Recent research has shed light on the extent of socioeconomic inequality in both colonial and contemporary societies, and that is where we begin. We will then review the various factors that explain the very high levels of inequality observed in the colonial world. The colonies were to a very large extent organized for the sole benefit of the colonizers, especially regarding social and educational investment. Inequalities of legal status were quite pronounced and involved various forms of forced labor. All of this was shaped—in contrast to slave societies—by an ideology based on concepts of intellectual and civilizational domination in addition to military and extractive domination. Furthermore, the end of colonialism was accompanied, as we will see, by debates about possible regional and transcontinental forms of democratic federalism. With the perspective afforded us by the passage of time, we can see that these debates are rich in lessons for the future, even if they have yet to bear fruit.

The Two Ages of European Colonialism

This is obviously not the place to put forward a general history of the various forms of colonial society, which would far exceed the scope of this book. More modestly, my objective is to situate colonial societies in the broader history of inequality regimes and to bring out those aspects that are most important for the analysis of the subsequent evolution of inequality.

Broadly speaking, it is common to distinguish between two eras of European colonization. The first begins around 1500 with the "discovery" of the Americas and of maritime routes from Europe to India and China and ends in the period 1800–1850, specifically with the gradual extinction of the Atlantic slave trade and the abolition of slavery. The second begins in the period 1800–1850, reaches a peak between 1900 and 1940, and ends with the former colonies' achievement of independence in the 1960s (or even the 1990s if one includes the special case of South Africa and the end of apartheid as an instance of colonialism).

To simplify, the first age of European colonization, between 1500 and 1800–1850, was based on a logic that is today widely recognized as military and extractive. It relied on violent military domination and forced displacement and/or extermination of populations, in particular in the form of the triangular trade and the development of slave societies in the French and British West Indies, the Indian Ocean, Brazil, and North America, as well as with the Spanish conquest of Central and South America.

The second colonial age, from 1800–1850 until 1960, is often said to have been kinder and gentler, especially by the former colonial powers who like to insist on the intellectual and civilizational aspects of the second phase of colonial domination. Although the differences between the two phases are significant, it is important to note that violence was scarcely absent from the second phase and that elements of continuity between the two eras are quite apparent. In particular, as we saw in the previous chapter, the abolition of slavery did not happen all at once but took most of the nineteenth century. Furthermore, slavery was supplanted by various forms of forced labor, which as we will see continued until the middle of the twentieth century, especially in the French colonies. We will also discover that, in terms of concentration of economic resources, postslave colonial societies figure among the most inegalitarian societies history has ever known, not far behind slave societies despite real differences of degree.

It is also common to distinguish between colonies with a significant population of European origin and colonies in which the European settler population was quite small. In the slave societies of the first colonial era (1500–1850), the proportion of slaves reached its highest levels in the French and British West Indies in the 1780s, with slaves accounting for more than 80 percent of the population of the islands and as much as 90 percent in Saint-Domingue (Haiti)—the highest concentration of slaves anywhere in the period and also the site of the first victorious slave rebellion in 1791–1793. Nevertheless, the proportion of Europeans in the West Indies in the eighteenth and nineteenth centuries was close to or above 10 percent, which is a lot compared with most other colonial societies. Slavery rested on total and complete domination of the slave population, which required a significant proportion of colonizers in the population. In the other slave societies that we studied in Chapter 6 and that proved more durable, the proportion of Europeans was even higher—two-thirds on average (compared to one-third slaves) in the southern United States with a minimum just above 40 percent whites (compared to 60 percent slaves) in South Carolina and Mississippi in the 1850s. In Brazil, the slave population was close to 50 percent in the eighteenth century and fell to around 20–30 percent in the second half of the nineteenth century (see Figs. 6.1–6.4).

In both the North American and "Latin" American cases, however, it is important to note that the question of European settlement raises two further issues: the brutal treatment of the native population and interbreeding.[1] In Mexico, for example, it has been estimated that the indigenous population in 1520 was between 15 and 20 million; as a result of military conquest, political chaos, and disease introduced by the Spaniards, the population fell to less than 2 million by 1600. Meanwhile, interbreeding among the indigenous and European populations as well as African populations grew rapidly, accounting for a quarter of the population by 1650, a third to a half by 1820, and nearly two-thirds in 1920. In the regions now occupied by the United States and Canada, the Amerindian population when Europeans first arrived has been estimated at 5 to 10 million before falling to less than a half million in 1900, by which time the population of European descent exceeded 70 million, so that

---

1. European subjection of indigenous populations to forced labor also plays an important (and long-neglected) role in the history of the continent, both in the regions that are now part of Chile and Peru and in Mayan regions and North America. See A. Reséndez, *The Other Slavery: The Uncovered Story of Indian Enslavement in America* (Harcourt, 2016).

the latter became ultra-dominant without significant interbreeding with either the indigenous or African populations.[2]

If we now turn to the empires of the second colonial era (1850–1960), the norm is that the European population was generally quite small or even minuscule, but again there was a great deal of diversity. Note first that European colonial empires in the period 1850–1960 attained much larger transcontinental dimensions than in the first colonial era—indeed, dimensions that were unrivaled in the entire history of humanity. At its peak in 1938, the British colonial empire encompassed a total population of 450 million, including more than 300 million in India (which is a veritable continent unto itself, and about which I will have more to say in Chapter 8); at the time, the metropolitan population of the United Kingdom itself was barely 45 million. The French colonial empire, which reached its zenith at the same moment, numbered around 95 million (including 22 million in North Africa, 35 million in Indochina, 34 million in French West and Equatorial Africa, and 5 million in Madagascar), compared with a little over 40 million in metropolitan France. The Dutch colonial empire comprised roughly 70 million people, mostly in Indonesia, at a time when the population of the Netherlands was barely 8 million. Bear in mind that the political, legal, and military ties that defined the borders of these various empires were highly diverse, as were the conditions under which censuses were conducted, so that the figures cited should be taken as approximate and valid only as indicators of orders of magnitude.[3]

Settler Colonies, Colonies Without Settlement

In most cases European settlement in these vast empires was quite limited. In the interwar years, the European (and mostly British) population of the vast British Raj never exceeded 200,000 (of whom 100,000 were British soldiers) or less than 0.1 percent of the total population of India (more than 300 million). These figures quite eloquently tell us that the type of domination that existed

---

2. On the main estimates of indigenous populations before the arrival of Europeans, see the online appendix (piketty.pse.ens.fr/ideology). The Mexican census of 1921 counted 60 percent of mixed blood *(mestizos),* 30 percent indigenous, and 10 percent "white." The country's multicultural identity is officially recognized by the constitutions, and these questions are no longer posed in current census questionnaires.

3. See the online appendix. The demographic data given here for the French, British, and Dutch empires also rely on the work of D. Cogneau and B. Etemad.

in India had little to do with that which existed in Saint-Domingue. In India, domination was of course based on military superiority, which was demonstrated in undeniable fashion in a number of decisive confrontations, but more than that, it rested on an extremely sophisticated form of political, administrative, police, and ideological organization as well as on numerous local elites and multiple decentralized power structures, all of which led to a kind of consent and acquiescence. Thanks to this organization and ideological domination, with a tiny population of colonizers the British were able to break the resistance and organizational capacity of the colonized—at least up to a point. This order of magnitude—a European settler population of 0.1–0.5 percent—is in fact fairly representative of many regions in the second colonial era (Fig. 7.1). For instance, in French Indochina in the interwar years and into the era of decolonization in the 1950s, the proportion of Europeans in French Indochina was barely 0.1 percent. In the Dutch East Indies (today Indonesia), the European population reached 0.3 percent in the interwar years, and we find similar levels in the same period in British colonies in Africa, such as Kenya and Ghana. In French West Africa (FWA) and French Equatorial Africa (FEA), the European population was about 0.4 percent in the 1950s. In Madagascar, the European population reached a comparatively impressive 1.2 percent in 1945 on the eve of the violent clashes that would lead to independence.

Among the rare examples of authentic settler colonies, one must mention the case of French North Africa, which, along with Boer and British South Africa, offers one of the few examples in colonial history of a confrontation between a significant European minority (roughly 10 percent of the total population) and an indigenous majority (of roughly 90 percent): there, domination was extremely violent and interbreeding virtually nonexistent. This pattern was quite different from what we see in British settler colonies (the United States, Canada, Australia, and New Zealand), where the indigenous population plummeted after the arrival of the Europeans (and there was almost no interbreeding), as well as Latin America, where there was a great deal of interbreeding between the native and European populations, especially in Mexico and Brazil.

In the 1950s, the European population, essentially of French origin but with Italian and Spanish minorities, accounted for nearly 4 percent of the total population in Morocco, 8 percent in Tunisia, and more than 10 percent in Algeria. In the Algerian case, European settlers numbered about 1 million on the eve of the war for independence out of a total population of barely 10 million. It was, moreover, a European population of fairly long standing, since

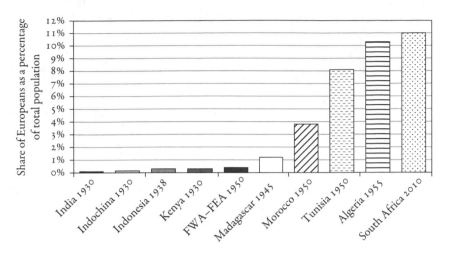

FIG. 7.1. The proportion of Europeans in colonial societies

Interpretation: The proportion of the population of European origin in colonial society between 1930 and 1955 was 0.1–0.3 percent in India, Indochina, and Indonesia, 0.3–0.4 percent in Kenya and French West Africa (FWA), 1.2 percent in Madagascar, nearly 4 percent in Morocco, 8 percent in Tunisia, 10 percent in Algeria in 1955 (13 percent in 1906, 14 percent in 1931). The proportion of whites in South Africa was 11 percent in 2010 (and between 15 and 20 percent from 1910 to 1990). *Sources and series:* piketty.pse.ens.fr/ideology.

the French colonization of Algeria began in 1830; the settler population began to grow quite rapidly in the 1870s. In the census of 1906, the European share of the population exceeded 13 percent and rose as high as 14 percent in 1936 before falling sharply to 10–11 percent in the 1950s owing to even more rapid growth of the indigenous Muslim population. The French were particularly well represented in the cities. In the 1954 census, there were 280,000 Europeans in Algiers compared with 290,000 Muslims for a total of 570,000. Oran, the second largest city in the country, had a population of 310,000, of whom 180,000 were European and 130,000 Muslim. The French colonizers, certain of their own righteousness, rejected independence for a country they regarded as their own.

Against all probability the French political class insisted that France would hold on to this particular colony ("Algeria is France"), but the settlers were wary of the government in Paris, which they suspected, not without reason, of being prepared to abandon the country to the independence forces. In 1958 French generals in Algeria attempted a putsch, which might have ended in an autonomous Algerian colony under the control of the settlers. But the events in

Algeria in fact led to General Charles de Gaulle's return to power in Paris, and the general was soon left with no choice but to put an end to the brutal war and accept Algerian independence in 1962. It is natural to compare these events with what happened in South Africa, where, after the end of British colonization, the white minority managed to hold on to power from 1946 until 1994 under the apartheid regime, about which I will say more later. The white minority in South Africa represented 15–20 percent of the population; by 2010 this had fallen to 11 percent (Fig. 7.1), owing to white departures and the rapid increase of the black population. This is a level quite close to that of French Algeria, and it is interesting to compare the level of inequality observed in both cases given the many differences and similarities between the two colonial systems.

Slave and Colonial Societies: Extreme Inequality

What can we say about the extent of socioeconomic inequality in slave and colonial societies, and what comparisons can be made with inequality today? Unsurprisingly, slave and colonial societies rank among the most inegalitarian ever observed. Nevertheless, the orders of magnitude and their variation in time in space are interesting in themselves and deserve to be examined closely.

The most extreme case of inequality for which we have evidence is that of the French and British slave islands in the late eighteenth century. Let's begin with Saint-Domingue in the 1780s, when slaves represented 90 percent of the population. Recent research allows us to estimate that the wealthiest 10 percent of the island's population—slaveowners (including some who resided partially or totally in France), white settlers, and a small mixed-race minority— appropriated roughly 80 percent of the wealth produced in Saint-Domingue every year, whereas the poorest 90 percent, which is to say the slaves, received (in the form of food and clothing) the equivalent in monetary value of barely 20 percent of annual production—more or less the subsistence level. Note that this estimate was carried out in such a way as to minimize inequality. It is possible that the share going to the top decile was in fact greater than 80 percent of the wealth produced, perhaps as high as 85–90 percent.[4] In any case, it could

---

4. See the online appendix. The available data allow us to estimate that French settlers and planters (about 5 percent of the population) claimed the equivalent of about 70 percent of the island's domestic production. The share going to people of mixed race (also 5 percent of the population) and the least badly treated slaves can be esti-

not have been much higher owing to the subsistence constraint. In other slave societies in the West Indies and Indian Ocean, where slaves generally represented 80–90 percent of the population, all available evidence suggests that the distribution of the wealth produced was not much different. In slave societies where the proportion of slaves was smaller, such as Brazil and the southern United States (30–50 percent, or as high as 60 percent in a few states), inequality was less extreme, with the top decile claiming an estimated 60–70 percent of annual income depending on the extent of inequality in the free white population.

Other recent research provides data for comparison with nonslave colonial societies. The available statistics are limited, primarily because tax systems in the colonies relied for the most part on indirect taxation. There were, however, some British and to a lesser extent French colonies in the first half of the twentieth century in which the competent authorities (governors and administrators theoretically under the supervision of the colonial ministry and the metropolitan government but in practice allowed a certain autonomy in circumstances that varied widely) applied progressive direct income taxes similar to those levied in the metropole. Statistics derived from those taxes have survived, especially for the interwar years and the period just before independence. Facundo Alvaredo and Denis Cogneau have worked on such data from the French colonial archives, while Anthony Atkinson has done the same with data from the British and South African colonial archives.[5]

In regard to Algeria, the available data allow us to estimate that the top decile's share was close to 70 percent of total income in 1930—hence a lower level of inequality than in Saint-Domingue in 1780 but significantly higher than in metropolitan France in 1910 (Fig. 7.2). Of course, this does not mean that the situation of the poorest 90 percent in colonial Algeria (essentially the Muslim population) was in any way close or comparable to that of the slaves

---

mated at 10–15 percent, depending on one's assumptions. In all cases, the top decile's share is 80 percent or higher, more than has ever been observed anywhere else.

5. For sources and hypotheses used, see the online appendix. For more detailed analyses, see F. Alvaredo, D. Cogneau, and T. Piketty, "Income Inequality under Colonial Rule. Evidence from French Algeria, Cameroon, Indochina and Tunisia, 1920–1960," WID.world, 2019; A. Atkinson, "The Distribution of Top Incomes in Former British Africa," WID.world, 2015; F. Alvaredo and A. Atkinson, Colonial Rule, *Apartheid and Natural Resources: Top Incomes in South Africa, 1903–2007* (CEPR Discussion Paper No. 8155, 2010).

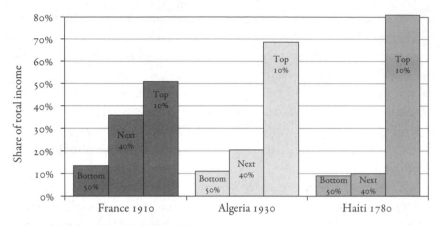

FIG. 7.2. Inequality in colonial and slave societies

Interpretation: The top 10 percent of earners received more than 80 percent of total income in Saint-Domingue (Haiti) in 1780 (where the population was 90 percent slaves and 10 percent Europeans, compared with 70 percent in colonial Algeria in 1930 (90 percent natives and 10 percent European settlers), and around 50 percent in metropolitan France in 1910. *Sources and series:* piketty.pse.ens.fr/ideology.

of Saint-Domingue. Among the crucial dimensions of social inequality are some that radically distinguish one inequality regime from another, starting with the right to mobility, the right to a private and family life, and the right to own property. Nevertheless, from the standpoint of distribution of material resources, colonial Algeria in 1930 was in an intermediate position between proprietarian France in 1910 and Saint-Domingue in 1780, perhaps a little closer to the latter than the former (although the lack of precision in the available data makes it difficult to be certain about this).

If we now broaden our spatial and temporal view and compare the share of wealth produced in one year that was appropriated by the wealthiest 10 percent, we find that slave societies such as Saint-Domingue in 1780 were the most inegalitarian in all of history, followed by colonial societies such as South Africa in 1950 and Algeria in 1930. Social-democratic Sweden around 1980 was one of the most egalitarian ever seen in terms of income distribution, so we can begin to make some judgments about the variety of possible situations. In Sweden, the top decile's share of total income was less than 25 percent, compared with 35 percent for Western Europe and around 50 percent for the United States in 2018; and for proprietarian Europe in the Belle Époque, the top decile's share of total income was around 55 percent for Brazil in 2018, 65 percent for the Middle East in 2018, roughly 70 percent

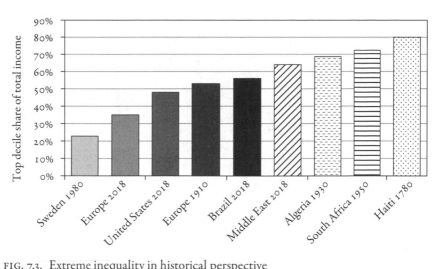

FIG. 7.3. Extreme inequality in historical perspective

Interpretation: Among the countries observed, the top decile's share of income ranged from 23 percent in Sweden in 1980 to 81 percent in Saint-Domingue (Haiti) in 1780 (where the population was 90 percent slaves). Colonial societies such as Algeria and South Africa in the period 1930–1950 rank among the most unequal societies in history, with about 70 percent of income going to the top decile, which included the European population. *Sources and series:* piketty.pse.ens.fr/ideology.

for colonial Algeria in 1950 or South Africa in 1950, and 80 percent for Saint-Domingue (Fig. 7.3).

If we look now at the share of the top centile (the wealthiest 1 percent), which enables us to include a larger number of colonial societies in the comparison (especially those with limited European populations, for which the available sources generally do not allow us to estimate the total income of the top decile), the terms of comparison are slightly different (Fig. 7.4). We find that some colonial societies stand out for an exceptionally high level of inequality at the peak of the distribution. Southern Africa is a case in point: the top centile's share was 30–35 percent in South Africa and Zimbabwe in the 1950s and more than 35 percent in Zambia. These were countries in which tiny white elites exploited vast landed estates or derived significant profits from other sectors such as mining. Furthermore, the top thousandth or ten-thousandth claimed an exceptionally large share. This was true to a slightly lesser extent in French Indochina. There, the top centile's share approached 30 percent, reflecting the very good pay of the colonial administrative elite as well as very high income and profits in sectors such as rubber (although the available data do not allow for a

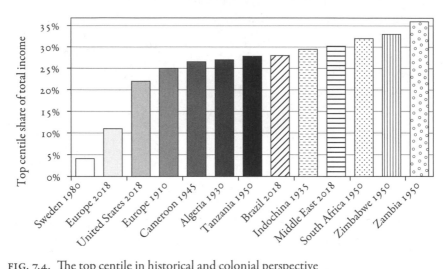

FIG. 7.4. The top centile in historical and colonial perspective

Interpretation: Of all societies observed (except slave societies) the top centile's share of income varied from 4 percent in Sweden in 1980 to 36 percent in Zambia in 1950. Colonial societies rank among the most inegalitarian ever seen. *Sources and series:* piketty. pse.ens.fr/ideology.

detailed breakdown). By contrast, in other colonial societies, we find that although the top centile's share was quite high (for example, 25 percent in Algeria, Cameroon, and Tanzania in the period 1930–1950), this was not very different from the levels observed in Belle Époque Europe or in the United States today, and it was distinctly lower than the levels seen today in Brazil and the Middle East (roughly 30 percent). As far as the top centile's share is concerned, all of these different societies are ultimately fairly similar, especially when compared to social-democratic Sweden in 1980 (with a top centile share below 5 percent) or Europe in 2018 (around 10 percent).

In other words, the summit of the income hierarchy (the wealthiest 1 percent and beyond) was not always all that elevated in colonial societies, at least when compared with very inegalitarian contemporary societies. Take colonial Algeria, for instance: the top centile's position relative to the average Algerian income at the time was not much higher than the top centile's position in metropolitan France compared with the average metropolitan income in the Belle Époque. Indeed, in strict standard-of-living terms, the top centile in Algeria was markedly inferior to the top metropolitan centile. By contrast, if one considers the top decile overall, then its distance from the rest of society was noticeably smaller in colonial Algeria than in France in 1910 (Figs. 7.2–7.3).

In fact, there are some societies in which a tiny elite of owners (roughly 1 percent of the population) stands apart from the rest of society by virtue of its wealth and lifestyle and other societies in which a broad colonial elite (roughly 10 percent of the population) differentiates itself from the indigenous masses. These parameters define very distinct inequality regimes and systems of power and domination, each with its own specific modes of conflict resolution.

More generally, it was not always the size of the income gap that differentiated colonial inequality from other inequality regimes but rather the identity of the victors—in other words, the fact that colonizers occupied the top of the hierarchy. Colonial tax archives do not always give a clear picture of the respective shares of colonizers and natives in different income tranches. Wherever the sources speak clearly, however—whether in North Africa, Cameroon, Indochina, or South Africa—the results are unambiguous. Although the European population was always a small minority, it always accounted for the vast majority of those with the highest incomes. In South Africa, where fiscal records in the apartheid period were tabulated separately by race, we find that whites always accounted for more than 98 percent of the taxpayers in the top centile. The other 2 percent were Asian (mostly Indian), not blacks, who accounted for less than 0.1 percent of the top earners. In Algeria and Tunisia, the data are not perfectly comparable, but the available indicators show that Europeans generally accounted for 80–95 percent of the top earners.[6] This was certainly not as small a percentage as in South Africa, but it nevertheless indicates that the economic domination of the colonizers was virtually absolute.

As for the comparison between Algeria and South Africa, it is interesting to note that Algeria is less inegalitarian in terms of the income distribution, but the difference is relatively small, especially if one looks at the top decile (Figs. 7.3–7.4). The white hyper-elite (top centile or thousandth) was certainly less prosperous in Algeria than in South Africa, but from the

---

6. The available records show that natives accounted for 5 percent of the highest earners (roughly the top centile) in Algeria and up to 20 percent in Tunisia. The estimates are not comparable, however, because Jews were classified as "Europeans" in Algeria (where the Crémieux decree of 1860 granted French nationality to "indigenous Israelites," some of whom had lived in North Africa since being expelled from Spain and the end of the *Reconquista*), in contrast to "Muslims." In Tunisia, Jews were counted as "non-European" along with Muslims, and they no doubt accounted for a large share (perhaps more than half) of the native high earners. See the online appendix.

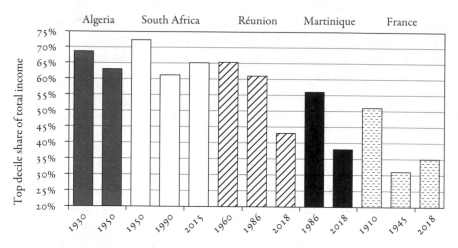

FIG. 7.5. Extreme inequality: Colonial and postcolonial trajectories

Interpretation: The top decile's share decreased in colonial Algeria between 1930 and 1950 and in South Africa between 1950 and 2018, while remaining at a level that ranks among the highest in history. In French overseas *départements* like Réunion and Martinique, income inequality has decreased significantly, while remaining higher than in metropolitan France. *Sources and series:* piketty.pse.ens.fr/ideology.

standpoint of the top decile the two countries were probably not so far apart. In both cases there was considerable distance between the white colonizers and the rest of the population. To be sure, the concentration of income seems to have decreased in Algeria between 1930 and 1950 as well as in South Africa between 1950 and 1990, but in both countries it remained extremely high (Fig. 7.5).

It is also striking that the top decile's share has increased in South Africa since the end of apartheid (we will come back to this point). Note, too, that the former French slave islands Réunion, Martinique, and Guadeloupe, which became French *départements* in 1946 (a century after the abolition of slavery in 1848), have remained extremely unequal in terms of income distribution. Consider Réunion, for example: fiscal archives recently studied by Yajna Govind show that the top decile's share of total income exceeded 65 percent in 1960 and was still above 60 percent in 1986—levels close to those observed in colonial Algeria and South Africa—before dropping to 43 percent in 2018, which is still much higher than in metropolitan France. The persistence of such a high level of inequality is explained in part by inadequate investment and by the existence of government officials who are very highly paid, at least by local standards, and who in many cases come from France.[7]

Maximal Inequality of Property, Maximal Inequality of Income

Before analyzing the roots of colonial inequalities and the reasons for their persistence, it will be useful to clarify the following point. When we discuss the issue of "extreme" inequality, we need to distinguish between the distribution of property and the distribution of income. In regard to inequality of property, by which I mean the distribution of goods and assets of all kinds that one is allowed to own under the existing legal regime, it is fairly common to observe an extremely strong concentration, with nearly all wealth owned by the wealthiest 10 percent or even the wealthiest 1 percent and virtually no property ownership by the poorest 50 or even 90 percent. In particular, as we saw in Part One, the ownership societies that flourished in Europe in the nineteenth and early twentieth centuries were characterized by extreme concentration of property. In France, the United Kingdom, and Sweden during the Belle Époque (1880–1914), the wealthiest 10 percent owned 80–90 percent of what there was to own (land, buildings, equipment, and financial assets, net of debt), and the wealthiest 1 percent alone owned 60–70 percent.[8] Extreme inequality of ownership can certainly pose political and ideological problems but raises no difficulty from a strictly material point of view. Strictly speaking, one can imagine societies in which the wealthiest 10 or 1 percent own 100 percent of all wealth. And that is not the end of it: large classes of the population can have negative wealth if their debts outweigh their assets. In slave societies, for example, slaves owe all their working time to their owners. The owning classes can therefore own more than 100 percent of the wealth because they own both goods and people. Inequality of wealth is above all inequality of power in society, and in theory it has no limit, to the extent that the owner-established apparatus of repression or persuasion (as the case may be) is able to hold society together and perpetuate this equilibrium.[9]

---

7. See Y. Govind, "Post-Colonial Inequality Trends: From the 'Four old colonies' to the French Overseas Departments," WID.world, 2019.
8. See esp. Figs. 4.1–4.2 and Figs. 5.4–5.6.
9. See the online appendix for examples of slave societies in which the top decile's share exceeded 100 percent of the value of nonhuman goods.

Income inequality is different. It refers to the distribution of the flow of wealth that takes place each year, a flow that is necessarily constrained to respect the subsistence of the poorest members of society, for otherwise a substantial segment of the population would die in short order. It is possible to live without owning anything but not without eating. Concretely, in a very poor society, where the output per person is just at the subsistence level, no lasting income inequality is possible. Everyone must receive the same (subsistence) income, so that the top decile's share of total income would be 10 percent (and the top centile's share 1 percent). By contrast, the richer a society is, the more it becomes materially possible to sustain a very high level of income inequality. For example, if output per person is on the order of one hundred times the subsistence level, it is theoretically possible for the top centile to take 99 percent of the wealth produced while the rest of the population remains at subsistence level. More generally, it is easy to show that the maximal materially possible level of inequality in any society increases with that society's average standard of living (Fig. 7.6).[10]

The notion of maximal inequality is useful because it helps us to understand why income inequality can never be as extreme as property inequality. In practice, the share of total income going to the poorest 50 percent is always at least 5–10 percent (and generally on the order of 10–20 percent), whereas the share of property owned by the poorest 50 percent can be close to zero (often barely 1–2 percent or even negative). Similarly, the share of total income going to the wealthiest 10 percent is generally no more than 50–60 percent, even in the most inegalitarian societies (with the exception of a few slave and colonial societies of the eighteenth, nineteenth, and twentieth centuries, in which this share rose as high as 70–80 percent), whereas the share of property owned by the wealthiest 10 percent regularly reaches 80–90 percent, especially in the proprietarian societies of the nineteenth and early twentieth centuries, and it could rapidly regain such levels in the neo-proprietarian societies in full flower today.

---

10. The notion of maximal inequality is quite close to the idea of "inequality frontier" used by B. Milanovic, P. Lindert, and J. Williamson ("Preindustrial Inequality," *Economic Journal,* 2011), except that I use shares of the top decile and centile instead of the Gini coefficient. To be clear, income can be temporarily negative (for instance, in case of operating losses), but consumption cannot be. In practice, the average income and average consumption of the poorest 50 percent coincide almost perfectly (one does not observe significant saving or dissaving on average, which reflects the fact that the average wealth of this group tends to be stable at a near zero or negative level). See the online appendix and Chap. 11.

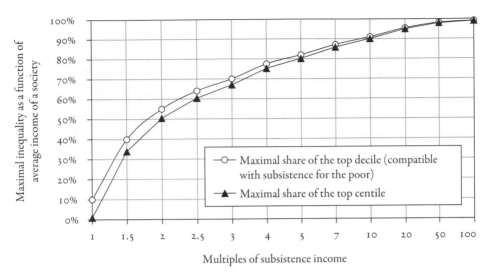

FIG. 7.6. Subsistence income and maximal inequality

Interpretation: In a society where the average income is three times the subsistence income, the maximal share of the top income decile (comparable with a subsistence income for the bottom 90 percent) is equal to 70 percent of total income, and the maximal share of the top centile (compatible with subsistence income for the bottom 99 percent) is 67 percent. The richer a society is, the higher the level of inequality it can achieve. *Sources and series:* piketty.pse.ens.fr/ideology.

The "material" determinants of inequality should not be exaggerated, however. In reality, history teaches us that what determines the level of inequality is above all society's ideological, political, and institutional capacity to justify and structure inequality and not the level of wealth or development as such. "Subsistence income" is itself a complex idea and not just a simple reflection of biological reality. It depends on representations fashioned by each society and is always a concept with many dimensions (such as food, clothing, housing, hygiene, and so on), which cannot be correctly measured by a single monetary index. In the late 2010s, it was common to situate the subsistence threshold at 1–2 euros per day; extreme poverty was measured at the global level as the number of people living on less than 1 euro per day. Available estimates show that per capita national income was less than 100 euros per month in the eighteenth and early nineteenth centuries (compared with 1,000 euros per month in 2020, with both amounts expressed in 2020 euros). This implies that a substantial fraction of the population was living not far above the subsistence level in the eighteenth century, a conclusion confirmed by the very high mortality rates and very short life expectancies observed for all age groups, but it also suggests that there was some room for maneuver, and hence that several different inequality regimes were possible.[11] More specifically, in Saint-Domingue, a prosperous island thanks to its production of sugar and cotton, the market value of output per capita was on the order of two or three times higher than the global average at the time, so that it was easy from a strict material point of view to extract a maximal level of profit. If a society's average per capita income exceeds four to five times the subsistence level, that is enough, moreover, for maximal inequality to reach extreme levels, where the top decile or centile can claim as much as 80–90 percent of total income (Fig. 7.6).

In other words, although it is indeed difficult for an extremely poor society to develop an extremely hierarchical inequality regime, a society does not have to be very rich to attain a very high level of inequality. Specifically, in strictly material terms, quite a number—perhaps most—societies that have existed since antiquity could have chosen extreme levels of inequality, comparable with those observed in Saint-Domingue, and today's wealthy societies could go even further (and some may do so in the future).[12] Inequality is determined primarily by ideological and political factors, not by economic or technological constraints. Why did slave and colonial societies attain such exceptionally high levels of inequality? Because they were constructed around specific political

---

11. See Figs. I.1–I.2. In other words, the world presumably moved from a global average income on the order of three times the subsistence income to an average income thirty times higher. These orders of magnitude are meant only to be suggestive, but I want to warn against overly mechanical interpretations: the price indices used for comparing purchasing power over the long run are incapable of accounting for the magnitude of the transformations that took place and the diversity and multidimensionality of individual situations. In statistical language, an average price index can conceal very different relative prices for prime necessities of life, which must be examined one by one if one wants to achieve a full understanding of how conditions of poverty evolved.

12. According to available estimates, and to the extent that such comparisons make sense, the average global income in antiquity was only a little lower than in the eighteenth century (thus on the order of one-third the subsistence level). In the wealthiest European, Asian, African, and Mesoamerican societies, average income was significantly higher than the global average and therefore quite sufficient to allow for a high level of maximal inequality. See the online appendix.

and ideological projects and relied on specific power relations and legal and institutional systems. The same is true of ownership societies, trifunctional societies, social-democratic and communist societies, and indeed of human societies in general.

Note, moreover, that while history has given us examples of societies that come close to the maximal level of income inequality in terms of the top decile's share (around 70–80 percent of total income in the most inegalitarian colonial and slave societies and 60–70 percent in today's most inegalitarian societies, especially in the Middle East and South Africa), the story of the top centile is different. There, the highest top centile shares amount to 20–35 percent of total income (Fig. 7.4), which is of course quite a high level but still quite a bit below the 70–80 percent of annual output that the top centile could in theory appropriate once average national income exceeds three to four times the subsistence level (Fig. 7.6). No doubt the explanation for this has to do with the fact that it is no simple matter to build an ideology along with institutions that would allow such a narrow group, just 1 percent of the population, to persuade the rest of society to cede control of nearly all newly produced resources. Maybe a handful of particularly imaginative techno-billionaires will be able to do so in the future, but to date no elite has managed such a feat. In the case of Saint-Domingue, which represents the absolute height of inequality in this study, we estimate that the top centile's share attained, at a minimum, 55 percent of the annual wealth produced, coming quite close to the theoretical maximum (Fig. 7.7). I must stress, however, that this calculation is somewhat contrived in that it includes among the top centile slaveowners who were in fact residing primarily in France rather than Saint-Domingue and who enriched themselves on the sales of goods exported from the island.[13] Perhaps this strategy of putting some distance between the top centile and the rest is in general a good way of making inequality more bearable than when it involves cohabitation in the same society. In the case of Saint-Domingue, however, it was not enough to prevent eventual revolt and expropriation.

---

13. I am assuming here that French owners who profited from goods exported from the island (roughly 55 percent of average economic value added between 1760 and 1790) were a tiny group of no more than a few thousand and hence less than 1 percent of the population of Saint-Domingue (more than 500,000 in 1790). Since the archives containing records of the compensation paid by Haiti to former slaveowners after 1825 (via the Caisse des Dépôts) have yet to be opened and studied systematically, it is difficult to say more. See the online appendix.

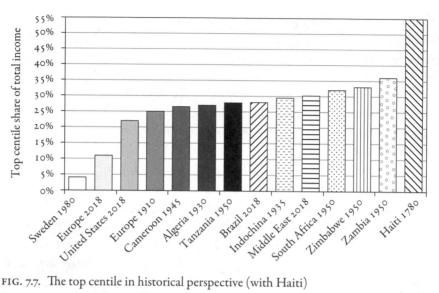

FIG. 7.7. The top centile in historical perspective (with Haiti)

Interpretation: If one includes slave societies such as Saint-Domingue (Haiti) in 1780, then the top centile share can go as high as 50–60 percent of total income. *Sources and series:* piketty.pse.ens.fr/ideology.

Colonization for the Colonizers: Colonial Budgets

We turn now to the question of the origins and persistence of colonial inequalities. Among the justifications of the inequalities associated with slavery, we saw in Chapter 6 that economic and commercial competition among rival state powers ranked high, along with denunciation of the hypocrisies of industrial inequality. These arguments also play a role in justifying postslavery colonial domination, but for the colonizers the main justification was always to insist on their *mission civilisatrice* (to use the standard French phrase, which translates into English as "civilizing mission"). From the standpoint of the colonizers, that mission depended first on keeping order and promoting a proprietarian (and potentially universal) model of development and second on a form of domination that saw itself as intellectual and founded on the diffusion of science and learning.[14] It is therefore interesting to study how the colonies

---

14. This duality of the civilizing mission (both military and intellectual, founded on both keeping order and maintaining spiritual supervision) is in some ways reminiscent of the trifunctional schema with its warrior and clerical elites: the ternary logic is simply expanded to encompass international and interstate relations.

were organized concretely, particularly with respect to their budgets, taxes, and legal and social systems; more generally, it will be helpful to examine the various development models that colonizers put in place. Unfortunately, research on these topics is limited, but enough is known to draw some preliminary conclusions.

Broadly speaking, an abundance of evidence shows that colonies were organized primarily for the benefit of the colonizers and the metropole and that any investment in social and educational improvements for the benefit of the indigenous population was extremely limited, not to say nonexistent. We find the same low levels of investment in France's so-called overseas territories, particularly in the West Indies and Indian Ocean, which have remained attached to France to this day; this may help to explain the persistence of glaring inequalities both within these territories and between them and metropolitan France. For example, French parliamentary reports from the 1920s and 1930s noted extremely low rates of schooling in Martinique and Guadeloupe and, more generally, the "lamentable" state of the school systems on both islands.[15] The situation gradually improved in both territories after they became *départements* in 1946; it also improved to a lesser extent in other French colonies in the 1950s, when the metropole was still hoping to hold on to pieces of its empire. But the accumulated lag was significant, and it would take half a century for the overseas *départements* to reduce inequalities to anything close to metropolitan levels (Fig. 7.5).

Recent work, especially that of Denis Cogneau, Yannick Dupraz, Elise Huilery, and Sandrine Mesplé-Somps, has given us a better understanding of colonial budgets in North Africa, Indochina, and the French West and Equatorial Africa and how they evolved in the late nineteenth and first half of the twentieth centuries.[16] The general principle of French colonization, at least in the second colonial empire (that is, from 1850 to 1960 or so), was that the colonies should be self-sufficient in budgetary terms. In other words, taxes paid in each colony should suffice to finance expenditures in that colony, no more and no less. There should be no fiscal transfer from the colonies to France or

---

15. See N. Schmidt, *La France a-t-elle aboli l'esclavage? Guadeloupe, Martinique, Guyane, 1830–1935* (2009), p. 340.

16. See esp. D. Cogneau, Y. Dupraz, and S. Mesplé-Somps, *Fiscal Capacity and Dualism in Colonial States: The French Empire 1830–1962* (EHESS and Ecole d'économie de Paris, 2018). See also E. Huilery, "The Black Man's Burden: The Costs of Colonization of French West Africa," *Journal of Economic History*, 2014.

from France to the colonies. And indeed, in formal terms, colonial budgets were balanced throughout the period of colonization. Taxes equaled expenditures, in particular in the Belle Époque (1880–1914) and in the interwar years (1918–1939), and more generally throughout the period 1850–1945. The only exception came in the period immediately prior to independence, which roughly coincides with the Fourth Republic (1946–1958), during which we find a modest fiscal transfer from France to the colonies.

It is important, however, to understand what "balanced" colonial budgets meant in the period 1850–1945. In practice, it meant that budgetary costs fell primarily on the colonized for the exclusive benefit of the colonizers. In terms of taxation, we find mainly regressive taxes, with higher rates on low incomes than on high incomes: consumption taxes, indirect taxes, and above all a *capitation,* or head tax, meaning a tax of a certain amount on each resident, whether rich or poor, without any consideration for the taxpayer's ability to pay. This is the least sophisticated form of taxation imaginable, which Ancien Régime France had largely done away with in the eighteenth century, even before the Revolution. Furthermore, these colonial budgets make no mention of *corvées,* or days of forced labor that colonized people owed to the colonial administration, about which I will say more later.

It also bears emphasizing that the level of fiscal extraction was relatively high in view of the poverty of the societies in question. From the available data about output levels (including self-produced foodstuffs), we estimate that in 1925 taxes amounted to nearly 10 percent of GDP in North Africa and Madagascar and more than 12 percent in Indochina, which is almost as high as in the metropole at the same time (where 16 percent of GDP went to taxes), and more than in France from 1800 to 1914 (less than 10 percent) as well as many poor countries today.

Last but perhaps most important, on the expenditure side we find that colonial budgets were designed for the exclusive benefit of the French and European population, in particular to provide very comfortable salaries for the governor, high colonial administrators, and police. In short, the colonized populations paid heavy taxes to finance the luxurious lifestyles of the people who came to dominate them politically and militarily. There was also some investment in infrastructure as well as meager spending on education and health, but most of that was intended for the colonizers. Generally speaking, the number of public officials in the colonies, especially teachers and doctors, was quite small, but they were exceptionally well paid compared to the average local income. Looking at the budgets for all the French colonies in 1925, we find, for example, that there were barely two civil servants for every 1,000 residents, but each of them was paid at roughly ten times the average per capita income. By contrast, in metropolitan France at that time, there were roughly ten civil servants per 1,000 residents, and each was paid about twice the average per capita income.[17]

In some cases, colonial budgets recorded separately salaries paid to civil servants from the metropole and those recruited from the indigenous population. In Indochina and Madagascar, for example, we find that Europeans represented roughly 10 percent of civil servants but received more than 60 percent of total salaries. Sometimes it is also possible to distinguish the amounts spent on different populations, especially for education, because the school systems open to the children of colonizers were usually strictly segregated from those reserved for native children. In Morocco, primary and secondary schools reserved for Europeans received 79 percent of the total educational expenditure in 1925 (although they accounted for only 4 percent of the population). In the same period less than 5 percent of native children attended school in North Africa and Indochina and less than 2 percent in FWA. It is particularly striking to note that this glaring inequality does not seem to have improved in the final stages of colonization, despite the fact that the metropole had begun to invest more resources in the colonies. In Algeria, budget records show that schools reserved for colonizers received 78 percent of total expenditure on education in 1925 and 82 percent in 1955, even though the war for independence had already begun. The colonial system operated in such an inegalitarian manner that it appears to have been largely resistant to reform.

Of course, one should take into account the fact that all educational systems at the time were extremely elitist, including in the metropole. As we will see later, educational expenditure is still to this day quite unequally distributed in terms of both a child's social origin and that child's early educational success (the two criteria are correlated, but not completely). Lack of both transparency and reformist ambition in this area is one of the many challenges that must be faced by anyone who hopes to reduce inequality in the future, and no country is really in a position to give lessons on this subject. In any case, the degree of educational inequality in colonial societies seems to have been exceptionally high, much more so than elsewhere. Take the case of Algeria in the early 1950s: we estimate that the 10 percent of primary,

---

17. See Cogneau, Dupraz, and Mesplé-Somps, *Fiscal Capacity and Dualism*, p. 35.

secondary, and tertiary students who benefited the most from social expenditure on education in each age cohort (meaning, in practice, children of colonizers) received more than 80 percent of all monies spent on education (Fig. 7.8). If we carry out the same calculation for France in 1910, which was extremely stratified in terms of education in the sense that the lower classes rarely progressed beyond the primary level, we find that the top 10 percent in terms of educational expenditure received only 38 percent of the total monies spent, compared with 26 percent for the least educated 50 percent of each age cohort. This is still a significant level of educational inequality, given that the second group is by construction five times as large as the first. In other words, eight times as much money was spent on each child in the top 10 percent compared with each child in the bottom 50 percent. Inequality of educational expenditure decreased significantly in France between 1910 and 2018, although today's system continues to invest nearly three times as much per child in the top 10 percent compared with the bottom 50 percent, which is rather astonishing for a system that is supposed to reduce social reproduction (we will come back to this when we study the criteria of a fair educational system). At this stage, note simply that educational inequality in colonial societies such as French Algeria were incomparably higher: the ratio of money spent per child of the colonizers to money spent per child of the colonized was forty to one.

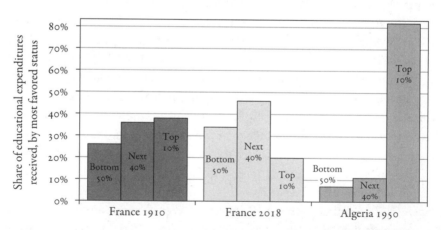

FIG. 7.8. Colonies for the colonizers: Inequality of educational investment in historical perspective

Interpretation: In Algeria in 1950, the most favored 10 percent (the colonizers) received 82 percent of total educational expenditure. The comparable figure for France was 38 percent in 1910 and 20 percent in 2018. *Sources and series:* piketty.pse.ens.fr/ideology.

During the final phase of colonization (1945–1960), the French state sought for the first time to invest significant amounts in the colonies. In decline, imperial France tried to promote a developmental perspective in the hope of persuading the colonies to remain part of an empire redefined as a social and democratic "French Union." But as we have seen, the apportionment of state expenditure in the colonies reproduced existing inegalitarian structures. Beyond that, one should not overstate the magnitude of the metropole's sudden generosity. In the 1950s, transfers from France to colonial budgets never exceeded 0.5 percent of the metropole's annual national income. Such sums, while not totally negligible, quickly aroused opposition from many sides in France.[18] These transfers were roughly of the same order (as a percentage of national income) as the net contribution of the wealthiest member states of the European Union (EU) (including France and Germany) to the EU budget in the decade 2010–2020; we will have more to say about what such amounts signify concretely when we look at the problems and prospects of European political integration.[19] As for the French colonial empire, it is not really correct to speak of "transfers to the colonies," given that these sums were mainly intended to pay expatriate French civil servants, who were handsomely remunerated and worked for the benefit of the colonizers. In any case, it is worth comparing the 0.5 percent of national income transferred from the metropole to civilian budgets in the colonies in the 1950s with the much larger sums (more than 2 percent of metropolitan national income) devoted to the military for the purpose of maintaining order in the colonies in the late 1950s. Apart from this final phase, moreover, it is worth noting that the sums allocated by Paris to the military to keep order and expand the colonial empire never exceeded 0.5 percent of annual metropolitan national income between 1830 and 1910. In some respects, this cost is remarkably low, given that the population of the empire at its peak was nearly 2.5 times that of the metropole (90 million compared with 40 million).[20] From this it should be clear that differences in levels

---

18. Note, however, that the famous slogan "la Corrèze plutôt que le Zambèze" (Corrèze, not Zambezi) was uttered by Jean Montalat, Socialist deputy for Corrèze, at the podium of the National Assembly in 1964 (hence after independence), during debate on the issue of postcolonial developmental aid.

19. See esp. Chaps. 12 and 16.

20. In the interwar years, colonial military expenditure ran about 0.5–1.0 percent of GDP. See Cogneau, Dupraz, and Mesplé-Somps, *Fiscal Capacity and Dualism*, p. 46.

of development and state and military capacity created a temptation to embark on ambitious colonial adventures at very low cost.

Slave and Colonial Extraction in Historical Perspective

On the question of "transfers" between the metropole and its colonies, it is also important to point out that it would be a significant error to limit ourselves to examining the government budget balance. The taxes paid in the colonies equaled government expenditure throughout the period 1830–1950, but this obviously does not mean that there was no "colonial extraction"—that is, no profit to the colonizing power. The first to profit from colonization were the governors and civil servants of the colonies, whose remuneration came from taxes paid by the colonized populations. More generally, the colonizers, whether employed as civil servants or in the private sector (for example, in the agricultural sector in Algeria or on rubber plantations in Indochina), often enjoyed much higher status than they would have had in the metropole. To be sure, life was not always simple; some colonizers were far from wealthy, and disillusionment was common. Think, for example, of the difficulties faced by the mother of writer Marguerite Duras, whose fields on the Pacific coast were constantly flooded; or of the misfortunes of the *petits blancs* (poor whites), who had to contend with the colonial *haute bourgeoisie,* both capitalists and officials, who harassed and extracted bribes from small farmers. Still, even the poor whites had chosen their own lot to a greater extent than the natives, and they enjoyed greater rights and opportunities simply by virtue of their race.

One also has to consider the private profit extracted from the colonies. In the first colonial era, the era of the Atlantic slave trade, the profit extraction was crude and unambiguous, and the profits took the form of cold hard cash. The sums at stake have been well documented, and they were considerable. In the case of Saint-Domingue, the profits extracted from the island by way of sugar and cotton exports surpassed 150 million *livres tournois* annually in the late 1780s. If one includes all colonies in the same period, available estimates suggest profits of roughly 350 million livres in 1790, at a time when French national income was less than 5 billion livres. Thus, more than 7 percent in additional national income (3 percent from Haiti alone) flowed into France from the colonies; this was a huge amount, especially in view of the fact that these sums benefited a very small minority. In addition, it was pure extraction after allowing for the costs of production (especially the cost of the imports needed to produce the goods), to buy and maintain the slaves (leaving aside the profits of the slave traders), and local consumption and investment by the planters. For the United Kingdom, profits from the slave islands in the 1780s were on the order of 4–5 percent of national income.[21]

During the second colonial era (1850–1960), the age of the great transcontinental empires, private financial profits took more complex but ultimately just as substantial forms, provided that we look at global investment overall and not just investment in a few slave islands. Earlier, we saw the importance of international investments in Parisian fortunes during the Belle Époque. In 1912, shortly before World War I, foreign assets accounted for more than 20 percent of total Parisian wealth, and those assets were highly diversified: they included both shares and direct investments in foreign firms, private bonds issued by firms to finance their international investments, and government bonds and other forms of state borrowing, which alone accounted for nearly half of the total.[22]

Let us turn now to the two major colonial powers of this era, the United Kingdom and France, and note the immense (and to this day unequaled) scope of the foreign investments held by residents of these two countries (Fig. 7.9).[23] In 1914, on the eve of World War I, the UK's net foreign assets (that is, the difference between the value of investments in the rest of the world and held by British citizens and the value of investments in Britain and held by citizens of the rest of the world) amounted to 190 percent (or nearly two years' worth) of the country's national income. French investors were not far behind, with net foreign assets worth more than 120 percent of French national income in 1914. These gigantic asset holdings in the rest of the world were much larger than those of other European powers, and in particular Germany, which plateaued at a little more than 40 percent of national income despite the country's remarkable industrial and demographic surge. This was partly because Germany lacked a significant colonial empire but more generally because it occupied a less important and more recent position in global commercial and financial networks. These colonial rivalries played a central role in exacerbating tensions

---

21. For details of these estimates, see the online appendix.
22. See Table 4.1.
23. The foreign assets included on Fig. 7.9 include all forms of assets, whether financial assets, direct investment, real estate, land or natural resources such as mining fields. In modern national accounts, foreign assets are all treated as financial assets (from a pure accounting perspective) as soon as they take place at an international level.

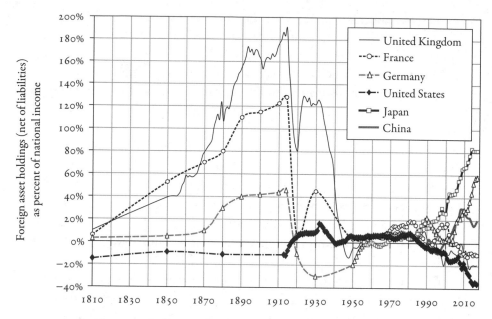

FIG. 7.9. Foreign assets in historical perspective: The Franco-British colonial apex
Interpretation: Net foreign assets (that is, foreign asset holdings by residents of each country, including its government) less assets in each country held by the rest of the world, came to 191 percent of national income in the United Kingdom in 1914 and 125 percent in France. In 2018, net financial assets amounted to 80 percent of national income in Japan, 58 percent in Germany, and 20 percent in China. *Sources and series:* piketty.pse. ens.fr/ideology.

between the powers, as in the Agadir Crisis of 1911. Wilhelm II ultimately accepted the Franco-British treaty of 1904 on Morocco and Egypt, but he obtained significant territorial compensation in Cameroon, which delayed the onset of war by a few years.

British and French foreign asset holdings increased at an accelerated pace during the Belle Époque, and it is natural to ask how long this rising trajectory might have continued had there been no war (a question to which I will return when we study the fall of ownership society). In any event, Franco-British holdings fell precipitously after World War I and definitively in the wake of World War II, due in part to expropriation (think of the famous Russian bonds, whose repudiation after the Russian Revolution of 1917 was particularly painful for French investors) but mostly to the fact that French and British investors were obliged to sell growing fractions of their foreign holdings and lend to their own governments to finance the wars.[24]

To gain a better understanding of the scope of foreign investment that the United Kingdom and France accumulated in the late nineteenth and early twentieth centuries, note that no country since then has ever held such large volumes of foreign assets in the rest of the world. For example, Japan accumulated significant foreign assets as a result of large commercial surpluses in the 1980s and beyond, as did Germany in the wake of unusually high trade surpluses since the mid-2000s, but in neither case did foreign holdings in 2018 exceed 60–80 percent of national income. That is a high level of foreign investment, quite different from the very low levels (close to zero) seen in the period 1950–1980 and significantly higher than China's current holdings (barely 20 percent of national income in 2018)—but still much lower than the Franco-British peak on the eve of World War I (Fig. 7.9).[25]

One can also compare Franco-British foreign assets in 1914 (one to two years of national income) to the total assets (financial, real estate, equipment, net of debt, foreign plus domestic) held by French and British citizens at the time, which amounted to six or seven years of national income of both countries combined. In other words, one-fifth to one-quarter of what people owned at the time was held abroad. The ownership societies that prospered in France and the United Kingdom in the Belle Époque thus rested in large part on foreign assets. The key point is that these assets earned considerable income: the average yield was close to 4 percent a year, so that income on foreign capital added about 5 percent to French national income and more than 8 percent to British national income. The interest, dividends, profits, rents, and royalties earned in the rest of the world thus substantially boosted the standard of living

---

24. Note that the negative position of Germany shown in Fig. 7.9 for the 1920s would be even more negative if we included the debts imposed by the Treaty of Versailles. In Chap. 10 I will return to the collapse of foreign investment in the period 1914–1945.

25. There are some oil-producing countries with higher accumulations, such as Norway, whose net foreign asset position exceeds 200 percent of national income, but this is a country whose economy is small compared with the global economy. Furthermore, the modest size of China's foreign holdings is partly due to the country's very high growth rate: assets that China accumulated a decade or two ago are small compared to its current GDP, particularly since China (like many oil-producing countries) has thus far been content to earn relatively low yields, often on US Treasury bonds. I will return to these issues in Chaps. 12 and 13.

in the two colonial powers or, more precisely, in certain segments of their population. To gauge the enormous size of the sums at stake, note that the 5 percent additional national income that France earned from its foreign possessions in the period 1900–1914 was approximately equal to the total industrial output of northern and eastern France, the most industrialized regions of the country. Hence this was a very substantial financial boost.[26]

From the Brutality of Colonial Appropriation to the Illusion of "Gentle Commerce"

It is striking to note that the financial profits that France and Britain reaped from their colonies were of roughly the same order in the periods 1760–1790 and 1890–1914: 4–7 percent of national income in the earlier period and 5–8 percent in the later. There are obviously important differences between the two periods, however. In the first colonial era, appropriation was brutal and intensive and concentrated in small territories: slaves were transported to the islands and put to work producing sugar and cotton, and enormous profits (of up to 70 percent of output in Saint-Domingue, including income earned by colonizers) were extracted from the wealth that was produced. The extractive efficiency was maximal, but the risk of revolt was serious, and it would have been difficult to generalize the system to global scale. In the second colonial era, the modes of appropriation and exploitation were more subtle and sophisticated: investors held stocks and bonds in many countries, from which they extracted a portion of the output for each region. To be sure, this portion was smaller than could be extracted under the slave regime, but it was far from negligible (often 5–10 percent of a country's production, sometimes even more), and more importantly, it could be applied in many more parts of the world or even to the entire globe. Ultimately, the scale of the second system dwarfed the first, and it might have grown even larger had its development not been interrupted by the eminently political shocks of the period 1914–1945. The first colonial era was ended by rebellions, and the second by wars and revolutions, themselves caused by frenetic competition among colonial powers and by violent social tensions born of the internal and external inequalities engendered by globalized ownership societies (at least in part; I will come back to this).

One might also be tempted to think that another difference between the two situations was that the slave trade and exploitation of slaves on the islands

---

26. For an analysis of these amounts, see the online appendix.

in the first colonial era were "illegal" (or at any rate "immoral"), while the French and British accumulation of foreign financial assets in the second colonial era was perfectly "legal" (and certainly more "moral"), having been accomplished in accordance with the virtuous and mutually profitable logic of "gentle commerce." The second colonial era did indeed justify itself in terms of a potentially universalistic (though in practice highly asymmetric) proprietarian ideology and a model of development and trade similar in certain respects to the current neo-proprietarian model, in which extensive cross-border financial holdings can in theory be beneficial to all. According to this virtuous, harmonious scenario, some countries can run large trade deficits (if, for example, they have good products to sell to the rest of the world or because they deem it necessary to build reserves for the future, as a hedge, for instance, against demographic aging or potential disaster), that leads them to accumulate assets in other countries—assets which of course then earn a fair remuneration. Otherwise, who would make the effort to accumulate wealth, and who would agree to abstain patiently from consumption? The problem is that this stark contrast between two eras of colonialism—one brutal and violently extractive, the other virtuous and mutually profitable—while admissible in theory fails to capture the subtler shades of reality.

In practice, a significant portion of French and British foreign holdings in the period 1880–1914 came directly from the compensation that Haiti was forced to pay in exchange for its freedom or that taxpayers in both countries were forced to pay to slaveowners deprived of their human property (which, as Victor Schoelcher liked to say, had been acquired "in a legal framework" and therefore could not be purely and simply expropriated without just indemnification). More broadly, a significant fraction of foreign assets consisted of public and private debt extracted by force—in many cases akin to military tribute. This was the case, for example, with the public debt imposed on China in the wake of the Opium Wars of 1839–1842 and 1856–1860. Britain and France held China responsible for the military confrontations (shouldn't the Chinese government simply have agreed to import opium?) and therefore compelled the Chinese to repay a heavy debt to compensate the aggressors for military costs they would have preferred to avoid and to encourage China to behave more docilely in the future.[27]

Through this device of "unequal treaties" the colonial powers were able to seize control of many countries and foreign assets. On the basis of a more or

27. I will come back to these episodes in Chap. 9.

less convincing pretext (such as a country's refusal to open its borders widely enough, or a riot in which European citizens were attacked, or a need to maintain order), a military operation would be mounted; this was followed by the colonial power demanding jurisdictional privileges or a financial tribute of some kind, payment of which would require seizure of administrative control over, say, customs, and then over the entire fiscal system so as to improve the yield to colonial creditors (in conjunction with steeply regressive taxes, which generated strong social tensions and in some cases authentic tax revolts against the occupier), leading ultimately to seizure of the entire country.

The case of Morocco is exemplary in this regard. Public opinion in Morocco in favor of assisting the country's Muslim neighbors in Algeria (conquered by France in 1830) compelled the sultan to offer refuge to Algerian rebel leader Abdelkader. This provided France with the ideal pretext to shell Tangiers and impose a first treaty on Morocco in 1845. Then Spain seized on a Berber revolt as a pretext to capture Tétouan and impose a heavy war indemnity in 1860; the resulting debt was subsequently refinanced through bankers in London and Paris, and repayment of these loans soon absorbed more than half of Morocco's customs revenues annually. One thing led to another, and France ultimately made Morocco a protectorate in 1911–1912 after invading much of the country in 1907–1909, officially to protect its financial interests and its citizens following rioting in Marrakech and Casablanca.[28] It is interesting to note that the conquest of Algeria in 1830 was justified by the alleged need to eradicate the Barbary pirates who threatened Mediterranean shipping at the time— pirates whom the *dey* of Algiers was accused of tolerating in his port, thus providing a pretext for the French *mission civilisatrice*. Another, no less serious motive was that, to supply grain to the expeditionary force dispatched to Egypt in 1798–1799, France had incurred a debt guaranteed by the *dey,* which first Napoleon and then Louis XVIII refused to repay, and this became a recurrent source of tension during the Restoration. Here is yet another illustration of the limits of proprietarian ideology when it comes to regulating both social relations and interstate relations: in a dispute, each side can use this ideology in its own way to justify its desire for wealth and power, which quickly leads to

---

28. On the cases of China and Morocco, see the online appendix and the recent work of B. Truong-Loï, *La dette publique chinoise à la fin de la dynastie Qing (1874–1913)* (master's thesis, Institut d'Etudes Politiques de Paris, 2015), and A. Barbe, *Public Debt and European Expansionism in Morocco, 1856–1956* (master's thesis, Paris School of Economics, 2016).

logical contradictions when it comes to defining norms of justice acceptable to all; conflicts then have to be resolved by the application of naked power and armed force.

Note, moreover, that such rough justice between states, and recurrent blurring of the lines between military tribute in the past and public debt in the present, can also be found within Europe itself. At the end of the long and complex process of German unification, from the German Confederation of 1815 to the North German Confederation of 1866, the new imperial German state availed itself of its victory in the Franco-Prussian War (1870–1871) to impose on France a heavy indemnity of 7.5 billion gold francs, equal to 30 percent of French national income at the time.[29] This was a significant amount, well beyond the military costs of the war, but France paid in full without a notable impact on its accumulated financial wealth—a sign of just how prosperous French property owners and savers were at the end of the nineteenth century.

The difference was this: while the European colonial powers sometimes imposed tributes on one another, when it came to imposing a highly lucrative domination on the rest of the world, they were usually allies—at least until their ultimate self-destruction by armed forces in the period 1914–1945. Although the justifications and forms of pressure have evolved, it would be wrong to imagine that such rough treatment of some states by others has totally disappeared or that naked power no longer plays a role in determining the financial fortunes of states. Consider, for example, the unrivaled ability of the United States to impose staggering sanctions on foreign firms as well as dissuasive commercial and financial embargoes on governments deemed to be insufficiently cooperative—an ability not unrelated to US global military dominance.

On the Difficulty of Being Owned by Other Countries

Some of France and Britain's foreign assets in the period 1880–1914 also came from the trade surpluses the two industrial powers had been able to run since the beginning of the nineteenth century. Several points call for clarification, however. First, it is not easy to say what trade flows would have looked like in the absence of armed domination and violence. This is obvious in the case of the opium exports forced on China in the wake of the Opium Wars, which

---

29. See the online appendix for an analysis of these amounts. The 7.5 billion gold francs included 5 billion francs of indemnity plus 2.5 billion to cover the costs of occupation.

contributed to the official trade surpluses of the first two-thirds of the nineteenth century. But it is also true for other exports, including textiles. Trade patterns were shaped by the international balance of power and by extremely violent interstate relations. The textile industry itself depended on supplies of cotton produced by slave labor, and exports benefited from punitive tariffs imposed on Indian and Chinese output, about which I will say more later.

To view nineteenth-century trade flows as straightforward consequences of "market forces" and "the invisible hand" is hardly serious and cannot explain the manifestly political transformations of the interstate system and global trade that actually occurred. In any event, if one takes the trade flows as given, the fact remains that the trade surpluses we can measure on the basis of available sources for the period 1800–1880 can explain only a small part (between a quarter and a half) of the enormous mass of foreign financial assets that Britain and France had accumulated by 1880. Most of those assets were therefore accumulated in other ways, whether by the quasi-military forms of tribute discussed earlier, uncompensated appropriations of one sort or another, or unusually high returns on certain investments.

Finally but perhaps most significantly, it is important to understand that accumulations of wealth such as France and Britain amassed in the period 1880–1914 and such as other countries may amass in the future, whether legally or illegally, morally or immorally, begin to follow an accumulative logic of their own once they attain a certain size.

At this point it is important to call attention to a fact that may not be sufficiently well known, although it is well attested by trade statistics from the era and was well known to contemporaries. In the period 1880–1914, the United Kingdom and France earned so much from their investments in the rest of the world (roughly 5 percent additional national income for France and more than 8 percent for the United Kingdom) that they could allow themselves to run persistent structural trade deficits (an average of 1–2 percent of national income for both countries) while continuing to accumulate claims on the rest of the world at an accelerated pace. In other words, the rest of the world labored to increase the consumption and standard of living of the colonial powers, even as it became increasingly indebted to those powers. This situation is like that of the worker who must devote a large portion of his salary to pay rent to his landlord, which the landlord then uses to buy the rest of the building while leading a life of luxury compared to the family of the worker, which has only his wages to live on. This comparison may shock some readers (which I think would be healthy), but one must realize that the purpose of property is to increase the owner's ability to consume and accumulate in the future. Similarly, the purpose of accumulating foreign assets, whether from trade surpluses or colonial appropriations, is to be able to run subsequent trade deficits. This is the principle of all wealth accumulation, whether domestic or international. If one wants to get beyond this logic of endless accumulation, one needs to equip oneself with the intellectual and institutional means to transcend the idea of private property—for example, the concept of temporary ownership and permanent redistribution of property.

Today, in the early twenty-first century, some people think that trade surpluses are an end in themselves and can continue indefinitely. This perception reflects a political and ideological transformation that is itself extremely interesting. It corresponds to a world in which a country wishes to create jobs for its people in export sectors while accumulating financial claims on the rest of the world. Yet today as in the past, those financial claims are not only intended to create jobs and bring prestige and power to the surplus country (even if those goals cannot be neglected); they are also meant to procure future financial income. This, of course, makes it possible to acquire not only additional assets but also goods and services produced by other countries without the need to export anything at all.

Consider the petroleum exporting countries, which are the most obvious contemporary example of countries amassing large amounts of foreign assets. It is obvious that these countries' oil and gas exports and attendant trade surpluses will not last forever. Their goal is precisely to accumulate enough financial claims on the rest of the world to be able to live in the future on the income from those investments and to import all sorts of goods and services from the rest of the world well after their stocks of hydrocarbons are completely exhausted. In the case of Japan—which currently holds the most impressive portfolio of foreign assets in the world (Fig. 7.9) thanks to the trade surpluses racked up by Japanese industry in past decades—it is possible that the country is on the brink of a phase of structural trade deficit (or at least the end of its accumulative phase). Germany and China will probably also face such turning points, once saving reaches a certain level and the aging of their populations has proceeded further than it has today. There is obviously nothing particularly "natural" about such evolutions. They depend on political and ideological transformations in the countries involved and on the way in which various state and economic actors perceive and interpret what is at stake.

I will come back to these questions and say more later about possible sources of future conflict. The important point for now is simply that international property relations are never simple, especially when they attain such huge proportions. In fact, property relations in general are always more complex than the fairy tales one reads in economics textbooks, where they are often presented as spontaneously harmonious and mutually advantageous. It is never simple for a worker to sacrifice a substantial portion of her wage to an owner's profit or a landlord's rent or for the children of renters to pay rents to the children of landlords. That is why property relations are always conflictual and always give rise to institutions whose purpose is to regulate their scope and transmissibility. Regulation can be achieved through union struggles or power-sharing mechanisms within firms, through laws governing wage setting and rent control or limiting the power of landlords to evict tenants, by setting the term of a lease or conditions of an eventual buyout, or by establishing estate taxes or other fiscal and legal devices to facilitate the acquisition of property by new social groups and limit the reproduction of wealth inequalities across generations.

When one country is required to pay another country profits, rents, and/or dividends over a long period of time, however, property relations can become even more complex and explosive. Constructing norms of justice acceptable to a majority through democratic deliberation and social struggle is already a complex enough process within a single political community; it becomes practically impossible when the owners of property are external to the community. In the most common and likely case, such external property relations will be regulated by violence and military force. In the Belle Époque, the colonial powers made ample use of gunboat diplomacy to ensure that interest and dividends would be paid on time and that no one would think of expropriating creditors. The military and coercive dimension of international financial relations and investment strategies also plays an essential role today, even though the interstate system has become much more complex. In particular, two of today's leading international creditors, Japan and Germany, are states without armies, whereas the two principal military powers, the United States and to a lesser degree China, are focused more on investing domestically than on accumulating external financial claims. This may be due to the continental dimensions of both of these states as well as to their demographic dynamism (which may be about to change in China and may someday change in the United States).

In any case, the Franco-British experience with foreign asset accumulation in the Belle Époque is rich in instruction for the future and for our overall understanding of the proprietarian inequality regime, especially in its international and colonial dimension. In this respect, it should be noted that the mechanisms of financial and military coercion developed by the colonial powers to extend the accumulation process over time applied not just to explicitly colonized territories but also to countries that were not (or have not yet been) colonized, such as China, Turkey (the Ottoman Empire), Iran, and Morocco. Indeed, when one studies the available sources of information regarding the international investment portfolios of the period, one finds that they extended far beyond the colonies in the strict sense.

Of the international financial assets held by Parisians in 1912, between a quarter and a third represented direct investment in the French colonial empire. The remaining assets originated in many other countries: Russia and Eastern Europe, the Levant and Persia, Latin America and China, and so on.[30] The newer parts of the colonial empire, such as French Equatorial Africa and French West Africa, were not always the most profitable in terms of financial income: they benefited mainly the colonial administrators and settlers who lived there and of course contributed to the prestige of the civilizing power, as segments of the French elite and population imagined it to be at the time.[31] We find similar portfolio diversification in the British case: British international portfolios earned very comfortable incomes, enough to finance a structural trade deficit with the rest of the world while continuing to amass claims at an accelerated pace. Nevertheless, certain parts of the British Empire were far less profitable than others and represented a broad civilizing mission or a strategy intended to benefit specific groups of owners and settlers rather than a strictly financial operation.[32] In sum, the inequality regime of the Belle Époque was justified by both proprietarian and civilizing arguments, both of which influenced subsequent developments in significant ways.

---

30. This estimate is rather imprecise, however, because many companies that issued stocks and bonds did business in numerous different countries.

31. One should be careful, however, to avoid the error (committed by J. Marseille) of interpreting the trade deficit of certain African colonies with respect to the metropole as a sign that the colonized populations were living at France's expense. In fact, those deficits were smaller than the military and civilian expenditures that went to the colonizers to pay for keeping order in the colonies and to finance the lifestyle of the settlers, not of the colonized populations. See Cogneau, Dupraz, and Mesplé-Somps, *Fiscal Capacity and Dualism;* Huilery, "The Black Man's Burden."

32. See L. Davis and R. Huttenback, *Mammon and the Pursuit of Empire. The Political Economy of British Imperialism, 1860–1912* (Cambridge University Press, 1986).

Metropolitan Legality, Colonial Legality

We turn now to the question of the origins of inequality in colonial societies and the reasons for its persistence. I have already discussed the role of colonial budgets in producing and perpetuating inequality in the colonies. Once colonized populations began to be heavily taxed primarily for the benefit of the colonizers, especially regarding educational investment, it is not surprising that existing inequalities were perpetuated. To the inequalities induced by the tax system and structure of public expenditures, however, we must add inequalities stemming from other aspects of the colonial regime starting with the legal system, which was substantially biased in favor of the colonizers. Specifically, in cases involving commercial, property, or labor law, the native and European populations did not have access to the same courts and did not compete economically on an equal footing.

We see this particularly brutal aspect of colonial inequality in the story of Sanikem, the heroine of Pramoedya Ananta Toer's splendid novel *This Earth of Mankind,* published in 1980. In 1875, near Surabaya in eastern Java, Sanikem's father hopes to obtain a promotion and amass a small nest egg by selling her at age 14 as a *nyae* (concubine) to Herman Mallema, a Dutch plantation owner. The young girl understands that the only person she will ever be able to count on is herself: "His arms with skin as rough as an iguana's were covered with blond hair as thick as my thighs." But Herman has his own problems: he has fled the Netherlands, his friends, and his wife, whom he accused of adultery, and before succumbing to alcoholism he tries to rebuild his life by teaching Sanikem Dutch so that she can read to him from the magazines that arrive by the carton from Holland. She quickly learns to run the Wonokromo plantation on her own, enduring many sacrifices and much mockery. She is glad to see her daughter Annelies in a relationship with a native, Minke, who has miraculously been admitted to the Dutch high school in Surabaya, while her son Robert compensates for the humiliation he suffers as a "half-breed" by venting his wrath on the natives with even greater fury than the pure whites. What Sanikem does not know, however, is that the fruits of her labor are not legally hers. Herman's legitimate son arrives from Holland, furious with his wretch of a father for having mixed his blood with that of the natives; shortly thereafter, Herman is found dead in a Chinese brothel. His son goes to a Dutch court in Surabaya to claim what is legally his and ends up in control of the plantation. Annelies is sent against her will to the Netherlands, where she succumbs to madness, while Sanikem and Minke, both crushed, remain in Java. With the coming of the twentieth century, only one option remains open to them: to join the long struggle for justice and independence.

Pramoedya Ananta Toer knows whereof he speaks: he spent two years in Dutch jails, 1947–1949, before coming to know the jails of Sukarno and Suharto in the 1960s and 1970s owing to his communist commitments and his defense of the Chinese minority in Indonesia. In his novel he dissects monetary inequalities in a period during which the gold standard and zero inflation vested money with social significance and gave property a solidity that nothing else could match. Sanikem's father had sold her to Mallema for 25 florins, "enough to allow a village family to live comfortably for 30 months." But this is not a classic European novel, and the essence of the matter lies elsewhere: the colonial inequality regime is based above all on inequalities of status, on ethnic and racial identity. Pure whites, "half-breeds," and natives do not have the same rights, and all are engulfed in a swirling mix of contempt and hatred with far-reaching consequences.

Recent research, especially the work of Emmanuelle Saada, has shown how the colonial powers in the twentieth century developed specific legal systems in their empires that allowed them to grant rights on the basis of carefully codified ethnic and racial categories, even though such classifications had supposedly been expunged from metropolitan law after the abolition of slavery. As an example, racial indications were dropped from census reports from Réunion and the French West Indies after 1848. Under a 1928 decree concerning "the status of children of mixed race born to legally unknown parents in Indochina," French nationality was awarded to any individual with at least one parent "presumed to be the French race," a provision that would lead courts to consider the physical and racial characteristics of individuals with business before them.

There were several schools of thought about such matters. Some colonial administrators doubted that "half-breeds," the fruit of fleeting encounters with "yellow women," could adapt socially and therefore rejected the policy of automatic naturalization. But many settlers, having themselves been involved in mixed couplings, insisted instead on the danger "of allowing men with our blood in their veins to wander footloose." It would be highly "imprudent," they argued, "to allow an anti-French party to be created and to arouse the scorn of the Annamites [Vietnamese], who blame us for abandoning people they regard as our sons." Another reason for considering racial criteria was the concern of colonial authorities to combat fraudulent acknowledgment of offspring. All signs are that this was quite rare (as were mixed-race births in general), but some feared that the practice might lead to "a veritable industry on the part of clever Europeans who had fallen into poverty and who might wish to gain some security for their old age" (as one lawyer put it at the time). In Madagascar, administrators worried about the difficulty of applying such a law, which had been designed for Indochina: How could a judge distinguish between the child of a Réunionnais father (a French citizen, even if not of the "French race") and the child of a Malagasy father (and therefore not a citizen but a native subject)? In any case, the decree was applied in Indochina: in the 1930s medical certificates were issued to confirm the mixed Franco-Indochinese race of certain children, and after World War II this led to the forced "repatriation" of thousands of minors of mixed race.[33]

Note, too, that while mixed marriages were in theory authorized in both the colonies and the metropole, the authorities sought to discourage them in practice, especially in cases in which a French woman wished to marry a native man. In 1917, when colonial workers came in large numbers to France from Indochina and other colonies and in some cases struck up relationships with French women working in the same factories, the Ministry of Justice sent out a circular urging mayors to do everything they could to prevent such relationships from ending in marriage. They were told to warn "rash or credulous compatriots about dangers of which they might be unaware," having to do not only with the suspected polygamy of their partners but also with their standard of living, "since native wages are inadequate to provide a decent life for a European woman."[34]

Beyond the question of mixed-race couples, there existed a whole parallel legal system in the colonies, often in direct contradiction with the principles on which the metropolitan legal system purported to be based. In 1910, the Haiphong Chamber of Commerce explained to the Ministry of Colonies why young Frenchmen accused of rape by native women should be treated with the utmost leniency: "In France, a peasant or worker who takes advantage of a neighbor woman *makes reparations;* and a man who by virtue of his position is able to abuse a younger or poorer woman contracts a debt that cannot be renounced. But without getting into any discussion of color or racial inferiority,

---

33. See the excellent book by E. Saada, *Les enfants de la colonie. Les métis de l'empire français, entre sujétion et citoyenneté* (La découverte, 2007), pp. 47, 147–152, 210–226; published in English as *Empire's Children: Race, Filiation, and Citizenship in the French Colonies,* trans. A. Goldhammer (University of Chicago Press, 2011).

34. See E. Saada, *Les enfants de la colonie,* pp. 45–46.

social relations are not the same between the young Frenchman who lands on these shores and the native women who are more often than not offered to him."[35]

In the case of Dutch Indonesia, Denys Lombard has shown the nefarious role played by the colonial statute of 1854, which strictly distinguished between "natives" and "oriental foreigners" (a category including Chinese, Indian, and Arab minorities). This distinction helped freeze identities and animosities permanently, whereas for more than a millennium the "Javanese crossroads," or "Insulindia," had stood out as a place where Hindu, Confucian, Buddhist, and Muslim cultures combined to form a unique mix. This syncretism may not have conformed to the European idea of globalization, but in the end it probably had a more lasting impact on the cultures of the region and on the "oriental Mediterranean" (from Jakarta to Canton and Phnom Penh to Manila) than the martial order imposed by the West.[36]

Legal Forced Labor in the French Colonies, 1912–1946

A particularly revealing case is that of legal forced labor (or at any rate forced labor in a form that sought to give the appearance of legality) in the French colonies from 1912 to 1946. Here we see the continuity that existed between

---

35. "In the case of a union between a European male and an Annamite woman, it may be asserted that seduction is extremely rare. . . . The Annamites, like the Chinese, have a legitimate wife and one or more concubines. The latter can be repudiated, and a woman who lives with a European is considered a concubine by the Annamites. . . . A European almost always takes a concubine with the consent of her parents, who generally receive a sum of money and who regard the temporary establishment of their daughter as perfectly respectable. In many other cases, the woman is introduced to the European by a procuress, who has purchased the girl from her parents. There is no rape: the concubines taken by Europeans are very rarely if ever virgins. There can be no question of seduction since an Annamite woman will never choose to live with a European without a pecuniary interest. Furthermore, the lack of fidelity among Annamite women and their all too common immorality would constitute a grave danger if they were allowed to sue their lovers, since for them coupling with a European is merely a business activity, which they regard as honorable but in which questions of sentiment play little part." See E. Saada, *Les enfants de la colonie*, pp. 45–46.

36. See D. Lombard, *Le carrefour javanais. Essai d'histoire globale (Les limites de l'occidentalisation; Les réseaux asiatiques; L'héritage des royaumes concentriques)* (EHESS, 1990).

slave society and colonial society as well as the importance of looking in detail at the legal and fiscal systems adopted by different inequality regimes. In Africa, all signs are that forced labor never really ended after the end of the slave trade and the beginning of the second colonial era; in other words, it continued throughout the nineteenth century. At the end of the century, as Europeans began to move further inland to exploit mineral and other natural resources, they made abundant use of forced labor, often under extremely brutal conditions. Controversies erupted in Europe in 1890–1891 and again in 1903–1904 as news spread of atrocities committed in the Belgian Congo, which from 1885 on was the personal property of Belgian King Leopold II. The Congo's rubber plantations relied on particularly violent methods to mobilize and discipline the local work force: villages were set ablaze and hands were cut off to save on bullets.[37] Ultimately, the Europeans demanded that the territory be transferred to Belgium in 1908, in the hope that parliamentary oversight would soften the regime.[38] Abuses in the French colonies were regularly denounced, and it was in this context that the Ministry of Colonies published a number of texts that sought to define a legal basis for "services" (*prestations,* but more commonly called *corvées*) that could be demanded of the citizens of French Africa.

The logic of the case was meant to be impeccable: the colonial administration counted on all citizens to pay taxes; some natives lacked sufficient resources to meet their tax obligations, hence they could be called on to pay their tax in kind in the form of unpaid days of labor. In practice, the problem was not simply that these *corvées* were levied on top of already onerous taxes in cash and in kind (taken from the harvest) paid by the colonized population but also that the

---

37. Severing of hands is regularly cited among the panoply of methods used to discipline labor and establish domination from the ternary societies of the eleventh century (see Chap. 2) to the colonial societies of the twentieth. In Chimamanda Ngozi Adichie's *Half of a Yellow Sun* (Farafina, 2006), the militant anticolonialist Richard writes a book entitled *The Basket of Hands* about British colonization in Nigeria; his lover Kainene destroys his manuscript, partly as vengeance for his infidelity but also to let him know that it would be best to leave this history to the Nigerians and return to fight for Biafra.

38. See V. Joly, "1908: Fondation du Congo Belge," in *Histoire du monde au 19e siècle,* ed. P. Singaravélou and S. Venayre (Fayard, 2017), pp. 381–384. In J. Richard, *Il est à toi ce beau pays* (Albin Michel, 2018), Richard relates the Congolese abuses and the problems that the African American militant Washington Williams has in making them known in the United States, where there was no interest at the time in enforcing racial equality.

use of unpaid labor opened the way to all kinds of abuses and was tantamount to legalizing those abuses in advance. The 1912 order "regulating native services in the Colonies and Territories of the Government of French West Africa" did establish certain safeguards, but oversight was lax. The order stipulated that "natives can be required to perform services related to the maintenance of lines of communication: roads, bridges, wells, and so on," as well as other infrastructure, including "the laying of telegraphic lines" and "public works of all kinds," all under the exclusive control of the lieutenant governor or commissioner in each colony. The text indicated that the order applied to "all individuals of the male sex, able-bodied and adult, with the exception of the elderly" (without specification of any age limit).[39] In theory, such "services" were limited to "12 days of [unpaid] labor" per person per year. Only legal services are recorded in the colonial archives, and these records are sufficient to substantially increase estimates of the fiscal pressure exerted by the colonial regime and to conclude that forced labor was an essential cog in the colonial system.[40]

Numerous accounts from the interwar years suggest that the number of days of unpaid labor actually demanded was in fact much higher. In case of necessity, the norm was thirty to sixty days in the French colonies, as well as in Belgian, British, Spanish, and Portuguese colonies. In the French case, the use of forced labor was especially scandalous in the tragic construction of the Congo-Ocean Railway between 1921 and 1935. The FEA administration initially agreed to provide some 8,000 local workers, which it thought it would be able to "recruit" from a 100-kilometer strip of land along the right of way. But the exceptionally high death rate among the workers and demonstrated dangerousness of the job frightened away recruits, and the colonial authorities went to the other end of the central Congo in search of "adult males." From 1925 on,

---

39. See *Journal official de l'Afrique occidentale française*, 1913, p. 70. The order specified that "services cannot be required in principle during periods of harvest and gathering" and "cannot take place at a distance greater than 5 km from the worker's village, unless those performing the service are provided with a ration in cash or in kind." In practice, the authorities could move anyone they wished from one end of the country to the other whenever they wished as long as they provided the "service workers" with a "ration."

40. For a recent analysis of these archives and debates, see M. van Waijenburg, "Financing the African Colonial State: The Revenue Imperative and Forced Labor," *Journal of Economic History*, 2018. See also I. Merle and A. Muckle, *L'indigénat. Genèses dans l'empire français, pratiques en Nouvelle-Calédonie* (CNRS éditions, 2019).

they had to organize raids into Cameroon and Chad. Numerous accounts were published of this "dreadful consumption of human lives," most notably André Gide's celebrated *Voyage au Congo* in 1927 and Albert Londres's *Terre d'ébène* in 1929.

International pressure on France then increased, especially from the International Labor Organization (ILO), which was founded in 1919, at the same time as the League of Nations, with a constitution containing the following preamble:

> Whereas universal and lasting peace can be established only if it is based upon social justice; And whereas conditions of labour exist involving such injustice, hardship and privation to large numbers of people as to produce unrest so great that the peace and harmony of the world are imperiled; and an improvement of those conditions is urgently required . . . ; Whereas also the failure of any nation to adopt humane conditions of labour is an obstacle in the way of other nations which desire to improve the conditions in their own countries.

What followed was a series of recommendations and reports concerning the duration and dangerousness of labor, setting of wages, and rights of workers and their representatives. Unfortunately, the ILO lacked the means and power to impose the sanctions it would have needed to enforce its recommendations.

During the 1920s, the ILO regularly summoned France to cease its use of unpaid labor and forced displacement of workers, which it said came close to a form of servile labor. But French authorities rejected these accusations, insisting that they had only recently extended to all "natives" (and not just the most "evolved," which was the word that the colonial administration used to designate the small minority of natives who had adopted a European lifestyle) the possibility of avoiding labor service by paying a cash fee. One of the favorite arguments of the French administration was that many of the allegations of forced labor, particularly on the Congo-Ocean Railway, in fact involved military conscription, which was one of the few forms of unpaid labor authorized by the ILO, provided that the military was not used to perform civilian tasks (the ILO suspected France of abusing this loophole). The French authorities, offended by this intrusion into what they regarded as their "national sovereignty," therefore refused to ratify the ILO convention in 1930. Unpaid forced labor in the form of "services" and conscriptions therefore continued in the French colonies until the end of World War II, for example, in the cacao plantations of the Ivory Coast. The decree of 1912 was not rescinded until

1946 in a very different political context, one that found France suddenly prepared to make whatever concessions were necessary to avoid the dismantling of its empire.

Late Colonialism: South African Apartheid, 1948–1994

The apartheid system in force in South Africa from 1948 to 1994 was no doubt one of the most extreme attempts to create a legal regime separating colonizers from colonized in a durable structure of inequality. My purpose here is not to write a history of apartheid but simply to call attention to a number of points of particular importance for a general history of inequality regimes. At the conclusion of the Boer War (1899–1902), in which the British with great effort ultimately carried the day against the descendants of the first Dutch settlers, the Union of South Africa was established and immediately set about unifying several previously separate territories. In some of these, most notably the British Cape Colony, the political regime was censitary rather than racial: blacks, coloreds (of mixed race), and Asians (mostly Indians) who were sufficiently wealthy had the right to vote and formed a small minority of the mostly white electorate.[41] But the Boers adamantly opposed extending this system to the rest of the Union, especially Transvaal, the Natal Colony, and the Orange Colony. Afrikaner elites moved quickly to intensify the system of discrimination with the adoption of the Native Labour Regulation Act of 1911, which controlled labor mobility by requiring every black laborer to carry a pass when leaving his zone of employment. The Natives Land Act of 1913 mapped out a series of "native reserves," which covered 7 percent of the country's territory (although blacks represented 80 percent of the population). Whites were not allowed to exploit land in the reserves, while Africans were of course forbidden to own or rent land in the "white zone."[42] These measures were radicalized when apartheid was officially established in 1948, and they were completed in 1950–1953 by the Population Registration Act, the Group Area Act, and the Separation of Amenities Act, all prior to the official end of British oversight in 1961.

Voting was also organized on a strictly racial basis: all whites and only whites had the right to vote without any wealth qualification. In the 1960s and 1970s,

---

41. See F. X. Fauvelle-Aymar, *Histoire de l'Afrique du Sud* (Seuil, 2006), pp. 382–395.

42. One finds similar native reserves in other colonial systems, for example, in French New Caledonia at the end of the nineteenth and early twentieth century. See G. Noiriel, *Une histoire populaire de la France* (Agone, 2018), pp. 431–435.

amid a wave of independence movements and in the middle of the Cold War, South Africans, facing strong criticism from abroad, debated the wisdom of reinstating voting rights for some blacks, with some sort of property qualification. The problem was that if one used the same tax or property threshold for whites and blacks, it would take an extremely high threshold to ensure a white majority, and this would mean depriving the white working and middle class of the right to vote; yet these classes had no intention of giving up their newly won political rights to wealthy blacks. If one lowered the threshold too much, however, blacks could well become the majority and take power. This was ultimately what happened after apartheid ended in 1990–1994. In 1994 Nelson Mandela was elected, something the Afrikaner population had long regarded as unthinkable until the determination of demonstrators in the townships, aided by international sanctions, forced them to agree to a change in the rules.

The end of apartheid and discrimination made advancement possible for a minority of blacks who joined the country's political and economic elite. For example, whereas blacks accounted for only 1 percent of the top centile of the income distribution in 1985, they accounted for nearly 15 percent in the period 1995–2000, mainly because blacks now had access to top government jobs and also because a portion of the white population left. Since that time, however, the proportion of blacks in the top centile has slightly decreased, falling to 13–14 percent in the 2010s. In other words, whites still represent more than 85 percent of the top centile (and nearly 70 percent of the top decile) although they account for a little over 10 percent of the total population.[43] South Africa has gone from a situation in which blacks were totally excluded from top jobs to one in which they are theoretically admitted but whites remain hyperdominant. It is also striking to discover that the gap between the top 10 percent of the income distribution and the rest of the population has increased in South Africa since the end of apartheid (Fig. 7.5).

This can be explained in part by the unusual configuration of South African politics, in which the African National Congress (ANC), the party that led the anti-apartheid struggle, continues to occupy a quasi-hegemonic position but has never adopted a genuine policy of wealth redistribution. No agrarian reform was introduced after the end of apartheid and no sufficiently ambitious fiscal reform was adopted; this means that the incredible inequalities due to black South Africans being confined to less than 10 percent of the territory

---

43. See the online appendix and the work of F. Alvaredo, A. Atkinson, and E. Morival.

for nearly a century (from the Natives Land Act of 1913 until 1994) have essentially remained in place. Indeed, the ANC has generally been dominated by factions with fairly conservative positions on issues of redistribution and progressive taxation, although social and political pressure in this direction has become stronger since the early 2010s.[44] It also bears emphasizing that the global ideological environment was hardly encouraging in the period 1990–2010. If a South African government had undertaken a land redistribution program, it would probably have triggered strong opposition from the white minority, in which case it is by no means certain that the support the ANC enjoyed in Western countries would have continued for long.

It is symptomatic, moreover, that in 2018–2019, when the ANC government discussed the possibility of agrarian reform, US president Donald Trump hastened to express his firm support for white farmers and ordered his administration to follow the matter closely. In his eyes, the fact that generations of blacks had been violently discriminated against and confined to reserves until the 1990s clearly did not justify any compensation: all that was old business that should promptly be forgotten. No parcel of land could be taken from whites and given to blacks because no one would know where to end such a process. In practice, however, one might think that no one could really oppose a democratically elected South African government that decided to redistribute wealth in the most peaceful way possible via agrarian reform and progressive taxation, as was done in many countries (especially in Europe and Asia) in the twentieth century.[45]

What the South African case demonstrates in its own particular way is, once again, the power of proprietarian inegalitarian mechanisms: the concentration of wealth in the country was built on a foundation of the most absolute racial inequality, but that concentration largely endured even after the advent of formal equality of rights, which plainly has not been enough to eliminate it. In most other colonial societies, the redistribution of land and other property was accomplished through the departure of the white community and a more or less chaotic process of nationalization. But when one attempts, as in South Africa, to arrange

---

44. In part under pressure from the black Economic Freedom Fighters (EFF) party, which has fought for redistribution of wealth, and also because some of the black bourgeoisie has joined the old what Afrikaner National Party, which became the Democratic Alliance in 1999. See A. Gethin, *Cleavage Structures and Distributive Politics* (master's thesis, Paris School of Economics, 2018), and the online appendix.

45. See Chaps. 5, 10–11.

for durable and peaceful cohabitation of the former ruling class in a violent colonial society with the classes they once ruled, one must then envisage other legal and fiscal mechanisms to achieve the desired redistribution.

The End of Colonialism and the Question of Democratic Federalism

Slave and colonial societies have left indelible traces on the structure of modern inequality, both between countries and within them. But I would like now to insist on a less well-known legacy of this long history. The end of colonialism led to debates about regional and transcontinental democratic federalism, and even if nothing concrete has yet emerged from these debates, they are nevertheless rich in instruction for the future.

The end of the French colonial empire is particularly interesting in this regard, as we know from Frederick Cooper's recent study.[46] In 1945, after the colonies helped the metropole liberate itself from four years of German occupation, it was quite clear to everyone (except perhaps a few European settlers) that there would be no going back to the colonial empire that had existed before the war. French authorities wanted to preserve the empire, but they knew that in order to do so there would have to be changes in the way it operated. In the first place, the metropole would need to adopt a more deliberate policy of investment and fiscal transfers to the colonies (which, as we have seen, did happen after the war despite a budgetary structure that continued to strongly favor the colonizers). Second and even more important, the political institutions of the colonies would need to be radically transformed. What is unusual about the French case is that between 1945 and 1960 the effort to overhaul political institutions in the colonies was led by a National Assembly that included elected representatives from both the metropole and the colonies. In practice, the basis of this representation was never one of numerical equality, because that would have threatened the supremacy of the metropole; this lack of sufficient institutional imagination is what undermined the whole effort. A better result might have been achieved by setting up a West African or North African federation before attempting to work toward transcontinental parliamentary sovereignty.

---

46. See the excellent book by F. Cooper, *Citizenship Between Empire and Nation: Remaking France and French Africa, 1945–1960* (Princeton University Press, 2014). See also F. Cooper, *Africa in the World: Capitalism, Empire, Nation-State* (Harvard University Press, 2014).

Still, the attempt to transform an authoritarian empire into a democratic federation was fairly novel (British colonies were never represented in either the House of Lords or the House of Commons) and deserves to be revisited.[47]

The National Constituent Assembly that was elected in October 1945 to draft a new French constitution included 522 deputies from metropolitan France and 64 deputies representing the various territories of the empire. This was far from numerical equality, since the population of metropolitan France was then about 40 million while that of the colonies was about 60 million (excluding Indochina, where the war for independence had already begun). What is more, the sixty-four colonial deputies were elected by separate colleges of settlers and natives in a highly inegalitarian manner. For instance, FWA elected ten deputies, four of whom were chosen by 21,000 settlers and the other six by some 15 million natives. Nevertheless, numerous African leaders did sit and play an important role in the French National Assembly from 1945 to 1960, including Léopold Senghor and Félix Houphouët-Boigny, who both served several terms as ministers in French governments. Senghor then went on to serve as president of Senegal from 1960 to 1980, while Houphouët-Boigny served as president of Ivory Coast from 1960 to 1993. It was at the behest of the latter that the Constituent Assembly in 1946 adopted a law abolishing all forms of forced labor in France's overseas territories and, in particular, the 1912 decree regarding "services" owed by natives—this was the least one could ask of a colonial power that claimed to want to recast its relations with its colonies on a basis of equality. And it was at the behest of Amadou Lamine-Gueye (future president of the Senegal Assembly from 1960 to 1968) that the Constituent Assembly passed a law establishing the French Union and bestowing French citizenship on every inhabitant of the empire.

The first constitution proposed by the Constituent Assembly was rejected in a close referendum vote (53–47 against) in May 1946. A new Constituent Assembly was then elected in June and drafted a second constitution, which was adopted in yet another close vote (also 53–47, but this time in favor) on October 1946. This became the constitution of the Fourth Republic, which remained in effect from 1946 to 1958. Among the criticisms that the Gaullists and the parties of the center and right had leveled at the first draft constitution was that it was too monocameral: it gave full powers to the National Assembly, and

---

47. In 1809–1812 Spain tried to organize a federal parliament that included representatives of its Latin American colonies, but the context was quite different, and the system never really had time to function.

the fear was that Socialist and Communist deputies would wield a majority of the votes in that chamber. The second draft constitution therefore attempted to counterbalance the National Assembly with a second chamber, the Council of the Republic, which, like the Senate in the (current) Fifth Republic, was to be elected by indirect suffrage and therefore structurally more conservative. A second factor—less well known but just as essential—played a crucial role in the debates: the first draft foresaw a single National Assembly that would include deputies from the entire French Union (comprising the metropole and its former colonies), leaving it up to legislators to determine its exact composition. This worried the most conservative metropolitan deputies (as well as some Socialists and Communists), who feared that the assembly would be full of "Negro chieftains." The critics also pointed out that voter lists were not ready and that Africans were illiterate, to which their opponents responded that the voter lists were ready enough when it was a question of collecting taxes and that the French peasantry had been just as illiterate in the early years of the Third Republic. In any event, the fear of a unicameral National Assembly that might ultimately opt for quasi-proportional representation of the former colonies and thus gradually deprive the metropole of its majority played a key role in the first proposal's narrow defeat in the May 1946 referendum.

The second constitution was also ambiguous, since the National Assembly included both metropolitan and overseas deputies in proportions to be set by legislators themselves. The difference was that the National Assembly was now balanced by a conservative Council of the Republic as well as by an Assembly of the French Union composed of 50 percent representatives of the metropole (to be chosen by the National Assembly and the Council of the Republic) and 50 percent representatives of the overseas territories (to be chosen by their future assemblies). The constitution also placed all military forces of the French Union under the government of the French Republic and ultimately the control of the National Assembly and Council of the Republic, with no more than a consultative role for the Assembly of the French Union. Even though the apportionment of seats in the National Assembly was left open, the whole structure left no doubt that the metropole would retain the vast majority of the seats and exercise regalian functions in the name of the French Union, which in spite of all the changes would remain an empire under French direction. Proponents of egalitarian democratic federalism thus saw their hopes dashed.[48]

---

48. The first proposed constitution also envisioned an Economic Council and a Council of the French Union, but these were to have been purely consultative

From the Franco-African Union to the Mali Federation

Many African leaders nevertheless continued to believe in the federal option. Black voters had massively supported the first proposed constitution in the May 1946 referendum, especially in Senegal and the West Indies, whereas whites had opposed it.[49] In particular, Senghor was convinced that the tiny, artificial nation-states such as Senegal and Ivory Coast that were emerging from the decolonization process would not be fully sovereign in economic terms. Only by becoming part of a large federal structure based on free circulation and fiscal solidarity as well as on an alliance between European socialist currents and African solidaristic and collectivist traditions would they be able to achieve harmonious economic and social development within the framework of global capitalism. In retrospect, of course, it is hard to imagine how a majority of French voters could have been induced to accept Franco-African federalism on a politically egalitarian basis. In the early 1950s, French officials regularly issued warnings like this one: "If we continue to increase the colonial presence in the National Assembly, we will end up with 200 polygamists legislating for French families." Pierre-Henri Teitgen, the chair of the MRP (the main center-right party), even offered the prognostication that equal political representation would lead to transfers that will "reduce the standard of living in the metropole by at least 25–30 percent."

A more realistic alternative to egalitarian Franco-African federalism might have been a West African political union (a monetary version of which now exists in the form of the CFA franc, which is still in use today but which offers nothing in the way of parliamentary or fiscal sovereignty). This might have led to some kind of Franco-African Assembly with jurisdiction over the flow of people, capital, and goods and some limited form of fiscal solidarity. This is what Senghor, recognizing that the French Union had reached an impasse, eventually proposed to Houphouët-Boigny and other West African leaders in

---

bodies under the control of the Assembly. On these debates, see F. Cooper, *Citizenship Between Empire and Nation,* pp. 42–61, 92–93, 148–151,187–189, 214–258.

49. It is interesting to note that when Réunion, Guadeloupe, and Martinique were made *départements* in 1945, with Communist support, some white planters advocated a segregationist independence model like that of South Africa. Gaston Monnerville, the grandson of a slave and deputy from Guiana, became president of the Council of the Republic and then of the Senate from 1947 to 1968; he came within six months of being the first mixed-race (interim) president of the French Republic after General de Gaulle resigned.

1955–1956. But it was already too late. The Africans were already preoccupied with consolidating government in their own countries, and in 1957–1958 Ivory Coast refused to participate in the building of any authentic West African institutions, thus paving the way to national independence without cross-border cooperation. In some cases, this led, decades later, to the development of exaggerated forms of national identity, such as *ivoirité*, despite the largely arbitrary character of the initial colonial borders. As for North Africa, the number of deputies granted to France's "Algerian *départements*" rose as high as 74 (close to what Algeria's population deserved) in 1958, with a total of 106 seats for all overseas territories still remaining in the French Community (which had replaced the French Union) out of a total of 579 deputies in the National Assembly, but the community was by then living its final days as Algerian rebels were already on the way to achieving independence.[50] Vestiges of this system survive to this day: in 2017 France's overseas *départements* elected twenty-seven of the 577 deputies in the National Assembly. Representation today is now entirely proportional to population but with less risk to the metropolitan majority in view of the small size of the overseas *départements*.

In 1958–1959 a number of African leaders (including Senghor) refused to accept the idea that 20 million West Africans could not achieve unity at a time when the much more populous nations of Europe were creating an economic and political union. In 1959 they launched the Mali Federation, which linked Senegal, Sudan (today's Mali), Upper Volta (today's Burkina Faso), and Dahomey (today's Bénin). This collapsed in 1960, partly because of lack of cooperation from Ivory Coast and Niger (which declined to join) and France (which continued to believe in its French Union) and partly because of unforeseen tax issues that arose between Senegal and Sudan (which was less wealthy but had more people, 4 million compared with Senegal's 2.5 million). In the end, Sudan remained as the only member of the federation and kept the name Mali. The main stumbling block was that each of these territories had begun to govern itself separately in 1945; their leaders met mainly in the National

---

50. In negotiations in 1946, the first Constituent Assembly allocated thirty-five seats to Algeria (fourteen for settlers, twenty-first for Muslims); Algerian leader Ferhat Abbas (who in 1962 became independent Algeria's first chief of state) demanded fifty-five seats (twenty for settlers and thirty-five for Muslims, although numerical parity would have given them 106); the second Constituent Assembly gave Algeria thirty seats (fifteen for settlers and fifteen for Muslims). In the eyes of many observers, war became inevitable from that point on. See F. Cooper, *Citizenship Between Empire and Nation,* p. 135.

Assembly and had not developed the habit of shared governance in the period 1945–1960.[51] Things might have gone differently if African and French political leaders had gambled in 1945 on a strong regional federalism and a more balanced and realistic relationship with what would soon cease to be the metropole. In the end, France decided in 1974 to put an end to free circulation of people born in the former colonies prior to 1960. And so ended the idea of transforming an authoritarian empire into a democratic federation. That chapter was closed.

When one rereads these debates decades later, it is particularly striking to note the many possible switch points where different routes might have been chosen. No one really knew how best to organize a large-scale federal political community any more than we know how to accomplish this today, but many people felt that retreating within the borders of small states with tiny populations was not necessarily the best solution. In retrospect, we can see a variety of federal solutions that might have worked, and this naturally leads us to take a fresh look at those that exist today and that (naysayers notwithstanding) will continue to evolve in the future. It is highly unlikely, for example, that the current institutional structure of the European Union will remain as it is eternally, and apart from a few American nationalists, most people think there are ways in which the United States can be improved. More generally, the challenge of constructing spaces for deliberation and political decision making on a regional and continental scale is one that concerns not only Africa, Latin America, and Asia but the entire planet in the twenty-first century. New forms of cooperation between Europe and Africa are more necessary than ever, particularly in relation to issues of migration. The democracy that currently exists at the level of the nations-states is not the end of history. Political institutions are and will always be undergoing perpetual transformation, particularly at the postnational level. Study of past switch points is the best way to prepare for those that lie ahead. We will come back to this, especially when we look at the conditions of a just frontier and at a democratic organization of international economic relations and migrations (Chapter 17).

---

51. F. Cooper, *Citizenship Between Empire and Nation*, pp. 328–421.

EIGHT

Ternary Societies and Colonialism: The Case of India

We turn now to the case of India, which is particularly important for our study. This is not just because the Republic of India has been the "largest democracy in the world" since the middle of the twentieth century and will soon become the most populous nation on the planet. If India plays a central role in the history of inequality regimes, it is also because of its caste system, which is generally regarded as a particularly rigid and extreme type of inequality regime. It is therefore essential that we understand its origins and peculiarities.

Apart from its historical importance, the caste system has left traces in contemporary Indian society much more prominent than the status inequalities stemming from the European society of orders (which have almost entirely disappeared except for largely symbolic vestiges such as hereditary peerages in the United Kingdom). Our task is therefore to understand whether these distinct evolutionary trajectories can be explained by longstanding structural differences between European orders and Indian castes or if they are better understood in terms of specific social and political trajectories and distinct switch points.

We will find that the trajectory of Indian inequality can be correctly analyzed only within a more general framework involving the transformation of premodern trifunctional societies. What distinguishes the Indian trajectory from the various European ones is the fact that state construction in the vast subcontinent followed an unusual path. Specifically, the process of social transformation, state construction, and homogenization of statuses and rights (which were particularly disparate in India) was interrupted by a foreign power, the British colonizer, which in the late nineteenth century sought to map the caste hierarchy to assert control over society. Its primary tool for doing this was the census, which was conducted every ten years from 1871 to 1941. An unanticipated consequence of the census was that it gave the caste hierarchy an administrative existence, which made the system more rigid and resistant to change.

Since 1947, independent India has tried to use the state's legal powers to cor-rect the legacy of caste discrimination, especially in access to education, gov-ernment jobs, and elective office. The government's policies, though far from perfect, are highly instructive, all the more so since discrimination exists ev-erywhere, not least in Europe, which has just begun to deal with ethnic and religious hostilities of the sort with which India has had to contend for centu-ries. The course of Indian inequality was profoundly altered by its encounter with the outside world in the form of a remote foreign power. Now, in turn, the rest of the world has much to learn from India's experience.

The Invention of India: Preliminary Remarks

As far back as we can go in the demographic sources, we find that the territory now occupied by the Republic of India and the People's Republic of China has always been home to more people than Europe and other parts of the world. In 1700, the population of India was about 170 million and that of China about 140 million, compared with 100 million in Europe. In the nineteenth and twentieth centuries China leapt ahead of India. Since China's adoption of a single child per family policy in 1980, however, its population has been shrinking, and by the end of the 2020s India should once again be the most populous country-continent on the planet. It will remain so for the rest of the twenty-first century, with nearly 1.7 billion citizens by 2050 if one believes the latest projections from the United Nations (Fig. 8.1). To explain the exceptional population densities in China and India, many authors have followed the lead of Fernand Braudel, who insisted in *Civilisation matérielle, économie et capi-talisme* on the importance of different dietary regimes: the reason for Europe's lower population density, Braudel argues, is that Europeans are too fond of meat, since it takes more acres to produce animal calories than to produce vegetable calories.

Our focus is on inequality, however. We have already seen the crucial importance of centralized state building in the evolution of structures of inequality. The first question to ask now is how did a population as large as India's (already 200 million by the end of the eighteenth century, when the population of the largest European country, France, was less than 30 million and already in the throes of revolution) manage to coexist peacefully in a single large state. The first answer is that Indian unity is actually a very recent development. India as a human and political community developed only grad-ually, following a complex social and political trajectory. Many state structures

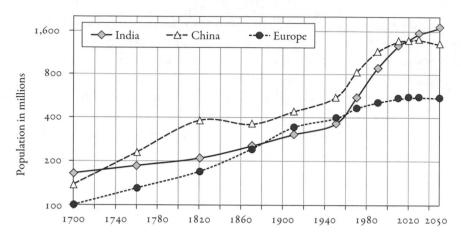

FIG. 8.1. Population of India, China, and Europe, 1700–2050

Interpretation: Around 1700, the population of India was about 170 million, of China 140 million, and of Europe 100 million (roughly 125 million if one includes the area corresponding to today's Russia, Belarus, and Ukraine). In 2050, according to UN forecasts, the population of India will be about 1.7 billion, of China 1.3 billion, and of Europe (EU) 550 million (720 million if one includes Russia, Belarus, and Ukraine). *Sources and series:* piketty.pse.ens.fr/ideology.

coexisted in India for centuries. Some of them extended over vast portions of the Indian subcontinent: for instance, the Maurya Empire in the third century BCE and the Mughal Empire, which even at its peak in the sixteenth and seventeenth centuries never covered all of present-day India and thereafter went into decline.

When the British Raj (as Britain's colonial empire in India was known) gave way to independent India in 1947, the country still comprised 562 princely states and other political entities under the tutelage of the colonizing power. To be sure, the British directly administered more than 75 percent of the country's population, and the censuses conducted from 1871 to 1941 covered the entire country (including the princely states and autonomous regions). The British administration nevertheless relied heavily on local elites and often did little more than maintain order. Infrastructure and public services were as rudimentary or nonexistent as in the French colonies.[1] It was left to independent India to achieve administrative and political unification after 1947 under a vibrant, pluralist parliamentary democracy. India's political practice was of

1. See Chap. 7.

course influenced by its direct contact with Britain and its parliamentary model. It is important to recognize, however, that India developed this form of government on a larger human and geographic scale than anything that preceded it in history. Europe is currently attempting to build a political organization on a large scale with the European Union and European Parliament (although Europe's population is less than half of India's and its political and fiscal integration is much less advanced). Meanwhile, the United Kingdom, which parted company with Ireland in the early twentieth century and may lose Scotland in the twenty-first, has had a hard time maintaining unity on the British Isles.

In the eighteenth century, when the British were preparing to push further inland, India was divided into a multitude of states led by Hindu and Muslim princes. Islam began to make inroads into northwest India as early as the eighth to tenth centuries, which led to the founding of the first kingdoms and then the seizure of Delhi by Turco-Afghan dynasties in the late twelfth century. The Delhi Sultanate then expanded and transformed itself in the thirteenth and fourteenth centuries, after which new waves of Turco-Mongol immigration led to the founding of the Mughal Empire, which dominated the Indian subcontinent from 1526 to 1707. The Mughal state, led from Agra and later Delhi by Muslim sovereigns, was multiconfessional and polyglot. In addition to the Indian languages spoken by the vast majority of the population and the Hindu elites, the Mughal court spoke Persian, Urdu, and Arabic. The Mughal state was a complex and shaky structure, clearly running out of energy by 1707 and permanently contested by Hindu kingdoms such as the Maratha Empire, initially located in present-day Maharashtra (centered on Mumbai) before extending its reach into northern and western India between 1674 and 1818. It was in this context of rivalry among Muslim, Hindu, and multiconfessional states and gradual decay of the Mughal Empire that the British slowly took control, first under the auspices of the shareholders of the East India Company from 1757 to 1858 and then under the authority of the Empire of India from 1858 to 1947. The Empire was directly linked to the British Crown and Parliament after the Sepoy Mutiny of 1857 showed London the need for direct administration. In 1858 the British seized the opportunity to depose the last Mughal emperor, whose empire had shrunk to a small territory in the neighborhood of Delhi but who still symbolized moral authority and a semblance of native sovereignty in the eyes of Hindu and Muslim rebels who had sought his protection for their efforts to mount a rebellion against the European colonizer.

Broadly speaking, the very long shared history of Hindus and Muslims in India, from the Delhi Sultanate of the late twelfth century to the ultimate fall

of the Mughal Empire in the nineteenth, gave rise to a unique cultural and political syncretism in the Indian subcontinent. A significant minority of India's
military, intellectual, and commercial elites gradually converted to Islam and
forged alliances with the conquering Turco-Afghans and Turco-Mongols,
whose numbers were quite small. As the Muslim sultanates extended their dominion into the center and south of India in the sixteenth century at the expense of the Hindu kingdoms, especially the Vijayanagara Empire (in today's
Karnataka), they forged close ties with Hindu elites and literary circles associated with the various courts, including Brahmin scholars working for Muslim
sultans and Persian chroniclers who frequented the palaces. Their ties to the
European colonizers were even closer, especially with the Portuguese who established colonies (most notably in Goa and Calicut) on the Indian coast after
1510 and who sought to overwhelm the Muslim kings and take up the cause of
the Vijayanagara Empire while refusing the emperor's offer of matrimony.[2]
Hostility between Hindus and Muslims also existed, especially since many who
converted to Islam came from the lower strata of Hindu society and saw conversion as a way to flee a particularly hierarchical and inegalitarian caste system.
Muslims are still overrepresented in the poorest segments of Indian society; in
Part Four of this book we will see that the attitude of Hindu nationalists toward
poor Muslims has been a key structural feature of Indian politics from the late
twentieth century to the present, in some respects comparable to recent conflicts in Europe (with the important difference that there have been Muslims
in India for centuries, whereas in Europe their presence dates back only a few
decades).[3]

At this stage, note simply that thanks to the imperial censuses conducted
every ten years from 1871 to 1941 and continued after independence from 1951
to 2011, we can measure the evolution of the country's religious diversity
(Fig. 8.2). We find that Muslims accounted for roughly 20 percent of the 250
million people enumerated in the first two censuses, in 1871 and 1881, and that
this proportion rose to 24 percent in 1931 and 1941 thanks to a higher birth
rate among Muslims. In 1951, in the first census organized by the independent
Republic of India, the proportion of Muslims fell to 10 percent owing to the

---

2. Portugal was willing to accept a Hindu princess but refused to offer a Portuguese princess. On these court intrigues, see the excellent book by S. Subrahmanyam, *L'éléphant, le canon et le pinceau. Histoires connectées des cours d'Europe et
   d'Asie 1500–1750* (Alma, 2016).
3. See Chaps. 14–16.

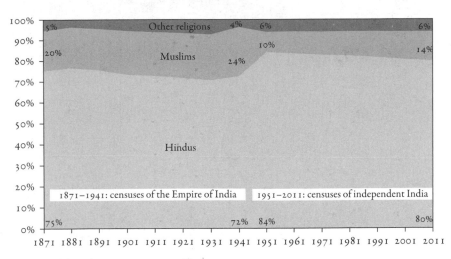

FIG. 8.2. The religious structure of India, 1871–2011

Interpretation: In the 2011 census, 80 percent of the population of India was declared Hindu, 14 percent Muslim, and 6 percent other religions (Sikhs, Christians, Buddhists, no religion, etc.). These figures were 75 percent, 20 percent, and 5 percent in the colonial census of 1871; 72, 24, and 4 percent in the census of 1941; 84, 10, and 6 percent in the first census of independent India in 1951 (after the partition with Pakistan and Bangladesh). *Sources and series:* piketty.pse.ens.fr/ideology.

partition of the country: Pakistan and Bangladesh, where most Muslims lived, ceased to be part of India and were therefore no longer included in the census, in addition to which there were large-scale movements of Hindus and Muslims after partition. Since then, the proportion of Muslims has risen slightly (again owing to a slightly higher birth rate), reaching 14 percent in the 2011 census out of a population of more than 1.2 billion.

Religions other than Hinduism and Islam have accounted for around 5 percent of the population in every census from 1871 to 2011. Among them we find mainly Sikhs, Christians, and Buddhists (in roughly comparable numbers), as well as individuals professing no religion at all (of whom there are very few—always less than 1 percent). Bear in mind, however, that colonial censuses and to a lesser extent those conducted after independence as well are based on a complex mix of self-declared identities and identities assigned by census agents and administrators. If a person did not clearly belong to a listed religion (Muslim, Sikh, Christian, or Buddhist), the default classification was generally "Hindu" (since Hindus accounted for 72–75 percent of the population in the colonial era and 80–84 percent in the era of independence), even

TABLE 8.1

The structure of the population in Indian censuses, 1871–2011

	1871	1881	1891	1901	1911	1921	1931	1941	1951	1961	1971	1981	1991	2001	2011
Hindus	75%	76%	76%	74%	73%	72%	71%	72%	84%	83%	83%	82%	81%	81%	80%
Muslims	20%	20%	20%	21%	21%	22%	22%	24%	10%	11%	11%	12%	13%	13%	14%
Other religions (Sikhs, Christians, Buddhists, etc.)	5%	4%	4%	5%	6%	6%	7%	4%	6%	6%	6%	6%	6%	6%	6%
Total	100%	100%	100%	100%	100%	100%	100%	100%	100%	100%	100%	100%	100%	100%	100%
Scheduled castes (SC)									15%	15%	15%	16%	17%	16%	17%
Scheduled tribes (ST)									6%	7%	7%	8%	8%	8%	9%
Total Indian population (millions)	239	254	287	294	314	316	351	387	361	439	548	683	846	1,029	1,211

Interpretation: The results indicated here are based on censuses conducted in the Empire of India from 1871 to 1941 and then in independent India from 1951 to 2011. The proportion of Muslims fell from 24 percent in 1941 to 10 percent in 1951 owing to the partition of Pakistan and Bangladesh. From 1951 on, the censuses recorded "scheduled castes" (SC) and "scheduled tribes" (ST)—untouchables and disadvantaged aborigines. *Sources and series:* piketty.pse.ens.fr/ideology.

when the person belonged to a pariah group subject to discrimination by Hindus, including lower castes, former untouchables, and aborigines.

The overwhelming "Hindu" majority is therefore partly artificial and masks immense disparities of status, identity, and religious practice within Hindu polytheism, especially since different groups do not enjoy the same level of access to ceremonies and temples. Islam, Christianity, and Buddhism purport to be egalitarian religions (in which everyone has access to God or wisdom in the same way, independent of origin or social class), at least in theory, since in practice those religions have also developed trifunctional and patriarchal ideologies that structure the social and political order and justify social inequalities and sexual division of labor and functions. Hinduism is more explicit in linking religion to social organization and class inequality. I will say more later about the way in which Hindu castes were defined and measured in colonial censuses as well as the way in which independent India has developed new categories, "scheduled castes" (SC) and "scheduled tribes" (ST), which account for roughly 25 percent of the population in the most recent censuses (Table 8.1). The purpose was of course to correct old discrimination but with the risk that these new categories could become permanent. Before taking up that question, we need to gain a better understanding of the origins of the caste system.

India and the Quaternary Order: Brahmins, Kshatriyas, Vaishyas, Shudras

In our study of European societies of orders, we learned that the earliest texts giving formal expression to the trifunctional organization of society, with a religious class (*oratores*), a warrior class (*bellatores*), and a laboring class (*laboratories*), were penned by bishops in England and France in the tenth and eleventh centuries.[4] The origins of the trifunctional idea in India date from much earlier. The functional classes in the Hindu system are called *varnas*, and the *varnas* appear as the four parts of the god Purusha in Sanskrit religious texts of the Vedic era, the oldest of which date from the second millennium BCE. But the fundamental text is the *Manusmriti*, or Code of Laws of Manu, a compendium of laws written in Sanskrit between the second century BCE and the second century CE and constantly revised and commented on ever since. This was a normative political and ideological text. Its authors described the way they thought society should be organized and specifically the way they

---

4. See Chap. 2.

thought the dominated and laborious classes should obey rules set by religious and warrior elites. It is in no sense a factual or historical description of Indian society at the time of its writing or at any time thereafter. That society encompassed thousands of social micro-classes and professional guilds, and the political and social order were constantly being challenged by revolts of the dominated classes and by the regular appearance of new warrior classes, which emerged from the ranks bearing new promises of harmony, justice, and stability—sometimes with effect, sometimes not, just as in Christian Europe and other parts of the world.

The heart of the Manusmriti is a description of the rights and duties of the several *varnas,* or social classes, whose role is defined in the first chapters. *Brahmins* functioned as priests, scholars, and men of letters; *Kshatriyas* were warriors responsible for maintaining order and providing security for the community; *Vaishyas* were farmers, herders, craftsmen, and merchants; and *Shudras* were the lowest level of workers, whose only mission was to serve the three other classes.[5] In other words, this was an explicitly quaternary rather than ternary system, in contrast to the theoretical trifunctional order of medieval Christendom. In practice, however, the Christian system included serfs until a relatively late date, at least the fourteenth century in Western Europe and almost to the end of the nineteenth in the East, so that the laboring class really included two subgroups (free workers and servile workers), as in India. Note, moreover, that the scheme set forth in the Manusmriti was theoretical; in practice, the line between Vaishyas and Shudras, workers of different status and unequal duties, was often blurry. Depending on the context, it is reasonable to think that the distinction roughly corresponded to the difference between farmers who owned their own land and landless rural workers, or, in Europe, to the distinction between free peasants and serfs.

After defining the four major social classes, the Manusmriti goes into great detail about the rituals and rules that Brahmins must obey as well as the conditions governing the exercise of royal power. In principle, the king is a Kshatriya, but he is supposed to choose a group of counselors consisting of seven or eight Brahmins, preferably the wisest and most learned of their class. He is urged to consult with them daily about affairs of state and finances and is admonished not to make major military decisions without the approval of the most illustrious Brahmin.[6] The Vaishyas and Shudras are more cursorily described. The

---

5. See *The Law Code of Manu,* trans. P. Olivelle (Oxford Classics, 2004), p. 19.
6. See *The Law Code of Manu,* pp. 106–110.

Manusmriti also contains detailed descriptions of how the courts are supposed to function in a well-ordered Hindu kingdom, along with a large number of civil, criminal, fiscal, and successoral rules pertaining to such matters as the share of an estate due to children of "mixed" marriages between members of different varnas (which were discouraged but not forbidden). The text seems to be addressed primarily to a sovereign seeking to establish a kingdom in a new territory but also pertains to existing Hindu kingdoms. Distant barbarians are mentioned, especially Persians, Greeks, and Chinese, and it is stipulated that they should be considered and treated as Shudras, even if they were Kshatriyas by birth, because they do not obey the law of the Brahmins. In other words, a noble foreigner is the same as a Shudra as long as he has not been civilized by a Brahmin.[7]

Many scholars have tried to determine the context in which this text was written, circulated, and used. The Manusmriti is said to be the collective work of a group of Brahmins (the name *Manu* refers not to the actual author of the text but to a mythical legislator from centuries prior to the drafting of the code) who supposedly drafted and then polished this theoretical corpus in stages starting in the second century BCE. The goal was clearly to restore the power of the Brahmins, which in the eyes of the drafters was the basis of social and political harmony in Hindu society, in the particularly fraught political circumstances that followed the fall of the Maurya Empire (322–185 BCE). Brahmin power had been challenged in the third century BCE by the conversion to Buddhism of Emperor Asoka (268–232 BCE). The first Buddha, Siddhartha Gautama, who supposedly lived in the late sixth and early fifth centuries BCE, was according to tradition the scion of a family of Kshatriyas, and his ascetic, meditative, and monastic way of life constituted a challenge to the traditional Brahminic clerical class. Even though Asoka seems to have relied on both traditional Brahmin priests and Buddhist ascetics, his conversion raised questions about some of the rites and animal sacrifices performed by the Brahmins. In fact, it was allegedly in reaction to competition from Buddhist ascetics and to enhance their prestige in the eyes of the other classes that the Brahmins became strict vegetarians.

In any case, the Manusmriti clearly expresses a desire to place (or replace) learned Brahmins at the heart of the political system. The authors plainly believed that the time had come to promote their preferred model of society by drafting and circulating a wide-ranging legal and political-ideological treatise.

---

7. See *The Law Code of Manu,* pp. 183, 284.

The other chief complaint that emerges from the text is related to the fact that the Maurya emperors themselves were descended from military leaders risen from the ranks and born into the lower class of Shudras. Brahmins leveled the same criticism at any number of the other dynasties that succeeded one another in northern India before and after Alexander the Great's invasion of the north-western Indian subcontinent in 326 BCE.

What the Manusmriti proposes is a social structure and rules intended to end the permanent chaos and restore order to the Hindu social and political system: Shudras are encouraged to remain in their place at the bottom of the social hierarchy while kings must be chosen among the Kshatriyas under the strict supervision of learned Brahmins.[8] In practice, the Brahmins' demand that kings be chosen from among the authentic Kshatriyas (which can be read more prosaically as a demand that kings and warriors submit to the wisdom of the Brahmins and that the ceaseless changes of political and military power should come to an end) would never be fully satisfied. As in European and all other human societies, the warrior elites of India's various regions would continue to battle one another for superiority, and the eternal task of the intellectuals, no less in India than anywhere else, would be to impose discipline on the warriors or, at the very least, insist on a modicum of respect for their vast knowledge.

The Brahmin discourse in the Manusmriti should of course be analyzed as the centerpiece of a bid for social and political dominance. As with the tri-functional schema put forward by bishops in medieval Europe, its primary objective was to see to it that the lower classes accepted their fate as workers subordinate to the priests and warriors. The Indian text added a further fillip: a theory of reincarnation. Members of the lowest varna, the Shudras, could in theory be reincarnated as members of higher varnas. Conversely, members of the first three varnas—Brahmins, Kshatriyas, Vaishyas—were twice-born: the ceremony by which they were initiated into their varna was regarded as a second birth, which entitled them to wear a sacred thread, the *yagyopavita,* across their breast. The logic here was in a sense the opposite of the logic of meritocracy, with its exaggerated emphasis on individual talent and merit. In the Brahminic system, each individual occupies an assigned place and works together with all the others like the various parts of a single body to ensure social harmony;

---

8. See P. Olivelle, "Introduction," in *The Law Code of Manu,* pp. xli–xlv. See also P. Olivelle, *Between the Empires: Society in India 300 BCE to 400 CE* (Oxford University Press, 2006); P. Olivelle and D. Davies, *Hindu Law. A New History of Dharmasastra* (Oxford University Press, 2018).

in a future life, however, the same individual might just as well occupy another place. The point was to ensure earthly harmony and avoid chaos while making use of acquired or inherited knowledge and skills; personal effort and discipline might be required, and individual advancement was not impossible, but the process must not lead to unbridled social competition, which would threaten the stability of the society. One finds in all civilizations the idea that strict assignment of social positions and political functions can serve as a check on hubris and ego; this is often used as a defense of hereditary hierarchies, especially in monarchic and dynastic systems.[9]

Brahminic Order, Vegetarian Diet, and Patriarchy

Like the Christian trifunctional schema, the Brahminic order expressed an ideal equilibrium of different forms of legitimacy. In both, the goal was to make sure that kings and warriors, the embodiment of brute force, did not neglect the wise counsel of learned clerics and that political power availed itself of the power of knowledge and intellect. Recall that Gandhi, who criticized the British for having taken once-fluid caste divisions and made them more rigid to better divide and conquer India, also took a rather respectful conservative position with respect to the Brahmin ideal.

Of course, Gandhi fought for a less inegalitarian, more inclusive society, particularly regarding the lower classes of Shudras and "untouchables," a category even lower than the Shudras which included those whom the Hindu order relegated to the margins, many of whom were engaged in occupations deemed unclean, such as the slaughter of animals or the tanning of animal hides. But Gandhi also insisted on the essential role of Brahmins—or at any rate those whom he took to behave like Brahmins, namely, without arrogance or greed but with kindness and magnanimity, using their knowledge and learning for the benefit of society. Himself a member of the twice-born Vaishya caste, Gandhi defended (in a number of speeches, especially one delivered in Tanjore in 1927) the functional complementarity that he believed to be the basis of traditional

---

9. Georges Dumézil, who sympathized with monarchists in the 1920s, summed up the argument this way in a 1986 interview: "The principle—not just monarchic but dynastic—that protects the highest position in the state from whims and ambitions seemed to me, and still seems to me, preferable to the ubiquity of election with which we have been living since Danton and Bonaparte." See D. Eribon, *Faut-il brûler Dumézil? Mythologie, science et politique* (Flammarion, 1992), p. 67.

Hindu society. By recognizing the principle of heredity in the transmission of talents and occupations, not as an absolute, rigid rule but as a general principle allowing for individual exceptions, the caste regime assigned a place to everyone, thus avoiding unbridled competition among social groups, the war of all against all, and therefore the kind of class warfare that existed in the West.[10] Gandhi was particularly wary of the anti-intellectual aspects of anti-Brahmin discourse. Although not a Brahmin himself, he associated himself through his personal practice with the Brahmin virtues of sobriety and wisdom, which he believed were indispensable for achieving general social harmony. He was also wary of Western materialism and its boundless thirst for wealth and power.

More broadly, Brahminic domination always had an intellectual and civilizing dimension, especially with respect to mores and diet. The slaughter of animals was prohibited, and the strict vegetarian diet reflected (then and now) not only an ideal of purity and asceticism but also a supposedly more responsible attitude toward nature and the future. Slaughtering a cow might make for a feast today but did nothing to lay the groundwork for the future harvests needed to feed the broader community over the long run. Brahmins also denied themselves the use of alcohol. Their moral code was strict, particularly with respect to women (widows were forbidden to remarry, and arranged marriages involving prepubescent girls and under strict parental control was the norm), whereas the lower castes were regularly accused of debauchery.

It is important to insist once again on the fact that the Manusmriti, like the medieval texts in which Christian monks and bishops set forth their descriptions of the trifunctional schema, was a theoretical account of a political-ideological ideal type, not a description of an actual society. The authors believed that one could and should seek to emulate this ideal, but the reality of power relations at the local level was always more ambiguous. In the high Middle Ages in Europe, the ternary schema was clearly understood to be an idealized normative construct conceived by a handful of clerics rather than an operational description of social reality. The actual elite was more complicated, and it was difficult to discern a single, unified nobility.[11] It was only in the final

---

10. On Gandhian ideology, see, for example, N. Dirks, *Castes of Mind: Colonialism and the Making of Modern India* (Princeton University Press, 2001), pp. 232–235, 298–299.

11. See, for example, F. Bougard, G. Bührer-Thierry, and R. Le Jan, "Les élites du haut Moyen Age: identités, stratégies, mobilités," *Annales. Histoire, Sciences Sociales*, 2013.

stages of transformation of trifunctional society—as revealed, for example, by the Swedish censuses of the mid-eighteenth century and beyond or, more generally, in the transition to absolutism, proprietarianism, and censitary voting in eighteenth- and nineteenth-century Europe, and especially in Britain and France—that the ternary categories began to harden even as they were about to disappear, culminating a long process at the center of which lay the construction of the centralized modern state and the unification of legal statuses.[12]

Similarly, in the Indian context, society was in practice composed of thousands of overlapping social categories and identities, partly reflected in specific occupational guilds and military and religious roles but also related to dietary and religious practices, some of which depended on access to different temples or sites. These thousands of distinct groups, which the Portuguese called "castes" *(castas)* when they discovered India in the early sixteenth century, were only loosely related to the four varnas of the Manusmriti. The British, whose knowledge of Hindu society came largely from books like the Manusmriti, one of the first Sanskrit texts translated into English at the end of the eighteenth century, met with great difficulty when it came to fitting these complex professional and cultural identities into the rigid framework of the four varnas. Yet fit them they did, especially the lowest and highest groups, because doing so seemed to them the best way to understand and control Indian society. From this encounter and this project of simultaneous understanding and domination came a number of essential features of today's India.

The Multicultural Abundance of the Jatis, the Quaternary Order of the Varnas

There is a great deal of confusion about the meaning of "caste," about which I want to be clear. The word "caste" is often used to refer to occupational or cultural micro-groups (called *jatis* in India), but in some cases it is also used to refer to the four major theoretical classes of the Manusmriti *(varnas)*. The two terms refer to two very different realities, however. The jatis are elementary social units with which individuals identify at the most local level of society. There are thousands of jatis across the vast Indian subcontinent corresponding to both specific occupational groups and specific regions and territories; they are often defined by complex mixtures of cultural, linguistic, religious, and culinary identities. In Europe one might speak of masons from the Creuse,

---

12. See Chaps. 2–5.

carpenters from Picardy, wet nurses from Brittany, chimney sweeps from Wales, grape harvesters from Catalonia, or dockworkers from Poland. One of the peculiarities of the Indian jatis—and probably the main distinctive feature of the Indian social system overall—is the persistence to this day of a very high degree of endogamy within jatis, although it is also the case that exogamous marriage has become much more common in urban milieus. The important point is that the jatis do not reflect any hierarchy of social identities. They are occupational, regional, and cultural identities, which are in some ways comparable with national, regional, and ethnic identities in the European or Mediterranean context; they serve as the foundation of horizontal solidarities and networks of sociability, not of a vertical political order like the varnas.

The confusion between jatis and varnas stems in part from Indian history itself: certain Indian elites tried for centuries to organize society hierarchically around the four varnas, and while they met with some success, it was neither total nor lasting. The confusion was compounded when the British colonizers tried to fit the jatis within the framework of the varnas and give the whole setup a stable, bureaucratic existence with the colonial government's stamp of approval. One consequence of this was to make certain social classifications considerably more rigid than they had been, starting with the Brahmins, a category that included hundreds of jatis of vaguely Brahminic priests and scholars whom the British were determined to treat as a single class throughout the subcontinent, partly to assert their own power at the local level but more importantly to simplify India's infinitely complex and indecipherable social reality—the better to dominate it.

Hindu Feudalism, State Construction, and the Transformation of Castes

Before turning to the censuses conducted by the British Raj, it will be useful to review what we know about Indian social structures before the arrival of the British in the late eighteenth and early nineteenth centuries and thus before the invention of "castes" in their colonial form. Our knowledge is limited, but it has progressed over the past few decades. Broadly speaking, recent work has shown that social and political relations in India were in constant flux from the fifteenth to the eighteenth centuries. The processes of change were probably not very different from those observed in Europe in the same period when the traditional trifunctional feudal system came into conflict with the construction of centralized states. In saying this I do not mean to deny the specificity of the Indian caste system or the inegalitarian political and ideological regime associated with it. Among its distinctive features were an emphasis on ritual and dietary purity, strong endogamy within jatis, and specific forms of separation and exclusion dividing upper from lower classes (untouchables). If we are to understand the variety of possible historical trajectories and switch points, however, we also need to insist on the features that the Indian and European cases share in common, especially in regard to trifunctional political organization and social conflict and transformation.

The European colonizers liked to depict the Indian caste system as frozen in time and totally alien because this allowed them to justify their civilizing mission and entrench their power. India's castes were the living incarnation of oriental despotism, utterly opposed to European realities and values: in this respect they constitute the paradigmatic example of an intellectual construct whose purpose was to justify colonial rule. Abbé Dubois, who in 1816 published one of the first works on "the mores, institutions, and ceremonies of the peoples of India"—a work based on the sparse testimony of a few late-eighteenth-century Christian missionaries—was firm in his conclusion. First, it was impossible to convert the Hindus, because they were under the influence of an "abominable" religion. Second, the castes provided the only means of disciplining such a people. This says it all: castes are oppressive, but use must be made of them for the purpose of imposing order. Many British, German, and French scholars ratified this view in the nineteenth century, and this understanding persisted to the middle of the twentieth century and sometimes beyond. Max Weber's work on Hinduism (published in 1916), like that of Louis Dumont's (published in 1966), described a caste system which in broad outline had not changed since the Manusmriti, topped by the eternal Brahmins, whose purity and authority no other social group had seriously contested.[13] Both authors relied primarily on classic Hindu texts and normative religious legal treatises, starting with the Manusmriti, which they frequently cited. Although their judgment of Hinduism was more measured than Abbé Dubois's, their approach remains relatively textual and ahistorical. They did not attempt to study Indian society as a conflictual and evolving sociopolitical process, nor

---

13. See M. Weber, *Hindouisme et bouddhisme* (1916); L. Dumont, *Homo hierarchicus. Le système des castes et ses implications* (1966). For Dumont, the recourse to the sacred and the religious to assign places in society gave Indian society its structure, and the rejection of this principle in European societies intoxicated by rationalism and war partly explains what went awry in the twentieth century.

did they explore sources that might have allowed them to analyze the transformations of that society. Instead, they sought to describe a society they assumed from the outset to be eternal and unchanging.

Since the 1980s a number of scholars relying on new sources have begun to fill in the gaps in our knowledge. Unsurprisingly, Indian societies turn out to have been complex and ever changing; they bear little resemblance to the frozen caste structures depicted by colonial administrators or to the theoretical varna system one finds in the Manusmriti. For example, Sanjay Subrahmanyam has compared Hindu and Muslim chronicles and other sources to study the transformations of power and court relations in Hindu kingdoms and Muslim sultanates and empires in the period 1500–1750. The multiconfessional dimension appears to be central to understanding the dynamics at work here; by contrast, scholars in the colonial era tended to treat the Hindu and Muslim societies of the subcontinent separately, as watertight entities governed by different social and political logics (when they did not simply ignore the Muslim societies altogether).[14] Among Muslim states, it is also important to distinguish between Shiite sultanates such as that of Bijapur and Sunni states such as the Mughal Empire, although we find in both similar elites, practices, and ideas about the art of governing pluralistic communities. Their methods of government were nevertheless quite different from those of the British colonizers, and none of these states ever organized a census comparable with the colonial censuses conducted by the British.[15]

In addition, Susan Bayly and Nicholas Dirks have shown that the military, political, and economic elites of Hindu kingdoms were frequently renewed by infusions of new blood and that the warrior classes often dominated the Brahmins rather than the other way around. More broadly, the social structures of both Hindu states and Muslim sultanates were shaped by property and power

---

14. See Subrahmanyam, *L'éléphant, le canon et le pinceau.* The same author has recently insisted, along with others, that the British conquest of India was the result of an uncertain process with multiple contingencies. It might have turned out differently, depending on the changing strategies of the various states involved (such as the hasty retreat from Delhi by Persian emperor Nadir Shah in 1739, in contrast to previous conquerors, thus leaving the way clear for the Europeans). See P. Singaravélou, *Pour une histoire des possibles. Analyses contrefactuelles et futurs non advenus* (Seuil, 2016), pp. 231–238.

15. For a recent analysis of socioeconomic and political-ideological transformation in the Hindu and Muslim kingdoms of Mysore and Gujarat, see also K. Yazdani, *India, Modernity and the Great Divergence: Mysore and Gujarat (17th to 19th C.)* (Brill, 2017).

relations similar to those observed in France and Europe. For example, we find systems in which several rents were paid on the same piece of land, with free peasants paying both local Brahmins and local Kshatriyas for their respective religious and regalian services, while some groups of rural workers, classified as Shudras, were not allowed to own land and were relegated to a status closer to serfdom. Relations among these groups had social, political, and economic—as well as religious—dimensions and evolved as the balance of political and ideological power shifted.

The case of the Hindu kingdom of Pudukkottai in southern India (present-day Tamil Nadu) is illuminating. There, a small, energetic local tribe, the *Kallars,* who elsewhere were considered a low caste and whom the British would later classify as a "criminal caste" (the better to subjugate them), seized power and set itself up as a new royal warrior nobility in the seventeenth and eighteenth centuries. In the end the Kallars forced the local Brahmins to swear allegiance to them, in exchange for which priests, temples, and Brahminic foundations were rewarded with tax-exempt land. Power relations of this sort are reminiscent of those that existed in feudal Europe between the Church and its monasteries on the one hand and new noble and royal classes on the other, regardless of whether the latter emerged through conquest or rose from the ranks, which happened regularly in both Europe and India. It is interesting to note that it was not until the British strengthened their hold on the Pudukkottai kingdom in the second half of the nineteenth century, at the expense of the Hindu warrior class and other local elites, that the Brahmins saw their influence increase and their preeminence recognized, which allowed them to impose their own religious, familial, and patriarchal norms.[16]

More generally, the collapse of the Mughal Empire around 1700 contributed to the rise of numerous Hindu kingdoms built around new military and administrative elites. To establish their dominance, these groups and their Brahmin allies then turned to the old ideology of the varnas, which enjoyed a certain renaissance in the late seventeenth and eighteenth centuries, all the more so because the new state forms made it possible to apply the religious, familial, and dietary norms of the upper castes on a much broader scale and in a more systematic fashion. The founder of the Maratha Empire, Shivaji Bhonsle, was initially a member of the Maratha peasant class who had served as a tax collector for Muslim sultanates allied with the Mughal Empire. After consolidating

---

16. See N. Dirks, *The Hollow Crown: Ethnohistory of an Indian Kingdom* (Cambridge University Press, 1987); Dirks, *Castes of Mind,* pp. 65–80.

power in an independent Hindu state in western India in the 1660s and 1670s, he demanded that local Brahmin elites recognize him as a twice-born Kshatriya. The Brahmins hesitated, some on the grounds that the authentic Kshatriyas and Vaishyas of ancient times had disappeared with the arrival of Islam. Shivaji ultimately obtained the recognition he wanted by way of a scenario with which we are by now familiar, one that was frequently replayed in both India and Europe: a compromise was struck between the new military elite and the old religious one to achieve the much-desired social and political stability. In Europe, one thinks of Napoleon Bonaparte being crowned emperor by the Pope, like Charlemagne a thousand years before him, before rewarding his generals, family, and loyal followers with titles of nobility.

In Rajasthan, new groups of Kshatriyas, the Rajputs, emerged in the thirteenth and fourteenth centuries from local landowning and warrior classes, on which Muslim sovereigns and later the Mughal Empire sometimes relied to maintain social order; some succeeded in negotiating their way to autonomous principalities.[17] The British also sought support among the upper classes or portions thereof, depending on their interests at the moment. In the case of Shivaji's kingdom, Brahmin ministers known as peshwas ultimately became hereditary rulers in the 1740s. But they got in the way of the East India Company, which decided to depose them in 1818 on the grounds that they had usurped a Kshatriya role to which they had no right, thereby winning the British the support of those who had taken a dim view of the unusual seizure of political power by Brahmin scholars.[18]

On the Peculiarity of State Construction in India

The conclusion that emerges clearly from this work is that Hindu varnas were no more solid in the seventeenth and eighteenth centuries than were European

---

17. Several theories have been proposed to explain the origin of the Rajputs. One, much favored during the colonial era, linked them to a foreign invasion in the era of the Huns and Scythians, after which they were supposedly incorporated into the Kshatriyas with the fall of the Gupta Empire. Others say that they were direct descendants of the Kshatriyas of the Vedic era or else former Brahmins who became Kshatriyas by assuming political power. See A. Hiltebeitel, *Rethinking India's Oral and Classical Epics: Draupadi among Rajputs, Muslims, and Dalits* (University of Chicago Press, 1999), pp. 441–442.

18. See S. Bayly, *Caste, Society and Politics in India from the 18th Century to the Modern Age* (Cambridge University Press, 1999), pp. 33–34, 56–63.

classes and elites in the Middle Ages, the Renaissance, or the Ancien Régime. The varnas were flexible categories that enabled groups of warriors and priests to justify their rule and paint an image of a durable and harmonious social order, whereas in reality that order evolved constantly as the balance of power shifted among social groups. All of this unfolded in a context of rapid economic, demographic, and territorial development accompanied by the emergence of new commercial and financial elites. Indian society in the seventeenth and eighteenth centuries thus appears to have been evolving just as much as European society. It is of course impossible to say how the various societies and states of the Indian subcontinent would have evolved in the absence of British colonization. It is not unreasonable to think, however, that status inequalities stemming from the ancient trifunctional logic would gradually have disappeared through the process of central state formation in the same way we have observed in Europe—and, as we will see in Chapter 9, in China and Japan.

Within this overall pattern, however, there exists a broad spectrum of possibilities. In the European case we have already noted the diversity of possible trajectories and switch points. In Sweden, for example, large property owners joined the old nobility in creating a political system (1865–1911) in which the number of votes a person could cast was strictly proportional to that person's wealth.[19] Had Brahmins and Kshatriyas been left to their own devices, they would no doubt have proved to be just as imaginative (perhaps by awarding votes on the basis of the number of diplomas or ascetic lifestyle or dietary habits, or simply on the basis of property and taxes paid) before being driven from power by a popular uprising. Because there are so many structural differences between Indian and European inequality regimes, the number of possible trajectories one can imagine is especially large.

If we take the long view, the main difference between India and Europe probably has to do with the role of Muslim kingdoms and empires. In vast swathes of the Indian subcontinent, regalian powers were exercised by Muslim sovereigns for centuries, in some cases from the twelfth or thirteenth centuries to the eighteenth or nineteenth. Under these conditions, the prestige and authority of the Hindu warrior class would clearly have suffered. In the eyes of many Brahmins, the authentic Kshatriyas had quite simply ceased to exist in many parts of the country, even though in practice the Hindu military classes often played supporting roles under Muslim princes or retreated into independent Hindu states and principalities like the Rajputs in Rajasthan. The relative

19. See Chap. 5.

retreat of the Kshatriyas also increased the prestige and preeminence of Brahmin intellectual elites; this retreat allowed the Brahmins to fulfill their religious and educational functions on which Muslim sovereigns (and later the British) relied to uphold the social order, often going so far as to validate and enforce judgments handed down by Brahmins concerning dietary or familial laws or access to temples, water, and schools, in some cases even imposing excommunication. Compared with other trifunctional societies not only in Europe but also in other parts of Asia (especially China and Japan) and around the world, this may have led to a certain imbalance between the religious and warrior elites, enhancing the importance of the former or even leading in some regions to a quasi-sacralization of the power of the Brahmins, which was temporal as well as spiritual. As we have seen, however, the balance of power could shift very quickly, leading to the emergence of new Hindu states backed by new military and political elites.

The second important difference between the Indian and European cases has to do with the fact that the Brahmins were a true social class unto themselves, with families and children, accumulated wealth and inheritances, whereas the Catholic clergy had to replenish its ranks from the other classes owing to the celibacy of priests. We saw how this led in the European society of orders to the emergence of ecclesiastical institutions and religious organizations (such as monasteries, bishoprics, and the like), which accumulated significant amounts of property on behalf of the clergy and thus also led to the development of sophisticated economic and financial rules.[20] This may also have made the European clerical class (which was not really a class) more vulnerable. The decisions to expropriate monasteries in Britain in the sixteenth century or to nationalize clerical property in France in the late eighteenth century were not easy, to be sure, but no hereditary class was affected. On the contrary: the nobility and bourgeoisie benefited substantially. In India, expropriation of Brahmin temples and religious foundations would have to have been more gradual, although the development of new nonreligious ruling classes in Hindu kingdoms in the eighteenth and nineteenth centuries again shows that it wouldn't have been impossible. In any case, we will see that when British colonization interrupted the autochthonous state construction process, census reports show that the Brahmin class commanded a very large share of the wealth as well as of educational, cultural, and professional resources.

---

20. See Chap. 2.

The Discovery of India and Iberian Encirclement of Islam

Before analyzing how the British sought to take the measure of India's castes with its colonial censuses in the nineteenth century, it will also be useful to remind the reader that Europe's discovery of India came in stages and originated in an unusual quest, based on quite limited knowledge. Much research, especially the work of Sanjay Subrahmanyam (based on systematic comparison of Indian, Arab, and Portuguese sources), has shown that Vasco da Gama's expedition in 1497–1498 was based on numerous misunderstandings.

During the second half of the fifteenth century, the Portuguese government was deeply divided over the issue of overseas expansion. One faction of the landed nobility was content with the success of the Reconquista and opposed to further action against Islam. But the Military Orders, especially the Orders of Christ and Santiago (to which da Gama's family belonged), having played a key role in mobilizing the lesser warrior nobility during the era of "reconquest" of Iberian territory from Islam, favored pursuing the Moors to the coast of Morocco and pushing them back as far as possible from Christian shores. The boldest warriors proposed further exploration of the African coast in order to outflank the Muslims to the south and east and ultimately link up with the mythical "Kingdom of Prester John." This apocryphal Christian kingdom, inspired by Ethiopia, played an important part in Europe's confused representations of global geography from the era of the Crusades (eleventh to thirteenth centuries) to the Age of Discovery, fostering hopes of ultimate victory over Islam. The ambitious strategy of encircling the Muslim enemy did not command unanimous support, however, and ideological conflict between the landed faction and the imperial anti-Islamic faction gave the Portuguese monarch pause. In the face of pressure from the Orders, which he wanted to keep tethered to the monarchy, the king finally decided in 1497 to send da Gama on his voyage with orders to round the Cape of Good Hope, which Bartolomeu Dias had discovered ten years earlier.

Thanks to surviving sailors' accounts (some of which lay undiscovered until the nineteenth century) and comparison with Arabic and Indian sources, it has been possible to reconstruct the various stages of the voyage in considerable detail.[21] After leaving Lisbon in July 1497, da Gama's three ships reached the

---

21. S. Subrahmanyan, *Vasco de Gama. Légende et tribulations du vice-roi des Indes* (Alma, 2012), pp. 159–207; published in English as *The Career and Legend of Vasco da Gama* (Cambridge University Press, 1997).

South African coast in November and then set sail slowly northward along the east coast of Africa, stopping at Muslim ports in Mozambique, Zanzibar, and Somalia in search of Christians, whom the Portuguese never found. At the time, Indian Ocean commerce was the province of Arabs, Persians, Gujaratis, Keralans, Malays, and Chinese, whose intersecting networks encompassed a vast multilingual region and brought large imperial and agrarian states (under the Vijayanagara, Ming, Ottomans, Safavids, and Mughals) into contact with small commercial coastal states (Kilwa, Ormuz, Aden, Calicut, Malacca). Disappointed by these unanticipated encounters and worried about the hostility of Muslim merchants, da Gama continued on his way, reaching the Indian coast in May 1498. A series of tense encounters and blunders ensued, most notably in Calicut (in present-day Kerala in the south of India). Da Gama visited Hindu temples that he mistook for the churches of a Christian kingdom, to the astonishment of the Brahmins, who were equally surprised by the very modest gifts tendered by a man who claimed to be representing the greatest kingdom in Europe. Da Gama finally returned to Lisbon under difficult conditions.

In July 1499 the king of Portugal proudly announced to his fellow Christian kings that the route to the Indies was open and that his envoy had discovered on the Indian coast a number of Christian kingdoms, including one in Calicut, "a city larger than Lisbon and inhabited by Christians."[22] It was several years before the Portuguese awoke to their mistake and realized that the sovereigns of Calicut and Kochi were Hindus who traded with Muslims, Malays, and Chinese; and before long these Hindu sovereigns were at war with one another over which of them would do business with the Christians. Da Gama returned to Kochi as viceroy of the Indies in 1523 to defend the Portuguese trading posts that were by then numerous in Asia. In the meantime, in 1500, Cabral had discovered Brazil (as da Gama had come close to doing in 1499 on his way back from India), and Magellan had sailed around the world in 1521.

It would take an even longer time for the nature of Portugal's imperial project to change. The messianic dimension—to promote Christianity over Islam—would continue to play a central role throughout the sixteenth century, especially after the founding of the Society of Jesus (Jesuits) in 1540. This outsized messianic motive explains, by the way, how a tiny country of barely 1.5

22. See Subrahmanyan, *Vasco de Gama,* pp. 193–196. This irreverent portrait of a Portuguese national hero, coming from a mischievous Indian writer, no less, triggered a stormy reaction among conservative Portuguese historians when the book was published.

million people could have set out to conquer the world, to say nothing of countries that not only had much larger populations but also were in many respects more advanced. The mercantile motive never entirely eclipsed the messianic. In the Dutch case, however, the mercantile motive was paramount: the Vereenigde Oostindische Compagnie (VOC, or Dutch East India Company), one of the first large joint-stock companies in the world, was founded in 1602. Over the course of the seventeenth century it would gradually take over many of Portugal's Asian trading posts.[23] In 1511 the Portuguese had occupied the strategic port of Malacca, ending the Muslim sultanate that had controlled a crucial strait on the maritime route connecting India to China, between today's Malaysia and the island of Sumatra (Indonesia). The Dutch took Malacca from the Portuguese in 1641 before ceding sovereignty to it as well as Singapore to the British in 1810.

Unlike the Portuguese, the Spanish built their empire on dry land: it grew rapidly, starting with the occupation of Mexico by Hernan Cortes in 1519 and of Cuzco and Peru by Francisco Pizarro in 1534. By the 1560s Spanish navigators had mastered the Pacific currents, enabling them to cross in both directions, thus linking Mexico to the Philippines and the Asian parts of the empire. In the early 1600s Mexico was truly the multicultural heart of the Spanish Empire, the place where "the four corners of the world" evoked by Serge Gruzinski came together at a time when states exerted less control over borders and identities than they would later. There, the mixing of blood among Mexican Indians, Europeans, Brazilian mulattos, Filipinos, and Japanese led to some astonishing *mises en abîme* by chroniclers writing in different languages and representing different cultures. The Catholic monarchy of Spain, which at its zenith absorbed Portugal under a single crown (1580–1640), once again faced Islam as its global rival, including in the Philippines and Moluccas (Indonesia)—where Muslims had gained a foothold shortly before the arrival of the Iberians and where Spanish soldiers had not expected to find their old European rivals so far from Grenada and Andalusia, from which they had just expelled the last infidels in 1492, the very year in which Columbus landed in Hispaniola (Saint-Domingue) while searching for the Indies.[24]

---

23. S. Subrahmanyan, *L'empire portugais d'Asie, 1500–1700* (Points, 1999); published in English as *The Portuguese Empire in Asia, 1500-1700: A Political and Economic History* (Longman, 1993).

24. See S. Gruzinski, *Les quatre parties du monde. Histoire d'une mondialisation* (La Martinière, 2004). In this illuminating book, Gruzinski also shows how Spain's

Domination by Arms, Domination by Knowledge

When Europeans arrived in India and found Muslim sultanates and empires playing a major role there, they naturally took the side of the Hindu kingdoms against their Muslim rivals. Religious, commercial, and military conflicts soon arose, however. After the messianic era came the mercantile era, embodied to perfection by the Dutch VOC and the British East India Company (EIC). These joint-stock companies, founded in the early 1600s, were much more than trading companies to which European monarchs had granted commercial monopolies. They were in fact private companies charged with exploiting vast regions of the world and maintaining order at a time when the boundary between public functions (such as tax farming) and lucrative state-licensed private businesses was extremely porous. In the middle of the eighteenth century, especially in the wake of English victories over Bengali armies in the 1740s, the EIC took de facto control of great swathes of the Indian subcontinent. The EIC maintained veritable private armies made up mainly of Indian soldiers paid from its coffers. It extended its control by taking advantage of the void left by the collapse of the Mughal Empire and the rivalry between contending Hindu and Muslim powers.

Nevertheless, the many abuses that the EIC committed on Indian soil quickly led to notorious scandals. By the 1770s members of Parliament were calling on the Crown to tighten its oversight of the EIC. One of the most outspoken critics was the conservative philosopher Edmund Burke, famous today for his *Reflections on the French Revolution* (1790). Burke insisted on the need to put an end to the corruption and brutality of the company's agents, and after a tense trial in the House of Commons in 1787 he succeeded in impeaching Warren Hastings, the former head of EIC and governor-general of Bengal. Although Hastings was ultimately acquitted by the House of Lords in 1795, British elites were increasingly convinced that Parliament needed to play a greater role in the colonization of India. It was felt that Britain's civilizing mission could proceed only on the basis of rigorous administration and solid knowledge and that sovereignty could no longer be delegated to a gang of greedy traders and mercenaries. Administrators and scholars were needed.

---

rapid victory in Mexico is explained not only by the diseases the Iberians brought with them but also by their intrusion into a specific inequality regime where they were able to spark revolt (because the forms of forced labor and domination used by the Aztec nobility had long been challenged, and the arrival of the Spaniards provided an alternative that led to the Aztecs' downfall).

Edward Saïd, in his book on the origins of "orientalism," showed how important this new colonial presence in Asia was. Henceforth domination was to depend not just on brute military force but more on cognitive, intellectual, and civilizational superiority.[25] Saïd notes that this cognitive moment, which followed the messianic and mercantilist eras, found its first embodiment in Bonaparte's Egypt expedition (1798–1801). Of course, there was no shortage of political, military, and commercial motives for this adventure, but the French were careful to insist on the scientific aspects of the campaign. Some 167 scholars, historians, engineers, botanists, draftsmen, and artists accompanied the soldiers, and their discoveries led to the publication between 1808 and 1828 of twenty-eight large-format volumes of "Descriptions of Egypt." The residents of Cairo, who rose up in late 1798 to drive out the French, were clearly not entirely convinced of the disinterested motives of these civilizing benefactors, any more than were the Egyptian and Ottoman soldiers who, with support from the British Navy, sent the expedition packing back to France in 1801. This episode nevertheless marked a historical turning point: henceforth colonization would more and more often be portrayed as a civilizing necessity, a service rendered by Europe to civilizations frozen in time and unable to evolve or to discover their own identities, much less preserve their historical legacy.

In 1802 François-René de Chateaubriand published his *Génie du christianisme,* followed in 1811 by *Itinéraire de Paris à Jérusalem,* both of which directed harsh criticism at Islam and justified the civilizing role of the Crusades.[26] In

---

25. See E. Saïd, *Orientalism,* 1st ed. (Vintage Books, 1978); also published as *Orientalism,* Penguin Modern Classics ed. (Penguin, 2003), with a new preface by the author.

26. "Of liberty they know nothing; of property they have none. Force is their God. When a long time has passed since the last appearance of the conquerors charged with carrying out the sentences imposed from on high, they have the air of soldiers without a captain, of citizens without legislators, of a family without a father. . . . The Moors several times came close to enslaving Christendom. And while this people seems to have been more elegant in its manners than other barbarians, in its religion, which permits polygamy and slavery, and its despotic and jealous temperament, it presented, as we were saying, an invincible obstacle to the enlightenment and happiness of humankind. The military orders of Spain, by combating these infidels, thus saved us from great misfortunes. . . . Some would accuse the knights of having chased infidels into their own homes, but they fail to say that these were, after all, just reprisals against peoples who had been the first to attack the Christian peoples: the Moors justify the Crusades. Did the disciples of the Koran remain quiet in the deserts of Arabia, or did they not bring their law and their ravages to the walls of Delhi and the

1833 the poet Alphonse de Lamartine published his famous *Voyage en Orient,* in which he theorized the European right to sovereignty over the Orient even as France was waging a brutal war of conquest in Algeria. No doubt these violent civilizational discourses can be read as a response to a major hidden European trauma. For a millennium, from the first Muslim incursions into Spain and France in the early eighth century to the decline of the Ottoman Empire in the eighteenth and nineteenth centuries, Christian kingdoms had feared that they might never see the end of the Muslim states that had seized control of the Iberian peninsula and Byzantine Empire and occupied much of the Mediterranean coast. This ancient but ultimately banished existential fear found clear expression in the writing of Chateaubriand, along with a centuries-old thirst for revenge, whereas Lamartine insisted more on the mission to preserve and civilize.

Saïd showed that the influence of orientalism on Western representations continued well after the colonial period. The refusal to historicize "oriental" societies, the insistence on essentializing them and portraying them as frozen in time, eternally flawed and structurally incapable of governing themselves—ideas that justify every kind of brutality in advance—continued, Saïd argued, to permeate European and American perceptions in the late twentieth and early twenty-first centuries: for example, at the time of the invasion of Iraq in 2003. Orientalism yielded scholarship and knowledge along with specific ways of looking at remote societies, specific modes of knowledge that for a long time explicitly served the political purposes of colonial domination and often continued to reflect their initial biases in postcolonial academia and society. Inequality is not simply a matter of social disparities within countries; it is also at times a clash of collective identities and models of development. Their respective merits and limitations might in theory be subjects for calm and constructive debate, but in practice they are often transformed into violent clashes of identity. This is as much the case today as in centuries past, despite important contextual changes. Hence it is essential to describe the historical genealogy of these conflicts to gain a better understanding of what is currently at stake.

British Colonial Censuses in India, 1871–1941

We turn now to the records of the censuses conducted by the British colonizers in the Indian Empire. Although the Sepoy Mutiny of 1857–1858 was quickly

---

ramparts of Vienna? Should one perhaps have waited until the lairs of these ferocious animals were once again occupied?" See Saïd, *Orientalism,* p. 172.

put down, it frightened the colonial authorities and convinced them of the need for direct administration. To that end, they needed a better understanding of India's land tenure systems in order to levy taxes. They also needed to know more about local elites and social structures, especially castes, which they only dimly understood but feared might foster group solidarity and thus lead to future revolts. The first experimental censuses were conducted in northern India in 1865 and 1869 in the "Northwestern Provinces" and in Oudh, which in the administrative subdivision of the early British Raj corresponded roughly to the Ganges valley and present-day Uttar Pradesh (population 204 million according to the 2011 census; already more than 40 million at the time of the first censuses). The census was then extended to the entire population of the Indian Empire in 1871—some 239 million people, of whom 191 million lived in areas under direct British administration and 48 million in principalities under British tutelage. The census was then repeated in 1881, 1891, and every ten years thereafter until 1941. After each census the authorities published hundreds of thick volumes presenting thousands of tables for every province and district, relating caste to religion, occupation, education, and in some cases land ownership. These volumes attest to the immensity of the undertaking, which involved thousands of census takers and covered vast expanses of territory—an eminently political enterprise. Questions were posed in the various Indian languages and then translated into English, eventually yielding thousands upon thousands of pages. These documents, together with the many reports and pamphlets that record the hesitations and doubts of colonial administrators and scholars, tell us at least as much about the nature of colonial rule as about the social realities of India.

The British initially approached the exercise through the prism of the four varnas of the Manusmriti but soon realized that these categories were not very useful. The individuals surveyed identified instead with the jatis, a broader and more fluid set of social classifications. The problem was that colonial administrators had no complete list of jatis, and the people they were interviewing had extremely diverse opinions about what jatis were most relevant and how they should be grouped. Many Indians must also have wondered why these strange British lords and their census-taking agents were so interested in their identities, occupations, and diets and so determined to have their views on social classifications and ranks. The 1871 census enumerated some 3,208 different "castes" (in the sense of jatis); by 1881 the number had risen to 19,044 distinct groups, including subcastes. The average population of each caste was less than 100,000 in the first census and less than 20,000 in the second. Often these "castes" were merely small local occupational groups present only in limited areas. It was very difficult to discern any order in such data, let alone produce knowledge of use on an imperial scale. To get an idea of the scope of the undertaking, try to imagine how an Indian sovereign taking control of Europe in the eighteenth or nineteenth centuries might have gone about conducting a census across the continent from Brittany to Russia and Portugal to Scotland, classifying people by occupation, religion, and dietary preferences. No doubt they would have invented categories that would surprise us today.[27] But the fact is that by producing these categories and using them to administer the country, the British colonizers exerted a deep and lasting impact on Indian identities and on the structure of Indian society itself.

Some colonial administrators also explored racialist explanations. They started with the premise that, according to certain Hindu myths, the varnas were rooted in racial differences from the era of conquest. Light-skinned Aryans from Iran, to the north, had supposedly invaded the Ganges valley before moving into southern India, perhaps early in the second millennium BCE; their descendants became Brahmins, Kshatriyas, and Vaishyas, according to the myths, while the darker-skinned natives and even blacks in the southernmost parts of the subcontinent became subjugated Shudras.[28] Many administrators and scholars therefore set about measuring skulls and jawbones and examining noses and skin textures in the hope of discovering the secret of India's castes. Herbert Risley, an ethnographer who was appointed census commissioner in 1901, argued that, if the British wished to beat the Germans in the area of racial research, a field in which German scholars were particularly active at the time, it was of the utmost strategic importance to study the races of India.[29] In practice, the racial approach yielded no tangible results because most castes exhibited thoroughly mixed ethnic and racial origins.

---

27. It is even more difficult to say what would have happened to the masons from Creuse, the carpenters from Picardy, and the grape pickers from Catalonia if an Indian colonizer had pigeonholed them accordingly and distributed rights and obligations for decades based on those classifications.

28. In Sanskrit, the word "varna" comes from the word for color. In the Ramayana, Rama triumphs over the demon Ravana and frees his beloved Sita only with the help of Hauman and an army of apes: this represents the union of all Indian people, from the blackest in the south to the whitest in the north, paving the way for the restoration of political order and harmony on earth (while at the same time bringing Sri Lanka under Indian domination).

29. Bayly, *Caste, Society and Politics in India,* p. 132.

Even earlier, in 1885, John Nesfield—an administrator who had been assigned the job of reflecting on new classifications that might better capture the reality of Indian society and who believed that castes should be thought of primarily as occupational groups—was already aware that racial theory was of little use in understanding castes. One had only to go to Benares, he remarked, where 400 young Brahmins were studying in the most prestigious Sanskrit schools. There, it was easy to see that they represented the full palette of skin colors from the entire subcontinent.[30] Risley had his own theory on the subject. For one thing, the Brahmins had mixed thoroughly with other castes between the time of the Aryan invasions, early in the second millennium BCE, and the time when the Manusmriti recommended strict endogamy (around the second century BCE). For another, competition with Buddhism, which was especially intense from the fifth century BCE to the fifth century CE, had ostensibly led the Brahmins to incorporate many lower-caste Indians into their ranks. Finally, many Hindu rajahs had allegedly created new classes of Brahmins over the centuries to cope with the indiscipline of existing Brahmins.

The testimony of administrators like Nesfield is generally much more instructive than that of racialist ethnographers like Risley and Edgar Thurston because the administrators reported on interesting exchanges with the populations they were charged with counting. To be sure, Nesfield's analysis reflects prejudices of his own as well as those of his interlocutors (who were drawn mainly from the upper castes), but those prejudices are themselves significant. For example, Nesfield explains that the aborigines and untouchables excluded themselves from the Hindu community by their behavior. Specifically, they were groups of hunters who lived in forests or on the outskirts of villages in a state of unimaginable filth, always on the brink of rebellion or plunder. They were denied access to temples because their morals were deplorable: they did not shrink from prostituting their own daughters when necessary. The topographic descriptions in this part of Nesfield's account suggest that he is talking about isolated aboriginal tribes rather than untouchables as such, although he doesn't always distinguish clearly between the two groups, particularly when he is discussing habitats on the outskirts of villages relatively far from the wooded and mountainous areas generally associated with aborigines. In any

---

30. See J. Nesfield, *Brief view of the Caste system of the North-western provinces and Oudh, together with an examination of names and figures shown in the Census Report 1882* (Allahabad, 1885), p. 75.

event, he is clearly referring to groups whose way of life was radically different from the norm.[31]

Nesfield adds that these pariah groups also included lesser agricultural castes whose morals and dietary customs linked them to the lowest of the low. He mentions in particular groups that still ate rodents such as nutrias and field rats, a deplorable practice proscribed centuries earlier by the Manusmriti. He also discusses certain occupational groups such as the *chamars* (tanners) and scavengers who collected human waste, garbage, and animal carcasses. According to Nesfield's informants, their morals were also questionable, and their frequent public drunkenness and regrettable promiscuity did not escape his notice. He is convinced, moreover, that the less prestigious social classes generally performed tasks requiring the least knowledge and skills, such as basket weaving, an activity that he notes is common not only among the very lowest castes in India but also among the Roma in Europe. Conversely, those higher up the social ladder engaged in more sophisticated work such as pottery making, weaving, and at the very top of the craft hierarchy, metallurgy, glass making, jewelry making, and stone cutting. This same hierarchy is observed in other walks of life: hunters are less prestigious than fishermen, who are themselves less prestigious than farmers and breeders.

The most important *Banyas* (merchants) lived by a moral code similar to that of the Brahmins; in particular, their widows were forbidden to remarry. Nesfield also remarks that the former Kshatriya warriors, now called Rajputs (a term that initially designated individuals of royal blood) or Chattris (derived from Kshatriyas and *kshatras,* a term designating the owner of a landed estate), had lost much of their prestige under Muslim and then British domination. Some found employment as soldiers or police in the colonial service while others lived on the rent from their land and still others vegetated. In addition, Nesfield points out that the Brahmins have long since branched out from their original activity as priests and taken up work as teachers, doctors, accountants,

---

31. One finds similar descriptions in the texts of Chinese travelers in Cambodia in the thirteenth century and in Javanese texts from the fifteenth century, which describe populations that are not integrated into the main society, barely speak the language of the "civilized," and live in the woods or on the outskirts of villages on whatever game they are able to kill; these texts also reflect the strong negative prejudices of the "civilized," sometimes tinged with hopes of integration. See D. Lombard, *Le carrefour javanais. Essai d'histoire globale,* tome 3, *L'héritage des royaumes concentriques* (EHESS, 1990), pp. 24–25.

and administrators while still collecting comfortable rents from others in their rural communities.

While recognizing that the administrative skills of the Brahmins were much more useful to the colonial authorities and that their talents were much better suited to modern times than those of the now-sidelined warriors, Nesfield argues that there are far too many Brahmins in relation to the services they render (up to 10 percent of the population in some parts of northern India). On the whole, he found that the Indian social hierarchy looked rather good apart from the excessive number of Brahmins, who truly abused their dominant position. The conclusion was obvious: the time had come for British administrators to replace them as the country's leaders.

Enumerating Social Groups in Indian and European Trifunctional Society

What statistical results can we glean from the census data? Broadly speaking, colonial administrators had no idea how to group the thousands of jatis into intelligible categories, so the presentation of the results varied greatly from one census to the next. Some administrators, including Nesfield, proposed abandoning the varnas almost entirely in favor of an entirely new set of occupational classifications based on trades and skills, which Nesfield proposed to develop for use throughout imperial India. In reality, what the British decided to do from 1871 to 1931 was to classify every local group they believed to be related to the Brahmins under the head "brahmin." Already in 1834 a survey had found 107 different Brahmin groups. In the communities that Nesfield studied, he, too, had distinguished numerous subgroups: the *acharjas* supervised religious ceremonies, the *pathaks* specialized in the education of children, the *dikshits* were in charge of initiation ceremonies for the twice-born, the *gangaputras* assisted priests, the *baidyas* served as physicians, the *pandes* were responsible for educating lower castes, and so on, to say nothing of the *khataks* and *bhats,* former Brahmins who became singers and artists, or again, the *malis,* a sophisticated agricultural caste specialized in the production of flowers and wreaths used in processions, who were sometimes counted as Brahmins. Nesfield estimated that only 4 percent of Brahmins were full-time priests, while 60 percent assisted in one way or another in religious functions to supplement their primary work as teachers, physicians, administrators, or landowners. In a sense this was a bourgeoisie of literate landowners who participated in the teaching of religion.

Across India, the proportion of the population categorized as Brahmins in British census reports was significant. In the census of 1881, we find 13 million Brahmins (including their families), or 5.1 percent of the total population of 254 million and 6.6 percent of the Hindu population of 194 million. Depending on the region and province, the proportion of Brahmins varied from barely 2 to 3 percent in southern India to roughly 10 percent in the Ganges valley and northern India, with Bengal (Calcutta) and Maharastra (Mumbai) close to the average (5–6 percent).[32] As for the Kshatriyas, the census reports do not give a total figure because the term was rarely used explicitly and the colonizers declined to revive it. By adding up the numbers for the various castes of Chattris and especially Rajputs, which accounted for most of the total, we arrive at a figure of 7 million Kshatriyas in 1881, which amounts to 2.9 percent of the total population and 3.7 percent of the Hindu population, again with regional variations but less marked than in the case of the Brahmins (northern India was a little above average, while southern India and other regions were a little below). All told, we find that the two highest castes accounted for 10 percent of the Hindu population in 1881 (6–7 percent for the Brahmins and 3–4 percent for the Kshatriyas). A half century later, in the census of 1931, the proportion of Brahmins had decreased slightly (from 6.6 to 5.5 percent) while that of Kshatriyas had increased slightly (from 3.7 to 4.1 percent), but the total barely budged. According to the census data, Brahmins and Kshatriyas together accounted for 10.3 percent of the Hindu population in 1881 and 9.7 percent in 1931 (Fig. 8.3).[33]

If one compares these numbers with those of the clergy and nobility in the United Kingdom and France from the sixteenth to the eighteenth centuries—countries in which the process of centralized state formation was already very well advanced—one finds that the Brahmins and Kshatriyas were still relatively numerous in late nineteenth-century and early twentieth-century India. According to available estimates, the clergy accounted for roughly 3 percent of the adult male population in France and Britain in the sixteenth century and

---

32. Detailed data from colonial reports of census results, together with links to the original documents, can be found in the online appendix (piketty.pse.ens.fr/ideology).

33. The proportion of Kshatriyas increased between 1881 and 1891, which may be due to the fact that the British had sought in the earliest two censuses mainly to identify the Brahmins. The two groups lost importance between 1891 and 1931 in a context where identification as a high-caste individual ceased to be an advantage and could even become a drawback. See Table 8.2.

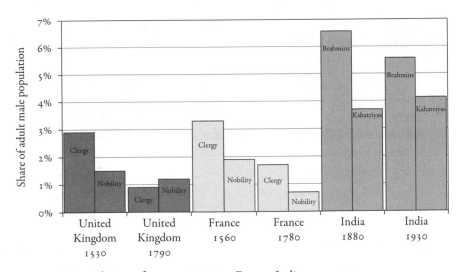

FIG. 8.3. The evolution of ternary societies: Europe-India 1530–1930

Interpretation: In the United Kingdom and France, the two dominant classes of trifunctional society (clergy and nobility) shrank between the sixteenth and eighteenth centuries. In India, the proportion—of Brahmins and Kshatriyas (old classes of priests and warriors), as measured by colonial British censuses, slightly decreased from 1880 to 1930 but remained significantly higher than in Europe in the sixteenth to eighteenth centuries. *Sources and series:* piketty.pse.ens.fr/ideology.

the nobility for less than 2 percent, for a total of less than 5 percent for the two privileged orders, compared with 10 percent for the Brahmins and Kshatriyas in late nineteenth-century India. The orders of magnitude are not dissimilar, however. Remember, too, that other European countries had much larger clerical and warrior classes in the eighteenth century than the United Kingdom or France. In Spain, we can estimate that the clergy accounted for 4 percent of the adult male population in 1750, while the lesser and greater nobility accounted for more than 7 percent, for a total of roughly 11 percent for the clerical and warrior classes, a level quite close to that observed in India in 1880.[34] Countries such as Portugal, Poland, and Hungary had noble classes that accounted by themselves for 6–7 percent of the population around 1800.[35] In terms of size, then, Indian and European trifunctional societies (with their regional variants) therefore appear to have been fairly similar, with differences

34. See Fig. 1.1.
35. See Fig. 5.2.

reflecting the different sociopolitical processes of state construction in the various subregions of both continents.

Literate Landowners, Administrators, and Social Control

The detailed census reports enable us to be more specific about several important characteristics of the populations surveyed. In Madras province in 1871, Brahmins accounted on average for 3.7 percent of the population, ranging from 1.5 to 13.1 percent depending on the district. We find that Brahmins were strongly dominant not only in the schools (70 percent of students in Madras were Brahmins) and learned professions (between 60 and 70 percent of teachers, physicians, lawyers, accountants, and astrologers in the province were Brahmins) but also among rural landowners: 40 percent of those classified as landowners were Brahmins (compared with only 20 percent Kshatriyas), and in some districts this figure ran as high as 60 percent. The administrator who commented on these results was even more explicit than Nesfield: according to him, Brahmin domination of the other classes was so oppressive that if the British were to leave the country, political chaos and rebellion would immediately ensue.[36] The comment is revealing: the British colonizers relied on local Brahmin elites to control and administer the country while denouncing their tyrannical hold to justify their own civilizing mission. Meanwhile, they overlooked the fact that the concentration of property and political power was at least as extreme in the United Kingdom, where absentee landlords had only recently allowed part of the population of Ireland to die of hunger and major upheavals lay just ahead.[37]

Other census reports confirmed this extreme concentration of both educational resources and wealth in the hands of those whom the British classified as Brahmins (or, more precisely, Brahmin males, because all signs are that Indian society was highly patriarchal). In 1891 the census found that only 10.4 percent of males in the British Raj were literate (and 0.5 percent of women). The only province in which literacy was high was Burma, where more than 95 percent of the population was listed as Buddhist (this being the only region in which Buddhism displaced Hinduism) and where the literacy rate reached 44.3 percent (but only 3.8 percent for women). Colonial administrators attributed this exceptional result to Buddhist monks and their schools. In reality,

---

36. See *Report on the 1871 Census of the Madras Presidency* (Madras, 1874), p. 363.
37. See Chap. 5.

no one can be sure to what extent the census takers were actually evaluating skills or simply recording their own prejudices or the prejudices of the family heads they consulted. The figures are nevertheless suggestive. In the 1911 census, the literacy rate among Brahmin women in Bengal was 11.3 percent (compared with 64.5 percent for Brahmin men). Although this was still not a very high rate, the progress was clear: Brahmin women now accounted for more than 60 percent of all literate women in the province, whereas Brahmin men accounted for only 30 percent of all literate men—still quite a high ratio.

In most provinces, we find that Brahmins were at least equal to and usually ahead of Rajputs and Chattris when it came to landownership. In terms of education, the gap was huge: Brahmins were way ahead of Kshatriyas, whose cultural and intellectual resources appear to have been very feeble (the literacy rate among male Rajputs in most provinces was 10–15 percent, barely more than the national average). Note, however, that Brahmin educational superiority varied from region to region: it was less noticeable in northern India (where Brahmins were very numerous and their literacy rate in some areas fell as low as 20–30 percent) than in southern India, where the Brahmins constituted a smaller elite (2–3 percent of the population compared with 10 percent) and where their literacy rate ran 60–70 percent or higher.

The only caste whose intellectual and educational capital equaled or sometimes even surpassed that of the Brahmins was the small group of *Kayasths,* which accounted for about 1 percent of the population (more than 2 percent in Bengal) and which colonial administrators found particularly intriguing. The Kayasths clearly ranked among the upper castes, but it seemed impossible to classify them as either Brahmins or Kshatriyas, so they were treated separately. There are various accounts of their origins, all largely unverifiable. According to one ancient legend, a Chattri queen in a difficult situation allegedly promised that her sons would become writers and accountants rather than warriors so that the enemy would spare their lives. More likely, the Kayasths may have issued from an ancient Kshatriya or Chattri lineage which decided that some of its sons should become scholars and administrators to free themselves from the tutelage of the Brahmins (a natural enough temptation, which must have arisen more than once in the history of India's dynasties and probably helped to renew the ranks of the Brahmins).

In any case, the Kayasths allowed themselves to consume alcohol, like the Kshatriyas but unlike the Brahmins; in the eyes of British administrators, this confirmed their complex origins. Apart from that, they resembled Brahmins in every respect and even surpassed them in educational achievement and access to high administrative posts and the learned professions. The Kayasths had reputedly been quick to learn Urdu in order to offer their services to the Mughal emperors and Muslim sultans, and they did the same with English to gain access to posts in the British colonial administration.

In any case, it is important to note that the caste censuses were not done solely to satisfy the orientalist curiosity and taste for exoticism of British and European scholars. Their main purpose was to aid the British in governing colonial India. They showed the British which groups they could rely on to fill high administrative and military posts and pay taxes. Such knowledge was especially crucial because British-born settlers accounted for an extremely small proportion of the population of India (never more than 0.1 percent).

Only an excellent organization could hold such an edifice together. At the bottom of the social ladder the caste census served another purpose: to identify those classes likely to pose problems, especially the "criminal castes," which were groups said to indulge in plunder and other deviant behavior. The Criminal Tribes and Castes Act, which set forth abbreviated procedures for arresting and imprisoning members of these groups, was regularly reinforced from 1871 to 1911.[38] Like the French in Africa,[39] the British made extensive use of forced labor in India, especially for building roads, and the caste censuses showed which groups were most suitable for "recruitment." Indeed, the British demonstrated a certain sophistication in the use of anti-mendicant laws to recruit labor. When landowners met with difficulty recruiting workers for tea and cotton plantations in the late nineteenth century, the authorities used these laws to crack down on beggars, boosting "hiring."[40]

Between the high administrative castes and the criminal and quasi-servile castes, there was a whole series of intermediate classes, especially the agricultural castes, which also played an important role in governing colonial India. In the Punjab, the Land Alienation Act of 1901 limited the purchase and sale of land to a specific group of agricultural castes, which the act also redefined. The official purpose of the act was to reassure certain classes of heavily indebted peasants whose land was in danger of being seized by creditors. The threat of rural unrest worried British authorities, especially because these same agricul-

---

38. See Dirks, *Castes of Mind,* pp. 181–182.

39. See Chap. 7.

40. See A. Stanziani, "Slavery in India," in *The Cambridge World History of Slavery,* ed. D. Eltis, S. Engerman, S. Drescher, and D. Richardson, vol. 4, *AD 1804–AD 2016* (Cambridge University Press, 2017), p. 259.

tural castes were an important source of recruits for the military. But the redefinition of these castes led to many conflicts during subsequent censuses: various rural groups demanded to be reclassified so that they, too, could acquire land, and their wishes were granted.[41]

The key point here is that the administrative categories created by the British to rule the country and assign rights and duties frequently bore little relation to actual social identities. Hence the policy of assigning identities profoundly disrupted existing social structures and in many cases solidified once-flexible boundaries between groups, thus fostering new antagonisms and tensions.

The colonial authorities were largely forced to abandon their initial ambition to divide the population according to the varnas of the Manusmriti. The Kshatriyas no longer really existed except as Rajputs (or Chattris, whose numbers were much smaller). As for the Vaishyas—the artisans, merchants, and free peasants of the Manusmriti—it was impossible to locate them as such: there were of course many local occupational groups that might have been included under this broad head, but these groups had no national identity except perhaps for the Banyas (merchants), whom the British authorities attempted to enumerate and classify as members of the twice-born Vaishya group.

During the first few censuses, colonial administrators were called on to arbitrate numerous conflicts that they themselves had helped to create but had no idea how to resolve, particularly when those conflicts had a religious dimension. In Madras, for example, the colonial authorities agreed to recognize the Nadar caste as Kshatriyas in the census of 1891. A small group of Nadars then used this newfound identity to enter the Minakshi temple of Kamudi, scandalizing the high castes in charge there. The colonial courts ultimately decided that the Nadars must pay the cost of the purification rituals made necessary by their intrusion. Similar conflicts erupted over the use of various public spaces for processions.

British authorities were particularly perplexed by groups that enjoyed high status in certain regions, such as the Kayasths in Bengal, the Marathas in the area of Mumbai, and the Vellalars near Madras, which by all appearances were high castes but had no relation to any of the varnas. Research has shown how, in the late nineteenth century, groups that initially had no clear high-caste identity, such as the Banyas, began to adopt very strict norms of familial or dietary purity (by prohibiting widows from remarrying, for example, or imposing very

---

41. See G. Cassan, "Identity-Based Policies and Identity Manipulation: Evidence from Colonial Punjab," *American Economic Journal,* 2014.

strict vegetarian diets and banning contact with less pure castes), thus moving themselves closer to the twice-born and the Brahmins, whose unified existence was acknowledged and rewarded by the census takers.[42]

Colonial India and the Rigidification of Castes

Although it is obviously impossible to say how India would have developed in the absence of colonization, one of the effects of the census and of the astonishing bureaucratization of social categories that attended it seems to have been that caste boundaries became considerably more rigid. By bestowing precise administrative significance on categories that previously did not exist at the national level, or at any rate existed not in such clear-cut and general form but primarily at the local level, British colonization not only interrupted the autochthonous development of an ancient trifunctional society but also redefined its contours.

In this respect, it is striking to note that the proportions of the high castes in the population remained virtually unchanged from 1871 to 1931 and indeed until 2014, despite considerable growth of the population (Fig. 8.4 and Table 8.2). Note that the census stopped recording high-caste membership in 1931. The British ultimately realized that they had helped to exacerbate identity conflicts and social boundary disputes and therefore changed their approach in the census of 1941. The governments of independent India sought to end discrimination on the basis of caste and therefore stopped asking questions about caste identity (except for the lowest castes, as we will see in a moment). Other surveys continued to ask questions about caste membership, however, and I have included here the results of postelection polls conducted after most Indian legislative elections from 1962 to 1914. The two sources are quite different: the censuses, conducted by official census takers, covered the entire population, while the postelection polls relied on the declarations of only a few tens of thousands of respondents.

Still, it is interesting to note that the various proportions remain virtually unchanged. The proportion of Brahmins in the Hindu population varied between 6 and 7 percent in censuses from 1871 to 1931; it remained at the same level from 1962 to 2014. The proportion of Kshatriyas (in practice mainly Rajputs) ranged from 4 to 5 percent in colonial censuses from the late nineteenth to the early twentieth century; it remained the same in postelection surveys in the late twen-

---

42. See Bayly, *Caste, Society and Politics in India,* pp. 217–232; Dirks, *Castes of Mind,* pp. 236–238.

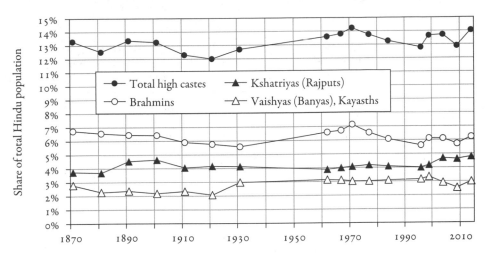

FIG. 8.4. The rigidification of upper castes in India, 1871–2014

Interpretation: The results indicated are based on British colonial censuses from 1871 to 1931 and on (self-declared) postelection surveys from 1962 to 2014. Note the relative stability over time of the proportion of people recorded as Brahmins (priests and scholars), Kshatriyas (Rajputs) (old warrior class), and other high castes: Vaishyas (Banyas) (artisans, merchants) and Kayasths (writers, accountants). Not counted here are local high castes such as the Marathas (about 2 percent of the population). *Sources and series:* piketty.pse .ens.fr/ideology.

tieth and early twenty-first centuries. In Figure 8.4 and Table 8.2 I have also indicated the proportions of Vaishyas (Banyas) and Kayasths: both groups represented 2–3 percent of the Hindu population throughout this period. If we consider the total for all high castes, including the latter two groups, we find that they accounted for 12–14 percent of the Hindu population throughout the period 1871–2014. If we add the Marathas (about 2 percent of the population) and other high castes present only in certain specific regions and whose classification as high castes has been the subject of numerous conflicts and controversies, we come to a total of 15–20 percent, depending on the definitions used.

What is at stake behind these numbers? To answer this question, we must first note that the consequences of these classifications changed radically over the course of the twentieth century. In the late nineteenth century, it was worth a lot to be recognized as a member of a high caste, not only for the symbolic prestige but also to gain access to certain temples, schools, fountains, wells, and other public places. In the late colonial period, especially in the interwar years,

TABLE 8.2

The structure of high castes in India, 1871–2014 (percentage of population)

	1871	1881	1891	1901	1911	1921	1931
Total high castes	13.3%	12.6%	13.4%	13.2%	12.3%	12.0%	12.7%
Brahmins (priests, scholars)	6.7%	6.6%	6.5%	6.4%	5.9%	5.8%	5.6%
Kshatriyas (Rajputs) (warriors)	3.8%	3.7%	4.5%	4.6%	4.1%	4.2%	4.1%
Other high castes: Vaishyas (Banyas), Kayasths	2.8%	2.3%	2.4%	2.2%	2.3%	2.1%	3.0%
Total Hindu population (millions)	179	194	217	217	228	226	247

Interpretation: The results indicated here are based on British colonial censuses from 1871 to 1931 and on postelection surveys from 1962 to 2014. One finds a relative stability over time of the proportion of people recorded as Brahmins (former class of clerics and scholars), Kshatriyas (Rajputs) (former warrior class), and other high castes: Vaishyas (Banyas) (artisans, merchants) and Kayasths (writers, accountants). Other local high castes such as Marathas are not counted here (about 2 percent of the population). *Sources and series:* piketty.pse.ens.fr/ideology.

the British authorities, under pressure from independence movements, began to abolish rules that discriminated against the lower castes, especially the untouchables, and began to put in place preferential access rules intended to correct for past discrimination. Only after independence in 1947, however, were the old discriminations definitively abolished and replaced by a systematic policy of "affirmative action" *(discrimination positive)*. John Hutton, census commissioner in 1931, observed that "Untouchables Excluded" signs were still commonplace in restaurants and barber shops in Madras in 1929.[43] In 1925 the independence leader Periyar (Periyar E. V. Ramasamy) quit the Congress Party because he thought it too timid in its battle to force the most conservative of the twice-born to open all temples to the lower castes and to end separate meals for Brahmin and non-Brahmin students in the schools. He thought the party should be asking for more, and at a faster pace.[44]

43. See J. Hutton, *Castes in India: Its Nature, Functions and Origins* (1946), pp. 197–199.
44. See Dirks, *Castes of Mind*, pp. 257–263.

1962	1967	1971	1977	1996	1999	2004	2009	2014
13.6%	13.8%	14.2%	13.7%	12.8%	13.6%	13.7%	12.8%	14.0%
6.6%	6.7%	7.1%	6.5%	5.6%	6.1%	6.1%	5.7%	6.2%
3.9%	4.0%	4.1%	4.2%	4.0%	4.2%	4.7%	4.6%	4.8%
3.1%	3.1%	3.0%	3.0%	3.2%	3.3%	2.9%	2.5%	3.0%
375	419	453	519	759	800	870	939	1,012

Bhim Rao Ambedkar, the first untouchable to earn degrees in law and economics at Columbia University and the London School of Economics and future drafter of the Indian constitution of 1950, met with great difficulty when he tried to open a law practice in India in the 1920s. He helped launch the movement of the Dalits (the word means "broken" in Sanskrit, and Ambedkar proposed it as the name for ex-untouchables). In 1927 he publicly burned the Manusmriti during a large Dalit rally at the cistern of Chavdar (Maharastra). Ambedkar subsequently invited Dalits to convert to Buddhism. He was convinced that only a radical challenge to the Hinduism could destroy the caste system and put an end to ancient discriminations. He strongly opposed Gandhi, who thought it highly disrespectful to burn the Manusmriti. Gandhi defended the Brahmins and the ideal of functional solidarity among the varnas and called upon the untouchables (whom he called "harijans," or children of god) to assume their place within the Hindu system. In the eyes of many high-caste Indians, this meant that they should also adjust their behavior and adopt familial, dietary, and hygienic norms that would bring them closer to the purity that the upper classes tried to incarnate (somewhat akin to the paternalistic attitude of the Victorian bourgeoisie in England, which sought to encourage sobriety and virtue in the British working class). Some twice-borns close to Gandhi went so far as to propose that untouchables, aborigines, and even Muslims symbolically convert to Hinduism to mark their full return to the Hindu community and embrace of purity.

By the 1920s, moreover, everyone sensed that the colonial system would probably not last forever, and the British had entered into negotiations to extend the right to vote while granting additional powers to elected Indian assemblies. The colonial authorities had already begun to establish separate property-qualified voter lists for Hindus and Muslims before World War I, specifically in Bengal in 1909; many scholars see this as the beginning of a process that would eventually lead to partition in 1947 and the creation of Pakistan and Bangladesh. In the late 1920s Ambedkar also defended the idea of separate electorates, but for Dalits and non-Dalit Hindus: in his view, this was the only way that the former untouchables could make their views heard, find representation, and defend their interests. Gandhi strongly opposed this and began a hunger strike. The two independence leaders ultimately reached a compromise with the Poona Pact of 1932: Dalits and non-Dalit Hindus would vote together for the same deputies, but some districts (proportionate to their share of the population) would be reserved for Dalit candidates only. This so-called system of "reservations" would be enshrined in the 1950 constitution and is still in force today.

At the time of the 1931 census, it was estimated that "outcasts," "tribes," and "depressed classes"—to use the terms that British administrators employed at the time to describe untouchables and other disadvantaged groups, which would later come to be called SCs and STs—encompassed some 50 million people, or 21 percent of the 239 million Hindus. In the late 1920s, independence activists launched anti-census boycotts in several provinces, urging people not to indicate any jati or varna to the census takers. Little by little, the system changed from one that had attempted in the late nineteenth and early twentieth centuries to identify high-caste elites (in some cases to reward them with explicit rights and privileges) to one in which the goal was to identify the lowest castes for the purpose of correcting past discrimination. In 1935, when the colonial government experimented with granting preferential access to certain public jobs to the SCs, it was found that some jatis who had mobilized in the 1890s to be recognized as Kshatriyas and thus to gain access to certain temples and public places were now mobilizing to be counted among the lowest castes.[45] This shows once again how fluid individual identities were and how easily they could adapt to the contradictory incentives created by the colonial authorities.

It is interesting to note that the first attempts to limit the monopoly of the privileged castes on university study and public service jobs were made in 1902 in the Maratha principality of Kolhapur. The king of Kolhapur had felt humiliated in front of his own court when the local Brahmins banned him from a ritual reading of the Vedas on the grounds that his Shudra background prohibited him from participating. Furious, he immediately ordered that 50 percent of the high posts in his administration be set aside for non-Brahmins. Similar movements developed in Madras with the creation of the Justice Party in 1916 and then in the principality of Mysore (Karnataka) in 1918, where the sovereign and non-Brahmin elites became increasingly resistant to the fact that Brahmins, who accounted for just 3 percent of the population, represented 70 percent of the university's student body and occupied the most important government posts, just as in Kolhapur. The Justice Party launched a similar movement in Tamil Nadu in 1921. In southern India, where Brahmin elites were sometimes treated as intruders from the north even though they had lived there for centuries (somewhat like the Chinese in Malaysia), these anti-Brahmin quotas took a fairly radical turn well before independence. By contrast, the Congress Party, whose ranks from Gandhi and Nehru on down included many representatives of the high castes of north India, always took a more moderate stance on "reservations." Yes, one had to help the lower castes progress, but that should not deprive the highest castes of any chance to demonstrate their talents for the benefit of all. It would take decades for these conflicts to fully ripen.

Independent India Faces Status Inequalities from the Past

Following independence in 1946, the Republic of India adopted the most systematic affirmative action policy ever attempted anywhere. The idea of "affirmative action" is often associated with the United States, but the reality is that the United States never adopted official quotas in favor of African Americans or other minorities. Preferential admissions to universities and other institutions always existed in a legal gray area on the margins of the system; affirmative action was a voluntary practice on the part of certain institutions and never a systematic national policy. By contrast, the Indian constitution of 1950

---

45. See Dirks, *Castes of Mind*, pp. 236–238.

explicitly established a legal framework designed to correct past discriminations under the aegis of the state. In a general sense, the constitution of 1950 began by abolishing all caste privileges and expunging all references to religion from the law. Articles 15–17 put an end to untouchability and banned all restrictions on access to temples and other public places.[46] Article 48 gave states broad latitude to regulate the slaughter of cows, however. Conflicts on this issue gave rise to many riots and lynchings of Dalits and Muslims, who were regularly accused of transporting the carcasses of improperly slaughtered animals. Article 46 provided the means to promote the educational and economic interests of SCs and STs—that is, former untouchables and disadvantaged aborigines. Articles 338–339 established commissions to handle the delicate task of deciding who should be classified as an SC or ST. Article 340 envisioned similar measures to support "other backward classes" (OBCs).

At first, only the commissions responsible for defining the SC and ST were actually implemented. The general principle was that groups classified as SC and ST should meet the following criteria: first, they should be objectively handicapped in terms of education, living conditions and housing, and job description (according to census data and other official surveys), and second, this socioeconomic backwardness and "material deprivation" should be due at least in part to specific discriminations suffered in the past. Implicitly, this referred to former untouchables and aborigines living on the fringes of traditional Hindu society (like those Nesfield described in his 1885 account). In practice, under the classifications established by these committees, which are reviewed periodically, successive censuses and surveys established that the SCs and STs accounted for about 21 percent of the Indian population between 1950 and 1970 and about 25 percent in the period 2000–2020.

In theory, social groups and former jatis of all religions could be awarded SC or ST status. In practice, Muslims were all but excluded (only 1–2 percent were SCs or STs). By contrast, nearly half of Buddhists were recognized as SC (especially after Ambedkar urged conversion from Hinduism) and nearly a third of Christians were recognized as ST (many aborigines and isolated tribes

---

46. In 1970, however, the Supreme Court dismissed a suit by Periyar, who wanted to eliminate the hereditary priesthood in Tamil Nadu and require equal access to all clerical functions. See Dirks, *Castes of Mind*, p. 263. For an analysis of spatial stratification and continuing discrimination between Brahmins and non-Brahmins in rural India in the 1950s, especially in relation to diet, see A. Beteille, *Caste, Class and Power: Changing Patterns of Stratification in a Tanjore Village* (1965).

had converted to Christianity during the colonial era, provoking misgivings among the colonial authorities that the conversions were insincere). The SC-ST classification opened the door to reserved places in the universities and civil service as well as to candidacies in reserved districts in federal legislative elections, the number of which was proportionate to the number of SC-ST in the population.

Article 340 of the constitution concerning the OBC took much longer to be concretely implemented. The problem was that the scope of this category was much broader: it included all social groups suffering from social or economic backwardness or material deprivation regardless of whether their situation could be attributed to past discrimination. The OBC might thus in theory include all Shudras—that is, the entire population except the SC-ST and the highest castes. Hence the lower and upper bounds of the OBC were difficult to determine; more than that, the threat to Indian elites was potentially much greater. As long as the quotas applied to no more than 20–25 percent of the available places (in the university, civil service, etc.), the Brahmins and other upper classes were not seriously threatened: their children's better grades would be enough to claim admission to the 75–80 percent of the places remaining. But if the quotas were double or triple that amount, as was the case in some southern Indian states even before independence, things would be different, especially given the relatively small number of university students and civil servants in a country as poor as India. A committee appointed to study the problem in the period 1953–1956 concluded that the OBC represented a minimum of 32 percent of the population; if one added to that the SC-ST quota, some 53 percent of places would be "reserved." The high castes reacted vehemently, and the federal government wisely decided to do nothing and to allow the states to experiment with their quotas, which they did on a large scale, especially in the south. By the early 1970s, most states had established affirmative action programs of one sort or another that went beyond the federal programs, especially in their treatment of the OBC.

Then, in 1978–1980, the Mandal Commission concluded that the implementation of the federal mechanisms envisioned by the constitution could be delayed no longer and estimated that the OBC entitled to benefit from the reservation quotas represented 54 percent of the population (rather than 32 percent—a sign, incidentally, of the great difficulty of defining the OBC and particularly their upper boundary). The federal government ultimately decided to implement the OBC reservations in 1989, which set off a wave of immolations among high-caste students who felt that their lives were ruined despite having earned higher grades than their OBC classmates. The Indian Supreme Court validated the measure in 1992 but stipulated that the quotas could not exceed 50 percent of the available places (including reservations for both OBC and SC-ST).

The commissions authorized to define the contours of the OBC were appointed, and since 1999 the National Sample Survey has officially tracked individuals classified as belonging to the group. The proportion of the population classified as OBC was 36 percent in 1999, 41 percent in 2004, and 44 percent in 2011 and 2014 (note the difference with the estimates of the Mandal Commission, which again shows the fluidity of this category). We thus find that, all told, in the mid-2010s, nearly 70 percent of the Indian population benefited from affirmative action aimed at either the SC-ST or the OBC (Fig. 8.5). Of the 30 percent who do not benefit, upper-caste Hindus (and, more generally, Hindus not classified as SC-ST or OBC) account for 20 percent, while Muslims, Christians, Buddhists, and Sikhs not classified as SC-ST or OBC account for a little less than 10 percent. Historically, these high-ranking social groups filled most of the places in the university and civil service. The stated goal of the "reservations" is precisely to ensure that the bottom 70 percent can have access to a substantial number of these places.

It is worth noting that the OBC category, unlike the SC-ST, is open to Muslims, a fact that contributed to the rise of the Hindu nationalist Bharatiya Janata Party (BJP). This party, with its rather outspoken anti-Muslim rhetoric, has attracted an electorate that is increasingly centered on the upper castes. This calls attention to the crucial interaction between the socioeconomic structure of electorates and the evolution of the redistributive mechanisms around which political and electoral conflict is organized. (I will return to this in Part Four.) Note, too, that in 1993 the Supreme Court of India introduced an income criterion for the application of quotas: if a caste or jati is included in the OBC, members of that group belonging to its "creamy layer" are excluded from the quotas, where the "creamy layer" is defined as consisting of individuals with an annual income above a certain threshold (set initially in 1993 at 100,000 rupees, which by 2019 had risen to 800,000 rupees, a level that in practice excludes less than 10 percent of the Indian population).

The issue is far from closed, however. In particular, the "creamy layer" criterion raises the key question of the relation between belonging to a socially and economically disadvantaged group (and, in the case of the SC-ST, a victim of past discrimination) and individual characteristics such as income or wealth. In the 2011 census, moreover, for the first time since the census of 1931, it was

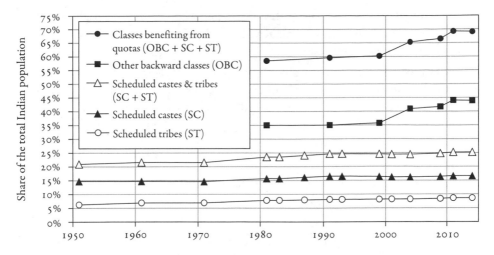

FIG. 8.5. Affirmative action in India, 1950–2015

Interpretation: The results indicated here are based on decennial censuses from 1951 to 2011 and National Sample Surveys (NSS) surveys 1983–2014. Quotes for access to universities and government jobs were established for the "scheduled castes" (SC) and "scheduled tribes" (ST) (former untouchables and disadvantaged aborigines) in 1950, before being extended in the 1980s to "other backward classes" (OBC) (former Shudras) by the Mandal Commission (1979–1980). The OBC were surveyed in the NSS only beginning in 1999, and the estimates shown here for 1981 and 1991 (35 percent of the population) are approximate. *Sources and series:* piketty.pse.ens.fr/ideology.

decided to collect information pertaining to all castes and jatis in order to begin an overall reevaluation of the socioeconomic characteristics of all groups in terms of education, employment, housing (walls and roofs of bamboo, plastic, wood, brick, stone, or concrete), income bracket, assets (refrigerator, cell phone, motor scooter, car), and even amount of land owned. The Socio-Economic and Caste Census (SECC) of 2011 thus marks a departure from the censuses conducted between 1951 and 2001, which collected similar socioeconomic information but without asking questions about castes and jatis (other than membership of the SC-ST). This fresh look at the problem could potentially lead to revision of the whole system of "reservations." The subject is explosive, however, and the detailed findings of the 2011 census remained inaccessible in 2019.

In late 2018 the Supreme Court decided to extend the "creamy layer" rule to the SC-ST, which was tantamount to saying that old status discriminations could not eternally justify measures of compensation. Given the high income threshold used, however, the impact of this decision will be limited. In early 2019, the Indian government (BJP) passed a measure to extend the benefit of reservations to high-caste individuals earning less than the threshold but without reducing the quotas for other groups. These issues will likely continue to be controversial in the decades ahead.

Successes and Limits of Affirmative Action in India

Did India's affirmative action policies reduce the inequalities associated with ancient status classifications or did they help solidify caste distinctions? This is a complex question, and we will come back to it in subsequent parts of this book, in particular when we study the transformations of the socioeconomic structure of political and electoral cleavages in the world's largest democracy.[47] Several remarks can already be formulated, however. First, the Indian case shows how essential it is to take a broad comparative and historical approach to the analysis of inequality regimes in the twenty-first century. The structure of inequality in present-day India is the product of a complex history involving the transformation of a premodern trifunctional society whose evolution was profoundly altered by its encounter with British colonizers—colonizers who decided to establish a rigid administrative codification of local social identities. The issue today is not to speculate about how India's inequality regime might have evolved without colonization. That question is largely unanswerable, because two centuries of British presence, first under the EIC (1757–1858) and then via direct administration (1858–1947), totally disrupted the previous developmental logic. The important question now is rather to determine the best way to overcome this very oppressive inegalitarian heritage, at once trifunctional and colonial.

The available evidence suggests that the policies India has pursued since independence have significantly reduced inequalities between the old disadvantaged castes and the rest of the population—more, for example, than inequalities were reduced between blacks and whites in the United States and much more than between blacks and whites in South Africa since the end of apartheid (Fig. 8.6). To be sure, these comparisons will hardly end the debate. The fact that blacks in South Africa earned less than 20 percent of what whites earned in the 2010s, whereas the SC and ST—the former untouchables and

---

47. See Chap. 16.

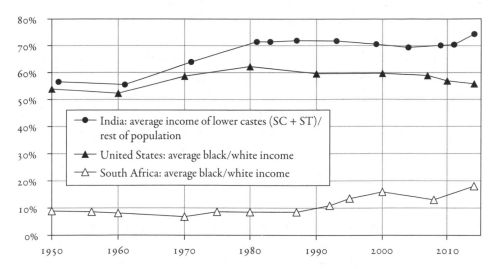

FIG. 8.6. Discrimination and inequality in comparative perspective

Interpretation: The ratio of average lower-caste income in India (scheduled castes and tribes, SC + ST, former untouchables and disadvantaged aborigines) to that of the rest of the population rose from 57 percent in 1950 to 74 percent in 2014. The ratio between average black and average white income went from 54 to 56 percent in the United States over the same period and from 9 to 18 percent in South Africa. *Sources and series:* piketty .pse.ens.fr/ideology.

disadvantaged aborigines—earn more than 70 percent of what the rest of the population earns, has to be seen in context, since the situations in the two countries are very different. Blacks represent more than 80 percent of the South African population, whereas the SC-ST account for 25 percent of the Indian population. In this respect, the comparison with blacks in the United States (12 percent of the population) is more relevant. It shows that India, starting from a similar point in the 1950s (with an income ratio of about 50 percent, as far as one can judge from imperfect data) was able to achieve a significantly greater reduction of inequality. However, the standard of living remains much lower in India than in the United States, which limits the relevance of the comparison. The available data also show that while individuals belonging to the old high castes (especially Brahmins) continue to enjoy greater income, wealth, and educational attainment than the rest of the population, the differences are much less pronounced than in other countries marked by strong status inequalities, such as South Africa (admittedly not a very high bar).[48]

More revealing still, perhaps, is that many studies have shown that the measures adopted in India through parliamentary democratic procedures had the effect of bringing the lower classes into electoral politics. In particular, the "reservation" of seats for the SC-ST in all federal legislative elections since the early 1950s encouraged all political parties to back candidates from those groups in numbers proportional to their share of the population, and it is highly unlikely that such a result could have been achieved in any other way.[49] In 1993, a constitutional amendment required states that had not already done so to reserve a third of leadership posts in *panchayats* (village councils) for women. Research has shown that experiments with female-led panchayats has helped to reduce negative stereotypes of women (as measured by reactions to identical political speeches read by male and female voices), which may be the most convincing proof of the usefulness of affirmative action in overcoming longstanding prejudices.[50] Indians are still debating whether or not to amend the constitution to reserve a third of the seats in federal legislative elections for women and how such new reservations should interact with existing reservations for SCs and STs.

More generally, concerning the political integration of disadvantaged classes and especially the OBC (which, unlike the SC and ST, do not benefit from reserved seats at the federal level), it is important to note the key role played

---

48. The average income of non-Brahmins in the 2010s was about 65 percent of the income of Brahmins (who accounted for a little more than 5 percent of the population, a smaller elite than white South Africans). See the online appendix and the data collected in N. Bharti, "Wealth Inequality, Class and Caste in India, 1951–2012," WID.world, 2018. On racial inequality in the United States, see R. Manduca, "Income Inequality and the Persistence of Racial Economic Disparities," *Sociological Science,* 2018; P. Beyer and K. Kofi Charles, "Divergent Paths: A New Perspective on Earnings Differences Between Black and White Men since 1940," *Quarterly Journal of Economics,* 2018.

49. See F. Jensenius, *Social Justice through Inclusion: The Consequences of Electoral Quotas in India* (Oxford University Press, 2017). The number of reservations evolved as a function of census data and redistricting. In 2014, 25 percent of voters in SC districts were SC, compared with 17 percent nationwide. SC-ST deputies do not appear to have voted differently from others in the same party or favored different socioeconomic policies, a result that some will see as disappointing and others as a sign of successful social integration in the parties and the political system.

50. L. Beaman, R. Chattopadhyay, E. Duflo, R. Pande, and P. Topalova, "Powerful Women: Does Exposure Reduce Bias?" *Quarterly Journal of Economics,* 2009.

since 1980 by the emergence of new parties focused on mobilizing the lower castes. This "caste democracy" has been studied by Christophe Jaffrelot.[51] Like elites in other countries, Indian elites, surprised by this phenomenon, have often reacted to these popular mobilizations from which they feel excluded by characterizing them as "populist." In 1993, one of the slogans of the BSP, a lower-caste party that took power in Uttar Pradesh in the 1990s and 2000s before finishing third in the 2014 federal elections (behind the Hindu nationalists of the BJP and the Congress Party), perfectly captured the anti-high-caste sentiment of its supporters: "Priest, merchant, soldier, boot them out forever."[52] In Part Four of this book we will see that this type of mobilization allowed for a high level of democratic participation as well as for the development of new class cleavages in the Indian electorate—cleavages that could not have been predicted from the politics of previous decades.

That said, it would be quite misleading to idealize the way the "reservations" system was used to reduce inequalities in India or, more generally, to idealize the way caste identities were instrumentalized in Indian politics. By construction, reservations in the universities, civil service, and elected bodies can only benefit a small minority of individuals within the most disadvantaged social classes. Individual advancement into top-end positions is very important, and it can justify recourse to a quota system, especially when the effects of discrimination and prejudice are as clearly demonstrated as they were in India. But it is not enough. To have achieved truly significant reductions of Indian social inequalities, it would have been necessary to invest massively in basic public services for the most disadvantaged classes (SC-ST and OBC combined), especially in the areas of education, public health, sanitary infrastructure, and transportation, ignoring ancient boundaries between status and religious groups.

In fact, investment was quite limited, not only in comparison with the rich countries but, more importantly, in comparison with India's Asian neighbors. In the mid-2010s, India's total public health budget amounted to barely 1 percent of national income, compared with more than 3 percent in China (and 8 percent in Europe). For Jean Drèze and Amartya Sen, the fact that

---

51. See C. Jaffrelot, *Inde: la démocratie par la caste. Histoire d'une mutation socio-politique 1885–2005* (Fayard, 2005). On the central importance of caste and ideas of how to overcome it in regimes based on status inequalities, see also C. Jaffrelot, "Partir de la caste pour penser les assignations statutaires," in C. Jaffrelot and J. Naudet, *Justifier l'ordre social* (Presses Universitaires de France, 2013).

52. See A. Teltumbe, *Republic of Caste: Thinking Equality in a Time of Neoliberal Hindutva* (Navayana, 2018), p. 346.

India's upper classes refused to pay the taxes that would have been required to finance essential social expenditures was in part a consequence of a particularly elitist and inegalitarian Hindu political culture (which the quota system in some ways served to hide). As a result, India—despite the undeniable successes of its model of parliamentary democracy, government of laws, and inclusion of the lower classes in the political and justice system—has lost ground in the areas of economic development and basic social welfare, even when compared with neighbors that were not especially well advanced in the 1960s and 1970s. If we look, for example, at indices of health and education for the 1970s, we find that India not only did less well than China and other communist countries such as Vietnam but also fell behind non-communist but less elitist countries such as Bangladesh.[53]

In the case of India, it is particularly striking to note that the glaring lack of sanitary infrastructure such as running water and toilets (according to available estimates, more than half the population was still defecating outdoors in the mid-2010s) has at times been coupled with stigmatizing political rhetoric and explicitly discriminatory measures toward the populations concerned.[54]

To these factors one must of course add the weight of the international environment. In an ideological and institutional context marked by heightened fiscal competition to attract private investors and appease the wealthiest taxpayers and by the unprecedented proliferation of tax havens, it became increasingly difficult in the 1980s and 1990s for the poorest countries, including India and the nations of sub-Saharan Africa, to establish norms of fiscal justice or to collect enough in taxes to finance an ambitious welfare state. I will have more to say about these issues in Part Three.[55] In India, however, the in-

---

53. J. Drèze and A. Sen, *An Uncertain Glory: India and Its Contradictions* (Princeton University Press, 2013). The contrast with the less alarmist evaluation the same authors made twenty years earlier is both justified and revealing: see J. Drèze and A. Sen, *India: Economic Development and Social Opportunity* (Oxford University Press, 1995).

54. In 2015, the BJP governments of the Rajasthan and Haryana limited access to elective office to individuals with toilets in their homes and sufficient education (a minimum of five years for women and eight for men), and these measures were validated by the Supreme Court. In 2018, a school admission form that asked whether parents had an "unclean occupation" (clearly aimed at the children of untouchables) caused a scandal and was finally abandoned in Haryana. See Teltumbe, *Republic of Caste,* pp. 57–75.

55. See esp. Chap. 13.

adequacy of spending on health and education for the most disadvantaged classes can also be related to older domestic factors. In particular, this failure should be seen in relation to the "reservations" granted to the lower castes after 1950. In the eyes of the favored progressive classes that supported the quota policy (particularly in the Congress Party), that policy had the great advantage of not costing anyone anything in taxes, and ultimately it worked, primarily to the detriment of the OBC. By contrast, a high-quality universal system of public health and education accessible to all, but especially to the SC-ST and OBC, would have cost a lot, and the taxes would have had to be paid by the most advantaged groups.

Property Inequalities and Status Inequalities

In addition to health and education, the other structural policy that might have contributed to a major reduction of social inequality in India is of course redistribution of property, especially farmland. Unfortunately, no agrarian reform was attempted or even considered at the federal level. Broadly speaking, both the constitution of 1950 and the principal political leaders of independent India took a relatively conservative approach to issues of property. This was true not only of the leaders of the Congress Party but also of Dalit leaders like Ambedkar, whose battle for "the annihilation of caste" (the title of his censured 1936 speech) involved such radical measures as separate electorates and conversion to Buddhism but eschewed any measures that might have undermined the property regime. This was partly due to his wariness of Marxists, who in the Indian context tended to reduce everything to the question of ownership of the means of production, which in Ambedkar's view led to neglect of the discrimination to which Dalit workers were subjected by non-Dalits in the textile factories of Mumbai and to the pretense that such problems would solve themselves once private property ceased to exist.[56]

Ambedkar aside, it is interesting to note that there were many debates in India in the 1950s and 1960s on the usefulness of agrarian reform as well as on the possibility of basing quotas on "objective" family characteristics such as income, wealth, education, and so on rather than caste. Such proposals encountered two main counterarguments: first, many people insisted that caste was a

---

56. On the conflicts and polemics between Ambedkar and leaders of the Communist Party of India (founded in 1925) in the interwar years, see Teltumbe, *Republic of Caste,* pp. 105–107.

key category for reducing social inequality and orienting government policy in India (both because caste played a real role in discrimination and because it was quite difficult to measure "objective" characteristics); and second, some feared that no one would know how to end agrarian reform once it began, besides which there was no certainty of reaching agreement about the best way to combine income, wealth, and other parameters to define reservation quotas and, more generally, to allocate shares under a policy of redistribution.[57]

All of these Indian debates are essential for our study for several reasons. First, we have already encountered more than once this fear that any redistribution of wealth or income would open Pandora's box and that it would be better never to open it than to face the problem of not being able to close it once opened. This argument has been used at one time or another in many different contexts to justify keeping property rights exactly as they have always been. We saw it raised during the French Revolution, in the British House of Lords, and in debates over the abolition of slavery and the need to compensate slaveowners. It therefore comes as no surprise to find it coming up again in India, where property inequalities were compounded by status inequalities. The problem was that the "Pandora's box argument" did nothing to palliate the sense of injustice among the disadvantaged or to alleviate the risk of violence. Indeed, since 1960, large parts of India have been rocked repeatedly by Naxalite-Maoist uprisings pitting landless peasants descended from the former untouchable and aboriginal populations against landowners of upper-caste descent.[58] These conflicts have unfolded against a background of land tenure and property relations largely unchanged since the days of Hindu feudalism as consolidated under the British, a legacy that still continues to feed the spiral of hostility based on identity and intercaste violence.[59]

---

57. Bayly, *Caste, Society and Politics in India*, pp. 288–293; Dirks, *Castes of Mind*, pp. 283–285.

58. The term "Naxalite" refers to the village of Naxalbari in northern Bengal, where in 1967 landless peasants seized rice stores belonging to a landlord to launch the movement. It has become synonymous with anti-government rebels of all kinds: for example, in 2018 there were arrests in Maharastra of "urban Naxalites" (in reality, pro-Dalit intellectuals, like those in the film *Court*, dir. C. Tamhane [Zeitgeist Films, 2014]). These followed controversial ceremonies marking the bicentennial of the battle of Koregaon (1818), which one side interpreted as a battle between Dalits and Maraths and the other as a battle against the pro-Dalit English.

59. See Bayly, *Caste, Society and Politics in India*, pp. 344–364; Teltumbe, *Republic of Caste*, pp. 179–202.

An ambitious agrarian reform, backed by a more redistributive tax system to pay for better health and educational services, would have helped to pull up the disadvantaged classes and reduce Indian inequalities. Research has shown that limited experiments with agrarian reform in states such as West Bengal after the Communist victory in the 1977 elections did result in significant improvements in agricultural productivity. In Kerala, the agrarian reform that began in 1964 coincided with the turn to a more egalitarian development model than in the rest of India, especially with respect to education and health. By contrast, those parts of India where land tenure was most inegalitarian and property most concentrated experienced the least rapid economic growth and social development.[60]

Social and Gender Quotas and the Conditions of Their Transformation

The Indian debates are also essential because they illustrate the need both to take antidiscrimination policy seriously (if need be by means of quotas) and to rethink and revise it constantly. When a group is the victim of longstanding, well-established prejudices and stereotypes, as women are more or less everywhere and as specific social groups (such as the lower castes in India) are in various countries, it is clearly not enough to base redistributive policies solely on income, wealth, or education. It may be necessary to resort to preferential access and quotas (like the "reservations" system in India) based directly on membership in disadvantaged groups.

In recent decades a number of countries have developed systems similar to India's, especially with respect to access to elective office. In 2016, seventy-seven countries were using quota systems to increase the representation of women in their legislative bodies, and twenty-eight countries were doing the same to encourage better representation of national, linguistic, and ethnic minorities in Asia, Europe, and around the world.[61] In wealthy democracies, a sharp decrease in the proportion of working-class representatives in the legislature has

---

60. See esp. A. Banerjee, P. Gertler, and M. Ghatak, "Empowerment and Efficiency: Tenancy Reform in West Bengal," *Journal of Political Economy*, 2002; A. Banerjee, L. Iyer, and R. Somanathan, "History, Social Divisions, and Public Goods in Rural India," *Journal of the European Economic Association*, 2005; A. Banerjee and L. Iyer, "History, Institutions, and Economic Performance: The Legacy of Colonial Land Tenure Systems in India," *American Economic Review*, 2005.

61. See Jensenius, *Social Justice through Inclusion*, pp. 15–20.

led to new thinking about forms of political representation, including the use of lotteries and "social quotas."[62] These ideas bear some resemblance to India's "reservations" system, a point to which I will return later.

We will also see how countries like France and the United States are just beginning to develop procedures for preferential access to secondary schools and universities. Since 2007, for example, admissions procedures to Paris lycées have been taking social background explicitly into account by awarding bonus points to students whose parents are low income or reside in underprivileged neighborhoods. This system was extended to higher education in France in 2018. Other criteria are sometimes considered, such as the student's region or school of origin. These devices resemble the reservations for SC-ST students at the federal level in India since 1950; even more the new admissions procedures introduced at some universities (such as Jawaharlal Nehru University in Delhi) in the 1960s go beyond the federal quotas by taking account not only SC-ST status but also gender, parental income, and region of origin.

The fact that India has been a pioneer on these issues attests to the country's desire to face up to its very heavy inegalitarian heritage, the product of status inequalities stemming from ancient trifunctional ideology solidified by British colonial codification. My point here is not to idealize the way independent India addressed this legacy but simply to note that it is possible to draw any number of conclusions from India's experience. In Europe and elsewhere, it has long been thought that affirmative action was unnecessary because people from different social classes enjoyed equal rights, particularly with respect to education. Today we see more clearly that such formal equality is not enough and must in some cases be complemented by more proactive measures.

In any event, the Indian experience also illustrates the risk that quotas may solidify identities and categories and underscores the need to invent more flexible and adaptable systems. In the Indian case, it is possible that the quotas adopted to help the SC-ST in the 1950s and then the OBC in the 1990s (after decades of colonial censuses and imposed identities) helped to solidify caste and jati identities. Marriage outside one's jati has certainly increased: according to available data, barely 5 percent of marriages involved spouses of different jatis in the 1950s in both rural and urban areas, but this had increased to 8 percent for rural and 10 percent for urban marriages by the 2010s. Recall that intra-jati marriage reflected the persistence of social solidarities within micro-groups

---

62. J. Cagé, *Le prix de la démocratie* (Fayard, 2018); published in English as *The Price of Democracy*, tr. Patrick Camiller (Harvard University Press, 2020).

sharing the same occupational, regional, cultural, and in some cases culinary characteristics rather than any vertical, hierarchical logic. For example, if one measures the probability of marriage to a person of similar educational attainment (or to a person with parents of similar educational attainment), one finds that the level of social homogamy in India, while quite high, is roughly of the same order as one finds in France and other Western countries.[63] Recall, moreover, that intermarriage rates between persons of different national, religious, or ethnic backgrounds are often extremely low in Europe and the United States (we will come back to this) and that Indian jatis in part reflect distinct regional and cultural identities. It is nevertheless reasonable to believe that intra-jati marriage, which remains quite high in India, reflects some degree of social closure and that excessive reliance on quotas and caste-based political mobilization strategies has contributed to perpetuating this.

Ideally, a quota system should anticipate the conditions under which it would ccasc to be necessary. In other words, "reservations" favoring disadvantaged groups should be phased out if and when they succeed in reducing prejudices. When quotas other than gender are involved, it also seems crucial to move as quickly as possible to objective socioeconomic criteria such as income, wealth, and education, as otherwise categories such as the SC-ST in India tend to solidify, which considerably complicates the development of norms of justice acceptable to all. It is possible that the Indian quota system is currently undergoing a major transformation and will gradually transition from a system based on old status categories to one based on income, assets, and other objectifiable socioeconomic criteria applicable to all groups. The transition is moving slowly, however, and may require a better system for gauging income and wealth together with a new tax system, about which I will say more later. In any case, taking the full measure of the successes and limitations of the Indian experience will be useful in thinking about how one might do more to overcome longstanding social and status inequalities in India and around the world.

---

63. See the online appendix and the comparisons in N. Bharti, *Wealth Inequality, Class and Caste in India, 1951–2012* (master's thesis, Paris School of Economics, 2018). See also A. Banerjee, E. Duflo, M. Ghatak, and J. Lafortune, "Marry for What? Caste and Mate Selection in Modern India," *American Economic Journal*, 2013. The surveys record the answers of several thousand to several tens of thousands of jatis and sub-jatis.

NINE

Ternary Societies and Colonialism: Eurasian Trajectories

In previous chapters we studied first slave societies and then postslave colonial societies, looking in particular at the cases of Africa and India. Before beginning our study of the crisis of proprietarian and colonial societies in the twentieth century, which we will do in Part Three, we must first complete our analysis of colonialism and its consequences for the transformation of non-European inequality regimes. In this chapter we will be looking specifically at the cases of China, Japan, and Iran and, more generally, at the way in which the encounter between European powers and the principal Asian state structures affected the political-ideological and institutional trajectories of these various inequality regimes.

We will begin by examining the central role played by rivalries among European states in the development of unprecedented levels of fiscal and military capacity in the seventeenth and eighteenth centuries, far beyond the capacities of the Chinese and Ottoman empires in the same period. This European state power, spurred by intense competition among states and sociopolitical communities of comparable size in Europe (especially France, the United Kingdom, and Germany), was largely responsible for the West's military, colonial, and economic domination, which for a long time was the characteristic feature of the modern world. We will then analyze the various ideological and political constructs that supplanted trifunctional society in Asia in the wake of the encounter with European colonialism. In addition to the Indian case, which we have already discussed, we will be looking at Japan, China, and Iran. Once again, we will find that many trajectories were possible, and this leads us to minimize the role of cultural or civilizational determinism and to emphasize instead the importance of sociopolitical developments and the logic of events in the transformation of inequality regimes.

Colonialism, Military Domination, and Western Prosperity

We have already touched at several points on the central role of slavery, colonialism, and the most brutal forms of coercion and military domination in the rise of European power between 1500 and 1960. It is hard to deny that pure force played a key role in the triangular trade that brought slaves from Africa to French and British slave colonies, the southern United States, and Brazil. The fact that the raw material extracted from slave plantations yielded considerable profits to the colonial powers and that cotton in particular played a central role in the takeoff of the textile industry is also well established. We have also seen that the abolition of slavery led to generous compensation for the slave-owners (in the Haitian case resulting in a heavy debt to France that was not repaid until 1950, and in the American case resulting in the denial of civil rights to the descendants of slaves until the 1960s—or in South Africa until the 1990s). Finally, we saw how postslave colonialism relied on various forms of legal and status inequality, including forced labor, which persisted in France's colonies until 1946.[1]

We turn now to the question of how European military domination, which gradually emerged in the seventeenth and eighteenth centuries and led to European hegemony in the nineteenth and early twentieth centuries, depended on the European states' development of an unprecedented level of fiscal and administrative capacity. Although the sources that would enable us to measure the tax revenues of all these countries prior to the nineteenth century are limited, certain facts are well established. In particular, recent research has shown that it is possible to collect reasonably homogeneous data on tax receipts for the major European countries and the Ottoman Empire from the early sixteenth to the nineteenth centuries.[2] The main difficulty is to compare the numbers in a meaningful way. Although the populations of the countries in question are relatively well understood, at least to a first approximation, the same cannot be said of their levels of economic activity, about which our information is woefully incomplete. It is also important to remember that many obligatory (or quasi-obligatory) payments at that time were made not to the state but to other actors, such as religious organizations, pious foundations, and

---

1. See Chaps. 6–7.
2. See the online appendix (piketty.pse.ens.fr/ideology); see also K. Karaman and S. Pamuk, "Ottoman State Finances in European Perspective, 1500–1914," *Journal of Economic History*, 2010.

local seigneuries or military orders, not only in Europe but also in the Ottoman Empire, Persia, India, and China; comparison along these lines might also be interesting. In what follows, however, attention will be focused solely on monies collected by the central government in the strict sense of the word.

One way to proceed would be to estimate the gold or silver equivalent of the sums collected by states in various currencies. Since all currencies at the time had a metallic base, this would give us a good idea of each state's capacity to pay for its policies by remunerating its soldiers, purchasing commodities, or financing the construction of roads and ships. What we find is a prodigious increase in the sums collected by European states between the early sixteenth and the late eighteenth centuries. In the period 1500–1550, the tax receipts of the major European powers such as France and Spain amounted to 100–150 tons of silver per year, roughly the same as the Ottoman Empire. At that time England was taking in barely fifty tons a year, partly owing to its smaller population.[3] In the centuries that followed these sums would grow spectacularly, mainly due to the intensifying rivalry between England and France: both countries were taking in 600–900 tons of silver in 1700, 800–1,100 tons in the 1750s, and 1,600–1,900 tons in the 1780s, leaving all other European powers far behind. Importantly, Ottoman tax receipts remained virtually unchanged from 1500 to 1780: barely 150–200 tons. After 1750, it was not only France and England that had a far greater tax capacity than the Ottoman Empire; so did Austria, Prussia, Spain, and Holland (Fig. 9.1).

These changes can be explained in part by population changes (recall that in the eighteenth century France was by far the most populous country in Europe) and changes in output (England, for instance, made up for its smaller population by producing more per capita). But the main reason for the increase in tax receipts was intensified fiscal pressure from European governments while Ottoman appetites remained stable. A good way to measure the intensity of taxation is to look at tax receipts per capita and compare the results with daily wages in urban construction. Urban construction wages are relatively well known and easy to compare across countries over a long period both in Europe

---

3. In the fourteenth and fifteenth centuries, the tax receipts of France and England were always below one hundred tons of silver a year, with many ups and downs linked to military conflicts and shifting territorial boundaries. See, for example, J.-P. Genet, "France, Angleterre, Pays-Bas: l'Etat moderne," in *Histoire du monde au XVe siècle,* ed. P. Boucheron, tome 1, *Territoires et écritures du monde* (Hachette Pluriel, 2012), pp. 248–249.

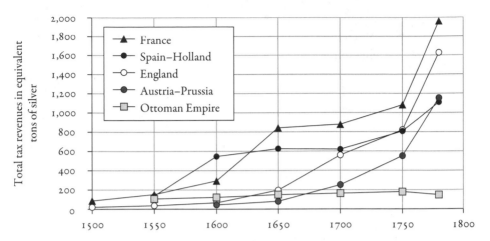

FIG. 9.1. State fiscal capacity, 1500–1780 (tons of silver)

Interpretation: In 1500–1550, tax receipts of the principal European states as well as the Ottoman Empire were equivalent to 100–200 tons of silver per years. In the 1780s, the tax receipts of England and France were between 1600 and 2000 tons of silver per year, while those of the Ottoman Empire remained below 200 tons. *Sources and series:* piketty .pse.ens.fr/ideology.

and the Ottoman Empire and to some extent in China. The available data are imperfect, but the orders of magnitude are quite striking. We find, for example, that per capita tax receipts amounted to two to four days of unskilled urban labor in the period 1500–1600 in Europe, the Ottoman Empire, and the Chinese empire. Tax pressure then intensified in Europe in the period 1650–1700. It rose to ten to fifteen days of wages in the period 1750–1780 and to nearly twenty days in 1850, following very similar trajectories in the major states, including France, England, and Prussia, where state and nation building (though begun much earlier) picked up speed in the eighteenth century. The growth of fiscal pressure in Europe was extremely rapid: although there was no clear difference between Europe, the Ottoman Empire, and China in 1650, the gap begins to widen around 1700 and becomes significant in the period 1750–1780 (Fig. 9.2).

Why did European states increase their fiscal pressure in the seventeenth and eighteenth centuries, and why did the Ottomans and Chinese not follow suit? To be clear, note that this level of fiscal pressure is still very low compared with modern times. As we will see in subsequent chapters, taxes and other obligatory payments in Europe and the United States did not exceed 10 percent of

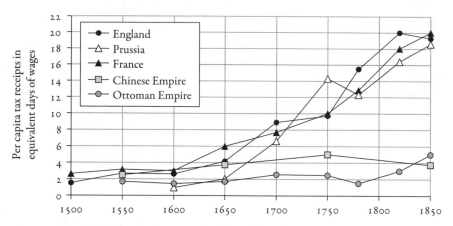

FIG. 9.2. State fiscal capacity, 1500–1850 (days of wages)

Interpretation: In 1500–1600, per capita tax receipts in Europe were equivalent to two to four days of unskilled urban labor; in 1750–1850 this rose to ten to twenty days of wages. Receipts remained around two to five days of wages in the Ottoman and Chinese Empires. With national income per capita of around 250 days of urban wages, this meant that receipts stagnated at 1–2 percent of national income in the Chinese and Ottoman Empires but rose from 1–2 to 6–8 percent in Europe. *Sources and series:* piketty. pse.ens.fr/ideology.

national income throughout the nineteenth century and until World War I before jumping upward between 1910 and 1980 and then stabilizing at between 30 and 50 percent of national income after 1980 (see Fig. 10.14). In the seventeenth and eighteenth centuries fiscal pressure was relatively low (never above 10 percent of national income) compared with modern times.

It is also interesting to note that the earliest estimates of national income (that is, the total income in cash and kind earned by the residents of a given country) appeared in the United Kingdom and France around 1700, thanks to authors such as William Petty; Gregory King; Pierre Le Pesant, sieur de Boisguilbert; and Sébastien Le Prestre de Vauban.[4] The purpose of their work

---

4. Recall that national income is equal to what we would today call gross domestic product (GDP; the sum of all goods and services produced in a given territory in a year less the cost of the goods and services required to produce them) minus depreciation of capital (which in practice amounts to 10–15 percent of GDP), plus or minus the net income received from abroad (which can be positive or negative for a given country but which sums to zero at the global level). The first

was to estimate the state's fiscal potential and consider possible reforms of the tax system at a time when everyone felt that the central state was increasing its fiscal pressure and needed to take a more rational, quantitative approach to its finances. Estimates of national income were based on calculations of surface area and agricultural output as well as on commercial and wage data (including wages in the construction sector), and they provide useful orders of magnitude. The national income and gross domestic product series based on seventeenth- and eighteenth-century data enable us to see overall levels and progressions, but the decade-by-decade changes are too uncertain to use here, which is why I prefer to express the evolution of tax receipts in terms of tons of silver and days of unskilled urban labor (units of measurement better adapted to statistical work on these periods). To clarify our thinking, however, we can say the following: the increase in per capita tax receipts that we see in France, the United Kingdom, and Prussia, from two to four days' wages in 1500–1550 to fifteen to twenty days' wages in 1780–1820, corresponds to an increase in total tax receipts from barely 1–2 percent of national income in the early sixteenth century to about 6–8 percent of national income in the late eighteenth century (Fig. 9.2).[5]

When the State Was Too Small to Be the Night Watchman

As rough as these approximations may be, the orders of magnitude are worth keeping in mind because they correspond to very different state capacities. A state that claims only 1 percent of national income has very little power and very little capacity to mobilize society. Broadly speaking, it can put 1 percent

British and French estimates of national income in the period 1690–1710 were later refined, especially during the French Revolution (see, for example, the work of Lavoisier on the "national wealth of France"). On the history of national accounts, see T. Piketty, *Capital in the Twenty-First Century*, translated by A. Goldhammer (Harvard University Press, 2014), chaps. 1–2. In Chap. 10 I will say more about the various measures of "national wealth" that were also developed after 1700.

5. See the online appendix. The national income calculations use the urban wage data cited here but in combination with many other sources of data on output and trade, which in theory can lead to a better estimate of true national income. But when the various basic sources are quite uncertain, aggregating them into a national income or GDP estimate does not always lead to clarity of debate; hence my choice and that of many other scholars to express tax receipts in terms of days of urban wages.

of the population to work on tasks it deems useful.[6] By contrast, a state that claims around 10 percent of national income as taxes can put about 10 percent of the population to work (or finance transfers or purchases of goods and equipment of a similar amount), which is a good deal more. Concretely, with tax receipts of 8–10 percent of national income, which is what European states were collecting in the nineteenth century, it is certainly not possible to pay for an elaborate educational, health, and welfare system (with free elementary and high schools, universal health insurance, retirement pensions, social transfer payments, and so on), which as we will see required much higher levels of fiscal pressure in the twentieth century (typically 30–50 percent of national income). By contrast, such sums are more than sufficient to allow the centralized state to pay for "night watchman" functions such as police forces and courts capable of maintaining order and protecting property at home along with equipping a military capable of projecting force abroad. In practice, when the fiscal pressure rose to around 8–10 percent of national income as in Europe in the nineteenth and early twentieth centuries, or even 6–8 percent as in the late eighteenth century, military expenses alone generally absorbed half of all tax revenues and in some cases more than two-thirds.[7]

By contrast, a state with barely 1–2 percent of national income in tax receipts is condemned to be a weak state, incapable of maintaining order and carrying out even the minimal functions of the night watchman state. By this measure, most states around the world were weak until relatively recent times; this is true of European states until the sixteenth century and of the Ottoman and Chinese states until the nineteenth century. More precisely, the latter were weakly centralized state structures, incapable of autonomously guaranteeing the security of people and property and of maintaining public order and enforcing respect for the rights of property throughout the territory supposedly under their control. In practice, to carry out these regalian tasks, these states relied

---

6. Assuming that people employed by the state (police, military, administrators, etc.) have on average the same level of skills and remuneration as the average person in the rest of society and that the equipment and supplies they need to do their jobs are also on the same order as the average.

7. These orders of magnitude are still valid for military budgets today, which run about 2 percent of national income in countries that are not very active militarily (as in Europe), more than 4 percent in the United States, and more than 10 percent in Saudi Arabia. Globally, military expenditure fell from more than 6 percent of global income in the early 1960s (the era of colonial wars and the Cold War) to just 3 percent in the 2010s. See the online appendix.

on various local entities and elites—seigneurial, military, clerical, and intellectual elites within the framework of trifunctional society in one of its many variants. Once European states developed a more significant fiscal and administrative capacity, new dynamics were set in motion.

Within the countries in question, the development of the centralized state coincided with the transformation of ternary societies into ownership societies, accompanied by the rise of proprietarian ideology and based on strict separation of regalian powers (henceforth the monopoly of the state) from property rights (supposedly open to all). Abroad, the capacity of European states to project force beyond their borders led to the formation first of slave and then of colonial empires and to the development of the various political-ideological constructs around which these were structured. In both cases, the processes by which fiscal and administrative capacities were constructed were inseparable from political-ideological developments. State capacities always developed with an eye to structuring domestic and international society (in the rivalry with Islam, for example); the process, unstable by nature, always involved social and political conflict.

To summarize, the development of the modern state involved two great leaps forward. The first unfolded between 1500 and 1800 in the leading states of Europe, which were able to increase their tax revenues from barely 1–2 percent of national income to about 6–8 percent. This process was accompanied by the development of ownership societies at home and colonial empires abroad. The second leap forward came in the period 1910–1980, when the rich countries as a group went from tax revenues of 8–10 percent of national income on the eve of World War I to revenues of 30–50 percent of national income in the 1980s. This transformation was accompanied by a broad process of economic development and historic improvement in living conditions and gave rise to various forms of social-democratic society. Within this general pattern different trajectories were possible. It proved difficult to extend the second leap forward to poorer countries in the late twentieth and early twenty-first centuries, as we will see later.

Back to the initial question: Why did the first leap forward, the development of an unprecedented fiscal capacity, take place in the leading European states in the period 1500–1800 and not in, say, the Ottoman Empire or Asia? There is no single answer to this question and no deterministic explanation. Nevertheless, one factor seems to have been particularly important: specifically, the political fragmentation of Europe into several states of comparable size, which led to intense military rivalries. From this another question naturally follows: What was the reason for Europe's political fragmentation compared with the relative unity of China or even (to a lesser degree) India? It is possible that geographical and physical barriers played a role in Europe, especially in Western Europe (where France is separated from its most important neighbors by mountains, seas, or rivers). Clearly, however, different states might have emerged on different parts of European soil or in other parts of the world had socioeconomic and political-ideological developments taken a different course.

Nevertheless, if we take as given the state borders that existed in 1500, and if we then examine the sequence of events that led to the near tenfold increase of European state fiscal capacity between 1500 and 1800 (Figs. 9.1–9.2), we find that each major increase in tax revenues corresponded to a need to recruit new soldiers and field more armies in view of the quasi-permanent state of war that existed in Europe at the time. Depending on the nature of the political regime and the socioeconomic structure of each country, these recruitment needs led to the development of extensive fiscal and administrative capacities.[8] Historians have focused mainly on the Thirty Years' War (1618–1648), the War of the Spanish Succession (1701–1714), and the Seven Years' War (1756–1763), the first European conflict of truly global scope since it involved the colonies in America, the West Indies, and India and laid the groundwork for revolutions in the United States, Latin America, and France. But in addition to these major conflicts, there was also a host of shorter, more localized wars. If we include all military conflicts across the continent in each period, we find that European countries were at war 95 percent of the time in the sixteenth century, 94 percent in the seventeenth century, and still 78 percent in the eighteenth century (compared with 40 percent in the nineteenth century and 54 percent in the twentieth century).[9] The period 1500–1800 was one of incessant rivalry among Europe's military powers, and this is what fueled the development of unprecedented fiscal capacity as well as numerous technological innovations, particularly in the areas of artillery and warships.[10]

---

8. See esp. K. Karaman and S. Pamuk, "Different Paths to the Modern State in Europe: The Interaction Between Warfare, Economic Structure, and Political Regime," *American Political Science Review,* 2013. See also M. Dincecco, "The Rise of Effective States in Europe," *Journal of Economic History,* 2015; M. Dincecco, *State Capacity and Economic Development* (Cambridge University Press, 2017).

9. C. Tilly, *Coercion, Capital, and European States, AD 990–1990* (Blackwell, 1990). See also N. Genniaoli and H. J. Voth, "State Capacity and Military Conflict," *Review of Economic Studies,* 2017.

10. On the scope of these technological innovations, see P. Hoffman, "Prices, the Military Revolution, and Western Europe's Comparative Advantage in Violence,"

By contrast, the Ottoman and Chinese states, which had fiscal capacities close to those of European states in the period 1500–1550 (Figs. 9.1–9.2), did not face the same incentives. Between 1500 and 1800 they ruled large empires in a relatively decentralized fashion and felt no need to increase their military capacity or fiscal centralization. Heightened competition among the medium-sized European states that were organizing themselves in this same period does indeed appear to have been the central factor in the development of specific state structures—structures that were more highly centralized and fiscally developed than the states emerging in the Ottoman, Chinese, and Mughal empires. In the beginning, European states developed their fiscal and military capacity primarily because of internal conflict in Europe, but ultimately this competition endowed these states with much greater power to strike states in other parts of the world. In 1550, the Ottoman infantry and navy comprised roughly 140,000 men, equal to the French and English forces combined (respectively, 80,000 men and 70,000 men). This equilibrium would be disrupted over the next two centuries, which were marked by endless wars in Europe. By 1780, Ottoman forces remained virtually unchanged (150,000 men), while the French and English armies and navies now numbered 450,000 (280,000 soldiers and sailors for France, 170,000 for England); in warships and firepower they also enjoyed marked superiority over potential enemies. To these numbers one must add 250,000 men for Austria and 180,000 for Prussia (states that had had no military to speak of in 1550).[11] In the nineteenth century, the Ottoman and Chinese empires were clearly dominated militarily by the states of Europe.[12]

Interstate Competition and Joint Innovation: The Invention of Europe

Is Western economic prosperity due entirely to the military domination and colonial power that European states exercised over the rest of the world in the eighteenth and nineteenth centuries? Clearly, it is very difficult to give a single

---

Economic History Review, 2011; P. Hoffman, "Why Was It Europeans Who Conquered the World?" *Journal of Economic History,* 2012.

11. Karaman and Pamuk, "Ottoman State Finances," p. 612.

12. In addition to these quantitative differences, it is important to stress the role of superior military organization (especially in naval matters) developed in intra-European warfare in previous centuries. See esp. C. Bayly, *The Birth of the Modern World, 1780–1914* (Oxford University Press, 2004).

answer to such a complex question, especially since military domination also fostered technological and financial innovations that proved useful in themselves. In the abstract, one can imagine historical and technological trajectories that would have enabled the countries of Europe to enjoy the same prosperity and the same Industrial Revolution without colonization: for instance, if planet Earth had been one vast European island-continent allowing no possibility of foreign conquest, no "great discovery" of other parts of the world, and no extraction of any kind. To conceive such a scenario would require a certain imagination, however, as well as a willingness to speculate boldly on the pace of technological innovation.

Kenneth Pomeranz has shown in his book on "the great divergence" how much the Industrial Revolution of the late eighteenth and nineteenth centuries—first in Britain and then in the rest of Europe—depended on large-scale extraction of raw material (especially cotton) and energy (especially in the form of wood) from the rest of the world—extraction achieved through coercive colonial occupation.[13] In Pomeranz's view, the more advanced parts of China and Japan had attained a level of development in the period 1750–1800 more or less comparable to corresponding regions of Western Europe. Specifically, one finds similar forms of economic development based in part on demographic growth and intensive agriculture (made possible by improved agricultural techniques as well as a considerable increase in cultivated acres thanks to land clearing and deforestation); one also finds comparable process of proto-industrialization, particularly in the textile industry. Subsequently, Pomeranz argues, two key factors caused European and Asian trajectories to diverge. First, European deforestation, coupled with the presence of readily available coal deposits, especially in England, led Europe to switch quite rapidly to sources of energy other than wood and to develop corresponding technologies. More than that, the fiscal and military capacity of European states, largely a product of their past rivalries and reinforced by technological and financial innovations stemming from interstate competition, enabled them in the eighteenth and nineteenth centuries to organize the international division of labor and supply chains in particularly profitable ways.

---

13. See the illuminating book by K. Pomeranz, *The Great Divergence: China, Europe, and the Making of the Modern World Economy* (Princeton University Press, 2000). For a global perspective on the exploitation of the world's natural resources between 1500 and 1800, see also J. Richards, *The Unending Frontier: An Environmental History of the Early Modern World* (University of California Press, 2003).

Regarding deforestation, Pomeranz insists that by the end of the eighteenth century Europe came close to confronting a very significant "ecological" constraint. Forests in the United Kingdom, France, Denmark, Prussia, Italy, and Spain had been shrinking rapidly for several centuries: whereas they had once covered 30–40 percent of the land area around 1500, by 1800 they had decreased to little more than 10 percent (16 percent in France, 4 percent in Denmark). At first, imported wood from still-forested areas in eastern and northern Europe partially made up for the loss, but these new supplies quickly proved to be insufficient. China also experienced deforestation between 1500 and 1800 but to a lesser degree than in Europe, in part because the more advanced regions were better integrated politically and commercially with the wooded inland regions.

In the European case, the "discovery" of America, the triangular trade with Africa, and commerce with Asia made it possible to overcome this ecological constraint. The exploitation of land in North America, the West Indies, and South America using slave labor imported from Africa produced the raw materials (wood, cotton, and sugar) that not only earned handsome profits for the colonizers but also fed the textile factories that began to develop rapidly in the period 1750–1800. Military control of long-distance shipping routes allowed for the development of large-scale complementarities. The profits earned by exporting British textiles and other manufactured goods to North America compensated the owners of the plantations that produced wood and cotton, who could then feed their slaves with a portion of their profits. Note that a third of the textiles used to clothe slaves in the eighteenth century came from India, while imports from Asia (textiles, silk, tea, porcelain, and so on) were paid for in large part with silver mined in America from the sixteenth century on. By 1830, British imports of cotton, wood, and sugar required the exploitation of more than 10 million hectares of cultivable land, according to Pomeranz's calculations, or 1.5–2 times all the cultivable land available in the United Kingdom.[14] If the colonies had not made it possible to circumvent the ecological constraint, Europe would have needed to find other sources of supply. One is of course free to imagine scenarios of historical and technological development that would have enabled an autarkic Europe to achieve a similar level of industrial prosperity, but it would take considerable imagination to envision fertile cotton plantations in Lancashire and soaring oaks springing from the soil outside Manchester. In any case, this would be the history of another world, having little to do with the one we live in.

---

14. See Pomeranz, *The Great Divergence*, pp. 211–230, 264–297, 307–312.

It seems wiser to take as given the fact that the Industrial Revolution emerged from Europe's intimate ties to America, Africa, and Asia and to think about alternative ways in which these relationships might have been organized. What happened, as we have seen, was that international relations were shaped by European military and colonial domination, which made possible the forced transfer of slave labor from Africa to America and the West Indies, the forcible opening of Indian and Chinese ports, and so on. But those relations did not have to be as they were; they might have been organized in countless other ways, allowing for fair trade, free migration of labor, and decent wages, had the political and ideological balance of power been other than it was. By the same token, it is possible to imagine many ways of structuring global economic relations in the twenty-first century under many different sets of rules.

Accordingly, it is striking to note how little Europe's successful military strategies and institutions in the eighteenth and nineteenth centuries resembled the virtuous institutions that Adam Smith recommended in *The Wealth of Nations* (1776). In that foundational text of economic liberalism, Smith advised governments to adhere to low taxes and balanced budgets (with little or no public debt), absolute respect for property rights, and markets for labor and goods as integrated and competitive as possible. In all these respects, Pomeranz argues, Chinese institutions in the eighteenth century were far more Smithian than the United Kingdom's. In particular, China's markets were much more integrated. The grain market operated over a much broader geographic area, and labor mobility was significantly greater. One reason for this was the continuing influence of feudal institutions in Europe, at least until the French Revolution. Serfdom persisted in Eastern Europe until the nineteenth century (whereas it had almost totally disappeared from China by the early sixteenth century). Furthermore, there were more restrictions on labor mobility in Western Europe in the eighteenth century, especially in the United Kingdom and France, owing to Poor Laws and the great latitude granted to local elites and seigneurial courts to impose coercive regulations on the laboring classes. Europe also suffered from the prevalence of ecclesiastical property, much of which could not be sold.

Last but not least, taxes were much lower in China: barely 1–2 percent of national income compared with 6–8 percent in Europe in the late eighteenth century. The Qing dynasty enforced strict budget orthodoxy: taxes paid for all expenses, and there was no deficit. By contrast, European states, starting with France and the United Kingdom, accumulated significant public debt despite their higher taxes, especially in wartime, because tax revenues were never enough to cover the exceptional expenses of war together with interest payments on the accumulated debt.

On the eve of the French Revolution, both France and the United Kingdom had amassed public debts close to a year's national income. By the end of the American Revolutionary and Napoleonic Wars (1792–1815), British public debt had soared to more than 200 percent of national income; the debt was so high that one-third of the taxes paid by British taxpayers between 1815 and 1914 (mainly by people of middle and low income) was devoted to repayment of the debt and interest (profiting the wealthy who had lent the government money to pay for the wars). We will come back to all this later when we look at the problems posed by public debt and its reimbursement in the twentieth and twenty-first centuries. At this stage, note simply that these colossal debts do not seem to have impeded European development. Like Europe's higher tax rates, its debts helped to build state and military capacity that proved decisive for increasing European power. To be sure, taxes and debts might have been used to pay for things more useful than armies in the long run (such as schools, hospitals, roads, and clean water). It also might have been preferable to tax the wealthy rather than allow them to become still wealthier by buying government bonds. In view of the era's violent interstate competition, and with political power in the hands of the wealthy, the choice was made to spend money on the military and to finance it with public debt, and this helped to secure European domination over the rest of the world.

On Smithian Chinese and European Opium Traffickers

In the abstract, Smith's tranquil, virtuous institutions might have made sense if all countries had adopted them in the eighteenth and nineteenth centuries (although he underestimated the usefulness of taxes for financing productive investment and neglected the importance of educational and social equality for economic development). But in a world in which some countries develop superior military capacity, the most virtuous are not always the ones who come out on top. The history of European-Chinese relations is a case in point. By the eighteenth century Europe had exhausted the supply of American silver with which it had paid for its trade with China and India, and Europeans feared they might have nothing to sell in exchange for imported silk, textiles, porcelain, spices, and tea from the two Asian giants. The British accordingly attempted to intensify their growing of opium in India to export to Chinese resellers and consumers who had developed a taste for it. The opium trade grew substantially over the course of the eighteenth century, and in 1773 the East India Company established its monopoly over the production and export of the drug from Bengal.

The Qing emperor, seeing the enormous increase in opium imports and under pressure from his bureaucracy and enlightened public opinion to stop it, tried to enforce a ban on the recreational use of opium in 1729. Subsequent emperors took a more proactive approach for obvious public health reasons. In 1839 the emperor ordered his envoy in Canton not only to end the traffic but also to burn existing opium stores without delay. In late 1839 and early 1840, the British press launched a vigorous anti-China campaign, which was paid for by opium dealers; articles denounced China's unacceptable violation of British property rights and attack on the principle of free trade. Unfortunately, the Qing emperor had seriously underestimated the UK's progress in increasing its fiscal and military capacity: in the First Opium War (1839–1842) Chinese forces were quickly routed. The British sent a fleet to shell Canton and Shanghai and forced the Chinese in 1842 to sign the first "unequal treaty" (as Sun Yat-sen would call it in 1924). The Chinese indemnified the British for the destroyed opium and war costs while granting British merchants legal and fiscal privileges and ceding the island of Hong Kong.

The Qing government nevertheless refused to legalize the opium trade. England's trade deficit continued to grow until the Second Opium War (1856–1860), and the sack of the summer palace in Beijing by French and British troops in 1860 finally forced the emperor to give in. Opium was legalized, and the Chinese were obliged to grant the Europeans a series of trading posts and territorial concessions and forced to pay a large war indemnity. In the name of religious freedom it was also agreed that Christian missionaries would be allowed to roam freely in China (while no thought was given to granting similar privileges to Buddhist, Muslim, or Hindu missionaries in Europe). The irony of history is this: owing to the military tribute that the French and British imposed on China, the Chinese government was obliged to abandon its Smithian budget orthodoxy and for the first time experiment with a large public debt. The debt snowballed, and the Qing were forced to raise taxes to repay the Europeans and eventually to cede more and more of their fiscal sovereignty, following a classic colonial scenario of coercion through debt, which we have already encountered elsewhere (in Morocco, for example).[15]

---

15. See Chap. 7. On the Opium Wars, see, for example, P. Singaravelou and S. Venayre, *Histoire du monde au XIXᵉ siècle* (Fayard, 2017), pp. 266–270.

Another important point about the very heavy public debts that European states took on to finance their internecine wars in the seventeenth and eighteenth centuries: these played an important role in the development of financial markets. This is true in particular of British debt issued during the Napoleonic wars, which to this day represents one of the highest levels of national debt ever attained (more than two years of national income or GDP, which was a lot, especially in view of the country's share of the global economy in 1815–1820). To sell this debt to wealthy and thrifty British subjects, the country had to develop a solid banking system and networks of financial intermediation. I have already alluded to the role of colonial expansion in creating the first global-scale joint-stock companies—the British East India Company and Dutch East India Company, companies that commanded veritable private armies and exercised regalian powers over vast territories.[16] The many costly uncertainties associated with maritime trade also encouraged the development of insurance and freight companies, which would have a decisive impact later on.

Public debt linked to European warfare also drove the process of securitization and other financial innovations. Some experiments in this area ended in resounding failure, starting with the famous bankruptcy of John Law in 1718–1720, which stemmed from competition between France and Britain to redeem their debts by offering the bearers of government bonds stock in colonial companies, some of whose assets were rather dubious (like those of the Mississippi company that triggered the collapse of Law's "Mississippi bubble"). At the time, most joint-stock companies derived their revenues from colonial commercial or fiscal monopolies; they were more a sophisticated, militarized form of highway robbery than a productive entrepreneurial venture.[17] In any case, by developing financial and commercial technologies on a global scale, Euro-

---

16. See Chap. 7.

17. The most grandiose project associated with John Law and the Mississippi bubble (1718–1720) was a company dreamed up by French merchants, who were to receive a monopoly on trade with the Americans with a capital of 80 million pounds sterling (about one year of British national income at the time). Several projects promised to discover the mythical kingdom of Ophir, which was reputed to be in possession of King Solomon's treasures and was generally believed to lie somewhere between today's Mozambique and Zimbabwe. Another project aimed to produce textiles in Africa and exchange them for slaves so as to adapt more quickly to the tastes of local merchants. See S. Condorelli, *From Quincampoix to Ophir: A Global History of the 1720 Financial Boom* (Bern University, 2019). See also A. Orain, *La politique du merveilleux. Une autre histoire du Système de Law* (Fayard, 2018).

peans created infrastructure and comparative advantages that would prove decisive in the age of globalized industrial and financial capitalism (in the late nineteenth and early twentieth centuries).

Protectionism and Mercantilism: The Origins of the "Great Divergence"

Recent research has largely confirmed Pomeranz's conclusions concerning the origins of the "great divergence" and the central role of military and colonial domination and the financial and technological innovations that went with it.[18] In particular, Jean-Laurent Rosenthal and R. Bin Wong insist that while Europe's political fragmentation has had largely negative effects over the very long run (illustrated by Europe's self-destruction in 1914–1945 as well as difficulties forming a European union after World War II or, more recently, facing up the financial crisis of 2008), it nevertheless allowed European states to gain the upper hand over China and the rest of the world from 1750 to 1900, thanks in large part to innovations stemming from military rivalries.[19]

Sven Beckert's work has also shown the crucial importance of slave extraction and cotton production in the seizure of control of the global textile industry by the British and other Europeans in the period 1750–1850. In particular, Beckert points out that half of the African slaves shipped across the Atlantic between 1492 and 1882 sailed in the period 1780–1860 (especially between 1780 and 1820). This late phase of accelerated growth in the slave trade and cotton plantations played a key role in the rise of the British textile industry.[20] Finally,

---

18. Note that the role of slave and colonial extraction in the development of industrial capitalism was already analyzed by numerous nineteenth-century observers (beginning with Karl Marx) as well as by Eric Williams (prime minister of Trinidad from 1956 to 1981) in E. William, *Capitalism and Slavery* (1944). By contrast, Max Weber, in *The Protestant Ethic and the Spirit of Capitalism* (1905), stressed cultural and religious factors, whereas Fernand Braudel in *Civilisation matérielle, économie et capitalisme* (1979) focused on the role of high finance in both Catholic and Protestant Europe. The recent work of Pomeranz, Parthasarathi, and Beckert is much less Eurocentric; it represents a return to Marx and Williams but with the richer tools and sources associated with global and connected history.

19. See J.-L. Rosenthal and R. Bin Wong, *Before and Beyond Divergence: The Politics of Economic Change in China and Europe* (Harvard University Press, 2011).

20. S. Beckert, *Empire of Cotton: A Global History* (Knopf, 2014). See also S. Beckert and S. Rockman, *Slavery's Capitalism: A New History of American Economic Development* (University of Pennsylvania Press, 2016).

the Smithian idea that the British and European advance was due to peaceful and virtuous parliamentary and proprietarian institutions has few champions nowadays.[21] Some researchers have collected detailed data on wages and output that should allow us to compare Europe, China, and Japan before and during "the great divergence." Despite the deficiencies of the sources, the available data confirm the thesis of a late divergence between Europe and Asia, which begins to take shape only in the eighteenth century, with minor differences among authors.[22]

Prasannan Parthasarathi emphasizes the key role played by anti-India protectionist policies in the emergence of the British textile industry.[23] In the seventeenth and eighteenth centuries, manufactured export products (such as textiles of all sorts, silk, and porcelain) came mainly from China and India, and they were largely paid for with silver and gold originating in Europe and America

---

21. To be clear, Adam Smith's views were in part normative and prospective. He did not claim that military power and slavery had played no role in Britain's prosperity (which would have been a difficult argument to make), but rather that the key to future wealth was respect for property rights and the laws of supply and demand. Similarly, D. North and B. Weingast defend a neo-proprietarian view centered on the protection of property rights and the virtues of British institutions (see esp. D. North and B. Weingast, "Constitutions and Commitment," *Journal of Economic History,* 1989), although they do not deny the importance of other factors. The approach developed by D. Acemoglu and J. Robinson, which was initially centered on the role of systems of property rights stemming from the Atlantic revolutions, was subsequently extended; they now insist on the role of "inclusive institutions," a broad notion that potentially encompasses many social, fiscal, and educational institutions. See, for example, D. Acemoglu and J. Robinson, *Why Nations Fail: The Origins of Power, Prosperity and Poverty* (Crown Publishers, 2012).

22. See, for example, S. Broadberry, H. Guan, and D. Daokui Li, "China, Europe and the Great Divergence: A Study in Historical National Accounting, 980–1850," *Journal of Economic History,* 2018. These authors conclude that the divergence of per capita output and average wage between China and the United Kingdom is clear starting in 1700, which is a little earlier than Pomeranz finds (he argues that wage parity between the more advanced parts of Europe and Asia persisted until 1750–1800) but "later than prior Eurocentric arguments." It is not clear, however, that the sources allow us to draw such precise conclusions, and it may be preferable to concentrate on specific regions of China and Europe (as Pomeranz does).

23. See the illuminating book by P. Parthasarathi, *Why Europe Grew Rich and Asia Did Not: Global Economic Divergence, 1600–1850* (Cambridge University Press, 2011).

(as well as Japan).[24] Indian textiles, especially print fabrics and blue calico, were all the rage in Europe and throughout the world. In the early eighteenth century, 80 percent of the textiles that English traders exchanged for slaves in West Africa were manufactured in India, and by the end of the century that figure still remained as high as 60 percent. Freight records show that Indian textiles in the 1770s alone accounted for a third of the cargo loaded in Rouen onto ships bound for Africa to barter for slaves. Ottoman records indicate that Indian textile exports to the Middle East were still greater than those bound for West Africa, which did not seem to pose any major problem for the Turkish authorities, who were more sensitive to the interests of local consumers.

European merchants soon realized that they stood to profit by stirring up hostility against Indian imports to advance their own transcontinental projects. In 1685 the British Parliament introduced customs duties of 20 percent on textile imports, and this rose to 30 percent in 1690 before imports of printed and dyed fabrics were simply banned in 1700. From that date on, only virgin fabrics were imported from India, which allowed British manufacturers to improve their techniques for producing colored fabrics and prints. Similar measures were approved in France while British import restrictions, including a 100 percent tariff on all Indian textiles in 1787, continued to be tightened throughout the eighteenth century. Pressure from Liverpool slave traders, who urgently needed quality textiles to expand their business on the African coast without depleting their metallic currency reserves, played a decisive role, especially between 1765 and 1785, a period during which the quality of English production improved rapidly. Only after acquiring a clear comparative advantage in textiles, most notably through the use of coal, did the United Kingdom begin in the mid-nineteenth century to adopt a more full-throated free trade rhetoric (though not without ambiguities, as in the case of opium exports to China).

The British also relied on protectionist measures in the shipbuilding industry, which was flourishing in India in the seventeenth and eighteenth centuries. In 1815 they levied a special tax of 15 percent on all goods imported on India-built ships; a subsequent measure provided that only English ships could import merchandise from east of the Cape of Good Hope to the United Kingdom. While it is difficult to suggest an overall estimate, it clear that, taken

---

24. According to available estimates, of 142 kilotons of precious metals (in silver equivalent) extracted between 1600 and 1800 (132 in America, ten in Japan), roughly twenty-three kilotons (20 percent) were exported to India. See Parthasarathi, *Why Europe Grew Rich*, pp. 46–47.

together, these protectionist and mercantilist measures, imposed on the rest of the world at gunpoint, played a significant role in achieving British and European industrial domination. According to available estimates, the Chinese and Indian share of global manufacturing output, which was still 53 percent in 1800, had fallen to 5 percent by 1900.[25] Again, it would be absurd to view this as the only possible trajectory leading to the Industrial Revolution and modern prosperity. For instance, one can imagine other historical trajectories that would have allowed European and Asian producers to grow at the same rate (or, together, at an even higher rate) without anti-India and anti-Chinese protectionism, without colonial and military domination, and with more balanced and egalitarian trade and interactions among different regions of the globe. This would certainly be a very different world from the one we live in. But the role of historical research is precisely to demonstrate the existence of alternatives and switch points and to show how choices are conditioned by the political and ideological balance of power among contending groups.

Japan: Accelerated Modernization of a Ternary Society

We turn next to the way in which the encounter with European colonial powers affected the transformation of the ternary inequality regimes prevalent in different parts of Asia before the arrival of Europeans. In Chapter 8 we saw how inequalities in precolonial India were structured by trifunctional ideology, with a kind of rough balance between military warrior elites (Kshatriyas) and clerical and intellectual elites (Brahmins) in a variety of evolving and unstable configurations whose development depended on the emergence of new warrior elites, on competition between Hindu and Muslim kingdoms, and on the shifting identities and allegiances of the jatis. We also saw how the British administration, by rigidifying castes through its colonial policies and censuses, contributed to the emergence of a unique inequality regime in India based on a novel mix of ancient status inequalities and modern inequalities of wealth and education.

The Japanese case is different from the Indian in many ways, but there are also numerous similarities. Japan in the Edo era (1600–1868) was a strongly hierarchical society with many social disparities and status rigidities of the trifunctional type, similar in some respects to those seen in Ancien Régime

---

25. See Parthasarathi, *Why Europe Grew Rich,* pp. 97–131, 234–235. See also Singaravelou and Venayre, *Histoire du monde au XIXe siècle,* pp. 90–92.

Europe and precolonial India. Society was dominated on the one hand by a warrior nobility, with *daimyos* (great feudal lords) at the top under the authority of the *shogun* (military leader), and on the other hand, by a class of *Shinto* priests and Buddhist monks (with degrees of symbiosis and rivalry between the two religions which varied over time). The distinctive feature of the Japanese regime in the Edo period was that the warrior class had assumed marked superiority over the others. After restoring order in 1600–1604 following decades of feudal warfare, the hereditary shoguns of the Tokugawa dynasty gradually ceased to be mere military captains and became the real political leaders of the country at the head of an administrative and judicial system centered in the capital Edo (Tokyo) while the emperor in Kyoto was reduce to the symbolic functions of a spiritual leader.

The legitimacy of the shogun and of the warrior class was seriously shaken, however, by the arrival in Tokyo Bay in 1853 of a fleet of heavily armed warships under the command of Commodore Matthew Perry of the United States. When Perry returned in 1854 with an armada twice the size of the first, reinforced by the ships of several European allies (Britain, France, the Netherlands, and Russia), the shogunate had no choice but to grant the commercial, fiscal, and jurisdictional privileges demanded by the coalition. This unmistakable humiliation initiated a phase of intense political and ideological reflection in Japan, resulting in the beginning of a new era, the Meiji, in 1868. The last Tokugawa shogun was deposed and the authority of the emperor was restored at the behest of a segment of the Japanese nobility and elite eager to modernize the country and compete with the Western powers. Japan thus offers an unusual example of accelerated sociopolitical modernization, which began with an imperial restoration (largely symbolic, to be sure).[26]

The reforms undertaken from 1868 on rested on several pillars. Old status distinctions were eliminated. The warrior nobility lost its legal and fiscal privileges. This reform affected not only the high aristocracy of daimyos (a very small

---

26. For the anthropologist Claude Lévi-Strauss, it was Japan's good fortune that its modernization took the form of a restoration: because the emperor and a segment of the old elite took power, he argues, industrial success was possible while maintaining respect for tradition, whereas the French revolutionary bourgeoisie was only good for occupying bureaucratic posts after dispossessing the old nobility (which was prepared to take a chance on capitalism). While this argument is not entirely convincing, it illustrates the pressing need to make sense of different national socioeconomic and political-ideological trajectories. See C. Lévi-Strauss, *L'autre face de la Lune. Écrits sur le Japon* (Seuil, 2011), pp. 75–76, 155–156; in English, *The Other Face of the Moon,* tr. J. M. Todd (Belknap Press, 2013).

group comparable in size to British lords) but also other warriors endowed with fiefs (revenues derived from village production); both groups received partial financial compensation. The constitution of 1889, inspired by the British and Prussians, provided for a house of peers (which allowed a select portion of the old nobility to retain a political role) and a house of representatives, initially elected on a property-qualified basis by barely 5 percent of adult males, before male suffrage was extended in 1910 and again in 1919, ultimately becoming universal in 1925. Women were given the right to vote in 1947, at which time the house of peers was abolished.[27]

According to the censuses by class carried out under the Tokugawa from 1720 on, the class of daimyos and warriors with fiefs represented 5–6 percent of the population, with considerable variation by region and principality (from 2–3 percent to 10–12 percent). The size of this group seems to have decreased in the Edo era, since the warrior class represented only 3–4 percent of the population in the census of 1868, at the beginning of the Meiji era, shortly before fiefs and the warrior class (except for peers) were abolished. Shinto priests and Buddhist monks accounted for 1–1.5 percent of the population. If we compare this with Europe in the sixteenth to eighteenth centuries, we find that the warrior class was larger in Japan than in France or the United Kingdom while the religious class was slightly smaller (Fig. 9.3).[28] As we have seen, other European countries, as well as certain subregions of India, had warrior and noble classes of a size close to or greater than that observed in Japan.[29] All things considered, these orders of magnitude are not very different and attest to a certain similarity among trifunctional societies, at least in terms of formal structure.

Beyond the abolition of fiscal privileges and forced labor, the reforms of the early Meiji era eliminated the many status inequalities that had existed among various categories of urban and rural workers under the previous regime. In particular, the new government officially ended discrimination against the *burakumin* ("hamlet people"), the lowest category of workers under the Tokugawa, whose pariah status was in some ways similar to that of untouchables and aborigines in India. It is generally believed that the burakumin

---

27. See, for example, E. Reischauer, *Histoire du Japon et des Japonais* (Seuil, 1997), tome 1, *Des origines à 1945*, pp. 164–196; originally published in English as *Japan: The Story of a Nation* (Knopf, 1981).

28. See the online appendix for detailed analysis of the data from Japanese censuses of the Edo and Meiji eras, collected with the help of G. Carré.

29. See Fig. 5.2 and Fig. 8.2.

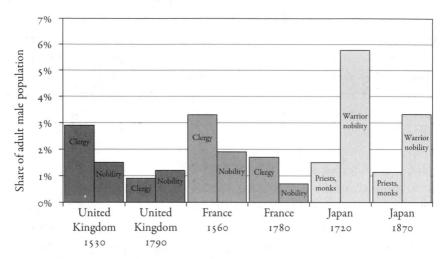

FIG. 9.3. The evolution of ternary societies: Europe-Japan 1530–1870

Interpretation: In the United Kingdom and France, the two dominant classes in trifunctional society (clergy and nobility) decreased in size between the sixteenth and eighteenth centuries. In Japan, the proportion of the warrior nobility (daimyo) and warriors endowed with fiefs was significantly higher than that of Shinto priests and monks, but it decreased sharply between 1720 and 1870, according to Japanese census data from the Edo and early Meiji eras. *Sources and series:* piketty.pse.ens.fr/ideology.

accounted for less than 5 percent of the population in the Edo era, but they were not usually counted in censuses; the category was officially abolished in the Meiji era.[30]

In addition, the Meiji regime developed a series of policies intended to promote accelerated industrialization and catch up with the Western powers. The central government's fiscal and administrative capacity was rapidly increased (with prefects and regions taking the place of daimyos and fiefs), and significant taxes were levied to finance investments in the social and economic development of the country, especially in the areas of transportation infrastructure (roads, railroads, shipping) and health and education.[31]

---

30. See G. Carré, "Les marges statutaires dans le Japon pré-moderne: enjeux et débats," *Annales. Histoire, Sciences Sociales,* 2011; T. Morishita, "Le Japon prémoderne: une société de statuts. Réflexions sur quatre décennies de débats," *Histoire, économie et société,* 2017.

31. According to some estimates, Japanese fiscal revenues were already fairly high (nearly 10 percent of national income, hence closer to European than to Chinese or Ottoman levels) in the middle of the nineteenth century, hence before the Meiji

Investment in education was truly spectacular. The intent was not only to train a new elite capable of rivaling Western engineers and scientists but also to bring literacy and education to the masses. With the elites, the motive was clear: to avoid Western domination. Japanese students who sailed from Kagoshima in 1872 to study in Western universities told their stories with no sugarcoating. While stopped at an Indian port on their way to Europe, they watched young Indian children reduced to diving into the ocean after small coins for the amusement of British settlers on the shore. From this they concluded that they had better study like mad in order to make sure that Japan would not experience the same fate.[32] Mass literacy and technical training were also seen as indispensable prerequisites for successful industrialization.

On the Social Integration of Burakumin, Untouchables, and Roma

The point here is not to idealize Meiji policies of social and educational integration. Japan remained an inegalitarian hierarchical society. Groups like the burakumin continued to struggle against real (albeit illegal) discrimination even after World War II, and traces of this oppressive legacy persist to this day (though to a much lesser extent than in the case of the lower castes in India). What is more, Japanese social integration went hand in hand with rising nationalism and militarism, which led to Pearl Harbor and Hiroshima.

For some Japanese nationalists, the long conflict with the West from 1854 to 1945 should be seen as the "Great War of East Asia" (as it is called in the military museum of the Yasukuni shrine in Tokyo), a war in which Japan, despite crushing defeats, led the way to the decolonization of Asia and the world. Proponents of this view emphasize Japanese support for independence movements in India, Indochina, and Indonesia during World War II and, more generally, the fact that Europe and the United States had never truly accepted the idea of an independent Asian power and would never have agreed to the end of colonial domination had it not been for the willingness of some Asians to fight. Despite brilliant military victories in China in 1895, Russia in 1905, and Korea in 1910—irrefutable proof of the success of Meiji-era reforms—Japan felt

---

era; they subsequently increased to more than 10 percent of national income. See T. H. Sng and C. Moriguchi, "Asia's Little Divergence: State Capacity in China and Japan before 1850," *Journal of Economic Growth*, 2014.

32. There is a monument honoring the Kagoshima students in the city's museum.

that it could never gain the full respect of the West or be admitted to the club of industrial and colonial powers.[33] In the eyes of Japanese nationalists, the ultimate humiliation was the West's refusal to incorporate the principle of racial equality into the Treaty of Versailles in 1919, despite repeated Japanese demands.[34] Even worse was the Washington Naval Conference (1921), which stipulated that the naval tonnage of the United States, United Kingdom, and Japan should remain frozen in the ratio 5–5–3. This rule condemned Japan to eternal naval inferiority in Asian waters no matter what industrial or demographic progress it made. The Japanese empire rejected the agreement in 1934, paving the way to war.

In 1940–1941, two increasingly antagonistic worldviews confronted each other: Japan demanded a full Western withdrawal from East Asia while the United States demanded a withdrawal of all colonial powers (including Japan) from China and deferred the broader issue of decolonization until later. When Roosevelt imposed an oil embargo on Japan, threatening to immobilize its army and navy in short order, Japanese generals felt that they had no choice but to attack Pearl Harbor. This Japanese nationalist view is interesting and in some respects comprehensible, but it omits one essential point: the people of Korea, China, and other Asian countries occupied by Japan do not remember the Japanese as liberators but as yet another colonial power exhibiting the same brutality as the Europeans (or in some cases worse, although this needs to be judged case by case, given the very high bar). The colonial ideology that seeks to liberate and civilize nations in spite of themselves generally leads to disaster, no matter what the color of the colonizer's skin.[35]

---

33. In his last film, *The Wind Rises,* dir. H. Miyazaki (Walt Disney Pictures, 2013), Hayao Miyazaki, the author of many splendid pacifist and feminist mangas, tenderly evokes the life of Jori Horikosui (the designer of the Mitsubishi A6M Zero fighter, which proved particularly lethal during World War II) and, more generally, the doubts of Japanese engineers who tried to win the esteem and respect of German and European engineers between the two world wars.

34. The Western powers, sure of their domination, frequently administered such insults in those days. In 1926, Brazil quit the League of Nations when it was refused a seat as a permanent member of the council. See B. Badie, *Nous ne sommes plus seuls au monde. Un autre regard sur l'"ordre international"* (La Découverte, 2016), p. 142.

35. Among other major examples of intra-Asian colonization in the modern era is the extension of the Kingdom of Viet Nam into Cambodia in 1806–1848. This project was part of an ambitious Vietnamization-Sinicization of the barbarian west, before the Khmer kings called on France for assistance in 1863. The French

If we leave aside the always bitter conflicts among colonial powers and ideologies and the memories of the colonized populations, it remains true that the policies of social and educational integration and economic development that Japan adopted in the Meiji era (1868–1912) and that demilitarized Japan continued to pursue after 1945 represent an experiment with the particularly rapid sociopolitical transformation of a premodern inequality regime. The success of Japan's proprietarian and industrial transition shows that the mechanisms at work have nothing whatsoever to do with Christian culture or European civilization.

Last but not least, the Japanese experience shows that proactive policies, especially regarding public infrastructure and investment in education, can overcome very strong and longstanding status inequalities in a matter of decades—inequalities that in other contexts are seen as rigid and unalterable. Although past discrimination against pariah classes has left traces, Japan nevertheless became over the course of the twentieth century a country whose standard of living is among the highest in the world and whose income inequality falls between European and US levels.[36] Japanese government policies intended to achieve socioeconomic and educational development and social integration between 1870 and 1940 were not perfect, but they were a good deal more effective than, for example, British colonial policy in India, which showed little concern with reducing social inequality or improving the literacy and skills of the lower castes. In Part Three of this book we will see that the reduction of social inequality in Japan was further assisted by an ambitious program of agrarian reform in the period 1945–1950 as well as by highly progressive taxation of top incomes and large estates (a policy that began in the Meiji period and continued in the interwar years but was reinforced after the defeat).

In the European context, the Roma are probably the group most directly comparable with the burakumin in Japan and the lower castes in India in terms of social discrimination. The Council of Europe uses the term "Roma" to describe any number of nomadic or sedentarized populations known by various other names (including Tziganes, Romani, Romanichels, Manouchians, Travelers, and Gypsies), most of which have lived in Europe for at least a millennium and can trace their origins back to India and the Middle East, despite a

---

needed no other excuse and took advantage of the invitation to begin their conquest of the entire Indochinese peninsula. See Singaravelou and Venayre, *Histoire du monde au XIXe siècle,* pp. 171–172.

36. See Fig. I.6.

great deal of racial mixing over the years.[37] By this definition, the Roma numbered between 10 and 12 million in the 2010s, or roughly 2 percent of the total population of Europe. This is a smaller proportion than the Japanese burakumin (2–5 percent) or the lower castes of India (10–20 percent) but still significant. One finds Roma in nearly every European country, especially Hungary and Romania, where Roma slavery and serfdom were abolished in 1856, after which the newly emancipated populations fled their old masters and scattered across the continent.[38]

Compared with the fate of the burakumin, untouchables, and aborigines, integration of the Roma was very slow. This can be explained in large part by the absence of adequate integration policies and above all by the fact that European countries have tried to shift responsibility for these groups to others. These excluded groups continue to be the object of prejudices regarding their allegedly alien way of life and supposed refusal to integrate when in fact they are subject to significant discrimination and little effort has been made to integrate them.[39] The case of the Roma is particularly interesting in that it can help Europeans, who are often prompt to give lessons to the rest of the world, to gain a better understanding of the difficulties that countries like Japan and India have faced in trying to integrate the burakumin or the lower castes—social groups that have faced prejudices similar to those confronting the Roma. Nevertheless, these countries have succeeded in overcoming prejudice through long-term policies of social and educational integration.

---

37. See, for example, I. Mendizabal et al., "Reconstructing the Population History of European Romani from Genome-wide Data," *Current Biology,* 2018.

38. Before 1856, the Roma were exploited by both nobles and monasteries. The 160th anniversary of the abolition of Roma slavery was celebrated in Romania and elsewhere in Europe in 2016. At several points I have stressed the complexity and porosity of the boundaries between slavery, serfdom, and other forms of forced labor (see esp. Chaps. 6 and 7). To answer the question of whether the Roma were slaves or serfs before 1856 would require detailed examination far beyond the scope of this book. The same can be said of the slavery-serfdom of the nobis in Korea, whose revolt, emancipation, and "debt" nullification in 1894 led to the fall of the Korean Empire and the invasion of the Japanese. See, for example, B. R. Kim, "Nobis: A Korean System of Slavery," *Slavery and Abolition,* 2003.

39. On the inadequacy of European policy with regard to the Roma, see, for example, EU Agency for Fundamental Rights, *Working with Roma: Participation and empowerment of local communities* (Publications Office of the European Union, 2018).

Trifunctional Society and the Construction of the Chinese State

Let us turn now to the way in which colonialism affected the transformation of the Chinese inequality regime. Throughout its history, until the revolution of 1911 that gave rise to the Republic of China, China was organized in terms of an ideological configuration that can be characterized as trifunctional, analogous to the trifunctional regimes found in Europe and India until the eighteenth or nineteenth centuries. However, one important difference has to do with the nature of Confucianism, which is closer to a civic philosophy than to a religion in the sense of Christian, Jewish, or Muslim monotheism or Hinduism. Kongfonzi (Latinized as Confucius) was a peerless scholar and teacher who lived in the sixth and early fifth centuries BCE. Born into a princely family buffeted by the constant conflict among the Chinese kingdoms, Confucius, according to tradition, crisscrossed China to deliver his lessons and demonstrate that peace and social harmony could be achieved only through education, moderation, and a search for rational and pragmatic solutions (which in practice were usually fairly conservative in terms of morals and included respect for elders, property, and property owners). As in all trifunctional societies, the moderation of scholars and men of letters was to play a central role in the political order, balancing the unruliness of the warriors.

Confucianism—*ruxue* in Chinese ("the teaching of the literati")—thus became official state doctrine in the second century BCE and remained so until 1911, even as it underwent a series of transformations and exchanged symbioses with Buddhism and Taoism. From time immemorial Confucian literati were seen as scholars and administrators who placed their vast stores of knowledge and competence, their understanding of Chinese literature and history, and their very strict domestic and civil morality at the service of the community, public order, and the state—rather than being seen as a religious organization distinct from the state. This was a fundamental difference between the Confucian and Christian versions of trifunctionality, and it offers one of the most natural explanations for the unity of the Chinese state in contrast to the political fragmentation of Europe (notwithstanding the Catholic Church's many attempts to bring the Christian kingdoms closer together).[40]

---

40. Roman Catholicism also sought to work toward European political unity: the spiritual power of the papacy found its official counterpart in the temporal power of the Holy Roman Empire (962–1806). In practice, this fragile, unstable political construct covered only a part of Christendom (mainly Germanic and Central Eu-

Some may also be tempted to compare Confucianism, which in the history of the Chinese empire functioned as a "religion of state unity," with modern Chinese communism, which in a different sense is also a form of state religion. They would argue, in other words, that the Confucian administrators and literati who served the Han, Song, Ming, and Qing emperors have simply evolved into officials and high priests of the Chinese Communist Party (CCP), serving the president of the People's Republic. Such comparisons are sometimes used to suggest that the Communist regime's efforts to achieve national unity and social harmony are merely a continuation of China's Confucian past. It was in this spirit that CCP leaders restored Confucius to a place of honor in the early 2010s—a rather remarkable turnabout, since the economic and social conservatism of Confucianism was much criticized during the Cultural Revolution and the campaign against "the four olds" (old things, old ideas, old culture, and old habits), landlords, and mandarins. Abroad but sometimes in China as well, the same historical parallel is often used in a negative sense to suggest that the Chinese government has always been authoritarian with immutable masses under the thumb of a millennial despotism that is a reflection of China's culture and soul: emperors and their mandarins have simply given way to Communist leaders and apparatchiks. Such comparisons are fraught with difficulties. They assume a continuity and determinism for which there is no evidence and prevent us from thinking about the complexity and diversity of China's past—and, indeed, the complexity and diversity of all sociopolitical trajectories.

The first problem raised by these comparisons is that the imperial Chinese state utterly lacked the means to be despotic. It was a structurally weak state with extremely limited fiscal revenues and little to no capacity for economic or social intervention or oversight compared with today's Chinese government. Available studies suggest that tax receipts under the Ming (1368–1644) and Qing (1644–1912) dynasties never exceeded 2–3 percent of national income.[41]

---

rope). More than that, the decisive difference between the Confucian literati who served the Chinese empire and the Christian clerics and bishops was that the latter served primarily the papacy (and not the emperor). The two powers were frequently in conflict, moreover, which contributed to the fragility of the whole edifice. Obviously, many other political-ideological, socioeconomic, and geographic factors also figure among the reasons why Europe was so fragmented compared to China.

41. Research suggests that the fiscal pressure was higher under the Song dynasty (960–1279) at a time when China was more divided politically (and during which

If we express per capita tax receipts in terms of days of wages, we find that the resources available to the Qing governments amounted to no more than a quarter to a third of the resources of European states in the late eighteenth and early nineteenth centuries (Fig. 9.2).

The recruitment of imperial and provincial functionaries (whom the Europeans called "mandarins") followed very strict procedures, including the famous examinations, which were given throughout the empire for thirteen centuries, from 605 to 1905. The examination system made a great impression on Western visitors to China and inspired similar efforts in France and Prussia. But the total number of Chinese functionaries was always quite small: in the middle of the nineteenth century there were barely 40,000 imperial and provincial officials, or 0.01 percent of the population (of around 400 million), and generally 0.01–0.02 percent of the population across the ages.[42] In practice, most of the resources of the Qing state were devoted to the warrior class and the army (as is always the case in states of such limited means), and what was left for civil administration, public health, and education was negligible. As we have seen, the Qing state in the eighteenth and early nineteenth centuries lacked the means to ban the use of opium within its borders. In practice, the Chinese administration operated in an extremely decentralized way, and imperial and provincial officials had no choice but to rely on the power of local warrior, scholar, and landowner elites over which they exerted very limited control, as was also the case in Europe and other parts of the world before the rise of the modern centralized state.[43]

Another point bears emphasizing: as in other trifunctional societies, the Chinese inequality regime relied on a complex and evolving relationship of

---

the empire developed a permanent navy, gunpowder, and paper money) before stabilizing at lower levels in the united neo-Confucian Ming and Qing eras (2–3 percent of national income in tax revenues compared with 5–10 percent earlier). See R. von Glahn, *The Economic History of China: From Antiquity to the Nineteenth Century* (Cambridge University Press, 2016), pp. 358–382.

42. According to official counts, the empire employed 24,653 functionaries (1,944 in the central government in the capital and 22,709 in the provinces) in the early Ming years (the late fourteenth century, when the population was around 100 million), or 0.02 percent of the population. See J. Gernet, "Le pouvoir d'État en Chine," *Actes de la recherche en sciences sociales,* 1997, p. 19.

43. One finds the same mythology in Spanish absolutism, said to be responsible for Iberian backwardness, when in fact the Spanish state in the eighteenth and nineteenth centuries lacked the capacity to enforce its decisions and was largely dependent on local clerical and noble elites.

compromise and competition between literary and warrior elites; the former did not dominate the latter. This is particularly clear in the era of the Qing dynasty, which began when Manchu warriors conquered China and seized control of Beijing in 1644. The Manchu warrior class arose in early seventeenth-century Manchuria and was organized under the "Eight Banners" system. Warriors were given rights to land and administrative, fiscal, and legal privileges denied to the rest of the population. The Manchus brought their military organization with them to Beijing and gradually integrated new Han Chinese elements into the Manchu warrior elite.

Recent research has shown that the warrior nobility of the Eight Banners (bannermen) included some 5 million people in 1720, or nearly 4 percent of the Chinese population of approximately 130 million. It is possible that this group grew from roughly 1–2 percent of the population at the time of the Manchu conquest in the mid-seventeenth century to 3–4 percent in the eighteenth century as the new regime was consolidated before declining in the nineteenth century. The sources are fragile, however, and there are many problems with such estimates—similar to those we encountered in estimating the size of the nobility in France and elsewhere in Europe in the seventeenth and eighteenth centuries—so that it is impossible to be precise in the absence of any systematic census data prior to the twentieth century (an absence indicative, by the way, of the weakness of the central imperial government).[44] The figures we have (which show bannermen accounting for 3–4 percent of the population in the eighteenth century) are relatively high compared with the size of the French and British nobility in the same period (Fig. 9.3) but are of the same order as Japan and India[45] and lower than the numbers for European countries where the military orders were large and territorial expansion was in progress, such as Spain, Hungary, and Poland.[46]

At the beginning of the Qing era, the bannermen were primarily stationed in garrisons near large cities. They lived on land rights and income skimmed from local production or paid by the imperial government. In the middle of the eighteenth century, however, the Qing government decided that the warrior nobility was too large and was costing too much to maintain. As in all tri-

---

44. See M. Elliott, C. Campbell, and J. Lee, "A Demographic Estimate of the Population of the Qing Eight Banners," *Études Chinoises*, 2016, for a detailed presentation of the sources and methods used.

45. See Fig. 8.2.

46. See Fig. 5.2.

functional societies, reform was a delicate matter as any radical move against the warrior nobility risked endangering the regime. In 1742 the Qing emperor tried to relocate some of the bannermen to Manchuria. In 1824 this policy took a new turn: with an eye to both cutting the budget and colonizing and exploiting northern China, the imperial government distributed land in northern China to some bannermen and at the same time encouraged non-nobles to move north and work for the new landowners. This was a difficult undertaking, and its scope remained limited on the one hand because most bannermen had no intention of allowing themselves to be shipped north so easily and on the other hand because the immigrant commoners were often better equipped to exploit the land than the nobles, giving rise to frequent tensions. In the early twentieth century, however, one finds interesting proprietarian micro-societies developing in northern Manchuria, where landowner-ship was highly concentrated in the hands of the old warrior nobility.[47]

Chinese Imperial Examinations:
Literati, Landowners, and Warriors

The Qing state was obliged to maintain a certain equilibrium between the warrior class and other Chinese social groups. In practice, however, it attended mainly to the balance among elites. This was true in particular of the organization of the imperial examination system, which was subject to constant reform over its lengthy history as the balance of power shifted among competing groups. The compromises that were struck are interesting because they reflect the search for a balance between the legitimacy of knowledge on the one hand and the legitimacies of wealth and military might on the other. In practice, officials were recruited in several stages. The first step was to pass the examinations that were given two years out of every three in the various prefectures of the empire; those who passed received a certificate *(shengyuan)*. This certificate did not lead directly to a public job but allowed the holder to sit for various other exams for the selection of provincial and imperial officials.

Holding the shengyuan also granted legal, political, and economic privileges (such as the right to testify in court or participate in local government) as well as considerable social prestige, even for those who never became officials. According to available research, based on exam archives and student lists,

---

47. See S. Chen, *State Sponsored-Inequality: The Banner System and Social Stratification in Northeast China* (Stanford University Press, 2017).

in the nineteenth century approximately 4 percent of adult males possessed a classical education (in the sense of having an advanced mastery of Chinese writing and traditional knowledge and having sat at least one examination for the shengyuan). Of this number, roughly 0.5 percent of adult males actually passed the exam and obtained the precious certificate. However, a second group of people had the right to sit directly for examinations leading to official jobs: those who had bought a certificate *(jiansheng)*. The size of this group increased in the nineteenth century: it represented 0.3 percent of adult males in the 1820s and nearly 0.5 percent in the 1870s, almost as many as those who had obtained the shengyuan.[48]

Recent research on the Jiangnan provincial archives has shown that this mechanism significantly increased social reproduction in the selection of officials: it allowed the sons of landowners and other wealthy individuals to have a chance of being recruited without passing the difficult shengyuan examination while at the same time yielding much-needed revenue for the state (which was the justification given for this practice). The archives show that social reproduction was also very high in the classical procedure: the vast majority of candidates who successfully passed the exam and were recruited as imperial or provincial officials had a father, grandfather, or other ancestor who had occupied a similar position; there were exceptions, however (about 20 percent of cases).[49]

The possibility of buying a shengyuan certificate existed because the Chinese state ran into budgetary problems in the eighteenth and nineteenth centuries; it can be compared to the French Ancien Régime practice of selling offices and charges and numerous other public functions as well as similar practices in many other European states. The difference in the Chinese case was that even those who purchased a certificate were in theory required to sit for the same exams as the others to qualify for official posts (although there was widespread suspicion that this final requirement was not always honored, it is

---

48. See Yifei Huang, "Social Mobility and Meritocracy: Lessons from Chinese Imperial Civil Service Examination" (PhD diss., California Institute of Technology, 2016), pp. 5–11, table 1.1. See also C. Chang, *The Chinese Gentry: Studies on their Role in Nineteenth-Century Chinese Society* (University of Washington Press, 1955). See also J. Osterhammel, *La transformation du monde. Une histoire globale du XIXᵉ siècle* (Nouveau monde éditions, 2017), pp. 1023–1027.

49. See Yifei Huang, "Social Mobility and Meritocracy." See also B. Elman, *Civil Examinations and Meritocracy in Late Imperial China* (Harvard University Press, 2013).

not possible to say to what extent these suspicions were justified). The Chinese system was perhaps more like the system for admission to the most prestigious US universities today, who openly admit that certain "legacy students" whose parents have made large enough gifts may receive special consideration in the admissions process. I will come back to this point later, as it raises many issues about what a fair admissions system and a just society might look like today and again illustrates the need to study inequality regimes in historical and comparative perspective, including comparisons across countries, periods, and institutions that might prefer not to be compared.[50]

As for Chinese imperial examinations, there is another crucial but relatively little-known aspect of the rules in force during the Qing era: roughly half of the 40,000-odd official posts (equal to about 0.01 percent of the total Chinese population in the nineteenth century and 0.03 percent of the adult male population) were reserved for bannermen.[51] In practice, members of the warrior class sat for special exams, sometimes in the Manchu language, to make up for their inadequate knowledge of classical Chinese; for certain posts their exams were similar to those taken by holders of real or purchased certificates but with places reserved for the bannermen. This Chinese version of the "reservations" system was very different from the Indian quota system, which favored members of the lower castes, and it extended well beyond qualifying exams for public service jobs. In each administrative department and job category, there were also quotas for members of the warrior aristocracy (Manchus and Hans) and for literati and landowners recruited through other channels.[52] These rules were often contested and permanently renegotiated, but broadly speaking, the warrior aristocracy managed to maintain its advantages until the fall of the empire in 1911, and the wealth privilege (linked to the purchase of certificates) was reinforced throughout the nineteenth and into the twentieth centuries, partly owing to the growing budgetary requirements of the Qing state (which had to pay off a growing debt to the European powers).

---

50. See esp. Chaps. 11 and 15.

51. The total number of posts open to holders of the shengyuan was thus barely 0.01 percent of the adult male population: the potential success rate was therefore about one in fifty certificate holders (0.5 percent of adult males), and one in 400 literati (4 percent of adult males). The funnel was even narrower because the central administration in Beijing accounted for fewer than 10 percent of official posts (versus 90 percent for territorial posts).

52. Elliott, Campbell, and Lee, "A Demographic Estimate of the Population of the Qing Eight Banners"; Chen, *State-Sponsored Inequality*.

Chinese Revolts and Missed Opportunities

To sum up, imperial Chinese society was highly hierarchical and inegalitarian and marked by conflicts among literate elites, landowners, and warriors. All available evidence suggests that these groups overlapped to a degree: the literary and administrative elites were also landowners who collected rents from the rest of the population just as the warrior elites did, and there were many alliances among these groups. The regime was far from static, however: not only was there elite conflict, but there were also many popular rebellions and revolutions, which might have taken China along trajectories other than the one it ultimately followed.

The bloodiest and most spectacular was the Taiping Rebellion (1850–1864). In the beginning this was a rebellion like many others, of poor peasants who refused to pay rent to landowners and who illegally occupied the land. Such revolts had always been common, but they proliferated and became more threatening to the regime after China's humiliating defeat at the hands of the Europeans in the First Opium War (1839–1842). In fact, the Taiping Rebellion came close to toppling the Qing empire in 1852–1854 in the early years of the movement. The rebels established a capital in Nanking, near Shanghai. In 1853 the regime issued a decree promising to redistribute land to families according to their needs and began to implement it in regions controlled by the rebels. On June 14, 1853, Karl Marx published an article in the *New York Daily Tribune* stating that the rebellion was on the brink of victory and that events in China would soon provoke turmoil throughout the industrial world, leading to a series of revolutions in Europe. The conflict quickly developed into a vast civil war in the heart of China, pitting imperial forces based in the north (and backed by a relatively weak state) against increasingly well-organized Taiping rebels in the south, in a country whose population had grown enormously over the previous century (from about 130 million in 1720 to nearly 400 million in 1840) despite being ravaged by opium and famine. According to available estimates, the Taiping Rebellion may have caused between 20 and 30 million military and civilian deaths between 1850 and 1864, or more than all the deaths in World War I (which claimed 15 to 20 million lives). Research has shown that the Chinese regions most affected by the rebellion never completely recovered from their population losses as fighting continued in rural areas more or less permanently until the fall of the empire.[53]

---

53. See esp. L. C. Xu and L. Yang, *Stationary Bandits, State Capacity, and Malthusian Transition: The Lasting Impact of the Taiping Rebellion* (World Bank Group, Policy Research Working Paper, 2018).

At first the Western powers took a neutral stance in the conflict. One reason for this was that the rebel leader compared himself with Christ and professed to be on a messianic mission, which won him sympathy in some Christian countries, especially the United States, where the public had a hard time understanding why the United States should support the Qing emperor (who was portrayed as reluctant to open his country to Christian missionaries). In Europe, some socialists and radical republicans saw the rebellion as a sort of Chinese equivalent of the French Revolution, but this view was less influential than the messianic image in the United States. But once the rebels began to challenge property rights and not only threaten trade disruptions but also halt China's repayment of its debts to the West (which the French and British had imposed after sacking Beijing in 1860), the European powers decided to take the side of the Qing government. Their support was probably decisive in the ultimate victory of imperial forces over the rebels in 1862–1864, right in the middle of the US Civil War (which in any case facilitated the European intervention, since American Christians were preoccupied by events at home).[54] If the rebels had triumphed, it is very hard to say how China's political structure and borders might have evolved.

By the end of the nineteenth century, the moral legitimacy of the Qing dynasty and China's warrior and mandarin elites had fallen very low in the eyes of the Chinese public. The country had been forced to accept a series of "unequal treaties" with the Europeans powers and found itself obliged to increase taxes sharply to repay the Westerners and their bankers what was effectively a military tribute, together with the accumulated interest.[55] In such a context, the 1895 defeat of China by Japan (which for millennia had been dominated militarily and culturally by China), together with Japanese incursions into Korea and Taiwan, appeared to signal the end of the road for the Qing.

In 1899–1901, the Boxer Rebellion, fomented by the "Righteous and Harmonious Fists," a secret society whose symbol was a clenched fist and whose goal was both to destroy feudal and imperial Manchu power and to expel the foreigners, nearly brought down the regime yet again. The Western powers, anxious for their territorial concessions, helped the Qing government put down the revolt and experimented in 1900–1902 with a novel form of international

---

54. See Singaravelou and Venayre, *Histoire du monde au XIXᵉ siècle*, pp. 286–288.
55. Between 1880 and 1910 China therefore had to run an increasing trade surplus to repay its debts. See von Glahn, *The Economic History of China*, p. 394, fig. 9.11.

government at Tianjin (a strategic port controlling access to Beijing). No fewer than ten colonial powers, already established in China or new to the feast, shared power in an administration charged with liquidating the last Boxer rebels. The archives of this astonishing government record the presence of particularly brutal and undisciplined French and German troops, who were repeatedly accused of rape and plunder by the local population; they were as violent and contemptuous toward the Chinese as they were toward the Indian soldiers that the British had brought in from the Raj (and with whom the Chinese themselves avoided contact as much as possible). Committees composed of representatives of the various powers had to resolve all sorts of complex economic and legal issues concerning supplies to the city and the creation of courts and brothels for the soldiers. After much debate, especially between the French and Japanese, the minimum age for Chinese prostitutes was set at age 13, although it had been raised from 13 to 16 in the United Kingdom in 1885. When it came time to leave and hand power back to the Qing government in 1902, the French soldiers who had stood out for their savagery confided their sadness in diaries and letters in which they lamented having to return to proletarian life in France after so many intoxicating and amusing months occupying China.[56]

The revolution of 1911 ultimately led to the fall of the empire and the founding of the Republic of China; Sun Yat-sen was elected its first president by an assembly of representatives gathered in Nanking. To explain the eventual triumph of the Communists and the transition from the bourgeois republic of 1911 to the People's Republic of 1949 after nearly four decades of virtual civil war between nationalists (who sought refuge in Taiwan in 1949) and Communists, as well as battles with Japanese and Western occupiers, it is tempting to mention the excessively conservative character of the regime that was founded in 1911–1912, which did not really reflect the aspiration of Chinese peasants for land redistribution and equality after decades and centuries of the Qing inequality regime. In fact, Sun Yat-sen was a republican Anglican and anti-Manchu physician but relatively conservative on economic and social issues, and most of the bourgeois revolutionaries of 1911 shared his respect for the es-

---

56. See especially the interesting diary of one Jacques Grandin, quoted in P. Singaravelou, *Tianjin Metropolis. Une autre histoire de la mondialisation* (Seuil, 2017), pp. 224–225, 281–299, 331–335. The occupying powers included the United Kingdom, France, the United States, Germany, Russia, Japan, Austria-Hungary, Italy, Belgium, and Denmark.

tablished order and property rights (once the old warrior class was stripped of its unwarranted privileges). The Chinese constitution of 1911 was in this respect not very innovative: it protected existing property rights and made peaceful legal redistribution virtually impossible, in contrast, for example, to the Mexican constitution of 1910 or the German constitution of 1919, which portrayed property as a social institution intended to serve the general interest and envisioned the possibility of legislative revision of existing property rights and far-reaching agrarian reforms or other limitations on the rights of existing owners.[57] President Sun Yat-sen was himself driven from power and replaced by imperial General Yuan Shikai in 1912 under pressure from Western countries, which felt that a strong military leader would be more likely to maintain order in China and ensure the continued fiscal flows needed to pay the principal and interest owed to the colonial powers.

In view of the complex sequence of events and political-ideological, military, and popular mobilizations in China in the period 1911–1949, however, it would not be very credible to see the advent of the People's Republic as an ineluctable, deterministic consequence of the shortcomings of the bourgeois republic of 1911–1912 and the profound centuries-old sense of injustice on the part of the anti-imperial, anti-landlord, and anti-mandarin peasantry. The situation might have evolved in any number of ways, perhaps even toward some form of social-democratic republic.[58] In Part Three we will also see that the advent of a Communist People's Republic in China left open (and continues to leave open) a range of possible political-ideological and institutional trajectories.[59] Like the transformation of any inequality regime, the transformation of China's trifunctional regime into a proprietarian and then a Communist regime must be seen as a set of sociopolitical experiments in which many available roads were not taken. By studying these missed opportunities we can learn a lot that may be useful in the future.

---

57. See Singaravelou and Venayre, *Histoire du monde au XIXᵉ siècle,* pp. 393–399. I will return to these constitutional and ownership issues later (see esp. Chap. 11 on the German constitutions of 1919 and 1949).

58. In the 1930s and early 1940s, many American diplomats and geopoliticians invested their hopes in a social democratic China to counterbalance the Soviet Union and the European colonial powers in organizing the postwar order. See O. Rosenboim, *The Emergence of Globalism: Visions of World Order in Britain and the United States, 1939–1950* (Princeton University Press, 2017), pp. 59–99.

59. See esp. Chap. 12.

An Example of a Constitutional Clerical Republic: Iran

We turn now to the case of Iran, which offers an unprecedented example of late constitutionalization of a clerical government with the creation in 1979 of the Islamic Republic of Iran, a fragile regime that has nevertheless survived as of this writing. The Iranian revolution, like all events of its type, was the result of a series of more or less contingent factors and events that could well have come together in a different way. The revulsion aroused by the last Shah of Iran, Mohammad Reza Pahlavi and his connivance with Western governments and their oil companies played a particularly important role, along with the tactical acumen of Ayatollah Khomeini. Leaving aside the logic of events, however, the important point is that the very possibility of a clerical republic in Iran was related to the specific form that the trifunctional structure took in the history of Sunni and Shiite Islam and, more specifically, the role of the Shiite clergy in the resistance to colonialism.[60]

Broadly speaking, Muslim societies have long been differentiated by the relative importance accorded to military and warrior elites on the one hand and clerical and intellectual elites on the other. From the beginning, Sunnis recognized the authority of the caliph, the temporal and military leader chosen to lead the *umma,* or Muslim community, whereas Shi'as followed the *imam,* the religious and spiritual leader recognized as a leader among the learned. Sunnis criticize Ali (the Prophet Muhammad's son-in-law, first imam and fourth caliph, along with his successor imams) for rejecting the authority of the caliphs and dividing the community. By contrast, Shi'as revere the authority of the first twelve imams and refuse to forgive the Sunnis for impeding their unifying efforts and supporting sometimes brutal caliphs who possessed no genuine knowledge of religion. After the occultation of the twelfth imam in 874, the leading Shiite *ulemas* (bodies of scholars) temporarily renounced temporal power and in the eleventh through thirteenth centuries published in Iraqi holy cities collections of traditional sayings and judgments attributed to the twelve imams. All believers are supposed to be equal in their efforts to imitate the ideal example of the imams.

The political-ideological equilibrium changed in the sixteenth century. Although the Shiite community was then confined to a few sites in western Iran, Iraq, and Lebanon (mainly among poor segments of the population, which re-

---

60. See the illuminating book by J. P. Luizard, *Histoire politique du clergé chiite, XVIIIe–XXIe siècles* (Fayard, 2014).

sponded to the imams' denunciation of princes and other powerful figures, thus establishing a bond between the Shiite clergy and disadvantaged social groups that persists to this day among Shiite minorities in Lebanon and Iraq), the Safavid dynasty sought, for both political and religious reasons, the support of Shiite ulemas to convert all of Persia to Shiism (which explains why Iran became the only Muslim country that is almost entirely Shiite).[61] Little by little, Shiite ulemas extended their power to interpret ancient precepts and justify the use of reason. Their political role increased further in the late eighteenth and early nineteenth centuries toward the end of the Safavid era and the beginning of the Qajar (1794–1925): for example, when the new sovereigns asked them to declare jihad against the Russians, for which the ulemas obtained in return confirmation of their right to pass judgment and collect taxes.

From their fiefs in Najaf (south of Baghdad, where the tomb of Ali is located), Karbala (site of the sacrifice of Ali's son Hussein), and Samarra (where the twelfth imam vanished),[62] the ulemas regularly defied Persian and Ottoman sovereigns whose actions they disapproved and set themselves up as veritable counterpowers. In the nineteenth century, a clear doctrine emerged: every Shiite had to follow a *mujahid;* the *marja* was the most learned of all *mujahideen;* and some *maraji* specialized in certain domains of wisdom or

---

61. The high Shiite clergy is still based primarily in Iran, Iraq, and Lebanon and "reigns" over approximately 170 million Shiites throughout the world (constituting 11 percent of all Muslims), accounting for 85 percent of the population of Iran, 75 percent in Bahrain, 55 percent in Iraq, 35 percent in Lebanon (but more than half of the Muslims in that country), roughly 15–20 percent in Pakistan and Afghanistan (and of Muslims in India), and generally less than 10 percent in other Muslim countries. See Luizard, *Histoire politique du clergé chiite,* pp. 40–41. Some authors insist that the *pishtras,* functional social classes in trifunctional Iran in the Zoroastrian period (first millennium BCE to early first millennium CE), accorded a preeminent place to the priestly class as opposed to the warrior class (see, for example, E. Sénart, *Les castes dans l'Inde. Les faits et le système* [1896], pp. 140–141). It would be risky, however, to link the power of the Iranian clerical class too strongly to this tradition, since conversion to Shiism also involved other regions. On debates over the process of Iran's conversion to Shiism, see I. Poutrin, "Quand l'Iran devint chiite. Religion et pouvoir chez les Safavides (16e–17e s.)," *Conversion/Pouvoir et religion,* 2017.

62. These three holy cities are located in Iraq. In Iran, only Mashhad can boast of the tomb of an imam. Fatima, the Prophet's daughter, and other imams are buried in Medina (Saudi Arabia), which is a source of great tension with the (Sunni) Saudi authorities during pilgrimages.

possessed special competences. The views of the marja are transmitted either by direct contact or through men who have heard them from the lips of the marja himself.

In general, there are no more than five or six living maraji throughout the Shiite world. To rise from mujahid to marja is the work of a lifetime and requires both wisdom and religious learning; by contrast, membership of Sunnite ulemas is based on official recognition by the temporal powers. Under the Persian and Ottoman Empires in the eighteenth to twentieth centuries, the Shiite clergy became virtual heads of state thanks to the extraterritorial status of the holy Shiite cities in Iraq and Iran where they exercised moral, fiscal, and military authority. Their status was not unlike that of the Papal states in medieval and modern Europe, with one important difference: the Shiite clerical class is a true social class unto itself, with matrimonial alliances uniting families of major ulemas (for example, Khomeini's grandson is married to a granddaughter of the marja Sistani, based in Najaf). Through these alliances the clergy control large amounts of property, although it is usually held on behalf of mosques, schools, and religious foundations and linked to the provision of social services.

On the Anticolonialist Legitimacy of the Shiite Clergy

While the Ottoman and Persian Empires were increasingly accused of giving in to the demands of the Christian colonial powers as well as succumbing to corruption themselves, the Shiite clergy stood out as the voice of the resistance, especially during the tobacco riots of 1890–1892. The great marja Shirazi, already quite popular for his relief work during the Mesopotamian famine of 1870, opposed the monopolies on tobacco, railroads, and natural resources granted to the English in 1890–1891 at a time when the Imperial Bank of Persia had fallen under the control of British creditors (the Ottoman Imperial Bank had been under the control of a Franco-British consortium since 1863). The ensuing riots and other expressions of popular discontent were such that the Shah had to give up his plans for a time in 1892.[63] Subsequently, the Western powers regained the upper hand, especially after the discovery of oil in 1908, the occupation of Iranian cities by English and Russian troops in 1911, and then the division of Ottoman territory between France and Britain in 1919–1920. But the Shiite clergy had stood out as a major anticolonial force and would reap the fruits of its resistance later on. In general, intense proselytizing in the

---

63. See Luizard, *Histoire politique du clergé chiite,* pp. 77–88.

late nineteenth century by Christian missionaries from the West (convinced of the superiority of their cultural and religious models) helped stimulate various forms of Hindu and Muslim religious revival from the early twentieth century on.[64] For example, the (Sunni) Muslim Brotherhood was founded in Egypt in 1928. It subsequently developed social services and fostered solidarity among the faithful that in some ways resembled the Shiite quasi-states, with one difference: the latter enjoyed the support of a much more organized religious hierarchy and clerical class.

After Iranian prime minister Mossadegh tried to nationalize the oil industry in 1951, the English and Americans instigated a coup in 1953 to bring the Shah back to power and above all reinstate the privileges of the Western oil companies. The Shah belonged to a family of soldiers who had risen from the ranks and had little to do with religion; after taking power in 1925, they were regularly accused of nepotism. In 1962 the regime tried to do away with the Shiite clergy once and for all by attacking its financial base: an agrarian reform forced the *waqf* (pious foundations) to sell their land. This led to huge rallies, to Ayatollah Khomeini's exile to Najaf from 1965 to 1978, and to increasingly violent repression.

Finally, in February 1979, the very unpopular Shah was forced to flee the country and cede power to Khomeini, who joined with the ulemas to promulgate a constitution for which there are few if any historical precedents. The 1906 Persian constitution had stipulated that any law passed by parliament had to be ratified by at least five mujahideen appointed by one or more marjas. But this rule was circumvented in 1908–1909, and the drafters of the 1979 constitution took care to ensure that the clergy's power would be firmly protected in the Islamic Republic of Iran. To be sure, the Majlis (parliament), Assembly of Experts, and president were to be elected by direct universal suffrage (including women, who obtained the right to vote in Iran in 1963). But only religious men (in principle with diplomas in theology or other sufficient religious education) could run for the eighty-six-member Assembly of Experts, the body that elected the Supreme Guide and could in theory remove him. In practice, there have only been two Supreme Guides: Ayatollah Khomeini from 1979 to his death in 1989 and Ayatollah Khamenei since 1989. The Guide clearly dominates the civil authorities, especially in times of serious crisis: he is the head of Iran's armies; he appoints senior military leaders and judges; and he arbitrates disputes among the executive, legislative, and judicial branches. In addition,

---

64. See Singaravelou and Venayre, *Histoire du monde au XIXᵉ siècle,* pp. 147–148.

the Guide directly appoints six of the twelve men of religion who make up the Council of Guardians (the six others must be approved by the Majlis after nomination by the judicial authorities, who are controlled by the Guide). The Council is the supreme constitutional body that controls the electoral system since it must approve all candidates for the Majlis, the Assembly of Experts, and the presidency.

Although there are many modern political regimes that grant full power to the military class (usually in the form of military dictatorships with relatively loose legal structures) and some constitutional regimes that grant the military special prerogatives within the context of a parliamentary system, especially in relation to budgets (examples include the current constitutions of Egypt and Thailand), the Iranian constitution is a case apart.[65] The clerical class has organized and codified its grip on political power in a very sophisticated way while leaving quite a bit of room for relatively open and pluralist elections or, at any rate, elections more open and pluralist than one finds in most political regimes in the Middle East.

Note, however, that the state power officially granted to Shiite religious leaders by the Iranian constitution has always aroused a great deal of suspicion in much of the clerical class, which has generally preferred to stay out of politics for fear of being caught up in its vagaries. This is particularly true of the highest marjas and other religious dignitaries in Iraq's holy cities as well as of the lower Shiite clergy and imams in Iran's mosques, who are mostly hostile to the current regime. Those religious leaders and theologians (or people passing themselves off as theologians) who make their careers in the Assembly of Experts, in politics, or in the state apparatus therefore constitute a distinct group, which should not be confused with the clergy as a whole.[66] It is interesting to note that the constitution of 1979 initially stipulated that only an authentic marja could be elected Supreme Guide of the Islamic Republic. But in 1989, when Khomeini (who had been awarded the title of marja during his exile in Najaf) died, no living marja met the conditions and wished to become Supreme Guide. Hence the decision was made to elect the current Guide, Ali Khamenei

---

65. For example, the Egyptian constitution of 2014 stipulates that the military budget is to remain secret (only a total figure is released to the public) and must be negotiated with army commanders. The Thai constitution of 2016 gives military commanders the power to appoint senators, who can bring down the government.

66. The only nonreligious leader to serve as president to date is Mahmoud Ahmadinejad (2005–2013), who was seen as stricter and more conservative than many presidents drawn from the clerical and religious class.

(who was only an ayatollah)—an outright breach of the constitution. The constitution was then retroactively amended in late 1989 to make Khamenei's election legal. Subsequently, the regime sought to persuade living marjas to recognize the Supreme Guide as a marja but without success.[67] This humiliating episode marked a clear divorce between Shiism's transnational religious authorities and the national governing bodies of the Islamic Republic of Iran.[68]

Egalitarian Shiite Republic, Sunni Oil Monarchies: Discourses and Realities

Today, the Iranian regime still tries to portray itself as more moral and egalitarian than other Muslim states, especially the Saudis and other Gulf oil monarchies, which Iran regularly accuses of instrumentalizing religion to hide the monopolization of natural resources by a family, dynasty, or clan. In contrast to those regimes, governed by princes, billionaires, and the newly rich, the Iranian regime claims to stand for republican equality among its citizens, without dynastic privilege of any kind, and for the wisdom of religious scholars and experts, regardless of their social origins.

Available data do in fact show that the Middle East today is the most inegalitarian region in the world.[69] This is primarily because the economic resources have been captured by oil states with small populations and, within those states, by very thin social strata. Among the fortunate few are the ruling families of Saudi Arabi, the Emirates, and Qatar, which for decades have relied on strict religious doctrine in certain respects (notably with regard to women) in the hope, perhaps, of covering up their financial misdeeds. In Part Three of this book I will return to this important feature of the current global inequality regime and more generally to the question of how to reduce inequalities at the regional and international level.[70]

---

67. See Luizard, *Histoire politique du clergé chiite,* pp. 217–230.
68. The regime does, however, continue to command a certain prestige among the religious owing to its regional standing and protection of Shiites, as well as to the memory of the war with Iraq (1980–1988), at a time when all the Western countries were supporting and arming Saddam Hussein, a member of the Sunni minority in Iraq (and not very religious), who had not hesitated to execute the grand marja of Najaf in 1980.
69. See Fig. I.4.
70. See esp. Chap. 13.

At this stage, note simply that such extreme levels of inequality cannot fail to engender enormous social and political tensions. The perpetuation of such regimes depends on a sophisticated repressive apparatus as well as on Western military protection, especially from the United States. If Western armies had not come to boot Iraqi forces out of Kuwait in 1991 and restore the emir's sovereignty over the country and its petroleum resources (as well as to protect the interests of US and European firms), it is likely that the redrawing of regional boundaries would not have ended there. Within Islam, the Shiite regime in Iran is not the only actor to denounce the corruption of the oil monarchies and the alleged connivance of Western infidels. Many Sunni citizens and political groups share this view, most of them pacifists and straining to make their voices heard, while a few engage in terrorist actions that have captured a large share of the world's headlines in recent years (especially organizations such as al-Qaeda and the Islamic State).[71]

Note, too, that the Iranian regime, rhetoric notwithstanding, is also quite opaque as to the distribution of its wealth. This lack of transparency, together with the suspicions of corruption that it arouses in the population, explains the extreme fragility of the regime today. The *pasdarans,* or Revolutionary Guards, under direct orders of the Supreme Guide, constitute a veritable state within the state and according to some estimates control 30–40 percent of the Iranian economy. The many pious foundations controlled by the Guide and his allies are also said to possess considerable assets, officially in support of their role in providing social services and assisting in the development of the country, but the virtually total absence of detailed information prevents any precise accounting and naturally arouses suspicion.[72] Iranian films give us occasional glimpses of what is going on, and the picture is not very reassuring. In *A Man of Integrity* (2017), Reza lives in fear that his house and land will be taken by a mysterious company close to the regime and to local authorities. He ends up distraught amid his dead fish. The director, Mohammad Rasoulof, was arrested

---

71. Recall that al-Qaeda is a Sunni terrorist group known primarily for its attacks on September 11, 2001, and relatively open to Shiites, whereas the Islamic State (Daech) is a territorial project that aims to establish a Sunni Caliphate "in Iraq and the Levant" (including a radical redrawing of the boundary between Iraq and Syria, which it came close to achieving between 2014 and 2018); Daech is violently opposed to Shiites in Iraq and throughout the region.

72. On recent changes in the regime, see esp. A. Chelly, *Iran, autopsie du chiisme politique* (Cerf, 2017); C. Arminjon Hachem, *Chiisme et Etat. Les clercs à l'épreuve de la modernité* (CNRS, 2013).

and stripped of his passport with no official reason given, and since then he has been living under threat of imprisonment.

Equality, Inequality, and Zakat in Muslim Countries

Broadly speaking, there is no denying that the promises of social, political, and economic equality that Islam has preached over the centuries, like those of Christianity, Hinduism, and other religions, have regularly ended in disillusionment. It is true, of course, that for millennia religions have supported the development of essential services at the local level. The clerical and intellectual classes associated with various religions (including Confucianism and Buddhism) also served to balance the power of warrior and military classes in trifunctional societies around the world. The messages of equality and universality promoted by religion have often been seen as possible avenues of emancipation for disadvantaged minorities, as evidenced, for example, by Hindu conversions to Islam (for which some Hindu nationalists today attack their Muslim fellow citizens).

But when it comes to organizing society and reducing inequality on a broader scale, the rigidity, conservativism, and contradictions of religious ideology, particularly regarding familial, legal, and fiscal matters, become glaringly apparent. Of course, we find in Islam as in all religions a certain attachment to the idea of social equality at the theoretical level, but the practical and institutional recommendations that flow from this are generally fairly vague. And they are often so malleable that they can be pressed into service by the conservative ideology of the moment. Take slavery, for example: Christianity proved to be quite capable of accommodating the slave system for centuries. We saw this in the attitude of popes and Christian kings in the Age of Discovery and in the social justifications of slavery offered by Thomas Jefferson and John Calhoun in the early nineteenth century, and we find the same fundamental ambiguities throughout the long history of Islam. In theory, slavery is condemned, especially when it involves coreligionists or Muslim converts. In practice, we find huge concentrations of Negros in many Muslim states from the days of the hegira onward, starting with the black slaves who toiled on Iraqi plantations in the eighth and ninth centuries during the "golden age" of the Abbasid Caliphate.[73] Today, in the early twenty-first century, Muslim theologians, like

---

73. See esp. A. Popovic, *La révolte des esclaves en Iraq au IIIe/IXe siècle* (1976); C. Coquery-Vidrovitch, *Les Routes de l'esclavage: Histoire des traites africaines* (Albin Michel, 2018), pp. 67–68.

nineteenth-century senators from Virginia and South Carolina, continue to supply learned explanations of why slavery, while unsatisfactory in the grand sweep of history, can be abolished only after extensive preparation with due attention to contemporary concerns and with the time needed to ensure that liberated slaves have sufficient skills and maturity to live without the oversight of their masters.[74]

As for taxation and social solidarity, Islam in principle proposes the obligation of the *zakat:* those among the faithful who have the means are supposed to contribute to help meet the needs of the community and its poorest members, ostensibly in proportion to their assets (in cash, precious metals, inventories, lands, harvests, livestock, and so on). The zakat is mentioned in several surahs (chapters) of the Koran, but in a somewhat vague way. Various formulations have been passed down through Muslim legal tradition, at times in contradictory terms. In the nineteenth century, in the Shiite regions of Iraq and Iran, the faithful were supposed to give from a fifth to a third of their income and a third of their inheritances to a mujahid of their choosing.[75] Note, however, that the amount actually paid was often quite small: in most Muslim societies, the zakat was generally the result of a direct dialogue between the individual, his conscience, and God, so a certain flexibility was essential. That is probably why no records of the zakat have survived from any Muslim society (Shiite or Sunni) and hence no documents that can be studied to see how much was actually given or how such gifts affected the distribution of wealth and income. In the case of the oil monarchies, gifts proportioned to the wealth of oil sheiks and billionaires could in fact provide substantial resources to the community while also yielding invaluable information about the distribution of wealth and its evolution. Note that the zakat was generally seen as a strictly proportional tax (with the same rate for rich and poor); in some cases there were two tranches (a certain amount of wealth was exempted, while a single rate was applied to the rest) but never an explicitly progressive tax with multiple tranches—the only way to ensure that the effort required of each contrib-

---

74. See, for example, T. Ramadan, *Le génie de l'Islam. Initiation à ses fondements, sa spiritualité et son histoire* (Archipoche, 2016), p. 47. In the same vein the author explains that while certain limitations on the rights of women (such as half-shares of inheritances) are certainly not satisfactory, they can be justified if men assume their roles and take good care of their women (p. 150).

75. See Luizard, *Histoire politique du clergé chiite,* pp. 38–39.

utor would depend on his ability to contribute, which might have offered a genuine prospect of wealth redistribution.[76]

The lack of transparency, progressivity, and redistributive ambition that we find in the zakat is, moreover, something we find in all religions. For example, the tithe that was paid in France under the Ancien Régime, which was given the force of law by the monarchy and seigneurial elites, was a strictly proportional tax.[77] Not until the debates of the French Revolution and later, in the twentieth century, do we see the emergence of explicitly progressive taxes allowing for more ambitious efforts of social justice and inequality reduction in societies that had by then become secular. We find the same type of conservatism in more recent religions such as the Church of Latter-Day Saints (Mormons), founded in 1830 by Joseph Smith on the basis of a revelation that enabled him to link the United States to the stories of Abraham and Jesus Christ; the Mormon church is today financed by a tithe of 10 percent on the income of the faithful.[78] These large payments have allowed the development

---

76. References to the zakat do however sometimes mention variable rates depending on the tax basis, such as "2.5 percent on sums of money and 5–10 percent of harvests." See Ramadan, *Le génie de l'Islam*, p. 127; see also A. D. Arif, *L'Islam et le capitalisme: pour une justice économique* (L'Harmattan, 2016), p. 70. The fact that the first rate seems to refer to a tax on a stock of capital and the second to a tax on an annual income flow (or else a product not immediately consumed or reinvested, according to some interpretations) adds to the confusion, especially since no comparison is made with actually existing taxes on income, estates, or wealth. In practice, the zakats seem to have varied a great deal with the context, the society, and local norms.

77. See Chap. 2.

78. According to the Book of Mormon, one of the Church of Jesus Christ of Latter-Day Saints' four sacred texts that include the Bible, a Jewish tribe fled Mesopotamia and later the coast of Arabia by ship and settled in America in the sixth century BCE. The story of what took place in biblical lands was supposedly recounted to the lost tribe directly by Jesus Christ, who visited America shortly after his resurrection. The corresponding tablets were then allegedly recovered by Joseph Smith in 1828 in western New York State. This way of associating a place with a community that sees itself as peripheral to the great monotheistic narrative was not unlike the way in which the Koran linked the Hejaz to the Jewish and Christian narrative (the Arabas are said to be descendants of Ishmael, who built the foundation of the Kaaba in Mecca with his father Abraham). This egalitarian aspect of the messianic narratives and this refusal to hierarchize territories and origins is an essential feature of these texts. On the social context of the emergence of Islam, see the classic book by M. Rodinson, *Mahomet* (Seuil, 1961).

of new forms of sharing and solidarity in a community of 16 million Mormons around the world (of whom nearly 7 million live in the United States, mainly in Utah). But the Mormon tithe is a strictly proportional tax, the finances of the church are unusually opaque, and everything is under the exclusive control of a college of twelve Apostles who serve for life (like the Catholic Pope and the justices of the US Supreme Court) and are based in the prosperous Mormon capital of Salt Lake City. The oldest Apostle automatically becomes the head of the church and its official Prophet. If one of the Apostles dies, the remaining eleven choose a successor. The current Prophet, Russell Nelson, assumed his post in 2018 at the age of 94, replacing his predecessor, who died at 91. Coincidentally, it may be worth noting that a papal bull issued in 1970 denied cardinals over the age of 80 the right to participate in the conclave that elects a new pope. Here is proof that any institution can evolve, even the most venerable.

Proprietarianism and Colonialism: The Globalization of Inequality

To recapitulate: in the first two parts of this book we have studied the transformation of trifunctional societies into ownership societies and the way in which the encounter with European colonial powers and ownership societies affected the evolution of ternary societies elsewhere in the world. We learned that most premodern societies, in Europe as well as in Asia, in Africa as well as in America, were organized around a trifunctional logic. Power at the local level was structured around, on the one hand, clerical and religious elites charged with the spiritual leadership of society and, on the other hand, warriors and military elites responsible for maintaining order in various evolving political-ideological configurations. Between 1500 and 1900, the formation of the centralized state went hand in hand with a radical transformation of the political-ideological devices that served to justify and structure social inequalities. In particular, trifunctional ideology was gradually supplanted by proprietarian ideology based on a strict separation of property rights (supposedly open to all) and regalian powers (henceforth the monopoly of the centralized state).

This movement toward proprietarianism, which accompanied the construction of the state and the development of new means of transportation and communication, also coincided with intensified contacts with remote parts of the world and far-flung civilizations that had previously almost entirely ignored one another. These encounters took place under plainly hierarchical and inegalitarian conditions, given the superior fiscal and military capacity that European states had developed because of their internal rivalries. This contact between European colonial powers and societies on other continents resulted in a variety of political-ideological trajectories, depending especially on the way in which the legitimacy of old intellectual and warrior elites was affected by these encounters. The modern world is a direct result of these processes.

There are many lessons that can be drawn from these historical experiences and trajectories, and I want to stress the great political, ideological, and institutional diversity of the means by which different societies structure social inequalities at both the local and the international level, in contexts marked by numerous rapid transformations. Think, for example, of the European strategy to outflank Islam along the African coast and the discovery of India (followed by codification of its castes); or of Europe's powerful fiscal-military states, which became fiscal-welfare states in the twentieth century; or of proprietarian ideologies; or of the audacious colonial joint-stock companies invented in Europe. Think of dietary purity, of multilinguistic and multiconfessional racial mixing; of social quotas and large-scale federal parliamentarism in India; of the lettered administrators who served the Chinese state and people and of Chinese imperial exams and Chinese Communist policies development policies; of Japan's shogunate and social integration strategies; and of the social role of the Shiite quasi-states, or the role of the Council of Guardians and other novel republican reforms invented in Iran. A good many of these political-ideological constructs and institutions have not survived. Others remain in an experimental state, and we have made no attempt to hide their weaknesses. The common point of all these historical experiences is that they show that there is never anything "natural" about social inequality. It is always profoundly ideological and political. Every society has no choice but to make sense of its inequalities, and the claim that inequality serves the common good is effective only if it has some degree of plausibility and some embodiment in durable institutions.

The objective of Parts One and Two—through which we have surveyed the history of trifunctional, proprietarian, slave, and colonial inequality regimes up to the turn of the twentieth century, with occasional excursions into more recent times—was not just to illustrate the political-ideological ingenuity of human societies. I also tried to show that it was possible to glean from history certain lessons for the future, concerning especially the capacity of various ideologies and institutions to achieve their objectives of political harmony and social justice. We saw, for example, that the proprietarian promise of greater diffusion of wealth, which found forceful expression during the French Revolution, collided with a very different reality: the concentration of property in France and Europe was greater on the eve of World War I than it had been a century earlier or under the Ancien Régime (Chapters 1–5). We noted the hypocrisy of civilizing rhetoric and of efforts to sacralize property and to justify racial and cultural domination in the development of colonial society. We saw the lasting effects of modern state codification of longstanding status inequalities (Chapters 6–9). Above all, the study of these various trajectories has afforded us a better understanding of the intertwined socioeconomic and political-ideological processes by which the various parts of the globe came into contact with one another and gave rise to the modern world. To go further, we must now analyze the way in which the events and ideologies of the twentieth century radically transformed the structure of inequality both within countries and at the international level.

THE GREAT TRANSFORMATION OF THE TWENTIETH CENTURY

TEN

The Crisis of Ownership Societies

In Parts One and Two of this book we studied the transformation of trifunctional societies (based on a tripartite division of clergy, nobility, and third estate and an overlapping of property rights and regalian powers at the local level) into ownership societies (organized around a strict separation of property rights, ostensibly open to all, and regalian powers, a monopoly of the centralized state). We also looked at the way in which the encounter with proprietarian colonial European powers affected the evolution of ternary societies in other parts of the world. In Part Three, we are going to analyze the way in which the twentieth century profoundly disrupted this structure of inequality. The century between the assassination of Archduke Ferdinand in Sarajevo on June 28, 1914, and the attack on New York on September 11, 2001, was one of hope for a more just world and more egalitarian societies and marked by projects that aimed at radical transformation of inequality regimes inherited from the past. These hopes were dampened by the depressing failure of Soviet Communism (1917–1991)—a failure that contributes to today's sense of disillusionment and to a certain fatalism when it comes to dealing with inequality. This can be overcome, however, provided that we follow the thread of this history back to its origin and fully absorb the lessons it has to teach. The twentieth century also marked the end of colonialism; indeed, this may have been its most important result. Societies and cultures that had previously been subject to military domination by the West now emerged as actors on the world stage.

We will begin this chapter by examining the crisis of ownership societies in the period 1914–1945. Then, in the next chapter, we will study the promises and limitations of the social-democratic societies that arose after World War II. We will then analyze the case of communist and postcommunist societies and finally the rise of hypercapitalist and postcolonial societies at the end of the twentieth and beginning of the twenty-first centuries.

Rethinking the "Great Transformation" of the First Half of the Twentieth Century

Between 1914 and 1945 the structure of global inequality, both within countries and at the international level, experienced a deep and rapid transformation. Nothing like it had ever been seen in the entire previous history of inequality. In 1914, on the eve of World War I, the private property regime seemed as prosperous and unalterable as the colonial regime. The countries of Europe, proprietarian and colonial, were at the peak of their power. British and French citizens boasted of portfolios of foreign assets unequaled to this day. Yet by 1945, barely thirty years later, private property had ceased to exist under the communist regime in the Soviet Union, and soon in China and Eastern Europe as well. It had lost much of its power in countries that remained nominally capitalist but were actually turning social-democratic through a combination of nationalizations, public education and health policies, and steeply progressive taxes on high incomes and large estates. Colonial empires were soon to be dismantled. The old European nation-states had self-destructed, and their reign had given way to a global ideological competition between communism and capitalism, embodied by two powers of continental dimension: the Union of Soviet Socialist Republics and the United States of America.

We will begin by measuring the extent to which income and wealth inequality decreased in Europe and the United States in the first half of the twentieth century, beginning with the collapse of private property in the period 1914–1945. Physical destruction linked to the two world wars played only a minor part in this collapse, though it certainly cannot be neglected in the countries most affected. The collapse was mainly the result of a multitude of political decisions, often taken in urgent circumstances; the common feature of these decisions was the intent to reduce the social influence of private property, whether by expropriation of foreign assets, nationalization of firms, imposition of rent and price controls, or reduction of the public debt through inflation, exceptional taxes on private wealth, or outright repudiation. We will also analyze the central role played by the introduction of large-scale progressive taxation in the first half of the twentieth century, with rates of 70–80 percent or more on the highest incomes and largest estates—rates that were maintained until the 1980s. From the distance afforded us by the passage of time, the evidence suggests that this historical innovation—progressive taxation—played a key role in reducing inequality in the twentieth century.

Finally, we will study the political-ideological conditions that made this historical turning point possible, especially the "great transformation" of attitudes toward private property and the market that Karl Polanyi analyzed in 1944 in his book of that title (a magisterial work, written in the heat of action, about which I will say more later).[1] To be sure, the various financial, legal, social, and fiscal decisions taken between 1914 and 1950 grew out of a specific series of events. They bear the mark of the rather chaotic politics of the period and attest to the way in which the groups in power at the time tried to cope with unprecedented circumstances, for which they were often ill-prepared. But, to an even greater degree, those decisions stemmed from profound and lasting changes in social perceptions of the system of private property and its legitimacy and ability to bring prosperity and offer protection against crisis and war. This challenge to capitalism had been in gestation since the middle of the nineteenth century before crystallizing as majority opinion in the wake of two world wars, the Bolshevik Revolution, and the Great Depression of the 1930s. After such shocks, it was no longer possible to fall back on the ideology that had been dominant until 1914, which relied on the quasi-sacralization of private property and the unquestioned belief in the benefits of generalized competition, whether among individuals or among states. The contending political forces therefore set out in search of new avenues, including various forms of social democracy and socialism in Europe and the New Deal in the United States. The lessons that can be drawn from this history are obviously relevant to what is happening today, especially since a neo-proprietarian ideology began to gain influence in the final decades of the twentieth century. This can be attributed in part to the catastrophic failure of Soviet Communism. But it can also be explained by the neglect of historical studies and the disciplinary divide between economics and history as well as by the shortcomings of the social-democratic solutions that were tried in the middle of the twentieth century and that stand today in urgent need of review.[2]

---

1. See K. Polanyi, *The Great Transformation: The Political and Economic Origins of Our Time* (1944). A Hungarian economist and historian, Polanyi fled Vienna for London in 1933, then emigrated to the United States in 1940. There, between 1940 and 1944, he wrote his classic analysis of the catastrophe ravaging Europe. For Polanyi, it was the ideology of the self-regulated market, which was beyond dominant in the nineteenth century, that led European societies to self-destruct in the period 1914–1945 and thus to questioning the basis of economic liberalism.

2. See Chap. 11.

The Collapse of Inequality and Private Property (1914–1945)

The fall of ownership society in the period 1914–1945 can be analyzed as a consequence of three challenges: the challenge of inequality within European ownership societies, which led to the emergence first of counterdiscourses and then of communist and social-democratic counter-regimes in the late nineteenth and first half of the twentieth centuries; the challenge of inequality among countries, which led to critiques of the colonial order and the rise of increasingly powerful independence movements in the same period; and finally, a nationalist and identitarian challenge, which heightened competition among the European powers and eventually led to their self-destruction through war and genocide in the period 1914–1945. It is the conjunction of these three profound intellectual crises (the emergence of socialism and communism, the twilight of colonialism, and the exacerbation of nationalism and racialism) with specific series of events that accounts for the radical nature of the challenge and the ensuing transformation.[3]

Before studying the mechanisms at work here and returning to the long-term political-ideological transformations that made these evolutions possible, it is important to begin by taking the measure of the historic reduction of socioeconomic inequalities and the decline of private property in this period. Let us begin with income inequality (Fig. 10.1). In Europe, the share of the top decile (the 10 percent of the population with the highest incomes) amounted to about 50 percent of total income in Europe in the nineteenth and early twentieth centuries until the beginning of World War I. It then began a chaotic fall between 1914 and 1945, eventually stabilizing at around 30 percent of total income in 1945–1950, where it stayed until 1980. European income inequality, which was significantly higher than that of the United States until 1914, fell below US levels during the so-called Trente Glorieuses 1950–1980, a period of exceptionally high growth (especially in Europe and Japan) and historically low levels of inequality. In addition, the revival of inequality since 1980 has been much stronger in the United States than in Europe so that in the late twentieth and early twenty-first centuries the United States has taken the lead—the reverse of the situation at the turn of the twentieth century.

When we look more closely at Europe, we find, first, that inequality collapsed between 1914 and 1945–1950 in all countries for which data are avail-

---

3. On these three challenges, see also Chap. 5.

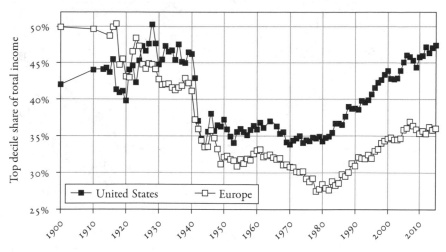

FIG. 10.1. Income inequality in Europe and the United States, 1900–2015

Interpretation: The top decile's share of total national income was on average around 50 percent in Western Europe in 1900–1910 before falling to around 30 percent in 1950–1980, then rising above 35 percent in 2010–2015. The increase of inequality was much stronger in the United States, where the top decile's share was 45–50 percent in 2010–2015, above the level for 1900–1910. *Sources and series:* piketty.pse.ens.fr/ideology.

able, and second, that while inequality has indeed increased since 1980, the magnitude of the increase varies widely from country to country (Figs. 10.2–10.3). For example, the trajectory of the United Kingdom is closest to that of the United States while income inequality in Sweden remains the lowest on the continent; Germany and France fall between these two extremes.[4] We find similar results if we look at the evolution of the top centile (instead of the top decile) share, with the US lead in inequality in recent decades even more marked by this measure. In subsequent chapters I will return to the general increase in inequality since 1980 and the reasons for the various trajectories and chronologies we observe in Europe and the United States.

---

4. The estimates given for income inequality in Europe in Figs. 10.1–10.3 are an average of the figures for the United Kingdom, Germany, France, and Sweden (which are the countries with the fullest long-term data sets). Other countries for which we have estimates going back to the turn of the twentieth century (especially the Netherlands, Denmark, and Norway) indicate similar evolutions. Japan also follows a similar trajectory over the long run, with a position between the United States and Europe for the most recent period. See the online appendix (piketty.pse. ens.fr/ideology), especially Figs. S1.6 and S10.1–S10.5. See also Fig. I.6.

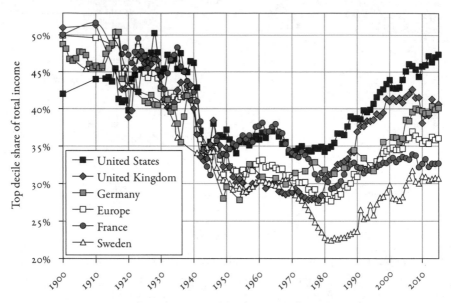

FIG. 10.2. Income inequality, 1900–2015: The diversity of Europe

Interpretation: The top decile's share of total national income averaged around 50 percent in Western Europe in 1900–1910 before falling to around 30 percent in 1950–1980 (or even 25 percent in Sweden), then rising above 35 percent in 2010–2015 (or even 40 percent in the United Kingdom). In 2015 the United Kingdom and Germany were above the European average, and France and Sweden were below. *Sources and series:* piketty.pse .ens.fr/ideology.

From European Proprietarianism to American Neo-Proprietarianism

At this stage, note simply that the levels of income inequality observed in the United States in the period 2000–2020 are very high, with the top decile claiming 45–50 percent of total income and the top centile, 20 percent. These levels are almost as high as those observed in Europe in 1900–1910 (around 50 percent for the top decile and 20–25 percent for the top centile, and even a little more in the United Kingdom). This does not mean, however, that the structure of inequality was exactly the same in the two periods. In Belle Époque Europe (1880–1914), the very high level of income inequality was the distinctive characteristic of ownership society. The highest incomes consisted almost entirely of income from property (rents, profits, dividends, interest, and so on), and it was the collapse of the concentration of property and of the largest fortunes that led to the decrease in top income shares and the disappearance of ownership society in its classic form.

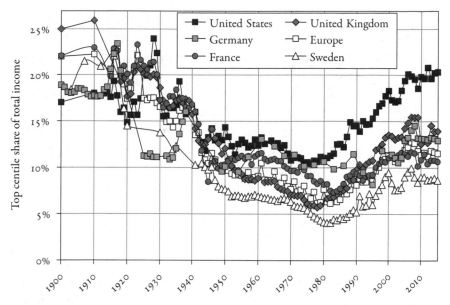

FIG. 10.3. Income inequality, 1900–2015: The top centile

Interpretation: The top centile's share of total national income was about 20–25 percent in Western Europe in 1900–1910 before falling to 5–10 percent in 1950–1980 (and less than 5 percent in Sweden), then climbing to about 10–15 percent in 2010–2015. The increase of inequality was much greater in the United States, where the top centile's share attained 20 percent in 2010–2015 and surpassed the 1900–1910 level. *Sources and series:* piketty.pse.ens.fr/ideology.

In the United States in 2000–2020, income inequality has a somewhat different origin. High incomes from capital still play a role at the top of the social hierarchy, all the more so because concentration of wealth has increased sharply in the United States since 1980. But this concentration of wealth remains somewhat less extreme than that observed in Europe in 1880–1914. Another factor is partly responsible for the high level of income inequality in the United States today—namely, the explosion of high salaries for top executives since 1980. Contrary to what interested parties would have you believe, this in no way implies that this form of inequality is more "just" or "meritocratic" than the other. As noted earlier, access to higher education in the United States is highly unequal, despite official claims of meritocratic rewards.[5] In Chapter 11 we will see that skyrocketing executive pay mainly reflects the absence of adequate countervailing power within firms and the decline of the moderating role

---

5. See Fig. I.8.

of fiscal progressivity. Simply put, the mechanisms and processes at work (both socioeconomic and political-ideological) are not exactly the same in neo-proprietarian US society in 2000–2020 as those that were at work in pre-1914 proprietarian societies.

As for the evolution of wealth inequality, remember that it was always much greater than income inequality. The share of private property owned by the wealthiest 10 percent reached 90 percent in Europe on the eve of World War I before decreasing in the interwar and postwar years to 50–55 percent in the 1980s, at which time it began to rise again (Fig. 10.4).[6] In other words, when wealth inequality fell to its historic low, its level was still comparable to the highest observed levels of income inequality. The same is true for the top centile (Fig. 10.5).[7] Paradoxically, the sources available today (in the era of big data) are less precise than those that were available a century ago due to the internationalization of wealth, the proliferation of tax havens, and above all, lack of political will to enforce financial transparency, so it is quite possible that we are underestimating the level of wealth inequality in recent decades.[8]

Two facts appear to be well established, however. First, the increased concentration of wealth in recent decades has been noticeably greater in the United States than in Europe. Second, despite the uncertainties, the level of wealth inequality in 2000–2020 appears to be somewhat less extreme than in Belle Époque Europe. In the United States the top decile share is 70–75 percent of all private property according to the latest data, which is obviously significant but still not as high as the 85–95 percent levels observed in France, Sweden, and the United Kingdom in the period 1900–1910 (Fig. 10.4). The top centile share in the United States in 2010–2020 is 40 percent, compared with 55–70 percent in France, Sweden, and the United Kingdom in 1900–1910 (Fig. 10.5). Given the rapid pace of change, however, it is not out of the question that the share of wealth belonging to the least wealthy 90 percent of the population will continue to decrease in decades to come. (In practice, moreover, most of what belongs to the bottom 90 percent is actually owned by what

---

6. The estimates of wealth inequality in Europe in Figs. 10.4–10.5 are based on averaging results for the United Kingdom, France, and Sweden. The other countries for which we have estimates going back to the early twentieth century (unfortunately, the sources are less numerous than for income) suggest similar evolutions. See the online appendix.

7. Note, moreover, that this high level of wealth inequality, much higher than for income inequality, is also found within each age cohort. See the online appendix.

8. On this lack of transparency and the political issues it raises, see Chap. 13.

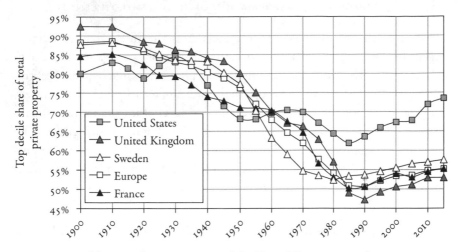

FIG. 10.4. Wealth inequality in Europe and the United States, 1900–2015

Interpretation: The top decile's share of total private property (real estate, professional, and financial assets, net of debt) was about 90 percent in Western Europe in 1900–1910 before falling to around 50–55 percent in 1980–1990, then rising again. The increase was much stronger in the United States, where the top decile's share approached 75 percent in 2010–2015, close to the 1900–1910 level. *Sources and series:* piketty.pse.ens.fr/ideology.

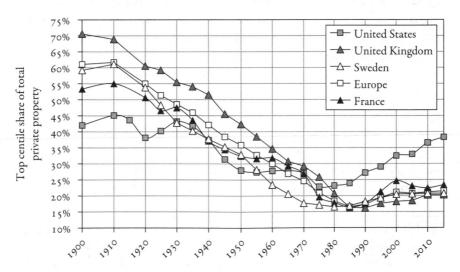

FIG. 10.5. Wealth inequality, 1900–2015: The top centile

Interpretation: The top centile's share of total private property was roughly 60 percent in Western Europe in 1900–1910 (55 percent in France, 70 percent in the United Kingdom) before falling to less than 20 percent in 1980–1990, then rising since that date. The rise of inequality was much stronger in the United States, where the top centile's share approached 40 percent in 2010–2015, close to the 1900–1910 level. *Sources and series:* piketty.pse.ens.fr/ideology.

I have called the "patrimonial middle class," that is, the fiftieth to ninetieth percentile of the wealth distribution, because the bottom 50 percent own virtually nothing). The United States might then attain the same hyperconcentration of wealth that we find in Europe in the late nineteenth and early twentieth centuries, compounded by an unprecedented level of inequality in labor income, in which case the neo-proprietarian United States could prove to be even more inegalitarian than Belle Époque Europe. But this is only one possible trajectory; as we will see, it is not impossible that new redistributive mechanisms will develop in the United States in the coming years.

The End of Ownership Society; the Stability of Wage Inequalities

As for Europe, I must emphasize the magnitude and historic significance of the deconcentration of wealth that took place between 1914 and the 1970s (Figs. 10.4–10.5). In particular, the top centile, which in 1900–1910 owned 55 percent of all private property in France, 60 percent in Sweden, and 70 percent in the United Kingdom, owned no more than 15–20 percent in any of these countries by the 1980s before rising to 20–25 percent (and perhaps, in reality, a little higher) in 2000–2020. This collapse of the share of the wealthiest is all the more striking because there was no sign that such an evolution was possible before the outbreak of World War I. In all European countries for which we have adequate wealth data, the concentration of property was extremely high throughout the nineteenth century and until 1914, with a slight upward trend and, at the end, an accelerating rate of increase in the decades prior to World War I.[9] The same is true for countries where we have income tax data that allow us to study the final decades of the nineteenth century: for example, Germany, in which from 1870 to 1914 we find a growing concentration of total income due to income derived from capital.[10] Wages did begin to rise slowly in the final decades of the nineteenth century and the first decade of the twen-

---

9. This was true of France, the United Kingdom, and Sweden. See Figs. 4.1–4.2 and Figs. 5.4–5.5. Available data for the United States in the nineteenth century are not perfect, but what we have also suggests a rising trend, albeit with the peculiarity that the composition of wealth changed markedly after the Civil War and the disappearance of slave wealth in the South. See the online appendix.

10. See C. Bartels, "Top Incomes in Germany, 1871–2014," *Journal of Economic History,* 2019; F. Dell, *L'Allemagne inégale. Inégalités de revenus et de patrimoine en Allemagne, dynamique d'accumulation du capital et taxation de Bismarck à Schröder 1870–2005* (EHESS, 2008).

tieth, which is a positive sign compared with the virtually total stagnation (or regression) of wages from 1800 to 1860 or so. Moreover, this dark era of industrialization contributed to the rise of socialist movements.[11] In any case, inequality remained quite high in 1870–1914, and the concentration of wealth and capital income even increased up to World War I.[12]

More generally, all signs are that the concentration of wealth was also very high in the eighteenth century and earlier within the framework of trifunctional society, where property rights often overlapped with regalian rights exercised by clerical and noble elites. Some research suggests that wealth inequality was on the rise in Europe between the fifteenth and eighteenth centuries and that the trend then continued in the nineteenth century as property rights were strengthened (as indicated by French estate data, along with other data from Britain and Sweden). Comparisons with periods prior to the nineteenth century are full of uncertainty, however, partly because the available data usually pertain to specific cities or regions and do not always cover the entire population of the poor and partly because the very notion of property was then associated

---

11. On wage stagnation prior to 1860 and on the strong resulting increase in the profit share of output, see R. Allen, "Engels' Pause: Technical Change, Capital Accumulation, and Inequality in the British Industrial Revolution," *Explorations in Economic History*, 2009. See also T. Piketty, *Capital in the Twenty-First Century*, trans. A. Goldhammer (Harvard University Press, 2014), pp. 7–11 and figs. 6.1–6.2. Many works attest to the intensification of labor and the deterioration of living conditions (as measured, for instance, by the height of recruits) during the first phase of the Industrial Revolution. See S. Nicholas and R. Steckel, "Heights and Living Standards of English Workers during the Early Years of Industrialization," *Journal of Economic History*, 1991. See also J. De Vries, "The Industrial Revolution and the Industrious Revolution," *Journal of Economic History*, 1994; H. J. Voth, "Time and Work in Eighteenth-Century London," *Journal of Economic History*, 1998.

12. The complex reality of the period 1870–1914 (with rising real wages but also increasing income and wealth inequality) helps us to gain a better understanding of the violent controversies that raged among European socialists in the period 1890–1910, especially in the Social Democratic Party of Germany (SPD), where Eduard Bernstein's revisionist theses (which challenged the Marxist theory of stagnating wages and ineluctable revolution) confronted the orthodox line of Karl Kautsky and Rosa Luxembourg (who castigated the reformism of Bernstein, a man prepared to collaborate with the regime and even become vice president of the Reichstag). From today's vantage, it appears that the wage increase was real (though modest) but that Bernstein was unduly optimistic about the diffusion of property and reduction of inequality.

with legal and jurisdictional privileges that are hard to quantify. In any case, the sources, though imperfect, indicate levels of wealth inequality in the fifteenth to eighteenth centuries significantly higher than those observed in the twentieth century.[13]

The decreasing concentration of wealth in the twentieth century was thus a major historical novelty, the importance of which cannot be overstated. Admittedly, wealth remained highly unequally distributed. But for the first time in the history of modern societies, a significant share of total wealth (several dozen percent and sometimes as much as half) was owned by social groups in the bottom 90 percent of the distribution.[14] People in the new property-owning strata might own their own homes or small businesses but did not have enough to live on income from their property alone; their wealth complemented their labor, which was their main source of income. The wealth was simply a sign of accomplishment, a symbol of status achieved through hard work. By contrast, the decline of the share of the wealthiest households, and in particular the collapse of the top centile (whose share was roughly divided by three over the course of the twentieth century in Europe), meant that there were many fewer people able to live on their rents, dividends, and interest alone. What happened was thus a transformation of the nature of property itself and, simultaneously, of its social significance. What was even more striking was that this process of diffusion of property and renewal of elites also coincided with an acceleration of economic growth, which had never before been as rapid as in the second half of the twentieth century. We need to understand this better.

---

13. See esp. G. Alfani's work on the evolution of wealth inequality in Italy and Holland between 1500 and 1800 (with top decile shares of 60–80 percent of total wealth and apparently rising, partly owing to the regressivity of the tax system). See esp. G. Alfani and M. Di Tullio, *The Lion's Share: Inequality and the Rise of the Fiscal State in Preindustrial Europe* (Cambridge University Press, 2019). See also the online appendix.

14. Archaeological research (including the work of Monique Borgerhoff Mulder) suggests that wealth concentration was limited in hunter-gatherer societies, where there was little wealth to accumulate and pass on compared with societies that arose after the invention of agriculture (in which property tended to become concentrated and quickly reached levels comparable to those observed in Europe in the fifteenth to eighteenth centuries). These results are fragile and apply only to very small societies, but they confirm in a way the historical uniqueness of the deconcentration of property that took place in the twentieth century. See the online appendix.

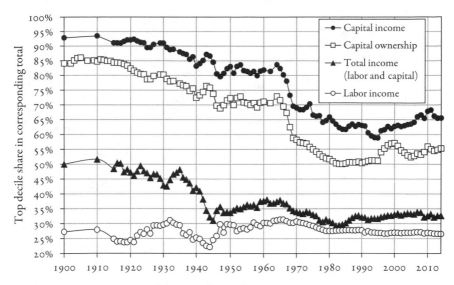

FIG. 10.6. Income versus wealth inequality in France, 1900–2015

Interpretation: In 1900–1910, the 10 percent with the most capital income (rents, profits, dividends, interest, etc.) received about 90–95 percent of the total income from capital; the 10 percent who received the most income from labor (wages, nonwage remuneration, pensions) received 25–30 percent of total labor income. The reduction of inequality in the twentieth century came entirely from deconcentration of property, while inequality of labor income changed little. *Sources and series:* piketty.pse.ens.fr/ideology.

Note, moreover, that this deconcentration of property (and therefore of the income derived from property) is the major reason for the reduction of income inequality in Europe over the course of the twentieth century. In the case of France, for example, we find that inequality of labor income (including both wages and nonwage income) did not decrease significantly in the twentieth century. If we ignore short- and medium-term variations, the share of the top decile has fluctuated between 25 and 30 percent of total labor income, and only the collapse of the inequality of capital income can explain the decrease of overall income inequality (Fig. 10.6)[15] The same is true if we look at the top centile share of labor income, which fluctuated between 5 and 8 percent in

---

15. An additional factor to consider is the decrease of the share of capital income in national income, from 35–40 percent in the late nineteenth and early twentieth centuries, to 20–25 percent in 1950–1970, and to 25–30 percent in 2000–2020. This evolution is largely the result of changes in the balance of power between capital and labor and in the negotiating capacities of both sides. See Piketty, *Capital in the Twenty-First Century,* chap. 6, and the online appendix.

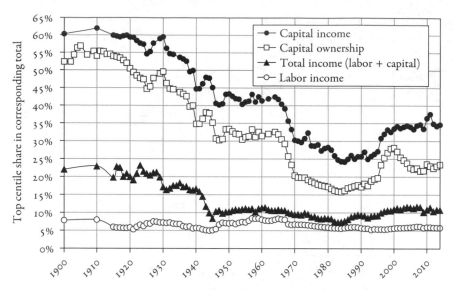

FIG. 10.7. Income versus wealth in the top centile in France, 1900–2015

Interpretation: In 1900–1910, the top centile of capital income (rents, profits, dividends, interest, etc.) claimed roughly 60 percent of the total; the top 1 percent of capital owners (real estate, professional and financial assets, net of debt) held roughly 55 percent of the total; the top centile of total income (labor and capital) received roughly 20–25 percent of the total; the top centile of labor income (wages, nonwage compensation, pensions) received roughly 5–10 percent of the total. Over the long run, the reduction of inequality is explained entirely by the deconcentration of wealth. *Sources and series:* piketty.pse.ens.fr/ideology.

France in the twentieth century with no clear trend, whereas the corresponding share of capital income fell, leading to a decrease in the top centile share of total income (Fig. 10.7).

One should be careful, however, not to exaggerate the stability of labor income inequality over the last century. If we look beyond the monetary dimensions of labor income and consider changes in the status of workers, stability of employment, social and union rights, and especially access to fundamental goods such as health, training, and pensions, we find that inequalities with respect to labor—particularly between different classes of workers—significantly decreased over the course of the twentieth century (I will come back to this). Nevertheless, from a strict monetary standpoint, which is of some significance in determining living conditions and power relations between individuals, inequalities of labor income remained fairly stable, and only the deconcentration of wealth and the income derived from it resulted in a reduction of overall income inequality. Available data for other European countries lead to similar conclusions.[16]

Decomposing the Decline of Private Property (1914–1950)

Let us now try to understand the mechanisms responsible for these changes, especially the disappearance of European ownership societies. Apart from the deconcentration of wealth, which stretched out over much of the twentieth century (from 1914 to the 1970s), it is important to note that the most sudden and striking phenomenon was the abrupt collapse of the total value of private property (relative to national income), which took place quite rapidly between 1914 and 1945–1950.

In the late nineteenth and early twentieth centuries, private capital was flourishing. The market value of all real estate, professional, and financial assets (net of debt) held by private owners fluctuated between seven and eight years of national income in France and the United Kingdom and around six years in Germany (Fig. 10.8). These sums included assets held abroad in in the colonies and elsewhere. The Belle Époque (1880–1914) was the high watermark of international investment, which on the eve of World War I surpassed the equivalent of a year's national income for France and nearly two years of national income for the United Kingdom, compared with less than half a year for Germany—still quite a lot in comparative historical terms but not all that much by contemporary European norms.[17]

Note, moreover, that the difference between the impressive international investments held by citizens of the two great colonial powers, France and Britain, and more limited German foreign holdings is roughly the same as the difference in total wealth, which illustrates the importance of the link between proprietarianism, colonialism, and more generally, the internationalization of economic and property relations. Apart from foreign assets, private property at the time breaks down into two halves of roughly comparable size: on the one hand, farmland and residential real estate (with the share of farmland declining considerably over time), and on the other hand, professional property (factories, warehouses, etc.) and financial assets (stocks, private and government bonds, and investments of all kinds).

---

16. See the online appendix.
17. See Fig. 7.9.

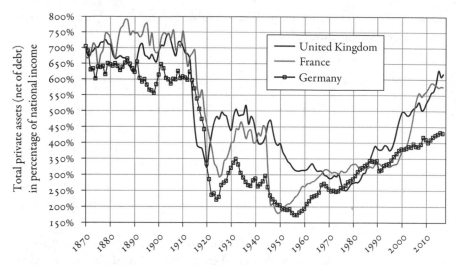

FIG. 10.8. Private property in Europe, 1870–2020

Interpretation: The market value of private property (real estate, professional and financial assets, net of debt) was close to six to eight years of national income in Western Europe from 1870 to 1914 before collapsing in the period 1914–1950 and stabilizing at two to three years of national income in 1950–1970, then rising again to five to six years in 2000–2010. *Sources and series:* piketty.pse.ens.fr/ideology.

To be clear from the outset, this indicator—the ratio of the market value of private property to national income—tells us nothing about wealth inequality. It is nevertheless useful for comparing the overall importance of private property and property relations in different societies across time and space. Of course, a high wealth-income ratio may indicate that large investments were made in the past to accumulate productive capital: clearing and improvement of land; construction of homes, buildings, and factories; and accumulation of machinery and equipment. In practice, a high ratio may also attest to the scope of opportunities for wealth appropriation that the existing legal and political regime affords to the owners of private property: colonial riches, natural resources, and patents and intellectual property. The market value of property reflects expected future gains and profits of all kinds. For a given unit of productive capital, what determines its value as property is the solidity of the rights guaranteed to its owners by the political system, together with the belief that those rights will be honored in the future. In any event, this indicator measures, to a certain extent, private property's influence in a given society: a low wealth-income ratio means that in principle a few years of saving should be enough to catch up with the current owners of property (or at any rate to achieve an average level of wealth). By contrast, a high ratio indicates that the gulf between owners and nonowners is more difficult to overcome.[18]

In this case, it is striking to note that the high levels of wealth observed in the ownership societies of the Belle Époque (1880–1914) are matched, to a first approximation, throughout the period 1700–1914. Many estimates of the total value of property were carried out in the late seventeenth and early eighteenth centuries, especially in the United Kingdom and France, by William Petty; Gregory King; Sébastien Le Prestre de Vauban; and Pierre Le Pesant, sieur de Boisguilbert; these were later refined during the French Revolution (by Antoine Lavoisier in particular) and then, throughout the nineteenth century, by numerous authors (including Patrick Colquhoun, Robert Giffen, Alfred de Foville, and William Colson). If we compare and contrast all these sources, we find that the total value of private property was generally six to eight years of national income throughout the eighteenth and nineteenth centuries, which is extremely high compared with later periods.[19] The composition of property was totally transformed over this period (as the importance of farmland declined and that of industrial and international assets increased), but property owners continued to thrive without interruption. The novels of Jane Austen and Honoré de Balzac, set in the period 1790–1830, illustrate the plasticity of property to perfection. It mattered little whether a fortune consisted of a landed estate, foreign assets, or government bonds, provided that it was solid enough and yielded the expected income and the social life that went with it.[20] Nearly a century later, in 1913, when Marcel Proust published *Swann's Way,* property had again changed its identity but remained just as indestructible, regardless of whether it took the form of a portfolio of financial assets or the Grand Hotel of Cabourg where the novelist liked to spend his summers.

---

18. If the ratio of private capital (measured at market value) and national income is two, then a savings rate of 10 percent applied to the average income is enough to become an average property owner after twenty years. If the ratio is eight, it would take eighty years. To get an idea of orders of magnitude, the national income of the United Kingdom and France was about 35,000 euros a year per adult in the 2010s; hence the ratio of five to six shown in Fig. 10.8 corresponds to average wealth per adult of roughly 200,000 euros. In subsequent chapters I will return to the actual structure of wealth (see esp. Fig. 11.17).

19. See the online appendix and Piketty, *Capital in the Twenty-First Century,* figs. 3.1–3.2.

20. See Chaps. 4–5.

All this would change very quickly, however. The total value of private property literally collapsed during World War I and in the early 1920s before recovering slightly later in the decade and collapsing again in the Great Depression, World War II, and the immediate postwar years, to the point where private property represented the equivalent of only two years of national income in France and Germany in 1950. The fall was a little less pronounced in the United Kingdom but still dramatic: British private property was worth a little over three years of national income in the 1950s, compared with more than seven in 1910. In every case the value of private property had been divided by a factor of two to three within the space of a few decades (Fig. 10.8).

To explain this collapse, we must take several factors into account. I presented a detailed quantitative breakdown in previous works, so here I will simply summarize the main conclusions, reserving more detailed discussion for the political-ideological context in which these changes took place.[21] Note that the many sources available for estimating the evolution of property in different periods (records of real estate and stock prices, censuses of buildings, land, and firms, etc.), despite their deficiencies, are good enough to clearly establish the principal orders of magnitude. In particular, physical destruction of houses, buildings, factories and other property during the two world wars, although considerable (especially due to the mass bombings conducted in 1944–1945, a shorter period than the fighting of 1914–1918 but over a wider geographic area and with much more destructive technology), can explain only part of the loss of property: between a quarter and a third in France and Germany (which is a lot), and at most a few percent in the United Kingdom.

The rest of the fall was due to two sets of factors of comparable magnitude, which we will analyze one at a time. Each explains a little more than a third of the total decrease in the ratio of private property to national income in France and German (and nearly half in the United Kingdom). The first set of factors includes expropriations and nationalizations and, more generally, policies aimed explicitly at reducing the value of private property and the power of

---

21. See Piketty, *Capital in the Twenty-First Century,* chaps. 3–5. For the most complete series breakdowns, see T. Piketty and G. Zucman, "Capital Is Back: Wealth-Income Ratios in Rich Countries, 1700–2010," *Quarterly Journal of Economics,* 2014, and the corresponding appendices. This work is based on a systematic examination of various sources and estimates of the total and structure of private and public property since the beginning of the eighteenth century. Note, too, that the fall indicated in Fig. 10.8 concerns not only the European countries but also Japan and to a lesser degree the United States (which started from a lower level).

property owners over the rest of society (for example, rent control and power sharing with worker representatives in firms). The other set of factors has to do with the low level of private investment and returns on those investments in the period 1914–1950, largely because much of private saving was lent to governments to pay for the wars, in return for bonds which lost most of their value due to inflation and other factors.

Expropriations, Nationalizations-Sanctions, and the "Mixed Economy"

Let us begin with expropriations. One striking example involves foreign (mainly French) investment in Russia. Before World War I, the alliance between the French Republic and the Russian Empire found material embodiment in huge bond issues by the Russian government and many private companies (such as railroads). Newspaper campaigns (often subsidized by bribes from the Tsarist regime) persuaded wealthy French investors of the solidity of the Russian ally and the safety of Russian bonds. After the Bolshevik Revolution of 1917, the Soviets decided to repudiate all these debts, which in its eyes had only prolonged the existence of the Tsarist regime (which was not entirely false). The United Kingdom, United States, and France sent troops to northern Russia in 1918–1920 in the hope of quelling the revolution, to no avail.

At the other end of the period in question, Nasser's decision to nationalize the Suez Canal in 1956 led to the expropriation of British and French shareholders who had owned the canal and collected dividends and royalties from its operation ever since its inauguration in 1869. Obedient to old habits, the United Kingdom and France dispatched troops to recover their assets. But the United States, worried about driving countries of the global south into the hands of the Soviets (particularly newly independent countries, which were quite likely to nationalize or expropriate property, especially that of the former colonial masters), chose to abandon its allies. Under pressure from both the Soviets and the Americans, the two former colonial powers were obliged to withdraw their troops and recognize what was henceforth apparent to everyone— namely, that the old proprietarian colonial world had ceased to exist.

The expropriations of foreign assets illustrate to perfection the political-ideological shift that took place in the world in the first half of the twentieth century. Between 1914 and 1950 it was the very concept of property that changed due to the effects of war and social and political conflict. Existing property rights, which had seemed unquestionably solid in 1914, had by 1950 given way to a more social and instrumental concept of property, according to which the purpose of productive capital was to further the cause of economic development, social justice, and/or national independence. Expropriations played an important role not only in reducing inequalities among countries (as former colonies and debtor nations reclaimed ownership of themselves) but also in reducing inequalities within Europe itself, since foreign investments were among the favorite assets of the rich, as we learned from our examination of Paris estate records.[22] The particularly high level of income inequality in the United Kingdom and France before World War I—compared with Germany, for example—can in large part be explained by the amount of income derived from foreign investments by wealthy British and French citizens. In this respect, the domestic inequality regimes one sees in Europe were closely related to the structure of inequality at the international and colonial level.

Note that there were also waves of nationalization (in some cases veritable nationalization-expropriations) in Europe to a degree that varied from county to country. In general, faith in private capitalism was strongly shaken by the economic crisis of the 1930s and the ensuing cataclysms. The Great Depression, triggered by the Wall Street crash of 1929, struck rich countries with unprecedented force. By 1932, a quarter of the industrial labor force was unemployed in the United States, Germany, United Kingdom, and France. The traditional laissez-faire doctrine of government nonintervention in the economy, which prevailed in all countries in the nineteenth century and to a large extent until the early 1930s, was durably discredited. A shift in favor of interventionism took place almost everywhere. Governments and people naturally demanded explanations from financial and economic elites that had enriched themselves while leading the world to the brink of the abyss. People began to imagine forms of "mixed economy" involving some degree of public ownership of firms alongside more traditional forms of private property or, at the very least, stronger public regulation and oversight of the financial system and of private capitalism more generally.

In France and other countries, this general suspicion of private capitalism was reinforced in 1945 by the fact that a substantial segment of the economic elite was suspected of collaboration with the Germans and of indecent profiteering during the Occupation (1940–1944). It was in this electrifying climate that the first wave of nationalizations took place during the Liberation: these involved mainly the banking sector, coal mines, and the automobile industry,

---

22. See Table 4.1.

including the famous "nationalization-sanction" of Renault. Louis Renault, the owner of the automobile firm, was arrested as a collaborator in September 1944, and his factories were seized by the provisional government and nationalized in January 1945.[23] Another type of sanction on capital was the national solidarity tax established by the law of August 15, 1945. This was a special progressive tax on both capital and gains made during the Occupation, a one-time tax whose extremely high rate was yet another shock to the fortunes of the individuals concerned. The tax was a lump-sum payment based on estimated wealth as of June 4, 1945, with rates as high as 20 percent for the largest fortunes, supplemented by an exceptional tax on capital gains between 1940 and 1945 at rates as high as 100 percent for those with the largest gains.[24]

In Europe these postwar nationalizations played an important role, resulting in very large public sectors in many countries in the period 1950–1970. In Chapter 11 we will consider the way in which Germany, Sweden, and most other northern European countries developed new forms of industrial organization and corporate governance after World War II. More specifically, the power of shareholders on boards of directors was reduced, while the power of employee representatives was increased (along with the power of regional governments and other public stakeholders in certain cases). This experience is particularly interesting because it illustrates the gap between the market value of capital and its social value. The record shows that these policies led to lower stock-market valuations of firms in these countries (which continue to this day), without hurting business or economic growth—quite the opposite: greater worker involvement in the long-term strategies of German and Swedish firms seems rather to have increased their productivity.[25]

23. C. Andrieu, L. Le Van, and A. Prost, *Les Nationalisations de la Libération: de l'utopie au compromis* (Fondations nationale des sciences politique, 1987), and T. Piketty, *Top Incomes in France in the Twentieth Century* (Harvard University Press, 2018), pp. 130–131.

24. In practice, because of inflation (prices having more than tripled between 1940 and 1945), this was tantamount to a 100 percent tax on all who had not lost enough during the war. For André Philip, an SFIO member of General Charles de Gaulle's provisional government, it was inevitable that this exceptional tax would hurt "those who had not grown richer and perhaps even those who had grown poorer in the sense that their wealth did not increase as rapidly as the general price level but who had still retained their wealth at a time when so many French people lost everything." See *L'année Politique, 1945–1945* (Éditions du Grand Siècle), p. 159.

25. I will come back to these issues in Chap. 11. Note that if one were to use book value (rather than market value) to measure the assets of German firms, their value

Finally, in addition to nationalizations and new forms of industrial power sharing, between 1914 and 1950 most European countries implemented a variety of policies for regulating real estate and financial markets, which had the effect of limiting the rights of property owners and reducing the market value of their assets. A case in point involves the development of rent control, which began during World War I. The scope of rent control expanded after World War II to the point where the real value of French rents in 1950 fell to one-fifth of what it had been in 1914, resulting in a comparable fall in the price of real estate.[26] These policies also reflected a profound shift in attitude regarding the legitimacy of private property and of inequalities stemming from property relations. In a period of very high inflation, unknown before 1914, in which real wages often had not returned to prewar levels, it seemed unreasonable that landlords should be allowed to continue to enrich themselves on the backs of workers and others of modest means who had just returned from the front. It was in this climate that various countries began to regulate rents, increase tenant rights, and enact protections against eviction; leases were extended, rent was fixed over long periods, and tenants were given preferential options to purchase their apartments, in some cases at a discount. At their most ambitious, such measures were similar in spirit to agrarian reform (discussed previously in regard to Ireland and Spain), where the goal was to break up the largest parcels of land and facilitate their purchase by the people who actually farmed them.[27] Broadly speaking, quite apart from any additional regulations, low real estate prices in the period 1950–1980 naturally facilitated access to ownership and spread wealth to new strata of society.[28]

---

would equal (or slightly exceed) the value of French and British firms in the period 1970–2020 in Fig. 10.8. By contrast, the very large increase in the stock market value of English and British firms since 1980 is large a consequence of the increased bargaining power of shareholders (and not of real investments). See the online appendix. See also Piketty, *Capital in the Twenty-First Century,* chap. 5, pp. 187–191, esp. fig. 5.6.

26. In France, the ratio of the rent index to the overall price index, with a base of one hundred in 1914, fell to around thirty to forty in 1919–1921 and ten to twenty in 1948–1950 before slowly rising thereafter to seventy in 1970–1980 and then back to one hundred in 2000–2010. See Piketty, *Top Incomes in France in the Twentieth Century,* p. 80, fig. 1.9.

27. See Chap. 5.

28. Note that the low value of German real estate (due in part to various rent control measures) also helps to explain the gaps observed in 2000–2020 in Fig. 10.8. More generally, if one could measure in perfectly comparable ways the social value of the capital stock (as opposed to its market value), in particular by taking into

Private Saving, Public Debt, and Inflation

Let us turn now to the role played by low private investment as well as inflation and public borrowing in the fall of private wealth between 1914 and 1950. Note first that throughout much of this period—not only the war years but also the 1930s—investment in low-priority civilian sectors was so feeble that it often failed to cover the cost of replacing worn equipment.[29] In the period 1914–1945 most private saving was invested in the growing public debt stemming from the costs of war and preparing for war.

In 1914, on the eve of World War I, public debt was equal to roughly 60–70 percent of national income in the United Kingdom, France, and Germany and less than 30 percent in the United States. After World War II, in 1945–1950, public debt attained 150 percent of national income in the United States, 180 percent in Germany, 270 percent in France, and 310 percent in the United Kingdom (Fig. 10.9). Note, moreover, that the total would have been even higher if part of the debt incurred in World War I had not been drowned out by inflation in the 1920s, especially in Germany and to a lesser degree in France. To finance this kind of increase in the public debt, savers in each country had to devote most of their savings not to their usual investments (in real estate, industry, or foreign assets) but almost exclusively to the purchase of treasury bonds and other public debt instruments. Wealthy people in Britain, France, and Germany gradually sold a large fraction of their foreign assets to lend the amounts needed by their governments, at times perhaps out of patriotism but also because they saw a good investment opportunity. In theory, their principal and interest were guaranteed by the full faith and credit of their own governments, and those same governments had always made good on their promises in the past. In some cases the loans were quasi-obligatory, particularly

---

account the effect of power-sharing policies on stock market values and of rent control on real estate value, it is likely that the levels of accumulation indicated in Fig. 10.8 for the period 2000–2020 would surpass those of 1880–1914. See the online appendix.

29. In other words, investment net of depreciation (the difference between raw investment and the depreciation of capital) was often negative. Note that in view of the growth of national income (which was low but not zero between 1913 and 1950), a steady and relatively large flow of net investment was necessary to maintain a high ratio of private capital to national income. For example, with a growth of 1 percent a year, a flow of 8 percent is required to maintain a capital/income ratio of eight. See Piketty, *Capital in the Twenty-First Century*, chap. 3.

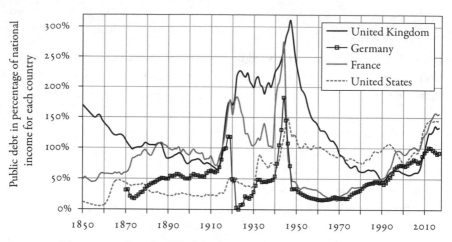

FIG. 10.9. The vicissitudes of public debt, 1850–2020

Interpretation: Public debt increased sharply after the two world wars to between 150 and 300 percent of national income in 1945–1950. It then fell sharply in Germany and France (owing to debt cancellations and high inflation) and more slowly in the United Kingdom and United States (moderate inflation, growth). Public assets (notably real estate and financial) varied less strongly over time and generally stood at about 100 percent of national income. *Sources and series:* piketty.pse.ens.fr/ideology.

in wartime, as governments required banks to hold large quantities of public debt and took steps to place a ceiling on interest rates.

Things did not turn out well: the private savings and proceeds of assets sales that investors placed in government bonds would soon melt away as quickly as snow on a sunny day as the "full faith and credit" that governments had promised bond owners gave way to other priorities. In practice, governments resorted to printing banknotes, and prices soared. During the eighteenth and nineteenth centuries, inflation had been close to zero (Fig. 10.10). The value of currency had been tied to its gold and silver content, and the purchasing power of a given quantity of precious metal remained virtually unchanged. This was true of both the pound sterling and the gold franc, which during the French Revolution supplanted the Ancien Régime's *livre tournois* but retained the same parity with gold, remaining unchanged from 1726 to 1914—proof, if proof were needed, of the continuity of the proprietarian regime. The equivalence of currency, whether livre or franc, with gold was so strong that early-nineteenth-century French novelists used both measures to delineate the boundaries between social classes, often passing from one to the other without noticing.[30]

---

30. See Piketty, *Capital in the Twenty-First Century*, pp. 102–109.

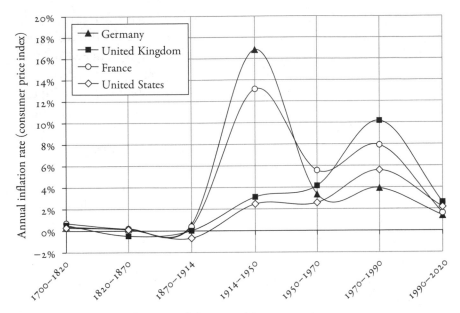

FIG. 10.10. Inflation in Europe and the United States, 1700–2020

Interpretation: Inflation was virtually zero in the eighteenth and nineteenth centuries before rising in the twentieth century. Since 1990 it has been on the order of 2 percent per year. Inflation was particularly strong in Germany and France from 1914 to 1950 and to a lesser degree in the United Kingdom, France, and the United States in the 1970s. *Note:* Average German inflation of roughly 17 percent from 1914 to 1950 omits the hyperinflation of 1923. *Sources and series:* piketty.pse.ens.fr/ideology.

World War I almost immediately put an end to this long period of monetary stability. As early as August 1914, the principal belligerents suspended convertibility of their currency into gold. Attempts to restore the gold standard in the 1920s did not survive the Depression.[31] All told, from 1914 to 1950 inflation averaged 13 percent a year in France (equivalent to a hundredfold increase in the price level) and 17 percent in Germany (a threehundredfold price increase).[32] In the United Kingdom and United States, which were less affected by the two world wars and less destabilized politi-

---

31. The gold standard introduced after World War II fared little better: established in 1946, it ended in 1971 when the convertibility of the dollar into gold was suspended.

32. This calculation excludes the year 1923 for Germany (during which prices multiplied by 100 million) and thus measures average inflation in the periods 1914–1922 and 1924–1950.

cally, the rate of inflation was significantly lower: barely 3 percent a year on average from 1914 to 1950. This nevertheless represented a threefold price increase after two centuries of near stability. In the case of the United Kingdom, however, this was not enough to eliminate the impressive public debt taken on during the wars, which explains why the British debt remained high in the period 1950–1970—until inflation of 10–20 percent in the 1970s finally melted it, too, away.

In France and Germany, the elimination of the debt was much more expeditious. By the early 1950s the once-enormous public debts of both countries had fallen below 30 percent of national income (Fig. 10.9). In France, inflation exceeded 50 percent a year for four consecutive years, from 1945 to 1948. The public debt automatically dwindled to nothing, as inflation proved to be a far more radical remedy than the exceptional tax on private wealth levied in 1945. The problem was that inflation also wiped out millions of small savers, leaving many of France's elderly in a state of endemic poverty in the 1950s.[33]

In Germany, where the hyperinflation of the 1920s had seriously destabilized social relations and turned the entire country upside down, there was greater wariness of the social consequences of rising prices, so more sophisticated methods of accelerated debt reduction were tried in 1949–1952. More specifically, the young Federal Republic of Germany established a variety of progressive and exceptional taxes on private wealth, which some Germans were required to pay for decades—in some cases until the 1980s.[34] Finally, West Germany benefited when the London Conference of 1953 suspended its foreign debt, which was later definitively canceled when Germany was reunified in 1991. Along with other measures, such as the exceptional taxes levied in 1952, this debt nullification enabled West Germany to concentrate on reconstruction in

33. To be sure, financial assets accumulated in the 1920s had already been largely wiped out by the collapse of the stock market. Nevertheless, the inflation of 1945–1948 came as an additional shock. The response was the *vieillesse minimum* (minimum old-age benefit) created in 1956 for the impoverished elderly and the development of old-age pensions (created in 1945 but gradually increased).

34. High progressive taxes on private property were also levied until the 1980s under so-called Lastenausgleich (burden-sharing) programs intended to compensate refugees from the east for losses incurred when borders changed. See M. L. Hughes, *Shouldering the Burdens of Defeat: West Germany and the Reconstruction of Social Justice* (University of North Carolina Press, 1999).

the 1950s and 1960s, substantially increasing the amounts available for social spending and investment in infrastructure.[35]

Liquidating the Past, Building Justice: Exceptional Taxes on Private Capital

It is worth noting that exceptional taxes on private property had been applied even earlier, after World War I, to reduce public debt in a number of European countries, including Italy, Czechoslovakia, Austria, and Hungary in the period 1919–1923, with rates up to 50 percent on the largest fortunes. One of the largest and most remunerative such taxes was the levy imposed in Japan in 1946–1947, with rates as high as 90 percent on the largest portfolios. France's national solidarity tax of 1945 also falls under this head, although its revenues went into the general budget (rather than being earmarked specifically for debt reduction).[36]

Compared with inflation, which shrinks everyone's savings by the same proportion, rich and poor alike, the advantage of exceptional taxes on private property is that they afford much greater latitude for distributing the burden, partly because the rate can vary with the amount of wealth (usually with an exemption for the smallest fortunes, with rates on the order of 5–10 percent for medium-sized fortunes and 30–50 percent or more for the largest fortunes); and partly because they are generally applied to private assets of all types, including buildings, land, and professional and financial assets. In contrast, inflation is a regressive tax on wealth. Those who hold only cash or bank deposits are hit the hardest, whereas the wealthy, most of whose assets are in real estate, professional equipment, or financial portfolios largely escape the effects of rising prices, unless other measures such as rent controls and asset price controls are also implemented. As for financial assets, bonds and other fixed-income

---

35. See G. Galofré-Vila, C. Meissner, M. McKee, and D. Stuckler, "The Economic Consequences of the 1953 London Debt Agreement," *European Review of Economic History*, 2018.

36. There were also debates around such measures in France and the United Kingdom in 1919–1923, but nothing came of them. For more of an overview of various experiments with taxation of private capital to reduce public debt, see B. Eichengreen, "The Capital Levy in Theory and Practice," in *Public Debt Management: Theory and History*, ed. R. Dornbusch and M. Draghi (Cambridge University Press, 1990). On these debates, see also J. Hicks, U. Hicks, and L. Rostas, *The Taxation of War Wealth* (Oxford University Press, 1941).

investments—beginning with government bonds themselves—are hit by inflation, but stocks, shares of partnerships, and other such investments, which are favored by the wealthiest, often escape the inflation tax because their prices tend to rise with the general price level. More generally, the problem with inflation is that it apportions gains and losses in a relatively arbitrary fashion, depending on who rebalances his or her portfolio at the right moment. Inflation is the sign of a society that is dealing with a serious distributive conflict: it wants to unburden itself of debts incurred in the past, but it cannot openly debate how the required sacrifices should be apportioned and prefers to rely on the vagaries of rising prices and speculation. The obvious risk of doing so is that a widespread sense of injustice will be created.

For this reason, it is not surprising that so many countries resorted to exceptional taxes on private property to reduce the debts incurred in World Wars I and II. I do not mean to idealize these efforts, which were carried out by governments ill-prepared for the task at a time when the information technologies we possess today did not exist. Nevertheless, these taxes worked and helped rapidly stifle significant public debates and pave the way for successful social reconstruction and economic growth in countries like Japan and Germany. In the German case, it is clear that the exceptional taxes on private wealth that were levied in 1949–1952 and continued into the 1980s were a much better way of reducing public debt than the hyperinflation of the 1920s, not only from an economic point of view but also from a social and democratic one.

Apart from the technical and administrative aspects of these measures, it is also important to emphasize the political-ideological transformations they reveal. One can of course find many examples of public debt cancellation in history from the most ancient times. But it was not until the twentieth century that progressive taxes were applied to capital on such a scale and in such a sophisticated manner. In medieval and modern Europe, sovereigns occasionally altered the metallic content of money to alleviate their debts.[37] In the late eighteenth century, at the time of the French Revolution, there was open debate about the wisdom of instituting a progressive tax on both income and wealth;

---

37. It is estimated that the gold and silver content of European coins was on average divided by a factor of 2.5–3 between 1400 and 1800, which corresponds to an inflation rate of 0.2 percent over 400 years, which in practice took the form of a series of phases of price stability punctuated by sudden devaluations of a few dozen percent. See C. Reinhart and K. Rogoff, *This Time Is Different: Eight Centuries of Financial Folly* (Princeton University Press, 2009), chap. 11.

top earners were briefly forced to lend the state up to 70 percent of their income in 1793–1794. In retrospect, this system looks like an anticipation of the one that would be adopted in many countries after the two world wars.[38] It was nevertheless insufficient. Because the Ancien Régime had failed to tax its privileged class early enough, it had accumulated a significant amount of debt, on the order of one year of national income, or even a year and a half if one includes the value of charges and offices, which was a way for the state to satisfy its immediate needs for cash in exchange for revenues to be extracted later from the population and hence was a form of public debt. In the end, the Revolution established a tax system that ended the privileges of the nobility and clergy but was strictly proportional and renounced the ambition to move toward a progressive tax. The public debt was significantly reduced, less by exceptional taxes than by the "*banqueroute des deux tiers*" (a two-thirds debt write-down decreed in 1797) and depreciation of the *assignats* (paper money issued by the revolutionary government), which in effect inflated prices, leaving the state with very little debt in 1815 (less than 20 percent of national income).[39]

Between 1815 and 1914, the countries of Europe thus embarked on a long phase of sacralization of private property and monetary stability, during which the very idea of not repaying a debt was considered totally taboo and unthinkable. Of course, the European powers often had rude manners, particularly when it came to imposing military tributes on one another or, more commonly, on the rest of the world. Once a debt was established, however—whether it was the debt imposed on the French by the allied monarchies in 1815 or by Prussia in 1871 or the debts owed by the Chinese Empire or the Ottoman Empire or Morocco to the United Kingdom and France—it was then essential for the operation of the system that the amount be repaid in full, at its equivalent in gold, or else military action would follow. The countries of Europe might well threaten one another with war and disburse significant amounts to prepare for conflict, but once there was a debt to be repaid, hostilities ceased and proprietarian powers agreed that debtors must respect the property rights of creditors. For example, when the Turks attempted to default on their debt in 1875, European high finance joined with governments in a coalition whose

---

38. See Table 3.1.
39. The subsequent increase in public debt between 1814 and 1914 was due mainly to exceptional measures such as war indemnities and the *milliard des émigrés* (emigré billion). See Chap. 4. See also Piketty, *Capital in the Twenty-First Century*, pp. 131–134.

purpose was to force the Ottomans to resume payments and sign the Treaty of Berlin, which they did in 1878. Defaults were still relatively common in the eighteenth century: in 1752, for example, Prussia refused to repay the Silesian loan to the British. But they became increasingly rare.[40] Defaults ceased altogether after the repudiations of the French Revolution, which, after years of hesitation, led de facto to proprietarian monetary stability in Europe.

The case of the United Kingdom is particularly significant in this regard. Its public debt exceeded 200 percent of national income in 1815 at the end of the Napoleonic wars. The country, which was of course governed at the time by a tiny group of wealthy men who stood to benefit directly, chose to devote almost a third of British tax revenues (which, thanks to the predominance of indirect taxes in this period, came mostly out of the pockets of modest and middle-class taxpayers) to the repayment of the principal and especially the interest on the huge debt (for the benefit of those who had lent money to pay for the wars, who mostly belonged to the top centile of the wealth distribution). What this shows is that it is of course technically possible to reduce such a sizable debt by running primary budget surpluses. In the United Kingdom from 1815 to 1914 the primary budget service fluctuated between 2 and 3 percent of national income, at a time when total tax revenues were less than 10 percent of national income and total spending on education was less than 1 percent. It is by no means certain that this use of public money was the best strategy for Britain's future. In any case, the problem was that this method of reducing the debt was also extremely slow. British public debt still exceeded 150 percent of national income in 1850 and 70 percent in 1914. The primary surplus, though large, was just enough to pay the interest on the debt; to reduce the principal it was necessary to wait until the effects of national income growth began to be felt (and growth was relatively rapid: more than 2 percent annually for a century). Recent research has shown that these interest payments contributed greatly to the increase of inequality and concentration of property in the United Kingdom between 1815 and 1914.[41]

The experience with reduction of the debt due to the wars of the twentieth century shows that it is possible to proceed differently. Debts of 200–300 percent of national income in 1945–1950 were reduced to almost nothing

---

40. Polanyi, *The Great Transformation*.
41. See the online appendix and V. Amoureux, *Public Debt and Its Unequalizing Effects: Explorations from the British Experience in the Nineteenth Century* (master's thesis, Paris School of Economics, 2014).

within a few years in the cases of France and Germany and in a little more than two decades in the case of the United Kingdom, which was slow compared with its French and German neighbors but a good deal faster than the century from 1815 to 1914 (Fig. 10.9). In retrospect, it is clear that the strategy of accelerated debt reduction is preferable: if the countries of Europe had pursued the nineteenth-century British strategy, they would have been saddled with heavy interest payments to the old propertied classes from 1950 until 2050 (or beyond), at the expense of programs designed to reduce social inequality and improve education and infrastructure—factors that contributed to the exceptional growth of the postwar years. In the heat of action, however, such issues are never easy to deal with, because countries faced with large public debts must arbitrate between two sets of a priori legitimate claims: those stemming from existing property rights and those of social groups without property whose needs and priorities are different (for social and educational investment, for example). I will say more later about the lessons that can be drawn from these experiences for resolving the problems posed by public debt in the twenty-first century.[42]

From Declining Wealth to Durable Deconcentration: The Role of Progressive Taxation

We have just examined the various mechanisms that explain the collapse of the total value of private property in Europe between 1914 and 1945–1950. This depended on several factors (destruction, expropriation, inflation) whose combined effects led to an exceptionally large fall in the ratio of private capital to national income, which reached its minimum between 1945 and 1950 or so and then gradually increased through 2020 (Fig. 10.8). We must now try to understand why this decrease in total wealth coincided with a sharp decrease in the concentration of wealth, which began in the period 1914–1945 and continued through the 1970s. In spite of the upward trend that can be seen since 1980, this deconcentration of wealth, and especially the fall of the top centile's share, remains the most significant feature of the long-term evolution (Figs. 10.4–10.5).

Why, then, did the overall decline of the wealth-income ratio in the period 1914–1950 coincide with a durable deconcentration of the wealth distribution? One might think that the decrease of the wealth-income ratio would have

---

42. See especially Chap. 16 on the European case.

affected fortunes of all sizes more or less equally and therefore would not have changed the share of the top decile or centile. I have already mentioned several reasons why large fortunes decreased more dramatically than smaller ones: specifically, the expropriation of foreign assets had a greater effect on large portfolios (which contained more foreign assets), and the exceptional and progressive taxes on private capital, which were established to liquidate public debts (or as sanctions for wartime collaboration or profiteering), deliberately focused on larger fortunes.

In addition to these specific factors, a more general mechanism was at work. At the end of World War I and throughout the interwar years, people with high incomes and large fortunes found themselves confronted with a permanent system of progressive taxation—that is, a tax system structured in such a way that individuals with high incomes and large fortunes paid more than the rest of the population. The subject of progressive taxation had been debated for centuries, especially toward the end of the eighteenth century and during the French Revolution, but no progressive tax system had ever been tried on a large scale or over a long period of time. In most European countries as well as in the United States and Japan, two types of progressive tax emerged: a progressive tax on total income (that is, the sum of wages and salaries, pensions, rents, dividends, interest, royalties, profits, and other income of all kinds), and a progressive tax on inheritance (that is, on all forms of wealth transmission via inheritances at death or *inter vivos* gifts, including land, buildings, professional and financial assets, or other forms of property).[43] For the first time in history, and virtually simultaneously in all countries, the taxes assessed on the highest incomes and largest estates were durably raised to very high levels on the order of dozens of percent.

The evolution of the top tax rates on income and inheritance in the United States, United Kingdom, Japan, Germany, and France is shown in Figs. 10.11–

---

43. In some countries, especially Germany, Sweden, and other northern European countries, a third form of progressive tax was also introduced early in the twentieth century—namely, a progressive annual tax on wealth (in addition to the inheritance tax paid at the time of wealth transmission to the next generation or to other inheritors). I will come back to this in Chap. 11. Also note that the English language distinguishes between the inheritance tax, assessed on each heir's share of a bequest, and the estate tax, assessed on the total wealth of the deceased, notwithstanding the division among heirs. The estate itself can be broken down into real estate and personal estate; the latter includes movable goods and financial assets. European countries generally use an inheritance tax, whereas the United States has an estate tax. For simplicity, we generally refer to both as the "inheritance tax" in what follows.

10.12, and from this we gain an initial idea of the extent of the upheaval.[44] In 1900, the rates assessed on the highest incomes and largest estates was everywhere below 10 percent; in 1920, rates stood between 30 and 70 percent on the highest incomes and between 10 and 40 percent on the largest estates. Top rates came down somewhat during the brief calm of the 1920s before rising again in the 1930s, especially after the election of Roosevelt in 1932 and the beginning of the New Deal. At a time when a quarter of the labor force was unemployed and governments needed revenues to pay for public works and new social policies, it seemed obvious that the most favored social categories would have to pay more, especially since they had prospered so spectacularly in previous decades (especially during the Roaring Twenties) while leading the country into crisis. Between 1932 and 1980 the top marginal income tax rate in the United States averaged 81 percent. Over the same period, the rate levied on the largest estates was 75 percent.[45] In the United Kingdom, where the Depression also resulted in a profound reevaluation of economic and financial elites, the rates applied in the period 1932–1980 averaged 89 percent on the highest incomes and 72 percent on the largest estates (Figs. 10.11–10.12).

In France, when the parliament finally approved a progressive income tax on July 15, 1914, the top rate was only 2 percent. The political and economic elites of the Third Republic had long blocked any such reform, which they deemed both harmful and unnecessary in a country as supposedly egalitarian as France—but not without a good deal of hypocrisy and bad faith (see Chapter 4). Then, during the war, the top rate was increased, subsequently rising again to 50 percent in 1920, 60 percent in 1924, and as high as 72 percent in 1925. It is particularly striking to learn that the decisive law of June 25, 1920, which raised the rate to 50 percent, was passed by the so-called Blue Horizon Chamber (one of the most right-wing chambers in the entire history of the Republic) and the so-called National Bloc majority, which consisted largely of deputies who before World War I had been most fiercely opposed to the creation of an income tax with a top rate of 2 percent. This complete reversal of

---

44. The top marginal rates shown here generally applied to only a small fraction of taxpayers, those who have the highest incomes and largest estates and who usually belonged to the top centile or even the top thousandth. But the fact is that this is precisely the level where the deconcentration of wealth and income was the highest. Later on I will discuss the evolution of effective tax rates at different levels of the distribution.

45. Note that these figures are solely for the federal income and estate tax, to which state taxes must be added, with additional rates on the order of 5–10 percent depending on the period.

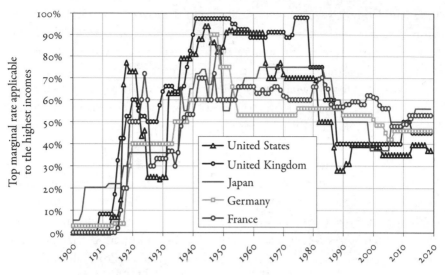

FIG. 10.11. The invention of progressive taxation, 1900–2018: The top income tax rate
Interpretation: The top marginal rate applicable to the highest incomes was on average
23 percent in the United States from 1900–1932, 81 percent from 1932 to 1980, and
39 percent from 1980 to 2018. In these same periods, top rates were 30, 89, and 46 percent
in the United Kingdom; 26, 68, and 53 percent in Japan; 18, 58, and 50 percent in Germany; and 23, 60, and 57 percent in France. Progressive taxation peaked at midcentury,
especially in the United States and United Kingdom. *Sources and series:* piketty.pse.ens.
fr/ideology.

deputies on the right of the political spectrum was due primarily to the disastrous financial situation caused by the war. Despite the ritual speeches on the
theme "Germany will pay!" everyone recognized that new tax revenues had to
be found. At a time when shortages of goods and liberal use of the printing
press had sent inflation soaring to levels unknown before the war, when workers
had yet to regain the purchasing power they enjoyed in 1914 and when several
waves of strikes threatened to paralyze the country in May and June of 1919 and
then again in the spring of 1920, political affiliations did not matter much in
the end. Money had to be found somewhere, and no one imagined for a moment that high earners would be spared. It was in this explosive political and
social context, marked by the Bolshevik Revolution of 1917, which much of the
French socialist and workers' movement supported, that the progressive tax
changed in nature.[46]

---

46. The rates shown in Fig. 10.11 do not include the 25 percent tax hikes intro-
    duced in 1920 for unmarried taxpayers without children and married taxpayers

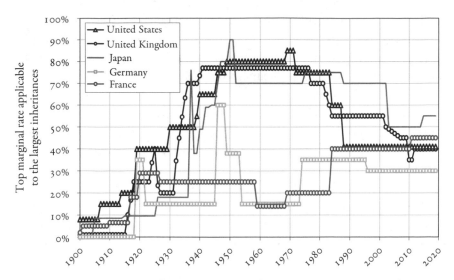

FIG. 10.12. The invention of progressive taxation, 1900–2018: The top inheritance tax rate

Interpretation: The top marginal rate applicable to the largest inheritances averaged 12 percent in the United States from 1900 to 1932, 75 percent from 1932 to 1980, and 50 percent from 1980 to 2018. Over the same periods, top rates were 25, 72, and 46 percent in the United Kingdom; 9, 64, and 63 percent in Japan; 8, 23, and 32 percent in Germany; and 15, 22, and 39 percent in France. Progressivity was maximal at midcentury, especially in the United States and United Kingdom. *Sources and series:* piketty.pse.ens. fr/ideology.

The effect of these very heavy tax shocks was to amplify and more importantly extend the effect of the other shocks sustained by the wealthiest people in the period 1914–1945. In fact, all the evidence available today suggests that this radical fiscal innovation was one of the main reasons why the decrease in

---

"who after two years of marriage still have no child" (if they were included, the top rate would be 62 percent in 1920 and 90 percent in 1925). This interesting provision of the law, which attests to the depth of the French trauma regarding low birth rates as well as the boundless imagination of the deputies when it came to expressing the country's hopes and fears through the tax code, would become the "family compensation tax" from 1939 to 1944 and then, from 1945 to 1951, part of the family quotient system (married couples without children, normally given two shares, fell to 1.5 shares if they still had no child "after three years of marriage"; note that the Constituent Assembly of 1945 prolonged by one year the grace period set by the National Bloc in 1920). For a detailed analysis of these episodes and debates, see Piketty, *Top Incomes in France in the Twentieth Century,* chap. 4.

total wealth led to a durable reduction of wealth inequality. It also explains why the reduction occurred gradually, as income and therefore the ability to save and replenish large fortunes was reduced by the increasing progressivity of the income tax and as the largest fortunes were whittled down over generations of bequests.

Recent research on Paris inheritance records from the years between the two world wars and after World War II has shown how the process worked at the individual level.[47] In the late nineteenth century and until the eve of World War I, the wealthiest 1 percent of Parisians enjoyed average capital incomes thirty to forty times larger than the income of the average worker. The tax these wealthy people paid on their incomes and inheritances did not exceed 5 percent, and they could save only a small fraction (between a quarter and a third) of the income from their property and still pass enough wealth to the next generation to ensure that their offspring could continue to enjoy the same standard of living (relative to the average wage, which was also rising). All this suddenly changed at the end of World War I. Because of the shocks sustained during the war (expropriation of foreign assets, inflation, rent controls) and the new income taxes (whose effective rate in the 1920s climbed to 30–40 percent for the wealthiest 1 percent of Parisians and to more than 50 percent for the wealthiest 0.1 percent), this group's standard of living fell to only five to ten times the average worker's wage. Under such conditions it became materially impossible to reconstitute a fortune comparable to prewar levels, even if one drastically cut back on expenditures and let go much of one's household staff (the number of servants, stable before the war, fell sharply in the interwar period). This became even more difficult as effective inheritance tax rates on this group rose gradually to 10–20 percent in the 1920s and to nearly 30 percent in the 1930s and 1940s.

Of course, this does not mean that all wealthy families ended in bankruptcy. As in the days of Balzac, Père Goriot, and César Birotteau, everything depended on where one invested and what returns one obtained, and these returns could be larger or smaller and were in any case especially volatile in this period of inflation, reconstruction, and recurrent crises. Some got rich and were able to maintain their standard of living. Others kept consuming for too long and depleted their fortunes at an accelerated rate because they could not accept that

---

47. See the online appendix and T. Piketty, G. Postel-Vinay, and J. L. Rosenthal, "The End of Rentiers: Paris 1842–1957," WID.world, 2018, for full data and results, which I summarize here.

it was no longer possible to live as they had before the war. What is certain is that it was inevitable, owing to the new progressive taxes on the highest incomes (which in practice meant incomes that consisted largely of returns on investments) and on the largest estates, that the average position of this social group would collapse between 1914 and 1950 and continue to fall thereafter, with no material possibility of returning to previous levels no matter how much they saved or how quickly they adapted to their new standard of living.

On the Anglo-American Origins of Modern Fiscal Progressivity

Things were not very different in the United Kingdom. Recall the crisis engendered by the vote on the "People's Budget" in 1909–1911: the Lords had initially rejected raising progressive taxes on the highest incomes and largest inheritances (the revenues of which were intended to pay for social measures for the benefit of the working class), which led to their downfall and the end of their political role.[48] The top rates were again increased at the end of World War I, at which point it became materially impossible for wealthy Britons to maintain their prewar standard of living. The difficult adjustment process is depicted, for example, in the television series *Downton Abbey,* which also alludes to the importance of the Irish question in undermining the proprietarian regime. But to cope with tax rates on top incomes (mainly from returns to capital in the forms of rents, interest, and dividends) that quickly rose to 50–60 percent in the 1920s and 1930s and with inheritance tax rates of 40–50 percent, wealthy Britons could not just slightly reduce the number of servants they employed. The only solution was to sell part of their property, and that is what happened at an accelerated rate in interwar Britain.

The great landed estates were the most affected, and these had historically been exceptionally concentrated. The scope and pace of land transfers in the 1920s and 1930s were unprecedented; nothing like it had been seen in Britain since the Norman conquest of 1066 and the dissolution of the monasteries in 1530.[49] But the impact was perhaps even greater on the enormous portfolios of foreign and domestic financial assets that wealthy Britons had accumulated in the nineteenth and early twentieth centuries; these were quickly picked apart, as can be seen in the spectacular collapse of the top decile's share of total British

---

48. See Chap. 5.

49. See D. Cannadine, *The Decline and Fall of the British Aristocracy* (Yale University Press, 1990), p. 89.

property holdings (Fig. 10.5). The depth of this collapse increased still further after World War II, when the top income tax rate rose beyond 90 percent and the top inheritance tax rate remained at 80 percent for decades, in the United States incidentally and in the United Kingdom (Figs. 10.11–10.12). When such rates are established, it is obvious that the goal is simply to eradicate this level of wealth or at any rate to make its perpetuation drastically more difficult (through exceptionally high rates on inherited property).

More broadly, it is important to note the key role played by the United States and United Kingdom in developing large-scale progressive taxation on both income and estates. Recent work has shown that in both countries it was not only the theoretical top marginal rate that was raised to unprecedented levels in the period 1932–1980; in fact, the effective tax rates actually paid by the wealthiest groups reached new heights. From the 1930s to the 1960s, the total tax paid (in all forms, direct and indirect) by the top 0.1 and 0.01 percent of people with the highest incomes fluctuated between 50 and 80 percent of their pretax income, whereas the average for the population as a whole was 15–30 percent and, for the poorest 50 percent, between 10 and 20 percent (Fig. 10.13). Furthermore, all signs are that the marginal rates of 70–80 percent also affected the pretax income distribution (which by definition does not show up in effective rates). Indeed, such high marginal rates made it almost impossible to maintain revenue from capital at this level (except by massive reductions of living standards or gradual sale of assets) and also had a major dissuasive effect on setting executive salaries at excessively high levels.[50]

As for the inheritance tax, it is striking to see that Germany and France applied rates of just 20–30 percent to the largest fortunes in the period 1950–1980, compared with rates of 70–80 percent in the United States and United Kingdom (Fig. 10.12). This can be explained in part by the fact that wartime

---

50. On this mechanism, see Chap. 11 and T. Piketty, E. Saez, and S. Stantcheva, "Optimal Taxation of Top Labor Incomes: A Tale of Three Elasticities," *American Economic Journal: Economic Policy,* 2014. Furthermore, the gradual disappearance of the highest incomes partly explains the fact that effective rates decreased on the top centiles and millimes between 1930–1950 and 1960–1970. The fact that top effective rates never equaled statutory marginal rates is also explained by the fact that governments chose to exclude certain types of income (such as capital gains), especially after 1960. For detailed series on effective rates by centile and type of tax, see the online appendix and T. Piketty, E. Saez, and G. Zucman, "Distributional National Accounts: Methods and Estimates for the United States," *Quarterly Journal of Economics,* 2018.

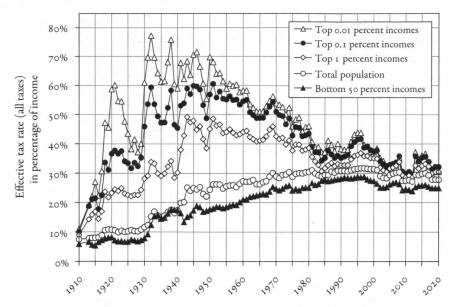

FIG. 10.13. Effective rates and progressivity in the United States, 1910–2020

Interpretation: From 1915 to 1980, the tax system in the United States was highly progressive, in the sense that effective tax rates (all taxes combined, in percent of total pretax income) were significantly higher for the highest incomes than for the population as a whole (especially the poorest 50 percent). Since 1980, the system has not been very progressive, with limited differences in effective rates. *Sources and series:* piketty.pse.ens.fr/ideology.

destruction and postwar inflation took a greater toll in Germany and France, which therefore had less need than the United States and United Kingdom to wield the tax weapon to transform the existing inequality regime.[51]

It is also striking to note that the only time Germany taxed the highest incomes at a rate of 90 percent was in the period 1946–1948, when German fiscal policy was set by the Allied Control Council, which was dominated in practice by the United States. Once Germany regained its fiscal sovereignty in 1949, successive governments chose to reduce this tax, which quickly stabilized at 50–55 percent (Fig. 10.11). As the Americans saw it in 1946–1948, the top rate of 90 percent was in no sense a punishment inflicted on German elites since the same rate was applied to American and British elites. According to

---

51. Note, however, that Japan, which also suffered greatly from wartime destruction, did impose very high inheritance taxes in the period 1950–1980 and continues to heavily tax the largest estates today.

the then-dominant ideology in the United States and United Kingdom, steeply progressive taxes were an integral part of the institutional tools that would form the basis of the postwar world order: free elections would need to be complemented by solid fiscal institutions to prevent democracy from being captured once again by oligarchical and financial interests. This may seem surprising, or ancient history, since the same two countries, the United States and United Kingdom, would set out in the 1980s to dismantle the progressive tax system, but this past is part of our common heritage. These transformations illustrate yet again the importance of political-ideological processes in the dynamics of inequality regimes. Many transitions are possible, and they can be rapid. Furthermore, there is no cultural or civilizational essence that disposes some countries to equality and others to inequality. There are only conflictual sociopolitical trajectories in which different social groups and people of different sensibilities within each society attempt to develop coherent ideas of social justice based on their own experiences and the events they have witnessed.

In the case of the United Kingdom, we have seen how the groundwork for progressive taxation and wealth and income redistribution was laid by social struggles that began in the early nineteenth century with the extension of the right to vote. It took a decisive turn toward the end of the century in debates around the Irish question and "absentee landlords," the rise of the labor movement, and finally the People's Budget and the fall of the House of Lords in 1909–1911.

As for the United States, we noted earlier how the Democratic Party, which was violently segregationist in the South, attempted in the 1870s and 1880s to federate the aspirations of working-class whites, small farmers, and recent Italian and Irish immigrants while attacking the selfishness of northeastern financial and industrial elites and calling for a more just distribution of wealth.[52] In the 1890s, the Populist Party (officially called the People's Party) ran candidates on a platform of land redistribution, credit for small farmers, and opposition to the influence of stockholders, owners, and large corporations on the federal government. The Populists never achieved power, but they did play a central role in the fight to reform the federal tax system, which led to the adoption in 1913 of the Sixteenth Amendment, followed by a vote that same year to adopt a federal income tax, and then, in 1916, a federal estate tax. Previously, neither tax had been authorized by the US Constitution, as the US Supreme Court pointed out in 1894 when it struck down a law approved by the Demo-

---

52. See Chap. 6.

cratic majority. Because it is not easy to amend the Constitution (amendments must be approved a two-thirds majority of both houses of Congress and then ratified by three-quarters of the states), strong popular mobilization was required, and the adoption of the amendment attests to the intensity of the demand for fiscal and economic justice. This was the period known in the United States as the Gilded Age, when industrial and financial fortunes were amassed on a previously unimaginable scale, and people worried about the power wielded by John D. Rockefeller, Andrew Carnegie, J. P. Morgan, and the like. The demand for greater equality became ever more insistent. The emergence of this new federal tax system based on direct progressive taxation of income and estates in a country financed primarily by customs duties—where the federal government had previously played a limited part—also owes a great deal to the role of the parties and especially the Democrats in mobilizing voters and interpreting their demands.[53]

It is interesting, moreover, to note that in the late nineteenth and early twentieth centuries, the United States was among the leaders of an international campaign in favor of the income tax. In particular, numerous books and articles published between 1890 and 1910 by the American economist Edwin Seligman in praise of a progressive income tax were translated into many languages and inspired passionate debate.[54] In a 1915 study of the distribution of wealth in the United States (the first comprehensive work on the subject), the statistician Willford King worried that the country was becoming increasingly inegalitarian and estranged from its original pioneer ideal.[55]

In 1919, the president of the American Economic Association, Irving Fisher, went further still. He chose to devote his "presidential address" to the question of inequality and bluntly told his colleagues that the increasing con-

53. On this subject see W. E. Brownlee, *Federal Taxation in America: A Short History* (Cambridge University Press, 2016). The authors emphasize the fact that the federal government (as well as the states) had long benefited from the sale of public lands in frontier regions, which may partly explain earlier resistance to taxes.

54. On this period and the debates in question, see, for example, P. Rosanvallon, *La société des égaux* (Seuil, 2011), pp. 227–233. See also N. Delalande, *Les Batailles de l'impôt. Consentement et résistances de 1789 à nos jours* (Seuil, 2011).

55. See W. I. King, *The Wealth and Income of the People of the United States* (Macmillan, 1915). The author, a professor of statistics and economics at the University of Wisconsin, collected imperfect but suggestive data on several American states, compared them with European estimates, and found the differences smaller than he initially imagined.

centration of wealth was on the brink of becoming America's foremost economic problem. If steps were not taken, the United States might soon become as inegalitarian as old Europe (which was seen as oligarchic in spirit and therefore contrary to the American way). Fisher was alarmed by King's estimates. The fact that "2 percent of the population owns more than 50 percent of the wealth" and that "two-thirds of the population owns almost nothing" seemed to him "an undemocratic distribution of wealth," which threatened the very foundation of American society. Rather than impose arbitrary restrictions on the share of profits or the return on capital—solutions that Fisher evoked the better to refute them, it would be preferable, he argued, to levy a heavy tax on the largest inheritances. More specifically, he broached the idea of a tax equal to one-third the value of the estate transmitted in the first generation, two-thirds in the second generation, and 100 percent if the legacy persisted for three generations.[56] This specific proposal was not adopted, but the fact remains that in 1918–1920 (under the presidency of Democrat Woodrow Wilson) rates of more than 70 percent were applied to the highest income bracket earlier than in any other country (Fig. 10.11). When Franklin D. Roosevelt was elected in 1932, the intellectual groundwork had long since been laid for establishing a far-reaching system of progressive taxation in the United States.

The Rise of the Fiscal and Social State

The inequality regime in Europe in the nineteenth century and until 1914 rejected progressive taxation and made do with limited overall tax revenues. In the eighteenth and nineteenth centuries European states were fiscally wealthy compared with the governing structures of previous centuries or with the contemporary Ottoman and Chinese states (see Chapter 9). But they were fiscally poor compared with the states of the twentieth century—a period that marked a decisive leap forward for the fiscal state. Beyond the question of progressive taxation, the rise of the fiscal and social state played a central role in the transformation of ownership societies into social-democratic societies.

The main orders of magnitude are the following. Total fiscal receipts, including all direct and indirect taxes, social contributions, and other obligatory

---

56. See I. Fisher, "Economists in Public Service," *American Economic Review*, 1919. Fisher took his inspiration largely from the Italian economist Eugenio Rignano. See G. Erreygers and G. Di Bartolomeo, "The Debates on Eugenio Rignano's Inheritance Tax Proposals," *History of Political Economy*, 2007.

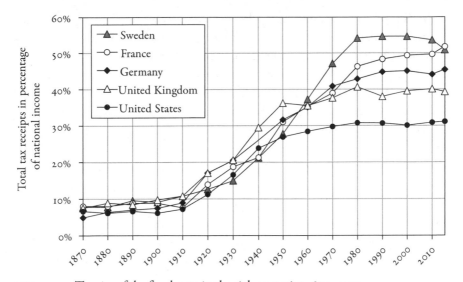

FIG. 10.14. The rise of the fiscal state in the rich countries, 1870–2015

Interpretation: Total tax receipts (all taxes, fees, and social contributions combined) amounted to less than 10 percent of national income in the rich countries in the nineteenth century and until World War I before rising sharply from 1910 to 1980, then stabilizing at levels that varied by country: around 30 percent in the United States, 40 percent in the United Kingdom, and 45–55 percent in Germany, France, and Sweden. *Sources and series:* piketty.pse.ens.fr/ideology.

payments of all kinds (at all levels of government, including central state, regional governments, social security administration, etc.), amounted to less than 10 percent of national income in Europe and the United States in the late nineteenth and early twentieth centuries. Tax revenues then rose to around 20 percent in the 1920s and 30 percent in the 1950s before stabilizing since the 1970s at levels that varied substantially from country to country: around 30 percent of national income in the United States, 40 percent in the United Kingdom, 45 percent in Germany, and 50 percent in France and Sweden (Fig. 10.14).[57] Note, however, that no rich country has been able to develop with tax revenues limited to 10–20 percent of national income and that no one

---

57. In the United States the bulk of the long-term increase went to federal tax revenues, which amounted to barely 2 percent of national income throughout the nineteenth century and up to 1914, then rose to 5 percent by 1930 and 15 percent by 1950 before stabilizing at around 20 percent since 1960. State and local tax revenues have remained stable at around 8–10 percent of national income since the late nineteenth century. See the online appendix.

today is proposing a return to nineteenth-century levels of taxation. Debate nowadays usually revolves around stabilizing the level of taxation or perhaps decreasing it slightly or increasing it more or less substantially; it is never about cutting taxes to a fourth or a fifth of their current level, which is what it would mean to return to the nineteenth century.

A great deal of research has shown that the rise of the fiscal state did not impede economic growth (a fact quite visible in Fig. 10.14). Indeed, the opposite is true: the fiscal state played a central role in the modernization and development of the economy in Europe and the United States over the course of the twentieth century.[58] The new tax revenues financed spending that was essential for development, including (in comparison with the past) massive and relatively egalitarian investment in health and education and social spending to cope with aging populations (such as pensions) and to stabilize economy and society in times of recession (by means of unemployment insurance and other social transfers).

If we average the data from various European countries, we find that the increase in tax revenues between 1900 and 2010 is explained almost entirely by the rise in social spending on education, health, pensions, and other transfer and income replacement payments (Fig. 10.15).[59] Note, too, the crucial importance of the period 1910–1950 in transforming the role of the state. In the early 1910s, the state maintained order and enforced respect for property rights both domestically and internationally (and in the colonies), as it had done throughout the nineteenth century. Regalian expenditures (on the army, police, courts, general administration, and basic infrastructure) absorbed nearly all tax revenues: roughly 8 percent of national income out of total revenues of 10 percent, and all other expenses combined amounted to less than 2 percent of national income (of which less than 1 percent went to education). By the early 1950s, the essential elements of the social state were already in place in Europe, with total

---

58. See esp. P. Lindert, *Growing Public: Social Spending and Economic Growth since the Eighteenth Century* (Cambridge University Press, 2004).

59. The series shown in Fig. 10.14 were obtained by averaging the main European countries for which we have adequate long-run data (United Kingdom, France, Germany, and Sweden). These orders of magnitude may be taken as globally representative for Western and Northern Europe. Note that total public expenditures may in practice be slightly higher than the tax revenues broken down here in view of nonfiscal revenues (such as user fees for access to certain public services) and debt (even though the primary deficit is generally close to zero on average over the long run, including interest on the debt). See the online appendix.

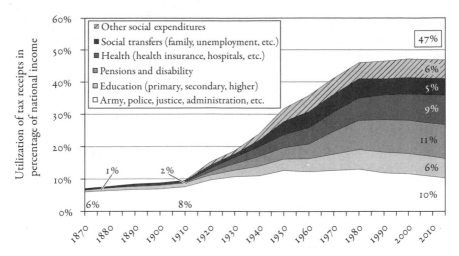

FIG. 10.15. The rise of the social state in Europe, 1870–2015

Interpretation: In 2015, fiscal receipts represented 47 percent of national income on average in Western Europe and were spent as follows: 10 percent of national income for regalian expenses (army, policy, justice, general administration, and basic infrastructure, such as roads); 6 percent for education; 11 percent for pensions; 9 percent for health care; 5 percent for social transfers (other than pensions); and 6 percent for other social expenses (housing, etc.). Before 1914, regalian expenses absorbed nearly all tax revenues. *Note:* The evolution depicted here is the average of Germany, France, United Kingdom, and Sweden (see Fig. 10.14). *Sources and series:* piketty.pse.ens.fr/ideology.

tax revenues in excess of 30 percent of national income and a range of educational and social expenditures absorbing two-thirds of the total, supplanting the previously dominant regalian expenses. This stunning change was possible only thanks to a radical transformation of the political-ideological balance of power in the period 1910–1950, years in which war, crisis, and revolution exposed the limits of the self-regulated market and revealed the need for social embedding of the economy.

Note, too, that in the period 1990–2020, the upward trend in pensions and health costs, in a context characterized by population aging and a freeze on total tax revenues, led inevitably to reliance on debt coupled with stagnation (or even a slight decrease) of public investment in education (Fig. 10.15). This is paradoxical at a time when there is so much talk about the knowledge economy and the importance of innovation and a growing proportion of each successive age cohort gains access to higher education (which is an excellent thing in itself but may entail enormous human waste and tremendous social frustration in the absence of proper financing). I will come back to this point later when I discuss the inadequacy of the social-democratic response to this fundamental challenge.

In theory, the fact that obligatory tax payments are close to 50 percent of national income shows that the public authorities (in their various incarnations) could employ half the working-age population at the average private-sector wage using the same machinery, locations, and so on and producing half of the country's gross domestic product. In practice, public employment at various levels of government and in schools, universities, hospitals, and so on accounted for about 15–20 percent of employment in West European countries in the period 2000–2020, compared with 80–85 percent of employment in the private sector. The reason for this is that most tax revenues are used not to pay public employees but to finance transfer payments (pensions, welfare, etc.) and to purchase goods and services from the private sector (buildings, public works, equipment, outsourcing, etc.).[60] Besides the ratio of tax revenues to national income (40–50 percent in Western Europe) and the ratio of public-sector employment to total employment (15–20 percent), there is a third way to measure the weight of the state, which is to measure its share of national capital. Using this measure, we will see that the state's share has decreased quite a lot over the past several decades and in many countries has become negative.[61]

On the Diversity of Tax Payments and the Role of Fiscal Progressivity

Note, moreover, that in practice the rise of the fiscal and social state has required the use of many different kinds of taxes. To raise tax revenues equal to 45 percent of national income, which is roughly the West European average for the past two decades, one could of course simply levy a single proportional tax of 45 percent on all income. Or one could levy a single progressive tax on income, with rates below 45 percent at the lower end of the income distribution and above 45 percent at the higher end, so that the weighted average comes out to

---

60. In 2017, public-sector employees (of the state, towns and regions, hospitals, etc.) accounted for 21 percent of total employment in France versus 79 percent for the private sector (12 percent self-employed and 67 percent employed by private-sector firms). See the online appendix for more on the complexity of these distinctions.

61. See Chap. 12.

45 percent.[62] In practice, tax revenues do not come from a single tax but from a multitude of taxes, fees, and contributions, which constitute a complex and incoherent system that is often opaque to taxpayers.[63] This complexity and opacity may render the system less acceptable to citizens, especially at a time when heightened tax competition tends to result in lower taxes for more mobile and favored social groups and gradual tax increases for the rest. Nevertheless, a single tax is not the answer, and the question of an ideal just tax deserves to be examined in detail, in all its complexity. There are in particular good reasons for seeking a balance between taxing flows of income and taxing stocks of wealth—reasons of justice as well as efficiency. I will say more about this later.[64]

At this stage I want mainly to emphasize the historic complementarity between the development of large-scale progressive taxation and the rise of the social state over the course of the twentieth century. The 70–80 percent tax rates on the highest incomes and largest estates between the 1920s and the 1960s admittedly affected only a small fraction of the population (generally, 1–2 percent of the population but in some cases barely 0.5 percent). All signs are that these taxes played an essential role in durably reducing the extreme

---

62. For example, the effective tax rate could be 30 percent on the bottom 50 percent weighted by income (which roughly corresponds to the bottom 80 percent of the current income distribution in Europe) and 60 percent on the top 50 percent weighted by income (which corresponds roughly to the top 20 percent of the current income distribution). We will see later that the current tax structure in France is considerably less progressive than this. See Fig. 11.19.

63. The current distribution of the tax burden in Europe is roughly the following: about a third of the total comes from income taxes (including taxes on corporate profits); a third comes from social security contributions and other deductions from income; and another third comes from indirect taxes (such as value-added taxes and other consumption taxes) together with wealth and inheritance taxes (less than a tenth of the total). The boundaries between these categories are somewhat arbitrary (especially between the first two: social contributions deducted from wages are not very different from income taxes in the narrow sense). The real issue is usually the overall progressivity of the whole tax package, together with the issue of what the money is used for and how the tax is governed, rather than what it is nominally called. Note, too, that the overall tax burden is significantly lower in the poorer countries of the European Union (barely 25–30 percent of national income in Romania and Bulgaria). See the online appendix.

64. See esp. Chaps. 11 and 17.

concentration of wealth and economic power that characterized Belle Époque Europe (1880–1914). By themselves, these top marginal tax rates would never have sufficed to generate the revenues necessary to pay for the social state, and it was essential to develop other taxes that would tap the whole spectrum of wages and incomes. It was the conjunction of two complementary visions of the purpose of taxation (to reduce inequalities and to pay state expenses) that made it possible to transform ownership societies into social-democratic societies.

Note in particular that between the 1920s and the 1960s there was a considerable gap between the average tax rate (20–40 percent of national income, trending upward) and the rate applied to the highest incomes and largest fortunes (70–80 percent or more). The system was clearly progressive, and people at the bottom or in the middle of the social hierarchy could understand that great effort was being demanded of those at the top, which served not only to reduce inequalities but also to generate support for the tax system.

The dual nature of the twentieth-century fiscal state (which combined significant progressivity with the resources to finance the social state) explains why the long-run decrease in the concentration of wealth did not hinder continued investment and accumulation. The accumulation of productive and educational capital since World War II has proceeded at a faster pace than was observed prior to 1914, partly because public channels of accumulation have replaced private ones and partly because increased accumulation by more modest social groups (which are less affected by progressive taxes) has made up for decreased accumulation by the rich. The situation in 1990–2020 was strictly the opposite, however: the average tax rate on the middle and working classes is equal to or greater than the tax rate at the top. This naturally tends to have the opposite effect: rising inequality, reduced support for the tax system, and low overall accumulation. We will come back to this in Chapter 11.

Ownership Societies, Progressive Taxation, and World War I

We come now to a particularly complex and delicate question. Could the extremely rapid rise of progressive taxation, with top rates of 70–80 percent in the 1920s, have taken place without World War I? More generally, would the ownership societies that seemed so solid and unshakable in 1914 have been transformed as rapidly without the unprecedented destructive violence that was unleashed between 1914 and 1918? Can one imagine a historical trajectory in which, without a global conflict, ownership society would have maintained its grip on Europe and the United States, to say nothing of the rest of the world, via colonial domination? And for how long?

Obviously, it is impossible to give any definite answer to such a "counterfactual" question.[65] The outbreak of the first global conflict so disrupted all existing social, economic, and political dynamics that it is now very difficult to imagine what might have happened had it not occurred. This counterfactual nevertheless has consequences for the way one thinks about redistribution and inequality in the twenty-first century, and it is possible to hazard some guesses and avoid the trap of deterministic thinking. Within the framework of this book—in which I stress the importance of political-ideological factors in the evolution of inequality regimes together with the interaction between long-term changes in thinking and the short-term logic of events—World War I can be seen as a major event, which opened the way to many possible trajectories. It is enough to look at the dramatic increase in the top income tax rate (Fig. 10.11) or the collapse of private wealth (Fig. 10.8) or of foreign asset values (Fig. 7.9) to see the profound and multifarious effects of the war on the colonialist and proprietarian inequality regime. The reduction of inequality and exit from the ownership society that took place in the twentieth century were not peaceful processes. Like most important historical changes, they were consequences of crises and of the interaction of those crises with new ideas and social and political struggles. But can one really say that similar developments might not have occurred in any case, possibly in conjunction with other crises, even if World War I had not happened?

Recent research has stressed the importance of wartime experience itself, and especially the role of mass military conscription in legitimizing progressive

---

65. Counterfactual history has a long tradition. In the first century CE, Titus Livy imagined what would have happened if Alexander the Great had headed west instead of east and conquered Rome. In 1776 Edward Gibbon imagined a (highly refined) Muslim Europe coming to pass after the defeat of Charles Martel at Poitiers in 732. In 1836 Louis Geoffroy imagined Napoleon as emperor of the world after defeating Russia and England in 1812–1814 and then conquering India, China, and Australia in 1821–1827 and finally winning the submission of the US Congress in 1832. In 2003 Niall Ferguson imagined a better world (in his view) in which British diplomats would have allowed Germany to crush France and Russia in 1914, leaving British and German empires to dominate the world in the twentieth century instead of the American and Russian empires. See Q. Deluermoz and P. Singaravélou, *Pour une histoire des possibles. Analyses contrefactuelles et futurs non advenus* (Seuil, 2016), pp. 22–37.

taxation and nearly confiscatory rates on the highest incomes and largest fortunes after the war. After so much working-class blood had been shed, it was impossible not to demand an unprecedented effort on the part of the privileged classes to liquidate the war debt, rebuild the country, and pave the way to a more just society. Some scholars go so far as to conclude that such steeply progressive taxes could not have been implemented without World War I; without a similar (and at this point improbable) experience of mass military conscription in the twenty-first century, it is argued, no such progressive tax will ever again see the light of day.[66]

As interesting as these speculations are, they strike me as overly rigid and deterministic. Rather than pretend to be able to identify the causal impact of any particular event, it seems to me more promising to see confluences of crises as endogenous switch points reflecting deeper causes. Each such switch point opens the way to a large number of possible future trajectories. The actual outcome then depends on how actors mobilize and seize on shared experiences and new ideas to change the course of events. World War I was not an exogenous event catapulted to Earth from Mars. It was arguably caused, at least in part, by very serious social inequalities and tensions in pre-1914 European society. Economic issues were also very powerful. As noted earlier, foreign investments were yielding 5–10 percent additional national income to France and the United Kingdom on the eve of the war, and this extra income was growing rapidly in the period 1880–1914; this can only have aroused envy. Indeed, French and British foreign investment increased so rapidly between 1880 and 1914 that it is hard to imagine how it could have continued at such a pace without stirring up tremendous political tensions, both within the possessed countries and among European rivals. Such large investment flows had consequences not only for French and British investors but also for the ability of countries to pursue fiscal and financial policies to ensure social peace.[67] Apart from the economic interests involved, which were anything but symbolic, it is important to note that the development of European nation-states heightened awareness of

---

66. See esp. K. Scheve and D. Stasavage, *Taxing the Rich: A History of Fiscal Fairness in the United States and Europe* (Princeton University Press, 2016). On the crucial role of war in the history of inequality, see W. Scheidel, *The Great Leveler: Violence and the History of Inequality from the Stone Age to the Twenty-First Century* (Princeton University Press, 2017).

67. V. I. Lenin, in his classic 1916 book *Imperialism, The Highest Stage of Capitalism,* used statistics on foreign investment to demonstrate the importance of the race for resources among rival colonial powers.

national identities and exacerbated national antagonisms. These colonial rivalries gave rise to identity conflicts like the one between French and Italian workers in southern France, which reinforced divisions between natives and foreigners; hardened national, linguistic, and cultural identities; and ultimately made war possible.[68]

Furthermore, the central role of World War I in the collapse of ownership society does not mean that we should neglect the importance of other major events of the period, including the Bolshevik Revolution and the Great Depression. These various crises might have unfolded differently and fit together in various ways, and the analysis of numerous countries and their varied trajectories shows that it is difficult to isolate the effects of the war from those of other events. In some cases, the role of World War I was decisive, as in the adoption of the income tax in France in July 1914.[69] But things were generally more complicated, which means that the effects of the war and mass conscription should be seen in a broader perspective.

For example, in the United Kingdom, progressive income and estate tax rates were put in place earlier, after the political crisis of 1909–1911, and hence before the outbreak of war (Figs. 10.11–10.12). The fall of the House of Lords had nothing to do with World War I or conscription, any more than did the dissolution of the monasteries in 1530, the French Revolution of 1789, the agrarian reform in Ireland in the 1890s, or the end of wealth-proportionate voting rights in Sweden in 1911 (see Chapter 5). The aspiration to greater justice and equality takes many historical forms and can thrive without experience of the trenches. The Japanese case was similar: the development of a progressive income tax was well under way before 1914, particularly when it came to taxing high incomes (Figs. 10.11–10.12). The Japanese case followed a logic of its own, related to the specificities of Japanese history, several aspects of which mattered more than World War I (see Chapter 9 for a fuller discussion).

---

68. One example is the deadly anti-Italian riots in Marseille in 1881 (a few years before the Aigues-Mortes massacre of 1893), after Italian workers were suspected of jeering a parade of French troops that had just seized control of Tunisia at Italy's expense. See G. Noiriel, *Une histoire populaire de la France* (Agone, 2018), pp. 401–405, who sees this event as one of the key moments in the politicization of the immigration issue in France.

69. Note, however, that the progressivity of the inheritance tax was increased in 1910 in connection with a search for ways to finance the law on peasant and worker pensions, which suggests that France would have adopted the income tax with or without the war. See Chap. 4.

On the Role of Social and Ideological Struggles in the Fall of Proprietarianism

As we have seen, social demand and popular mobilization for fiscal justice in the United States increased sharply in the 1880s. The lengthy process that led to the adoption of the Sixteenth Amendment in the United States in 1913 pre-dated World War I, and the war did not seem to influence Irving Fisher's 1919 speech or President Roosevelt's decision in 1932 to raise top tax rates to reduce the concentration of property and the influence of the wealthy. In other words, one shouldn't exaggerate the political effects of World War I in the United States: the war was mainly a European trauma. For most people in the United States, the Wall Street crash and the Great Depression (1929–1933) were much more powerful shocks. John Steinbeck's *Grapes of Wrath* recounts the suffering of Oklahoma farmworkers and sharecroppers who lose everything and find themselves mistreated and exploited in California work camps. This tells us more about the climate that led to the New Deal and Roosevelt's progressive tax policies than any stories coming out of the trenches of northern France. It is reasonable to think that any financial crisis similar to that of 1929 would have sufficed to bring about political changes similar to the New Deal even if there had been no world war. Similarly, while World War II without a doubt played an important role in justifying new tax hikes on the ultrarich—especially the Victory Tax Act of 1942 (which raised the top marginal rate to 91 percent)[70]—the fact is that the change in attitude on taxation began much earlier in Roosevelt's term at the height of the Depression in the early 1930s.

The Bolshevik Revolution also had a major impact. It forced capitalist elites to radically revise their positions on wealth redistribution and fiscal justice, especially in Europe. In France in the 1920s, politicians who had refused to vote for a 2 percent income tax in 1914 suddenly turned around and approved rates of 60 percent on the highest incomes. One thing that emerges clearly from debate on the bill is how afraid the deputies were of revolution at a time when general strikes threatened to engulf the country and a majority of delegates to the French Section of the Workers' International (SFIO, or Socialist) Congress in Tours voted to support the Soviet Union and join the new Communist

---

70. To justify the tax increases of the Victory Tax Act, the government even called upon Donald Duck, the hero of the famous 1943 cartoon "Taxes Will Bury the Axis."

international bloc led by Moscow.[71] Compared with the threat of widespread expropriation, a progressive tax suddenly seemed less frightening. The quasi-insurrectional strikes that took place in France in the period 1945–1948 (especially in 1947) had a similar effect. To those who feared a Communist revolution, higher taxes and social benefits seemed the lesser evil. It is true, of course, that the Russian Revolution was itself a consequence of World War I. Even so, it is highly unlikely that the Tsarist regime would have endured indefinitely had there been no war. The war also played a key role in the expansion of voting rights in Europe. For example, universal male suffrage was instituted in the United Kingdom, Denmark, and Holland in 1918 and in Sweden, Italy, and Belgium in 1919.[72] There again, however, it seems likely that a similar evolution would have taken place without the war: there would have been other crises and, more significantly, other popular and collective mobilizations.

We earlier saw the importance of social struggles in the Swedish case. It was the social-democratic workers' movement whose exceptional mobilization in the period 1890–1930 led to the transformation of the extreme Swedish proprietarian regime (in which a single wealthy citizen could in some cases cast more votes in local elections than all the other residents of the town combined) into a social-democratic regime with steeply progressive taxes and an ambitious welfare state. World War I, in which Sweden did not participate, seems to have played a very minor role in these developments. Note, moreover, that Sweden's progressive tax rates remained relatively moderate during World War I and the 1920s (20–30 percent). Only after the social democrats gained a firm grip on the reins of power firmly in the 1930s and 1940s did the rates applied to the highest incomes and largest estates rise to 70–80 percent, where they remained until the 1980s.[73]

---

71. At the Congress of Tours in 1920, the majority of delegates chose to quit the SFIO and create the French Section of the Communist International (SFIC), which would eventually become the French Communist Party (PCF). The latter took control of the party newspaper, *L'Humanité*. By contrast, a majority of socialist deputies chose to remain in the SFIO, which was attacked as "bourgeois" and centrist by the Communists.

72. It was also in 1919 that Germany—where (as in France) all adult males had had the right to vote since 1871 but not in private—moved to a secret ballot. In practice, the nonsecret ballot could limit the right to vote in places where the influence of local elites was powerful.

73. See Chap. 5 and the online appendix, Figs. S10.11a–12a.

Italy offers another example of a distinctive political trajectory. The fascist regime that came to power in 1921–1922 had little taste for progressive taxes. The rates applied to the highest incomes held steady at 20–30 percent throughout the interwar years before suddenly jumping up to more than 80 percent in 1945–1946, when the fascist regime gave way to the Republic of Italy and when both the Communist and Socialist Parties were quite popular. In 1924, Mussolini's government actually decided to abolish the estate tax altogether, flying in the face of what was happening everywhere else; in 1931, it was reinstated, albeit at a very low rate of 10 percent. After World War II, the rates applied to the largest estates were immediately raised to 40–50 percent.[74] This confirms the hypothesis that political mobilization (or its absence) was the main reason for changes in the tax structure and the structure of inequality.

To recapitulate: the end of ownership society was due more than anything else to a political-ideological transformation. Reflection and debate around social justice, progressive taxation, and redistribution of income and wealth, already fairly common in the eighteenth century and during the French Revolution, grew in amplitude in most countries in the late nineteenth and early twentieth centuries, owing largely to the very high concentration of wealth generated by industrial capitalism as well as to educational progress and the diffusion of ideas and information. What led to the transformation of the inequality regime was the encounter between this intellectual evolution and a range of military, financial, and political crises, which were themselves due in part to tensions stemming from inequality. Along with political-ideological changes, popular mobilizations and social struggles played a central role, with specificities associated with each country's particular national history. But there were also common experiences, increasingly widely shared and interconnected

---

74. See the online appendix, Figs. S10.11b–12b. Note that progressive tax rates in Germany, which had been raised quite a bit in the 1920s, were kept at high levels under the Nazis. On the other hand, Nazi policies contributed to higher industrial profits (especially in strategic sectors) and wage hierarchies, which led to a significant increase of income inequality (especially the top centile share) between 1933 and 1939, in contrast to other countries (see the online appendix and Fig. 10.3). In an international context marked by significant reduction of social inequalities, Fascism and Nazism were more concerned with fighting foreign enemies and establishing order and hierarchy than with reducing inequality within their national communities.

throughout the world, which could accelerate the spread of certain practices and transformations. Things will probably be much the same in the future.

On the Need for Socially Embedded Markets

In *The Great Transformation,* Karl Polanyi proposed a magisterial analysis of the way in which the ideology of the self-regulated market in the nineteenth century led to the destruction of European societies in the period 1914–1945 and ultimately to the death of economic liberalism. We know now that this death was only temporary. In 1938 liberal economists and intellectuals met in Paris to lay the groundwork for the future. Aware that pre-1914 liberal doctrine had lost its sway, worried about the success of economic planning and collectivism, and transfixed by the impending rise of totalitarianism (a word seldom used at the time), these men set out to reflect on a possible renaissance of liberal thought, which they proposed to call "neoliberalism." Among the participants in the Walter Lippmann Colloquium (named for the American essayist who convoked this gathering in Paris) were people of many different points of view, some of whom were close to social democracy while others—including Friedrich von Hayek, whose ideas would inspire Augusto Pinochet and Margaret Thatcher in the 1970s and 1980s, and about whom I will say more later on[75]—called for a return to economic liberalism plain and simple. For now, let us dwell a moment on Polanyi's thesis, which has much to tell us about the collapse of ownership society.[76]

When Polanyi wrote *The Great Transformation* in the United States between 1940 and 1944, Europe was pursuing its self-destructive and genocidal instincts to their ultimate end, and faith in self-regulation was at a low ebb. As the Hungarian economist and historian saw it, nineteenth-century civilization rested on four pillars: the balance of power, the gold standard, the liberal state, and the self-regulated market. Polanyi showed in particular how absolute faith

---

75. On Hayek's authoritarian proprietarianism, see Chap. 13. For a critical analysis of the papers from the 1938 Lippmann Colloquium and their aftermath, see S. Audier, *Le colloque Lippmann. Aux origines du "néo-libéralisme"* (Le bord de l'eau, 2012); S. Audier, *Néo-libéralismes: une archéologie intellectuelle* (Grasset, 2012).

76. Polanyi does not explicitly use the term "ownership society," but that is what he has in mind. In particular, he stresses the quasi-sacralization of private property in the period 1815–1914. Broadly speaking, I think the term "proprietarianism" better captures what is at stake here than "liberalism," which plays on the ambiguity between economic liberalism and political liberalism.

in the regulatory capacity of supply and demand poses serious problems when applied unreservedly to the labor market, in which the equilibrium price (wages) is literally a matter of life and death for flesh-and-blood human beings. In order for the supply of labor to decrease and its price to rise, human beings must disappear; this was more or less the solution envisioned by British land-owners in the Irish and Bengali famines. For Polanyi, who in 1944 believed in the possibility of democratic (noncommunist) socialism, the market economy had to be socially embedded. In the case of the labor market, this meant that wage setting, worker training, limits on labor mobility, and collectively financed wage supplements were all matters to be settled by social and political nego-tiation outside the sphere of the market.[77]

Similar problems of social embeddedness arise in connection with the mar-kets for land and natural resources, supplies of which are finite quantities and can be depleted. Hence it is illusory to think that supply and demand alone can ensure rational social utilization via the market. More specifically, it makes no sense to give all power to the "first" owners of land and natural capital and even less sense to guarantee their power until the end of time.[78] Finally, regarding the money market, which is intimately linked to state finances, Polanyi shows how the belief in self-regulation, coupled with the broadening of the scope of the market and the generalized monetization of economic rela-tions, leaves modern society in a very fragile condition. That fragility abruptly manifested itself in the interwar years. In a world whose economy had been entirely monetized and given over to the market, the collapse of the gold stan-dard and the ensuing disruption of the global financial system had incalculable consequences which burst into the open in the 1920s. Entire classes of people were reduced to poverty by inflation while speculators amassed fortunes, which fed demands for strong, authoritarian governments, most notably in Germany.

---

77. Polanyi, without seeking to idealize the British Poor Laws, stressed the fact that before the reforms of 1795 and 1834 they included not only limitations on mobility but also wage supplements indexed to grain prices and financed locally. In the nineteenth century, industrial elites promoted the idea of a self-regulated single market encompassing the entire nation. Polanyi is not entirely clear, however, about the territorial scope he had in mind (nation-state, Europe, Europe-Africa, world) and by what means he proposed to regulate labor mobility and wage setting in the postwar period. See Polanyi, *The Great Transformation,* chaps. 6–10.

78. Note, however, that Polanyi is silent about remedies: he does not explicitly discuss public ownership, agrarian reform, redistribution of wealth, or progressive taxa-tion. His book is more an account of collapse than of reconstruction.

Flights of capital brought down governments in France and elsewhere, under conditions and with a rapidity unknown in the nineteenth century.

Imperial Competition and the Collapse of European Equilibrium

Finally, Polanyi pointed out that the ideology of self-regulation also applied to the balance of power in Europe. From 1815 to 1914, people thought that the existence of European nation-states of comparable size and power, all committed to the defense of private property, the gold standard, and the co-lonial domination of the rest of the world, would suffice to guarantee the continuation of the process of capital accumulation and the prosperity of the continent and the world. The hope of balanced competition applied in partic-ular to the three "imperial societies" (Germany, France, and the United Kingdom), each of which sought to promote its territorial and financial power and cultural and civilizational model on a global scale while taking no notice of the fact that their hunger for power had desensitized them to the social inequalities that were undermining them from within.[79] As Polanyi notes, this further application of the theoretical principle of self-regulated competi-tion was the most fragile of all. The United Kingdom signed a treaty with France in 1904 to divide Egypt and Morocco and then another with Russia in 1906 to do the same with Persia. Meanwhile, Germany consolidated its alli-ance with Austria-Hungary, leaving two sets of hostile powers confronting each other and no alternative to total war.

At this point it is important to stress the obvious effects of demographic shifts. For centuries the major nation-states of Western Europe had populations of roughly equal size. From the fifteenth to eighteenth centuries this contrib-uted to military competition, early state centralization, and financial and tech-nological innovation.[80] Nevertheless, several major shifts in relative standing occurred within this broad equilibrium (Fig. 10.16). In the eighteenth century, France was by far the most populous country in Europe, which partly explains its military and cultural dominance. Specifically, in 1800, France (with a popu-lation of roughly thirty million) was 50 percent larger than Germany (with a

---

79. See the stimulating analysis by C. Charle, *La crise des sociétés impériales. Allemagne, France, Grande-Bretagne, 1900–1940. Essai d'histoire sociale comparée* (Seuil, 2001).

80. See Chap. 9.

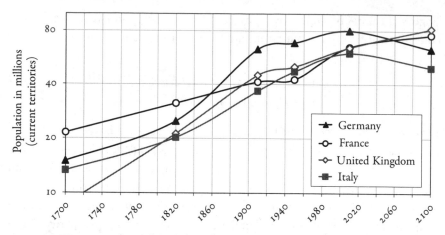

FIG. 10.16. Demography and the balance of power in Europe

Interpretation: Germany, the United Kingdom, Italy, and France have had roughly similar populations for centuries: each country had around 20–30 million people in 1820 and 60–80 million in 2020. There have been frequent changes in relative position, however: in 1800 France was 50 percent larger than Germany (31 million vs. 22 million); in 1910, Germany was 50 percent larger than France (63 million vs. 41 million). According to UN predictions, the United Kingdom and France should be the largest countries by 2100. *Sources and series:* piketty.pse.ens.fr/ideology.

little over twenty million)—and Germany, to boot, was not yet unified.[81] It was in this context that Napoleon sought to build a European empire under the French banner. Then France's population virtually ceased to grow for a century and a half (by 1950 the population was just a little over 40 million), for reasons that are not fully understood but that seem to be related to de-Christianization and very early success with birth control.[82] By contrast, Germany experienced accelerated demographic growth in the nineteenth

---

81. The estimates shown in Fig. 10.16 cover the present-day territory of each country and should be read as indicating orders of magnitude rather than precise values. See the online appendix.

82. Low birth rates and de-Christianization (as measured by birth records and baptismal acts) seem to have begun in the period 1750–1780 and to have been more advanced in *départements* where more priests rallied to the Revolution. No other country experienced such an early demographic transition. See T. Guinnane, "The Historical Fertility Transition," *Journal of Economic Literature,* 2011; T. Murphy, "Old Habits Die Hard (Sometimes): What Can Department Heterogeneity Tell Us about the French Fertility Decline?" *Journal of Economic Growth,* 2015.

century, in addition to which it achieved political unity under the aegis of the kaiser. By 1910, Germany's population was 50 percent larger than that of France: more than 60 million Germans compared with barely 40 million French.[83] I do not mean to suggest that such demographic shifts were the sole cause of repeated military conflict between the two countries, but clearly the changes in relative population gave people ideas.

At the end of World War I, France saw an opportunity to avenge its defeat in the Franco-Prussian War (1870–1871) and demanded enormous reparations from Germany. The history is well known, although the amounts and their significance are often left unsaid. In fact, the sums officially demanded of Germany were totally unrealistic. Under the Treaty of Versailles (1919), the terms of which were clarified by the Reparation Commission in 1921, Germany was supposed to pay 132 billion gold marks, or more than 250 percent of Germany's 1913 national income and roughly 350 percent of German national income in 1919–1921 (in view of the fall in output between the two dates).[84] Note that this is approximately the same proportion of national income as the debt imposed on Haiti in 1825 (roughly 300 percent), which dragged Haiti down until 1950—with one important difference, namely, the much greater size of Germany's national income on both the European and global scale.[85] From the standpoint of the French authorities, this amount was justified. After the defeat of 1871, France had paid Germany 7.5 billion gold francs, roughly 30 percent of its national income, and the damage suffered in World War I was far, far greater. The French and British negotiators also insisted that both countries needed to recover sums in keeping with the enormous public debts they had contracted with their wealthy and thrifty citizens, whom at that point they fully intended to reimburse in keeping with the sacred promise that had been made to those who paid for the war.

---

83. Within the 1913 borders, the population gap between Germany (67 million) and France (39 million) was even larger than that indicated here (63 million versus 41 million). The German population was at that point growing by nearly a million a year. See the online appendix.

84. See the online appendix. I did not include debts arising from the Treaty of Versailles in the German public debt series shown in Fig. 10.9 (or in the series on foreign financial assets shown in Fig. 7.9), partly because this would have required a change of scale and partly because it would also have been necessary to count French and British assets, which would be largely artificial, since their reimbursement never really began.

85. See Chap. 6.

Nevertheless, the sums demanded placed Germany in a state of eternal dependency on its conquerors, especially France. One doesn't have to be a great statistician to understand this (or to understand the growing demographic gap between the two countries), and German politicians in the interwar years made it their business to explain the implications to German voters. With an interest rate of 4 percent, mere payment of the interest on a debt of 350 percent of national income would have required Germany to transfer something on the order of 15 percent of its output in the 1920s and 1930s just to pay the interest, without even beginning to reimburse the principal. Unsatisfied with the pace of payment and frustrated by the small value of Germany's foreign assets (which the French and British allies had immediately seized and divided up in 1919–1920, along with Germany's meager colonies), the French government sent troops to occupy the Ruhr in 1923–1925, with the goal of helping themselves directly to the output of German factories and mines. Had not Prussian troops occupied France until 1873, until the tribute of 1871 was paid in full? The comparison was not very valid, partly because France in the 1870s was flourishing when compared with devastation of 1920s Germany and partly because the sums demanded of Germany were more than ten times greater. It nevertheless convinced many French people, who had also been sorely tried by the conflict. The occupation of the Ruhr had little effect other than to spur resentment in Germany as the country fell victim to hyperinflation and output languished 30 percent below 1913 levels. Germany's debts were finally canceled in 1931 as the entire world was sinking into the Great Depression, and any prospect of reimbursement vanished forever. We now know, of course, that all this merely laid the groundwork for Nazism and World War II.

The most absurd thing about France's relentless pursuit of repayment, which was vigorously criticized at the time by the most lucid British and American observers, was that French political and economic elites realized in the 1920s that the payment of such sums by Germany could have undesirable effects on the French economy.[86] To reimburse the annual equivalent of 15 percent of its output, Germany would have needed to realize, year after year, a trade surplus

---

86. On the slowly dawning awareness of the undesirable effects of German transfers, see, for example, A. Sauvy, *Histoire économique de la France entre les deux guerres* (Fayard, 1965–1975). This book, though rather out of date, is nevertheless an interesting contribution by the man who was finance minister Paul Renaud's adviser in 1938 (and a staunch opponent of the Popular Front and the forty-hour week) before becoming the leading thinker of the movement to repopulate France in the postwar era.

of 15 percent of its output: in economic terms this is an accounting identity. A German trade surplus of that size threatened to impede the restarting of French industrial production, thus limiting job creation and increasing unemployment in France. In the nineteenth century, states paid military tribute without worrying about such economic consequences. Tribute payments were seen as pure financial transfers between states, leaving each of them to work things out with their property owners, savers, taxpayers, and workers (especially the former).

In a world where the various sectors of national economies were in competition with one another for global markets, however, this was no longer the case. Financial transfers affected trade and could therefore have negative effects on economic activity, employment, and ultimately the working class in certain sectors. Governments were just beginning to be concerned with promoting industrial development, full employment, and good jobs and with raising the level of national output itself. In fact, in a society concerned solely with increasing domestic output and employment, even if it meant running indefinite trade surpluses with the rest of the world without ever using them, there would be strictly no interest in imposing a financial tribute on a neighboring country (because that would reduce its purchases of one's own output). A world in which governments value output and employment is very different ideologically and politically from a world based on property and the income from property. The world that collapsed between 1914 and 1945 was one of colonial and proprietarian excess, a world in which elites continued to think in terms of increasingly exorbitant colonial tributes and failed to understand the terms and conditions of possible social reconciliation.[87]

From Abnormal Military Tribute to a New Military Order

The tribute of 300 percent or more of German national income is important because it was directly in line with previous practice and, in this sense, perfectly justified in the eyes of British and especially French creditors and also because it brought the system to the breaking point. This episode convinced an important segment of the German public that a nation's survival in the industrial and

---

87. Note, incidentally, that the world of productivist and mercantilist excess (in which trade surpluses became an end in themselves, partly perhaps to protect countries against international financial markets and their reversals) is in its own way just as absurd as the world of proprietarian and colonial excess. I will come back to this in Chap. 12.

colonial age depended above all on the military power of the state; only with a strong military could they hold their heads high. When one reads Adolf Hitler's *Mein Kampf* today, what is most chilling is not the sick anti-Semitic element, which is well known and expected, but the quasi-rational analysis of international relations and the speed with which the electoral process can accredit reasoning like Hitler's and put such a frustrated man in power. The opening lines say it all: "As long as the German nation is unable even to band together its own children in one common State, it has no moral right to think of colonization as one of its political aims."

A little further on, Hitler distinguishes clearly between commercial and financial colonialism, which allows a nation to enrich itself on profits earned in the rest of the world, and continental and territorial colonialism, in which a people can invest in and develop its own agricultural and industrial activity. He rejects the former model, that of the British and French empires, which he compares to "pyramids standing on their points." These are countries with minuscule metropolitan territories (and in the case of France a declining population as well, as Hitler repeatedly remarks). They try to capture the profits of vast, far-flung colonies forming a disparate and, in Hitler's eyes, fragile whole. By contrast, the power of the United States rests on a strong and unified continental base inhabited by a people less homogeneous than the Germans, to be sure, but sharing strong German and Saxon roots. The territorial strategy, Hitler concludes, is sounder than the strategy of commercial and financial colonialism, especially for the German people, who are growing rapidly in number. For the sake of coherence, Germany's territorial expansion must take place on European soil, not just in Cameroon, because "no divine will" made it necessary for "one people to possess more than fifty times as much territory as another" (Russia was the target here).

In this work, written in prison in 1924 during the occupation of the Ruhr and published in two volumes in 1925–1926, a few years before the seizure of power by the National Socialist German Workers' Party (NSDAP, or Nazi Party), Hitler also expressed his contempt for social democrats, educated elites, frightened bourgeois, and pacifists of every stripe, who dared to claim that Germany's salvation might come from contrition and internationalism; only through force and rearmament could a united German people and its unified German state exist in the modern industrial world.[88] On this point it is hard

---

88. Hitler's contempt for intellectuals seems to have derived from his belief that they were both pacifist and ineffectual: "A people of scholars, when they are physically

to deny that he has absorbed the lessons of history and of Europe's rise from 1500 to 1914, which did indeed rely on military and colonial domination and gunboat diplomacy.[89] His contempt for France, a country in demographic decline bent on destroying Germany by imposing a despicable tribute (the amount of which is repeatedly mentioned), is reinforced by the fact that the French occupier has brought in "hordes of Negroes" who, he says, have "unleashed their lust" on the banks of the Rhine (no doubt referring to colonial troops he may have heard about or encountered). The possibility of a "Negro republic in the heart of Europe" is a repeated refrain.[90] Leaving aside his tirades against blacks and Jews, Hitler's main goal is to convince the reader that internationalists and pacifists are cowards and that only absolute unity of the German people behind a strong state will make Germany great again. He denounces the cowardly leaders who failed to take up arms against the French occupier in 1923–1924 and concludes by telling the reader that the NSDAP is henceforth prepared to accomplish its historic mission. What is most chilling, of course, is that this strategy was crowned with success until it ultimately encountered a superior military and industrial force.[91]

---

degenerated, irresolute and cowardly pacifists, will not conquer heaven, nay it will not even be able to assure its existence on this globe." He also denounced the alleged propensity of the intellectual class to reproduce itself and to exhibit social contempt: "One will immediately object that the cherished son of a higher State official for example cannot be expected to become, let us say, a craftsman, because some other boy whose parents were craftsmen, seems more able. This may be true for today's evaluation of manual work. For this reason the folkish State will have to arrive at an attitude that is different in principle in regard to the conception of work. It will have to break, if necessary through centuries of education, with the injustice of despising physical labor." For further information, see the online appendix.

89. See Chap. 9.

90. Hitler goes so far as to accuse the French of preparing a "great replacement" coupled with a vast project of racial mixing. If their colonial policy continues, "the last vestiges of Frankish blood will disappear" and "a vast mixed-race state will extend from the Congo to the Rhine." See also the astonishing references to meetings with groups working for the national liberation of India and Egypt, with which Hitler found it hard to identify.

91. According to available estimates, the German occupier extracted 30–40 percent of French output between 1940 and 1944. Given the degree of violence and genocidal malevolence involved, it may be that the calculations of extractive efficiency make no sense. See F. Occhino, K. Oosterlinck, and E. White, "How Much Can a

In *La trahison des clercs* (*The Treason of the Clerks,* 1927), the essayist Julien Benda accused "clerics" (a class in which he included priests, scientists, and intellectuals) of having succumbed to nationalist, racist, and classist passions. After more than 2,000 years of moderating political passions and quenching the ardor of warriors and rulers ("since Socrates and Jesus Christ," as he put it), the clerical class had failed to oppose the European death instinct and the unprecedented rise of identity conflict in the twentieth century when they had not stirred up antagonism themselves. While he reserved a special animus for German clergymen and professors, who in his view had been the first to succumb to the sirens of war and nationalism during World War I, it was the entire European clerical class he had in his sights.

In 1939, the anthropologist and linguist Georges Dumézil published *Mythes et dieux des Germains (Myths and Gods of the Germans),* an "essay of comparative interpretation," in which he analyzes the relationship of ancient German mythology to Indo-European religious concepts and representations. In the 1980s Dumézil was caught up in a nasty polemic in which he was accused of conniving with Nazis or at the very least participating in an anthropological justification of the warrior spirit said to have come from the East. In reality, he was a French conservative of monarchical leanings who could not really be accused of Hitlerist sympathies or Germanophilia. In his book on trifunctional ideology he sought to show that ancient Germanic myths were structurally unbalanced by hypertrophy of the warrior class and an absence of a true sacerdotal or intellectual class (in contrast to the Indian case, for example, where the Brahmins generally dominated the Kshatriyas).[92]

These references to trifunctional logics in the interwar years may seem surprising. Once again, they illustrate the need to make sense of structures of inequality and the way they evolve, in this case, through the emergence of a new warrior order in Europe. They also remind us that proprietarian ideology never really stopped trying to justify inequality in the trifunctional key. Europe's eco-

---

Victor Force the Vanquished to Pay? France under the Nazi Boot," *Journal of Economic History,* 2008.

92. Dumézil's general thesis (founded on the analysis of ancient myths, a method that, as we saw in the case of India, is not always well suited to analyzing sociohistorical change and that tends to petrify supposed civilizational differences) was that Germano-Scandinavian myths and religions were excessively focused on the warrior cult and neglected the trifunctional equilibrium that one finds in both the Italo-Celtic and Indo-Iranian worlds. See D. Eribon, *Faut-il brûler Dumézil? Mythologie, science et politique* (Flammarion, 1992), pp. 185–206.

nomic takeoff owed little to its virtuous and peaceful proprietarian institutions (recall the European drug traffickers and the Chinese Smithians I discussed in Chapter 9). It owed much more to the ability of European states to maintain order to their advantage at the international level as they relied both on military domination and on their supposed intellectual and civilizational superiority.

The Fall of Ownership Society and the Transcendence of the Nation-State

To recapitulate: nineteenth-century European ownership societies were born of a promise of individual emancipation and social harmony, a promise associated with universal access to property and to the protection of the state; they replaced premodern trifunctional societies, characterized by inequalities of status. In practice, ownership societies largely conquered the world thanks to the military, technological, and financial power they derived from intra-European competition. They failed for two reasons: first, in the period 1880–1914 they attained a level of inequality and concentration of wealth even more extreme than that which existed in the Ancien Régime societies they purported to replace; and second, the nation-states of Europe ultimately self-destructed and were replaced by other states of continental dimension organized around new political and ideological projects.

In *The Origins of Totalitarianism,* a book written in the United States between 1945 and 1949 and published in 1951, Hannah Arendt tried to analyze the reasons why various European societies destroyed themselves. Like Polanyi, she believed that the collapse of 1914–1945 could be seen as a consequence of the contradictions of unbridled and unregulated European capitalism in the period 1815–1914. She laid particular stress on the fact that Europe's nation-states had in a sense been transcended by the globalized industrial and financial capitalism they had helped to create. Given the planetary scale and unprecedented transnational scope of trade, capital accumulation, and industrial growth, states were no longer able to control and regulate economic forces or their social consequences. For Arendt, the principal weakness of social democrats in the interwar years was precisely that they had still not fully integrated the need to transcend the nation-state. In a sense, they were alone in this. The colonial ideologies on which the British and French empires rested did transcend the nation-state in the phase of accelerated expansion (1880–1914). Empires were a way of organizing global capitalism through large-scale imperial communities and strongly hierarchical civilizational ideology, with the superior metropole at the center and the subordinate colonies on the periphery. They would soon be undermined, however, by centrifugal forces of independence.

For Arendt, the political projects of the Bolsheviks and Nazis succeed because both relied on new postnational state forms adapted to the dimensions of the global economy: a Soviet state spanning a vast Eurasian territory and combing pan-Slavic and messianic Communist ideologies at the global level; and a Nazi state based on a Reich of European dimensions drawing on pan-German ideology and racialized hierarchical organization led by those who were most capable. Both promised their people a classless society in which all enemies of the people would be exterminated, with one major difference: the Nazi *Volksgemeinschaft* allowed every German to imagine himself as a factory owner (on the global scale), whereas Bolshevism promised that everyone could become a worker (a member of the universal proletariat).[93] By contrast, the failure of the social democrats was, according to Arendt, due to their inability to conceive of new federal forms and their willingness to settle for a facade of internationalism when their actual political project was to build a welfare state within the narrow limits of the nation-state.[94]

This analysis, aimed at the French Socialists, German Social Democrats, and British Labourites of the late nineteenth and early twentieth centuries, is all the more interesting in that it remains quite pertinent for understanding the limitations of postwar social-democratic societies, including in the second half of the twentieth century and beyond. It is also relevant to the debates of 1945–1960, concerning not only the construction of a European economic community but also the transformation of the French colonial empire into a democratic federation at a time when many West African leaders were very much aware of the difficulties that tiny "nation-states" like Senegal and Ivory Coast would face in developing a viable social model in the context of global capitalism.[95] It is relevant, too, to the glaring inadequacies of the current European Union, whose feeble attempts to regulate capitalism and establish new norms

93. H. Arendt, *The Origins of Totalitarianism,* Part 3: *Totalitarianism* (1951; Harcourt, 1973).

94. In passing, Arendt mentions a limited French attempt to include representatives of the colonies in its parliament, in contrast to the United Kingdom. See H. Arendt, *The Origins of Totalitarianism,* Part 2: *Imperialism* (1951; Harcourt, 1976).

95. See Chap. 7.

of social, fiscal, and environmental justice have yet to be crowned with success and which is regularly accused of doing the bidding of more prosperous and more powerful economic actors.

Nevertheless, Arendt left wide open the question of the form and content of the new federalism. Her hesitation anticipates difficulties that would emerge more clearly later. Was what she had in mind a federalism that would seek to reduce inequalities and transcend capitalism, or was it a federalism intended to prevent the overthrow of capitalism and constitutionally enshrine economic liberalism? In the years that followed the publication of her essay, Arendt more than once expressed growing faith in the American model as the only political project truly grounded in respect for individual rights, whereas European political processes were in her view stuck in a Rousseauian-Robespierrist search for the general will and social justice—a search that led almost inevitably to totalitarianism. This vision is expressed with particular clarity in her *Essay on Revolution,* published in 1963 at the height of the Cold War, in which she sought to unmask the true nature of the French Revolution and rehabilitate the American, previously unjustly neglected in her view by European intellectuals keen on equality and insufficiently concerned about liberty.[96] Arendt's profound skepticism about Europe no doubt owes a great deal to her personal history and to the context of the time, and it is very hard to know how she, who died in 1975, would have judged today's United States and European Union. Nevertheless, her very negative conclusions as to the very possibility of democratic social justice is in the end rather close to the position taken in 1944 by another

---

96. It is interesting to note that Arendt attributes the success of the American constitutional model to the relative initial equality of pioneer society (if one excepts slaves, whose case Arendt skips over quickly), which in her view enabled it to remove the question of class inequality and social justice from political discussion. (In Arendt's view, these questions cannot be peacefully resolved in the political sphere.) By contrast, the inegalitarian soil of the old regime in Europe gave rise, she argues, to an obsession with the social question and class violence. See H. Arendt, *On Revolution* (Viking, 1963). Previously, she had compared the unleashing of modern anti-Semitism—in her view, a consequence of the fact that by the late nineteenth century nation-states and their banks no longer needed the transnational networks of Jewish bankers to issue their debt—to the violence unleashed against the nobility in the French Revolution, the noble class long since having become useless, so that it was now possible to exact vengeance. See H. Arendt, *The Origins of Totalitariansim,* Part 1: *Antisemitism* (1951; Harcourt, 1979). For Arendt, only the new world seems to be able to escape the eternal resentments bequeathed by history.

celebrated European exile—Friedrich von Hayek, who in his essay *The Road to Serfdom* explains in substance that any political project based on social justice leads straight to collectivism and totalitarianism. He was writing at the time in London, and the British Labour Party, which was on the verge of taking power in the 1945 elections, was uppermost in his mind. In retrospect, this judgment seems harsh and almost incongruous from someone who a few decades later was prepared to support the military dictatorship of General Augusto Pinochet.

Federal Union Between Democratic Socialism and Ordoliberalism

These debates about federalism and its uncertainties and the transcendence of the nation-state are highly instructive. They also enable us to understand why discussions of federalism, which were common in the 1930s and 1940s, did not lead anywhere. The year 1938 witnessed the launch of the Federal Union movement in the United Kingdom. Soon there were hundreds of sections throughout the country. Adherents saw union as the way to avoid war.[97] Among the movement's various proposals were a federal democratic union between Britain and its colonies, a US-UK union, and a union of European democracies against Nazism. In 1939, New York journalist Clarence Streit wrote a book entitled *Union Now,* in which he proposed a transatlantic federation of fifteen countries governed by a House of Representatives with membership proportional to population and a Senate of forty members (eight for the United States, four for the United Kingdom, four for France, and two for each of the twelve other countries). In 1945 he went so far as to propose a world federation with a convention to be elected by universal suffrage (with each of the nine regions of the globe divided into fifty districts and an overrepresentation of Western powers) that would then elect a president and council of forty members in charge of nuclear disarmament and redistribution of natural resources.[98] The Charter of the United Nations, adopted in 1945, provided for a General Assembly consisting of one representative for each country and a Security

---

97. On these debates, see the illuminating book by O. Rosenboim, *The Emergence of Globalism: Visions of World Order in Britain and the United States, 1939–1950* (Princeton University Press, 2017), pp. 100–178. See also Q. Slobodian, *Globalists: The End of Empire and the Birth of Neoliberalism* (Harvard University Press, 2018).

98. The two-stage election procedure was intended to avoid national biases. The initial proposal also reserved seats for experts and intellectuals, but that idea was scrapped.

Council with five permanent members with veto power and ten additional members elected by the General Assembly.[99] It was heavily influenced by the federalist debates of the 1930s and 1940s.

During the interwar years many people felt that the old colonial empires were close to collapse; the Great Depression had shown how interdependent the world's economies were, highlighting the need for new collective regulations; and the advent of long-distance air travel had brought the different regions of the world dramatically closer together.[100] In such conditions many people felt emboldened to imagine novel forms of political organization for the world to come.

In this connection, the British Federal Union movement and the debates it stimulated are particularly noteworthy. Initiated by young activists who saw federalism as a way of accelerating independence and providing a framework for peaceful political cooperation, the movement soon drew the support of academics like William Beveridge (the author of the celebrated 1942 report on social insurance which paved the way for the Labour Party to establish the National Health Service in 1948) and Lionel Robbins (of a much more liberal persuasion). The union movement inspired a proposal by Winston Churchill in June 1940 to create a Franco-British Federal Union, which the French government, then in refuge in Bordeaux, rejected, preferring instead to award full powers to Marshal Philippe Pétain. While several members of the government openly stated their preference for "becoming a Nazi province rather than a British dominion," it must be noted that the institutional content of the proposed federal union was rather vague, apart from a firm commitment to full Franco-British military cooperation and a complete merger of all remaining land, sea, and colonial forces not yet under German control.

Earlier, in April 1940, a group of British and French academics had met in Paris to study how a potential federal union might work, first at the Franco-British level and then at the European level, but no agreement was reached. The view most steeped in economic liberalism was that of Hayek, who had left

---

99. Since Resolution 1991 was adopted in 1963 by the General Assembly, the ten elected members of the Security Council include five members from Africa, Asia, and the Pacific; two members from Latin America; two from Western Europe; and one from Eastern Europe.

100. In 1943, Wendell Wilkie (the Republican candidate defeated by Roosevelt in 1940) published *One World,* an optimistic and colorful account of a world tour by airplane he had made in 1942 to meet political leaders and citizens from around the globe. See Rosenboim, *The Emergence of Globalism,* pp. 4–5.

Vienna for London, where he had been teaching at the London School of Economics since 1931 (Robbins had recruited him). Hayek favored a purely commercial union based on the principles of competition, free trade, and monetary stability. Robbins took a similar line but also envisioned the possibility of a federal budget and, in particular, a federal estate tax in case free trade and free circulation of persons did not suffice to spread prosperity and reduce inequality.

Other members of the group held views much closer to democratic socialism, starting with Beveridge, an adept of social insurance, and the sociologist Barbara Wooton, who proposed federal taxes on income and estates with a top rate of 60 percent and a ceiling on incomes and inheritances above a certain cutoff value. The meeting ended with an avowal of disagreement as to the economic and social content of any prospective federal union, although participants expressed the hope that a military union might be completed as quickly as possible. Wooton later spelled out her proposals more fully in two books, *Socialism and Federation* (1941) and *Freedom Under Planning* (1945). It was partly in response to Wooton that Hayek published *The Road to Serfdom* (1944). While acknowledging that the book might cost him many friends in his adopted country, he nevertheless felt it necessary to alert the British public to the danger he believed the Labour Party and other collectivists posed to freedom. He also warned against the Swedish Social Democrats, the new darling of the progressives, noting that Nazi economic interventionism had also been hailed in its day before people realized the threat it posed to freedom (a judgment to which history has not been kind, given Sweden's success).[101] These debates around a federal union spurred responses from across Europe. In 1941, Altiero Spinelli, a Communist activist held at the time in one of Mussolini's prisons, took inspiration from them to write his "Manifesto for a Free and United Europe," also known as the Ventotene Manifesto (for the name of the island where he was held).[102]

---

101. See F. Hayek, *The Road to Serfdom* (Routledge, 1944), pp. 3–10, 66–67, where Hayek warns his British readers about Labour's "platform for a planned society," which was adopted in 1942; indications dating from the 1930s that full realization of the Labour platform might imply the delegation of considerable power from Parliament to the bureaucracy; and the immunization of reforms against possible changes of government by giving them constitutional status.

102. In 1984, Spinelli was the author of a proposal to reform the institutions of the European Union, which was adopted by the European Parliament (of which he was a member). I will say more about this in Chap. 16.

These debates about federalism and the uncertainties associated with it are of fundamental importance because they are still with us. The fall of ownership society raises one key question: What is the appropriate political level for transcending capitalism and regulating property relations? Once the choice has been made to organize economic, commercial, and property relations at the transnational level, it seems obvious that the only way to transcend capitalism and ownership society is to work out some way of transcending the nation-state. But exactly how can this be done? What precise form and content can one give to such a project? In the following chapters we will see that the answers given to these questions by the political movements of the postwar period were limited in significant ways, particularly at the European level, and more generally in the various economic and trade agreements that were developed to organize globalization both during the Cold War (1950–1990) and in the postcommunist years (1990–2020).

ELEVEN

Social-Democratic Societies:
Incomplete Equality

In the previous chapter we examined how ownership societies that seemed so prosperous and solid on the eve of World War I collapsed between 1914 and 1945. The collapse was so complete that nominally capitalist countries actually turned into social democracies between 1950 and 1980 through a mixture of policies including nationalizations, public education, health and pension reforms, and progressive taxation of the highest incomes and largest fortunes. Despite undeniable successes, however, these social-democratic societies began to run into trouble in the 1980s. Specifically, they proved unable to cope with the rampant inequality that began to develop more or less everywhere around that time.

In this chapter we will focus on the reasons for this failure. In the first place, attempts to institute new forms of power sharing and social ownership of firms remained confined to a small number of countries (especially Germany and Sweden). This avenue of reform was never explored as fully as it might have been, even though it offered one of the most promising responses to the challenge of transcending private property and capitalism. Second, social democracy did not have a good answer to one pressing question: how to provide equal access to education and knowledge, particularly higher education. Finally, we will look at social-democratic thinking about taxation, especially progressive taxation of wealth. Social democracy did not succeed in building new transnational federal forms of shared sovereignty or social and fiscal justice. Today's globalized economy is one in which regulation in all its forms has been undermined by free trade and free circulation of capital, instituted by agreements to which social democrats consented or even instigated. In any case they had no alternative to offer. The resulting heightened international competition has gravely endangered the social contract (and consent to taxation) on which the social-democratic states of the twentieth century were built.

On the Diversity of European Social Democracies

In the period 1950–1980, the golden age of social democracy, income equality settled at a level noticeably lower than in previous decades in the United States and United Kingdom, France and Germany, Sweden and Japan, and nearly every European and non-European country for which adequate data are available.[1] This reduced inequality was due in part to destruction occasioned by war, which hurt those who owned a great deal much more than those who owned nothing. But a much more important reason for the reduction of inequality was a set of fiscal and social policies that made societies not only more egalitarian but also more prosperous than they had ever been before. To all of these societies we may therefore apply the label "social-democratic."

Let me be clear from the outset: I am using the terms "social-democratic society" and "social democracy" rather broadly to describe a set of political practices and institutions whose purpose was to socially embed (in Polanyi's sense) private property and capitalism. In the twentieth century, these practices and institutions were adopted by many noncommunist countries both in Europe and elsewhere, some of which explicitly called themselves social-democratic while others did not. In a narrower sense, only Sweden was ruled more or less continuously by an official social-democratic party (the Swedish Social Democratic Party, or SAP) from the early 1930s to the present (with occasional interludes of so-called bourgeois parties in power after the banking crisis of 1991–1992, about which I will say more later). Sweden is thus the quintessential social democracy, the country that conducted the longest experiment with this type of government. The Swedish case is all the more interesting in that Sweden was, prior to the reforms of 1910–1911, one of the most inegalitarian societies in the world, with voting power concentrated in a tiny stratum of the wealthy.[2] But from 1950 to 2000 it was the country that claimed the largest share of national income as taxes and had the highest social spending in Europe until France caught up with it in the early 2000s. The notion of social democracy I use in this book is best captured by these indicators, which measure the extent of the fiscal and social state.[3]

---

1. See Figs. 10.1–10.2, and the online appendix (piketty.pse.ens.fr/ideology), Figs. S10.1–S10.2.
2. See Chap. 5.
3. See Figs. 10.14–10.15.

In Germany, the Social Democratic Party (SPD), which by the end of the nineteenth century was the leading social-democratic party in Europe in terms of membership, has only been in power intermittently since the end of World War II. Its influence on the development of the German social state was nevertheless considerable, so much so that the Christian Democratic Union (CDU), which held power continuously from 1949 to 1966, adopted the "social market economy" as its official doctrine. In practice, proponents of the social market economy acknowledge the importance of social insurance and accept some degree of power sharing between shareholders and unions. Note, moreover, that the SPD decided at its Bad Godesberg convention in 1959 to drop all references to nationalizations and Marxism. Thus, there was a certain programmatic convergence of the two leading German parties of the postwar era, both of which were searching for a new developmental model that would enable them to rebuild the country after the Nazi catastrophe—a model that one might characterize as "social-democratic." Nevertheless, substantial differences remained between the SPD and CDU: they disagreed, for example, about the extent and organization of the social welfare and pension system. But both accepted a broad general framework that included high taxes and social spending compared with the pre–World War I period, to which no political party wished to return (in Germany or any other European country). The political landscape therefore resembled Sweden's, where the "bourgeois" parties never radically challenged the social state created by the SAP even when they came to hold power after 1991. It also resembled the postwar political landscape of other central and northern European countries with powerful social-democratic parties (such as Austria, Denmark, and Norway).

I also apply the term "social-democratic" (in the broad sense) to various other postwar state models such as those of the United Kingdom, France, and other European countries. These countries have parties that call themselves Labour, Socialist, or Communist and do not explicitly claim the "social-democratic" label. In the United Kingdom, the Labour Party has its own distinctive history, with roots in the trade union movement, Fabian socialism, and British parliamentarism.[4] Labour followed a distinctive political path: it won

---

4. The Fabian Society, founded in 1884 to promote a gradual reformist transition to democratic socialism without a revolutionary conflagration (hence the choice of namesake, the Roman general Fabius, an adept of the war of attrition in the third century BCE), is still today one of the "socialist societies" affiliated with the Labour Party. The Fabians Beatrice and Sidney Webb founded the London School of Economics in 1895; William Beveridge directed it from 1919 to 1937. On the intellec-

a large majority in Parliament in 1945, and Clement Attlee's government proceeded to establish the National Health Service and lay the foundation of the
British social state. Despite subsequent challenges, most notably from the
Tories led by Margaret Thatcher in the 1980s, Britain's fiscal and social state
remained large in the first two decades of the twenty-first century (with tax
revenues of 40 percent of national income, less than the 45–50 percent that
one finds in Germany, France, and Sweden but significantly higher than the
mere 30 percent in the United States).

In France, the socialist movement split permanently at the Congress of
Tours (1920) into a Communist Party (PCF) that supported the Soviet Union
and a Socialist Party (PS) that preferred democratic socialism. The two parties
shared power with the Radical Party in the Popular Front government elected
in 1936.[5] They later played a central role in establishing *la Sécurité sociale,* the
French health and pension system, which was adopted after the Liberation in
1945. Like other postwar policies, including the nationalization of many firms
and the expansion of the role of unions in collective bargaining, wage setting,
and workplace organization, the social security system was partly inspired by
the 1944 program of the Conseil National de la Résistance. The Socialists and
Communists again governed together in 1981 following the victory of the
Union of the Left. In the French context, the label "social-democratic" has often
been attacked as a synonym for "centrist," partly owing to the competition (and
verbal one-upmanship) between Socialists and Communists. For instance, nationalizations formed the backbone of the left program in 1981, at a time when
the German SPD had long since renounced the practice. In France, "social democracy" was often equated with renunciation of any real ambition to transcend capitalism. Be that as it may, the social and fiscal system that France
adopted after World War II puts it in the broad family of European social-
democratic societies.[6]

---

tual history of the Labour Party, see M. Bevir, *The Making of British Socialism*
(Princeton University Press, 2011).

5. The Radical Party (actually called the Republican, Radical, and Radical-Socialist
Party) included the more radical republicans from the first decades of the Third
Republic. It championed "social reform with respect for private property" and op-
posed nationalizations. More conservative than the Socialists and Communists on
socioeconomic issues, it lost its central place in the French political system after
World War II. Until 1971, the PS was generally known as the SFIO (from the
French initials for French Section of the Workers' International).

6. For a classic study of social-democratic models and of the French case, see A. Ber-
gounioux and B. Manin, *La social-démocratie ou le compromis* (Presses universita-

The New Deal in the United States: A Bargain-Basement Social Democracy

One might also characterize as "social-democratic" (very broadly speaking) the social system established in the United States in the 1930s under Franklin D. Roosevelt's New Deal. This was extended by Lyndon B. Johnson's War on Poverty in the 1960s. Compared with its European counterparts, however, the social-democratic society that the Democratic Party built in the United States was a bargain-basement version of social democracy, for reasons we will need to understand better. Concretely, European levels of taxation and social spending easily eclipsed those of the United States in the period 1950–1980; no such gap had existed in the nineteenth or early twentieth centuries.[7] In contrast to what became the postwar European norm, for example, the United States never established universal health insurance. Medicare and Medicaid, which Congress passed in 1965, are reserved for people over 65 and the poor, respectively, leaving uninsured workers not poor enough to qualify for Medicaid and not rich enough to pay for private coverage. To be sure, there has been much discussion of Medicare for All in recent years, and it is not out of the question that such a reform will pass someday.[8] Since 1935 the Social Security system has provided pensions and unemployment insurance to Americans. Though less generous than similar programs in Europe, these services have been around longer. As we saw in Chapter 10, income and inheritance taxes were more steeply progressive in the United States than in most European countries in the period 1932–1980. It may seem paradoxical that the United States was more egalitarian than Europe in terms of fiscal progressivity yet less ambitious with respect to its social state; we will look closely at this.

---

ires de France, 1979). On the diversity of European social democracy, see H. Kitschelt, *The Transformation of European Social Democracy* (Cambridge University Press, 1994). See also G. Esping-Andersen, *The Three Worlds of Welfare Capitalism* (Princeton University Press, 1990).

7. See Fig. 10.14.

8. The Affordable Care Act, or "Obamacare" (2010), was intended to make private insurance compulsory with subsidies for those who needed them. Implementation has proved difficult, largely because of opposition from Republican states and because Supreme Court decisions make it difficult for the federal government to impose social programs on the states. More ambitious proposals (including "Medicare for All") are now being advocated by a growing number of Democratic leaders.

There were also many non-European societies that developed social systems comparable to European social democracies in the period 1950–1980; for example, Latin America, and especially Argentina.[9] It might also be tempting to see many newly independent countries, such as India between 1950 and 1980, as vaguely belonging to the democratic socialist universe. Bear in mind, however, that India, like most countries in southern Asia and Africa, still had fairly low tax revenues (10–20 percent of national income, sometimes even less than 10), and the trend in the 1980s and 1990s was downward (I will come back to this). It is therefore very difficult to compare such countries to European social democracies. In subsequent chapters, moreover, we will study communist and postcommunist societies and their influence on perceptions of the social-democratic state. More generally, in Part Four, we will take a detailed look at the evolution of voting patterns and "social-democratic" coalitions in Europe, the United States, and other parts of the world, which will help us gain a better understanding of the specificities of these various trajectories and political constructs.

On the Limits of Social-Democratic Societies

At this stage, note simply that in most parts of the world, whether it be social-democratic Europe, the United States, India, or China, inequality has increased since 1980, with a strong rise in the top decile's share of total income and a significant drop in the share of the bottom 50 percent (Fig. 11.1).[10] Within this broad global landscape, it is true that between 1980 and 2018 inequality increased the least in the social-democratic societies of Europe. In this sense, the European social-democratic model seems to offer greater protection than other models (especially the meager American social state) from the inegalitarian pressures of globalization at work since the 1980s. Nevertheless, it is quite clear that a significant change has occurred compared with earlier periods: 1914–1950 saw a historic drop in inequality, while 1950–1980 was a period of

---

9. In Argentina and to a lesser degree in Brazil (where inequality was much greater), tax receipts in 1950–1980 reached a level intermediate between the United States and Europe (30–40 percent of national income). By contrast, Mexico and Chile continued to take in much less in taxes (less than 20 percent of national income). See the online appendix and the work of M. Morgan.

10. Europe, for the purposes of Fig. 11.1, includes both the western and eastern parts of the continent (a total of 540 million people). If we focus on Western Europe, the difference with the United States is even clearer. See Fig. 12.9.

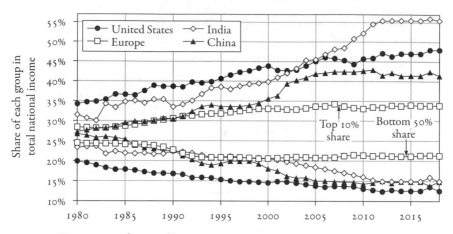

FIG. 11.1. Divergence of top and bottom incomes, 1980–2018

Interpretation: The top decile share increased in all parts of the world. It ranged from 27 to 34 percent in 1980 and from 34 to 56 percent in 2018. The share of the bottom 50 percent decreased: it was between 20 and 27 percent and is now between 12 and 21 percent. The divergence of top and bottom incomes is general, but its amplitude varies with the country: it is greater in India and the United States than in China and Europe (EU). *Sources and series:* piketty.pse.ens.fr/ideology.

stabilization.[11] In a context of increasing fiscal and social competition, which European social-democratic governments themselves did much to create and which has created many problems for African, Asian, and Latin American countries seeking to develop viable social models, it is not out of the question that the inegalitarian trend of the post-1980 period may grow stronger in the future. In addition, most of the countries of the Old Continent have had to contend with growing nationalist and anti-immigrant sentiment since 2000. Clearly, European social democracy cannot afford to rest on its laurels.

Furthermore, the egalitarian character of the period 1950–1980 should not be exaggerated. For example, if we compare the case of France (which is fairly representative of Western Europe) and the United States, we find that the share of national income going to the bottom 50 percent has always been significantly smaller than the share going to the top 10 percent (Fig. 11.2). At the turn of the twentieth century, the top decile claimed 50–55 percent of total income, and the bottom five deciles had gotten about one-quarter of that (around 13 percent of total income). Since the first group is by definition one-fifth the size of the second, this means that the average income of the top decile was twenty times

---

11. See Figs. 10.1–10.2.

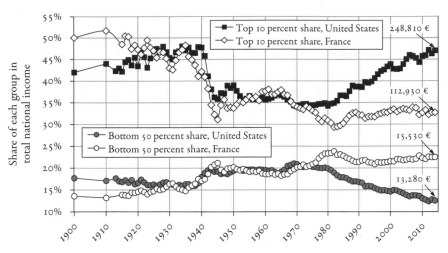

FIG. 11.2. Bottom and top incomes in France and the United States, 1910–2015

Interpretation: Income inequality in the United States in 2010–2015 exceeded its level in 1900–1910, whereas it was reduced in France (and Europe). In both cases, however, inequality remained high: the top decile, one-fifth the size of the bottom 50 percent, still received a much larger share of total income. The incomes shown are average annual incomes for each group in 2015 euros (at purchasing power parity). *Sources and series:* piketty.pse.ens.fr/ideology.

that of the bottom 50 percent. In the 2010s, this ratio was nearly eight: the average income of the top decile in 2015 was 113,000 euros per adult, compared with 15,000 euros for the bottom 50 percent. Clearly, then, social-democratic society may be less unequal than the ownership society of the Belle Époque or than other social models around the world, but it remains a highly hierarchical society in economic and monetary terms. As for the United States, we find that the ratio is close to twenty: nearly 250,000 euros for the top decile compared with barely 13,000 euros for the bottom half. Later we will see that taxes and transfers only slightly improve this situation for the bottom half of the US population today (and that the gap between the United States and Europe is due to the gap prior to taxes and transfers).

Public Property, Social Property, Temporary Property

For all these reasons, it is important to take a fresh look at what social-democratic societies have achieved as well as the limits of those achievements. Social-democratic institutions, including the legal system (especially corporate and labor law), the social insurance system, the educational system, and the tax system, were often put in place under emergency conditions (whether in the immediate aftermath of World War II or during the Depression) and never really conceived as a coherent whole. Countries generally relied on their own experience and took little account of the experiences of others. Sharing and mutual learning were sometimes important, as in the case of setting high top rates on progressive income and inheritance taxes, but played a more limited role when it came to setting social policy or designing the legal system.

Our first priority will be to look at the property regime. To simplify, there are three ways of moving beyond private ownership of firms and shareholder omnipotence. The first is public ownership: either the central government, a regional, state, or town government, or an agency under public control can replace private shareholders and take ownership of the firm. The second is social ownership: the firm's workers participate in its management and share power with private (and possibly public) shareholders, potentially replacing private shareholders entirely. The third is what I propose to call temporary ownership: the wealthiest private owners must return part of what they own to the community every year to facilitate circulation of wealth and reduce the concentration of private property and economic power. This could take the form of, for example, a progressive tax on wealth, which would be used to finance a universal capital endowment for each young adult. We will look more closely at this option later.[12]

To sum up: public ownership uses state power to balance the power of private property. Social ownership seeks to share power and control of the means of production at the firm level. Temporary ownership allows private property to circulate and prevents the persistence of excessively large holdings.

History suggests that these three ways of transcending private property are complementary. In other words, the key to transcending capitalism permanently is to rely on a mix of public ownership, social ownership, and temporary ownership. Communist societies of the Soviet type sought to rely almost exclusively on public ownership, indeed, on hypercentralized state ownership of nearly all firms and fixed capital—an experiment that ended in abject failure. Social-democratic societies took a more balanced approach, relying to a degree on all three remedies, but their efforts were insufficiently ambitious and systematic, particularly in regard to social and temporary ownership. Nationalization and state ownership were all too often the primary focus of policy, and ultimately even this option was abandoned after the fall of communism, with

---

12. See Chap. 17.

nothing worthy of the name to replace it. Hence in the end social democrats almost entirely gave up even thinking about moving beyond private property.

More generally, it is important to note that each of these three ways of transcending private ownership comes in many variants, offering endless scope for political, social, and historical experimentation. My intention here is not to close the debate but rather to open it up and reveal its full complexity. For instance, there are many forms of public ownership, some more democratic and participatory than others. What matters is how the corporate governance of public firms is organized. Are users, citizens, and other stakeholders represented on boards of directors? How are administrators appointed by the state or other public entities, and how is their work monitored? Public ownership can be perfectly justifiable, and it has demonstrated its superiority over private ownership in many sectors, including transportation, health, and education, provided that governance is transparent and responsive to the needs of citizens and users. As for temporary ownership and the universal capital endowment, these may require the institution of some new form of progressive wealth tax, with which we have little experience to date. I will come back to this in greater detail later. Finally, social ownership and power sharing between employees and stockholders can also be organized in many ways, some of which have been practiced in a number of European countries since the 1950s. We will start there.

Sharing Powers, Instituting Social Ownership: An Unfinished History

Germany and Sweden, and more generally the social-democratic societies of Germanic and Nordic Europe (especially Austria, Denmark, and Norway), are the countries that have gone furthest in the direction of co-management (from the German *Mitbestimmung,* sometimes translated as "codetermination"), which is a specific form of social ownership of firms and institutionalized power sharing between workers and shareholders. To be clear, co-management is not an end in itself. We can go beyond it. But we need first to study this important historical experience in order to gain a better understanding of possible next steps.

The German case is particularly interesting in view of the importance of the German social and industrial model for European social democracy.[13] A

---

13. For a recent analysis of German co-determination, see E. McGaughey, "The Co-determination Bargains: The History of German Corporate and Labour Law," *Columbia Journal of European Law,* 2017. See also S. Silvia, *Holding the Shop Together:*

1951 law made it mandatory for large firms in the coal and steel industries to reserve half the seats (and voting rights) on their boards of directors for representatives of their employees (generally elected from union slates). In concrete terms, this meant that workers on the board could vote on all of the firm's strategic choices (including nomination and removal of top executives and certification of financial results) and have the same access to the same documents as the directors chosen by the shareholders. In 1952, another law made it mandatory for large firms in other sectors to set aside one-third of their board seats for worker representatives. These two laws, adopted under Christian Democratic Chancellor Konrad Adenauer (1949–1963), also contained extensive provisions concerning the role of factory committees and union delegates in collective bargaining, especially in regard to wage setting, the organization of work, and occupational training.

The laws were further extended when the Social Democrats came to power in Bonn between 1969 and 1982 (under Willy Brandt and Helmut Schmidt). In 1976 an important law on co-management was passed. In its main outlines this law remains unchanged to this day. It requires all firms with more than 2,000 employees to reserve half their board seats (and voting rights) for worker representatives (one-third for firms with between 500 and 2,000 employees). These seats and voting rights are assigned to the worker representatives as such, regardless of worker participation in the firm's capital. When workers do own shares in the company (either as individuals or through a pension fund or other collective structure), they may hold additional board seats, potentially commanding a majority. The same is true if a local government, the federal state, or some other public body holds a minority share of the stock.[14]

It is important to note that this system, which was given legal force by the laws of 1951–1952 and 1976, is above all the result of the very strong mobilization of German unions since the late nineteenth and early twentieth centuries, combined with Germany's specific historical trajectory. While these rules are widely accepted in Germany today, including by employers, they were strongly contested in the past by German shareholders and owners, who gave in only after intense social and political struggles waged under historical circumstances

---

German Industrial Relations in the Postwar Era (Cornell University Press, 2013). The German *Mitbestimmung* system can be translated as "codetermination" or "co-management." The latter seems more expressive in English.

14. For example, in 2019, the state of Lower Saxony held 13 percent of Volkswagen's shares, and the firm's statutes guarantee it 20 percent of the voting rights.

in which the balance of power between workers and shareholders was a little less skewed than usual. It was in the aftermath of World War I, in the very unusual (and at times insurrectional) climate of the period 1918–1922, that the German workers' movement succeeded for the first time in negotiating with employers new rights related to factory committees, union delegates, and wage-setting procedures. These were later incorporated in the 1922 law on collective bargaining and worker representation.

It was also under pressure from the unions and the Social Democrats that the Weimar Constitution of 1919 instituted a much more social and instrumental concept of property than any previous constitution. In particular, the Constitution of 1919 specified that property rights and their limits would henceforth be defined by law, which meant that property was no longer considered a sacred natural right. The text explicitly envisioned the possibility of expropriations and nationalizations if "the good of the community" required it under terms set by law. The law also stipulated that land ownership should be organized in relation to explicit social objectives.[15] The German Fundamental Law of 1949 includes similar language, to the effect that property rights are legitimate only insofar as they contribute to the well-being of the community. The text explicitly mentioned socialization of the means of production in terms that opened the way to measures such as co-management.[16] In many countries, the demand for power sharing in firms, and more generally for redefining ownership and redistributing wealth, have encountered the objection that they are unconstitutional and violate property rights said to be absolute and unlimited; the German Fundamental Law makes this objection moot.

After being suspended by the Nazis from 1933 to 1945, the rights granted to unions by the German law of 1922 were reinstated under the Allied occupation. During reconstruction, from 1945 to 1951, the unions, once again in a relatively powerful position, succeeded in negotiating new rights with employers in the steel and energy sectors, including equal representation in the governing instances of firms. These new rights, obtained through negotiation and struggle,

---

15. Article 155: "The distribution and utilization of the land are controlled by the state in such a way as to prevent abuses and achieve the objective of ensuring that every family has a healthy place to dwell, corresponding to its needs.... Land required to satisfy needs resulting from a shortage of housing... or to develop agriculture may be expropriated."

16. Article 15: "The soil and land, natural resources and the means of production, may be placed under a regime of collective ownership or other forms of collective management by a law."

were simply incorporated into the 1951 law. It is worth noting that the 1952 law was seen by German trade union federations (especially the Confederation of German Trade Unions [DGB]) as a disappointment, even a step backward.[17] Worker participation in boards of directors (outside the coal and steel industries) was limited to one-third (in practice, two or three seats), whereas the unions were agitating for universal adoption of the principle of equal representation of shareholders and workers. The law also envisioned separate elections for blue- and white-collar workers, which in the eyes of the unions was tantamount to dividing the firm's employees and weakening their voice.

Successes and Limitations of German Co-Management

Broadly speaking, it is important to emphasize that one of the main limitations of German co-management is that worker-shareholder parity is in some ways a trap unless workers or the state also own shares in the company. With parity, the directors chosen by the shareholders hold the decisive vote when it comes to choosing the firm's top executives or deciding on its investment or recruitment strategy. This decisive vote is cast by the chairman of the board, who is always a representative of the shareholders. Another key point to bear in mind is that most German firms are governed not by a single board of directors (as is the case in most other countries) but by a two-headed structure consisting of an oversight committee and a directorate. Worker representatives hold half the seats on the oversight committee, but the shareholders, who have the decisive vote, can name as many members of the directorate as they wish, and this is the operational leadership of the firm. A recurrent demand of German unions, who remain dissatisfied with the system to this day, is for parity in the directorate as well: in other words, worker representatives should be allowed to choose half of the company's management team and not just the personnel manager or director of human resources (a post often filled by a union representative in large German firms, which already marks a significant departure from standard practice in other countries). These debates show that social ownership and co-management, as currently embodied, should not be regarded as finished solutions. On the contrary, they are still largely unfinished projects, history in progress, whose logic has not been pursued all the way to the end.

---

17. On these debates, see McGaughey, "The Codetermination Bargains." See also C. Kerr, "The Trade Union Movement and the Redistribution of Power in Postwar Germany," *Quarterly Journal of Economics,* 1954, pp. 556–557.

In the case of Sweden, the law of 1974, extended in 1980 and 1987, reserves a third of board seats for workers in firms with twenty-five or more employees.[18] Since Swedish firms are governed by a single board of directors, this representation, though a minority, sometimes results in more effective operational control than the German parity in oversight committees (which are farther removed from effective management of the firm). The Swedish rules also apply to much smaller firms than the German rules, which are applicable only to firms with 500 or more employees (very restrictive in practice). In Denmark and Norway, workers are entitled to a third of board seats in firms of more than thirty-five and fifty employees respectively.[19] In Austria, the proportion is also one-third, but the rule applies only to firms with more than 300 employees, which considerably limits the scope of its application (almost as much as in Germany).

Regardless of the limitations of German and Nordic co-management as it has been practiced since the end of World War II, all signs are that the new rules have somewhat shifted the balance of power between shareholders and employees and encouraged more harmonious and ultimately more efficient economic development (at least in comparison with firms in which workers enjoy no board representation). In particular, the fact that the unions help to define the firm's long-term strategy and are given access to all the documents and information they need for that purpose leads to greater employee involvement in the firm and thus to higher productivity. The presence of workers on boards of directors has also helped to limit wage inequality and in particular to control the vertiginous growth of executive pay seen in some other countries. Specifically, in the 1980s and 1990s, executives in German, Swedish, and Danish firms had to make do with far less fabulous raises than their English and US counterparts, yet this did not harm their firms' productivity or competitiveness— quite the contrary.[20]

---

18. More precisely, the current law provides two seats in firms of 25–1,000 employees and three seats in firms with more than 1,000 employees, which, given the size of boards of directors, usually corresponds to about a third of the seats in both cases.

19. In both cases, workers are entitled to half the number of directors elected by shareholders or exactly one-third of the total. Firms with thirty to fifty employees are also entitled to a paid director in Norway. See the online appendix.

20. See E. McGaughey, *Do Corporations Increase Inequality?* (Transnational Law Institute Think! Paper 32, King's College London, 2016). Later we will discuss other determinants of executive pay, especially the degree of fiscal progressivity.

The criticism that a minority presence of workers on boards of directors simply leads to ratification of decisions taken unilaterally by shareholders and therefore reduces union combativeness also appears to be unjustified. To be sure, the co-management system needs to be improved and surpassed. Nevertheless, all countries where it has been introduced have also established collective bargaining systems affording workers representation through factory committees, union delegates, and other entities composed solely of workers and responsible for negotiating directly with management over working conditions and wages (regardless of whether the managers have been approved by boards with worker membership). In Sweden, after the Social Democrats came to power in the 1930s, the unions were quick to take advantage of these entities for capital-labor negotiations. Similar institutions made it possible to develop a true worker "status" with a guaranteed wage income (generally in the form of a monthly wage instead of work paid by the task or the day, as in the nineteenth century) and protection against unjustified dismissal (which also encouraged workers to identify with the long-term interests of their firms) in nearly all developed countries, even where workers were not represented on company boards.[21] But obtaining board seats offered an additional channel of influence. This is particularly true at times of industrial and union decline and is part of the reason why the German and Nordic social and economic model has been more resilient since the 1980s.[22] To sum up, co-management has been one of the most highly developed and durable means of institutionalizing the new balance of power between workers and capital. It came into being in the mid-twentieth century as the culmination of a very long process involving union struggles, worker militancy, and political battles, which dated back to the middle of the nineteenth century.[23]

---

21. On the slow constitution of a "salaried worker" status and veritable "salaried society," *(société salariale),* see R. Castel, *Les métamorphoses de la question sociale* (Folio, 1995), pp. 594–595. It was not until 1969–1977, for example, that monthly pay became the norm in France. See also R. Castel and C. Haroche, *Propriété privée, propriété sociale, propriété de soi* (Pluriel, 2001).

22. See McGaughey, *Do Corporations Increase Inequality?*

23. Among the many works devoted to this history, see S. Bartolini, *The Political Mobilization of the European Left, 1860–1980: The Class Cleavage* (Cambridge University Press, 2000). For an analysis of European worker networks and early forms of mutual aid and strike funds dating back to the 1860s, especially in connection with the First International, see N. Delalande, *La lutte et l'entraide. L'âge des solidarités ouvrières* (Seuil, 2019).

On the Slow Diffusion of German and Nordic Co-Management

To recapitulate: In the Germanic and Nordic countries (notably Germany, Austria, Sweden, Denmark, and Norway) worker representatives fill between a third and a half of the seats on the boards of directors of the largest firms whether or not they own any part of the firm's capital. In Germany, which led the way on these matters, this system has been in place since the early 1950s. Despite the widely acknowledged success of the German and Nordic social and industrial model, which is noted for producing a high standard of living, high productivity, and moderate inequality, other countries until recently had not followed suit. In the United Kingdom, United States, France, Italy, Spain, Japan, Canada, and Australia, private firms continue to be governed by immutable corporate bylaws: in all these countries, a general assembly of shareholders continues to elect the entire board of directors according to the principle "one share, one vote," with no representation for employees (except in a few cases that have a merely consultative representation, without voting rights).

Things began to change slightly in 2013, when France passed a law requiring firms with more than 5,000 employees to set aside one board seat out of twelve for a worker representative. This new French rule was nevertheless quite limited compared to the German and Nordic systems (limited in terms of both the number of worker representatives and the scope of firms covered).[24] Of course, it is not out of the question that coverage will be increased in the coming decade, not only in France but also in the United Kingdom and United States, where some fairly ambitious and innovative proposals have recently been discussed by Labour and Democratic politicians respectively. If France, Britain, and the United States were to move more decisively in this direction, it is possible that this would lead to a more global diffusion of the model. Nevertheless, as of 2019, if one excepts the meager single board seat introduced in France in 2013, power-sharing and co-management arrangements remain confined to the Germanic and Nordic countries. Co-management is a trademark of Rhenish and Scandinavian capitalism, not of Anglo-American capitalism (or French, Latin, or Japanese capitalism). How can we explain such slow and limited

---

24. More precisely, the law created one paid directorship when the board of directors consisted of fewer than twelve members and two seats when the board was larger. The 2013 law was to apply to firms with more than 5,000 employees in France or more than 10,000 throughout the world; these thresholds were reduced in 2015 to firms employing more than 1,000 workers in France or 5,000 throughout the world.

diffusion of the co-management model compared with the rapid and wide-spread diffusion of large-scale progressive taxation after World War I?

The first explanation is that the decision to give workers voting rights without any corresponding participation in the firm's capital constituted a fairly radical conceptual challenge to the very idea of private property, which shareholders and owners have always strenuously opposed. It is easy, even for parties with a relatively conservative economic outlook, to defend a certain theoretical diffusion of ownership. For instance, the French Gaullists promoted the idea of "participation" (in the double sense of employee share ownership and potential profit sharing, but without voting rights). Conservatives in Britain and Republicans in the United States have regularly championed the idea of employee stock ownership; this idea was floated in the 1980s, for example, when Thatcher privatized publicly owned firms. But to change the rules linking ownership of capital to the power to decide what use to make of one's property (a power taken to be absolute in classic definitions of property) and to create voting rights for people who own nothing—these are from a conceptual standpoint highly destabilizing actions, even more so (arguably) than progressive taxation. In Germany and the Nordic countries, such a drastic revision of corporate law and the law of property was possible only in very specific historic circumstances, characterized by unusually strong mobilization of trade unions and social-democratic parties.

The second explanation, which complements the first, is precisely that the political and social forces in other countries did not have the same determination as in Germany for reasons related to the political-ideological trajectory of each country. In France, it is often thought that the enduring socialist preference for nationalizations (which, for example, formed the centerpiece of the Union of the Left program in the 1970s) and the lack of appetite for co-management stem from the supposed statist ideology of French Socialism and its weak ties to the union movement. It is indeed striking that no measure to set aside board seats for worker representatives was proposed between 1981 and 1986, when the Socialists had an absolute majority in the National Assembly. The role of union delegates in negotiating wages and working conditions was expanded, and certain steps were taken to promote decentralization and participation in other sectors (such as increasing the autonomy of local governments), but the link between shareholding and decision-making power within firms was not touched. By contrast, the sweeping program of nationalizations in 1982 sought to complete the nationalizations of the Liberation by incorporating nearly the entire banking sector and major industrial conglomerates in the public sector, which meant appointing directors chosen by the government in place of directors elected by shareholders. In other words, French Socialists believed that the state and its high civil servants were perfectly capable of taking over the boards of directors of all key industries but that worker representatives had no place among them.

Then, in 1986–1988, the Gaullist and liberal parties returned to power in a new context of privatization and deregulation under Thatcher and Reagan, while at the same time the Communist bloc was slowly crumbling. This led to the privatization of most of the companies that had been nationalized between 1945 and 1982. The privatization movement continued, moreover, in the legislatures of 1988–1993, 1997–2002, and 2012–2017, during which the Socialists were in power, yet still no Germano-Nordic-style co-management was ever attempted, apart from the timid and belated law of 2013.[25] French Socialists and Communists might also have pushed from co-management in 1945–1946, but they chose instead to concentrate on other battles, including nationalizations and social security, for example.

It is not clear, however, whether the lack of appetite for co-management can be attributed to the weakness of French trade unionism. True, the workers' movement in France was less powerful and less organized than in Germany or the United Kingdom and less closely tied to French political parties.[26] Still, the unions and social mobilizations did play an important role in French political history (especially in 1936, 1945, 1968, 1981, 1995, and 2006). Furthermore, Germano-Nordic co-management did not spread to the United Kingdom either, even though the Labour Party has from its inception been structurally tied to powerful British trade union movement. The more likely explanation

---

25. François Mitterrand, in a "letter to the French" written in 1988, promised "neither-nor" (neither new nationalizations nor new privatizations). His reelection hinged on this promise of social peace, coupled with his denunciation of police violence against student demonstrators (opposed to the increase in registration fees) and of the suppression of the wealth tax.

26. The looser ties between unions and parties in France are often attributed to the fact that democracy and universal suffrage preceded social democracy and trade unionism in France (whereas the opposite is to a large extent true in Germany and the United Kingdom); hence, there is a certain wariness on the part of the unions (which were long subject to the ban on professional organizations and guilds enacted in 1791 and were not legalized until 1883) toward parliament and government. See, for example, M. Duverger, *Les partis politiques* (Armand Colin, 1951), pp. 33–34.

for the shared British and French aversion to co-management is that both French Socialists and British Labourites long believed that nationalization and state ownership of large firms was the only way to truly alter the balance of power and move beyond capitalism. This is obvious in the French case (as the Common Program of 1981 indicates), but it is just as obvious for the United Kingdom. The famous Clause IV of the Labour Party's constitution of 1918 set "common ownership of the means of production" as the party's central goal (or so it was interpreted). As recently as the 1980s Labour platforms were still promising further nationalizations and indefinite extension of the public sector, until New Labour under Tony Blair finally succeeded in 1995 in eliminating any reference to the property regime from Clause IV.[27]

Socialists, Labourites, Social Democrats: Intersecting Trajectories

From this point of view, it was the SPD that was the exception. Although the French and British parties waited until the fall of the Soviet Union in 1989–1991 to renounce nationalizations as a central tenet of their programs, the German Social Democrats had already endorsed co-management in the early 1950s and abandoned nationalizations at Bad Godesberg in 1959. In the interwar years things were different: nationalizations were at the heart of the SPD program in the 1920s and 1930s, and, like its French and British counterparts, the party showed little interest in co-management.[28] If things changed in 1945–1950, it was because of Germany's unique political-ideological trajectory.

---

27. In fact, the Clause IV of 1918 opened the way to various forms of ownership, since it stated the party's objective as follows: "To secure for the workers by hand or by brain the full fruits of their industry and the most equitable distribution thereof that may be possible upon the basis of the common ownership of the means of production, distribution and exchange, and the best obtainable system of popular administration and control of each industry or service." The clause adopted in 1995 reads as follows: "The Labour Party is a democratic socialist party. It believes that by the strength of our common endeavour we achieve more than we achieve alone, so as to create for each of us the means to realise our true potential and for all of us a community in which power, wealth and opportunity are in the hands of the many, not the few, where the rights we enjoy reflect the duties we owe, and where we live together, freely, in a spirit of solidarity, tolerance and respect."

28. The same was true before World War I, in particular when Bernstein's "revisionist" faction was outvoted at the Congress of Hanover in 1899. See Chap. 10.

Not only had the very bitter clashes between the SPD and the Communist Party of Germany (KPD) in the interwar years left deep traces,[29] but the West-German Social Democrats had every reason in the 1950s to wish to set themselves apart from the Communists in the East and the idea of state ownership. The traumatic experience of hypertrophied state power under the Nazis no doubt also contributed to discrediting nationalizations and state ownership in the eyes of the SPD and the German public, or at the very least to enhancing the appeal of co-management as a solution.[30]

In any case, it is interesting to note that the abandonment of any reference to nationalizations in the 1990s did not lead either the French Socialists or the British Labour Party to embrace the co-management agenda. In the period 1990–2010 neither party exhibited the slightest desire to transform the property regime. Private capitalism and the "one share, one vote" principle appeared to have become unsurpassable horizons, at least for the time being. Both parties contributed to this state of mind by privatizing some state enterprises and by supporting the free flow of capital and the race to cut taxes.[31] In the French case, the fact that co-management ultimately resurfaced in the timid law of 2013 owed a great deal to the demands of certain unions (especially the French Democratic Confederation of Labor [CFDT]) and above all to the increasingly obvious success of the German industrial sector. In the late 2000s and early 2010s, when references to Germany and its economic model were ubiquitous, partly for good reasons, it became increasingly difficult for French employers and shareholders to reject co-management out of hand and to insist that the presence of workers on corporate boards would sow chaos.[32] The timid advance of 2013—timid by comparison with decades-old German and Nordic

---

29. In the decisive 1930–1932 elections, the SPD (Social Democrats) and KPD (Communists) together won more votes than the NSDAP (Nazis): 37 percent of the votes and 221 seats for the SPD and KPD in the November 1932 elections versus 31 percent of the votes and 196 seats for the NSDAP. But the inability of the two left-wing parties to unite allowed the Nazis to take power.

30. On the intellectual context, see McGaughey, "The Codetermination Bargains."

31. The French Socialists in 1997–2002 and the British Labour Party in 1997–2010 also pursued other reforms, including the reduction of the work week (for the French) and educational reform (for the British). But regarding the key issues of the property regime and the international financial regime, both the Socialists and the Labourites adopted a fairly conservative stance.

32. By contrast, Germany's economic difficulties, associated with reunification in the 1990s and early 2000s, probably slowed the diffusion of co-management.

practices—tells us a great deal about the political and ideological resistance at work, as well as about the often quite national character of the process of policy experimentation and learning.

In the British case, the need for new approaches in the fight against rising inequality, coupled with the change in the Labour Party's leadership in 2015 (partly because of dissatisfaction with the Blairite line and the country's inegalitarian drift), has contributed in recent years to the development of a new political approach. The party is more open to nationalizations (public enterprises are now thought to be desirable in some sectors such as transportation and water supply, reflecting a new pragmatism compared with the preceding era), a new system of labor law, and new forms of corporate governance. The growing popularity of worker representation on boards of directors, an idea that has also been canvased among previously skeptical Democrats in the United States as well as certain British Conservatives, can be explained by the fact that co-management is a social measure that costs the public treasury nothing—a particularly valued quality in these days of growing inequality and rising deficits. For all these reasons, good and bad, it is likely that these issues will continue to be debated in the coming years, although it is impossible at this stage to say when change might occur.

From a European Directive on Co-Management to Proposition "2x + y"

Before we turn to these new prospects, however, it is important to emphasize that the various political-ideological trajectories I have just rehearsed are simply the ones that actually came to pass. Many other paths might have been taken, because the history of property regimes, like the history of inequality regimes in general, contains numerous switch points and should not be seen as linear or deterministic.

One particularly interesting case involves the so-called $2x + y$ proposal discussed in the United Kingdom in 1977–1978. In 1975 Labour Prime Minister Harold Wilson commissioned a report from a commission chaired by historian Allan Bullock and composed of jurists, trade unionists, and employers. The commission's conclusions were submitted in 1977. The inquiry was a response to a request from the European Commission, which, under pressure from Germany, was considering a European directive on corporate governance. A draft published by the Brussels authorities in 1972 proposed that all firms with more than 500 employees should have at least one-third of their directors representing workers. Revised drafts were published in 1983 and 1988, but in the end the whole project was abandoned for want of a majority of European countries willing to vote for it.[33] I will say more later about how EU rules make it almost impossible to adopt common policies of this type (for reforms of the fiscal and social system as well as the legal system); only a profound democratization of EU institutions can change this. It is nevertheless interesting that a proposal for a European model of power sharing between workers and shareholders did reach a relatively advanced stage in the 1970s and 1980s.

In any case, the Bullock Commission proposed in 1977 that the Labour government adopt the so-called $2x+y$ system.[34] Concretely, in every firm with more than 2,000 employees, shareholders and workers were both to elect a number x of board members, and the government would then top off the board by naming y independent directors, who would cast the decisive votes in case of a stalemate between shareholder and worker representatives. For example, a board of directors might consist of five shareholder representatives, five worker representatives, and two representatives of the government. The numbers x and y could be set by the firm's bylaws, but the latter could not affect the overall structure or the fact that the board of directors alone had the right to make the most important decisions (such as naming the firm's executives, approving its financial reports, distributing dividends, and so on). Unsurprisingly, shareholders and the City of London's financial community outspokenly opposed the proposal, which radically challenged the usual assumptions of private capitalism, potentially going much farther than German or Swedish co-management. By contrast, there was strong support from the unions and the Labour Party, with no compromise in sight.[35] In the fall of 1978, James Callaghan, the new Labour prime minister who replaced Wilson in 1976, seriously contemplated calling a snap election at a time when the polls were predicting a Labour victory. In the end, he decided to wait another year. The country was immobilized by numerous strikes during the "Winter of Discontent"

---

33. The so-called Draft Fifth Company Law Directive also suffered from the fact that the 1972 version favored the German model of dual governance. The 1983 and 1988 versions dropped this but preserved strong representation of workers on corporate boards (from a third to a half of the seats), without success. See the online appendix.

34. On this proposal and the history of these debates, see E. McGaughey, "Votes at Work in Britain: Shareholder Monopolisation and the 'Single Channel,'" *Industrial Law Journal*, 2018.

35. Union and employer representatives had clashed within the Bullock Commission, and it was the jurists and academics who cast the deciding votes in favor of the majority report.

(1978–1979) in a period of high inflation. The Tories, led by Margaret Thatcher, won the election in 1979, and the project was definitively buried.

Beyond Co-Management: Rethinking Social Ownership and Power Sharing

In Part Four I will return to the question of how one might move toward a new form of participatory socialism in the twenty-first century, drawing on the lessons of history and, in particular, combing elements of social and temporary ownership.[36] At this stage, I simply want to indicate that social ownership— that is, power sharing within the firm—can potentially take forms other than German or Nordic-style co-management. This history is far from over, as any number of recent proposals and debates suggest.

Broadly speaking, one key issue concerns the extent to which it is possible to overcome the automatic majority that shareholders enjoy under the German system of co-management. The Bullock Commission's $2x+y$ proposal is one answer to this question, by assigning a major role to the state. This might work with very large firms (where it would be tantamount to making local and national governments minority shareholders), but it might be problematic to apply such a system to hundreds of thousands of small and medium firms.[37] One important limitation of the German system is that it applies only to large firms (with more than 500 employees), whereas Nordic co-management applies much more broadly (to firms with more than thirty, thirty-five, or fifty salaries depending on the case). Since the majority of workers work for small firms, it is essential to find solutions applicable to companies of all sizes.[38]

As a complement to ideas like "$2x+y$," one might also want to encourage employee shareholding, which could add seats to those already held by workers

---

36. See Chap. 17.
37. It could be problematic unless the procedures for appointing public board members are spelled out and steps are taken to ensure that the system functions in a satisfactory manner (which is not necessarily impossible but would require concrete historical experimentation).
38. In 2017, 21 percent of private-sector workers in France worked for firms with fewer than ten employers, 40 percent for firms with 10–250 employees, 26 percent for firms with 251–5,000 employees, and 13 percent for firms with more than 5,000 employees. Self-employment accounted for 12 percent of employment, compared with 21 percent in the private sector (state, municipalities, and hospitals) and 67 percent in the private sector (all types of firms and associations combined). The figures for other European countries are comparable. See the online appendix.

without shares, opening the way to worker majorities. Several Democratic senators proposed bills in 2018 to require US firms to set aside 30–40 percent of their board seats for worker representatives.[39] Passage of such a law would be revolutionary in the United States, where nothing of the kind has ever existed. There is a certain tradition of employee stock ownership, however, although the influence of the patrimonial middle class has decreased in recent decades as the concentration of wealth has skyrocketed. Fiscal policies less favorable to the highest earners and wealthiest individuals, together with incentives for employee stock ownership, could change this.[40] Proposals like the one I will discuss later (for a progressive wealth tax coupled with a universal capital endowment) could also create new majorities, alter the balance of power, and equalize participation in the economy. Still, the movement to set aside board seats for workers has not gotten very far in the United States, where it does little good to point to the success of co-management in Germany or Scandinavia or, for that matter, anywhere outside the United States. It might help, however, to call attention to the fact that there is an old (and largely forgotten) Anglo-American tradition of limiting the power of large shareholders: in the early nineteenth century, British and American companies often placed limits on the voting rights of large stockholders.[41]

Recent British debates have also suggested new ways of moving beyond existing co-management models. In 2016, for example, a collective of jurists published a "Labor Law Manifesto," which was partly incorporated into the official platform of the Labour Party. The goal was to revise large parts of labor and corporate law to encourage greater worker participation and improve working conditions and pay while enhancing social and economic efficiency.

---

39. Although limited to large firms, these bills were novel in the American context. The "Reward Work Act" bill (March 2018) would have required listed firms to set aside at least a third of their board seats for worker representatives elected on the basis of "one worker, one vote." The "Accountable Capitalism Act" bill (August 2018) envisioned 40 percent of "employee directors" for the largest firms (with annual revenues of more than $1 billion), whether listed or not, and would also have required a three-fourths majority of the board to approve political donations (since the Supreme Court had ruled that corporate donations could not be forbidden). Neither of these bills has been adopted so far, but the fact that they are openly discussed in the US Congress is already a major novelty.

40. See J. Blasi, R. Freeman, and D. Kruse, *The Citizen's Share: Putting Ownership Back into Democracy* (Yale University Press, 2013). See also J. Ott, *When Wall Street Met Main Street: The Quest for an Investors' Democracy* (Harvard University Press, 2011).

41. See Chap. 5.

The manifesto proposed that workers immediately be given a minimum of two board seats (typically 20 percent of the total). The most original proposal was that board members should be elected by a mixed assembly of shareholders and workers.[42] In other words, workers should be considered members of the firm on the same footing as shareholders—that is, as actors involved in its long-term development. As such, they would enjoy voting rights in a mixed assembly responsible for choosing the firm's board. Initially, workers would be given 20 percent of the voting rights in this assembly, but this would gradually be increased (possibly to 50 percent or more). These rules would apply, moreover, to all firms, regardless of size, including the smallest; in this respect the manifesto departed from the experience of other countries and offered the potential of involving all workers, not just the employees of large firms.

One virtue of such a system, according to the authors, is that it would oblige would-be directors to address the concerns of both workers and shareholders. Rather than represent solely the interests of one group or the other, directors elected by such a mixed assembly would have to present long-term strategies based on the aspirations and understandings of both. If workers were also shareholders, either individually or through some collective entity such as a pension fund, new dynamics might emerge.[43]

Cooperatives and Self-Management: Capital, Power, and Voting Rights

Mention should also be made of ongoing reflection on the governance of cooperatives and nonprofit organizations such as associations and foundations, which play a central role in many sectors, including education, health, culture, universities, and media. One of the main limits on the development of coop-

---

42. E. McGaughey, "A Twelve-Point Plan for Labour, and a Manifesto for Labour Law," *Industrial Law Journal,* 2017. See also K. Ewing, J. Hendy, and C. Jones, eds., *A Manifesto for Labour Law* (Institute of Employment Rights [IER], 2016); J. Hendy, K. Ewing, and C. Jones, eds., *Rolling Out the Manifesto for Labour Law* (IER, 2018), pp. 32–33.

43. See also the propositions of I. Ferreras, *Firms as Political Entities: Saving Democracy through Economic Bicameralism* (Cambridge University Press, 2017), who envisions firms governed by an assembly of workers and an assembly of shareholders, with neither taking precedence over the other, in the manner of democracies with bicameral legislatures. The advantage would be to encourage actors to reach mutually advantageous compromises; the risk is deadlock.

eratives has been excessive structural rigidity. In the classic cooperative, each member has one vote. This structure is perfectly appropriate for certain types of project, in which each participant does the same amount of work and contributes the same amount of resources. Historically, cooperatives have also demonstrated their ability to manage natural resources in an egalitarian way.[44]

This structure can lead to complications in many situations, however: for example, when investors in a new venture contribute different amounts to the project. This can be a problem for both large and small ventures. Take a person who wants to open a restaurant or an organic food store and has $50,000 to invest. Suppose the business has three employees: the founder and two other people she recruits to work with her but who contribute no capital. With a strictly egalitarian cooperative structure, each worker would have one vote. The two new hires, who may have joined the business the week before or may be thinking of leaving to start their own businesses the following week, can outvote the founder on all sorts of matters, even though she invested all her savings and may have been dreaming about the business for years. Such a structure might be appropriate in some situations, but to impose it in every case would be neither just nor efficient. Individual aspirations and career paths vary widely, and any power-sharing arrangement must take this diversity into account rather than stifle it. In Chapter 12 I will say more about this important topic in connection with communist and postcommunist societies.

More generally, for projects involving more workers or a more diversified capital structure, there is nothing wrong with giving more votes to individuals who supply more capital, provided that workers are also represented in decision-making bodies (perhaps through representatives chosen according to the rules of the German co-management model or perhaps through a mixed assembly of workers and shareholders) and provided that everything possible is done to reduce inequalities of wealth and to equalize access to economic and social life. One can also set a ceiling on the number of votes that any one stockholder can cast or create several different classes of voting rights.[45]

---

44. See D. Cole and E. Ostrom, eds., *Property in Land and Other Resources* (Lincoln Institute of Land Policy, 2011). See also F. Graber and F. Locher, eds., *Posséder la nature. Environnement et propriété dans l'histoire* (Editions Amsterdam, 2018).

45. This was done in the eighteenth and nineteenth centuries in both political assemblies and shareholder assemblies. One could apply the "one share, one vote" principle across the board, or alternatively, one could group shareholders according to their wealth or capital and define several classes of voting rights. See Chap. 5.

For example, it was recently proposed to create a class of "nonprofit media companies," with a ceiling on the voting rights of the largest donors and corresponding extra voting rights for smaller donors (such as journalists, readers, crowdfunders, and so on). For instance, one might decide that only a third of individual contributions above 10 percent of the firm's total capital should be granted voting rights.[46] The idea is that it might make sense to give more votes to a journalist or reader who invests $10,000 rather than $100, but it is best to avoid giving all the power to a deep-pocketed investor who invests $10 million to "save" the paper. A firm of this type would be between a traditional joint-stock company, based on the "one share, one vote" principle, and a foundation, association, or other nonprofit to which contributions do not give rise to voting rights (at least not directly).

Initially conceived for the media sector and for a setting in which financial contributions take the form of (nonrecoverable) gifts, a model of this kind might work well for cooperatives in other sectors and might also be applicable in cases where contributions of capital were recoverable. In general, there is no reason to restrict oneself to a choice between a pure cooperative model (one person, one vote) and a pure shareholder model (one share, one vote). The important point is that one needs to experiment with new mixed forms on a large scale. In the past, the idea of worker-managed firms aroused high hopes, for example, in France in the 1970s (where the watchword was *autogestion*). But many projects did not get much beyond the slogan stage and led nowhere for want of concrete plans.[47] Any discussion of new enterprise structures must include plans for amending the way nonprofit ventures are taxed. In most countries, tax benefits for giving mostly favor the rich, whose preferences in charity, culture, arts, education, and sometimes politics are de facto subsidized by less well-to-do taxpayers. In Part Four I will say more about how the tax system can be changed to encourage more democratic and participatory outcomes by allowing each citizen to give the same amount to nonprofit ventures of his or her choosing, possibly including gifts to sectors not previously exempt from taxation (such as the media or ventures in sustainable development).

To recapitulate: In the nineteenth century and until World War I, the dominant ideology sacralized private property and owners' rights. Then, from 1917

46. J. Cagé, *Saving the Media*, trans. A. Goldhammer (Harvard University Press, 2016).

47. On the debates surrounding *autogestion*, see, for example, P. Rosanvallon, *Notre histoire intellectuelle et politique, 1968–2018* (Seuil, 2018), pp. 56–77.

to 1991, new thinking about the forms of property was blocked by the bipolar opposition of Soviet Communism and American capitalism. One was either for unlimited state ownership or for full private shareholder ownership. This helps to explain why alternatives such as co-management and self-management were not explored as fully as they might have been. The fall of the Soviet Union inaugurated a new period of unlimited faith in private property from which we have not yet completely emerged but which is beginning to show serious signs of exhaustion. Just because Soviet Communism was a disaster does not mean that we should stop thinking about property and how it might be transcended. The concrete forms of property and power are constantly being reinvented. It is time to take a fresh look at this history, starting with the German and Nordic experiments with co-management, and to ask how these might be generalized and extended to viable, innovative, and participatory forms of self-management.

Social Democracy, Education, and the End of US Primacy

We come now to one of the principal challenges that social-democratic societies must face today, namely, the issue of access to skills and training, especially higher education. Property is important, but education has also played a central role in the history of inequality regimes and the evolution of social and economic inequalities both within and between countries. Two points deserve particular attention. First, throughout much of the twentieth century, the United States has held a significant lead in education over Western Europe and the rest of the world. This US advantage dates back to the early nineteenth century and beyond, and it explains much of the large gap in productivity and standard of living that one observes through most of the twentieth century. In the late twentieth century, the United States lost this lead and witnessed the appearance of a new stratification with respect to education: significant gaps in educational investment separated the lower and middle classes from those with access to the most richly endowed universities. Looking beyond the United States, I will stress the fact that no country has responded in a fully satisfactory way to the challenge of transitioning from the first educational revolution to the second—that is, from the revolution in primary and secondary education to the revolution in tertiary education. This failure is part of the reason why inequality has risen since 1980 and why the social-democratic model (and the electoral coalition that made it possible) seems to have run its course.

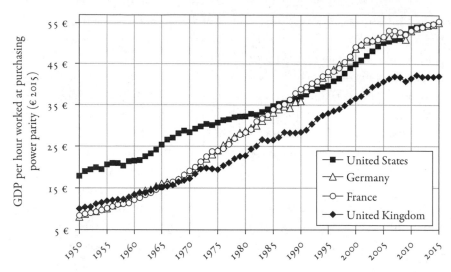

FIG. 11.3. Labor productivity, 1950–2015 (2015 euros)

Interpretation: Labor productivity, measured by GDP per hour worked (in constant 2015 euros at purchasing power parity), rose from 8 euros in Germany and France in 1950 to 55 euros in 2015. Germany and France caught up (or slightly passed) the United States in 1985–1990, whereas the United Kingdom remains 20 percent lower. *Sources and series:* piketty.pse.ens.fr/ideology.

Let us begin with American primacy. In the early 1950s, labor productivity in Germany and France was barely 50 percent of the US level. In the United Kingdom it was less than 60 percent. Then Germany and France surpassed the United Kingdom in the 1960s and 1970s and ultimately caught up with the United States in the 1980s. German and French productivity subsequently stabilized at roughly the same level as the United States after 1990, while British productivity stagnated at a level 20 percent lower (Figs. 11.3–11.4).

These graphs call for several remarks. First, the productivity measures shown in Figs. 11.3 and 11.4, namely gross domestic product (GDP) divided by total hours worked, are far from completely satisfactory. The very notion of "productivity" is problematic and calls for further discussion. The word might seem to convey an injunction to produce more and more forever and ever, which makes no sense if the result is to make the planet unlivable. Hence instead of reasoning in terms of GDP, it would be far better to use net domestic product—deducting for depreciation and damage to capital, including natural capital—but currently available national accounts do not allow us to do this. Although this does not affect the comparisons we focus on here, its importance

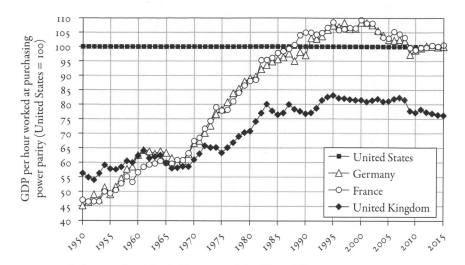

FIG. 11.4. Labor productivity in Europe and the United States

Interpretation: Labor productivity, measured by GDP per hour worked (in constant 2015 euros at purchasing power parity), was half of US productivity in Western Europe in 1950. Germany and France caught up (or slightly surpassed) the United States in 1985–1990, while the United Kingdom remained 20 percent lower. *Sources and series:* piketty.pse. ens.fr/ideology.

for analyzing inequality in the global economy of the twenty-first century remains fundamental.[48]

Second, it is fairly complex to measure in a reliable and comparable way the number of hours worked in different countries. Since the 1960s there have been of course many surveys that allow us to estimate hours worked per week, vacation time, and other essential data. But these surveys are seldom completely consistent across time and space, and they are far less numerous and comprehensive for years before 1960. In this book I have used data on hours worked compiled by international statistical agencies. These are the best estimates we have, but their accuracy should not be exaggerated. The main fact to bear in mind (which is reasonably well documented) is that the number of hours worked per job was approximately the same in Western Europe and the United States until the early 1970s (1900–2000 hours per year per job); however, a significant gap opened up in the 1980s. By the mid-2010s, the number of hours worked per job per year was 1,400–1,500 in Germany and France; 1,700 in the United Kingdom; and nearly 1,800 in the United States. These differences

48. See Chap. 13.

reflect both the shorter work week and longer vacations in Germany and France.[49]

Note that working time has decreased over the long run (including in the United Kingdom and to a lesser extent in the United States), which seems logical. As productivity rises, it is natural to work fewer hours to spend more time with family and friends, to discover the world and other people, and to seek entertainment and culture. It may be that this is indeed the goal of technological and economic progress and that the objective of improving the quality of life is better served by the trajectories we see in Germany and France than by those of Britain and the United States. What is the ideal rate of reduction of work time? What is the best way to organize work? These are extremely difficult questions to answer, and I do not intend to do so here. The downward trend in working hours is an eminently political question, which always involves social conflict and ideological change.[50] Note simply that in the absence of national legislation or collective bargaining for the entire work force, or at least the work force of an

---

49. The series used are those of the OECD and the US Bureau of Labor Statistics (BLS). To simplify, an annual duration of 2,000 hours corresponds to 40 hours per week × 50 weeks (two weeks of vacation), while an annual duration of 1,500 hours corresponds roughly to 35 hours per week × 43 weeks (seven weeks of vacation). The average duration in Germany was 1,370 hours per job in 2015 (versus 1,470 in France, 1,680 in the United Kingdom, and 1,790 in the United States), which also reflects the extent of part-time employment. See the online appendix. Available historical research indicates that working durations were significantly shorter in the United States between 1870 and 1914 and then converged with Europe during the interwar period before exceeding European levels after 1970. See M. Huberman and C. Minns, "'The times they are not changing': Days and Hours of Work in Old and New Worlds, 1870–2000," *Explorations in Economic History,* 2007.

50. For example, the reduction of the legal work week in France to thirty-five hours between 1997 and 2002 coincided with increasingly flexible hours for the lowest-paid workers and a prolonged freeze in disposable income; it turned out to be of greater benefit to management than to workers (with managers receiving additional vacation time). In the United Kingdom and United States, the relatively small decrease in working hours in recent decades coincided with a sharp decline in trade union membership (and failure of government to compensate) and an especially sharp increase in wage inequality. A full analysis of the different national trajectories with respect to work-time reduction and restructuring is beyond the scope of this book.

entire sector of the economy, it is historically extremely rare to see major reductions of working hours.[51]

Note, finally, that the notion of productivity used here, though highly imperfect and unsatisfactory, is more subtle than a simple market-based notion of productivity. In particular, the productivity of the government and nonprofit sectors is taken into account because their "output" is reflected in GDP through production costs; this is equivalent to assuming that the "value" society assigns to teachers, doctors, and so on is equal to the amount of taxes, subsidies, and contributions required to pay for their services. This probably results in underestimation of GDP in countries with an extensive public sector, but the bias is smaller than if the nonmarket sector were simply ignored.

The United States: An Early Leader in Primary and Secondary Education

Returning to the American lead in productivity and its slow reduction after 1950 (Figs. 11.3–11.4), note first that Europe's low productivity level compared with that of the United States actually dates back to a time well before the middle of the twentieth century. The gap was certainly aggravated by destruction and disruption of Europe's productive apparatus in two world wars, but the important fact is that it was already fairly large in the late nineteenth and early twentieth centuries. In France and Germany, GDP per capita or per job was 60–70 percent of the US level in 1900–1910. The gap with the United Kingdom was smaller, around 80–90 percent. But the fact is that Britain—which had enjoyed the highest productivity in the world through most of the nineteenth century thanks to the lead established in the first Industrial Revolution (owing largely to British domination of the global textile industry)—had clearly fallen behind the United States by the first decade of the twentieth century, having lost ground at an accelerating rate over the decades prior to World War I.

---

51. The reason for this is that it is difficult for an individual worker to negotiate over working hours along with a tendency to aim for a certain standard of living: no worker wants to be the first to sacrifice his disposable income; even if collectively, workers would prefer more leisure time. The decrease observed in the number of hours worked by the self-employed following legislation applicable only to wage workers suggests that the second factor is of some importance. The data available to resolve these questions are imperfect, however.

The evidence suggests that these old, persistent, and growing (at least until the 1950s) productivity gaps were due in large part to America's historic advance in training its workers. At the beginning of the nineteenth century, the US population was small compared with the populations of Europe, but a larger proportion of Americans went to school. The data we have, mostly taken from census reports, indicates that the primary schooling rate (defined as the percentage of children ages 5 to 11, both male and female, attending primary school) was nearly 50 percent in the 1820s, 70 percent in the 1840s, and more than 80 percent in the 1850s. If we exclude the black population, the primary schooling rate for whites was more than 90 percent by the 1840s. At the same time, the comparable rate was 20–30 percent in the United Kingdom, France, and Germany. In all three countries it was not until the period 1890–1910 that we find the near-universal primary education that the United States had achieved half a century earlier.[52] America's educational advance is explained in part by its Protestant religious roots (Sweden and Denmark were not far behind the United States in the first half of the nineteenth century) but also by more specific factors. Germany was slightly ahead of France and the United Kingdom in primary schooling in the mid-nineteenth century but far behind the United States. Another reason for the American lead was a phenomenon we see today among migrants. Individuals in a position to emigrate to the United States in the eighteenth and nineteenth centuries were on average better educated and more inclined to invest in the education of their children than the average European of the time, even controlling for geographic and religious origins.

America's lead in education, which is very clear at the primary level in the period 1820–1850, coincided with a much more rapid expansion of male suffrage. Alexis de Tocqueville already noticed the connection in 1835: for him, the diffusion of education and landownership were the two fundamental forces responsible for the flourishing of the "democratic spirit" in the United States.[53]

---

52. See the online appendix for the various sources used. The schooling rates cited here are taken from the data in J. Lee and H. Lee, "Human Capital in the Long-Run," *Journal of Development Economics,* 2016, which relies on many earlier works.

53. "But, from the beginning, the originality of American civilization was most clearly apparent in the provisions made for public education. . . . Municipal magistrates were made responsible for seeing that parents sent their children to school. They were authorized to impose fines on any parent who refused to do so. If resistance continued, society, putting itself in the place of the family, might seize the child and deprive its father of natural rights so egregiously abused." Alexis de Toc-

In fact, we find that the rate of participation of adult white males in US presidential elections rose from 26 percent in 1824 to 55 percent in 1832 to 74 percent in 1844.[54] Of course, women and African Americans continued to be denied the right to vote (until 1965 for many African Americans). Nevertheless, one had to wait until the end of the nineteenth century or in some cases the beginning of the twentieth to see similar extension of male suffrage in Europe.[55] Participation in local elections progressed at the same pace, which in turn contributed to greater public support for financing public schools through local taxes.

The key point here is that America's educational lead would continue through much of the twentieth century. In 1900–1910, when Europeans were just reaching the point of universal primary schooling, the United States was already well on the way to generalized secondary education.[56] In fact, rates of secondary schooling, defined as the percentage of children ages 12–17 (boys and girls) attending secondary schools, reached 30 percent in 1920, 40–50 percent in the 1930s, and nearly 80 percent in the late 1950s and early 1960s. In other words, by the end of World War II, the United States had come close to universal secondary education. At the same time, the secondary

---

queville, *Democracy in America,* trans. A. Goldhammer (Library of America, 2004), pp. 46–47.

54. For detailed data by state, see S. Engerman and K. Sokoloff, "The Evolution of Suffrage Institutions in the New World," *Journal of Economic History,* 2005, p. 906, table 2.

55. See Fig. 5.3. The contrast is particularly striking with Latin America (esp. Brazil, Mexico, Argentina, and Chile), where the participation rate of adult white males in elections remained below 10–20 percent until 1890–1910. See Engerman and Sokoloff, "The Evolution of Suffrage Institutions in the New World," pp. 910–911, table 3. On the slow transition from a mercantilist-absolutist ideology to a proprietarian-censitary ideology among Argentine elites in the nineteenth century related to the recomposition of wealth (from silver export to a large agricultural surplus), see J. Adelman, *Republic of Capital: Buenos Aires and the Legal Transformation of the Atlantic World* (Stanford University Press, 1999). On the absence of an inequality leveling period in Latin America during the twentieth century (similar to Europe or the United States), see J. Williamson, "Latin American Inequality: Colonial Origins, Commodity Booms or a Missed Twentieth Century Leveling," *Journal of Human Development and Capabilities,* 2015.

56. See, in particular, C. Goldin, "America's Graduation from High School: The Evolution and Spread of Secondary Schooling in the Twentieth Century," *Journal of Economic History,* 1998; C. Goldin, "The Human Capital Century and American Leadership: Virtues of the Past," *Journal of Economic History,* 2001.

schooling rate was just 20–30 percent in the United Kingdom and France and 40 percent in Germany. In all three countries it is not until the 1980s that one finds secondary schooling rates of 80 percent, which the United States had achieved in the early 1960s. In Japan, by contrast, the catch-up was more rapid: the secondary schooling rate attained 60 percent in the 1950s and climbed above 80 percent in the late 1960s and early 1970s.[57]

Interestingly, voices began to be raised in Europe in the late nineteenth century, especially in the United Kingdom and France, about the lack of investment in education. Many people had begun to see that the world domination of the two colonial powers was fragile. There was of course an obvious moral and civilizational purpose in broadening access to education, but beyond that there was a relatively new idea in the air that skills would play a central role in future economic prosperity. In retrospect, it is clear that the second Industrial Revolution, which took place gradually between 1880 and 1940 with the rise of the chemical and steel industries, automobile manufacturing, household appliances, and so on, was much more demanding in terms of skills than the first. In the first Industrial Revolution, concentrated in coal and textiles, it was enough to mobilize a relatively unskilled work force, which could be overseen by foremen and a small number of entrepreneurs and engineers familiar with the new machines and production processes. Crucially, the whole system relied on the capitalist, colonialist state to organize the flow of raw materials and the global division of labor.[58] In the second Industrial Revolution it became essential for growing numbers of workers to be able to read and write and participate in production processes that required basic scientific knowledge, the ability to understand technical manuals, and so on. That is how, in the period 1880–1960—first the United States and then Germany and Japan, newcomers to the international scene—gradually took the lead over the United Kingdom and France in the new industrial sectors.

In the late nineteenth and early twentieth centuries, the United Kingdom and France were too confident of their lead and their superior power to take the full measure of the new educational challenge. In France, the trauma of military defeat at the hands of Prussia in 1870–1871 played a decisive role in accelerating the process. In the 1880s the Third Republic passed laws making

---

57. See the online appendix. The available sources are imperfect, but the orders of magnitude and especially the gaps between countries are well established.
58. See Chap. 9.

schooling compulsory and centralizing financing of the primary schools, which had a definite positive effect on primary schooling rates. But it was relatively late in the day, coming as it did after a long period of slow progress in literacy and primary schooling rates, which began in the eighteenth century and gradually accelerated in the nineteenth.[59]

In the United Kingdom, worry about the lack of educational investment began to manifest itself in the middle of the nineteenth century. The country's political and economic elites remained unconcerned, however, as they were convinced that British prosperity depended above all on the accumulation of industrial and financial capital and on the solidity of proprietarian institutions. Recent work has shown that the results of the British census of 1851 were manipulated to minimize the educational gulf that was opening between the United Kingdom and other countries, especially the United States and Germany. In 1861, an official parliamentary report proudly announced that nearly all children under the age of 11 were in school, but it was contradicted a few years later by a field survey that found that only half of those children were in fact attending classes.[60]

Minds began to change after the North defeated the South in the US Civil War. British and French elites interpreted it as the triumph of educational superiority, just as they would later interpret Prussia's victory over France in 1871. Nevertheless, budget statistics show that educational investment in the United Kingdom continued to lag until World War I. In 1870, public expenditure on education (at all levels) represented more than 0.7 percent of national income in the United States compared with less than 0.4 percent in France and 0.2 percent in the United Kingdom. In 1910, the comparable figures were 1.4 percent for the United States compared with 1 percent for France and

---

59. After the expulsion of the Protestants in 1685, a first royal edict of 1698 required every parish to have a school to teach the catechism and develop a written religious culture. The use of tax money to pay for compulsory education was approved in 1792–1793 but never applied. In 1883, local governments *(communes)* were required to pay teachers, with supplementary funding by the state after 1850; the state took full responsibility for paying teachers in 1889 (the same year in which the practice of having priests issue certificates of morality to schoolteachers was ended). See F. Furet and J. Ozouf, *Lire et écrire. L'alphabétisation des Français de Calvin à Jules Ferry* (Editions de Minuit, 1977). See also A. Prost, *Histoire de l'enseignement en France, 1800–1967* (Armand Colin, 1968).

60. See D. Cannadine, *Victorious Century: The United Kingdom, 1800–1906* (Viking, 2017), pp. 257, 347.

0.7 percent for the United Kingdom.[61] By comparison, recall that from 1815 to 1914 the United Kingdom spent 2–3 percent of national income year in and year out to serve the interests of its sovereign bondholders, which illustrates the gap between the importance assigned to proprietarian ideology versus that ascribed to education. Recall, too, that public expenditure on education was close to 6 percent of national income in the major European countries in the period 1980–2020.[62] This shows how much things changed over the course of the twentieth century as well as the potential for divergence between countries and for inequality between social groups within an overall pattern of rising investment in education. The British system in particular remains one of strong social and educational stratification, with stark differences between lavishly endowed private schools and garden-variety public schools and high schools—differences that explain some of Britain's lag in productivity despite additional school spending since the late 1990s.[63]

US Lower Classes Left Behind Since 1980

How did the United States, which pioneered universal access to primary and secondary education and which, until the turn of the twentieth century, was significantly more egalitarian than Europe in terms of income and wealth distribution, become the most inegalitarian country in the developed world after 1980—to the point where the very foundations of its previous success are now in danger? We will discover that the country's educational trajectory—most notably the fact that its entry into the era of higher education was accompanied by a particularly extreme form of educational stratification—played a central role in this change.

Care should be taken not to overstate the importance of a country's egalitarian roots. The United States has always entertained an ambiguous relationship with equality: more egalitarian than Europe in some respects but much more inegalitarian in others, especially owing to its association with slavery. As noted earlier, moreover, American "social democracy" can trace its

---

61. See P. Lindert, *Growing Public: Social Spending and Economic Growth since the Eighteenth Century* (Cambridge University Press, 2005), vol. 2, pp. 154–155.

62. See Fig. 10.15.

63. Total educational expenditure in the United Kingdom today is close to that of other European countries (such as Germany, France, and Sweden): around 6 percent of national income. See the online appendix.

ideological origins to a form of social nativism: the Democratic Party was long the segregationist party when it came to blacks and the egalitarian party when it came to whites.[64] In Part Four we will take a closer look how electoral coalitions in the United States and Europe evolved in the twentieth and early twenty-first centuries. In particular, we will analyze the extent to which these differences help to explain why the development of the social and fiscal state was more limited in the United States than in Europe and whether similar racial and ethno-religious factors play a comparable role in the European context in the future.

In any case, as recently as the 1950s inequality in the United States was close to or below what one found in a country like France, while its productivity (and therefore standard of living) was twice as high. By contrast, in the 2010s, the United States has become much more inegalitarian while its lead in productivity has totally disappeared (Figs. 11.1–11.4). The fact that European countries like Germany and France have caught up in terms of productivity is not entirely surprising. Once those countries developed a large fiscal capacity in the postwar period and began investing significant resources in education and, more generally, in social spending and public infrastructure, it was only to be expected that they would overcome the educational and economic lag. The rise of inequality in the United States is more puzzling. In particular, while the standard of living of the poorest 50 percent of Americans was higher than that of the equivalent group in Europe in the 1950s, the situation had totally turned around by the 2010s.

Note from the outset that there are many reasons for the collapse of the relative position of America's lower classes; the evolution of the educational system is only one of them. The entire social system and the way workers are trained and selected must bear a share of the blame. But I want to stress that my use of the word "collapse" is no exaggeration. The bottom 50 percent of the income distribution claimed around 20 percent of national income from 1960 to 1980, but that share has been divided almost in half, falling to just 12 percent in 2010–2015. The top centile's share has moved in the opposite direction, from barely 11 percent to more than 20 percent (Fig. 11.5). For comparison, note that while inequality has also increased in Europe since 1980 with a significant rise in the top centile's share and a fall in the share of the bottom half—which has by no means gone unnoticed in a general climate of sluggish growth—the orders of magnitude are not the same. In particular, the share of total income going

64. See Chap. 6.

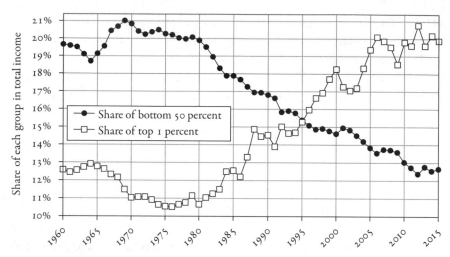

FIG. 11.5. The fall of the bottom 50 percent share in the United States, 1960–2015

Interpretation: The share of the bottom 50 percent of the income distribution fell from about 20 percent of total income in the United States in the 1970s to 12–13 percent in the 2010s. During the same period, the top centile share rose from 11 percent to 20–21 percent. *Sources and series:* piketty.pse.ens.fr/ideology.

to the bottom 50 percent in Europe remains significantly larger than the share going to the top centile (Fig. 11.6).

Note, too, that there is absolutely no reason to think that this divergence between the United States and Europe was inevitable. The two regions are comparable in size, with the US population around 320 million in 2015 and the West European population around 420 million. Levels of development and productivity are similar. Labor mobility is higher in the United States owing to its greater linguistic and cultural homogeneity, which is widely believed to contribute to income convergence. The United States collects taxes at the federal level (both income and estate taxes) and conducts major federal social programs (such as pensions and health insurance), which is not the case in Europe. Clearly, countervailing factors linked to social, fiscal, and educational policies at the national level in Europe played a more important role.[65]

It is now well known that the explosion of inequality in the United States since 1980 was due to an unprecedented increase in very high incomes, especially the famous "1 percent." Indeed, for the top centile's share of total income

---

65. In the next chapter we will also see that inequality in Europe is significantly lower than the United States even if one includes Eastern Europe. See Fig. 12.8.

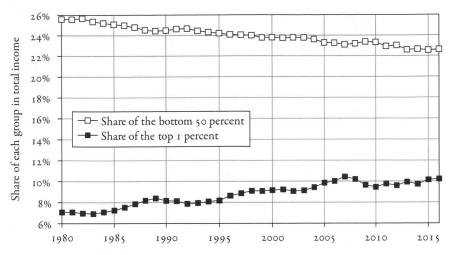

FIG. 11.6. Low and high incomes in Europe, 1980–2016

Interpretation: The share of the bottom 50 percent by income fell from 26 percent of total income in Western Europe in the early 1980s to 23 percent in the 2010s. Over the same period, the share of the top centile rose from 7 percent to 10 percent. *Sources and series:* piketty.pse.ens.fr/ideology.

to exceed the share of the bottom 50 percent, it is necessary and sufficient for the average income of the first group to be fifty times higher than the average income of the second. This is precisely what happened (Fig. 11.7). Until 1980, the average income of the top centile was on the order of twenty-five times the average income of the bottom 50 percent (roughly $400,000 a year for the top centile versus $15,000 for the bottom 50 percent). In 2015, the average income of the top centile is more than eighty times that of the bottom 50 percent: $1.3 million versus $15,000 (all amounts expressed in constant 2015 dollars).

Without a doubt, however, the most striking phenomenon here was not the rise of the one percent but the fall of the bottom 50 percent. Again, this was in no way inevitable: the increase of the top centile share could have come at the expense of those just below them, the people in the ninetieth to ninety-ninth percentile or of the middle 40 percent (fiftieth to ninetieth percentile). But the fact is that it came almost entirely at the expense of the bottom 50 percent. It is particularly depressing to discover that the disposable income of the bottom 50 percent has stagnated almost completely in the United States since the late 1960s. Before taxes and transfers, the average income of the bottom 50 percent averaged about $15,000 per adult per year in the late 1960s, and it is still at roughly the same level in the late 2010s (in 2015 dollars), a

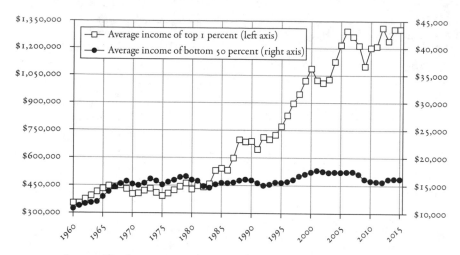

FIG. 11.7. Low and high incomes in the United States, 1960–2015

Interpretation: In 1970, the average income of the poorest 50 percent was $15,200 per year per adult, and that of the richest 1 percent was $403,000, for a ratio of 1 to 26. In 2015, the average income of the poorest 50 percent was $16,200 and that of the richest 1 percent was $1,305,000, for a ratio of 1 to 81. All amounts are in 2015 dollars. *Sources and series:* piketty.pse.ens.fr/ideology.

half-century later. This is quite remarkable, especially in view of the significant changes in the US economy and society during this time (including a sharp rise in productivity). In a context notable for rampant deregulation of the financial system, this wage stagnation inevitably increased the indebtedness of the poorest households and the fragility of the banking system, which contributed to the financial crisis of 2008.[66]

If we now take taxes and transfers into account, we find that the situation of the bottom 50 percent improves only slightly (Fig. 11.8).[67] We look first at the results obtained if we limit ourselves to cash transfers, including food

---

66. M. Bertrand and A. Morse, "Trickle-Down Consumption," *Review of Economics and Statistics,* 2016; M. Kumhof, R. Rancière, and P. Winant, "Inequality, Leverage and Crises," *American Economic Review,* 2015. On the history of credit regulation in the United States, see L. Hyman, *Debtor Nation: The History of America in Red Ink* (Princeton University Press, 2011); L. Hyman, *Borrow. The American Way of Debt. How Personal Credit Created the American Middle Class and Almost Bankrupted the Nation* (Vintage Books, 2012).

67. The results summarized here were obtained by combining a variety of available sources: tax records, household surveys, and national accounts. See T. Piketty, E. Saez, and G. Zucman, "Distributional National Accounts: Methods and Evidence

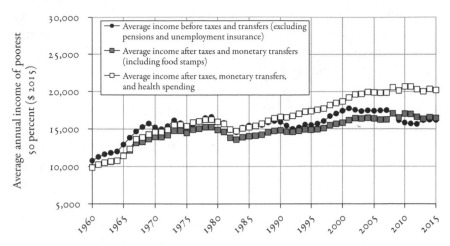

FIG. 11.8. Low incomes and transfers in the United States, 1960–2015

Interpretation: Expressed in constant 2015 dollars, the average annual income before taxes and transfers of the poorest 50 percent stagnated around $15,000 per adult between 1970 and 2015. The same is true after taxes (including indirect taxes) and monetary transfers (including food stamps), with taxes and transfers roughly balancing each other out. It rises to $20,000 in 2010–2015 if one includes transfers in kind in the form of public health spending. *Sources and series:* piketty.pse.ens.fr/ideology.

stamps, which are not cash strictly speaking but nevertheless allow more freedom of use than most transfers in kind. We find that average income is not very different after taxes and transfers, which means that the taxes paid by the bottom 50 percent (notably in the form of indirect taxes) are roughly equal to the cash transfers they receive (including food stamps).[68]

---

from the United States," *Quarterly Journal of Economics,* 2018. See the online appendix for the detailed series.

68. The principal cash transfer to the poor (excluding food stamps) is the Earned Income Tax Credit (EITC), which is a negative tax similar to the *prime d'activité* in France, the purpose of which is to increase the disposable income of low-paid workers. The extension of the EITC and tax decreases subsequent to the 2008 crisis explain why post-tax-and-transfer income rose slightly above pre-tax-and-transfer income. As in other countries, the pre-tax-and-transfer income considered here includes public pensions (minus the corresponding contributions), without which retiree income would be artificially low. If we look only at the working-age population, we find the same stagnation of the average income of the bottom 50 percent over the past half century. See Piketty, Saez, and Zucman, "Distributional National Accounts," p. 585, fig. 4. Furthermore, the decrease in the progressivity of the income tax implies that the gap between effective tax rates on the

If we now include reimbursements from Medicare and Medicaid, we find that the post-tax-and-transfer income of the bottom 50 percent did increase somewhat, from roughly $15,000 in 1970 to $20,000 in 2015 (Fig. 11.8). Over such a long period of time, however, this not only represents a very limited improvement in living standards; it is also hard to interpret. To be sure, this $5,000 of "additional income" for health expenses does represent an improvement in people's lives in an era of longer life expectancy (less so in the United States than in Europe, however, particularly for the lower classes). But this increase in transfers also reflects the rising cost of health care in the United States, which in practice means higher pay for physicians, higher profits for pharmaceutical companies, and so on—these groups have prospered in recent decades. Concretely, the additional $5,000 a year for the bottom 50 percent corresponds to roughly one week's pretax income for a caregiver belonging to the top income decile and roughly one day of income for a caregiver belonging to the top centile. This should clarify the difficulties of interpretation that arise when one looks at transfers in kind and not just in cash.[69]

On the Impact of the Legal, Fiscal, and Educational System on Primary Inequalities

In any event, it is clear that no transfer policy (whether in cash or in kind) can deal satisfactorily with such a massive distortion in the distribution of primary incomes (that is, incomes before taxes and transfers). When the share of primary income going to the bottom 50 percent is nearly halved in the space of just forty years and the share going to the top 1 percent is doubled (Fig. 11.5), it is illusory to think that the change can be compensated simply by ex post redistribution. Redistribution is essential, of course, but one also needs to think about policies capable of modifying the primary distribution, which means making deep changes to the legal, fiscal, and educational system to give the poorest people access to better paying jobs and ownership of property.

---

bottom 50 percent and top 1 percent has greatly shrunk compared with the period 1930–1970. See Piketty, Saez, and Zucman, "Distributional National Accounts," p. 599, fig. 9a, and this work, Fig. 10.13.

69. One might also include other transfers in kind (such as spending on education and law enforcement), but it then becomes even more difficult to impute and interpret them in a satisfactory way. See the online appendix for detailed results.

The various inequality regimes that we find in history are characterized above all by their primary distribution of resources. This is true of trifunctional and slave societies as well as colonial and ownership societies. It is also true of the various types of social-democratic, communist, postcommunist, and neo-proprietarian societies that arose in the twentieth and early twenty-first centuries. For example, if the United States is now more inegalitarian than Europe, it is solely because primary incomes are more unequally distributed there. If we compare levels of inequality before and after taxes and transfers in the United States and France, as measured by the ratio between the average income of the top 10 percent and the bottom 50 percent, we find that taxes and transfers reduce inequality by comparable amounts in both countries (indeed, slightly more in the United States) and that the global inequality gap is explained entirely by the difference observed before taxes and transfers (Fig. 11.9).[70] In other words, it is at least as essential to look at "predistribution" policies (which affect primary inequality) as at "redistribution" policies (which reduce inequality of disposable income for a given level of primary inequality).[71]

Given the complexity of the social systems involved and the limitations of the available data, it is difficult to precisely quantify the degree to which different institutional arrangements explain variations of primary inequality over time and space. It is nevertheless worth trying to describe the principal

---

70. As for the United States, the estimates for France were obtained by combing a variety of available sources: tax records, household surveys, and national accounts. See A. Bozio, B. Garbinti, J. Goupille-Lebret, M. Guillot, and T. Piketty, "Inequality and Redistribution in France 1990–2018: Evidence from Post-Tax Distributive National Accounts (DINA)," WID.world, 2018. The results are identical with other indicators of inequality (such as the Gini coefficient) or if we separate out different age groups (by excluding retirees, for example). See the online appendix for detailed series.

71. The results given here confirm the importance of the notion of "predistribution" (see M. O'Neill and T. Williamson, "The Promise of Predistribution," *Policy Network,* 2012; A. Thomas, *Republic of Equals: Predistribution and Property-Owning Democracy* [Oxford University Press, 2017]). Note, however, that this idea has sometimes been instrumentalized to minimize the importance of redistribution and especially progressive taxes (which was not the intention of its promoters). By contrast, I emphasize the usefulness of progressive taxation (with rates as high as 70–90 percent on astronomical incomes) as one of the most important institutions for influencing "predistribution." I develop this point further in this and subsequent chapters.

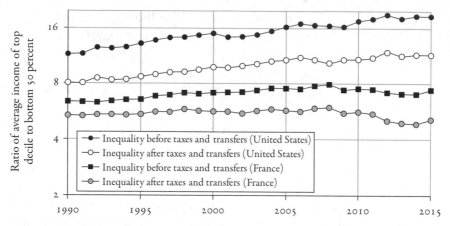

FIG. 11.9. Primary inequality and redistribution in the United States and France

Interpretation: In France, the ratio of average income before taxes and transfers of the top decile to the bottom 50 percent rose from 6.4 in 1990 to 7.4 in 2015. In the United States, the same ratio rose from 11.5 to 18.7. In both countries, taking account of taxes and monetary transfers (including food stamps and housing allowances) reduces inequality by 20–30 percent. *Note:* The distribution is annual income per adult. *Sources and series:* piketty.pse.ens.fr/ideology.

mechanisms at work. The legal system plays an essential role, especially in the areas of labor and corporate law. The importance of collective bargaining, unions, and, more generally, rules and institutions involved in wage setting has already been discussed. For example, the presence of worker representatives on company boards (under the Germano-Nordic co-management system) tends to limit extravagant executive pay; indeed, it generally results in more compressed and less arbitrary pay scales.[72] The minimum wage and its evolution also play a central role in explaining variations in wage inequality across time and space. In the 1950s and 1960s, the United States had by far the highest minimum wage in the world. In 1968–1970 the federal minimum wage was more than $10 an hour in today's dollars. Since 1980, however, the failure to raise the minimum wage regularly gradually eroded its value in real terms: in

---

72. For an analysis of the role of pay scales (and especially minimum and maximum wages) in securing workers and increasing their investment in the firm, especially where the bargaining power of employers is strong, see T. Piketty, *Capital in the Twenty-First Century* (Harvard University Press, 2014), chap. 9, pp. 307–314. See also H. Farber, D. Herbst, I. Kuziemko, and S. Naidu, *Unions and Inequality Over the Twentieth Century: New Evidence from Survey Data* (Princeton University, Working Papers 620, 2018).

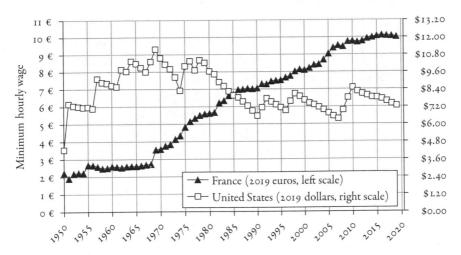

FIG. 11.10. Minimum wage in the United States and France, 1950–2019

Interpretation: Converted into 2019 purchasing power, the federal minimum wage rose from $4.25 in 1950 to $7.24 per hour in 2019 in the United States, while the national minimum wage (SMIG in 1950, then SMIC after 1970) rose from €2.23 in 1950 to €10.03 per hour in 2019. The two scales represent purchasing power parity ($1.20 to 1€ in 2019). *Sources and series:* piketty.pse.ens.fr/ideology.

2019 it was only $7.20, representing a 30 percent decline in purchasing power over half a century—remarkable for a country at peace and growing economically. This reversal attests to the magnitude of the political-ideological changes that took place in the United States since the 1970s and 1980s. Over the same period, the French minimum wage rose from barely 3 euros an hour in the 1960s to 10 euros in 2019 (Fig. 11.10), advancing at roughly the same rate as the average productivity of labor (Fig. 11.3).

Many works have shown that the drop in the minimum wage in the United States contributed strongly to the declining position of low-wage workers since the 1980s in a general climate of decreased worker bargaining power. The federal minimum wage fell so much relative to the general productivity level, moreover, that several states raised their minimum wage to a much higher level without hurting employment. For example, the minimum wage in California in 2019 is $11 an hour and will gradually rise to $15 by 2023. Similarly, the high federal minimum wage from the 1930s to the 1960s, in a context of high US productivity and skill levels, helped to reduce wage inequality while employment remained high. Recent work has shown that the extension of the minimum wage in the 1960s to sectors in which African American labor was employed more intensively (including agriculture, which had been excluded from the federal minimum wage law in 1938, partly because of hostility from southern Democrats) strongly contributed to reducing wage discrimination and the wage gap between blacks and whites.[73]

It is interesting to note that several European countries were relatively slow to adopt a national minimum wage. The United Kingdom did so only in 1999 and Germany in 2015. These countries previously relied solely on wage negotiations at the firm and sector level, which could result in high minimum wages but with variations from sector to sector. Changes in the structure of employment, especially the decline of industrial employment and the gradual shift to services coupled with a lower unionization rate, have gradually reduced the role of collective bargaining since the 1980s. This is probably part of the reason for greater reliance on a national minimum wage.[74] While the minimum wage is an indispensable tool, it is no substitute for wage bargaining and power sharing at the branch and firm level; these could take new forms in the future.

In addition to the legal system (labor and corporate law), the tax system can also have a decisive impact on primary inequalities. This is obviously the case for the inheritance tax. A progressive wealth tax that could be used to finance a universal capital endowment might have a similar effect. Taxing wealth leads to structural reductions of wealth inequality in each new generation, which also helps to equalize investment opportunities and thus the future distribution of labor and capital income. More surprisingly, perhaps, the progressive income tax has also had a very strong impact, not only on after-tax inequality but also on primary inequality (before taxes and transfers).

First, higher tax rates on large incomes helped to limit the concentration of saving and capital accumulation at the top of the distribution, while reduced tax rates in the middle and bottom of the distribution contributed to the diffusion of property. In addition, one of the main consequences of the extremely high marginal rates (70–90 percent) on top incomes between 1930 and 1980, especially in the United States and United Kingdom,[75] was to put an end to

---

73. See E. Derenoncourt and C. Montialoux, *Minimum Wages and Racial Inequality* (Harvard University, Working Paper, 2018).

74. In the late 1960s, the United States had the highest real minimum wage in the world. In the late 2010s, the minimum wage is significantly higher in Germany, the United Kingdom, France, Holland, Belgium, Australia, and Canada. See L. Kenworthy, *Social-Democratic Capitalism* (Oxford University Press, 2019), p. 206, fig. 7.12. The Nordic countries continue to rely on wage bargaining.

75. See Fig. 10.11.

the most extravagant executive pay. By contrast, the sharp reduction of top tax rates in the 1980s strongly contributed to the skyrocketing of executive pay. Indeed, if one looks at the evolution of executive pay in listed companies in all the developed countries since 1980, one finds that variations in tax rates explain much of the variation in executive pay—much more than other factors such as sector of activity, firm size, or performance.[76] The mechanism at work seems to be linked to the way executive pay is determined and to the bargaining power of executives. How does an executive persuade other relevant actors (including direct subordinates, other employees, shareholders, and members of the firm's compensation committee) that a pay raise is justified? The answer is never obvious. In the 1950s and 1960s, the top executives of major British and American firms had little interest in fighting for huge raises, and other actors were reluctant to grant them because 80–90 percent of any raise would have gone directly to the government. In the 1980s, however, the nature of the game changed completely. The evidence suggests that executives began to devote considerable effort to persuading others that enormous raises were warranted, which was not always difficult to do, since it is hard to measure how much any individual executive contributes to the firm's success. What is more, compensation committees were often constituted in a rather incestuous fashion. This also explains why it is so difficult to find any statistically significant correlation between executive pay and firm performance (or productivity).[77]

Since the 1980s, moreover, US production has become more and more concentrated in the largest companies (not just in the information technology sector but across the economy). This increased the bargaining power of executives in the leading firms in each sector and enabled them to compress the bottom and middle portions of the pay scale and increase the profit share of value-added.[78] This growing concentration reflects the weakness of antitrust

---

76. See T. Piketty, E. Saez, and S. Stantcheva, "Optimal Taxation of Top Labor Incomes: A Tale of Three Elasticities," *American Economic Journal: Economic Policy,* 2014.

77. See Piketty, Saez, and Stantcheva, "Optimal Taxation," in particular, figs. 3, 5, and A1 and tables 2–5.

78. See, for example, M. Pursey, "CEO Pay and Factor Shares: Bargaining Effects in US Corporations, 1970–2011" (Paris School of Economics, 2013). See also M. Kehrig and N. Vincent, *The Micro-Level Anatomy of the Labor Share Decline* (National Bureau of Economic Research, NBER Working Papers 25275, 2018); E. Liu, A. Mian, and A. Sufi, *Low Interest Rates, Market Power, and Productivity Growth* (National Bureau of Economic Research, NBER Working Papers 25505, 2019).

policies, the failure to keep up with changing industrial conditions, and above all, the lack of political will on the part of successive administrations to take any action against monopolies. The reasons for this include an ideological context favorable to laissez-faire, heightened international competition, and perhaps a campaign financing system biased in favor of large corporations and their leaders (I will come back to this).

Higher Education and the New Educational and Social Stratification

Last but perhaps not least, in addition to the legal and tax systems, the educational system also plays a crucial role in shaping primary inequalities. In the long run, it is access to skills and diffusion of knowledge that allow inequality to be reduced both within countries and at the international level. Technological progress and transformation of the structure of employment mean that the productive system demands ever higher levels of skill. If the supply of skills does not evolve to meet this demand—for example, if some social groups fail to increase or even decrease their investment in education while others devote an increasing share of their resources to training—wage inequality between the two groups will tend to increase, no matter how good the legal or tax system in place.

The evidence strongly suggests that growing educational investment has played a central role in the particularly sharp increase of income inequality in the United States since the 1980s. In the 1950s and 1960s, the United States was the first country to have achieved nearly universal secondary education. In the 1980s and 1990s, Japan and most countries in Western Europe caught up. All of these countries have now entered the age of mass higher education, in which a growing proportion of each new age cohort attends college or university. In the mid-2010s, the tertiary schooling rate (defined as the percentage of young adults of age 18–21 enrolled in an institution of higher learning) is 50 percent or more in the United States and all the countries of Western Europe and approaching 60–70 percent in Japan and Korea.[79] The educational

---

Awareness of the outsized influence of private monopolies in the United States may be on the rise, as indicated, for example, by the increasingly contentious debates around the need for some sort of public control of major information technology firms such as the so-called GAFA (Google, Apple, Facebook, and Amazon).

79. See the online appendix.

and symbolic order has been turned upside down. In the past, higher education was the privilege of a small fraction of the population: still less than 1 percent at the turn of the twentieth century and less than 10 percent until the 1960s. In the wealthy countries, majorities of the younger generations are now college graduates, and eventually majorities of the entire population will be as well. The process is well under way: given the rate of generational replacement, we find that the proportion of the adult population with a college degree, which is currently 30–40 percent in the United States and in the most advanced European and Asian countries, will rise to 50–60 percent a few decades from now.

This educational upheaval is the source of new kinds of inequality, both between and within countries. The United States lost its educational lead in the 1980s. Many studies have shown how the slowdown in educational investment in the United States contributed to the increase of education-related income inequality since the 1980s and 1990s.[80] Note, too, that the financing of primary and secondary education, though very largely public (as in most developed countries), is extremely decentralized in the United States. It depends essentially on local property taxes, which can lead to significant inequality depending on the wealth of the community. Compared with European and Asian countries, where the financing of primary and secondary education is generally centralized at the national level, secondary education in the United States is therefore somewhat less universal than elsewhere. Nearly everyone finishes high school, but the variation in the quality and financial resources of different high schools is quite large.

Furthermore, recent research has shown that access to higher education in the United States is largely determined by parental income. More specifically, the probability of attending university in the mid-2010s was 20–30 percent for children of the poorest parents, increasing almost linearly to 90 percent for the children of the richest parents (see Fig. I.8). Similar data for other countries, though quite incomplete (which is itself problematic), suggest that the slope of the curve is less steep. In addition, research comparing the relative income of parents and children shows a particularly steep curve (hence a very low intergenerational mobility rate) in the United States compared with Europe,

---

80. See especially C. Goldin and L. Katz, *The Race Between Education and Technology: The Evolution of US Educational Wage Differentials, 1890–2005* (Belknap Press, 2010). See also Piketty, *Capital in the Twenty-First Century,* chap. 9, pp. 305–307.

especially the Nordic countries.[81] Note, too, that the intergenerational correlation between the position of parents in the income hierarchy and that of children has increased sharply in the United States in recent decades.[82] This significant decrease in social mobility, which contrasts so flagrantly with hypothetical talk about "meritocracy" and equality of opportunity, attests to the extreme stratification of the American educational and social system. It also demonstrates the importance of subjecting political-ideological rhetoric to systematic empirical evaluation, which the available sources do not always permit us to do with sufficient comparative historical perspective.

The fact that access to higher education in the United States is strongly linked to parental income can be explained in many ways. In part it reflects a preexisting stratification: since primary and secondary education is already highly inegalitarian, children from modest backgrounds are less likely to satisfy the admissions requirements of the more highly selective universities. It also reflects the cost of private education, which has attained astronomical heights in the United States in recent decades. More broadly, while all developed countries pay for primary and secondary education almost exclusively with public funds, there is much greater variation in the financing of higher education. Private financing pays 60–70 percent of the cost in the United States and nearly 60 percent in the United Kingdom, Canada, and Australia— compared with an average of 30 percent in France, Italy, and Spain, where tuition is generally lower than in the United States and United Kingdom, and less than 10 percent in Germany, Austria, Sweden, Denmark, and Norway, where higher education is in principle virtually free, just like primary and secondary education (Fig. 11.11).[83]

---

81. In terms of intergenerational mobility, France and Germany seem to fall between the least mobile countries (the United States and United Kingdom) and the most mobile countries (Nordic countries). See the online appendix.

82. J. Davis and B. Mazumder, *The Decline of Intergenerational Mobility after 1980* (Federal Reserve Bank of Chicago, Working Paper WP-2017-5, 2017). See also R. Chetty, D. Grusky, M. Hell, N. Hendren, R. Manduca, and J. Narand, "The Fading American Dream: Trends in Absolute Income Mobility Since 1940," *Science*, 2017; F. Pfeffer, "Growing Wealth Gaps in Education," *Demography*, 2018.

83. We find similar diversity in other parts of the world. Private financing is fairly extensive in Japan and Korea as well as Chile and Colombia but limited in China, Indonesia, and Turkey as well as Argentina and Mexico. The share of private financing in primary and secondary education is quite low everywhere (10–20 percent at most). See the online appendix, Fig. S11.11.

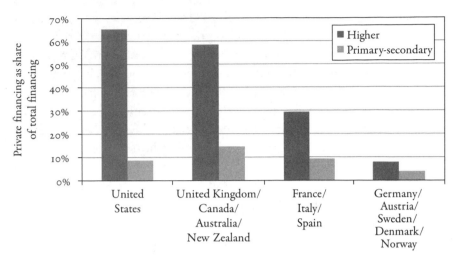

FIG. 11.11. Share of private financing in education: Diversity of European and American models

Interpretation: In the United States, private financing represented 65 percent of total (private and public) financing in higher education and 9 percent of total financing of primary and secondary education. The shares of private financing of higher education vary strongly with country, with an Anglo-American model, a south European model, and a north European model. Private financing is relatively insignificant in primary and secondary education everywhere (2014–2016 figures). *Sources and series:* piketty.pse.ens.fr /ideology.

In the US case, the importance of private financing of higher education has had two key consequences: first, the best American universities are very rich (which allows them to attract some of the best foreign researchers and students), and second, the system of higher education is extremely stratified. If one considers all resources (public and private) available for higher education, the United States continues to lead the world.[84] The problem is that the gap between the resources available to the best universities and those available to less well-endowed public universities and community colleges has grown to abyssal proportions in recent decades. This inequality has been exacerbated by

---

84. The total resources devoted to higher education amount to roughly 3 percent of national income in the United States, compared with 1–1.5 percent in Europe. (Italy spends the least, behind Spain, France, Germany, Sweden, Denmark, and Norway in ascending order.) This figure includes spending on scientific and academic research and on research institutes (spending on universities in the narrow sense is barely 0.5 percent of national income). See the online appendix.

the financial dynamics of global capitalism. The universities with the largest endowments have earned higher yields on their investments than those with smaller endowments, which has widened the gap between them.[85] If one looks at the available international rankings, as imperfect as they are, it is striking to see that American universities are ultra-dominant among the top twenty in the world but fall well below European and Asian universities if one looks at the top 100 or top 500.[86] It is likely that the international renown of the wealthiest US universities masks the internal imbalance of the system as a whole. That imbalance would probably be even clearer if US universities were not so attractive to students from the rest of the world. This is a new form of interaction between the global inequality regime and domestic inequality not seen in earlier periods.

Can One Buy a Place in a University?

Furthermore, inequality of access to higher education in the United States is aggravated by the fact that the wealthiest parents can in some cases use financial contributions to win admission to the best universities for children who would not otherwise qualify. Admissions procedures often include not very transparent "legacy preferences" (that is, special advantages for the children of graduates of the institution in question). Unsurprisingly, the American universities where such preferences are allowed claim that the number of students

---

85. The 850 American universities with capital endowments earned an average real return of 8.2 percent a year between 1980 and 1990 (after correcting for inflation and deducting management fees), with the 498 least well endowed (endowments of less than $100 million) earning 6.2 percent, while the sixty best endowed (with endowments greater than $1 billion) earned 8.8 percent; Harvard, Yale, and Princeton averaged 10.1 percent. The share of the sixty best endowed universities increased from 50 percent of the total endowment in 1980 to more than 70 percent in 2010. These gaps seem to be due to economies of scale: access to the most remunerative investments (unlisted foreign shares, derivatives on raw materials, etc.) is available only to the largest portfolios. See Piketty, *Capital in the Twenty-First Century*, pp. 447–450, table 12.2.
86. According to the Academic Ranking of World Universities, 2018 ed., by Shanghai Rankings, sixteen of the top twenty universities are American and four are European, while sixty-nine of the top 200 are American, eighty European, forty Asian-Oceanian, and ten from the rest of the world. Of the top 500, 139 are American, 195 European, 133 Asian-Oceanian, and thirty-three from the rest of the world.

thus favored is ridiculously small—in fact, so tiny that it would be pointless to name them publicly or to explain the algorithms and procedures used to winnow applicants. Indeed, it is likely that the numbers are small and that these opaque practices play a quantitatively less important role than other mechanisms (such as the decentralized public financing of primary and secondary education and the high tuitions and high yields on endowments) in explaining the overall inequality of the system.

The question nevertheless deserves close attention, for several reasons. First, research has shown that the practices may be somewhat less marginal than the universities claim. It turns out that gifts by graduates to their former universities are abnormally concentrated in years during which their children are of an age to apply for admission.[87] Furthermore, the lack of transparency is in itself clearly problematic, all the more so in that the new class of inheritors (the beneficiaries of greater US inequality in recent decades) stands out more and more conspicuously in the social landscape; this may stoke resentment of elites.[88] The lack of transparency shows that the universities are not prepared to defend what they are doing in public; this can only encourage serious doubts about the overall fairness of the system.

It is also striking to discover that American university faculty are increasingly inclined to justify these practices and the secrecy that surrounds them because they are effective in raising funds from the generous billionaires who finance their research and teaching. This ideological evolution is interesting, because it raises a more general question: Exactly how far should the power of money extend, and what institutions and procedures can set limits on that power? We have run into this type of question before: for example, in considering the Swedish practice of awarding voting rights in proportion to wealth in the period 1865–1911.[89] In the present case, the more apt comparison might be with the imperial Chinese exam system in the

---

87. See J. Meer and H. Rosen, "Altruism and the Child Cycle of Alumni Donations," *American Economic Journal: Economic Policy,* 2009.

88. Note an expression in the United States to refer to heirs blessed with all privileges: "trust-fund babies." In 2018, a boy band (Why Don't We, or WDW) composed a song entitled "Trust Fund Baby." The boys in the band, from Minnesota and Virginia, explained that they wanted independent girls who knew how to fix cars and take care of things on their own, unlike "trust fund babies"—heiresses born with silver spoons in their mouths who think of nothing but money.

89. See Chap. 5.

Qing era, which allowed wealthy elites to purchase places for their children (in addition to setting aside places for the children of the old warrior class), which undoubtedly weakened the regime and undermined its moral and political legitimacy.[90]

Last but not least, the flagrant lack of transparency in the admissions procedures of America's leading universities is of concern to all countries because it raises this fundamental challenge: How to define educational justice in the twenty-first century? For example, suppose one wants a quota system with extra points to encourage better representation of disadvantaged social classes, as in India.[91] If every university keeps its admissions algorithm secret, and if that algorithm awards extra points to the children of the rich rather than to the disadvantaged while admissions officials claim that the practice is very rare and must be kept secret, how is democratic deliberation supposed to proceed—especially when the issue is so delicate and complex, affecting the futures of children from lower, middle, and upper classes, and when it is so difficult to construct a standard of justice acceptable to the majority? Yet authorities in the United States have been able to impose much stricter rules and standards on universities in the past.[92] As always, history shows that nothing is foreordained.

On Inequality of Access to Education in Europe and the United States

As noted, inequality of access to education is quite significant in the United States. It is also significant in Europe. Indeed, throughout the world one finds a wide gap between official rhetoric about equality of opportunity, the "meritocratic" ideal, and so on and the reality of unequal access to education for different social groups. No country is in a position to give lessons on the subject. Indeed, the advent of the era of higher education has posed a structural challenge to the very idea of educational equality everywhere.

In the era of primary and secondary education, there was a fairly obvious rule of thumb for educational equality: the goal was to achieve first universal

---

90. See Chap. 9.
91. See Chap. 8.
92. On relations between Harvard and the state of Massachusetts, see N. Maggor, *Brahmin Capitalism: Frontiers of Wealth and Populism in America's First Gilded Age* (Harvard University Press, 2017), pp. 26–28, 96–104.

primary education and then universal secondary education so that every child would receive roughly the same grounding in basic knowledge. With tertiary education, however, things became much more complicated. For one thing, it is not very realistic to think that every child will grow up to receive a PhD, at least not any time soon. Indeed, there are many paths to higher education. In part, this diversity reflects the variety of fields of knowledge and the range of individual aspirations, but it lends itself to hierarchical organization. This in turn influences social and professional hierarchies after graduation. In other words, the advent of mass higher education poses a new kind of political and ideological challenge. One has to live with some degree of permanent educational inequality, especially between those who embark on long courses of study and those who opt for shorter courses. Obviously, this in no way precludes thinking about how to allocate resources more justly or how to devise fairer rules for access to different curricula. But the challenge is more complex than that of achieving strict equality in primary and secondary education.[93]

In Part Four we will see that this new educational challenge is one of the main factors that led to the breakdown of the postwar social-democratic coalition. In the 1950s and 1960s, the various European social-democratic and socialist parties as well as the Democratic Party in the United States scored their highest percentages of the vote among less educated social groups. In the period 1980–2010, this voting pattern was reversed, and the same parties did best among the better educated. One possible explanation, which we will explore in greater detail later, has to do with changes in the policies backed by these parties, which gradually came to be seen as more favorable to the winners in the socio-educational competition.[94]

At this stage, note simply that even though the educational system is on the whole more egalitarian in Europe than in the United States, European countries too have found it quite difficult to cope with the challenge of educational expansion in recent decades. For instance, it is striking to note that public spending on education, which increased rapidly over the course of the twentieth century from barely 1–2 percent of national income in 1870–1910 to 5–6 percent in the 1980s, subsequently plateaued (Fig. 10.15). In all the countries of Western Europe, whether Germany or France, Sweden or the United

---

93. On the ideological challenge of higher education, see also E. Todd, *Où en sommes-nous? Une esquisse de l'histoire humaine* (Seuil, 2017).

94. See Chaps. 14–15.

Kingdom, we find educational investment stagnating between 1990 and 2015 at about 5.5–6 percent of national income.[95]

This stagnation can of course be explained by the fact that public spending in general stopped growing in this period. In a context marked by the structural and all-but-inevitable increase in spending on health and pensions, some people felt that it was essential to hold the line on educational spending or even decrease it somewhat in relation to national income, relying more instead on private financing and tuition fees. Alternatively, one might have considered (and might in the future still consider) a limited tax increase to pay for additional investment in education, tapping all levels of income and wealth in a fair and equitable manner. In other words, tax competition between countries, combined with the perceived impossibility of devising a fair tax system, may explain both the stagnation of educational investment and the recourse to deficit spending.

In any case, it is important to note how paradoxical this spending freeze was. Just as the developed countries were moving into the era of mass higher education and as the proportion of each age cohort attending college was rising from barely 10–20 percent to more than 50 percent, public spending on education came to a standstill. As a result, some who had believed in the promise of expanding access to higher education—often people of modest or middle-class background—found themselves confronted with dwindling resources and absence of opportunities after graduation. Note, moreover, that even when college is free or nearly free and most of the cost is borne by the government, true equality of access to higher education is nevertheless not guaranteed. Students from privileged backgrounds are often better placed to enter more promising courses of study, thanks both to their family heritage and to prior access to better schools and high schools.

The French case offers a particularly striking example of educational inequality within an ostensibly free and egalitarian public system. In practice, the public resources invested in elitist tracks that prepare students for the so-called *grandes écoles* (the most prestigious institutions of higher education) are two to three times greater per student than the resources invested in less elitist tracks. This longstanding stratification of the French system became flagrant in the era of mass higher education, especially because promises to equalize in-

---

95. See the online appendix. The data we have for comparing educational budgets between countries are far from perfect, but the break with previous periods is quite clear.

vestment in less privileged primary, middle, and high schools were never kept; this gave rise to very strong social and political tensions. Beyond the French case, educational justice requires transparency about resource allocation and admissions procedures. This is a fundamental issue, which will become increasingly urgent around the world in years to come. I will have much more to say about it later on.[96]

Educational Equality, the Root of Modern Growth

Note, finally, that the stagnation of educational investment in the rich countries since the 1980s may help to explain not only the rise of inequality but also the slowing of economic growth. In the United States, per capita national income grew at a rate of 2.2 percent per year in the period 1950–1990 but slowed to 1.1 percent in the period 1990–2020. Meanwhile, inequality increased, and the top income tax rate fell from an average of 72 percent in the period 1950–1990 to 35 percent in the period 1990–2020 (Figs. 11.12–11.13). In Europe, we also find that growth was strongest in the period 1950–1990, when inequality was lower and fiscal progressivity greater (Figs. 11.14–11.15). In Europe, the exceptional growth of 1950–1990 can be attributed in part to the need to make up ground lost during the two world wars. This does not apply to the United States, however: growth in the period 1910–1950 was stronger than in 1870–1910 and growth in the period 1950–1990 was even more rapid than in 1910–1950, but the growth rate then fell by half in the period 1990–2020.

This stark historical reality has much to teach us. In particular, it rules out a number of mistaken diagnoses. First, strongly progressive taxes are clearly no obstacle to rapid productivity growth, provided that the top rates apply to sufficiently high levels of income and wealth. If rates on the order of 80–90 percent were applied to everyone even slightly above the mean, for instance, it is quite possible that the effects would be different. But when the top rates apply only to very high levels of income and wealth (typically in the top centile or half centile), the historical evidence suggests that it is quite possible to combine highly progressive taxes, low inequality, and high growth. The strongly progressive tax system that was put in place in the twentieth century helped end the extreme concentration of wealth and income observed

---

96. See especially Chaps. 13, 14, and 17. On inequality of investment in different tracks in France, see Fig. 7.8. See also S. Zuber, *L'inégalité de la dépense publique d'éducation en France: 1900–2000* (EHESS, Paper, 2003), and the online appendix.

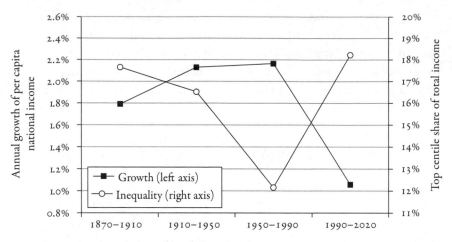

FIG. 11.12. Growth and inequality in the United States, 1870–2020

Interpretation: In the United States the growth of per capita national income fell from 2.2 percent per year from 1950 to 1990 to 1.1 percent from 1990 to 2020, while the top centile share of national income rose from 12 to 18 percent in the same period. *Sources and series:* piketty.pse.ens.fr/ideology.

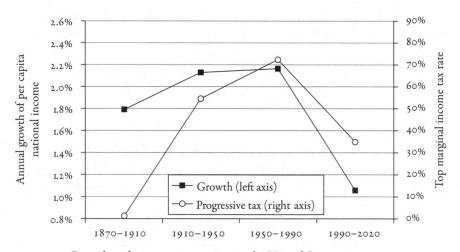

FIG. 11.13. Growth and progressive taxation in the United States, 1870–2020

Interpretation: In the United States, annual growth of per capita national income fell from 2.2 percent from 1950 to 1900 to 1.1 percent from 1990 to 2020, whereas the top marginal income tax rate fell in the same period from 72 percent to 35 percent. *Sources and series:* piketty.pse.ens.fr/ideology.

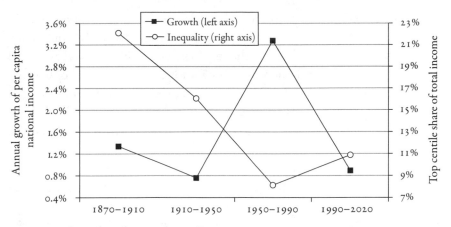

FIG. 11.14. Growth and inequality in Europe, 1870–2020

Interpretation: In Western Europe, growth of per capita national income fell from 3.3 percent in 1950–1990 to 0.9 percent in 1990–2020, while the top centile share of national income rose over the same period from 8 to 11 percent (average for Germany, United Kingdom, and France). *Sources and series:* piketty.pse.ens.fr/ideology.

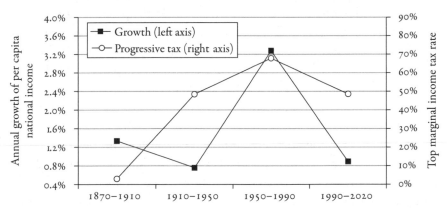

FIG. 11.15. Growth and progressive tax in Europe, 1870–2020

Interpretation: In Western Europe, annual growth of per capita national income fell from 3.3 percent in 1950–1990 to 0.9 percent in 1990–2020, while the top marginal income tax rate fell over the same period from 68 to 49 percent (average for Germany, the United Kingdom, and France). *Sources and series:* piketty.pse.ens.fr/ideology.

in the late nineteenth and early twentieth centuries, and this reduction of inequality opened the way to stronger growth than ever before. At a minimum, this should convince everyone that the very high level of inequality that existed before World War I was in no way necessary for growth, as much of the elite claimed at the time. Everyone should also agree that the conservative Reagan revolution of the 1980s was a failure: growth in the United States fell by half, and the notion that it would have fallen even more in the absence of conservative reforms is not very plausible.[97]

Last but not least, the historic role played by America's educational lead in the nineteenth and much of the twentieth centuries shows how crucial egalitarian investment in training and education was. Why was the United States more productive than Europe in the nineteenth and early twentieth centuries, and why did its economy grow faster? Not because property rights were better protected or because taxes were lower; taxes were low everywhere, and property rights were nowhere better protected than in France, the United Kingdom, and elsewhere in Europe. The key point is that the United States in the nineteenth and twentieth centuries had a fifty-year head start on Europe in terms of universal primary and later secondary education. This advance ended toward the end of the twentieth century, and with it ended the productivity gap. At a more general level, the period 1950–1990 saw an exceptionally high level of educational investment in all the rich countries, much higher than in previous periods, which may help to explain the unusually high level of growth. By contrast, the stagnation of educational investment in the period 1990–2020, even as more and more students headed to university, is consistent with slower productivity growth.

To sum up: in the light of the history of the past two centuries, educational equality played a more important role in economic development than the sacralization of inequality, property, and stability. More generally, history demonstrates the recurrent risk of an "inequality trap," which many societies have faced throughout the ages. Elite discourse tends to overvalue stability, and especially the perpetuation of existing property rights, whereas development often requires a redefinition of property relations and opening up of opportu-

---

97. The idea that Reaganism was a success is based in part on a complex political-ideological construct, which has a lot to do with America's success in the political and military competition with the Soviet Union (an outcome which itself had little to do with American economic and fiscal policy in the Reagan years), and somewhat less to do with the reduced gap between US and European growth (which would certainly have happened without Reagan, because the postwar catch-up phase had ended).

nities to new social groups. The refusal of British and French elites to redistribute wealth and invest in education and the social state continued until World War I. This refusal rested on sophisticated ideological constructs, as is also the case in the United States today.[98] History shows that change can come only when social and political struggle converges with profound ideological renewal.

Social Democracy and Just Taxation: A Missed Opportunity

Let us turn now to the question of just taxation, which will lead to the question of transcending the nation-state. We have seen the difficulties that social-democratic societies encountered when they tried to redefine the norms of just property and education after 1980, when the basic agenda of nationalizations ceased to be attractive and the world entered the era of higher education. The same political-ideological limitations hampered new thinking about taxes. Parties of the left—Social Democrats, Socialists, Labour, Democrats—tended to neglect fiscal doctrine and just taxation. The dramatic rise of progressive income and inheritance taxes in the period 1914–1945 generally came about as an emergency response and was never fully integrated into party doctrine, either intellectually or politically. This partly explains the fragility of the fiscal institutions that were put in place and the challenges that were raised against them in the 1980s.

Broadly speaking, the socialist movement grew as a response to the question of the property regime, with the goal of nationalizing privately owned firms. This focus on state ownership of the means of production, which remained strong among French Socialists and British Labourites until the 1980s, tended to foreclose thinking about other issues, such as progressive taxes, co-management, and self-management. In short, faith in state centralization as the only way to transcend capitalism sometimes led to neglect of tax-related issues, including what should be taxed and at what rates as well as issues of power sharing and voting rights within firms.

Among the shortcomings of social-democratic reflection on tax issues, two points warrant special mention. First, parties of the left failed to foster the kind

---

98. For other examples of the "inequality trap," such as the Netherlands in the seventeenth and eighteenth centuries (where the commercial elite largely captured the state, and especially public finances, for its own benefit via accumulation of debt, blocking development), see B. van Bavel, *The Invisible Hand? How Market Economies Have Emerged and Declined Since AD 500* (Oxford University Press, 2016).

of international cooperation needed to protect and extend progressive taxation; indeed, at times they contributed to the fiscal competition that has proved devastating to the very idea of fiscal justice. Second, thinking about just taxation too often neglected the idea of a progressive wealth tax, despite its importance for any ambitious attempt to transcend private capitalism, particularly if used to finance a universal capital endowment and promote greater circulation of wealth. As we will see in what follows, just taxation requires striking a balance among three legitimate and complementary forms of progressive taxation: taxes on income, inheritance, and wealth.

Social Democracy and the Transcendence of Capitalism and the Nation-State

Twentieth-century social democracy was always internationalist in principle but much less so in political practice. As we saw in Chapter 10, this was the critique that Hannah Arendt leveled at the social democrats of the first half of the twentieth century in 1951. It could equally well be extended to their successors in the second half of the century. After 1950, social-democratic movements focused on building the fiscal and social state within the narrow framework of the nation-state. Although they achieved undeniable success, they did not really try to develop new federal or transnational political forms (such as social, democratic, and egalitarian counterparts to the transnational colonial, Bolshevik, and Nazi regimes analyzed by Arendt). Because social democracy failed to achieve postnational solidarity or fiscality (as the absence of a common European fiscal and social policy attests), it weakened what it had built at the national level, endangering its social and political base.

At the European level, various social-democratic and socialist movements did of course steadfastly support efforts to develop the European Coal and Steel Community in 1952, followed by the European Economic Community (EEC) created by the Treaty of Rome in 1957, and finally the European Union, which succeeded the EEC in 1992. This series of political, economic, and trade agreements, consolidated by treaty after treaty, paved the way to an unprecedented era of peace and prosperity in Europe. Cooperation made this possible, initially by regulating competition in major areas of industrial and agricultural production. The contrast is striking between the 1920s, when French troops occupied the Ruhr to exact payment of a debt-tribute equivalent to 300 percent of German GDP, and the 1950s, when France, Germany, Italy, and the Benelux countries (Belgium, the Netherlands, and Luxembourg) coordinated their production of coal and steel to stabilize prices and ensure the smoothest possible postwar reconstruction. In 1986 the Single European Act established the principle of free circulation of goods, services, capital, and people in Europe (the "four freedoms").[99] Then the Maastricht Treaty of 1992 established not only the European Union but also a common currency for those countries that wanted it (the euro came into use by banks in 1999 and entered general circulation in 2002). Since then, member states have increasingly relied on EU institutions to negotiate trade agreements between Europe and the rest of the world in a context of rapidly expanding international economic openness. Scholars have accurately described the construction of Europe in the period 1950–2000 as a "rescue of the nation-state," a political form that to many people seemed doomed in 1945–1950. In fact, at first the EEC and then the EU allowed Europe's old nation-states to coordinate their output and trade, initially among themselves and then with the rest of the world while maintaining their role as central political players.[100]

Despite its successes, the European construction suffered from many limitations, which today threaten to turn large numbers of people against the entire project as illustrated by the Brexit referendum of 2016. Over the past few decades, the feeling has spread that "Europe" (a word that has come to refer to the bureaucracy in Brussels, ignoring all previous phases of the process) penalizes the lower and middle classes for the benefit of the wealthy and large corporations. This "Euroskepticism" has also fed on hostility to immigration and a sense of lost status (compared with the colonial era in some places or the communist era in others). In any case, European governments have been unable to cope with the combination of rising inequality and lower growth since the 1980s. What are the reasons for this resounding failure? First, Europe has relied almost exclusively on a competitive model pitting region against region and person against person, which has benefited groups perceived to be more mobile. Second, member states have been unable to agree on any kind of common fiscal or social policy. This failure is itself a result of the decision to require unanimity in fiscal matters, a decision perpetuated in treaty after treaty from the 1950s to the present.[101]

---

99. Note in passing that the "four freedoms" established by the Single European Act of 1986 are rather different from the "four freedoms" evoked by Franklin D. Roosevelt in his famous State of the Union speech in 1941: freedom of speech and expression, freedom of worship, freedom from want, and freedom from fear.

100. See esp. A. Milward, *The European Rescue of the Nation-State* (Routledge, 2000).

101. A single state, such as Luxembourg or Ireland, is enough to block any common fiscal policy. I will come back to this question in greater detail in Chap. 16.

To date, the construction of Europe has been based largely on the hypothesis that free competition and free circulation of goods and capital should suffice to achieve general prosperity and social harmony—on the conviction that the benefits of fiscal competition between states outweigh the costs (the benefits coming from the fact that competition is supposed to prevent states from becoming too bloated or giving in to redistributive fantasies). These hypotheses are not totally indefensible from a theoretical point of view. Indeed, it is not easy to build a political structure with the legitimacy to levy taxes, particularly on a scale as large as Europe. Yet the same hypotheses are also vulnerable to criticism, especially in view of the recent rise of inequality and the dangers it entails as well as the fact that political communities of comparable or larger size, such as the United States and India, have long since adopted common fiscal policies in a democratic framework. The fact that European integration strategy since the 1950s has been based on the construction of a common market can also be explained by the history of the previous decades. In the interwar years, the rise of protectionism and noncooperative mercantilist strategies made the crisis worse. In a way, the ideology of competition is a response to the crises of the past. Yet by proceeding in this way, Europe's builders forgot another lesson of history: the steady rise of inequality in the years 1814–1914, which demonstrated the need to embed the market in a web of social and fiscal regulations.

It is particularly striking that European social democrats (in particular the German Social Democrats and French Socialists), even though they have regularly held power (sometimes simultaneously) and been in a position to rewrite existing treaties, never formulated a specific proposal to replace the unanimity rule for fiscal policy making. No doubt they were not entirely convinced that the (genuine) complications of a common fiscal policy were worth the trouble. Admittedly, creating a federal structure appropriate to Europe and its old nation-states will be anything but simple. Nevertheless, there are many conceivable ways in which a democratic European federation might have agreed on a common tax policy—a prospect that was already contemplated in 1938–1940 in debates about the Federal Union (Chapter 10). This could quickly become a reality in the years and decades to come (I will come back to this).

However, the fact remains that the unanimity rule and fiscal competition led in the period 1980–2020 to rampant "fiscal dumping" in which countries competed for business by undercutting one another's tax rates—particularly with respect to corporate tax rates, which gradually fell from 45–50 percent in most countries in the 1980s to just 22 percent on average across the EU in 2018, while overall tax revenues remained stable. Furthermore, there is no guarantee that the long-term decline in corporate tax rates has ended.[102] Rates could still drop toward 0 percent or even become subsidies to attract investment, as is sometimes already the case. Although European states need corporate tax revenues to finance their social benefits, they have been world leaders in reducing corporate taxes, far more than the United States (where corporate taxes, like income and estate taxes, are levied for the most part at the federal level). This attests to the importance of tax competition as well as to the central role of political and electoral institutions for fiscal outcomes.[103] The fact that the construction of Europe has become synonymous with the defense of "free and undistorted competition" and that the EU is widely perceived as a force hostile or indifferent to the development of the social state also explains why the British Labour Party was divided in the 1972 referendum about whether the United Kingdom should join the EU and again in the 2016 Brexit referendum. Yet between those two dates the party proposed nothing that might have changed the perception of the European Union.[104]

Rethinking Globalization and the Liberalization of Capital Flows

Recent research has also shown the central role played by European social democrats and especially the French Socialists in liberalizing capital flows in Europe and the world since the late 1980s.[105] Burnt by the difficulties they faced

---

102. See European Commission, *Taxation Trends in the European Union,* 2018 ed. (Publications Office of the European Union, 2018), p. 35, graph 17. Some states such as France still have statutory tax rates of 30 percent or more, while Ireland and Luxembourg have rates of 10 percent or less. In a perfectly coordinated international fiscal system, it might be nothing more than a simple withholding against each shareholder's progressive individual income tax obligation. In practice, given the absence of coordination and exchange of information concerning the ultimate beneficiary and the many opportunities for tax avoidance and evasion, the corporate tax is often the sole tax for which payment is actually guaranteed. See Chap. 17.

103. The US federal corporate tax rate was 45–50 percent until the 1980s; it fell to 30–35 percent under Reagan. It then remained stable at 35 percent from 1992 to 2017 (with an addition 5–10 percent in state taxes) before falling to 21 percent under Trump in 2018. This may lead to a new race to the bottom with European and other countries.

104. On British disappointment with respect to social Europe, see A. B. Atkinson, *Inequality: What Can Be Done?* (Harvard University Press, 2015).

105. R. Abdelal, *Capital Rules: The Construction of Global Finance* (Harvard University Press, 2007). This work relies on accounts by officials at the time (especially

in implementing the nationalizations of 1981, the ill-timed stimulus of 1981–1982, and the exchange controls of 1983, which would have affected the middle class without reducing capital flight by the wealthy, the French Socialists decided in 1984–1985 on a radical change in their economic and political strategy. In the wake of the Single European Act of 1986, they gave in to the demands of the German Christian Democrats for complete liberalization of capital flows, which led to a 1988 European directive that was later incorporated into the Maastricht Treaty of 1992. Its terms were subsequently borrowed by the Organization for Economic Co-operation and Development (OECD) and the International Monetary Fund (IMF) and became a new international standard.[106] According to the accounts of the principal actors in the process, the concessions made by the French Socialists to German demands (which were intended to guarantee full "depoliticization" of monetary and financial questions) were seen as acceptable compromises in exchange for German agreements to a single currency and a shared federal sovereignty over the future European Central Bank (ECB).[107] In fact, the ECB became the only truly federal European institution (neither the German nor the French representative can veto decisions of the majority of the board of directors). As we will see, this allowed it to play a significant role in the aftermath of the 2008 financial crisis.

It is not clear, however, that the principal actors involved fully understood the long-run consequences of completely liberalizing capital flows. The problem was not just short-term flows—the "hot money" that Roosevelt denounced in 1936 and whose destabilizing effects were obvious in the 1930s (especially in the Austrian banking crisis of 1931). These had been regulated, for good reason, between 1945 and 1985 but then liberalized to such an extent that they were partly to blame for the Asian crisis of 1997.[108] More generally, liberalization of

---

Jacques Delors and Pascal Lamy). See also N. Jabko, *L'Europe par le marché. Histoire d'une stratégie improbable* (Sciences Po, 2009).

106. The insistence of German Christian Democrats on free circulation of capital is often associated with Ordoliberalism. It was incorporated into many bilateral treaties signed by the Federal Republic of Germany in the 1950s and 1960s. See, for example, L. Panitch and S. Gindin, *The Making of Global Capitalism: The Political Economy of American Empire* (Verso, 2012), pp. 116–117.

107. The goal was also to reduce the cost of public borrowing on international financial markets. But there was no time for all these different objectives to be spelled out and explicitly debated.

108. The 1997 crisis led the IMF to reevaluate European rules on short-term capital flows and to rely instead on more flexible principles allowing certain capital

capital flows becomes a problem if it is not accompanied by international agreements providing for automatic exchanges of information about who owns cross-border capital assets along with coordinated and balanced policies to regulate and tax profits, income, and wealth. The problem is precisely that when the world moved in the 1980s to free circulation of goods and capital on a global scale under the influence of the United States and Europe, it did so without any fiscal or social objectives in mind, as if globalization could do without fiscal revenues, educational investments, or social and environmental rules. The implicit hypothesis seems to have been that each nation-state would have to deal with these minor problems on its own and that the sole purpose of international treaties was to arrange for free circulation and prevent states from interfering with it. As is often the case with historical turning points of this kind, the most striking thing is how unprepared decision makers were and how much they had to improvise. Note, by the way, that the economic and financial liberalization that began in the 1980s was not entirely due to the conservative revolutions in the United States and United Kingdom: French and German influences also played a central role in these complex developments.[109] The role played by numerous financial lobbies from several European countries (such as Luxembourg) should also be stressed.[110]

Note, too, that the inability of postwar social democracy to organize the social and fiscal state on a postnational scale was not limited to Europe; we find

---

controls in the spirit of the Bretton Woods accords of 1944. See Abdelal, *Capital Rules*, pp. 131–160.

109. By the same token, the role of German Ordoliberalism should not be overstated. There is also a strong French liberal tradition quite prevalent in the nineteenth and early twentieth centuries, especially in the interwar years, and revived in the 1960s and 1970s by Valéry Giscard d'Estaing, first as secretary of state and then minister of finance more or less continuously from 1959 to 1974 and later as president from 1974 to 1981. In 2001–2004 Giscard chaired the Convention on the Future of Europe, which led to the proposed European Constitutional Treaty (ECT), which de facto sacralized free circulation of capital and the principle of unanimity on tax issues. The ECT was rejected in France in a 2005 referendum but later adopted by parliamentary vote after slight changes in the form of the Lisbon Treaty of 2007. I will say more later about these European treaties and rules. See esp. Chaps. 12 and 16.

110. See S. Weeks, "Collective Effort, Private Accumulation: Constructing the Luxembourg Investment Fund, 1956–1988" (presentation, Accumulating Capital: Strategies of Profit and Dispossessive Policies conference, Paris, France, Thursday, June 6, 2019).

it in all parts of the world. Attempts to organize regional unions in Latin America, Africa, and the Middle East ran afoul of similar difficulties. We saw earlier how West African leaders, already aware in 1945–1960 of the difficulties their tiny nation-states would face in finding their place and developing viable social models within global capitalism, unsuccessfully sought to develop new types of federations—most notably the Mali Federation consisting of Senegal, Dahomey, Upper Volta, and present-day Mali (see Chapter 7). The ephemeral United Arab Republic (1958–1961), a union of Egypt and Syria (and briefly Yemen), also reflects awareness of the fact that a large community is needed to control the economic forces of capitalism. In this context, the European Union plays a special role owing to the wealth of its members and the potential to inspire emulators by its success.

Furthermore, the magnitude of the European social and fiscal state, which claimed 40–50 percent of national income as taxes in the period 1990–2020,[111] implies that questions of fiscal justice and consent to taxation should play a crucial role. But consent has been sorely tested, partly because European tax systems are so complex and lack transparency (because they have developed in stages and have never been reformed and rationalized as much as they could have been) and partly because of heightened fiscal competition and lack of coordination between states, which tends to favor those social groups that have already benefited the most from the globalization of trade.

In this connection, bear in mind that the concentration of wealth and income from capital, though less extreme than in the Belle Époque (1880–1914), remained quite high in the late twentieth century and remains high today, higher than the concentration of income from labor (see Figs. 10.6–10.7). This implies that the highest incomes consist in large part of income from wealth, especially dividends and interest on financial capital (Figs. 11.16–11.17). Inequalities of capital and labor income both remain high, but the orders of magnitude are not at all the same. In regard to capital income, the bottom 50 percent account for only 5 percent of all capital income in France in 2015, compared with 66 percent for the top decile (Fig. 11.18). As for labor income, the bottom 50 percent receive 24 percent of the total, or nearly as much as the 27 percent going to the top decile (who are of course one-fifth as numerous). Note, too, that the high concentration of wealth and of the income derived from it is not skewed by the age profile of the wealthy; it can be found in every age cohort,

---

111. See Figs. 10.14–10.15.

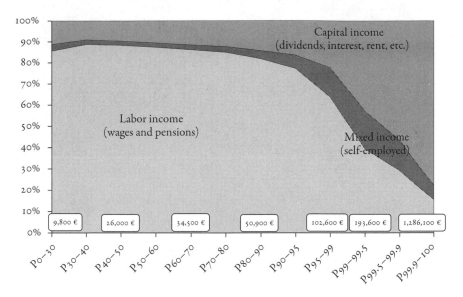

FIG. 11.16. Composition of income in France, 2015

Interpretation: In France in 2015 (as in most countries for which data are available), low and medium incomes consist mainly of labor income, and high incomes mainly of capital income (especially dividends). *Note:* The distribution shown here is annual income per adult before taxes but after pensions and unemployment insurance. *Sources and series:* piketty.pse.ens.fr/ideology.

from the youngest to the oldest. In other words, wealth diffuses only very slowly with age.[112]

In view of this very high concentration of wealth (especially financial wealth), it is easy to see why liberalizing capital flows without exchange of information or fiscal coordination can undermine the overall progressivity of the tax system. Beyond the race to the bottom on taxing corporate profits, many European countries allowed dividends and interests to escape progressive taxation in the period 1990–2020. This in turn allowed wealthy people to pay

---

112. The concentration is particularly strong in the 20–39 age group, with 62 percent of the wealth held by the 10 percent wealthiest in this group in France in 2015 (because of the importance of inheritances among the few wealthy people in this group) compared with 53 percent in the 40–59 age group, 50 percent in the 60-and-over group, and 55 percent for the population as a whole. In each age group, the poorest 50 percent own almost nothing (barely 5–10 percent of total wealth in all cases). See the online appendix, Fig. S11.18. For detailed results on age profiles and wealth structure by age group, see B. Garbinti, J. Goupille-Lebret, and T. Piketty, "Accounting for Wealth Inequality Dynamics: Methods and Estimates," WID.world, 2016.

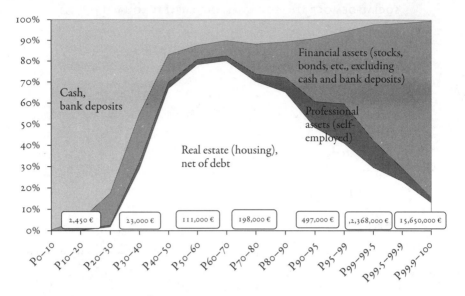

FIG. 11.17. Composition of property in France, 2015

Interpretation: In France in 2015 (as in all countries for which data are available), small fortunes consist primarily of cash and bank deposits, medium fortunes of real estate, and large fortunes of financial assets (mainly stocks). *Note:* The distribution shown here is wealth per adult (couples' wealth is divided in half). *Sources and series:* piketty.pse.ens. fr/ideology.

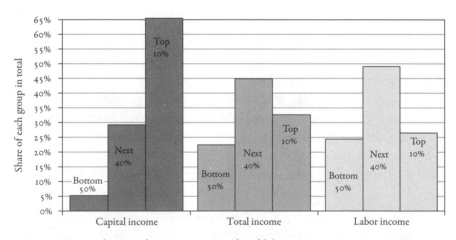

FIG. 11.18. Inequalities with respect to capital and labor in France, 2015

Interpretation: The top decile of capital income accounts for 66 percent of total capital income, compared with 5 percent for the bottom 50 percent and 29 percent for the middle 40 percent. For labor income, these shares are respectively 27, 24, and 49 percent. *Note:* The distributions shown here are income per adult (couples' income is divided in half). *Sources and series:* piketty.pse.ens.fr/ideology.

less on their income than a person earning an equivalent amount entirely from labor—a radical change in perspective compared with earlier periods.[113]

In fact, if one tries to calculate a comprehensive profile of the tax structure, it turns out that progressivity has decreased significantly since the 1980s. This follows automatically from the fact that the average tax rate has remained stable while rates on the highest income brackets have declined.[114] This general factor has been aggravated by various exemptions. In France, the overall tax rate is 45–50 percent on the bottom 50 percent, 50–55 percent on the middle 40 percent, and 45 percent within the wealthiest 1 percent (Fig. 11.19). In other words, taxes are slightly progressive from the bottom to the middle of the distribution but regressive at the top. This is a result of the importance of indirect taxes in France (value-added tax, energy tax, and so on) and of social contributions paid by the lowest earners, with a progressive income tax for the middle and upper-middle classes. For the wealthiest individuals, the progressive tax is not heavy enough to compensate for the lower indirect taxes and social contributions due to numerous exemptions for capital income. The regressivity at the top would be slightly less significant if we measured taxes paid as a function of the taxpayer's position in the wealth distribution (rather than the income distribution) or if we combined both distributions, which would probably be the best method. Note, finally, that none of these estimates take into account the tax optimization strategies of the rich or the use of tax havens, which also leads to underestimation of the regressivity at the top.[115]

Of course, the fact that the lower and middle classes pay significant amounts of tax is not a problem in itself. If one wants to pay for a high level of social spending and educational investment, everyone must bear part of the burden. But if citizens are to consent to the taxes they must pay, the tax system must be transparent and just. If the lower and middle classes have the impression that they are paying more than the rich, there is an obvious risk that fiscal consent will be withheld and that the social contract on which social-democratic societies rest will gradually disintegrate. In this sense, the inability of social

---

113. When the progressive income tax was created in the early twentieth century, the main objective was to tax high capital incomes, and most countries had tax laws favorable to income from labor, such as the French *cédulaire* system. In the 1960s and 1970s, the United States and United Kingdom taxed capital income ("unearned income") at a higher rate the labor income ("earned income").

114. See Figs. 10.11–10.13.

115. For detailed results, see Bozio et al., "Inequality and Redistribution in France 1990–2018." See the online appendix for a discussion of methods.

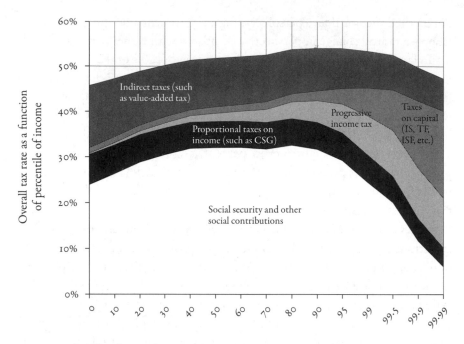

FIG. 11.19. Profile of tax structure in France, 2018

Interpretation: In France in 2018, the overall tax rate was roughly 45 percent for the lowest income groups, 50–55 percent for the middle and upper-middle groups, and 45 percent for the highest income groups. *Note:* The distribution shown here is annual income for adults aged 25 to 60 working at least part time. *Sources and series:* piketty.pse.ens.fr /ideology.

democracies to transcend the nation-state is the main weakness that is undermining them from within.

The United States, Europe, and the Property Tax: An Unfinished Debate

We have discussed the problem of transcending the nation-state and establishing common taxes and new forms of transnational fiscal cooperation. Now we must delve into the question of just taxation. Broadly speaking, debate about just taxation since the eighteenth century has centered on the idea of progressivity, that is, taxing the poor at a low rate which increases gradually as one moves up the scale of income or wealth. Many progressive tax proposals were debated during the French Revolution.[116] Progressive taxes were introduced on a large scale on all continents in the twentieth century.[117] This general schema is important, but it does not exhaust the subject because the general idea of progressive taxation hides several different realities.

Broadly speaking, there are three major categories of progressive tax: progressive income tax, progressive inheritance tax, and progressive wealth tax. Each has its justifications and can be seen as complementary to the other two. The progressive income tax falls in principle on all income received in a given year, regardless of its source, including both labor income (wages, pensions, self-employed earnings, and so on) and capital income (dividends, interest, rents, profits, and so on). Each person can thus be taxed as a function of his or her resources at a given point in time and therefore current capacity to contribute to public expenditures. The inheritance tax, which usually includes gifts, is assessed whenever wealth is passed from one generation to the next; it can therefore be used to reduce intergenerational perpetuation of fortunes, thereby reducing the concentration of wealth.[118] The wealth tax, which may also go by the name property tax or tax on capital or fortune, is assessed annually on the total value of goods a person owns, which can be seen as a more revealing and stable (and in some respects less manipulable) index of the taxpayer's capacity to contribute to public expenditure than annual income. It is also the only way to achieve a permanent redistribution of wealth and true circulation of capital.

History suggests that the ideal tax system should seek to strike a balance among these three a priori legitimate forms of progressive taxation, making use of available historical knowledge. This is not an easy goal to achieve, however, because success requires broad social and political engagement with the issues, which (it is true) concern everyone but whose apparent technical complexity can lead even the best intentioned people to rely on others (who, unfortunately, may not be altogether disinterested).

In practice, we find that nearly all developed countries adopted progressive income and inheritance taxes in the late nineteenth or early twentieth centuries, with low rates at the bottom of the wealth and income distributions and rates typically as high as 60–90 percent at the very top.[119] In contrast, countries

---

116. See Table 3.1.
117. See Figs. 10.11–10.12.
118. See Chap. 10 for the distinction between the inheritance tax and the estate tax.
119. See Figs. 10.11–10.12.

have followed very disparate and hesitant courses with respect to the wealth tax. In a number of countries, exceptional progressive taxes on private wealth have played an important role. Experience with a permanent annual progressive wealth tax is more limited, but the topic has been much debated in both the United States and Europe; there is much to learn from these debates, as well as from occasional attempts to implement such a tax in practice. All signs are that the progressive wealth tax will become a central issue in the twenty-first century owing to the increased concentration of wealth since the 1980s.[120] Furthermore, as I will explain in detail at the end of this book, a true progressive wealth tax can be used to finance a universal capital endowment and a more egalitarian investment in education. Taken together, these measures could help to counter the inegalitarian and identarian tendencies that we see in globalized capitalism today.

The Progressive Wealth Tax, or Permanent Agrarian Reform

Let us begin by analyzing the case of exceptional taxes on private property. After World War II, a number of exceptional taxes were assessed on real estate and/or professional and financial assets for the purpose of liquidating government debt, most notably in Japan, German, Italy, France, and various other European countries. Assessed just once, these taxes applied rates close to or equal to zero on small to medium fortunes but were as high as 40–50 percent or more on the largest fortunes.[121] Despite their shortcomings, including especially the virtual absence of international coordination, these levies on the whole proved to be a great success in the sense that they permitted rapid liquidation of very large debts (in a more just and controlled manner than could have been achieved through a chaotic inflationary process). What is more, the resources derived from these one-time taxes could be used to pay for postwar reconstruction and investments in the future.

In a sense, agrarian reform can also be seen as a type of exceptional tax on private wealth: an agrarian reform policy might involve the seizure of very large tracts of land (perhaps as much as 40–50 percent, often covering entire regions) in order to break it up into small parcels for redistribution to individual farmers. Unsurprisingly, agrarian reform programs frequently give rise to intense social and political struggles. Earlier, I discussed land redistribution during the French

---

120. See Figs. 10.4–10.5 and 10.8.
121. See Chap. 10.

Revolution, agrarian reform in Spain, and the seizure of land owned by absentee landlords in Ireland, which was followed by a redefinition of Irish property rights in the late nineteenth and early twentieth centuries.[122] The large-scale agrarian reforms carried out in Japan and Korea in 1947–1950 are widely considered to have been great successes. They paved the way to a relatively egalitarian distribution of farmland and were combined with social and educational investment strategies that led to subsequent economic takeoff and a consensus development strategy.[123] As noted earlier, moreover, the agrarian reforms carried out in India, especially western Bengal in the late 1970s and 1980s (though unfortunately more timid), nevertheless had very positive effects in terms of productivity.[124] By contrast, agrarian reform in Latin America, especially in Mexico after the revolution of 1910, ran afoul of strong resistance from landowners and very cumbersome and often chaotic political processes.[125]

In general terms, an important limitation of agrarian reform (and, more broadly, of exceptional wealth taxes) is that it offers only a temporary solution to the issue of concentration of wealth and of economic and political power. That is why a permanent and annual progressive wealth tax is necessary. Although the tax rates on the highest concentrations of wealth are of course lower in the case of a permanent tax than an exceptional one, they can still be high enough to shift ownership of large amounts of wealth and prevent it from becoming reconcentrated. If such a tax were used to finance a universal capital

---

122. See Chaps. 3 and 5.

123. See, for example, J. You, "Land Reform, Inequality, and Corruption: A Comparative Historical Study of Korea, Taiwan, and the Philippines," *Korean Journal of International Studies,* 2014. See also T. Kawagoe, *Agricultural Land Reform in Postwar Japan: Experience and Issues* (World Bank, Working Paper WPS 2111, 1999). See also E. Reischauer, *Histoire du Japon et des Japonais* (Seuil, 1997), vol. 2, pp. 22–30. Reischauer, a former US ambassador to Japan who was deliberately condescending to the Japanese and hardly suspect of socialist sympathies, expresses pleasure with the success of agrarian reform and equalization of property at a time when the West was locked in competition with communism.

124. See Chap. 8 and the references to the work of A. Banerjee. The land redistribution in western Bengal followed the 1977 victory of the Left Front (led by the Communist Party of India), which remained in power until 2011.

125. In Mexico, where it is estimated that 1 percent of the population owned more than 95 percent of the land on the eve of the 1910 revolution, agrarian reform unfolded over the period 1910–1970. See S. Sanderson, *Land Reform in Mexico, 1910–1980* (Elsevier, 1984); P. Dorner, *Latin American Land Reforms in Theory and Practice: A Retrospective Analysis* (University of Wisconsin Press, 1992).

endowment for every young adult, it would be tantamount to a permanent and continuous agrarian reform but applied to all private capital and not just farmland.

Of course, it is plausible to argue that land (or natural resources in general) is a special case when it comes to redistribution, since no one made the land or other natural resources, which can be thought of as the common wealth of humankind. Indeed, most countries have special laws pertaining to ownership of underground resources, based on different ideas of communal sharing and appropriation. If a person were to discover in his backyard a new natural resource of exceptional value, essential to preserving life on Earth, and everyone on the planet were about to die unless this new substance were shared immediately, then it is likely that the political and legal system would be amended to allow for such redistribution, whether the fortunate owner of the lucky backyard likes it or not. It would be a mistake, however, to think that such questions arise only in connection with natural resources. Suppose the same lucky individual were to awake from his siesta one day with an idea for a magical medicine that would save the planet; the case for legitimate redistribution of this miracle drug would be just as strong. The question is not so much whether an item of property is a shared natural resource or a private good developed by a single individual, as all wealth is fundamentally social. Indeed, all wealth creation depends on the social division of labor and on the intellectual capital accumulated over the entire course of human history, which no living person can be said to own or claim as his or her personal accomplishment.[126] The important question to ask is rather this: To what extent does the general interest, and in particular the interest of the most disadvantaged social groups, justify a given level of wealth inequality, regardless of the nature of the wealth in question?[127] In any case, it would be illusory to think that one could establish a just society by effecting one great agrarian reform, redistributing all land and natural resources in an equitable manner once and for all, and then allowing everyone to exchange and accumulate wealth however they please until the end of time.

---

126. This "solidaristic" concept of property as social property was proposed in the 1890s by Léon Bourgeois and Émile Durkheim as justification for a progressive income and estate tax. See R. Castel, *Les métamorphoses de la question sociale. Une chronique du salariat* (Fayard, 1995), pp. 444–449.

127. I will say more about this (imperfect) definition of justice in Part Four. See Chap. 17.

In the late nineteenth century, at the height of the Gilded Age, Americans worried about the growing concentration of wealth and the increasing power of large trusts and their shareholders. The autodidact writer Henry George scored a major success with his *Progress and Poverty,* published in 1879, in which he denounced private ownership of land. In edition after edition over subsequent decades, millions of copies were sold as readers devoured George's exuberant attacks on the people who had arrogated to themselves the ownership of America's soil, which had originally been divided up according to the whims of the monarchs of England, France, and Spain and even the Pope. Even as he attacked monarchs, Europeans, and property in general, George denounced the claims of landlords to compensation, going so far as to compare them to the slaveowners who had demanded hefty compensation when the British abolished slavery in 1833–1843.[128] Yet when it came to proposing a solution for the country's ills, George in the end showed himself to be fairly conservative. He proposed taking care of everything with a proportional tax on property in land, equal to the total rental value of the land free of any construction, drainage, or other improvement, thus allowing each person to benefit from the fruits of his own labor.[129] He did not envision any tax on bequests, thus leaving open the possibility of a future reconcentration of wealth in assets other than land. Furthermore, his proposal was impractical because it was virtually impossible to determine the value of unimproved land devoid of the many improvements introduced over the years (unless one was willing to accept a perpetually shrinking tax). This explains why no consideration was ever given to putting George's proposal into practice. But his book contributed to a revolt against inequality that ultimately led to the adoption of a progressive income tax in 1913 and a progressive estate tax in 1916.

A half century after George published his book, the issue of a property tax returned to the agenda in the United States with the debate over proposals by Louisiana's Democratic Senator Huey Long. Incensed by the power of stockholders in large corporations, Long tried in the early 1930s to outflank

---

128. See H. George, *Progress and Poverty* (1879), pp. 342–359. On the question of compensation, see Chap. 6.

129. Concretely, Henry George's proposal was a tax on the income from land at a rate equal to 100 percent of its rental value (whether actually rented or not) or, equivalently, a tax on capital equal to, say, 4 percent of the land's value (assuming a rental value of 4 percent).

Roosevelt on his left on the issue of progressive taxes, explaining that progressive taxes on income and inheritances were not enough to solve the country's problems. In 1934 he published a brochure laying out his plan to *Share Our Wealth: Every Man a King.* The heart of his program was a steeply progressive tax on all private fortunes valued at more than $1 million (around seventy times the average person's wealth at the time) so as to guarantee each family "a share in the wealth of the United States" at least equal to a third of the national average. To complement this he also proposed higher top income and estate tax rates to pay for higher pensions for elderly people with small savings as well as reduced working hours and an investment plan aimed at restoring full employment.[130] Born into a poor white family in Louisiana, Long was a colorful character, authoritarian and controversial, who announced his intention to challenge Roosevelt in the 1936 Democratic primary. Partly in response to the pressure, Roosevelt included in the Revenue Act of 1935 a "wealth tax," which was in fact a surtax on income with a rate of 75 percent on the highest incomes. Long's popularity was at its height in September 1935 (with more than 8 million members of local "Share Our Wealth" committees and record audiences of 25 million for his radio broadcasts) when he was shot dead by a political opponent in the Louisiana State Capitol in Baton Rouge.

---

130. Long envisioned a progressive wealth tax starting at $1 million (seventy times the average individual wealth at the time) and marginal rates rising gradually to 100 percent, with a maximum wealth of $50 million (3,500 times the average), while noting that the scale could be adjusted if necessary to set the maximum at $10 million (700 times the average). His main goal was to guarantee every American family a fortune of one-third the average ($5,000 for an average of $15,000), and he was careful to make clear that he had nothing against private wealth as long as it remained reasonable and not obscene. The program was riddled with religious references questioning how a small minority had gotten hold of most of the country's wealth. "God invited us all to come and eat and drink all we wanted. He smiled on our land and we grew crops of plenty to eat and wear. He showed us in the earth the iron and other things to make everything we wanted. He unfolded to us the secrets of science so that our work might be easy. God called: 'Come to my feast.' Then what happened? Rockefeller, Morgan, and their crowd stepped up and took enough for 120 million people and left only enough for 5 million of all the other 125 million to eat. And so many millions must go hungry and without these good things God gave us unless we call on them to put some of it back." See the online appendix.

On the Inertia of Wealth Taxes Stemming from the Eighteenth Century

Let us turn now to historical experiments with annual wealth taxes. It is useful to distinguish two groups of countries. In the first group—consisting of the United States, France, and the United Kingdom—the idea of a progressive annual wealth tax long met with stiff resistance from property owners so that the proportional wealth taxes inherited from the eighteenth and nineteenth centuries were never really reformed. By contrast, in the period 1890–1910, the Germanic and Nordic countries—Germany, Austria, Switzerland, Sweden, Norway, and Denmark, the same countries that introduced power sharing between stockholders and employees—introduced a progressive annual wealth tax, usually at the same time as progressive taxes on income and inheritance.

Let's start with the first group, especially the United States. Although the proposals of Henry George and Huey Long were never enacted, the property tax has played a central role in US fiscal history. It is one of the principal sources of funding for states and municipalities today. Of course, there are many different kinds of property tax. If assessed at a low proportional rate on all property, regardless of its value, it is not much of a threat to people of great wealth, who may well prefer it to an income tax. This is the case with the property tax in the United States as well as the land tax (*contribution foncière*, today's *taxe foncière*) established during the French Revolution, which French property owners viewed as the ideal tax throughout the nineteenth century because its rate was low, it was minimally intrusive, and it encouraged accumulation and concentration of wealth. Along with the inheritance tax, the real estate tax remained the French government's main source of revenue until World War I.[131] The US equivalent was the property tax, which also dates from the late eighteenth century; it was the principal direct tax in the United States in the nineteenth and early twentieth centuries, with the specific feature that it was assessed by states and municipalities and not by the federal government, whose tax revenues remained limited until the creation of the federal income tax in 1913. In France, the real estate tax ceased to be used to finance the central government and became a local tax in 1914, when the income tax was established.

Both the real estate tax *(taxe foncière)* and the property tax, which still exist today as local taxes yielding substantial revenues (2–2.5 percent of national income in both France and the United States in the 2010s), are assessed not only

---

131. See Chap. 4.

on housing but also on professional equipment used as productive capital by firms, including office buildings, storage lots, warehouses, and so on.[132] The main difference between a progressive wealth tax and the real estate tax or property tax is that the latter have always been strictly proportional. In other words, the tax rate is the same whether one owns a single house or a hundred houses.[133] The fact that professional assets are taxed at the level of the firm that owns and uses them (or rents them to other users) and not at the level of the shareholder who owns the firm also implies that it is never necessary to list all the properties owned by a given person in a single tax statement (which is comforting for those who own many properties, who might otherwise worry that the tax could quickly become progressive rather than proportional). The fact that the tax is local offers an additional guarantee against any effort to redistribute.[134] Note, however, that both the French real estate tax and the US property tax are based on the same fiscal philosophy, namely that wealth should be taxed as such, independent of income. No one has ever suggested that a person who owns dozens of apartment buildings or houses or lots or warehouses should be exempt from the property tax or real estate tax because he or she derives no income from the properties (because they are not rented or used). Even if the consensus is rather confused because knowledge of both the tax system and the income and wealth distributions is often highly imperfect, there is in fact a consensus that the owner of a property should either pay the property tax or real estate tax or sell the property to someone who can make better use of it.[135] In other words, the principle is that wealth should be taxed as such

---

132. Revenue from the French land tax in 2018 was about 40 billion euros (2 percent of national income), while the US property tax yielded $500 billion (more than 2.5 percent of national income).

133. The current rate is about 0.5–1 percent of the value of a property in France and the United States (with variations by state and town). Given the fact that the total value of private property is around five to six years of national income in both countries in the 2010s (see Figs. 10.8 and S10.8 in the online appendix), it is easy to see how receipts can amount to several percent of national income despite exemptions.

134. Give the competition among local governments to attract wealthy taxpayers, only a tax levied at the national or federal level could be steeply progressive.

135. In 2007–2011, the French government tried to put in place a so-called tax shield, that is, a ceiling on the total amount of tax any individual should be required to pay in relation to that person's income (as opposed to wealth). Only the land tax paid on the taxpayer's principal residence was included in this total.

because it is a measure of the taxpayer's ability to pay that is more durable and less manipulable than income.

The second essential difference between a general progressive wealth tax (ideally including all forms of property) and a real estate or property tax is that the latter leaves many types of assets untouched—especially financial assets, which constitute the lion's share of the largest fortunes (Fig. 11.17). Of course, it is quite misleading to say that the real estate tax or the property tax falls exclusively on residential property: it also applies to offices, lots, warehouses, and other real estate owned by firms, and shareholders in these firms are therefore also affected. Still, the resulting tax rate on financial assets is much lower than the tax rate on real estate, partly because financial assets invested abroad or in government bonds are totally exempt[136] and partly because many things that constitute the value of investments in domestic firms escape all or part of the tax (including machinery and equipment as well as intangible assets such as patents).[137] This hodgepodge is not the result of any preconceived plan. It is the fruit of particular historical processes and specific political-ideological mobilizations (or the absence thereof) around the issue of a wealth tax.

Note, moreover, that the US property tax, as its name suggests, has at times been more ambitious than the French real estate tax. There is considerable variation in the nature of the various property taxes assessed across the United States. Depending on the state or municipality, the property tax may apply not only to "real property" (such as land and buildings, from vacant lots to homes, apartment buildings, office buildings, warehouses, and so on) but also to "personal property" (including cars, boats, furniture, cash, and even financial assets). At the moment, the most common type of property tax applies only to real property, but this has not always been the case.

In this connection, the very lively debates that took place in Boston in the late nineteenth century, recently studied by Noam Maggor, are particularly interesting.[138] At the time, the property tax levied in the capital of Massachusetts, where much of the country's high financial and industrial aristocracy resided, fell on both real and personal property, including the financial

---

136. Foreign assets may of course be subject to a land or property tax in the countries where they are invested.

137. Machinery and equipment are sometimes included in the property tax or partially taxed via other local business taxes such as the now-defunct *taxe professionnelle* in France. In practice, such assets are in general taxed at much lower rates than real estate.

138. See Maggor, *Brahmin Capitalism,* esp. pp. 76–95 and pp. 178–203.

portfolios of the Boston elite, which were full of investments in other US states and foreign countries. Wealthy Bostonians were up in arms against this tax. They pointed out that they were already paying heavy taxes in the places where their capital was invested, and they demanded that the property tax be limited to real estate, which they saw as a nonintrusive index of their capacity to pay; this was the way things were done in Europe, most notably France.[139] To support their case, they called upon the help of economists and tax experts from nearby universities, especially Harvard, who praised the wisdom of European tax systems. Thomas Hills, the chief tax assessor of the city of Boston from 1870 to 1900, saw things differently, however. In 1875 he published a white paper showing that real estate accounted for only a tiny fraction of the wealth of the richest Bostonians and that exempting their financial assets from taxation would result in an enormous revenue loss. This would do much harm to the city, which was expanding rapidly at the time, with new waves of Irish and Italian immigrants filling its suburbs, requiring major public investments.[140] The political balance of power at the time was such that the broad wealth tax was maintained. But the debate continued in the 1880s and 1890s, and the wealthy finally carried the day in the early 1900s as various types of personal property were gradually removed from the purview of the property tax. Exemptions were granted to one type of financial asset after another, until in 1915 the Boston property tax was finally limited to real property only.[141]

These debates are particularly interesting because they illustrate the variety of possible trajectories and switch points. A key element in the controversy was the lack of cooperation between states and municipalities, which refused to

---

139. Though not necessarily everywhere in Europe: to believe Victor Hugo in *L'archipel de la Manche,* the real estate tax in Guernsey in the nineteenth century fell on the overall wealth of the taxpayer, which the novelist, who was as usual curious about everything, found quite surprising, since he was used to the French system. See V. Hugo, *Les travailleurs de la mer* (1866; Folio, 1980), p. 67.

140. Another political battle at the time had to do with extending the city limits to incorporate recently urbanized areas and formerly independent towns. Hills defended this extension, while wealthy residents of central Boston opposed it so as not to have to share the city's tax revenues with surrounding communities. See Maggor, *Brahmin Capitalism.* This episode once again illustrates the structural linkage of the tax regime to the political regime and the boundary regime.

141. On the political and administrative process that led eventually to complete exemption of personal property in 1915, see Maggor, *Brahmin Capitalism.* See also C. Bullock, "The Taxation of Property and Income in Massachusetts," *Quarterly Journal of Economics,* 1916.

share information about who owned what. One way to overcome these contradictions would have been (or might be in the future) to levy a coordinated property tax at the federal level and transform it into a true progressive tax on individual net worth. The choice that the United States made in 1913–1916 was different: the federal government concentrated on federal income and estate taxes, while the annual wealth tax (generally limited to real estate and assessed at a flat rate) was left to states and municipalities.[142]

In the end, both the US property tax and the French real estate tax, neither of which has been comprehensively reformed since the eighteenth century (that is, since the proprietarian-censitarian era), remain today as egregiously regressive taxes, which simply take no account of financial assets and liabilities. Assume for instance that the property tax (or the real estate tax) due for a house worth $300,000 is $3,000—that is, 1 percent of the value of the property. Consider now a person who owns this house but with a mortgage of $270,000 so that his or her net worth is only $30,000. For her, the tax payment will be 10 percent of her net wealth ($3,000 divided by $30,000). Imagine now someone who owns a stock portfolio worth $2.7 million together with this same house (and no mortgage), so that his net worth is $3 million. With the property tax system current applied in the United States, or the land tax system *(taxe foncière)* applied in France, this person would still pay the same tax ($3,000), although this makes only 0.1 percent of his net worth ($3,000 divided by $3 million). Such a regressive tax system is hard to justify and contributes to undermining fiscal consent and making economic justice seem impossible. It is also striking to discover that surveys on this subject show that most people would prefer a mixed tax system based on both income and net wealth (including both real estate and financial assets, which respondents logically regard as equivalent in terms of fiscal justice).[143] The only possible (but relatively

---

142. On the way property-owning elites were able to mobilize against the extension of property taxation in the nineteenth-century United States, both in the north (where the main issue from the elites' viewpoint was to avoid the taxation of financial assets) and in the south (where the primary concern of property-owning classes was to avoid what they feared could become an excessive taxation of slave property), see E. Einhorn, *American Taxation, American Slavery* (University of Chicago Press, 2006).

143. R. Fisman, K. Gladstone, I. Kuziemko, and S. Naidu, *Do Americans Want to Tax Capital? Evidence from Online Surveys* (National Bureau of Economic Research, NBER Working Paper 23907, 2017). Specifically, the survey presents pairs of income and wealth and asks what people think would be a fair tax. For a given

nihilistic and factually false) justification for not taking financial assets and liabilities into account is that people with financial assets have so many opportunities for tax avoidance that there is no choice but to exempt them entirely from the wealth tax. In fact, financial institutions have long been required to report interest and dividends on financial assets, and there is no reason why they should not be required to report the value of the assets themselves (and not just the income that flows from them). This could be extended to the international level by amending existing treaties concerning capital flows.[144] Remember, too, that the exceptional taxes on private wealth successfully levied in Germany, Japan, and many other countries after World War II obviously applied to financial assets. It would have been totally incongruous to have proceeded otherwise, since the purpose of these taxes was to tap the wealth of the well-to-do.

Collective Learning and Future Prospects for Taxing Wealth

All signs are that this long history is far from over. The existing system is a consequence of sociopolitical processes shaped primarily by the balance of political-ideological power and the mobilization capacities of the various parties in contention, and it will continue to evolve in the same way. The key point is this: the very sharp rise in wealth inequality in the United States in the period 1980–2020, combined with mediocre growth, has created the conditions for a challenge to the conservative ideological turn of the 1980s. Since the mid-2010s, leading Democrats have increasingly called for a return to 70–80 percent top marginal rates on the highest incomes and largest fortunes. The most outspoken of all was Bernie Sanders, who narrowly lost to Hillary Clinton in the 2016 Democratic presidential primary: he proposed a top marginal rate of 77 percent on the largest estates (in excess of $1 billion).

In anticipation of the 2020 presidential election, some Democratic candidates have begun to speak of creating the first US wealth tax, for instance, with a rate of 2 percent on fortunes of $50 million to $1 billion and 3 percent on

---

income (say, $100,000 per year), respondents felt that people with a net worth of $1 million should pay more in taxes than those who owned nothing and less than those with a net worth of $10 million. The same is true if one varies income for a fixed net worth.

144. I will have more to say on this. See esp. Chaps. 13 and 17.

wealth beyond $1 billion, to quote Elizabeth Warren's proposal of early 2019.[145] The Warren plan includes an exit tax of 40 percent for anyone who decides to give up US citizenship and transfer his or her wealth to another country. The tax would apply to all assets, with no exemptions, and impose dissuasive sanctions on individuals and governments unwilling to share relevant information about assets held abroad.

It is impossible to say at this stage if or when such a proposal might become law and what form it would take if it did. The suggested 3 percent rate on fortunes greater than $1 billion suggests a clear intention to put wealth back into circulation. This rate implies that a static fortune of $100 billion would return to the community after a couple of decades. In other words, the largest fortunes would only temporarily reside in the hands of any given individual. In view of the average rate of increase of large fortunes, however, one would need to consider higher rates on larger wealth holdings: at least 5–10 percent or maybe several dozens percent on multibillionaires so as to facilitate a fast renewal of fortune and power.[146] It might also be preferable to link the rates on the largest fortunes to the much-needed reform of the property tax (with the possibility of reducing the property tax on people with mortgages or seeking to purchase a first home).[147] In any case, these debates are far from over, and their outcome will depend largely on the ability of participants to relate recent developments to past experiences.

In other countries we find a similar need to place current debates in historical perspective. In France as in the United States, there were numerous

---

145. Warren's proposal would apply to individuals with wealth more than one hundred times the US average (of roughly $500,000 per couple and $250,000 per adult), or less than 0.1 percent of the population but holding 20 percent of total wealth, which would yield substantial tax revenues, estimated at more than 1 percent of national income. See E. Saez and G. Zucman, *How Would a Progressive Wealth Tax Work?* (University of California, Berkeley, Paper, 2019); E. Saez and G. Zucman, *The Triumph of Injustice: How the Rich Dodge Taxes and How to Make Them Pay* (Norton, 2019).

146. See Table 17.1.

147. Some researchers recently proposed a high proportional tax (of 7 percent) on all assets in order to force frequent reallocation of property. See E. Posner and E. G. Weyl, *Radical Markets: Uprooting Capitalism and Democracy for a Just Society* (Princeton University Press, 2018). Given the complete absence of progressivity, however, such a proposal might lead to greater concentration rather than diffusion of wealth. (In any case, the chief goal claimed by the authors is to facilitate rapid reallocation of land and goods.)

debates in the late nineteenth and throughout the twentieth centuries about establishing a true progressive wealth tax. There was discussion before World War I, indeed early in 1914, but by the summer of that year the emergency had arrived, and in view of the ideological resistance aroused by the idea of an annual wealth tax, the Senate opted for a general income tax instead. In the 1920s, debate within the Cartel of the Left led nowhere, both because the Radicals did not wish to worry smallholders and because the Socialists were more interested in nationalizations than in tax reform. Indeed, this ideological bias acted as a constant brake on any socialist or social-democratic thinking about a progressive wealth tax: for centrist parties the idea was terrifying, while for parties farther to the left, attached to the idea of state ownership of the means of production, it lacked the power to mobilize the masses. In 1936, at the time of the Popular Front, the Communists agreed to participate in the government; they favored a progressive wealth tax with rates ranging from 5 percent on fortunes of 1 million francs to 25 percent on fortunes larger than 50 million francs (respectively, ten and 500 times the average wealth at the time). But the parliamentary majority depended on the Radicals, who refused to vote for this bill, which they saw as a Trojan horse for socialist revolution. Many other proposals were floated subsequently, especially by the General Confederation of Labour (CGT) in 1947 and by Socialist and Communist deputies in 1972.

Finally, after the Socialists won the presidential and legislative elections in 1981, a "tax on large fortunes" (IGF) was passed by the Socialist-Communist majority, but in 1986 it was repealed by the Gaullist-liberal majority and then subsequently restored by the Socialists as a "solidarity tax on wealth" (ISF) after the 1988 elections.[148] Later, I will come back to the way the government elected in 2017 set about replacing the ISF in 2018 with a tax on real estate (IFI), with complete exemption for financial assets and therefore the bulk of the largest fortunes.[149] At this point, note simply that the very strenuous opposition aroused by this reform suggests that the story is far from over. In any case, bear in mind that the IGF (1982–1986) and ISF (1989–2017) never concerned more than a small minority of taxpayers (less than 1 percent of the population) and

---

148. For a detailed analysis of Socialist and Communist programs and debates on progressive wealth taxes from the interwar years to the 1980s, see T. Piketty, *Top Incomes in France in the Twentieth Century* (Harvard University Press, 2018), pp. 367–380. Regarding Joseph Caillaux's proposal in 1914 and the 1947 and 1972 bills, see J. Grosclaude, *L'impôt sur la fortune* (Berger-Levrault, 1976), pp. 145–217.

149. See esp. Chap. 14.

that rates were very low (generally 0.2 to 1.5–2 percent), with many exemptions. The result was that the real estate tax *(taxe foncière),* which in broad outline remained more or less unchanged since the 1790s, continued to be the main French wealth tax.[150]

Intersecting Trajectories and the Wealth Tax

In the United Kingdom, Labour governments led by Harold Wilson and later James Callaghan came close to passing a progressive wealth tax in 1974–1976. Urged on by economist Nicholas Kaldor, Labour concluded in the 1950s and 1960s that the tax system based on progressive income and estate taxes needed to be completed by an annual progressive tax on wealth for reasons of both justice and efficiency. In particular, this seemed to be the best way to gather information about the distribution of wealth and its evolution in real time and thus to combat avoidance of the estate tax by way of trusts and similar devices. Labour's platform in the successful 1974 election campaign included a progressive tax with a rate of 5 percent on the largest fortunes. But the plan ran into trouble, not only because of opposition from the treasury but also because of the consequences of the oil crisis and the ensuing inflation and monetary crisis of 1974–1976 (which led to IMF intervention in 1976), and was ultimately abandoned.[151]

The United Kingdom thus stands with the United States as the country that has achieved the highest level of fiscal progressivity with respect to income and inheritance yet has never experimented with an annual progressive wealth tax. Recent British experience with the so-called mansion tax bears mention, however. Although the British system of local taxing of houses is particularly regressive, the country does stand out for a strongly progressive system of taxes on real estate transactions. The tax paid on a real estate transaction is zero for transactions up to £125,000, 1 percent for transactions between £125,000 and £250,000, and 4 percent on transactions above £500,000. In 2011, a new 5 percent tax was created for sales of properties with a value greater than £1 million

150. On the eve of the 2018 reform, the ISF yielded revenues of about 5 billion euros (less than 0.3 percent of national income), compared with 40 billion euros from the *taxe foncière* (more than 2 percent of national income).
151. See H. Glennerster, *A Wealth Tax Abandoned: The Role of UK Treasury 1974–6* (London School of Economics, CASE Paper 147, 2011).

("mansions").[152] It is interesting to note that this 5 percent tax, introduced by a Labour government, was at first harshly criticized by Conservatives, who, after coming to power themselves, enacted a 7 percent transaction tax on properties worth more than £2 million. This shows that in a context of rising inequality, especially when wealth is highly concentrated and it is difficult for many people to gain access to the housing market, the need for a more progressive wealth tax can make itself felt across traditional party lines. It also points to the need for a comprehensive reassessment of property and wealth taxes: instead of such high transaction taxes, it would be more just and efficient to have an annual wealth tax with lower rates but based on total asset holdings of all types.

Finally, I should mention the Germanic and Nordic countries, which for the most part did not go as far as the United Kingdom or United States in imposing progressive income and estate taxes but were early to complement those two taxes with annual progressive wealth taxes. Prussia established an annual progressive tax on total wealth (including land, buildings, and professional and financial assets, net of debt) as early as 1893, shortly after it enacted a progressive income tax in 1891. Saxony did the same in 1901, and other German states followed suit, leading to the enactment of a federal wealth tax in 1919–1920.[153] Sweden enacted a progressive wealth tax in 1911, again coinciding with the progressive income tax reform.[154] In other countries in this group (such as Austria, Switzerland, Norway, and Denmark), similar systems combining

---

152. More precisely, the rate is 0 percent when the property is worth less than £125,000, 1 percent when it is worth £125,000–250,000, 3 percent between £250,000 and £500,000, 4 percent between £500,000 and £1 million, 5 percent between £1 million and £2 million (a new tax introduced in 2011), and 7 percent above £2 million (introduced in 2012). This progressive system is fairly surprising if one considers that such transaction fees are proportional in most countries (including France) and that the local "council tax," which replaced the "poll tax" in 1993 (and cost Margaret Thatcher her post) was in reality almost as regressive as the latter (the rate of the council tax rose far less than proportionately to the rental value of the main residence). On this, see Atkinson, *Inequality*, pp. 197–199, fig. 7.3.

153. On the evolution of the German tax system since 1870, see F. Dell, *L'Allemagne inégale. Inégalités de revenus et de patrimoine en Allemagne, dynamique d'accumulation du capital et taxation de Bismarck à Schröder 1870–2005* (EHESS, 2008).

154. The Swedish system was unique in imposing a joint tax on income and wealth from 1911 to 1947 before evolving into two separate systems in 1948. For details, see G. Du Rietz and M. Henrekson, "Swedish Wealth Taxation (1911–2007)," in

progressive taxes on income, wealth, and inheritance were put in place in the same period, generally between 1900 and 1920. Note, however, that these wealth taxes, which generally applied to barely 1–2 percent of the population with rates ranging from 0.1 to 1.5–2 percent (and up to 3–4 percent in Sweden in the 1980s), played a significantly less important role than the income tax.

It is also very important to note that these taxes were repealed in most of these same countries in the 1990s or early 2000s (with the exception of Switzerland and Norway, where they remain in place), partly because of tax competition (in a period marked by liberalized capital flows in Europe after the late 1980s) and an ideological context marked by the conservative revolution in the United States and United Kingdom and the fall of the Soviet Union. In addition to these well-known factors, we should also note the decisive (and instructive) importance of errors in the initial design. Conceived before World War I, at a time when the gold standard was still in effect and inflation was unknown, these Germano-Nordic wealth taxes were mostly based not on the market value of real and financial assets (with an index to prevent unduly abrupt increases or decreases in the amount of tax assessed) but rather on cadastral values—that is, values periodically recorded at intervals of, say, ten years, when all property was inventoried. While such a system is viable in times of zero inflation, it was quickly rendered obsolete by the very high inflation seen in the wake of the two world wars and in the postwar period. Such inflation is already the source of serious problems for a proportional wealth tax (such as the French real estate tax and the US property tax). In the case of a progressive tax, where the problem is to determine who is above each threshold of taxation and who is not, relying on values recorded in the relatively distant past on the basis of comparable local or neighborhood prices is untenable. It was because of this inequity that the German constitutional court suspended the wealth tax in 1997: taxpayers were no longer equal before the law because of inflation. The political coalitions that have held power in Berlin since then have had other priorities than reforming the wealth tax, for reasons we will come back to later.

Finally, note the specific role of the Swedish banking crisis of 1991–1992 in the country's political-ideological evolution (which had a significant impact on other countries, given the emblematic role of Swedish social democracy). The extreme gravity of the crisis, in which the main Swedish banks nearly went under, raised questions about banking regulation, monetary policy, and the role

---

Swedish Taxation: Developments Since 1862, ed. M. Henrekson and M. Stenkula (Palgrave, 2015), pp. 267–302.

played by capital flows. This led to a general critique of the alleged excesses of Sweden's social and fiscal model and, more broadly, to a sense that the country found itself in a very precarious position in a world that had gone over to globalized financial capitalism. For the first time since 1932 the Social Democrats were driven from power and replaced by the Liberals, who in 1991 exempted interest and dividends from taxation and strongly reduced the progressivity of the progressive wealth tax. This tax was finally abolished by the Liberals in 2007, two years after the Social Democrats abolished the estate tax, which may be surprising but reflected the degree to which a country the size of Sweden can be gripped by the fear of fiscal competition as well as the perception that the Swedish egalitarian model is so firmly established that it no longer needs such institutions. There is nevertheless reason to believe that such radical reform of tax policy can have fairly substantial inegalitarian consequences in the long run; this may also help to explain why Swedish Social Democrats appeal more and more to the relatively well-off and less and less to their traditional popular electorate.[155]

We will come back to these questions in Part Four, when we examine the evolution of voting patterns and of political conflict in the major parliamentary democracies. At this stage, several lessons can be drawn. Broadly speaking, social democracy, for all its successes, has suffered from a number of intellectual and institutional shortcomings, especially with respect to social ownership, equal access to education, transcendence of the nation-state, and progressive taxation of wealth. On the last point, we have traced a number of trajectories, with multiple switch points. Policies have been highly inconsistent, and there has been too little sharing of experiences across countries. No doubt this is partly because political movements and citizens have not fully engaged with these issues. Recent developments reflect considerable hesitation: on the one hand, rising inequality of wealth clearly calls for the development of new forms of fiscal progressivity; on the other hand, there is a widespread perception that pitiless tax competition justifies less progressivity, even if it contributes to greater inequality.

In reality, refusing to have a rational debate about a progressive wealth tax and pretending that it is wholly impossible to make the largest fortunes contribute to the common good and that the lower and middle classes have no choice but to pay in their place strike me as a very dangerous political choice. All history shows that the search for a distribution of wealth acceptable to the

---

155. See Chap. 16.

majority of people is a recurrent theme in all periods and all cultures. The thirst for fiscal justice grows stronger as people become better educated and better informed. It would be surprising if things were different in the twenty-first century and these debates were not once again central, especially at a time when the concentration of wealth is increasing. To prepare for this, it is best to begin by delving into past debates—the better to move beyond them. If we are not willing to do this, we risk making people wary of any ambitious effort to achieve fiscal and social solidarity and encouraging instead social division and ethnic and national hostility.

TWELVE

Communist and Postcommunist Societies

Thus far, we have analyzed the fall of ownership society between 1914 and 1945 and the way in which the social-democratic societies that were constructed in the period 1950–1980 entered a period of crisis in the 1980s. For all its successes, social democracy proved unable to cope adequately with the rise of inequality because it failed to update and deepen its intellectual and political approach to ownership, education, taxation, and above all the nation-state and regulation of the global economy.

We turn now to the case of communist and postcommunist society, primarily in Russia, China, and Eastern Europe. The goal is to analyze communist society's place in the history and future of inequality regimes. Communism, especially in its Soviet form as the Union of Socialist Soviet Republics (USSR), was the most radical challenge that proprietarian ideology—its diametrical opposite—ever faced. Whereas proprietarianism wagered that total protection of private property would lead to prosperity and social harmony, Soviet Communism was based on the complete elimination of private property and its replacement by comprehensive state ownership. In practice, this challenge to the ideology of private property ultimately reinforced it. The dramatic failure of the Communist experiment in the Soviet Union (1917–1991) was one of the most potent factors contributing to the return of economic liberalism since 1980–1990 and to the development of new forms of sacralization of private property. Russia, in particular, became a symbol of this reversal. After three-quarters of a century as a country that had abolished private property, Russia now stood out as the home of the new oligarchs of offshore wealth— that is, wealth held in opaque entities with headquarters in foreign tax havens: in the game of global tax evasion, Russia became a world leader. More generally, postcommunism in its Russian, Chinese, and East European variants has today become hypercapitalism's best ally. It has also inspired a new kind of disillusionment, a pervasive doubt about the very possibility of a just economy, which encourages identitarian disengagement.

We will begin by analyzing the Soviet case, especially the reasons for the failure of communism and the inability to imagine any form of economic or social organization other than hypercentralized state ownership. We will also study the Russian regime's kleptocratic turn since the fall of Communism and its place in the global rise of tax havens. We will then look at the case of China, who took advantage of Soviet and Western failures to build a dynamic mixed economy with which it was able to make up the ground lost under Maoism. In addition, the Chinese regime raises fundamental questions for Western parliamentary democracies. The answers it proposes, however, require a degree of opacity and centralism incompatible with effective regulation of the inequalities produced by private property. Finally, we will examine the postcommunist societies of Eastern Europe, their role in the transformation of the European and global inequality regime, and the way in which they reveal the ambiguities and limitations of the economic and political system currently in place in the European Union.

Is It Possible to Take Power Without a Theory of Property?

To study the Soviet Communist experience (1917–1991) today is first of all to try to understand the reasons for its dramatic failure, which still weighs heavily on any new attempt to think about how capitalism might be overcome. The Soviet failure is also one of the main political-ideological factors responsible for the global rise of inequality in the 1980s.

The reasons for this failure are numerous, but one is obvious. When the Bolsheviks took power in 1917, their action plan was not nearly as "scientific" as they claimed. It was clear that private property would be abolished, at least when it came to the major industrial means of production, which in any case were relatively limited in Russia at that time. But how would the new relations of production and property be organized? What would be done about small production units and about the commercial, transport, and agricultural sectors? How would decisions be made, and how would wealth be distributed by the gigantic state planning apparatus? In the absence of clear answers to these questions, power quickly became ultra-personalized. When results failed to measure up to expectations, reasons had to be found and scapegoats designated, which led to accusations of treason and capitalist conspiracies against the Communist state. The regime then resorted to purges and imprisonments, which to some extent continued until its downfall. It is easy to proclaim the abolition of private property and bourgeois democracy but more complex (as well as more interesting) to draw up detailed blueprints for an alternative political, social, and economic system. The task is not impossible, but it requires deliberation, decentralization, compromise, and experimentation.

My purpose is not to blame Marx or Lenin for the failure of the Soviet Union but simply to observe that before the seizure of power in 1917, neither they nor anyone else had envisioned solutions to the crucial problems involved in organizing an alternative society. To be sure, in *Class Struggles in France* (1850) Marx did warn that the transition to communism and a classless society would require a phase of "dictatorship of the proletariat," during which all means of production would need to be placed in the hands of the state. The term "dictatorship" was hardly reassuring. But in reality this formula really said nothing about how the state should be organized, and it is very difficult to know what Marx would have recommended had he lived to see the Revolution of 1917 and its aftermath. As for Lenin, we know that shortly before his death in 1924 he favored the New Economic Policy (NEP), which envisioned an extended period of reliance on a regulated market economy and private property (even if the modes of regulation remained largely undefined). Joseph Stalin, wary of anything that might slow the process of industrialization, chose to avoid these complexities: in 1928 he ended the NEP and ordered immediate collectivization of agriculture and full state ownership of the means of production.

The absurdity of the new regime became quite apparent in the late 1920s when the government moved to criminalize independent workers who did not fit readily into standard categories but were nevertheless essential to urban life and the Soviet economy. Among those stripped of civil rights (including the right to vote and, above all, the right to rations, which made survival difficult) were not only members of the old Tsarist military and clerical classes but also anyone "deriving income from private commerce or wholesale activities" as well as anyone "hiring a worker for the purpose of earning a profit." In 1928–1929, some 7 percent of the urban and 4 percent of the rural population were thus included on so-called *listenzii* lists for engaging in prohibited activities. In practice, this measure targeted a whole population of carters, food sellers, craftsmen, and tradespeople.

In their applications for rehabilitation, which involved endless bureaucratic paperwork, these people described their "little lives" and scant possessions—nothing more than a horse and cart or a humble food stand—and professed their bewilderment at being targeted by a regime they supported and whose forgiveness they implored.[1] The absurdity of the situation stemmed from the

---

1. See N. Moine, "Peut-on être pauvre sans être un prolétaire? La privation de droits civiques dans un quartier de Moscou au tournant des années 1920–1930," *Le Mouvement social*, 2001.

fact that it is obviously impossible to organize a city or a society solely with authentic proletarians, if "proletarian" is defined as a worker in a large factory. People need to eat, dress, move about, and find housing, and these things require large numbers of workers in production units of various sizes, sometimes quite small, which can be organized only in a fairly decentralized way. Society depends on each person's knowledge and aspirations and sometimes requires small businesses funded with private capital and employing a handful of workers.

The 1936 Constitution of the USSR, promulgated at a time when it was believed that these deviant practices had been definitively eradicated, instituted "personal property" alongside "socialist property" (meaning state property, including collective farms and cooperatives strictly controlled by the state). But personal property consisted solely of possessions acquired with the income from one's work, as opposed to "private property," which consisted of ownership of the means of production and therefore implied exploitation of the work of others, which was completely banned, no matter how small the production unit. To be sure, exceptions to the rule were regularly negotiated: for instance, collective farmworkers were allowed to sell a small part of their production at farmers' markets, and Caspian Sea fishermen were permitted to sell part of their haul for their own benefit. The problem was that the regime devoted considerable time to undermining and renegotiating its own rules, partly out of ideological dogmatism and wariness of subversive practices and also because it needed scapegoats and "saboteurs" to blame for its failures and for the frustrations of its people.

At the time of Stalin's death in 1953, more than 5 percent of the adult Soviet population was in prison, more than half for "theft of socialist property" and other minor larceny, the purpose of which was to make their daily lives more bearable. This was the "society of thieves" described by Juliette Cadiot—a symbol of the dramatic failure of a regime that was supposed to emancipate the people, not incarcerate them.[2] To find a similar incarceration rate, one would have to look at the black male population of the United States today (about 5 percent of adult black males are in prison). Looking at the United States as a whole, about 1 percent of the adult population was behind bars in 2018, enough to make the country the unchallenged world leader in this

---

2. See J. Cadiot, *La société des voleurs. La protection de la propriété socialiste sous Staline* (EHESS, 2019). See also J. Cadiot, "L'affaire Hain. Kyiv, hiver 1952," *Cahiers du Monde Russe*, 2018.

category in the early twenty-first century.[3] The fact that the Soviet Union had an incarceration rate five times as high in the 1950s says a great deal about the magnitude of the human and political disaster. It is particularly striking to discover that the incarcerated were not just dissidents and political prisoners; the majority were economic prisoners, accused of stealing state property, which was supposed to be the means of achieving social justice on earth. Soviet prisons were full of hungry people who pilfered from their factories or collective farms: petty thieves accused of stealing a chicken or a fish and factory managers accused of corruption or embezzlement, often wrongly. Such people became targets of officials determined to brand "thieves" of socialist property as enemies of the people and were subject to five to twenty-five years of hard labor for minor thefts and capital punishment for more serious offenses. Interrogation and trial transcripts allow us to hear the voices and justifications of these alleged thieves, who do not hesitate to challenge the legitimacy of a regime that failed to keep its promise of improving living conditions.

It is interesting to note that one paradoxical consequence of World War II was that the Soviet regime briefly adopted a somewhat more expansive concept of private property, at least on the surface. This had to do with postwar Russian demands for indemnification and compensation for Nazi destruction and pillage in occupied parts of Russia between 1941 and 1944. Under international law at that time private losses would receive more generous indemnities than public losses. Soviet commissions therefore methodically set about collecting testimony about damage to private property, including losses by small production units that had supposedly been abolished by the constitution of 1936. In practice, however, this invocation of private property was essentially a rhetorical strategy that the regime deployed on the diplomatic and legal front, usually without direct consequences in terms of actual restitution to the individuals said to have suffered the losses.[4]

---

3. By comparison, the incarceration rate (in percent of the adult population) is currently 0.7 percent in Russia, 0.3 percent in China, and less than 0.1 percent in all the countries of Western Europe. See the online appendix (piketty.pse.ens.fr/ideology).

4. See N. Moine, "La perte, le don, le butin. Civilisation stalinienne, aide étrangère et biens trophés dans l'Union soviétique des années 1940," *Annales. Histoire, sciences sociales,* 2013; N. Moine, "Evaluer les pertes matérielles de la population pendant la Seconde guerre mondiale en URSS : vers la légitimation de la propriété privée?" *Histoire et mesure,* 2013.

On the Survival of "Marxism-Leninism" in Power

Given these depressing results, it is natural to ask how the Soviet regime could have stayed in power for so long. Clearly its repressive capacity is part of the answer, but as with all inequality regimes, one must also consider its persuasive capacity. The fact is that "Marxist-Leninist ideology," on which the Soviet ruling class relied to maintain itself in power, had, for all its weaknesses, a number of strengths. The most obvious was the comparison with the previous regime. Not only had the Tsarist regime been deeply inegalitarian; it had also failed dismally to develop Russia's economy, society, and schools. The Tsarist government relied on noble and clerical classes directly descended from premodern trifunctional society. It abolished serfdom in 1861, only a few decades before the Russian Revolution of 1917. At that time serfs still accounted for nearly 40 percent of the population. At the time of abolition, the imperial government decreed that former serfs must pay an annual indemnity their former owners until 1910 in return for their freedom. The spirit was similar to that of the financial compensation awarded to slaveowners when the United Kingdom abolished slavery in 1833 and France in 1848, except that the serfs lived in the Russian heartland rather than on remote slave islands.[5] Although most payments ended in the 1880s, the episode places the Tsarist regime and Russian Revolution in perspective by reminding us of the extreme forms that the sacralization of private property and the rights of property owners sometimes took before World War I (regardless of the nature and origin of the property).

With the Tsarist government as point of comparison, the Soviet regime had no difficulty portraying its project as one that held out greater promise for the future in terms of both equality and modernization. And in spite of repression, ultra-centralization, and state appropriation of all property, public investment in the period 1920–1950 clearly did lead to rapid modernization that brought the Soviet Union closer to Western European levels, especially in the areas of infrastructure, transportation, education (and literacy), science, and public health. Within a few decades the Soviet regime had considerably reduced the concentration of income and wealth while raising the standard of living, at least until the 1950s.

With respect to income inequality, recent work has shown that the top decile's share of national income remained fairly low throughout the Soviet period, around 25 percent from the 1920s to the 1980s, compared with

5. See Chap. 6.

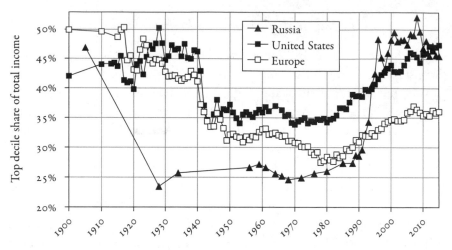

FIG. 12.1. Income inequality in Russia, 1900–2015

Interpretation: The top decile share of total national income averaged 25 percent in Soviet Russia, lower than in Western Europe or the United States, before rising to 45–50 percent after the fall of communism, surpassing both Europe and the United States. *Sources and series:* piketty.pse.ens.fr/ideology.

45–50 percent under the Tsars (Fig. 12.1). The top centile's share decreased to around 5 percent of total income in the Soviet era compared with 15–20 percent before 1917 (Fig. 12.2). To be sure, such estimates have their limits. The available data on monetary incomes have been corrected to reflect the in-kind benefits available to the privileged classes in the Soviet regime (including access to special stores, vacation centers, and so on), but such corrections are by their nature approximate.[6] In the end, the data on income inequality in the Soviet period mainly demonstrate the fact that the Communist regime did not structure its inequalities around money. For one thing, capital income, which constitutes a large share of the income of high earners in other societies, was totally absent in the Soviet Union. For another, the pay differences between a worker, an engineer, and a government minister were relatively small.[7] This

---

6. If we looked only at monetary income, the top decile's share would be barely 20 percent of total income (rather than 25 percent) and the top centile's less than 4 percent (instead of 5 percent). See the online appendix and F. Novokmet, T. Piketty, and G. Zucman, "From Soviets to Oligarchs: Inequality and Property in Russia, 1905–2016," WID.world, 2017; also in *Journal of Economic Inequality,* 2018.

7. Specifically, a top centile share of 4–5 percent means that the average income of the best paid 1 percent was four to five times that of the average income overall and

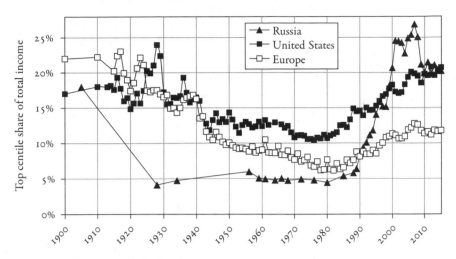

FIG. 12.2. The top centile in Russia, 1900–2015

Interpretation: The top centile share of total national income averaged 5 percent in Soviet Russia, lower than in Western Europe or the United States, before rising to 20–25 percent after the fall of communism, surpassing both Europe and the United States. *Sources and series:* piketty.pse.ens.fr/ideology.

was an essential characteristic of the new regime, which would have lost all internal ideological coherence and forfeited all legitimacy if it had begun paying its leaders salaries and bonuses one hundred times the pay of ordinary workers.

However, this should not obscure the fact that the regime organized its inequalities in other ways by offering in-kind benefits and privileged access to certain goods to its officials. These are difficult to take fully into account. There were also stark status differences: the mass incarceration of whole classes of people is only the most extreme instance of this; there was also a sophisticated internal passport system, which restricted the mobility of some, including the ability of peasants, who suffered greatly from the collectivization of agriculture and the forced march toward industrialization, to migrate to the cities. Suspect or condemned groups were confined to certain areas, and workers were prevented from moving if planners felt that they were needed in certain places or that there was insufficient housing to accommodate them elsewhere.[8] It

---

generally eight to ten times that of the wages of the lowest paid (which are generally close to half the overall average income).

8. N. Moine, "Le système des passeports à l'époque stalinienne. De la purge stalinienne au morcellement du territoire (1932–1953)," *Revue d'histoire moderne et contemporaine,* 2003.

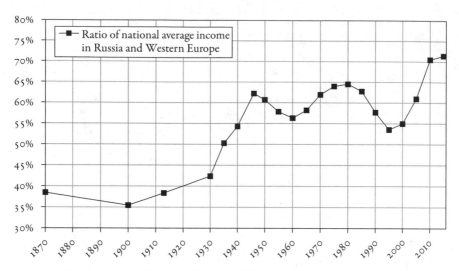

FIG. 12.3. The income gap between Russia and Europe, 1870–2015

Interpretation: Expressed in terms of purchasing power parity, the national income per adult in Russia was 35–40 percent of the Western European average (Germany, France, and the United Kingdom) from 1870 to 1980, before rising from 1920 to 1950, then stabilizing at about 60 percent of the Western European level from 1950 to 1990. *Sources and series:* piketty.pse.ens.fr/ideology.

would be misleading to try to integrate all these aspects of Soviet inequality into a single quantitative index based on monetary income. In my view, it is best to indicate what is known about monetary inequality while insisting on the fact that this was only one dimension of Soviet inequality (and not necessarily the most significant one); the same is true of other inequality regimes.

As for the evolution of the standard of living under Soviet rule, once again the evidence is incomplete. According to the best available estimates, the standard of living, as measured by per capita national income, stagnated in Russia in the period 1870–1910 at around 35–40 percent of the West European level (defined as the average of the United Kingdom, France, and Germany); it then rose gradually in the period 1920–1950 to about 60 percent of the West European level (Fig. 12.3). Although these comparisons should not be viewed as perfectly precise, the orders of magnitude may be taken as significant. There is no doubt that Russia began to catch up with Western Europe between the Revolution of 1917 and the 1950s. Some of this was of course due to the fact that Russia started out so far behind. Its progress was made more visible by the poor performance of the capitalist countries in the 1930s, when production collapsed in Western Europe and the United States, while the planned Soviet economy continued full speed ahead. For both structural and conjunctural reasons, then, it was possible in the 1950s to see the Soviet Union's results as globally positive.

Over the next four decades (1950–1990), however, Russian national income stagnated at about 60 percent of the West European level (Fig. 12.3). This was clearly a failure, especially in view of the rapid advance in level of education during this period in Russia (as well as elsewhere in Eastern Europe), which should normally have led to continuation of the catch-up process and gradual convergence with Western Europe. The fault must therefore lie with the organization of the system of production. The frustration was even greater because the scientific, technological, and industrial achievements of the communist regimes were abundantly praised in the 1950s and 1960s both inside and outside the communist bloc. In the eighth edition (1970) of Paul Samuelson's celebrated economics textbook, used by generations of North American students, it was predicted on the basis of observed trends in the period 1920–1970 that Soviet gross domestic product (GDP) might surpass that of the United States sometime between 1990 and 2000.[9] During the 1970s, however, it became increasingly clear that the catch-up process had ground to a halt and that the Russian standard of living had stagnated compared to that of the capitalist countries.

It is also possible, moreover, that these comparisons underestimate the actual gap in standard of living between East and West, particularly at the end of the period. Indeed, if the poor quality of consumer goods (such as household appliances and cars) available in the communist countries is taken into account in the price indices used in these comparisons, it is quite possible that the gap grew even wider in the 1960s and afterward. Another complication stems from the bloated Soviet military sector, which represented as much as 20 percent of GDP during the Cold War, compared with 5–7 percent in the United States.[10] To be sure, the concentration of material investments and intellectual resources in strategic sectors did lead to spectacular successes, such as the launching of the first Sputnik satellite in 1957, to the consternation of the United States. But none of that can mask the mediocrity of living conditions for ordinary citizens and the increasingly glaring backwardness relative to the capitalist countries in the 1970s and 1980s.

---

9. See P. Samuelson, *Economics,* 8th ed. (McGraw-Hill, 1970), p. 831.
10. See, for example, M. Mann, *The Sources of Social Power* (Cambridge University Press, 2013), vol. 4, p. 182.

The Highs and Lows of Communist and Anticolonialist Emancipation

In view of the significant differences between Eastern and Western methods of tallying production and accounting for income as well as the multidimensional character of the gaps, the best way to measure how bad conditions in Soviet Russia were is probably to use demographic data. The numbers show a worrisome stagnation of life expectancy from the 1950s on. Indeed, in the late 1960s and early 1970s we even find a slight decrease in life expectancy for men, which is unusual in peacetime; in addition, infant mortality rates stopped decreasing.[11] These figures point to a health system in crisis. In the 1980s, the efforts of Mikhail Gorbachev, the last president of the Soviet Union, to reduce alcohol abuse played an important role in the decline of his popularity and the ultimate collapse of the regime. Soviet Communism, once celebrated for rescuing the Russian people from Tsarist misery, had become synonymous with rampant poverty and shortened lives.

On the political-ideological level, the Soviet Union suffered in the 1970s from loss of the prestige it had enjoyed in the postwar era. In the 1950s the Soviet Union's international reputation was enhanced by the decisive role it had played in the victory over Nazism and by the fact that, through the Communist International which it controlled, it was the only political and ideological force that stood in clear and radical opposition to colonialism and racism. In the 1950s, racial segregation was still widely practiced in the southern United States. It was not until 1963–1965 that American blacks mobilized to force the Democratic administrations of John F. Kennedy and Lyndon B. Johnson (who had no desire to send troops into the South to defend blacks) to grant civil and voting rights to African Americans. South Africa introduced and then reinforced apartheid in the 1940s and early 1950s with a series of laws intended to confine blacks to the townships and preventing them from setting foot in other parts of the country (Chapter 7). The South African regime, close to Nazism in its racialist inspiration, was supported by the United States in the name of anticommunism. It was not until the 1980s that international sanctions were imposed on South Africa, despite opposition from the Reagan administration in the United States, which continued until

---

11. See E. Todd, *La chute finale. Essai sur la décomposition de la sphère soviétique* (R. Laffont, 1976).

1986 (when Reagan used his veto to try to thwart Congressional disapproval of apartheid but was overridden).[12]

In the 1950s, the decolonization movement had just begun, and France was on the verge of waging a fierce war in Algeria. While the Socialists participated in the government and supported increasingly violent operations to "maintain order" in Algeria, only the Communist Party spoke out unambiguously in favor of immediate independence and withdrawal of French troops. At that key point in time, the communist movement seemed to many intellectuals and to the international proletariat to be the only political force in favor of organizing the world on an egalitarian social and economic basis, while colonialist ideology continued to prefer an inegalitarian, hierarchic, racialist logic.

In 1966, a newly independent Senegal organized in Dakar a "World Festival of Negro Arts." This was an important event for the pan-African movement and the idea of "negritude," a literary and political concept elaborated by Léopold Senghor in the 1930s and 1940s. Senghor, a writer and intellectual, became the first president of Senegal in 1960 after trying in vain to form a broad West African federation.[13] All the major powers, capitalist as well as communist, responded to the invitation and sought to make a good impression. At the Soviet stand, a delegation from Moscow displayed a brochure setting forth its convictions and political analyses. Russia, unlike the United States and France, did not need slavery to industrialize, this document argued. It was therefore in a better position to forge development partnerships with Africa on an egalitarian basis.[14] This claim apparently surprised no one because it seemed so natural at the time.

By the 1970s, this Soviet moral prestige had almost totally dissipated. The era of decolonization was over, black Americans had obtained their civil rights, and antiracism and racial equality were among the values to which the capitalist countries laid claim now that they had become postcolonial and social-democratic. Of course, racial issues and the question of immigration would soon play a growing role in European and American political conflict in the 1980s and 1990s. I will say much more about this in Part Four. But the fact

---

12. At the end of a long congressional battle, Reagan vetoed the Comprehensive Anti-Apartheid Act passed by the US Congress, but Congress overrode the veto, and the bill became law.

13. See Chap. 7.

14. See *Dakar 66: Chroniques d'un festival panafricain* (exhibition, Musée du quai Branly, Paris, February 16–May 15, 2016).

remains that by the 1970s the communist camp had lost its clear moral advantage on these issues, and critics of communism could now focus on its repressive and carceral policies, its treatment of dissidents, and its poor social and economic performance. In the television series *The Americans,* Elizabeth and Philip are KGB (the USSR's Committee for State Security) agents operating in the United States in the early 1980s. Elizabeth has an affair with a black American activist, which shows that she remains more sincerely attached to the communist ideal than Philip, the Soviet agent posing as her husband, who wonders why he is doing what he is doing as the end of the Soviet regime draws near. Broadcast between 2013 and 2018, this series shows how much things had changed since the days when Soviet Communist was widely regarded as a champion of antiracism and anticolonialism.[15]

A similar though less dramatic shift occurred with feminism. In the period 1950–1980, when the patriarchal ideology of the housewife reigned supreme in the capitalist countries, communist regimes took the lead in advocating equality between men and women, particularly in the workplace. Support was offered in the form of public day care and preschools as well as contraception and family planning. This positioning was not free of hypocrisy, to judge by the fact that political leadership in the communist countries was as male-dominated as anywhere else.[16] Still, soviets and other parliamentary assemblies in the Soviet Union and Eastern Europe were up to 30–40 percent female in the 1960s and 1970s, at which time women made up less than 5 percent of parliaments in Western Europe and the United States. Of course, assemblies in the communist countries had limited political autonomy and were often chosen by elections in which there was only one candidate or perhaps a token

---

15. In January 1988, when apartheid was still in force, the Cuban air force intervened in Angola against South African tanks. "We decided to resolve the problem at our own risk, as allies of Angola," Castro explained on July 26, 1991, with Nelson Mandela in attendance. Mandela, who had come to express "a great debt of gratitude to the Cuban people," stressed the historic significance of the defeat that "destroyed the myth of the invincibility of the white oppressor," which was "a turning point in the struggle" against apartheid. See the collection of speeches by F. Castro and N. Mandela, *Cuba et l'Afrique: La victoire de l'égalité* (Bègles, 2018).

16. The history of communist attitudes toward contraception is also far from straightforward. The USSR was the first country to legalize abortion in 1920 but prohibited it in 1936 (Stalin took a hard natalist line), then legalized it again in 1955.

opposition candidate, with the Communist Party holding nearly all the real power. The inclusion of female candidates therefore had only limited consequences for the reality of power and its distribution.

In any case, the proportion of female representatives abruptly fell from 30–40 percent to little more than 10 percent in Russian and Eastern Europe in the 1980s and 1990s, roughly the same level as in the West or even slightly below.[17] By the way, it is worth noting that China and several other countries in South and Southeast Asia were well ahead of the West in regard to the proportion of female representatives in the 1960s and 1970s. In Chimamanda Ngozi Adichie's novel *Half of a Yellow Sun,* which is set in Nigeria in the early 1960s on the eve of the Nigerian civil war, the intellectual Igbo Odenigbo is passionate about his newly independent country's politics. He follows the news as a citizen of the world, from the struggle for racial equality in Mississippi to the Cuban revolution, to say nothing of the election of the first female prime minister in Ceylon. In the 1990s the Western countries would take up the feminist cause, like so many others before it, with varying degrees of sincerity and effectiveness when it came to achieving actual equality between the sexes (I will come back to this).

Communism and the Question of Legitimate Differences

To return to the Soviet attitude toward poverty, it is important to try to understand why the government took such a radical stance against all forms of private ownership of the means of production, no matter how small. Criminalizing carters and food peddlers to the point of incarcerating them may seem absurd, but there was a certain logic to the policy. Most important was the fear of not knowing where to stop. If one began by authorizing private ownership of small businesses, would one be able to set limits? And if not, would this not lead step by step to a revival of capitalism? Just as the proprietarian ideology of the nineteenth century rejected any attempt to challenge existing property rights for fear of opening Pandora's box, twentieth-century Soviet ideology refused to allow anything but strict state ownership lest private property find its

---

17. See the interesting data in S. Carmichael, S. Dilli, and A. Rijpma, "Gender inequality since 1820," in *How Was Life? Global Well-Being Since 1820,* ed. J. van Zanden, J. Baten, M. d'Ercole, A. Rijpma, C. Smith, and M. Timmer (Organisation for Economic Co-operation and Development [OECD], 2014), p. 238, fig. 12.9.

way into some small crevice and end up infecting the whole system.[18] Ultimately, every ideology is the victim of some form of sacralization—of private property in one case, of state property in another; and fear of the void always looms large.

With the advantage of hindsight and knowledge of the twentieth century's successes and failures, it is possible to outline new ideas—such as participatory socialism and temporary shared ownership—with which it might be possible to go beyond both capitalism and the Soviet form of communism. Specifically, one can imagine a society that allows privately owned firms of reasonable size while preventing excessive concentration of wealth by means of a progressive wealth tax, a universal capital endowment, and power sharing between stockholders and employees. Historical experience can teach us to set limits and map boundaries. Of course, history cannot tell us with mathematical certainty what the perfect policies are in every situation. Instead, the lessons we draw must be subject to permanent deliberation and experimentation. Still, history can teach us where to begin in order to move ahead. For example, we now know that the top centile's share of total wealth can fall from 70 to 20 percent without impeding growth (quite the contrary, as Western European experience in the twentieth century shows). We know from experience with Germanic and Nordic versions of co-management that employee and shareholder representatives can each control half the voting rights in a firm and that such power sharing can improve overall economic performance.[19] The path from these concrete experiences to a fully satisfactory form of participatory socialism is complex, especially since it is hard to draw the line between small production units and large ones. Indeed, it is indispensable to conceptualize the entire system and to think about how firms of different sizes, from the smallest to the largest, might be flexibly regulated and taxed.[20] Nevertheless, history is suffi-

---

18. In *Land and Freedom* (1995), Ken Loach depicts a village council in Spain in 1936. There is conflict over communal land: Does it belong to the government or to individuals? This exacerbates squabbling among anarchists, Stalinists, and Trotskyists and inevitably strengthens the enemy: Franquists, clergy, and landlords.

19. See Chaps. 10–11.

20. In practice, employment and output are divided in a very balanced way among firms of different sizes (with, for example, about 20 percent of private-sector jobs in firms of fewer than ten employees, 20 percent between ten and fifty employees, 20 percent between fifty and 250 employees, and so on). This necessitates a range of solutions in regard to power sharing and ownership of these various structures. See Chap. 11.

ciently rich in lessons that we can draw from it many ideas about possible paths forward.[21]

Why did Bolshevik leaders reject the path of decentralized participatory socialism in the 1920s? It was not just because they lacked the experimental knowledge gained over the course of the twentieth and early twenty-first centuries, concerning most notably the successes and limitations of social democracy. Nor was it solely because they worried about the complexities mentioned earlier. To have a clear idea of the virtues of decentralization, one also has to articulate a clear vision of human equality—a vision that fully recognizes the many legitimate differences among individuals, especially with respect to knowledge and aspirations, and the importance of these differences in determining how social and economic resources are deployed. Soviet Communism tended to neglect the importance and especially the legitimacy of such differences, probably because it was in the grip of an industrial and productivist illusion. Specifically, if one believes that human needs are few in number and relatively simple (for, say, food, clothing, housing, education, and medical care) and can be satisfied by providing virtually identical goods and services to everyone (partly on the reasonable ground that all human beings share fundamentally the same hopes), then decentralization may seem unimportant. A centrally planned society and economy should be able to do the job, allocating every material and human resource as needed.

In fact, however, the problem of social and economic organization is more complex. It cannot be reduced to satisfying a basic set of simple, homogeneous needs. In all societies—whether in Moscow in 1920 or Paris or Abuja in 2020—individuals "need" an infinite variety of goods and services to lead their lives and fulfill their hopes and aspirations. Of course, some of these "needs" are artificial or exploitative or harmful or polluting and therefore inimical to the basic needs of others, in which case their expression must be limited through collective deliberation, laws, and institutions. But much of this diversity of human needs is legitimate, and if the central government attempts to suppress it, the government risks becoming oppressive to both individuality and individuals. In 1920s Moscow, for example, some people preferred, because of their personal history or social habits, to live in certain neighborhoods or eat certain foods or wear certain clothes. Others had come to own a cart or food stand or to possess certain specific skills. The only way such legitimate differences could be expressed and made to interact with one another would have been

---

21. See Chap. 17.

through decentralized organization. A centralized state could not do the job, not only because no state could ever gather enough relevant information about every individual but also because the mere attempt to do so would negatively affect the social process through which individuals come to know themselves.

On the Role of Private Property in a Decentralized Social Organization

Workers' cooperatives were often discussed in debates around the NEP in 1920s Russia as well as in the 1980s in connection with Gorbachev's *perestroika* (economic restructuring). Yet even cooperatives cannot respond fully to the challenges posed by the diversity of human needs and aspirations. Recall our discussion in Chapter 11 of the individual who wanted to open a restaurant or an organic grocery store. We saw there that it would not have made much sense to accord the same decision-making power to the person who had invested all her savings and energy in getting such a project off the ground as to the person hired as an employee the day before, who might be dreaming of starting his own business, in which it would make just as little sense to take away his primary role. Such individual differences with respect to both projects and aspirations are legitimate, and they will continue to exist even in a perfectly egalitarian society in which each person starts out with strictly the same economic and educational capital. In that case they would simply reflect the diversity of human aspirations, subjectivities, and personalities and the range of possible individual histories. Indeed, private ownership of the means of production, correctly regulated and limited, is an essential part of the decentralized institutional organization necessary to allow these various individual aspirations and characteristics to find expression and in due course come to fruition.

Of course, the resulting concentration of private property and the power that flows from it will need to be rigorously debated and controlled and should not exceed what is strictly necessary; this could be accomplished through devices such as a steeply progressive wealth tax, a universal capital endowment, and fair power sharing between a firm's employees and shareholders. As long as private property is viewed in such purely instrumental terms, without sacralization of any kind, it is indispensable, provided that one agrees that the ideal socioeconomic organization must respect the diversity of aspirations, knowledge, talent, and skills that constitutes the wealth of humankind. By contrast, criminalizing every form of private property, down to the carter's cart and the food vendor's stand, as the Soviet authorities tried to do in the 1920s, comes down to assuming that this diversity of aspirations and subjectivities is of limited value when it comes to organizing production and building an industrial economy.

Finally, one additional element of complexity is worth pointing out. In practice, legitimate differences of aspiration have often been used rhetorically to justify quite dubious inequalities. For instance, parental preferences for different types of schools and curricula are often cited as justifications for inequality between schools and for disadvantaging children whose parents are less skilled at deciphering the codes and choosing the most promising schools and courses. A reasonable solution to this problem might be to banish market competition from the sphere of education and supply adequate and equal funding to all schools, which is what most countries have in fact done, at least at the primary and secondary level.[22] In general, the rules appropriate to each sector should be decided by collective democratic deliberation. When a good or service is reasonably homogeneous—for instance, when a given community can agree on the knowledge and skills that every child of a certain age ought to have—then there is little need for competition among the units producing that good or service (much less for private profit-generating ownership of the means of production); indeed, competition may well prove harmful in such circumstances. By contrast, in sectors where there is a legitimate diversity of individual aspirations and preferences—for instance, in the supply of clothing or food—then decentralization, competition, and regulated private ownership of the means of production are justified.

This reflection on the extent of legitimate differences is of course complex. It is too simple to say that private ownership is the solution to every problem or, conversely, that it should be criminalized in all circumstances. The question must be dealt with, however, if the goal is to rethink property as temporarily private but ultimately social in the framework of a global strategy of emancipation designed not to reproduce the fatal errors of Soviet Communism.

Postcommunist Russia: An Oligarchic and Kleptocratic Turn

In contrast to the Soviet Union, a "society of petty thieves," postcommunist Russia is a society of oligarchs engaged in grand larceny of public assets. Let us begin with a glance back at recent history. The dismantling of the Soviet Union and its productive apparatus in 1990–1991 led directly to a sharp decline in the

---

22. See Fig. 11.11.

standard of living in 1992–1995. In the late 1990s per capita income began to climb until in the 2010s it stood at about 70 percent of the West European level in terms of purchasing power parity (Fig. 12.3) but at half that level using current exchange rates (owing to the weakness of the ruble). On the whole, although the situation has improved since the end of communism, the results have been mediocre, especially since inequality increased dramatically in the 1990s (Figs. 12.1–12.2).

It is important to note that it is very difficult to measure and analyze income and wealth in postcommunist Russia because the society is so opaque. This is due in large part to decisions taken first by the governments headed by Boris Yeltsin and later by Vladimir Putin to permit unprecedented evasion of Russian law through the use of offshore entities and tax havens. In addition, the postcommunist regime abandoned not only any ambition to redistribute property but also any effort to record income or wealth. For example, there is no inheritance tax in postcommunist Russia, so there are no data on the size of inheritances. There is an income tax, but it is strictly proportional, and its rate since 2001 has been just 13 percent, whether the income being taxed is 1,000 rubles or 100 billion rubles.

Note, by the way, that no other country has gone as far as Russia in rejecting the very idea of a progressive tax. In the United States, the Reagan and Trump administrations did make reduction of top marginal tax rates a central plank in their platforms in the hope of stimulating economic activity and entrepreneurial spirits, but they never went so far as to reject the principle of progressive taxation itself: tax rates on the lowest income brackets remain lower in the United States than rates on the highest brackets, which Republican administrations reduced to 30–35 percent when they had the chance, but not to 13 percent.[23] A flat tax of 13 percent would trigger vigorous opposition in the United States, and it is hard to imagine an electoral or ideological majority willing to approve such a policy (at least for the foreseeable future). The fact that Russia did opt for such a tax policy shows that postcommunism is in a sense the ultimate form of the inegalitarian ultra-liberalism of the 1980s and 1990s.

Note, too, that there were no progressive income or inheritance taxes in the communist countries (or, if there were, their role was minor), because central planning and state control of firms allowed the state to set wages and incomes directly. When planning was abandoned and firms were privatized, however, progressive taxation could have played a role similar to the role it played in the

---

23. See Fig. 10.11.

capitalist countries in the twentieth century. The fact that this did not happen demonstrates once again how little countries share experiences and learn from one another.

As usual, the lack of a political commitment to progressive taxation coincided in Russia with a particularly opaque fiscal administration. The available tax data are extremely limited and rudimentary. With Filip Novokmet and Gabriel Zucman, however, we were able to access certain sources, which allowed us to show that official estimates, which are based on self-declared survey data and ignore top incomes almost entirely, seriously underestimate the increase of income inequality since the fall of communism. Concretely, the data show that the top decile's share of total income, which was just over 25 percent in 1990, rose to 45–50 percent in 2000 and then stabilized at that very high level (Fig. 12.1). Even more dramatic was the increase in the top centile's share from barely 5 percent in 1990 to about 25 percent in 2000, a level significantly higher than the United States (Fig. 12.2). Peak inequality was probably achieved in 2007–2008. The highest Russian incomes have probably declined since the crisis of 2008 and the imposition of economic sanctions on Russia after the Ukraine crisis of 2013–2014, although the level remains extremely high (and is no doubt underestimated owing to the limitations of the available data). Thus, in less than ten years, from 1990 to 2000, postcommunist Russia went from being a country that had reduced monetary inequality to one of the lowest levels ever observed to being one of the most inegalitarian countries in the world.

The rapidity of postcommunist Russia's transition from equality to inequality between 1990 and 2000—a transition without precedent anywhere else in the world according to the historical data in the WID.world database—attests to the uniqueness of Russia's strategy for managing the transition from communism to capitalism. Whereas other communist countries such as China privatized in stages and preserved important elements of state control and a mixed economy (a gradualist strategy that one also finds in one form or another in Eastern Europe), Russia chose to inflict on itself the famous "shock therapy," whose goal was to privatize nearly all public assets within a few years' time by means of a "voucher" system (1991–1995). The idea was that Russian citizens would be given vouchers entitling them to become shareholders in a firm of their choosing. In practice, in a context of hyperinflation (prices rose by more than 2,500 percent in 1992) that left many workers and retirees with very low real incomes and forced thousands of the elderly and unemployed to sell their personal effects on the streets of Moscow while the government offered large blocks of stock on generous terms to selected individuals, what had to happen did happen. Many Russian firms, especially in the energy sector, soon fell into the hands of small groups of cunning shareholders who contrived to gain control of the vouchers of millions of Russians; within a short period of time these people became the country's new "oligarchs."

According to the classifications published by *Forbes,* Russia thus became within a few years the world leader in billionaires of all categories. In 1990, Russia quite logically had no billionaires, because all property was publicly owned. By the 2000s, the total wealth of Russian billionaires listed in *Forbes* amounted to 30–40 percent of the country's national income, three or four times the level observed in the United States, Germany, France, and China.[24] Also according to *Forbes,* the vast majority of these billionaires live in Russia, and they have done particularly well since Vladimir Putin came to power in the early 2000s. Note, moreover, that these figures do not include all the Russians who have accumulated not billions but merely tens or hundreds of millions of dollars; these Russians are far more numerous and more significant in macroeconomic terms.

In fact, what has distinguished Russia in the period 2000–2020 is that the country's wealth is largely in the hands of a small group of very wealthy individuals who either reside entirely in Russia or divide their time between Russia and London, Monaco, Paris, or Switzerland. Their wealth is for the most part hidden in screen corporations, trusts, and the like, ostensibly located in tax havens so as to escape any future changes in Russia legal and tax systems (although Russian authorities have not shown themselves to be particularly vigilant). The use of screens, cutouts, and other legal subterfuges to place assets outside the legal jurisdiction of a given country while affording solid guarantees to the owners and while the actual economic activity of the firm takes place inside the country is a general characteristic of the economic, financial, and legal globalization that has taken place since the 1980s.[25] This has occurred because the international treaties and accords that Europe and the United States agreed on to liberalize capital flows in this period did not include any regulatory mechanisms or provisions for exchanges of information that would have allowed states to establish appropriate fiscal, social, and legal policies and

---

24. See the online appendix and Novokmet, Piketty, and Zucman, "From Soviets to Oligarchs," fig. 2.

25. K. Pistor, *The Code of Capital: How the Law Creates Wealth and Inequality* (Princeton University Press, 2019).

cooperative structures for coping with this new environment (see Chapter 11). Responsibility for this state of affairs is therefore broadly shared. But even within this general landscape, Russian abuse of the system has attained unheard-of proportions, as recent work by legal scholars has shown.[26]

When Offshore Assets Exceed Total Lawful Financial Assets

Note, too, that in terms of macroeconomic significance of capital flight, Russia is also in a league of its own. Because of the very nature of financial dissimulation, it is of course difficult to give a precise accounting. In Russia, however, the very magnitude of the sums involved simplifies things somewhat, as does the fact that the country enjoyed enormous trade surpluses in the period 1993–2018: Russia's annual trade surplus averaged 10 percent of GDP over this twenty-five-year period, or a total of nearly 250 percent of GDP (2.5 years of national product). In other words, since the early 1990s, Russian exports, especially gas and oil, massively exceeded Russian imports of goods and services. In principle, then, the country should have accumulated enormous financial reserves of roughly the same amount. This is what we see in other petroleum-exporting countries such as Norway, whose sovereign wealth fund held assets in excess of 250 percent of GDP in the mid-2010s. But Russia's official reserves in 2018 amounted to less than 30 percent of GDP. Something like 200 percent of Russian GDP has therefore gone missing (and this does not even take into account the income those assets should have produced).

Official Russian balance-of-payments statistics reveal other astonishing features. Public and private assets invested abroad seem to have obtained remarkably mediocre yields, with large capital losses in some years, whereas foreign investments in Russia invariably earned exceptional yields, especially in view of fluctuations in the value of the ruble, which would partly explain why the country's net wealth position vis-à-vis the rest of the world did not increase more. It is quite possible that these statistics hide operations linked to capital flight. In any case, even if we accept these yield differentials as legitimate, the

---

26. See D. Nougayrède, "Outsourcing Law in Post-Soviet Russia," *Journal of Eurasian Law,* 2014; D. Nougayrède, "Yukos, Investment Round-Tripping and the Evolving Public-Private Paradigm," *American Review of International Arbitration,* 2015; D. Nougayrède, "The Use of Offshore Companies in Emerging Market Economies: A Case Study," *Columbia Journal of European Law,* 2017. See also T. Gustafson, *Wheel of Fortune: The Battle for Oil and Power in Russia* (Harvard University Press, 2012).

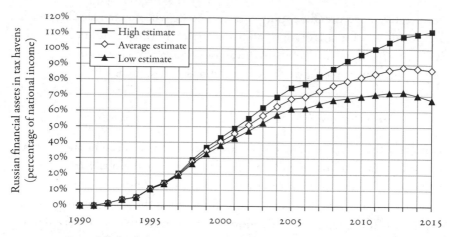

FIG. 12.4. Capital flight from Russia to tax havens

Interpretation: By examining the growing gap between cumulative Russian trade surpluses (nearly 10 percent a year on average from 1993 to 2015) and official reserves (barely 30 percent of national income in 2015), and using various hypotheses about yields obtained, one can estimate that the amount of Russian assets held in tax havens was between 70 and 110 percent of national income in 2015, with an average value of around 90 percent. *Sources and series:* piketty.pse.ens.fr/ideology.

fact remains that the official reserves in the balance-of-payments data are still much too low. Using these very conservative assumptions, one can estimate that cumulative capital flight from 1990 to the mid-2010s amounts to roughly one year of Russian national income (Fig. 12.4). To be clear, this is a minimum estimate; the actual figure might be twice as high or even higher.[27] In any event, this minimum estimate implies that the financial assets tucked away in tax havens are roughly equal to the total amount of all financial assets legally owned by Russian households inside Russia (roughly one year of national income). In other words, offshore property has become at least as important in macroeconomic terms as legal financial property—and probably is more important. In a sense, then, illegality has become the norm.

There are also other sources that reveal (or confirm) the magnitude of Russian capital flight and, more generally, the unprecedented growth of tax havens around the world since the 1980s. For instance, one can look at inconsistencies in international financial statistics. In theory, looking at a country's balance of payments should allow us to measure financial flows and in partic-

---

27. For details about this estimate, see Novokmet, Piketty, and Zucman, "From Soviets to Oligarchs," pp. 19–23.

ular inward and outward flows of capital income (dividends, interest, and profits of all kinds). In principle, the total of all positive and negative flows should sum to zero every year at the international level. Of course, the complexity of the accounting may result in small discrepancies, but these should be both positive and negative and even out over time. Since the 1980s, however, there has been a systematic tendency for outward capital income flows to exceed inward flows. From these and other anomalies it is possible to estimate that in the early 2010s, financial assets held in tax havens and not registered in other countries amounted to nearly 10 percent of total global financial assets. All signs are that this has only increased since then.[28]

Furthermore, by exploiting data made public by the Bank for International Settlements (BIS) and the Swiss National Bank (SNB) on countries where assets are held, one can estimate each country's approximate share of offshore assets held in tax havens relative to the total (lawful and unlawful) assets held by residents of each country. The results are as follows: "only" 4 percent for the United States, 10 percent for Europe, 22 percent for Latin America, 30 percent for Africa, 50 percent for Russia, and 57 percent for the petroleum monarchies (Fig. 12.5). Once again, these should be regarded as minimum estimates. These calculations exclude (or only partially account for) real estate and shares in unlisted companies.[29] Note, by the way, that financial opacity is a problem everywhere, particularly in the less developed countries, for which it is an obstacle to state building and to finding a standard of fiscal justice acceptable to a majority of citizens.

The Origins of "Shock Therapy" and Russian Kleptocracy

Why did postcommunist Russia go from the land of soviets and (monetary) income equality to the land of oligarchs and kleptocrats? It is tempting to see this as a "natural" swing of the pendulum: traumatized by the Soviet failure, the country moved energetically in the opposite direction, that of ruthless capitalism. This explanation cannot be totally wrong, but it leaves out a lot

---

28. See G. Zucman, "The Missing Wealth of Nations: Are Europe and the US Net Debtors or Net Creditors?" *Quarterly Journal of Economics,* 2013; G. Zucman, *The Hidden Wealth of Nations* (University of Chicago Press, 2017); G. Zucman, "Global Wealth Inequality," *Annual Review of Economics,* 2019.

29. See G. Zucman, "Taxing Across Borders: Tracking Personal Wealth and Corporate Profits," *Journal of Economic Perspectives,* 2014; A. Alstadsæter, N. Johannesen, and G. Zucman, "Who Owns the Wealth in Tax Havens? Macro Evidence and Implications for Global Inequality," *Journal of Public Economics,* 2018.

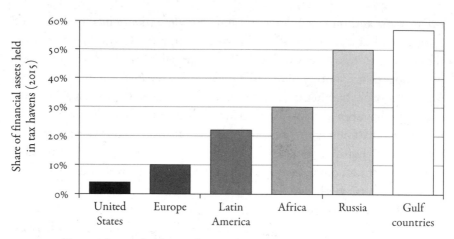

FIG. 12.5. Financial assets held in tax havens

Interpretation: By exploiting anomalies in international financial statistics and break-downs by country of residence from the Bank for International Settlements (BIS) and the Swiss National Bank (SNB), one can estimate that the share of financial assets held in tax havens is 4 percent for the United States, 10 percent for Europe, and 50 percent for Russia. These figures exclude nonfinancial assets (such as real estate) and financial assets unreported to BIS and SNB, and should be considered minimum estimates. *Sources and series:* piketty.pse.ens.fr/ideology.

and is too deterministic. There was nothing "natural" about Russia's post-communist transformation, any more than the transformation of any other inequality regime. There were many choices available in 1990, as there always are. Rather than rehearse the various deterministic accounts, it is more interesting to see what happened as the fruit of contradictory and conflictual socioeconomic and political-ideological processes, which could have taken any number of paths and turned out differently had the balance of power and capacity for mobilization of the various contending groups been different.

In the early 1990s, with Russia in a state of extreme weakness, there was brief but intense struggles about the choice of "shock therapy" for the post-Soviet transition. Among the proponents of shock therapy were many representatives of Western governments (especially the United States) and international organizations based in Washington, such as the World Bank and the International Monetary Fund. The general idea was that only an ultra-rapid privatization of the Russian could ensure that the changes would be irreversible and prevent any possibility of a return to communism. It is no exaggeration to say that the dominant ideology among economists working for these institutions in the early 1990s was much closer to Anglo-American capitalism in the Reagan-Thatcher mold than to European social democracy or Germano-Nordic co-management. Most Western advisers working in Moscow at the time were convinced that the Soviet Union had sinned by an excess of egalitarianism; hence, any possible increase of inequality in the wake of privatization and shock therapy should be considered a relatively minor worry.[30]

With the advantage of hindsight, however, we can see that the levels of (monetary) inequality observed in Soviet Russia in the 1980s were not very different from those observed at the same time in the Nordic countries, especially Sweden: in both cases the top decile claimed about 25 percent of total income and the top centile 5 percent, which never prevented Sweden from ranking among the countries with the highest standard of living and highest productivity levels in the world (see Figs. 10.2–10.3). Thus, the problem was not so much excessive equality as the way the economy and production were organized, which involved central planning and total abolition of private ownership of the means of production. It is reasonable to think that if Russia had adopted Nordic-style social-democratic institutions with a highly progressive tax system, an advanced system of social protection, and co-management by unions and shareholders, it would have been possible to preserve a certain level of equality while raising the level of productivity and standard of living. The choice that Russia made in the 1990s was very different: a small group of people (the future oligarchs) was offered the opportunity to take possession of most of the country's wealth with a flat income tax of 13 percent (and no inheritance tax), which allowed them to entrench their position; contrast this with the adoption by most Western countries of progressive income and inheritance taxes in the twentieth century. It is sometimes shocking to discover the degree to which historical memory is lacking and just how little countries are able to share and learn from each other's experiences. It is especially shocking when the people and institutions responsible for these failures are supposed to be the very ones whose presumed purpose is to further international cooperation through shared knowledge and expertise.

It would be a mistake, however, to attribute Russia's political-ideological choices solely to outside influences. Internal disagreements also mattered. In the late 1980s, Mikhail Gorbachev tried without success to promote an economic model that would preserve the values of socialism while encouraging

---

30. For a book reflecting this state of mind, see M. Boycko, A. Shleifer, and R. Vishny, *Privatizing Russia* (MIT Press, 1995).

contributions from cooperatives and regulated (though ill-defined) forms of private ownership. Other groups inside the Russian government, particularly within the security apparatus, did not share Gorbachev's views. In this respect, Vladimir Putin's analyses in interviews conducted by (the very pro-Putin) film-maker Oliver Stone in 2017 are particularly revealing. Putin mocks Gorbachev's egalitarian illusions and his obsession with saving socialism in the 1980s, especially his liking for "French Socialists" (an approximate but significant reference, since French Socialists at the time represented what was most socialist in the Western political landscape). In substance, Putin concluded that only an unambiguous renunciation of egalitarianism and socialism in all their forms could restore Russia's greatness, which depended above all on hierarchy and verticality in both politics and economics.

It is important to stress the fact that this trajectory was not foreordained. The post-Soviet economic transition took place in particularly chaotic circumstances, with no real electoral or democratic legitimacy. When Boris Yeltsin was elected president of the Russian Federation by universal suffrage in June 1991, no one knew exactly what his powers would be. The pace of events accelerated after the failed Communist putsch of August 1991, which led to the accelerated dismantling of the Soviet Union in December. Economic reforms then proceeded at full throttle, with the liberalization of prices in January 1992 and "voucher privatization" in early 1993. All this took place without new elections so that key decisions were imposed by the executive on a hostile parliament, which had been elected in March 1990 during the Soviet era (when only a handful of non-Communist candidates were allowed to run). This was followed by a violent clash between the president and parliament, which was settled by force in the fall of 1993 when the parliament was shelled and then dissolved. With the exception of the presidential election of 1996, which Yeltsin won with just 54 percent of the vote in the second round against a Communist candidate, no genuinely contested election has taken place in Russia since the fall of the Soviet Union. Since Putin came to power in 1999, the arrest of political opponents and clamp down on the media have left Russia under de facto authoritarian and plebiscitarian rule. The fundamentally oligarchic and inegalitarian orientation of policy since the fall of communism has never really been debated or challenged.

To sum up, Soviet and post-Soviet experience demonstrates in a dramatic way the importance of political-ideological dynamics in the evolution of inequality regimes. The Bolshevik ideology that dominated after the revolution of 1917 was relatively crude, in the sense that it was based on an extreme form of hypercentralized state rule. Its failures led to steadily increasing repression and a historically unprecedented rate of incarceration. Then the fall of the Soviet regime in 1991 led to an extreme form of hypercapitalism and an equally unprecedented kleptocratic turn. These episodes also demonstrate the importance of crises in the history of inequality regimes. Depending on what ideas are available when a switch point arrives, a regime's direction may turn one way or another in response to the mobilizing capacities of the various groups and discourses in contention. In the Russian case, the country's postcommunist trajectory reflects in part the failure of social democracy and participatory socialism to develop new ideas and a workable plan for international cooperation in the late 1980s and early 1990s, when the hypercapitalist and authoritarian-identitarian conservative agendas were in their ascendancy.

If we now look to the future, it is legitimate to ask why the countries of Western Europe have been so uninterested in the origins of Russian wealth and so tolerant of such massive misappropriations of capital. One possible explanation is that they were partly responsible for the shock therapy approach to the transition and benefited from infusions of capital invested by wealthy Russians in West European real estate, financial firms, sports teams, and media. This is obviously true not only of the United Kingdom but also of France and Germany. There is also the fear of a violent response by the Russian government.[31] Still, instead of imposing trade sanctions, which affect the entire country, a better solution would be to freeze or severely penalize financial and real estate assets of dubious origin.[32] One might then be able to influence Russian public opinion, since the Russian people themselves were the first victims of the kleptocratic turn. If European governments have not been more proactive, it is no doubt because they worry about not knowing where it will end if they begin to question past appropriations of common resources by private individuals (this is the Pandora's box syndrome that we have encountered several times before).[33] Nevertheless, Europe might be better equipped to solve

---

31. In a sense, Russia (or at any rate its elites) has as much to lose in the fight against tax havens and financial opacity as the United States has in the struggle against global warming (see Chap. 13).

32. Trade sanctions were imposed on Russia in the wake of its annexation of Crimea and of Russian military intervention in eastern Ukraine in 2014. That crisis followed an attempt by Ukraine to align itself commercially and politically with Europe rather than with Russia.

33. European courts have at times been receptive to claims against "ill-gotten" wealth. For example, a French court ordered the seizure of property belonging to

many of the other problems it faces if it were to engage more energetically in the fight against financial opacity by insisting on the creation of a true international register of financial assets.

On China as an Authoritarian Mixed Economy

We turn now to communism and postcommunism in China. It is well known that China drew lessons from the USSR's failures as well as from its own mistakes in the Maoist era (1949–1976), during which the attempt to completely abolish private property and to initiate a forced march toward collectivization and industrialization ended in disaster. In 1978 the country began experimenting with a novel type of political and economic regime, which rests on two pillars: a leading role for the Chinese Communist Party (CCP), which has been maintained and even reinforced in recent years, and the development of a mixed economy based on a novel balance between private and public property, which has proved to be durable.

We begin with the second pillar, which is essential for understanding the specificities of the Chinese case. Another advantage of this choice is that the contrast with Western experience is illuminating. The best way to proceed is to pull together data from all available sources concerning the ownership of firms, farmland, residential real estate, and financial assets and liabilities of all kinds in order to estimate the share of property owned by the government (at all levels). The results are shown in Fig. 12.6, which compares China's evolution with that of the leading capitalist countries (United States, Japan, Germany, United Kingdom, and France).[34]

---

members of the family of Teodoro Obiang, the ruler of Guinea. This shows, by the way, that it is technically quite possible to freeze or expropriate assets. See T. Piketty, *Capital in the Twenty-First Century* (Harvard University Press, 2014), pp. 446–447. Russian misappropriation of capital is so extensive, however, that judicial tools are not enough; fiscal tools are also required. It is also possible that the courts are more likely to become involved where the theft involves natural resources (like the Guinean forests at the root of Obiang's wealth) in a very poor country; or it may also be that wealth is more suspect when it belongs to someone with black skin.

34. For details on sources and methods, see T. Piketty, G. Zucman, and L. Yang, "Capital Accumulation, Private Property and Rising Inequality in China, 1978–2015," WID.world, 2017; also in *American Economic Review*, 2019. See the online appendix.

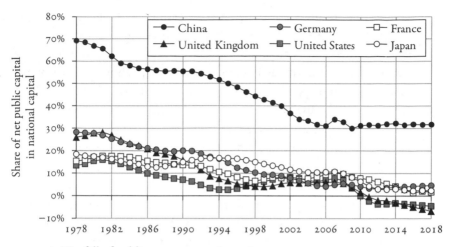

FIG. 12.6. The fall of public property, 1978–2018

Interpretation: The share of public capital (public assets net of debt including all public assets: firms, buildings, land, investments, and financial assets) in national capital (total public and private) was roughly 70 percent in China in 1978; it then stabilized at around 30 percent in the mid-2000s. It was 15–30 percent in the capitalist countries in the 1970s and is near zero or negative in the late 2010s. *Sources and series:* piketty.pse.ens.fr/ideology.

The main conclusion is that the public share of capital was close to 70 percent in China in 1978, when economic reforms were inaugurated, but then fell sharply in the 1980s and 1990s before stabilizing at around 30 percent since the mid-2000s. In other words, the gradual privatization of Chinese property ended in 2005–2006: the relative shares of public and private property have barely moved since then. Because the Chinese economy has continued to grow at a rapid rate, private capital has obviously continued to increase: new land has been improved and new factories and apartment buildings have continued to be built at a breakneck pace, but publicly owned capital has also continued to increase at roughly the same rate as privately owned capital. China thus appears to have settled on a mixed-economy property structure: the country is no longer communist since nearly 70 percent of all property is now private, but it is not completely capitalist either because public property still accounts for a little more than 30 percent of the total—a minority share but still substantial. Because the Chinese government, led by the CCP, owns a third of all there is to own in the country, its scope for economic intervention is large: it can decide where to invest, create jobs, and launch regional development programs.

It is important to note that the 30 percent public share of capital is an average that hides very large difference between sectors and asset categories. For instance, residential real estate is almost entirely privatized. In the late 2010s, the government and firms owned less than 5 percent of the housing stock, which has become the leading private investment of Chinese households with sufficient means. This has caused the price of real estate to skyrocket, especially since other savings opportunities are limited and the public retirement system is underfunded and shaky. By contrast, the government held 55–60 percent of the total capital of firms in 2010 (including both listed and unlisted firms of all sizes in all sectors). This share has remained virtually unchanged since 2005–2006. In other words, the state and party continue to maintain tight control over the productive system—indeed, tighter than ever with respect to the largest firms.[35] Since the mid-2000s there has been a significant decrease in the share of firm capital held by foreign investors, which has been offset by an increase in the share held by Chinese households (Fig. 12.7).[36]

From the 1950s to the 1970s, the capitalist countries were also mixed economies, with important variations from country to country. Public assets took many forms, including infrastructure, public buildings, schools, and hospitals; in addition, many firms were publicly owned, and there was public financial participation in certain sectors. Furthermore, public debt was historically low owing to postwar inflation and government measures to reduce debt, such as exceptional taxes on private capital or even outright debt cancellation (see Chapter 10). All told, the share of public capital (net of debt) in national capital was generally 20–30 percent in the capitalist countries in the period 1950–

---

35. See J. Ruet, *Des capitalismes non alignés. Les pays émergents, ou la nouvelle relation industrielle du monde* (Raisons d'agir, 2016). The author also stresses a continued state role in industry in India, Brazil, and Indonesia (less extensive than in China but more extensive than in Europe, the United States, and Japan). In Russia, the share of public capital in national capital fell much more rapidly than in China, but it remained significant, roughly 15–20 percent in the late 2010s, despite capital flight. The reason for this is the extent of natural resources and the continued existence of some very large public energy firms. See F. Novokmet, T. Piketty, L. Yang, and G. Zucman, "From Communism to Capitalism: Private vs. Public Property and Inequality in China and Russia," *American Economic Association Papers & Proceedings*, 2018.

36. For detailed series by asset category, see Piketty, Zucman, and Yang, "Capital Accumulation," figs. 5–6, and the online appendix.

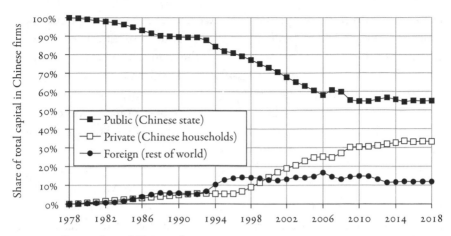

FIG. 12.7. Ownership of Chinese firms, 1978–2018

Interpretation: The Chinese state (at all levels of government) in 2017 held roughly 55 percent of the capital of Chinese firms (both listed and unlisted, of all sizes in all sectors), compared with 33 percent for Chinese households and 12 percent for foreign investors. The share of the latter has decreased since 2006 and that of Chinese households has increased, while the share of the Chinese state has stabilized at around 55 percent. *Sources and series:* piketty.pse.ens.fr/ideology.

1980.[37] In the late 1970s, available estimates show a level of 25–30 percent in Germany and the United Kingdom and 15–20 percent in France, the United States, and Japan (Fig. 12.6). To be sure, these levels are lower than the share of public capital in China today but not by much.

The difference is that the Western countries have long since ceased to be mixed economies. Owing to privatization of public assets (for instance, in the utilities and telecommunications sector), limited investment in sectors that have remained public (especially education and health), and the steady increase of public indebtedness, the share of net public capital in national capital has shrunk to virtually zero (less than 5 percent) in all the major capitalist countries; in the United States and United Kingdom, it is negative. In other words,

---

37. To gauge orders of magnitude, net public capital generally amounted to a year of national income (around 150 percent of national income for public assets and barely 50 percent for public debt) at a time when total private wealth (also net of debt) was close to three years of national income. See Fig. 10.8. See also the online appendix and T. Piketty and G. Zucman, "Capital Is Back: Wealth-Income Ratios in Rich Countries, 1700–2010," *Quarterly Journal of Economics,* 2014, for detailed series by country.

in the latter two countries, public debts exceed the total value of public assets. This is a striking fact, and I will say more later about its significance and implications. At this stage, note simply how rapid the change has been. When I published *Capital in the Twenty-First Century* in 2013/2014, the latest available complete data sets pertained to the years 2010–2011; among developed countries, only Italy had public debt that exceeded public capital.[38] Six years later, in 2019, with data available through 2016–2017, the United States and United Kingdom have also entered the realm of negative public wealth.

By contrast, China appears to have settled on a permanent mixed economy. Of course, it is impossible to predict how things will evolve in the long run: the Chinese case is in many ways unique.[39] The country is in the throes of debate about further privatizations, and it is difficult to predict what the outcome will be. For the foreseeable future the current equilibrium will most likely continue, especially since the demand for change is coming from opposing ideological camps and taking contradictory forms. A number of "social-democratic" intellectuals are demanding new forms of power sharing and decentralization with an important role for worker representatives and independent trade unions (which currently do not exist) and a diminished role for the party officials at both the state and local level.[40] By contrast, business circles are demanding further privatizations and reinforcement of the role of private shareholders and market mechanisms with an eye to moving China closer to a capitalist model of the Anglo-American type. Meanwhile, CCP leaders feel they have good reasons to oppose both sides, whose proposals they fear might threaten the country's harmonious and balanced growth in the long run (as well as reduce their own role).

---

38. See Piketty, *Capital in the Twenty-First Century,* chap. 5, pp. 183–187 and fig. 5.5.
39. Recall that in a very different political-ideological and socioeconomic context, ecclesiastical organizations held 25–30 percent of all property in Europe in the sixteenth to eighteenth centuries (for example, in France and Spain as well as in Britain until the dissolution of the monasteries). This gave them the means to structure society and orient its moral and material development. See Fig. 2.3. The comparison is suggestive but can hardly be used to predict the future of the Chinese model.
40. See, for example, the work of the economist and historian Qin Hui, collected and translated in *The Chinese Economy,* July–October 2005. On Qin's career since the Cultural Revolution, see Qin Hui, "Dividing the Big Family Assets," *New Left Review,* 2003.

Before going further, several points deserve to be highlighted. In general, it is important to keep in mind that the very definitions of public and private property are not set in stone. They depend on specific features of each legal, economic, and political system. The temporal evolutions and international comparisons shown in Fig. 12.6 indicate rough orders of magnitude, but the precision of the data should not be overestimated.

For example, Chinese farmland was partly private before the 1978 reforms, in the sense that it could be passed on from parents to children (along with improvements to the land), provided that the children remained officially rural residents. China has a system of residential registration and mobility control under which every Chinese citizen holds an official residence permit, the *hukou,* which designates the holder as a rural or urban resident. A rural resident can work in a city and retain ownership of farmland but only if the migration is temporary. If the person wishes to move permanently to the city and satisfies the requirements (primarily years of residence), he may ask for his rural *hukou* to be converted into an urban one, which is often necessary for spouse and children to have access to schools and public services (such as health care). However, he must then forfeit ownership of any village land, including any capital gains on the land, which can be considerable because of rising land prices (which explains why some urban migrants prefer to hold on to their rural *hukou*). If the land is forfeited, it reverts to the local government, which can reassign it to other individuals who hold a rural *hukou* for that particular village. Such land is therefore a form of property somewhere between private and public; the exact rules governing its ownership have evolved over time, and we have tried to take this into account in our estimates, but the results are inevitably approximate.[41]

Negative Public Wealth, Omnipotence of Private Property

More generally, it is important to note that the notion of public capital used in these estimates is quite restrictive, in the sense that it is largely dependent on concepts and methods normally used for estimating the value of private

41. In view of changes in the law, we estimate that the public share of farmland fell gradually from 70 percent in 1978 to 40 percent in 2015. If we had worked with other assumptions, the effect on the overall evolution of Chinese property structure would have been small (owing to the limited value of farmland compared to capital in firms and urban real estate). See Piketty, Zucman, and Yang, "Capital Accumulation."

property. The only public assets included are those that can be exploited economically or sold, and their value is evaluated in terms of the market price they would fetch if sold. For example, public buildings such as schools and hospitals are counted if there are examples of similar assets being sold at market prices that can be observed (or estimated in terms of the price per square foot of similar buildings).[42] In all these estimates we have followed the official rules of national accounting as set forth by the United Nations.[43] I will say more about these rules in Chapter 13. They raise many issues, especially in regard to natural resources, which are not included in official national accounts until they begin to be exploited commercially. This inevitably results in underestimating the depreciation of natural capital and overestimating the real growth of GDP and national income, since growth depletes existing reserves while contributing to air pollution and global warming, neither of which is reflected in official national accounts.

At this stage, two points are worth mentioning. First, if one were really determined to assign a value to all public assets in the broadest sense of the term, including all aspects of man's natural and intellectual patrimony (which very fortunately has not been fully privately appropriated, at least not yet)—encompassing everything from landscapes, mountains, oceans, and air to scientific knowledge, artistic and literary creations, and so on—then it is quite obvious that the value of public capital would be far greater than that of all private capital, no matter what definition one attached to the notion of "value."[44]

---

42. By contrast, unique assets, for which no comparable sales have been recorded to date, such as the Louvre or Eiffel Tower, are not counted or are counted on the basis of hypothetical values (based on surface area or replacement cost), which in practice seriously underestimates their potential market value.

43. The so-called System of National Accounts (SNA) 2013 rules. The SNA rules are revised every ten years or so by a consortium of international organizations and statistical agencies, and in principle all countries should abide by them. For the Western countries, the estimates indicated in Fig. 12.8 are taken from official national accounts. For China, where there is no official wealth accounting, we have applied the same definitions to data taken from various available primary sources. See the online appendix.

44. Even if we limited the scope to the contribution of immaterial capital, scientific and technological knowledge, and human skills to GDP (as currently defined), we would end up with a capitalized value roughly twice the total value of private property (because the labor share in national accounts is generally at least twice the capital share). Such a narrow-minded calculation of public capital would in any case omit experiences generally regarded as life's most desirable (such as

In the present case, it is by no means certain that such an effort of generalized accounting would make any sense or be in any way useful for public debate. Nevertheless, it is important to bear one essential fact in mind: the total value of public and private capital, evaluated in terms of market prices for national accounting purposes, constitutes only a tiny part of what humanity actually *values*—namely, the part that the community has chosen (rightly or wrongly) to exploit through economic transactions in the marketplace. I will discuss this point in detail in Chapter 13 in connection with the issues of global warming and knowledge appropriation.

Second, because natural capital has an inherent tendency to depreciate, the share of public capital (in the restricted sense of marketable assets) in official national accounts underestimates the magnitude of ongoing changes. The fact that public capital (in the narrow sense) has fallen to zero or below in most capitalist countries is extremely worrisome (Fig. 12.6). Indeed, it significantly reduces the maneuvering room of governments, especially when it comes to tackling major issues such as climate change, inequality, and education. Let me be clear about the meaning of negative public capital such as we find today in the official national accounts of the United States, United Kingdom, and Italy. Negative capital means that even if all marketable public assets were sold— including all public buildings (such as schools, hospitals, and so on) and all public companies and financial assets (if they exist)—not enough money would be raised to repay all the debt owed to the state's creditors (whether direct or indirect). Concretely, negative public wealth means that private individuals own, through their financial assets, not only all public assets and buildings, on which they collect interest, but also a right to draw on future tax receipts. In other words, total private property is greater than 100 percent of national capital because private individuals own not only tangible assets but also taxpayers (or some of them, at any rate). If net public wealth becomes more and more negative, a growing and potentially significant share of tax revenues could go to pay interest on the debt.[45]

---

breathing pure mountain air, profiting from works inherited from the past, etc.), which fortunately are not included in GDP or national income.

45. In strictly theoretical terms, there is no limit on how negative public wealth can go. Strictly speaking, one could reach a point where private individuals through their financial assets owned the totality of all future tax revenues or even the totality of everyone else's income, so that everyone would de facto be working for the bond-holders. This happened frequently in ancient times (when slavery was a conse-

There are several ways to analyze how this situation came to pass and what it portends for the future. The fact that net public capital fell to zero or below in nearly all the rich countries in the 1980s reflects a profound political-ideological transformation of the regime that existed in the period 1950–1970, when governments owned 20–30 percent of national capital. Capitalists found this situation untenable and decided to reassert control. Previously, in the 1950s, after two world wars and a Great Depression, governments faced with the challenge of communism had chosen to rapidly shed public debt stemming from the past to give themselves room to invest in public infrastructure, education, and health; they also nationalized previously private firms. By the 1980s, however, the ideological perspective had shifted. More and more people came to believe that public assets would be better managed outside the public sphere and should therefore be privatized. The decline of public capital was the result.

Note, moreover, that the increase in the total value of private property, which rose from barely three years of national income in the 1980s to five or six in the 2010s, far outweighed the decrease of public wealth.[46] In other words, the rich countries remain rich, but their governments chose to become poor. Recall, too, that on average the public debt of the rich countries (United States, Europe, and Japan) is held by residents of those countries, in the sense that their net wealth is positive: the value of financial assets in the rest of the world held by these countries is significantly greater than the value of assets of each country held by the rest of the world.[47]

---

quence of heavy debt or military tribute; see Chap. 6). Without going so far, it is clear that net public capital could become even more negative in the future.

46. See Fig. 10.8 and the online appendix, Fig. S10.8. Privatizations and the declining value of public assets explain only part of the increase in private wealth (between a fifth and a third, depending on the country). The rest was due to the accumulation of savings in a context of slower growth and, above all, rising real estate and stock market prices, a rise due in part to changes in the legal and political regime favorable to property owners. See Chap. 10 and the online appendix for a detailed breakdown.

47. The positions of Japan and Germany are positive, those of the United States and United Kingdom negative, and those of other European countries close to balance. The official position of the entire group is slightly negative, but if one includes assets held in tax havens by private owners from the rich countries, all signs are that the actual position is significantly positive. See Zucman, "The Missing Wealth of Nations."

Embracing Debt and Renouncing Fiscal Justice

Why did public debt increase? To answer this question requires a more complex analysis. In the abstract, there are all sorts of reasons for accumulating public debt. For instance, there might be a glut of private savings, poorly invested for the short or long term. Or the government might see opportunities for physical investment (in infrastructure, transportation, energy, and so on) or intangible investment (in education, health care, or research) that promises to yield a social benefit greater than that of private investment or than the rate of interest at which the government can borrow. The problem is primarily one of how much to borrow and what the rate of interest is. If the debt is too large or the interest rate too high, the resulting debt burden can cripple the state's ability to act on behalf of its people.[48]

In practice, rising public debt in the 1980s was in part the consequence of a deliberate strategy intended to reduce the size of the state. Reagan's budget strategy in the 1980s may be taken as a typical example: it was decided to sharply reduce taxes on top earners, which added to the deficit, and this increased the pressure to cut social spending. In many cases, tax cuts for the rich were financed by the privatization of public assets, which in the end amounted to a free transfer of ownership: the wealthy paid $10 billion less in taxes and then used that $10 billion to buy government bonds. The United States and Europe have continued to pursue this same strategy to this day, increasing inequality and encouraging concentration of private wealth.[49]

More generally, the debt increase can also be seen as a consequence of the perceived impossibility of a just tax. When the highest earners and wealthiest individuals cannot be made to pay their fair share, and when the lower and middle classes become increasingly reluctant to give their consent to the tax

---

48. On average, in the period 1970–2015, the interest on the public debt was equivalent to the secondary deficit in nearly all the rich countries (with the exception of Italy, where interest dominated), which corresponds to a virtually zero primary deficit (despite a sharp increase of total debt over the period). See the online appendix. In Chap. 16 I will say more about European budget rules and the notions of primary and secondary deficit.

49. For a recent (and highly controversial) example, see the proposal to privatize Groupe ADP, who owns the Paris airports. Approved by the French government in 2019, this plan is supposed to yield 8 billion euros, which will partly replace the yearly 5 billion euros lost through suppression of the wealth tax (ISF) and the progressive tax on capital income.

system, indebtedness becomes a tempting way out. But where does it lead? There is an important historical precedent: at the end of the Napoleonic Wars, the United Kingdom was saddled with a public debt in excess of two years of national income (equivalent to a third of all British private property), and net public wealth was seriously in the red. As noted earlier, the dilemma was resolved by running significant budget surpluses (amounting to roughly one-quarter of tax revenues) or, to put it another way, by having modest and middling British taxpayers transfer their earnings to bondholders for nearly a century, from 1815 to 1914. At the time, however, only the wealthy had the right to vote and held all political power (at least at the beginning of the period), and proprietarian ideology was more persuasive than it is today. Today, people are or should be aware that many countries quickly shed the debt that burdened them after two world wars, and it seems unlikely that middle- and lower-class taxes will be that patient. At the moment, however, the issue is less salient than it might be owing to the abnormally low rate of interest on most public debt. This state of affairs may not last, however, in which case the debt issue will quickly become a major factor in the reconfiguration of social and political conflict, especially in Europe. I will come back to this point.

Note, finally, the striking contrast between China's trajectory and the trajectories of the Western countries in the first decades of the twenty-first century. While the share of public capital in total national capital has remained stable at around 30 percent in China since 2006, the financial crisis of 2007–2008 (which was caused by excessive deregulation of private finance and contributed to further private enrichment) has reduced public wealth in the West even more.

The point is of course not to idealize public property in China, much less to pretend to know the "ideal" share of public capital in a just society. Once the state assumes responsibility for producing certain goods and services (such as education and health care), it stands to reason that it would hold a share of productive capital correlated with its share of total employment (say, 20 percent). This is an inadequate rule of thumb, however, because it ignores the state's potential role in using debt to channel savings toward the preservation of natural capital and the accumulation of nonphysical capital. The real question has to do with the forms of governance and power sharing associated with public and private property, which must be continually questioned, reevaluated, and reinvented. In the Chinese case, the mode of governance of public property is notable for its vertical authoritarian character and can hardly be taken as a universal model.

That said, there remains something paradoxical about the recent collapse of public wealth in the West in the wake of the financial crisis. Market deregulation made many people rich, governments went into debt to mitigate the severity of the recession and to save private banks and other firms, and in the end private wealth continued to grow, leaving lower- and middle-class taxpayers to foot the bill for decades to come. These episodes had deep repercussions on perceptions of what can and cannot be done in terms of economic and monetary policy—repercussions of which we have probably not yet seen the end.

On the Limits of Chinese Tolerance of Inequality

Back to inequality in China: How has the income distribution changed since the beginning of the process of economic liberalization and privatization of property in 1978? The available sources indicate a very sharp increase of income inequality from the time the reforms began until the mid-2000s, when the situation stabilized. In the late 2010s, China, to judge by the share of national income going to the top 10 percent and the bottom 50 percent, is only slightly less inegalitarian than the United States and significantly more so than Europe, whereas it was the most egalitarian of the three regions at the beginning of the 1980s (Fig. 12.8).

If we compare China to the other Asian giant, India, it is clear that since the early 1980s China has been both more efficient in terms of growth and more egalitarian in terms of income distribution (or, rather, less inegalitarian, in the sense that concentration of income has increased less dramatically than in India).[50] As noted earlier in the discussion of India (see Chapter 8), one reason for this difference is that China has been able to invest more in public infrastructure, education, and health care. China achieved a much higher level of tax revenues than India, where basic health-care and educational services remain notoriously underfinanced. Indeed, in the 2010s, China has nearly matched Western levels of taxation, taking in roughly 30 percent of national income in taxes (and roughly 40 percent if one includes profits from public firms and sale of public lands).[51]

These Chinese successes are well known, and they lead many people to conclude that the regime will go unchallenged as long as it continues to achieve this level of economic success (and can continue to rely on the fact that many Chinese fear that the country will split apart if not ruled with a firm hand). But there

---

50. See Fig. 11.1.

51. See B. Naughton, "Is China Socialist?" *Journal of Economic Perspectives,* 2017, fig. 1. See also Piketty, Zucman, and Yang, "Capital Accumulation," table A313.

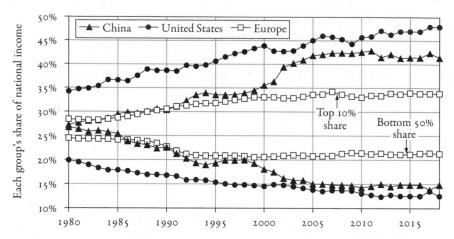

FIG. 12.8. Inequality in China, Europe, and the United States, 1980–2018

Interpretation: Income inequality increased sharply in China between 1980 and 2018, but it is still below that of the United States (though higher than Europe), according to available sources. *Sources and series:* piketty.pse.ens.fr/ideology.

may be limits to the Chinese people's tolerance of inequality. First, the fact that China so quickly became so much more inegalitarian than Europe was by no means inevitable and clearly represents a failure for the regime. In the 1980s, the level of income inequality was close to that of the most egalitarian countries in Europe, such as Sweden. The same is true of wealth inequality, which shows, by the way, how inegalitarian the privatization process was. The top decile's share of total private wealth was 40–50 percent in the early 1990s, below that of Sweden and other European countries; in the 2010s it is close to 70 percent, a level close to that of the United States and only slightly lower than Russia's.[52]

Now, to go from Swedish to American levels of inequality in the space of a few decades is not an insignificant change for a country like China, which officially continues to promote "socialism with Chinese characteristics." For some Chinese businessmen, who have long felt that such slogans have no real social or economic significance, this hardly matters because they find the Anglo-American model of capitalism so attractive. But for "social-democratic" intellectuals and much of the population, this extremely rapid rise of inequality is a problem, especially since no one knows where it will end. Given that Europe has demonstrated the possibility of achieving prosperity while limiting inequality, it is not clear why Chinese socialism should tolerate levels of in-

52. See Fig. 13.8.

equality on a par with American capitalism.[53] The situation raises questions about the way privatization was conducted, about redistributive policies in China, and more generally, about the reorientation of the reform process.

The existence of an internal passport and migration restrictions in China, especially between rural and urban zones when free circulation of labor has become the norm in Europe, may also help to explain China's high level of inequality. More specifically, economic reform has primarily benefited urban centers, while rural areas have not reaped the gains they had hoped for. Modifications of the system over the decades have not proved sufficient to reduce the differences between urban and rural areas. Mobility restrictions are not the only reason for this because similar inequalities exist within urban zones (and to a lesser extent within rural zones).[54] Furthermore, despite easing of *hukou* restrictions, the system remains quite authoritarian, and in recent years it has been augmented by a potentially far more intrusive system of social control, including the awarding of "social grades" and "social credit" based on massive data collection through social networks. Recent research suggests that less advantaged social groups are less tolerant of these procedures, whose repressive aspects and connection with other social control policies also deserve to be emphasized.[55]

On the Opacity of Inequality in China

The stabilization of Chinese inequality since the mid-2000s might suggest that the worst of the increase is over. Bear in mind, however, that Chinese income and wealth data are extremely opaque. The estimates shown in Fig. 12.8 are the

---

53. On the fears aroused by rising inequality in China, see, for example, Shi Li, H. Sato, and T. Sicular, eds., *Rising Inequality in China: Challenges to a Harmonious Society* (Cambridge University Press, 2013).

54. See Piketty, Zucman, and Yang, "Capital Accumulation."

55. See G. Kostka, *China's Social Credit Systems and Public Opinion: Explaining High Levels of Approval* (Freie Universität Berlin, SSRN, 2018). See also Xiaojun Yan, "Engineering Stability: Authoritarian Political Control over University Students in Post-Deng China," *China Quarterly,* 2014; A. Nathan, "The Puzzle of the Chinese Middle Class," *Journal of Democracy,* 2016. On the way in which massive accumulation of personal data and individual grading seeks to define itself as a morally acceptable form of capitalist accumulation and extraction of economic value, see M. Fourcade, "The Fly and the Cookie: Alignment and Unhingement in 21st-century Capitalism," *Socio-Economic Review,* 2017 ; M. Fourcade and K. Healy, "Seeing Like a Market," *Socio-Economic Review,* 2017.

most reliable we could establish on the basis of currently available Chinese sources. But the sources are flawed and full of holes, so it is quite possible that we are underestimating both the level and evolution of Chinese inequalities. In theory, China has a progressive tax system. It was established in 1980, shortly after the beginning of the economic reforms, and its marginal rates range from 5 percent on the lowest brackets to 45 percent on the highest (the rates have not changed since 1980).[56] Compared with the 13 percent flat tax in post-Soviet Russia, the Chinese system is therefore much more progressive, at least in theory.

The problem is that no detailed data about the Chinese income tax have ever been published. The only information regularly made public is the figure for total revenue. It is impossible to know how many taxpayers pay the tax each year, how many are in each tax bracket, or by how much the number of high-income taxpayers has increased in a particular city or province. The answers to such questions would help us to understand how the gains of Chinese growth have been distributed over the years. They might also help to realize that the tax laws are not always being applied as rigorously at the local level as they are supposed to be.[57] In 2006 the Chinese fiscal authorities published a bulletin requiring all taxpayers with incomes above 120,000 yuan (less than 1 percent of the adult population at the time) to fill out a special declaration, which was to be used in the fight against corruption. The results of this national survey were published from 2006 to 2011 but in a rudimentary form: only the total number of taxpayers above the threshold was indicated, sometimes together with their aggregate income, without any further breakdown. Publication was ended in 2011. It has been possible to find similar data in publications by regional tax authorities (in some cases with different thresholds, such as 500,000 yuan or 1 million yuan) in certain provinces between 2011 and 2017, but the information is irregular and inconsistent.

Such is the fragmentary nature of the data we have used. Though sadly incomplete, these data have allowed us to revise substantially upward official Chinese measures of inequality and its evolution—measures based solely on

---

56. On the establishment and (extremely opaque) operation of the Chinese income tax since 1980, see T. Piketty and N. Qian, "Income Inequality and Progressive Income Taxation in China and India," *American Economic Journal: Applied Economics,* 2009.

57. For instance, we know that some provinces and cities have been granted special income tax exemptions, but little is known about such practices.

household declarations, which included very few households at this level of income.[58] The estimates obtained can be compared with those for Europe and the United States (which are based on much more detailed data, including tax records) in a more plausible and satisfactory way than could be done before (Fig. 12.8). Still, the Chinese estimates obviously remain quite fragile and may underestimate both the level and evolution of inequality in China. The fact that the authorities stopped publishing national data on high-income taxpayers in 2011 is especially worrisome. In some ways, public information about the workings of the income tax system is even scarcer in China than in Russia, which is setting the bar quite low.[59] Although lack of transparency about inequality is a global problem (about which I will say more in Chapter 13), it is clear that Russia and China are more opaque than most.

As for the recording and measurement of wealth in China, the situation is even worse than for income. In particular, there is no Chinese inheritance tax and therefore no data of any kind concerning inheritances, which greatly complicates the study of wealth concentration. It is truly paradoxical that a country led by a communist party, which proclaims its adherence to "socialism with Chinese characteristics," could make such a choice. As long as the extent of private wealth remained limited, the absence of an inheritance tax was not very surprising. But now that two-thirds of Chinese capital is in private hands (Fig. 12.6), it is surprising that those who have benefited most from privatization and economic liberalization are allowed to pass all of their wealth on to their children without any tax, even a minimal one. Recall that after much variation over the course of the twentieth century, the tax rates applied to the largest estates settled between 30 and 55 percent in the leading capitalist countries (United States, United Kingdom, Japan, Germany, and France) in the period 2000–2020.[60] In Japan the top rate was even raised from 50 to 55 percent

---

58. For detailed comparisons between the official and corrected series, see T. Piketty, G. Zucman, and L. Yang, "Capital Accumulation, Private Property and Rising Inequality in China, 1978–2015," WID.world 2017, *American Economic Review* 2019 and the online appendix.

59. The fiscal data that Russia has made public for the period 2008–2017 have at least one merit: they include a large number of brackets (including one for people earning more than 10 billion rubles), although the concept of income used is not very clear and is in many ways inconsistent. See Novokmet, Piketty, and Zucman, "From Soviets to Oligarchs."

60. See Fig. 10.12.

in 2015. In the other capitalist countries of East Asia, there are high inheritance taxes: for example, in South Korea the top rate is above 50 percent.

So we find ourselves in the early twenty-first century in a highly paradoxical situation: an Asian billionaire who would like to pass on his fortune without paying any inheritance tax should move to Communist China. A case that speaks volumes is that of Hong Kong, which had a high inheritance tax when it was a British colony but abolished it in 2005, shortly after it was handed back to the People's Republic of China in 1997. In Taiwan, many businessmen favor integrating the country into the People's Republic to do away with the inheritance tax. This tax competition in East Asia, partly driven by China, tends to reinforce the global trend while contributing to rising inequality in the region.[61]

The Hong Kong case illustrates a novel and particularly interesting trajectory. In the first place, it is the sole case of a capitalist country that became more inegalitarian by joining a Communist regime.[62] Second, Hong Kong's position as a financial center played a key role in the development of China. In particular, it enabled wealthy Chinese to move capital outside the country more easily than they could have done through the banking system of the People's Republic of China. It also allowed large Chinese firms and the Chinese government itself to invest abroad and conduct foreign transactions more nimbly than they could have done otherwise. To date there is no evidence to suggest that capital flight from China was anywhere near as massive as what was observed in the Russian case. But given the extent of corruption in China, the tenuous nature of many of the property rights acquired through privatization, and the fact that the rapid growth of recent decades may not continue, capital flight may increase in the future and undermine the regime from within.[63]

China: Between Communism and Plutocracy

The political system imposed on Hong Kong also illustrates the ambiguities of the Chinese regime, theoretically inspired by communism but in practice

---

61. On this see N. Kim, "Top Incomes in Korea, 1933–2016," WID.world, 2018; C. T. Hung, "Income Inequality in Hong Kong and Singapore, 1980–2016," WID. world, 2018; C. Chu, T. Chou, and S. Hu, "Top Incomes in Taïwan, 1977–2013," WID.world, 2015.
62. See Hung, "Income Inequality in Hong Kong and Singapore."
63. See M. Pei, *China's Crony Capitalism: The Dynamics of Regime Decay* (Harvard University Press, 2016).

sometimes closer to a certain type of plutocracy. Until 1997, the governor of Hong Kong was appointed by the Queen of England. The colony was governed by a complex system of assemblies elected by indirect suffrage; in practice it was governed by committees dominated by economic elites. It was not an explicitly censitary system like those found in the United Kingdom and France in the nineteenth century (or until 1911 in Sweden, where the number of ballots a person could cast was proportional to that person's wealth),[64] but the effect was similar: power was essentially vested in the business elite. This proprietarian-colonialist system was only slightly modified when Hong Kong was handed over to Communist China. Today, Hong Kong holds nominally free elections, but candidates must first be approved by a nominating committee appointed by the authorities in Beijing and in practice controlled by Hong Kong business elites and other pro-Chinese oligarchs.

In the abstract, one can imagine a world in which China would join with Europe, the United States, and other countries to establish a more transparent financial system that would put an end to all tax havens, whether located in Hong Kong, Switzerland, or the Cayman Islands. This may someday come to pass. Broad segments of the Chinese population are scandalized by the country's plutocratic turn. Some intellectuals have proposed social-democratic measures in direct contradiction with the policies preferred by the regime, while others have worked on new ways to combat inequality since the repression of the Tiananmen Square demonstrations in 1989.[65] At the moment, however, it is clear that we are still a long way from seeing such changes in China.

When questioned about these issues, Chinese officials and intellectuals close to the government often explain that the authorities are aware of the risk of capital flight such as occurred in Russia and that China will soon develop new forms of progressive income, inheritance, and wealth taxes. These predictions have yet to be borne out, however. A second response, no doubt more revealing, is that China has no need of such Western-style fiscal solutions, which are complex and often ineffective, and will need to invent its own remedies, like the merciless battle that the CCP and state authorities have waged against corruption.

Indeed, Xi Jinping (whose name was added in 2018 to the preamble of the Chinese constitution alongside Mao Zedong and Deng Xiaoping) has written

---

64. See Chap. 5.
65. See S. Veg, *Minjian: The Rise of China's Grassroots Intellectuals* (Columbia University Press, 2019).

abundantly about "socialism with Chinese characteristics," and nowhere in these theoretical texts does one find any reference to progressive taxes, systems of co-management or self-management, or power sharing within firms. By contrast, one finds many assertions to the effect that the "invisible hand" of the market needs to be firmly counterbalanced by the "visible hand" of the government, which must detect and correct every abuse. Xi Jinping frequently alludes to the danger of a "potential degeneration of the party," "owing to the duration of its exercise of power," which only "an implacable struggle against corruption" can prevent.[66] The prospect of "new silk roads" is discussed at length, allowing Xi to discreetly but insistently develop the idea of a Chinese-led globalization, which would establish benevolent commercial ties between different parts of the world without political interference. This would at last put an end to Europe's mad colonial ambitions and the damaging "unequal treaties" imposed on China and other countries. Geopolitically, a Eurasian power bloc with China at its center would ultimately relegate America to its proper place on the world periphery.

When it comes to concrete institutions for regulating inequality, ending injustice, and controlling corruption, however, it is clear that "socialism with Chinese characteristics" means nothing very specific. We are told that the "visible hand" of the government and party must be "implacable," but it is difficult to find out exactly what this means. It is not clear that imprisoning oligarchs or state officials who have too conspicuously and scandalously enriched themselves is enough to meet the challenge. In the fall of 2018, film star Fan Bingbing was arrested after a star television news anchor revealed that she had a secret contract under which she was paid 50 million yuan, whereas her official pay was only 10 million yuan. The affair attracted a great deal of attention, and the government saw an ideal opportunity to show that it was prepared to take on excessive inequality and the cult of money. The case is certainly interesting, but there is good reason to doubt that inequality in a country of 1.3 billion people can be controlled simply by means of public denunciation and imprisonment without any systematic registration and taxation of wealth and estates, while journalists, citizens, and trade unions are prevented from developing the means to investigate abuses and the police arrest anyone who shows too much interest in wealth accumulated by people with close ties to the government. Nothing guarantees that the Chinese regime will be able to avoid a kleptocratic fate similar to Russia's.

---

66. See Xi Jinping, *La gouvernance de la Chine* (anthology), Beijing, 2014, pp. 137–141, 470–475.

On the Effect of the Cultural Revolution on the Perception of Inequality

All things considered, the Chinese government apparently does not take very seriously the fact that a society based on private property, without sufficient fiscal and social safeguards, risks attaining a level of inequality that may prove harmful in the long run, as European experience in the nineteenth and first half of the twentieth centuries shows. This is probably yet another manifestation of the sense of being exceptional and refusing to learn from the experiences of others from which so many societies have suffered throughout history.[67] Another historical and political-ideological factor specific to China should also be mentioned, however: namely, the extraordinary violence of the Maoist period and in particular the Cultural Revolution, which had a profound influence on perceptions of inequality and particularly of family transmission processes. China has only recently emerged from a major traumatic experience, in which the effort to interrupt the intergenerational reproduction of inequality took a particularly radical form with the arrest and ostracism of anyone whose family background was linked in any way to the former imperial landlord or intellectual classes. Large segments of Chinese society, including much of today's ruling class, saw grandparents or other relatives killed or harshly treated during the Cultural Revolution. After such a violent repudiation of the transmission process, for which so many families paid dearly, the logic of accumulation has reasserted itself in China, at least for now.

In *Brothers* (2006), the Chinese novelist Yu Hua describes the intersecting destinies of two brothers to evoke the radical transformation of values in China from the time of the Cultural Revolution (when descendants of former landlords were hunted down and chastity was promoted) to the 2000s, when there was nothing that could not be bought or sold. This includes factories and land eagerly exchanged for cash by greedy local party officials to fake breasts and hymens used to manufacture contestants for a Virgin Beauty Contest for the delectation of the new Chinese man, who was eager to profit from everything the world had to offer, to say nothing of filling the pockets of the contest's promoters. Once the economy was opened up and businesses were privatized, the watchword was "anything goes" as long as regional GDP statistics continued

---

67. Take, for example, France before 1914, when the political and economic elites of the Third Republic argued that France was so egalitarian (thanks to the French Revolution) that it had no need of the fiscal reforms already adopted by Germany and the United Kingdom. See Chap. 4.

to soar. Li Guangtou (called Baldy Li in the English translation) and Song Gang, both born in 1960, are half-brothers. Li is clearly the less honest of the two, and it is he who becomes a billionaire. He starts out in the 1980s in the scrap business by recycling metal and manufacturing cardboard, makes a fortune in the 1990s by selling freighter loads of used Japanese suits (which replace the now-unfashionable Mao jackets), and in the 2000s becomes a multimillionaire who dresses in Armani and contemplates paying for a ride to the moon on a spaceship. In the end, however, he seems almost more likable than Song Gang, who allows himself to be ground to bits by the evolving system.

The Cultural Revolution (1966–1976), which is hard on both brothers, is portrayed as an attempt to reshape minds while blaming scapegoats for the failure of agricultural and industrial collectivization to yield the anticipated Great Leap Forward in the 1950s and 1960s. Song's father, who is the pride and joy of both boys with his red armband and enthusiastic Communist spirit, is soon arrested, and the family home is searched. As the son of a landlord and himself a teacher, Song's father embodies the former ruling class, which (whether it knows or not) is sabotaging the revolution because it is contemptuous of the people, of whom it knows nothing. The Red Guards make it their mission to remind the boy's father that it is through cultural and ideological transformation that China will atone for its deeply inegalitarian past. For all their ideological zeal, the Red Guards also display a flair for practical realities: when they come to search the house, they empty all the closets in search of land deeds, "ready to be pulled out should there be any change of regime." They do not find any, but Song Fanping is lynched anyway. The two boys, assisted by Tao Qing, wheel his body home through the streets of Lui Town in a cart. Beyond the drama of the tale, the book allows the reader to gauge the magnitude of the disturbing political-ideological transformation that led within a few decades from the Cultural Revolution to Chinese hypercapitalism, from the socialist-made "White Rabbit" caramels that delighted the young boys in the late 1960s and early 1970s (when only the district commander of the People's Army was entitled to a new bicycle) to the "great national gold rush" of the 1990s, with its juicy business deals, and ultimately to today's China, in which newly rich billionaires dream of traveling to the moon.[68]

---

68. Note, too, the importance in *Brothers* of public toilets and mediocre sanitary facilities to evoke the misery of the 1960s and 1970s (and also to allow the young criminal Li Guangtou to exchange his knowledge of the female anatomy for bowls of three-flavored noodles).

On the Chinese Model and the Transcendence of
Parliamentary Democracy

Note, moreover, that the Chinese regime survives by capitalizing on the weaknesses of other models. Having learned from the failures of the Soviet and Maoist regimes, the Chinese have no intention of repeating the errors of the Western parliamentary democracies. In this respect, it is highly instructive to read the regime's official newspaper, the *Global Times,* especially since the Brexit referendum and the election of Donald Trump. One finds lengthy and repeated denunciations of the West's nationalist, xenophobic, and separatist deviations and of the explosive cocktail of vulgarity, reality TV, and the money-is-king mentality to which so-called free elections inevitably lead—so much for the marvelous political institutions that the West wants to impose on the rest of the world. The paper also emphasizes the respect with which Chinese leaders treat other world leaders, especially those of the African nations that the president of the United States, the supposed "leader of the free world," has called "shithole countries."

Reading all this is instructive and raises questions about the supposed civilizational and institutional superiority of Western electoral democracies. There is obviously something absurd about the idea that "Western" democratic institutions have achieved some sort of unique and unsurpassable perfection. The parliamentary regime, with universal suffrage and elections every four or five years to choose representatives who then have the power to make law, is a specific, historically determined form of political organization. It has its virtues but also its limits, which must be constantly questioned and transcended.[69] Among the criticisms traditionally leveled at Western institutions by communist regimes such as the Russian and Chinese, two warrant particular attention.[70] First, equal political rights are illusory when the news media are captured by the power of money, which gives the wealthy control over minds and

---

69. On this see J. Goody, *The Theft of History* (Cambridge University Press, 2006), Chap. 9. The author notes that the historical pathways leading to these institutions were to some degree halting and contingent and in no way a reflection of distinct civilizational essences. For instance, the United States would probably not have granted African Americans the right to vote in the 1960s if they had constituted a majority of the population (or even too large a minority), and the country might today be governed by a regime close to South African apartheid (p. 252).

70. Another general criticism should be added to these two. We have mentioned it before and will come back to it again: in Western parliamentary regimes, laws

political ideology and thus tends to perpetuate inequality. The second criticism is closely related to the first: political equality remains purely theoretical if the way political parties are financed allows the wealthy to influence political platforms and policies. The fear that the wealthy will capture the political process has been especially potent in the United States since the 1990s and even more so since the Supreme Court gutted American campaign finance laws.[71] The problem is actually much broader in scope, however.

Indeed, the implications of how the media and political parties are financed have never really been fully thought through. Admittedly, many countries have passed laws that seek to limit media monopolies and regulate political financing. But these laws are often quite inadequate, falling far short of what would be required to ensure equal participation in politics, to say nothing of the many setbacks regulatory efforts have suffered in recent decades (especially in the United States and Italy). By drawing on the lessons of history, however, one can identify new approaches, including the idea of establishing nonprofit and participatory media companies and working toward equality in the financing of political movements.[72] I will come back to these issues in Part Four.[73]

In any event, the capture of the media or political parties by the forces of money is not a reason to do away with elections or to require candidates to be approved by a committee on the basis of their compatibility with the party in power. Communist leaders in Russia and Eastern Europe did use such arguments to keep themselves in power by ensuring that there would be no authentic competition at the ballot box. History shows that this is the wrong way to oppose the power of money.

---

usually must conform to a fairly rigid constitution and pass muster with constitutional judges, which often has the effect of protecting existing property rights.

71. Of the many works dealing with the capture of American politics by the wealthy, see especially J. Hacker and P. Pierson, *Winner-Take-All Politics: How Washington Made the Rich Richer—and Turned its Back on the Middle Class* (Simon and Schuster, 2010); K. Schlozman, S. Verba, and H. Brady, *The Unheavenly Chorus: Unequal Political Voice and the Broken Promise of American Democracy* (Princeton University Press, 2012); T. Kuhner, *Capitalism v. Democracy: Money in Politics and the Free Market Constitution* (Stanford University Press, 2014); L. Bartels, *Unequal Democracy: The Political Economy of the New Gilded Age* (Princeton University Press, 2016).

72. See esp. J. Cagé, *Saving the Media,* trans. A. Goldhammer (Harvard University Press, 2016); J. Cagé, *Le prix de la démocratie* (Fayard, 2018); also in English as *The Price of Democracy,* trans. P. Camiller (Harvard University Press, 2020).

73. See Chap. 17.

History also has many examples of regimes that used the power of money over the democratic process as a reason to clamp down on the political process by, for example, transforming the media into propaganda instruments, ostensibly to counter the competing propaganda spread by the private media. In some cases, the results of elections have simply been ignored. Think, for example, of the "Bolivarian" regime in Venezuela under Hugo Chavez (1998–2013) and Nicolas Maduro (2013–). This regime portrays itself as a new type of "plebiscitary socialism," in the sense that it has used the proceeds from its sale of petroleum in a more egalitarian and social manner than previous governments (which is not setting the bar very high given the oligarchic practices of previous regimes, but it is still important), while relying on personalized, authoritarian, hypercentralized statist rule periodically validated by elections and direct dialogue with "the people." Think of the famous television program *Alo presidente,* in which Chavez spoke directly to the people for the better part of every Sunday (his record was more than eight hours). After winning numerous elections and surviving a coup attempt in 2002 (with US support for the putschists), to say nothing of other episodes that would far exceed the scope of this book, the regime was finally defeated unambiguously in the 2015 legislative elections. It refused to accede to the decision of the voters, however, leading to a serious and violent crisis against a background of hyperinflation and economic collapse, which continues as of this writing (2019).[74]

Chavez's relation to the media is interesting because there is no doubt that the leading private media in Venezuela (as in most countries in Latin America and throughout the world) have often been biased in favor of the worldview of their owners (as well as the interests of their financial backers, mostly linked

---

74. The government tried to institute a new constituent assembly in 2017, but the opposition refused to participate in the new elections. The president of the assembly elected in 2015 declared himself president in 2018 with support from the United States and other Western countries (while Maduro received support from China and Russia). New elections may take place in 2019. For an analysis of the Chavez years, see K. Roberts, *Changing Course in Latin America: Party Systems in the Neoliberal Era* (Cambridge University Press, 2014). In the author's view, the disintegration and brutalization of the Venezuelan party system, which had been relatively stable, can be linked to the spectacular train wreck that followed the 1988 elections: the center-left Democratic Action (AD) party won the election with an attack on the International Monetary Fund but then proceeded within a few months to make drastic budget cuts, leading to bloody riots in Caracas in 1989 followed by the removal from office of the AD president for corruption in 1993 and the election in 1998 of Chavez (the man behind another coup attempt in 1992).

to hyper-inegalitarian exploitation of petroleum resources in partnership with the major Western firms). Still, to use this state of affairs as a pretext to take control of public media and then reject the results of an election that fails to turn out as hoped is not a satisfactory response. In the end, such tactics only reinforce the proprietarian ideology they claim to combat. As the present situation makes clear, for hypercentralized power to ride roughshod over democratic institutions resolves nothing. A more promising approach is to radically reform the system for financing and governing the media and political parties so that each person has an equal opportunity to express him- or herself ("one person, one vote" rather than "one dollar, one vote") while respecting the diversity of points of view and the need for alternation. I will come back to this.

Electoral Democracy, Borders, and Property

The role of money in the financing of the media and political parties is an important issue but by no means the only grounds on which Western parliamentary democracies can be criticized. Suppose the problem of equal access to the media and political financing were fully resolved. Western democratic theory would still need to deal with three major conceptual shortcomings: namely, the lack of a theory of borders, a theory of property, and a theory of deliberation.

The border question is obvious: over what territory and to what human community is the law of the majority supposed to apply? Can a city, neighborhood, or family decide by majority vote to secede from the political community, reject the law of the majority, and become a legitimate sovereign state unto itself, governed by the majority of the tribe? The fear of endless and unlimited separatist escalation has often been used by authoritarian regimes as their main argument for refusing elections. This is true of the Chinese regime, which derives its identity largely from its ability to keep the peace in a community of 1.3 billion human beings, in contrast to Europe, which has always been torn by tribal hatreds. In the eyes of the Chinese regime, this is a sufficient reason to reject so-called free elections, which in reality merely spur identitarian and nationalist passions. This Chinese response is interesting, but once again it is a brittle response to a genuine question. A more satisfactory answer might take the form of a transnational theory of democracy based on social-democratic federalism and the construction of norms of socioeconomic justice at the regional and ultimately global level. This task is anything but simple, but there are not many other options.[75]

---

75. See Chaps. 16–17.

The question of property poses an equally difficult challenge to Western democratic theory. Can the majority pass laws that totally redefine and immediately redistribute rights to property? In the abstract, of course, it might make sense to set rules and procedures (such as qualified majority voting) to lend a degree of permanence to certain aspects of the legal, social, fiscal, and educational system. The goal would be to avoid sudden changes but not to block social and economic change altogether when the need is widely felt. The problem is that this argument has often been exploited by proprietarian ideologies to constitutionally enshrine rules that preclude any possibility of peaceful legal change, even when wealth has become hyperconcentrated or where it was initially acquired in an especially dubious or even totally indefensible manner.[76]

Note, too, that this same stability argument has also been used by various one-party states to justify placing certain decisions (such as public ownership of the means of production) outside the scope of electoral debate or even to dispense with elections altogether (or to require prospective candidates to obtain the approval of party committees). This has been true of regimes other than strictly communist ones. After achieving independence, for example, some African countries established one-party states, at least temporarily, in some cases to avoid secession and civil war and in others because it was impossible to judge the effects of certain social or economic policies after a period of just four or five years.[77] Without going that far, the pension and health insurance systems that one finds in most European social democracies are governed by complex systems that grant large roles to social security administrations and trade unions. This has helped to immunize these systems against changes of government: a sufficiently large and durable parliamentary majority could regain control, but it would take a particularly large measure of democratic legitimacy to do so. More generally, there are good reasons to ponder the merits of granting more substantial constitutional protections to social rights, educational justice, and fiscal progressivity.

To all these legitimate and complex questions, the Chinese regime has one answer: namely, that reliance on solid intermediary bodies such as the CCP

---

76. Recall the debates during the French Revolution over the appropriation of noble estates or the Irish question in the United Kingdom in the nineteenth century (Chaps. 3–5), slave and colonial appropriations (Chaps. 6–9), or the appropriation of natural resources and public companies by Russian and Chinese oligarchs discussed in the present chapter.

77. See Goody, *The Theft of History*, p. 251.

(with a membership of roughly 90 million in 2015, or 10 percent of the adult population) makes it possible to organize the process of deliberation and decision making so as to achieve a stable, harmonious, and rational development model that is protected from the identitarian instincts and centrifugal forces rampant in the Western electoral supermarket. This position was forcefully articulated at a 2016 colloquium organized by the Chinese authorities on "the role of political parties in global economic governance," and it is regularly discussed on the website of the *Global Times*.[78] Note that the very large membership of the CCP is roughly comparable to the participation in presidential primaries in the United States and France (about 10 percent of the adult population in the most recent primaries in both countries). Active membership of Western political parties is much lower (at most a few percent of the population).[79] Participation in legislative and presidential elections is much higher, however (generally more than 50 percent, although there has been an alarming decline in recent decades, particularly in the working-class population).[80]

In every case, the Chinese argument rests on the idea that deliberation and decision making within an organization such as the CCP will be more profound and rational than Western-style democracy in the public square. Instead of relying on a few minutes of the voters' superficial attention every four or five years, as in the West, China's party-managed democracy is supposed to be guided by a significant minority of the population, made up of party members (about 10 percent of the adult population) who are fully involved and informed and who deliberate collectively and in depth for the good of the country as a whole. Such a system, it is argued, is better equipped to strike reasonable compromises in the interests of the nation and the entire community, particularly when it comes to questions of borders and property.

Hu Xijin, the current editor-in-chief of the *Global Times,* has given an account of his career which illustrates the Chinese belief in the ability of party-managed democracy to deal more effectively with border questions

---

78. See the online appendix for documents circulated at the 2016 colloquium. Reading the *Global Times* is probably the best way to become familiar with Chinese arguments on these issues.

79. The notion of a party "activist" is itself being redefined as are other forms of participation (reduced frequency of section meetings, rise of online militancy), all in a context in which the traditional parties are in a state of collapse (for example, in Italy and France).

80. I will come back to this decrease in participation in Part Four.

than electoral democracy. As a young student, Hu was deeply involved in the Tiananmen demonstrations of 1989. He tells of being traumatized by the sudden dismantling of the Soviet Union and even more by the separatist and tribal wars that tore apart the former Yugoslavia, which brought home to him the need for the party to play a peacemaking role and the impossibility of leaving such decisions to the voters' whimsical passions.[81]

Note, too, that a standard (and well-honed) Chinese criticism of pro-democracy militants in Hong Kong is that they are selfish, especially when they oppose (or express doubts about) immigration from the People's Republic of China. In other words, the accusation is that the Hong Kong democrats' supposed love of democracy and "free" elections is actually intended to keep the privileges they enjoy in their city-state enclave entirely to themselves. In fact, only a minority within the Hong Kong movement call for independence; the movement's main demand is for democracy in a federal China that allows free circulation of people and political pluralism—a demand that is rejected out of hand by the CCP.[82]

On the Single-Party State and the Reformability of Party-Managed Democracy

Another key CCP argument is that the party represents all strata of the population. Even if only a minority are active members, it is a minority more motivated and determined than the average Chinese citizen (because party members are carefully selected and must prove their continued dedication) as well as more profoundly representative than Western parties and electoral democracies allow. In fact, according to available data, of the 90 million members of the CCP in 2015, 50 percent were workers, employees, or peasants; 20 percent retirees; and 30 percent administrators or technical managers in state firms.[83]

---

81. See interview with Hu Xijin: H. Thibault and B. Pedroletti, "Chine: le 'Global Times,' porte-parole décomplexé," *Le Monde,* October 18, 2017.

82. On the complexity of the political-ideological evolution of the Hong Kong democratic movement, see S. Veg, "The Rise of 'Localism' and Civic Identity in Post-handover Hong Kong: Questioning the Chinese Nation-State," *China Quarterly,* 2017.

83. C. Li, "China's Communist Party-State: The Structure and Dynamics of Power," in *Politics in China: An Introduction,* 2nd ed., ed. W. Joseph (Oxford University Press, 2014), pp. 203–205, fig. 6.4. See also C. Li, *Chinese Politics in the Xi Jinping Era: Reassessing Collective Leadership* (Brookings, 2016), pp. 42–44.

Admittedly, managers are overrepresented (they constitute only 20–30 percent of the population), but the gap is not very wide and certainly narrower than in most Western countries.[84]

These arguments for the superiority of Chinese party-managed democracy are interesting and potentially convincing in strictly theoretical terms, but they nevertheless run into a number of serious difficulties. First, it is quite difficult to know what role workers, employees, and peasants really play in the actual functioning of the party at the local level. At the highest level—that of the National People's Congress (NPC), which is the primary legislative body in the Chinese constitution, and to an even greater extent at the level of its Standing Committee, which wields the real power at the NPC's annual meetings—we find that Chinese billionaires and the world of business in general are dramatically overrepresented.[85]

The Western press often harps on these points as evidence of the hypocrisy of the Chinese regime, which is closer to plutocracy than to communism with its deliberative, socially representative cells. The critique is on the mark. Note, however, that the available data are far from precise. The wealthy are undeniably overrepresented in the NPC but perhaps not much more than in the US Congress (which is not particularly reassuring). Still, the overrepresentation of the wealthy seems much greater than what we see in Europe, where the disadvantaged classes are severely underrepresented in parliament, but it is the intellectual professions rather than businessmen and wealthy who are overrepresented.[86] In any case, there is little support at this stage for the notion that Chinese-style party-managed democracy is more representative than Western electoral democracy.

---

84. Until the 1970s, Western socialist, communist, and social-democratic parties relied on large battalions of working-class militants, but since then their membership has shifted largely toward managers and intellectual professions (and so did their electorate). See Part Four, Chap. 14–16.

85. The NPC comprises some 3,000 members and meets only ten days a year, whereas the Standing Committee has 175 members (elected by the NPC) and remains in session year-round under a mandate approved during the NPC's annual session. Under the terms of the Chinese constitution, the NPC wields extensive powers (to pass laws, elect the president of the People's Republic, and so on), and it is elected by all Chinese citizens. In practice, the vote has several layers of indirectness, and all candidates at each level must be approved by committees controlled by the CCP.

86. See Piketty, *Capital in the Twenty-First Century*, pp. 534–537.

Furthermore, as things currently stand, the idea that deliberation within an enlightened minority of party members is somehow more profound poses a major problem. There is no record of these deliberations, so that Chinese citizens (much less anyone outside China) cannot form their own opinions of what was actually discussed or how decisions were taken and therefore cannot judge the ultimate legitimacy of the party-led deliberative model. Things could be done differently: debates among party members could be made entirely public, and decisions and candidate selections could be subject to genuinely open, competitive votes. At this point, however, there is no sign that the Beijing regime will evolve in this direction anytime soon.

There are interesting historical examples of single-party systems that eventually allowed candidates from other parties and opinion groups. Senegal, for instance, was a one-party state from independence until the constitutional reform of 1976 but eventually authorized selected parties of other ideological stripes to present candidates. It was a foregone conclusion that the Socialist Party (the party of President Senghor when Senegal was a one-party state) would win the first pseudo-free elections in the 1980s, but the playing field was gradually leveled and eventually Abdoulaye Wade's Senegalese Democratic Party won in 2000. Without idealizing the Senegalese case, it does show that political transitions can follow many pathways.[87]

To sum up, China's party-managed democracy has yet to demonstrate its superiority over Western electoral democracy, owing in part to its flagrant lack of transparency. The very sharp increase of inequality in China and the extreme opacity of Chinese data also raise serious doubts about the degree to which the lower classes are actually involved in the supposedly representative deliberative process that the CCP claims to embody. Nevertheless, China's many criticisms of Western political systems should be taken seriously. The power of money over the media and parties and the structural difficulty of dealing with the problems of borders and property rights are important issues, as is the fact that parliamentary institutions are increasingly dominated by closed circles of insiders in both the European Union and the United States. What is more, traditional representative mechanisms need to be complemented by arrange-

---

87. See R. B. Riedl, *Authoritarian Origins of Democratic Party Systems in Africa* (Cambridge University Press, 2014). The author supports the view that transitions organized by the former single party (as in Senegal and Ghana) are generally more successful than those that come about when the single ruling party collapses (as in Benin).

ments allowing for true deliberation and participation rather than just casting a ballot every four or five years. There is always a need to reinvent democracy in its concrete forms, and to that end it is useful to compare different models and historical experiences, assuming that the comparison can be conducted without prejudice or nationalist arrogance.

Eastern Europe: A Laboratory of Postcommunist Disillusionment

We turn now to communist and postcommunist societies in Eastern Europe. Communism's imprint on Eastern Europe is not as deep as its imprint on Russia, partly because the communist experience was shorter and partly because most East European countries were more highly developed than Russia was when communism arrived. In addition, most of the East European countries that were communist in the period 1950–1990 joined the European Union in the early 2000s. Being integrated in a politically and economically prosperous region helped to close the gap in standard of living somewhat more quickly and encouraged political stabilization around elected parliamentary regimes. Nevertheless, the process has also given rise to increasingly powerful frustrations and misunderstandings within the EU, so that Europe has become a veritable laboratory of postcommunist disillusionment.

To begin with, let's focus on the more positive aspects. First, it is particularly striking that if one measures income inequality for all of Europe (East and West combined), it is of course higher than in Western Europe alone but still significantly lower than in the United States (Fig. 12.9). The gap between average income in the poorest and richest EU member states—between, say, Romania or Bulgaria and Sweden or Germany—is of course substantial: larger, for instance, than the gap among US states. But this gap has shrunk, and, more importantly, inequality within European states (in both East and West) is sufficiently smaller than inequality within US states such that overall inequality across Europe is much lower than inequality across the United States. Specifically, the bottom 50 percent of the income distribution in Europe receives 20 percent of total income, compared with barely 12 percent in the United States. Note, moreover, that the gap would be even larger if one included Mexico and Canada with the United States. Such a comparison would make sense, partly because then the total populations would be closer and partly because the North American countries, like the European countries, are members of a customs union. Of course, social, economic, and political integration is more limited in North America than in the European Union, which provides so-

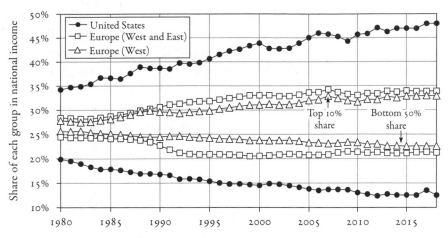

FIG. 12.9. Regional inequality in the United States and Europe

Interpretation: Income inequality is higher when one combines Eastern and Western Europe (population 540 million) than if one looks only at Western Europe (420 million) and excludes Eastern Europe (120 million), given the persistent average income gaps between West and East. In any case, inequality is much smaller than in the United States (population 320 million). *Sources and series:* piketty.pse.ens.fr/ideology.

called structural funds to less developed regions and allows free circulation of workers; at the moment, the latter seems totally out of the question in North America.

The fact that income inequality is lower in the former communist countries of Eastern Europe than in the United States or post-Soviet Russia is due to several factors, most notably the existence in Eastern Europe of relatively highly developed egalitarian systems of education and social protection inherited from the communist period. In addition, the transition from communism proceeded more gradually and in a less inegalitarian fashion than in Russia. For example, in Poland (a country that opted, along with the Czech Republic, for "shock therapy" in the 1990s), the transition was actually much more gradual and peaceful than in Russia. To be sure, the Poles did apply voucher privatization to small business in the period 1990–1992, especially in the retail and crafts sectors, but this was not extended to large firms until 1996 and even then only gradually as the new legal and fiscal systems took effect, which made it possible to limit the tendency for a small group of oligarchs to capture most of the shares, as was the case in Russia. The postponement of the privatization of large firms, initially planned to take place quickly after passage of the law of 1990, came about in response to vigorous opposition from the

Solidarność (Solidarity) union, more than from the former Communist Party, which became the Social Democratic Party (SLD) and played a leading role during the transition.[88] Recent work has shown that this gradualism contributed to the success of the Polish transition and to the strong growth observed between 1990 and 2018.[89]

Nevertheless, while the East European transition from communism was undoubtedly a success compared with Russia's turn to oligarchy and kleptocracy, it is important to put things in perspective. First, while inequality did not skyrocket as in Russia, it did increase sharply in all the countries of Eastern and Central Europe. The top decile's share of national income was less than 25 percent in 1990 and roughly 30–35 percent in 2018 in Hungary, the Czech Republic, Bulgaria, and Romania and as high as 35–40 percent in Poland. The share of the bottom 50 percent fell in similar proportions.[90] The degree to which the countries of the East have caught up with those of the West should also not be exaggerated. The average income in Eastern Europe (in terms of purchasing power parity) has indeed risen from 45 percent of the European average in 1993 to 65–70 percent in 2018. But in view of the decrease in output and income that followed the collapse of the communist system in the period 1980–1993, the level attained by the late 2010s still remains well below West European levels and is not that different from East European levels in the 1980s (about 60–65 percent, as far as the available data allow us to judge).[91]

---

88. The SLD, in power in 1993–1997 and 2001–2005, played a major role in Poland's postcommunist transition before disintegrating in the 2005 elections and giving way to a contest between the conservative liberals of the Civic Platform (PO) and the conservative nationalists of the Law and Justice Party (PiS). See Chap. 16.

89. See M. Piatkowski, *Europe's Growth Champion: Insights from the Economic Rise of Poland* (Oxford University Press, 2018), pp. 193–195. The author also stresses the positive role played by the egalitarian educational system inherited from the communist period, which helped break down the hyper-inegalitarian social structure that was still in place in the interwar years.

90. See the online appendix, and T. Blanchet, L. Chancel, and A. Gethin, "How Unequal Is Europe? Evidence from Distributional National Accounts, 1980–2017," WID.world, 2019, fig. 9. See F. Alvaredo et al., *World Inequality Report 2018* (Harvard University Press, 2018); also available online at https://wir2018.wid.world/; and F. Novokmet, *Between Communism and Capitalism. Essays on the Evolution of Income and Wealth Inequality in Eastern Europe 1890–2015 (Czech Republic, Poland, Bulgaria, Croatia, Slovenia, Russia)* (EHESS, 2017).

91. See the online appendix and Blanchet, Chancel, and Gethin, "How Unequal Is Europe?" fig. 4.

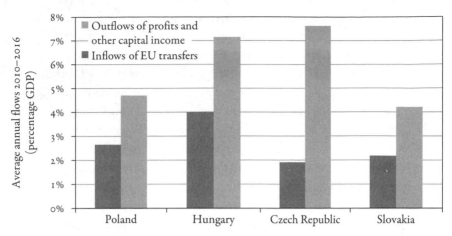

FIG. 12.10. Inflows and outflows in Eastern Europe, 2010–2016

Interpretation: Between 2010 and 2016, the annual flow of EU transfer payments (difference between payments received and contributions to the EU budget) averaged 2.7 percent of GDP for Poland, while over the same period outflows of profits and other capital income (net of corresponding inflows) averaged 4.7 percent of GDP. For Hungary the same figures were 4.0 and 7.2 percent. *Sources and series:* piketty.pse.ens.fr/ideology.

These mixed results help us to understand why frustration and incomprehension have grown in the European Union over the past two decades. The euphoria that followed the integration of the Eastern bloc countries into Europe rapidly gave way to disappointment and recrimination. In West European eyes, the citizens of the East have no cause for complaint. They benefited from joining the EU, which rescued them from the bad pass in which communism had left them—not to mention that they received and continue to receive generous public transfers from the West. Indeed, if one looks at the differences between monies received (especially structural funds) and monies paid as recorded by Eurostat (the official EU statistical agency), one finds that countries like Poland, Hungary, the Czech Republic, and Slovakia received net transfers of 2–4 percent of GDP between 2012 and 2016 (Fig. 12.10). By contrast, the largest West European countries, starting with Germany, France, and the United Kingdom, paid out net transfers on the order of 0.2–0.3 percent of GDP—a fact that proponents of Brexit trumpeted in the campaign ahead of the 2016 referendum.[92] In view of these generous outlays, West Europeans find it difficult

---

92. The total budget of the European Union is about 1 percent of European GDP. It draws on payments proportion to the gross national income (GNI) of each

to understand the frustration and rancor of the East and the election—particularly in Hungary and Poland—and of nationalist governments openly contemptuous of Brussels, Berlin, and Paris.

Perceptions in the East are totally different. There, many people believe that their income has stagnated because the powers that dominate the EU have placed Eastern Europe in a position of permanent economic subordination, leaving them in the position of second-class citizens. A story widely believed in Warsaw, Prague, and Budapest is that Western (especially German and French) investors exploited their countries for the enormous profits to be made from pools of cheap labor. Indeed, after the collapse of communism, Western investors did gradually become owners of much of the capital of the former Eastern bloc: about a quarter if one considers the entire capital stock (including real estate) but more than half if one looks only at firms (and even greater if one considers only large firms).

Filip Novokmet's illuminating work shows that inequality in Eastern Europe has not grown as much as in Russia or the United States largely because much of the substantial return on East European capital goes abroad (as it did before communism, when much of the Eastern capital stock was already owned by German, French, and Austrian investors).[93] Basically, it was only during the communist era that Eastern Europe was not owned by Western investors. But the region was then dominated militarily, politically, and ideologically by its giant neighbor to the east, a still more painful situation to which no one wants to return. This intractable dilemma is no doubt part of the reason for the disarray.

The consequences of these cross-border capital holdings for income flows are far from negligible. National accounts data indicate that outflows from profits and other capital income (interest, dividends, etc.) net of corresponding inflows averaged 4–7 percent of GDP between 2010 and 2016, which substantially exceeds the inward flow of EU funds in Poland, Hungary, the Czech Republic, and Slovakia (Fig. 12.10).

---

member state. The budget is jointly approved by the European Parliament and the European Council (consisting of heads of state, who must vote unanimously). See the online appendix for budget details.

93. See Novokmet, *Between Communism and Capitalism*. Individual country studies are available on WID.world. See the online appendix.

On the "Naturalization" of Market Forces in the European Union

Of course, the above comparison of the two flows is not meant to imply that joining the EU was a bad deal for these countries (despite what nationalist leaders sometimes say). The outflow of profits is the result of investments made (and in some cases of advantageous privatizations), which may have increased overall productivity and therefore the wage level in Eastern Europe. Still, wages have not increased as rapidly as hoped, in part because of the bargaining power of Western investors, who can threaten to withdraw their capital if profits are too low; this has helped to limit wage hikes.

In any case, the flows are large enough for the question to be raised. The level of wages and profits is not decreed from on high. It depends on prevailing institutions, rules, and union bargaining power in each country as well as on taxes and regulations (or their absence) at the European level (especially since it is difficult for a small country to influence the forces that determine wages). The question is especially pertinent in a historical context where the wage share of value added by firms has been trending downward in Europe and indeed globally since the 1980s, while the profit share has been rising. This phenomenon can be attributed in part to the evolution of the respective bargaining power of firms and unions.[94] Different European institutions and wage rules might have led (and might still lead) to higher wages in Eastern Europe and therefore to a significant reduction in the outward flow of profits. The potential macroeconomic impact is quite large—of the same order as the flows into Eastern Europe from the European Union.[95] The question therefore cannot be dismissed out of hand. It is hard to deny that the countries of Western Europe have derived substantial commercial and financial benefits from the integration of the Eastern bloc into the European Union (this is especially true of Germany, largely because of its geographical location and industrial specialization). Therefore, the question of how to share the resulting profits is legitimate

---

94. On the various factors explaining the declining wage share, see the online appendix. See also Piketty, *Capital in the Twenty-First Century,* chap. 6, and L. Karabarbounis and B. Neiman, "The Global Decline of the Labor Share," *Quarterly Journal of Economics,* 2014.

95. For example, if the outflow of profits from Hungary or the Czech Republic were reduced by 30 percent, those countries would gain 2–3 percent of GDP annually. See Fig. 12.10.

and important, especially since those profits have contributed to Germany's unprecedented trade surplus.[96]

Europe's dominant powers, especially Germany and France, tend to ignore this issue of private profits flowing out of Eastern Europe entirely, however. The implicit assumption is that the "market" and "free competition" automatically yield a just distribution of wealth, and transfers that depart from this "natural" equilibrium are seen as an act of generosity on the part of the winners (on this view, only transfers of public funds count as "transfers," whereas flows of private profits are considered part of the "natural" functioning of the system). In reality, relations of ownership and production are always complex, especially within human communities as large as the EU, and cannot be regulated by the "market" alone. They always depend on specific institutions and rules, which are based on particular sociohistorical compromises; these include the legal, fiscal, and social systems, labor law, corporate law, and worker bargaining power. The fact that the European Union is based primarily on free circulation of capital and goods and regional competition without much in the way of common fiscal and social policy inevitably affects the level of wages and profits; the current state of affairs tends to favor the most mobile actors (hence investors and owners rather than workers).

The tendency of dominant economic actors to "naturalize" market forces and the resulting inequalities is common, both within and between countries. It is particularly striking in the European Union and in the period 1990–2020 led to bafflements and misunderstandings not only between East and West but also between North and South. These threatened the European project, especially during the Eurozone debt crisis and periods of speculation on interest rates. The Maastricht Treaty of 1992, which set the rules governing the common currency, was silent about the usefulness of combining the public debt of member states or harmonizing tax systems. The compromise that was struck among the various countries involved consisted in postponing these complex political questions until later and concentrating instead on simple rules such

---

96. German and French exports and imports were similar until the 1990s (around 20–25 percent of GDP), but Germany's trade flows doubled in the period 1995–2015 (to 40–45 percent in 2015), while France's increased much less (to 30 percent in 2015), more in line with the overall global evolution of trade. The reason for the difference has to do with the deep integration of Germany's production system with Eastern Europe. This has coincided with a significant increase in Germany's trade surplus and corresponding accumulation of foreign financial assets. See the online appendix and Fig. S12.10. See also Fig. 7.9.

as setting deficit limits and above all on the makeup and powers of the European Central Bank (ECB), a powerful federal institution whose decisions need only a simple majority to be approved.[97] In the first few years after the introduction of the euro in 1999, the assumption was naturally that the common currency was here to stay. Quite logically, interest rates converged to virtually identical levels for all Eurozone member states. Between 2002 and 2008, interest on ten-year sovereign bonds was roughly 4 percent not only for Germany and France but also for Italy, Spain, Portugal, and Greece. This situation, though not surprising as long as markets remained calm, would not prevail for long, however.

Indeed, in 2007–2008, as the financial crisis triggered by the collapse of subprime mortgages in the United States and the failure of Lehman Brothers deepened, and after the ECB itself helped to create a panic around Greek debt, interest rates on European sovereign debt began to diverge widely.[98] The rates demanded of the countries deemed to be the safest and most solid (such as Germany and France) fell to less than 2 percent while those demanded of Italy and Spain rose to 6 percent (and even as high as 12 percent for Portugal and 16 percent for Greece in 2012). As always with financial markets, market movement due to speculation became a self-fulfilling prophecy: once the market

---

97. The Governing Council of the ECB consists of the governors of the central banks of Eurozone member states (one seat per country) and a six-member directorate (consisting of the president, vice president, and four other members) appointed for eight years by the European Council under qualified majority voting (55 percent of the states representing 65 percent of the population), which generally increases the representation of the large countries on the Governing Council. In 2019, the directorate has representatives from Italy, Spain, France, Germany, Belgium, and Luxembourg. The euro, introduced as money of account for banks and firms on January 1, 1999, and in general circulation since January 1, 2002, was adopted by eleven of fifteen EU member states in 1999 and is today used by nineteen of twenty-eight member states.

98. See the online appendix, Fig. S12.11. "Subprimes" are ultra-risky mortgages whose issuance was encouraged by financial deregulation in the United States. Lehman Brothers was a major US investment bank, and its failure in September 2008 triggered the worst financial panic since 1929, until the Federal Reserve intervened massively to prevent a series of cascading bank failures. In late 2009, the ECB declared that it would no longer accept Greek sovereign debt as collateral if the ratings agencies downgraded it, which was tantamount to placing the fate of the common currency in the hands of agencies that had not distinguished themselves for honesty in previous years. This encouraged a wave of speculation on European sovereign debt.

anticipates that a country is going to have to pay higher interest on its future debt, the question of potential insolvency arises, which reinforces the determination of bond buyers to demand still higher interest rates. In view of the growing financialization of the economy and the increased role of speculative capital (which, by the way, it would be wise to regulate more strictly), only determined action by central banks and governments could stem the panic. This is what happened in 2011–2012, when the ECB and the leaders of France and Germany finally realized that there was no other option if the euro was to be saved. Their action came too late, however, to prevent a serious recession in Greece and southern Europe and a slowing of economic activity throughout the Eurozone.[99]

In the next chapter I will say more about recent changes in the role of central banks and their place in today's hyper-financialized world—a question that extends well beyond the Eurozone.[100] At this stage, note simply that the ECB's belated intervention coincided with a new budgetary agreement, which tightened deficit rules;[101] a European Stability Mechanism (ESM) financed by member states in proportion to their GDP and authorized to lend to countries under attack by speculators was also created by a separate treaty in 2012.[102] In concrete terms, the ESM enabled wealthy countries such as Germany and France to lend to Greece at rates below those demanded by financial markets (which were astronomical at the time) but still well above the (near-zero) rates at which these generous lenders could themselves borrow. People in Germany and France often imagine that they helped the Greeks: they look at market prices (in this case interest rates) and see any deviation from them as an act of generosity. Greeks interpret these events very differently: they see the handsome margins that their French and German lenders enjoyed after imposing a

---

99. See the online appendix, Figs. S12.12a–S12.12c. Because of the slowing of the European economy in 2011, it was not until 2015 that Eurozone GDP returned to its 2007 level (whereas the United States, despite being the origin of the crisis, was already 10 percent above its 2007 level); it was not until 2018–2019, moreover, that Eurozone GDP per capita returned to its pre-crisis level.

100. See esp. Figs. 13.12–13.13.

101. The Treaty on Stability, Coordination, and Governance (TSCG), signed in 2012, set a maximum deficit of 0.5 percent—compared with 3 percent under the Maastricht Treaty (1992)—together with a system of automatic sanctions if the rules were not respected (which has not really functioned, however). See the online appendix and Chap. 16.

102. The European Stability Mechanism was also created by a separate treaty in 2012.

heavy dose of austerity on their country, which consequently suffered from sky-rocketing unemployment, especially among the young (not to mention the ensuing clearance sale of Greek public assets, often to the benefit of German and French property owners).

To sacralize market prices and the resulting inequalities is a simple way of looking at things. It avoids having to worry about what might happen if Pandora's box were opened—a recurrent fear that we have touched on several times already. It is always tempting for the most powerful economic actors to defend market forces. Yet their defense is selfish and short-sighted. As Karl Polanyi observed in *The Great Transformation*,[103] markets are always socially and politically embedded, and their sacralization only exacerbates nationalistic and identitarian tensions. This is especially true of the labor and money markets, which set wages and interest on sovereign debt. Young Greeks and Hungarians are no more responsible for their countries' sovereign debt and for the market interest rates they pay than young Bavarians or Bretons are for the interest they earn. If Europe has nothing more to offer than market relations, it is by no means certain that it will hold together permanently. By contrast, if Greeks, Hungarians, Bavarians, and Bretons began to think of themselves as members of the same political community, with equal rights to deliberate and approve common social regulations, laws, and tax systems and with common procedures for setting wages and progressive income and wealth tax rates and so on, it might then be possible to transcend differences of identity and rebuild Europe on a postnational socioeconomic basis. I will say more later about the European treaties and the possibility of revising them to work toward a truly social-democratic project embodying norms of justice acceptable to the majority.[104]

Postcommunism and the Social-Nativist Trap

Let us return now to the specific political-ideological situation of postcommunist Eastern Europe, notably in relation to the rise of social nativism. There is no doubt that all the postcommunist countries are suffering from widespread disillusionment in the wake of rising inequality and, more generally, in regard to the question of whether capitalism can be regulated and transcended. In Eastern Europe, as in Russia and China, many people feel that they have paid

---

103. See Chap. 10.
104. See esp. Chap. 16.

the price for the ill-considered promises of past communist and socialist revolutionaries, and they are generally skeptical of anyone who gives the impression of wanting to pursue similar fantasies yet again. One can of course regret that such reactions often lack subtlety and precision and tend to confuse very different historical experiences. As noted earlier, the fact that Soviet Communism failed dramatically cannot alter the fact that Swedish social democracy was a great success, and it is unfortunate that postcommunist Russia (or Eastern Europe) did not try to establish social-democratic institutions rather than turn to inegalitarian oligarchy. Nevertheless, the fact remains that disillusionment is very deeply rooted in all postcommunist societies; today's neo-proprietarian ideology rests on it, as does, more generally, a certain form of economic conservatism.

In the particular case of Eastern Europe, this general factor is reinforced by the fact that the countries in question are small in terms of both population and natural resources, which limits their possibilities for pursuing autonomous development strategies. By contrast, Russia and China are countries of continental dimensions, and this allows them more scope to do as they wish (for better or for worse). In addition, the countries of Eastern Europe are integrated into the European Union, which has no common fiscal policy or strategy for reducing inequality; fiscal competition between member states also severely limits options for redistribution and offers smaller countries strong incentives to become virtual tax havens.

Taken together, these factors explain why socialist and social-democratic parties have virtually disappeared from the electoral chessboard in the East. Poland is the paradigmatic case: there, the contest is now between the conservative liberals of the Civic Platform (PO) and the conservative nationalists of Law and Justice (PiS). Both parties are fairly conservative economically, especially on the issue of fiscal progressivity, but PO portrays itself as pro-European while PiS harps on nationalism, claiming that Poland is treated as a second-class country. Above all, PiS defends what it sees as traditional Polish and Catholic values, including opposition to abortion and same-sex marriage, and denies any Polish anti-Semitism or complicity in the Shoah (to the point of making it a criminal offense to search for evidence to the contrary). It has also tried to assert control over the media and courts (which the party claims are threatened by liberal values) and stands firmly opposed to any immigration from outside Europe. The migrant crisis of 2015, when Germany briefly opened its doors to Syrian refugees, was an important and revealing moment in this political reconfiguration. It allowed a faction of PiS to take a strong stand against a proposal, briefly entertained by EU leaders, to impose refugee quotas on all member states. It was also an opportunity to attack PO, whose former leader, Donald Tusk, had become president of the European Council, as a vassal of overlords in Brussels, Berlin, and Paris.[105] At the same time, PiS sought, not without success, to portray itself as the champion of the lower and middle classes by promoting redistributive social policies and attacking the rigidity of EU budget rules. In the end, the ideological stance of PiS is in some ways similar to the "social nativism" we encountered previously in our discussion of the Democratic Party in the United States in the late nineteenth and early twentieth centuries,[106] despite many differences, beginning with postcommunist disillusionment. What is certain in any case is that the confrontation of conservative nationalists with conservative liberals, which we also see in Hungary and other East European countries, has little in common with the "traditional" left-right conflict between social democrats and conservatives that defined politics in Western Europe and the United States during much of the twentieth century.

In Part Four I will delve into these political-ideological transformations in greater detail. I see them as essential for understanding the evolution of inequality and the possibility of reconstituting an egalitarian and redistributive coalition in the future. At this stage, note that the clash between conservative liberals and conservative nationalists is not simply a curiosity of postcommunist Eastern Europe. It is one of the possible trajectories toward which political conflict may move in many Western democracies, as recent developments in France, Italy, and the United States suggest. Broadly speaking, it is one of the forms that ideological conflict may take in societies that take the reduction of socioeconomic inequalities off the table while opening up the space for identitarian conflict. The only way to overcome such contradictions is to work toward a novel internationalist political platform to achieve greater equality.

---

105. On the relation of the European Council to other EU institutions, see Chap. 16.
106. See Chap. 6.

THIRTEEN

Hypercapitalism: Between Modernity and Archaism

In Chapter 12 we looked at the role of communist and postcommunist societies in the history of inequality regimes, especially in relation to the resurgence of inequality since the 1980s. Today's world is a direct consequence of the great political-ideological transformations that inequality regimes experienced over the course of the twentieth century. The fall of communism led to a certain disillusionment concerning the very possibility of a just society. Disillusionment led to retreat and to the defense of national, ethnic, and religious identities; this must be overcome. The end of colonialism gave rise to new, ostensibly less inegalitarian economic relations and migration flows between different regions of the world, but the global system remains hierarchical and not sufficiently social or democratic, and new tensions have arisen both within and between countries. Finally, proprietarian ideology has returned in a new form, which I call neo-proprietarian despite the many differences between the old version and the new. But the neo-proprietarian regime is less unified and more fragile than it might appear.

In this chapter we will study several of the major inegalitarian and ideological challenges that all societies face today, with an emphasis on the potential for change and evolution. We will begin by looking at the various types of extreme inequality that exist in the world today, as old and new logics come together. We will then ask why our economic and financial system has become increasingly opaque, particularly with respect to recording and measuring income and wealth. In a world that regularly celebrates the era of "big data," this may come as a surprise. It reflects a dereliction of duty on the part of government authorities and statistical agencies. Worse, it greatly complicates the task of organizing an informed global debate about inequality and other major issues, beginning with climate change, which could serve as a catalyst for a new politics. After that, we will review other fundamental global challenges related to inequality: the persistence of strong patriarchal inequalities between men and women, which only vigorous proactive measures can overcome; the paradoxical pauperization of the state in developing countries as a consequence of trade liberalization imposed without sufficient preparation or political coordination; and finally, the new role of monetary creation since 2008, which has deeply altered perceptions of the respective roles of governments and central banks, taxes and monetary creation, and, more generally, of the idea of a just economy. All of this will help us to understand today's neo-proprietarianism and what needs to be done to overcome it.

Forms of Inequality in the Twenty-First Century

The most obvious characteristic of today's global inequality regime is that societies around the world are more intensely interdependent than ever before. Globalization is of course a very long-term process. Relations among the different regions of the world have been gradually expanding since 1500. Violence was often involved, as in the era of slavery and colonialism. But at other times trade and cultural exchange took more peaceful forms. In terms of commerce, immigration, and finance, the world achieved a remarkable level of integration during the Belle Époque (1880–1914). But since then, globalization has attained another level altogether in the era of hypercapitalism and digital technology (1990–2020). International travel has become routine, and images, texts, and sounds can now be transmitted instantaneously to the four corners of the earth. New information technologies have given rise to previously unknown forms of cultural, sociopolitical, and political-ideological exchange and interdependence. These changes have taken place, moreover, against a background of rapid demographic growth and broad rebalancing. The United Nations predicts that the global population will reach 9 billion in 2050: 5 billion in Asia, 2 billion in Africa, 1 billion in the Americas, and less than 1 billion in Europe (Fig. 13.1).

Such interconnectedness is not incompatible with a great social and political diversity, however. According to available sources, the top decile's share of total income is less than 35 percent in Europe but close to 70 percent in the Middle East, South Africa, and Qatar (Fig. 13.2). If we look at the share of national income going to the bottom 50 percent, the next 40 percent, and the top 10 percent (or 1 percent), we find large variations between countries. In the least inegalitarian countries, the top decile share is "only" 1.5 times as large as that of the bottom 50 percent, compared with seven times as large in the most inegalitarian countries (Fig. 13.3). The top centile share is half that of the bottom 50 percent in the most egalitarian countries (which is quite a lot, considering that the top centile is one-fiftieth the size) but more than triple the bottom 50 percent's share in the most inegalitarian countries (Fig. 13.4). These figures

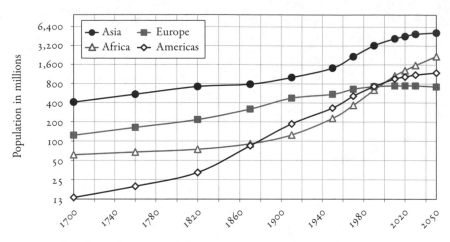

FIG. 13.1. Population by continents, 1700–2050

Interpretation: In 1700, the global population was about 600 million, of whom 400 million lived in Asia and the Pacific, 120 million in Europe and Russia, 60 million in Africa, and 15 million in America. In 2050, according to UN projections, it will be about 9.3 billion, with 5.2 billion in Asia/Pacific, 2.2 in Africa, 1.2 in the Americas, and 0.7 in Europe/Russia. *Sources and series:* piketty.pse.ens.fr/ideology.

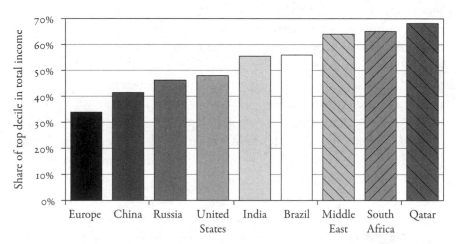

FIG. 13.2. Global inequality regimes, 2018

Interpretation: In 2018, the top decile share of national income was 34 percent in Europe, 41 percent in China, 46 percent in Russia, 48 percent in the United States, 55 percent in India, 56 percent in Brazil, 64 percent in the Middle East, 65 percent in South Africa, and 68 percent in Qatar. *Sources and series:* piketty.pse.ens.fr/ideology.

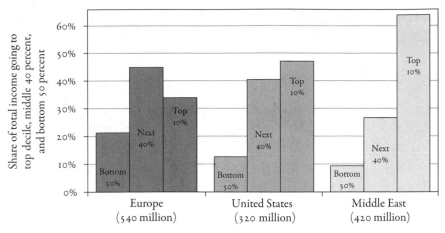

FIG. 13.3. Inequality in Europe, the United States, and the Middle East, 2018

Interpretation: The top decile's share of total income is 64 percent in the Middle East (population 420 million) compared with 9 percent for the bottom 50 percent. In Europe (enlarged EU, pop. 540 million), these shares are 34 and 21 percent, and in the United States (pop. 320 million), 47 and 13 percent. *Sources and series:* piketty.pse.ens. fr/ideology.

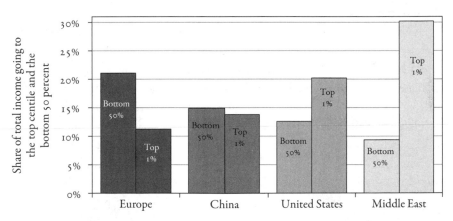

FIG. 13.4. Global inequality regimes, 2018: The bottom 50 percent versus the top 1 percent

Interpretation: The top centile's share of total income is 30 percent in the Middle East compared with 9 percent for the bottom 50 percent. In Europe, these two shares are 21 and 11 percent; in China, 15 and 14 percent; and in the United States, 20 and 13 percent. *Sources and series:* piketty.pse.ens.fr/ideology.

show why it is a mistake to compare countries only in terms of macroeconomic averages (such as gross domestic product [GDP] per capita). Equivalent averages can conceal totally different realities in terms of income distribution among different social groups.

These regional differences are important and instructive, and they may be helpful for understanding what kinds of social and fiscal institutions are useful for keeping inequality down (as Europe has done). Bear in mind, however, that inequality levels are high and rising nearly everywhere (including in Europe).[1] Hence it is not a very good idea to use such data to explain to Europe's lower and middle classes that, because their lot is so enviable compared to the rest of the world, they must make sacrifices. Unfortunately, people at the top of the global income and wealth distribution (and the politicians they support) often invoke such arguments to justify sacrifices in their favor. Rhetoric of this kind may be politically effective, but it is also dangerous. Most Europeans are perfectly well aware that the level of inequality in Europe is lower than in South Africa, the Middle East, Brazil, and the United States. To argue that immutable laws of economics require them to accept the kinds of inequality that exist elsewhere (a totally fantastic and baseless assertion, which in no way helps to clarify the issues) is surely the best way to persuade them to turn against globalization.

A more relevant comparison for European citizens is to note that while income inequality in Europe decreased considerably over the course of the twentieth century, it has increased sharply since the 1980s.[2] To be sure, the increase has been smaller than that observed elsewhere, but it still represents a clear and well-documented reversal of the previous trend, for which there is no obvious justification. Indeed, the increase of inequality has coincided with a decrease in the growth rate.[3] Furthermore, inequality remains extremely high in absolute terms. In fact, the concentration of wealth in Europe has always been stunning, and it has been increasing since the 1980s: the bottom 50 percent owns barely 5 percent of the wealth, while the top 10 percent owns 50–60 percent.[4]

Turning now to the regions of the world where inequality is highest, it is interesting to note that they contain several distinct types of political-ideological

---

1. See Fig. I.3.
2. See Figs. 10.1–10.5.
3. See Fig. 11.4.
4. See Figs. 4.1–4.2, Figs. 5.4–5.5, and Figs. 10.4–10.5.

regime (Fig. 13.2).[5] First, one finds countries with a legacy of status inequality and discrimination based on race, colonialism, or slavery. This is the case in South Africa, which ended apartheid in the early 1990s, and in Brazil, which was the last country to abolish slavery at the end of the nineteenth century.[6] The racial dimension and history of slavery may also help to explain why the United States is more unequal than Europe and has had greater difficulty building social-democratic institutions.[7]

The Middle East: Pinnacle of Global Inequality

Sharing the pinnacle of the global inequality hierarchy is the Middle East, whose inequality has more "modern" roots in the sense that it is linked not to past racial divisions or a history of slavery but to the concentration of petroleum resources in small countries with modest populations compared to the region as a whole.[8] This oil, exported around the world, is being transformed into permanent financial wealth via financial markets and the international legal system. This sophisticated system is the key to understanding the exceptional level of inequality in the region. For instance, Egypt, a country of 100 million people, annually spends on its schools 1 percent of the combined petroleum revenues of Saudi Arabia, the United Arab Emirates, and Qatar, whose populations are tiny.[9]

Inequality in the Middle East is also closely connected to the borders laid down by the French and British at the end of World War I as well as to the

---

5. See also L. Assouad, L. Chancel, and M. Morgan, "Extreme Inequality: Evidence from Brazil, India, the Middle East and South Africa," WID.world, 2018; also published in *AEA Papers and Proceedings,* 2018.

6. See Chaps. 6–7. On the long-term impact of slavery on inequality in Brazil, see T. Fujiwara, H. Laudares, and F. Valencia, "Tordesillas, Slavery and the Origins of Brazilian Inequality" (working paper, February 25, 2019), https://economics .ucdavis.edu/events/papers/copy_of_416Valencia.pdf.

7. See Chaps. 10–11. I will come back to this in Part 4 (esp. Chap. 15).

8. The Middle East is defined here as the region stretching from Egypt to Iran and from Turkey to the Arabian Peninsula, with a population of about 420 million. For a detailed presentation of these estimates, see F. Alvaredo, L. Assouad, and T. Piketty, "Measuring Inequality in the Middle-East 1990–2016: The World's Most Unequal Region?" WID.world, 2018; also published in *Review of Income and Wealth,* 2019.

9. See T. Piketty, *Capital in the Twenty-First Century,* trans. A. Goldhammer (Harvard University Press, 2014), pp. 537–538.

military protection that Western powers subsequently provided to the oil monarchies. Without that protection, the political map would probably have been redrawn several times, notably after the invasion of Kuwait by Iraq in 1990.[10] The 1991 military intervention, whose purpose was to restore Kuwait's oil to its emirs and to promote Western interests, coincided with the collapse of the Soviet Union, which facilitated Western intervention (now that there was no longer a rival superpower to contend with). These events marked the beginning of the new political-ideological era of hypercapitalism. They also illustrate the fragility of the compromise that was struck at the time. A few decades later, the Middle Eastern inequality regime epitomizes the explosive mixture of archaism, hyper-financialized modernity, and collective irrationality typical of recent times. It bears traces of the logic of colonialism and militarism; it contains reserves of petroleum that would be better kept in the ground to prevent global warming; and its wealth is protected by the extremely sophisticated services of international lawyers and financers, who find ways to put it beyond the reach of covetous have-nots. Finally, note that the oil monarchies of the Persian Gulf are, together with postcommunist Russia, the countries that make most extensive use of the world's tax havens.[11]

The estimates of Middle Eastern inequality shown in Fig. 13.2 should be seen as lower limits owing to the limitations of the available sources and the hypotheses needed to interpret them. The measurement of inequality in the Middle East is complicated by the extreme difficulty of obtaining data about income and wealth, particular in the oil monarchies. The evidence suggests, however, that wealth in these states is very highly concentrated, both within the native population and between natives and foreign workers (who make up 90 percent of the population of Qatar, the Emirates, and Kuwait and 40 percent of the population of Saudi Arabia, Oman, and Bahrain). For want of sufficient data, the estimates given here are based on very conservative hypotheses about within-country inequalities; it is primarily the very wide gaps between coun-

---

10. See Chap. 9.

11. See Fig. 12.5. Note that wealthy people who live in authoritarian inequality regimes without progressive taxes must still worry about possible shifts in public opinion and the sociopolitical balance of power. In 2017 the Saudi heir apparent, Crown Prince Mohammed bin Salman, imprisoned the leading Saudi billionaires (including members of the royal family and the prime minister of Lebanon) in the Riyadh Ritz-Carlton and stripped them of their property, a reminder that even in these proprietarian regimes, there are always factions contending for power.

tries that give rise to the differences depicted here. By adopting alternative (and very likely more realistic) hypotheses, one would arrive at estimates of top decile shares on the order of 80–90 percent (rather than 65–70), especially for Qatar and the Emirates—a level of inequality close to that of the most inegalitarian slave societies ever observed.[12]

There is little doubt that the extreme inequality observed in the Middle East has heightened tensions and contributed to the region's persistent instability. In particular, the wide gap between the reality of the situation and officially proclaimed religious values (based on principles of sharing and social harmony within the community of believers) is quite likely to provoke allegations of illegitimacy and lead to violence. In the abstract, a democratic federal regional organization such as the Arab League or some other political organization could allow wealth to be shared while coordinating vast investments in a better future for the region's youth. For the time being, however, little has been done in this direction.[13] Why not? Not only because of the limitations of the strategies of regional actors but also because the wider world lacks the requisite political and ideological vision. In particular, the Western powers as well as private interests in Europe and the United States see advantages in maintaining the status quo, especially when the oil monarchies buy their weapons and offer financial support to their sports teams and universities. Yet in this as in other cases, strict respect for existing power relations and property rights has failed to yield a viable model of development. Indeed, Western actors have every reason to look beyond their short-term financial interests in order to promote a democratic, social, federalist agenda that would allow these contradictions to be overcome. Ultimately, it was the refusal to contemplate new egalitarian postnational solutions that gave rise to reactionary and authoritarian political projects in Europe in the first half of the twentieth century; the same is true of the Middle East in the late twentieth and early twenty-first centuries.[14]

---

12. See Alvaredo, Assouad, and Piketty, "Measuring Inequality in the Middle-East," figs. 9a–9b, and the online appendix. On inequality in slave and colonial societies, see Figs. 7.2–7.3.

13. There have been attempts to redraw borders and build new state structures but thus far only in the form of Saddam Hussein's expansionary authoritarian dictatorship (1990–1991) and the attempt by the so-called Islamic State (ISIS) to restore the caliphate with all its ancient militaristic and misogynistic brutality (2014–2019).

14. See Chap. 10 and Hannah Arendt's analyses of Europe.

Measuring Inequality and the Question of Democratic Transparency

Along with global warming, the rise of inequality is one of the principal challenges confronting the world today. Whereas the twentieth century witnessed a historic decline in inequality, its revival since the 1980s has posed a profound challenge to the very idea of progress. What is more, the challenge of inequality is closely related to the climate challenge. Indeed, it is clear that global warming cannot be stopped or at least attenuated without substantial changes in the way people live. For such changes to be acceptable to the majority, the effort demanded must be apportioned as equitably as possible. The need for fair apportionment of the effort is all the more obvious because the rich are responsible for a disproportionate share of greenhouse gas emissions while the poor will suffer the worst consequences of climate change.

For these reasons, the issue of democratic transparency regarding inequalities of income and wealth is of paramount importance. Without intelligible indices based on reliable and systematic sources, it is impossible to have a reasoned public debate at the national level, much less at the regional or global level. The data presented in this book are drawn in large part from the World Inequality Database (WID.world), an independent consortium supported by a number of research centers and international organizations whose main objective is precisely to facilitate public debate about inequality on the basis of the most complete available data.[15] The information in the database is the result of systematic comparison of available sources (including national accounts, household surveys, tax and estate records, and so on). With this information we have been able to provide the first comprehensive map of global inequality regimes and their evolution. Note, however, that despite the best efforts of everyone involved, the currently available sources remain fragmentary and insufficient. The main reason for this is that the data made public by governments and statistical agencies suffer from considerable limitations. Indeed, economic and financial opacity have increased in recent years, especially with

---

15. See the discussion in the Introduction. Initially launched by researchers in the early 2000s, the WID.world network now encompasses some one hundred researchers in more than seventy countries on all continents and works closely with many other centers and organizations specialized in the study of inequality such as the Center for Economic Growth, the Commitment to Equality, the Luxembourg Income Study, and the United Nations Development Programme. See F. Alvaredo et al., *World Inequality Report 2018* (Harvard University Press, 2018); also available online at https://wir2018.wid.world/.

respect to accounting for capital income and financial assets. This may seem paradoxical at a time when modern information technology should in theory facilitate greater transparency. The failure in some cases reflects a veritable surrender by governments, fiscal authorities, and statistical agencies; more than that, it reflects a political-ideological refusal to take the issue of inequality seriously, particularly when it comes to wealth inequality.

Let us begin with the question of the indices used to describe and analyze the distribution of income and wealth. These should be as intuitive as possible so that everybody can understand them. That is why it is preferable to use indices such as the share of total income (or wealth) accruing to the bottom 50 percent, the middle 40 percent, and the top 10 percent. Every citizen can take from these figures a fairly concrete idea of what each distribution means (Figs. 13.2–13.4).

To compare inequality between countries, an especially simple and expressive index is the ratio between the share of the top 10 percent (or top 1 percent) and that of the bottom 50 percent. This reveals quite significant differences between countries. For instance, we find that the ratio of the top decile's share of income to that of the bottom 50 percent is roughly eight in Europe, nineteen in the United States, and thirty-five in South Africa and the Middle East (Fig. 13.5). The ratio between the top centile's share and that of the bottom 50 percent is currently about twenty-five in Europe, eighty in the United States, and 160 in the Middle East (Fig. 13.6). The advantage of this type of index is twofold: it is very easy to understand, and it can be directly related to fiscal and social policy. In particular, citizens can form their own opinions about how different tax rates might modify the distribution of income.[16] The same is true if one looks at the concentration of wealth and the potential for wealth redistribution: the share of wealth claimed by different groups shows immediately how a redistribution of property rights would affect each group's holdings.

By contrast, indices such as the Gini coefficient, often used in official inequality statistics, are much more difficult to interpret. The Gini coefficient is a

---

16. Figs. 13.2–13.6 reflect income including pensions and unemployment insurance (after deduction of related taxes) but before other transfers and direct or indirect taxes. Accounting for other taxes and transfers reduces inequality by 20–30 percent (as measured, for instance, by the ratio between the top decile and bottom 50 percent shares) in Europe and the United States. See Fig. 11.9. There is less tax-driven redistribution in South Africa or the Middle East (where inequality would be reduced by less than 10 percent or perhaps not at all, given the lack of progressive taxes and the preponderance of indirect taxes), which would increase the intercountry differences in Figs. 13.5–13.6. See the online appendix.

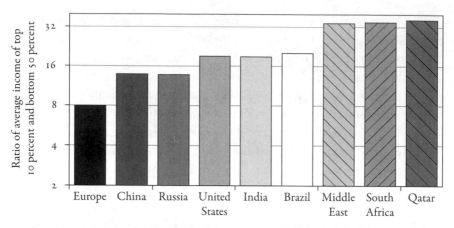

FIG. 13.5. Inequality between the top 10 percent and the bottom 50 percent, 2018

Interpretation: In 2018, the ratio of the average income of the top decile and that of the bottom 50 percent was 8 in Europe, 14 in China and Russia, 19 in the United States and India, 20 in Brazil, 34 in the Middle East, 35 in South Africa, and 36 in Qatar. *Sources and series:* piketty.pse.ens.fr/ideology.

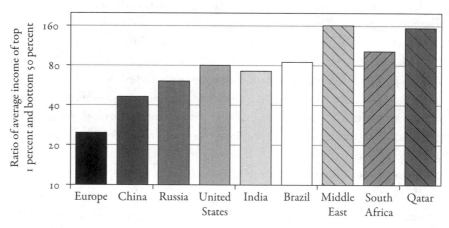

FIG. 13.6. Inequality between the top 1 percent and the bottom 50 percent, 2018

Interpretation: In 2018, the ratio between the average income of the top centile and that of the bottom 50 percent was around 25 in Europe, 46 in China, 61 in Russia, 80 in the United States, 72 in India, 85 in Brazil, 161 in the Middle East, 103 in South Africa, and 154 in Qatar. *Sources and series:* piketty.pse.ens.fr/ideology.

number between zero and one, with zero representing total equality and one representing total inequality. It tells us nothing about which social groups are responsible for differences in the index over time or between countries. Broadly speaking, the Gini coefficient masks flesh-and-blood social conflict between different groups in the income or wealth hierarchy and often obscures ongoing changes.[17] For instance, inequality strongly increased between the middle and the top of the distribution at the global level since 1980 while it declined between the bottom and the middle, so that a synthetic indicator like the Gini coefficient could wrongly give the impression that we live in an era of complete distributional stability and balanced growth.[18] Furthermore, the Gini coefficient is generally calculated on the basis of data that inherently tend to underestimate the degree of inequality—most notably, household surveys in which income and wealth are self-declared; such surveys often absurdly understate the income and wealth of people at the top of the distribution. For these reasons, indices like the Gini coefficient frequently conceal flaws (or outright aberrations) in the underlying data or at the very least cast a discreet veil over the difficulties involved.[19]

Another frequently used approach is simply to ignore the part of the distribution that lies above a certain threshold, such as the ninetieth percentile (above which lies the top decile). One then divides the ninetieth percentile level by the median level (which corresponds to the fiftieth percentile) or the tenth percentile level (below which lies the bottom decile).[20] The problem with this approach is that it amounts to neglecting a significant part of the distribution: the top decile's share of total income is generally 30–70 percent, but its share of total wealth is generally 50–90 percent. If such a large share of income or wealth is simply swept under the rug, the transparency of democratic debate suffers, and the credibility of government statisticians and agencies is impaired.

---

17. See Piketty, *Capital in the Twenty-First Century,* pp. 266–269.
18. See the discussion of the "elephant curve" in Fig. I.5.
19. The percentile and decile data presented in this book can of course be used to calculate Gini coefficients, which are also given in the WID.world database, even though they are less expressive than the decile and centile shares. By contrast, from Gini coefficients alone one cannot derive decile and centile data (which are often not published in analyses based on the Gini coefficient or similar coefficients and indices, such as the Theil index).
20. These ratios, sometimes designated as P90/P50 or P90/P10, would therefore be equal to one (suggesting complete equality) in a society in which the top 5 percent claimed all income or wealth while the bottom 95 percent were all approximately equal.

On the Absence of Fiscal Transparency

Apart from the choice of indices, the most important question for the measurement of inequality is obviously the availability of sources. The only way to obtain a comprehensive view of inequality is to compare different sources (including national accounts, household surveys, and fiscal data), which shed complementary light on different segments of the distribution. Experience has shown that fiscal data, though highly imperfect, generally improve the quality of measurement substantially by correcting the data at the top end of the distribution (which surveys always seriously underestimate). This is true even in countries where the fiscal authorities lack the means to control fraud and where income tax data are rudimentary. For instance, as we saw in Chapter 12, although tax data from Russia and China are seriously incomplete and unsatisfactory, we were able to use this information to make substantial upward revisions to official inequality measures (based exclusively on surveys), yielding more plausible (though still probably low) estimates. In India and Brazil, thanks to the help of many researchers, citizens, and journalists, governments and agencies recently agreed to open up previously inaccessible records, and this has added to our knowledge of income inequality in those countries.[21] Similarly, recent work on Lebanon, Ivory Coast, and Tunisia has shown that the use of tax data resulted in considerable improvement over previously available measures of inequality.[22] In all these countries, data from current income tax reports—though flawed and disregarding the fact that much income probably goes untaxed—led to substantial upward revisions of official measures of

---

21. On the case of India, see L. Chancel and T. Piketty, "Indian Income Inequality 1922–2015: From British Raj to Billionaire Raj?" WID.world, 2017. India stands out for having completely ceased to publish fiscal statistics from 2002 to 2016 at the height of the "information age." On Brazil, see M. Morgan, "Falling Inequality Beneath Extreme and Persistent Concentration: New Evidence on Brazil Combining National Accounts, Surveys and Fiscal Data, 2001–2015," WID.world, 2017. This work has revealed strong growth in top income shares in recent years. In the case of the United States, the use of tax data has demonstrated the historic rise of inequality in recent decades. See T. Piketty and E. Saez, "Income Inequality in the U.S., 1913–1998," *Quarterly Journal of Economics,* 2003; T. Piketty, E. Saez, and G. Zucman, "Distributional National Accounts: Methods and Estimates for the United States," *Quarterly Journal of Economics,* 2018.
22. See L. Assouad, "Rethinking the Lebanese Economic Miracle: The Concentration of Income and Wealth in Lebanon 2005–2014," WID.world, 2017; L. Czajka, "Income Inequality in Cote d'Ivoire 1985–2014," WID.world, 2017; R. Zighed, "Income Inequality in Tunisia 2003–2016," WID.world, 2018.

inequality. It should therefore be clear that widely used official measures, based as they often are on self-declared household surveys, understate inequality to a significant degree, and this systematic distortion can substantially bias public debate.[23]

The use of tax sources, however imperfect, can also reveal poor enforcement of tax laws and inefficiency in their application. Research can thus equip society with the tools to mobilize and demand better fiscal enforcement. Take China, for example. If the authorities were to publish data on the number of taxpayers in each income bracket, in city after city and year after year, with details about the sources of income for those in the highest brackets, it would no doubt be possible to fight corruption more effectively than with the methods currently being used. Fiscal transparency links the measurement of inequality to the challenge of mobilizing people politically to transform the government.

Unfortunately, pressuring governments and tax authorities to open up their tax records is not enough to resolve all the problems. There is another issue: the evolution of the international fiscal and legal system has also reduced the quality of the available data. The free circulation of capital in conjunction with the absence of adequate international coordination on tax-related matters (and especially the lack of any requirement to share information about cross-border wealth holdings) has led some countries, especially in Europe, to adopt special preferential rules for taxing capital income (such as flat tax systems). In practice, this has resulted in a deterioration in the quality of sources that allow us to link an individual's labor income to his or her capital income. This impoverishment of the European sources does not augur well for what is likely to happen in less wealthy countries. The difficulty of measuring income inequality is only compounded when it comes to measuring wealth inequality, about which even less is known, as we will see shortly.

Social Justice, Climate Justice

Let us take a closer look at the notion of income, whose inequality we are trying to measure, and in particular at the difficulties we encounter when we try to account fully for the degradation of the environment. To measure a country's

---

23. By "official" measures I mean measures published by government statistical agencies. I should note explicitly that blame for the resulting lack of transparency lies with the political authorities and the flaws in available tax data; it is not the fault of the people working for these statistical agencies, who are often the first to demand better access to the sources.

economic prosperity, it is broadly preferable to rely on national income rather than GDP. Recall the key differences between the two: national income is equal to GDP minus depreciation of capital (also called consumption of fixed capital) plus net income from abroad (or minus net outflow, as the case may be). For example, a country whose entire population was occupied reconstructing a capital stock destroyed by a hurricane could have a high GDP but zero national income. The same would be true if all the country's output went abroad to remunerate the owners of its capital. The notion of GDP reflects a production-centered view and does not worry about the degradation of capital (including natural capital) or about the distribution of income and wealth. For these various reasons, national income is clearly a more useful notion. It is also more intuitive: national income per capita corresponds to the average income that citizens of the country actually earn.[24]

The problem is that available estimates do not allow us to correctly measure the depreciation of natural capital.[25] In practice, official national accounts do register an upward trend in the depreciation of capital. Globally, consumption of fixed capital amounted to slightly more than 10 percent of global GDP in the 1970s but rose to nearly 15 percent in the late 2010s.[26] In other words, national income was about 90 percent of GDP in the 1970s but only 85 percent

---

24. National income is also called "net national product" or "net national income" (as opposed to "gross national product" or "gross national income," which takes foreign income into account but does not deduct consumption of capital). For a brief history of these terms and of national accounting, see Piketty, *Capital in the Twenty-First Century,* chap. 1. National income per capita corresponds to average income before taxes and transfers. It is also equal to average income after taxes and transfers if one considers public expenditures on education, health, and so on as transfers in kind.

25. This is only the most serious problem; there are others about which I do not have the space to elaborate here. In particular, the question of the boundary between private household consumption and so-called intermediate consumption by firms (which in practice can be used as additional private consumption and is not taken into account in the calculation of national income or inequality, even though the phenomenon can assume massive proportions at the top of the distribution) might deserve much more attention in the future. It is quite possible that this bias leads to significantly underestimating inequality.

26. This upward trend is observed in all regions, especially in the rich countries. See T. Blanchet and L. Chancel, "National Accounts Series Methodology," WID.world, 2016, fig. 2.

today.[27] This rising depreciation reflects the accelerated obsolescence of certain types of equipment, such as machinery and computers, which need to be replaced more often today than in the past.[28]

In principle, these estimates should also include the consumption of natural capital. In practice, this runs into difficulties of several kinds. Consider, first, available estimates of annual extraction of natural resources from 1970 to 2020, including hydrocarbons (oil, gas, coal), minerals (iron, copper, zinc, nickel, gold, silver, etc.), and wood. It turns out that these flows were substantial (generally 2–5 percent of global GDP, depending on the year) and that they varied considerably with time (as prices changed) and country. Calculations are based on the annual value of the material extracted net of any replenishment (very slow for hydrocarbons and minerals, somewhat less so for forests). Many uncertainties bedevil the data.[29]

---

27. By definition, net national income from and to other countries balances out at the global level (provided that one includes flows passing through tax havens). In practice, these net foreign income flows (which are primarily flows of capital income and secondary flows of income form temporary labor abroad) are less important than depreciation: they are generally between −2 and +2 percent of GDP, and usually between −1 and +1 percent. There are, however, countries where so much of the capital is owned by foreign investors that the outflows are larger: 5–10 percent of GDP or even more (these are usually poor countries, in sub-Saharan Africa, for example). They may also be countries that relied heavily on foreign investment, such as Ireland, where the outflow exceeds 20 percent of GDP, and, by contrast, countries where inflows can go as high as 5–50 percent of GDP, such as France and the United Kingdom in the Belle Époque or oil-exporting countries such as Norway today. See the online appendix.

28. For a capital stock on the order of 500 percent of GDP, a consumption of fixed capital of 10 percent corresponds to an average depreciation of 2 percent per year, while a consumption of fixed capital of 15 percent per year corresponds to an average depreciation of 3 percent per year. In practice, depreciation varies considerably with asset type: it may be less than 1 percent a year for buildings or warehouses and more than 20–30 percent a year for certain types of machinery.

29. Net annual extractions can go as high as 10–20 percent of GDP for petroleum-exporting countries and many poor countries (especially in Africa). See the online appendix for the available series and associated uncertainties. See also E. Barbier, "Natural Capital and Wealth in the 21st Century," *Eastern Economic Journal,* 2016; E. Barbier, *Nature and Wealth: Overcoming Environmental Scarcity and Inequality* (Palgrave, 2015). See also G. M. Lange, Q. Wodon, and K. Carey, *The Changing Wealth of Nations 2018: Building a Sustainable Future* (World Bank, 2018), p. 66, fig. 2B3.

The first problem is to evaluate these flows in terms of market values, which is probably not the best choice. The social cost of natural resource extractions should be factored in, especially the impact of CO_2 and other greenhouse gas emissions on global warming. Such estimates are by their nature highly uncertain. In 2007, the *Stern Review* estimated that global warming could eventually reduce global GDP by 5 to 20 percent.[30] The acceleration of global warming over the past decade could lead to even larger snowball effects.[31] As noted in Chapter 12, it is not clear that it always makes sense to try to quantify things in monetary terms. In this case, it might be a better idea to set climate targets that are not to be exceeded and then to deduce the consequence in terms of maximum permissible emissions and the policies needed to meet that goal, including (but not limited to) setting a "price on carbon" and imposing a carbon tax on the worst polluters. In any case, it is essential to reason in the future in terms of national income rather than GDP growth and to account for the consumption of fixed capital on the basis of plausible estimates of the true social cost of natural resource extraction (possibly with a range of estimates based on different methodologies).[32]

The second difficulty is that national accounts as developed to date include natural resources only from the point at which they begin to be exploited economically. In other words, if a company or a country begins exploiting a deposit in 2000 or 2010, the value of the reserves in question generally appears in estimates of public or private wealth in official national accounts only as of 2000 or 2010.[33] It will not appear in estimates for 1970 or 1980, even though

---

30. See N. Stern, *The Stern Review: The Economics of Climate Change* (Cambridge University Press, 2007).

31. See, for example, V. Masson-Delmotte et al., eds., *Global Warming of 1.5°C* (Intergovernmental Panel on Climate Change [IPCC], 2018), and all the reports of the IPCC/GIEC at www.ipcc.ch.

32. Using national income instead of GDP was one of the recommendations in J. Stiglitz and Members of a UN Commission of Financial Experts, *The Stiglitz Report: Reforming the International Monetary and Financial Systems in the Wake of the Global Crisis* (The New Press, 2010), but thus far to no effect.

33. The notion of national wealth accounts (which include stocks of assets and liabilities of various economic actors as opposed to traditional national accounts, which focus on annual flows of output and income) is fairly new and evolving rapidly. It was generalized at the international level by the new System of National Accounts (SNA) standards adopted in 1993 and 2008. It is still being developed in many countries and will evolve in the future as various social, economic, and political actors mobilize. See the online appendix.

the deposit in question was obviously already there. This has the potential to severely distort the measure of the evolution of total private wealth (as a percentage of national income or GDP) over the entire period.[34] Research under way in countries rich in natural resources (such as Canada) shows that this is enough to completely transform the long-term picture; some data series need to be recalculated retrospectively.[35] This illustrates once again a conclusion I have already emphasized several times—namely that the increase in the total value of private property often reflects an increase in the power of private capital as a social institution and not an increase in "the capital of mankind" in the broadest sense.

We encounter the same set of issues with respect to the private appropriation of knowledge. If a company were some day to obtain the rights to the Pythagorean theorem and begin collecting royalties from every schoolchild using it, its stock market capitalization would probably be substantial, and total global private wealth would increase accordingly, even more so if other aspects of human knowledge could be similarly appropriated. Nevertheless, mankind's capital would not increase one iota, since the theorem has been known for millennia. This hypothetical case might seem extreme, but it is not dissimilar to that of private companies like Google, which has digitized public libraries and archives, opening up the possibility of some day billing for access to resources that were once free and public and thereby generating significant profits (potentially far beyond the investment required). Indeed, the stock market value of technology firms includes patents and knowhow that might not exist were it not for basic research financed with public money and accumulated over decades. Such private appropriation of common knowledge could increase dramatically in the coming century. What happens will depend on the evolution of legal and tax systems and on the social and political response.[36]

---

34. See Fig. 10.8, and the online appendix.
35. See the online appendix. See also E. Barbier, "Natural Capital and Wealth in the 21st Century."
36. See A. Kapczynski, "Four Hypotheses on Intellectual Property and Inequality" (Yale Law School, Working Paper Prepared for the SELA Conference, July 11–14, 2015); G. Krikorian and A. Kapczynski, *Access to Knowledge in the Age of Intellectual Property* (Zone Press, 2010). See also J. Boyle, "The Second Enclosure Movement and the Construction of the Public Domain," *Law and Contemporary Problems,* 2003; D. Koh, R. Santaeulàlia-Llopis, and Y. Zheng, "Labor Share Decline and Intellectual Property Products Capital," working paper, 2018.

On Inequality of Carbon Emissions Between
Countries and Individuals

Finally, the third and probably most important difficulty is that it is imperative to take environmental inequalities into account, both in terms of damages caused and damages suffered. In particular, carbon emissions are not solely the responsibility of the countries that produce hydrocarbons or the countries that host factories generating significant emissions. Consumers in the importing countries, particularly the wealthiest of them, bear part of the responsibility as well. By using available data on the income distribution in various countries together with surveys that allow us to associate income with consumption profiles, it is possible to estimate how responsibility for carbon emissions is distributed among the world's people. The principal results are shown in Fig. 13.7. These estimates reflect both direct emissions (from transportation and home heating, for example) and indirect emissions; that is, emissions incurred in the use and production of goods consumed by individuals in different countries as well as in the shipment of those goods from the place of origin to the place of consumption.[37] Looking at all carbon emissions in the period 2010–2018, we find that North America and China are each responsible for about 22 percent of global emissions, Europe for 16 percent, and the rest of the world for about 40 percent. But if we focus on individuals responsible for the heaviest emissions, the distribution changes completely. The 10 percent of the world's people responsible for the highest emissions emit on average 2.3 times the global average; together they account for 45 percent of global emissions. Of these emissions, North America represents 46 percent, Europe 16 percent, and China 12 percent. If we look at emissions greater than 9.1 times the global average, which gives us the top centile of emitters (who account for 14 percent of total emissions, more than the bottom 50 percent combined), North America (essentially the United States) represents 57 percent, versus 15 percent for Europe, 6 percent for China, and 22 percent for the rest of the world (including 13 percent for the Middle East and Russia and barely 4 percent for India, Southeast Asia, and sub-Saharan Africa).[38]

---

37. For a detailed account of methods and results, see also L. Chancel and T. Piketty, "Carbon and Inequality: From Kyoto to Paris. Trends in the Global Inequality of Carbon Emissions and Prospects for an Equitable Adaptation Fund," WID.world, 2015. See also L. Chancel, *Insoutenables inégalités. Pour une justice sociale et environnementale* (Les petits matins, 2017).
38. For results by country, see Chancel and Piketty, "Carbon and Inequality," table E4.

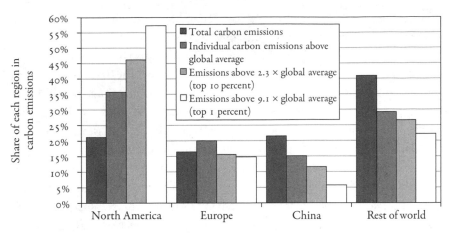

FIG. 13.7. The global distribution of carbon emissions, 2010–2018

Interpretation: The share of North America (United States and Canada) in total (direct and indirect) carbon emissions is 21 percent on average in 2010–2018 but 36 percent if one looks at individual emissions greater than the global average (6.2 tonnes CO_2 per year), 46 percent for emissions above 2.3 times the global average (the top 10 percent of world emitters, responsible for 45 percent of all emissions, compared to 13 percent for the bottom 50 percent of world emitters), and 57 percent of those emitting more than 9.1 times the global average (the top 1 percent of emitters, responsible for 14 percent of all emissions). *Sources and series:* piketty.pse.ens.fr/ideology.

This extremely high concentration of the highest emitters in the United States is a result of both higher income inequality and a way of life that is particularly energy intensive (owing to large homes, highly polluting vehicles, and so on). Of course, these results alone will not persuade people around the world to agree on who should make the greatest effort. In the abstract, given the facts about who is to blame, it would not be illogical for the United States to compensate the rest of the world for the damage it has done to global well-being, which is potentially considerable (bearing in mind that global warming may eventually lead to a loss of 5–20 percent of global GDP, if not more). In practice, it is quite unlikely that the United States would spontaneously undertake to do this. By contrast, it is not totally fanciful to think that the rest of the world might some day demand an accounting and impose sanctions to compensate for the damage it has suffered. To be sure, the extent of the damage due to global warming is such that this could lead to violent political tensions between the United States and the rest of the world.[39] In any case, the search for a

39. In particular, it would be naïve to think that the balance of power (including its military aspects) will play no role. US president Donald Trump regularly explains

compromise and for norms of justice acceptable to the majority will necessitate shared awareness of how emissions are distributed globally.

The high level of individual emissions inequality also has consequences for climate policy at the national level. It is often argued that the best way to combat global warming is to levy a carbon tax proportional to emissions together with setting building and pollution standards and investing in renewable energy. For instance, a recent report suggested that carbon dioxide emissions should be taxed at a rate of up to $100 a ton between now and 2030 to meet the criteria set by the Paris Accords of 2015.[40] That is, each country should set up an additional tax of $100 per ton on all emissions.[41] The problem with such a proportional tax on carbon is that it can be quite socially unjust, both within and between countries. In practice, many households with low to middling incomes are required to spend a higher proportion of their income on transportation and heating than are wealthier households, particularly in areas where there is inadequate or no mass transportation or where homes are not insulated. A better solution would be to levy a higher tax on those who produce higher levels of emissions. For instance, one might offer an exemption to households emitting less than the global average and place a tax of $100 a ton on emissions above the average, then $500 a ton on emissions above 2.3 times the average and $1,000 (or more) on emissions above 9.1 times the average.

I will come back to the question of a progressive carbon tax in Chapter 17, where I consider what a just tax system might look like. At this stage, note simply that no policy will succeed in combating global warming unless it tackles

---

that global warming is a fantasy invented to extract a ransom from his country and demands that his "allies" pay a high price for the military shield generously provided by the United States. Nevertheless, the relative importance of the United States (which currently accounts for 4 percent of the world's population and 15 percent of global GDP) will decline in the decades to come so that economic and commercial rules developed by the rest of the world will become increasingly important.

40. N. Stern and J. Stiglitz, *Report of the High-Level Commission on Carbon Prices* (Carbon Pricing Leadership Coalition, 2017).

41. In practice, there is major confusion associated with the fact that the carbon tax is supposed to be added to existing taxes on energy (such as the gas tax), which allegedly correct other negative effects of energy usage (such as air pollution and traffic jams). The problem is that all of this is usually fairly opaque and raises suspicions that the government is using the environment as an excuse to raise taxes to finance priorities unrelated to the environment (which unfortunately is frequently the case).

the issues of social and fiscal justice. There are several ways to work toward a progressive, durable, and collectively acceptable carbon tax. At a minimum, all proceeds of the carbon tax must be put toward financing the ecological transition, particularly by compensating the hardest-hit low-income families. One could also explicitly exempt electricity and gas consumption up to a certain threshold and impose higher taxes on those consuming more than the limit. And one could set higher taxes on goods and services associated with elevated emissions: air travel, for example.[42] What is certain is that if one does not take inequality seriously, major misunderstanding is likely, and this could block any hope of achieving an effective climate policy.

In this respect, the so-called revolt of the *gilets jaunes,* or yellow vests, in France in late 2018 is especially emblematic. The French government had planned to increase its carbon tax sharply in 2018–2019 but chose to abandon the idea in the wake of this violent protest movement. The affair was particularly badly handled, almost to the point of caricature. Only a small part (less than a fifth) of the additional carbon tax revenues were to be applied to the ecological transition and measures of compensation, with the rest going to finance other priorities, including major tax cuts for the social groups with the highest income and greatest wealth.[43]

Note, too, that the various forms of carbon tax currently levied in France and Europe contain numerous exemptions. For instance, kerosene is totally exempt from the carbon tax under European competition rules. What this means is that people of modest means who drive to work every morning must pay the full carbon tax on the gasoline they use, but wealthy people who fly off for a weekend vacation pay no tax on the jet fuel they consume. In other words, the carbon tax is not even proportional: it is hugely and blatantly regressive, with lower rates on those responsible for the highest emissions. Examples like this, widely publicized during the winter 2018–2019 protests in France, played an important role in persuading demonstrators that French climate policy was mainly a pretext to force them to pay higher taxes and that

---

42. In view of observed usage patterns of air travel by country and income group, a proportional tax on air tickets would yield a distribution close to that of a carbon tax applicable only to consumers responsible for more than the global average level of emissions. For a more progressive result, one would have to assess a higher tax on frequent travelers. See Chancel and Piketty, "Carbon and Inequality," table E4, and the online appendix.

43. Owing to the elimination of the wealth tax (ISF) and its replacement by a real estate tax (IFI). I will say more about this in the next chapter.

French and European authorities cared more about the haves than the have-nots.[44] Of course, no matter what climate policy is adopted, there will always be people who oppose it. Clearly, however, it only strengthens the opposition if no effort is made to design a more just carbon tax. What this episode shows is once again the crucial need for new forms of transnational taxation, in this instance a true European tax system. If European governments continue to operate as they have always done—on the principle that the benefits of fiscal competition always outweigh the (real but manageable) costs and complications of a common tax policy—they will very likely face further tax revolts in the future and fatally compromise their climate policy. By contrast, the political movement to do something about climate change, which is gaining strength among the young, might change the political equation regarding democratic transparency and transnational fiscal justice.

On the Measurement of Inequality and the Abdication of Governments

It is paradoxical that in the so-called age of big data, public data on inequality are so woefully inadequate. Yet that is the reality, as is clear from the extreme difficulty of measuring the distribution of wealth. I alluded earlier to the inadequacy of the data on income distribution. The situation is even worse with respect to wealth, especially financial assets. To put it in a nutshell, statistical agencies, tax authorities, and, above all, political leaders have failed to recognize the degree to which financial portfolios have been internationalized and have not developed the tools needed to assess the distribution of wealth and to follow its evolution over time. To be clear, there is no technical obstacle to developing such tools; it is purely a political and ideological choice, the reasons for which we will try to unravel.

Of course it is possible, by exploiting and systematically comparing all currently available sources (national accounts, survey data, and tax records), to paint in broad strokes the way in which the concentration of wealth has evolved in the various regions of the world. The main results are shown in Figs. 13.8 and 13.9, which describe the evolution of the top decile and top centile shares of total wealth in France, the United Kingdom, the United States, India, China, and Russia. The oldest series are from France, where abundant estate tax rec-

---

44. Another oft-cited example was the exemption for fuel used by international freighters.

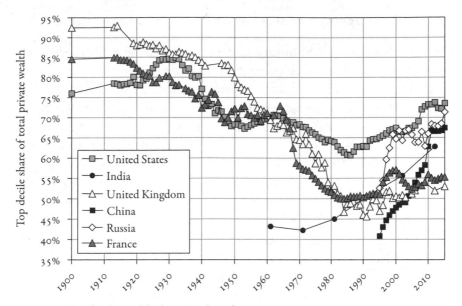

FIG. 13.8. Top decile wealth share: Rich and emerging countries

Interpretation: The top decile share of total private wealth (real estate, professional and financial assets, net of debt) has increased sharply in China, Russia, India, and the United States since the 1980s and increased to a lesser degree in the United Kingdom and France. *Sources and series:* piketty.pse.ens.fr/ideology.

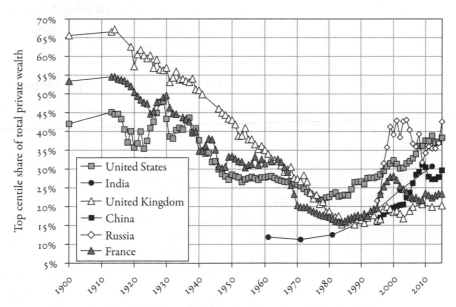

FIG. 13.9. Top centile wealth share: Rich and emerging countries

Interpretation: The top centile share of total private wealth (real estate, professional and financial assets, net of debt) has increased sharply in China, Russia, India, and the United States since the 1980s and increased to a lesser degree in the United Kingdom and France. *Sources and series:* piketty.pse.ens.fr/ideology.

ords enable us to trace the history all the way back to the French Revolution (see Chapter 4). The available sources concerning the United Kingdom and other European countries (such as Sweden) are less precise but also enable us to work back to the beginning of the nineteenth century (see Chapter 5). For the United States, the data take us back to the late nineteenth and early twentieth centuries, and the quality improves after the creation of the federal estate tax in 1916. In India, the available sources (mainly surveys of estates) begin in the 1960s. In China and Russia, it is only since the wave of privatizations in the 1990s that it has become possible to analyze the evolution of the wealth distribution.

The big picture is relatively clear. In the Western countries, the concentration of wealth diminished sharply after World War I and remained low until the 1970s, then turned upward in the 1980s.[45] Wealth inequality rose more in the United States and India than in France or the United Kingdom, as did income inequality. The increase in the concentration of wealth was particularly large in China and Russia in the wake of privatization. While this overall pattern is well established, it is important to keep in mind that there are many aspects of recent developments that remain unclear. Paradoxically, the data in Figs. 13.8–13.9 for the last three decades (1990–2020) are undoubtedly less accurate than the data for the entire period (1900–2020). This is partly because the quality of the sources is not as good as it used to be and partly because the authorities have not developed the tools needed to follow the internationalization of wealth.

As for income, the sources from which we can glean information about wealth are of several kinds. First, there are national accounts: by combining the balance sheets of firms with many surveys and inventories of production, wages, housing, and so on, statistical agencies produce estimates of GDP, national income, and financial and nonfinancial assets held by households, governments, and firms. In addition to problems associated with accounting for the degradation of national capital, which I discussed earlier, the main limitation of the national accounts is that, by design, they are concerned only with aggregates and averages and not with distribution. Nevertheless, they do provide the most complete and internationally comparable estimates of both total national income and total private and public wealth, and it is natural to begin with these

---

45. Recall that the concentration of wealth was very high in Europe throughout the nineteenth century and was even trending upward in the decades before World War I. See Figs. 4.1–4.2 and Figs. 5.4–5.5.

totals before delving into their distribution. Household surveys are one of the main sources for studying distributions. Their strength is that they pose dozens of questions about the composition of income and wealth as well as other individual characteristics not generally available in tax data (such as level of education and professional and family background). The disadvantage is that the answers that respondents give, in the absence of any sanction or verification, are often inaccurate, particularly at the top end of the distribution where income and wealth are generally hugely understated. This is already highly problematic when it comes to measuring income inequality, but with wealth, which is much more highly concentrated (with the top decile generally holding 50 to 90 percent), it is clearly crippling.

The most important surveys of wealth are conducted jointly by statistical agencies and central banks. This makes sense, given that central banks are the public institutions most directly concerned with the evolving structure of assets and liabilities. The monetary and financial policies of central banks have a major influence on the evolution of asset prices and yields as well as on their distribution at the individual level on the one hand and the firm and government level on the other. The oldest and most complete wealth survey is the Survey of Consumer Finances, which the US Federal Reserve has conducted every three to four years since the 1960s with tens of thousands of participating households. In Europe, the European Central Bank (ECB) has since 2006 coordinated wealth surveys in the various countries of the Eurozone with an eye to harmonizing methods and questionnaires, which were totally incompatible prior to the creation of the euro in 1999–2002.[46] In both the United States and Europe, central bank statisticians have made real efforts to improve the reliability of these surveys. Unfortunately, the task is beyond their reach. It is unfortunately impossible to measure the distribution of wealth, especially financial assets, properly on the basis of self-declared surveys. Despite all the efforts to improve the results, the total wealth declared in the Household Finance and Consumption Survey (HFCS) coordinated by the ECB is at most 50–60 percent of the total estimated in national accounts. This is primarily the result of understatement of wealth by respondents at the top of the distribution, particularly in regard to financial assets. In a nutshell, the ECB prints hundreds of billions of euros (indeed, trillions of euros, as we will see later) to influence the

---

46. The first wave of the Household Finance and Consumption Survey (HFCS) coordinated by the ECB was in 2010 and the second in 2014 (with about 80,000 participating households in various countries).

European economy and the formation of asset prices, but it does not know how to measure the distribution of all that wealth correctly.

Overcoming Opacity: A Public Financial Register

What is particularly distressing about this situation is that the problem can easily be solved by developing better tools. Indeed, it would suffice to correlate survey data with data from financial institutions and tax authorities concerning financial assets. Real estate ownership has long been recorded not only in deed registries but also by tax authorities charged with collecting the property tax in the United States or the real estate tax *(taxe foncière)* in France. One of the main institutional innovations of the French Revolution was to establish a national cadastre (property register) covering all real estate (agricultural and nonagricultural land, homes, buildings, warehouses, factories, shops, offices, and so on). Similar reforms were introduced in most countries: in a sense, this marked the birth of ownership society. The centralized state assumed responsibility for recording and protecting property rights, supplanting the noble and clerical classes that had previously regulated power and property relations in premodern trifunctional societies (see Chapters 3–4). This process coincided with the development of the legal infrastructures required to organize relations of exchange and production on a wider scale than in the past.

Financial assets are in fact recorded in various ways that could be tracked. The problem is that governments have largely left responsibility for this in the hands of private financial intermediaries. In each country (or continent) there are private institutions that serve as central repositories (custodian banks) for financial assets. Their function is precisely to keep track of the ownership of nonphysical assets issued by companies (such as stocks, bonds, and other financial instruments). The goal is to make sure that no two individuals can both claim ownership of the same financial assets, which for obvious reasons would complicate the workings of the economy. The best known custodian banks are the Depository Trust Company in the United States and Clearstream and Eurostream in Europe.[47] The fact that this function is discharged by private companies, which incidentally have in recent years drawn complaints about the opacity of their operations, raises a number of problems. Governments in the United States and Europe could easily decide to nationalize them or at a min-

---

47. The repository function is sometimes linked to the clearing house function, which is to facilitate secure transactions when assets are bought and sold.

imum to regulate them more closely to establish a true public register of financial assets. They could then establish rules to allow the identification of the ultimate holders of each asset (that is, the physical person exercising effective control, beneath the veil of shell companies and other complicated financial structures), which is not always the case today because of the way custodian banks operate.[48]

While it would be desirable for such a financial register to cover the widest possible expanse of territory—Europe, say, or Europe and the United States, or Europe and Africa, and ultimately the entire globe—it is important to point out that each state can make progress toward the final goal without waiting for others to act. Specifically, each country can immediately impose regulations on companies doing business within its borders. Each government could, for instance, require companies to provide detailed information about their stockholders. Indeed, rules of this sort exist already for both listed and unlisted firms, but they could be significantly reinforced and systematized in light of the possibilities offered by new information technologies.

Furthermore, tax authorities have for a long time required banks, insurance companies, and financial institutions to transmit information about interest, dividends, and other financial income received by taxpayers. In many countries, this information appears automatically in pre-filled tax statements sent to taxpayers for verification along with information about other third-party income (such as wages and pensions). The new technology makes it possible to automate monitoring procedures that were previously hit-and-miss. In principle, technology should make it possible to tabulate detailed information about financial income and the assets from which it derives. This information could be used both to ensure more efficient tax collection and to produce statistics on the distribution of wealth and its evolution.

To date, however, political choices have limited the potential positive effects of new technology. For one thing, bank reporting requirements often omit

---

48. On the (difficult but surmountable) technical problems in establishing a Global Financial Register (GFR), see Alvaredo et al., *World Inequality Report*, pp. 294–298. See also D. Nougayrède, "Towards a Global Financial Register? Account Segregation in Central Securities Depositories and the Challenge of Transparent Securities Ownership in Advanced Economies" (presentation, Columbia Law School Blue Sky workshop, April 2017). See also Piketty, *Capital in the Twenty-First Century*, pp. 518–524; G. Zucman, *The Hidden Wealth of Nations* (University of Chicago Press, 2015); T. Pogge and K. Mehta, *Global Tax Fairness* (Oxford University Press, 2016).

various forms of financial income subject to special rules.[49] Exemptions of this kind seem to have proliferated in recent decades, especially in Europe. In some cases, income from financial assets is taxed separately at a flat rate rather than the progressive rates applicable to other types of income (especially wages).[50] In theory, it should be entirely possible to separate the mode of taxation from the transmission of information. In practice, whenever financial income of a certain type—and especially a flat tax—is made subject to special rules, the relevant information generally disappears from tax statements and published statistics, thus decreasing the quality of the public data and democratic transparency as to capital income, even though modern information technology should have the opposite effect.[51] On top of that, there has been a clear degradation of the quality of inheritance data (which in some cases is disappearing), so it is no exaggeration to say that published wealth statistics have become much poorer in recent years.

Furthermore, the automatic transmission of information from banks to tax authorities is generally limited to the income from financial assets, whereas it could easily include information about the assets themselves. In other words, using information from financial institutions and real estate registries, the tax authorities could easily compile pre-filled wealth statements, just as the French authorities do now with income statements. Instead, the ECB and European statistical agencies rely entirely on self-declared wealth surveys so that it is com-

---

49. For instance, the pre-filled tax statements in use in France since the early 2010s omit interest and dividends on a form of investment called *assurance-vie* (a long-term financial investment that has been in widespread use in France for decades precisely because it benefits from tax exemptions and has nothing to do with "life insurance" in the usual sense), as long as certain requirements regarding holding duration are met. The rules themselves have varied over time, so that much of the value of this potentially useful source of information is lost.

50. "Dual taxation" of labor and capital income (with a flat rate on capital income) was adopted first in Sweden in 1991 after the banking crisis (see Chap. 11), then in Germany in 2009 and in France in 2018. In practice, these reforms often go along with continued exemptions for certain types of financial incomes (such as the *assurance-vie* in France).

51. For instance, the German reform of 2009 had the effect of hiding information about capital income and making it very difficult for researchers to gauge the evolution of total (income plus capital) income inequality. On this subject, see C. Bartels and K. Jenderny, "The Role of Capital Income for Top Income Shares in Germany," WID.world, 2015; C. Bartels, "Top Incomes in Germany, 1871–2014," WID.world, 2017, also published in *Journal of Economic History,* 2018.

pletely impossible to track the evolution of the composition of wealth (and especially financial assets) in the Eurozone; hence the ECB cannot even study the effects of its own policies. We find the same statistical backwardness in the United States. The Federal Reserve's wealth surveys, although more homogeneous and of overall better quality than their European counterparts, also rely entirely on self-declaration with no verification against bank or administrative data, which greatly limits accuracy, particularly when it comes to tracking the portfolios of the wealthiest taxpayers.

On the Impoverishment of Public Statistics in the Information Age

This situation is all the more surprising in that the use of tax and administrative data has become standard practice in the measurement of the income distribution. In the United States, there is a very broad consensus around the idea that self-declared income declarations are not sufficiently accurate and must be complemented by tax data from filed income tax returns. Indeed, it was the use of tax data that established the very sharp increase of inequality after 1980 (an increase that was underestimated in survey data). In Europe, many statistical agencies recognized the limitations of self-declared income surveys and therefore decided decades ago to move to a mixed model. One starts with survey data, which provides social, demographic, occupational, and educational data not available from tax records, but one then adds data from official tax records to provide accurate information about the income of the households responding to the survey. Since these official records reflect data transmitted by firms, government agencies, and financial institutions to the tax authorities, this mixed model is widely seen as more reliable and satisfactory than the self-declared model.[52] When it comes to wealth, however, the countries of Europe (as well as the United States) behave as though surveys alone suffice, even though the evidence shows that self-declared wealth is even less reliable than self-declared income.

How can we explain this, and, more generally, how can we explain why the era of "big data" and modern information technology has also witnessed an

---

52. The mixed model has been used by the National Institute of Statistics and Economic Studies in France since 1996 in its so-called ERFS surveys (employment surveys combined with tax data and information on social transfers). The Nordic countries also have a long tradition of using administrative and tax records in their surveys.

impoverishment of public statistics, especially regarding the measurement of wealth and its distribution?

Note first that this is a complex phenomenon, with multiple causes. For instance, when tax authorities moved to digital technology in the 1980s, this was in some cases accompanied by a paradoxical loss of statistical memory.[53] In my view, however, another piece of the explanation has to do with a certain political fear of transparency and the demands for redistribution that might result from it. Indeed, to lend credibility to the system I have just described (combining a public financial register with pre-filled wealth declarations), it would be ideal to link it to a tax on wealth. In the beginning, this could be a simple registration fee (of 0.1 percent per year or less, for instance), which each asset owner would be required to pay to record his or her ownership of the asset and thus enjoy the protections of the national and international legal system. The government would then have the tool it needs to make the distribution of wealth transparent, and this information would become available for public debate and democratic deliberation, which might (or might not) lead to more substantial progressive wealth tax rates or other redistributive policies.[54] Fear that events would take this course is, I think, one key reason why political leaders have been unwilling to support transparency about the distribution of wealth.

This unwillingness is extremely dangerous, I believe, not only for Europe and the United States but also for the rest of the world. Among other things, it takes away an essential tool for understanding the reality of inequality and developing policies to reduce it. These anti-democratic choices make it impossible to develop ambitious international egalitarian programs and ultimately hasten the retreat within the borders of the nation-state and the rise of identi-

---

53. In France and many other countries, the tax authorities ceased to publish the voluminous statistical bulletins that they had been assiduously publishing since the nineteenth century but no longer considered necessary for their own work because what they needed was stored in their computers. Unfortunately, they neglected the problem of storing those digital records for posterity so that there is paradoxically less information available for the post-1990 period than for previous eras. See the online appendix.

54. It would also be indispensable to release public information on the amounts of taxes actually paid (on assets as well as on asset incomes) by bracket of total wealth holdings. In principle, if automatic transmissions of banking information were adequately enforced, this type of information could be released by each tax administration as well as at the international level.

tarian reaction. Succinctly stated, if we do not acquire the transnational tools to reduce socioeconomic inequalities, and especially inequality of wealth, then political conflict will inevitably center on questions of national identity and borders. I will have much more to say about this in Part 4.

If the rejection of transparency is bad, how do we get beyond it? First, we need to gain a better understanding of its political-ideological roots. In general terms, the underlying ideology is fairly close to the proprietarian ideology that was dominant throughout the nineteenth and into the early twentieth centuries. Adherents stubbornly refused to open Pandora's box by questioning the distribution of wealth, for fear that once opened, it could never be closed again. One of the novelties of today's neo-proprietarianism is precisely that Pandora's box was opened in the twentieth century as many countries experimented with a variety of redistributive solutions. In particular, the failure of communism is regularly invoked in both postcommunist and capitalist countries as an object lesson—a warning as to where any ambitious redistributive project is likely to end up. But this is to forget that the economic and social success of the capitalist countries in the twentieth century depended on ambitious and largely successful programs to reduce inequality, and in particular on steeply progressive taxes (Chapters 10–11). Why has this lesson been forgotten? Lack of historical memory is one reason, and disciplinary divisions in the academy are another, but these can be overcome. In the twentieth century, exceptional one-time levies on the largest fortunes (in real estate and above all financial assets) played a crucial role in eliminating existing public debt and turning attention from the past to the future, especially in Germany and Japan. It may be tempting to say that the circumstances were unique and that these experiences cannot be repeated. But the reality is that extreme inequality recurs again and again; to deal with it, societies need institutions capable of periodically redefining and redistributing property rights. The refusal to do so in as transparent and peaceful a manner as possible only increases the likelihood of more violent but less effective remedies.

Neo-Proprietarianism, Opacity of Wealth, and Fiscal Competition

Neo-proprietarianism refuses to be transparent about wealth. Opacity is maintained by a specific set of legal and institutional arrangements, which allow free circulation of capital but require no common system of registration or taxation of property. For much of the nineteenth century, proprietarianism depended on censitary suffrage; that is, limited property-qualified access to the polls. Only the wealthiest people enjoyed the right to vote so that the risk of political redistribution of property was quite limited. Today, the international neo-proprietarian legal regime complements constitutional protections of property rights and in a sense serves as a substitute for the censitary system. The refusal of transparency is sometimes justified by the idea that data about property ownership could be used in nefarious ways by dictatorial governments. In Europe, however, this argument has little weight. European banks have long shared information with their countries' tax authorities, which enjoy reputations for neutrality in systems where the rule of law is unchallenged. The argument that transparency leads to government abuse reminds one of Montesquieu, the owner of the highly lucrative post of president of the Parlement of Bordeaux, who argued for maintaining the jurisdictional privileges of the nobility on the grounds that a centralized legal system would inevitably lead to despotism.[55]

A potentially more convincing argument, which has played a key role in the rejection of a common European tax system, is that taxes in Europe are already too high and that only intense fiscal competition among governments keeps them from increasing without limit. Besides being anti-democratic, this argument has numerous other problems. If Europeans could vote for common taxes in the framework of a common democratic assembly, it is by no means certain that they would vote for unlimited tax increases. It is just as likely that they would vote for a different tax system altogether: for example, a system that would tax high incomes and large fortunes more heavily in order to alleviate the burden on the lower and middle classes (a burden created by the continuous increase in indirect and direct taxes and contributions on wages and pensions). Bear in mind that there was enough trust among these same European states to establish a common currency and a powerful European Central Bank with the authority to create trillions of euros by simple majority vote of its Governing Council, with minimal democratic control. To reject transparency of ownership and common democratic taxes is particularly dangerous, since it also leaves the ECB itself in the position of conducting monetary policy without reliable data on the distribution of wealth in Europe and its evolution.[56]

---

55. See Chap. 3.
56. I will return to the subject of central banks (especially the ECB), whose primary function is to ensure the solvency and stability of the banking system and not to influence the distribution of wealth among households. Nevertheless, the actions of the central bank have a profound influence on asset prices and the distribution

In principle, progress toward greater transparency after the financial crisis of 2008 should have been facilitated by announcements made at various international summits (such as the G8 and G20) concerning the need to combat tax havens and fiscal opacity. Some countries did take concrete steps: for example, in 2010 the United States passed the Foreign Account Tax Compliance Act, which in theory requires financial institutions around the world to transmit to relevant tax authorities all information concerning their customers' bank accounts and asset holdings. In practice, such measures do not go far enough, however, and nothing has been done about replacing custodian banks with a public financial register. What efforts to date have demonstrated, though, is that progress is possible with adequate sanctions, such as the threat to cancel the licenses of Swiss banks to operate in the United States (which helped to eliminate some of the more glaring abuses). In this regard, Europe unfortunately stands out more for its declarations of good intentions than for real action. One important reason for this is that all decisions on tax matters in the European Union are stymied by the rule of unanimity.

In recent years Europe has been hit by a number of financial and fiscal scandals. For instance, in November 2014, the LuxLeaks story broke just as Jean-Claude Juncker was taking office as president of the European Commission. An international consortium of journalists published leaked documents from the period 2000–2012, which showed how the government of Luxembourg had entered into a series of confidential agreements (called tax letters) with private firms. Under the terms of these agreements, negotiated in private, large companies were granted the right to pay taxes below official rates (which were already quite low in Luxembourg). As it happens, the prime minister of Luxembourg from 1995 to 2013 was none other than Jean-Claude Juncker, who also served as the grand duchy's finance minister and as president of the Eurogroup (the council of finance ministers of the Eurozone).

No one was really surprised to learn that Luxembourg countenanced tax evasion—nor did this discovery prevent the European People's Party, an alliance of Christian Democratic and center-right parties, from designating Juncker as its candidate for the Commission presidency—but the scope of the practice was breathtaking. In Chapter 12, I noted that Chinese tax authorities publish no data to show that they are actually enforcing the ostensible tax code. What went on in Luxembourg was not very different. Caught red-handed, Juncker

---

of wealth, and it is not acceptable to conduct monetary policy with inadequate tools for measuring wealth.

admitted the facts of the case. He explained in substance that while these practices may not have been very satisfactory from a moral point of view, they were perfectly legal under Luxembourg's tax laws. In several interviews with European newspapers, he justified what was done on the grounds that Luxembourg had been hit hard by deindustrialization in the 1980s and needed a new development strategy for his country. What he hit upon was a strategy based on the banking sector, "tax dumping," financial opacity, and siphoning of tax revenues from Luxembourg's neighbors.[57] He promised not to do it again, however, and the leading parties of the European Parliament (including not only his own center-right party but also the liberals and the social democrats sitting on the center-left) chose to reward him with their confidence.

Similar consortiums of journalists subsequently broke other scandals, including Swiss Leaks in 2015 and the Panama Papers in 2016–2017, which disclosed widespread use of tax havens and other occult practices. These revelations demonstrated the extent of the cheating, even in countries reputed for efficient tax administration, such as Norway. Using data from the Swiss Leaks and Panama Papers in conjunction with Norwegian tax records (which were made available for study) and data from random tax audits, researchers were able to show that tax evasion was rare among people with little wealth but amounted to nearly 30 percent of the taxes due on the largest 0.01 percent of fortunes.[58]

In the end, it is hard to know how these various affairs affected European public opinion, especially in the case of Juncker, who occupied the highest political office in the European Union from 2014 to 2019. What is certain is that no decision was taken in those years to develop a public financial register, to harmonize taxes on the most mobile taxpayers, or in a more general sense, to take steps to make sure that such scandals would not happen again. All this

---

57. See interview with J. C. Juncker, "Le Luxembourg n'avait pas le choix, il fallait diversifier notre économie," *Le Monde,* November 28, 2014.
58. See A. Alstadsæter, N. Johannesen, and G. Zucman, "Who Owns the Wealth in Tax Havens? Macro Evidence and Implications for Global Inequality," *Journal of Public Economics,* 2018; A. Alstadsæter, N. Johannesen, and G. Zucman, "Tax Evasion and Inequality," *American Economic Review,* 2019; A. Alstadsæter, N. Johannesen, and G. Zucman, "Tax Evasion and Tax Avoidance" (University of California, Berkeley, Working Paper, 2019). See also Alvaredo et al., *World Inequality Report,* fig. 27.1, and G. Zucman, "Global Wealth Inequality," *Annual Review of Economics,* 2019, figs. 8–9.

created the impression that the fight for fiscal justice and for higher taxes on major economic actors was not really a priority for the EU. This is dangerous, in my view, because it inevitably encourages anti-European sentiment among the lower and middle classes and provokes nationalist and identitarian reactions from which nothing positive can come.

On the Persistence of Hyperconcentrated Wealth

Let us return now to the measurement of the concentration of wealth and its evolution. In the absence of a public financial register and information from financial institutions, we have to make do with incomplete data. Combining household surveys with income and inheritance tax data is the best way to proceed. The curves shown in Figs. 13.8–13.9 for the United States, France, and the United Kingdom are based on this mixed method. To test the consistency of the results, we also compared them with data from the very top end of the distribution provided by magazines such as *Forbes,* which has been compiling annual lists of the world's billionaires since 1987.

For the United States, the income tax method yields results quite close to those found by *Forbes* while the inheritance tax method yields a smaller (though still significant) increase (as does the uncorrected household survey).[59] There are two apparent reasons for this: first, the inheritance tax has been less carefully audited than the income tax in the United States since the 1980s,[60] and second, the so-called mortality multiplier method becomes less accurate as the population ages.[61] The capitalization method applied to the income tax data also suffers from certain limitations, and the results obtained are not entirely

---

59. For a detailed analysis, see E. Saez and G. Zucman, "Wealth Inequality in the United States since 1913: Evidence from Capitalized Income Tax Data," *Quarterly Journal of Economics,* 2016.

60. In particular, various ways of avoiding the estate tax—most notably the use of family trusts and other legal devices for reducing the value of estates or hiding them behind pseudo-philanthropic facades—are tolerated. It may also be that income taxes are more closely monitored because of their importance in financing the federal government.

61. The mortality multiplier method involves weighting inheritance tax data by the inverse of the mortality rate for each age tranche in the analysis, correcting for mortality differentials by class of wealth. The method works less well to the extent that mortality is concentrated in older age cohorts. See the online appendix.

satisfactory.[62] In general, both methods (mortality multiplier and capitalization) are second-best solutions: it would be far better to have direct information from financial institutions and tax authorities about the wealth of living taxpayers rather than be forced to make inferences from the amount of capital income and size of estates. For the United Kingdom, the tax data on capital income have deteriorated so much since the 1980s that one has to rely on estate tax data alone, whereas up to the 1970s one can use both methods and compare the results for consistency.[63] Finally, in the case of France, both methods yield similar evolutions, globally consistent with the *Forbes* classifications.[64] There has, however, been a dramatic deterioration in the quality of the inheritance tax data for France in recent decades.[65] To be sure, the situation is even worse in countries that have abolished the inheritance tax, where information is totally lacking.[66]

---

62. The capitalization method involves dividing data on capital income (interest, dividends, and so on) by the average rate of return for the associated asset. This method has the advantage of using available tax data concerning taxpayers with very high capital income (not well captured by household surveys), but it does not do a good job of accounting for differential yields within a given asset class. See the online appendix.

63. For a detailed analysis, see F. Alvaredo, A. Atkinson, and S. Morelli, "Top Wealth Shares in the UK over More Than a Century (1895–2014)," WID.world, 2016. For a meticulous comparison of the results obtained with both methods in the period 1920–1975, see A. Atkinson and A. Harrison, *The Distribution of Personal Wealth in Britain* (Cambridge University Press, 1978).

64. For a detailed analysis, see B. Garbinti, J. Goupille-Lebret, and T. Piketty, "Accounting for Wealth Inequality Dynamics: Methods and Estimates for France (1800–2014)," WID.world, 2017. Data from the wealth tax (ISF) indicate similar trends. See Chap. 14.

65. For many years the French inheritance tax data were among the best in the world. With this information it was possible to study the evolution of wealth concentration in France since the French Revolution (Chap. 4). After the inheritance tax was made progressive in 1901, the authorities published more detailed information on estate size, type of assets, age, kinship, and so on, from 1902 to 1964. Since the 1970s, however, the annual records have disappeared. The authorities now publish data only every four to five years, and the samples are too small and too mediocre in quality. As a result, we know less about inheritances in France today than we did a century ago. See the online appendix.

66. As is the case in Sweden since 2007 and Norway since 2014. The Nordic system for recording wealth, which used to be quite advanced, has been partially dismantled. The recent financial scandals may have begun to change this, but things are still far from where they should be. I will say more in Chap. 16 about the paradoxical situation of the Nordic countries.

All in all, despite these difficulties, the curves shown in Figs. 13.8–13.9 for the United States, United Kingdom, and France over the last few decades can be considered to be reasonably consistent and accurate, at least to a first approximation. For the other countries shown (China, Russia, and India), there is no sufficiently detailed income tax data (and there is no inheritance tax data at all), so we are reduced to using the *Forbes* classifications to correct the household survey data at the top end of the distribution.

The results obtained probably bear some resemblance to reality, but I want to stress how unsatisfactory it is to have to rely on such a nebulous "source." To be sure, published wealth rankings in all countries show dramatic changes in recent decades, and these changes on the whole seem consistent with what we are able to measure using other available sources. Note that, according to *Forbes,* the world's largest fortunes have grown at a rate of 6–7 percent a year (correcting for inflation) from 1987 to 2017—that is, three to four times as fast as average global wealth and roughly five times as fast as average income (Table 13.1).

Obviously, such differences cannot persist indefinitely unless one assumes that the share of global wealth owned by billionaires will eventually approach 100 percent, which is neither desirable nor realistic. Most likely, a political reaction will set in well before this occurs. The spectacular growth of large fortunes may have been accelerated by the privatization of many public assets between 1987 and 2017, not only in Russia and China but also in the Western countries and around the world, in which case this evolution may slow in coming years (to the extent that there are fewer and fewer assets to privatize). The legal imagination being what it is, however, it may not be a good idea to count on this. Furthermore, the available data suggest that the gap was equally large in the two subperiods, 1987–2002 and 2002–2017, despite the financial crisis, which suggests that there are deep structural factors at work. It is possible that financial markets are structurally biased in favor of the largest portfolios, which are able to earn real returns higher than others—as high as 8–10 percent a year for the largest US university endowments in recent decades.[67] Furthermore, all available evidence suggests that the world's largest fortunes have made very advantageous use of clever tax-avoidance strategies, which enable them to earn returns higher than smaller fortunes can.

The concepts and methods used by magazines like *Forbes* to establish these classifications are so vague and imprecise as to be useless for delving more deeply

---

67. See Chap. 10.

TABLE 13.1

The rise of top global wealth holders, 1987–2017

Average real annual growth rate, 1987–2017 (corrected for inflation)	World	US, Europe, China
The 1/100 millionth richest (*Forbes*)	6.4%	7.8%
The 1/20 millionth (*Forbes*)	5.3%	7.0%
The 0.01 percent richest (WID.world)	4.7%	5.7%
The 0.1 percent richest (WID.world)	3.5%	4.5%
The 1 percent richest (WID.world)	2.6%	3.5%
Average wealth per adult	1.9%	2.8%
Average income per adult	1.3%	1.4%
Total adult population	1.9%	1.4%
GDP or total income	3.2%	2.8%

Interpretation: From 1987 to 2017, the average wealth of the 100 millionth richest people in the world (about thirty out of 3 billion adults in 1987 and about fifty out of 5 billion in 2017) grew by 6.4 percent a year globally, and the average person's wealth grew by 1.9 percent a year. The skyrocketing of the largest fortunes was even more marked if one looks only at the United States, Europe, and China. *Sources and series:* piketty.pse.ens.fr/ideology.

into these questions.[68] The fact that the global debate about inequality is partly based on such "sources" and that even public authorities sometimes invoke them is symptomatic of a widespread failure of public institutions to meet the challenge of measuring wealth inequality.[69] These are key democratic issues, however, and the public has begun to take notice of them, including in the United States. There, as I noted in Chapter 11, rising inequality has led to calls for more progressive taxes and in turn to demands for greater statistical transparency.[70]

---

68. See Piketty, *Capital in the Twenty-First Century,* pp. 440–447.

69. The ECB has done some work to correct its HFCS survey with information about billionaires taken from magazines. See, for example, P. Vermeulen, *How Fat Is the Top Tail of the Wealth Distribution?* (European Central Bank, ECB Working Paper 1692, 2014). The attempt is interesting, but the result is far from satisfactory. It would be much better if European governments, tax authorities, and statistical agencies provided systematic and accurate data rather than rely on press surveys.

70. For example, the Schumer-Heinrich bill—Measuring Real Income Growth Act, introduced in Congress in 2018—seeks to require the federal government to establish distributional national accounts.

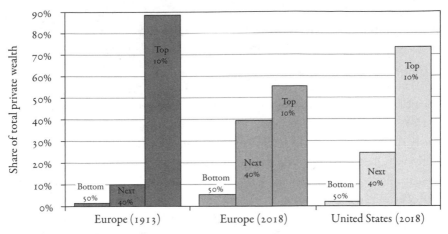

FIG. 13.10. The persistence of hyperconcentrated wealth

Interpretation: The top decile of private wealth owners in Europe owned 89 percent of all private wealth (average of the United Kingdom, France, and Sweden) in 1913 (compared with 1 percent for the bottom 50 percent), 55 percent in Europe in 2018 (compared with 5 percent for the bottom 50 percent), and 74 percent in the United States in 2018 (compared with 2 percent for the bottom 50 percent). *Sources and series:* piketty.pse.ens. fr/ideology.

To recapitulate, the resurgence of wealth inequality coupled with increased financial opacity is an essential feature of today's neo-proprietarian inequality regime. Although the twentieth century witnessed a deconcentration of wealth that allowed the emergence of a patrimonial middle class, wealth remained quite unequally distributed, with the bottom 50 percent of the distribution owning a negligible share of the total (Fig. 13.10). The sharp increase of the top decile share, especially in the United States, reflects a gradual and worrisome erosion of the share owned by the rest of the population. The lack of diffusion of wealth is a central issue for the twenty-first century, which may undermine the confidence of the lower and middle classes in the economic system—not only in poor and developing countries but also in rich ones.

On the Persistence of Patriarchy in the Twenty-First Century

The hypercapitalist societies of the early twenty-first century are quite diverse. Of course, they are connected to one another by the globalized and digitalized capitalist system. But every country also bears traces of its own particular political-ideological trajectory, whether it be social-democratic, postcommunist, postcolonial, or petro-monarchical. Generally speaking, today's inequality regimes combine elements of modernity and archaism. Some institutions and discourses are new, while others reflect a return to old beliefs, including a quasi-sacralization of private property.

Among the most archaic and traditionalist survivals is patriarchy. Most societies throughout history have known one form or another of male domination, especially with regard to political and economic power. This was obviously the case in premodern trifunctional society where warrior and clerical elites were also male, no matter what the civilization or religion. It was also the case in nineteenth-century proprietarian society. Given the increased role of the centralized state with its codes and laws, the scope of male domination in proprietarian society even grew or at any rate became more systematic in its application. Feminist demands raised during the French Revolution were quickly silenced and forgotten, and Napoleon's Civil Code of 1804 bestowed all legal power on the male paterfamilias and property owner, in all families, rich or poor, throughout France.[71] In many Western countries, including France, it was not until the 1960s and 1970s that married women were allowed to sign work contracts or open bank accounts without their husband's approval or that the law ceased to treat male and female adultery differently in divorce. The battle for women's right to vote was long and conflictual and is not over yet. Women were successful in New Zealand in 1893, in the United Kingdom in 1928, in Turkey in 1930, in Brazil in 1932, in France in 1944, in Switzerland in 1971, and in Saudi Arabia in 2015.[72]

With this lengthy history in mind, people sometimes imagine that a consensus exists today, especially in the West, concerning equality between men and women and that the issues of patriarchy and male domination are behind us. The reality is more complex. If one looks at the percentage of females among top earners (whether salaried or self-employed), one finds that women have indeed made progress. In France, the proportion of women among the top income centile increased from 10 percent in 1995 to 16 percent in 2015. The

---

71. In the United Kingdom the Reform Bill of 1832 (Chap. 5) made it clear that the right to vote was for men only, although there were (rare) cases of women who owned property (especially widows or single women) inscribed on voter lists in previous centuries, depending on local customs and power relations.

72. In some cases women's suffrage was granted in stages. In the United Kingdom, for example, women over the age of 30 who met a property ownership condition obtained the right to vote in 1918; in 1928 the conditions were changed to be the same as for men (over the age of 21 and no property qualification).

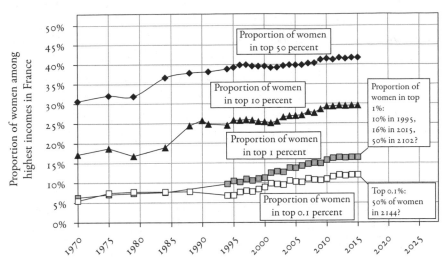

FIG. 13.11. The persistence of patriarchy in France in the twenty-first century

Interpretation: The proportion of women in the top centile of the labor income distribution (wages and nonwage labor income) rose from 10 percent in 1995 to 16 percent in 2015 and should reach 50 percent in 2102 if the 1994–2015 trend continues. For the top 0.1 percent, parity could be delayed until as late as 2144. *Sources and series:* piketty.pse.ens.fr/ideology.

problem is that this evolution has been extremely slow. If it continues in the coming decades at the same rate as in the period 1995–2015, women will account for half of the top income centile in 2102. If one does the same calculation for the top 0.1 percent, one finds that parity will not be achieved until 2144 (Fig. 13.11).

It is striking to note that the figures are almost exactly the same for the United States in terms of both level and rate of increase. Specifically, men accounted for 90 percent of the top income centile in 1990 and about 85 percent in the mid-2010s.[73] In other words, the very sharp increase in the share of national income going to the top centile primarily concerns men. In this respect, male domination is not going away any time soon. For all countries for which similar data are available, we find the same marked male dominance among the top income group and relatively slow progress toward parity.[74]

---

73. See Piketty, Saez, and Zucman, "Distributional National Accounts," fig. 7.

74. Unfortunately, limited access to sources means that we do not have perfectly comparable data for all countries. It is possible that more accurate data would reveal important differences. For instance, recent estimates for Brazil show that the proportion of women among the top income centile in the period 2000–2015 may be

There are several reasons for this slow progress. First, the historical prejudice against women is significant, particularly when it comes to holding positions of responsibility and power. I alluded earlier to experiments in India in which the same political speeches were read by male and female voices: those read by women were systematically judged to be less credible, but this bias was smaller in towns that had been led by a women because the post was "reserved" for a woman chosen by lot.[75]

It bears emphasizing, moreover, that the period 1950–1980 was a sort of golden age of patriarchy in Western culture. For the lower and middle class as well as the upper class, it was the era of the housewife as feminine ideal: the goal for every woman was to give up any thought of earning money through a professional career in order to stay at home with the children. Indeed, we are only just emerging from this period. In France in 1970, for example, women aged 30–55 earned on average one-quarter of what men earned for work outside the home. In other words, nearly 80 percent of all wages went to men because women suffered from both a lower rate of participation in the work force and lower pay if they did work.[76] It was a world in which women were responsible for domestic work and for bringing warmth and affection to the home in a cold industrial age but were de facto excluded from money matters. Of course, many tasks were assigned to women (especially childcare and other emotional labor), but managing the household budget was not one of them. The situation has evolved considerably since then, but the average pay gap remains quite high: to be sure, in 2015, it was "only" 25 percent at the beginning of working life in 2015, but owing to differences in career trajectories and opportunities for promotion, it was greater than 40 percent at age 40 and 65 percent at age 65, which also implies enormous inequalities of pension income.[77]

---

as high as 25–30 percent and hence significantly higher than in France or the United States. See M. Morgan, *Essays on Income Distribution Methodological, Historical and Institutional Perspectives with Applications to the Case of Brazil (1926–2016)* (PhD diss., Paris School of Economics and EHESS, 2018), p. 314, fig. 3.8.

75. See L. Beaman, R. Chattopadhyay, E. Duflo, R. Pande, and P. Topalova, "Powerful Women: Does Exposure Reduce Bias?" *Quarterly Journal of Economics,* 2009.

76. In self-employed occupations (farmer, craftsman, merchant), it was long the custom not to declare the wife's work, even if she worked the same hours as her husband (in addition to her household work), so that women enjoyed no pensions and no social rights.

77. The widely reported estimates of male-female wage gaps for a particular job on the order of 15–20 percent tend to underestimate these inequalities because by defini-

To accelerate the convergence process, proactive measures are needed. For example, one might consider quotas or "reservations" of certain jobs for women, as in India, not only for elective office (where such quotas already apply in many countries) but also for higher-level jobs in firms, government offices, and universities. There is also a need to rethink how working time is organized and how professional life relates to family and personal life. Many men who earn the highest pay rarely see their children, family, friends, or the outside world (even when they have the means to live otherwise, in contrast to less well-paid workers). Solving the problem by giving women incentives to live similar lives is not necessarily the best choice. Research has shown that the professions in which male-female equality has progressed the most are those in which work is organized so as to give individuals more control over their schedules.[78]

In addition, the increase in the concentration of wealth has had specific consequences for gender inequality. First, the division of assets among siblings or within couples has become particularly important. While there may in theory be laws requiring equal partition among brothers and sisters or between husbands and wives, there are many ways to get around them: for instance, through the evaluation of professional assets.[79] In countries like France, it has become increasingly common for couples to form between individuals who bring comparable amounts of property (and not just equivalent incomes and levels of education) to the marriage.[80] In a way, this represents a return to the world of Balzac and Austen, even if the level of patrimonial homogamy today is not

---

tion they do not take into account the fact that men and women do not fill the same jobs. For profiles of male-female inequality by age from 1970 to 2015, see the online appendix, Fig. S13.11. See also B. Garbinti, J. Goupille-Lebret, and T. Piketty, "Income Inequality in France: Evidence from Distributional National Accounts," WID.world, 2017 (also published in *Journal of Public Economics*, 2018), for detailed results.

78. See, for example, C. Goldin and L. Katz, *The Most Egalitarian of All Professions: Pharmacy and Evolution of a Family-Friendly Occupation* (National Bureau of Economic Research, NBER Working Paper 18410, 2012). On the role of family disruptions to career trajectories, see H. Kleven and C. Landais, "Gender Inequality and Economic Development: Fertility, Education and Norms," *Economica*, 2017.

79. C. Bessière and S. Gollac, "Un entre-soi de possédant·e·s. Le genre des arrangements patrimoniaux dans les études notariales et cabinets d'avocat·e·s," *Sociétés contemporaines*, 2017; C. Bessière, "Reversed Accounting. Legal Professionals, Families and the Gender Wealth Gap in France," *Socio-Economic Review*, 2019.

80. N. Frémeaux, "The Role of Inheritance and Labor Income in Marital Choices," *Population*, 2014.

as high as it was in the nineteenth century.[81] In view of the very rapid increase of professional homogamy in recent decades (also called assortative mating—a phenomenon that has played a very important role in the rise of inequality between couples in the United States and in Europe), it is entirely possible that patrimonial homogamy will continue to increase in the twenty-first century.[82]

The last few decades have also witnessed a very important parallel development of separate property both in marriages and civil unions. In theory, this could be a logical complement of greater professional equality between men and women and more distinctive career patterns.[83] In practice, given that income inequality within couples remains high—partly due to interruption of the wife's career following childbirth(s)—the shift to separate property has mainly benefited men. This phenomenon has contributed to a paradoxical increase of wealth inequality between men and women (especially after divorce or separation) since the 1990s, in contrast to the relative convergence of labor income.[84] These changes, which have been too little studied, once again illustrate the central role of the legal and tax systems in determining the structure of inequality regimes. They also show how wrong it would be to think that the movement toward greater gender equality is somehow "natural" and irreversible. In Part Four I will say more about the role of gender inequality in the evolution of political cleavages.

---

81. See P. Mary, *Inheritance and Marriage in Paris: An Estimation of Homogamy (1872–1912)* (master's thesis, Paris School of Economics and EHESS, 2018).

82. D. Yonzan, "Assortative Mating over Labor Income and Its Implication on Income Inequality: A US Perspective 1970–2017" (presentation, City University of New York, Inequality Seminar Series, 2018); B. Milanovic, *Capitalism, Alone: The Future of the System That Rules the World* (Belknap Press of Harvard University Press, 2019), p. 40, fig. 2.4.

83. In France, the default matrimonial regime (with marriage becoming less popular over time) is that community property is limited to goods acquired after marriage, which are shared equally (along with income) while property inherited or owned before the marriage remains separate. This asymmetry is usually justified by a strong division of labor and low professional income for the wife.

84. On these long-term evolutions, see N. Frémeaux and M. Leturcq, "Prenuptial Agreements and Matrimonial Property Regimes in France (1855–2010)," *Explorations in Economic History,* 2018; N. Frémeaux and M. Leturcq, "The Individualization of Wealth: Evidence from France" (Working Paper, 2016), https://lagv2017 .sciencesconf.org/file/310896.

On the Pauperization of Poor States and the Liberalization of Trade

We turn now to an issue of particular importance to the evolution of the global inequality regime in the twenty-first century: the relative and paradoxical pauperization of the poorest states in recent decades, particularly in sub-Saharan Africa and South and Southeast Asia. There has in general been a good deal of variation in the rate at which poor countries have closed the gap with rich countries since the 1970s. The China-India comparison has already been discussed at length. We saw that China not only grew faster than India but also generated less inequality, probably because it invested more in education, health, and necessary developmental infrastructure.[85] More generally, we have seen that economic development has historically always been closely associated with state building. The constitution of a legitimate government capable of mobilizing and allocating major resources while retaining the confidence of the majority is the fundamental prerequisite of successful development and the hardest to achieve.

In this connection, it is striking to discover that the poorest states in the world became poorer in the period 1970–2000; things improved very slightly between 2000 and 2020 but did not return to their initial level (which was already very low). More precisely, if we divide the countries of the world into three groups and look at the average tax revenues of the poorest group (which consists mainly of African and South Asian countries), we find that tax receipts fell from nearly 16 percent of GDP in 1970–1979 to less than 14 percent in 1990–1999 and then rose to 14.5 percent in 2010–2018 (Fig. 13.12). Not only are these extremely low levels; they also conceal important disparities. In many African countries, such as Nigeria, Chad, and the Central African Republic, tax revenues are just 6–8 percent of GDP. As noted when we analyzed centralized state formation in today's developed countries, this level of tax revenue is just enough to maintain order and basic infrastructure but not enough to finance significant investments in education and health care.[86] At the same time, we find that tax revenues in the richest countries (essentially in Europe and North America plus Japan) have continued to increase, rising from an average of about 30 percent of GDP in the 1970s to 40 percent in the 2010s.

---

85. See esp. Chaps. 8 and 12.
86. See Figs. 10.14–10.15.

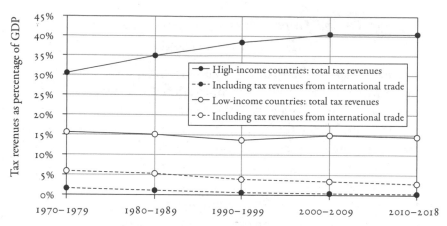

FIG. 13.12. Tax revenues and trade liberalization

Interpretation: In low-income countries (bottom third: sub-Saharan Africa, South Asia, etc.), tax revenues fell from 15.6 percent of GDP in 1970–1979 to 13.7 percent in 1990–1999 and 14.5 percent in 2010–2018, partly because of the uncompensated decrease in customs duties and other taxes on international trade (which brought in 5.9 percent of GDP in the 1970s, 3.9 percent in the 1990s, and 2.8 percent in 2010–2018). In high-income countries (top third: Europe, North America, etc.), customs duties were already very low at the beginning of the period and tax revenues continued to rise before stabilizing. *Sources and series:* piketty.pse.ens.fr/ideology.

To explain the peculiar trajectory of the poor countries, we must of course consider the fact that state building is a lengthy and complex process. In the late 1960s and early 1970s, most of the sub-Saharan African countries had just emerged from colonization. These newly independent states faced significant challenges in terms of internal and external consolidation, in some cases contending with separatist movements as well as rates of demographic growth that no Western country ever faced. The tasks were immense, and no one expected tax revenues to jump to 30 or 40 percent of GDP in the space of a few years (besides which there would have been undesirable effects had they done so). Nevertheless, the fact that tax revenues actually *decreased* between 1970 and 2000 (by nearly 2 percent of GDP) is a historical anomaly, which greatly handicapped the development of efficient social states in these countries in the crucial post-independence decades. This anomaly calls for an explanation.

Recent work has shown that this post-independence decrease of tax revenues was closely tied to an unusually rapid liberalization of trade, which was in part imposed by the rich countries and international organizations during the

1980s and 1990s, leaving the poor countries without the time or support necessary to replace what they used to take in as customs duties with new taxes (such as taxes on income or property).[87] In the 1970s, customs duties and other taxes on international trade accounted for a very large share of total tax revenue in the poor countries: nearly 6 percent of GDP. This was by no means an unusual situation: it was the same in Europe in the nineteenth century. Customs duties are the easiest taxes to collect, and it is natural to rely on them in the early phases of development. But the Western countries were able to reduce tariffs very gradually and at their own pace as they developed other types of taxes capable of replacing the revenue from customs duties while increasing total revenue. The poorest countries on the planet, especially in sub-Saharan Africa, faced a very different situation: their receipts from customs duties suddenly plunged to less than 4 percent of GDP in the 1990s and to less than 3 percent in the 2010s, and their governments were initially unable to make up for these losses.

My point is not to place the entire responsibility for what happened in Africa on the shoulders of the former colonial powers. The development of any tax system depends primarily on the nature of domestic sociopolitical conflict. Nevertheless, it was very difficult for the poorest countries in the world to resist the pressure of the rich countries for accelerated trade liberalization, especially in the ideological climate of the 1980s, which tended to disparage the state and progressive taxation, particularly under the so-called Washington consensus led by the US government and international organizations based in Washington (such as the World Bank and International Monetary Fund).

In a more general sense, it bears emphasizing that all the points previously made about the lack of economic and financial transparency in the rich countries have even more serious consequences in the poor countries. In particular, the regime of heightened fiscal competition and free capital flows without political coordination or automatic exchange of bank information—a regime promoted by the United States and Europe since the 1980s—has proved extremely undesirable and damaging for poor countries, especially in Africa. According to available estimates, assets held in tax havens represent at least 30 percent of total African financial assets—three times higher than in Europe.[88] It is not easy to persuade people to consent to taxes and construct new collective norms of fiscal justice in an environment where many of the

---

87. J. Cagé and L. Gadenne, "Tax Revenues and the Fiscal Cost of Trade Liberalization, 1792–2006," *Explorations in Economic History*, 2018.

88. See Fig. 12.5.

wealthiest taxpayers can avoid paying taxes by stashing their assets abroad and escaping to Paris or London if the necessity arises. On the other hand, an ambitious program of legal and fiscal cooperation with the rich countries and greater international transparency regarding financial assets and the profits of multinational firms could allow the poorest countries to develop their state and fiscal capacities under far better conditions than presently exist.

Will Monetary Creation Save Us?

One of the most dramatic changes since the financial crisis of 2008 is the new role of central banks in creating money. This change has profoundly altered perceptions of the respective roles of the state and central banks, taxes and money; more generally, it has changed the way people think about what a just economy means. Before the crisis, the prevailing wisdom was that it was impossible, or at any rate not advisable, to ask central banks to create huge amounts of money in a short space of time. In particular, this was the understanding on which Europeans agreed to create the euro in the 1990s. After the "stagflation" of the 1970s (a mixture of economic stagnation, or at any rate slow growth, with high inflation), it was not too difficult to convince people that the euro should be managed by a central bank with as much independence as possible and a mandate to keep inflation positive but low (under 2 percent) while interfering as little as possible in the "real" economy; these were the terms under which the Maastricht Treaty was agreed in 1992. After the crisis of 2008, however, central banks around the world suddenly took on a new role, sowing great confusion in Europe and elsewhere. It is important to understand what happened.

To clarify the terms of the discussion, let us begin by examining the evolution of the balance sheets of the principal central banks from 1900 to 2018 (Fig. 13.13). The balance sheet of a central bank lists all the loans it has made to other economic actors, generally through the banking system, and all the financial assets and securities (mainly bonds) it has purchased on financial markets. Most of these loans and bond purchases take place by way of purely electronic monetary creation by the central bank, without any actual printing of banknotes or minting of coins. To simplify the discussion and clarify the mechanisms involved, it is best to begin by imagining an entirely digital monetary economy—that is, an economy in which money exists only as virtual signs in bank computers and all transactions are settled electronically by credit card (which is not far from being the case already, so that describing today's real economy would require few changes to the description I will give here).

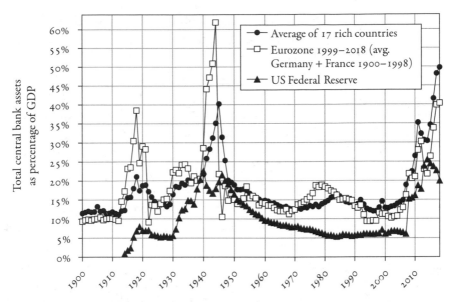

FIG. 13.13. The size of central bank balance sheets, 1900–2018

Interpretation: The total assets of the European Central Bank rose from 11 percent of Eurozone GDP on the last day of 2004 to 41 percent on the last day of 2018. The 1900–1998 curve is the average of the French and German central banks, with peaks of 39 percent in 1918 and 62 percent in 1944). The total assets of the Federal Reserve (created in 1913) rose from 6 percent of United States GDP in 2007 to 26 percent at the end of 2014. *Note:* The rich country average includes Australia, Belgium, Canada, Denmark, Finland, France, Germany, Holland, Italy, Japan, Norway, Portugal, Spain, Sweden, Switzerland, the United Kingdom, and the United States. *Sources and series:* piketty.pse.ens.fr/ideology.

On the eve of the financial crisis of 2007–2008, the balance sheet of the US Federal Reserve represented the equivalent of a little more than 5 percent of US GDP, while that of the ECB was close to 10 percent of Eurozone GDP. Both balance sheets consisted primarily of short-term loans to banks, usually with terms of a few days or at most a few weeks. Lending to banks in this way is the traditional function of a central bank in periods of calm. Deposits and withdrawals of funds from private bank accounts depend on the decisions of millions of individuals and businesses, so daily deposits and withdrawals never precisely balance each other to the exact dollar or euro. Banks therefore lend to one another on a very short-term basis to keep the payment system in balance, and the central bank maintains the stability of the whole system by injecting liquidity as needed. These loans—both interbank loans and loans from the central bank to private bank—are generally liquidated within a few days or weeks and leave no lasting trace. The whole business is a purely technical financial operation, essential to the stability of the system but generally of little interest to outside observers.[89]

After the bankruptcy of Lehman Brothers in September 2008 and the ensuing financial panic, things changed completely, however. The world's major central banks devised increasingly complex money-creation schemes collectively described by the enigmatic term "quantitative easing" (QE). In concrete terms, QE involves lending to the banking sectors for longer and longer periods (three months, six months, or even a year rather than a few days or weeks) and buying bonds issued by private firms and governments with even longer durations (of several years) and in much greater quantities than before. The Federal Reserve was the first to react. In September-October 2008 its balance sheet increased from the equivalent of 5 percent of GDP to 15 percent; in other words, the Fed created money equivalent to 10 percent of US GDP in a few weeks' time. This proactive stance would continue in subsequent years: the Fed's balance sheet had risen to 25 percent of GDP by the end of 2014; since then it has declined slightly, but it remains substantially larger than it was before the crisis (20 percent of GDP at the end of 2018 compared with 5 percent in mid-September 2008). In Europe the reaction was slower. The ECB and other European authorities took longer to understand that massive intervention by the central bank was the only way to stabilize financial markets and reduce the "spread" between the interest rates of the various Eurozone countries.[90] Since then, ECB purchases of public and private bonds have accelerated, however, and the ECB's balance sheet stood at 40 percent of Eurozone GDP at the end of 2018 (Fig. 13.13).[91]

There is a fairly broad consensus that this massive intervention by central banks prevented the Great Recession of 2008–2009, the worst downturn of

---

89. In particular, the fact that the ECB's balance sheet was twice that of the Fed on the eve of the crisis (a gap that continues to this day) mainly reflects the fact that banks and bank loans to firms play a more important role in financing the European economy (whereas the United States relies more on financial markets).

90. In large part this slow reaction by the ECB also explains the Eurozone debt crisis that began in 2009–2010 and the second dip in European economic activity in 2011–2012, while the US recovery continued. See Chap. 12 and the online appendix, Figs. S12.11–S12.12.

91. The ECB balance sheet was 4.7 trillion euros at the end of 2018 (or 40 percent of the Eurozone GDP, 11.6 trillion euros). For comparison, it was 1.5 trillion euros at the beginning of 2008, so 3.2 trillion euros were created in less than ten years. See the online appendix for detailed series.

the postwar period in the rich countries (with an average 5 percent decrease of activity in the United States and Europe), from turning into an even deeper crisis comparable to the Great Depression of the 1930s (which saw decreases of 20–30 percent in the major economies between 1929 and 1932). By avoiding cascading bank failures and acting as "lender of last resort," the Fed and ECB did not repeat the errors that the central banks committed in the interwar years, when orthodox "liquidationist" thinking (based on the idea that bad banks must be allowed to fail so that the economy can restart) helped push the world over the edge of the abyss.

That said, the danger is that these monetary policies, by avoiding the worst, gave the impression that no broader structural change in social, fiscal, or economic policy was necessary. Nevertheless, the fact is that central banks are not equipped to solve all the world's problems or to serve as the ultimate regulator of the capitalist system (let alone move beyond it).[92] To combat excessive financial deregulation, rising inequality, and climate change, other public institutions are necessary: laws, taxes, and treaties drafted by parliaments relying on collective deliberation and democratic procedures. What makes central banks so powerful is their ability to act extremely rapidly. In the fall of 2008, no other institution could have mobilized such massive resources in so short a time. In a financial panic, war, or extremely serious natural catastrophe, monetary creation is the only way for public authorities to act quickly on the scale required. Taxes, budgets, laws, and treaties require months of deliberation, to say nothing of the time required to assemble the necessary political majorities

---

92. It is interesting to note that the anti-liquidationist consensus of 2008 was in part a consequence of the "monetarist" reinterpretation of the crisis of 1929. In denouncing the Fed's tight-money policy and ensuing deflation in the early 1930s, Milton Friedman concluded that a proper monetary policy (designed to ensure steady moderate inflation) would have sufficed to avoid the Depression and restart the economy. In other words, no need for the New Deal, Social Security, or the progressive income tax to regulate capitalism: a wise Fed should be enough. In the United States in the 1960s—while some Democrats dreamed of completing the work of the New Deal but many people were beginning to worry about the decline of the United States relative to a then rapidly growing Europe—this simple, powerful political message had an enormous impact. The work of Friedman and the Chicago School encouraged suspicion of the growing role of the state and influenced the climate that led to the conservative revolution of the 1980s. See M. Friedman and A. Schwartz, *A Monetary History of the United States, 1857–1960* (Princeton University Press, 1963); and Piketty, *Capital in the Twenty-First Century,* pp. 547–553.

to support them; this may require new elections, with no guarantee of the outcome.

If the ability to act quickly is the strength of central banks, it is also their weakness: they lack the democratic legitimacy to venture too far beyond their narrow sphere of expertise in banking and finance. In the abstract, there is nothing to stop central banks from enlarging their balance sheets by a factor of ten or even more. Recall, for example, that total private wealth (comprising real estate and professional and financial assets, net of debt) in the hands of households in the 2010s was roughly 500–600 percent of national income in most of the rich countries (compared with barely 300 percent in the 1970s).[93] From a strictly technical standpoint, the Fed or the ECB could create dollars or euros worth 600 percent of GDP and attempt to buy all the private wealth of the United States or Western Europe.[94] But this would raise serious issues of governance: central banks and their boards of governors are no better equipped to administer all of a country's property than were the Soviet Union's central planners.

Neo-Proprietarianism and the New Monetary Regime

Without going quite that far, it is entirely possible that central bank balance sheets will continue to grow in the future, particularly in the event of a new financial crisis. It bears emphasizing that the financialization of the economy has attained phenomenal proportions in recent decades. In particular, the extent of cross-firm and cross-country financial holdings has increased significantly more rapidly than the size of the real economy and net capital. In the Eurozone, the total value of the financial assets and liabilities of the various institutional actors (financial and nonfinancial firms, households, and government) amounted to more than 1,100 percent of GDP in 2018 compared with barely 300 percent in the 1970s. In other words, even if the ECB balance sheet is now 40 percent of Eurozone GDP, this amounts to only 4 percent of the financial assets in circulation. In a sense, central banks have simply adapted to rampant financialization, and the increase in the size of their balance sheets has simply allowed them to maintain a certain capacity for action on the prices of financial assets, which has increased their tentacular reach many times over.

---

93. See Fig. 10.8, and the online appendix, Fig. S10.8.
94. In practice, some private owners would want to keep what they own so that this policy would result in an enormous increase of asset prices and therefore creation of money in excess of what would be necessary to acquire all private wealth.

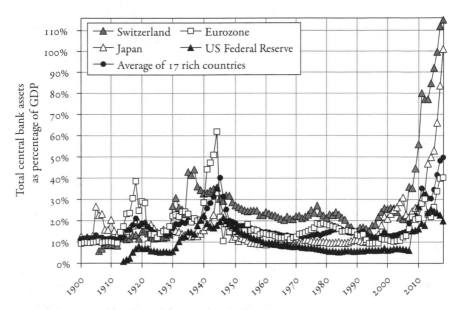

FIG. 13.14. Central banks and financial globalization

Interpretation: Total central bank assets of the rich countries rose from 13 percent of GDP on average on the last day of 2000 to 51 percent on the last day of 2018. The central bank assets of Japan and Switzerland exceeded 100 percent of GDP in 2017–2018. *Note:* The rich country average includes Australia, Belgium, Canada, Denmark, Finland, France, Germany, Holland, Italy, Japan, Norway, Portugal, Spain, Sweden, Switzerland, the United Kingdom, and the United States. *Sources and series:* piketty.pse.ens.fr/ideology.

If circumstances require, the ECB and Fed could be forced to go even farther. Indeed, the Bank of Japan and the Swiss National Bank both have balance sheets in excess of 100 percent of GDP (Fig. 13.14). This has to do with the peculiarities of each country's financial situation.[95] It is nevertheless impossible to rule out that similar things will someday happen to the Eurozone or the United States. Financial globalization has assumed such proportions that it may lead those responsible for setting monetary policy step by step toward decisions that would have been unthinkable only a few years before.

---

95. In Japan, public debt is more than 200 percent of GDP but is cross-held by various public agencies (especially retirement funds) and the central bank. In Switzerland, the central bank chose to deal with the enormous international demand for Swiss francs as a reserve asset (without any relation to the actual size of the Swiss economy) by creating a large amount of money to avoid an excessive appreciation of the exchange rate.

These changes pose numerous problems, however. First, the real priority should no doubt be to reduce the size of private balance sheets rather than engage in a race to keep up with them. A situation in which all economic actors are to some degree indebted to one another and in which the total size of the financial sector (assets and liabilities combined) is growing faster than the real economy cannot continue forever; it leaves both economy and society in a very fragile state.[96]

Second, the long-term real effects of these "unconventional" monetary policies are not well understood, and it is quite possible that they will increase the inequality of financial returns and the concentration of wealth. When central bank balance sheets attained comparable heights (of 40–90 percent of GDP) in the aftermath of World War II, the creation of such large volumes of money coincided with significant inflation. Economies then became trapped in wage-price spirals, to which governments contributed by increasing public-sector wages; this inflationary process helped to reduce the value of public debt to virtually nothing, which encouraged investment and accelerated postwar reconstruction.[97] Nothing like this is true in the current period. Wages are virtually frozen in both the public and private sector, and consumer price inflation has been extremely low since the crisis of 2008, especially in the Eurozone (where inflation is barely 1 percent a year); it would very likely have turned negative without monetary intervention.

Although monetary creation has not increased consumer prices, it has contributed to the increase of certain asset prices while at the same time creating large "spreads" (differences in the yield of similar assets). Indeed, the nominal interest rates on German and French public debt is close to zero, and real rates

---

96. See A. Turner, *Between Debt and the Devil: Money, Credit, and Fixing Global Finance* (Princeton University Press, 2016). See also C. Durand, *Le capital fictif. Comment la finance s'approprie notre avenir* (Les prairies ordinaires, 2014); A. Tooze, *Crashed: How a Decade of Financial Crisis Changed the World* (Penguin, 2018).

97. The curve for the Eurozone in Fig. 13.13 actually depicts the Franco-German average for the period before 1999. This is broken down in Fig. S13.13 (online appendix). In 1956–1946, the Bank of France's balance sheet was 80–90 percent of GDP and the Bundesbank's was 40–50 percent. During each of the two world wars, direct loans to governments to finance the war played a central role in the evolution of central bank balance sheets. See, for example, E. Monnet, *Controlling Credit: Central Banking and the Planned Economy in Postwar France, 1948–1973* (Cambridge University Press, 2018), p. 67, fig. 1. The key difference compared with the present period is that those loans went immediately to pay new expenses.

are negative. This is partly due to the fact that the ECB has bought so much public debt to try to reduce the spreads between the sovereign debt of different countries. In addition, new prudential rules require that a substantial portion of each bank's capital must consist of safe assets. Finally, many global financial actors use the sovereign debt of Western countries as safe reserves, which they think they need in a general climate of fear in which every country is afraid that it might become the target of a financial panic (and therefore wants to keep extra reserves on hand, just in case).

In a sense, one might say that these near-zero rates reflect a situation where it is impossible to "get rich while sleeping" (at least with very safe assets). This marks a sharp difference from the past and from the classic proprietarianism of the nineteenth century and the era of the gold standard when the real return on public debt was generally 3–4 percent (albeit with a decrease in the decades before 1914 due to overaccumulation of capital, which led to a frenetic search for higher yields abroad or in the colonies). Today, interest rates on sovereign debt are close to zero, but this does not mean however that everyone is earning zero return on capital. In practice, it is small and medium savers who are earning near-zero (or negative) returns on their bank accounts, while larger investors with better information about the movements of certain asset prices (sometimes caused by central banks but even more by swollen private balance sheets) still manage to make gains. For example, the returns on large endowments (such as those of universities) and the growth rates of the biggest fortunes seem not to have been affected by the near-zero returns on safe sovereign debt: both seem to be growing at rates on the order of 6–8 percent a year, partly thanks to sophisticated financial products not available to smaller investors.[98]

Last but not least, this monetary activism attests to the many roadblocks that governments face in other policy areas such as financial regulation, taxes, and budgets. This is true in the United States, where the structure of partisan conflict and a dysfunctional Congress have made it increasingly difficult to pass laws or even just to agree on a budget (hence the repeated shutdowns of the federal government). It is still more obvious in Europe, whose federal institutions are even more dysfunctional than those of the United States. Given the impossibility of agreeing on even a minimal common budget (because each EU member state has veto power), the EU's capacity for action is quite limited. The EU budget is approved by unanimous vote of the European Council for a

98. See Chap. 11 and the online appendix concerning returns on university endowments.

period of seven years, with a concurring majority vote by the European Parliament. Funds are drawn primarily from member states, which pay in proportion to their gross national income. The annual EU budget for the period 2014–2020 amounts to just 1 percent of EU GDP.[99] By contrast, member-states' budgets amount to 30–50 percent of GDP, depending on the country. The US federal budget is 20 percent of GDP, compared with less than 10 percent for individual states and other local governments.[100]

To recapitulate: The European Union is a financial midget, paralyzed by the unanimity rule in tax and budget matters. The ECB is therefore the only powerful federal institution in Europe. It can take decisions by a simple majority vote, and it was on this basis that it increased the size of its balance sheet by nearly 30 percent of European GDP between 2008 and 2018. In other words, the ECB created every year on average a volume of money equal to almost 3 percent of European GDP, which is nearly three times the total budget of the EU. These figures clearly indicate the importance of the political and institutional regime in determining economic and financial dynamics. More than that, they show the extent to which the swelling of the money supply is due to fear of democracy and just taxation. What this means is that because European governments cannot agree on common taxes, a common budget, a common debt, and a common rate of interest—which would require an EU governed by a democratic parliament rather than by the mere agreement among heads of state that for the time being takes the place of authentic governance—the ECB's Governing Council is called upon to solve problems for which it does not have the tools.

This loss of direction is worrisome and cannot last very long. Even though monetary policy is supposedly a technical matter beyond the understanding of ordinary citizens, the amounts involved are so huge that they have begun to alter perceptions of the economy and finance. Many citizens have quite understandably begun to ask why such sums were created to bail out financial institutions, with little apparent effect in jump-starting the European economy, and

---

99. This is approximately the same level as previous budgets and as the budget currently under negotiation for the period 2021–2027. The EU budget is secondarily financed by a percentage of value-added tax revenues from each country and by meager customs fees levied on goods and services entering the European Union. See the online appendix.

100. See Chap. 10. In the nineteenth and early twentieth centuries, the US federal budget was about 2 percent of GDP (thus closer to the present-day EU than to the present US federal budget).

why it shouldn't be possible to mobilize similar resources to help struggling workers, develop public infrastructure, or finance large investments in renewable sources of energy. Indeed, it would by no means be absurd for European governments to borrow at current low interest rates to finance useful investments, on two conditions: first, such investments should be decided democratically, in parliament with open debate, and not by a Governing Council meeting behind closed doors; and second, it would be dangerous to lend credence to the notion that every problem can be resolved by printing money and taking on debt. The principal instrument for mobilizing resources to undertake common political projects was and remains taxation, democratically decided and levied on the basis of each taxpayer's economic resources and ability to pay, in total transparency.

In July 2013, the British rock band Muse gave a concert at the Olympic Stadium in Rome. The title song, "Animals," explicitly referred to the fact that "quantitative easing" was invented to save the bankers. The lead singer, Matt Bellamy, alluded to the "masters of the universe" who speculate on the lives of ordinary people. He dedicated the song "to all the Fred Goodwins of the world" (referring to the banker deemed responsible for the failure of the Royal Bank of Scotland in 2008 but who nevertheless left the bank with a golden parachute). At that moment a terrifying-looking banker took the stage and began distributing banknotes to the crowd. As the singer explained in an interview, "We don't take a stance, we express the confusion of our time."[101] And the confusion is indeed considerable. Quantitative easing and the bloating of the financial sector avoided the fundamental issues and encouraged people to give up hope of any possibility of achieving a just economy. This is one of the principal contradictions of today's neo-proprietarian regime. It is urgent to move beyond it.

Neo-Proprietarianism and Ordoliberalism: From Hayek to the EU

To review: Today's neo-proprietarian ideology relies on grand narratives and solid institutions, including the story of communism's failure, the "Pandorian" refusal to redistribute wealth, and the free circulation of capital without regulation, information sharing, or a common tax system. Nevertheless, it is also

---

101. See the *Evening Standard,* May 24, 2013: "This is going to be our Zoo TV" (interview with the band Muse). In 2017 the singer Matt Bellamy declared that he had voted for Brexit.

important to bear in mind that this political-ideological regime has many weaknesses, or to put it the other way around, there are many forces pushing to change and to overcome it. Financial opacity and rising inequality significantly complicate the response to the challenge of climate change. More generally, they give rise to social discontent, to which the only solution is greater transparency and more redistribution, without which identitarian tensions will grow increasingly strong. Like all inegalitarian regimes, this one is unstable and evolving.

Broadly speaking, I think it is important not to overestimate the internal coherence of neo-proprietarianism and its political-ideological matrix, especially in the context of the European Union. It is commonplace to associate the EU with ordoliberalism, a doctrine according to which the essential role of the state is to guarantee the conditions of "free and undistorted" competition, or with the constitutional and consciously authoritarian liberalism of Friedrich von Hayek. Indeed, the circumvention of parliamentary democracy, government by automatic rules, and the principle that all member states must unanimously agree on fiscal matters (which de facto prevents any common tax system) all betray an obvious kinship with ordoliberal and Hayekian ideas. Still, I think it is important to place these influences in context and not to exaggerate the intellectual or political consistency of the European construct, which is a product of many intersecting influences and not the result of a fixed, preconceived plan. The institutional and political-ideological structure of the EU is still largely unfinished. It may take any of a number of different paths in the future, and it could reconstitute itself in concentric circles or around a number of separate nuclei with greater or lesser degrees of political, social, and fiscal integration; what happens will be determined by power relations; social, political, and financial crises; and the debates that take place in the meantime.

To see what differentiates the present-day European Union (or, more generally, today's world) from systematic and consistent neo-proprietarianism, it may be useful to look at the treatise that Hayek published between 1973 and 1982 entitled *Law, Legislation and Liberty,* which is perhaps the clearest statement of triumphant self-conscious proprietarianism.[102] Recall that we encountered Hayek earlier in connection with the debates of 1939–1940 about a pro-

---

102. The work is in three volumes: *Rules and Order* (published in 1973), *The Mirage of Social Justice* (1979), and *The Political Order of a Free People* (1979). It was then revised and republished as a single volume in 1982: F. Hayek, *Law, Legislation and Liberty: A New Statement of the Liberal Principles of Justice and Political Economy* (Routledge, 1982). Here I cite the 1982 edition.

posal for a Franco-British union and the Federal Union movement, as well as in connection with his book *The Road to Serfdom* (1944), in which he warned against the risk of totalitarianism inherent, in his view, in any project based on the illusion of social justice and departing from the principles of liberalism pure and simple. His critique was aimed at the British Labour and Swedish Social Democratic parties of the day, which he suspected of seeking to undermine individual liberties. In retrospect this may come as a surprise, since Hayek would later become an active supporter of General Augusto Pinochet's ultra-liberal military dictatorship in Chile in the 1970s and 1980s (while also supporting and serving as an adviser to Margaret Thatcher's government in the United Kingdom). Reading *Law, Legislation and Liberty* (hereafter abbreviated as *LLL*) is an instructive exercise because it sheds light on the overall coherence of Hayek's thought. After moving to London in 1931, Hayek joined the faculty of the University of Chicago in 1950 (the temple of the "Chicago Boys," the young economists who would later advise the Chilean dictator). In 1962 he returned to Europe, where he taught at the University of Freiburg (the historic home of ordoliberalism) and the University of Salzburg until his death in 1992 at the age of 93. In the 1950s, he turned his attention to political and legal philosophy, from which he mounted his defense of what he then considered to be the threatened values of economic liberalism.

In *LLL* Hayek clearly expresses the proprietarian fear of redistribution of any kind: if one begins to question existing property rights or gets caught up in the works of progressive taxation, it will be impossible to know where to stop. Hayek credits the Florentine historian and statesman Francesco Guicciardini, responding in 1538 to a proposed progressive tax, with being the first to state this "Pandorian" idea clearly and the first to dismiss out of hand the whole idea of progressive taxation. Alarmed by the marginal rates in excess of 90 percent then being levied in the United States and United Kingdom and convinced that the final victory of collectivism was near, Hayek had already proposed in an earlier work that the very idea of progressive taxation should be constitutionally prohibited. According to his proposal, the tax rate on the highest incomes in any given country should not exceed the average overall tax rate, which was equivalent to saying that the tax system could be regressive (with a lower rate on top incomes than on the rest of the population) but certainly not progressive.[103] In general, Hayek was convinced that liberalism had taken a wrong turn in the eighteenth and nineteenth centuries by entrusting so much

---

103. See F. Hayek, *The Constitution of Liberty* (University of Chicago Press, 1960), vol. 7, pp. 430–450. Hayek noted that the income tax could be slightly progressive

legislative power to elected parliaments, to the detriment of rights (especially property rights) established in the past. He opposed constructivist rationalism, which claimed to be able to redefine rights and social relations *ex nihilo,* and defended evolutionary rationalism, based on respect for preexisting rights and social relations. He insisted that "law precedes legislation" and that neglect of this wise principle almost inevitably leads to the emergence of a "supreme legislator" and therefore to totalitarianism.[104]

In the final volume of *LLL,* he pushes this argument still further by proposing an entirely new basis for parliamentary democracy, which would drastically limit the power of any future political majority. He envisioned a vast federal politics based on strict respect for property rights. To be sure, "governmental assemblies" could be elected at the local level on the basis of universal suffrage, with the proviso that civil servants, retirees, and more generally, anyone receiving transfers of public funds should be denied the right to vote. Importantly, the sole power of these assemblies would be to administer state services at the local level; they would not be allowed to modify the legal system, which is to say property rights, civil or commercial law, or the tax code, in any way. Such fundamental and quasi-sacred laws should be decided, Hayek argued, by a competent "legislative assembly" at the federal level, whose membership should be decided in such a way that it would not be subject to the whims of universal suffrage. In his view, this supreme assembly should consist of persons aged 45 or over, chosen to serve fifteen-year terms after having demonstrated their abilities and professional success. He seems to have hesitated about the wisdom of explicitly reintroducing property qualifications for voting, eventually opting instead for a strange formula involving election by professional clubs "such as Rotary Clubs," where wise men would be able to mingle regularly before electing the wisest of them above the age of 45. The Supreme Court, made up of former members of this assembly, would have full power to arbitrate conflicts of competence among local governmental assemblies and to declare a state of emergency in case of social unrest.[105] The overall goal was

---

in order to compensate for the possible regressivity of indirect taxes, but no more than that, for fear of not knowing where to stop.

104. See Hayek, *Law, Legislation and Liberty,* vol. 1, pp. 83–144.

105. See Hayek, *Law, Legislation and Liberty,* vol. 3, pp. 109–132. Note that local governmental assemblies would be allowed to modify the general level of taxes, but only by applying a flat coefficient to the rules, rates, and tax brackets decided by the legislative assembly and hence without the ability to modify the relative rates applied to different social groups.

clearly to reduce to a minimum the power of universal suffrage and its caprices and in particular to muzzle youth, with its socialistic fantasies, which Hayek found particularly troubling in the climate of the 1970s, not only in Chile but also in Europe and the United States.[106]

Hayek's position is interesting as an illustration of an extreme version of neo-proprietarianism and its contradictions. At bottom, the only regime fully consistent with proprietarianism is the censitary regime (that is, a regime in which political power is explicitly vested in property owners, who are said to be the only people with the wisdom and capacity to see into the future and legislate responsibly). Hayek demonstrates a certain imagination in arriving at the same result without explicitly invoking property qualifications for voting, but that is what he really has in mind. What separates the European Union as an institutional and political-ideological construct from Hayek's avowed neo-proprietarianism should also be clear. The institutions of the EU can and should be deeply transformed, and in particular the rule of unanimity on fiscal matters should be abolished. To achieve this, however, we must stop thinking of Europe as a coherent and invincible ordoliberal or neo-proprietarian conspiracy and view it instead as an unstable, precarious, and evolving compromise. More specifically, the European Union is still searching for a parliamentary form appropriate to its history. The rule of unanimity on fiscal matters is unsatisfactory. Although it is true that the heads of state and finance ministers who sit on the key European councils are ultimately designated through the process of universal suffrage, giving each of them veto power leads to perpetual blockage. Yet moving to qualified majority voting and strengthening the power of the European Parliament (the traditional federalist solution) does not solve all the problems—far from it. I will come back to this (see esp. Chapter 16).

The Invention of Meritocracy and Neo-Proprietarianism

The neo-proprietarianism that has emerged over the past several decades is a complex phenomenon; it is not merely a return to the proprietarianism of the nineteenth and early twentieth centuries. In particular, it is linked to an extreme

---

106. In numerous interviews given at the time, Hayek explained that he preferred an authoritarian regime such as Pinochet's that respected the rules of economic liberalism and the rights of property more than a self-styled democratic regime that trampled on those rights. See, for example, the interview he gave to *El Mercurio* in April 1981: "Personally, I prefer a liberal dictatorship to a democratic government without liberalism." See G. Chamayou, *La société ingouvernable. Une généalogie du libéralisme autoritaire* (La Fabrique, 2018), pp. 219–220.

form of meritocratic ideology. Meritocratic discourse generally glorifies the winners in the economic system while stigmatizing the losers for their supposed lack of merit, virtue, and diligence. Of course, meritocracy is an old ideology, on which elites in all times and places have always relied in one way or another to justify their dominance. Over time, however, it has become increasingly common to blame the poor for their poverty. This is one of the principal distinctive features of today's inequality regime.

For Giacomo Todeschini, the idea of "the undeserving poor" can be traced back to the Middle Ages and perhaps more generally to the end of slavery and forced labor and the outright ownership of the poor classes by the wealthy classes. Once the poor man became a subject and not simply an object, it became necessary to "own" him by other means and specifically in the realms of discourse and merit.[107] This new vision of inequality, which became commonplace, may have been related to another medieval innovation studied by Todeschini: the invention of new forms of ownership and investment and their validation by Christian doctrine.[108] In other words, these two aspects of "modernity" may be correlated: once the rules of the economy and property become subordinated to principles of justice, the poor become responsible for their own fate, and they must be made to understand this.

Nevertheless, as long as the proprietarian order was built first upon the trifunctional regime and later upon the censitary regime, meritocratic discourse played a limited role. With the advent of the industrial age and the new threats to the elite posed by class struggle and universal suffrage, the need to justify social differences on the basis of individual abilities became more pressing. For instance, in 1845, Charles Dunoyer, a liberal economist and prefect under the July Monarchy, wrote a book entitled *On the Freedom of Labor,* in which he vigorously opposed all obligatory social legislation: "The effect of the industrial regime is to destroy artificial inequalities, but only in order to highlight natural inequalities." For Dunoyer, these natural inequalities included differences of physical, intellectual, and moral capabilities; they were at the heart of the new innovation economy that he saw wherever he looked and justified his rejection of state intervention: "Superiorities are the source of everything great

---

107. See G. Todeschini, "Servitude et travail à la fin du Moyen Âge: la dévalorisation des 'salariés' et les pauvres peu méritants," *Annales. Histoire, Sciences Sociales,* 2015. See also G. Todeschini, *Au pays des sans-noms. Gens de mauvaise vie, personnes suspectes ou ordinaires du Moyen Âge à l'époque moderne* (Verdier, 2015).
108. See Chap. 2.

and useful. Reduce everything to equality and you will have reduced everything to inaction."[109]

But it was above all when the era of higher education began that meritocratic ideology assumed its full proportions. In 1872, Émile Boutmy founded the École Libre des Sciences Politiques, to which he ascribed a clear mission: "Obliged to submit to the law of the majority, the classes that call themselves superior can preserve their political hegemony only by invoking the law of the most capable. Because the walls of their prerogatives and tradition are crumbling, the democratic tide must be held back by a second rampart made up of brilliant and useful merits, of superiority whose prestige commands obedience, of capacities of which it would be folly for society to deprive itself."[110] This incredible statement deserves to be taken seriously: it means that it was the survival instinct of the upper classes that led them to abandon idleness and invent meritocracy, without which they ran the risk of being stripped of their possessions by universal suffrage. No doubt the climate of the times played a part: the Paris Commune had just been put down, and universal male suffrage had just been restored. In any case, Boutmy's statement deserves credit for pointing out an essential truth: it is a matter of vital importance to make sense of inequality and to justify the position of the winners. Inequality is above all ideological. Today's neo-proprietarianism is all the more meritocratic because it can no longer be explicitly censitary, unlike the classical proprietarianism of the nineteenth century.

In *The Inheritors* (1964; English edition 1979), Pierre Bourdieu and Jean-Claude Passeron analyzed the way in which the social order was legitimized by the higher educational system of that time. In the guise of individual "merit" and "talent," social privilege was perpetuated because disadvantaged groups lacked the codes and other keys to social recognition. The number of students in higher education had exploded, and educational credentials had begun to play a growing role in the structure of social inequality. But the lower classes were almost totally excluded: less than 1 percent of the children of farmworkers attended college compared with 70 percent of the children of factory managers

---

109. See C. Dunoyer, *De la liberté du travail, ou simple exposé des conditions dans lesquelles les forces humaines s'expriment avec le plus de puissance* (Guillaumin, 1845), pp. 382–383.

110. E. Boutmy, *Quelques idées sur la création d'une Faculté libre d'enseignement supérieur* (1871). See also P. Favre, "Les sciences d'Etat entre déterminisme et libéralisme. Emile Boutmy (1835–1906) et la création de l'Ecole libre des sciences politiques," *Revue française de sociologie*, 1981.

and 80 percent of the children of independent professionals. An openly segregationist system, like the one that was beginning to disappear in the United States in 1964 when *The Inheritors* was originally published, could hardly have been more exclusionary than this; except the cultural and symbolic domination that one saw in France was portrayed as the result of free choice, where everyone theoretically enjoyed equal opportunities. That is why Bourdieu and Passeron preferred to compare the French system to the system of reproduction of the wizard caste among the Omaha tribe studied by anthropologist Margaret Mead, where young men of any background were presumably free to try their luck. They were then required "to withdraw into solitude, fast, return and recount their visions to the elders, only to be told, if their families did not belong to the elite, that their visions were not authentic."[111]

The issue of educational injustice and meritocratic hypocrisy has only gained in importance since the 1960s. Access to higher education has expanded significantly but remains highly stratified and inegalitarian, and there has been no serious investigation of the resources actually allocated to different groups of students or to pedagogical reforms that might provide more authentic equality of access. In the United States, France, and most other countries, the praise heaped on the meritocratic model is rarely based on close examination of the facts. The goal is usually to justify existing inequalities with no consideration of the sometimes glaring failures of the existing system or of the fact that lower- and middle-class students do not have access to the same resources or courses as the children of the upper classes.[112] In Part Four we will see that educational inequality is one of the main causes of the disintegration of the "social-democratic" coalition over the past few decades. Socialist, Labour, and social-democratic parties have gradually come to be seen as increasingly favorable to the winners in the educational contest while they have lost the support they used to enjoy among less well-educated groups in the postwar period.[113]

It is interesting to note that the British sociologist Michael Young warned against just such developments as long ago as 1958. After helping to draft and enact the Labour platform of 1945, he became estranged from the party in the 1950s because it had failed, in his view, to push its program forward, particularly in regard to education. One thing that particularly worried Young was the

---

111. See P. Bourdieu and J. P. Passeron, *Les héritiers. Les étudiants et la culture* (Minuit, 1964), p. 10.
112. See Fig. I.6 and Chap. 11.
113. See Chaps. 14–16.

extreme stratification of the British system of secondary education. He published an astonishingly prescient work entitled *The Rise of the Meritocracy, 1870–2033: An Essay on Education and Equality.*[114] He imagined a British (and global) society increasingly stratified on the basis of cognitive capacity, closely (but not exclusively) related to social origins. In his book the Tories have become the party of the highly educated and have restored the power of the House of Lords thanks to the new domination of intellectuals. Labour has become the party of "Technicians," which must contend with the "Populists." The latter consists of the lower classes, furious at having been relegated to the socioeconomic backwaters in a world where science has decreed that only a third of the population is employable. The Populists cry in vain for educational equality and unification of the school system through "comprehensive schools" offering equal training and equal resources to all young Britons. But the Tories and Technicians join forces to reject their plea, having long since given up any egalitarian ambitions. The United Kingdom ultimately succumbs to a populist revolution in 2033. There the story ends, because the sociologist-reporter who is recounting the tale is killed in the violent riots that ravage the country. Young himself died in 2002, too early to see his fiction overtaken by reality, but he was wrong on at least one point: in the first two decades of the twenty-first century it was Labour, not the Tories, that became the preferred party of the well educated.[115]

From the Philanthropic Illusion to the Sacralization of Billionaires

Today's meritocratic ideology glorifies entrepreneurs and billionaires. At times this glorification seems to know no bounds. Some people seem to believe that Bill Gates, Jeff Bezos, and Mark Zuckerberg single-handedly invented computers, books, and friends. One can get the impression that they can never be rich enough and that the humble people of the earth can never thank them enough for all the benefits they have brought. To defend them, sharp lines are drawn between the wicked Russian oligarchs and the nice entrepreneurs

---

114. It is generally accepted that Young's droll yet profound fable marked the first use of the term "meritocracy."

115. See Chap. 15. The irony is that Young was appointed to the House of Lords by the Labour government in 1978 and sat there until 2002 (while manifesting his opposition to Blairism).

from Seattle and Silicon Valley, while all criticism is forgotten: their quasi-monopolistic behavior is ignored as are the legal and tax breaks they are granted and the public resources they appropriate.

Billionaires are such fixtures of the contemporary imagination that they have entered into fiction, which fortunately maintains more ironic distance than do the magazines. In *Destiny and Desire* (2008), Carlos Fuentes paints a portrait of Mexican capitalism and its attendant violence. We meet a cast of colorful characters, including a president who sounds like an ad for Coca-Cola but is ultimately a pitiful political timeserver whose power is risible compared with the eternal power of capital, embodied in an omnipotent billionaire who strongly resembles the telecommunications magnate Carlos Slim, the richest man not only in Mexico but also in the world from 2010 to 2013 (ahead of Bill Gates). Two young people hesitate between resignation, sex, and revolution. They end up being murdered by a beautiful, ambitious woman who covets their inheritance and who has no need of a Vautrin to tell her what she needs to do to get it—proof, if proof were needed, that violence has been cranked up a notch since 1820. Inherited wealth, coveted by all who are born outside the privileged family circle but destructive of the personalities of those born within it—is at the heart of the novelist's meditation. The book occasionally alludes to the baleful influence of the *gringos,* the Americans who own "thirty percent of Mexico" and make inequality even harder to bear.

In *L'empire du ciel* (Heaven's Empire), a novel published in 2016 by Tancrède Voituriez, a Chinese billionaire has an ingenious idea for changing the climate. By taking a few thousand feet off the top of the Himalayas, he can arrange for the Indian monsoon to waft over China and get rid of the nasty shroud of pollution hanging over Beijing. Communists or not, billionaires think that anything goes, are enamored of geoengineering, and detest nothing so much as simple but unpleasant solutions (such as paying taxes and living quietly).[116] In *All the Money in the World* (TriStar Pictures, 2017), Ridley Scott portrays J. Paul Getty, the world's richest man in 1973 and so stingy that he is

---

116. Note that in the era of *Le Transperceneige: Intégrale,* the splendid graphic novel published by Jacques Lobb and J. M. Rochette (Casterman, 1984) and adapted for the screen as *Snowpiercer* (dir. Bong Joon-Ho [Radius-TWC, 2014]), climatic disasters were resolved by class struggle: the proletariat at the back of the bus has to get rid of the privileged to save humanity. In *The Handmaid's Tale,* a novel published by Margaret Atwood (McClelland and Stewart, 1985) and adapted as a TV series in 2017 by Hulu, the United States establishes a theocratic dictatorship when fertility drops because of pollution and toxic waste. Mexicans and

willing to run the risk that the Italian mafia will cut off his grandson's ear rather than pay a large ransom (even with a tax deduction). The film showed a billionaire so petty and antipathetic that today's moviegoers, used to seeing wealth celebrated and entrepreneurs depicted as amiable and deserving, felt somewhat embarrassed by it.

Several factors help to explain the force of today's ideology. As always, there is fear of the void. If one accepts the idea that Bill, Jeff, and Mark could be happy with $1 billion each (instead of their $300 billion joint net worth) and would no doubt have lived their lives in exactly the same way even if they had known in advance that this was as rich as they would get (which is quite plausible), then some will ask, "But where does it end?" Historical experience shows that such fears are exaggerated: redistribution can be done in a methodical, disciplined way. But the lessons of history are of no avail: some people will always remain convinced that it is too risky to open Pandora's box. The fall of communism is also a factor. The Russian and Czech oligarchs who buy athletic teams and newspapers may not be the most savory characters, but the Soviet system was a nightmare and had to go. Nevertheless, people are increasingly aware that the influence of billionaires has grown to proportions that are worrisome for democratic institutions, which are also threatened by the rise of inequality and "populism" (to say nothing of the riots Michael Young anticipated for 2033).

Another important factor contributing to the legitimation of billionaires is what one might call the philanthropic illusion. Because the state and its tax revenues have grown since the 1970s-1980s to unprecedented size, it is natural to think that philanthropy (altruistic private financing in the public interest) ought to play an increased role. Indeed, precisely because of the size of the government, it is legitimate to demand greater transparency about what taxes are levied and how the revenues are spent. In many sectors, such as culture, media, and research, it may be a good idea to have mixed public and private financing channeled through a decentralized network of participatory organizations. The problem is that philanthropic discourse can be deployed as part of a particularly dangerous anti-state ideology. This is especially true in poor countries, where philanthropy (and in some cases foreign aid from rich countries) can be a means of circumventing the state, which contributes to its pauperization. The fact is that in poor countries the state is anything but omnipotent. In most cases,

---

Canadians, long aware that their neighbors could be sanctimonious and at times oppressive, did not expect that they would go this far.

its tax revenues are extremely limited and indeed quite a bit smaller than the revenues that the rich countries enjoyed when they were developing.[117] For the billionaire or even the less well-endowed donor, it may be pleasant to be in a position to set a country's priorities in health care and education. Still, nothing in the history of the rich countries suggests that this is the best method of development.

Another point about the philanthropic illusion is that philanthropy is neither participatory nor democratic. In practice, giving is extremely concentrated among the very wealthy, who often derive significant tax advantages from their gifts. In other words, the lower and middle classes subsidize through their taxes the philanthropic preferences of the wealthy—a novel form of confiscation of public goods and control derived from wealth.[118] A different model might be better. If citizens could participate equally in a collective social process of defining the public good along the lines of the egalitarian model of political party financing that I discussed earlier, it might be possible to move beyond parliamentary democracy.[119] Along with educational equality and widespread ownership of property, this will figure in the discussion of participatory socialism that I will present in Chapter 17.

---

117. See Fig. 13.12 and Fig. 10.14.

118. See, for example, R. Reich, *Just Giving: Why Philanthropy Is Failing Democracy and How It Can Do Better* (Princeton University Press, 2018).

119. See J. Cagé, *Le prix de la démocratie* (Fayard, 2018), chap. 12; in English, *The Price of Democracy,* trans. P. Camiller (Harvard University Press, 2020).

PART FOUR

RETHINKING
THE DIMENSIONS
OF POLITICAL CONFLICT

{ FOURTEEN }

Borders and Property:
The Construction of Equality

In Parts One through Three of this book, we studied the transformation of inequality regimes from premodern trifunctional and slave societies into today's hypercapitalist and postcommunist societies, with proprietarian, colonial, social-democratic, and/or communist societies as intermediate stages. In each instance I emphasized the political-ideological dimension of the transformation. Each inequality regime is associated with a corresponding theory of justice. Inequalities need to be justified; they must rest on a plausible, coherent vision of an ideal political and social organization. Every society therefore needs to answer a series of conceptual and practical questions about the boundaries of the community, the organization of property relations, access to education, and the apportionment of taxes. The answers given to these questions in the past were not always robust. Most have not withstood the test of time and have been replaced by other answers. It would nevertheless be wrong to think that today's ideologies, based in one way or another on the sacralization of financial opacity and merited wealth, are any less outlandish or more likely to last.

In the age of representative democracy and universal suffrage, political-ideological conflicts around the question of just inequality continue. Criticism can be expressed through demonstrations and revolutions, or it can be couched in pamphlets and books. But conflict can also be expressed at the ballot box: people vote for different political parties and coalitions, depending on their worldviews and socioeconomic positions. Some also choose not to vote, which is in itself a declaration. Elections leave clues about people's political beliefs and their evolution. These clues are often ambiguous and hard to interpret, but still, voting records provide richer and more systematic information than one finds in societies where there are no elections.

In Part Four we are going to study precisely this type of information. In particular, we are going to analyze the way in which the "classist" structure of political and electoral cleavages was radically transformed between the social-democratic era (1950–1980) and the hypercapitalist and postcolonial era (1990–2020). In the first period, the least favored classes *(classes populaires)*[1] identified with parties of the broad left, whether Socialist, Communist, Labour, Democratic, or Social Democratic. This ceased to be the case in the second period, during which left-wing political parties and movements became parties of the educated; in some places they are also becoming the parties of voters with higher incomes and greater wealth.[2] This evolution reflects the failure of the postwar social-democratic coalition to update its political agenda, specifically in regard to fiscal, educational, and international issues. It also shows that egalitarian coalitions are complex political-ideological constructs. Numerous social and ideological cleavages, beginning with conflicts about boundaries and property, always divide electorates. It is not easy to overcome these divisions and unite less advantaged voters with different histories and backgrounds (urban and rural, salaried and self-employed, native and immigrant, etc.) unless specific sociohistorical and political-ideological conditions are met.

In this chapter we will begin by studying the case of France. In subsequent chapters we will look first at the United States and United Kingdom and then at other representative democracies in Western and Eastern Europe, as well as non-Western cases such as India and Brazil. Comparing the different trajectories of each of these countries will help us to understand why these changes occurred and give us insight into possible future dynamics. We will also look at an important recent development: social nativism, which is a consequence of postcommunist disillusionment, inadequate reflection on the structure of globalization, and the difficulty of accommodating to postcolonial diversity. Social nativism is a trap. Under what conditions can it be avoided? One way of coping with this new identitarian threat might be to work toward what I call social federalism and participatory socialism. We will consider both in the final chapters.

---

1. Translator's note: The French text uses the phrase *classes populaires,* for which there is no good English equivalent. What is meant here is roughly the bottom 50 percent of the social hierarchy, a concept that is deployed throughout this book. It is not accurately captured by "working class" or "lower class." It may include a variety of social groups with many disparate characteristics in terms of education, income, and wealth, as the text makes clear. Hence the translation will resort to the circumlocution used here, "least favored classes" or "disadvantaged classes."
2. See Fig. I.9.

Deconstructing Left and Right: The Dimensions
of Sociopolitical Conflict

There are many reasons why electoral and political cleavages can never be reduced to a single dimension, such as an opposition between "poor" and "rich." In the first place, political conflict is above all ideological, not "classist." It opposes worldviews—systems of beliefs about a just society, which cannot be reduced to individual socioeconomic characteristics or class membership. For a given set of individual attributes, there will always exist a wide variety of possible opinions, which will be influenced by individual and family histories, encounters and exchanges, reading, reflection, and subjective responses. "What is the ideal organization of society?" is too complicated a question to allow a deterministic relation between "class position" and political beliefs. Of course, I do not mean to say that political beliefs are entirely arbitrary. On the contrary, I am convinced that history has much to teach us about the shape of an ideal property or tax regime or educational system. But these issues are so complex that the only hope of real and lasting progress is through collective deliberation in which the variety of individual experiences and ideas of the just society are represented, and these can never be reduced to class position. The way in which organizations such as political parties and movements, trade unions, and other associations translate individual aspirations to equality and emancipation into political programs plays a crucial role in determining how individuals participate and engage in politics.

Furthermore, the very notion of social class must be seen as profoundly multidimensional. It involves every aspect of a person's occupation: the sector and status of the work, wages and other forms of labor income, skills, professional identity, hierarchical position, and ability to take part in decision making and in the organization of production. Class also depends on levels of training and education, which partly determine access to different occupations, forms of political participation, and social interactions and, along with family and personal networks, help to determine cultural and symbolic capital. Finally, social class is closely related to wealth. Today as in the past, whether or not one owns real estate or professional or financial assets has numerous consequences. For instance, it determines whether one must devote an important part of one's lifetime income to paying rent, which other people collect. Property ownership also implies the ability to purchase goods and services produced by others, which is yet another important determinant of social class; indeed, wealth is a determinant of social power in general. For instance, it has a direct impact on one's ability to start a business and hire other people to work in a hierarchical and asymmetrical setting toward the realization of a plan. Wealth also enables individuals to support the projects of others and perhaps even to influence politics by financing parties and/or news media.

Apart from occupation, education, and wealth, the social class with which an individual identifies may also be influenced by age, gender, (real or perceived) national or ethnic origin, and religious, philosophical, dietary, or sexual orientation. Class position is also characterized by level of income, which is a complex and composite attribute since it depends on all the other dimensions. In particular, income includes both labor income (wage and nonwage) and capital income (rent, interest, dividends, capital gains, profits, etc.). It therefore depends on occupation, level of education, and property, especially since wealth, which can be used to pay for education and training or to finance professional investments, partly determines access to certain occupations and therefore to income from those occupations.

This multidimensionality of social cleavages is essential for understanding the evolution the political and electoral cleavage structure (Figs. 14.1–14.2). To

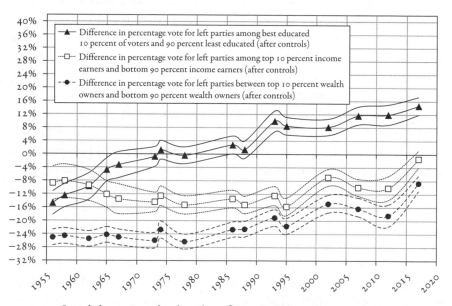

FIG. 14.1. Social cleavages and political conflict in France, 1955–2020

Interpretation: In 1950–1970, the vote for left parties (Socialist, Communist, Radical, Green) was associated with less educated, lower income, and less wealthy voters; in 1990–2010 it was associated with better educated voters. *Note:* Thin lines indicate 90 percent confidence levels. *Sources and series:* piketty.pse.ens.fr/ideology.

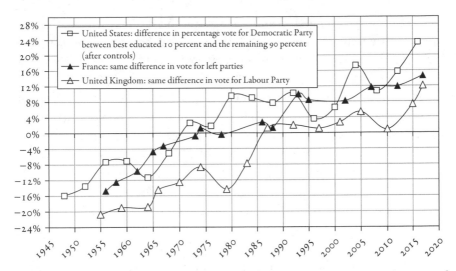

FIG. 14.2. Electoral left in Europe and the United States, 1945–2020: From the party of workers to the party of the educated

Interpretation: In 1950–1970, the vote for the Democratic Party in the United States, for left parties (Socialists, Communists, Radicals, Greens) in France, and for Labour in the United Kingdom was associated with less educated voters. In 1990–2010 it became associated with better educated voters. *Sources and series:* piketty.pse.ens.fr/ideology.

begin, consider voting patterns in the social-democratic era—roughly 1950–1980. In nearly all Western countries, the various dimensions of social cleavage were politically aligned. In other words, people at the bottom of the social hierarchy tended to vote for socialist, communist, or (broadly) social-democratic parties or movements, regardless of the dimension considered (education, income, or wealth); furthermore, occupying a low rank in several dimensions had a cumulative effect on one's vote. This was true not only for explicitly social-democratic parties such as the German Social Democratic Party (SPD) or Swedish Social Democratic Party (SAP) but also for the Labour vote in the United Kingdom and the Democratic vote in the United States, as well as for left-wing parties of various stripes (Socialist, Communist, Radical, or Green) in countries where the left was historically divided into several parties, such as in France.[3] In contrast, the vote for the Republican Party in the United States,

---

3. The word "left" is used here to refer to parties that use the word to designate themselves and is not assumed to be an eternal and unalterable essence. I will come back to this.

the Conservative Party in the United Kingdom, and various parties of the right and center-right in other countries was larger among the more highly educated, higher paid, and wealthier, with cumulative effects for voters highly placed along all three axes.

The structure of political conflict in the period 1950–1980 was "classist" in the sense that it pitted less advantaged social classes against more advantaged social classes, regardless of the axis considered. In contrast, political conflict in the period 1990–2020 involves a system of multiple elites: one coalition is backed by the more highly educated while the other enjoys the support of the wealthiest and highest paid (although less and less clearly, as elites transition from the latter coalition to the former). Note, moreover, that in all countries in the classist era we find a very clear gradation in the degree of political cleavage associated with the three dimensions of social stratification. Wealth is the most divisive dimension: people without property voted heavily for social-democratic (or equivalent) parties, while conversely, wealthy people rarely did. Education exerted a similar influence in the period 1950–1980 but to a significantly smaller degree: the less well educated were more likely to vote for social-democratic (or equivalent) parties, while the opposite was true for the better educated, but the gap was much less pronounced than in the case of wealth. Logically enough, income fell between these two extremes: it was less divisive than wealth but more divisive than education.

This gradation in the degree of politicization of these three dimensions of social cleavage is clearly visible in the case of France (Fig. 14.1); it also exists in all the other countries studied. In the French case, if we look at the percentage of people voting for parties of the left among the wealthiest 10 percent and the poorest 90 percent of the population, we find a very marked gap on the order of 25 percentage points for the period 1950–1980. Take, for instance, the French presidential election of 1974. After a very tight election campaign in a period of great social turmoil, the candidate of the Union of the Left, François Mitterrand, narrowly lost in the second round with 49 percent of the vote, compared with 51 percent for his right-wing opponent, Valéry Giscard d'Estaing. Mitterrand won nearly 52 percent of the votes of people in the bottom 90 percent of the wealth distribution, however, compared with just 27 percent of the votes of the top 10 percent—a gap of twenty-five points.

If we now look at the percentage of people voting for the same parties among the top 10 and bottom 90 percent of the income distribution (as opposed to the wealth distribution), we find a gap of 10 to 15 percentage points in the period 1950–1980. Although this is a large difference in absolute terms, the income effect is nevertheless smaller than the wealth effect.[4]

The Left-Wing Vote Since 1945: From the Workers'
Party to the Party of the Educated

It is quite striking to discover that the educational effect has completely reversed since 1980. In the 1950s and 1960s, the vote for left-wing parties was significantly smaller among the 10 percent of the population with the highest levels of education than among the 90 percent with the lowest. Over the next two decades the size of this gap diminished, however, and then it changed sign. In the 1990s and 2000s, the vote for left-wing parties was significantly higher among the best educated 10 percent than among the less well-educated 90 percent, again with a gap of 10–15 percentage points but in the opposite direction (Fig. 14.1).

In short, in the postwar years, the people who voted left were likely to be less well-educated salaried workers, but over the past half century this has changed, and they now are more likely to be people with higher levels of education, including managers and people in intellectual professions.

In this and subsequent chapters, I will try to document this radical transformation in greater detail and above all try to understand its origins, significance, and consequences. At this stage, several points need to be made explicit. First, this same basic structure of political conflict (with an identical gradation of wealth, income, and educational effects) and same basic evolution since World War II are found in all Western democracies, including the United States, United Kingdom, Germany, and Sweden (with variants that we will examine). For instance, in regard to the United States, if one looks at the gap in the vote for the Democratic Party between the best educated 10 percent and the remaining 90 percent, one finds approximately the same evolution as in the vote for left-wing parties in France (Fig. 14.2). The same is true of the Labour vote in the United Kingdom. The British seem to have lagged slightly behind France and the United States (see below), but ultimately the basic pattern is identical. Labour, which long identified itself as the workers' party, has de facto become the party of the educated, whom it attracts in greater number than the Tories. Michael Young,

---

4. For detailed breakdowns by income and wealth deciles, see Figs. 14.12–14.13.

as prescient as he was in *The Rise of Meritocracy* (published in 1958), nevertheless failed to anticipate such a complete reversal.[5]

It is particularly striking to note the similarity of the change in the United States and Europe, given that the political-ideological origins of the party systems are totally different. In the United States, the Democratic Party was the party of slavery and segregation before it became the party of the New Deal, greater socioeconomic equality, and civil rights. From the end of the Civil War on, the transformation was gradual and steady, without a sharp break.[6] By contrast, in Europe, the various left-wing parties were in one way or another the heirs of socialist, communist, or social-democratic traditions and ideologies, committed to one degree or another to collectivization of the means of production. Furthermore, the socioeconomic contexts in which they competed were virtually devoid of racial and ethnic divisions (at least within Europe, not including the colonies). In Europe, moreover, there was diversity among left-wing parties. For instance, in France, there was a sharp division between the anti-Soviet Socialist Party and the pro-Soviet Communist Party. In Britain, the Labour Party was unified and for a long time favorable to nationalizations while in Sweden and Germany the social-democratic parties had long since converted to co-management.[7] Despite all these differences, we find a similar pattern of evolution in all cases, and this calls for explanation.

Indeed, the similarity of trajectories across countries suggests that any narrowly national hypothesis should be viewed with a skeptical eye. More global explanations, based in particular on the reasons why members of less favored social groups increasingly feel less well represented (not to say abandoned) by the electoral left, are a priori more plausible. Specifically, I have in mind the inability of (broadly) social-democratic postwar coalitions to update their programs sufficiently, particularly in regard to developing convincing norms of justice adapted to the age of globalization and higher education. The shift in the global ideological climate that followed the failure of communism in the Soviet Union and Eastern Europe also seems to have been an important factor in this change, owing to a certain disillusionment with the very idea that a more just economy and a real and durable reduction of inequality were even possible.

In dealing with such complex changes, however, it is impossible to rule out a priori many other potential explanations, such as the growing importance of

---

5. See Chap. 13.
6. See Chap. 6.
7. See Chap. 11.

new cultural, racial, or immigration-related cleavages in postcolonial societies. To understand these transformations, we must carefully examine the trajectory of change in each country, being careful not to exaggerate our ability to imagine how things might have taken a different course.

Toward a Global Study of Electoral and Political-Ideological Cleavages

Before proceeding further, I should say a bit more about the sources on which this type of analysis is based and acknowledge their limits as well as their strengths. The results shown in Figs. 14.1–14.2 and the other graphs in this and subsequent chapters are the fruit of joint research based on an original and systematic exploitation of postelection survey data in a variety of countries over the past several decades. These surveys were generally conducted by consortia of universities and research centers, in some cases in conjunction with the media, to study electoral behavior. Representative samples of the population were questioned about their votes and motivations, usually in the days following an election. The surveys included questions about individual sociodemographic and economic characteristics: age, sex, place of residence, occupation, sector of employment, level of education, income, assets, religious practice, origins, and so on. These instruments thus offer direct evidence of the socioeconomic structure of the electorate in each country and how it changed over time.

The sources suffer from a number of shortcomings, however. First, postelection surveys are a relatively recent invention. In particular, they do not allow us to study elections prior to World War II. We will begin with detailed studies of the United States, France, and the United Kingdom, where fairly elaborate surveys have been conducted since the late 1940s or early 1950s. The records are sufficiently well preserved to allow satisfactory analysis of the structure of the electorate for nearly all US presidential elections since 1948 and all British and French legislative elections since 1955 or 1956.[8] Comparable surveys have

8. For the United States we rely on the American National Election Studies (ANES), which have been conducted since 1948. For the United Kingdom the most complete accounts are those of the British Election Study (BES). In France, most of the surveys since 1958 have been conducted in partnership with the Fondation Nationale des Sciences Politiques (FNSP) and its various research centers (especially Le Centre de recherches politiques de Sciences Po, known as CEVIPOF). The files are archived and available through various portals, such as the Inter-university Consortium for Political and Social Research (ICPSR); ANES; Centre de données

also been conducted in Germany and Sweden since the 1950s as well as in most European and non-European representative democracies (including India, Japan, Canada, and Australia) since the 1960s or 1970s. In the new democracies of Eastern Europe, it is possible to study the evolution of electoral cleavages since the 1990s or 2000s. In Brazil, one can do the same from the fall of the military dictatorship and return to elections in the late 1980s. In South Africa, surveys begin in the mid-1990s with the fall of apartheid. Clearly, then, with postelection surveys it is possible to work one's way around the world.[9] However, the available data do not allow us to study elections from the nineteenth or first half of the twentieth centuries, for which other methods and materials are needed.[10]

The other import limitation of the survey-based method is the limited sample size (generally around 4,000–5,000 people for each sample). This technical point is important: it implies that we cannot use this source to study small variations from election to election because these are generally too small

---

socio-politiques (CDSP)/Archives de données issues de la statistique publique (ADISP), and the Comparative Study of Electoral Systems (CSES). These post-election studies should not be confused with exit polls, which usually rely on shorter, more rudimentary questionnaires, although sometimes larger samples are used as in the National Exit Polls (NEP) conducted in the United States since 1972, which I used as a check of the robustness of the results obtained with the ANES. See the online appendix (piketty.pse.ens.fr/ideology).

9. Detailed results from the analysis of these survey data, along with computer code for transforming the raw data into the series presented here, are available in the online appendix. See also T. Piketty, "Brahmin Left vs Merchant Right: Rising Inequality and the Changing Structure of Political Conflict (Evidence from France, Britain and the US, 1948–2017)," WID.world, 2018; A. Gethin, C. Martinez-Toledano, and T. Piketty, "Political Cleavages and Inequality. Evidence from Electoral Democracies, 1950–2018," WID.world, 2019; A. Banerjee, A. Gethin, and T. Piketty, "Growing Cleavages in India? Evidence from the Changing Structure of the Electorates 1962–2014," WID.world, 2019; F. Kosse and T. Piketty, "Changing Socioeconomic and Electoral Cleavages in Germany and Sweden 1949–2017," WID.world, 2019; A. Lindner, F. Novokmet, T. Piketty, and T. Zawisza, "Political Conflict and Electoral Cleavages in Central-Eastern Europe, 1992–2018," WID.world, 2019.

10. In practice, for periods prior to World War II, one can compare voting data at the local level (towns, counties, etc.) with census data or administrative or tax records also available at the local level. This geo-electoral method has its limits (since there is no information about individual voting), but it is the only way to push the investigation further back in time. Later I will discuss some examples of using this method, which André Siegfried magisterially pioneered in 1913.

to be statistically significant. By contrast, the long-term evolutions on which we will concentrate here are very significant, as the confidence intervals shown in Fig. 14.1 indicate.[11] In particular, the complete reversal of the educational cleavage between the two periods, 1950–1980 and 1990–2020, in which the left goes from being the choice of the less educated to that of the better educated, is extremely significant, not just in France but everywhere. The samples are also large enough to allow reasoning in terms of "all other things being equal." In other words, we can isolate the effects of education by controlling for the effects of other individual attributes, which are often correlated with education (but not systematically).[12] Note, too, of course, that election surveys, like any source involving self-declared information, may suffer from biases in the answers given by respondents. Specifically, we often find a slight overrepresentation of responses in favor of winning parties and coalitions as well as a slight underrepresentation of the vote for minority or stigmatized political movements (or movements perceived as such).[13] Nevertheless, there is no reason to think that these biases affect vote differentials between social groups, much less the evolution of these differentials over time, which recur in survey after survey and country after country and therefore appear to be well established.[14]

---

11. The confidence intervals are slightly larger at the beginning of the period because of the smaller sample sizes ($n = 2,000–3,000$ rather than $n = 4,000–5,000$). They are not shown on subsequent graphs to simplify the presentation, but one should keep in mind that small variations of two to three points or less are generally not significant.

12. For example, the effects of education in Figs. 14.1–14.2 are measured after controlling for other factors (including sex, age, family situation, income, and wealth). Similarly, the income effects shown in Fig. 14.1 control for sex, age, family situation, education, and wealth. The same is true of wealth effects. The evolutions would be similar in the absence of controls but are reinforced when we take controls into account. See the online appendix, Figs. S14.1a and S14.2a, as well as the discussion below.

13. For instance, the Communist vote was underrepresented in French surveys from the 1950s and 1960s, primarily to the benefit of the Socialist vote, with a total left-wing vote virtually identical to the result actually observed. The vote for the (far right) Front National was understated in surveys and polls in the 1990s and 2000s but is barely understated at all in the 2010s.

14. The survey data are generally reweighted to reproduce the exact results of the vote (while preserving the national representativeness and sociodemographic structure of the sample), and the reweighted data are used to estimate the results presented here. The observed trends in differentials by education, income, wealth, etc., are identical if one uses the raw (un-reweighted) data. See the online appendix.

Note, moreover, that Figs. 14.1–14.2 focus on a specific indicator (namely, the vote differential between the top 10 percent and the bottom 90 percent), but the evolutions would be similar if one measured the cleavages with a different indicator, such as the 50 percent best educated compared to the 50 percent least well educated (and the same for income and wealth). Or one could compare those with college degrees to those without or those with high school diplomas to those without.[15]

In short, despite their limitations, postelection surveys confirm the robustness of the results shown in Figs. 14.1–14.2. I will return to this point when I discuss the detailed results for France, the United States, United Kingdom, and other countries.

The surveys and results discussed thus far also enable us to determine the degree to which the three dimensions of social stratification are correlated. Note that the correlation is not systematic: there are always people with a high level of education but not much wealth, for instance, while others with little education may be quite wealthy. Social classes constitute a multidimensional space. Of course, there is a central diagonal consisting of groups disadvantaged or advantaged on all axes at once (to the extent that individual attributes can be ordered vertically, which is not always the case). But class is a complex phenomenon resulting from many different trajectories. Individuals can occupy different positions on different axes (sometimes only slightly different, sometimes more so). In every society, these differences of position, combined with differences of trajectory, belief, and representations for a given social position, define a complex, multidimensional social space. If the three dimensions considered here (education, income, and wealth) were perfectly correlated, then by definition it would be impossible to present results like those shown in Fig. 14.1: all three curves would coincide exactly. According to the postelection survey data, the correlation among these three dimensions seems to have remained roughly constant over the entire period 1950–2020 (with perhaps a slight increase toward the end of the period, as far as one can judge on the basis of imperfect data).[16] In other words, the evolutions in question cannot be explained

---

15. See the online appendix, Figs. S14.1b–S14.1c and S14.12b–S14.2c.

16. Specifically, the correlation coefficients between level of education, income, and wealth appear to be relatively stable according to postelection survey data from France, the United States, and United Kingdom over the period 1948–2017 (with coefficients of 0.3–0.4 for education and income, 0.2–0.3 for income and wealth, and 0.1–0.2 for education and wealth). A coefficient of zero indicates no correlation, while a coefficient of one indicates perfect correlation. See the online ap-

by a sudden decrease in the correlation of education, income, and wealth. The important change is therefore political-ideological in nature (rather than socioeconomic). It is related primarily to the ability of political organizations and electoral coalitions to unite or divide the various dimensions of social inequality.

Internationalizing the Study of Ethno-Racial Cleavages and Social Nativism

Note, finally, that the results presented here build upon an important body of work in political science. In the 1960s, the political scientists Seymour Martin Lipset and Stein Rokkan proposed a multidimensional analysis of electoral cleavages as a way of analyzing party systems and their evolution. They argued that modern societies began with two great revolutions: the national revolution (which led to the construction of nation-states with centralized governments) and the industrial revolution. Out of these two revolutions came four major political cleavages, whose relative salience varied from country to country: (1) a cleavage between center and periphery (central regions or areas close to the capital and regions perceived as peripheral); (2) a cleavage between the central government and churches; (3) a cleavage between agricultural and industrial sectors; and (4) a cleavage related to ownership of the means of production, pitting workers against employers and owners.[17]

For instance, Lipset and Rokkan used these ideas to explain the British party system circa 1750, which pitted Tories (conservatives) against Whigs (liberals). The former were rural, landed elites jealous of their local power while the latter were urban business elites more reliant on the central state. This battle unfolded in an era when only a few percent of the population enjoyed the right to vote, so that the only form political and electoral conflict could take was between elites. The advent of universal suffrage and the industrial cleavage led to the

---

pendix. Because of the limited number of observations and the imperfection of the variables available for the different dimensions, however, this source tends to slightly underestimate these correlations and does not allow us to identify possible changes within this overall stability. More refined data (not including electoral variables) suggests a possible increase in these correlations since the 1980s. I will come back to this.

17. See S. Lipset and S. Rokkan, "Cleavage Structures, Party Systems and Voter Alignments: An Introduction," in *Party Systems and Voter Alignments: Cross-national Perspectives,* ed. S. Lipset and S. Rokkan (Free Press, 1967).

replacement of the Whig Party (which became the Liberal Party in 1859) by the Labour Party between 1900 and 1950.[18] Lipset and Rokkan also insist on the importance of religious and educational issues in the constitution of European party systems in the nineteenth and first half of the twentieth centuries: proponents of a secular state clashed, often violently, with defenders of a continuing role for ecclesiastical institutions (especially in France, Italy, and Spain). In most countries this had a lasting impact on party structures (with separate Protestant and Catholic parties emerging in some countries, such as Germany and the Netherlands). The cleavages studied by Lipset and Rokkan continue to play an important role to this day.

The approach developed here differs from theirs, however, in two essential details. First, with the advantage of hindsight and recently available sources, I have been able to identify profound transformations in the structure of electoral and sociopolitical cleavages that have taken place since the 1950s. To pinpoint these changes, I propose to classify voters by their position in the educational, income, and wealth hierarchies and to make systematic use of the postelection surveys that have been conducted regularly since 1945. Of course, deciles of education, income, or wealth do not translate directly into social and class identities as they manifest themselves in politics and history. But just as with the measurement of inequality, this terminology has the advantage of allowing comparison of electoral cleavages in very different types of society over long periods of time. In other words, educational, income, and wealth deciles make precise historical comparisons possible, whereas occupational classifications do not (because they change significantly over time).[19]

Second, one limitation of the framework proposed by Lipset and Rokkan is that it completely ignores the question of ethno-racial cleavages. This may seem paradoxical, since their work was published in the 1960s, at the height of the civil rights battle in the United States. Contrary to what may have been

---

18. On the role played by the Liberal Party, progressive taxation, and the Irish question in the transformation of British politics in the late nineteenth and early twentieth centuries, see Chap. 5.

19. In particular, the notion of "working class," which is often used in the study of evolving political cleavages based on postelection surveys, clearly does not have the same meaning in a society where industry accounts for 40 percent of employment as in one where it accounts for only 10 percent. Educational, income, and wealth deciles may not be as meaningful at any given moment as the occupational categories often used, but they allow us to compare societies that would otherwise be incomparable. Ideally, both sets of terminology could be used together. I will come back to this.

thought at the time, this dimension of political conflict has not disappeared.[20] It has actually grown stronger, both in the United States where the race factor is often cited as a reason for the gradual shift of the white working-class vote from the Democratic to the Republican Party in the half century since the 1960s and in Europe where conflicts over issues of identity and immigration have taken on new salience since the rise of anti-immigrant parties since the 1980s and 1990s. All too often studies of these issues focus separately on either Europe or the United States. Work on the US party system tends to concentrate exclusively on what is happening there (which unfortunately is true of much work in the United States in general).[21] Research on Europe is similarly skewed, probably in part because the US party system seems radically different and therefore undecipherable or at any rate hard to compare.[22] European observers never cease to be amazed that the pro-slavery party of the nineteenth century gradually turned into the New Deal party of Roosevelt in the twentieth century and then into the party of Barack Obama in the twenty-first century, and some worry about the significance of that history and its possible implications.

Comparative analysis of the role of ethno-racial cleavages in Europe and the United States (as well as in several non-Western democracies) can nevertheless clarify the evolution of political cleavages on both sides of the Atlantic and shed light on possible future trajectories. In particular, this approach will enable us to analyze the risk of a social-nativist turn in various countries and

---

20. The approach that Lipset and Rokkan introduced in the 1960s is largely centered on European—indeed northern European—party systems (as they developed in the nineteenth and first half of the twentieth centuries), partly because of the influence of Rokkan, a Norwegian, and probably also because Lipset, an American, was hoping for a gradual attenuation of racial cleavages.

21. For example, the numbering of successive US party systems since its independence is a specifically American exercise. There are of course good reasons for this, given the obvious idiosyncrasies of the US trajectory. See Chap. 6 for a rapid presentation of the US party systems.

22. In particular, the very interesting work devoted to the rise of anti-immigrant parties and cleavages over identity and migration in Europe (in some cases going so far as to introduce this new systemic cleavage dimension into the Lipset-Rokkan framework) generally do not refer to the role of racial cleavages in the development of the US party system. See, for example, S. Bornschier, *Cleavage Politics and the Populist Right* (Temple University Press, 2010). See also H. Kitschelt, *The Transformation of European Social Democracy* (Cambridge University Press, 1994); H. Kitschelt, *The Radical Right in Western Europe* (University of Michigan Press, 1995).

to study the conditions under which socioeconomic cleavages may regain their ascendancy over ethno-racial conflict.

Renewal of Political Parties, Declining Electoral Participation

Let us turn again to the case of France and the transformation of the French electorate since the end of World War II. We will be looking at both legislative and presidential elections. From 1871 to the present, there have been legislative elections in France at roughly five-year intervals, first under universal male suffrage and then, since 1944, under universal suffrage. Compared with the United States and United Kingdom, France stands out for the very large number of its political parties and more or less permanent transformation of party structures. In the United States, a two-party system—Democrats versus Republicans—has dominated since the middle of the nineteenth century, although within each party there have always been many factions. Candidates are selected by a system of primaries, and there have been deep and lasting transformations of the ideological orientations of each bloc. In the United Kingdom, the bipartite Liberal-Conservative system of the nineteenth and early twentieth centuries was supplanted in 1945 by a bipartite Labour-Conservative system, again with numerous complications that I will discuss later coupled with profound ideological and programmatic changes. In practice, the contrast between the multipartite French system and the bipartite British and American systems has more to do with institutional differences rather than with the supposedly broader range of ideological diversity in France. Among those institutional differences are the respective electoral systems of each country, but one can of course see electoral systems themselves as reflections of different concepts of political pluralism and their embodiment in political parties.[23]

Since my primary purpose here is to study the evolution of electoral and political-ideological cleavages in a long-term historical and comparative perspective, I will begin by focusing on the distribution of votes between two sets

---

23. The US system (single-round uninominal) tends to concentrate votes on the candidates of the two leading parties, whereas the French system (two-round uninominal) allows a larger number of parties to emerge and persist. Two classic studies of electoral systems and party systems are M. Duverger, *Les partis politiques* (Armand Colin, 1951), and A. Lijphart, *Electoral Systems and Party Systems: A Study of Twenty-Seven Democracies, 1945–1990* (Oxford University Press, 1994).

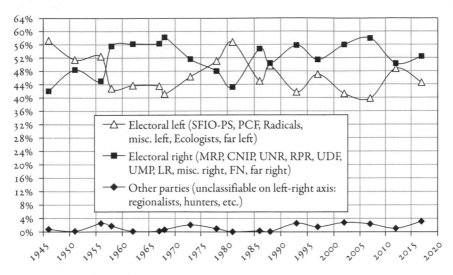

FIG. 14.3. Legislative elections in France, 1945–2017

Interpretation: The scores obtained for the parties of left (Socialists, Communists, Radicals, ecologist, etc.) and the parties of the right (combing all parties or the center-right, right, and far right) ranged from 40 to 58 percent of the vote in the first round of legislative elections in the period 1945–2017. *Note:* The score obtained by the LREM-MoDem coalition in 2017 (32 percent of the vote) is divided equally between center-right and center-left (see Figs. 14.4–14.5). *Sources and series:* piketty.pse.ens.fr/ideology.

of parties that took part in French legislative elections in the period 1945–2017. To simplify matters, I propose to call one group of parties the "electoral left" and the other the "electoral right" (Fig. 14.3). In the period that concerns me here, the electoral left included the Socialist, Communist, and Radical Parties, joined at times by an ecological party along with other small parties classified as center-left, left, or extreme left (Fig. 14.4). Similarly, the electoral right included the Gaullist party and various other political formations classified as center-right, right, or extreme right (Fig. 14.5). The justification for grouping parties in this way is that the goal is to compare the French cleavage structure with that observed in the two-party US and UK systems. I have simply classified the various French parties based on where voters place them on a left-right scale in postelection surveys, which I take to be the least arbitrary way of dividing the electorate into two roughly equal halves.[24] Furthermore, the results

---

24. All postelection surveys in France since 1950 include questions about the left-right position of the various political parties (usually on a scale of 1–7 or 1–10). On the

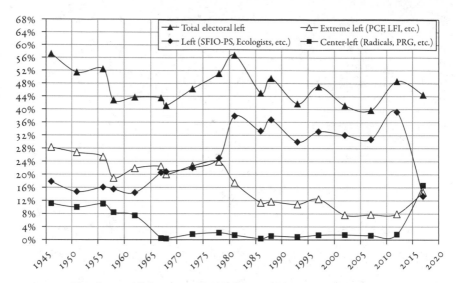

FIG. 14.4. The electoral left in France: Legislatives, 1945–2017

Interpretation: The total score obtained by the left parties (Socialists, Communists, Radicals, Ecologists, etc.) varied from 50–57 percent of the vote in the first round of French legislative elections in the period 1945–2017. *Note:* The vote obtained by the LREM-MoDem coalition in 2017 (32 percent of the vote) is divided equally between center-right and center-left. *Sources and series:* piketty.pse.ens.fr/ideology.

are consistent with the way the parties describe themselves. The only parties excluded from this classification are those that voters either refuse to place on a left-right scale or else rank inconsistently. In practice, these are small regionalist parties or single-issue parties (like the Hunters Party), which did not receive more than 4 percent of the vote in any legislative election, whereas the left and right blocs each received 40–58 percent (Fig. 14.3).[25]

basis of the average score assigned by voters, the Communist Party is unambiguously to the left of the Socialist Party, followed by the parties of the center, center-right, right, and finally, extreme right. Voters also position themselves in the same way: Communist voters place themselves to the left of Socialist voters, who place themselves to the left of centrist voters, and so on. See the online appendix.

25. In the 2017 legislative elections, the coalition of La République en Marche (LREM) and Le Mouvement Démocratique (MoDem), which won 32 percent of the first-round vote, was classified by voters as centrist (relative to the other parties), and in Figs. 14.3–14.5 I have divided its vote equally between center-right and center-left. I will come back to this point.

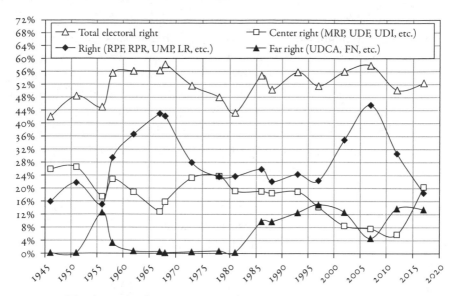

FIG. 14.5. The electoral right in France: Legislatives, 1945–2017

Interpretation: The total score obtained by the parties of the right (including center-right, right, and far right) varied from 50 to 58 percent of the votes in the first round of French legislative elections in the period 1945–2017. *Note:* The score obtained by the LREM-MoDem coalition in 2017 (32 percent of the vote) has been divided evenly between the center-right and center-left. *Sources and series:* piketty.pse.ens.fr/ideology.

It is important to note, however, that these categorizations are largely artificial. Within each broad party group there has always existed a very broad range of opinions and sensibilities (which is also true of the major British and American parties). In fact, the structure of political-ideological conflict is as a general rule highly multidimensional. In particular, there is disagreement about matters related to property (which include fiscal policy and other measures to reduce inequality) and to borders (including immigration policy). Of course, there are times when one dimension or another becomes the primary focus of electoral competition and therefore influences how voters perceive the relative positions of the parties. Because political-ideological is multidimensional and the dimensions are not perfectly correlated, equilibria are generally precarious, unstable, and temporary.

This is indeed the case in France today in the late 2010s. As we will see later, this is clearly a period in which the principal axis of electoral and political conflict is being redefined. One sign of this is the vehement rejection of terminology related to old political cleavages (especially "left" and "right," terms that are even more indignantly repudiated than usual—a sign that their meaning is shifting). To understand how we got to this point, however, it will be useful to begin by studying the evolution of the left-right cleavage in France since 1950 and to compare it with the Democratic-Republican and Labour-Conservative cleavages in the United States and United Kingdom.

Indeed, the designations "left" and "right" have always been a site of intense political-linguistic conflict. Some speakers use these words positively to define their own identities or pejoratively sense to discredit their enemies. Others reject them as no longer applicable (which does not prevent new axes of conflict from emerging). My goal here is not to settle disputes about terminology, police language, or expound the deep nature of the "authentic left" or "authentic right." To do any of these things would make little sense, especially since "left" and "right" clearly have no fixed eternal meaning. They are sociohistorical constructs, which structure and organize political-ideological conflict and electoral competition in specific historical contexts. First used during the French Revolution to refer to political groups seated on the left and right sides of the chamber, specifically in relation to their position on the question of perpetuating or ending the monarchy, the notions of left and right have been the object of constant struggle and perpetual redefinition ever since. In particular, disputes over the meaning of left and right are likely to arise when there is disagreement about political strategies that claim to transcend the conflicts of the past and introduce new political cleavages. At this stage, my goal is simply to study the evolution of left and right as electoral descriptions. How have specific groups and parties embodied the notions of left and right in elections since the end of World War II? I will also compare the evolution of electoral cleavage structures across countries during this period.

It is also interesting to consider electoral behavior in the second rounds of those French presidential elections from 1965 to 2012 in which a candidate of the right faced a candidate of the left (Fig. 14.6). In these contests, voters faced a binary choice, which is perforce reductive but also revealing. It turns out that the results for presidential elections confirm those derived from legislative elections.[26] The latter have the advantage of extending over a longer

---

26. I mainly used the results of the first rounds of legislative elections (because some seats are filled after the first round and there is no second-round vote) and the results of the second rounds of presidential elections (in which turnout is higher). When legislative elections took place in the same year and the presidential election ended in a left-right duel, the results shown in Figs. 14.1–14.2 (and after) concern the second

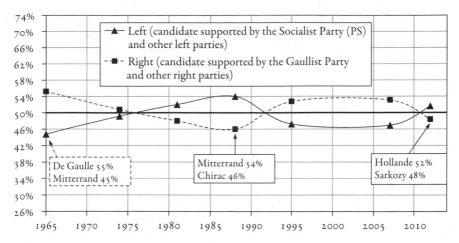

FIG. 14.6. Presidential elections in France, 1965–2012

Interpretation: The scores obtained in the second rounds of French presidential elections (where left faced right) are as follows: 1965 (De Gaulle 55 percent, Mitterand 45 percent), 1974 (Giscard 51 percent, Mitterrand 49 percent), 1981 (Mitterrand 52 percent, Giscard 48 percent), 1988 (Mitterrand 54 percent, Chirac 46 percent), 1995 (Chirac 53 percent, Jospin 47 percent), 2007 (Sarkozy 53 percent, Royal 47 percent), 2012 (Hollande 52 percent, Sarkozy 48 percent). The other second rounds involved the right, center, and far right and are not shown here: 1969 (Pompidou 58 percent, Poher 42 percent), 2002 (Chirac 82 percent, Le Pen 18 percent), 2017 (Macron 66 percent, Le Pen 34 percent). *Sources and series:* piketty.pse.ens.fr/ideology.

period and give a more accurate picture of the multiparty nature of French political life.[27]

Finally, note that although French parties changed significantly, particularly toward the end of the period, voter turnout nevertheless decreased. In presidential elections the decrease is less noticeable: it fell from 80–85 percent in

---

round of the presidential election (for example, for 2012, with almost identical results for the legislatives). The 2017 presidential election was a key turning point, for which I used the votes from the first round. I will say more about this later.

27. The first French presidential election with universal (male) suffrage took place in 1848, but the winner decided to crown himself emperor and eliminate elections entirely. Between 1871 and 1962 the president was elected by the legislature and had limited powers. Election of the president by universal suffrage was restored by General Charles de Gaulle in 1962 by referendum and applied since 1965; the powers of the presidency were strengthened as well. In contrast to legislative elections (where all candidates winning more than 12.5 percent of the registered electorate in the first round can remain in the running), only the two top candidates can continue on to the second round in the presidential.

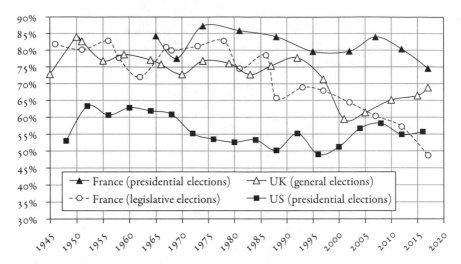

FIG. 14.7. The evolution of voter turnout, 1945–2020

Interpretation: Voter turnout has been relatively stable at around 80–85 percent in presidential elections since 1965 (with a slight drop to 75 percent in 2017). The decrease was much sharper in legislative elections, where turnout was 80 percent until the 1970s but less than 50 percent in 2017. Turnout fell in the United Kingdom before climbing again in 2010. In the United States it has generally fluctuated at around 50–60 percent. *Sources and series:* piketty.pse.ens.fr/ideology.

the period 1965–2012 to 75 percent in 2017. The decrease was greater in legislative elections where the participation rate of 75–80 percent from the 1950s to the 1980s fell to 60–65 percent in the 2000s and to less than 50 percent in 2017 (Fig. 14.7).[28] Note that participation in general elections in the United Kingdom was also around 75–80 percent from the 1950s to the 1980s but fell quite rapidly in the 1990s (to about 60 percent in the early 2000s) and then climbed again in the 2010s (to almost 70 percent in 2017). In the United States, voter turnout has always been relatively low, so the decrease is less marked: it was about 60–65 percent in the 1950s and 1960s and has fluctuated around 50–55 percent since the 1970s.[29]

---

28. The turnout rates shown are for the first round of legislative elections and the second round of presidential elections (which are generally higher, for the reasons indicated above).

29. Note a peak of 58 percent when Obama was first elected in 2008. The turnout rates for the United States in Fig. 14.7 are for presidential elections. Participation in senate and congressional elections is generally much lower (especially in midterms).

On the Declining Turnout of the Less Advantaged Classes

The next point is especially important: it is striking to note that turnout rates are linked to inequality. Turnout remains high among socially advantaged voters but declines among less advantaged voters (Fig. 14.8). Using postelection surveys from the United States, United Kingdom, and France for the period 1948–2017, we can relate turnout rate to individual socioeconomic characteristics. In the United States, where overall turnout is generally low, we find that turnout has always been much higher among voters belonging to the top 50 percent of the income distribution compared with turnout among those in the bottom 50 percent; the gap has ranged from 12 to 20 percentage points over the past sixty years. We find a similar gap if we use level of education, occupation, or wealth. Whatever the criterion used, we find that abstention is higher among less advantaged groups.

In the United Kingdom and France between 1950 and 1980, turnout was high among all classes. Specifically, the difference between the turnout rate of those in the top 50 percent of the income distribution and those in the bottom 50 percent was barely 2–3 percentage points. In other words, all social categories

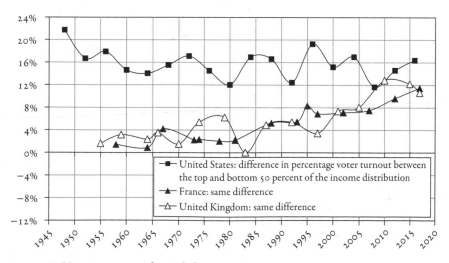

FIG. 14.8. Voter turnout and social cleavages, 1945–2020

Interpretation: In the period 1950–1970, voter turnout in France and the United Kingdom was barely 2–3 percent higher in the top 50 percent of the income distribution than in the bottom. This gap subsequently increased and attained 10–12 percent in the 2010s, approaching US levels. *Sources and series:* piketty.pse.ens.fr/ideology.

voted at practically the same rate (close to 80 percent). By contrast, from the 1990s on, as overall turnout declined, we find that the social gap increased. In the 2010s, in both France and the United Kingdom, the gap between the turnout rate of the top 50 percent of the income distribution and that of the bottom 50 percent was 10–12 percentage points, a level approaching that of the United States (Fig. 14.8). Here again, we find similar gaps if we look at education, occupation, or wealth.[30]

I will come back to this declining turnout of the less advantaged classes, which is of central importance to the argument of this book. It has been quite persistent in the United States over the last half century. In France and the United Kingdom it first appeared in the period 1990–2020, following a period of relatively egalitarian voter turnout from 1950 to 1990. It is natural to interpret this change by positing that the less advantaged classes felt less well represented by the political parties and platforms on offer in the second period than in the first. In this connection, it is striking to note that the accession to power of Tony Blair's "New Labour" in 1997–2010 and of the French Socialist Party in 1988–1993 and 1997–2002 coincided with a particularly sharp drop in the turnout of the less advantaged classes.

Note that the turnout rates given here are based on the number of registered voters (since the unregistered generally are not included in postelection surveys). Of those theoretically eligible to vote, as many as 10 percent commonly go unregistered, and this percentage is even higher among the less advantaged classes, especially African Americans in the United States, who are prevented from registering in some states by a variety of regulations and procedures (such as requirements to provide proof of identity or laws excluding convicted felons from the rolls).[31] The French postelection surveys for 2012 and

---

30. More precisely, due to sample sizes and data limitations, participation rates look similar in terms of income, education, and wealth. More complete data might reveal larger gaps for one dimension or another. Note, too, that the participation gaps shown for France concern presidential elections and are still higher for legislative elections (12–15 percentage points in 2012–2017 for the gap between the top and bottom 50 percent, a level virtually identical to that observed in the United States and higher than in the United Kingdom). See the online appendix.

31. Until the mid-1960s, it was practically impossible for African Americans to register to vote in the southern states (owing to so-called literacy tests administered in a totally biased way by white officials). Changes to federal law in 1964–1965 put an end to the worst abuses but still allowed states to influence the social and racial composition of voter lists in more indirect ways.

2017 include data from which it possible to demonstrate the existence of very large social biases regarding voter registration.[32]

Ultimately, the declining turnout of the less advantaged classes in the period 1990–2020 illustrates one good aspect of the "classist" cleavage structure of the period 1950–1980. In the abstract, it is neither a good thing nor a bad thing that political conflict is organized along classist lines, in which one party or coalition attracts the votes of the least advantaged (on any dimension: education, income, or wealth) and the other attracts the votes of the more advantaged. One might even argue that an electoral system split along purely class lines suggest a certain failure of democracy. Elections in such a system come down to a clash of antagonistic interests and would no longer reflect a broad range of opinions and experiences.[33] Note, however, that the classist cleavages of the period 1950–1980 left a good deal of room for diverse individual trajectories and subjectivities: individuals with the lowest levels of education, income, and wealth tended on average to vote more often for parties of the left, but the relation was far from systematic.

Classist electoral conflict had at least one positive feature: it mobilized all social categories in equal proportions.[34] Matters of redistribution were very much a part of political debate: this was the era of the welfare state, which put in place systems of social insurance and progressive taxation. Left and right

---

32. Those two surveys showed that 6 percent of French nationals living in France were unregistered, with a rate of only 4 percent among managers and the most highly educated to 10 percent among workers and the least highly educated (as well as 11 percent of people aged 18–25 and only 2 percent among those over 65). See the online appendix. This additional bias is not shown in Fig. 14.8 (which shows only registered voters) because this information is not available for previous years.

33. In his *Essai sur l'application de l'analyse à la probabilité des décisions rendues à la pluralité des voix* (1785), the Marquis de Condorcet, Nicolas de Caritat, aptly summed up this ambiguity of the electoral system: if every individual possesses information and experiences of common interest, then majority rule is a way of aggregating this information, and it is in no one's interest to prefer dictatorship over elections, which Condorcet envisioned as a kind of "jury." On the other hand, if an election is a mere confrontation of antagonistic interests, majority rule can lead to chaotic "cycles," and the majority can be shown to prefer every possible decision over every other one. See the online appendix.

34. At least in Europe. The fact that the US electoral regime never allowed such a high degree of social mobilization may be related to the fact that the New Deal was less ambitious in its social experimentation than European social democracies. See Chap. 11.

coalitions brought their different experiences and aspirations to the table. It would be naïve to describe the choices that emerged as fully democratic, because many asymmetries remained in the distribution of political power and influence. Still, all classes participated. By contrast, what has emerged in the period 1990–2020 is an electoral regime of competing elites. Social cleavages remain at the center of political conflict (because one coalition attracts the votes of the better educated while the other attracts the highest earners and wealthiest individuals), but debate about redistribution has largely been obliterated, and the less advantaged classes have substantially decreased their participation. This can hardly be seen as a positive development.

On the Reversal of the Educational Cleavage: The Invention of the Party of the Educated

We come now to what is surely the most striking evolution in the long run; namely, the transformation of the party of workers into the party of the educated. Before turning to explanations, it is important to emphasize that the reversal of the educational cleavage is a very general phenomenon. What is more, it is a complete reversal, visible at all levels of the educational hierarchy. Take, for example, the legislative elections of 1956, in which the parties of the left (Socialists, Communists, and Radicals) did extremely well in France, together capturing nearly 54 percent of the vote. Among voters without a diploma or whose highest diploma was an elementary school leaving certificate and who comprised 72 percent of the electorate at the time. The parties of the left captured an even higher portion of the vote—57 percent (Fig. 14.9)— among voters without a diploma or whose highest diploma was an elementary school leaving certificate and who comprised 72 percent of the electorate at the time. The left captured 49 percent of the vote among voters with a secondary-school diploma of one kind or another and who comprised 23 percent of the electorate in 1956. By contrast, the left parties claimed only 37 percent of the vote of those with a tertiary degree, who at the time made up only 5 percent of the electorate.

Could this be a statistical accident due to a small sample size or specific features of this particular election? The answer is no. Although the sample size is not as large as one might like, the vote differentials are highly statistically significant. Furthermore, we find exactly the same profile—the higher the level of education, the less likely the left-wing vote—in all elections in this period, in survey after survey, without exception, and regardless of the ambient political

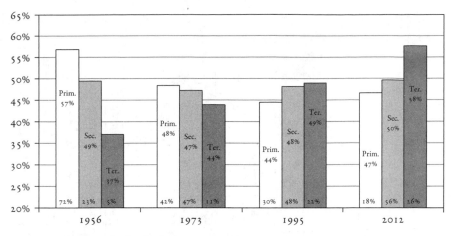

FIG. 14.9. Left vote by level of education in France, 1956–2012

Interpretation: In the 1956 legislative elections, 57 percent voters with a primary school education or less (72 percent of the electorate) voted for the left versus 50 percent for those with secondary diplomas (23 percent of the electorate) and 37 percent with tertiary diplomas (5 percent of the electorate). In the 2012 presidential elections, this educational cleavage had completely reversed: the left candidate obtained 58 percent of the vote of those with tertiary degrees in the second round versus 47 percent of those with at most a primary diploma (18 percent of the electorate). *Sources and series:* piketty.pse.ens.fr/ideology.

climate. Specifically, the 1956 profile is repeated in 1958, 1962, 1965, and 1967.[35] Not until the 1970s and 1980s does the shape of the profile begin to flatten and then gradually reverse. The new norm emerges with greater and greater clarity as we move into the 2000s and 2010s.

For example, in the presidential election of 2012, which Socialist François Hollande won over right-wing candidate Nicolas Sarkozy by 52 to 48 percent, we find that the left owed its victory entirely to better educated voters. Among individuals with no diploma or at most a primary diploma, who accounted for 18 percent of the electorate in 2012, the Socialist candidate obtained only 47 percent of the vote (Fig. 14.9). His score was 50 percent among voters with a secondary diploma (56 percent of the electorate) and 58 percent among those with a tertiary degree (26 percent of the electorate in 2012). Again, could this be a coincidence, perhaps related to the personality of the candidates? No. We

---

35. See online appendix, Fig. S14.9a.

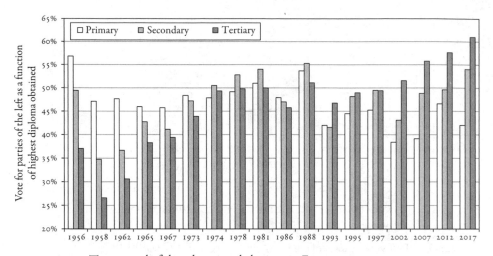

FIG. 14.10. The reversal of the educational cleavage in France, 1956–2017

Interpretation: In the 1950s and 1960s, the vote for the parties of the left (Socialists, Communists, Radicals, Greens) was highest among voters with at most a primary school leaving certificate and lower for those with secondary or tertiary degrees. In the 2000s and 2010s, the situation was precisely the opposite. *Sources and series:* piketty.pse. ens.fr/ideology.

find exactly the same profile in all elections in this period: 2002, 2007, 2012, and 2017.[36]

More generally, when we look at the profiles of the left-wing vote in France by level of education over the entire period 1956–2017, it is striking to see how gradual and steady the change has been over these six decades. The profile is systematically decreasing from the beginning of the period to the middle, flattens out between 1970 and 2000, and then turns sharply upward toward the end of the period in the 2000s and 2010s (Fig. 14.10).

Several points call for clarification. First, all the results presented here on the vote breakdown pertain solely to voters. If one adds the fact that turnout of the less educated decreased toward the end of the period, the change is even more dramatic. In particular, it means that the support of the less educated for left-wing parties decreased even more sharply than is indicated in Fig. 14.10.

Second, it is important to add that the reversal of the overall educational cleavage occurred not just across the three educational levels considered—

---

36. See online appendix, Fig. S14.9b. I will say more later about the peculiarities of the 2017 election, which in terms of educational cleavage is right in line with the previous votes.

primary, secondary, and tertiary—but also within each category. For example, among individuals with secondary diplomas, we find that, at the beginning of the period, those with the *baccaluréat* (that is, who completed the long secondary curriculum) were less likely to vote for the left than those with only a *brevet* (which is normally awarded at age 15 as opposed to 18 for the *bac*).[37] At the end of the period, this has turned around: individuals with the *bac* were more likely to vote for the left than those whose secondary schooling ended earlier. The same is true among those with tertiary degrees, who can be broken down into smaller groups in surveys from the 1970s and beyond, as university education broadened and diversified. In particular, one can distinguish between those with short degrees, requiring only two or three years after the *bac*, and those with long degrees (*maîtrises, diplômes d'études avancées, grandes écoles* in business or science, etc.). In the elections of 1973, 1974, and 1978, when individuals with higher degrees generally tended to vote for parties of the right, this tendency was particularly pronounced among those with long degrees. This was also true in 1981 and 1988, but the gap was smaller. From the 1990s on, and even more clearly in the 2000s and 2010s, the cleavage reversed. The higher the tertiary degree, the more likely its holder was to vote for the left. This was true not only in 2012 when the Socialist candidate made his highest scores among those with long tertiary degrees but also in all other elections in this period.[38]

On the Robustness of the Reversal of the Educational Cleavage

Note, moreover, that this complete reversal of the educational cleavage also exists within each age cohort. More generally, it can be found in groups sharing similar sociodemographic and economic characteristics. Begin with the effect of age. One might think that the high percentage of individuals with tertiary

---

37. The *brevet* and other equivalent diplomas are issued when a student finishes the *college* (in principle, at age 15), whereas the *baccalauréat* is issued upon finishing the *lycée* (in principle, at age 18) and carries with it access to higher education.

38. See the online appendix, Fig. S14.10. If we could distinguish between degrees in different disciplines or between different *grandes écoles,* it would probably be possible to show interesting variations of these patterns and their evolutions. Unfortunately, the sample sizes of the surveys and the questionnaires used (which group all individuals with long tertiary degrees together) make this impossible.

degrees voting for the Socialist candidate in 2012 was due not to the educational effect as such but rather to the fact that people with tertiary degrees are more likely to be younger and the young are more likely to vote for the left. This is true to some extent, and it helps to explain why the left-wing vote gap between those with and without tertiary degrees decreases slightly with age, but one can show that the age effect is relatively weak. Indeed, there are many young people without degrees and many older people with them, so the two effects can be clearly distinguished. In the end, the data show unambiguously, in survey after survey, that the educational effect within each age cohort is of roughly the same magnitude as in the population as a whole. Furthermore, the slight age bias has always been present: the young have always tended to vote more strongly for the left and are also more likely to have a higher educational level than the average for the whole population; this is true in the 1950s and 1960s as well as in the 2000s and 2010s. Technically, the curve obtained with age as a control variable is always slightly below the curve obtained without the control (because part of the educational effect is linked to age), but to a first approximation this effect has been constant over time, so that controlling for age has virtually no effect on the magnitude of the trend observed over the past half century, which in this sense seems to be quite robust (Fig. 14.11).[39]

Note, moreover, that the same general effect of age on voting is also found in other representative democracies; in no case does it alter the conclusion about the reversal of the educational cleavage. Specifically, we find that from the 1950s to the 2010s voters aged 18–34 were generally more likely than voters over age 65 to vote for left-wing parties in France, for the Democratic Party in the United States, and for the Labour Party in the United Kingdom. The reason for this is that the ideological positioning of these parties was generally more favorable to the aspirations of youth (in particular in regard to lifestyle and religion) whereas the parties of the right took positions more compatible with the views of older voters. Note, however, that the vote gap between younger and older voters was quite volatile in all three countries: it was particularly pronounced in the United States in the 1960s, in France in the 1970s, and in the United Kingdom in the late 2010s; by contrast, it was much weaker (or even negligible) in other periods, especially after a prolonged term in office for the parties of

---

39. All technical details on these statistical regressions, along with computer code for reproducing the results from the raw data, are available in the online appendix. See also Piketty, "Brahmin Left vs Merchant Right."

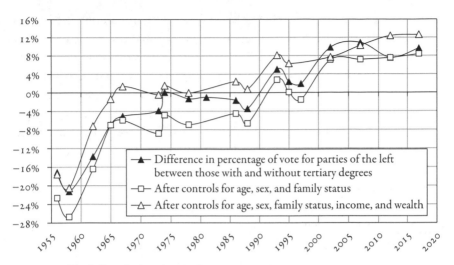

FIG. 14.11. The left and education in France, 1955–2020

Interpretation: In 1956 the parties of the left (Socialists, Communists, and Radicals) obtained a score seventeen points lower among voters with tertiary degrees than among those without; in 2012, the difference was eight points in the opposite direction. Using controls does not affect the trend, only the level. *Sources and series:* piketty.pse.ens.fr/ideology.

the left.[40] In any case, although this volatility of the youth vote is interesting, it has no effect on the basic tendency in which we are mainly interested here; namely, the complete reversal of the educational cleavage.

---

40. See the online appendix, Fig. S14.11a. The gap even became slightly negative in the United States between 1980 and 1984: voters aged 18–34 were slightly more likely to vote for Reagan than were those over age 65, which is the only example of this type of reversal in any US, French, or UK election in the period 1948–2017. By contrast, the vote gap in favor of Labour between those aged 18–34 and those over age 65 rose to nearly 40 percentage points in 2015–2017, compared with 25–30 points for the French left in the 1970s and 15–20 points for the Democrats in the 1960s (as well as in 2008–2012). The size of these gaps remains roughly the same after controlling for socioeconomic variables (such as sex, education, wealth, parents' occupation, etc.) but decreases sharply if one controls for religion and religious practices, with the coefficients of some variables even changing signs, as in France in recent years: among declared Catholics, younger people (who are admittedly rare) are more likely to vote for the right than older people. On this point, see Piketty, "Brahmin Left vs Merchant Right," Fig. 2.2g.

In Fig. 14.11 I have also included sex and marital status among the control variables. This again has little impact on the educational effect: the reversal of the educational cleavage occurs among both men and women as well as both single and married individuals. It is worth noting that postelection surveys also confirm that women have been moving leftward over the long run. In the 1950s and 1960s, women were far more likely to vote for the right than men, especially in France and the United Kingdom and to a lesser extent in the United States. This bias decreased over the 1970s and 1980s and then reversed slightly in France and the United Kingdom (where women were a little more likely than men to vote for the left in the decades after 1990); in the United States the reversal was more pronounced.[41] To account for this change, some researchers have emphasized the importance of rising divorce and separation rates and of the number of women—especially single mothers—living in economically precarious circumstances.[42] More generally, this evolution reflects deep socioeconomic and political-ideological transformations regarding family structure, combined with the growing salience of the issue of gender equality. Workplace equality gradually emerged as the goal of many women, supplanting the patriarchal ideal of the housewife (which many women had internalized in the 1950s and 1960s); this feminist demand was championed primarily by parties of the left.[43] As we saw in Chapter 13, however, gender-related income and wealth inequality remains quite high.

Finally, I also used income and wealth as control variables. As with age, controlling for income and wealth slightly alters the curve but not the underlying trend (Fig. 14.11). In other words, the reversal of the educational cleavage— that is, the fact that the more highly educated became more likely to vote for

---

41. See the online appendix, Fig. S14.11b.

42. See L. Edlund and R. Pande, "Why Have Women Become Left-Wing? The Political Gender Gap and the Decline in Marriage," *Quarterly Journal of Economics,* 2002. See also R. Inglehart and P. Norris, "The Developmental Theory of the Gender Gap: Women's and Men's Voting Behavior in Global Perspective," *International Political Science Review,* 2000.

43. Note that controlling for socioeconomic variables (such as education, income, wealth, parents' occupation, etc.) has very little effect on the tendency of women to vote for the right in the 1950s and 1960s—a tendency that we find in all categories at the time. By contrast, controlling for religion and religious practice practically eliminates this effect entirely: among declared believers, women were not more likely to vote for the right than men. It may be that more overt religiosity among women in the 1950s and 1960s was itself linked to a system of beliefs about the maternal role in family life and child-rearing. See Piketty, "Brahmin Left vs Merchant Right," Fig. 2.2c.

the left in the period 1990–2020—is a phenomenon that exists at every level of income and wealth.[44] I also included many other control variables, such as parents' occupation, geographic location, and population of place of residence. None of these variables affected the reversal of the educational cleavage. We also find the same result when, instead of comparing individuals with and without tertiary degrees, we compare those with either tertiary or secondary degrees and those without, or the best educated 10 percent with the remaining 90 percent, or the best educated 50 percent with the other 50 percent.[45] Given that the educational cleavage has changed direction and increased in magnitude at every level of education (or, to put it another way, given that the left-wing vote gap used to decrease with rising education but now increases), it makes little difference how one breaks down levels of education: the same reversal exists no matter how one does the calculation.

Reversal of the Educational Cleavage; Redefinition of Occupational Cleavages

If we now look at different occupations and sectors of activity, we find that the reversal of the educational cleavage is particularly striking for certain categories of work. Among the less educated individuals who voted strongly for parties of the left in the 1950s and 1960s but ceased to do so in the period 1990–2020, blue-collar workers stand out. The collapse of the working-class vote for socialist, communist, and social-democratic parties in Europe and for the Democrats in the United States and Labour in the United Kingdom is a well-known phenomenon that exists in all Western countries.[46] The most obvious

---

44. Note that controlling for income and wealth raises the level of the curve, which is logical, given that higher levels of education are correlated with higher income and wealth and that higher income and wealth generally strengthen the tendency to vote for the right. The effect is similar to the age effect but in the opposite direction (Fig. 14.11).

45. See the online appendix, Figs. S14.11c–S14.11d.

46. In particular, the Alford index is a classical measure of the difference between workers and the rest of the population in the vote for social-democratic parties (or for Labour, Democrats, or Socialists, depending on the context). The Alford index was very high in all Western countries in the 1950s and 1960s (as high as 40–50 percentage points in Nordic countries like Sweden and Norway, where the social-democratic vote among workers was as high as 70–80 percent). It gradually decreased in the 1980s and 1990s and dropped to almost zero in the 2000s and 2010s (in some

explanation for this is that workers increasingly feel that the parties that were supposed to represent them have been less and less successful at doing so, especially in a context of falling industrial employment and globalization without sufficient collective regulation.

By contrast, certain highly educated groups continue to vote left (or have become more likely to vote left), including teachers, mid-level and supervisory personnel in the public sector, healthcare professionals, and individuals working in cultural professions. In other words, the reversal of the educational cleavage did not take place in a void or an unchanging environment. It occurred in rapidly changing societies, characterized by an unprecedented increase in the average level of training and access to secondary and higher education, coupled with an equally unprecedented expansion of service-sector employment.

It would nevertheless be a mistake to reduce the reversal of the educational cleavage to changes in the voting patterns of specific occupational groups (such as industrial workers and teachers). We find the same reversal in specific occupational groups and sectors of the economy. For example, among private-sector workers (or, more narrowly, nonindustrial private-sector workers or also among public-sector workers), we find that the less educated were more likely than the better educated to vote for parties of the left between 1950 and 1970, while the opposite is true between 1990 and 2020. It is not just industrial workers who have stopped voting for the left: disaffection is just as pronounced among less educated service workers. Unfortunately, the limitations of the data do not allow us to study the interaction between the occupational and educational effects with as much precision as we would like.[47] But we have enough

cases even going negative). See R. Alford, "A Suggested Index of the Association of Social Class and Voting," *Public Opinion Quarterly*, 1962; S. Bartolini, *The Political Mobilization of the European Left, 1860–1980: The Class Cleavage* (Cambridge University Press, 2000); G. Evans, *The End of Class Politics? Class Voting in Comparative Context* (Oxford University Press, 1999); R. Inglehart and P. Norris, *Trump, Brexit and the Rise of Populism* (Harvard University, HKS Working Paper No. RWP16–026, August 2016), fig. 7. The limitation of this type of index is that the definition of "worker" varies widely by country and period, and the proportion of the working population so classified has also evolved substantially over time.

47. More specifically, the tendencies indicated in Figs. 14.11 and S14.11c–S14.11d are not affected by including controls for sector of activity (public, private, and self-employed) or occupational category (blue-collar, white-collar, supervisory, and other). Note, however, that the occupational categories included in the surveys changed frequently between 1950 and 2010, and the small sample sizes seriously limit the possibilities for studying interaction effects. See the online appendix.

information to conclude that the reversal of the educational cleavage is a general phenomenon not limited to a particular sector or political party.[48]

The Electoral Left and the Less Advantaged Classes: Anatomy of a Divorce

How can we explain why the electoral left, which in the 1950s and 1960s was the party of workers and other less advantaged groups, became the party of the highly educated in the 1990s and 2000s? We will not be able to answer this question fully until we have examined the trajectories of the United States, United Kingdom, and other countries, along with the many processes that may have contributed to this complex evolution. To simplify matters, it may be useful to divide the explanations into two broad categories: one based on a social hypothesis, the other on a nativist hypothesis (the two are not mutually exclusive). The social hypothesis, which I regard as by far the more important and convincing of the two, is that the less advantaged classes came to feel more and more abandoned by the parties of the left, which increasingly drew their support from other social categories (notably the better educated). By contrast, the nativist hypothesis holds rather that the parties of the left were abandoned by the less advantaged classes, which were fatally drawn to the sirens of racism and anti-immigration. The latter hypothesis is particularly widespread in the United States where it is often (correctly) pointed out that disadvantaged southern whites began a slow transition to the Republican Party after the Democrats took up the cause of racial equality and desegregation in the 1960s. Furthermore, a great deal of research on both Europe and the United States highlights the existence of growing cleavages around immigration and multiculturalism, which have allegedly driven a wedge between the less advantaged

---

48. In the French left, the vote for the Communist Party always drew more heavily on the less advantaged and less well educated than did the Socialist vote. But both electorates shifted toward the more highly educated to a similar degree (at least to a first approximation and allowing for the limited sample sizes, which limit what it is possible to say), and the overall evolution was accelerated by the shrinking size of the Communist share of the vote. In any case, the central fact is that one observes the same reversal of the educational cleavage in countries where the electoral left was never structured in this way (such as the United States and United Kingdom). Hence this evolution must have deeper political and intellectual roots.

classes and the electoral left.[49] This hypothesis deserves to be taken seriously, and I will examine it closely in what follows. There is no denying that in recent decades, nativist, racist, and anti-immigrant themes have been exploited to the hilt by parties of the traditional right (starting with the Republican Party in the United States and the Conservative Party in the United Kingdom) as well as by new movements of the far right that have mobilized around these issues (for which the archetype is the Front National in France).

Nevertheless, the nativist hypothesis poses numerous problems and, in my view, fails to give a correct account of the observed changes. The key fact is that the reversal of the educational cleavage is a long-term phenomenon that began in the 1960s and 1970s, not only in the United States but also in France and the United Kingdom, which was well before the immigration cleavage became truly salient in Europe. It is obviously very convenient for the elites to explain everything by stigmatizing the supposed racism of the less advantaged. However racism is not more "natural" among the least favored classes than among the well-offs. If the less advantaged truly supported anti-immigrant movements, their turnout should be at a peak today. The fact that it is very low clearly shows that many less advantaged voters are not satisfied with the choices presented to them. Finally, when we come to examine the whole range of countries for which we possess comparable data, we will find that the educational cleavage has also reversed in places where the immigration cleavage plays virtually no role. All this argues in favor of the social hypothesis—that is, the idea that the less advantaged classes feel abandoned by the parties of the center-left. Indeed, nativist discourse has fastened on this sense of abandonment in the hope of winning over these disillusioned voters.

The "Brahmin Left" and the Question of Social and Educational Justice

Let us try now to better understand the significance of the social hypothesis in the French case. Look again at the evolution observed from the legislative elections of 1956 to the presidential elections of 2012 (Fig. 14.9). In 1956,

---

49. See H. Kitschelt, *The Radical Right in Western Europe* (Michigan University Press, 1995); S. Bornschier, *Cleavage Politics and the Populist Right* (Temple University Press, 2010). See also R. Inglehart, *Modernization and Postmodernization: Cultural, Economic and Political Change in 43 Societies* (Princeton University Press, 1997); Inglehart and Norris, *Trump, Brexit and the Rise of Populism.*

72 percent of voters had no diploma beyond primary school. In 2012, only 18 percent of voters fit this description. In other words, the vast majority of the children and grandchildren of the less educated voters of 1956 were able to remain in school longer, some to earn secondary diplomas and others tertiary degrees of one kind or another. What is striking is that among those children and grandchildren, those who managed to make it to university (and particularly those who earned the more advanced university degrees) are the ones who continued to vote for the parties of the left with the same frequency as the less educated voters of 1956. Those who settled for secondary diplomas (especially those who obtained only a *brevet* and did not go all the way to the *baccalauréat*) were clearly less enthusiastic about voting for those same parties. Those who "remained" at the primary level or quit before finishing primary school massively deserted the parties of the left.

A natural explanation for this disaffection with the electoral left is the perception that the parties of the left totally changed in nature and adopted completely new platforms. Briefly put, the social hypothesis is this: that the less educationally advantaged classes came to believe that the parties of the left now favor the newly advantaged educated classes and their children over people of more modest backgrounds. There is much evidence in favor of this hypothesis, which suggests that it is not a mere impression but has a solid basis in fact. It bears emphasizing that this major political-ideological and programmatic shift was steady, gradual, and largely unforeseen; it also coincided with a significant expansion of educational opportunity. In other words, the electoral left was transformed from the workers' party into the party of the educated (which I propose to call the "Brahmin left"). This transformation was unwitting; it was not the result of any single person's decision.[50] Indeed, it is easy to understand why those who improved their social status through education and particularly through public schooling would in many ways feel grateful to the parties of the left, which always stressed the importance of education as a means to emancipation and social advancement.[51] The problem is that many who succeeded in this way developed smug and condescending attitudes toward the rest of the

---

50. Of course, certain individual actors had more opportunities to influence this trajectory than most other voters and citizens. Here, I simply want to stress the fact that this long-term evolution was due to many actors and did not follow any preestablished plan.

51. We cannot tell from postelection survey data whether a given individual was educated publicly or privately, nor do we have information about fields of study and different degrees. We do, however, see the same reversal of the educational cleavage

population; or, to put it more charitably, they did not inquire too deeply into whether official "meritocratic" pronouncements corresponded to reality or not. Thus, the former workers' party became the party of the winners of the educational system and gradually moved away from the disadvantaged classes, much as Young had imagined when he foresaw the widening gulf between "technicians" and "populists" in his premonitory fictional account of 1958.[52]

Conflict between the new disadvantaged classes, which gradually deserted the parties of the left, and the new educated classes of the "Brahmin left" has taken a variety of forms in recent decades (and continues to this day). The two groups differ regarding how public services are organized; how cities, suburbs, and rural areas are financed; what cultural activities are supported; and how the transportation infrastructure is designed and maintained. We also see conflict between large cities, especially Paris and its environs, where many of the highly educated now live, and smaller cities and rural areas that are less well integrated into the global economy.[53] The issue of financing high-speed rail service (TGV), which is so expensive that it is used mainly by the favored classes of the big cities, and the concomitant closing of local lines linking smaller cities and towns, is another clear example of this kind of cleavage. Issues of taxation and apportionment of the fiscal burden have also become quite salient, especially since the 1980s and 1990s, when the left in power played an important role in liberalizing capital flows without insisting on concomitant exchanges of information or social and fiscal coordination. This benefited the wealthy and mobile while increasing the tax burden on classes perceived to be immobile (which were hit with higher indirect and payroll taxes).[54]

Finally, conflict between the less advantaged categories and the "Brahmin left" is also rooted in the organization of the educational system itself. Bear in mind that French schools and universities are extremely stratified and inegalitarian. Primary and secondary curricula have gradually been unified in the sense that, in theory, all children have had access since the 1970s to the same oppor-

---

in countries where private higher education plays a greater role, such as the United States, which shows the plasticity of the new meritocratic ideology.

52. Chap. 13.

53. An important and readily apparent symbol of the change is the fact that Paris swung sharply left in the 1990s and 2000s (with a Socialist winning a majority in every mayoral race since 2001—whereas the city voted strongly on the right in the 1970s and 1980s). We see similar changes in many other prosperous metropolises such as London and New York.

54. See Chap. 11.

tunities, with identical programs and financing for all primary schools and *collèges* (junior high schools), at least up to the age of 15.[55] By contrast, three separate types of *lycées* (high schools) remain: general, technological, and professional. In practice, these strongly reproduce existing social cleavages. Even more serious is the extremely hierarchical nature of the French system of higher education. On the one hand there are the so-called *grandes écoles,* which prepare students for careers in science, business, and public service. To gain access to these schools, students normally attend special preparatory classes. These schools are highly selective and elitist; graduates often go on to fill executive positions in both the public and private sector as well as top jobs in management, engineering, and the civil service.[56] On the other hand, there are universities, which historically have not been allowed to select their students: in principle, any student with a *baccalauréat* is automatically admitted. And there are also so-called technological universities (IUTs), which offer shorter curricula of two to three years.

In practice, the children of the advantaged classes are overrepresented in the preparatory classes and the *grandes écoles,* which benefit from public financing two to three times as high per student as in the universities, where most children of the less advantaged classes end up. To justify this system, a slogan was invented: "republican elitism." This is supposed to be a good thing. The existence of elitism is acknowledged, but it is justified as "republican" because it is supposed to serve the general interest and is based on merit and

---

55. The minimum age for leaving school was raised from 14 to 16 in 1967 (applicable to students born in 1953 or later), but it was not until 1973 that the *collège unique* (that is, identical junior high school curricula for all students) was put in place. Previously, children of the less advantaged classes, once they obtained their primary school leaving certificate at age 11 or 12, were often placed in special "terminal studies" sections of the junior high schools until age 15. See the illuminating work of J. Grenet, *Démocratisation scolaire, politiques éducatives et inégalités* (EHESS, 2008); J. Grenet, "Is Extending Compulsory Schooling Alone Enough to Raise Earnings? Evidence from French and British Compulsory Schooling Laws," *Scandinavian Journal of Economics,* 2013.

56. Since the nineteenth century, the preparatory classes for the *grandes écoles* have been based in the best general *lycées,* so that the whole system is completely separate from the universities. Sciences Po (to which I alluded in Chap. 13 in discussing the uninhibited hypermeritocratic elitism of its founder Emile Boutmy in 1872) serves in practice as something like a preparatory school for the École Nationale d'Administration (ENA), whose creation in 1945 capped off the *grande école* system. Four of six presidents of France since 1974 are graduates of the ENA.

equality of opportunity. Hence it presumably has nothing in common with the hereditary privileges enjoyed by the elites of the Ancien Régime. Like any ideological system, this one has a certain prima facie plausibility. All societies need to select the individuals who will occupy posts of responsibility, and to do so by means of competitive examinations and the investment of significant public resources might seem to be fairer than selection on the basis of high tuition fees and parental gifts.[57] Nevertheless, the French educational system can be seen as particularly inegalitarian and hypocritical. Because there is boundless faith in exams as the basis of a just inequality, the fate of an individual can be decided by performance in school at the age of 18 or 20. It is also difficult to justify the fact that far greater public funds go to socially advantaged students than to students from less privileged backgrounds. Ultimately, the result of such policies is to exacerbate rather than diminish existing differences between families.

In fact, the electoral left, having become the party of the educated, has also become the advocate and champion of republican elitism, even more so than the "bourgeois" parties that the left opposed when it was the party of workers. Led by the Socialist Party, the electoral left has held power repeatedly since the early 1980s (a little more than half the time all told). Each time it commanded parliamentary majorities that should have enabled it to transform French higher education.[58] For example, it could have decided to make structural changes by investing as much per student in the universities as in the *grandes écoles*. Why did the Socialists not do this? Probably because they felt that the elitist structure of higher education financing was justified or else because they preferred to spend the money on other priorities (including lower taxes for the advantaged classes).[59]

All told, looking at the allocation of resources throughout the educational system (primary, secondary, and tertiary), we find that the current system invests nearly three times as much public money in each child belonging to the top decile in terms of educational expenditure as in each child in the bottom 50 percent.[60] These significant educational inequalities, which largely overlap social inequalities, are due both to differences in access to secondary and higher

---

57. Like the US system. See Chap. 11.
58. The Socialist Party led the government and commanded an absolute majority of deputies in the National Assembly (sometimes alone, sometimes in conjunction with Communist, Radical, or Green allies) in 1981–1986, 1998–1993, 1997–2002, and 2012–2017.
59. Corporate taxes were reduced in 1988–1993, income taxes were cut in 2000–2002, and various employer charges were reduced in 2012–2017.
60. See Fig. 7.8. See also Fig. 17.1.

education and to inequalities of spending within the system. Note, moreover, that due to lack of adequate data, these estimates understate the degree of these inequalities. In particular they are based on the hypothesis that all children benefit from the same average expenditure for each year spent in primary or secondary schooling. The evidence suggests, however, that spending on children of the least advantaged groups is also lower at these levels.

To be more specific, a number of researchers have shown that socially disadvantaged schools, *collèges,* and *lycées* were assigned less experienced teachers. They also had more temporary teachers and unreplaced absences, despite the fact that the effects of these shortcoming on students have been convincingly shown to be both negative and significantly higher for less advantaged students.[61] For example, if we look at public *collèges* in the Paris region, we find that the percentage of (untenured) contract and novice teachers was barely 10 percent in Paris and in the most advantaged *départements* such as Hauts-de-Seine, but it was as high as 50 percent in disadvantaged *départements* such as Val-de-Marne and Seine-Saint Denis.[62] Of course, the same is true in most Organisation for Economic Co-operation and Development (OECD) countries (which is scarcely reassuring): students from privileged backgrounds are more likely to be taught by experienced, tenured teachers than those from disadvantaged backgrounds, who are often taught by substitute or contract teachers. Research has shown, however, that the gaps are particularly high in France.[63]

On the Need for New Norms of Educational Justice

Hypocrisy in this realm is particularly extreme, since on the one hand French governments have established priority education zones (which have existed in France since the 1980s), in which certain schools are designated as particularly

---

61. See, for example, A. Benhenda and J. Grenet, "Stay a Little Longer? Teacher Turnover, Seniority and Quality in French Disadvantaged Schools" (presentation, Teachers College, Columbia University, April 21, 2016); A. Benhenda, *Absence, Substitutability and Productivity: Evidence from Teachers* (working paper, Paris School of Economics, November 2017).

62. See H. Botton and V. Miletto, *Quartiers, égalité, scolarité. Des disparités territoriales aux inégalités scolaires en Ile-de-France* (National Council for School System Evaluation [CNESCO], 2018). See also P. Caro, *Inégalités scolaires d'origine territoriale en France métropolitaine* (CNESCO, 2018).

63. See Organisation for Economic Co-operation and Development (OECD), *Effective Teacher Policies: Insights from PISA* (Programme for International Student Assessment [PISA] and OECD Publishing, 2018).

disadvantaged and in need of extra support, while on the other hand more resources are in fact allocated to schools in more advantaged areas. To be sure,
bonus systems for teachers have been set up in some priority education zones.
But all signs are that these (rather opaque) mechanisms are not sufficient to
compensate for more than a small part of the enormous gaps due to the fact
that the poorer schools have a much higher proportion of inexperienced and
contract teachers. If we were to look at the total resources devoted to each student as a function of the social position of the parents, it is highly likely that
we would find that the most substantial amounts went to the most privileged
students and schools and particularly to the most prestigious big-city *lycées,*
whose faculties contain the highest proportions of experienced teachers with
advanced degrees.

Recent research has lifted part of the veil. If one calculates the average salary
of a teacher at any level (primary school, *collège,* or *lycée*), considering not only
bonuses paid in priority education zones but also all other supplemental pay
(for seniority, level of education, tenured or contract status, etc.), one finds that
the higher the percentage of students from privileged social classes, the higher
the average teacher pay. The relationship is strictly increasing in both *collèges*
and *lycées.* The average number of students per class is also higher in the more
privileged schools, and the two effects balance out so that the average expenditure per pupil is almost constant. Nevertheless, the more privileged *collège*
and *lycée* students arguably receive a better treatment: there are more of them
per class, but the average level of the students is higher, and they have more
experienced, better trained, and better paid teachers.[64] In any case, the very fact
that such information is not published regularly so that it can serve as the basis
of an evolving and verifiable educational reform policy raises serious questions.

---

64. At the *collège* (junior high school) level, average teacher pay (including bonuses) is less than 2,400 euros a month in the 10 percent of schools with the
smallest percentage of socially advantaged students, rising to nearly 2,800 euros
a month in the 10 percent of schools with the most advantaged students. In the
lycées, average pay ranges from 2,700 euros a month for teachers in the most disadvantaged 10 percent of *lycées* to 3,200 euros a month in the 10 percent most advantaged. At the *collège* level, the class size effect is more important for the most
disadvantaged 10 percent of schools while expenditure per student is almost exactly constant across the remaining 90 percent. See A. Benhenda, "Teaching Staff
Characteristics and Spendings per Student in French Disadvantaged Schools"
(presentation, University College London, Institute of Education, and Paris School
of Economics, April 2019).

This is all the more unfortunate because a transparent, avowed effort to channel additional resources to the least advantaged schools (especially at the primary level) could substantially reduce social inequality with respect to scholastic success.[65]

Quite apart from the issue of inequality of resources, it is also important to note that social segregation in the French educational system has increased dramatically. Of the 85,000 pupils registered in the 175 Parisian *collèges* (junior high schools), 16 percent come from the least advantaged classes. But if one looks at the geographic distribution, it turns out that some *collèges* have fewer than 1 percent of disadvantaged students while others have more than 60 percent. Among the *collèges* almost entirely closed to the less advantaged classes, the vast majority are private and nearly a third of Paris *collégiens* attend them, and yet—this is one of the astonishing peculiarities of the French system—they are almost entirely financed by public funds, even though they retain the right to select their students as they wish with no obligation to conform to any common rules.[66] We also find many public *collèges* with only a few percent of less advantaged students, while in other public *collèges* only a few Métro stops away nearly half the students are disadvantaged.[67] The reasons for

---

65. See T. Piketty and M. Valdenaire, *L'impact de la taille des classes sur la réussite scolaire dans les écoles, collèges et lycées français. Estimations à partir du panel primaire 1997 et du panel secondaire 1995* (Ministère de l'éducation nationale, 2006). The doubling of funds for elementary classes in priority education zones as of the fall of 2017 is clearly a step in the right direction. Note, however, that this measure was calibrated to cost as little as possible (roughly 200 million euros or 0.4 percent of the total national education budget; see the online appendix). By itself it will not compensate for the existing gaps affecting the least advantaged students at all levels of the educational system (see Chap. 17, Fig. 17.1).

66. Another astonishing peculiarity of the public-private French system (surprising in view of the French readiness to lecture other countries about the virtues of *laïcité*, the idiosyncratic French version of separation of church and state) is that the public primary schools allow a weekly break for catechism class (on Thursdays from 1882 to 1972 and subsequently on Wednesdays). Not only does the absence of Wednesday classes do particular harm to the least advantaged students, the system also has very negative effects on professional equality between men and women. See C. Van Effenterre, *Essais sur les normes et les inégalités de genre* (EHESS and Paris School of Economics, 2017). A tentative reform to hold classes Monday through Friday as in other countries was attempted in 2012–2017, but in 2017 Wednesdays without classes were restored.

67. See J. Grenet, "Renforcer la mixité sociale dans les collèges parisiens" (presentation, Paris School of Economics, June 22, 2016).

this include significant residential segregation, recourse to private schools to escape the confines of public districting, and most important of all, the absence of any public policy that seeks to change the situation. Yet recent experiments have shown that better designed and more transparent assignment algorithms could achieve more thorough social mixing.[68]

I do not claim that these factors by themselves are sufficient to account for the reversal of the educational cleavage over the past few decades or for the fact that the least advantaged classes feel less and less well represented by the parties of the left. Clearly, however, such glaring educational inequalities may have made people wary of the Socialists in power and lent credence to the belief that they cared more about the better educated and their children than about children from more modest backgrounds.

Since the financial crisis of 2008, educational budgets have stagnated, adding to the frustration, particularly among disadvantaged youth who had been led to believe that working to obtain a *baccalauréat* would open the doors to higher education and employment. In fact, whereas barely 30 percent of each age cohort obtained the *bac* in the 1980s, that figure rose to 60 percent by 2000 and to nearly 80 percent in 2018, partly thanks to a very sharp increase in the number of technological *bacs*. The number of university students increased by 20 percent from 2008 to 2018, rising from barely 2.2 million to nearly 2.7 million. Unfortunately, resources did not increase commensurately: in real terms, budgets increased only 10 percent, which means that the budget per student decreased by 10 percent.[69] Note that the resources per student in the elitist and selective schools where most students came from advantaged groups were maintained. By contrast, students in the regular universities had to study in conditions that fell far short of the promises that had been made to them. For instance, despite the rapid growth of the number of students with technological or professional *bacs,* the number of places in the so-called university institutes of technology (IUT) increased very little, for want of resources. This created tensions, which were exacerbated by the fact that students with the general *bac* also sought to fill these places; many of them came from advantaged backgrounds but failed to get into a preparatory class for the *grandes écoles* and chose to go to an IUT rather than to a general university

---

68. See G. Fack, J. Grenet, and A. Benhenda, *L'impact des procédures de sectorisation et d'affectation sur la mixité sociale et scolaire dans les lycées d'Ile-de-France* (Institut des Politiques Publiques, 2014).

69. See the online appendix, Fig. S14.11e.

(where guidance is hard to come by and job opportunities after graduation are sometimes wanting).

This explosive situation became the subject of a recent TV series, *Le Baron noir* (2016), which features a rather unsavory Socialist president aided by a slightly corrupt deputy from the Nord, Philippe Rickwaert, who tries to buff up the government's image with a symbolic measure of educational justice. To that end, he supports the demands of a group of students from the downscale Paris suburbs. These students, who have graduated with the less prestigious *bac professionnel,* want a number of places set aside for them in the so-called technological universities (IUTs), from which they feel they have been unfairly displaced by students with the more prestigious *bac général.* Rickwaert goes so far as to don a worker's coveralls when he defends the measure in the National Assembly, explaining that by championing the disadvantaged classes he is putting "the social" back in socialist and doing honor to the left. But these tactics displease the party's *jeunesse dorée,* the militants of the Young Socialist Movement, who, as is only to be expected, have graduated from the capital's fanciest *lycées généraux.* To torpedo the movement of their suburban rivals, they go so far as to infiltrate one of their meetings. Shortly thereafter, the leader of the suburban students is compromised by a photograph proving that he is close to accepting a position on a list of right-wing candidates in an upcoming European parliamentary election. This is taken as proof that only young socialists from the classier *lycées* are fit to defend the values of the Brahmin left, which the upstarts from the downscale suburbs are prepared to comprise by complicity with the merchant right.

This series also deserves credit for highlighting another factor that will surely play a growing role in future debates about educational justice: the algorithms used to assign students to different educational tracks. Not so long ago (and to this day in some countries), it was common for parents to use personal connections to get their children into preferred high schools and universities. It is hard to deny that compared to this, impersonal algorithms represent progress toward greater social justice and democracy—but only if they are designed in a transparent manner with abundant input from citizens, which is far from the case today. In 2018, the Post-Bac Admissions (APB) algorithm was replaced by a new algorithm called Parcoursup, which established social quotas for admission to the preparatory classes leading to the *grandes écoles;* this has the potential to result in a more socially just selection process. But the parameters on which the Parcoursup quotas are based remain completely obscure, and only scholarship students are eligible, which disadvantages students whose parents' earnings are just slightly above the scholarship cutoff (this is also the case with the Affelnet system by which students are assigned to *lycées*). If one hopes to achieve norms of justice acceptable to the majority, it would no doubt be better to design a system that factors in social origin in a more gradual and continuous manner and, above all, does so more transparently. It is interesting to note that India, which makes broad use of quotas and "reservations," is in some ways more advanced in dealing with these issues than are the Western countries.[70] Properly used, such democratic tools can break the deadlock in which debate about education has been stuck for decades. I will come back to this.

On Property, from Left and Right

We turn now to the evolution of electoral cleavages involving inequalities of income and wealth. Let us begin by examining the vote profile of the electoral left as a function of income from the 1950s to the 2010s (Fig. 14.12). It is striking to observe that this profile has consistently been relatively flat across the lower 90 percent of the income distribution (with little variation in the average support for parties of the left), but with support for the left falling off sharply among the highest paid 10 percent, particularly from the 1950s through the 1970s. For example, in the 1978 legislative elections, the electoral left won more than 50 percent of the vote in most income deciles, but this figure drops sharply in the top decile and dips to less than 20 percent among the top centile.[71] From the 1990s on, the slope steadily decreases. In the 2012 presidential election, the Socialist candidate won almost 50 percent of the vote in the top income decile and nearly 40 percent in the top centile.

This flattening of the curve is a logical consequence of the fact that the highly educated now vote more heavily for the left. Note, however, that until the 2010s high earners continued to prefer parties of the right, in contrast to the highly educated. In the 1990s, in other words, the partisan cleavage structure shifted to a system of two elites: the highly educated voted left, while high

---

70. See Chap. 8.

71. The questionnaires used in postelection surveys generally included at least ten to fifteen income tranches, with detailed tranches for top incomes, which allows us to deduce the very sharp gradient at the top of the distribution. The method used— which is to estimate deciles and centiles by assuming fixed vote structures within each income tranche (or wealth or education tranche), thus ignoring any gradient within tranches—leads, however, to minimizing slopes and reversals. See the online appendix.

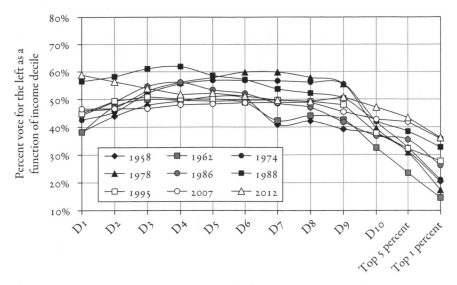

FIG. 14.12. Political conflict and income in France, 1958–2012

Interpretation: In 1978, the parties of the left (Socialist, Communist, Radical, Green) obtained 46 percent of the vote among the bottom income decile, 38 percent in the middle decile, and 17 percent among the top 1 percent. More broadly, the profile of the left-wing vote is fairly flat across the bottom 90 percent of the income distribution and sharply decreasing in the top 10 percent, especially early in the period. *Note:* D1 refers to the bottom 10 percent of the distribution, D2 to the next 10 percent, and D10 to the top 10 percent. *Sources and series:* piketty.pse.ens.fr/ideology.

earners voted right (Fig. 14.1).[72] The key question is how long this will last. It may be that in the future the highly educated will tend to earn the highest incomes and possess the largest fortunes and perhaps draw to their coalitions high-income and high-wealth individuals who do not hold advanced degrees so that both elites will end up in the same party. This possibility cannot be ruled out, and we will see that it is close to becoming a reality in France and the United States. But things are actually more complex. There are two main reasons why the highly educated and the highly paid do not necessarily vote for the same parties. This was the case in both the presidential and legislative elections of 2012, and it may continue to be the case in the future (which does not mean that the two elites cannot agree on many issues, such as setting a low priority on reducing inequality).

72. This is true if one looks at raw profiles (without controls) and even truer after controls. See the online appendix, Figs. S14.1a–S14.1c.

First, for a given level of education, those who are more successful at monetizing their education in the form of higher pay are clearly more likely to vote for the right. The data do not allow us to determine why they earn more: it may be because they chose more remunerative careers (in the private rather than the public sector, say, or a higher-paying job within a given sector) or because they were more successful in winning promotions and getting ahead. But in any case, they are more likely to vote for the right, perhaps because they see it as in their own best interest in that right-wing parties generally favor lower taxes on high incomes or because they hold a worldview according to which income is the reward for individual effort. In other words, the Brahmin left and the merchant right do not share precisely the same experiences and aspirations. The Brahmin left values scholastic success, intellectual work, and the acquisition of diplomas and knowledge; the merchant right emphasizes professional motivation, a flair for business, and negotiating skills. Each group invokes an ideology of merit and just inequality, but the type of effort expected is not exactly the same—nor is the reward for that effort.[73]

Second, at any given level of education, some individuals may have higher incomes than others because they own capital that produces income (rent, interest, dividends, etc.) and allows them to engage in professions that require substantial investment or perhaps even run a company (possibly a family firm). In fact, it is generally the case in all periods and all countries for which adequate data are available that wealth is a much stronger determinant of electoral preference than either income or education. In particular, the curve showing the vote for parties of the left as a function of wealth is much more steeply sloped than the corresponding curve for income (Fig. 14.13). For example, in the 1978 legislative elections, the left's share of the vote fell to just over 10 percent in the top wealth centile (nearly 90 percent of whom therefore voted for the right), compared with 70 percent in the bottom income decile. In other words, property ownership appears to be an almost irresistible determinant of political attitude: the wealthiest asset holders virtually never vote for the left, while those

---

73. For a theoretical model analyzing how belief in effort adapts to individual trajectories, which can then be used to explain the effect of mobility on political attitudes, see T. Piketty, "Social Mobility and Redistributive Politics," *Quarterly Journal of Economics,* 1995. This framework can be extended to a situation in which there are two mechanisms of social promotion (professional effort and scholastic effort), which can then lead to two systems of meritocratic belief and account for a political regime with multiple elites. See T. Piketty, "Brahmin Left vs Merchant Right," section 5.

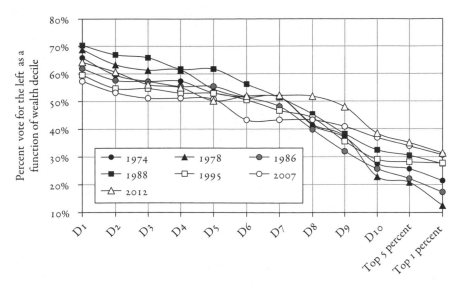

FIG. 14.13.   Political conflict and property in France, 1974–2012

Interpretation: In 1978, the parties of the left (Socialists, Communists, Radicals, Greens) obtained 69 percent of the vote of the bottom wealth decile, 23 percent of the middle decile, and 13 percent of the top centile. More broadly, the profile of the left-wing vote as a function of wealth slopes strongly downward (much more so than the income curve), especially early in the period. *Note:* D1 refers to the bottom wealth decile, D2 to the next, and D10 to the top decile. *Sources and series:* piketty.pse.ens.fr/ideology.

who not own anything seldom vote for the right. The relation between voting and wealth grew weaker after 1970 but still remains much stronger than the relation between voting and income.[74]

---

74. The curves in Fig. 14.13 begin in the 1970s because it is only after 1978 that we have detailed questionnaires on ownership of different types of assets. On this very innovative survey, see J. Capdevielle and E. Dupoirier, "L'effet patrimoine," in *France de gauche, vote à droite?* ed. J. Capdevielle, É. Dupoirier, G. Grunberg, É. Schweisguth, and C. Ysmal (Presses de la Fondation nationale des sciences politiques [FNSP], 1981). Among the more significant works on the relation between wealth and voting, see also M. Persson and J. Martinsson, "Patrimonial Economic Voting and Asset Value: New Evidence from Taxation Register Data," *British Journal of Political Science,* 2016; M. Foucault, R. Nadeau, and M. Lewis-Beck, "Patrimonial Voting: Refining the Measures," *Electoral Studies,* 2017; M. Foucault, "La France politique des possédants et des non-possédants," in *La démocratie de l'entre soi,* ed. P. Perrineau and L. Rouban (Presses de la FNSP, 2017). The results presented here are perfectly consistent with those studies, except that I try to compare the size of

The decisive role of wealth in determining political attitudes will come as no surprise. In the nineteenth and twentieth centuries, the property regime was the central issue of political-ideological conflict. Only since the end of the twentieth century has the issue of education and the type of educational regime assumed comparable importance. Historically, the political regime that emerged from the French Revolution was built around the defense of private property (with limited redistribution), as noted earlier.[75] In his *Tableau politique de la France de l'ouest sous la Troisième République,* published in 1913, André Siegfried carefully and systematically studied legislative votes from 1871 to 1910, canton by canton, relating the vote to taxes paid in proportion to agricultural acreage and to the results of a vast ministerial survey of public and private schooling of girls. His conclusions are perfectly clear. In cantons where land redistribution during the French Revolution enabled peasants to acquire small plots, they voted for republican parties, which at the time stood on the left of the political spectrum (notably the Radical Party, so called because it was the most radically republican).

By contrast, in cantons where the land remained concentrated in the hands of large property owners, often of noble origin, and where the Catholic Church remained influential, particularly through its control of schools, voters favored conservative and monarchist candidates. In the most conservative cantons, such as Léon in northwest Brittany, there were even astonishing legislative battles between priests and aristocrats, including one contest that pitted Abbé Gayrault against the Comte de Blois in 1897. So deep was the attachment of the people to local religious elites that the representatives of the old clerical class often emerged victorious from these contests. Siegfried described a world in which the old trifunctional order still held sway, reassuring citizens who continued to turn to the château and the presbytery for leadership. They were wary of what Parisian republicans had in mind for them because they had no concrete, practical knowledge of what republican government might mean.[76]

---

the wealth effect with that of the income and education effects and, above all, to consider these questions in a comparative historical perspective.

75. See esp. Chaps. 3–4.

76. Siegfried also discusses the pressure that landlords could bring to bear on farmers and sharecroppers, and priests on parents. The trifunctional order could be oppressive when it needed to be. Like Arnoux (see Chap. 2), Siegfried did not hide the fact that his sympathies lay with the priests, their schools, and their charities rather than with the nobles. He also notes that priests were more likely to support the income tax in the Chamber of Deputies (indeed, more likely than republicans of the center-right,

The Left and the Self-Employed: A Twentieth-Century Chronicle of Suspicion

The world that Siegfried describes was on the point of disappearing as he wrote, however. As a good republican of the center-left, he worried about the modest breakthroughs of the "collectivists" in western France, especially among workers in the arsenals of Brest and sardine fishermen in Concarneau. Elsewhere in France, however, Socialist candidates were making more significant progress. Between the two world wars, the Socialist and Communist Parties, which had split at the Congress of Tours in 1920, gradually gained the ascendancy over the Radicals, whom they drove toward the center. After World War II the Radicals were eliminated almost entirely. When it came to private property, Socialist and Communist ideology was quite a bit more subversive than that of the Radicals or republicans of the center-left. Whereas the Radicals had been champions of smallholders, peasants, merchants, and the self-employed of all kinds, and of "social reform respectful of private property," notably by way of the income tax sponsored by Joseph Caillaux, the Socialists and Communists advocated collectivization of the means of production, especially in the industrial sector. Until the 1980s their platforms always included calls for the nationalization of key industries. Throughout the twentieth century they did try to persuade self-employed small businessmen that they had no intention of doing them harm and that people of modest wealth had nothing to fear. But in the absence of definite and reassuring propositions, suspicion of Socialists and Communists remained strong among the self-employed and indeed would continue so until very recently.

This wariness among peasants, small businessmen, craftspeople, and other independents largely accounts for the relatively flat profile of the left-wing vote as a function of income up to the ninetieth percentile (Fig. 14.12). From the 1950s until the 1970s and beyond, the lower income deciles consisted in large part of independent workers, whose income was certainly low but who nevertheless owned a small amount of property (a field, a farm, or a store) and were extremely suspicious of the plans of the collectivists. The weight of independents, and especially peasants, explains the particularly flat profile of the left-wing vote in France in the period 1950–1980; in the United Kingdom and

who favored complete laissez-faire). See A. Siegfried, *Tableau politique de la France de l'Ouest sous la Troisième République* (1913), pp. 89–92, 240–251.

United States this same profile slopes much more markedly downward in the lower nine deciles than it does in France.[77]

In retrospect, such outlandish fear of the parties of the left may bring a smile to the lips. French Socialists and Communists never had either the power or the intention to turn farms and shops into Soviet-style *kolkhozes, sovkhozes,* and *gastronoms* (as the quite un-gastronomic chain of state-run supermarkets was called in the Soviet era). But they also never had the opportunity to explain clearly what their long-term intentions were with respect to small and medium private property or how they conceived its role in the ideal society they envisioned. This ambiguity and uncertainty on the question of property are by no means minor matters. They are at the root of major rifts between Socialists and Communists and between both parties and the rest of society (starting with the self-employed). They go a long way toward explaining why the Social Democrats and Communists in Germany were never able to join forces against the Nazis in the 1930s, and why Radicals, Socialists, and Communists were unable to form durable coalitions in the interwar years (apart from the important but ephemeral Popular Front of 1936–1938). This serious conflict around the property regime and support for the Soviet model (as well as colonialism) also largely explains why the Socialists often governed in so-called third-force coalitions with the Radicals and the center-right between 1947 and 1958. Since these coalitions excluded both the Communists and the Gaullists, this choice was tantamount to governing from the center.[78]

Beyond the existential fear of expropriation of small property owners, it is important to note that the parties of the left themselves contributed to the climate of suspicion and conflict, especially in debates over taxes—particularly the income tax—where they took positions much more favorable to wage workers than to the self-employed. Recall that the income tax adopted in 1914–1917 included both a general tax on income (based on total income from all sources) and a so-called cedular tax that was levied separately on different

---

77. See Figs. 15.5 and 15.13.
78. Note, however, that the brief joint presence of Socialists and Communists in the National Assembly in 1945–1946 had a decisive impact: the social security system was established and the senatorial veto was abolished in the constitution of the Fourth Republic (this veto had been used to block many social and fiscal reforms in the Third Republic). Communist deputies also played a key role in reinforcing the progressivity of the income tax by eliminating the deduction for the previous year's tax payment. On these debates in 1945, see T. Piketty, *Top Incomes in France in the Twentieth Century,* trans. S. Ackerman (Harvard University Press, 2018), pp. 301–304.

types of income (wages, self-employment income, profits, interest, etc.).[79] The cedular tax on wages was much lower than on self-employment income. Wage earners enjoyed significant deductions, so that only 10–15 percent of the highest paid actually paid this tax, while the self-employed paid tax on their full income, which they were required to declare in detail. Angered by such flagrant injustice, peasants, merchants, craftsmen, and other modest self-employed individuals energetically mobilized and won various concessions and compensations in the 1920s and 1930s. But wage earners, defended by the Socialists and Communists, rejected the idea of applying identical rules to both groups because this would have implied higher taxes on workers with low to modest wages, which they regarded as unacceptable, and therefore preferred sticking with a blatantly unfair arrangement.[80]

This situation continued after World War II. The tax reforms of 1948 and 1959 were supposed to unify the system with common rules applied to income of all types, but there were actually special deductions for wage earners, who were also exempt from paying the *taxe proportionnelle*.[81] This issue was also largely responsible for a violent antitax and pro-small-business protest movement, which resulted in a Poujadist surge in the 1956 legislative elections.[82] In

79. See Chap. 4.

80. This issue was a matter of recurrent conflict between, on the one hand, the Socialists and Communists and, on the other, the Radicals, who were traditionally more favorable to smallholders and independents. In parliamentary debates in 1907–1908, Caillaux strenuously defended the idea of a neutral tax on overall income so that "executives of large corporations" would not be treated more favorably than "humble craftsmen" and "humble merchants." He even said that "the schoolteacher, tax collector, and railway employee are often rich in the eyes of the small farmer or small businessman." See Piketty, *Top Incomes in France*, pp. 212–213.

81. For a detailed analysis of these legislative evolutions and corresponding political conflicts, see Piketty, *Top Incomes in France*, pp. 304–318. See also N. Mayer, *La boutique contre la gauche* (Presses de Sciences Po, 1986). On the structure of political conflict over property (especially real estate), see also H. Michel, *La cause des propriétaires. Etat et propriété en France, fin XIXe–XXe siècle* (Belin, 2006).

82. In July 1953, Pierre Poujade, a stationer in Saint-Céré in the Lot Valley, led the first protest of merchants and craftsmen from his small town against tax agents. A few months later, he founded the Union for the Defense of Merchants and Craftsmen (UDCA). Poujadist agitation reached its peak in 1954–1955, with multiple "commando operations" intended to assist small businessmen facing bankruptcy owing to the voracity of the tax collectors. The UDCA declared a "tax strike" in January 1955, and in the January 1956 elections the movement achieved its highest score (leading to the formation of a sizable Poujadist parliamentary group,

the eyes of the Socialists and Communists, the favorable treatment of salaried workers was justified by the fact that the self-employed were all too inclined to understate their income, which wage earners could not do. The argument is understandable, but it was also clearly destined to fail. Instituting a special exemption to compensate wage earners for the fraud allegedly committed by the self-employed would obviously do nothing to decrease fraud nor would it help to develop norms of fiscal justice acceptable to all. Though technical in appearance, these debates played a central role in structuring the electoral cleavage between salaried workers and the self-employed in the twentieth century.[83] Fiscal antagonism between rural and urban areas also played an important role in defining political identities in the nineteenth century.[84] What these conflicts show is that the question of social and fiscal justice cannot be dealt with in the abstract, independent of its institutional and administrative setting. A just tax must be constructed historically and politically on the basis of information about the ability of different taxpayers to share the overall burden. For this, one needs to be able to record and evaluate the wealth and income of people whose situations and economic activities may vary widely.

Strengths and Weaknesses of the "Brahmin Left" and "Merchant Right"

With the end of Soviet communism and bipolar confrontations over private property, the expansion of educational opportunity, and the rise of the "Brahmin left," the political-ideological landscape was totally transformed.

---

including Jean-Marie Le Pen). The Poujadists attacked measures that favored workers, especially "Parisian managers," which in their eyes proved that the "modernizing central government" and its "heartless technocrats," regardless of political label, did not care about the fate of small independent producers. None of this should be allowed to distract from Poujade's very real anti-Semitism, which was caricatured in the "Poujadolf" cover of *L'Express,* a weekly magazine much read by Parisian managers and highly educated wage earners at the time.

83. The 20 percent deduction for workers (on top of another 10 percent reduction for "professional costs"), which was eventually extended to the self-employed, was finally rescinded and integrated into the tax schedule in 2005.

84. For example, in 1848, peasants who owned modest plots were not happy about land tax increases approved early in the year by the new republican government. This was one reason why rural voters heavily favored Louis-Napoléon Bonaparte, who had opposed those tax increases and preferred indirect taxes on city dwellers. See G. Noiriel, *Une histoire populaire de la France* (Agone, 2018), pp. 353–354.

Within a few years the platforms of left-wing parties that had advocated nationalization (especially in the United Kingdom and France), much to the dismay of the self-employed, had disappeared without being replaced by any clear alternative. A dual-elite system emerged, with on one side, a "Brahmin left," which attracted the votes of the highly educated, and on the other side, a "merchant right," which continued to win more support from both highly paid and wealthier votes (Fig. 14.1). We will find this same cleavage structure in the United States, the United Kingdom, and other Western countries. This balance, though robust in some respects, is fragile in others and therefore extremely unstable.

The strength of the Brahmin-merchant duo is that the two sides embody complementary values and experiences. They share certain characteristics, including a certain conservatism when it comes to maintaining the existing inequality regime. The Brahmin left believes in rewarding scholastic effort and talent; the merchant right, on the other hand, emphasizes business talent. The Brahmin left seeks to accumulate diplomas, knowledge, and human capital; the merchant right accumulates cash and financial assets. On some points there are differences. The Brahmin left may prefer somewhat higher taxes than the merchant right: for instance, to pay for the *lycées, grandes écoles,* and cultural and artistic institutions to which it is attached.[85] But both camps are strongly attached to the existing economic system and to globalization as it is currently organized, which ultimately serves the interests of both intellectual elites and economic and financial elites.

At bottom, the Brahmin left and merchant right embody two different forms of legitimacy. Indeed, this system of dual elites in a sense represents a return to the deep logic of premodern trifunctional society based on power sharing between intellectual and warrior elites, except that the warriors have been replaced by merchants (because security of goods and persons is now assured by the centralized state). The Brahmin left and merchant right can either alternate in power or govern together in a coalition of elites. An interesting example of coalition-formation was the 2017 election in France, in which center-

---

85. In the French context, the fact that prestigious private *lycées* and their preparatory classes benefit from the same public funds as their public counterparts can, however, create a certain solidarity between those whose children go to Sainte-Geneviève (a *lycée* favored by the merchant right) and those whose children go to Louis-le-Grand (favored by the Brahmin left) and who often find themselves together later in one of the *grandes écoles.*

left joined with center-right; I will say more about this in a moment. As the highly educated become wealthier, it is even possible that there will be a socio-economic fusion of the two elites to the point where a single party representing both will be the logical outcome. In late-nineteenth-century India, the Brahmins were both the best educated and the largest property owners.[86] Since individuals from different elites tend to make different career choices (with one group choosing, say, work in the public sector or cultural professions and the other private-sector marketing and finance), it may be that the two elites will never fuse completely, however.

While this political equilibrium is clearly quite potent, it is also extremely precarious. As noted earlier, one symptom of this weakness is the withdrawal of the less advantaged classes (Figs. 14.7–14.8). One might interpret this cynically as a boon to the elites: the less the lower classes turn out for elections, the easier it is for the upper classes to maintain their hold on power. But in the long run the risk is that this will undermine the legitimacy of elections and of the political regime itself, opening the way to violent revolution and authoritarian government. In a broader sense, it is clear that the whole postwar political cleavage structure and system of electoral coalitions is in danger of collapse. What remains of the "electoral left" is fractured by deeper and deeper rifts between a pro-market center-left and a more radical wing that favors redistribution and seeks new answers to the challenge of rising inequality. I will say more later about how emerging forms of participatory socialism and social federalism might respond to this challenge. The "electoral right" is equally divided between a pro-market center-right and a more radical nativist and nationalist right, which sees identitarian retreat and anti-immigrant social nativism as the proper response to the challenges of a global economic system run amok. We turn next to the new identitarian cleavages, which will lead us to the four-way division of the electorate seen in France in 2017.

On the Return of Identitarian and Religious Cleavages in France

To begin with, note that the existence of important identitarian and religious cleavages is hardly new in France. The division between Catholics and seculars, which partially overlapped conflicts around property and between rural

---

86. See Chap. 8. I will come back to this point in Chap. 16, when we study electoral cleavages in relation to caste in present-day India.

peasants and urban workers, played a central role in the nineteenth and much of the twentieth centuries.[87] This internal border separating believers from non-believers, even within the less advantaged classes, further complicated the task of organizing socioeconomically coherent political coalitions. If classist political cleavages did develop after the war, it was partly because religious and identitarian cleavages had begun to fade. But it was also because the challenges of two world wars, the crisis of the 1930s, and communism had accustomed people to the idea that a higher level of social and economic intervention was needed. This gave the Socialists and the Communists what they needed to win their battle with the Radicals—their rival in the interwar years—and to convince voters that the time had come for new socioeconomic policies. The issue of the property regime then took precedence over boundary questions.

In recent decades, identitarian and religious cleavages of a new type have developed in France and other European countries as anti-immigrant movements have gathered momentum. These movements oppose immigration from outside Europe, especially Muslims from Arab countries. If we look at the evolution of religious practice in France as declared in postelection surveys since 1967,[88] we find that the proportion of respondents answering "no religion" has increased significantly, from 6 percent in 1967 to 36 percent in 2017 (Fig. 14.14). A majority of the electorate continues to declare itself Catholic, but its size has shrunk from 91 percent in 1976 to 55 percent in 2017. In other words, Catholics once made up an overwhelming majority of the electorate, but now they are merely a relative majority. If we focus on voters below the age of 50, we find that those without religion outnumber Catholics in the 2012 survey (44 to 42 percent).[89] Furthermore, practicing Catholics (defined as those who said

---

87. André Siegfried's work reminds us that the Catholic sensibility was long linked to defense of the old trifunctional order (or at any rate a strong attachment to the role of local elites, symbolized by the château and presbyter). This was the local proprietarian order that existed before the formation of the centralized state. The important point is that this was a political-ideological attachment, which rested on plausible beliefs in an ideal educational, proprietarian, and social organization partly linked to socioeconomic interests but not reducible to them.

88. The 1958 and 1962 surveys did not contain questions about religious practice.

89. These figures are respectively 55 and 24 percent if one focuses on voters below age 35 in the same survey. These results are consistent with those obtained from larger surveys of religious practices. See, for example, the National Institute for Demographic Studies (INED), "Trajectories and Origins" (TeO) Survey, website, n.d., https://teo-english.site.ined.fr.

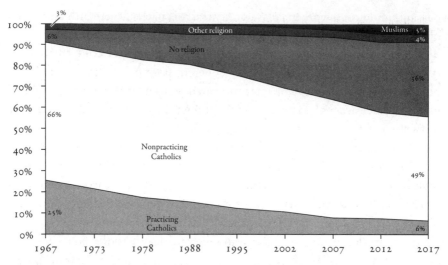

FIG. 14.14. The religious structure of the French electorate, 1967–2017

Interpretation: From 1967 to 2017, the proportion of the electorate declaring itself to be practicing Catholic (that is, attending church at least once a month) decreased from 25 percent to 6 percent. Nonpracticing Catholics decreased from 66 percent to 49 percent, individuals declaring themselves without religion increased from 6 percent to 36 percent, other religions (Protestant, Jewish, Buddhist, etc., excluding Islam) rose from 3 to 4 percent, and self-declared Muslims rose from 1 to 5 percent. *Sources and series:* piketty.pse.ens.fr/ideology.

they went to church at least once a month) have almost totally disappeared: they accounted for less than 6 percent of voters in 2017. The remaining 49 percent claim to have a Catholic identity but practice little if at all.[90]

Not only did the number of people declaring "no religion" increase sharply, but also between 1967 and 2017, there was a smaller but still significant increase in the number of people practicing religions other than Catholic. In 1976, fewer than 3 percent of respondents practiced another religion, mainly Protestant (roughly 2 percent) or Jewish (roughly 0.5 percent); all other religions (Islam, Buddhism, Hinduism, etc.) accounted for less than 0.5 percent. Muslim voters

---

90. The questionnaires do allow us in some cases to distinguish between those who do not practice at all and those who attend services on major holidays (such as Easter and Christmas) or for family occasions (weddings, baptisms, funerals, etc.). But this information is imprecise and not continuous, so I chose to stay with the homogeneous criterion presented here.

still represented less than 1 percent of the electorate in 1988, at which time they began to be counted separately from other religions in postelection surveys. They still represented less than 2 percent of the electorate in 1997, climbing to 3 percent in the elections of 2002 and 2007 and then 5 percent in 2012 and 2017.[91] Among voters stating their faith as Muslim, the vast majority appear to practice infrequently, like the vast majority of Catholics.[92]

To be clear, these numbers apply only to registered voters—hence, French citizens (and therefore likely to be at least second-generation immigrants) who have taken the trouble to register.[93] Other surveys suggest that people defining themselves as Muslims represented roughly 6–8 percent of the population residing in France.[94] We find comparable levels in other West European countries, specifically the United Kingdom and Germany. The proportion of Muslims in France is smaller than but comparable in magnitude to the proportion of

---

91. The proportions of Protestants (1.5–2 percent) and Jews (barely 0.5 percent) remained relatively stable while the proportion of other religious groups, including Buddhists, Hindus, and so on, slightly increased from 0.5 to 1–1.5 percent, with variations from survey to survey and not necessarily statistically significant in view of the small sample size. The increase of the share of Muslim voters from barely 0.5 percent in 1988 to roughly 5 percent in 2012 and 2012 is highly significant, however.

92. Using the same criterion (participation in a religious ceremony at least once a month), we find that the proportion of practicing Muslims was about 15–25 percent between 1995 and 2017 (with slight variations from survey to survey). This is slightly higher than the same figure for Catholics (roughly 10–15 percent over the same period), but this leaves 75–85 percent of nonpracticing Muslims (compared with roughly 85–90 percent of nonpracticing Catholics).

93. The most recent postelection survey (e.g., 2012) cover the entire population (which enables us to determine that registration rates vary strongly with age and occupation), but more detailed questions (concerning religion and origins in particular) are put only to the sub-sample of registered voters.

94. The TeO Survey carried out in 2008–2009 found that roughly 8 percent of the resident population aged 18–50 to be of the Muslim faith. See C. Beauchemin, C. Hamel, and P. Simon, eds., *Trajectoires et origines. Enquête sur la diversité des populations en France* (INED, 2015), p. 562, table 1. According to a survey conducted in 2016, roughly 6 percent of the resident population aged 15 and over declared itself to be of "the Muslim faith." This figure would rise to 7 percent if one included people of "Muslim culture" and to 8.5 percent if one included children (owing to larger family sizes). See H. El Karoui, *L'Islam, une religion française* (Gallimard, 2018), pp. 20–26. These categories are fluid and vague, however, and the results obtained depend on the questionnaire and the way in which individual identities, which are multiple and complex, are deduced from the questions asked and the terms used. The same is true for individuals identified as Jewish or Catholic.

Muslims in India (10 percent in the 1951 census, 14 percent in that of 2011), with the important difference that Hindus and Muslims have coexisted in India since the thirteenth century whereas religious pluralism is a relatively recent phenomenon in Western Europe.[95] By contrast, the proportion of Muslims is small in Poland, Hungary, or in the United States (less than 1 percent).

What is the effect of religious cleavages on voting? Two facts stand out. First, if we begin by setting aside religions other than Catholic, we find that the gap between Catholic voters and those professing "no religion" has always played a very important role in French politics. This was obviously the case during the Third Republic, especially in the period 1871–1910 studied by André Siegfried, who among other things looked at the relation between private school attendance, the pattern of land ownership, and the vote for Catholic candidates.[96] Religion continued to have a major impact on voting in the period 1960–1980: only 10–20 percent of practicing Catholics voted for parties of the left (Socialists, Communists, Radicals, and Greens), compared with 70–80 percent of voters claiming "no religion" (Fig. 14.15). Nonpracticing Catholics have always occupied an intermediate position between these two groups. To find a socioeconomic factor with an effect on voting as dramatic as that of religion, one would have to compare the vote of the bottom wealth decile with that of the top centile (Fig. 14.13). But not all "no religion" voters are poor, nor are all practicing Catholics rich—far from it.

If we consider all Catholic voters (both practicing and nonpracticing), their propensity to vote for parties of the right in the period 1960–1980 was roughly 40 percentage points higher than that of voters without religion. This is an important and highly statistically significant effect. If we control for all socioeconomic variables, this gap falls to about thirty points. This stems from the fact that Catholics are on average older, better paid, and above all significantly wealthier than "no religion" voters.[97] Nevertheless, most of the gap (about three-quarters) appears to be due to political-ideological rather than just socioeconomic factors.[98] The roughly thirty- or forty-point difference (after and before applying controls, respectively) persisted throughout the period 1960–1980 but then gradually decreased to twenty to twenty-five points in the

---

95. On the evolution of the Indian religious structure, see Fig. 8.2.

96. See A. Siegfried, *Tableau politique de la France de l'Ouest*.

97. See online appendix, Figs. S14.15a–S14.15b, for complete results.

98. This is consistent with Siegfried's analysis, which found that poor peasants voted for Catholic candidates in conservative cantons.

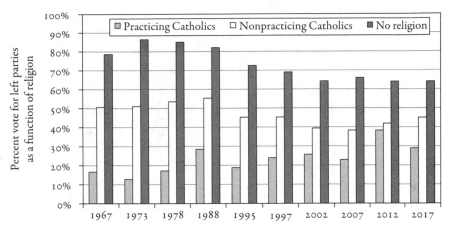

FIG. 14.15. Political conflict and Catholicism in France, 1967–2017

Interpretation: Voters declaring themselves to be practicing or nonpracticing Catholics were always less likely to vote for the left than those declaring themselves without religion, but the gap has decreased over time. *Sources and series:* piketty.pse.ens.fr/ideology.

period 1990–2010. This is still a large gap compared with the ten- to twenty-point gap generally associated with socioeconomic variables (Figs. 14.1–14.2).

The Rise of Nativism and the Great Political-Religious Upheaval

We turn now to the great upheaval in politics and ideology caused by the advent of new forms of religious diversity in France (and more generally in Western Europe, as we will see later). Historically, religious diversity was associated with a higher vote for the parties of the left. In the 1960s and 1970s, for example, we find that Protestants and Jews had a propensity to vote for the left that fell between that of nonpracticing Catholics and that of voters without religion (Fig. 14.16). These two religious minorities maintained the same intermediate position from the 1960s to the 2010s.[99]

---

99. The available data also indicate that Protestant voters were generally closer to nonpracticing Catholics while Jewish voters were closer to those without religion (even though this seems to be less so at the end of the period). Because of the small sample sizes, however, we cannot go beyond this general statement (which is valid to a first approximation from the 1960s to the 2010s) to study differences between these two groups in greater detail.

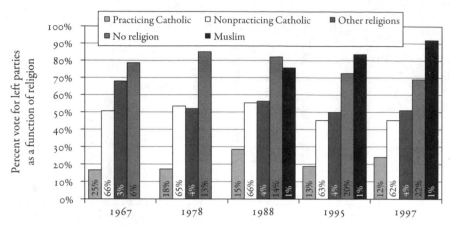

FIG. 14.16. Political conflict and religious diversity in France, 1967–1997

Interpretation: Voters declaring themselves Muslim were significantly more likely to vote for parties of the left than voters without religion after 1997. Before 1988, Muslims are classified with other religions (Protestant, Jewish, Buddhist, Hindu, etc.) and account for less than 1 percent of the electorate. *Sources and series:* piketty.pse.ens.fr/ideology.

As for Muslim voters, whose behavior the postelection surveys allow us to study from 1988 on, we find a much clearer tendency to vote for the left. In the elections of 1988 and 1995, roughly 70–80 percent of Muslims voted for parties of the left—approximately the same as unreligious voters (the small sample size does not allow us to say more). From 1997 on, including the elections of 2002, 2007, 2012, and 2017, we find that Muslim voters voted massively for parties of the left at levels of 80–90 percent in survey after survey (Figs. 14.16–14.17). Although the samples are of limited size, the effects are highly significant, and they recur in election after election. The gap between the vote for left-wing parties of Muslim and non-Muslim voters was roughly 40–50 percentage points throughout the period 1995–2017, with a confidence interval of five points at the end of the period. Only a small part (barely a tenth) of the difference can be explained by other voter characteristics that might account for a left-wing vote (such as lower income or wealth).[100]

---

100. See the online appendix, Figs. S14.17–S14.18, for complete results. In 2017, the 91 percent score obtained by candidates of the left and the center was divided as follows: 66 percent for Mélenchon and Hamon together and 25 percent for Macron, which seems consistent with the candidates' attitudes toward immigration and redistribution (Table 14.1). This strong left vote, particularly in favor of LFI,

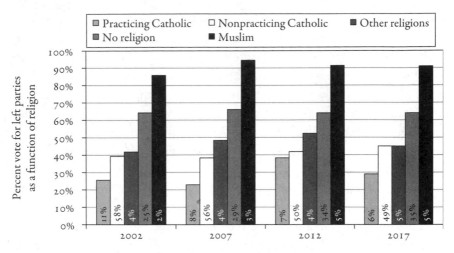

FIG. 14.17. Political conflict and religious diversity in France, 2002–2017

Interpretation: 80–90 percent of voters declaring themselves Muslim voted for parties of the left in all French elections since 1990. Before 1988, Muslims were classified with other religions (Protestant, Jewish, Buddhist, Hindu, etc.) and accounted for less than 1 percent of the electorate. *Sources and series:* piketty.pse.ens.fr/ideology.

These results call for several comments. First, there is no socioeconomic variable that yields a vote as lopsided as the 80–90 percent Muslim vote for parties of the left (except, perhaps, the 80–90 percent vote of the very wealthy for parties of the right in the 1970s: Fig. 14.13). Later, however, we will see that 80–90 percent of African Americans have regularly voted for the Democratic Party in the United States since the 1960s, and 80–90 percent of Muslim voters in the United Kingdom have regularly voted for Labour since the 1980s. In the next chapter, I will discuss the similarities and differences between these different forms of politicization of (perceived) ethno-religious cleavages.

At this stage, note simply that the main explanation for why 80–90 percent of Muslims vote for parties of the left is fairly clear: Muslim voters see the parties of the right as extremely hostile toward them. For decades the Front National (FN), which has won roughly 10–15 percent of the vote in legislative elections and 15–20 percent of the vote in presidential

---

was also observed in 2017 in the fascinating ethnographic survey undertaken by S. Beaud: *La France des Belhoumi. Portraits de famille (1977–2017)* (La Découverte, 2018), especially among young women with North African origins, while men appear to be less politicized and more disillusioned.

elections from the late 1980s to the present (and even as much as 25–30 percent in regional and European elections in 2014–2015), has been overt in its hostility to immigrants from outside Europe, and similar hostility has been evident in the harder-right factions of the more mainstream center-right and right parties. The early successes of the FN in the 1980s came after the party campaigned on an unambiguously nativist platform, announced in a leaflet first distributed before the 1978 legislative elections: "A million unemployed is a million too many immigrants! France and the French first! Vote Front National!" Although the leaflet did not say so, the fact that its vitriol was aimed only at immigrants from outside Europe and not at white Europeans was clear to everyone.

Over the past several decades, the heart of the FN platform has always been to end immigration, close the borders, and reform the code of nationality so that the children of non-European immigrants cannot become French citizens.[101] Furthermore, the FN clearly hints that once it is in power, it will be quite possible to "send back" all undesirable immigrants and their offspring, even if it means retroactively stripping citizenship from people whose behavior is deemed unsatisfactory (according to criteria to be set by the new government). It is important to note the extreme vindictiveness of this position, which comes down to redrawing the boundaries of the nation retroactively and expelling individuals who have never lived anywhere but in France. In fact, mass cancellations of citizenship and deportations have been carried out in the past, not only in France and elsewhere in Europe during World War II[102] but also in the United States in the 1930s.[103] History shows that when people

---

101. Since 1889, the general rule in France has been that a person born in France of foreign parents acquires French citizenship at age 18 provided that certain conditions are met (regarding duration of residence, education, and in some cases a statement of desire to become French). These rules have been the subject of debate and various reforms. The other pillar of French nationality law is the so-called double *jus solis* instituted in 1851: any person born in France of parents born in France automatically becomes a French citizen at birth. See P. Weil, *Qu'est-ce qu'un Français? Histoire de la nationalité française depuis la Révolution* (Grasset, 2002).

102. With the law of July 22, 1940, the French state sought to revisit the status of all citizens naturalized since 1927—nearly 1 million people in all, including many Jews. See C. Zalc, *Dénaturalisés. Les retraits de nationalité sous Vichy* (Seuil, 2016).

103. It is estimated that 1–1.5 million Mexican Americans were forcibly deported between 1929 and 1936 (often with support from the government). Some 60 percent of them were US citizens. See Chap. 6.

are angry, they are sometimes willing even in "democratic" countries to hand control of the government to leaders prepared to resort to such measures. Note, too, that the risks of escalation after a party like the FN comes to power are high, especially since the promises about the economic benefits to be expected from deporting immigrants have no basis in reality.[104] To cope with the ensuing frustration, the next step would probably be to attack the stigmatized groups even more harshly, possibly leading to unimaginable levels of civil violence.

In the face of such rhetoric and threats, it is hardly surprising that the people most directly affected (namely, Muslim voters) choose to vote for the parties most diametrically opposed to the far right, namely, the parties of the left. Yet it is striking to see how the advent of ethno-religious diversity in France in the wake of postcolonial immigration in the 1960s and 1970s, followed by the rise of a nativist ideology violently opposed to that diversity in the 1980s and 1990s, totally disrupted the usual structure of political conflict. Traditionally, practicing Catholics were the voters most likely to vote for the right, followed by nonpracticing Catholics, then members of religious minorities (Protestants and Jews), and finally—least likely to vote for the right—people professing "no religion," who have been voting left in France since the French Revolution. The fact that practicing Muslims, many of whom are quite conservative on issues such as family values, are now more likely to vote for the parties of the left than are people without religion speaks volumes about the magnitude of the upheaval.

Note, too, that in 2013 the Socialist government legalized same-sex marriage, which all the surveys show is disliked by both practicing Catholics and practicing Muslims. But this did not prevent more than 90 percent of Muslim voters from voting for parties of the left and the center in 2017, just as they had done in 2012 and previous elections, before the passage of the law.[105] The obvious interpretation is that while the issue of same-sex marriage is important,

---

104. In particular, the idea that "immigration" is costing France a fortune (which is obviously nonsense over the long run in view of the substantial portion of the population that has foreign roots) has no basis in fact: the taxes paid by recent immigrants are equal to or even slightly greater than the benefits they receive. See, for example, E. M. Mouhoud, *L'immigration en France. Mythes et réalités* (Fayard, 2017), pp. 72–76. For international comparisons, see also A. Banerjee and E. Duflo, *Good Economics for Hard Times* (Public Affairs, 2019), pp. 18–50.

105. I will say more later about the breakdown of the vote in 2017.

it ultimately carried little weight compared with the existential threat that the FN and its nativist ideology represented in the eyes of Muslim voters.[106]

Religious Cleavages, Cleavages Over Origins: The Discrimination Trap

Since 2007, French postelection surveys have included questions about origins. We can therefore distinguish electoral cleavages based on religious identity from those based on family trajectories and immigration. In practice, these are very different, but earlier surveys tell us nothing about how they differ. Take, for example, the results for 2012. Respondents were asked to state whether they had "one or more parents or grandparents of foreign origin."[107] Among registered voters, 72 percent answered that they had no foreign grandparent, while 28 percent said that they had at least one. Of those 28 percent, 19 percent stated that they were of European ancestry (of whom nearly two-thirds came from either Spain, Italy, or Portugal), while 9 percent said they had ancestors outside Europe. In nearly 65 percent of those cases, those ancestors lived in North Africa (Algeria, Tunisia, or Morocco), while about 15 percent were from sub-Saharan Africa, for a total of 80 percent from the African continent.[108]

Looking now at the structure of the vote, we find that voters of foreign but European origin voted exactly the same way as those without foreign origins: 49 percent preferred the Socialist candidate in the second round of the 2012 election compared with 77 percent of voters of non-European origin (Fig. 14.18).

---

106. According to postelection surveys after the presidential elections of 2002 and 2017, 100 percent of Muslim voters voted against the FN in the second round. To be sure, the samples are limited (between 100 and 300 Muslim voters depending on the survey and sample size). Nevertheless, the fact that not a single Muslim in either sample voted for either Jean-Marie or Marine Le Pen in either election says a great deal about the depth of the conflict. See the online appendix for complete results.

107. The exact meaning of the term "foreign origin" was not specified: it was left to each respondent to decide whether it means nationality at birth or naturalized citizenship, birthplace of place of residence, and so on.

108. There was room to declare two different foreign origins, which nearly 10 percent of the relevant respondents did, in every possible combination. The results described here are based on the first answer and would be similar if one considered all answers. These results are consistent with those obtained in the TeO Survey, though not precisely comparable owing to difference of scope and questionnaires. See Beauchemin, Hamel, and Simon, *Trajectoires et origines,* Tables 1–3, pp. 37–41.

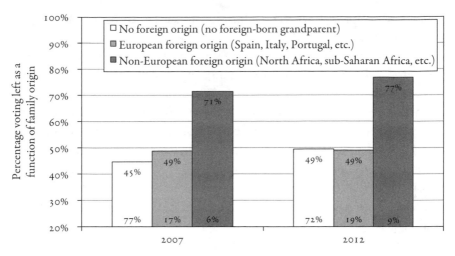

FIG. 14.18. Political attitudes and origins in France, 2007–2012

Interpretation: In 2012, the Socialist candidate obtained 49 percent of the vote among voters with no foreign origin (no foreign-born grandparent), 49 percent of the vote among voters of European foreign origin (primarily Spain, Italy, or Portugal), and 77 percent among voters of non-European origin (in practice, primarily North Africa and sub-Saharan Africa). *Sources and series:* piketty.pse.ens.fr/ideology.

This effect is independent of religion, moreover, which is especially important because the relation between non-European origin and religious identity is more complex than one might imagine. For example, of those claiming a North African background, fewer than 60 percent declare themselves to be Muslims.[109] From this we can determine that respondents of North African or sub-Saharan African origins voted massively for parties of the left, including not just Muslims but also Christians and those without religion. Interaction between the two dimensions, religion and foreign origins, strengthens this effect. In other words, a voter of North African origin but without religion is much more likely to vote for a party of the left than a voter of French or European ancestry, all other socioeconomic characteristics being

109. More precisely, of those reporting North African origins, 58 percent declare themselves to be Muslims, 6 percent Jews, 10 percent Catholics, 2 percent Protestants or other religions, and 24 percent no religion. Of those reporting sub-Saharan African origins, 40 percent declare themselves to be Muslims, 30 percent Catholics, 10 percent Protestant or other religions, and 20 percent no religion.

equal. But this propensity to vote for the left is even stronger if the voter in question is also Muslim.[110]

This cumulative effect would make little sense if it were only a matter of individual political preferences (regarding, say, family values or same-sex marriage). The only reasonable explanation is that these voters see the parties of the right, and especially the far right, as especially hostile to Islam. Indeed, there are many reasons to think that this perception is accurate. Anti-Muslim discourse played an important role in European colonial ideology, especially in France, from the early nineteenth century on.[111] More generally, it is important to recall the very old roots of today's nativist ideologies. In the interwar years, fear of what is today called "the great replacement" (the idea that Europe could someday be dominated by foreigners) was an important element of Nazi ideology.[112] Before World War I, colonial ideologues (such as Pierre Paul Leroy-Beaulieu in France) propounded the theory that the historical supremacy of the "white race" and "Christian civilization" required the export of Europe's surplus population to the rest of the world, failing which Europe itself might be invaded and bastardized.[113] In France, the far right redefined itself in the period 1950–1980 around the rejection of decolonization. Among its founders were many (including Jean-Marie Le Pen) who had absolutely refused to countenance the end of France's colonial domination of Algeria. From the

---

110. Concretely, in 2012, the Socialist candidate's score among Muslim voters was 42 percentage points higher than his score among other voters. This gap decreases to thirty-eight points if one controls for age, sex, family situation, education, income, and parental wealth and occupation and to twenty-six points if one also controls for foreign origins (broken down by geographical region: Italy, Spain, Portugal, other European, North Africa, sub-Saharan Africa, other non-European). See the online appendix, Fig. S14.18. Because of the limited sample size, it is not possible to proceed farther with this type of analysis.

111. The antagonism between Christianity and Islam goes back much further to the time of the Crusades and the Age of Discovery, which was partly motivated by a strategy of encircling the Muslim enemy. See Chap. 7.

112. Hitler was particularly concerned that the black troops he saw stationed on the banks of the Rhine would someday penetrate the heart of Europe. See Chap. 10.

113. See H. Le Bras, *L'invention de l'immigré. Le sol et le sang* (Éditions de L'Aube, 2014). Recall that slaveholding elites in the United States in the early nineteenth century (starting with Jefferson) could imagine an end to slavery only if all the slaves were sent back to Africa because they found it impossible to conceive of living in peace on a footing of equality with former slaves. See Chap. 6.

beginning the FN did particularly well with former French colonists repatriated from Algeria, many of whom settled in the south of France.[114] Hostility to the "Muslims" who had won their independence in 1962, putting an end to nearly a century and a half of French rule (1830–1962), was for obvious reasons particularly strong among this group.

Research has shown that Muslims are discriminated against in France and Europe, especially in the job market.[115] It is well established that for a given level of education, immigrants from North Africa and sub-Saharan Africa face unusual difficulties in finding work, experience higher unemployment, and are paid less.[116] Other recent research has shown that the probability of being called for a job interview is much lower if a Muslim-sounding first name is mentioned on the candidate's curriculum vitae (CV); this remains true after controlling for educational level, professional experience, and foreign origin.[117] To overcome prejudices of this type, comparable with prejudices faced by women and minorities in other countries, various solutions are conceivable, include a quota or "reservations" system like the one India has set up to assist groups historically subject to discrimination. What the Indian experience shows, however, is that quotas can stigmatize certain groups unless one takes care to anticipate their effects. In the French and European context, the risk that quotas would

---

114. According to one survey of repatriated settlers *(pieds-noirs),* the FN garnered 55 percent of their votes in the Alpes-Maritimes in the period 1980–1990. See E. Comtat, "Traumatisme historique" et vote Front national: l'impact de la mémoire de la Guerre d'Algérie sur les opinions politiques des rapatriés," *Cahiers Mémoire et Politique,* 2018, table 2.

115. As well as the housing market.

116. See, for example, Y. Brinbaum, D. Meurs, and J. L. Primon, "Situation sur le marché du travail: statuts d'activité, accès à l'emploi et discrimination," in *Trajectoires et origines,* ed. Beauchemin, Hamel, and Simon, pp. 203–232.

117. For example, given two candidates of Lebanese origin, one with the first name "Mohammed" is less likely to be granted an interview than one with the first name "Michel." The effect is large: given two young applicants with similar CVs, fewer than 5 percent of those with Muslim first names are called for interviews compared with 20 percent of the others. Mentioning participation in the Muslim scouts causes response rates to drop sharply, while participating in the Catholic or Protestant scouts causes them to rise. Jewish names are also discriminated against but much less so than Muslim names. The study is based on 6,000 representative jobs in small and medium businesses. See M. A. Valfort, *Discriminations religieuses à l'embauche: une réalité* (Institut Montaigne, 2015).

exacerbate identity conflicts and hostility to Muslims is real.[118] It might be better to impose severe penalties for discrimination on the basis of religion or national origin and to develop means of detecting instances of such discrimination. In any case, it is clear that the advent of postcolonial diversity and the emergence of novel nativist ideologies have given rise to a type of inequality and political conflict unknown in Europe just a few decades ago.

Borders and Property: An Electorate Divided Four Ways

To review, over the past few decades the electoral left has turned into the Brahmin left, which is itself increasingly divided between a pro-market (center-left) faction and a more radical pro-redistribution faction (some would say that it is simply less right-wing). Meanwhile, the electoral right has split into a pro-market center-right and a nativist and nationalist right. In the end, it is clear that the whole system of "classist" cleavages, together with the left-right political structure of the period 1950–1980, has gradually broken down. Recomposition is currently under way. As we will soon discover by looking at countries other than France, this redefinition of the dimensions of political conflict can take different forms. It would be a mistake to see these developments in a deterministic light. The system of political cleavages can evolve in quite different ways depending on the strategies of the actors and the ability of contending social groups to mobilize support and ideas.

The state of political-ideological conflict in France in the late 2010s illustrates to perfection the indeterminacy and profound instability of the system. Briefly stated, the electorate has fractured into four approximately equal parts: an ideological bloc that can be characterized as egalitarian internationalist, another that can be described as inegalitarian internationalist, a third that can be called inegalitarian nativist, and finally, an egalitarian nativist bloc. This decomposition is crude in part because political conflict is more than two-dimensional and in part because each axis of disagreement includes a subtle gradation of positions and subpositions that cannot be reduced to points on a

---

118. In India, quotas were initially intended to benefit only Hindu groups that suffered from discrimination ("scheduled castes" and "scheduled tribes") and excluded Muslims (even though they were just as poor and equally discriminated against in many regions) because including them would no doubt have aroused virulent opposition. Only in a second phase were quotas extended to "other backward classes," including Muslims. See Chap. 8. What is more, this evolution had a decisive influence on the transformation of India's political cleavages and party system. See Chap. 16.

straight line. But the analysis given here, in terms of two principal axes—borders and property—is useful for clarifying ideas.

To divide the electorate along these two dimensions, we can use responses to the following two questions. Postelection surveys asked registered voters whether they agreed or disagreed with the following assertion: "There are too many immigrants in France." In 2017, 56 percent of respondents said they agreed; 44 percent disagreed.[119] In the period 2000–2020 the percentage of those who agreed varied from 50 to 60 percent (versus 40 to 50 percent of those who disagreed), largely as a function of the business cycle. For instance, 61 percent thought there were too many immigrants in 2002; this figure fell to 49 percent in 2007, when unemployment and the vote for the FN touched bottom then rose to 51 percent in 2012 and 56 percent in 2017.[120]

The second question concerns the reduction of inequality between rich and poor. In the questionnaires, the statement is formulated in deliberately aggressive terms: "To establish social justice, one must take from the rich and give to the poor." If this had been phrased more mildly, more respondents might have approved, but the advantage of putting it this way is that it divides the electorate into two roughly comparable halves. In 2017, 52 percent agreed that one must "take from the rich and give to the poor" (versus 48 percent who disagreed). The proportion of pro-poor voters (as defined by this question) was 56 percent in 2007 and 60 percent in 2012. The decrease from 2012 to 2017 can be interpreted as a sign of greater acceptance of the claim that tax competition has made redistribution impossible; alternatively, it might reflect disappointment with the results achieved by the incumbent Socialist president.[121]

---

119. To simplify, I grouped those who responded "agree" or "strongly agree" in one group and "disagree" or "strongly disagree" in the other, excluding those who did not respond (fewer than 5 percent).

120. This question has been included in postelection surveys since 1988. In the late 1980s and 1990s (when unemployment was at a peak), the proportion of anti-immigrant voters (as defined by this question) was 70–75 percent. See the online appendix, Fig. S14.19a. The decrease in anti-immigrant sentiment between the period 1985–2000 (70–75 percent) and 2000–2020 (50–60 percent) is partly due to generational change and the rise of antiracist movements. It would be a mistake to think that it has to do with lower salience for the issue of immigration. Indeed, it may reflect heightened conflict around this issue, with two camps of comparable size mobilized around opposing positions.

121. See the online appendix, Fig. S14.19b. In 2002, the question was formulated differently, in terms of "reducing the gap between the poor and the rich." Sixty-three percent deemed this to be extremely important or very important, compared with

To sum up: in the late 2010s, questions about immigration on the one hand and the rich and poor on the other divided the electorate, in each case, into two parts of roughly equal size. If these two dimensions of political conflict had aligned—that is, if the answers to both questions had been perfectly correlated—the electorate itself would have fallen into two roughly equal parts, and electoral conflict would have been two-sided rather than four-sided.[122]

But the two dimensions did not align: the answers to the two questions were almost totally uncorrelated so that the electorate can be analyzed as falling into four roughly equal parts (Fig. 14.19). In 2017, 21 percent of voters can be classified as "egalitarian internationalists" (pro-immigrant, pro-poor); 26 percent are "inegalitarian nativists" (anti-immigrant, pro-rich); 23 percent are "inegalitarian internationalists" (pro-immigrant, pro-rich), and 30 percent are "egalitarian nativists" (anti-immigrant, pro-poor). Note in particular that the relative weight of these parts can change rapidly within a few years' time depending on the state of political debate, notable events, and representation of those events in the media. Furthermore, the imprecision of the survey questions allows us only to identify broad ideological families with fluid boundaries rather than perfectly precise or structured positions. Note, finally, that the small differences in size among the four groups are not statistically significant, especially in 2007 and 2017.[123]

It so happens that these four ideological "quarters" found almost perfect embodiment in four electoral "quarters" in the first round of the 2017 presidential election (Tab. 14.1). The egalitarian internationalist bloc captured 28 percent of the vote, led by the "radical left" candidate Jean-Luc Mélenchon and his movement La France Insoumise (LFI) with 20 percent, complemented

---

37 percent who considered it "somewhat important" or "not very important." More broadly, it should be noted that no question in the surveys was formulated in exactly the same way from the period 1950–1970 to the period 2000–2020, which sets obvious limits to the analysis (which is one reason for paying close attention to the transformation of the education, income, and wealth cleavages, which are at least comparable over time and space). Ideally, it would obviously be preferable to have specific and identical questions about inequality, wealth, taxes, the educational system, and so on.

122. A priori, this could take two forms: an egalitarian internationalist camp versus an inegalitarian nativist camp, or an inegalitarian internationalist camp versus an egalitarian nativist camp.

123. See the online appendix, Fig. S14.19c.

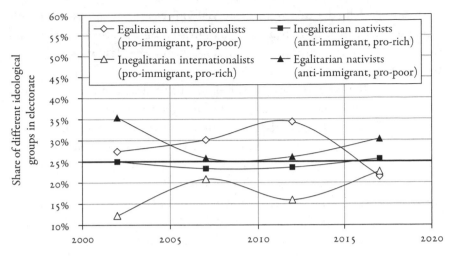

FIG. 14.19. Borders and property: The four-way ideological divide in France

Interpretation: In 2017, 21 percent of voters can be classed as "egalitarian internationalists" (they do not believe that there are too many immigrants and favor reducing inequality between rich and poor); 26 percent are "inegalitarin nativists" (who believe that there are too many immigrants and one should not reduce inequality between rich and poor); 23 percent are "inegalitarian internationalists" (pro-immigrant, pro-rich); and 30 percent are "egalitarian nativists" (anti-immigrant, pro-poor). *Sources and series:* piketty.pse.ens.fr/ideology.

by the candidate of the left wing of the Socialist Party, Benoît Hamon, who finished with 6 percent, and two candidates of the far left, with 2 percent.[124] It is reasonable to describe this bloc as egalitarian internationalist in the sense that, relative to the three other groups, the 28 percent of the electorate who supported it believe most strongly that France could be more open to immigrants (only 32 percent think that there are too many, compared with 56 percent on average) and that more should be done to redistribute from rich to poor (69 percent of egalitarian internationalists consider this to be desirable, compared with 52 percent on average of all four groups). Note, too, that this

---

124. On the issues of redistribution from rich to poor, internationalism, and defense of immigrants, Nathalie Arthaud, the candidate of Lutte Ouvrière (LO), and Philippe Poutou, the candidate of the Nouveau Parti Anticapitaliste (NPA), were the most radical. In the 2019 European Parliament elections, the joint statement last presented by these two candidates advocated a Socialist United States of Europe as a first step toward a Universal Socialist Republic.

is a relatively well-educated group (only Macron's electorate surpasses it in this dimension and then by only a small margin) but also relatively poorly paid (only Le Pen's electorate is worse in this respect) and even less wealthy (poorer than Le Pen's electorate).

The inegalitarian internationalist bloc won 24 percent of the vote behind the candidacy of Emmanuel Macron, who emerged from the pro-market wing of François Hollande's Socialist government (which he served from 2012 to 2016, first as principal economic adviser and then as minister of the economy). His candidacy was backed by his own movement, La République en Marche (LRM), which was joined by MoDem, a party of the center-right, as well as the more centrist and well-to-do segment of the old Socialist electorate. I call this bloc inegalitarian internationalist, because it was less opposed to immigration than the average voter but definitely not convinced of the need to take from the rich to give to the poor. This group was highly educated as well as both better paid and wealthier than average. As for economic and fiscal policy, its main thrust after coming to power in 2017–2018 was to abolish the wealth tax (ISF) and the progressive tax on capital income, paying for both by increasing indirect taxes on motor fuels, a measure it was forced to rescind in late 2018 to placate the "yellow vests" (see Chapter 13).[125]

The inegalitarian nativist bloc took 22 percent of the vote behind François Fillon (20 percent), along with three minor right-wing candidates (2 percent).[126] This was the bourgeois and traditional Catholic right, 62 percent of which was hostile to immigration but above all strongly opposed to any redistribution from rich to poor (of which 73 percent wanted no part). Its voters were slightly less well educated than those of the LRM-MoDem bloc, but they were also wealthier and better paid. Destined for victory before being undermined by a corruption scandal, Fillon lost to Macron, and since the election, a significant portion of his electorate has supported Macron's government, not least because the abolition of the ISF, enacted by Macron, was a symbolic measure that much of the right had wanted for quite some time but had never been able to pass.[127]

---

125. As for Macron's postelection immigration policies—supposedly "less opposed" to immigration (but in reality extremely restrictive and conservative)—I will say more in Chap. 16.

126. The candidacies of François Asselineau, Jacques Cheminade, and Jean Lassalle are hard to classify and had only a limited impact on the overall structure of the vote.

127. In 1986 the right abolished the tax on large fortunes (*impôt sur les grandes fortunes* or IGF), which the left had passed in 1981. But losing the 1988 presidential election convinced the parties of the right that it would be unwise to attack this

Finally, the egalitarian nativist bloc took 26 percent of the vote behind the candidacies of Marine Le Pen, who represented the FN (21 percent), and Nicolas Dupont-Aignan, who represented the sovereignist right (5 percent) and who threw his support to Le Pen in the second round. This electorate was more favorable than the average voter to redistribution from rich to poor (61 percent versus 51 percent), but its principal characteristic was extreme hostility to immigrants (91 percent believed that there were too many in France). These voters were also significantly less educated than those of the three other groups (the percentage with tertiary degrees was half that of the others), and their income was the lowest of the four. By contrast, they were somewhat wealthier than those who voted for Mélenchon and Hamon (but much less wealthy than Macron and Fillon voters).

Finally, it is important to note that the electorate contained a "fifth quarter" not shown in Table 14.1: the abstentionists (22 percent of registered voters did not vote in the first round). This group was characterized by low education and income and much lower wealth than the four voting groups.[128] From an ideological standpoint, this was by far the least politicized group; abstainers seldom responded to the survey questions about redistribution and immigration.[129]

---

popular tax when the left reinstated it in 1990 under a new name, *impôt sur la fortune* (ISF). In 2007, however, Nicolas Sarkozy enacted a so-called tax shield (a ceiling on the total amount a taxpayer with a given income could be asked to pay). The effect of this was to exempt many of the rich from much of the burden of the ISF. But Sarkozy had to rescind this unpopular measure a few months before the 2012 elections while at the same time sharply reducing the rates of the ISF (the top rate, applicable to fortunes above 17 million euros, was decreased from 1.8 to 0.5 percent). This measure never went into effect: the Socialist government, elected in 2012, partially restored rates to their previous levels. The top rate was nevertheless reduced to 1.5 percent on fortunes above 10 million euros on the grounds that interest rates had fallen. The argument is odd, since large fortunes are not invested in sovereign bonds, and their rate of increase indicates much higher rates of return (see Chap. 13, Table 13.1).

128. Only 41 percent of abstentionists owned their own homes, compared with 48 percent of Mélenchon/Hamon voters, 51 percent of Le Pen/Dupont-Aignan voters, 69 percent of Macron voters, and 78 percent of Fillon voters. Furthermore, only 19 percent had tertiary degrees and only 8 percent earned more than 3,000 euros a month, which placed them at the level of the Le Pen/Dupont-Aignan electorate. See the online appendix.

129. The nonresponse rate on these two questions was close to 50 percent among abstentionists, compared with 10 percent for voters. Those who did answer were more pro-poor (54 percent) and anti-immigrant (64 percent) than average, but the difference was less pronounced than for the four voting groups.

TABLE 14.1

Political-ideological conflict in France in 2017: An electorate divided into four quarters

2017 presidential election (first round)	All voters	Mélenchon/Hamon ("egalitarian internationalist vote")	Macron ("inegalitarian internationalist vote")	Fillon ("inegalitarian nativist" vote)	Le Pen/Dupont-Aignan ("egalitarian nativist" vote)
"There are too many immigrants in France" (% agree)	100%	28%	24%	22%	26%
	56%	32%	39%	62%	91%
"To establish social justice, one must take from the rich and give to the poor" (% agree)	51%	67%	46%	27%	61%
Tertiary degree (%)	33%	39%	41%	36%	16%
Monthly income > 4,000€ (%)	15%	9%	20%	26%	8%
Homeownership (%)	60%	48%	69%	78%	51%

Interpretation: In 2017, 28 percent of first-round voters voted for Mélenchon/Hamon; 32 percent of them believed there were too many immigrants in France (compared with 56 percent on average for all voters) and 67 percent said that one must take from the rich and give to the poor (compared with 51 percent on average). This was ideologically the "egalitarian internationalist" (pro-immigrant, pro-poor) vote, where Macron's electorate was "inegalitarian internationalist," Fillon's was "inegalitarian nativist" (anti-immigrant, pro-rich), and that of Le Pen/Dupont-Aignan was "egalitarian nativist" (anti-immigrant, pro-poor). *Note:* The votes for Arthaud/Poutou (2 percent) and Asselineau/Cheminade/Lassalle (2 percent) were added to the votes for Mélenchon/Hamon and Fillon respectively. *Sources and series:* piketty.pse.ens.fr/ideology.

On the Instability of the Four-Way
Division of the Electorate

This division of the electorate into four quarters calls for several remarks. First, the presidential election of 2017 was clearly the unforeseen culmination of a long process of disintegration of the classist cleavages and left-right divide that defined the period 1950–1980. The two traditional coalitions, the electoral left and electoral right, were now divided by deep social and ideological cleavages. A four-way division of the electorate represents this complexity better than a binary or unidimensional view.

Second, it is quite unusual to find four candidates winning 20–24 percent of the vote each in the first round of an election in which only the top two candidates qualify for the second round. As a general rule, strategic voters will tend to vote for the two candidates leading the pre-election polls. One finds occasional three-way races, but such close four-way contests are extremely rare.[130] What this suggests is that the social and ideological differences that led to this four-way division of the electorate were strong enough to overcome the normal urge to vote strategically. In the end, Macron and Le Pen narrowly beat the two other candidates to reach the second round, which therefore pitted the inegalitarian internationalist bloc against the egalitarian nativists.[131] Clearly, however, the scores of the four top first-round contenders were so close that any two of the four could have ended up in the second round.

In the future, this four-way division could evolve into a three-way structure organized around three ideological families: liberalism, nationalism, and socialism.[132] This could happen if, for instance, the economically more liberal

---

130. Two months before the election, polls showed the two main candidates of the egalitarian internationalist bloc were running even, but then the vote shifted to Mélenchon, who was the more radical and pugnacious of the two during the debates. Strategic voting thus did its part to reduce the number of candidates in a position to qualify for the second round from five to four. But it did not eliminate two of the remaining four.

131. The inegalitarian internationalists scored a clear victory (66–34 percent) because the vast majority of the French electorate considered the anti-immigrant position of the FN to be extreme.

132. For a stimulating analysis of the tripartite liberal-nationalist-socialist division of the political-ideological space, see B. Karsenti and C. Lemieux, *Socialisme et sociologie* (EHESS, 2017). Briefly, liberalism sacralizes the market and the disembedding of the economy, nationalism responds by reifying the nation and ethno-

segment of Fillon's electorate were captured by Macron, while the more anti-immigrant segment turned to Le Pen. An evolution along these lines may already have begun, as illustrated by the European elections of 2019.[133] In the 2017 election, the ideological divisions among the four quarters of the electorate were sufficiently well defined that each found its own candidate.

Clearly, then, the current system of political cleavages is quite unstable. The principle axis of political-ideological conflict is being redefined, and it is possible to imagine several future trajectories, depending on the ability of contending groups to mobilize and on the depth of their respective convictions and ideas. In the next chapter, we will see that the situation is comparable in the United States. In the 2016 presidential election, for example, the final duel would have been quite different if the Democratic primary process had chosen the pro-redistribution candidate, Bernie Sanders, rather than the centrist Hillary Clinton. As in the 2017 French election, it is hard to say what the outcome would have been if these contests and debates had not taken place; in any case, future political-ideological developments would have probably been deeply affected by them.

The 2017 French election was a turning point, in which the old cleavage structure finally broke down in ways consistent with previous changes, most notably the rise of the Brahmin left and the dual elite. In fact, in the graphs presented in the chapter on the long-term evolution of the socioeconomic structure of the electorate, I defined the electoral left of 2017 as the 52 percent of the electorate that voted for the Mélenchon/Hamon and Macron blocs, as opposed to the 48 percent who voted for Fillon and Le Pen/Dupont-Aignan. These coalitions were totally artificial: the 2017 contest was more of a four-way battle (Tab. 14.1). But this way of looking at things is useful precisely because it shows that the 52 percent who voted for Mélenchon, Hamon, or Macron in 2017 were only slightly higher in educational level (and a bit higher still in terms of income and wealth) than the electoral left of 2012 or earlier elections (Figs. 14.1 and 14.10–14.11).[134] What took place in 2017 was thus the culmination of

---

national solidarities, and socialism promises emancipation through education and knowledge.

133. It could also happen if the segment of Macron's support that came from the left were to return to the left, which to some extent is also already happening.

134. More specifically, the 52 percent who voted for Mélenchon/Hamon/Macron in 2017 were very close to the 53 percent who voted in 2012 for the candidates of the left (44 percent) and center-right (François Bayrou, 9 percent) and not very different from the 52 percent who voted for Hollande in the second round in 2012.

a process already under way for several decades. The outcome revealed just how unstable the new dual-elite configuration is. The wealthier segment of the Brahmin left voted for Macron, consummating the break with the less wealthy segment of the old electoral left, which turned to either Mélenchon or Hamon. The old electoral right, which really ceased to be a viable electoral coalition once the FN and nativist ideology moved to center stage, seems more divided than ever between pro-market and anti-immigrant camps.

Yellow Vests, Carbon, and the Wealth Tax: The Social-Nativist Trap in France

There are of course several different ways of describing the recompositions currently under way and developments that may occur in the future. The new electoral bloc that has formed around Macron and the LRM and MoDem can be seen as a "bourgeois bloc" that will reconcile the Brahmin left with the merchant right.[135] In sociological terms, it is quite clear that this coalition brings together the most highly educated, best paid, and wealthiest voters of both the center-left and center-right. Some would describe the new coalition as "progressive." They like this term because it can be contrasted with "nationalist": progressives see nationalists as "backward" because they reject both globalization and Europe and because their aggressive attitudes and "deplorable passions" encourage hostility not only to immigrants but also to "entrepreneurs." Progressives particularly resent it when these "backward" opponents attack entrepreneurs as "fat cats" who should be required to pay their fair share, whereas in the progressive view the entrepreneurial class creates jobs and therefore diligently contributes to the common good.

Interestingly, this way of looking at the political battlefield as a clash between progressives and nationalists is also favored by the nativist camp, which is only too glad to reverse the terms so that the nativists are the good guys and the progressives the bad.[136] For Le Pen and the FN, the new conflict is between globalists and patriots. Globalists are nomadic elites, without roots, always

---

135. I take the expression "bourgeois bloc" from B. Amable and S. Palombarini, *L'illusion du bloc bourgeois. Alliances sociales et avenir du modèle français* (Raisons d'agir, 2017).

136. The progressive-nativist division to some degree also overlaps the open versus closed society confrontation pushed by Tony Blair and New Labour in the late 1990s and early 2000s.

ready to squeeze workers and hire cheap immigrant labor while patriots defend the interests of the less advantaged classes against the threats of hypercapitalist mongrelized globalization without borders or fatherland. The problem is that this binary vision of political conflict, which suits those who place themselves at the center of the contest, is both misleading and dangerous.

It is misleading because the reality of the current political-ideological conflict in France and most other countries is profoundly multidimensional. In particular, the electorate contains an egalitarian internationalist bloc, whose shape and size varies with context. More than the other segments of the electorate, it champions both internationalism and equality, defending immigrant workers of all origins and promoting redistribution of wealth from rich to poor. Can this camp attract a majority? The question is as open today as it has always been. The answer depends on whether it is possible to develop what I call a social-federalist platform, by which I mean a program designed to enable redistribution and internationalism to reinforce each other. To ignore this possibility, to think that political conflict in the future will inevitably pit progressives against nationalists (or globalists against patriots), is to forget that electorates are often divided four ways (or sometime three ways), as in France in 2017–2019. Not only can four-way divisions evolve in any number of directions, but also the boundaries dividing these four groups are porous and changeable.

More than that, binary division (progressive-nationalist or globalist-patriot) is dangerous, because it casts nativist ideology with its potential for violence as the only possible alternative. The aim of such a rhetorical strategy is of course to keep the "progressives" in power indefinitely. In reality, however, it runs the risk of hastening the success of the "nationalists," especially if they are able to develop a social-nativist ideology: in other words, an ideology combining social and egalitarian objectives for the "native" population with violent exclusion of "nonnatives" (like the Democratic Party in the United States in the late nineteenth and early twentieth centuries).[137] The ideology of the FN has been moving in this direction for several decades now, and the risk is that the events of 2017–2019 (especially the "yellow vests" crisis) will accelerate the transfor-

---

137. In the French and European context, "nonnatives" may be non-European immigrants, especially Muslims. In the US context, they may be blacks. The Democratic Party, which had been the party of slavery, redefined itself in the late nineteenth and first half of the twentieth centuries as a social-nativist party: more social and egalitarian than the Republicans with respect to the white population (especially white immigrants from Europe, such as Irish and Italians) but aggressively segregationist toward blacks; see Chap. 6. I will later discuss the risks of this type of evolution in Europe in this century; see Chap. 15–16.

mation. In the 1980s, the FN was already aggressively anti-immigrant, but in social and economic dimensions its ideology was relatively elitist, which made it less dangerous. Specifically, the party continues to bears traces of the Poujadist antitax influence of its early years: until the late 1980s it called for complete elimination of the income tax.[138] Then, in the 1990s and 2000s, the FN took a social turn, stepping up its defense of low-wage workers and of the system of social protection (provided it was reserved for the native-born). At a time when the Brahmin left seemed to be abandoning the disadvantaged classes, this helped to expand the FN's electoral base.[139] So, for example, in 2017–2019 the FN first opposed abolition of the wealth tax and then called for its restoration, whereas it had itself favored the elimination of all forms of progressive taxation only a few decades earlier.

Of course, the sincerity and depth of the FN's conversion on social and fiscal matters should not be overstated; it owed a great deal to opportunism. Basically, the FN program emphasizes the exclusion of immigrants and the endless benefits to be expected from such exclusion, and the nationalist retreat it favors would likely lead to increased fiscal dumping for the benefit of the rich, as has happened in the United States since the election of Donald Trump (I will come back to this). Nevertheless, this rhetoric could pay off, and the risk of France's falling into a social-nativist trap as a result of the Macron government's uninhibited pursuit of policies favorable to the wealthy is quite real. The fact that the carbon tax increases of 2017–2018 (ultimately rescinded in 2019) actually served to finance not the ecological transition but the abolition of the wealth tax (and other taxes on the wealthy) tends to validate the allegations of hypocrisy that nativists have traditionally directed at "globalists."

Europe and the Disadvantaged Classes: The Grounds for a Divorce

The policies that have been pursued since 2017, and especially the way in which the issue of the European Union has been instrumentalized to justify tax cuts for the wealthy, also increase the risk that the middle and disadvantaged classes

---

138. Jean-Marie Le Pen, who founded the FN in 1972, was elected a deputy on a Poujadist ticket in 1956.
139. Of the many works devoted to the FN's changing discourse and to the social and geographic composition of its electorate, see esp. G. Mauger and W. Pelletier, eds., *Les classes populaires et le FN. Explications de vote* (Croquant, 2016). See also H. Le Bras, *Le pari du FN* (Autrement, 2015).

will form an anti-European front in years to come. Of course, there is nothing new about instrumentalizing Europe for the benefit of the wealthy. As noted earlier, the complete liberalization of capital flows, without common fiscal regulation or automatic sharing of information about cross-border financial asset holdings, has contributed to escalating fiscal competition to the advantage of the mobile since the 1980s. The perception of the European Union as a place of competition of all against all, of benefit primarily to the upper classes, helps to explain the disaffection of the disadvantaged, which manifested itself in France during the 1992 referendum on the Maastricht Treaty and then again in the 2005 referendum on the European Constitutional Treaty.

These two elections are important because they reveal the depths of the divorce. In the 1992 referendum, which was primarily about creating the euro, "yes" won by a slim margin, 51 to 49 percent, thanks mainly to a last-minute intervention by the Socialist president after several polls predicted a victory for "no." The fact remains that the outcome depended entirely on the vote of the privileged classes. Data from postelection surveys shows clearly that the 30 percent of voters with the highest levels of education, income, and wealth voted heavily for "yes," while the 60 percent at the bottom voted clearly for "no" (Fig. 14.20). The 2005 referendum was about bringing the various European treaties together in a single treaty that would serve as a constitution for the European Union based on the principles of "free and undistorted competition," free circulation of capital, goods, and people, and continuation of the rule of unanimity on fiscal matters (which would thus have been institutionally enshrined). It was curtly rejected by French voters, 55 to 45 percent. The available data show that the top 20 percent (and especially the top 10 percent) in terms of education, income, and wealth voted "yes" with a large margin in 2005, whereas the bottom 80 percent massively favored "no."

These two referenda are revealing because the very clear "classist" structure of the vote, regardless of the dimension considered (education, income, or wealth), was different from that of the left-right blocs that still existed at the time. It was the well-to-do of the center-left and center-right, the "Brahmin left" and "merchant right," who came together to push the European project forward, well before the attempt to form a political alliance in the shape of a "bourgeois bloc" that one saw in 2017.

How to explain this divorce between the disadvantaged classes (in the broadest sense) and the construction of the European Union? The most plausible explanation, in my view, is the (largely justified) perception that the European Single Market primarily benefited the most powerful actors and the most advantaged social groups. Indeed, it is difficult to deny that tax

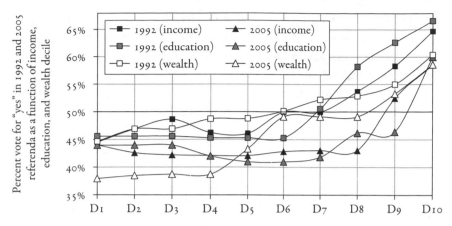

FIG. 14.20. The European cleavage in France: The 1992 and 2005 referenda

Interpretation: In the 1992 referendum on the Maastricht treaty ("yes" won with 51 percent) as in the 2005 referendum on the European Constitutional Treaty ("yes" lost with 45 percent), the vote was strongly skewed socially: the top income, education, and wealth deciles voted strongly for "yes," while the bottom deciles voted for "no." *Note:* D1 refers to the bottom decile, D2 to the next, and D10 to the top. *Sources and series:* piketty.pse.ends.fr/ideology.

competition among the countries of Europe has led them to distort their tax structures in such a way as to benefit of the most mobile actors to the detriment of the disadvantaged.[140] The idea that the socially disadvantaged are spontaneously and irrationally nationalist (or even racist), which conveniently allows "progressive" elites to justify their civilizing mission, can scarcely withstand analysis. For example, the postelection survey of 1958 contains questions about maintaining French colonial rule in Algeria and West Africa. In both cases we find that workers were the most likely to favor immediate independence in keeping with the egalitarian internationalism championed at the

---

140. Recent work has shown that tax competition alone can result in a substantial loss of income and well-being (10–20 percent depending on the estimates) for the poorest 50 percent of Europeans. See M. Munoz, "How Much Are the Poor Losing from Tax Competition? Estimating the Welfare Effects of Fiscal Dumping in Europe," WID.world, 2019. It is very difficult (if not impossible) to say whether this loss is greater or smaller than the gains due to trade integration, especially since those gains vary greatly from sector to sector and depend on whether one's position is more that of a worker or a consumer. As for possible gains from financial integration, the available studies suggest much smaller benefits (less than 1 percent of national income). See P. O. Gourinchas and O. Jeanne, "The Elusive Gains from International Financial Integration," *Review of Economic Studies,* 2006.

time by the Communist and Socialist Parties. The highly educated took a wait-and-see attitude, while the self-employed were the most supportive of keeping Algeria French and continuing French colonial rule in Africa (perhaps because they identified more with the repatriated colonists and the property they had lost in the colonies).[141] The poor are no more spontaneously nationalistic than the rich: nationalism is historically, socially, and politically constructed and deconstructed.

After such socially skewed votes, and especially after the rejection of the European Constitutional Treaty in 2005, one might have thought that there would be a change of political direction in France and Europe. Until the European Union is clearly and visibly seen to serve the cause of social and fiscal justice (for instance, by imposing a European tax on high incomes and large fortunes), it is difficult to imagine an end to the bitter divorce that has alienated the disadvantaged classes from the European project.[142]

On the Neo-Proprietarian Instrumentalization of Europe

Unfortunately, no reorientation of this sort took place. The main provisions of the (rejected) 2005 European Constitutional Treaty were incorporated into the Treaty of Lisbon (2007), which, in order to avoid the hurdle of another referendum, was put to a vote by the French National Assembly, which duly ratified it. To be sure, the "no" coalition is itself full of contradictions and did not propose any specific alternative draft that might have served as the basis of a new treaty. Still, it is dangerous to so willfully ignore a verdict so clearly expressed at the ballot box and to refuse to countenance any constructive political alternative (such as a more just tax system). In the 2012 French presidential election, the Socialist candidate vaguely evoked the possibility of renegotiating the new budget treaty (Treaty on Stability, Coordination, and Governance), signed only a few months earlier, which had led to a considerable tightening of deficit rules.[143] But in the end nothing came of this discussion, which was not based on any precise proposal on the French side.

---

141. Note, however, that answers to these questions about independence on the whole revealed little cleavage from a socioeconomic standpoint. See the online appendix.

142. Full disclosure: I voted "yes" in 1992 (my first vote) and, along with others with my educational profile, in 2005 in the hope that a more social and fiscal Europe would finally come. Such trusting expectation, which many shared, seems to me increasingly dangerous and difficult to support, however.

143. See Chap. 12. I will come back to the issue of treaty reform in Chap. 17.

What has happened over the past few years has only widened the breach between the European Union and the disadvantaged classes. In particular, the Macron government (elected in 2017) calls itself pro-European but, like its predecessors, has instrumentalized the European project in the service of policies that quite blatantly favor the rich. In the fall of 2017, the new government enacted two fiscal measures: it transformed the wealth tax (*impôt sur la fortune,* or ISF) into a real estate tax (*impôt sur la fortune immobilière,* or IFI) and instituted a flat tax on capital income (in place of the progressive tax on wages and other income). Both measures were largely described as a response to European competition. To be sure, the president also justified both measures by invoking a metaphor of Alpine climbers, in which the person "at the head of the rope" pulls up everyone else on his team: in other words, tax cuts for the rich (portrayed by the president as the most deserving and useful members of society) will eventually find their way to the rest of the population. This was a French version of Ronald Reagan's trickle-down economics of the 1980s or the portrayal of the rich as "job creators" by Donald Trump and the Republican Party. Still, the French context being very different from the American, one may doubt that Macron's rope-climber ideology would by itself have led to the fiscal measures of 2017 without the additional argument that European tax competition made reform imperative.[144]

It is important to add that, despite the government's rhetoric, these two tax reforms are quite unpopular in France. Every opinion poll conducted in 2018–2019 shows that the vast majority of respondents favored reinstating the ISF. But the government has stood firm, explicitly using Europe as a pretext and thereby running the risk of exacerbating hostility to the kind of European integration it favors.

As for the ISF, another argument was advanced in support of the government's reform: namely, the idea that financial assets are by their very nature more likely to promote job creation than nonfinancial assets (like real estate). The problem with this argument is that it makes no sense: financial investments in other countries create no jobs in France, whereas the construction of a house or apartment building creates jobs at once. As a general rule, there is no connection between the legal form of an investment (financial asset or real estate

---

144. In Chap. 16 I will say more about the striking similarity of the Trump and Macron tax policies.

asset) and its social or economic efficiency.[145] By contrast, there is a very clear connection with wealth: nearly all of the largest fortunes are held in the form of financial assets so that exempting financial assets from the ISF is tantamount to abolishing the wealth tax on the wealthiest individuals without clearly saying so while pretending that the goal was to stimulate new investment and job creation.[146]

In reality, the only logically plausible justification for exempting financial assets is of an entirely different nature: it is based on the idea that financial assets cannot be taxed because they can magically disappear and thus avoid the tax collector. This was in fact the key argument that was widely invoked. If it were true, the implication would be that the only option is a regressive tax falling solely on the real estate of the middle class because financial assets, where the wealthy put most of their money, are impossible to tax. This belief, profoundly nihilistic and pessimistic as to our collective capacity to create just rules and institutions, poses two major problems. First, the assertion that huge amounts of financial assets were spirited out of France in order to avoid the wealth tax (ISF) is not supported by any serious evidence. Even though enforcement of the ISF was far from perfect, the fact is that the number and amount of assets have increased significantly since the 1990s. Indeed, the value of financial assets declared by people in the highest tax brackets has increased even more sharply than the value of real estate, which has itself increased more rapidly than gross domestic product (GDP) and income in recent decades.[147] Total

---

145. Of course, buying an apartment from a previous owner produces no new investment, but neither does buying a financial asset from a previous owner. The alleged link between type of asset and stimulus of additional investment is logically and empirically untenable.

146. See Fig. 11.9. Recall, too, that the principal tax on wealth in France and elsewhere is the proportional tax on real estate (*taxe foncière* in France or property tax in the United States), which in effect is a very regressive tax on net wealth.

147. For a detailed analysis of the various sources available for measuring the evolution of the French wealth distribution, see B. Garbinti, J. Goupille-Lebret, and T. Piketty, "Accounting for Wealth Inequality Dynamics: Methods and Estimates for France," WID.world, 2017. Data from wealth declarations indicate trends similar to those found in declarations of income and inheritances. It is important, however, to point out that very little public information has been released about the ISF since its creation because political leaders and bureaucrats want to maintain a monopoly over information they deem to be sensitive. In addition, the upper ranks of the French ministries of economy and finance have evinced a certain hostility to the wealth tax on principle.

receipts from the ISF quadrupled between 1990 and 2018, while nominal GDP only doubled.[148] This increase also reflects a general rise in the level and concentration of wealth (and especially in the size of the largest financial portfolios) throughout the world since the 1980s.[149] In any case, the point is that the assumption of a massive capital flight induced by ISF does not stand.

Last but not least, even if we assume that financial assets flowed out of France (which they definitely did not), the logical conclusion is that the French government should have taken steps to combat the practice. It is totally baseless to assume that nothing can be done to register or monitor financial assets. Financial institutions are legally required to transmit information about interest and dividends to the tax authorities. In France, taxpayers receive income tax statements with information about their income from various sources already filled in, but this practice has never been extended to wealth tax statements even though French banks know about the financial assets they hold for their clients. This is a political choice, not a technical necessity.[150] There is no reason why pre-filled wealth tax statements could not have been introduced in France (which would have broadened the coverage of the ISF and increased returns even more); meanwhile, the government could have worked harder to encourage adoption of a similar tax by other countries. To that end, it could have pressed for new treaties on the free circulation of capital requiring automatic transmission of data to the tax authorities; the United States imposed such

---

148. See the online appendix, Fig. S14.20. The transformation of the ISF into the IFI divided receipts by four in 2018–2019, roughly returning to the 1990 level.

149. See Figs. 13.8–13.9 and Table 13.1.

150. Note that the Hollande government elected in 2012 (partially) restored the ISF rates that Sarkozy had cut but never rescinded the decision of the previous government to raise the threshold of the ISF from 0.8 to 1.3 million euros and to eliminate the detailed reporting requirement under 3 million euros. Since then, wealth of 1.3–3 million euros (about half of those subject to the tax) simply indicate a figure for aggregate wealth, which the tax authorities have no way of checking. The contrast with the pre-filled forms system of income taxes (especially for wage earners) is striking. The refusal to set up a system of pre-filled wealth tax forms while the Socialists were in power (2012–2017) is especially surprising, because the government quickly found itself enmeshed in the Cahuzac affair, named for the Socialist minister of the budget, Jérôme Cahuzac, who avoided the wealth tax by failing to declare his Swiss bank accounts (uncovered by diligent journalists, not by the tax authorities). One might have expected that this would lead to efforts to make the system more transparent and to pre-filled statements.

requirements on Switzerland and other countries in 2010.[151] As for residential and professional assets located in France and, more generally, the assets of firms doing business or having economic interests in France, it is up to the French government alone to decide whether their owners must register with the tax authorities.[152] The fact that the French government did not undertake any of these reforms demonstrates quite clearly that, for political and ideological reasons, it had other objectives, even if it tried to hide these behind a facade of technical objections (which served only to heighten suspicion of its motives).

Recall that heavy progressive taxes were often levied on large concentrations of financial wealth in the twentieth century—for example, in Germany, Japan, and other countries after World War II; this alleviated public debt and created space for investment in the future.[153] And it was done without the benefit of today's information technology. At a time when rising inequality and rapid climate change threaten the entire planet, to say that financial assets cannot be taxed because their owners cannot be forced to comply with the law is both unconscionable and a sign of historical ignorance. In any case, it is dangerous to instrumentalize European tax competition and EU and international treaties in order to promote policies biased in favor of the rich. Doing so can only stir up anti-EU and anti-globalization sentiments and sow disillusionment about the very possibility of a just economy. This is precisely the kind of nihilism that encourages identitarian retreat and leads straight into the social-nativist trap. We will soon consider the conditions under which this fate might be avoided, but first we must look beyond France and analyze the extent to which the transformations of the political cleavage structure that we have observed there can also be found elsewhere.

---

151. See Chap. 13.
152. I will come back to this point in Chap. 17.
153. See Chap. 10.

FIFTEEN

Brahmin Left:
New Euro-American Cleavages

In Chapter 14 we studied the transformation of political cleavages in France since World War II. In particular, we saw how the "classist" structure of the period 1950–1980 gradually gave way to a system of multiple elites in the period 1990–2020. At the heart of that system were the party of the highly educated (the "Brahmin left") and the party of the highly paid and wealthy (the "merchant right"), both of which alternated in power. The very end of the period witnessed an attempt to create a new electoral bloc in France bringing those two elites together; it is too soon to say whether this will last.

To gain a better understanding of the dynamics and possible future developments, in this chapter I turn to the United States and United Kingdom. It is striking to discover how much these two countries, despite everything that differentiates them from France, have since 1945 followed a path broadly similar to the French. Nevertheless, the differences are also important—and revealing. I will continue this comparative approach in Chapter 16, in which I will look at other West and East European democracies along with several non-Western democracies such as India and Brazil. Comparing the different trajectories of all these countries will help us to understand the reasons for the transformations they experienced and what might lie ahead. In particular, I will consider in the final chapter the conditions under which it might be possible to avoid the social-nativist trap. I will also outline a form of social federalism and participatory socialism that could help to confront the new identitarian menace.

The Transformation of the US Party System

We begin with the United States, proceeding as we did for France by examining how the socioeconomic structure of the vote for the Democratic and Republican Parties changed from 1945 to the present. In the US case we have postelection surveys from 1948 on. These surveys allow for a relatively detailed

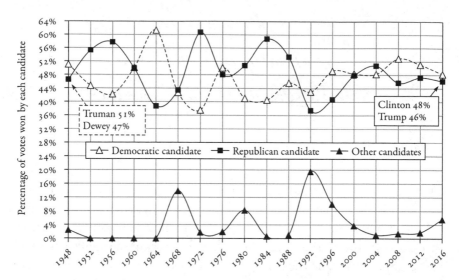

FIG. 15.1. Presidential elections in the United States, 1948–2016

Interpretation: The scores obtained by the candidates of the Democratic and Republican Parties in US presidential elections from 1948 to 2016 generally varied from 40 to 60 percent of the total popular vote. The scores obtained by third-party candidates have usually been low (less than 10 percent of the vote), except for George Wallace in 1968 (14 percent) and H. Ross Perot in 1992 and 1996 (20 and 10 percent). *Sources and series:* piketty.pse.ens.fr/ideology.

analysis, whose main conclusions I will present here.[1] I will focus on the structure of the vote in presidential elections from 1948 to 2016. These are the elections from which the national dimension of political conflict emerges most clearly.[2] In most presidential elections in this period the two major parties received between 40 and 60 percent of the vote, and races were usually fairly tight (Fig. 15.1). Third-party candidates usually captured less than 10 percent of the vote, with the exception of the southern segregationist governor of Alabama, George Wallace, who got 14 percent of the vote in 1968 and the busi-

---

1. As for France, the complete results of my analysis, along with computer code for transforming the raw data files into the series presented here, are available in the online appendix (piketty.pse.ens.fr/ideology). See also T. Piketty, "Brahmin Left vs Merchant Right: Rising Inequality and the Changing Structure of Political Conflict (Evidence from France, Britain and the US, 1948–2017)," WID.world, 2018.

2. House of Representatives and Senate elections in the United States often have a much stronger local dimension. In addition, turnout is usually lower (especially in midterm elections) than in presidential elections.

nessman Ross Perot, who garnered 20 percent in 1992 and 10 percent in 1996. In what follows I will focus on the Democrat-Republican cleavage and ignore the vote for third-party candidates.

Our first finding is that the educational cleavage has totally reversed. In the 1948 presidential election, the result is quite clear: the more educated the voter, the more likely to vote Republican. Specifically, 62 percent of voters with only a primary education or without a high school diploma, who constituted 63 percent of the US electorate at the time, voted for Harry Truman, the Democratic candidate (Fig. 15.2). Of those with high school diplomas (31 percent of the electorate), Truman scored barely 50 percent. Of those with college degrees (6 percent of the electorate), just over 30 percent voted Democratic, and the score was even lower among those with master's or higher degrees (more than 70 percent of whom voted for the Republican candidate, Thomas Dewey). Things were not much different in the 1960s: the higher the level of education, the lower the Democratic vote. The educational cleavage begins to flatten out in the 1970s and 1980s, however. Then, from the 1990s on, the higher the level

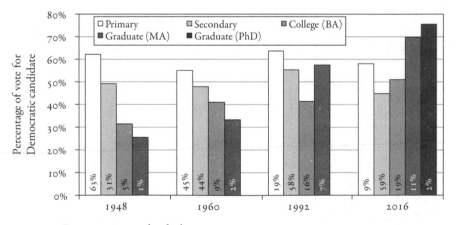

FIG. 15.2. Democratic vote by diploma, 1948–2016

Interpretation: In 1948, the Democratic candidate (H. Truman) won 62 percent of the vote among voters with a primary education (no high school diploma) (63 percent of the electorate at the time) and 26 percent of the vote among voters with advanced degrees (1 percent of the electorate at the time). In 2016, the Democratic candidate (H. Clinton) won 45 percent of the vote among those with high school diplomas (59 percent of the electorate) and 75 percent of the vote among those with a doctorate (2 percent of the electorate). As in France, the electoral cleavage totally reversed between 1948 and 2016.

Note: BA: bachelor's degree or equivalent; MA: master's degree or law or medical school degree; PhD: doctorate. *Sources and series:* piketty.pse.ens.fr/ideology.

of education, the more likely to vote Democratic, particularly among those with advanced degrees.

For example, in the 2016 presidential election, voters with doctoral degrees (2 percent of the electorate) voted 75 percent of the time for the Democrat, Hillary Clinton, while fewer than 25 percent voted for the Republican, Donald Trump. Now, the important point is that this was not a whim of intellectuals who suddenly quit the Republican Party because it failed to choose a reasonable candidate. It was rather the culmination of a structural evolution that began half a century earlier. Indeed, if one looks at the gap in the Democratic vote between those with and without college degrees, one finds that it has grown slowly but steadily since the 1960s. Clearly negative in the period 1950–1970, it rose toward zero in the period 1970–1990, then turned distinctly positive after 1990 (Fig. 15.3).

The evolution is even more dramatic if one looks at the gap between the most highly educated 10 percent and the remaining 90 percent (Fig. 15.4). This is because voting of the college-educated also turned around. In the 1950s and 1960s, the more advanced the diploma, the more likely the holder would vote

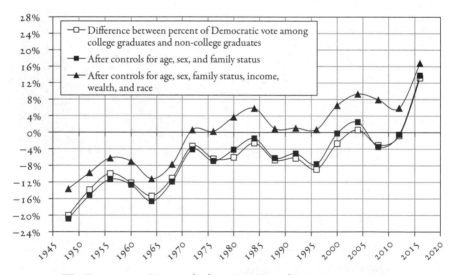

FIG. 15.3. The Democratic Party and education: United States, 1948–2016
Interpretation: In 1948, the Democratic candidate obtained a score 20 percent lower among college graduates than among nongraduates; in 2016, the same figure was fourteen points higher. Controlling for other variables affects levels but does not change the trend. *Sources and series:* piketty.pse.ens.fr/ideology.

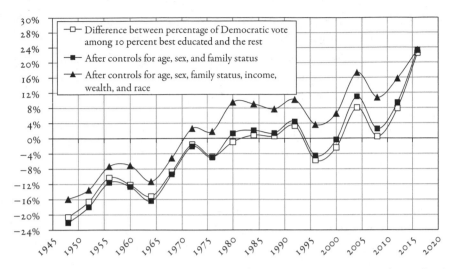

FIG. 15.4. The Democratic vote in the United States, 1948–2016: From the workers' party to the party of the highly educated

Interpretation: In 1948 the Democratic share of the vote among the best educated 10 percent was twenty-one points lower than his share of the other 90 percent of the electorate; in 2016, the same figure was twenty-three points higher than for the rest of the electorate. Controlling for other variables affects the levels but not the trend. *Sources and series:* piketty.pse.ens.fr/ideology.

Republican. In the 2000s and 2010s, the reverse is true: those with bachelor's degrees (obtained after three or four years of study at a college or university) are more likely to vote Democratic than those who have only a high school diploma, but they are less enthusiastically Democratic than those with a master's or a medical or law school degree, and even they are outdone by those with PhDs.[3] We also find the same evolution if we look at the gap between the Democratic vote for the most highly educated 50 percent and the remaining 50 percent.[4]

As in France, we also find that if we control for other socioeconomic variables, the basic pattern remains the same; these findings appear to be extremely robust. In the US case, it turns out that controlling for other variables raises the level of the curve. The primary reason for this is the racial factor (Figs. 15.3–15.4).[5]

---

3. As in the case of France, it would be interesting to be able to make even finer distinctions by type of university and discipline, but the surveys do not allow this, both because the sample sizes are too small and because of the survey questionnaire.
4. See the online appendix for detailed series.
5. See Fig. 14.11 for the French case.

Because the effect of race is roughly of the same size throughout the half century under investigation, it has no effect on the underlying trend.[6]

It is striking to see how similar the US and French results are. Like the left-wing parties in France, the Democratic Party in the United States transitioned over half a century from the workers' party to the party of the highly educated. The same is true of the Labour Party in the United Kingdom and of various social-democratic parties in Europe (for instance, in Germany and Sweden). In all these countries, the expansion of educational opportunity coincided with a reversal of the educational cleavage in the voting structure. Although the general educational level in the United States was relatively advanced compared with Europe in the 1950s, the majority of the electorate did not yet have a college or even a high school diploma. In 1948, 63 percent of voters had not finished high school, and 94 percent did not have a college degree. Most of these voters identified as Democrats. Clearly, many of the children and grandchildren of those voters experienced upward mobility in terms of education. And the striking fact is that, just as in France, those who rose the most continued to vote Democratic whereas those who were less successful in their educational careers tended to identify more with the Republican Party (Fig. 15.2).[7]

Will the Democratic Party Become the Party of the Winners of Globalization?

Why did the Democratic Party become the party of the educated? Before attempting to answer this question, it is interesting to see how the structure of the Democratic electorate evolved in terms of income. Because education is an important determinant of income, it is natural to expect that the party of the highly educated will also have become the party of the highly paid. And indeed, we do observe an evolution of this sort. In the period 1950–1980, the profile of the Democratic vote as a function of income was clearly decreasing (the higher the

---

6. Black voters are highly likely to vote Democratic throughout the period under study (I will come back to this). Since they are (on average) also less educated, this tends to reduce the estimated effect of education on the Democratic vote. When we control for other variables (for both white and black voters), the educational effect on Democratic vote therefore stands out even more clearly.

7. See Figs. 14.9–14.10 for the French case. Note that in the United States, high school dropouts were more likely to vote Democratic than those with high school diplomas in 2016. But this is a small group (9 percent of the electorate), and this effect is due primarily to the fact that many of the dropouts belong to minority groups.

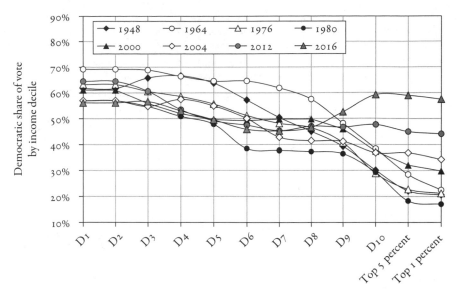

FIG. 15.5. Political conflict and income in the United States, 1948–2016

Interpretation: In 1964, the Democratic candidate won 69 percent of the vote of the lowest income decile, 37 percent of the vote of the top income decile, and 22 percent of the vote of the top income centile. Generally, the profile of the Democratic vote is decreasing with income, particularly earlier in the period. In 2016, for the first time, the profile reversed: the top decile voted 59 percent Democratic. *Sources and series:* piketty. pse.ens.fr/ideology.

income decile, the lower the Democratic vote). Then the curve flattened out in the 1990s and 2000s. Finally, in 2016, for the first time in the history of the United States, we find that the Democratic Party won more votes among the top 10 percent of US earners than did the Republican Party (Fig. 15.5).

Does it follow, however, that the Democratic Party is on its way to becoming the party of the winners of globalization, like the new inegalitarian internationalist coalition in France? This is without a doubt one possible path forward. The reality is more complex, however, and I think it is important to emphasize the diversity of possible trajectories and variety of potential switch points ahead. Political-ideological transformation depends above all on the balance of power of the contending groups and their relative capacity for mobilization, and there is no justification for a deterministic analysis. In the French case, we saw that the highly educated class did not perfectly coincide with the highly paid class, in part because people with equivalent levels of education may choose more

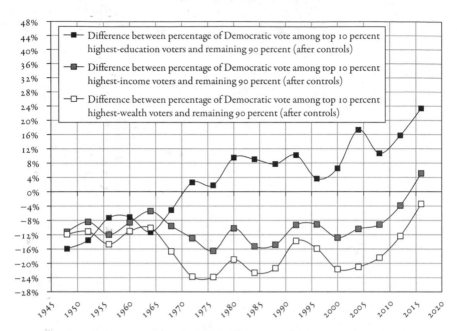

FIG. 15.6. Social cleavages and political conflict: United States, 1948–2016

Interpretation: In the period 1950–1970, the Democratic vote was associated with voters with lower levels of education, income, and wealth. In the period 1980–2010 it came to be associated with highly educated voters. In the period 2010–2020, it is close to being associated with high-income and wealthy voters as well. *Sources and series:* piketty.pse.ens.fr/ideology.

or less lucrative career paths (or experience different degrees of success in a given path), and in part because achieving a high income also depends in part on possessing some wealth, which is not fully correlated with level of education.

In fact, the available data suggest that high wealth has always been strongly associated with voting Republican and remained so in 2016 with Trump as the candidate, even though the strength of the relationship decreased (Fig. 15.6).[8]

---

8. The education, income, and wealth effects shown in Fig. 15.6 are after application of controls. The raw trends move in the same direction, but it is not until 2000 that the sign of the educational effect turns positive (for reasons already explained in the French case, the control variables tend to separate education effects more clearly from income and wealth effects). Recall, moreover, that because of small sample sizes, year-to-year variations are not significant, but long-term evolutions are quite significant. See the online appendix, Figs. S15.6a–S15.6d for the different variants with confidence intervals.

In other words, the US party system in the period 1990–2020 has become a system of multiple elites, with a highly educated elite closer to the Democrats (the "Brahmin left") and a wealthier and better paid elite closer to the Republicans ("merchant right"). This regime may be on the verge of turning into a classist confrontation in which these two elites merge in support of the Democratic Party, but the process is still incomplete and may yet change direction of a variety of reasons.

It bears emphasizing, moreover, that serious limitations of the available data make it very difficult to know the exact structure of the US vote. According to the data, the top centile of the income distribution was less likely to vote for Hillary Clinton than the top decile as a whole (Fig. 15.5). But the sample sizes and questionnaires make it impossible to be perfectly precise about this. In addition, the information we have about wealth from the US postelection surveys is quite rudimentary (and much more limited than in the French case) so that the estimates shown here should be treated with caution. It appears that the wealthiest voters continued to show a slight preference for the Republican candidate in 2016, but the gaps are so much reduced that uncertainty remains (Fig. 15.6).[9]

Among the factors that may encourage continued political-ideological evolution along these lines and lead to a gradual unification of elites, the evolution of the socioeconomic structure of inequality in the United States deserves to be mentioned. First, top incomes have increased sharply in the United States since the 1980s, and the beneficiaries, many of whom are highly educated and successful in their careers, have been able to accumulate a great deal of wealth in a short period of time. This means that the highly paid elite and the wealthy elite coincide to a greater degree now than was the case prior to 1980.[10] Second,

---

9. In France, postelection surveys since 1978 have included detailed questions about types of assets owned (real estate, stocks and bonds, professional assets, etc.). In the United States, apart from a few surveys in specific years in which more detailed wealth data were collected (which incidentally allow us to conclude that the wealth effect on the Republican vote was as pronounced as on the right-wing vote in France), the questionnaires in most of the US surveys asked only about real estate, which limits the precision of the estimates shown in Fig. 15.6.

10. For example, according to recent estimates, 30 percent of individuals in the top decile of labor income also belonged to the top decile of capital income in 2017, compared with only 15 percent in 1980. See B. Milanovic, *Capitalism, Alone* (Harvard University Press, 2019), p. 37, fig. 2.3. Note, however, that these two dimensions are still imperfectly correlated.

the fact that the system of higher education has become extremely costly for students (to say nothing of the fact that parental gifts are sometimes a factor in admission) is a structural factor contributing to the unification of the Brahmin and merchant elites. As noted earlier, the probability of access to higher education in general is strongly correlated with parental income in the United States.[11] Recent studies of admissions to the best US universities have shown that most of them draw a larger proportion of their students from families in the top centile of the income distribution than from families in the bottom 60 percent (which means that children of the top centile are at least sixty times more likely to be admitted than children of the latter group).[12] The fusion of educational and patrimonial elites will of course never be complete at the individual level, if only because of the diversity of aspirations and career choices. Nevertheless, compared with countries where the commodification of higher education is less advanced, the United States is probably the place where a political unification of elites is most likely to occur.[13]

It is also important to note that political parties and campaigns are for the most part privately financed in the United States. Now that the Supreme Court has eliminated the ban on corporate contributions, there is an obvious risk that candidates will represent the interests of financial elites.[14] Furthermore, this affects both the Republicans and Democrats. Note, interestingly, that it was the Democratic Party (in Barack Obama's 2008 campaign) that for the first

---

11. See Fig. I.9.

12. In particular, this is the case for the thirty-eight most selective US universities. See R. Chetty, J. Friedman, E. Saez, N. Turner, and D. Yagan, *Mobility Report Cards: The Role of Colleges in Intergenerational Mobility* (National Bureau of Economic Research, NBER Working Paper No. 23618, July 2017).

13. In France, the correlation between income and wealth does not appear to have increased over time; it has remained fairly stable and even decreased at the top of the distribution because of the increasing role of inheritance. See the online appendix.

14. See the many works cited in Chap. 12. Research has shown that both parties tend to respond more to the preferences of elites than to those of more modest voters. See M. Gilens, *Affluence and Influence* (Princeton University Press, 2012); B. Page and M. Gilens, *Democracy in America? What Has Gone Wrong and What We Can Do About It* (University of Chicago Press, 2017). T. Frank speaks of the Democrats' neglect of class conflict. See T. Frank, *What's the Matter with Kansas? How Conservatives Won the Heart of America* (Holt, 2004). This neglect feeds into what K. Cramer calls the "politics of resentment" among more modest voters: K. Cramer, *The Politics of Resentment: Rural Consciousness in Wisconsin and the Rise of Scott Walker* (University of Chicago Press, 2016).

time chose to renounce public funding to avoid limits on the amount it could spend from private contributions.[15]

Nevertheless, other factors cast doubt on the long-term viability of a transformation of the Democratic Party into the party of the winners of globalization in all its dimensions: educational as well as patrimonial. First, the presidential debates of 2016 showed the degree to which cultural and ideological differences remain between the Brahmin and merchant elites. Whereas the intellectual elite stressed values of level-headed rationality and cultural openness, which Barack Obama and Hillary Clinton sought to project, business elites favored deal-making ability, cunning, and virility, of which Donald Trump presented himself as the embodiment.[16] In other words, the system of multiple elites has not yet breathed its last because at bottom it rests on two different and complementary meritocratic ideologies. Second, the 2016 presidential election showed the risk that any political party runs if it becomes too blatantly identified as the party of the winners of globalization. It then becomes the target of anti-elitist ideologies of all kinds: in the United States in 2016, this allowed Donald Trump to deploy what one might call the nativist merchant ideology against the Democrats. I will come back to this.

Last but not least, I do not believe that this evolution of the Democratic Party is viable in the long run because it does not reflect the egalitarian values of an important part of the Democratic electorate and of the United States as a whole. Dissatisfaction was obvious in the 2016 Democratic primaries, in which the "socialist" senator from Vermont, Bernie Sanders, ran neck-and-neck with Hillary Clinton despite the fact that Clinton enjoyed much greater support from the media. As mentioned earlier, the 2020 presidential contest now under way shows that nothing is written in advance, and some Democrats are now openly proposing a strongly progressive tax on large fortunes (especially financial wealth).[17] The history of every inequality regime studied in this book

---

15. Under the US system of public financing of presidential campaigns, established in 1976, candidates who accept public funds must agree to limits on total campaign spending. They can also decide to forgo public funding (as Obama did for the first time in 2008), in which case the ceiling no longer applies. See J. Cagé, *The Price of Democracy* (Harvard University Press, 2020).

16. Note that the recourse to overtly anti-intellectual and anti-Brahmin leaders like Donald Trump is not limited to the US Republican Party: the European right has gone in a similar direction as shown by the choice of a Silvio Berlusconi in Italy or a Nicolas Sarkozy in France.

17. See Chap. 11.

shows that the ideologies deployed to justify inequality must have some minimum degree of plausibility if they are to survive. In view of the very rapid growth of inequality in the United States and the stagnation of the standard of living of the majority, it is unlikely that a political-ideological platform centered on the defense of the neo-proprietarian status quo and the celebration of the winners of globalization can last for long. As in France and elsewhere, the question facing the United States is rather one of possible alternatives to the status quo: more specifically, a choice between some form of nativist ideology and some form of democratic, egalitarian, and internationalist socialism.

On the Political Exploitation of the Racial Divide in the United States

For obvious reasons, the question of political exploitation of the racial divide has a long history in the United States. Slavery was in a sense congenital with the American Republic: recall that eleven of the first fifteen presidents were slaveowners. The Democratic Party was historically the party of slavery and states' rights—especially the right to preserve and extend the slave system. Thomas Jefferson thought abolition possible only if the freed slaves could be sent back to Africa because he believed that peaceful coexistence with them on US soil was impossible. Slavery's principal theoreticians, such as Democratic Senator John Calhoun of South Carolina, never tired of denouncing the hypocrisy of northern industrialists and financiers, who they said pretended to care about the fate of blacks but whose only objective was to turn them into proletarians to be exploited like the others. Abraham Lincoln's victory on a "free soil" platform in the 1860 presidential elections led to the secession of the southern states, the Civil War, and then the occupation of the South by federal troops. But in the 1870s segregationist Democrats regained control in the South and imposed strict racial segregation (since it was impossible to send all blacks back to Africa). The Democratic Party also gained support in the North by championing the cause of the poor and of newly arrived immigrants against Republican elites. In 1884 they regained the presidency and in subsequent decades alternated regularly with Republicans on the basis of a social-nativist platform (segregationist and differentialist with respect to blacks but more social and egalitarian than the Republicans when it came to whites).[18]

---

18. See Chap. 6 for a more detailed analysis.

That is more or less how things stood when Franklin D. Roosevelt, a Democrat, was elected president in 1932. At the federal level, of course, the new economic and social policies enacted under the New Deal benefited poor blacks as well as poor whites. But Roosevelt continued to rely on segregationist Democrats in the South, where many blacks were denied the right to vote. The first postelection surveys conducted after the presidential elections of 1948, 1952, 1956, and 1960 showed that black voters in the North were slightly more likely to vote for Democrats than for Republicans.[19] It was not until the John F. Kennedy and Lyndon B. Johnson administrations of the 1960s that the Democrats, partly against their will and under pressure from African American civil rights activists, wedded the cause of civil rights and won the massive support of the black electorate. In all presidential elections from 1964 to 2016, roughly 90 percent of blacks have voted for the Democratic candidate (Fig. 15.7). We even find peaks above 95 percent in 1964 and 1968, in the heat of the battle over civil rights, as well as in 2008, when Barack Obama was elected for the first time. Thus, the Democratic Party, which had been the party of slavery until the 1860s and then the party of racial segregation until the 1960s, became the preferred party of the black minority (along with abstention).

By contrast, the Republican Party, having been the party that freed the slaves, became in the 1960s the last refuge of those who had a hard time accepting the end of segregation and the growing ethnic and racial diversity of the United States. In the wake of George Wallace's fruitless third-party run in 1968, southern Democrats who supported segregation began a slow migration

---

19. There are no postelection surveys for the period 1870–1940, but from results observed at the local level there is no doubt that the majority of the black electorate (where it was allowed to vote) often supported Republican candidates. For example, a Republican governor elected with black votes briefly held office in Louisiana in the early 1870s until segregationist Democrats quickly regained control of the situation (see Chap. 6). Note, however, that northern Democrats soon adopted platforms and assumed an identity very different from their southern segregationist allies, which allowed them to equal or beat their Republican rivals among black voters (particularly since Republicans were not much interested in this segment of the electorate). Gallup polls for the presidential elections of 1932, 1936, 1940, and 1944 have been preserved but are unfortunately much more rudimentary than the postelection surveys carried out from 1948 on. Nevertheless, they allow us to discern a Democrat-Republican electoral structure quite similar to that observed from 1948 to 1960, with the vote for Roosevelt concentrated in the lower and lower-middle class (both black and white); among the well-to-do, Roosevelt voters were in the clear minority. See the online appendix.

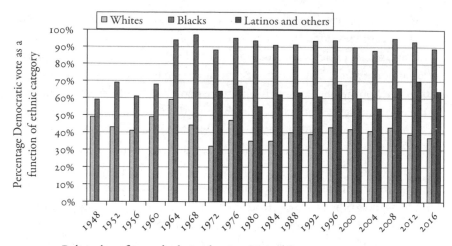

FIG. 15.7. Political conflict and ethnic identity: United States, 1948–2016

Interpretation: In 2016, the Democratic candidate won 36 percent of the vote of white voters (70 percent of the electorate), 89 percent of the vote of African American voters (11 percent of the electorate), and 64 percent of the vote of Latinos and those declaring themselves to be of other ethnicities (19 percent of the electorate, of which 16 percent are Latinos). In 1972, the Democratic candidate won 32 percent of the white vote (89 percent of the electorate), 82 percent of the African American vote (10 percent of the electorate), and 64 percent of other categories (1 percent of the electorate). *Sources and series:* piketty.pse.ens.fr/ideology.

to the Republican Party. There is no doubt that this "racist" vote (or "nativist" vote, to employ a more neutral term) played an important role in most subsequent Republican victories, especially Richard Nixon's in 1968 and 1972, Ronald Reagan's in 1980 and 1984, and Trump's in 2016.

Note, moreover, that the ethno-racial structure of the United States, as measured both by the US census and the postelection surveys, has changed considerably over the past half century. From the presidential election of 1948 to that of 2016, blacks have represented about 10 percent of the electorate. Other "ethnic minorities" accounted for a little over 1 percent in 1968 but thereafter increased sharply to 5 percent in 1980, 14 percent in 2000, and 19 percent in 2016. These are mainly people who declare themselves to be "Hispanic or Latino" according to the terms of the census and surveys.[20] All told, in the 2016

---

20. Latinos accounted for roughly 16 percent of the electorate in 2016, compared with 3 percent for other minorities (notably Asian). For a long time US censuses assigned identities (especially during the slave era) but gradually moved toward self-declared

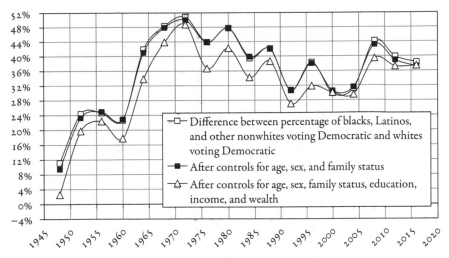

FIG. 15.8. Political conflict and racial cleavage in the United States, 1948–2016

Interpretation: In 1948, the Democratic vote was eleven points higher among African American and other minority voters (9 percent of the electorate) compared with whites (91 percent of the electorate). In 2016, the Democratic vote was thirty-nine points higher among African Americans and other minorities (30 percent of the electorate) than among whites (70 percent of the electorate). Controlling for other socioeconomic variables has a limited impact on this gap. *Sources and series:* piketty.pse.ens.fr/ideology.

election won by Trump, "minorities" accounted for 30 percent of the electorate (11 percent black, 19 percent Latinos and other minorities), compared with 70 percent white; the white share will diminish in the coming decades. Note, too, that Latinos and other minorities have always voted strongly in favor of Democratic candidates (55–70 percent) but not as strongly as blacks (90 percent). As for whites, since 1968 a majority of white voters have voted Republican: if only whites had voted, not a single Democratic president would have been elected in the last fifty years (Fig. 15.7).

Note, moreover, that only a small part of the massive minority vote in favor of Democratic candidates since the 1960s can be explained by socioeconomic characteristics of the electorate. The roughly forty-point gap between the minority and white votes for Democrats decreases very slightly over time owing to the increasing relative share of Latinos but remains extremely high (Fig. 15.8).

identity with the possibility of choosing among several categories. See P. Schor, *Compter et classer. Histoire des recensements américains* (EHESS, 2009).

The obvious explanation for this very stark electoral behavior is that minorities, especially the black minority, perceive the Republicans as violently hostile to them.

"Welfare Queens" and "Racial Quotas": The Republicans' Southern Strategy

Of course, no Republican candidate—not Nixon or Reagan or Trump—has ever explicitly proposed reinstating racial segregation. But they have openly admitted former proponents of segregation into their ranks. To this day, they have continued to tolerate white supremacist movements, at times appearing with their leaders. This was clear after the events of 2017 in Charlottesville, Virginia, when President Trump said that he saw "good people on both sides" of a demonstration pitting neo-Nazis and remnants of the Ku Klux Klan against protesters.[21]

Many segregationist Democrats eventually left the party and joined the Republicans: for example, Strom Thurmond, who served as a Democratic senator from South Carolina from 1954 to 1967 and then as a Republican from 1964 to 2003. A great advocate of the cause of states' rights (that is, the right of the southern states to continue to practice segregation and more generally not to enforce federal laws and executive orders deemed too favorable to blacks and other minorities), Thurmond symbolized the transfer of these issues from the Democratic Party (which had been their standard bearer from the early nineteenth to the middle of the twentieth centuries) to the Republicans. In 1948, worried about the influence that northern pro–civil rights Democrats had already begun to exert on the Democratic Party, Thurmond ran for president as a dissident segregationist Democrat under the banner of the ephemeral "States' Rights Democratic Party" (commonly known as "Dixiecrats").[22]

---

21. The fact that in 2018 Trump immediately voiced support for white South African farmers after rumors of agrarian reform circulated in South Africa (see Chap. 7) was also a perfectly clear message addressed to white supremacists.

22. In 2002, on Thurmond's hundredth birthday (he was still a senator), Trent Lott, a Republican senator from Mississippi and Republican leader in the Senate, publicly declared: "I want to say this about my state. When Strom Thurmond ran for president, we voted for him. We're proud of it. And if the rest of the country had followed our lead, we wouldn't have had all these problems over all these years, either." Because of this overtly pro-segregationist reference to the 1948 elections, Lott was forced to resign his leadership position, although he remained a senator. See S. Engel, "History

The situation grew tenser after the Johnson administration tried to force the southern states to end segregation, especially in schools, after 1964. Barry Goldwater, the Republican candidate in the 1964 election, opposed the Civil Rights Act. Although he lost to Johnson, he took up the cause of the South and its opposition to the federal government. To circumvent the hostility of southern state governments, Johnson promoted programs such as Head Start, which in effect funneled federal money directly to local nonstate organizations so as to fund day care and health centers in disadvantaged neighborhoods, many of them black.[23] Nixon won the 1968 election by opposing such federal interference. In particular, he stood against any generalization of timid experiments with busing, which sought to mix children from black and white neighborhoods in the same schools, and brandished the threat of racial quotas that would allow blacks to take the place of allegedly better qualified whites in universities and government jobs.[24] The Republicans' "southern strategy" paid off handsomely in the 1972 presidential election, in which Nixon captured the votes that had gone to Wallace in 1968. He was triumphantly reelected over the Democrat George McGovern, a strong opponent of the Vietnam War and proponent of new social policies intended to cap off Roosevelt's New Deal and Johnson's War on Poverty, which Nixon successfully opposed.

Since Nixon, Republican candidates have resorted to more subtle, coded attacks on social policies alleged to lavish money on the African American population. It was common, for instance, to attack "welfare queens," code for "single black mothers." This term was used by Ronald Reagan in the 1976

of Racial Politics in the United States," in J. Roemer, W. Lee, K. Van der Straeten, *Racism, Xenophobia, and Distribution: Multi-Issue Politics in Advanced Democracies* (Harvard University Press, 2007), pp. 41–43.

23. See M. Bailey and S. Danziger, eds., *Legacies of the War on Poverty* (Russell Sage Foundation, 2013). See also E. Cascio, N. Gordon, and S. Reber, "Paying for Progress: Conditional Grants and the Desegregation of Southern Schools," *Quarterly Journal of Economics,* 2010; E. Cascio, N. Gordon, and S. Reber, "Local Responses to Federal Grants: Evidence from the Introduction of Title I in the South," *American Economic Journal: Economic Policy,* 2013; M. Bailey, S. Sun, and B. Timpe, *Prep School for Poor Kids: The Long-Run Impact of Head Start on Human Capital and Economic Self-Sufficiency* (University of Michigan, working paper, 2018).

24. Such measures were never really tried in the United States. The hostility of many southern whites and the absence of adequate mobilization against them also explain the lack of any compensation or redistribution of land for discrimination suffered during centuries of unremunerated work under slavery, despite the forty acres and a mule offered to blacks at the end of the Civil War (see Chap. 6).

Republican primaries and then again in the 1980 campaign. Reagan was a fervent supporter of Goldwater in the 1964 campaign, during which he launched his political career by speaking on behalf of the Republican candidate. Reagan also opposed the Civil Rights Act of 1964 and the Voting Rights Act of 1965, which he attacked as unnecessarily humiliating to southerners and excessively intrusive.[25] Broadly speaking, exploitation of racial issues played an important role in the movement leading to the triumph of the "conservative revolution" in the 1980s.[26] The new conservative ideology that developed around Goldwater in 1964, Nixon in 1972, and Reagan in 1980 was based on both virulent anticommunism and strident opposition to the New Deal and to the growing power of the federal government and its social policies. Those social policies were charged with encouraging the alleged laziness of people of color (a canard endlessly repeated since the abolition of slavery). The money spent on the modest welfare state that the United States had established in the New Deal and New Frontier eras was said to be wasteful and intrusive and above all a diversion from the more important demands of the Cold War and national security, which the "socialistic" Democrats were accused of neglecting, while Republicans promised to restore American greatness.

These episodes are important because they remind us that Donald Trump's position on racial issues (as indicated by his remarks after the white supremacist demonstrations in Charlottesville in 2017 and his comments on statues of Confederate generals) has to be seen in the context of a long Republican tradition dating back to the 1960s. What is new is that in the meantime other minorities have also become important. Trump therefore attacks Latinos, whom he describes in particularly unflattering terms. To stop them from coming into the United States he wants to build a huge wall, a symbol of the importance he ascribes to the border issue. During his 2016 campaign and since his elec-

---

25. Engel, "History of Racial Politics in the United States," pp. 57–62.

26. As for Ronald Reagan, it is worth noting that in his career as an actor, he had the opportunity to play a number of roles compatible with the southern view of history. *Santa Fe Trail,* a film he made in 1940 with Errol Flynn and Olivia de Haviland, is set in Kansas in 1854, where a fanatic abolitionist sows terror and is prepared to sacrifice his own children for the sake of his political passions. The moral of the story is clear: southerners do not really treat their slaves so badly, so it is better to seek a compromise and gradual solution to allow the system to evolve for the better. Fortunately, some young and pragmatic officers from West Point (including Reagan's character) understand this and do not give in to the dangerous temptation represented by John Brown.

tion he has attacked virtually every nonwhite group in the United States, especially the Muslim minority (despite its small numbers on US soil).

Electoral Cleavages and Identity Conflicts: Transatlantic Views

European countries, and especially France, have long been intrigued by racial cleavages in the United States and their role in America's exotic politics and partisan dynamics. In particular, it has always been hard for Europeans to understand how the Democratic Party could have gone from the pro-slavery and segregationist party to the party of minorities while the Republican Party, which once counted so many abolitionists in its midst, became the racialist and nativist party, which minorities massively reject. In fact, these surprising transformations and comparisons are highly instructive. They can help us to understand changes currently under way and therefore to anticipate some possible political-ideological trajectories in the years to come, not only in the United States but also in Europe and other parts of the world.

It is particularly striking to see that electoral cleavages due to identity conflicts are today comparable in magnitude on both sides of the Atlantic. In the United States, the gap between the black and Latino vote for the Democratic Party and the vote of the white majority has been about 40 percentage points for the past half century; controlling for variables other than race barely changes this finding (Figs. 15.7–15.8). In France, we found that the gap between the Muslim vote and the vote of the rest of the population for parties of the left (themselves undergoing redefinition) has also been about 40 percentage points for several decades now, and controlling for other variables again has little effect.[27] In both cases the cleavage defined by racial or religious identity is immense—much greater, for instance, than the gap between the vote of the top income decile and that of the bottom 90 percent, which in both France and the United States is generally on the order of ten to twenty points. In the United States we find that since the 1960s, in election after election, 90 percent or more of African American voters have voted for the Democratic Party (and barely 10 percent for the Republicans). In France, 90 percent of Muslims vote in election after election for the parties of the left (and barely 10 percent for the parties of the right and extreme right).

---

27. See Figs. 14.16–14.17 and the online appendix, Figs. S14.17a–S14.17b.

Apart from these formal similarities (which would have astonished a French observer if one had predicted them a few decades ago), it is important to note the differences between the two countries. In the United States, the black minority is in large part descended from slaves, and the Latino minority is largely the product of immigration from Mexico and Latin America. In France, the Muslim minority is the product of postcolonial immigration, primarily from North Africa and to a lesser extent from sub-Saharan Africa. To be sure, the two cases share an important point in common. In both countries, a white majority of European origin, which long wielded uncontested power over the nonwhite population (whether by slavery, segregation, or colonial domination), must now cohabit with nonwhites in a single political community. Disagreements must be settled at the ballot box, in principle on the basis of (at least formally) equal rights. In the long run of human history, this is clearly a radically new phenomenon. For centuries, relations between populations from different regions of the world were limited to military domination and brute force or else to commercial relations largely structured by the balance of military power. The fact that we are now witnessing, within the confines of a single society, relations of a quite different kind—based on dialogue, cultural exchange, intermarriage, and the emergence of unprecedented mixed identities—is an undeniable sign of civilizational progress. The resulting identity conflicts have been exploited for political purposes, and this has given rise to significant challenges, which need to be examined closely. Nevertheless, even a rapid comparison of today's intergroup relations with those observed in the past suggests that we need to keep the magnitude of current difficulties in perspective and refrain from idealizing the past.

Beyond this general similarity between the US and French situations, however, it is clear that the identity conflicts in the two countries take very specific forms. In terms of electoral cleavages, what is most striking about the United States is that Latinos and other (nonblack) minorities (henceforth lumped together as "Latinos"), which currently account for about 20 percent of the electorate, fall somewhere between white and blacks in voting behavior. For instance, 64 percent of Latinos voted for the Democratic candidate in 2016, compared with 37 percent of whites and 89 percent of blacks. This intermediate position has not changed much since 1970 (Fig. 15.7). How it evolves in the future will have a decisive impact on the structure of political conflict in the United States in view of the increasing weight of minorities in general (30 percent of the electorate in 2016 if one groups together blacks, Latinos,

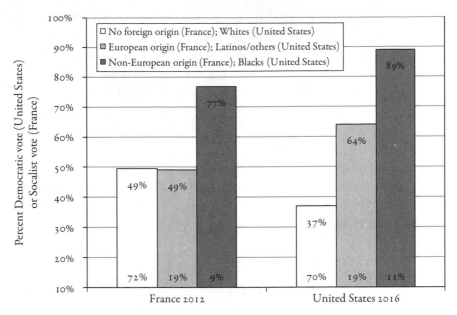

FIG. 15.9. Political conflict and origins: France and United States

Interpretation: In 2012, the Socialist candidate in the second round of the French presidential election obtained 49 percent of the vote of those with no foreign origin (no foreign-born grandparent) and of those with European foreign origin (primarily Spain, Italy, and Portugal) and 77 percent of the vote of those with non-European foreign origin (primarily North Africa and sub-Saharan Africa). In 2016, the Democratic candidate in the US presidential election obtained 37 percent of the white vote, 64 percent of the vote of Latinos and others, and 89 percent of the African American vote. *Sources and series:* piketty.pse.ens.fr/ideology.

and other minorities) and the declining importance of the white majority (70 percent in 2016).[28]

By contrast, in France, we find that people of European foreign origin vote on average the same way as those who declare themselves to be of French descent. For example, in the 2012 presidential election, 49 percent of both groups voted for the Socialist candidate in the second round, compared with 77 percent of voters of non-European foreign origin (Fig. 15.9). Note, too, that people who

---

28. The increased weight of Latinos and other minorities has coincided with a widening of the gap between Democrats and Republicans on the question of immigration since 2000. The positions of the two electorates were fairly close in the period 1980–2000. See R. Eatwell and M. Goodwin, *National Populism: The Revolt Against Liberal Democracy* (Penguin, 2018), p. 150, fig. 4.2.

declare themselves to be of foreign origin (defined as having at least one foreign-born grandparent) accounted for about 30 percent of the French electorate in the 2010s, roughly the same as "minorities" in the United States. But this analogy is purely formal. In particular, voters who declared themselves to be of European origin—primarily from Spain, Portugal, and Italy and roughly 20 percent of the population—do not see themselves and are not perceived as a "minority," much less as a "Latino" minority. Similarly, voters who declared themselves to be of non-European foreign origin—in practice mainly from North Africa and sub-Saharan Africa and roughly 10 percent of the population—are in no way a homogeneous group, much less an ethnic or religious category. Many say they have no religion. Indeed, this group only partially overlaps the group of people who identify as Muslims.[29]

On the Fluidity of Identities and the Danger of Fixed Categories

One key difference between the United States and France (and Europe more generally) has to do with the fact that ethno-religious cleavages in France are more fluid that racial cleavages in the United States. According to the "Trajectories and Origins" (TeO) survey conducted in France in 2008–2009, for example, more than 30 percent of respondents with a parent of North African descent are children of mixed couples (in which one parent is not of foreign origin).[30] When intermarriage levels are this high, clearly the very idea of "ethnic" identity has to be quite flexible. Origins and identities are constantly mixing, as we see for instance, in the very rapidly changing relative popularity

---

29. Voters declaring themselves to be of the Muslim faith accounted for roughly 5 percent of the electorate in the 2010s. See Fig. 14.17.

30. The proportion of mixed couples is 30 percent for individuals of Moroccan or Tunisian origin and 35 percent for those of Algerian origin—roughly the same as for individuals of Portuguese origin. The equivalent figure is more than 60 percent for individuals of Spanish or Italian origin but only 10 percent for those of Turkish origin. See C. Beauchemin, B. Lhommeau, and P. Simon, "Histoires migratoires et profils socioéconomiques," in *Trajectoires et origines. Enquête sur la diversité de la population française,* ed. C. Beauchemin, C. Hamel, and P. Simon (INED, 2015), p. 54, fig. 6. On the increase of mixed marriages involving North African immigrants between 1970 and 2000, see E. Todd, *Le Destin des immigrés. Assimilation et ségrégation dans les démocraties occidentales* (Seuil, 1994), pp. 302–304.

of first names from generation to generation.[31] It would not make much sense to ask such people to say whether they wholly identify with this or that "ethnic" group. That is why there is a fairly broad consensus in France, and to a certain extent in Europe (although the United Kingdom is in an intermediate situation, as we will see in a moment), that it is not appropriate to ask people what "ethnic" group they identify with. To require an answer to such a question would be unfair to those who see their origins and identity as mixed and multidimensional and who aspire simply to live their lives without having to show their papers and declare their "ethnic" identity. People can of course volunteer to answer questions in specific, noncompulsory surveys about their origins and about the birthplace of their parents or grandparents or their religious, philosophical, or political beliefs. But that is very different from requiring them to identify with an ethnic or racial group on a census form or mandatory administrative procedure.

In the United States, the business of assigning identities has very different historical roots. In the slave era and beyond, census agents assigned a "black" identity to slaves and their descendants, generally in accordance with the "one-drop rule": if a person had a single black ancestor, no matter how many generations back, that person was considered "black." Until the 1960s, many southern states prohibited interracial marriage. The US Supreme Court made that illegal in 1967. Intermarriage has increased considerably since then, including marriage between blacks and whites: 15 percent of African Americans were in mixed marriages in 2010 (compared with barely 2 percent in 1967).[32] Still, the obligation to declare ethno-racial identity in the United States, in censuses and other surveys, has probably sharpened lines between groups, even though identities are much less clear-cut in reality.

---

31. According to the TeO survey, only 23 percent of individuals of Maghrebin origin have a traditional Arab-Muslim first name by the third generation. The survey also shows that convergence occurs not because immigrants adopt traditional French first names but because both immigrants and natives adopt "international" first names with which people of different backgrounds can identify (such as Mila, Louna, Sarah, Inès, Yanis, Nael, Liam, Ethan, Adam, Rayan, etc.). See B. Coulmont and P. Simon, "Quels prénoms les immigrés donnent-ils à leurs enfants en France?" *Populations et sociétés,* 2019.

32. The proportion of mixed marriages (among couples married in 2015) was 25–30 percent for Latinos and Asians and about 10 percent for whites. See G. Livingston and A. Brown, "Intermarriage in the U.S. 50 Years after Loving v. Virginia," *Pew Research Center,* May 18, 2017.

Despite these important differences of national context, identity issues are currently being exploited in both the United States and France (and elsewhere in Europe), and the resulting political cleavages are of comparable magnitude. The exploited prejudices and cultural stereotypes are not exactly the same in the two cases, but there are common elements. In the United States, a term like "welfare queen" is meant to stigmatize both the alleged laziness of the single mother and the absence of the father. In France, racists accuse individuals of Maghrebi or African background of irrepressible criminal tendencies. Immigrants are often suspected of abusing the welfare system. They are also associated with unpleasant "noise and smells," even by political leaders not of the far right but of the center-right.[33]

This type of racist discourse calls for several responses. First, many studies have shown that allegations of minority abuse of the welfare system are baseless. On the other hand, many studies have shown that minorities and non-European immigrants are discriminated against in the workplace: given equal levels of education, the minority applicant is less likely to be hired than the white applicant.[34] Although studies of this kind will never convince everyone, they can and should be more widely publicized and brought to bear in public debate.[35]

---

33. In his unfortunately notorious speech at Orléans on June 19, 1991, Jacques Chirac said that "our problem is not with foreigners but with an overdose of foreigners. It may be true that there are no more foreigners now than there were before the war, but they are not the same, and that makes a difference. Having a Spaniard, Pole, or Portuguese working in your country is one thing, but they don't cause as many problems as Muslims or blacks. . . . What do you expect from a French worker who lives in the Goutte-d'Or where I was walking with Alain Juppé three or four days ago, who works with his wife, and the two of them make about 15,000 francs a month, and who sees on the stairs of his subsidized apartment house a family with a father, three or four wives, and twenty-some kids, and which rakes in 50,000 francs a month in welfare payments, naturally without working! [sustained applause] Add to that the noise and the smells [sustained laughter], and you know, the French worker on his stairway goes a little crazy. He blows a gasket. That's the way it is. And you have to understand that. If you were there, you'd react the same way. And it's not racist to say that." (Excerpts available via the Institut National de l'Audiovisuel.) This speech inspired the song "Noise and Smells" by the Toulouse rock group Zebda in 1995.

34. See the works cited in Chap. 14.

35. For instance, it seems reasonable to relate the discrimination against certain minorities in the legal job market to their disproportionate participation in lucrative illegal work (such as drug trafficking). In any case, this is more reasonable than accusing them of an innate and eternal propensity to criminality. Unfortunately, such arguments are unlikely to convince those who do not want to be convinced

It is also important, I think, to note that identity conflicts are fueled by disillusionment with the very ideas of a just economy and social justice. In Chapter 14, we saw that the French electorate was divided into four nearly equal parts by the conjunction of two issues: immigration and redistribution. If redistribution between the rich and the poor is ruled out (not just in the realm of political action but sometimes even in the realm of debate) on the grounds that the laws of economics and globalization strictly prohibit it, then it is all but inevitable that political conflict will focus on the one area in which nation-states are still free to act, namely, defining and controlling their borders (and if need be inventing internal borders). Even though we are living in a postcolonial world, identify conflict is not inevitable. If it sometimes seems that way, part of the reason, I think, is that the fall of communism extinguished all hope of truly fundamental socioeconomic change. If we want our politics to be about something other than borders and identity, we must therefore bring the issue of a just distribution of wealth back into public debate. I will have more to say about this.

The Democratic Party, the "Brahmin Left," and the Issue of Race

We come now to a particularly complex and important issue. In the US context, it is tempting to explain the "Brahminization" of the Democratic Party by the growing importance of racial and identity cleavages since the 1960s. The argument goes like this: disadvantaged whites left the Democratic Party because they refused to accept that their party had become the champion of blacks. On this view, it is nearly impossible for disadvantaged blacks and whites to join forces in a viable political coalition in the United States. As long as the Democratic Party was overtly racist and segregationist, or at any rate as long as disagreement on racial issues between northern and southern Democrats remained muted (broadly speaking, until the 1950s), it was possible to enlist the support of disadvantaged whites. But once the party ceased to be antiblack, it became almost inevitable that it would lose lower-class whites to the Republican Party,

---

(especially those who derive a moral or material benefit from their culturalist, essentialist, or frankly racist beliefs). On the overrepresentation of North Africans and Africans in French prisons, see F. Héran, *Avec l'immigration. Mesurer, débattre, agir* (La découverte, 2017), pp. 221–231. This overrepresentation is significant, though less so than the overrepresentation of blacks in American prisons (where the overall incarceration rate is ten times that of Europe; see Chap. 12).

which had no choice but to fill the racist void left vacant by the Democrats. In the end, the only exception to this iron law of American politics will have been the period 1930–1960, the era of the New Deal coalition, which somehow managed to keep disadvantaged whites and blacks together in the same party at the cost of some tenuous compromises and, even then, only under exceptional conditions (the Great Depression and World War II).

To my mind, this theory is too deterministic and ultimately not very convincing. The problem is not just that it depends on the notion that the disadvantaged classes are by their very essence permanently racist. As noted in the French case, the working class is no more naturally or eternally racist that the middle class, the self-employed, or the elite. More importantly, the theory is unconvincing because it fails to account for the observed facts. First, although there is no denying that racial issues played a key role in the flight of southern whites from the Democratic Party after 1963–1964,[36] the reversal of the educational cleavage since the 1950s occurred throughout the United States, in both North and South, independent of attitudes on racial issues. Furthermore, it unfolded slowly and steadily from the 1950s to the present (Figs. 15.2–15.4). It is difficult to explain such a long-term structural evolution in terms of a change of position of the Democratic Party on racial issues—a change that came about quite rapidly in the 1960s and whose effects on the black vote and the differential between the minority vote and the white vote were in any case immediate (Figs. 15.7–15.8).

One final but very important point: the same reversal of the educational cleavage also occurred in France, with a magnitude and chronology virtually identical to the United States (Figs. 14.2 and 14.9–14.11). We will also find the same basic trend in the United Kingdom, Germany, Sweden, and all the Western democracies. In these countries there was no civil rights movement and nothing comparable to the radical repositioning of the Democratic Party on racial issues in the 1960s. To be sure, one could point to the rising importance of the cleavage around immigration and identity in France, the United Kingdom, and elsewhere in Europe. But this cleavage begins to play a central role only much later, in the 1980s and 1990s, and cannot explain why the educational cleavage began to turn around much earlier, in the 1960s.

---

36. See I. Kuziemko and E. Washington, "Why Did the Democrats Lose the South? Bringing New Data to an Old Debate," *American Economic Review*, 2019. The authors show that changes of party affiliation in the South in the 1960s are explained primarily by attitudes on racial questions, independent of income or education.

Finally, we will see later that the educational cleavage also turns around in countries where the cleavage with respect to immigration never played a central role.

It therefore seems to me more promising to look for more direct explanations. If the Democratic Party has become the party of the highly educated while the less educated have fled to the Republicans, it must be because the latter group believes that the policies backed by the Democrats increasingly fails to express their aspirations. Furthermore, if such a belief is sustained for half a century and shared across so many countries, it cannot be a simple misunderstanding. Hence it seems to me that the most likely explanation is the one I began to develop for France. To summarize: the Democratic Party, like the parties of the electoral left in France, changed its priorities. Improving the lot of the disadvantaged ceased to be its main focus. Instead, it turned its attention primarily to serving the interests of the winners in the educational competition. From the turn of the twentieth century until the 1950s, the ambitions of the Democratic Party were strongly egalitarian, not only in tax policy but also with respect to education. Its goal was to ensure that everyone in every age cohort would receive not just a primary but also a secondary education. On this and other social and economic issues, the Democrats seemed to be clearly less elitist and more concerned with the disadvantaged (and ultimately with the prosperity of the country) than the Republicans.

Between 1950–1970 and 1990–2010, that perception was totally transformed. The Democratic Party became the party of the educated in a country where the university system is highly stratified and inegalitarian and the disadvantaged have virtually no chance of gaining admission to the most selective colleges and universities. In such circumstances, and in the absence of structural reform of the system, it is not abnormal that the least advantaged feel abandoned by the Democrats. The Republicans' skill in exploiting racial issues and above all in exploiting the fear of loss of status among disadvantaged whites surely explains part of their electoral success. In 1972, when McGovern proposed a federal minimum income to be paid for by an increase in the progressivity of the inheritance tax, Nixon supporters whispered that he was proposing yet another form of welfare for African Americans. Similarly, one reason for hostility to Obama's healthcare reform, the 2010 Affordable Care Act (popularly known as Obamacare), was that whites did not want to pay for health insurance for minorities. In general, the race factor has often been cited (rightly) among the structural reasons why social and fiscal solidarity are weaker in the United States than in Europe and why the United States has no equivalent to the European welfare state.[37] But it would be a mistake to reduce everything to the race factor, which cannot explain why we find an almost identical reversal of the educational cleavage on both sides of the Atlantic. If Democrats are now seen as serving the interests of the highly educated rather than the disadvantaged, it is above all because they never came up with an appropriate response to the conservative revolution of the 1980s.

Lost Opportunities and Incomplete Turns: From Reagan to Sanders

In the 1980 election campaign, Ronald Reagan succeeded in persuading Americans to accept a new account of their own history. To a country plagued by doubt after the Vietnam War, Watergate, and the Iranian Revolution, Reagan promised a return to greatness. His recipe was simple: cut federal taxes and make them less progressive. It was the New Deal and its confiscatory taxes and socialistic policies that had sapped the energy of American entrepreneurs and allowed the countries that had lost World War II to catch up with the United States. Reagan had rehearsed these themes during the 1964 Goldwater campaign as well in his 1966 race for governor of California, where he repeatedly explained that the "Golden State" could no longer be "the welfare capital of the world" and that no country in the world had ever survived paying a third of its gross domestic product (GDP) in taxes. In 1980 and 1984—in a country obsessed by fear of decline; the Cold War; and the rapid growth of Japan, Germany, and the rest of Europe—Reagan successfully parlayed these issues into a victory in the presidential race. The top federal income tax rate, which had averaged 81 percent from 1932 to 1980, was cut to 28 percent by the 1986 tax reform, the quintessential Reagan-era reform.[38]

From the vantage point of 2019, the effects of Reagan's reforms seem quite dubious. Growth of per capita national income fell by half in the three decades following Reagan's term (compared with the previous three or four decades). Since the goal of the reforms was to boost productivity and growth, this can

---

37. See Roemer, Lee, and Van der Straeten, *Racism, Xenophobia, and Distribution.* See also A. Alesina, E. Glaeser, and B. Sacerdote, *Why Doesn't the United States Have a European-Style Welfare State* (Brookings Institution, Brookings Papers on Economic Activity No. 2, 2001); A. Alesina and E. Glaeser, *Fighting Poverty in the US and Europe: A World of Difference* (Oxford University Press, 2004).

38. See Fig. 10.11.

hardly be counted a satisfactory outcome. In addition, inequality skyrocketed, so much so that the bottom 50 percent of the income distribution has seen no income growth since the early 1980s, which is totally unprecedented in US history (and fairly uncommon for any country in peacetime).[39]

And yet the Democratic presidents who followed Reagan, Bill Clinton (1992–2000) and Barack Obama (2008–2016), never made any real attempt to revise the narrative or reverse the policies of the 1980s. In particular, in regard to the reduction of the progressive income tax (whose top marginal rate fell to an average of 39 percent from 1980 to 2018, half its level in the period 1932–1980) and the de-indexing of the federal minimum wage (which led to a clear loss of purchasing power since 1980),[40] the Clinton and Obama administrations basically validated and perpetuated the basic thrust of policy under Reagan. This may be because both Democratic presidents, who lacked the hindsight we have today, were partly convinced by the Reagan narrative. But it may also be that acceptance of the new fiscal and social agenda was partly due to the transformation of the Democratic electorate and to a political and strategic choice to rely more heavily on the party's new and highly educated supporters, who may have found the turn toward less redistributive policies personally advantageous. In other words, the "Brahmin left," which is what the Democratic Party had become by the period 1990–2010, basically shared common interests with the "merchant right" that had ruled under Reagan and George H. W. Bush.[41]

The fall of the Soviet Union in 1990–1991 was clearly another political-ideological factor that played a key role in the United States, Europe, and elsewhere in this period. In some ways this validated the Reagan strategy of restoring US power and the capitalist model. The collapse of the communist

---

39. See Figs. 11.5 and 11.12–11.13.

40. See Fig. 11.10.

41. On this point, it is important to remember that many Democratic representatives and senators voted for the Tax Reform Act of 1986, which reflects both a certain opportunism and a fairly weak attachment to the idea of a progressive tax. Hence it is not very surprising that the Clinton administration (1992–2000) only partially restored the progressivity of the tax system. The TV series *The West Wing*, which was broadcast from 1999 to 2006, delighted in exposing the Clinton line: the president is as progressive as one might wish and a Nobel prizewinner in economics but at best lukewarm about raising taxes on the wealth. He nevertheless agrees to veto a Republican attempt to abolish the inheritance tax (which they caricature as the "death tax," as Bush Republicans did in the fall of 2001 when this episode was televised).

countermodel was undoubtedly a powerful reason for the renewal of faith—in some cases unlimited faith—in the self-regulated market and private ownership of the means of production. It was also one of the reasons why Democrats in the United States and Socialists, Labourites, and Social Democrats in Europe largely gave up thinking about ways to embed the market and transcend capitalism in the period 1990–2010.

As usual, however, it would be a mistake to interpret these trajectories in a deterministic fashion. These long-term intellectual and ideological shifts were important, but there were also many switch points where things might have taken a different course. For instance, the 1978 tax revolt in California, which was in some ways a harbinger of Reagan's successful run for the presidency two years later,[42] began with skyrocketing real estate prices in California in the 1970s, which led to sharp and largely unanticipated increases in the property taxes paid by homeowners. These tax hikes were often staggering, and they were a problem because the sudden increase in house prices was not accompanied by a corresponding increase in the income needed to pay the tax. Taxpayer resentment was even greater because the property tax is proportional: all homeowners pay the same rate, regardless of how many financial assets they own or how much debt they owe. Hence homeowners with low incomes and buried in debt still found themselves burdened with huge tax increases.[43] Discontent with this situation was cleverly exploited by conservative antitax activists, whose agitation led to the passage in June 1978 of the famous Proposition 13, which set a permanent ceiling on the property tax of 1 percent of the value of the property. This law, still in force today, has limited funding for California schools and led to repeated state budget crises.

Apart from its importance in the rise of Reaganism, this episode is interesting because it shows how very short-term phenomena (such as the spike in real estate prices in the 1970s and the success of a campaign for an antitax referendum) can combine with longer-term intellectual and ideological failures (in this case, failure to think about transforming property taxes into progressive taxes on all assets, both real estate and financial, net of debt) to produce major political changes. As in the case of the progressive income tax, it is important to be able to tax net wealth at different levels depending on whether an individual has amassed a fortune of $10,000, $100,000, $1 million, or $10 mil-

---

42. Reagan won California by large margins in 1980 and 1984.

43. Recall that the property tax in the United States (like its French equivalent, the land tax) has barely been reformed or modernized since the early nineteenth century. See Chaps. 4 and 11.

lion.[44] All surveys show that citizens favor such a progressive tax.[45] It is also essential to index the brackets of any wealth tax to the evolution of asset prices to prevent the tax from increasing automatically just because asset prices rise, without any prior debate, justification, or decision. In the case of the 1978 California tax revolt, the damage was even greater because the referendum put an end to revenue sharing between rich and poor school districts, which the California Supreme Court had authorized in 1971 and 1976 (in the so-called *Serrano* decisions) and which enjoyed widespread popular support at the time.[46]

Several recent developments suggest that the phase of US politics that began with Reagan's election in 1980 is about to end. First, the 2008 financial crisis showed that deregulation had gone too far. Second, growing awareness of the extent of the increase of inequality since 2000 and of wage stagnation since 1980 has gradually increased people's willingness to reevaluate the Reagan turn. Both of these factors have helped to open up political and economic debate in the United States, as the very close 2016 Democratic primary race between Hillary Clinton and Bernie Sanders shows. As noted previously, in the 2020 presidential campaign, several candidates (including Sanders and Senator Eliz-

---

44. The property (or land) tax as it works today is even worse because a person with wealth of $10,000 (say, a house worth $500,000 and a mortgage of $490,000) and another with wealth of $10 million (a house worth $500,000 and a financial portfolio worth $9.5 million) pay not only the same rate but the same amount of property tax (because financial assets and debts are ignored).

45. See R. Fisman, K. Gladstone, I. Kuziemko, and S. Naidu, *Do Americans Want to Tax Capital? Evidence from Online Surveys* (National Bureau of Economic Research, NBER Working Paper No. 23907, October 2017). Opinion polls also show very strong support for various forms of a progressive wealth tax.

46. On this point see I. Martin, "Does School Finance Litigation Cause Taxpayer Revolt? Serrano and Proposition 13," *Law & Society Review*, 2006; I. Martin, *The Permanent Tax Revolt: How the Property Tax Transformed American Politics* (Stanford University Press, 2008). See also J. Citrin and I. Martin, eds., *After the Tax Revolt: California's Proposition 13 Turns 30* (Institute of Governmental Studies Press, 2009). More generally, the impact of reforms from the 1970s on that was intended to reduce inequality of resource allocation to primary and secondary schools within states was counterbalanced by the increase of income and wealth inequality between school districts and states so that the concentration of school financing has actually increased in recent decades. C. Bonneau, *The Concentration of Educational Investment in the US (1970–2018), with a Comparison to France* (EHESS, working paper, 2019). On reforms attempted at the state level, see C. Jackson, R. Johnson, and C. Persico, "The Effects of School Spending on Educational and Economic Outcomes: Evidence from School Finance Reforms," *Quarterly Journal of Economics*, 2016.

abeth Warren) have proposed restoring the progressivity of the income and inheritance taxes and creating a federal wealth tax.[47] Revenue produced by such a wealth tax could be invested in the educational system, especially in public universities, whose finances have suffered greatly compared with those of the best private universities. There have also been proposals to share power and voting rights between employees and shareholders on the boards of directors of private US firms as well as to create a universal health insurance plan (Medicare for All), as is the norm in Europe (with better results at lower cost than the current US system provides).[48]

It is much too soon to say what will come of these developments. I think it is important, however, to insist on two things: first, the total reversal of the educational cleavage is not going to be undone overnight, and second, it is extremely important to reform the educational system. The Democratic Party has become the party of the highly educated in a country with a hyper-stratified inegalitarian educational system. Democratic administrations never did anything to change this (nor did they even say how they might go about changing if they ever commanded a majority for doing so). Such a situation can only breed mistrust between the disadvantaged classes and the hypereducated Democratic elite, who might as well be living in different worlds. Trump rode a wave of distrust for the "Brahmin" elite to win the election (without proposing any tangible solutions to the country's problems other than building a wall on the Mexican border and cutting his own taxes, for all the good either will do).[49] The answer is not simply to increase investment in public universities. Basic changes in the admissions policies of both private and public universities are needed, including common rules to improve the chances of currently disadvantaged groups. In general, without bold and clearly comprehensible reforms, it is hard to see how the disadvantaged classes, always somewhat alienated from politics in the United States, can be brought back into the process.[50]

---

47. See Chap. 11.
48. Recall that Hillary Clinton campaigned for universal health insurance in the 2008 Democratic primary while Barack Obama opposed it on the grounds that such a reform would be too interventionist. Ultimately, the Affordable Care Act adopted in 2010 was both less ambitious and more complex (and not necessarily any more popular).
49. In the next chapter I will say more about the nativist-business ideology of people like Trump and his European counterparts and discuss the possibility of a social-nativist evolution.
50. See Figs. 14.7–14.8.

The Transformation of the British Party System

Let us turn now to the case of the United Kingdom. Using postelection surveys as in France, we can study the structure of the electorate in British elections since the mid-1950s. Compared with the United States, the bipartite system in Britain is more complex and fluctuating. When we look at the distribution of votes for the main parties in legislative elections from 1945 to 2017, we find that although the Labour Party and the Conservative Party were dominant, the situation is more complex than in the United States (Fig. 15.10).

In the 1945 elections, Labour won 48 percent of the vote compared with 36 percent for the Tories; the two parties together thus claimed 84 percent of the vote. Despite the prestige garnered from having stewarded the country to victory in World War II, the Conservatives, led by Winston Churchill, were decisively beaten, and Labour's Clement Attlee became prime minister. The 1945 election was of fundamental importance in both British and European

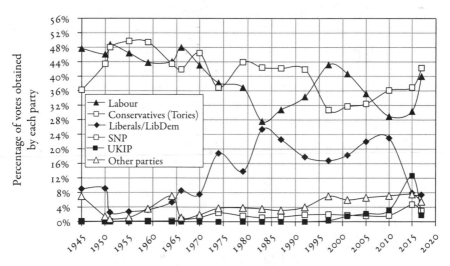

FIG. 15.10. Legislative elections in the United Kingdom, 1945–2017

Interpretation: In the 1945 legislative election, Labour won 48 percent of the vote and the Conservatives 36 percent (for a total of 84 percent of the vote for the two main parties). In the 2017 elections, the Conservative Party won 42 percent of the vote and Labour 40 percent (for a total of 82 percent). *Note:* Liberals/LibDem: Liberals, Liberal Democrats, SDP Alliance. SNP: Scottish National Party. UKIP: UK Independence Party. Other parties include green and regionalist parties. *Sources and series:* piketty.pse. ens.fr/ideology.

electoral history. It was the first time that the Labour Party by itself won a majority of seats in the House of Commons, which enabled it to assume power and enact its program to establish the National Health Service (NHS), institute an ambitious social insurance system, and significantly increase the progressivity of income and inheritance taxes. Furthermore, the 1945 election turned the two-party system in Britain upside down: throughout the eighteenth and nineteenth centuries the two main parties had been the Tories (or Conservatives) and the Whigs (renamed the Liberals in 1859). Barely thirty years after the People's Budget, which marked the Liberals' victory over the House of Lords in 1909–1911, Labour came to power in 1945 following several decades of intense competition with the Liberals, whom they permanently replaced as the main alternative to the Conservatives. The country that had been the most aristocratic of all at the turn of the twentieth century, the one in which the trifunctional schema had formed a symbiotic relationship with the logic of proprietarianism, also became the country in which a self-avowed party of the working class now held power.[51]

The Liberals would never regain their previous role. They eventually redefined themselves as Liberal Democrats and then as an SDP-Liberal alliance in the 1980s after a split in the Labour Party.[52] After winning 10–25 percent of the vote in the period 1980–2010, the Liberal Democrats fell back to less than 10 percent in the 2015 and 2017 elections. In 2017, the Conservatives led by Theresa May won 42 percent of the vote while Labour, led by Jeremy Corbyn, won 40 percent, for a total of 82 percent for the two major parties; the remaining votes were shared by the LibDems, the UK Independence Party (UKIP), the Scottish National Party (SNP), and green and regionalist parties. As in the United States, I will focus on the evolution of the structure of the vote for the two main parties, Labour and Conservative, in the period 1955–2017.[53]

---

51. On the People's Budget and the end of the House of Lords, see Chap. 5.

52. The Social-Democratic Party, or SDP, was created in 1981 by centrist Labour dissidents; it joined the Liberal Democrats in 1988.

53. The first large-scale postelection survey whose results were properly archived dates from 1963 in the United Kingdom (versus 1948 in the United States and 1958 in France), but the 1963 survey contains questions about the 1955 and 1959 elections, which I present here (just as the 1958 French survey contained questions about the 1956 elections). All details about these surveys, along with computer code for transforming raw data into final results, are available in the online appendix.

The first finding is that, over the past half century, the Labour Party, like the Democrats in the United States, has also become a party of the highly educated. In the 1950s the Labour vote among the highly educated was 30 percentage points lower than among the rest of the population. In the 2010s it was the reverse: ten points higher among those with tertiary degrees compared with the rest of the population. As in France and the United States, this reversal of the educational cleavage has affected all levels of education (not only between primary, secondary, and tertiary levels but also within the secondary and tertiary groups). The reversal has been slow and steady over six decades, and the basic trend is barely affected when we control for age, sex, and other individual socioeconomic characteristics (Figs. 15.11–15.12).

Compared with the French and US cases, however, the British evolution takes place slightly later. At the beginning of the period, the Labour vote is concentrated among the less educated at the beginning of the period, and it is not until the very end that the more highly educated clearly swing over to the

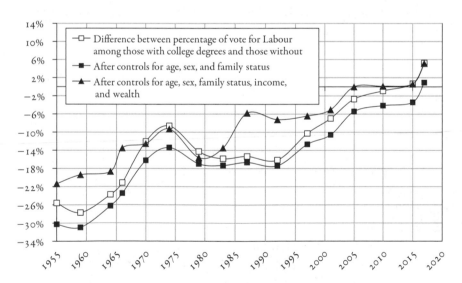

FIG. 15.11. Labour Party and education, 1955–2017

Interpretation: In 1955, the Labour Party scored twenty-six points lower among those with college degrees compared to those without; in 2017, it scored six points higher among those with college degrees compared to those without. Controlling for other variables affects the levels but does not alter the trend. *Sources and series:* piketty.pse. ens.fr/ideology.

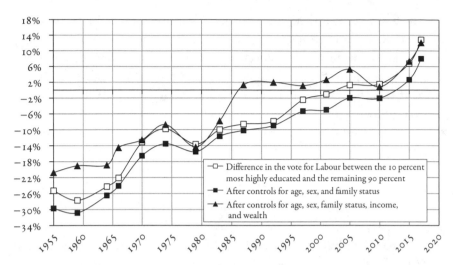

FIG. 15.12. From the workers' party to the party of the highly educated: The Labour vote, 1955–2017

Interpretation: In 1955, the Labour Party scored twenty-five points lower among the most highly educated 10 percent than among the other 90 percent of voters; in 2017, its score was thirteen points higher among the most highly educated 10 percent. Controlling for other variables affects levels but does not alter the trend. *Sources and series:* piketty.pse.ens.fr/ideology.

Labour side (Fig. 15.13).[54] This relative lag reflects an important reality—namely, that the Labour vote is still more of a working-class vote than either the Democratic vote in the United States or the Socialist and Communist votes in France.

It is interesting, moreover, to note that the authentically working-class British Labour party long frightened some of Britain's intellectual elite. The most famous example is that of John Maynard Keynes, who in a 1925 article explained why he could never vote for Labour and would continue, come what may, to vote for the Liberals. In sum, he worried about Labour's lack of intellectuals worthy of the name (and no doubt economists in particular) to keep the masses in line: "I do not believe that the intellectual elements in the Labour Party will ever exercise adequate control; too much will always be decided by those who do not know at all what they are talking about. . . . I incline to

54. See Fig. 14.2, for the same graph after controls have been applied, and the online appendix, Figs. S14.2a–S14.2c for other variants. The slight temporal shift can be seen in all cases.

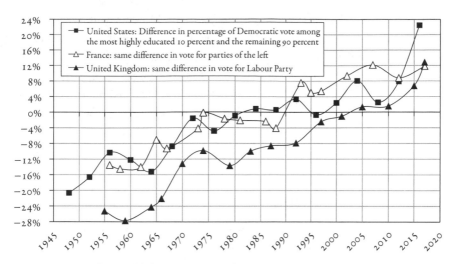

FIG. 15.13. The electoral left in Europe and the United States, 1945–2020: From the workers' party to the party of the highly educated

Interpretation: In the period 1950–1970, the vote for the Democratic Party in the United States, for the parties of the left (Socialists-Communists-Radicals-Greens) in France, and for the Labour Party in the United Kingdom was associated with less educated voters; in the period 1990–2010, it came to be associated with more highly educated voters. The British evolution slightly lags the French and American but goes in the same direction. *Sources and series:* piketty.pse.ens.fr/ideology.

believe that the Liberal Party is still the best instrument of future progress."[55] Note that Hayek, whose political point of view was quite different from Keynes's, also worried a great deal about handing power to the Labour Party— or to the Swedish Social Democrats. In his view, there was a danger that both would quickly more toward authoritarian rule and trample individual liberties underfoot; he therefore did his best to warn his intellectual friends against the dangerous sirens to which he believed they had succumbed.[56]

---

55. See J. M. Keynes, "Am I a Liberal?" *The Nation & Athenaeum,* 1925. This is the text of a speech that Keynes gave at the Liberal Summer School in Cambridge in 1925 (reprinted in J. M. Keynes, *Essays in Persuasion* [1931]). Keynes died in 1946, at about the same time that the Liberal Party was in rapid decline, so it is difficult to know if and when he would have ended up joining Labour.

56. See Chap. 10. Unlike Keynes, Hayek was also wary of the Liberals, who he thought had become dangerously left-wing and interventionist, especially under the influence of economists and intellectuals like Keynes.

By contrast, recall that the Labour sociologist Michael Young worried in the 1950s that his party, by failing to undertake a sufficiently ambitious egalitarian reform of Britain's horribly hierarchical educational system, would eventually alienate the less educated classes and become a party of "technicians" pitted against the masses of "populists." But even he never imagined that the Labour Party would ultimately displace the Conservatives as the party of the highly educated.[57]

On the "Brahmin Left" and the "Merchant Right" in the United Kingdom

Somewhat later than in France and the United States, the Labour Party thus also became a "Brahmin left" of a sort, racking up its best results among the highly educated. I turn now to the evolution of electoral cleavages as a function of income. In the period 1950–1980, we find a very marked income cleavage in the United Kingdom: the lower a voter's income, the more likely that voter was to vote for Labour, while the top income deciles voted heavily Conservative. This disparity was particularly clear in the 1979 election, which Margaret Thatcher won on a platform of anti-union measures, privatizations, and tax cuts for top earners in a time of economic crisis and high inflation. According to the available data, fewer than 20 percent of voters in the top income decile voted Labour in 1979, compared with 25 percent in 1955 and 1970. In every case the Conservatives won 75–80 percent of the vote in the top income decile (Fig. 15.14).

Compared to France, the income cleavage has historically been more pronounced in the United Kingdom. In France, the profile of the vote for parties of the left (Socialists, Communists, Radicals, and Greens) is relatively flat through the bottom 90 percent of the income distribution, falling off only in the top decile.[58] If we look at the detailed survey data by sector of activity, we find that the difference is explained mainly by the fact that in France there are more self-employed individuals, and especially farmers, whose income is not always very high but who often own professional assets and are wary of the left-wing parties. In the United Kingdom, the agricultural and self-employment sectors shrank earlier than in France, and most workers are wage earners; hence the classist cleavage is more pronounced, especially with respect to income. This

---

57. See Chap. 13.
58. See Fig. 14.12.

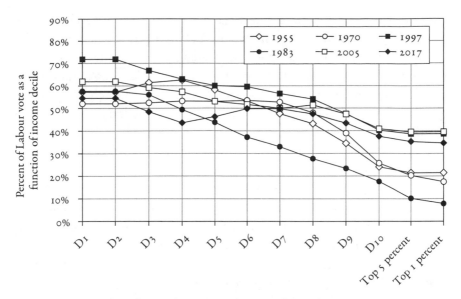

FIG. 15.14. Political conflict and income in the United Kingdom, 1955–2017

Interpretation: The profile of the Labour vote as a function of income decile is strongly decreasing, particularly in the top income decile, especially in the period 1950–1990. *Sources and series:* piketty.pse.ens.fr/ideology.

also explains why the educational cleavage was historically less pronounced and turned around earlier in France than in the United Kingdom: the self-employed (particularly self-employed farmers) are a large and relatively less educated group that has never voted strongly for the left.

As for income effects, we also find a fairly clear temporal evolution in the United Kingdom starting in the 1980s–1990s, exactly the same as in France and the United States. In particular, higher-income voters voted more heavily for Tony Blair's New Labour in the period 1997–2005 than they had voted for Labour previously. That may seem logical, given that New Labour also attracted more and more votes among college-educated people and its fiscal policies were relatively favorable to high earners. Just as the Clinton (1992–2000) and Obama (2008–2016) administrations had validated and perpetuated the Reagan reforms of the 1980s, New Labour governments in the period 1997–2010 largely validated and perpetuated the fiscal reforms of the Thatcher era.[59] Compared

---

59. For example, the top income and inheritance tax rates were both cut from 75 percent in 1979 to 40 percent in the 1980s and remained there to this day for the inheri-

with the Conservative Thatcher and Major governments, however, the New Labour Blair and Brown governments invested more public funds in the educational system. But they also sharply increased university tuitions when they took office, a move that was hardly favorable to students of modest background.[60] Ultimately, these policies point toward a rapprochement of the "Brahmin left" and "merchant right" in the United Kingdom.

The change of Labour Party leadership eventually shook things up, however. In the 2015 and 2017 legislative elections, we find that higher-income voters were much more likely to vote Conservative so that the gap between the educational effect and the income effect increased (Fig. 15.15).[61] This can be explained in various ways, and the available data do not allow us to choose one explanation over another. First, Labour's policy preferences changed significantly after Jeremy Corbyn was elected party leader in 2015. The party now envisions more redistributive tax measures than in the New Labour era and has turned to the left in other ways as well. This may have frightened wealthier voters. On the other hand, the Labour platform now includes policies that may be more appealing to voters from lower income groups. These include measures favorable to unions, giving more power to worker representatives and providing for power sharing between workers and shareholders on boards of directors, comparable with German and Nordic co-management, which has never been tried in the United Kingdom.[62] Finally, Labour is now calling for completely

---

tance tax and until 2009 for the income tax (after which it rose to 40 percent in 2010 and then dropped again to 45 percent in 2013). See Figs. 10.11–10.12.

60. The maximum tuition that British universities could charge was raised to 1,000 pounds in 1998, 3,000 pounds in 2004, and finally to 9,000 pounds in 2012. The share of tuition in the total resources of British universities is close to 1920 levels and approaching American levels. See the interesting historical series established by V. Carpentier, "Public-Private Substitution in Higher Education: Has Cost-Sharing Gone Too Far?" *Higher Education Quarterly*, 2012.

61. See the online appendix, Figs. S15.15a–S15.15d for the different variants (especially before and after controls) and confidence intervals. The British wealth data are more precise than the American. In particular, we know whether families that own their homes still have mortgages or not, and we know for certain whether they own stocks, particularly in surveys carried out after the privatizations of the 1980s. This allows us to determine that wealth effects systematically favor the Conservative vote (more so than income effects and much more than education), just as in France. The wealth data remain fragile, however (and less precise than the French data), and the variations should be treated with caution.

62. See Chap. 11 for an analysis of these issues.

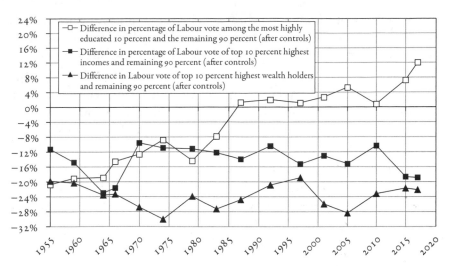

FIG. 15.15. Social cleavages and political conflict: United Kingdom, 1955–2017

Interpretation: In the period 1950–1990 the Labour vote was associated with low levels of education, income, and wealth; since 1990 it has come to be associated with high levels of education. *Sources and series:* piketty.pse.ens.fr/ideology.

free higher education (as in Germany and Sweden)—a complete about-face from the tuition increases New Labour enacted in 1997 and 2010. For obvious reasons, this proposal seems to have been particularly popular among young working-class voters in the 2017 election.[63]

We must also consider the effect of the 2016 Brexit referendum, in which 52 percent of the British electorate voted to leave the European Union, on the 2017 parliamentary elections. Although Corbyn's personal position on Brexit may have been ambiguous or lukewarm, the Labour Party officially favored "Remain." This was also the position of more than 90 percent of Labour MPs, compared with roughly half of Conservative MPs. In any case, the Labour vote overall was more pro-Europe than the Conservative vote (the Tories having initiated the 2016 referendum). This may have been one reason for the particularly high vote for Labour in 2017 among those with university degrees,

63. The difference between the Labour vote of those under age 35 and those over age 65 was forty points in the 2017 legislative elections—the largest gap observed since 1945, not only in the United Kingdom but also compared with the equivalent figures for the left parties in France and the Democratic Party in the United States since World War II. See the online appendix, Fig. S14.11b.

a large majority of whom opposed Brexit. Note that higher-income voters, who were also troubled by Brexit, nevertheless fled Labour in 2017 probably because the left turn instigated by Corbyn worried them even more than Brexit did. In the end, the vote for Labour in 2017 was highest among middle-income people with university degrees. I will say more later about the structure of the Brexit vote and the future of the European Union, which is becoming the central political-ideological issue both in the United Kingdom and on the continent.

To sum up, if we compare the general evolution of the cleavages observed in various countries as a function of education, income, and wealth, we find not only striking commonalities but also significant differences, especially at the very end of the period. In the United Kingdom, the divergence of the educational effect from the income and wealth effects increases in 2015–2017 (Fig. 15.15). By contrast, in the 2016 US presidential election, the income and wealth effects converge with the educational effect: wealthier and higher-income voters join those with higher degrees in voting Democratic (Fig. 15.6). Clearly, the stark contrast between the strategies of the Labour Party and the Democratic Party play an important role. Labour's pro-redistribution turn under Corbyn drove higher-income voters away from the party and attracted more modest-income voters, whereas the centrist line of the Democratic Party under Hillary Clinton had the opposite effect. If Democratic primary voters had chosen Sanders rather than Clinton, the vote structure might have been closer to that observed in the United Kingdom. France represents a third possibility. Because of its two-round voting system and historically fragmented political parties, the more prosperous elements of the old electoral left and right joined together in a new coalition of the highly educated with the wealthiest and highest paid, enabling Emmanuel Macron to win the presidency in 2017.[64]

These three situations are quite different from one another. They are interesting because they demonstrate that nothing is written in advance. In particular, everything depends on the mobilization strategies of the parties and the political-ideological balance of power. Admittedly, the underlying trends in all three countries are similar because the classist left-right party systems of the postwar era have given way to a system of dual elites consisting of a "Brahmin left" attractive to the highly educated and a "merchant right" attractive the wealthy and highly paid. But within this general pattern, many distinct trajec-

---

64. See Fig. 14.1 and Table 14.1.

tories are possible because the new system is extremely fragile and unstable. The "Brahmin left" is divided between pro-redistribution and pro-market wings, and the "merchant right" is just as divided between a faction tempted by the nationalist or nativist line and another that would prefer to maintain a primarily pro-business, pro-market orientation. Depending on which tendency wins out in each camp or on what new syntheses emerge, different trajectories are possible. The effects of turning one way or another are potentially long lasting. I will come back to this in Chapter 16 when I look at other countries and other electoral configurations.

The Rise of Identity Cleavages in the Postcolonial United Kingdom

We turn now to the question of identity cleavages in the United Kingdom. At first sight, the data and the realities they reflect seem relatively similar to the French case. Let us begin by looking at data on voters' declared religions, which can be found in British postelection surveys since the 1950s. With this information we are able to follow the evolution of the religious cleavage in parliamentary elections from 1955 to 2017.

Our first finding is that the United Kingdom, like France, was largely a country of one religion and one ethnicity until the 1960s. In the 1964 elections, 96 percent of the electorate professed to belong to one Christian denomination or another; 3 percent declared no religion, and only 1 percent claimed some other religion (mostly Jews, with a very small number of Muslims, Hindus, and Buddhists).[65] The proportion of individuals declaring "no religion" grew dramatically from the late 1960s on, however, rising from 3 percent of the electorate in 1964 to 31 percent in 1979 and 48 percent in 2017. The progression was even more rapid than in France where the proportion of voters with no declared religion rose from 6 percent in 1967 to 36 percent in 2017.[66]

---

65. The 96 percent of declared Christian voters in 1964 broke down as follows: 65 percent Anglican, 22 percent other Protestant denominations, and 9 percent Catholic. Among voters describing themselves as Christian, Anglicans have always been most likely to vote Conservative, followed by other Protestants, and then Catholics (who were roughly as likely to vote Labour as those claiming no religion). One finds similar cleavages in elections from 1955 to 2017 and equivalent cleavages between Protestant and Catholic votes for Republicans and Democrats in the United States. See the online appendix for detailed results.

66. See Fig. 14.14.

Importantly, the "no religion" grew much more than in the United States, which in general remains significantly more religious than Europe.[67]

As for other religions, we find that fewer than 1 percent of UK voters declared themselves to be Muslims in 1979; this figure rose to 2 percent in 1997, 3 percent in 2010, and roughly 5 percent in 2017. The increase is virtually identical to what we see in France, where the comparable figure rose from barely 1 percent in 1988 to 2 percent in 2002, 3 percent in 2007, and 5 percent in 2017. To be sure, the geographical origins of the two countries' Muslims populations are very different: most French Muslims come from North Africa (Algeria, Tunisia, or Morocco) while most British Muslims come from South Asia (mainly Pakistan, India, and Bangladesh). The effects of different colonial and postcolonial histories are obvious. The fact remains that these two countries, which had the largest colonial empires on the planet from the nineteenth century to the 1950s, had little experience with coexistence of their native Christian populations with substantial numbers of Muslims on their home soil before the 1970s.[68] Then, in the period 1990–2020, the proportion of Muslim voters

---

67. In US postelection surveys, the proportion of voters without religion was less than 5 percent until the 1960s and stands at around 20 percent in the 2010s. The remaining 80 percent are divided among various Christian denominations, except for 1.5 percent declaring themselves to be Jewish and less than 1 percent for other religions. Other indicators also attest to the greater (Christian) religiosity of the United States. For example, 80 percent of the adult population claimed to believe in God in 2015 compared with 51 percent on average in the European Union (with wide variations: 18 percent in Sweden, 27 in France, 37 in the United Kingdom, 44 in Germany, 74 in Italy, and 79 in Poland), 88 percent in Brazil, and 94 percent in Turkey. See M. Jouet, *Exceptional America: What Divides Americans from the World and from Each Other* (University of California Press, 2017), p. 90, table 3.

68. There have been Muslim and African minorities in European societies much earlier than this, of course, but their numerical size remained quite small (less than 0.1 percent of the population). For example, there were 2,000–3,000 Muslims in Berlin in the interwar years. See D. Motadel, "Worlds of a Muslim Bourgeoisie: The Socio-Cultural Milieu of the Islamic Minority in Interwar Germany," in *The Global Bourgeoisie: The Rise of the Middle Classes in the Age of Empire,* ed. C. Dejung, D. Motadel, and J. Osterhammel (Princeton University Press, 2019). See also D. Motadel, ed., *Islam and the European Empires* (Oxford University Press, 2014). Note that a French census of people of color in 1777 counted a total of 5,000 people. Anxiety ran high, however, since an edict was issued in 1763 banning mixed marriages and another was issued in 1777 banning all persons of color (including free persons) from French soil. See G. Noiriel, *Une histoire populaire de la France* (Agone, 2018), pp. 182–185.

gradually rose to about 5 percent—not a very high number in absolute terms but somewhat more substantial than the previously negligible figure.

As in France, these figures for the United Kingdom apply only to registered voters. If we consider the entire resident population of the United Kingdom, independent of nationality and voter registration status, the proportion of declared Muslims was according to various sources close to 7–8 percent in the late 2010s, thus roughly the same proportion as in France. In the United Kingdom, the proportion of voters declaring a religion other than Christianity or Islam also increased, reaching as high as 3–4 percent in the 2010s (nearly 2 percent Hindu, less than 1 percent Jewish, and less than 1 percent Buddhist and other religions).

If we now look at how voting behavior varied as a function of declared religion in the United Kingdom (Fig. 15.16), we find results quite similar to those observed in France.[69] Historically, voters without religion were more likely to vote Labour than were Christian voters, although the gap was less pronounced than in France. It turns out that 80–90 percent of Muslims have voted regularly for Labour since the 1980s, just as French Muslims have voted consistently in large numbers for the parties of the left.[70] The gap between this and the average vote of other voters has been close to 40 percentage points. As in France, socioeconomic variables account for only a small part of this difference.[71]

One peculiarity of the British data is that UK postelection surveys have included questions about ethnic self-identification since 1983. By contrast, the British surveys never ask about grandparents' country of origin so that it is not possible to compare French and British results for the recent period on this dimension. More specifically, the British questionnaires allow respondents to classify themselves as "White," "African-Caribbean," "Indian-Pakistani," and "other" (which includes Chinese, Arab, "other Asian," etc.).[72] For example, in

---

69. See Figs. 14.15–14.17.

70. As for other religions, self-declared Hindus voted in roughly the same way as Muslims (70–90 percent for Labour), whereas voters of other religions (Jews, Buddhists, etc., with no breakdown available) were closer to the average for the rest of the population. With limited sample sizes we can say no more. Islam and Hinduism are treated separately from other religions in postelectoral questionnaires from 1983 on (with information about the 1979 vote in the 1983 questionnaire). See the online appendix for complete results.

71. See the online appendix.

72. The question is phrased as follows: "Please choose one option that best describes your ethnic group or background." The list of possible answers has evolved somewhat

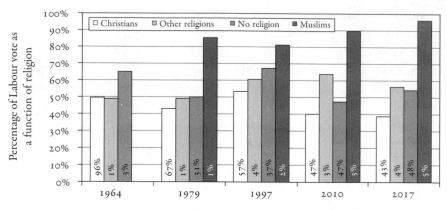

FIG. 15.16. Political conflict and religious diversity in the United Kingdom, 1964–2017
Interpretation: In 2017, the Labour Party won 39 percent of the vote of voters declaring themselves to be Christian (Anglicans, other Protestants, Catholics), 56 percent among voters of other religions (Jewish, Hindu, etc., except Islam), and 96 percent among Muslims. *Sources and series:* piketty.pse.ens.fr/ideology.

the 2017 postelection survey, of those who agreed to answer this question, 89 percent declared themselves to be white, 3 percent African Caribbean, 6 percent Indian Pakistani, and 2 percent "other." Of the whites, 41 percent voted for Labour, compared with 81 percent of African Caribbeans, 82 percent of Indian Pakistanis, and 68 percent of other ethnic groups (Fig. 15.17). Once again, in other words, there is a significant cleavage of the vote of a magnitude similar to that observed in France for individuals who declare one or more grandparents of North African or sub-Saharan African origin.[73] Note, too, that a significant proportion of the British electorate refused to answer the question—5 percent in 2017 or nearly a third of those who declared themselves to be nonwhite. These may be people of foreign origin, whether mixed race or not, who do not identify with any of the proposed categories, or more generally they may be people who do not identify with any specific ethnic

over time. The category "White" used here groups together the responses "English/British/White." Respondents could also answer "Mixed/Multiple ethnic groups," specifying "Mixed White/Black Caribbean" or "Mixed White/Black African" (categories here are included under "African-Caribbean" without effect on the results in view of the small numbers involved) or "White and Asian" (here classed as "other"). See the online appendix.

73. See Fig. 14.18.

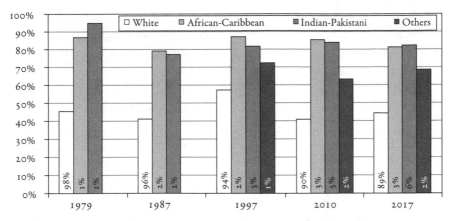

FIG. 15.17. Political conflict and ethnic categories in the United Kingdom, 1979–2017

Interpretation: In 2017, the Labour Party won 44 percent of the votes of those declaring themselves to be "white," 81 percent of "African-Caribbeans," 82 percent of "Indian-Pakistani-Bangladeshis," and 69 percent of "others" (including "Chinese," "Arabs," etc.). In 2017, 5 percent of the electorate refused to answer the question about ethnicity, and 77 percent of them voted for Labour. *Sources and series:* piketty.pse.ens.fr/ideology.

group or who deem the question to be inappropriate. In any case, we find that 77 percent of this group voted for Labour, and controlling for socioeconomic variables does not change this. In my view, these results illustrate the problems with ethnic classifications, which force people to put themselves in boxes with which they do not identify; this risks hardening the boundaries between groups.[74]

In the British case, note that 98 percent of the electorate declared itself to be white in the early 1980s and that the 2 percent nonwhite population was already voting for Labour at a level of 80–90 percent.[75] More broadly, even though the cleavage over immigration did not become truly significant in the United Kingdom until the 1980s–1990s, we observe the first signs of significant

---

74. My point is not to praise the French treatment of diversity. It is good to have various studies of discrimination (such as the regular TeO studies, which collect information about the birthplace of parents and grandparents). Penalties for discrimination need to be significantly increased (and new tools for detecting discrimination need to be perfected and used in conjunction with surveys). Nevertheless, the fact remains that asking people to identify their "ethnicity" in postelection and census surveys tends to highlight group boundaries, which seems counterproductive.

75. The results for 1979 shown in Fig. 15.17 reflect the 1979 vote as declared retrospectively in the 1983 postelection survey; the results are similar for 1983.

politicization of the issue from the late 1960s on. Compared with France, where politicization of the issue of immigration from outside Europe began with the creation of a new party (the Front National), in the United Kingdom the process unfolded largely within the two-party system as anti-immigrant sentiment began to be more and more overtly expressed within the Conservative Party.[76] In the postwar period, British governments had tried to maintain the Commonwealth by encouraging free circulation of people among the countries of the former empire. Specifically, the British Nationality Act of 1948 allowed citizens of any Commonwealth country to settle in the United Kingdom and claim British nationality. Free circulation was also among the founding principles of the Communauté Française and Union Française, which France created in the hope of transforming its former colonial empire into a democratic and egalitarian federation between 1946 and 1962.[77] In practice, however, in the early 1960s both countries began to restrict immigration from their former colonies. In the United Kingdom, the main sources of immigration in the 1950s and 1960s were the Caribbean, India, and Pakistan (and to a lesser degree East Africa). Although the influx was moderate, it was still large compared with the interwar period and before. The first restrictions were put in place in 1961, and these were followed by tougher measures in 1965 and 1968.

The Politicization of Immigration in the United Kingdom from Powell to UKIP

The politicization of the issue took a new turn in 1968 when the outspoken conservative MP Enoch Powell began to rail against non-European immigrants. In a widely publicized speech, Powell declared that "rivers of blood" would flow in the United Kingdom if the influx of immigrants continued. He alluded to race riots in the United States and worried that his country would experience the same fate if it continued on its present path.[78] In the 1979 election campaign,

---

76. Several parties formed with the express purpose of capturing the anti-immigrant vote: the British National Front in the 1960s and 1970s, the British National Party in the 1990s and 2000s, and more recently, the UK Independence Party, which focused mainly on the European question, however. See below. None of these was very successful in parliamentary elections owing to the nature of the electoral system.

77. See Chap. 7.

78. See R. Dancygier, "History of Racism and Xenophobia in the United Kingdom," in Roemer, Lee, and Van der Straeten, *Racism, Xenophobia, and Distribution,* pp. 130–165.

the immigration issue played a significant role. Just as exploitation of the racial and identity cleavage in the United States was one element of the Republican strategy that brought Richard Nixon to the White House in 1968 and 1976 and Ronald Reagan in 1980, the immigration and identity cleavage also figured in the strategy that culminated in Margaret Thatcher's victory in the United Kingdom.

Furthermore, questions about "race relations" in the 1979 postelection survey quite clearly revealed how voters reacted to the politicization of the issue. Of the Conservative voters polled, nearly 70 percent said that the only way "to improve race relations" was to end immigration, while just over 30 percent said that the solution was to create more jobs and housing. By contrast, nearly 60 percent of Labour voters ranked creation of jobs and housing first.[79] When asked which of the two parties was more likely to reduce the influx of immigrants, 35 percent of voters did not respond, but of those who did respond, the answer was clear: 63 said the Conservative Party and only 2 percent Labour.

In the 1980s and 1990s, the hope of Labour (and some Tory) voters that new social and economic policies might allow for both openness to immigration and greater social harmony was put to a rude test. Margaret Thatcher, who had toughened her line on immigration in the 1979 campaign, further slashed the social budget while clamping down on immigration. After New Labour came to power in 1997, it inherited both parts of Thatcher's approach. After the attacks of September 11, 2001, as Tony Blair's government prepared to join the United States in the invasion of Iraq in 2003–2004, the Labour government passed emergency anti-terror laws, which in practice allowed the police

---

79. The exact question was the following: "In order to improve race relations in this country, should we stop immigration, or have more jobs/housing in large cities?" This question was not asked again in the same form in subsequent surveys, so it is impossible to say how the answer would have evolved. It is important in general to underscore the degree to which the analysis of political-ideological transformations is limited by the nature of the materials available in postelection surveys. For study the evolution of ideologies, one can also use party manifestos and programs collected, for instance, by the Comparative Manifesto Project, which show how party programs have moved sharply to the right since the 1980s, not only on immigration but also on economic issues, including for social-democratic, labor, and socialist parties. On this point see A. Gethin, *Cleavage Structures and Distributive Politics* (master's thesis, Paris School of Economics, 2018), p. 12, fig. 1.2. But party manifestos are also relatively imprecise and difficult to compare across time and space.

to expedite the arrest and expulsion of thousands of undocumented immigrants. In *Americanah,* a novel by Chimamanda Ngozi Adichie, this is the moment when Obinze, having heard nothing from Ifemelu since her departure for the United States, decides to try his chances in the United Kingdom. Although he has a degree from a Nigerian university, he finds himself scrubbing toilets in England. In order to work, he has to use the national insurance number of Vincent Obi, a fellow Nigerian of more modest social background, in exchange for which Obi demands 35 percent of his wages: the Nigerian social hierarchy has been stood on its head. To avoid a new wave of immigrant roundups organized by Interior Minister David Blunkett, Obinze decides to go the route of a sham marriage, arranged by greedy Angolans. But he ignores Obi's demand that he must now pay 45 percent of his wages instead of 35 percent. Furious, Obi denounces him to his employer, and he is arrested on his wedding day and deported to Nigeria, wounded not only by the condescending looks of Europeans toward Africans who dare to take their fate into their own hands but also by the vile behavior to which immigrants are reduced by the white man's laws.

Recall that the 1990s and 2000s, especially while New Labour was in power (1997–2010), were also years during which voter turnout fell sharply in the United Kingdom and specifically among the disadvantaged classes.[80] Clearly, many voters were not satisfied with the choice they were offered between Labour and Tories, who inevitably promised even more security and tighter immigration controls and criticized the supposed softness of Labour on these issues.

In the early 2010s, the politicization of immigration took a new turn in the United Kingdom. Attention shifted to some extent to the European question. The financial crisis of 2008 increased resentment and frustration throughout Europe. In France, the Front National, which had fallen to a nadir in the 2007 elections, rose to new heights in 2012 and 2017. In Britain, UKIP indiscriminately attacked both immigration and the European Union with renewed ardor, especially after the EU was enlarged to Eastern Europe in 2004 (when Poland, Hungary, the Czech Republic, and Slovakia joined) and again in 2007 (with the inclusion of Romania and Bulgaria). This led to an influx of immigrants from the East, who under EU rules could now circulate freely throughout

80. See Figs. 14.7–14.8.

the European Union, just as Commonwealth workers had done in Britain after the war.[81]

The Divorce Between the European Union and the Disadvantaged Classes

The Conservative Party then decided it would be a good idea to open a debate about a possible withdrawal of the United Kingdom from the EU. In part this was a response to growing pressure from some party members and from the electorate. UKIP scored 2 percent in the 2005 parliamentary elections and 3 percent in 2010. It then leapt to 13 percent in 2015. Meanwhile, it did even better with 27 percent of the vote in the 2014 European parliamentary elections, which entitled the party to send a large contingent to the European Parliament. Because of Britain's voting system, however, the pressure to withdraw from the EU remained manageable: UKIP won only a single seat in Westminster in the 2015 elections. But to ensure his reelection, Prime Minister David Cameron saw to it that the party platform would include a promise to hold a referendum on Britain's continued membership in the European Union. After his reelection, he therefore organized the promised vote on Brexit, which took place in 2016. Before the vote, Cameron announced that he had secured from other member states the concessions he wanted, although he had never made his demands public either before or after the 2015 elections on the pretext that keeping them secret was a smart way to obtain the best deal from his partners. Satisfied with the results of his negotiations, he called upon the country to vote for "Remain." But many remained dubious, and 52 percent voted to "Leave."

Accordingly, from 2016 to 2019, the United Kingdom and European Union have been engaged in interminable negotiations over new treaties that will supposedly govern the future relationship between the continent and the British Isles (or, rather, some of them, since the Republic of Ireland will remain in the

---

81. The enlargement treaties of 2004 and 2007 increased the number of EU member states from fifteen in 2003 to twenty-five in 2004 and twenty-seven in 2007. They allowed old member states to impose temporary restrictions on the free circulation of workers from the new member states, but all such restrictions had to be lifted by 2011 at the latest. In practice, the restrictions were gradually lifted between 2004 and 2011, depending on the country.

European Union, while Scotland is again considering the future possibility of a secession referendum to be followed by application for EU membership as an independent state). One thing seems agreed upon: full-fledged free circulation of workers will not be part of any new treaty. But that does not settle the issue of future migration rules, nor does it deal with the status of British subjects living in the European Union (or Europeans living and working in the United Kingdom). As for free movement of goods, services, and capital, the big question is the extent to which the United Kingdom will be required to apply EU regulations and whether it will be able to sign separate trade agreements with the rest of the world. The problem is that none of these complexities were discussed in the debate leading up to the referendum. The exact nature of the accord to be signed in case of a "Leave" victory was never made clear, any more than the terms on which Britain might "Remain."

At this stage it is impossible to predict how relations between the United Kingdom and the European Union will evolve, nor is it possible to predict how the treaties governing the internal functioning of the European Union may be transformed in the future. Nevertheless, it is important to emphasize that many trajectories are possible and that the current organization of the European Union could change radically. It is too easy to criticize the feckless and opportunistic political decisions that led to Brexit or to castigate British voters for their supposed nationalism. Events could have unfolded differently and may yet follow a different course in the future. But the fact that Brexit was even possible is a sign of the serious inadequacy of the European project as shaped to date by leaders from many countries (including of course both Labourites and Tories from the United Kingdom but also leaders from France, Germany, and all the other member states).

If one looks at the structure of the 2016 Brexit vote as a function of education, income, and wealth, the results are extremely clear. In each of these three dimensions, more modest voters opted massively for "Leave" while the 30 percent at the top strongly supported "Remain" (Fig. 15.18). Those with more education were even more attached to the European Union than those with more wealth—part of the reason for which may be that the wealthy think they stand to benefit if the United Kingdom is transformed into a tax haven (a prospect touted by some Tory Brexiters).[82] Ultimately, the most striking finding

---

82. The wealth data in the postelection surveys are not sufficient to permit study of this point with satisfactory precision.

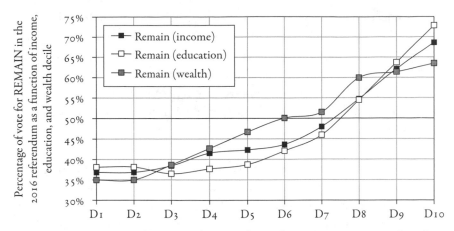

FIG. 15.18. The European cleavage in the United Kingdom: The 2016 Brexit referendum
Interpretation: In the 2016 Brexit referendum (in which "Leave" won with 52 percent of the vote), the vote was strongly skewed socially: the top income, education, and wealth deciles voted strongly for "Remain," while the lower deciles voted for "Leave." *Note:* D1 designates the lowest 10 percent of each distribution, D2 the next lowest, and D10 the top 10 percent. *Sources and series:* piketty.pse.ens.fr/ideology.

is that the European issue caused a significant cleavage between the lower, middle, and upper classes on all three dimensions of social stratification (education, income, and wealth). This result is all the more spectacular because this classist voting pattern had disappeared from normal elections: in the period 1990–2020 the party system became a system of dual elites (with the Labour Party attracting those with more education and the Conservative Party attracting the wealthier and higher paid).

The extremely socially skewed result of the 2016 Brexit referendum is also particularly striking because we find exactly the same vote profile in the French referenda of 1992 and 2005 on the Maastricht Treaty and the European Constitutional Treaty.[83] Although these three votes were separated by decades and took place in different countries, the pattern is the same: a complete divorce between the less advantaged classes and the European project. In both the United Kingdom and France in the period 1990–2020, Europe has become the issue that unites, on one side, the Brahmin left and merchant right (educational and business elites) and on the other side, the lower and middle classes (joined

83. See Fig. 14.20.

in their rejection of Europe as currently constituted, even though they have no specific alternative in mind). As noted earlier in the discussion of the French case, it is quite unsatisfactory and unconvincing to explain this cleavage as the result of the supposedly irrepressible racist and nationalist instincts of the lower classes. The disadvantaged are no more spontaneously racist than the elites: everything depends on the sociopolitical content of the internationalist project that is being proposed.

Now, the fact is that the European project is based primarily on competition between countries and individuals and on the free circulation of goods, capital, and workers. There has been no attempt to develop the tools necessary to achieve greater social and fiscal justice. In this sense, the European Union operates differently from other regional partnerships and federations, such as the United States of America and the Indian Union. In both of those cases we find federal budgets and progressive income taxes, which can certainly be improved but are nevertheless far more ambitious than anything found in the European Union.[84] The EU federal budget is minuscule: about 1 percent of European GDP, compared with 15–20 percent of GDP in India and the United States. There is no federal tax in the European Union, whereas in India and the United States the taxes levied on the most important economic actors, including the progressive income and inheritance taxes and corporate taxes, are systematically centralized at the federal level. By contrast, the European Union is a regional political organization in which virtually the only common bond is the principle of pure and perfect competition.

The problem is that fiscal and social competition between member states primarily benefits the most powerful actors. In particular, Brexit illustrates the limits of a model based on free circulation of workers without common, truly constraining social and fiscal rules. In a way, the limited British and French experiments with free circulation of citizens of their former colonies in the 1950s and 1960s also demonstrate the need for common social and political regulation to accompany freedom of movement. If the European Union does not succeed in transforming itself so as to embody an alternative to its current project, built around simple and transparent measures of social and fiscal justice, it is unlikely that the disadvantaged classes will change their mind. The

---

84. One might also mention the People's Republic of China, which functions similarly but is not an electoral political regime, so that it is more natural to compare the European Union to the United States or India (or Brazil).

risk then—and it is considerable—is that other countries will try to exit; or, alternatively, that people under the influence of nativist, identitarian ideologies will seize control of the European project. Before delving further into possible ways out of these impasses, we must first complete our overview of the transformation of electoral cleavages in other countries beyond the United Kingdom, United States, and France. In the next chapter we will therefore look at other Western and non-Western democracies, specifically in Europe and India.

SIXTEEN

Social Nativism: The Postcolonial Identitarian Trap

In the previous chapters, we looked at the transformation of political and electoral cleavages in the United Kingdom, United States, and France since World War II. In particular, we saw how, in all three countries, the "classist" party systems of the period 1950–1980 gradually gave way in the period 1990–2020 to systems of multiple elites, in which a party of the highly educated (the "Brahmin left") and a party of the wealthy and highly paid (the "merchant right") alternated in power. The very end of the period was marked by increasing conflict over the organization of globalization and the European project, pitting the relatively well-off classes, on the whole favorable to continuation of the status quo, against the disadvantaged classes, which are increasingly opposed to the status quo and whose legitimate feelings of abandonment have been cleverly exploited by parties espousing a variety of nationalist and anti-immigrant ideologies.

In this chapter, we will begin by verifying that the evolutions observed in the three countries studied thus far can also be found in Germany, Sweden, and virtually all European and Western democracies. We will also analyze the singular structure of political cleavages in Eastern Europe (especially Poland). This illustrates the importance of postcommunist disillusionment in the transformation of party systems and the emergence of social nativism, which can be seen as a consequence of a world that is at once postcommunist and postcolonial. We will consider the extent to which it is possible to avoid the social-nativist trap and outline a form of social federalism adapted to the European situation. We will then study the transformation of political cleavages in non-Western democracies, notably India and Brazil. In both cases we will find examples of incomplete development of cleavages of the classist type, which will help us to gain a better understanding of both Western trajectories and the dynamics of global inequality. Finally, with all these lessons in mind, we will turn in the final chapter to the elements of a program for creating, in a transnational perspective, new forms of participatory socialism for the twenty-first century.

From the Workers' Party to the Party of the Highly Educated: Similarities and Variants

To be clear from the outset: we will not be able to treat each of the subsequent cases in as much detail as we studied France, the United States, and the United Kingdom, partly because to do so would take us beyond the scope of this book and partly because the necessary sources are not available for all countries. In this chapter, I will begin with a relatively succinct presentation of the main results currently available for the other European and Western democracies. I will then analyze in greater detail the results for India (and in somewhat less detail for Brazil). Not only does India's democracy include more voters than all the Western democracies combined, but study of the structure of the Indian electorate and of the transformation of India's sociopolitical cleavages from the 1950s to the present illustrates the urgent need to go beyond the Western framework if we are to gain a better understanding of the political-ideological determinants of inequality as well as the conditions under which redistributive coalitions can be assembled.

In regard to Western democracies, the principal conclusion is that the results obtained for the United Kingdom, United States, and France are representative of a much more general evolution. First, we find that the reversal of the educational cleavage took place not only in the three countries already studied but also in the Germanic and Nordic countries that constitute the historic heart of social democracy: Germany, Sweden, and Norway (Fig. 16.1). In all three countries, the political coalition associated with the workers' party in the postwar decades (which did particularly well among more modest voters) became the party of the educated in the late twentieth and early twenty-first centuries, achieving its highest scores among those who obtained higher degrees.

In Germany, for example, we find that, in the period 1990–2020, the vote for the Social Democratic Party (SPD) and other parties of the left (especially Die Grünen and Die Linke) was five to ten points higher among highly educated voters than among the less educated, whereas it was around fifteen points lower in the period 1950–1980. To make the results as comparable as possible across time and space, I will focus here on the difference between the vote of the 10 percent most diplomaed voters and the 90 percent least diplomaed (after controlling for other variables). Note, however, that as in the French, American, and British cases, the trends are similar if one compares voters with and without college degrees or the 50 percent most educated with the 50 percent

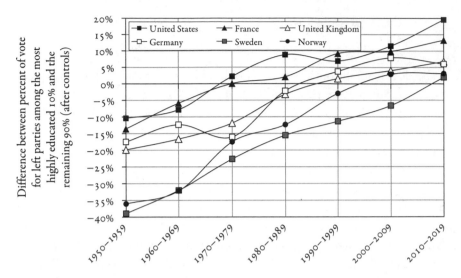

FIG. 16.1. The reversal of the educational cleavage, 1950–2020: United States, France, United Kingdom, Germany, Sweden, and Norway

Interpretation: In the period 1950–1970, the vote for Democrats in the United States and for various left parties in Europe (labor, social-democratic, socialist, communist, radical, and ecologist) was higher among less educated voters; in the period 2000–2020, it was higher among more educated voters. The change came later in Nordic Europe but went in the same direction. *Note:* "1950–59" includes elections from 1950 to 1959, and "1960–69" includes those from 1960 to 1969, and so on. *Sources and series:* piketty.pse.ens.fr/ideology.

least educated, both before and after controlling for other variables.[1] In the case of Germany, note that the amplitude of the reversal of the educational cleavage is almost identical to that observed in the United Kingdom (Fig. 16.1). Note, too, the role played by the emergence of the Greens (Die Grünen) in shaping the German trajectory. From the 1980s on, the ecological party has attracted a substantial share of highly educated voters. Yet one still sees a reversal of the educational cleavage (though less pronounced at the end of the period) if one focuses exclusively on the SPD vote.[2] Broadly speaking, al-

---

1. For a detailed analysis of the results for Germany and Sweden, see the online appendix (piketty.pse.ens.fr/ideology) and F. Kosse and T. Piketty, "Changing Socioeconomic and Electoral Cleavages in Germany and Sweden 1949–2017," WID. world, 2019.
2. See the online appendix, Fig. S16.1.

though the institutional structure of parties and factions varies widely from country to country as we saw in comparing France with the United States and United Kingdom, it is striking to see how limited the effect of these differences is on the basic trends that interest us here.

In Sweden and Norway, the politicization of the class cleavage in the postwar period stands out starkly. Specifically, the social-democratic vote among the 10 percent most highly educated voters was on the order of thirty to forty points lower than among the remaining 90 percent in 1950 to 1970. By contrast, this same gap was on the order of fifteen to twenty points in Germany and the United Kingdom and ten to fifteen points in France and the United States (Fig. 16.1). This shows the degree to which the Nordic social-democratic parties were built around an exceptionally strong mobilization of the working class and manual laborers.[3] This mobilization was necessary, moreover, to overcome the particularly extreme proprietarian inequality that persisted into the twentieth century (particularly in Sweden, where the electoral system weighted votes in proportion to wealth); it led to the establishment of unusually egalitarian societies in the postwar period.[4] Nevertheless, both in Sweden and Norway we find an erosion of this electoral base, which begins in the 1970s and continues throughout the period 1990–2020. Less educated voters little by little withdrew their confidence from the social democrats, which by the end of the period were racking up their highest scores among the highly educated. To be sure, compared with what we see in the United States and France and to a lesser degree in the United Kingdom and Germany, the social-democratic vote did hold up better among the disadvantaged classes in Sweden and Norway. But the basic tendency, which has been under way now in all countries for more than half a century, is clearly the same.

The postelection surveys available in each country do not always allow us to go all the way back to the 1950s. The types of survey that were conducted and the state of the surviving records are such that in many cases we cannot begin systematic comparison until the 1960s or even the 1970s or 1980s. The sources we have gathered nevertheless allow us to conclude that the reversal of

---

3. As in Germany and France, I have included in Fig. 16.1 not only the main social-democratic or labor party (the SAP in Sweden and the Arbeiderpartiet in Norway) but also other parties of the left (socialists, communists, etc.) and ecologists. If one focuses exclusively on the SAP, one still finds an extremely clear reversal of the educational cleavage. See the online appendix, Fig. S16.1.

4. On the Swedish case, see Chap. 5.

the electoral cleavage is an extremely general phenomenon in Western democracies. In nearly all the countries studied, we find that the vote profile of left-wing parties (labor, social-democratic, socialist, communist, radical, and so on, depending on the country) has reversed over the past half century. In the period 1950–1980, the profile was decreasing with educational level: the more educated the voter, the less likely he or she was to vote for the parties of the left. This gradually turned around in the period 1990–2020: the more highly educated the voter, the more likely to vote for the parties of the left (whose identity had clearly changed in the meantime)—increasingly so as time went by. We find this same evolution in countries as different as Italy, the Netherlands, and Switzerland as well as Australia, Canada, and New Zealand (Fig. 16.2).[5] When the questionnaires and surveys allow, we also find results comparable with those obtained for France, the United States, and the United Kingdom regarding the evolution of the vote profile as a function of income and wealth.[6]

Within this general scheme, several countries exhibit distinct variations owing to their socioeconomic and political-ideological configurations. These specific trajectories deserve more detailed analysis, which would take us far beyond the scope of this book.[7] I will say more later, however, about Italy, a textbook case of advanced decomposition of a postwar party system leading to the emergence of a social-nativist ideology.

---

5. For a comparative analysis of the results obtained in twenty-one countries, see the online appendix and A. Gethin, C. Martinez-Toledano, and T. Piketty, "Political Cleavages and Inequality. Evidence from Electoral Democracies, 1950–2018," WID.world, 2019.

6. In particular, unlike the vote profile as a function of education, which reversed in nearly all countries, the profile as a function of income remained decreasing (though less and less so), giving rise to a system of multiple elites of the "Brahmin left" versus "merchant right" type. See the online appendix, Fig. S16.2.

7. The very similar evolutions of the structure of electoral cleavages in so many different countries shows that certain common factors are ultimately more important than the national specificities that are often invoked. But as important as this general scheme is, it should not be allowed to mask the many national and regional political-ideological variants that contribute to the basic trend. For example, variants of electoral behavior linked to family structure can explain many local variations without undermining the basic similarity. On the links between family structure and political ideology, see these two classic studies: H. Le Bras and E. Todd, L'invention de la France (Hachette, 1981); E. Todd, L'invention de l'Europe (Seuil, 1990); L'origine des systèmes familiaux (Gallimard, 2011).

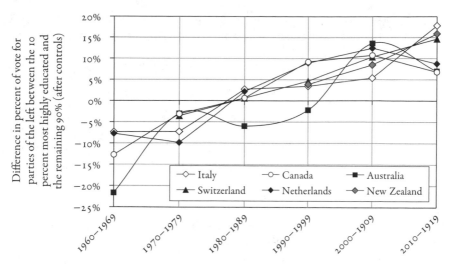

FIG. 16.2. Political cleavage and education, 1960–2020: Italy, the Netherlands, Switzerland, Canada, Australia, and New Zealand

Interpretation: In the period 1950–1970, the vote for Democrats in the United States and for various left parties in Europe (labor, social-democratic, socialist, communist, radical, and ecologist) was higher among less educated voters; in the period 2000–2020, it was higher among more educated voters. We find the same result in the United States and Europe, Canada, Australia, and New Zealand. *Note:* "1960–1969" includes elections between 1960 and 1969, "1970–1979" includes elections between 1970 and 1979, and so on. *Sources and series:* piketty.pse.ens.fr/ideology.

The only real exception to this general evolution of the cleavage structure of electoral democracy in the developed countries is Japan, which never developed a classist party system of the sort observed in the Western countries after World War II. In Japan, the Liberal Democratic Party (LDP) has held power almost continuously since 1945. Historically, this quasi-hegemonic conservative party has done best among rural farm voters and the urban bourgeoisie. By placing postwar reconstruction at the center of its program, it bridged the gap between the economic and industrial elite and traditional Japanese society. It was a complicated moment, marked by the US occupation and extreme anticommunism induced by the proximity of Russia and China. By contrast, the Democratic Party usually did best among modest-to-middling urban wage-earners together with more highly educated voters, who were eager to contest the US presence and the new moral and social order represented by the LDP. It was never able to constitute an alternative majority, however.[8] More generally, the specific structure of Japanese political conflict should be seen in relation to long-standing cleavages around nationalism and traditional values.[9]

Rethinking the Collapse of the Left-Right Party System of the Postwar Era

To recapitulate: Compared with the very high concentration of income and wealth observed in the nineteenth century and until 1914, income and wealth inequality fell to historically low levels in the period 1950–1980. This was due in part to the shocks and devastation of the period 1914–1945, but a more important cause of change was the far-reaching critique to which the dominant proprietarian ideology of the nineteenth and early twentieth centuries was subjected. Between 1950 and 1980, new institutions and social and fiscal policies were created for the express purpose of reducing inequality: these included mixed public-private ownership, social insurance, progressive taxes, and so on.[10] During this period, the political systems of all the Western democracies were structured around a "classist" conflict between left and right, and political debate centered on redistribution. The social-democratic parties (broadly understood to include the Democratic Party in the United States and various coalitions of social-democratic, labor, socialist, and communist parties in Europe) drew their support mainly from the socially disadvantaged classes, while the parties of the right and center-right (including the Republicans in the United States and various Christian-democratic, conservative, and conservative-liberal parties in Europe) drew their support mainly from the socially advan-

---

8. See A. Gethin, "Cleavages Structures and Distributive Politics" (master's thesis, Paris School of Economics, June 2018), pp. 89–100. See also K. Mori McElwain, "Party System Institutionalization in Japan," in *Party System Institutionalization in Asia,* ed. A. Hicken and E. Martinez Kuhonta (Cambridge University Press, 2015), pp. 74–107.

9. In *The Silent Cry* (Kodansha International, 1967 [Japan]; English trans. J. Bester, Kodansha International, 1981), Kenzaburo Oe magnificently evokes the complexity and violence of relations between the intellectual elites and the poorer classes in Japan, particularly in relation to the urban-rural cleavage, traditional values, and the question of modernization of the country since the beginning of the Meiji era (1868), to say nothing of the role played by the island nation's geopolitical position, its relation to the United States, and the antagonisms aroused by the presence of Korean laborers.

10. See Chaps. 10–11.

taged. This was true regardless of which dimension of social stratification—income, education, or wealth—one looked at. This classist structure of political conflict became so widespread in the postwar decades that many people came to believe that no other form of political organization was possible and that any deviation from this norm could only be a temporary anomaly. In reality, this classist left-right structure reflected a particular historical moment and was the product of specific socioeconomic and political-ideological conditions.

In all the countries studied, this left-right system has gradually broken down over the past half century. In some cases the names of the parties have remained the same, as in the United States, where the labels "Democrat" and "Republican" endure despite their countless metamorphoses. Elsewhere, parties have sometime updated their nomenclature, as in France and Italy in recent decades. But whether the names have changed or remained the same, the structure of political conflict in the Western democracies in 1990–2020 no longer has much to do with that of the period 1950–1980. In the postwar period, the electoral left was everywhere the workers' party, but in recent decades it has become the party of the educated (the "Brahmin left"): the more educated the voter, the more likely to vote for the left. In all the countries studied, less educated voters have little by little ceased to vote for the parties of the left, leading to a complete reversal of the educational cleavage; the same voters have sharply reduced their participation in the political process.[11] When a divorce of such magnitude occurs in so many countries as the result of a long-term process extending over six decades, it is clear that something real is happening and that this cannot be attributed to some unfortunate misunderstanding.

The decomposition of the postwar left-right system and in particular the fact that the disadvantaged classes gradually withdrew their confidence from the parties to which they had given their support in the period 1950–1980 can be explained by the fact that those parties failed to adapt their ideologies and platforms to the new socioeconomic challenges of the past half century. Two of those challenges stand out: the expansion of education and the rise of a global economy. With the unprecedented growth of higher education, little by little the electoral left became the party of the highly educated (the "Brahmin left") while the electoral right remained the party of the highly paid and wealthy (the "merchant right"), though less so over time. As a result, the social and fiscal policies of the two coalitions have converged. Furthermore, as commercial, financial, and cultural exchanges began to develop on a global scale, many

---

11. Figs. 16.1–16.2 and Figs. 14.8–14.9.

countries experienced the pressure of heightened social and fiscal competition, which benefited those with the most educational capital on the one hand and the most financial capital on the other. Yet the social-democratic parties (in the broadest sense of the term) never really revised their redistributive thinking so as to transcend the limits of the nation-state and meet the challenges of the global economy. In a sense, they never responded to the critique Hannah Arendt proposed in 1951 when she observed that to regulate the unbridled forces of global capitalism, new forms of transnational politics would need to be developed.[12] Instead, the social-democratic parties contributed in the 1980s–1990s to liberalize the flow of capital everywhere without regulation, compulsory information sharing, or common fiscal policy (even on the European level).[13]

Other important factors explaining the decomposition of the postwar party system include the end of the old colonial empires; the growth of trade and increasing competition between the old industrial powers and the poor but developing countries where labor was cheap; and finally, the influx of immigrants from the former colonies. Taken together, these factors contributed in recent decades to the emergence of unprecedented identitarian and ethno-religious political cleavages, especially in Europe. New anti-immigrant parties arose on the right while existing parties (such as the Republicans in the United States, the Conservatives in the United Kingdom, and various traditional right-wing parties on the continent) took a tougher line on immigration-related issues. Two points should be noted, however. First, the decomposition of the classist left-right structure of the postwar period unfolded very gradually; it began in the 1960s, well before the immigration cleavage became salient in most Western countries (which generally did not happen until the 1980s and 1990s and in some cases even later). Second, when we look at the various Western countries, what stands out is that, over the past half century, the reversal of the educational cleavage proceeded nearly everywhere at the same pace and without apparent relation to the magnitude of cleavages over race or immigration (Figs. 16.1–16.2).

In other words, while it is clear that anti-immigrant parties (and anti-immigrant factions within older parties) have exploited identity cleavages in recent decades, it is just as clear that the reversal began for other reasons. A more satisfactory explanation is that the disadvantaged classes felt abandoned by the

12. See Chap. 10.
13. See Chap. 11.

social-democratic parties (in the broadest sense) and that this sense of abandonment provided fertile ground for anti-immigrant rhetoric and nativist ideologies to take root. As long as the absence of redistributive ambition responsible for this sense of abandonment remains uncorrected, it is hard to see what might prevent that fertile ground from being exploited further.

Finally, an additional reason for the collapse of the left-right system of the postwar era is undoubtedly the fall of Soviet Communism and the ensuing shift in the political-ideological balance of power. For many years the mere existence of a communist countermodel put pressure on capitalist elites and political parties that had long been hostile to redistribution. But it also limited the redistributive ambitions of the social-democratic parties, which were de facto integrated into the anticommunist camp and therefore felt little incentive to seek an internationalist socialist alternative to capitalism and private ownership of the means of production. Indeed, the collapse of the communist countermodel in 1990–1991 convinced many political actors, especially among social democrats, that redistributive ambition had become superfluous. Markets, they now believed, were self-regulating, and the new goal of political action was to extend them as far as possible, both within Europe and around the world. The 1980s and 1990s were the crucial years when many key measures were decided, beginning with the complete liberalization of capital flows (without regulation). This effort was to a large extent led by social-democratic governments, and social-democratic parties remain unable even today to perceive alternatives to the situation they themselves created.

The Emergence of Social Nativism in Postcommunist Eastern Europe

The case of Eastern Europe clearly illustrates the role played by postcommunist disillusionment and the ideology of competitive markets in the collapse of the postwar party system (based on a clear left-right cleavage). In the transition to democracy following the collapse of communism in Eastern Europe, former ruling parties transformed themselves into social-democratic parties, in some cases fusing with newly emerged political movements and in others splintering and then recombining with them. Although much of the public remained hostile to the old parties (for understandable reasons related to their past errors), former state bureaucrats and managers of state enterprises affiliated with those parties often exercised important responsibilities in the early stages of the transition.

Consider, for example, the Democratic Left Alliance (SLD), which held power in Poland from 1993 to 1997 and again from 2001 to 2005. Eager to forget the communist past and join the European Union, the SLD adopted a platform that was social-democratic in name only. Its first priority was to privatize firms and open Polish markets to competition and investment from Western Europe, thus forcing the country to meet the criteria for EU admission as rapidly as possible. To attract capital, and in the absence of the slightest fiscal harmonization at the European level, a number of East European countries, including Poland, also set very low tax rates on corporate profits and high incomes in the 1990s and early 2000s.

Yet when the postcommunist transition was complete and Poland finally joined the European Union, the results did not always live up to expectations. Income inequality increased sharply, and large segments of the population felt left behind. German and French investments often generated large profits for shareholders while promised raises for wage-earners failed to materialize. This fostered strong resentment of the dominant powers within the EU, which were always quick to remind the Poles of the generous transfers of public funds they had received while forgetting that the reverse flow of private profits out of Poland (and other East European countries) significantly exceeded the influx of public transfers.[14] In addition, since the 1990s, political life in Eastern Europe has been scarred by a large number of financial scandals, often linked to privatizations and involving individuals close to the party in power. Several corruption cases (such as the Rywin Affair in Poland in 2002–2004) revealed alleged links between the media and political and economic elites.[15]

Such was the deleterious climate in which the SLD went down to defeat in the 2005 Polish elections, in which the party received barely 10 percent of the vote and the "left" was virtually wiped off the political map. Since then, political conflict in Poland has revolved around the conservative liberals of the Civic Platform (PO) on one side and the conservative nationalists of the Law and Justice Party (PiS) on the other. It is striking to see how the electorates of these two parties have evolved along classist lines since the early 2000s. In the elections of 2007, 2011, and 2015, the conservative liberals of Civic Platform

---

14. See Fig. 12.10.
15. Lew Rywin, a well-known Polish film producer, was convicted of attempting to extort millions of euros from Agora, the leading Polish media company. Invoking the name of the incumbent prime minister, Rywin tried to get Agora to pay him to back an amendment to a law governing radio and television broadcasting.

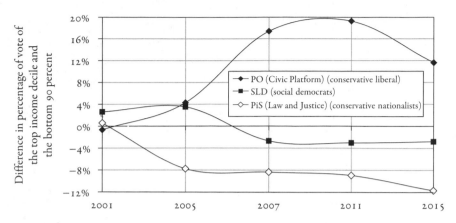

FIG. 16.3. Political conflict and income in Poland, 2001–2015

Interpretation: Between 2001 and 2015, the PO (Civic Platform) (conservative liberal) vote shifted toward higher income groups, whereas the PiS (Law and Justice) (conservative nationalist) vote shifted toward lower-income voters. *Sources and series:* piketty.pse. ens.fr/ideology.

did best among highly paid and highly educated voters while the conservative nationalists of PiS appealed mainly to the less well paid and less educated. SLD voters occupy an intermediate position, although the party scarcely registers in the current political lineup.[16] Their income is slightly below average, and their educational level slightly above, but the cleavage is smaller than with either the PO or PiS (Figs. 16.3–16.4).[17]

In Brussels, Paris, and Berlin, officials often worry that PiS seems hostile to the EU which PiS party leaders frequently accuse of treating Poland like a second-class partner. By contrast, Eurocrats love PO because it is always quick to endorse EU decisions and rules and religiously adheres to the principle of "free and undistorted competition." PiS is rightly accused of championing authoritarian government and traditional values: for instance, it vehemently opposes abortion and same-sex marriage.[18] Note, however, that since PiS came

16. In the 2007, 2011, and 2015 elections, the SLD captured less than 10 percent of the vote, compared with 30–40 percent each for the PO and PiS.

17. For a detailed presentation of these results, see A. Lindner, F. Novokmet, T. Piketty, and T. Zawisza, "Political Conflict and Electoral Cleavages in Central-Eastern Europe, 1992–2018," WID.world, 2019.

18. Remember that since 2015 the president of the European Council has been Donald Tusk, who served as prime minister of Poland and leader of PO from 2007 to 2014. See Chap. 12.

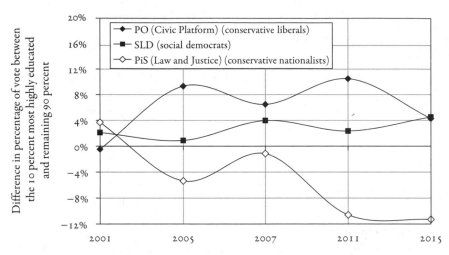

FIG. 16.4. Political conflict and education in Poland, 2001–2015

Interpretation: Between 2001 and 2015, the PO (Civic Platform) (conservative liberal) vote shifted toward more highly educated groups, while the PiS (Law and Justice) (conservative nationalist) vote shifted toward the less educated. *Sources and series:* piketty. pse.ens.fr/ideology.

to power in 2015, it has also enacted fiscal and social measures to help people of low income, including a sharp increase of family benefits and pension hikes for the poorest retirees. By contrast, PO, in power from 2005 to 2015, generally preferred policies that favored the well-to-do. In short, PiS has been readier to flout budget rules than PO and more willing to spend on social programs.

Thus, PiS developed an ideology that one might characterize as "social-nationalist" or "social-nativist," offering redistributive social and fiscal measures together with an intransigent defense of Polish national identity (deemed to be under threat from unpatriotic elites). The issue of immigration from outside Europe took on new importance in the wake of the refugee crisis of 2015, which provided PiS with an opportunity to voice its vigorous opposition to an EU plan to relocate immigrants throughout Europe (a plan that was quickly abandoned).[19] Note, however, that the classist structure of the PO and PiS

---

19. The 2015 refugee crisis arose after civil war broke out in Syria in 2012–2014, sending nearly 1 million Syrians fleeing to Europe (an influx that amounted to 0.2 percent of the EU population of 510 million). Most of these ended up in Germany. EU member states then decided to stanch the plow by signing an agreement with Turkey in 2016; in return for financial aid, Turkey agreed to keep most refugees

electorates was already in place before the issue of immigration really figured on the political agenda.

Unfortunately, it is not possible at this stage to systematically compare the evolution of the electoral cleavage structure in the various countries of Eastern Europe since the postcommunist transition of the 1990s owing to the inadequacy of the available postelection surveys.[20] Circumstances varied widely from country to country, and there was rapid turnover of political movements and ideologies. Social nativism has been spreading, with a mixture of strong hostility to non-European immigration (which has become the symbol of what the much-reviled Brussels elites would like to surreptitiously impose, despite the fact that the actual numbers of refugees are extremely small compared with the European population) and with a variety of social policies intended to show that the social-nativist parties care more about the lower and middle classes than do the pro-European parties.

The Hungarian case is in some ways similar to the Polish. Since 2010 the country has been governed by the conservative nationalist party Fidesz and its leader Victor Orban, who has without a doubt become one of the most prominent proponents of social-nativist ideology in Europe. Although officially a member of the European Peoples' Party, the same parliamentary group to which the German Christian Democratic Union (CDU) and other "center-right" parties belong, Orban did not hesitate to plaster his country with provocative anti-refugee posters in 2015 along with giant billboards denouncing the alleged nefarious influence of George Soros, a Hungarian-born billionaire said to symbolize a conspiracy of globalized Jewish elites against the peoples of Europe. For the "social" component of its program, Fidesz (like PiS) increased family benefits, which for obvious reasons served as a symbol of social nativism.[21] The

---

fleeing Syria in camps on its soil. We will see later that the flow of migrants entering the European Union has actually decreased since the economic crisis of 2008. The wide media coverage of "columns of immigrants" crossing the Balkans to reach Germany and Northern Europe—coverage that was intensely exploited by political parties—had a profound impact on the way the crisis was seen.

20. For an analysis of the available materials, see Lindner et al., "Political Conflict and Electoral Cleavages in Central-Eastern Europe."

21. Family benefits and other pro-natalist social and fiscal policies reduce inequality (a system providing equal allotments for each child is more of a boost for low-income families than for higher-income families) while also expressing the need to increase the country's population without bringing in immigrants. PiS's and Fidesz's family policy since 2015 can be compared with the bonus of $10,000 per child (starting

Hungarian government also created subsidized jobs aimed at putting the unemployed back to work under the control of local governments and mayors loyal to the ruling party. Fidesz also sought to encourage Hungarian entrepreneurs and companies by offering government contracts in exchange for political fealty. These measures demonstrated Fidesz's readiness to resist EU budget and competition rules, in contrast to its political rivals, especially the social democrats, who were regularly accused of marching to orders from Brussels.[22]

It is worth recalling the circumstances in which Fidesz came to power in 2010. In 2006 (as in 2002), the social-democratic Hungarian Socialist Party, or MSZP (a direct descendant of the Hungarian Socialist Workers' Party, or MSZMP, which had ruled from 1956 to 1989 and then been reorganized as the MSZP in 1990) won a narrow victory over a coalition led by Fidesz, whose popularity was rapidly increasing. The social-democratic leader—Ferenc Gyurcsany, who served as prime minister of Hungary from 2004 to 2009—was also an entrepreneur and one of the wealthiest men in the country, having amassed a fortune out of the privatizations of the 1990s. Shortly after his reelection in 2006, he gave a speech to party leaders that was supposed to remain confidential but somehow leaked to the media. In it, Gyurcsany candidly explained how he had lied for months to secure his victory, in particular concealing from voters planned budget cuts, which he regarded as inevitable. Social spending was to be slashed and the health care system overhauled. The news came as a bombshell; an unprecedented wave of demonstrations ensued. Orban saw the scandal as the long-awaited proof of the social democrats' shameless hypocrisy and shrewdly exploited the chaos. For Fidesz, which began as a conservative nationalist movement, the situation provided a perfect opportunity to demonstrate that it was more sincerely devoted to the disadvantaged than the so-called social democrats, who had in reality become pro-market elitist liberals. Gyurcsany was ultimately forced to resign in 2009 in circumstances further complicated by the financial crisis of 2008 and the imposition of budgetary austerity

---

with the second child) introduced in Russia in 2007, which apparently had a significant effect on the birth rate. See E. Yakovlev and I. Sorvachev, "Short-Run and Long-Run Effects of Sizable Conditional Child Subsidy" (presentation, Paris School of Economics, Applied Economics Lunch Seminar, September 18, 2018).

22. In practice, this did not prevent Fidesz from exercising lingering liberal-authoritarian instincts in response to economic issues. For instance, in late 2018, the government enacted a law reinforcing the power of employers to force workers to work overtime.

throughout Europe. This sequence culminated in 2010 with the ultimate collapse of the social democrats and the triumph of Fidesz, which then easily won the legislative elections of 2014 and 2018.[23]

The Emergence of Social Nativism: The Italian Case

It would be quite wrong to think of the development of social nativism as a specifically East European phenomenon without implications for Western Europe or the rest of the world. Eastern Europe should rather be seen as a laboratory where conditions were perfect for the combination of two ingredients that we also find in only slightly less extreme forms elsewhere. Together, these two factors give rise to social nativism: first, a strong sense of postcommunist and anti-universalist disillusionment leading to extreme identitarian withdrawal, and second, a global (or European) economy that prevents the establishment of coordinated, effective, and nonviolent policies of social redistribution and inequality reduction. In this light, it is particularly instructive to look at how a social-nativist coalition was formed in Italy after the legislative elections of 2018.

Compared with other Western democracies, Italy is distinctive in several ways. For one thing, the Italian postwar party system imploded in the wake of financial scandals unearthed by the anti-Mafia judges who conducted the Mani Pulite (Clean Hands) investigation in 1992. This led to the downfall of the two parties that had dominated Italian politics since 1945: the Christian Democrats and the Socialists. On the right of the political spectrum, the Christian Democrats were replaced in the 1990s by a complex and changing set of parties, including Silvio Berlusconi's conservative-liberal Forza Italia and the Lega Nord (Northern League). The Lega was initially a regionalist antitax party, which advocated fiscal autonomy for "Padania" (northern Italy) and opposed transfer payments to the south, a region deemed to be lazy and corrupt. Since the refugee crisis of 2015, the Lega has become a nationalist anti-immigrant party devoted to ridding the country of foreigners. Lega leaders regularly denounce

---

23. The coalition led by Fidesz (which included the Christian Democratic People's Party, or KDNP) won 53, 45, and 49 percent of the vote in the elections of 2010, 2014, and 2018 respectively versus 24, 19, and 12 percent for the MSZP (whereas the two blocs had been close to equal at 41–43 percent each in 2002 and 2006). These two groups are flanked on the right by Jobbik (with about 20 percent of the vote in the most recent elections). Jobbik is even more violently opposed than Fidesz to black and Muslim immigrants (even though they are totally absent in Hungary).

the alleged invasion of Italy by blacks and Muslims, who they claim threaten to take over the peninsula. The party appeals to anti-immigrant voters among the least favored classes, especially in the north, where it has also retained a base of antitax voters from the ranks of management and the self-employed.

On the left the situation is no less complicated. The collapse of the Socialist Party in 1992 and its ultimate dissolution in 1994 inaugurated a cycle of political realignment and renewal. The Italian Communist Party (PCI), long the most powerful in Europe along with its French counterpart, was hard-hit by the fall of the Soviet Union and chose in 1991 to transform itself into the Democratic Left Party (PDS). The PDS then joined other movements to create the Democratic Party (PD) in 2007, with the ambition of unifying "the left," like the Democratic Party in the United States. In 2013, the party organized an internal election to choose its new leader. The winner, Matteo Renzi, became prime minister in 2014 and served in that post until 2016 as the head of a coalition led by the PD.

What happened on the left went beyond name changes. The left electorate (Socialist Party, or PS; PCI; PDS; PD) has been totally transformed in recent decades. In the 1960s and 1970s these parties racked up their highest scores among the disadvantaged classes, but that is no longer the case. In the 1980s and 1990s, the PS and PCI (and later the PDS) obtained their best results among the highly educated. This trend continued in the 2000s and 2010s. In the 2013 and 2018 elections, the vote for the PD was twenty points higher among the highly educated than among the rest of the population.[24] The PD's policies, especially the loosening of restrictions on layoffs ("Jobs Act") enacted by Renzi soon after he took power, provoked strong opposition from the unions and huge demonstrations (a million people took to the streets of Rome in October 2014), which made the party even less popular among workers. Renzi's reforms received strong public support from Christian Democratic German Chancellor Angela Merkel, and they would not have been approved by the Italian parliament had the PD not entered into a de facto coalition with Forza Italia. These developments convinced many Italian that the PD no longer had much to do with the postwar Socialist and Communist Parties that figured in its pedigree.

The latest arrival on the Italian political scene was the Movimento Cinque Stelle (or Five-Star Movement—M5S). Founded in 2009 by the humorist

---

24. See Fig. 14.2. For detailed results on educational cleavages in Italian elections, see the online appendix and Gethin et al., "Political Cleavages and Inequality."

Beppe Grillo, M5S portrays itself an antisystem, antielitist party that cannot be placed on the usual left-right spectrum. One of its signature issues is a universal basic income. Compared with the PD, the M5S runs up its highest scores among less educated voters, among the disadvantaged classes in the south, and among the disillusioned of all the other parties, who are drawn to the movement's promises to spend more on social measures and develop neglected regions. Within a few years, M5S had capitalized on discontent with the former governing parties, starting with Forza Italia and the PD, and had begun winning a quarter to a third of the vote in each new election.

In the legislative elections of 2018, the electorate divided into three large blocs: M5S got 33 percent of the vote, the PD 23 percent, and a coalition of right-wing parties 37 percent.[25] The right-wing coalition was quite heterogeneous because it included the anti-immigrant Lega (17 percent), the conservative-liberal Forza Italia (14 percent), and a number of smaller conservative nationalist parties (6 percent). Since no single bloc obtained a majority of the seats, a coalition was necessary to form a government. An M5S-PD alliance was briefly considered, but mutual suspicion made this impossible. M5S and the Lega, which had already joined forces to oppose Renzi's Jobs Act both in parliament and in the streets in 2014, ultimately reached an agreement to govern the country on the basis of a synthesis of their two platforms, including both the guaranteed minimum income advocated by M5S and the uncompromising anti-refugee policy championed by the Lega.[26] The heterogeneous nature of this coalition agreement is reflected in the structure of the government: Luigi di Maio, the young leader of M5S, became the minister of economic development, labor, and social policy, which is responsible for overseeing the minimum income, territorial development, and public investment in the south while Matteo Salvini, the leader of the Lega, occupies the strategic post of minister of the interior, from which in the summer of 2018 he launched several spectacular anti-immigration operations, including closing all Italian ports to humanitarian ships engaged in rescuing refugees adrift on the Mediterranean.

The M5S-Lega coalition that has ruled Italy since 2018 is clearly a social-nativist alliance; it naturally calls to mind the PiS government and Poland and

---

25. The remainder of the vote (7 percent) went to small parties independent of the three major polls. In the 2016 elections, M5S received 26 percent of the vote, the PD 30 percent, and the coalition of the right 29 percent.

26. This compromise was never very coherent because the Lega proposed cutting the taxes needed to pay for the universal basic income. I will come back to this point.

the Fidesz government in Hungary. Of course, there is no guarantee that this coalition will survive. Either of the two pillars on which it stands could collapse, bringing down the whole edifice. Relations between the two governing parties are very tense, and all indications are that the nativists are on the verge of emerging as the dominant partner in the coalition. Salvini's sallies against refugees have made him increasingly popular and may allow the Lega to outstrip M5S in the next elections or even to win an absolute majority. In any case, the mere fact that such a social-nativist coalition could come to power in an old West European democracy like Italy (the third-largest economy in the Eurozone) shows that the phenomenon is not limited to postcommunist Eastern Europe. Social-nativist leaders in several countries, including Orban and Salvini, have not been shy about publicizing their shared antielitist attitudes and common view of Europe's future in both immigration and social policy.[27]

On the Social-Nativist Trap and European Disillusionment

It is natural to ask whether a similar political-ideological coalition could emerge in other countries, especially France. This would have significant consequences for the political equilibrium of the European Union. When we look at the distribution of votes in the 2018 Italian elections, we find three voting blocs (or four, if we distinguish between the two components of the right bloc, the Lega and Forza Italia, which split over the question of alliance with M5S). This configuration of Italy's ideological space has some important points in common with the four-part division we saw in the 2017 French presidential election as well as some significant differences.[28] In the French context, the closest equivalent to the M5S-Lega alliance would be a hypothetical alliance between the radical left, La France Insoumise (LFI), and the Front National (which in 2018

---

27. For instance, during a joint press conference in Milan in August 2018, the Hungarian prime minister declared: "We proved that immigration could be stopped on land, he is proving that it can be stopped on the sea." The Italian minister of the interior responded: "Today begins a common journey that will be followed by numerous other stages in the coming months to focus on the right to work, health, and security. Everything that the European elites refuse to give us." C. Ducourtieux, J.-B. Chastand, and M. Nasi, "Migrants: Viktor Orban et Matteo Salvini prennent Emmanuel Macron pour cible," *Le Monde,* August 29, 2018. The European elections of 2019 also confirmed that the nativist wing of the Italian coalition was on the verge of gaining the upper hand over M5S.

28. See Table 14.1 and Fig. 14.19.

renamed itself the Rassemblement National, or RN). At this stage, an LFI-RN alliance seems out of the question, however. The RN electorate includes voters most fiercely opposed to immigration while the LFI electorate (on the evidence of 2017) includes the voters most favorable to immigration.[29] The social and redistributive policies favored by LFI voters and party leaders, such as progressive taxation, are directly descended from the historical policies of the socialist and communist left. The RN draws on a very different ideological corpus, which makes it hard to imagine any way that the two parties could agree on a common plan of action, at least in the near future. Despite many attempts to win respectability and bury its historic origins (in Vichy, colonialism, and Poujadism), even to the point of changing its name, the RN remains the heir of a movement that the vast majority of LFI voters regard as untouchable.[30]

Nevertheless, the rapidity of change in Italy suggests a need for caution in anticipating what trajectories might be possible in the medium term. Several things made the social-nativist alliance of 2018 possible in Italy. One was the damage done by the collapse of the postwar party system in 1992. As the integrity of all the postwar parties was called into question, people lost faith in the old faces and promises to the point where they could no longer find their political bearings. Ideologies that had once seemed solid shattered into a thousand pieces, and previously unthinkable alliances became acceptable.[31]

One reason why the social-nativist cocktail became thinkable in Italy has to do with specific features of the Italian immigration controversy. Because of its geographical situation, Italy became the destination of choice for large

---

29. I am referring here to the "egalitarian internationalist" quarter of the 2017 presidential electorate, which includes not only LFI but the other parties of the left (although most of the votes went to the LFI candidate for tactical reasons related to the possibility of access to the second round). See Table 14.1.

30. The same is true of the party leadership, which has always stood for welcoming immigrants.

31. The series *1992*, an Italian political drama broadcast in 2015, offers an illuminating and instructive view of that key year in Italian political history and helps us to understand the lengthy process of political decomposition. We meet Leonardo Notte, a dishonest but likable press agent who assists in Berlusconi's rise. We also meet Pietro Bosco, a battered veteran of the Gulf War, who somewhat by accident finds himself elected to parliament on the Lega Nord ticket, in a milieu of old Roman politicians and their wheeling and dealing. Had the drama unfolded twenty-five years later, Bosco might have wound up in the M5S instead of the Lega.

numbers of refugees fleeing Syria and Africa via Libya.[32] The other countries of Europe, always prompt to lecture the rest of the world—including Italy—on the need for generosity, mostly refused to consider any plan to apportion responsibility for the refugees in a rational and humane way. France showed itself to be particularly hypocritical on this score: French border police were ordered to turn back any immigrants attempting to cross from Italy. Since 2015, France has admitted only one-tenth as many refugees as Germany.[33] In the fall of 2018, the French government decided to close its ports to the humanitarian vessels turned away by Italy, and it went so far as to refuse to allow the Aquarius to sail under a French flag, condemning the ship chartered by the humanitarian organization SOS Méditerranée to remain tied up in port while refugees drowned at sea. Salvini had a field day attacking the attitude of France and particularly its young president Emmanuel Macron, elected in 2017, who in Salvini's eyes was the very embodiment of Europe's hypocritical elite. French hypocrisy thus became his justification for cracking down on immigrants in Italy.

The charge of hypocrisy is of course one of the classic rhetorical devices of the anti-immigrant right. The Front National and other parties of its ilk have always denounced the self-righteousness of elites quick to defend open borders as long as they do not have to bear the consequences.[34] But rhetoric of this type (pioneered in France by Jean-Marie Le Pen in the 1980s) is usually convincing only to those who already believe because it is clear that those who use it are interested mostly in stirring up hatred as a stepping stone to power for

---

32. Libya had been plunged into chaos in 2008 by the joint Franco-British invasion, which can be compared for both lack of preparation and devastating consequences to the Anglo-American invasion of Iraq in 2003 (although the human cost of the latter invasion was significantly larger).

33. See the online appendix. The official position of the French government, first under François Hollande and then Macron, was that, although the so-called Dublin Accord (under which any demand for political asylum must be examined in the country where the applicant first set foot on European soil) needed to be reformed, reform was unfortunately impossible because Poland and Hungary refused to agree to it, and therefore France would continue to send refugees back to Italy. If Germany had taken the same position in 2015, it would not have admitted more than a million refugees.

34. As noted earlier, the Democrat John Calhoun made similar accusations of hypocrisy against the industrial and financial elites of the North, whom he charged with calling for the abolition of slavery only to secure a cheap, readily exploitable, and easily discardable work force for their factories. See Chap. 6.

themselves. In Salvini's case, in the context of a Europe-wide conflict over immigration with a particularly bitter clash between France and Italy, the charge of hypocrisy has acquired a certain plausibility. The specific nature of this conflict is part of the reason for the Lega's growing popularity in Italy. It also helps to explain why the M5S, although relatively moderate on the refugee issue, could agree to a coalition with the Lega: the tough anti-immigrant line could be presented as part of a broader attack on elite hypocrisy.

Last but perhaps not least, the social-nativist coalition in Italy is fueled by a widespread distaste for European rules and in particular European budgetary rules, which allegedly prevented Italy from investing and from recovering from the 2008 crisis and the purge that followed. Indeed, it is hard to deny that the European decision, pushed by Germany and France in 2011–2012, to impose deficit reduction throughout the Eurozone led to a disastrous "double-dip" recession and a sharp spike in unemployment, especially in the south.[35] It is also clear that Franco-German conservatism on the issue of pooling public debt and establishing a common interest rate at the European level—a policy change that would be consistent with having a common concurrency and would protect the countries of the south from speculation in the financial markets—is due largely to the fact that France and Germany would prefer to continue enjoying the benefits of near-zero interest rates by themselves, even if it means leaving the European project at the mercy of the markets in any future financial crisis.

Of course, the alternatives proposed by the Lega and M5S are far from perfect or well thought out. Some in the Lega seem to be contemplating an exit from the euro and return to the lira, which would allow for debt reduction through moderate inflation. The majority of Italians worry about the unpredictable consequences of such a move, however. Most leaders and voters of the Lega and M5S would prefer a change of Eurozone rules and of the policy stance of the European Central Bank (ECB). If the ECB could print trillions of euros to save the banks, people ask, why can't it help Italy by deferring its debt until better times return? I will say more later about these complex and unprecedented debates, which remain underdeveloped. What is certain is that answers to these questions cannot be postponed indefinitely. Social discontent with the EU and deep incomprehension of the authorities' inability to muster the same energy and deploy the same resources to help large numbers of people as they did to save the financial sector will not magically disappear.

---

35. See Chap. 12.

The Italian case also shows that the sense of disillusionment with Europe, which the Lega shares with M5S, can serve as a powerful bond for a social-nativist coalition. What makes the Lega and its leader Matteo Salvini so dangerous is precisely Salvini's ability to combine nativist rhetoric with social rhetoric—attacks on immigrants with attacks on speculators and financiers— and to wrap all of it up in a critique of hypocritical elites. A similar formula could be used to build social-nativist coalitions in other countries, including France, where disillusionment with Europe runs high among supporters of both the far left and the far right. The fact that Europe is so often instrumentalized for the pursuit of antisocial policies, as was clear in the sequence of events leading up to the Yellow Vest crisis of 2017–2019 (which followed abolition of the wealth tax in the name of European competition, financed by a carbon tax that fell heavily on the poorer half of the population), unfortunately makes such an evolution plausible. Indeed, if the nativist party opportunistically tones down its anti-immigrant rhetoric and concentrates instead on social issues and resistance to the European Union, it is not out of the question that we could someday see a social-nativist coalition similar to the Lega-M5S coalition in Italy coming to power in France.

The Democratic Party: A Case of Successful Social Nativism?

Some readers, even among those generally hostile to anti-immigrant politics, might nevertheless be tempted to welcome social-nativist movements in Europe. After all, wasn't the Democratic Party that backed the New Deal in the United States in the 1930s and ultimately supported the civil rights movement in the 1960s and elected a black president in 2008 originally an authentic social-nativist party? Having supported slavery and contemplated sending slaves back to Africa, the Democratic Party reconstructed itself after the Civil War around a social-differentialist ideology, combining very strict segregation in the South with a relatively egalitarian social policy for whites (especially white Italian and Irish immigrants and indeed the white working class generally). In any case, whatever its shortcomings, Democratic social policy was certainly more egalitarian than Republican social policy. Yet it was not until the 1940s that the Democratic Party tried to do something about the segregationist element within it, which it finally purged in the 1960s under pressure from the civil rights movement.

With this example in mind, one might imagine a trajectory in which PiS, Fidesz, the Lega, and the Rassemblement National follow a similar course in the coming decades, offering relatively egalitarian social measures to "native Europeans" combined with a very harsh crackdown on non-European immigrants and their children. Later, perhaps half a century or more in the future, the nativist component would fade away or perhaps even transform itself to the point of embracing diversity once conditions were right. There are several problems with this idea, however. First, before becoming the party of the New Deal and civil rights, the Democratic Party did a great deal of damage. From the 1870s to the 1960s, Democrats in the South imposed segregation on blacks, kept black children from attending the same schools as whites, and supported or covered up lynchings organized by the Ku Klux Klan and similar vigilante groups. It makes no sense to suggest that there was no other path to the New Deal and the Civil Rights Act. There are always alternatives. Everything depends on the ability of political actors to mobilize and search for them.[36]

In the current European context, the potential damage if social nativists were to take power would likely be of the same order. Indeed, the damage has already begun where social nativists currently hold power: not only have they cracked down on immigrants in their own countries, but they have also pressured timorous governments elsewhere in Europe to enact more restrictive immigration policies. Meanwhile, thousands of migrants die in the Mediterranean and hundreds of thousands molder in camps in Libya and Turkey. If the social-nativist parties were free to do as they wished, they might very well turn to more violent attacks on non-European immigrants and their descendants living in Europe, retroactively stripping them of nationality and deporting them, as purportedly democratic regimes have done in the past in both Europe and the United States.[37]

What is more, there are serious reasons to doubt that today's social-nativist movements are capable of enacting genuinely redistributive policies. In the late nineteenth and early twentieth centuries, the Democratic Party in the United States helped develop tools for social redistribution, including the federal income and inheritance taxes enacted in 1913–1916 and social insurance (pensions

---

36. For instance, the federal troops that occupied the South at the end of the Civil War could easily have imposed desegregation. In fact, they tried (too shortly), and it is not difficult to imagine a sequence of events and individual actions that might have ended in success. Similarly, Republicans might have won the White House since the 1960s without resorting to the racial attacks that Richard Nixon, Reagan, and Trump used so effectively, if only they had searched for more ambitious political and ideological alternatives.

37. See Chap. 14.

and unemployment) and minimum wage programs in the 1930s—and remember that under Democratic leadership the United States led the way in progressive taxation, raising top marginal rates to the highest levels ever seen anywhere in the period 1930–1980.[38] Contrast this record with the rhetoric and accomplishments of PiS in Poland, Fidesz in Hungary, and the M5S-Lega alliance in Italy. It is striking to see that none of these parties has proposed any explicit tax increase on the wealthy, even though they sorely need the revenue to finance their social policies. True, PiS did reduce certain tax deductions beneficial to people with high incomes so that they ended up paying somewhat more than before, but the Polish government still has not dared to raise tax rates on the wealthy.[39]

Interstate Competition and the Rise of Market-Nativist Ideology

In Italy, it is noteworthy and revealing that M5S agreed to include the Lega's campaign proposal for a "flat tax" (a legacy of the Lega's origins as an antitax party) in its coalition agreement with Salvini's party. If this measure were fully implemented, it would mean that every taxpayer, no matter how high his or her income, would pay the same flat rate—thus completely dismantling the progressive tax system. This would result in an enormous loss of tax revenue, the benefits of which would go to people of middle-to-high income but which would be paid for by increased public borrowing, on the model of Ronald Reagan's tax reforms of the 1980s. Because this would pose a serious problem for a heavily indebted country like Italy, this part of the coalition's reform program has been postponed and will no doubt be enacted only in some very limited form with a reduction of top marginal rates rather than complete elimination of progressive taxation. Nevertheless, the fact that M5S could have agreed to such a proposal says a great deal about the movement's lack of ideological backbone. It is hard to see how one can possibly finance an ambitious basic income proposal and a vast program of public investment while eliminating progressive taxes on top incomes.

Why do today's social nativists lack appetite for progressive taxation? There are several possible explanations. It may be that they do not want to be associated with the legacy of the social-democratic, socialist, Labour (United

---

38. See Chaps. 10–11.
39. See the online appendix.

Kingdom), or New Deal left. M5S has embraced the idea of a universal basic income, which it sees as innovative and modern, but rejects the progressive tax system that could finance it, which it finds complicated and tired. Another point that bears emphasizing is the degree to which the ECB's policy of massive monetary creation since 2008 has changed people's perceptions. Because the ECB created trillions of euros to save the banks, it is difficult for social nativists to admit that complex and potentially unjust and evadable new taxes are needed to pay for a universal basic income or new investment in the real economy. One finds repeated references to the need for just monetary creation in the rhetoric of M5S, the Lega, and other social-nativist movements. Until European governments propose a more convincing means of mobilizing resources, such as a European tax on the wealthy, the idea of paying for social expenditures by contracting new debt and creating new money will continue to attract strong support among social-nativist voters.

The lack of appetite for progressive taxes is also a consequence of several decades of antitax propaganda and sanctification of the principle of competition of all against all. Today's hypercapitalist economy is one of heightened interstate competition. Competition to attract high earners and wealthy capitalists already existed in the late nineteenth and early twentieth centuries. But it was less intense than competition today. This was partly because the means of transportation and information technology were different back then. More importantly, the international treaties that have defined the global economy since the 1980s have ensured that the new technology would be used to protect the legal and fiscal privileges of the rich rather than the majority. That technology could be used instead to create a public financial register, which would allow countries that so desire to impose redistributive taxes on transnational wealth and the income it generates. Such a system is not only possible but also desirable: it would replace existing treaties, which allow the capital to circulate freely, with new treaties that would create a regulated system built on the public financial register.[40] But this would require substantial international cooperation and ambitious efforts to transcend the nation-state, especially on the part of smaller countries (such as the nations of Europe). Nativist and nationalist parties are by their very nature not well equipped to achieve this kind of cross-border cooperation.

Therefore, it seems quite unlikely that today's social-nativist movements will develop ambitious plans for progressive taxation and social redistribution. The

---

40. See Chaps. 11, 13, and 17.

most probable outcome is that once they arrive in power, they will find themselves (whether they like it or not) caught up in the mechanism of fiscal and social competition and thus be forced to do whatever it takes to promote their national economies. Only for opportunistic reasons did the Rassemblement National in France oppose abolition of the wealth tax during the Yellow Vest crisis. If the RN were to come to power, it would likely cut taxes on the rich to attract new investment, not only because such a course would be in keeping with its old antitax instincts and its ideology of national competition but also because its hostility to international cooperation and a federal Europe would force it to engage in fiscal dumping. More generally, the disintegration of the EU (or just the reinforcement of state power and anti-migrant ideology within the EU) to which the accession of nationalist parties to power could lead would intensify social and fiscal competition, increase inequality, and encourage identitarian retreat.[41]

On Market-Nativist Ideology and Its Diffusion

In other words, social nativism is highly likely to lead in practice to a market-nativist type of ideology. In the United States, Donald Trump has clearly gone this route. In the 2016 presidential campaign, Trump tried to give his politics a social dimension by portraying himself as the champion of the American worker, whom he described as the victim of unfair competition from Mexico and China and as citizens abandoned by Democratic elites. But the actual policies of the Trump administration have combined more or less standard nativist measures (such as reducing the influx of immigrants, building a border wall, and supporting Brexit and nativist governments in Europe) with tax cuts for the rich and multinational corporations. Reagan's 1986 Tax Reform Act featured a reduction of the top marginal income tax rate (to 28 percent, later

---

41. A more optimistic view is the following: the disintegration of the European Union and the demise of its rules regarding budgets, finance, and competition could revive the old left-right competition. The left bloc would once again enjoy some room to maneuver and could propose new social and ecological policies, while the right bloc would be free to pursue a pro-business and anti-immigration agenda. This is the implicit hypothesis underlying B. Amable and S. Palombarini, *L'illusion du bloc bourgeois. Alliances sociales et avenir du modèle français* (Raisons d'agir, 2017). But there is reason to believe that the return to the nation-state would lead instead to intensified interstate competition, of which the primary beneficiaries would be the nativist and nationalist parties.

raised to 35–40 percent under George H. W. Bush and Bill Clinton but never restored to previous levels). The tax reform that Trump negotiated with Congress in 2017 pushed this logic even further by focusing cuts on corporations and "entrepreneurs." The federal corporate tax rate, which had been 35 percent since 1993, was abruptly cut to 21 percent in 2018, with an amnesty on profits repatriated from abroad. This reduced corporate tax receipts by half and very likely triggered a global race to the bottom on corporate taxes, an essential component of public finance.[42] On top of that, Trump obtained an additional tax reduction focused specifically on self-employed entrepreneurs (like himself), whose business income will henceforth be taxed at a maximum rate of 29.6 percent, compared with 37 percent on top salaries. The combined impact of these two measures is that the rate at which the wealthiest 0.01 percent of taxpayers (including the 400 richest people in the country) are taxed has for the first time fallen below the rate assessed on people lower down in the top centile or even the top thousandth; top rates are sinking closer and closer to the effective rate paid by the poorest 50 percent.[43] Trump also sought complete elimination of the progressive tax on inheritances, but Congress refused to go along with him on that point.

It is particularly striking to note the similarity between the tax reforms enacted by presidents Trump and Macron in 2017. In France, in addition to elimination of the wealth tax (ISF) discussed previously, the new government passed a gradual reduction of the corporate tax from 33 to 25 percent and also cut the tax on dividend and interest income to 30 percent (compared with the 55 percent rate on the highest salaries). The fact that a purportedly nativist government like Trump's adopted a tax policy similar to that of a supposedly more internationalist government like Macron's shows that political ideologies and practices have converged to a considerable degree. The rhetoric varies:

---

42. The corporate tax rate in the United States was 45–50 percent from the 1940s to the 1980s before dropping to 34 percent in 1988–1992 and then rising to 35 percent in 1993–2017 (to which one must add state taxes of 5–10 percent). Until 2018, the United States had resisted the race to the bottom on corporate taxes that began in Europe. See Chap. 11. The sudden cut to 21 percent risks restarting the race to the bottom.

43. See E. Saez and G. Zucman, *The Triumph of Injustice: How the Rich Dodge Taxes and How to Make Them Pay* (Norton, 2019). These conclusions follow from strict application of the tax code without even considering the various methods of tax avoidance employed by the very rich.

Trump praises "job creators" while Macron prefers to speak of the "climbers at the head of the rope" ("premiers de cordée"). Ultimately, however, both adhere to an ideology according to which the competition of all against all requires offering ever greater tax cuts to the most mobile taxpayers while the masses are exhorted to honor their new benefactors, who bring innovations and prosperity (while omitting to mention that none of this would exist without public support for education and basic research and private appropriation of public knowledge).

Meanwhile, both the French and US governments risk increasing inequality and contributing to the feeling of the lower and middle classes that they have been left to face the consequences of globalization on their own. Trump tries to win them over by claiming that he is doing a better job than the Democrats of stopping immigration and is far more vigilant when it comes to opposing unfair competition from abroad.[44] He cleverly portrays "job creators" as more useful than the Democrats' intellectual elites when it comes to winning the global economic war the United States is waging against the rest of the planet.[45] Trump regularly denounces intellectuals as condescending and hectoring, always ready to follow the latest cultural fad no matter how threatening to American values and society. In particular, he loves to denounce the newfound passion for the climate: the idea of climate change is "a hoax," he says, invented by scientists, Democrats, and foreigners jealous of American prosperity and

---

44. In practice, the new trade agreement negotiated with Mexico and Canada in 2018 is a carbon copy of the previous North American Free Trade Agreement (NAFTA), with just enough minor symbolic differences to lend plausibility to the idea that something has changed, such as the addition of a clause marginally increasing the percentage of automobile parts manufactured by workers paid more than $16 an hour, with a sanction of just 2–4 percent in customs duties in case of violation. In financial terms, the measure is totally insignificant compared with the corporate tax cuts approved in 2017.

45. Just as Reagan's election in 1980 can be linked in mind and spirit to the book that Milton Friedman published in 1963 with Anna Schwartz on the monetary history of the United States (the bible of monetarist economics; see Chap. 12), Trump's election in 2016 can be linked to a deeply Trumpian book that Samuel Huntington published (*The Clash of Civilizations and the Remaking of the World Order* [Simon and Schuster, 1996]). In sum, Huntington proposed that the ideological conflict between capitalism and communism would give way to a war of cultures and identities, which he took to be fixed, ahistorical essences (the "West" versus Islam, Hinduism, etc.).

greatness.[46] Anti-intellectual sentiments have also been mobilized by nativist governments in Europe and India, illustrating the crucial need for more education and for citizen appropriation of scientific knowledge.[47]

The French president has made the opposite wager. He hopes to hold on to power by branding his opponents as nativists and antiglobalists, betting that a majority of the French believe in tolerance and openness and will therefore vote against the social nativists when the moment of truth arrives (in any case, by then the social nativists will have turned into market nativists a la Trump). At bottom, both ideologies insist that there is no alternative to tax cuts benefiting the rich and that the progressive-nativist cleavage is the only remaining axis along which political conflict can occur.[48] Both are based on misleading simplifications and a healthy dose of hypocrisy. Indeed, it is still possible for individual countries to pursue ambitious programs of redistribution, even small countries like those found in Europe.[49] If even small states can redistribute, the federal government in the United States has all the power it needs to enforce its fiscal policies—provided it can muster the necessary political will.[50] Furthermore, there is nothing to prevent efforts to develop greater international cooperation, especially on tax issues, for the purpose of achieving more equitable and durable economic growth.

---

46. Trump's anti-Brahminism is also clear in fiscal measures targeting university presidents (who are paid too much compared with "job creators," according to Trump) and taxing tuition rebates for graduate students as wages (a measure that ultimately did not pass). By contrast, Trump's demands that nations benefiting from US military protection pay for services rendered is a clear throwback to the old warrior class and the military tributes it received in the premodern trifunctional order.

47. Note than in Italy, M5S and the Lega have also agreed on anti-vaccination legislation as punishment for allegedly know-it-all elites (and rapacious pharmaceutical companies). PiS in Poland and BJP in India regularly accuse scholars of abusing the Polish or Indian nation by questioning established truths. Bolsonaro in Brazil has engaged in similar criticism of scholars.

48. This cleavage is in reality rather artificial in light of the French government's actual immigration and climate policies.

49. As shown, for example, by the fact that tax receipts from the French wealth tax and the declared tax base both increased significantly from 1990 to 2018, despite fiscal competition and lax enforcement. See Fig. S14.20.

50. As shown by measures like the Foreign Account Tax Compliance Act (2010), which put pressure on Swiss banks to reveal hidden assets, or Elizabeth Warren's proposed wealth tax (with an exit tax of 40 percent on individuals who renounce US citizenship and try to take their wealth abroad). See Chap. 11.

On the Possibility of Social Federalism in Europe

The most natural way to escape the social-nativist trap would be to develop social federalism in one form or another. International cooperation and political integration can achieve social justice and redistribute wealth by democratic means. Unfortunately, such a harmonious and nonviolent reform of European institutions is not the most likely outcome. It is probably more realistic to prepare for somewhat chaotic changes ahead: political, social, and financial crises could tear the European Union apart or destroy the Eurozone. Whatever lies ahead, reform is essential. No one envisions a return to autarky, and new treaties will therefore be necessary and, if possible, more satisfactory than the existing ones. Here I will focus on the possibility of social federalism in the European context. The lessons are of more general import, however, partly because European social and fiscal policies can have an important impact on other parts of the world and partly because similar forms of transnational cooperation may be applicable to other regions (such as Africa, Latin America, or the Middle East) as well as to relations between regional organizations.

The European Union is a novel and sophisticated attempt to organize an "ever closer union among the peoples of Europe." In practice, however, European institutions, established in stages from the Treaty of Rome (1957), which constituted the European Economic Community (EEC), to the Maastricht Treaty (1992) establishing the EU and the Lisbon Treaty (2007), which set current EU rules, have mainly sought to organize a vast market and guarantee free circulation of goods, capital, and workers but not to arrive at a common social or fiscal policy. Recall the basic principles on which these institutions operate.[51] Broadly speaking, in order for decisions taken by the European Union,

---

51. See also Chaps. 11 and 12. The reference to "ever closer union" is taken from the first sentence of the preamble to the Treaty on the Function of the European Union, adopted in Lisbon in 2007 along with the Treaty on European Union. These two texts, which came into effect only gradually between 2009 and 2014, constitute the current legal foundation of the European Union. They were supplemented in 2012–2013 by the budget treaty (TSCG), which set new deficit rules, and by the European Stability Mechanism (ESM). The treaties adopted in Lisbon in 2007 are essentially the same as those rejected in France in the 2005 referendum on the European Constitutional Treaty (Chap. 14). They were simply cleaned up: the term "constitution" was eliminated, the principle of "free and undistorted competition" in the old preamble was replaced by "fairness in competition," and most importantly, the whole thing was ratified by parliament rather than by refer-

whether regulations, directives, or other legislative acts, to take effect, they must be approved by the two institutions that share legislative power: first, the European Council, which consists of heads of state and government (and which also meets, as the Council of the European Union, at the ministerial level depending on the issue under discussion, so there can be a council of ministers of finance, ministers of agriculture, and so on); and second, the European Parliament, which since 1979 has been elected by universal suffrage and represents the member states on the basis of population (with overrepresentation of smaller states).[52] Decisions are prepared and promulgated by the European Commission, which acts as a kind of executive body and European government with a president of the Commission as its head and Commissioners in charge of various domains appointed by the Council, which consists of heads of state and government, and then approved by the Parliament.

Formally, the setup resembles a classic federal parliamentary structure with an executive and two legislative chambers. Two particular features make the EU arrangement very different, however. One is the key role played by the unanimity rule and the other is the fact that the council of ministers is totally unsuited for parliamentary deliberation of a pluralistic, democratic kind.

Recall first that most important decisions require a unanimous vote of the council of ministers. In particular, unanimity is required in all matters relating to taxes, the EU budget, and systems of social protection.[53] As for regulation of the internal market, free circulation of goods, capital, and people, and trade agreements with the rest of the world, which are ultimately the matters at the heart of the European project, the rule of "qualified majority voting" applies.[54]

---

endum. For links to these various texts, which are worth consulting, see the online appendix. See also D. Chalmers, G. Davies, and G. Monti, *European Union Law: Text and Materials* (Cambridge University Press, 2014).

52. Technically, the legislative function is exercised by the council of ministers in the relevant area (along with the European Parliament), while the European Council (consisting of heads of state and government under the authority of a President of the European Council who is named by them) focuses on the broad orientation of policy and treaty reform. But because ministers generally act under the authority of their heads of government, the difference is more legal and practical than truly political.

53. The unanimity rule also applies in the areas of foreign policy and common security, police cooperation, admission of new member states, European citizenship, and so on.

54. The qualified majority rule is as follows: a decision is adopted if it is supported by 55 percent of the countries representing at least 65 percent of the population of the European Union. This rule, adopted after lengthy debate, is the principal innovation

But once any matter touching on common fiscal, budgetary, or social policy—and especially anything touching on taxation or the public finances of the member states—is at issue, the unanimity rule applies. Concretely, this means that every country has veto power. For instance, if Luxembourg, with a population of half a million or barely a tenth of a percent of the total EU population of 510 million, wants to tax corporate profits at zero percent at the expense of its neighbors, nobody can stop it from doing so. Any country, no matter how small—be it Luxembourg, Ireland, Malta, or Cyprus—can block any tax measure that comes up. Moreover, since the treaties guarantee free circulation of capital with no obligation of fiscal cooperation, conditions are ripe for a race to the bottom. Fiscal dumping is the result, and the beneficiaries are those whose capital is most mobile.

Furthermore, the absence of any common tax or budget is what makes the European Union more of a commercial union or international organization than a true federal government. In the United States or India, the central government also has a bicameral legislature, but it has the power to levy taxes for collective projects. In both cases, federal income, inheritance, and corporate taxes bring in revenues of about 20 percent of gross domestic product (GDP), compared with barely 1 percent for the European Union, which in the absence of any common tax system depends on contributions by member states set by unanimous agreement.

On the Construction of a Transnational Democratic Space

Can this be changed? One possibility would be to allow fiscal and budget issues to be decided by qualified majority vote. Leave aside the fact it would not be easy to persuade the small countries to give up their fiscal veto. It would probably take a coalition of countries exerting very strong pressure on the others and threatening them with significant sanctions. In any case, even if one succeeds in imposing the qualified majority rule on all twenty-eight member states (soon to be twenty-seven if the United Kingdom goes through with Brexit, which as of this writing remains uncertain) or if a smaller group of countries agrees to forge ahead on some other basis, the problem remains that the council

---

of the Treaty on European Union adopted in Lisbon in 2007 (and before that in the now-defunct European Constitutional Treaty). It has been in effect since 2014. Previously, a system based on assigning a certain number of votes to each country was used. This was reviewed periodically and was the subject of constant controversy.

of finance ministers (or heads of government) is totally unsuited to the task of developing a true European parliamentary democracy.

The reason is simple: the council is a body consisting of one representative per country. As such, it is designed to pit the (perceived) national interests of member states against one another. In no way does it allow for pluralist deliberation or the construction of a majority based on ideas rather than interests. In the Eurogroup,[55] the German finance minister alone represents 83 million citizens, the French finance minister 67 million, the Greek finance minister 11 million, and so on. Under these conditions, it is simply impossible to deliberate tranquilly. The representatives of the large countries cannot allow themselves to be publicly placed in the minority on a fiscal or budgetary matter of importance to the home country. As a result, decisions of the Eurogroup (or of any of the European bodies consisting of ministers or heads of state and government) are almost always unanimous, taken under the cover of consensus following deliberation behind closed doors. In these bodies, none of the usual rules of parliamentary debate apply. For example, there are no procedural rules governing amendments, speaking time, or the manner of voting. It makes no sense that such bodies can decide tax policy for hundreds of millions of people. Since at least the eighteenth century and the age of Atlantic Revolutions we have known that the power to levy taxes is the quintessential parliamentary power. Setting tax rules, deciding who and what can be taxed and how much, requires free and open public debate under the watchful eye of citizens and journalists. All shades of opinion in every country need to be fully represented. By its very nature, a council of finance ministers cannot satisfy these requirements.[56] To recapitulate: European institutions, in which ministerial councils currently play the central and dominant role, relegating the European Parliament to a supporting role, were designed to regulate the broad market and conclude intergovernmental agreements; they were not designed to make fiscal and social policy.

A second possibility, which is widely supported by European leaders who favor a federal system, would be to transfer all power to approve new taxes to

---

55. Although the term "Eurogroup" is not mentioned in any of the treaties, it has come to designate the council of finance ministers of the Eurozone, a body that took on an important role in the aftermath of the financial crisis of 2008–2009.

56. Remember that the decision inopportunely taken behind closed doors by the Eurogroup after the financial crisis of 2008–2009 explains why Europe absurdly fell back into recession in 2011–2012. See Chap. 12 and the online appendix, Figs. S12.12a–S12.12c. The poor performance of the Eurogroup shows how ill suited it was to the job.

the European Parliament. Elected by direct universal suffrage, subject to the usual rules of parliamentary debate, and taking decisions by majority vote, the European Parliament is clearly better suited than the ministerial councils to deliberate on new taxes and budgets. Although this is clearly a better option than the first, several difficulties remain. We need to consider all the implications and understand why this option is unlikely to succeed. First, note that one essential step to creating a viable European democracy is to completely rewrite the rules governing the lobbies that currently loom so large in Brussels politicking, whose lack of transparency raises serious problems.[57] Second, transferring fiscal sovereignty to the European Parliament would mean that the political institutions of the member states would not be directly represented in the vote on European taxes.[58] This would not necessarily be problematic, and such bypassing of national institutions already happens in other contexts, but the point nevertheless calls for careful consideration.

In the United States, the federal budget and taxes, like other federal laws, must be approved by the Congress, whose members are elected for the purpose and do not directly represent the political institutions of the individual states. Bills must be approved in identical terms by both the House of Representatives and the Senate. Seats in the House are apportioned according to the population of each state while two senators from each state (regardless of size) sit in the Senate. This system, in which neither chamber takes priority over the other, is not a model of its kind and frequently leads to deadlock. But it does function, more or less, perhaps because there exists a certain equilibrium among states of different sizes.[59] In India there are also two chambers: the Lok Sabha,

---

57. On this subject see S. Laurens, *Les courtiers du capitalisme. Milieux d'affaires et bureaucrates à Bruxelles* (Agone, 2015).

58. To date, not even the most federalist proposals for European reform have gone that far. In particular, the treaty instituting the European Union that the European Parliament adopted in 1984 (the so-called Spinelli plan) accorded an important role to the Parliament, which was to have the power to appoint and remove Commissioners and to examine and amend laws and directives proposed by the Commission while leaving intact the requirement that such laws and directives must also be approved in identical terms by the council of ministers of member states (possibly by qualified majority vote). The optimistic federalist hypothesis (still entertained today) is that the council would ultimately bow to majority decisions by the European Parliament even though it would retain its formal right of veto over parliamentary decisions.

59. In particular, it makes no sense to compare the US Senate to the European Council. The equivalent of the European Council would be a senate composed of the governors of the individual states, where two states, say California and New York, accounted for half of the country's GDP, which is roughly the situation of Germany

or House of the People, directly elected by citizens with districts carefully drawn to ensure proportional representation of the population throughout the country and the Rajya Sabha, or Council of States, whose members are elected indirectly by the legislatures of the states and territories of the Indian Union.[60] Laws must in principle be approved in identical terms by both chambers, but in case of disagreement it is possible to convene a joint session to agree on a final text, which in practice gives a clear advantage to the Lok Sabha owing to its numerical superiority.[61] In addition, when it comes to fiscal and budgetary measures ("money bills"), the Lok Sabha automatically has the last word.

Nothing stands in the way of imagining a similar solution for Europe: the European Parliament could have the last word on European taxes and a European budget financed by those taxes. There are, however, two key differences that render such a solution unsatisfactory. First, it is unlikely that the EU's twenty-eight member states would agree to delegate fiscal sovereignty, at least initially. Therefore, those states that wish to forge ahead would need to be allowed to constitute a subchamber of the European Parliament. This could happen, but it would mean a fairly sharp break with the remaining member states. Second, and more important, assuming that all twenty-eight countries are in agreement or that some subgroup is prepared to forge ahead, one key difference remains between the European Union and the United States or India: the nation-states of Europe existed as such before the EU. In particular, each member state is free via its own national parliament to ratify or reject international treaties. In addition, these national parliaments—be it the Bundestag in Germany, the Assemblée Nationale in France, or any of the others—have been voting for decades (in some cases since the nineteenth century) on taxes and budgets; over the years, these have grown to considerable proportions, on the order of 30–40 percent of GDP.

---

and France in the Eurozone. Such a system would probably function very poorly, and the two governors would probably meet often without coming to any agreement. The comparison sometimes made between the Bundesrat (which represents the German Länder) is also not very convincing. Note that US senators have been directly elected by universal suffrage only since passage of the Seventeenth Amendment in 1913. Previously they were chosen by state legislatures.

60. The members of the Rajya Sabha are chosen from lists presented by the parties and are not themselves members of the state legislatures.

61. The Lok Sabha has 545 members, and the Rajya Sabha, 245. In practice, the joint session procedure has been used only three times since the adoption of the Constitution of 1950, including once in 1963 to pass the law prohibiting dowries.

With the taxes approved by these national parliaments, Europe's nation-states were able to implement novel social and educational polices, pioneering an immensely successful new model of development. They achieved the highest standard of living ever attained while limiting inequality (at least compared with the United States and other parts of the world) and providing relatively equal access to health and education. These national parliaments will continue to exist and continue to levy taxes and approve budgets. No one believes that all decisions should be made in Brussels or that EU spending should jump overnight from 1 to 40 percent of GDP, supplanting all national, regional, and local budgets and social insurance programs. Just as the property regime should be decentralized and participatory, the political regime should also be as decentralized as possible and involve actors on all levels.

Building European Parliamentary Sovereignty on National Parliamentary Sovereignty

For these reasons, if one wants to construct a truly transnational democratic space appropriate to Europe as currently constituted, one had better allow some role for national parliaments. One possibility might be to create a European Assembly (EA) composed partly of representatives of participating national parliaments and partly of members of the European Parliament (MEPs). Each participating country would be represented in proportion to its population, and each political party would be represented in its national delegation in proportion to its representation in the home-country parliament or the European Parliament, as the case may be. These questions of apportionment are too complex to be settled here. One proposal that has emerged as a working hypothesis from recent discussions is that the EA should consist of 80 percent members of national parliaments and 20 percent MEPs.[62]

The advantage of this proposal, which is based on a draft Treaty on the Democratization of Europe (T-Dem),[63] is that it can be adopted by countries that wish to do so without modifying existing European treaties. Although it

---

62. See the "Manifesto for the Democratization of Europe," published in December 2018 and available at M. Bouju, L. Chancel, A.-L. Delatte, S. Hennette, T. Piketty, G. Sacriste, and A. Vauchez, "Manifeste pour la Démocratisation de l'Europe," website, www.tdem.eu. See also M. Bouju, L. Chancel, A. L. Delatte, S. Hennette, T. Piketty, G. Sacriste, and A. Vauchez, *Changer l'Europe, c'est possible!* (Seuil, 2019).

63. The draft of this treaty, the Treaty on the Democratization of Europe (T-Dem), is also available at www.tdem.eu.

would be best if it were adopted by as many countries as possible—especially Germany, France, Italy, and Spain (which by themselves account for 70 percent of the population and GDP of the Eurozone)—there is nothing to prevent a smaller subset of countries from moving forward to form, say, a Franco-German Assembly or a Franco-Italo-Belgian Assembly.[64] In any case, this EA would be granted the power to approve four important common taxes: a tax on corporate profits, a tax on high incomes, a tax on large fortunes, and a carbon tax. To complement these taxes, the Assembly would also vote on a common budget. Assuming tax revenues of, say, 4 percent of GDP, the money could then be apportioned as follows: half would revert to the member states for their own use (for instance, to reduce taxes on the lower and middle classes, which have thus far borne the brunt of European fiscal competition) while the other half would finance research, education, and the transition to renewable sources of energy, with an additional portion set aside to defray the cost of welcoming new immigrants.[65]

---

64. Broadly speaking, there is nothing to prevent countries that wish to sign bilateral or multilateral treaties from doing so while respecting their other commitments. Because the fiscal competences discussed here are not EU competences, the Democratization Treaty could be adopted without violating existing rules. For a legal analysis of these issues, see S. Hennette, T. Piketty, G. Sacriste, and A. Vauchez, *How to Democratize Europe* (Harvard University Press, 2019). Note that the so-called Elysée treaty, providing for bilateral cooperation between France and Germany, was renewed in 2019, at which time a Franco-German parliamentary assembly consisting of one hundred members drawn from the French Assemblée Nationale and the German Bundestag was created. For now, this assembly is purely consultative, but there is nothing to prevent it from being granted the kinds of decision-making competences discussed here.

65. The proposed taxes include a 15 percent tax on corporate profits (together with a 22 percent minimum on corporate taxes at the national level, for a total of 37 percent); a common tax on high incomes of 10 percent on incomes above 200,000 euros and 20 percent above 400,000 euros (on top of the 40–50 percent currently applied at the national level, for a total of 60–70 percent for the highest incomes); a common tax on large fortunes of 1 percent above 1 million euros and 2 percent above 5 euros million (on top of existing property, land, and other national wealth taxes, which could be complemented by a common tax on inheritances of 10 percent above 1 million euros and 20 percent above 2 million euros); and a common carbon tax (with an initial price of 30 euros per ton, to be reevaluated annually). All details are available at www.tem.eu. These proposals are meant simply to orient thinking about what kind of budget a European Assembly might adopt; they should in no sense be taken as representing an ideal of fiscal progressivity on high incomes and large fortunes (about which I will say more in the next chapter; see Tab. 17.1).

These suggestions are merely meant to be illustrative; obviously it would be up to the EA to set its own priorities and levy taxes accordingly.[66]

The key point is to create a European space for democratic deliberation and decision making in which it would be possible to adopt strong measures of fiscal, social, and environmental justice. As we saw in analyzing the structure of the French and British referendum votes in 1992, 2005, and 2016, the breach between Europe and the disadvantaged classes has grown to significant proportions.[67] Without concrete, visible measures to demonstrate that the European project can be made to serve the goal of greater fiscal and social justice, it is hard to see how this can change.

The T-Dem proposal does not depend on any particular composition of the EA: for example, 50 percent of its members could be drawn from national parliaments rather than 80 percent. Deciding on the precise makeup of the EA will require broad debate and deep reflection. Technically, the system proposed here could even work with zero percent national deputies, in which case the EA would simply be a subset of the current European Parliament (including only MEPs from countries willing to proceed with this plan). If enough countries agreed to move in this direction and entrust fiscal sovereignty to a subset of the European Parliament, then it would represent a significant improvement over the status quo. In my view, however, reducing the proportion of national deputies too much (below 50 percent, say) would entail significant risks. The most obvious of these is that if a national parliament strongly disagreed with the fiscal and social policies adopted by the EA, it could always decide to withdraw from the project and repudiate the authorizing treaty. Since no one denies that national parliaments retain sovereignty in ratifying (and therefore repudiating) international treaties—this is one of their most important powers—it seems strange to deny them the right to participate in voting on European taxes.[68]

---

66. For example, the European Assembly could also decide simply to return all revenues to its member states, in which case the arrangement would simply allow member states to tax their most powerful economic actors more effectively at the federal level to reduce the fiscal pressure on the lower and middle classes, which would already be a fine achievement.

67. See Fig. 14.20 and Fig. 15.18.

68. The hypothetical possibility of amending the constitutions of European countries to prevent them from leaving the European Union or repudiating various European and international treaties seems unrealistic for the foreseeable future. It would arouse fierce and probably irresistible opposition in Germany, France, and elsewhere. In the United States, the US Constitution did not allow the South to secede, but that did not stop them from trying. In Europe, the only conceivable

More importantly, if national parliaments were deeply involved in the composition of the EA, this would have the effect of transforming national legislative elections into European elections. If national deputies were strongly represented in the EA, it would be impossible for parties and candidates standing in national elections to keep on blaming Brussels for everything that goes wrong while claiming that they have nothing to do with EU institutions (the favorite sport, unfortunately, of many European political leaders). If a subset of national deputies were to represent their party in the EA, they would have to explain in their national campaigns what European-level policies they intended to support (including taxes, budgets, and amounts to be returned to the national treasury).[69] National political life would thus be profoundly Europeanized. For this reason, I think that the project of building European parliamentary sovereignty on top of national sovereignty is ultimately a more ambitious form of federalism than the alternative project, which is to construct a European Parliament entirely independent of national parliaments.[70] Above all, this novel way of constructing transnational parliamentary sovereignty seems better adapted to European political and historical realities: Europe is quite different in this respect from other countries with federal systems (such as the United States, India, Brazil, Canada, and Germany, among others). Hence a new approach is required.[71]

---

treaties at this point are those based on voluntary and reversible decisions of the member states. Obviously, this does not mean that things will always be this way.

69. Presumably, each political party would send deputies well versed in these matters to the European Assembly. The EA would meet less often than national parliaments (perhaps one week a month) and could schedule its sessions so as to conflict as little as possible with national parliamentary sessions.

70. The fact that the European Parliament, prior to its election by direct universal suffrage in 1979 when its role was purely consultative, consisted of representatives of national parliaments probably explains the reluctance of many of the most convinced federalists (particularly among MEPs) to approve of involving the national parliaments in a federalist project. The proposal I present here clearly goes in this direction, however, because the proposed European Assembly consists in part of national deputies and has the last word on European budgets and taxes (which are the most important elements of federal sovereignty). Hence the situation would be totally different from that which existed before 1979. Concertation with the European Council is envisioned, but in case of disagreement it is the Assembly that decides. See the Treaty on the democratization of Europe (www.tdem.eu), article 8.

71. The approach I take here builds European sovereignty on national political institutions but not on national governments (as has been done until now). Rather, I look to national parliaments (which represent the full range of opinions and allow for

Rebuilding Trust and Developing
Common Norms of Justice

The T-Dem proposal would also place a strict ceiling on transfer payments between states signing the agreement. The purpose of this provision is not only to facilitate acceptance of the proposal but also to signal that the main objective is to reduce inequality within countries. This might seem like a technical point, or even a blemish, but in view of the climate of distrust that currently prevails in Europe, it is doubtless the only way of making progress.

Under the current EU budget framework, the European Commission annually publishes each country's "budget balance"—that is, the difference between what it contributes to the total EU budget (currently around 1 percent of GDP) and the amount it receives in return. In the period 1998–2018, the largest net contributors were Germany, France, and the United Kingdom, with net contributions of 0.2–0.3 percent of GDP, depending on the year.[72] The issue of transfers to the European Union played a significant role in the Brexit campaign.[73] The new budget envisioned under the current T-Dem proposal (4 percent of GDP or more) would supplement the current EU budget for the states signing the agreement. To reduce the risk of rejection, the proposal envisions that the difference between monies received from the signatory states and monies returned to those same states under the supplementary budget should not exceed 0.1 percent of GDP.[74] Of course, this figure could be raised or lowered if the signatories agree without altering the substance of the proposal.

This is a crucial point because the fantasy of a "transfer union" has become a major impediment to fresh thinking about the EU. Since the crisis of 2008, German political leaders in particular have been quick to decry any hint of a *Transferunion*. Members of Chancellor Merkel's Christian Democratic Union have led the way, but the Social Democrats have not been far behind, and they

---

deliberation and decision by majority vote). Joschka Fischer gave a speech at Humboldt University in 2000 based on similar premises but received little in the way of reply from the French government at the time.

72. See the online appendix.

73. In particular, Nigel Farage, the leader of UK Independence Party, spent the entire campaign totaling up the amounts transferred to Europe that could have been used to pay for the National Health Service. Of course, he seriously inflated the numbers to make his point.

74. Treaty on the democratization of Europe (www.tdem.eu), article 9.

have been joined by others in northern Europe (especially in the Netherlands). The argument is that every proposal to levy a common European tax or increase the common EU budget is an attempt by the countries of southern Europe, including France (which is said to be badly managed), to lay hands on the wealth painstakingly produced by the virtuous and hard-working Europeans of the north. This is not the place to explain how such distrust reached this level, which at times resembles an identity conflict. No doubt the French government's recurrent tendency to complain about European budget rules that it helped to define (without proposing new rules to replace them) has long been irritating to Germans and others. Remember, too, that the Greek debt crisis began when Greek officials revealed that they had been seriously understating their country's deficit—a cause of significant mistrust.[75] On the other hand, it is clear that the German view—that all of Europe's problems could be solved if only every country would adopt the German model—makes no sense at all: if every country in Europe ran a trade surplus the size of Germany's, the rest of the world could not absorb it. In any case, focusing exclusively on public transfers is not the right way to look at things. There are large flows of private money between states as well, with much of it going to countries like Germany that have invested heavily and profitably in their neighbors. Recall that the outflow of private profits from Eastern Europe vastly exceeds the inflow of public transfers.[76] In the future, it will be important to consider the flows of capital and profits made possible by the integration of the European economy (and the way in which these are affected by current laws and fiscal policies) to avoid focusing exclusively on public balances.[77]

In any event, given the state of mistrust that currently exists in Europe after ten years of financial crisis in which every country has felt misused by the others, it is highly unlikely that any German (or French or other) government could persuade its citizens to transfer fiscal and budgetary authority to a European Assembly without setting a ceiling on any transfers that might result. If raising

---

75. In late 2009, the Greek government announced that its deficit was 12.5 percent of GDP and not 3.7 percent as previously stated. See Chalmers, Davies, and Monti, *European Union Law,* pp. 704–753, for a narrative of events and European responses.

76. See Fig. 12.10 and the online appendix, Fig. S12.10.

77. Note that private flows are partly considered already in the sense that contributions to the European budget (and annual balances) are calculated on the basis of gross national income (GNI), which is equal to GDP corrected by net income flows to and from other countries.

the proposed ceiling of 0.1 percent turns out to be possible, so much the better.[78] But the transfer ceiling should not be used as an excuse to reject the T-Dem proposal, which would remain useful even if explicit transfers were banned outright. The reason for this is that average incomes are not very different within the principal countries of the Eurozone, so the real goal is to reduce inequality within (rather than between) countries.[79] In other words, the lower and middle classes in all countries (including Germany) have much to gain from a more just tax system: for example, a system that would tax large companies at higher rates than small ones, high incomes and large fortunes at higher rates than low incomes and small fortunes, and heavy carbon emitters at higher rates than low carbon emitters. To sum up, the mere fact of establishing more just taxes within each country and protecting against the risk of fiscal competition (because the new taxes would be applied simultaneously in several countries) would in itself constitute decisive progress, even without any transfers.

Furthermore, the calculation of public transfers should of course exclude expenditures and investments by one country for the benefit of all, such as money spent on preventing climate change or housing refugees or educating students from other signatory states. Since the purpose of the common budget is to pay for public goods that will benefit all signatories, citizens of each country should see themselves as members of one and the same political community and view the common budget as something of benefit to all; one might then hope that over time the very concept of balancing each country's contributions against its rebates would cease to be meaningful. Until then, however, one has to accept that trust must be built gradually, lest nationalist reflexes derail the plan.

Ending the Permanent European Public Debt Crisis

The social-federalist project presented here is driven by an ambition to achieve fiscal, social, and environmental justice. The goal is to enable a community of states (in this instance in Europe, but the idea could easily be extended to other contexts) to show that internationalism can lead to more just public policy and not simply to the merciless competition usually associated with European integration (and globalization more generally). In the specific context of the Eurozone, where nineteen countries chose to create a common currency while

---

78. For example, a raise to 0.5 or 1 percent or even higher if agreement could be reached.

79. This is obviously less true outside the Eurozone: if the countries of Eastern Europe are included, then significant transfers and investment flows must be factored in.

maintaining nineteen separate public debts and nineteen different interest rates, our proposal also includes the possibility (if the European Assembly so decides) of borrowing at a common rate of interest.[80]

Once again, in view of the climate of mistrust alluded to earlier, it is important to be clear to avoid misunderstanding and to allow for progress. The point is not to mutualize debt. In other words, it is not to take Germany's debt (64 percent of GDP in 2018) and throw it into the same basket as Italy's debt (132 percent of GDP) and then to ask German and Italian taxpayers to pay off the total amount with no regard to who threw what into the basket. Not that this idea is totally preposterous on its face: young Italians are no more responsible than young Germans for the debt they inherited from their forebears. The point is simply that no German party could possibly win if it assented to debt mutualization. If we are to achieve transnational justice and redraw European borders, we must consider history and politics when dealing with the debt or any other major issue. Specifically, our proposal for dealing with European public debt is inspired by the 2012 German debate on a "public debt redemption fund," with one important difference: we rely on a democratic body, the European Assembly, rather than an automatic rule to decide the pace at which the debt will be repaid.[81] In other words, the EA could decide to pool all or part of the debt of signatory countries in a joint refinancing fund and decide each year, as bonds come due, what portion of the debt to refinance by issuing new bonds. Each country's debt would be placed in a separate account, however, to be serviced by that country's taxpayers but at a rate of interest identical for all. That is the key point.

This point may seem technical, but in reality it is fundamental. Indeed, it was the chaotic course of interest rate spreads between the various countries of the Eurozone that led to the European debt crisis (even though European public debt on the eve of the crisis was no higher than that of the United States, Japan, or the United Kingdom). Why did the Eurozone perform so poorly after the economic crisis of 2008? Because of a lack of organization and an inability to create a common Eurobond. The crisis began in the private financial sector

---

80. Bouju et al., "Manifesto for the Democratization of Europe," article 10.

81. In the German proposal for a "redemption fund" (a rather moralistic name), the goal was to reduce total outstanding debt to 60 percent of GDP over a period of twenty to thirty years at a rate (and therefore a primary budget surplus) to be decided in advance. But it is neither realistic nor wise to lock such a decision in without regard to changing economic circumstances.

in the United States, but the Eurozone alone must bear the blame for transforming it into a persistent crisis of public debt. The consequences have been dramatic, particularly in terms of rising unemployment, identitarian retreat, and growing anti-immigrant sentiment. Prior to the crisis, however, European integration seemed to be succeeding: unemployment was down, the extreme right was in retreat, and migrant flows were higher than in the United States.[82]

The emergency measures to which the Eurozone countries agreed to cope with the debt crisis did nothing to resolve the long-term issues, however, and they will need to be revisited in one way or another (unless their terms are simply ignored, which will only make everyone unhappy and exacerbate tensions). The new rules set by the 2012 budget treaty (the Treaty on Stability, Coordination and Governance in the Economic and Monetary Union, or TSCG) stipulate that, in theory, deficits must not exceed 0.5 percent of GDP.[83] Barring "exceptional circumstances," failure to obey the debt and deficit rules is supposed to be met with an automatic penalty. In practice, however, the rules are so absurd that they are unenforceable. The deficit in question is the secondary deficit; that is, the deficit after payment of interest on public debt. If a country's public debt equals 100 percent of GDP and the interest rate is 4 percent, it needs to realize a primary surplus of 3.5 percent of GDP to stay within the rules. In other words, taxpayers must pay more in taxes than they receive back in government spending, with a gap between the two equal to 3.5 percent of GDP, possibly for decades.

In the abstract, the approach envisioned by the TSCG is not illogical: once one rules out exceptional measures such as debt restructuring and cancellation,

---

82. According to UN demographic and migration data, the net flow of migrants into Europe (minus returns) reached 1.4 million a year between 2000 and 2010 and then fell to 0.7 million between 2010 and 2018 despite the refugee spike in 2015. In the United States, which recovered more quickly than Europe from the 2008 recession, the flow remained stable (1 million a year from 2000 to 2010, 0.9 million from 2010 to 2018). See the online appendix, Fig. S16.4. On average, migratory flows into the rich countries were barely 0.2–0.3 percent a year in the period 2000–2020. What is new is that these flows are occurring in a context of demographic stagnation: the annual birth rate is below 1 percent of the population in many rich countries, which means that an inflow of 0.2–0.3 percent a year can over time noticeably alter the composition of the population. Recent experience shows that this can lead to political exploitation of identity differences, especially if policies to promote job creation, new housing, and necessary infrastructure are absent.

83. Except in countries where the debt is "significantly lower than 60 percent of GDP," where the deficit can go as high as 1 percent. See TSCG, Article 3.

if inflation is near zero and growth limited, then running large primary surpluses is the only way to pay down debt on the order of 100 percent of GDP over a period of decades. The social and political consequences of such a choice have to be borne in mind, however. Running large primary surpluses means decades of devoting huge resources to repaying principal and interest on bonds held in the portfolios of wealthy investors while the country forgoes investment in the transition to clean energy, medical research, and education.

In practice, the TSCG rules have never been and never will be enforced. For example, in the fall of 2018, a new crisis erupted between the European Commission and the social-nativist government in Italy. The Italians wanted to increase their deficit to 2.5 percent of GDP, whereas the previous government had promised 1.5 percent. The Commission objected, and a compromise was struck, allowing Italy to run a deficit set officially at 2 percent of GDP but in reality probably somewhere between 2 and 2.5 percent (in any case, significantly above the official limit of 0.5 percent, which no one seemed to take seriously). Given that interest on the debt currently represents about 3 percent of Italian GDP, this means that the country is running a primary surplus of 0.5 to 1 percent of GDP, which is not insignificant: with such a sum Italy could double (or even triple) its total spending on higher education (of just over 0.5 percent of GDP).

Some might find it reassuring to say that the required primary surplus would have been much larger had the Commission and the Eurogroup decided to apply the rules more strictly and to rejoice in such flexibility. But the truth is that it makes no sense to lay down such hyper-rigid rules only to ignore them because they are so absurd, thus ending up with a murky compromise negotiated behind closed doors without open deliberation.[84] Still, one might make do with a requirement that future primary surpluses should be positive but small (less than 1 percent of GDP). In other words, debtor countries could be asked from now on to levy taxes sufficient to cover their spending plus a little bit more, but they would not be expected to pay off old debt at a rapid rate. Such a solution would be tantamount to postponing repayment of the old debt to the distant future (which could be seen as a reasonable compromise). In practice, however, none of this is ever spelled out clearly, and what is expected of one country is not the same as what is expected of another.

---

84. The best proof that the new budgetary rules are not taken seriously is that many European leaders continue to refer to "the 3 percent rule," apparently unaware that the new deficit target is 0.5 percent. This also illustrates the urgent need to bring these issues back within the realm of democratic debate.

In 2015, a clear political decision was made to humiliate Greece, which in the eyes of European (and especially German and French) authorities had elected a "radical left" party, Syriza (a coalition of communist, socialist, and green parties to the left of Pasok, the Greek socialist party, which had been discredited by having held power between 2009 and 2012 at the height of the financial crisis). Having won the election, Syriza sought to soften the terms of the austerity policy imposed on Greece by Europe's leaders. But to avoid handing Syriza a symbolic victory, which European leaders feared might lead to a contagious spread of left-wing resistance (especially in Spain, where Podemos was on the rise), they decided to force the new Greek government to accept an even harsher austerity policy, requiring a primary surplus target of 3 percent of GDP even though Greek output had fallen 25 percent below its 2007 peak.[85] Meanwhile, Europe's leaders ignored the fact that Syriza, for all its faults, was an internationalist party, open to Europe and supportive of immigrants arriving on Greek shores. It would have been wiser to work with the new Greek government to develop a more just fiscal policy for the EU, which might have included higher taxes on wealthy Greeks—and wealthy Germans and French as well.[86]

---

85. See Chap. 12 and the online appendix, Fig. S12.12c. For good measure, in July 2015 Greece was threatened with expulsion from the Eurozone if it refused these conditions (despite the absence of any legal grounds for such a threat).

86. The hostility aroused by Syriza was due in part to the clumsiness of its leaders, who at times during the 2015 crisis gave the impression of seeking special exemptions from the rules for the benefit of Greece alone, whereas resolving the Eurozone's public debt crisis actually called for a global solution applicable to Italy, Portugal, and other countries as well as the establishment of parliamentary bodies in which the influence of each country (including Greece) would have been limited. Nevertheless, all signs are that if European (and especially French and German) leaders had proposed a global response aimed at achieving social justice, Syriza's leaders would have been the first to embrace it. Ultimately, the hostility aroused by Syriza attests to a more general ideological climate of postcommunism and very deep conservatism on economic and financial matters. In particular, East European leaders were often the most hostile to Syriza, which they suspected of retailing socialist-communist promises similar to those for which they had paid the price in the past (in a very different context). They also resented the arrogance that the older member of the European club displayed toward the newcomers (identity conflicts are always close to the surface in Europe). In this respect, the fact that Angela Merkel was born in East Germany was not incidental to her conservatism on these issues (coupled with significant historical amnesia, in that

The European approach to the Greek crisis may have disheartened the radical left, but it emboldened the radical right: three years later, in 2018, a social-nativist government came to power in Italy. This was a coalition held together mainly by hostility to foreigners, but because of Italy's size, European officials were obliged to take a more conciliatory line in dealing with it.[87]

Although today's interest rates on sovereign debt are unusually low—a situation that may not last forever—interest payments on the debt currently amount to 2 percent of Eurozone GDP (the average deficit is 1 percent, and the primary surplus is 1 percent). In other words, more than 200 billion euros a year is being spent on interest payments, compared with a paltry 2 billion euros invested in the Erasmus student exchange program. Is this really the best way to achieve a better future? If such sums were devoted to education and research, Europe could lead the world in innovation, surpassing the United States. In any case, there should be a democratic forum for debating such choices. If there is another financial crisis, or even just an increase in interest rates, the flaws in the budget rules laid down in 2012 will quickly give rise to an explosive situation: the rules will be impossible to enforce, and latent tensions and hostilities among countries will rise to the surface because there is no legitimate democratic institution for seeking a better compromise.[88]

Germans conveniently forgot the debt cancellations from which they benefited in the 1950s) as well as to her willingness to open the gates to Syrian political refugees.

87. Small countries like Greece and Portugal can find themselves forced to accept high primary surplus targets (currently 3–4 percent) lest they find themselves in an even worse situation if forced out of the Eurozone (in view of the small size of their domestic markets and their vital need of European developmental assistance). In a country like Italy, any attempt to impose too high a primary surplus would probably give rise to irresistible internal pressure to exit the European Union. By definition, a primary budget balance means that a country can cover its expenses with its tax revenues and has no need of financial markets (reinforcing the temptation of autarky).

88. The ultimate circumvention of democracy was probably the 2012 treaty establishing the European Stability Mechanism (ESM). Loans from the ESM are conditional upon signing memoranda with the ECB, the Commission, and the International Monetary Fund regarding reforms to be undertaken by the country receiving the loan. These reforms can involve all kinds of issues (including health, education, pensions, and taxes), all without parliamentary oversight or public deliberation. See Chalmers, Davies, and Monti, *European Union Law*, pp. 741–753.

Relying on the History of the Debt; Finding New Solutions

The solution I am proposing here is to place our trust in parliamentary democracy. Open, pluralistic, public deliberation is the only way to achieve the legitimacy necessary for such decisions and to respond in real time to the changing economic, social, and political situation. It is time to reconsider the erroneous belief first enshrined in the Maastricht Treaty of 1992 (and compounded by the TSCG of 2012) that Europe, merely by applying automatic budgetary rules, can have a common currency without parliamentary democracy, a common debt, or common taxes. Under the proposed plan, the European Assembly would be competent to decide on a common refinancing rate for all or part of the debt of member states as well as for rescheduling debt and deciding the pace at which it will be repaid. Countries wishing to benefit from the common bond and common rate of interest must agree to accept the will of the majority of the EA (in which the influence of each country will be limited by design). If a country wishes to retain full sovereignty over its debt and deficit, then it will not be allowed to benefit from the common interest rate. As for the pooled portion of the debt, the EA will be free to choose how payments of principal and interest will be scheduled and serviced.[89] One solution might be to require member states to maintain a primary budget balance: tax revenues are exactly equal to expenditures, neither more nor less. This would amount to a rescheduling of existing debt over a long time horizon. If interest rates on the common debt are low (and kept there, whatever the financial markets do, by the action of the ECB, which will naturally purchase a significant share of the common debt)[90] and nominal growth is significantly higher in the future (which is not guaranteed), then the stock of past debt would gradually shrink in relation to GDP over the decades to come.[91]

---

89. There is no need to formally amend the TSCG because the rules it established would not apply to the common bond that would be issued by the states signing the T-Dem democratization treaty.

90. The T-Dem proposal also provides for increased oversight of the ECB and the European Monetary System, including public hearings and confirmation of nominations, compared with what currently exists. See Bouju et al., "Manifesto for the Democratization of Europe," articles 12–17.

91. With primary budget balance, the stock of debt increases at the rate of interest (since interest is paid by issuing new debt) while GDP increases at the nominal growth rate (the sum of real growth plus inflation). Hence the ratio between the two decreases if the nominal growth rate is higher than the rate of interest. How-

Some might be tempted to engrave the rule of primary budget balance in stone.[92] After all, once the possibility of democratically levying just taxes exists and the EA is authorized to tax high incomes and large fortunes in all signatory states, the idea of collecting just enough in taxes to cover all expenditures is an excellent principle to follow—as a general rule. The problem is that in certain circumstances—an economic crisis, say, leading to a large temporary decrease in tax revenues—such a rule is clearly too rigid. The same is true when long-term interest rates are unusually low (as they are now, partly because private investors are short of investment opportunities),[93] and governments, conversely, are in a position to promote strategic investments. Top priorities among those strategic investments include the transition to renewable sources of energy, the fight against global warming, research, and education.[94] To what extent are governments capable of identifying suitable investment opportunities and channeling funds to where they will do the most good? This is of course

---

ever, if two are equivalent (say 2 percent a year), then the stock of debt does not decrease as a percentage of GDP.

92. Note that such a rule would in any case be less constraining than the 0.5 percent secondary deficit required by the TSCG.

93. Today's low long-term interest rates are also a result of new prudential rules (which for excellent reasons require private financial institutions to hold large amounts of the safest public debt—though without reducing their unprecedentedly large private balance sheets) especially because there are few financial instruments as safe as US and European public debt (which can give a lasting advantage to these countries in a situation in which the share of the global economy deemed less safe is growing and, with it, the amount of savings in search of safe investment opportunities).

94. For an interesting project that would allow willing EU member states to set up a Bank for Climate and Biodiversity (in conjunction with the European Investment Bank and the ECB), see the proposed "Treaty Establishing a Union for Climate and Biodiversity," made public in 2019 under the auspices of the so-called Finance-Climate Pact: Pacte Finance-Climat, "Treaty Establishing a Union for Climate and Biodiversity" (2019), https://www.pacte-climat.net/wp-content/uploads/2019/03/Treaty_Finance_Climate_Pact.pdf. More broadly, it bears emphasizing that the T-Dem was built primarily around the issue of fiscal justice and in particular around the idea of a European Assembly able to levy common taxes to finance a balanced budget. Many issues (particularly financial and banking issues) are barely touched on. The goal is not to end discussion but to open it up around a specific project, which can then be amended and extended with other ideas such as those contained in the Finance-Climate Pact (which, by contrast, may put too much emphasis on banking and borrowing and not enough on fiscal justice and democratization).

a very complex question. Still, we need to create public bodies with the legitimacy to make such decisions. Absent evidence to the contrary, there is no reason to think that we can do better than pluralistic, public deliberation in a parliamentary setting followed by a vote of representatives elected under the most egalitarian possible conditions. The idea that it might be preferable to replace democratic decision making with rigid and automatic rules expresses a nihilistic disillusionment with democracy (which no historical experience justifies).[95]

In practice, the European Assembly could also decide to hasten the liquidation of debt by adopting specific measures such as exceptional progressive taxes on private wealth. Such measures played an important positive role at the end of World War II: they allowed public debt to be reduced quickly, creating room for public investment in reconstruction and growth, especially in Germany and Japan.[96] In hindsight, the most problematic aspect of the panoply of methods used in the postwar period was undoubtedly the recourse to inflation, which did contribute to rapid reduction of the debt but at the price of eating away the savings of the lower and middle classes. In light of such experience, it seems reasonable to maintain the ECB's mandate to keep inflation low and to focus on other proven methods of debt reduction, this time taking advantage of explicit coordination at the European level both to reschedule debt (relying on the ECB to keep interest rates very low) and to levy exceptional taxes (by way of the EA). The EA could decide to reschedule debt, for instance by delaying repayment until the countries of the Eurozone return to levels of employment and growth comparable to those of the pre-crisis period (especially in southern Europe but also throughout the Eurozone). The EA could also decide to delay repayment of the debt until sufficient progress has been made toward other goals, such as combating climate change. This could fairly easily be justified.[97]

---

95. That said, the challenges of transnational democracy are themselves real and unprecedented. If primary budget balance is a necessary condition for moving in the direction of mutualized interest on European public under the democratic supervision of a European Assembly, this would mark a clear improvement over the current situation.

96. See Chap. 10.

97. In practice, rescheduling debt with low (or near-zero) interest and nonindexing to real growth or inflation leads to a significant decrease in the value of the debt in relation to GDP within a few decades, which drains the drama from the issues raised by partial or total cancellation of the debt. For example, this is what happened

To conclude, I want to emphasize that my purpose is not to decide in advance what course should be followed. It is simply to illustrate the need for a democratic body of incontestable legitimacy such as the European Assembly, which would draw on both national parliaments and the European Parliament and be empowered to take the complex decisions that the situation requires. The idea that the significant problems raised by European public debt can be resolved by the kind of automatic budget rules included in the TSCG of 2012, which assumes that lower- and middle-class taxpayers will quietly agree to pay the taxes required to achieve large primary budget surpluses for decades to come, is totally unrealistic. Since 2008, the debt crisis has exacerbated existing tensions among the countries of Europe. In the end, it sowed reciprocal misunderstanding and mistrust among the countries primarily responsible for the construction of the European Union, most notably Germany, France, and Italy. The potential remains for serious political disturbances or even disintegration of the Eurozone. If we go on pretending to resolve these problems behind closed doors, in meetings of heads of state and ministers of finance in which naked power takes precedence over reason, then new crises are likely to erupt. Only the constitution of a true transnational parliamentary democracy offers the possibility of an open and thorough examination of the various options available in the light of historical experience. Without such a thorough examination, no lasting solution is possible.

On the Political Conditions for a Social-Federalist Transformation of Europe

The advantage of the social-federalist approach just outlined is that it would allow a core group of European countries that wished to move toward a stronger political and fiscal union to do so without undermining the current European Union of twenty-seven or twenty-eight member states. Call this new union the European Parliamentary Union, or EPU, to distinguish it from the current European Union (EU). Ideally, the core group of EPU members would include the four largest countries of the Eurozone (Germany, France, Italy, and Spain); at a minimum, two or three of these countries would be needed to make the

---

with the German foreign debt, which was frozen in 1953 by the London conference and ultimately canceled in 1991. See Chap. 10. The creditors in that case were a consortium of Western countries and banks. In the proposal outlined here, it would be mainly the ECB and certain special-purpose entities (such as the ESM).

EPU viable. Of course, it would be best if all the countries of the Eurozone joined up right away, but some non-Eurozone countries might be more eager to join.[98] Regardless of whether the initial core group consists of five, ten, or twenty countries, there is no reason why it could not peacefully and durably coexist with the EU for as long as it takes to convince all EU member states to join the EPU, at which point the two entities could merge. During the transitional phase, the member states of the EPU would participate in both its institutions (including the European Assembly, which would approve the EPU budget and taxes) and the institutions of the EU. If EPU members successfully demonstrate that their more empowered union can achieve greater fiscal, social, and environmental justice that the existing EU, then hopefully most EU member states would eventually, if not immediately, want to sign up.

Such a peaceful transition, though desirable, is unfortunately not the only imaginable scenario. In practice, it is likely that states that have invested heavily in fiscal dumping, such as Luxembourg and Ireland, would fiercely resist. Not only would they refuse to participate in the project; more than likely they would try to sabotage it by arguing that the EPU somehow violated existing treaties. They might even bring suit before the Court of Justice of the European Union (CJEU) on the grounds that only a general revision of the European treaties (requiring a unanimous vote of member states) can end the rule of fiscal unanimity and create a European Assembly allowing decisions by majority vote. The argument that unanimity is required to end the rule of unanimity may seem particularly specious and high-handed, but the national interests at stake (or perceived to be at stake) are so enormous that it would be a mistake to think that such arguments would not be made. The CJEU did validate the intergovernmental treaties signed in 2012 to cope with the financial emergency after determining that there existed no other legal way to respond to the crisis. So it is possible that it would respond in the same way to the Treaty on the Democratization of Europe (or a similar text) on the grounds that there is no other way to deal with the democratic and social emergency.[99] That said, law is not

---

98. For example, it is quite possible that some East European countries (where broad segments of the public reject the conservative-nativist evolution of their homelands as indicated by the high rate of abstention, especially in Poland) and Nordic countries would want to join the EPU before countries like Luxembourg and Ireland, whose governments have invested all their political capital since the 1990s in explaining that their future lies in fiscal dumping.

99. For an analysis of this point, see Hennette et al., *How to Democratize Europe*, pp. 46–52. The TSCG and ESM treaties were designed as simple intergovernmental treaties signed outside the general framework conceived for the revision of

an exact science, so there is no guarantee that the CJEU would approve, in which case the states backing the EPU would have no choice but to renounce the existing EU treaties so as to force other countries to negotiate new ones.

Furthermore, regardless of how the T-Dem or any similar text comes into effect, any attempt by the core countries to establish a common tax system would almost inevitably give rise to tensions with the countries that chose to remain outside. In particular, during the transitional phase, if the EPU decided to tax corporate profits, high incomes, large fortunes, and carbon emissions, it would need to make certain requests of nonmembers for information about cross-border profit flows, income, financial asset holdings, and carbon content of traded goods. Past experience suggests that it would not be easy to obtain their cooperation on such matters. Trade sanctions would likely have to be imposed to obtain the desired information. For example, in regard to taxing corporate profits, one way to deal with the lack of adequate international cooperation might be to apportion the profits of multinational corporations on the basis of the amount of goods and services sold in different countries (independent of the location where the profits are officially—and often fictitiously—reported).[100] All signs are that if the larger countries of the Eurozone imposed sanctions on Luxembourg and Ireland, those countries would quickly yield.[101] But the will to play hardball is indispensable, especially since the sanctioned countries would surely denounce the sanctions as violations of existing treaties.[102]

---

the European treaties, and some states refused to participate (notably the United Kingdom and the Czech Republic), which did not stop the CJEU from approving the method.

100. On this system, which has always been used to allocate taxable profits among the states of the United States and could be applied by the United States or European countries to other countries, see Saez and Zucman, *The Triumph of Injustice*. The larger the core group of the EPU, the more likely it will be to secure significant international cooperation. But the important point is that any country could on its own tax profits fictitiously recorded in noncooperating countries.

101. For example, in 2010, the United States did not need to withdraw the licenses of Swiss banks operating in the United States. The passage of a law providing for such sanctions in case of noncooperation was enough to induce the Swiss to change their banking laws to allow information about accounts held by US citizens to be transmitted automatically to US tax authorities.

102. In particular, apportionment of taxable profits on the basis of sales is equivalent to imposing tariffs on exports of goods and service, except that the tariffs in question are proportional to profits earned at the global level (a firm that makes no profit would not be taxed).

Consider, for example, the US threat in 2010 to withdraw the banking licenses of Swiss banks doing business in the United States. This threat broke a negotiating deadlock, compelling the Swiss government to amend its laws to allow banks to transmit to US tax authorities information about accounts held in Switzerland by US citizens. In Europe, if Germany, France, and Italy were to make similar threats against Luxembourg or Switzerland, the threatened countries would surely protest that sanctions are inconsistent with current European treaties. Unfortunately, such sanctions may be necessary to change the status quo, and they would probably need to be enforced for some period of time before having any real impact.

To sum up, the real obstacle is neither legal or institutional; it is primarily political and ideological. The central question is whether the countries that are suffering most from tax competition—chiefly large countries such as France, Germany, Italy, and Spain—consider the issue important enough to justify a proactive strategy that might include punitive sanctions against states that refuse to cooperate (which might require a unilateral exit from existing treaties). To date, the approach taken by most governments and parties, including socialist and social-democratic parties of one stripe or another, has been to regard tax competition as a problem, to be sure, but a problem that unfortunately cannot be solved as long as Luxembourg, Ireland, and all other countries refuse to give up their veto power. But it has been clear for some time that such an approach leads nowhere. Unfortunately, the governments of the large countries have thus far not felt that the issue was important enough to risk dividing the EU by creating separate political institutions (such as the European Assembly I am proposing) for a subset of countries prepared to move forward. Their hesitation is understandable. But ultimately the risks inherent in the status quo—namely, a definitive and potentially fatal breach between the disadvantaged classes and the proponents of the European project—seem to be greater. Furthermore, the construction of a transnational parliament exercising fiscal sovereignty by way of democratic deliberation is likely to be a fragile process, and it is therefore almost inevitable that it should begin with a small number of countries; only after it has demonstrated its viability need it be extended to the others. In other words, if the process (which would have been easier had it begun sooner) is delayed until all twenty-seven or twenty-eight member states are ready to move forward, it will probably never get started at all.[103]

---

103. The process could have been initiated when the EEC consisted of just six countries (France, Germany, Italy, Belgium, the Netherlands, and Luxembourg) from

Why has the process not already begun? Ultimately, the reason is no doubt that many political leaders and parties, especially in Germany and France and not only of the center-right but also of the center-left, continue to believe that the benefits of fiscal competition (in pressuring states to hold down spending at a time when taxes are already at historically high levels) outweigh the costs of the endless race to the bottom (which benefits those whose capital is most mobile) or at least do not justify the significant political complications that would arise from trying to end it.[104] Another equally important ideological factor is that the European project has long relied on the sacrosanct right of states to enrich themselves through trade and free circulation of goods, capital, and people and then further enrich themselves by siphoning off their neighbors' tax base. In reality, that sacrosanct right does not exist: it is a consequence of a very specific ideological interpretation of the history and politics of the European Union, whose benefits to the upper class in all the member states (including France and Germany) far outweigh any benefits accruing to the lower and middle classes of Ireland and Luxembourg. But leaders have insisted on that right for so long that it has come to be perceived as legitimate.[105]

Finally, although readiness to renounce existing treaties is no doubt a necessary condition for reaching agreement on new ones, it is by no means sufficient. Since the crisis of 2008, various political parties such as Podemos in Spain and LFI in France have toyed with the idea of threatening to exit as a way of forcing the EU to agree to new policies, especially in the area of fiscal and social harmonization.[106] The problem is that these parties have not thus far

---

1957 to 1972. No doubt these countries were preoccupied with other challenges, such as decolonization and the reconstruction of their political systems on the basis of a viable left-right competition at the national level.

104. As I indicated earlier, it is possible to meet the concern about high tax levels by returning to member states all or part of the revenues from common taxes, mainly to finance tax cuts for the lower and middle classes. If need be, this could be included in the treaty; although this is not the most desirable option, it would still represent a major improvement over the status quo.

105. Another factor accounting for the slowness of the movement toward a European Union with a parliament allowed to levy taxes is related to the fact that among the very highly educated elite (and especially among economists) a certain distrust of elected assemblies has emerged, coupled with a growing attraction to governance by unelected committees and rules decided by such committees.

106. The strategy is often formulated as Plan A versus Plan B: Plan A calls for agreement on certain treaty changes while Plan B threatens exit or disobedience in case of failure of Plan A, with the ultimate goal of forging a new agreement with a smaller number of countries. Various versions of the Plan A/Plan B approach were

indicated precisely what new political system they would like to see established in Europe. In short, we know what treaties they would like to renounce but not what treaties they would like to endorse in their place. The problem with this strategy is that is easily caricatured as anti-European, as it has been since 2008 by German and French governments, which in effect instrumentalize the European project to impose their inegalitarian ideology and refusal to consider common taxes at the European level. This is a powerful argument for discrediting these upstart parties in the eyes of a public worried about the prospect of dismantling the EU—an effective strategy for keeping them out of office.

Furthermore, if one of these parties were somehow to come to power in France, for example, the accumulated mistrust between member states (and between France and Germany in particular) could trigger a chaotic and uncontrollable breakdown of the European treaties. Resentment and misunderstanding among countries could ultimately outweigh their attachment to the European ideal. Another risk, in my view at least as likely as the first, is that devotion to Europe would keep the European Union together but, in the absence of any specific commitment to new institutions or precise plans for fiscal and social harmonization, would end in an insipid, disappointing compromise, especially if there is no prior public debate and citizens fail to grapple with these complex yet eminently political questions.[107]

The Separatist Trap and the Catalan Syndrome

What is at stake in the social-federalist transformation of Europe extends far beyond the boundaries of Europe itself. The question is whether a different organization of the global economy is possible. Can the treaties that currently govern free trade and customs unions be replaced by a broader set of interna-

---

developed in the wake of the 2015 Greek crisis and the threats of the German government (and particularly its finance minister) to exclude Greece from the Eurozone to force the Greek government to accede to Germany's wishes.

107. To be clear, I am not saying that it would be enough for a French government to be elected on a platform of remaking the European Union to impose its wishes on other countries. By contrast, it is clear that a French politician who simply declares his desire to renegotiate certain European treaties, as the Socialist candidate did in the 2012 presidential campaign without offering the slightest indication of what he wished to obtain, will not be in a very strong position to get what he wants once elected.

tional accords based on a model of durable and equitable development, with concrete and attainable goals of fiscal, social, and environmental justice? In the absence of such accords, the risk is that the race to the bottom will continue: fiscal dumping will increase; inequality will continue to rise; and xenophobic, identitarian, anti-immigrant political parties will continue to exploit the situation in their pursuit of power.

Another risk involves what one might call the separatist trap. An example of this can be seen in the attempt to organize a referendum on self-determination in Catalonia in 2017. It is striking to see the degree to which regionalist sentiment in Catalonia varied with income and education. When Catalonian voters were asked whether they supported the demand for greater regional autonomy (potentially leading to independence), it turned out that support increased with increasing income and education: support for the regionalist idea ran as high as 80 percent of those polled in the top decile of income or education compared with 40–50 percent among the bottom five deciles (Figs. 16.5–16.6). If we look only at voters supporting a referendum of self-determination (and thus eliminate those favoring greater autonomy within Spain), we find that the cleavage is even more pronounced: support for independence is dramatically higher among the upper classes, particularly those with the highest incomes.[108] Note, too, that support for self-determination increased sharply after the economic crisis, which hit Spain hard after 2009, with a second dip in 2011–2013 after austerity policies were imposed at the European level. Only 20 percent of Catalan voters favored self-determination in 2008, compared with 32 percent in 2011 and 35 percent in 2016.[109] It was because of this rapid increase of support for self-determination that the Catalan government organized an independence referendum in 2017

---

108. See the online appendix, Figs. S16.5–S16.6. See also A. Gethin, C. Martinez-Toledano, and M. Morgan, "Rising Inequalities and Political Cleavages in Spain," WID.world, 2019.

109. All told, 57 percent of Catalan voters in 2008 favored the idea of greater regional autonomy (potentially including self-determination), compared with 61 percent in 2011 and 59 percent in 2016. Between 2008 and 2016, the proportion of those favoring increased regional autonomy within Spain (but without self-determination) decreased while the percentage favoring self-determination increased, even though Catalan obtained greater autonomy in 2010 (as we will see). Note that the questions posed in the survey referred to a regime applicable to all Spanish regions. If one looks at answers to questions specifically dealing with Catalonia, support for self-determination by Catalan voters is ten points higher (up to 45–50 percent in 2017–2018).

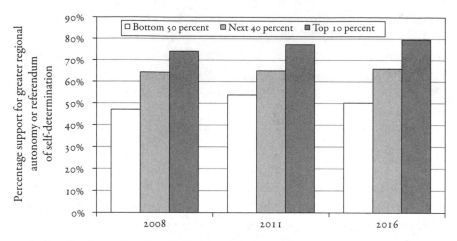

FIG. 16.5. Catalan regionalism and income, 2008–2016

Interpretation: In 2008, 47 percent of Catalan voters belonging to the bottom 50 percent of the income distribution supported greater regional autonomy or a referendum of self-determination (answers to both questions were added), compared with 64 percent of the next 40 percent and 74 percent of the top 10 percent. *Sources and series:* piketty.pse.ens.fr/ideology.

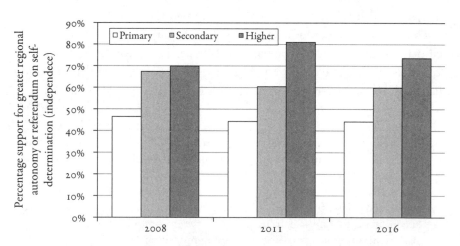

FIG. 16.6. Catalan regionalism and education, 2008–2016

Interpretation: In 2016, 44 percent of Catalan voters with only a primary education supported greater regional autonomy or a referendum on self-determination (independence). The two scores were added. Compare this with 60 percent among those with secondary diplomas and 74 percent of those with tertiary degrees. *Sources and series:* piketty.pse.ens.fr/ideology.

against the will of the government in Madrid; the election was boycotted by parties in favor of keeping Catalonia in Spain, and this precipitated a serious constitutional crisis, which is still ongoing.[110]

It is quite striking to discover that Catalan regionalism is much more pronounced among those with more advantages. It is instructive to compare the social profile of the Catalan vote with the profiles observed in the referenda on Europe conducted in France in 1992 and 2005 and in the United Kingdom in 2016. In all cases we find that the advantaged classes voted heavily for Europe while the disadvantaged rejected it.[111] These vote profiles are perfectly consistent, moreover, since the advantaged classes that supported Catalan independence (or increased autonomy) had no desire to quit the EU—quite the opposite. They wanted Catalonia to remain in the EU but as an independent state so as to continue to benefit from commercial and financial integration with Europe while keeping Catalan tax revenues in Catalonia.

Of course, it would be wrong to reduce Catalan regionalism to a fiscal motive. Cultural and linguistic factors are also important, as is the memory of Francoism and the brutality of the central government in Madrid. Still, the issue of fiscal autonomy played a key role in the Catalan regionalist movement, especially since Catalonia is wealthier on average than the rest of Spain. It is natural to think that the wealthiest taxpayers were particularly exasperated by the thought that some of what they paid in taxes was being transferred to other regions. By contrast, the lower and middle classes may be somewhat more sensitive to the virtues of social and fiscal solidarity. Note, however, that Spain is already a country with one of the most decentralized tax systems in the world, even when compared with much larger federal states. Specifically, since 2011, the income tax has been shared equally between the federal government and the regions.[112] There are many problems with such a

---

110. In the September 2017 independence referendum, "yes" won by 90 percent versus 8 percent for "no" and 2 percent blank, but the participation rate was only 42 percent.

111. See Fig. 14.20 and Fig. 15.18.

112. In 2018, the federal government taxed income at rates of 9.5 percent (for incomes below 12,450 euros) to 22.5 percent (for incomes above 60,000 euros). If a region decides to apply these same rates, then taxpayers in that region would pay total income taxes of 19 to 45 percent, with revenues divided fifty-fifty between Madrid and the region. Each region can also set its own tax brackets and its own additional rates, higher or lower than federal rates. In any case, it keeps the additional revenue and does not have to share it with other regions. These new fiscal

system: it undercuts the very idea of solidarity among citizens and pits region against region, which is particularly problematic when it comes to a tool like the income tax, which is supposed to make it possible to reduce inequality between rich and poor regardless of regional or professional identity.[113]

By way of comparison, in the United States the income tax has always been mainly a federal tax, even though the population is seven times as large as Spain's and despite the American penchant for decentralization and states' rights. Since the creation of the federal income tax in 1913, it has been the main tool for achieving fiscal progressivity, applying the highest rates to the highest incomes.[114] No doubt the wealthy taxpayers of California (a state almost as populous as Spain, with six times the population of Catalonia) would have liked to keep half of the income tax paid by the state's highest earners for themselves and their children, but they never succeeded in doing so (and never really tried, since the idea would have been interpreted as a secessionist declaration of war). Or consider an example closer to Spain: in the German Federal Republic the income tax is exclusively federal. The Länder are not allowed to levy additional taxes or keep any of the revenue for themselves, no matter what the taxpayers of Bavaria may think. To be clear, there is nothing necessarily wrong with levying additional taxes at the regional or local level, provided they remain moderate. But Spain, by choosing to divide income tax revenues fifty-fifty with the regions, probably went too far and now finds

---

decentralization rules were put in place in 2010 for Catalonia and the other regions of Spain. On the other hand, in 2010 the Spanish constitutional court invalidated other aspects of the new autonomy statute (such as the regionalization of justice, a controversial provision) that Catalonia approved by referendum in 2006 after negotiation with the Spanish parliament, which then had a socialist majority. This episode contributed to the hardening of pro-independence sentiment.

113. This system of internal competition has also led since 2011 to tax fraud by wealthy individuals and companies, which for tax purposes misrepresent their residence or place of business, potentially undermining the progressivity of the tax system. See D. Agrawal and D. Foremny, "Relocation of the Rich: Migration in Response to Top Tax Rate Changes from Spanish Reforms," *Review of Economics and Statistics,* 2019.

114. Admittedly, top marginal federal income tax rates have varied widely over time (from an average of more than 80 percent between 1930 and 1980 to around 40 percent since the 1980s), but the fact is that the federal income tax has always played a more important redistributive role than the additional income taxes enacted by the states (generally between 5 and 10 percent).

itself in a situation where some Catalans would like to keep 100 percent for themselves by becoming independent.

Europe also bears heavy responsibility for the Catalan crisis. In addition to its calamitous handling of the Eurozone crisis, to the detriment of Spain in particular, the European Union has for decades been promoting a development model based on the idea that it is possible to have everything at once: an integrated European and global market without any genuine obligation of solidarity or financing of public goods. Under such conditions, why shouldn't Catalonia try its luck and become a tax haven like Luxembourg? For many pro-independence Catalans, that is indeed the goal: as an independent state, Catalonia could keep all of its tax revenues for its own development while at the same time cutting taxes on foreign investors to draw new capital into the region. Not having to share revenues with the rest of Spain would make it that much easier to cut taxes on foreigners. There is no doubt that the politics of Catalan independence would have been totally different if the EU had had a federal budget comparable to that of the United States, financed by progressive federal income and inheritance taxes. If the taxes paid by high earners in Catalonia went to the EU federal budget, just as the US income tax goes to the US federal budget, Catalonia would have only a limited financial interest in separating from Spain. To escape the bonds of fiscal solidarity, it would need to exit Europe with the risk of being barred from the vast European market, the cost of which would be prohibitive in the eyes of many pro-independence Catalans. I am not claiming that the Catalan regionalist and independence movement would then immediately disappear or that it should disappear. But it would be seriously weakened, and its focus would turn to cultural, linguistic, and educational issues, which are important and complex, rather than being obsessed with tax issues and obscure bargains between regions. The Catalan crisis in its present form is a symptom of a Europe that pits region against region in a race to the bottom with no fiscal solidarity whatsoever. Every country seeks advantage for itself by undercutting its partners. The Catalan case shows how the organization of the political system is intimately intertwined with the issues of inequality, borders, and property rights.

Ideological Dissonance, Fiscal Dumping, and the Small-Country Syndrome

The temptations of fiscal competition can be strong, even in communities not initially inclined that way ideologically. Before Luxembourg became a tax haven, it had no particular ideological disposition to assume that role.[115] But once globalization (and in particular the treaties governing the free circulation of capital) developed in such a way as to make this strategy appealing, the temptation became too strong to resist. Small countries are particularly susceptible because the amount of (real or fictitious) investment they can hope to attract is quite large relative to the size of their economies. Neighboring countries may have large tax bases, which can more than make up for whatever domestic revenues may be lost by cutting taxes on the wealthy.[116]

The Swedish case offers a particularly extreme example of ideological dissonance.[117] During the Swedish banking crisis of 1991–1992, Swedes realized that a small country in a world of major financial flows and capital movements is quite exposed and vulnerable. The crisis might have been seen as an occasion to reconsider the dangers of the financial deregulation of the 1980s. In practice, however, it was instrumentalized by people who had believed for decades that the Swedish social model had been pushed too far, that the social democrats had been in power too long, and that it was time for the country to move toward the new Anglo-American liberal model that had emerged from the conservative revolution of the 1980s. The conservative liberals briefly came to power in 1991–1994, long enough to sharply reduce the progressivity of Swedish income and wealth taxes and to institute a flat tax of 30 percent on interest and dividends, which for the first time were exempted from the progressive tax regime. Conservative ideology continued to make inroads in the

---

115. See, for example, the statements by Jean-Claude Juncker cited in Chap. 11.

116. Note, too, that under current European law, it is quite possible to cut taxes only on new taxpayers enticed into the country, for instance, by using the special tax regime for the "stateless," as Denmark has recently done. See H. Kleven, C. Landais, E. Saez, and E. Schultz, "Migration and Wage Effects of Taxing Top Earners: Evidence from the Foreigners' Tax Scheme in Denmark," *Quarterly Journal of Economics,* 2014.

117. A somewhat different example of dissonance is provided by Norway, a country that likes to portray itself as social-democratic and environmentally conscious but that did not hesitate to extract hydrocarbons that should have been left in the ground (if one worries about global warming) to accumulate vast financial reserves. In the series *Occupied* (Netflix, 2015), guilt ultimately leads Norway to stop pumping oil, which triggers a Russian invasion to restart the flow, with the support of a European Union more concerned about its energy supply than about the climate. The EU is depicted as especially cowardly, notably in the person of a not very inspiring French European Commissioner.

1990s and 2000s, and in 2005 and 2007 the progressive tax on inheritances and wealth were abolished.[118]

The Swedish decision to abolish the inheritance tax in 2005, at practically the same time as Hong Kong (2006), illustrates the strength of the "small-country syndrome." Larger countries such as Germany, the United Kingdom, France, Japan, and the United States have all maintained the progressive inheritance tax, assessing rates of 30–55 percent on the largest estates in the late 2010s.[119] But Sweden's social democrats decided it would be a good idea to eliminate any tax on intergenerational wealth transfers, even though Germany's Christian Democrats, Britain's Conservatives, France's Gaullist liberals, and even US Republicans judged it preferable to keep them with reduced but still substantial rates on the largest fortunes.[120] During Swedish debates on these issues, the fear of capital leaks toward other countries of the region played an essential role. Whether justified or exaggerated, these fears did not induce the Swedish government to push for reform of the directives on the circulation of capital or for greater fiscal cooperation in Europe. As in the case of Catalonia, the solution was nevertheless simple: it would have sufficed to levy a progressive tax at the EU level. The fact that the Swedish social democrats never considered making such a proposal shows the degree to which the ideological and political agenda of social democracy remains confined for the moment to the nation-state. To be sure, Sweden remains more egalitarian than other countries thanks to an advanced system of social insurance financed by substantial taxes and social contributions assessed on the entire population as well as to a free

---

118. See Chap. 11 and G. Du Rietz, M. Henrekson, and D. Waldenstrom, "Swedish Inheritance and Gift Taxation (1885–2004)," in *Swedish Taxation: Developments since 1862,* ed. M. Henrekson and M. Stenkula (Palgrave, 2015). The conservative-liberal government of 1991–1994 also had an impact on the educational system, where competition was encouraged. On the influence of some Swedish economists on the liberal turn of the early 1990s, see A. Lindbeck, P. Molander, T. Persson, O. Peterson, A. Sandmo, B. Swedenborg, and N. Thygesen, *Turning Sweden Around* (MIT Press, 1994).

119. See Fig. 10.12, and the online appendix, Figs. S10.12a–S10.12b. There was an attempt to abolish the inheritance tax in the United States under George W. Bush in 2001–2002 and then again under Trump in 2017–2018, but these attempts did not succeed because some Republicans believed they went too far. But the tax threshold was raised significantly, reducing the effectiveness of the tax.

120. In Sweden, it was the social democrats who abolished the inheritance tax in 2005 while it was the liberal conservatives who abolished the wealth tax in 2007 (they were in power from 2006 to 2014).

and high-quality educational system (including higher education). Still, the abolitions of 2005–2007 increased inequality at the top of both the wealth and income distributions in Sweden since 2000 and may ultimately weaken the Swedish model.[121] This resistance to international cooperation made it more difficult to maintain progressive taxes elsewhere, including both rich countries and poor and emerging ones.[122]

What is more, the "small-country syndrome" may spread to larger countries. As emerging economies claim an ever greater share of the global economy, which has grown to unprecedented size, nearly all countries are small in relation to the global economy, including France, Germany, the United Kingdom, and even to a certain extent the United States. For many Conservative leaders, the purpose of Brexit is precisely to turn the United Kingdom into a tax haven and lightly regulated financial center (a postindustrial conversion process that in some respects began in the 1980s). Absent a social-federalist turn, globalization is likely to have the same effect in many other countries.

The Social-Localist Trap and the Construction of the Transnational State

It will not be easy to follow the social-federalist route to building a transnational governmental authority. For that reason, some political movements may be tempted by a social-localist strategy—promoting equality and economic alternatives at the local level. For instance, the Catalan independence movement includes a minority left-wing faction that sees Catalonia as more friendly to social experimentation than the government in Madrid (and that also wants to break with the Spanish monarchy and turn Catalonia into a republic). Unfortunately, it is quite possible that this left-wing group would be outflanked

---

121. The abolitions of 2005–2007 also reflected the perception of some Swedish social-democratic leaders that the country had become so egalitarian that it would not have been useful to tax the very wealthy. They may have forgotten that the country was extremely inegalitarian until the beginning of the twentieth century and that maintaining substantial social equality over the long run requires appropriate institutions. On Sweden's hyper-inegalitarian past, see Chap. 5.

122. The Swedish case was widely instrumentalized in the French debate on abolition of the wealth tax in 2017–2018. It may be exploited again to abolish the inheritance tax. The effect on less developed countries has been even greater because on their own they lack the means to influence the global system of registering and taxing wealth.

and dominated in any future Catalan state by conservative liberals wedded to a very different model of development (of the tax haven variety).

It is of course perfectly legitimate to promote a social-localist agenda, particularly since action at the local and municipal level can indeed offer opportunities to reshape social and property relations complementary to what can be achieved at the central level. Still, it is important that local action be conducted within a more general social-federalist framework. To clear up ambiguities about the various forms of Catalan regionalism and distinguish itself from those who simply want to keep regional tax revenues for themselves and their children, the pro-independence republican left should make clear that it favors common progressive wealth and income taxes at the European level. Just because the path to social federalism is complex is not a reason to be unclear about the broader strategy—quite the contrary.

The broader strategy is especially important because when it comes to the kinds of political action that social localism inspires, there are often fairly obvious limits to what can be achieved unless those actions are complemented by higher level regulations and policies. Take, for example, a recent effort to keep Google out of Berlin. As a result of anti-Google demonstrations, the company decided not to build a new campus in the Kreuzberg district of Berlin. This "campus," like others that Google already operates in London, Madrid, Seoul, São Paulo, Tel Aviv, and Warsaw, was to occupy an old red-brick factory and serve as a place for meetings, events, and training for information technology professionals. The local associations that organized the "Fuck Off Google" movement could legitimately proclaim victory. They had persuasively led the charge against real estate speculation, higher rents, and evictions of low-income families—which, for this already gentrifying neighborhood, would be the inevitable consequences of Google's decision to move in, even though it paid virtually no taxes in Germany and other countries where it earned most of its profits. This successful effort to block Google, a large-scale tax evader, drew a great deal of attention in Berlin, where the Christian Democrats blamed the governing coalition of SPD, Greens, and Die Linke for creating a climate "hostile to entrepreneurs" (which the coalition denies).[123]

Mobilizations of this type raise complex issues. Of course, it is close to unbearable to hear the CDU use the word "entrepreneur" to describe a corporation that pays virtually no taxes, especially since the party has led the federal

---

123. See T. Wieder, "A Berlin, le mouvement 'Fuck Off Google' plus fort que Google," *Le Monde,* October 26, 2018.

government in Germany (Europe's leading economic power) from 2005–2019 without doing anything to make Google accountable. But it is also clear that local mobilizations like the one in Berlin are not enough, partly because other cities will undoubtedly welcome a "Google campus" and partly because the real goal is to be able to tax and regulate a company of Google's size at the European level. And the fact is that the SPD, Greens, and Die Linke have thus far proposed no common plan of action that would make it possible to, say, levy a European tax on the profits of the largest corporations or, at a minimum, a Franco-German tax or a tax levied by the largest possible subset of EU member states. Sticking to social localism and refusing to join an ambitious social-federalist movement also offers adversaries particularly effective lines of attack.

In other contexts, especially in the United States, it is sometimes easier to go from a social-localist commitment to a social-federalist one. Consider the example of Alexandria Ocasio-Cortez (known as AOC), a Democrat from New York who was elected to the House of Representatives in November 2018. A member of the Democratic Socialists of America, AOC took a leading role in the fight to prevent Amazon from building a new headquarters in Brooklyn. As in Berlin, the movement zeroed in on the fact that the company not only pays virtually no tax on its profits but was asking for generous public subsidies, which various cities interested in hosting the new headquarters were competing to provide. Amazon's refusal to allow any union representation added fuel to the fire. The conflict ended when Amazon decided not to go ahead with the Brooklyn project in January 2019. To no one's surprise, Republican and Trumpist pressure groups unleased their wrath against AOC.[124] Unlike the anti-Google activists in Berlin, an elected representative like AOC can champion policies to regulate of large corporations and can also vote for progressive federal taxes (AOC is among those supporting a marginal income tax rate

---

124. One such group was the "Job Creators Network," which supported Trump's corporate tax cuts and "the fight against socialism" (its website features the headline "JCN's Next Mission: Fighting Socialism"). In early 2019 the JCN financed a campaign to plaster the walls of New York with posters attacking AOC: "Amazon Pullout: 25,000 Lost NYC Jobs. $4 Billion in Lost Wages. $12 Billion in Lost Economic Activity for NY. Thanks for Nothing, AOC!" The theme of fighting socialism has also become a top priority of the White House Council of Economic Advisors (as is evident from the report "The Opportunity Costs of Socialism" that the CEA published in October 2018). This shows that the threat of socialism is taken seriously and that significant material resources have been mobilized in the ideological battle.

above 70 percent on the highest incomes).[125] In the European context, by contrast, no such social-federalist platform is even possible unless people mobilize both to transform Europe's institutions and to build transnational coalitions to that end.

The Construction of Indian Political Parties and Cleavages

We have just taken a relatively detailed look at the conditions under which social federalism might develop in Europe and how it might provide a way out of the social-nativist trap. While the European case offers some lessons of general applicability, it remains a fairly special case. If we wish to gain a better understanding of the transformation of political cleavages and the structure of political-ideological conflict in large federal communities as well as of the risk of identitarian withdrawal in electoral democracies, it is absolutely essential that we not confine our attention to Europe and the United States alone. For that reason we will now turn our attention to political cleavages in India and Brazil.

The evolution of the party and cleavage structure of the Indian Union is particularly interesting, in part because it is the largest parliamentary federal republic in the world (with 1.3 billion citizens, compared with 510 million in the European Union and 320 million in the United States) and in part because, as we will see, the Indian party system has evolved since the 1960s toward a classist system while Western electoral democracies have evolved in the opposite direction. The Indian case is highly instructive because it shows that the construction of egalitarian coalitions and classist cleavages can follow a number of different paths and does not depend on exceptional events (such as the two world wars and the Great Depression in the West). This decentering of our gaze outside the West is also essential for rethinking the issue of federalism and deepening our understanding of the identity and ethno-religious cleavages that have emerged in Europe in recent decades. Comparable cleavages exist in India, which has a much longer experience of multiconfessionalism. It is instructive to compare the ways in which these issues are politicized in different countries.

In India's first elections after independence and the partition of Pakistan in 1947, the Congress Party (the Indian National Congress, or INC) played a clearly dominant role. Founded in 1885, INC had led India to independence

---

125. It remains to be seen whether this new rhetoric will lead to real change if the Democrats win the next election (which is not a sure thing, to judge by the record of past Democratic administrations).

by peaceful parliamentary means and therefore enjoyed great legitimacy. The Congress Party had always held a "secularist" multiconfessional view of India and insisted on respect for all religions (whether Hindu, Muslim, Christian, Sikh, Buddhist, Jewish, or atheist). It was also under Congress leadership that the Constitution of 1950 established a system of quotas and "reservations" aimed at giving former untouchables and aboriginal tribes ("scheduled castes/scheduled tribes," or SC/ST) access to higher education, public employment, and elective office. The intent of these policies was to rid the country of the inegalitarian heritage of the old caste system, which British colonialism had helped to rigidify. In practice, Congress relied on traditional local elites, often drawn from the highest castes, especially the Brahmin literati (like the Nehru-Gandhi family). INC combined a certain progressivism with various forms of social and political conservativism with respect to issues of property and education as indicated by the absence of real agrarian reform in India and insufficient investment in public services, health, and education for the socially disadvantaged.[126]

In the legislative elections of 1951, 1957, and 1962, INC took 45 to 50 percent of the vote, enough to win a comfortable majority in the Lok Sabha given the fragmentation of the opposition and the nature of the voting system.[127] The rest of the votes were scattered among a host of ideologically very different parties: regionalists, communists, nationalists, socialists, and so on, none of which seriously threatened the dominance of the Congress Party. In the 1957 and 1962 elections, the country's second leading party was the Communist Party of India (CPI), which took roughly 10 percent of the vote at the federal level.[128] The Hindu nationalists of Bharatiya Jana Sangh (BJS, or party of Hindu people) finished third, with less than 7 percent of the vote. INC's unchallenged dominance began to crumble in the 1960s and 1970s. The Congress vote fell below 40 percent, and it lost power for the first time in 1977 with the victory of the Janata Party (party of the people). But this was an ad hoc anti-INC coalition of

---

126. See Chap. 8.

127. A uninominal one-round system as in the United Kingdom and the United States.

128. In 1964, the CPI split into several parties, including the CPI and the CPI(M), mainly over the issue of the Russia-China spit and political strategy (whether to ally with the INC or pursue an independent strategy). The CPI(M) has held power in a number of Indian states since the 1970s, including West Bengal and Kerala, generally as the leader of a "Left Front" or "Left Democratic Front" coalition involving several left-wing parties.

left- and right-wing opponents of Indira Gandhi's Congress with no real common program.[129] It did not last. INC bounced back, more united and coherent than before, and regained power in the 1980 elections. All in all, India was governed virtually without interruption by INC and by prime ministers of the Nehru-Gandhi family for four decades, from the late 1940s to the late 1980s.[130]

After the first phase of Indian democracy, which the Congress Party dominated from 1950 to 1990, came the second phase (1990–2020), characterized by the gradual development of a true multiparty system with parties alternating in power at the federal level. When we look at the results obtained by the various parties in elections to the Lok Sabha, we find that INC's position began deteriorating around 1990: from 40 percent of the vote in 1989, its score fell to 20 percent in 2014. If we count the various centrist parties allied to Congress, however, the 2014 score comes to around 35 percent—much reduced from the postwar decades but still substantial (Fig. 16.7).[131]

Since 1990, India has witnessed the rise of the Bharatiya Janata Party (BJP).[132] Over time the BJP has become a vast and well-oiled political machine. It describes itself as "the largest political party in the world."[133] The BJP

---

129. Faced with growing social protest of many varieties, Indira Gandhi declared a state of emergency from 1975 to 1977, which temporarily united all the malcontents against her in the 1977 elections.

130. The successive prime ministers were Jawaharlal Nehru from 1947 to 1964, followed by his daughter Indira Gandhi from 1966 to 1977 and then 1980 to 1984, and then Rajiv Gandhi, who held the post from 1984 to 1989 after his mother was assassinated by her Sikh bodyguards in 1984. Note that the Nehru-Gandhi family is not related to Mahatma Gandhi, who joined the INC between the wars and remained a member until he was assassinated by a Hindu nationalist in 1948.

131. As allies of Congress we include the parties that frequently joined coalitions with the INC, especially as part of the United Progressive Alliance (UPA): the National Congress Party, Dravida Munnetra Kazhagam, Telangana Rashtra Samithi, and Biju Janata Dal. See A. Banerjee, A. Gethin, and T. Piketty, "Growing Cleavages in India? Evidence from the Changing Structure of the Electorates, 1962–2014," WID.world, 2019.

132. The name BJP can be translated as "party of the Hindu people" or "party of the Indian people." Since *Bharata* is the traditional name of India in Sanskrit and the BJP promotes an ideology that clearly stresses India's Hindu identity, the first translation seems preferable.

133. The BJP officially claims this title, pointing out that in 2015 its membership exceeded 110 million (see www.bjp.org), compared with about 90 million for the Chinese Communist Party (see Chap. 12).

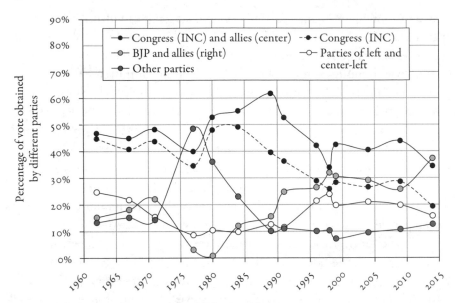

FIG. 16.7. Legislative elections in India (Lok Sabha), 1962–2014

Interpretation: In the 2014 legislative elections, the Congress Party (INC) and allied centrist parties won 34 percent of the vote (19 percent for the INC alone), the BJP (Hindu nationalists) and allied right-wing parties won 37 percent, and the parties of the left and center-left (SP, BSP, CPI, etc.) 16 percent, and other parties 13 percent. *Note:* In the 1977 legislative elections (after the state of emergency), Janata Dal grouped both left and right opponents of the INC and is here classed with "other parties." *Sources and series:* piketty.pse.ens.fr/ideology.

(like its predecessor, the BJS) is also the political and electoral arm of a huge Hindu missionary organization, the Rashtriya Swayamsevak Sangh (RSS), which is a federation of various youth movements ranging from a Hindu version of the Boy Scouts to actual paramilitary organizations.[134] Founded in 1925, the RSS is an organization whose ideology is in many ways the exact opposite of the ideology of INC (founded in 1885). Whereas INC proposed to unite India on the basis of secularism and religious diversity, the RSS has always preached a strictly Hindu and violently anti-Muslim version of nationalism. For instance, one of the founders of RSS, M. S. Golwalkar, alluded to an "800-year war" between Hindus and Muslims in a text that he wrote in 1939 that is one of the movement's foundational documents. In it, he explained how Islam

---

134. RSS translates to "National Volunteer Organization."

had profoundly handicapped the development of Hinduism and of Indian civilization more generally; a civilization, Golwalkar bluntly explained, which over the millennia has achieved a degree of refinement and sophistication never rivaled by Christianity or Islam.[135] Feelings of humiliation and the need for revenge after nearly two centuries of British colonial rule also played a crucial role.

To encourage the rebirth of Hindu civilization, the RSS and BJP have proposed an elaborate vision of the ideal society, which clearly cannot be reduced to religious hostility. Specifically, the principles of social harmony and moderation, embodied in vegetarianism and respect for traditional families, the Hindu religion, and Sanskrit culture, play an essential role in the doctrines they espouse. Nevertheless, hostility to Islam is never very far below the surface. The increasingly violent riots that the RSS and other Hindu religious organizations began to foment in 1984 with an eye to rebuilding a Hindu temple at Ayodhya (Uttar Pradesh), the mythical city of the god Rama as described in the Ramayana, played a central role in the BJP's rise. The destruction of the Babri Masjid (a sixteenth-century mosque) by Hindu activists in Ayodhya in 1992, following years of violence backed by the RSS and BJP then in power in the region, marked a decisive step.[136] Numerous similar riots ensued and continue to plague

---

135. See M. S. Golwalkar, *We, or Our Nationhood Defined* (1939), pp. 49–50. Golwalkar's vehement opposition to Islam and Hindu nationalism call to mind Chateaubriand's remarks in his 1802 *Génie du christianisme* (see Chap. 7). The RSS and BJP have at times used anti-Christian rhetoric and participated in anti-Christian actions (notably directed against Christian missionaries and their efforts to convert certain aboriginal tribes). But in the Indian context it was naturally the rivalry with Islam, which over the centuries had attracted numerous converts from the lower castes, that played the central role (see Chap. 8). Another classic RSS theme is that Hinduism, owing to its sense of moderation, respect for the planet, and vegetarianism, is the only viable alternative to Western ideologies and particularly to the opposition between capitalism and communism.

136. The RSS, which was briefly banned in 1948 after Gandhi was assassinated by a former member of the organization, was banned again in 1992 after members of the group participated in the destruction of the mosque. It was rehabilitated the following year, however, when the courts found that direct involvement of RSS leaders in organizing the riots had not been proven. According to Hindu activists, the Babri Masjid was built in the sixteenth century on a site formerly occupied by a temple dedicated to Rama. Archeological excavation has shown that many structures were built in the neighborhood of the site without definitively settling the matter.

the country.[137] In the BJP's 2019 campaign manifesto, the promise to rebuild a temple of Rama on the site of the Ayodhya mosque is still listed among the party's top priorities.[138]

In addition to the two main electoral blocs led by INC and BJP, there is a persistent third bloc consisting of parties of the left and center-left (Fig. 16.7). This group includes not only the various communist parties (CPI, CPI[M] [Marxist], and so on) but also a large number of parties that describe themselves as socialist or social-democratic, such as the Samajwadi Party (SP, a socialist party descended from the secularist branch of the Janata Party coalition of 1977–1980 and its brief rebirth as Janata Dal in 1989–1991) as well as lower-caste parties such as the Bahujan Samaj Party (BSP, "party of the majoritarian society"), about which I will say more later.[139] These parties play a central role in certain states and receive about 20 percent of the vote at the federal level. Ideologically, they are generally closer to INC than to the BJP but do not officially endorse either camp. The SP and BSP formed an explicit alliance in the 2019 elections. Whether they will join Congress or not is one of the key political questions facing India today.[140]

Indian Political Cleavages: Between Class, Caste, and Religion

We turn next to the question of how the structure of India's various electorates has evolved in relation to their respective ideologies. Let us begin with the vote for the BJP and its allies as a function of caste and religion (Fig. 16.8).[141]

---

137. In addition to destroying mosques, the principal motives of anti-Muslim riots have to with the illegal slaughter of animals and failure to respect certain holidays. See Chap. 8.

138. See BJP, *Sankalp Patra: Lok Sabha 2019* (Shahdol, India, 2019), https://www .bjp.org/en/manifesto2019, section on "Cultural Heritage." The case is still in the courts, with new excavations under way to determine how the site might be shared between Hindus and Muslims.

139. This group includes the following parties: CPI, CPI(M), SP, BSP, Janata Dal (United), Janata Dal (Secular), Rashtriya Janata Dal, and All India Trinamool Congress. See Banerjee, Gethin, and Piketty, "Growing Cleavages in India?"

140. In practice, the two coalitions, SP-BSP and INC-allies avoid running against each other in some states and strategic districts where alliance against the BJP and its allies seems indispensable, but they have not yet come to the point of concluding an explicit national alliance.

141. For a detailed presentation of the results and the postelection surveys used, see the online appendix and Banerjee, Gethin, and Piketty, "Growing Cleavages in

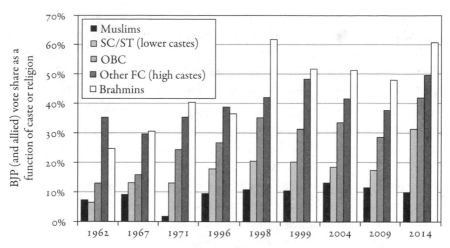

FIG. 16.8. The BJP vote by caste and religion in India, 1962–2014

Interpretation: In 2014, 10 percent of Muslim voters voted for the BJP (Hindu nationalists) and allied parties, compared with 31 percent of the SC/ST (scheduled castes/scheduled tribes, lower castes), 42 percent of OBC (other backward classes, intermediate castes), 49 percent of other FC (forward castes, high castes excluding Brahmins), and 61 percent of Brahmins. *Sources and series:* piketty.pse.ens.fr/ideology.

Broadly speaking, we find that there has always been a very strong cleavage in the structure of the BJP vote. Unsurprisingly, voters identifying as Muslim have never been tempted to vote for the BJP (barely 10 percent of them do so). In other words, 90 percent of Muslim voters have always voted for parties other than the BJP. In view of the BJP's violent anti-Muslim rhetoric, this is hardly surprising. Within the Hindu electorate, we find that the BJP vote has always been an increasing function of caste, in the sense that the likelihood that a voter will vote for the BJP or its allies is systematically lower among the lowest castes, especially the former untouchables and members of aboriginal tribes (SC/ST). It is slightly higher among the "other backward classes" (OBC), and it peaks among the highest castes, especially Brahmins. For instance, in the 1998 and 2014 elections, we find that 60 percent of Brahmins voted for the BJP.

India?" Records of the postelection surveys have been kept from 1962 to 2014, although some files are unfortunately missing and some surveys from the 1980s and early 1990s are defective.

To interpret these results properly, remember that Muslim voters represented 10–15 percent of the Indian population from 1960 to 2010, compared with 25 percent for the SC/ST, 40–45 percent for the OBC, and 15 percent for the high castes (6–7 percent Brahmins).[142] Note, moreover, that it is fairly logical that the BJP electorate is so tilted toward the higher castes. This cleavage reflects the widespread perception among the lower castes that Hindu nationalists attach great value to the traditional social order and to the symbolic and economic domination of the high castes. In particular, the BJP and its allies have often opposed quota systems that favor the lower castes, which they see as an unhelpful cause of division within a supposedly harmonious Hindu society as well as a reduction of the number of places for their children in universities, public employment, and elective office. In view of these positions, it is not surprising that the castes benefiting from the "reservations" system (SC/ST and OBC) are not generally drawn to the BJP.

Looking next at the vote for Congress and its allies as well as for the parties of the left and center-left, we find profiles that are the inverse of those we saw in the BJP vote (Figs. 16.9–16.10). The propensity to vote for INC and parties of the left is highest among Muslim voters, slightly lower among low-caste voters (SC/ST and OBC), and sharply lower among high-caste voters, especially Brahmins. At first sight, this reflects the fact that Congress and the parties of the left have always championed a secularist idea of India, notably by coming to the defense of Muslims against the BJP. They have also fought to reduce inequality between the lower castes and the upper castes by backing various quota systems.

Several points deserve further comment, however. First, the magnitude of the observed cleavages is striking. Among Muslim voters we regularly find votes of 50–60 percent in favor of INC and its allies and 20–30 percent for the parties of the left and center-left (for a total of 80–90 percent). The levels observed among lower-caste voters (especially SC/ST) are nearly as high. By contrast, high-caste support for these parties is very low, particularly toward the end of the period.

---

142. See Figs. 8.2–8.5 and Tables 8.1–8.2. Voters of other religions (Christians, Buddhists, Sikhs, etc.; roughly 5 percent of the population) voted on average in a way similar to Muslims and the low castes. The sample sizes are too small, however, to analyze their behavior separately, and they have been omitted from the analysis presented here. See Banerjee, Gethin, and Piketty, "Growing Cleavages in India?"

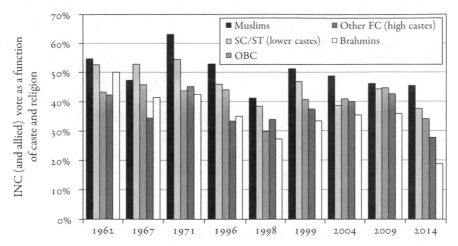

FIG. 16.9. Congress party vote by caste and religion in India, 1962–2014

Interpretation: In 2014, 45 percent of Muslims voters voted for Indian National Congress (INC) and allied parties, compared with 38 percent of SC/ST (scheduled castes/scheduled tribes, lower castes), 34 percent of OBC (other backward classes, intermediate castes), 27 percent of other FC (forward castes, high castes excluding Brahmins), and 18 percent of Brahmins. *Sources and series:* piketty.pse.ens.fr/ideology.

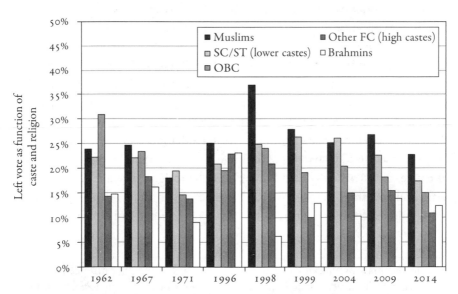

FIG. 16.10. The left vote by caste and religion in India, 1962–2014

Interpretation: In 2014, 23 percent of Muslim voters voted for parties of the left/center-left (SP, BSP, CPI, etc.), compared with 17 percent of SC/ST (scheduled castes/scheduled tribes, lower castes), 15 percent of OBC (other backward classes, intermediate castes), 11 percent of other FC (forward castes, high castes excluding Brahmins), and 12 percent of Brahmins. *Sources and series:* piketty.pse.ens.fr/ideology.

It is particularly interesting to note that in the 1960s (and probably also in the 1950s, although the absence of postelection surveys prior to 1962 makes it impossible to be precise), the Congress Party enjoyed substantially higher support among high-caste voters, especially Brahmins, who were more likely to vote for INC than were the other high castes (Kshatriyas, Rajputs, Banyas, and so on) in the 1962 and 1967 elections (Fig. 16.9). This reflects the fact that in the early decades of the Indian Republic, INC was a quasi-hegemonic party, which captured a very high proportion of the vote—around 40–50 percent on average, among all social groups, including local elites and in particular Brahmins, the caste from which the Nehru-Gandhi family sprang and which played a key role in organizing the party at the local level both before and after independence.[143] In the 1960s, Congress was still doing nearly as well among Brahmins as among Muslims and lower-caste Hindus. Since then, the profile of INC vote has been totally transformed. Support from the high castes fell away in the 1970s and 1980s and even more between 1990 and 2010 as the upper-caste vote was captured by the BJP. In the 2014 elections, the structure of the Congress vote no longer bore any relation to that of the 1960s: Muslim and lower-caste voters continued to place their confidence in INC, but support fell off rapidly in the higher levels of the caste hierarchy.

To sum up: over the past half century, India gradually moved from a system in which one party, Congress, was quasi-hegemonic, owing to its role in achieving independence (which won it the support of all social classes), to a "classist" party system, in which the Hindu nationalists of the BJP receive a disproportionate share of upper-caste votes while Congress and the parties of the left capture the bulk of the lower-caste vote. In other words, while the classist system has been disappearing in the Western democracies, which are increasingly characterized by systems of multiple elites (a "Brahmin left" that captures the votes of the highly educated and a "merchant right" that appeals to the well paid and wealthy), a classist system has emerged in India as the higher castes (Brahmins, warriors, and merchants) have quit Congress and joined the BJP.

---

143. In the 1946 provincial elections organized by the British, with a censitary suffrage (under which about 20 percent of the adult population enjoyed the right to vote), Congress won 80 percent of the seats, of which nearly 50 percent were occupied by Brahmins, provoking the rage of B. R. Ambelkar. See A. Teltumbde, *Republic of Caste* (Navayana, 2018), p. 143. On the subject of Ambelkar, the political leader of the lower castes, who was at odds with Congress in the 1930s and 1940s, see Chap. 8.

The Difficult Emergence of Classist Cleavages in India

One key point remains to be clarified, however. Can the electoral cleavages observed in India really be described as "classist," or should they rather be called "casteist"—that is, more closely related to caste and religious identity than to socioeconomic characteristics? There is no simple answer to this question, in part because there is a high degree of correlation among the variables involved and in part because the available data are not adequate to yield a clearer answer.

Consider the correlation among the key variables. Remember that the high castes were on average more highly educated than the rest of the population and also had higher incomes and greater wealth. In particular, individuals who identified themselves as Brahmins, who were already more educated and owned more property in the colonial era, remained at the top of all three hierarchies in the late twentieth and early twenty-first centuries. Other high-caste individuals were distinctly less educated but almost always high in the income and wealth distributions. By contrast, Muslims on average remain fairly low in all three dimensions, scarcely higher than the SC/ST, while the OBC fall in between those two groups and the high castes.[144] In other words, the caste hierarchy used to represent the electoral cleavages in Figs. 16.6–16.8 roughly corresponds to the socioeconomic hierarchy based on educational level, income, and wealth.[145]

Nevertheless, while the two hierarchies overlap on average, they do not perfectly coincide at the individual level. In other words, there are many high-caste voters, including Brahmins, who are less educated and have lower incomes and less wealth than many OBC, Muslim, or SC/ST voters. Note, too, that the correlations among the three dimensions of social inequality vary from state to state (for example, the proportion of high-caste individuals is higher in northern India than in southern India), and the politicization of caste and class also varies widely from region to region. To clarify things, the most natural way to proceed is to introduce control variables so that we can reason in terms of "other things being equal." Unfortunately, Indian postelection surveys do not contain variables that would allow us to correctly measure income and wealth

---

144. See Chap. 8 and N. Bharti, "Wealth Inequality, Class and Caste in India, 1951–2012," WID.world, 2018.

145. With one important difference: Muslim voters vote more to the left than the SC/ST, whereas they stand slightly higher in the socioeconomic hierarchy.

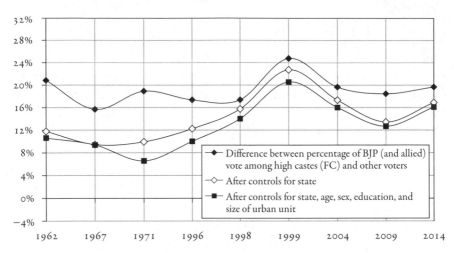

FIG. 16.11. The BJP vote among the high castes, 1962–2014

Interpretation: In the period 1962–2014, high-caste voters (FC, or forward castes) always voted more heavily than others for the BJP (and allies) before and after application of control variables. The caste effect (after controls) seems to have increased over time. *Sources and series:* piketty.pse.ens.fr/ideology.

(on a comparable basis over time). If we introduce controls for state, age, sex, education, and urban size, we obtain the following results.

Looking first at the BJP vote among the high castes (relative to other voters), we find that introducing controls somewhat reduces the magnitude of the "high-caste effect." It remains quite strong, however, and even increases over time (Fig. 16.11). We obtain a comparable result when we look at the BJP vote among the lower castes (SC/ST) relative to other voters (Fig. 16.12). Finally, the religious cleavage between Hindus (of all castes) and Muslims is barely diminished when we introduce controls; what is more, it strongly increases over time (Fig. 16.13).

It is hard to say how these results might change if we had better socioeconomic control variables (especially for income and wealth). Clearly, the religious cleavage would remain, which is not very surprising, given the BJP's very antagonistic attitude toward Muslims. Given the small effect of introducing controls (other than for region), it seems likely that the caste effect would also remain quite pronounced. The fact that caste can have an effect on voting independent of socioeconomic characteristics is in any case not very surprising given the importance of caste-based quotas in the Indian debate. If redistribution in India were based primarily on income and wealth—for

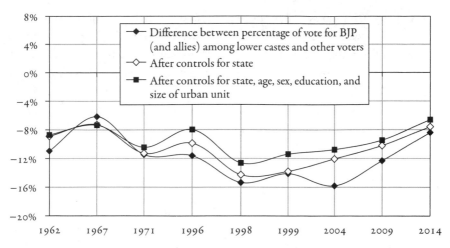

FIG. 16.12. The BJP vote among the lower castes, 1962–2014

Interpretation: In the period 1962–2014, low-caste voters (SC/ST, scheduled castes/scheduled tribes) were always less likely than others to vote for the BJP (and allies) both before and after application of controls. *Sources and series:* piketty.pse.ens.fr/ideology.

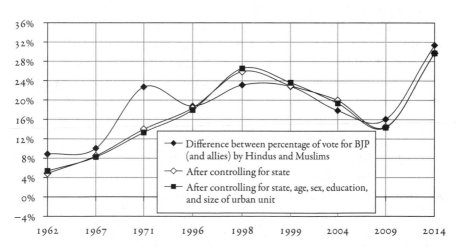

FIG. 16.13. The BJP and the religious cleavage in India, 1962–2014

Interpretation: In the period 1962–2014, Hindu voters (of all castes: SC/ST, OBC, and FC) were always more likely than Muslim voters to vote for the BJP (and allies) before and after application of controls. The size of the religious cleavage has significantly increased over time. *Sources and series:* piketty.pse.ens.fr/ideology.

example, by using taxes and money transfers dependent on those variables—or if preferential admission to universities and public employment depended on parental income or family wealth (rather than on caste as such), then it would be more surprising that caste remains the principal determinant of political cleavages. But since India makes limited use of social redistribution policies based on income and wealth, and quotas play a key role in structuring political conflict, the fact that politicization depends more on caste than on class should not be surprising.

On the Perception of a Common Fate
Among the Disadvantaged Classes

These results are particularly instructive for a Western observer because they show that electoral cleavages are historically and political constructed. They depend on the mobilization strategies of the parties and on the tools available for social redistribution. They are not fixed for all time and may evolve as political and ideological constructs change in complex ways. Note, too, that in contrast to what we find in recent decades in Europe and the United States where the white working class tends not to vote for the same parties as the Muslim or black minorities, in India lower-caste Hindus vote for the same parties as the Muslim minority (namely, Congress and the parties of the left). This again is valuable information because it shows that racism and Islamophobia are no more natural among the disadvantaged classes than among the elite. These attitudes are historically and socially constructed and depend on the tools available for building social solidarity and on the mobilization strategies of all parties.

In the Indian case, if low-caste Hindus and Muslims vote for the same parties, it is not just because both groups see themselves as targets of the high castes and Hindu nationalists of the BJP. It is also because the quota system has created de facto solidarity between the OBC and Muslims. The new quotas implemented in 1990 in favor of the OBC had important consequences. Recall that the original postwar "reservations" system covered only the former untouchables and aboriginal tribes (SC/ST). The constitution of 1950 did anticipate its extension to "OBC," but the issue was so explosive that it was not until 1990 that the new quotas were actually implemented following the proposals of the Mandal Commission (1978–1980).[146] The key point is that, unlike the quotas

---

146. The decisive contribution of the governments led by the Janata Party in 1977–1980 and by Janata Dal in 1989–1991 was to create this commission and introduce the

benefiting the SC/ST from which Muslims were excluded, the 1990 "reservations" favoring the OBC applied to both disadvantaged Hindus and disadvantaged Muslims. A system was established to gauge the living conditions and material needs of various social groups, based mainly on employment, housing, assets, and land (and not religion). An identical income ceiling was set for all groups: anyone who made more than that was ineligible for quota benefits.[147]

The new quotas were fiercely opposed by the higher castes, which feared, not without reason, that precious places would be taken from their children. The BJP was particularly hostile to the new system, which not only disadvantaged the children of its electorate but also awarded some of their places to the reviled Muslim minority. By contrast, among the disadvantaged, the new system played a key role in fostering a community of interests and fates between Hindus and Muslims, which came together in defense of the system. Several political parties emerged to defend the rights of the lower castes (SC/ST and Hindu and Muslim OBC) against the historical high-caste monopoly of India's top posts. I am thinking in particular of the lower-caste party BSP, whose name is usually translated as "party of the majoritarian society." Created in 1984 to defend the interests of the disadvantaged and denounce the privileges of the upper classes, the BSP—led by the charismatic Kumari Mayawati, the first women descended from the former untouchables (SC) to head a regional government in India—formed an alliance with the socialist SP (Samajwadi Party) in the 1993 regional elections to oust the BJP from power in Uttar Pradesh. These electoral clashes have continued from the 1990s to the present and have had a significant impact on the country.[148]

Whatever the limitations of a political program based on "reservations," and despite the sometimes chaotic nature of the coalitions associated with the spate

OBC quotas. See Chap. 8 and especially C. Jaffrelot's analyses of democratization by caste in India. To a large extent, the disintegration of the Janata Party coalition in 1980 was a result of the clash between Mandal and Mandir: the secularist and socialist parties chose to support the process initiated by the Mandal Commission, which led to the OBC quotas, while the Hindu nationalists quit the coalition and created the BJP, with the symbolic goal of building a Hindu temple (Mandir) in Ayodhya. See S. Bayly, *Caste, Society and Politics in India from the Eighteenth Century to the Modern Age* (Cambridge University Press, 1999), pp. 297–300.

147. The threshold for belonging to the "creamy layer" is currently 800,000 rupees per year (which excludes about 10 percent of the population). See Chap. 8.

148. Recall that Uttar Pradesh (in northern India) is the most populous Indian state (with 210 million people in 2018) and that elections in the region are widely covered by the Indian media.

of new parties, the fact remains that the emergence of parties representing the lower castes in the period 1990–2020 has played a decisive role in the politicization of inequality and mobilization of the disadvantaged classes. In a sense, just as the New Deal program of public works and social insurance helped to create a community of interests between disadvantaged blacks and whites in the United States (at least for a time), the reservations in favor of the OBC have created solidarity between disadvantaged Hindus and Muslims in India.

Classist Cleavages, Identitarian Cleavages: The Social-Nativist Trap in India

To what extent will classist cleavages and redistributive issues shape Indian democracy in the decades ahead? Although it is obviously impossible to foresee how things will evolve, various hypotheses are possible. There are contradictory forces at work. Several factors tend to reinforce identitarian cleavages. The fact that quota systems play so central a role in Indian politics is problematic. Quotas of course have their place in a broader set of social and fiscal policies, but by themselves they are not enough. Furthermore, "reservations" can lead to endless conflicts over the boundaries of subcastes and *jatis*, which may perpetuate and exacerbate identity conflicts.

In recent decades, moreover, the BJP has deliberately tried to deepen the religious cleavage and stir up hostility against Muslims. Having tried in vain to block the quotas in favor of the OBC in the 1990s, the BJP gradually changed its strategy in the 2000s and 2010s. Aware that it could not win a majority solely by appealing to high-caste voters, the party embarked on a campaign to win over disadvantaged Hindus. This strategy took concrete form when Narendra Modi became party leader. Modi was the first BJP leader to come from the OBC rather than from one of the high castes. Under his leadership the party won the 2014 elections. If one looks at the evolution of the vote structure, it is striking to see how much the BJP and its allies increased their share of the SC/ST and OBC vote in that election (Fig. 16.8). In effect, the BJP successfully split the lower-caste Hindu vote off from the Muslim vote. The split was not as severe in some states, such as Uttar Pradesh, where the lower-caste parties successfully unified the disadvantaged electorate, but the strategy clearly worked in many northern Indian states, including Modi's home state of Gujarat (Fig. 16.14).[149]

---

149. Broadly speaking, party dynamics vary widely at the state level, where we find variable combinations of classist and casteist cleavages. In Delhi, the INC won in

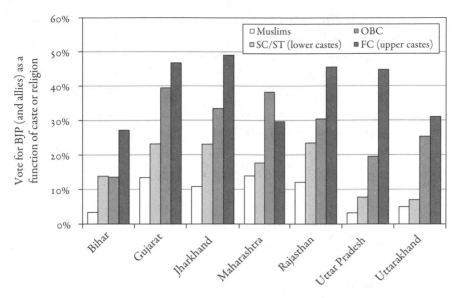

FIG. 16.14. The BJP vote by caste, religion, and state in India, 1996–2016

Interpretation: In all Indian states, the BJP (and allies) did better among FC voters (forward castes, high castes) than among OBC (other backward classes, intermediate castes), SC/ST (scheduled castes/scheduled tribes, lower castes), and Muslims. *Note:* The results indicated here show the average of regional election results from 1996 to 2016. *Sources and series:* piketty.pse.ens.fr/ideology.

The BJP's strategy of wooing the lower-caste Hindu vote rests on several pillars.[150] Modi of course has emphasized his modest background as a humble tea seller in Gujarat (which borders on Pakistan). He joined the RSS at the age of eight. The Congress Party, he insisted, was not only run by a dynasty of the privileged but also incapable of defending India from both its domestic enemies (Muslims) and its foreign enemy (Pakistan). In this connection, it is important to remember that the partition of Pakistan and the subsequent exchange

---

1998, 2003, and 2008 with support from the BSP and by relying on the disadvantaged and immigrant populations whereas the BJP (who won in 1993) did best among wealthy and anti-immigrant voters. See the illuminating book by S. Kumar, *Changing Electoral Politics in Delhi. From Caste to Class* (Sage, 2013). The citizens' anticorruption party—the Aam Aadmi Party—largely claimed the heritage and electorate of the INC-BSP to defeat the BJP in 2013 and 2015—a victory that earned it the implacable antipathy of the federal government.

150. For an illuminating analysis of BJP strategy in the 2014 elections and afterward, see C. Jaffrelot, *L'Inde de Modi. National-populisme et démocratie ethnique* (Fayard, 2019).

of Hindu and Muslim populations has left deep scars.[151] The conflict is in a sense still ongoing in the state of Jammu and Kashmir, whose ties to India are challenged by Muslim separatists who, according to India, use Pakistan as a rear base for preparing acts of terrorism. During the anti-Muslim riots that Modi and the BJP fomented in Gujarat in 2002—the most violent disturbances India had seen since 1947—tracts were circulated accusing the Muslim population, quite implausibly, of preparing an insurrection in case of a Pakistani invasion.[152] India has been permanently traumatized, moreover, by the Muslim terror attacks in Delhi in 2000–2001 and in Mumbai in 2008–2009 (carried out by Pakistani and Indian commandos).[153]

The idea that India's Muslim population of some 180 million—some of whom had ancestors who became Muslims as long ago as the eleventh century—somehow bears responsibility for these terror attacks (or that they were actively preparing for a Pakistani invasion) of course makes no sense, any more than the repeated allegations that Congress and the parties of the left are colluding with Islamist jihadis. But in a context where everyone is seeking explanations of truly traumatic events, it is unfortunately quite common to look

---

151. On this subject, see M. J. Akbar, *India: The Siege Within. Challenges to a Nation's Unity* (UBS Publishers Distributors, 1996).

152. The riots began after Hindus returning from Ayodhya (where they had demonstrated in favor of building a temple dedicated to Rama) died when their train was attacked by projectiles launched from a Muslim neighborhood. Modi, who was then chief minister of Gujarat, publicly accused the entire Muslim community of collective responsibility and implicitly urged his followers to riot. Modi's stirring of religious conflict contributed to his regular reelection as chief minister of Gujarat from 2001 to 2014 and served as a launching platform for the 2014 federal elections. See Jaffrelot, *L'Inde de Modi*, pp. 69–75. See also C. Thomas, *Progroms et ghetto. Les musulmans dans l'Inde contemporaine* (Karthala, 2018).

153. In 2018, ten years after the Mumbai attacks, 80 percent of people polled continue to rank Islamist terror as the principal threat facing the country. Modi—unlike his predecessor, the BJP's Atal Vajpayjee—has always refused to participate in public ceremonies celebrating the end of Ramadan, which he sees as an "appeasement strategy" comparable with Chamberlain's way of dealing with the Nazis. In the 2014 elections, Modi compared the ballot weapon to "bows and arrows under the Moghuls" and regularly referred to Rahul Gandhi as *shehzada* (heir apparent of the Muslim dynasties under the Moghuls). He never misses an opportunity to fan the flames of religious antagonism or to evoke past Muslim domination of India. See Jaffrelot, *L'Inde de Modi*, pp. 124–143.

for accomplices and scapegoats.[154] In such a climate, it is hardly surprising that the attack by Muslim separatists on Indian police in Pulwama (Jammu and Kashmir) a few months before the 2019 elections, followed by air raids on camps in Pakistan (an ideal opportunity for Modi to show his strength), had a decisive impact on the campaign to the advantage of the BJP.[155]

Note that the political issues raised by the exacerbation of the religious cleavage do not end with violence and rioting. In two states—Gujarat and Maharastra—where the BJP has held power, laws were passed to put pressure on Muslims (and to a lesser extent on Christians and Buddhists). The government tightened regulations on the slaughter of animals (extending the religious prohibition from cows to all cattle, violations of which have become a pretext for recurrent lynchings) and on religious conversion (Hindu nationalists argued that the old rules were too lax, leading to abuse by Muslim and Christian missionaries; young Muslims were accused of practicing "love jihad" by seducing gullible Hindu girls). What is ultimately at stake in these controversies is quite clearly the definition of who does and does not belong to the national community. Since 2014, BJP and RSS officials have made many statements showing that their goal is to challenge the very existence of secularism and multiconfessionalism in India, despite guarantees written into the 1950 constitution (which thus far the BJP has been unable to amend for lack of the required two-thirds majority).[156] School and university curricula are being revised to present the entire history of India in an exclusively Hindu and anti-Islamic light.

---

154. Although the situation in France is admittedly less violent, though more and more agitated, the charge that journalists from Mediapart were somehow complicit with Islamist extremism or even with the authors of the 2015 attack on Charlie Hebdo, or more generally, the routine accusations of "Islamo-leftism" leveled at any individual or political movement that defends Muslims and non-European immigrants against the xenophobic, anti-immigrant, anti-refugee right, clearly draw on the same inspiration as the strategy of the BJP.

155. The BJP rose sharply in the polls after these events.

156. In 2017, RSS leader Mohan Bhagwat defended the Hindu reconversion movement known as Ghar Wapsi ("coming back home") as follows: "India's Muslims are also Hindus. . . . We are bringing back our brothers who have gone astray. They did not leave us of their own volition. They were stolen, spirited away. . . . Now the thief has been caught, and everyone knows that my property is in his possession. I am going to take it back, and there is no reason to make a big thing out of this. . . . We need not fear. Why should we be afraid? We are not foreigners. This is our homeland. This is our country. This is the Hindu Rashtra." See Jaffrelot, *L'Inde de Modi*, pp. 172–173.

This is a debate about the very boundaries of the community, and in this case the frontier is internal: Hindu nationalists are arguing that only some members of the community are legitimate, and the rest must either submit or leave.

Boundary conflicts such as these have taken other forms in other contexts. In the United States in the nineteenth century there was talk of sending blacks back to Africa.[157] Then, from 1865 to 1965, the solution was segregation, designed to keep blacks out of white space. Latinos with US citizenship were expelled in veritable pogroms in the 1930s, and children born to undocumented immigrants are threatened today. In Europe, debate has focused on the rules for acquiring citizenship, the legitimacy of past naturalizations, and even the possibility of stripping the nationality of undesirable immigrants and their children and then deporting them. The issues and circumstances vary from case to case, but all illustrate the way in which conflicts over the boundaries of the community come to take precedence over issues of ownership and redistribution, which presuppose agreement on the contours of the community.

The Future of the Classist Cleavage and of Redistribution in India: Intersecting Influences

Despite the forces conspiring to deepen identitarian and religious cleavages, it is important to note that other, no less powerful forces are pushing in the opposite direction. First, the BJP's pro-market, pro-business economic strategy, which was supposed to strengthen India's international position, has led in practice to an extremely inegalitarian distribution of the fruits of growth. The BJP thus finds itself facing the same type of dilemma as Trump and the Republicans in the United States. Since much of the electorate is deriving little benefit from globalization and pro-business policies, one option open to these parties is to turn up the identitarian rhetoric, be it anti-Muslim or anti-Latino, and indeed they have done so. But availing themselves of this option affords other parties the opportunity to propose more appealing alternatives. In the Indian context, it is interesting to note that in the 2019 campaign, the Congress Party proposed a basic income policy: the Nyuntam Aay Yojana (NYAY).[158] The amount proposed was 6,000 rupees per month per household, the equivalent of about 250 euros in purchasing power parity (or one-third that amount at

---

157. Such talk led to the creation of Liberia, although the forced return of blacks never reached the level envisaged by its promoters. See Chap. 6.

158. *Nyuntam Aay Yojana* means system of guaranteed minimum income.

the current exchange rate), which in India is a considerable sum since the median monthly income is less than 400 euros per household. This basic income would go to the poorest 20 percent of the population. The cost would be significant (a little over 1 percent of GDP) but not prohibitive.

In any case, this proposal deserves credit for highlighting the need for redistribution and taking a step beyond the old system of quotas and "reservations," which despite having allowed some lower-caste individuals to attend university, find public jobs, and seek elective office, is by itself not enough. By design, measures like the basic income also encourage disadvantaged groups— whatever their origin or religion—to think of themselves as sharing a common fate. Like other basic income proposals, however, this one should not be regarded as a miracle solution or panacea. Public spending on health in India has stagnated in recent years, and spending on education has actually decreased (as a percentage of GDP).[159] These are precisely the areas in which India has fallen behind China, which has somehow found the resources necessary to improve education and health, on which future development depends.[160] It is important to strike the right balance between reducing poverty and investing in growth-enhancing social programs.

Another important shortcoming of the Congress Party proposal is that it says very little about how it should be financed. What is particularly unfortunate is that this could have been an opportunity for INC to rehabilitate progressive taxation and finally turn the page on its neoliberal phase. In the 1980s and 1990s, the Congress government, under the influence of Reagan and Margaret Thatcher so common in those years, chose to sharply reduce the progressivity of the income tax, which contributed to skyrocketing inequality.[161] No doubt afraid of vicious attacks from the BJP and its business backers if it proposed higher taxes on top earners and large firms, Congress pretended that the

---

159. Health expenditures have stagnated at 1.3 percent of GDP on average between 2009–2013 and 2014–2018 while investment in education fell from 3.1 to 2.6 percent. See N. Bharti and L. Chancel, "Tackling Inequality in India: Is the 2019 Election Campaign Up to the Challenge?" WID.world, 2019.

160. See Chap. 8.

161. See A. Banerjee and T. Piketty, "Top Indian Incomes, 1922–2000," *World Bank Economic Review*, 2005; L. Chancel and T. Piketty, "Indian Income Inequality, 1922–2015: From British Raj to Billionaire Raj?" WID.world, 2017. Income taxes on top earners were cut under both Rajiv Gandhi (1984–1989) and P. V. Narasimha Rao (1991–1996). See also J. Crabtree, *The Billionaire Raj: A Journey Through India's New Gilded Age* (Tim Duggan Books, 2018).

measure could be financed by growth alone, with no new taxes. As comprehensible as this choice was, it undermined the credibility of the proposal and would have limited INC's ability to invest more in health and education had it won, as during its previous stints in government.

Furthermore, without potent measures of fiscal and social justice for which demand in India is high, a more explicit alliance between INC and the parties of the left (such as the CPI, SP, and BSP) seems unlikely. Yet in view of the evolution of voting patterns and electorates in recent decades, such an alliance seems natural as a way of countering the BJP and its allies. In particular, the Congress electorate has become quite similar to the electorate of the parties of the left, in contrast to that of the BJP (Figs. 16.8–16.10). It is also interesting to note that the new alliance (Gathbandan) forged during the campaign between the socialist and lower-caste parties (SP and BSP) resulted in a joint proposal calling for the creation of India's first federal wealth tax, which would bring in roughly enough revenue to pay for the NYAY (basic income) proposed by Congress.[162]

Given the climate of heightened worries about national security in which the campaign unfolded, which benefited the BJP, and owing to the weakness of the other parties (Congress and left), which did not really form a coalition, the Hindu nationalists were reelected in 2019.[163] Debate on these issues will continue in the years ahead. The outcome will become increasingly important to the rest of the world, partly because of India's growing share of the global economy and partly because the debate revolves around issues of identity and inequality similar to those that are roiling the Western democracies. Two key differences stand out, however, and these are particularly instructive for other countries. First, although the importance of the classist cleavage has declined

---

162. The 2019 SP-BSP proposal called for a federal wealth tax of 2 percent on fortunes above 25 million rupees (roughly 1 million euros in purchasing power parity). This would affect about 0.1 percent of the Indian population (or 10 million people) and bring in revenues of roughly 1 percent of GDP. See the online appendix. Note that the introduction of a national minimum income in France in 1988 (*revenu minimum d'insertion*, or RMI) also coincided with the introduction of a new wealth tax (ISF), receipts from which largely covered the cost of the RMI.

163. The BJP and its allies in the National Democratic Alliance (NDA) had 336 of 545 seats in the previous Lok Sabha (281 of which belonged to the BJP); they won 352 (of which 303 belonged to the BJP) in 2019.

in the West since 1980, it has increased in India since 1990.[164] Second, while the white working class has parted company with black and Muslim minorities in Western democracies, in India the Hindu and minority Muslim classes vote for the same parties.[165] Several future trajectories are conceivable, ranging from intensification of conflicts of identity, religion, and inequality to the advent of a secularist redistributive coalition. Whatever choice Indians make and whatever new balance of power emerges among India's parties will have an impact well beyond India's borders.

Note, too, that India's affirmative action "reservations" system, enshrined in the 1950 constitution, is itself being reshaped and redefined. It was initially intended to afford greater upward social mobility to the lower castes (untouchables and aboriginal tribes). The goal was to use quotas to attenuate the persistent effects of a very oppressive heritage of inequality from the old caste society and its rigidification under the British. In 1990, the system was extended to "OBC," and in 1993 a parental income threshold was introduced for deciding who was eligible under the quota system (regardless of class or caste origin). This threshold was extended to the former untouchables and aborigines (SC/ST) in 2018. The BJP, finding itself unable to reduce the quotas open to the lower classes as much as it wished, passed a law in 2019 establishing new quotas for high-caste individuals (including Brahmins), whose parental income fell below the new threshold, at the expense of high-caste individuals with incomes above that level.[166] Interestingly, the BJP decided to do this because a

---

164. Note, too, that the lower classes in India still turn out heavily in Indian elections (sometimes more heavily than the well-to-do), in contrast to what we have found to be the case in Western democracies in recent decades. Some scholars see this as a consequence of a state so weak that the wealthy do not need to mobilize to protect themselves from it. See K. Kasara and P. Suryanarayan, "When Do the Rich Vote Less than the Poor and Why? Explaining Turnout Inequality Around the World," *American Journal of Political Science,* 2015. It may also be that the new lower-caste parties such as the BSP are able to turn out the vote effectively.

165. The same is true of the Christian, Buddhist, Sikh, and other minorities, although the numbers are smaller.

166. See Chap. 8. A constitutional amendment adopted in January 2019 created an additional quota of 10 percent (above the 50 percent of places reserved for SC/ST and OBC) for groups not previously covered by quotas (meaning, in practice, the high castes), whose annual income fell below the threshold of 800,000 rupees. In practice, this income threshold (which excluded about 10 percent of the population) was linked to other criteria having to do with the size of housing and amount of land owned. These rules were supposed to be enforced with the help of a new

large part of its electorate consisted of impoverished upper-caste individuals whose socioeconomic status and educational level were too low to derive full benefit from the country's economic growth. It was adopted by a nearly unanimous vote of the Lok Sabha. These developments suggest that in the future the quota system will likely be transformed from a system based on caste and *jati* to one based more on parental income, wealth, and other socioeconomic criteria.

At a time when Western societies are questioning the low representation of the disadvantaged in the most selective educational institutions, legislative bodies, and top political and administrative posts, India's evolving ways of dealing with such problems deserve close scrutiny, not to idealize or condemn them but to learn from them.[167] To be sure, there is no substitute for adequately financed educational and health services open to all coupled with ambitious policies to reduce income inequality and redistribute wealth. Still, it is possible to justify ways of compensating for social origins in student admissions and selection procedures in conjunction with these other policies.[168]

Conversely, the political-ideological evolutions that take place in Europe and the United States will have a decisive impact on India's future trajectory as well. I have already alluded to the effect of the conservative revolution of the 1980s in the United States and United Kingdom on tax policy in the rest of the world, including India. There will be more of the same in the future. Today, when the SP and BSP propose a progressive wealth tax as a way of paying for the Congress Party's basic income proposal, the BJP can easily argue that these are socialist fantasies that no other country is currently applying and that India's prosperity depends above all on stability of the social order and the property regime. If Europe were to turn in earnest toward social federalism, or if the United States were to return to the steeply progressive tax system it so successfully applied in the past (as more and more Democrats are advocating), then the debate in India and elsewhere would likely take a different turn. By the same token, if the rich countries continue to undercut one another in a race to the bottom on taxes, it will be that much more difficult for a coalition like that of the SP-BSP to persuade the Indian public, given the business commu-

---

and much more reliable system for recording income and wealth. See Bharti and Chancel, "Tackling Inequality in India."

167. See Chap. 8 for a more detailed discussion of India's experiments with quotas and reservations.

168. I will come back to this in the next chapter.

nity's strong opposition to the wealth tax and its role in financing the parties and the media. In that case, the BJP will likely take an even harder line toward Muslims. The world's various inequality regimes are more intimately related than ever before.

The Incomplete Politicization of Inequality in Brazil

In India we have just seen an example of a democracy in which a post-independence party system evolved in recent decades in a classist direction—the opposite of what we found in our study of Western democracies. Obviously, we cannot study the transformation of cleavage structures in all non-Western post-colonial societies. This would take us far beyond the scope of this book. Brazil is nevertheless an interesting case, in which we once again see a classist party system emerging in the period 1989–2018 with important consequences for re-distribution and significant interactions with other parts of the world.

Recall that Brazil was the last country in the Euro-Atlantic world to abolish slavery in 1888. Thereafter the country remained one of the most inegalitarian in the world. Not until the end of the military dictatorship (1964–1985) and the constitution of 1988 was the right to vote extended to all with no educational restriction.[169] The first presidential election under universal suffrage took place in 1989, and the former union worker Luiz Inácio Lula da Silva, backed by the Workers' Party (PT), qualified for the second round, in which he took 47 percent of the vote. In 2002 he was triumphantly elected with 61 percent of the second-round vote, and in 2006 he was reelected by the same margin despite having been mercilessly mocked by traditional Brazilian elites for his lack of education. Although some said that he was not worthy of representing the country abroad, Lula's election marked the beginning of the era of universal suffrage in Brazil. After Dilma Rousseff replaced Lula as the PT candidate, the party continued to win elections, although with shrinking margins (56 percent in 2010, 52 percent in 2014). Finally, in 2018, the nationalist conservative Jair Bolsonaro won with 55 percent of the second-round vote versus 45 percent for PT candidate Fernando Haddad, marking a new turn in Brazil's political history.[170]

---

169. The postslavery constitution of 1891 stipulated that illiterates would not be allowed to vote, and this provision was perpetuated in the constitutions of 1934 and 1946. In 1950, more than 50 percent of the adult population still could not vote. See Chap. 6.

170. The 2018 election took place in unusual circumstances. Lula, designated as his party's candidate, was in prison and prevented by the courts from running.

It is interesting to observe that the structure of the PT electorate and of the Brazilian party system more generally developed gradually over the three decades following the end of the dictatorship. At its inception in the 1980s, the PT did best among industrial workers, lower- to middle-class urban employees, and intellectuals who had mobilized against the dictatorship.[171] Because the lowest levels of education and income were found primarily in rural areas and poor regions, the PT electorate in the 1990s had a slightly higher level of education than the national average (but a slightly lower average income). In short, when the military dictatorship ended, as when independence came in India, the structure of the vote was not inherently classist. Only after Lula came to power did the social composition of the PT clearly change. In the 2006, 2010, 2014, and 2018 elections, PT always did best among less educated and lower-income voters (Fig. 16.15).[172] The evolution was equally dramatic at the regional level. The poorest regions of the country, particularly in the northeast, voted more and more heavily for the PT while the wealthier regions gradually turned away from the party. In the 2014 and 2018 elections the Nordeste continued to deliver large majorities for Rousseff and Haddad while the south (including São Paulo) decisively rejected the party. This social and geographic cleavage coincided with a very pronounced racial cleavage. After 2006 we find that voters identifying as black or mixed race (a little more than half of the population) were much more likely to support the PT than those who identified as white, even after controlling for other socioeconomic characteristics.[173]

The fact that the PT vote evolved in this direction is consistent with the policies the party pursued while in power. From 2002 on, PT governments

---

171. Lula had been a unionized worker in the industrial region of São Paulo, while Rousseff spent three years in prison under the military dictatorship before attending university.

172. As in India, the postelection surveys available in Brazil do not allow us to break down the vote by wealth. For a detailed presentation of the results for Brazil, see A. Gethin, *Cleavage Structures and Distributive Politics* (master's thesis, Paris School of Economics, June 2018), pp. 29–41; A. Gethin and M. Morgan, "Brazil Divided: Hindsights on the Growing Politicization of Inequality," WID.world, 2018.

173. See A. Gethin, "Cleavage Structures and Distributive Politics," p. 38, fig. 3.5. Note that the education and income effects shown in Fig. 16.15 are estimated after controlling for other variables (including region and race). Without controls, the effect of belonging to the top educational or income decile would be approximately twice as high (on the order of fifteen to twenty points rather than six to ten). See the online appendix, Fig. S16.15.

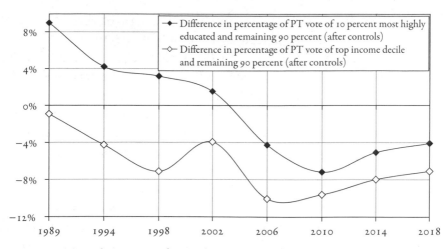

FIG. 16.15. The politicization of inequality in Brazil, 1989–2018

Interpretation: In the period 1989–2018, voting for the PT (workers' party) in Brazil became more and more clearly associated with lower levels of income and education, which was not the case in the first elections after the end of the military dictatorship. *Sources and series:* piketty.pse.ens.fr/ideology.

focused their efforts on reducing poverty, specifically through the social transfer program known as Bolsa Familia. The income of Brazilians in lower-income groups, particularly in the poorest regions of the country, rose sharply, which made Bolsa Familia and PT very popular among farm workers, poor peasants, domestic servants, low-paid service and construction workers, and so on. By contrast, among the employers of such workers, these social programs were often seen as very costly and as incitements to disruptive wage demands. PT governments also significantly increased the minimum wage, whose real value had fallen sharply under the dictatorship but which was restored in the 2010s to the level of the 1950s and early 1960s.[174] The PT also developed programs

---

174. See M. Morgan, *Essays on Income Distribution Methodological, Historical and Institutional Perspectives with Applications to the Case of Brazil (1926–2016),* (PhD diss., Paris School of Economics and EHESS, 2018), p. 106, fig. 3.5, and pp. 135–316, figs. 3.24–3.25. In retrospect, it is clear that it was the 1964 coup, backed by the United States against labor president João Goulart (who had been minister of labor in 1953 at the end of the Vargas era, during a period of important wage hikes), that put an end to the era of inequality reduction in Brazil (1945–1964). The military seized power largely to end what was seen as a socialistic trend subversive of Brazil's proprietarian social order.

to offer preferential access to universities for disadvantaged blacks and persons of mixed race, previously underrepresented on university campuses.

There is little dispute that these redistributive policies, in conjunction with the widening of the class cleavage, drove traditional Brazilian elites to seek ways to regain control of the situation. This desire led to the impeachment and removal of Rousseff in 2016 and then to the election of Bolsonaro in 2018. Bolsonaro portrays himself as the leader who will put an end to the country's drift toward socialism. He does not hide his sympathy for the military dictatorship or his zeal for restoring the social order, respecting property rights, and maintaining security. Like Trump, he relies on the exploitation of racial cleavages and nostalgia for white supremacy in a country in which "whites" are officially no longer in the majority.[175] Despite this, it is clear that the erosion of popularity that comes naturally with holding power in any democracy also played a role in the PT's demise, as did the obvious limitations of the policies it pursued between 2002 and 2016. The party failed to make a serious assault on Brazil's corruption problem, to which it contributed by accepting secret payments in a country where the financing of political parties and the media has never been adequately regulated. To be sure, these deficiencies were related to the fact that Brazil's electoral system and institutions make it very difficult to form a parliamentary majority. Despite repeated massive presidential victories, with substantially more than 50 percent of the second-round vote from 2002 to 2010, the PT could never muster a majority of deputies in support of its policies. It had to bargain with other political groupings to pass laws and approve its budgets.[176] Nor did the PT ever clearly explain the need for greater transparency in public life and for campaign finance reform so that it gave the impression of accommodating to the existing system, with all its flaws.

---

175. In the 2010 census, individuals identifying as "white" represented only 48 percent of the population, compared with 54 percent in 2000. In the states of southern Brazil, whites remain in the majority, however. They account for 70–80 percent of the population of the state of São Paulo and of the states close to Uruguay and Argentina, compared with barely 20–30 percent in the state of Bahia and in the Nordeste.

176. The bargaining occurred because the system under which the Brazilian federal congress is elected makes it very difficult for one party to win a majority (even when it wins more than 60 percent of the vote in the second round of the presidential election, as PT did in 2002 and 2006). In particular, the Brazilian National Congress is chosen by proportional representation at the state level, which leads to a proliferation of regional parties.

Note, too, that the PT's record in reducing inequality had its pluses and minuses. Although people at the lower end of the income spectrum clearly benefited from its policies with an increase in the share of national income going to the bottom 50 percent between 2002 and 2015, this improvement came entirely at the expense of the middle class, or more precisely, of those situated between the bottom 50 percent and the top 10 percent of the income distribution; those in the top 10 percent lost nothing and were able to maintain their position (which in Brazil's case is an unusually powerful one). Indeed, the top 1 percent of the income distribution increased its share of national income between 2002–2015: it remained twice as large as the share of the bottom 50 percent.[177] These disappointing and paradoxical results are easy to explain: the PT never attempted real fiscal reform. The middle class, not the wealthy, paid for its social policies, for the simple reason that the PT never attacked the country's regressive tax structure: Brazil has high indirect and consumption taxes (of up to 30 percent on electric bills, for example) while for historical reasons there is little in the way of progressive taxation of income or wealth (for instance, the tax on the largest inheritances is capped at 4 percent).

Once again, these policy shortcomings stem not only from doctrinal and ideological limitations but also from the absence of an adequate parliamentary majority. Whether in Brazil, Europe, or the United States, it is impossible to reduce inequality as much as one would like without also transforming the political, institutional, and electoral regimes. Note, too, as in India, the importance of outside influences. Quite clearly, it would have been much easier for Lula and the PT to forge ahead with progressive taxes on income and wealth had such tax policies enjoyed widespread international approval, as they might in the future.[178] On the other hand, the current race to the bottom among

---

177. According to available estimates, the share of national income going to the bottom 50 percent rose from 12 to 14 percent in Brazil between 2002 and 2015 while that of the next 40 percent fell from 34 to 32 percent and that of the top 10 percent remained stable at 56 percent. At the same time, the share going to the top 1 percent rose from 26 to 28 percent. See M. Morgan, "Falling Inequality beneath Extreme and Persistent Concentration: New Evidence on Brazil Combining National Accounts, Surveys and Fiscal Data, 2001–2015," WID.world, 2017, figs. 3–4.

178. Note that the reduction of inequality in Brazil in the period 1945–1964 took place at a time when the international ideological context was much more favorable to progressive taxation and redistribution.

countries engaged in tax competition with one another might reinforce the inegalitarian and identitarian orientation of Bolsonaro and his nationalist conservative backers, as it has encouraged Modi and the BJP in India.

Identity and Class Cleavages: Borders and Property

The Brazilian case, like the Indian, shows why it is essential to look beyond the West to understand the political dynamics associated with inequality and redistribution. In the period 1990–2020, as the left-right classist cleavage that had prevailed in Europe and the United States from 1950 to 1980 was crumbling and on the verge of collapse, other types of classist cleavage were emerging in India and Brazil, each following its own specific sociopolitical path and exhibiting its own specific fragilities and potentialities. The variations among these different trajectories show that political and ideological conflict is fundamentally multidimensional.

In every case we have studied, we can clearly distinguish two types of cleavage: one identitarian, the other classist. The identitarian cleavage revolves around the question of borders—that is, the boundaries of the political community with which one identifies and the ethno-religious origins and identities of its members. The classist cleavage revolves around issues of socioeconomic inequality and redistribution and especially the issue of wealth. These cleavages take different forms in Europe and the United States, India and China, Brazil and South Africa, and Russia and the Middle East. But we find both dimensions in most societies, usually with multiple ramifications and subdimensions.

Broadly speaking, the classist cleavage can win out only if the identitarian cleavage can be overcome. In order for political conflict to revolve around inequalities of wealth, income, and education, there must first be agreement about the boundaries of the political community. But the identitarian cleavage is not simply invented by politicians who seek to instrumentalize it to gain power (even if it is easy to identify such politicians in all societies).

The boundary question is fundamental and complex. In a global economy in which different societies are linked by flows of many kinds—commercial, financial, migratory, and cultural—but continue to function as separate political communities, at least in part, it is crucial to describe how those societies dynamically interact. In the postcolonial world, groups of human beings who had never previously had much contact (other than through war or colonial domination) have begun to mix and interact within the confines of a single society. This marks an important step forward for human civilization, but it has also given rise to new identity cleavages.

At the same time, the collapse of communism has at least temporarily stifled hopes for achieving a just economy and transcending capitalism by striving for greater social and fiscal justice. In other words, as the identity cleavage deepened, the class cleavage receded. This is surely the main reason for the rise of inequality since the 1980s. Technological and economic explanations miss the crucial point, which is that economic and property relations can always be organized in more than one way, as exemplified by the extraordinary political and ideological diversity of the inequality regimes we have studied in this book.

We find the same pattern in virtually every region of the world: the identity cleavage deepened and conflicts over boundaries intensified while the wealth cleavage weakened and criticism of wealth became muted. Yet although the pattern may be the same, the variations from society to society remain significant. No deterministic explanation can account for such diversity; what matters are social and political mobilization strategies. Here, the long-term comparative perspective is essential. Inequality regimes were extensively transformed well before the two world wars of the twentieth century. To argue that similar shocks are necessary before inequality can again be so dramatically reduced is to read the past in a very conservative and misleading fashion. The cases of India and Brazil show that identity cleavages need not take precedence over class cleavages. In both countries, disadvantaged classes were able to overcome differences of origin and identity in order to join forces in political coalitions built around seeking more redistributive policies. Everything depends on equipping groups of different origins and identities with the institutional, social, and political tools they need to recognize that what unites them outweighs what divides them.

Studying other national electoral patterns would yield further confirmation of this general fact.[179] The case of Israel is probably the most extreme example of an electoral democracy in which identity conflict has taken precedence over everything else. The relation of the Jewish population to the Palestinian and Israeli Arab populations has become virtually the only significant political issue.

---

179. Note, too, that the multidimensionality of political-ideological conflict is also a factor in countries that are not pluralist electoral democracies, such as China, Russia, Egypt, and Saudi Arabia. But it is harder to see there except in fleeting ways, which makes the collective learning process even more difficult.

In the period 1950–1980, the Israeli Labor Party dominated the party system; one of its main goals were to reduce socioeconomic inequality and foster novel cooperative practices. But because it was unable to come up with a viable political solution acceptable to all constituent communities, which would have required either the creation of a Palestinian state or a novel form of binational federal government, Labor has all but disappeared from the Israeli political scene, leaving more security-minded factions to outbid one another in an endless round of escalation after escalation.[180] In the Muslim countries, the religious and social dimensions of electoral conflict have combined in different ways at different times. In Turkey in the period 1950–1970, the Kemalist Republican People's Party (CHP) was both more secular and more popular among lower-class voters. Those voters differed with more religious voters over agrarian reform and redistribution of land to poor peasants, measures opposed not only by landlords but also by groups determined to protect land held by religious organizations (along with the social role those organizations played). In the period 1990–2010, the Party of Justice and Development (AKP) won over a substantial share of lower-class voters with a program of Muslim and nationalist revival while the CHP vote shifted more toward the cities.[181] In Indonesia, agrarian reform played a similar but more lasting role.[182] I alluded earlier to the absence of land reform in South Africa, where the existence

---

180. The Labor vote, which was quite high among the lower classes in the 1960s, began to center on the more highly educated in the 1980s, apparently reflecting both the transformation of the global ideological context (the turn away from socialism) and the evolving cleavage between Israelis of European and North American origin (Ashkenazim) and those of Middle Eastern and North African origin (Mizrahim and Sephardim). See Y. Berman, "The Long-Run Evolution of Political Cleavages in Israël, 1969–2015," WID.world, 2018. Note, moreover, the near-total absence of fiscal data on income and wealth in Israel despite the country's parliamentary Labor tradition.

181. F. M. Wuthrich, *National Elections in Turkey. People, Politics and the Party System* (Syracuse University Press, 2015).

182. In the early 1960s, some traditional elites transferred land to religious foundations *(waqf)* to avoid agrarian reform, and similar strategies continued to influence the geographic voting patterns for Islamist parties in 2000–2010. See S. Bazzi, G. Koehler-Derrick, and B. Marx, *The Institutional Foundations of Religious Politics: Evidence from Indonesia* (Sciences Po, working paper, 2018). See also P. J. Tan, "Explaining Party System Institutionalization in Indonesia," in *Party System Institutionalization in Asia,* ed. A. Hicken and E. Martinez Kuhonta (Cambridge University Press, 2015), pp. 236–259.

of a hegemonic post-apartheid party has complicated the emergence of any type of class cleavage.[183] By bringing all these cases together and looking closely at many different historical experiences, we gain a better idea of the complex interactions between cleavages based on income and wealth and cleavages based on ethno-religious identity. Looking beyond the West, we find that historical trajectories varied widely with respect to these two dimensions.

Still, despite all these cultural, national, and regional differences, the global ideological context should not be neglected. We saw this in the cases of India and Brazil: the ability of local political forces to promote credible redistribution strategies and give voice to class differences depended in important ways on ideological evolutions in the Western countries.[184] Given the economic, commercial, and financial weight of the United States and the European Union and their decisive influence on the legal framework within which the global economy operates, the political-ideological transformations under way in both regions will be crucial. What happens in China and India and in the medium run in Brazil, Indonesia, or Nigeria will also play a growing role as the world's ideologies become increasingly interconnected. What is certain is that the influence of ideology is not about to decrease— quite the contrary. Questioning of the property regime and the system of borders has never been more intense. Uncertainty about how to respond to recent changes has never been greater. We live in an era that wants to see itself as postideological but is in reality saturated in ideology. Nevertheless, I am convinced that the history recounted in this book can serve as the basis for new thinking about participatory internationalist socialism. The past can teach us how to restructure property regimes and borders to move us closer to a just society and quell the identitarian menace. I will explore these ideas further in the final chapter of the book.

---

183. See Chap. 7.
184. Other cases touched on in this chapter also illustrate the importance of foreign influences on party dynamics. The Cold War heritage and crushing of communist and socialist movements slowed the formation of class cleavages and encouraged the emergence of religious parties not only in Indonesia but also in Malaysia, Thailand, and Turkey. In South Africa, the defense of white landlords by Western governments (and most recently by Donald Trump) impeded ambitious agrarian reform. In Israel, it is obvious that the structure of political conflict could change completely if the United States and European Union decided to force a political settlement of the Israel-Palestine conflict.

The Dead Ends and Pitfalls of the Populism Debate

Before I do that, however, I need to clarify one bit of terminology. In this book I have deliberated avoided invoking the notion of "populism." The reason is simple: the concept is not useful for correctly analyzing the evolutions currently under way. The political-ideological conflicts we see in various parts of the world are profoundly multidimensional. In particular, they involve both cleavages over borders and cleavages over the property regime. "Populism," a word used ad nauseam in public debate, mixes everything up in one indigestible stew.

All too often, the notion is instrumentalized by political actors to designate whatever they do not like and from which they wish to dissociate themselves. It is taken for granted that any party that is anti-immigrant or hostile to foreigners should be regarded as "populist." But parties that call for higher taxes on the wealthy are also characterized as "populist." And if a party dares to suggest that public debt need not be repaid in full, then clearly it deserves to be called "populist" as well. In practice, the term "populism" has become the ultimate weapon in the hands of the objectively privileged social classes, a means to dismiss out of hand any criticism of their preferred political choices and policies. Gone is the need for any debate about novel social and fiscal arrangements or alternative ways of organizing globalization. It is enough to brand dissenters as "populists" to end all discussion with a clear conscience and foreclose debate. In France, for example, it has become commonplace since the 2017 presidential election to classify voters who opted for either Jean-Luc Mélenchon or Marine Le Pen in the first round as "populists," neglecting the fact that Mélenchon voters were on average the most open to immigration of all voters while Le Pen voters were the most fiercely hostile.[185] In the United States, it was not uncommon in 2016 to classify both the internationalist socialist Bernie Sanders and the nativist businessman Donald Trump as "populists." In India, one might characterize as "populist" both Modi's anti-Muslim BJP and the socialist, communist, and lower-caste parties that take a diametrically opposite tack. In Brazil, the label "populist" has been applied to both the authoritarian conservative Bolsonaro movement and the workers' party of former president Lula.

To my mind, the term "populism" should be strictly avoided because it does not help us to understand the world. In particular, it is silent about the multidimensionality of political conflict and about the fact that attitudes toward

---

185. See Fig. 14.1.

wealth and borders can diverge sharply. It is important to distinguish carefully among the various dimensions of political conflict and to analyze carefully and rigorously the political and institutional responses on offer. The debate about populism is vacuous: it licenses a lack of precision. A low point was reached in the debate about public debt during the Eurozone crisis. Any politician, demonstrator, or citizen who dared to suggest that sovereign debt might not be fully and immediately repaid became straightaway the target of pundits: no more "populist" idea was imaginable.

Yet all these enlightened pundits appeared to be almost totally ignorant of the history of public debt, not least the fact that debt had been canceled many times over the centuries and particularly in the twentieth century, often with success. Debt in excess of 200 percent of GDP weighed on any number of countries in 1945–1950, including Germany, Japan, France, and most other countries of Europe, yet it was eliminated within a few years by a combination of one-time taxes on private capital, outright repudiation, rescheduling, and inflation. Europe was built in the 1950s by wiping away past debt, thereby allowing countries to turn their attention to the younger generation and invest in the future. Of course, every situation is different, and we must seek new solutions to resolve our current debt problems in constructive ways, drawing on the successes of the past and circumventing their limitations, as I have tried to show. But for critics who know virtually nothing about history to dismiss as "populist" those who seek to launch a necessary and unavoidable debate is simply unacceptable. To be sure, the leaders of the Lega and M5S in Italy and of the "Yellow Vests" in France who have called for referenda on debt cancellation may not fully appreciate the complexity of the issue, which cannot be settled by a simple "yes" or "no." There is an urgent need for debate on the fiscal, financial, and institutional arrangements necessary to reschedule the debt because it is "details" like these that determine whether debt reduction comes at the expense of the wealthy (by way of a progressive wealth tax, for example) or of the poor (by way of inflation). The social demand to do something about the debt may be confused, but it is also legitimate, and the response should be not to shut down debate but rather to open it up in all its complexity.

To conclude, note that the worst consequence of the populism debate may be that it fosters new identity conflicts and impedes constructive deliberation. Although the term is usually used pejoratively, it is sometimes taken up by those accused of being populists as a badge of identity. This clouds the issue even further because the positive use of the term is just as nebulous as the negative one. For instance, some anti-immigrant movements brandish the term "populist" to show that they take the side of "the people" (who are assumed to be unanimous in their hostility to immigration) against the "elite" (who are said to favor open borders everywhere). Some would-be "radical" left movements (such as Podemos in Spain and LFI in France) have also taken up the term "populist," not always prudently, to set themselves apart from other "left" (socialist or social-democratic) parties, which they accuse of having betrayed the working class. There are better ways to make such a critique than by using a loaded, totemic, and dangerously polysemic word like "populist." In practice, the term pits "the people" against "the elite" (financial, political, or media as the case may be) while avoiding any discussion of what institutions (e.g., at the European level) are needed to alleviate the condition of the disadvantaged. At times "populism" is used to deny the importance of ideology: the implicit assumption is that pure force is all that matters and that institutional details can be settled once "the people" have asserted their strength and carried the day.[186]

The history of all the inequality regimes studied in this book proves the opposite. Historical changes of great magnitude occur when the logic of events comes together with short-term mobilizations and longer-term institutional and intellectual changes. In the late nineteenth and early twentieth centuries, the People's Party in the United States played a useful role not because it laid claim to the name "populist" (which in itself was neither necessary nor sufficient) but because it was part of a fundamental political and ideological shift that culminated in the Sixteenth Amendment to the US Constitution and the creation of the federal income tax in 1913—a tax that would become one of the most progressive in history and make it possible to finance the New Deal and reduce inequality.

---

186. In this connection, it is striking to see the degree to which works associated with "left populism" avoid dealing with the question of what kinds of institutions are needed to transcend capitalism. Although some of these books are quite interesting, they avoid tackling the social-federalist issues raised in this chapter and also eschew discussion of the property regime, voting rights within firms, and progressive wealth taxes. See, for example, E. Laclau, *La raison populiste* (FCE, 2005); J. L. Mélenchon, *L'ère du peuple* (Fayard, 2014); C. Mouffe, *Pour un populisme de gauche* (Albin Michel, 2018). These works start with the assumption that the first priority is to heighten the antagonism between people and the elite to mobilize voters tired of the false alternative between left and right (and sometimes attracted by xenophobic rhetoric). The implicit hypothesis is that questions of programmatic and institutional content (concerning, say, Europe or the property regime) will be dealt with once a new balance of power among parties has been achieved.

For all these reasons, I think it is important to be wary of the dead ends and pitfalls of the "populism" debate and focus instead on content and, specifically, on new thinking about the property regime; fiscal, social, and educational systems; and the organization of borders. In other words, we should be thinking about the social, fiscal, and political institutions that can help to create a just society and allow class cleavages once again to take priority over identity cleavages.

SEVENTEEN

Elements for a Participatory Socialism for the Twenty-First Century

In this book I have tried to present a reasoned history of inequality regimes from early trifunctional and slave societies to modern hypercapitalist and postcolonial ones. All human societies need to justify their inequalities. Their histories are organized around the ideologies they develop to regulate, by means of complex and changing institutional arrangements, social relations, property rights, and borders. The search for a just inequality is of course not exempt from hypocrisy on the part of dominant groups, but every ideology contains plausible and sincere elements from which we can derive useful lessons.

In the last few chapters, I have tried to highlight the significant dangers posed by the rise of socioeconomic inequality since 1980. In a period marked by internationalization of trade and rapid expansion of higher education, social-democratic parties failed to adapt quickly enough, and the left-right cleavage that had made possible the mid-twentieth-century reduction of inequality gradually fell apart. The conservative revolution of the 1980s, the collapse of Soviet communism, and the development of neo-proprietarian ideology vastly increased the concentration of income and wealth in the first two decades of the twenty-first century. Inequality has in turn heightened social tensions almost everywhere. For want of a constructive egalitarian and universal political outlet, these tensions have fostered the kinds of nationalist identity cleavages that we see today in practically every part of the world: in the United States and Europe, India and Brazil, China and the Middle East. When people are told that there is no credible alternative to the socioeconomic organization and class inequality that exist today, it is not surprising that they invest their hopes in defending their borders and identities instead.

Yet the new hyper-inegalitarian narrative that has taken hold since the 1980s is not ordained by fate. While it is partly a product of history and of the communist debacle, it is also a consequence of the failure to disseminate knowledge, of disciplinary barriers that are too rigid, and of insufficient citizen appropriation of economic and financial issues, which are too often left to others.

The study of history has convinced me that it is possible to transcend today's capitalist system and to outline the contours of a new participatory socialism for the twenty-first century—a new universalist egalitarian perspective based on social ownership, education, and shared knowledge and power. In this final chapter, I will attempt to gather up some of the elements that I believe will help us to progress toward this goal, based on the lessons of the past highlighted in previous chapters. I will begin by looking at the conditions of just ownership. New forms of social ownership will need to be developed, along with new ways of apportioning voting rights and decision-making powers within firms. The notion of permanent private ownership will need to be replaced by temporary private ownership, which will require steeply progressive taxes on large concentrations of property. The proceeds of the wealth tax will then be parceled out to every citizen in the form of a universal capital endowment, thus ensuring permanent circulation of property and wealth. I will also consider the role of progressive income taxes, universal basic incomes, and educational justice. Finally, I will look at the issue of democracy and borders and ask how it might be possible to reorganize the global economy so as to favor a transnational democratic system aimed at achieving social, fiscal, and environmental justice.

To be perfectly frank, it would be absurd for anyone to claim to have perfectly satisfactory and convincing answers to such complex questions or to present ready-made, easily applicable solutions. That is obviously not the purpose of the pages that follow. The whole history of inequality regimes shows that what makes historical change possible is above all the existence of social and political mobilizations for change and concrete experimentation with alternative arrangements. History is the product of crises; it never unfolds as textbooks might lead one to expect. Nevertheless, it seems useful to devote this final chapter to the lessons one can draw from the available sources and to the positions I would be inclined to defend if I had all the time in the world to deliberate. I have no idea what the crises to come might look like or what ideas will be drawn upon to propose new paths forward. But there is no doubt that ideology will continue to play a central role, for better and for worse.

Justice as Participation and Deliberation

What is a just society? For the purposes of this book, I propose the following imperfect definition. A just society is one that allows all of its members access to the widest possible range of fundamental goods. Fundamental goods include education, health, the right to vote, and more generally to participate as fully as possible in the various forms of social, cultural, economic, civic, and political life. A just society organizes socioeconomic relations, property rights, and the distribution of income and wealth in such a way as to allow its least advantaged members to enjoy the highest possible life conditions. A just society in no way requires absolute uniformity or equality. To the extent that income and wealth inequalities are the result of different aspirations and distinct life choices or permit improvement of the standard of living and expansion of the opportunities available to the disadvantaged, they may be considered just. But this must be demonstrated, not assumed, and this argument cannot be invoked to justify any degree of inequality whatsoever, as it too often is.

This imprecise definition of the just society does not resolve all issues—far from it. But to go further requires collective deliberation on the basis of each citizen's historical and individual experience with participation by all members of society. That is why deliberation is both an end and a means. The definition is nevertheless useful because it allows us to lay down certain principles. In particular, equality of access to fundamental goods must be absolute: one cannot offer greater political participation, extended education, or higher income to certain groups while depriving others of the right to vote, attend school, or receive health care. Where do fundamental goods such as education, health, housing, culture, and so on end? That is obviously a matter for debate and cannot be decided outside the framework of a particular society in a particular historical context.

To my way of thinking, the interesting questions arise when one begins to look at the idea of justice in particular historical societies and to analyze how conflicts over justice are embodied in discourse, institutions, and specific social, fiscal, and educational arrangements. Some readers may find that the principles of justice I set forth here are similar to those formulated by John Rawls in 1971.[1] There is some truth to this, provided one adds that similar principles can be found in much earlier forms in many civilizations: for instance, in Article I of the Declaration of the Rights of Man and the Citizen of 1789.[2]

---

1. Especially his "difference principle": "Social and economic inequalities are to be to the greatest benefit of the least advantaged members of society." This formula, taken from J. Rawls, *Theory of Justice* (1971), was repeated in J. Rawls's *Political Liberalism* (1993). The theory is sometimes summarized as "maximin" (the ultimate social objective is to maximize minimum well-being), even though it also insists on absolute equality of fundamental rights.

2. "Men are born and remain free and equal in rights. Social distinctions can only be based on common social utility." The second part of this proposition has often

Nevertheless, grand declarations of principle like those formulated during the French Revolution or in the US's Declaration of Independence did nothing to prevent the persistence and exacerbation of large social inequalities in both countries throughout the nineteenth and into the twentieth centuries, nor did they prevent the establishment of systems of colonial domination, slavery, and racial segregation that endured until the 1960s. Hence it is wise to be wary of abstract and general principles of social justice and to concentrate instead on the way in which those principles are embodied in specific societies and concrete policies and institutions.[3]

The elements of a participatory socialism that I will present below are based primarily on the historical lessons presented in this book—especially the lessons that can be drawn from the major transformations of inequality regimes that took place in the twentieth century. In reflecting on how to apply those lessons, I have had in mind today's societies, the societies of the early twenty-first century. Some of the items discussed below demand significant state, administrative, and fiscal capacities if they are to be implemented, and in that sense they are most directly applicable to Western societies and to the more developed non-Western ones. But I have tried to think about them in a universal perspective, and they may gradually become applicable to poor and emerging countries as well. The proposals I examine here derive from the democratic socialist tradition, notably in the emphasis I place on transcending private ownership and involving workers and their representatives in corporate governance (a practice that has already played an important role in German and Nordic social democracy). I prefer to speak of "participatory socialism" to emphasize the goal of participation and decentralization and to sharply distinguish this project from the hypercentralized state socialism that was tried in the twentieth century in the Soviet Union and other communist states (and is still widely practiced in the Chinese public sector). I also envision a central role for the educational system and emphasize the themes of temporary ownership

---

been interpreted as opening the way to just inequality. See T. Piketty, *Capital in the Twenty-First Century,* trans. A. Goldhammer (Harvard University Press, 2014), pp. 479–481.

3. The principal limitation of the Rawlsian approach is that it remains fairly abstract and says nothing precise about the levels of inequality and fiscal progressivity the principles imply. Thus Friedrich A. von Hayek was able to write in the preface to *Law, Legislation, and Liberty* (1982) that he felt close to Rawls and his "difference principle," which in practice has often been used to justify high levels of inequality to act as a useful incentive (on the basis of little evidence).

and progressive taxation (bearing in mind that progressive taxes played an important role in British and American progressivism and were widely debated though never implemented during the French Revolution).

In view of the largely positive results of democratic socialism and social democracy in the twentieth century, especially in Western Europe, I think that the word "socialism" still deserves to be used in the twenty-first century to evoke that tradition even as we seek to move beyond it. And move beyond it we must if we are to overcome the most glaring deficiencies of the social-democratic response of the past four decades. In any case, the substance of the proposals we will discuss matters more than any label one might attach to them. It is perfectly comprehensible that for some readers the word "socialism" will have been permanently tarnished by the Soviet experience (or by the actions of more recent governments that were "socialist" in name only). Therefore, they would prefer a different word. Nevertheless, I hope that such readers will at least follow my argument and the propositions that flow from it, which in fact draw on experiences and traditions of many kinds.[4]

Note, finally, that the options defended here reflect the following thought experiment. Suppose that we have unlimited time for debate in an immense global agora. The subject of debate is how best to organize the property regime, fiscal and educational systems, borders, and the democratic regime itself. The choices I make below are the ones I would defend in such a setting on the basis of the historical knowledge I acquired to write this book and in the hope of persuading the largest possible number of people that these are the policies that should be implemented. However useful such a thought experiment might be, it is clearly artificial in several respects. First, no one has unlimited time for debate. In particular, political movements and parties often have very little time to communicate their ideas and proposals to citizens, who in turn have limited

---

4. Some of the ideas presented here, in particular on the subject of circulation of property and taxation of inheritances and wealth, are similar in spirit to the ideas of authors in the French Solidarist Socialist tradition such as Léon Bourgeois and Émile Durkheim (see Chap. 11). Note, too, the proximity to the notion of "property-owning democracy" developed by James Meade. The problem is that this notion (like Rawls's concepts) has at times been invoked for conservative purposes. See, for example, B. Jackson, "Property-Owning Democracy: A Short History," in *Property-Owning Democracy: Rawls and Beyond,* ed. M. O'Neill and T. Williamson (Blackwell, 2012). By design, the options defended here are based on the historical experience of many countries since the nineteenth century and therefore combine a number of intellectual traditions.

patience for hearing them (often for good reasons, because people have other priorities in life besides listening to their political arguments).

Last but not least, if this endless deliberation were ever to take place in reality, I would no doubt have reason to revise the positions I am about to defend, which inevitably reflect the limited range of arguments, data, and historical sources to which I have been exposed to date. Each new discussion further enriches the fund of material on which I base my reflections. I have already revised my positions profoundly as a result of the readings, encounters, and debates in which I have been fortunate to participate, and I will continue to revise my views in the future. In other words, justice must always be conceived as the result of ongoing collective deliberation. No book and no single human being can ever define the ideal property regime, the perfect voting system, or the miraculous tax schedule. Progress toward justice can occur only as the result of a vast collective experiment. As history unfolds, the experience of each individual must be brought to bear in the widest possible deliberation. The elements I will explore here are meant merely to indicate possible paths for experimentation, derived from analysis of the histories recounted in the preceding chapters.

On the Transcendence of Capitalism and Private Property

What is just ownership? This is the most complex and central question we must try to answer if the goal is to define participatory socialism and imagine the transcendence of capitalism. For the purposes of this book, I have defined proprietarianism as a political ideology based on the absolute defense of private property; capitalism is the extension of proprietarianism to the age of large-scale industry, international finance, and more recently to the digital economy. At bottom capitalism rests on the concentration of economic power in the hands of the owners of capital. In principle, the owners of real estate capital can decide to whom they wish to rent and at what price while the owners of financial and professional capital govern corporations according to the principle of "one share, one vote," which entitles them, among other things, to decide by themselves whom to hire and at what wage.

In practice, this strict capitalist model has been altered and modified in various ways, and the notion of private property has therefore evolved since the nineteenth century, owing to changes in the legal and social system and the tax system. Changes in the legal and social system limited the power of the owners of property: for instance, renters were given long-term guarantees against evictions and rent increases, and some were even granted the right to purchase at a low price apartments or land that they had occupied for a sufficiently long period of time—a veritable redistribution of wealth. Similarly, the power of shareholders in firms was strictly limited by labor codes and social legislation; in some countries, worker representatives were granted seats and voting rights alongside shareholders on boards of directors, a move that if carried to its logical conclusion would amount to a veritable redefinition of property rights.

The tax system also curtailed the rights of property owners. Progressive inheritance taxes, which attained rates as high as 30–40 percent in most developed countries in the twentieth century (and 70–80 percent in the United States and United Kingdom for many decades) amounted in practice to transforming permanent ownership into temporary ownership. In other words, each generation is allowed to accumulate considerable wealth, but part of that wealth must be returned to the community at that generation's passing or shared with other potential heirs, who thus get a fresh start in life. Furthermore, progressive income taxes, assessed at rates comparable to the inheritance tax (or even higher in the United Kingdom and United States), which historically were directed at high capital incomes, also made it increasingly difficult to perpetuate large fortunes across generations (without a significant reduction in expenditure).

In order to transcend capitalism and private property and bring participatory socialism into being, I propose to rely on and improve these two instruments. Briefly, much more can be done with the legal and fiscal systems than has been done thus far: first, we can establish true social ownership of capital by more extensive power sharing within firms, and second, we can make ownership of capital temporary by establishing progressive taxes on large fortunes and using the proceeds to finance a universal capital endowment, thus promoting permanent circulation of property.

Sharing Power in Firms: An Experimentation Strategy

Begin with social ownership. Systems for sharing voting rights within firms have existed in Germanic and Nordic Europe since the late 1940s and early 1950s. Workers' representatives hold half the seats on boards of directors in German companies and a third of the seats in Sweden (including small business in the Swedish case), regardless of whether they own any capital.[5] These so-called

---

5. See Chap. 11 for a more detailed analysis.

co-management (or codetermination) arrangements were the result of hard-fought battles waged by unions and their political allies. The struggle began in the late nineteenth century. The balance of power began to shift after World War I and changed decisively after World War II. Substantial changes in the law went hand in hand with major constitutional innovations. Specifically, the German constitutions of 1919 and 1949 adopted a social definition of the rights of ownership, which took into account the general interest and the good of the community. Property rights ceased to be held sacred. Though shareholders initially fought these changes tooth and nail, the new rules have now been in force for more than half a century and enjoy widespread public approval.

All available evidence shows that co-management has been a great success. It has encouraged greater worker involvement in shaping the long-term strategies of employers and counterbalanced the often harmful short-term focus of shareholders and financial interests. It has helped the Germanic and Nordic countries to develop an economic and social model that is more productive and less inegalitarian than other models. It should therefore be adopted without delay in other countries in its maximal version, with half the board seats in all private firms, large or small, given to workers.[6]

As promising as Germano-Nordic co-management is, it suffers from numerous limitations, starting with the fact that shareholders have the decisive vote in case of a tie. Two possible improvements are worth considering. First, if wealth inequality is reduced by way of progressive taxation, capital endowments, and circulation of property, which I will discuss in due course, workers may be able to acquire shares in their firm and thus shift the balance of power by adding shareholder votes to the half they already hold as members of the board. Second, the rules apportioning votes on the basis of capital invested should also be rethought. As noted earlier, it would not be in the general interest to entirely eliminate the link between capital invested and economic power in the firm, at least in the smallest companies. If a person invests all her savings in a project of passionate interest, there is nothing wrong with her being able to cast more votes than a worker hired the day before, who may be setting aside his earnings to develop a project of his own.[7]

---

6. Depending on the country, the legal system, and the size of a firm, the body responsible for setting the overall direction of the company may by a simple oversight committee or management council rather than a board of directors in the usual sense.

7. See Chaps. 11 and 12.

Might it not be justifiable, however, to place a ceiling on the votes of large shareholders in major corporations? One recent proposal along these lines concerns "nonprofit media organizations": investments beyond 10 percent of a firm's capital would obtain voting rights corresponding to one-third of the amount invested, with the voting rights of smaller investors (including journalists, readers, crowd funders, and so on) augmented accordingly.[8] Initially conceived for nonprofit media organizations, this proposal could be extended to other sectors, including profit-making ones. A good formula might be to apply a similar vote ceiling to investments above 10 percent of capital in firms above a certain size.[9] The justification for this is that there is no reason why a large firm should leave power concentrated in the hands of a single individual and deprive itself of the benefits of collective deliberation.

Note in passing that many organizations in both the private and public sector function perfectly well without shareholders. For instance, most private universities are organized as foundations. The generous donors who contribute to their capital may derive some benefit from their contributions (such as preferential admission for their children or even a seat on the board), which incidentally should be regulated more strictly. There are other problems with this model, which ought to be corrected.[10] Nevertheless, donors are in a much weaker position than shareholders. Their contributions become part of the university's capital, and compensation such as seats on the board can be withdrawn at any time; with shareholders and their heirs this is not possible. Yet contributors continue to give, and private universities continue to function. To be sure, attempts have been made to organize universities as profit-making corporations (think of Trump University), but the results have been so disastrous

---

8. See J. Cagé, *Saving the Media,* trans. Arthur Goldhammer (Harvard University Press, 2016). Profit taking would not be allowed (nor could shares beyond a certain threshold be sold). In exchange, investors in the media could be granted tax deductions similar to those granted to contributors to nonprofit organization in education and the arts. I will say more later about taxing contributions.

9. For example, the investment threshold above which vote reductions apply could be set at 90 percent for small firms (fewer than ten employees), decreasingly gradually to 10 percent for larger firms (more than one hundred employees). Obviously, these thresholds are open to debate and experimentation, and the numbers given here should not be taken as definitive.

10. This educational model has given rise to growing inequalities in the university system, which should be corrected. I will come back to this.

that the practice has virtually disappeared.[11] This clearly shows that it is not only possible to drastically limit the influence of investors but also that organizations often work better when investor power is limited. Similar observations could be made about the health, culture, transportation, and environmental sectors, which will likely play a central role in the future. In general, the idea that the "one share, one vote" model of corporate organization is indisputably the best cannot withstand close scrutiny.

Reducing wealth inequality and capping large shareholder voting rights are the two most natural ways of extending the Germano-Nordic co-management model. There are others, such as a recent British proposal to have some board members elected by a mixed assembly of shareholders and workers.[12] This could allow novel deliberations to unfold and new coalitions to emerge, breaking out of the stereotypical roles that co-management sometimes forces on participants. But the debate does not end there: concrete experimentation is the only way to develop new organizational forms and social relations. What is certain is that there are many ways to improve on co-management as it currently exists so that social ownership and corporate power sharing can contribute to the goal of transcending capitalism.

Progressive Wealth Taxes and Circulation of Capital

Social ownership and shared voting rights in firms are important tools for transcending capitalism, but by themselves they are not enough. Once one accepts the idea that private property will continue to play a role in a just society, especially in small and medium firms, it becomes essential to find institutional arrangements that will prevent unlimited concentration of ownership which does not serve the general interest, regardless of the reasons for such concentration. In this respect, the lessons of history are quite clear: the extreme concentration of wealth that we observe in nearly all societies (and especially in Europe) up to the early twentieth century, when the wealthiest 10 percent owned 80–90

---

11. Why have such attempts failed? Perhaps because the profit motive tends to undermine the values of disinterestedness and intrinsic motivation that are essential to the educational enterprise. For similar reasons, experiments with offering students monetary bonuses based on exam results have generally produced very negative results (with intensive cramming on frequently posed questions and accelerated loss of competence in other areas). See the online appendix (piketty.pse.ens.fr/ideology).

12. See Chap. 11.

percent of all property (and the wealthiest 1 percent owned 60–70 percent), did not serve the general interest at all. The clearest proof of this assertion is that the very significant reduction of inequality that followed the shocks and political-ideological changes of the period 1914–1945 did not inhibit economic development. The concentration of wealth was significantly lower after World War II (with the top decile reduced to owning around 50–60 percent and the top centile 20–30 percent) than before 1914, yet growth accelerated.[13] Whatever the wealthy of the Belle Époque (1880–1914) may have thought to the contrary, extreme inequality was not the necessary price of prosperity and industrial development. Indeed, all signs are that the excessive concentration of wealth exacerbated social and nationalist tensions while blocking the social and educational investments that made the balanced postwar development model possible. Furthermore, the increased concentration of wealth that we have seen since the 1980s in the United States, Russia, India, and China and to a lesser extent in Europe shows that extreme wealth inequality can reconstitute itself for many different reasons, from profiteering on privatizations to the fact that large portfolios earn higher returns than small ones, without necessarily yielding higher growth for the majority of the population—far from it.[14]

To prevent a return to such extreme wealth concentration, progressive taxes on inheritances and income must again play the role that they used to play in the twentieth century when rates in the United States and United Kingdom ran as high as 70–90 percent on the highest incomes and largest fortunes for decades—decades in which growth rose to unprecedented levels.[15] Historical experience shows, however, that inheritance and income taxes alone are not enough; they need to be complemented by a progressive annual tax on wealth, which I see as the central tool for achieving true circulation of capital.

There are several reasons for this. First, the wealth tax is more difficult to manipulate than the income tax, particularly for the very wealthy, whose taxable income is often a small fraction of their wealth, while their actual economic income accumulates in family holdings or special-purpose vehicles. If a progressive income tax is the only available tool, it is almost inevitable that wealthy individuals will pay risibly small taxes compared to the size of their fortunes.[16]

---

13. See Figs. 10.4–10.5 and Figs. 11.12–11.15.

14. See Figs. 13.8–13.9 and Table 13.1.

15. See Figs. 10.11–10.12.

16. For instance, Warren Buffett paid $1.8 million in federal income tax in 2015 on a fortune estimated at $65 billion or a tax rate of 0.003 percent of his wealth. See E.

Note, moreover, that wealth is in itself an indicator of capacity to contribute to common expenditures—an indicator at least as relevant and consistent as annual income, which can vary for all sorts of reasons (some of which are irrelevant to deciding what a just tax should be). For example, if a person owns important properties (such as houses, apartments, warehouses, and factories) that for one reason or another legitimately generate no significant income, perhaps because they have been set aside for some purpose or have not been maintained, he should still be required to pay taxes. In fact, in all countries where there is a tax on real estate (whether housing or offices or professional equipment of any kind), such as the property tax in the United States or the *taxe foncière* (real estate tax) in France, no one would think of exempting large owners (whether private individuals or firms) on the grounds that they derive no income from their property.[17] But these taxes date from the eighteenth or nineteenth centuries, and for historical reasons many types of assets are exempt (such as intangible and financial assets). What is more, the tax is strictly proportional: the same tax rate is applied to all assets, no matter how large the portfolio to which they belong. Hence the redistributive effect is much smaller than it would be if total assets of all kinds (net of debt) were taxed at progressive rates.[18]

Saez and G. Zucman, *The Triumph of Injustice* (Norton, 2019), pp. 155–156. Public data on billionaires in other countries, such as Liliane Bettencourt in France in the early 2010s, paint a similar picture: taxable income of a few million euros compared with a fortune of several billion. One possibility would be to apply the income tax schedule to an "economic income" estimated on the basis of wealth (for example, by assuming a realistic yield), but this would require accurate declaration and registration of wealth (and not simply of income).

17. Except where the property owned is of little value. But no one would think of giving a property tax exemption to the owner of numerous apartment buildings, warehouses, or offices on the grounds that she was not deriving significant income from them when it would suffice to sell a small portion of the property to pay the tax. What is more, this would contribute to circulating wealth into the hands of more dynamic owners. This is the classic argument in favor of the property tax, independent of income, and it is relevant here to a certain extent. If the whole system depended on capital owned, then a firm making temporary losses would pay as much tax as another making enormous profits (on equivalent capital), which could push the first firm into bankruptcy for the wrong reasons. That is why an ideal tax system should always strike a balance between taxing property and taxing income.

18. On the history of property taxes in the eighteenth and nineteenth centuries and debates surrounding them, see Chaps. 4 and 11.

Compared with the progressive inheritance tax, which is also a tax on wealth (in that it depends solely on ownership and not on income), the advantage of the annual wealth tax is that it can adapt much more quickly to changes in wealth and in the ability of each taxpayer to pay. There is no need to wait for Mark Zuckerberg or Jeff Bezos to turn 90 years old and pass their wealth to their heirs in order to collect taxes. The inheritance tax is by its very nature not a good tool for taxing newly amassed fortunes. The annual wealth tax is better suited to the task, especially in view of today's longer life expectancy. Note, moreover, that current wealth taxes (such as the property or real estate tax), for all their limitations, have always generated more revenues than inheritance taxes, yet they are less unpopular. Indeed, it is striking to see how unpopular inheritance taxes are in all surveys, while property and income taxes are relatively well tolerated. Progressive wealth taxes (such as the ISF in France or the "millionaire tax" mentioned in US polling on the subject) are very popular.[19] In other words, taxpayers would prefer to pay an annual tax on the order of 1–2 percent of the value of their property over a period of decades rather than having to pay 20–30 percent when they pass their estate on to their heirs.

Of course, the hostility of some lower- and middle-class taxpayers to the inheritance tax may be due to a misperception of the actual incidence of that tax (a misperception that those hostile to progressive taxation naturally do what they can to sustain). But it also reflects a comprehensible fear on the part of people who have recently purchased property and who may have limited cash reserves and financial assets that their children will be obliged to pay a lump-sum tax so large that they may be forced to sell the property (be it a home, a vacation house, or a small business) in order to pay the tax.[20] In fact, when one considers all these aspects of the issue, it seems reasonable that the annual prop-

---

19. On this subject, see A. Spire, *Résistance à l'impôt, attachement à l'Etat* (La Découverte, 2018). This survey also shows that lower- and middle-class taxpayers have a fairly accurate understanding of the overall low progressivity of the tax system and of the regressivity at the top (given the weight of indirect taxes such as value-added taxes, gas taxes, and so on and of social security taxes on low and medium wages as well as opportunities for tax avoidance and manipulation at the top of the hierarchy) as well as the inequality of access to certain public expenditures (such as education and health). See also M. Forse and M. Parodi, "Les Français et la justice fiscale," *Revue de l'OFCE,* 2015. On the tax structure and the issue of progressivity, see Fig. 11.19.

20. On the composition of small, medium, and large fortunes, see Fig. 11.17.

erty tax should play a larger role than the inheritance tax (in terms of tax revenue), provided that the annual tax is made progressive.[21]

The Diffusion of Wealth and the Universal Capital Endowment

Last but not least, a progressive wealth tax is an indispensable tool for ensuring a greater circulation of wealth and broader diffusion of property than in the past. To be sure, the progressive inheritance and income taxes that were developed in the twentieth century significantly reduced income and wealth inequality in Europe, the United States, and Japan. Despite the historical importance of this change, it is important not to lose sight of the fact that wealth nevertheless remained extremely concentrated. In Europe, the top decile's share of private wealth decreased from 80–90 percent in 1900–1910 to 50–60 percent in 2010–2020. Not only is that still a considerable share for just 10 percent of the population, but the fact is that the beneficiaries of this reduction of wealth inequality were almost exclusively people in the fiftieth to ninetieth percentile (whose share rose from barely 10 percent to 30–40 percent of the total). By contrast, the diffusion of wealth never really touched the bottom 50 percent, whose share of total private wealth has always been around 5–10 percent (or even lower) in all countries and periods for which data are available.[22] Since the 1980s, moreover, the share of private wealth held by the disadvantaged classes (the bottom 50 percent of the distribution) and by the patrimonial middle class (as I call the next, or "middle," 40 percent—the fiftieth to ninetieth percentile of the distribution) has shrunk nearly everywhere. This is true in particular in the United States, where the share of wealth owned by the well-to-do (the top decile) has risen above 70 percent in the 2010s. It is also the case in Europe, though to a lesser degree, as well as in India, China, and Russia, where the concentration of wealth is rapidly approaching that of the United States (or surpassing it, in the case of Russia).[23]

---

21. In theoretical terms, when one introduces credit constraints or future variations in asset values and yields (unpredictable at the moment of transmission), it becomes preferable to collect a large share of the inheritance tax in the form of an annual wealth tax. See E. Saez and T. Piketty, "A Theory of Optimal Inheritance Taxation," *Econometrica*, 2013.

22. See Figs. 4.1–4.2 and Figs. 5.4–5.5. Furthermore, we find the same low share (around 5–10 percent) for the bottom 50 percent of each age cohort. See the online appendix, Fig. S11.18.

23. See Figs. 10.4–10.5 and Figs. 13.8–13.10.

This limited diffusion of wealth implies that the bottom 50 percent have minimal opportunity to participate in economic life by creating and running a business. This is not the ideal of participation that a just society should strive to achieve. Many attempts have been made to diffuse wealth more broadly, including agrarian reform intended to break up large farms of hundreds or thousands of acres to allow more modest farmers to work their own land and reap the fruits thereof instead of paying rent to landlords. The French Revolution witnessed a number of more or less ambitious efforts of land reform, although poor peasants were not always the primary beneficiaries.[24] More ambitious agrarian reforms have been carried out in other countries over the past two centuries: in Ireland and Spain in the late nineteenth and early twentieth centuries, in Mexico after the revolution of 1910, in Japan and Korea after World War II, and in certain Indian states (such as West Bengal or Kerala) in the 1970s and 1980s.[25]

Agrarian reform has thus played a significant role in diffusing wealth in a variety of contexts. Yet if faces a number of structural problems. First, there is no obvious reason why wealth redistribution should be limited to property in land (other than simplicity, especially in largely rural societies). In practice, different forms of capital are complementary, and the hyperconcentration of other assets (such as equipment, tools, warehouses, offices, buildings, cash, and financial assets of all kinds) poses similar problems to the concentration of landed wealth. In particular, it leads to hyperconcentration of economic power in the hands of a few. Furthermore, agrarian reformers tend to assume that it will suffice to redistribute property once and for all, after which economic development will proceed harmoniously forever after. Historical experience shows, however, that extreme inequality of wealth tends to reproduce itself in other forms as the agrarian societies of the past give way to societies based on industrial and financial wealth and real estate. Wealth can become reconcentrated for many reasons, including economic upheavals that benefit a minority (such as profitable privatizations or technological revolutions) and various cumulative mechanisms that allow the largest initial stakes to grow more rapidly

---

24. See Chaps. 3 and 4.
25. See Chaps. 5 and 11. By contrast, in the United States and South Africa, no land was redistributed to former slaves (despite their having worked for centuries without pay and despite promises of "forty acres and a mule" made to encourage the slaves to rise up against the confederacy at the end of the Civil War) or to victims of apartheid (about which debate continues). See Chap. 6.

than smaller fortunes (by achieving higher yields, using market power, or pursuing strategies of legal and fiscal optimization).

If one truly wants to diffuse wealth so as to allow the bottom 50 percent to acquire significant assets and participate fully in economic and social life, it is therefore essential to generalize and transform agrarian reform into a permanent process affecting the whole panoply of private capital. The most logical was to proceed would be to establish a capital endowment to be given to each young adult (at age 25, say), financed by a progressive tax on private wealth. By design, such a system would diffuse wealth at the base while limiting concentration at the summit.

The Progressive Tax Triptych: Property, Inheritance, Income

To clarify these ideas, I have indicated in Table 17.1 what a tax system capable of financing such a universal endowment might look like. In the broadest terms, the tax system of the just society would rest on three principal progressive taxes: a progressive annual tax on property, a progressive tax on inheritances, and a progressive tax on income.[26] As indicated here, the annual property tax and the inheritance tax would together yield about 5 percent of national income,[27] all of which would be used to finance the capital endowment. The progressive income tax, which would include social security taxes and a progressive carbon tax, would yield about 45 percent of national income, which would be used to finance all other public expenditures, including the basic income and, above all, the welfare state (which would cover health, education, pensions, and so on).[28] I will begin by discussing the wealth component—that is, the progressive

---

26. Over the course of history, annual property taxes (based on property owned) have gone by a variety of names, such as property tax, wealth tax, capital tax, tax on fortune, real estate tax, and so on. See Chap. 11. I prefer to speak of a property tax *(impôt sur la propriété)* because it emphasizes the importance of property as a social relation. The progressive property tax that I envision is based on all forms of property (real estate, business and financial assets, net of debt). Later, I will also say more about the role of corporate taxes, which are included here under the head of the progressive tax on income.

27. Of which roughly 4 percent would come from the annual property tax and 1 percent from the inheritance tax.

28. In the tax system presented here, there are no indirect taxes (except when needed to correct an externality, as with the carbon tax, which I will discuss later). Broadly speaking, indirect taxes (such as the VAT) are extremely regressive, and I prefer to

TABLE 17.1

Circulation of property and progressive taxation

Progressive property tax (financing the capital endowment to each young adult)			Progressive income tax (financing the basic income scheme and the social and ecological state)	
Multiple of average wealth	Annual property tax (effective rate)	Inheritance tax (effective rate)	Multiple of average income	Effective tax rate (including social taxes and carbon tax)
0.5	0.1%	5%	0.5	10%
2	1%	20%	2	40%
5	2%	50%	5	50%
10	5%	60%	10	60%
100	10%	70%	100	70%
1,000	60%	80%	1,000	80%
10,000	90%	90%	10,000	90%

Interpretation: The proposed tax system includes a progressive tax on property (annual tax + inheritance tax) financing a capital endowment for each young adult and a progressive income tax (including social contributions and a progressive tax on carbon emissions) financing the basic income and the social and ecological state (health, education, pensions, unemployment, energy, etc.). This system of circulating property is one of the constituent elements of participatory socialism, with voting rights on corporate boards shared fifty-fifty between workers and stockholders. *Note:* In the example shown here, the progressive tax on property brings in roughly 5 percent of national income (allowing a capital endowment equivalent to 60 percent of the average wealth at age 25) while the progressive income tax brings in roughly 45 percent of national income (allowing an annual basic income equivalent to 60 percent of average income after taxes—5 percent of national income) and the social and ecological state (40 percent of national income).

taxes on property and inheritances and the universal capital endowment. I defer discussion of the income and welfare state component until later.

Several points call for further comment. The figures given here are for illustrative purposes only. Setting precise parameters will require extensive discussion and broad democratic deliberation; it is not my intention to end all debate with this book.[29] Note, too, that the wealth component includes a rela-

---

replace them eventually with progressive taxes on property, inheritance, and income.

29. The thresholds, rates, and revenues indicated in Table 17.1 are calculated on the basis of average income and wealth distributions observed in the United States and Europe in the 2010s. Because the thresholds are expressed in multiples of average

tively ambitious version of the capital endowment. Specifically, with revenues on the order of 5 percent of national income from the property and inheritance taxes, it is possible to pay for an endowment of approximately 60 percent of average adult wealth to be given to each young adult at age 25.[30]

Consider an example. In the rich countries (Western Europe, United States, Japan), average private wealth in the late 2010s was roughly 200,000 euros per adult.[31] Thus, the capital endowment would amount to 120,000 euros. In essence, this system would provide every individual with the equivalent of an inheritance. Today, owing to the extreme concentration of wealth, the poorest 50 percent receive virtually nothing (barely 5–10 percent of average wealth); the richest 10 percent of young adults inherit several hundreds of thousands of euros, while others receive millions or tens of millions. With the system proposed here, every young adult could begin his or her personal and professional life with a fortune equal to 60 percent of the national average, which would open up new possibilities such as purchasing a house or starting a business. Note that this system of public inheritance for all would guarantee every individual a sum of capital at the age of 25, whereas private inheritance entails considerable uncertainty as to the age at which children will inherit from their parents (owing

wealth and average income and because wealth and income distributions are fairly similar in India, China, and Russia (to a first approximation), the tax schedules that would need to be applied in those countries to yield equivalent revenues (in proportion to national income) would also be fairly similar. The goal here is to fix orders of magnitude, not to provided definitive results. In countries where wealth and income are more concentrated (like the United States), the highest rates could be reduced slightly and still yield the same revenues. By contrast, they would have to be increased slightly in countries where concentration is lower (as in Europe). See the online appendix.

30. The size of a generation (that is, the number of persons reaching age 25 every year) is approximately 1.5 percent of the adult population in Europe, the United States, and China and slightly higher in India (where life expectancy is lower). For example, in France, each generation represents 750,000–800,000 individuals out of an adult population of roughly 50 million (and a total population of 67 million in 2018). Total private wealth is on the order of five to six years of national income in these countries. A capital endowment of 60 percent of average wealth per adult is therefore equivalent to 3–3.5 years of average national income per adult for a total cost on the order of 5 percent of national income if that sum is distributed every year to 1.5 percent of the adult population.

31. For an average national income on the order of 35,000–40,000 euros per year per adult (for a wealth/income ratio on the order of five to six). On the distribution and composition of wealth by type of asset and resources, see Figs. 11.16–11.17.

to wide variance in age of death and age at which parents have children). In practice, this means that children are inheriting later and later in life. Note, too, that the system proposed here would greatly reduce the average age of wealth holders, which could infuse new energy into society and the economy.[32]

The system I am proposing has a long pedigree. In 1795, Thomas Paine, in his book *Agrarian Justice,* proposed an inheritance tax to finance a basic income.[33] More recently, Anthony Atkinson proposed using the receipts from a progressive inheritance tax to finance a capital endowment for every young adult.[34] The principal novelty of my proposal is to use the proceeds of both an inheritance tax and an annual property tax to pay for the capital endowment; this would make much larger endowments possible and ensure permanent circulation of wealth.[35] Note that the sums I am proposing to mobilize to finance the capital endowment are substantial (5 percent of national income) and would entail a significant increase of both the property and inheritance taxes for the wealthiest individuals.[36] Still, this is a small amount compared

---

32. Currently, average wealth at age 25 is barely 30 percent of average wealth per adult (and very unequally distributed). See the online appendix. Note that the public inheritance system proposed here would still be of interest in a society where wealth was perfectly egalitarian within generations, in the sense that it would equalize inheritance ages and the average age of wealth holders and therefore the distribution of economic power.

33. See Chap. 3. See also the stimulating book by P. Van Parijs and Y. Vanderborght, *Basic Income: A Radical Proposal for a Free Society and a Sane Economy* (Harvard University Press, 2017).

34. See A. Atkinson, *Inequality* (Harvard University Press, 2015). The originality of Atkinson's proposal, which I draw on and extend here, is that the capital endowment should be coupled to an ambitious basic income plan (rather than be seen as a substitute for one). For interesting proposals regarding both the basic income and capital endowment, see Van Parijs and Vanderborght, *Basic Income,* and B. Ackerman and A. Alstott, *The Stakeholder Society* (Yale University Press, 1999).

35. In Atkinson's proposal, the capital endowment finance by the inheritance tax, even after that tax was increased, would amount to barely 5–10 percent of average wealth (10,000–20,000 euros in the United Kingdom or France), a sum close to the average inheritance received today by the poorest 50 percent, which would be a significant boost. Under my proposal, an endowment financed by both an inheritance tax and an annual wealth tax would come to 60 percent of average wealth (or 120,000 euros in the United Kingdom or France today).

36. Currently, wealth taxes in the form of the US property tax or the French real estate tax yield 2–3 percent of national income while the inheritance tax yields less than 0.5 percent. On average in the European Union, the various types of wealth tax

with the total tax bill (here set at 50 percent of national income). In the abstract, there is nothing to prevent an even more ambitious system of capital endowment than I am proposing here; for example, one might consider a transfer equal to the average wealth per adult in any given society.[37]

In my view, this system should be used together with the new rules for power sharing on corporate boards and caps on the influence of large shareholders, which I discussed earlier. That way, the diffusion and rejuvenation of wealth will have an even greater effect on the distribution of economic power.

On the Return to Fiscal Progressivity and Permanent Land Reform

I turn now to the progressive tax rates and schedules needed to finance all of these innovations. I propose that the rates to be assessed on the largest inheritances and highest incomes should be on the order of 60–70 percent on fortunes or incomes greater than ten times the average wealth or income and on the order of 80–90 percent for those above one hundred times the average (Table 17.1).[38] These rates are consistent with those assessed in the twentieth century in a number of countries (including the United States and United Kingdom in the period 1930–1980). In retrospect, we can see that those decades witnessed some of the strongest growth ever observed.[39] It therefore

---

(whether collected annually or at the time of death or on transactions) yield nearly 3 percent of national income. See European Commission, *Taxation Trends in the EU*, 2018 ed. (Publications Office of the European Union, 2018), p. 41, Graph 22. In the system proposed here, the annual property tax would yield roughly 4 percent of national income and the inheritance tax 1 percent for a total of 5 percent but with much greater progressivity than existing taxes, which would make it possible to reduce taxes on the lower and middle classes.

37. In particular, even if the inheritance tax will never be as important as the annual property tax and even if it is carefully explained and made especially transparent, it is natural to think of increasing it somewhat in the future in view of the growing share of inherited wealth in total wealth in recent years. See F. Alvaredo, B. Garbiti, and T. Piketty, "On the Share of Inheritance in Aggregate Wealth: Europe and the USA, 1900–2010," *Economica*, 2017.

38. One might want to set tax brackets in terms of the median rather than the average. The problem is that the median income is often very close to zero, so this wouldn't make much sense. Furthermore, measuring income and wealth relative to the average gives a better idea of the amount of revenue and extent of redistribution involved.

39. See Figs. 11.12–11.15.

seems reasonable to try such high rates again.[40] To do so would indicate a clear determination to reduce inequality and break with Reaganism, which could have an important effect on transforming the structure of electoral and political conflict.

The most innovative aspect of the new taxes I am proposing, which of course call for further discussion, relates to the annual progressive wealth tax. Looking to the past, we find that wealth taxes tended to be rather haphazardly designed. Taxes like the property tax in the United States or the real estate tax in France, which originated in the nineteenth century, generally have effective rates today of about 1 percent. They generally do not factor in financial assets (which constitute the bulk of large fortunes) or debt (which is of course a heavier burden on the less wealthy). Hence they are in fact steeply regressive wealth taxes, with much higher effective rates on the smallest fortunes than on the largest ones.[41] As for the wealth taxes that were tested in the twentieth century, especially in Germanic and Nordic Europe as well as in France in recent decades with the ISF, rates have generally varied from 0 percent for the smallest fortunes to 2–3 percent for the largest.[42]

Where land reform was implemented, implicit tax rates on the largest estates were sometimes a great deal higher. For example, if agrarian reformers decide that all farms of 500 acres or more must be redistributed to landless peasants, then the effective tax rate on a 2,000-acre property works out to 75 percent.[43] Hypothetically, one might imagine that all of Ireland belonged

---

40. Furthermore, if one tries to model that various effects at work (on equality, mobility, and incentives to work and save) with all the caution and rigor appropriate to such exercises, one can show that the ideal inheritance tax (for a Rawlsian type of social objective) should assess very high rates (70–80 percent or more) on the largest inheritances. See Saez and Piketty, "A Theory of Optimal Inheritance Taxation." Similarly, the optimal rate on the highest incomes is above 80 percent. See T. Piketty, E. Saez, and S. Stantcheva, "Optimal Taxation of Top Labour Incomes: A Tale of Three Elasticities," *American Economic Journal*, 2014.

41. Note that a proportional tax of 1 percent on all private wealth (including financial assets, which amounts to 500–600 percent of national income) would bring in 5–6 percent of national income in revenue, which shows that there is nothing extravagant about the revenues I am anticipating from the progressive property tax.

42. See Figs. 11.12–11.15.

43. Note that the tax rates shown in Table 17.1 are expressed in terms of effective rates directly applicable at the level of wealth or income considered (with a linear progression of the effective rate between the indicated levels). For implicit marginal rates corresponding to each bracket, see the online appendix.

to one person or that a single individual possessed a formula of infinite value to all mankind, in which case common sense would clearly dictate a re-distribution rate close to 100 percent.[44] When one-time taxes were levied on real estate and financial capital at the end of World War II, rates as high as 40–50 percent (or even higher) were applied to the largest fortunes.[45]

The tax schedule shown in Table 17.1 for the progressive property tax tries to combine these previous experiments in a consistent way. The tax rate is 0.1 percent for wealth below the national average, rising gradually to 1 percent at twice the national average, 10 percent at one hundred times the national average, 60 percent at 1,000 times the national average (or 200 million euros if the average wealth per adult is 200,000 euros), and 90 percent at 10,000 times the national average (which would be 2 billion euros). Compared with the current system of taxing property at a flat rate, which is in use in a number of countries, this schedule would result in a substantial tax decrease for the 80–90 percent of least wealthy people and would therefore make it easier for them to acquire property. By contrast, the wealthiest people would face very heavy tax increases. The 90 percent tax on billionaires would immediately reduce their wealth to one-tenth of what it was and reduce the share of national wealth held by billion-aires to a level below what it was in the period 1950–1980.[46]

I want to emphasize once again that the tax rates indicated here are for il-lustrative purposes only; they should be subject to collective deliberation and extensive experimentation. One of the virtues of the progressive property tax

---

44. See Chap. 11. The metaphor of a treasure of infinite value was explored in the film *Black Panther* (dir. R. Coogler, Marvel Studios, 2018). The small African country of Wakanda decides in the end to allow the planet to share in its wealth (which consists of vibranium, a substance that the nation was able to profit from thanks to its research and wise organization) in contrast to Norway with its pol-luting hydrocarbons.

45. See Chap. 11.

46. See the online appendix. In the United States, the share of top 0.001 percent of the wealth distribution (around 2,300 people out of a total adult population of 230 million) was 6 percent of total wealth in the late 2010s (or roughly 6,000 times the average wealth for each member of this group), compared with about 1 percent in the period 1950–1980 (roughly 1,000 times the average). The share of the top centile (roughly 2.3 million people) reached 40 percent in the late 2010s (around forty times the average) compared with 20–25 percent in 1950–1980 (twenty to twenty-five times the national average). The proposed tax schedule would immedi-ately reduce the share of the top 0.001 percent to its previous level and would have the same effect on the top 1 percent after ten to fifteen years.

is to promote transparency in regard to wealth. In other words, establishing such a tax, possibly with lower rates than those indicated here, would yield more information about the rate of growth of fortunes of different sizes, and rates could then be adjusted as necessary to achieve whatever goal of wealth deconcentration society chooses to set. The evidence available at this stage shows that the largest fortunes have been growing at rates on the order of 6–8 percent a year since the 1980s.[47] This suggests that tax rates of at least 5–10 percent are necessary to reduce the concentration of wealth at the top of the distribution or at least to stabilize it.[48] Note, too, that it is not strictly necessary (absent some special emergency) to tax the largest fortunes immediately at rates of 60 to 90 percent: rates of 10–20 percent would achieve the same result within a few years. The rates indicated in Table 17.1 are intended to show the range of possibilities and stimulate debate.

Note, finally, that it is in any case essential that the progressive property and inheritance taxes proposed here apply to overall wealth—that is, the total value of real estate and business and financial assets (net of debt) held or received by a given individual, without exception.[49] Similarly, the progressive income tax should apply to total income, including income from both labor (wages, pensions, nonwage income, etc.) and capital (dividends, interest, profits, rents, etc.).[50]

---

47. See Table 13.1.
48. See Saez and Zucman, *The Triumph of Injustice*, pp. 204–208 for simulations analyzing how much wealth concentration in the United States would be decreased by rates of 5 percent on wealth about $1 billion and 8 percent above $100 billion.
49. In general, inheritances can be taxed either on the basis of the amount received by each heir or of the total value of the estate bequeathed by the deceased. I prefer the first method, and it is the one I have chosen here: progressive rates are applied on the basis of total transfers throughout an individual's life, including both gifts and inheritances. A person who receives during the course of his life the equivalent of 0.5 times the average wealth (100,000 euros) would pay an inheritance tax of 5 percent (5,000 euros) and would thus receive a total inheritance of 215,000 euros (including the capital endowment of 120,000 euros). A person receiving twice the average wealth (400,000 euros in France currently) would pay a tax of 20 percent (80,000 euros) for a total inheritance of 440,000 euros when the endowment is added. By contrast, a person receiving five times the national average (1 million euros) would pay a tax of 50 percent (500,000 euros), leaving a total inheritance of 620,000 euros when the endowment is factored in. The rates indicated in Table 17.1 are for illustrative purposes only and call for extensive discussion.
50. When applying the tax schedules indicated here, the joint income of couples can be divided in half since the brackets are defined in terms of individual income and

History shows that if different types of assets and different forms of income are not treated identically by the tax code, taxpayers will respond by optimizing, creating a sense of injustice that can undermine the system, not only technically but also by making it less democratically acceptable.[51] In particular, it would make little sense to exempt specific types of assets from the property or inheritance tax, because to do so would only encourage tax avoidance.[52]

Toward Social and Temporary Ownership

To recapitulate: the model of participatory socialism proposed here rests on two key pillars: first, social ownership and shared voting rights in firms, and second, temporary ownership and circulation of capital. These are the essential tools for transcending the current system of private ownership. By combining them, we can achieve a system of ownership that has little in common with today's private capitalism; indeed, it amounts to a genuine transcendence of capitalism.

These proposals may seem radical. In fact, they are the culmination of an evolution that began in the late nineteenth and early twentieth centuries. Both power sharing in firms and progressive taxation originated in that period. In recent decades, this evolution has come to a halt, in part because social democrats failed to innovate and internationalize their project and in part because the dramatic collapse of Soviet-style communism plunged the world into a phase of unlimited deregulation and abandonment of all egalitarian ambitions in the 1980s (Russia and its oligarchs are no doubt the most glaring illustration of this change).[53] The skill with which the resulting political-ideological vacuum was

---

wealth. In my view, compensation for children is best handled by adopting a system of basic income plus family allotments rather than by tax deductions.

51. For instance, setting lower rates on capital income than on labor income (as Sweden did in 1991) led to totally fictitious and economically useless shifting of income between different categories; for example, from salaries to dividends. On this subject, see Saez and Zucman, *The Triumph of Injustice;* they propose to tax all capital income (including undistributed corporate profits and capital gains) at the same rates as labor income.

52. In particular, the idea of granting exemptions to "productive" capital is undercut by the fact that capital is always productive in one way or another, just as labor is: for instance, having a roof over one's head is at least as useful as having offices or warehouses for producing goods and services. If one begins by exempting this or that type of capital or labor on the grounds that it is productive, one risks ending up very quickly with nothing left to tax.

53. See Chap. 12.

filled by the promoters of the conservative revolution of the 1980s and of the nationalist anti-immigrant line in more recent times did the rest. Since the crisis of 2008, however, the first glimmers of a new movement have become visible, and many proposals for new forms of power sharing and progressive taxation have emerged and are being debated widely.[54] Of course, neo-proprietarian ideology remains tenacious, and nativist retreat remains tempting, but there has been clear change. The proposals I am making here merely add to that movement, which I have tried to set in a broad historical perspective.

In particular, the notion of temporary ownership embodied in the progressive property tax described above is ultimately just an extension of forms of temporary ownership implicit in the progressive inheritance and income taxes that were tried in the twentieth century. In general, these fiscal institutions looked at property as a social relation, which therefore had to be regulated as such. The idea that strictly private property exists and that certain people have an inviolable natural right to it cannot withstand analysis. The accumulation of wealth is always the fruit of a social process, which depends, among other things, on public infrastructures (such as legal, fiscal, and educational systems), the social division of labor, and the knowledge accumulated by humanity over centuries. Under such conditions, it is perfectly logical that people who have accumulated large amounts of wealth should return a fraction of it to the community every year: ownership thus becomes temporary rather than permanent. Ultimately, the only real argument against this logic is the "Pandora's box argument" to which I have alluded several times: namely, that any challenge to private property will inevitably unleash uncontrollable chaos so that it is better never to open the box. But the experience of the twentieth century showed that this argument is bogus: not only are steeply progressive taxes compatible with rapid growth; more than that, they are an important component of a developmental strategy based on relatively equal access to education and an overall reduction in inequality.

Once again, I want to stress that the purpose of citing the lessons of history is to suggest possible avenues of experimentation, not ready-made solutions. On issues like power sharing in corporations, progressive taxation, and permanent circulation of wealth, thinking will not change until successful experiments show that the innovations I am proposing can work. This is the way it has always been when it comes to changing inequality regimes.[55]

---

54. See Chap. 11.
55. I am thinking here of large-scale experimentation to be undertaken after new governments have come to power. I am not neglecting the importance of local experi-

On Transparency of Wealth in One Country

Ideally, the return to social progressivity and the implementation of a progressive property tax should take place in as broad an international setting as possible. It would be best to establish a public financial register that would allow governments and tax authorities to exchange all pertinent information about the ultimate owners of the financial assets issued in various countries. Such registers exist already, but they are largely in the hands of private intermediaries. However, there is no reason why governments in Europe, the United States, and elsewhere could not agree to change the terms of certain treaties to require the recording of assets in a public register; there is no technical obstacle to doing so.[56]

I will say more later about how one might think about transforming the legal foundations of the global economy and rewriting the treaties that regulate commercial and financial exchanges to foster a form of social federalism at the global level. At this stage, I simply want to point out that governments have considerable freedom to maneuver. They can make progress toward reducing inequality and establishing more just forms of ownership without waiting for international cooperation to be achieved. This is obvious for very large states such as the United States and China (and soon for India). In the United States there is no doubt whatsoever that the federal government, if it has the will to do so, has the means to enforce any decisions it makes in regard to taxes. I alluded earlier to the threat of US sanctions on Swiss banks in 2010, which led immediately to changes in Swiss banking laws.[57] This could be done much more systematically.

Note, too, that much of US tax law applies to US citizens no matter where they live. In other words, anyone wishing to escape the US tax authorities would have to give up US citizenship or even in some cases give up doing business in the United States (or even doing business in dollars, directly or indirectly, anywhere in the world). This can become very costly for an individual or business.[58] To sum up: whether the United States will or will not move to a more

---

mentation in producing new knowledge, but my view is that only truly large-scale experiments can bring about decisive changes in perceptions.

56. See Chap. 13.

57. See Chap. 11.

58. The ability of the US federal government to enforce its decisions is often used on behalf of business interests or in the geopolitical interest of the United States (sometimes in ways that come close to exacting what in the past would have been called military tributes). An instance of this is the use of sanctions to punish Euro-

progressive tax structure (possibly including a progressive property tax leading to circulation of capital as described above) is a purely political and ideological question; there is no technical reason why it cannot be done.

It is also important to note that while smaller states, such as France, obviously have more to gain from international cooperation, they, too, have a great deal of room to maneuver if they wish to pursue new policies at the national level. Not only can they adopt new rules concerning power sharing and voting rights in firms (as countries such as Germany and Sweden did decades ago, without waiting for other countries to move); they can also adopt progressive property taxes and take other steps to reduce inequality of income and wealth. This is important, especially since it runs counter to the fatalistic view, common in recent decades, that globalization imposes one unique policy on everyone (which just happens to be the policy that proponents of this view favor). Such fatalism is largely responsible for the abandonment of ambitious economic reforms and the retreat into nativism and nationalism. In practice, however, receipts from the French wealth tax (ISF) more than quadrupled between 1990 and 2018, growing more than twice as fast as gross domestic product (GDP), which is a fairly clearly sign that it is possible to levy such a tax in one country and derive significant revenues from it.[59] This was true, moreover, even though enforcement of the wealth tax was always notoriously lax. Audits were woefully inadequate, and successive governments chose to allow individuals to declare their own assets without systematic checks, although they could have instituted a system based on pre-filled wealth declarations using information about financial assets supplied by banks and other financial institutions (while relying on the existing real estate register, with valuations updated to reflect recent transactions). Such pre-filled declarations are already standard practice in the case of the income tax. Had this been done, receipts from the ISF would have grown even more rapidly.

More generally, there is no reason why a medium-sized state (such as France) cannot move toward greater wealth transparency even in the absence of international cooperation. This is obviously true for real estate located inside the

---

pean firms accused of circumventing US embargos on Iran and other countries. This state capacity could easily be used on behalf of more universal objectives, such as enforcing a steeply progressive tax on the highest incomes and largest fortunes.

59. See Chap. 14, and the online appendix, Fig. S14.20. Recall, too, that large holdings of financial assets added value more rapidly than real estate, which itself grew faster than GDP.

country, whether it is housing or business real estate (offices, factories, warehouses, shops, restaurants, etc.). More generally, it is also true for all firms doing business in the country or having economic interests there. Take the case of the French real estate tax *(taxe foncière)*. Like the US property tax and similar levies in other countries, this tax must be paid by anyone who owns real estate (residential or business) on French soil.

Note that the real estate tax must be paid by property owners (individuals and firms) whether they themselves are based in France or abroad (or are held by individuals based in France or abroad). Currently, the amount of the real estate tax does not depend on the identity of the owner or the owner's total wealth (since it is a strictly proportional tax) so that the tax authorities have no need of additional information (other than the name of the owner or entity to whom the bill should be sent). But the authorities could easily require corporations, holding companies, foundations, and other legal entities listed as owners to submit the names of their shareholders and the number of shares owned by each, failing which punitive sanctions would be applied.[60] With this information, coupled with information on financial assets submitted by banks and other financial institutions, tax authorities could easily transform the real estate tax into a progressive tax on individual net wealth, automatically accounting for all residential and business property in France, whether owned directly or by way of stock, partnership shares, or other types of financial intermediation. The tax authorities could also require all firms doing business in France or having economic interests in the country to submit information about their owners if such information would be useful for enforcing fiscal legislation.[61]

---

60. The most obvious sanction to apply to a firm or other legal entity is the progressive rates applicable to individual owners, as if the firm were owned entirely by a single individual (in the absence of further information).

61. Stockholders in publicly listed firms are recorded by (private) custodial banks and other institutions. Any company that refused to take the steps necessary to transmit adequate information about their stockholders to the fiscal authorities would be subject to sanctions proportional to the damage done (which could be based on available estimates of the international wealth structure or on sales and services invoiced in France, as in the case of the corporate tax; see Chap. 16). Stockholders in unlisted companies are generally known to the companies themselves, but other problems may arise, such as the difficulty of evaluating the share price (which could be estimated on the basis of company books or on the valuations of comparable listed companies).

Such wealth transparency would make it possible to establish a uniform progressive tax on property (a direct descendant of the existing real estate tax and former wealth tax) while sharply decreasing taxes on people of modest means or without property and increasing taxes on those who already own large amounts.[62] For example, a person who owned a home or business valued at 300,000 euros but with a debt of 250,000 euros would be taxed on the basis of her net wealth of only 50,000 euros, which with a progressive schedule such as the one shown in Table 17.1 would result in a tax close to zero and therefore a significant tax cut compared with the current real estate tax. By contrast, another person who owned a similar property worth 300,000 euros together with a financial portfolio worth 2 million euros, who currently pays the same real estate tax as the former (which says a great deal about the absurdity, injustice, and archaic nature of the current fiscal system, which dates all the way back to the turn of the nineteenth century), would face a sharp increase in his wealth tax.[63]

With such a system, the only tax avoidance strategy available to the owners of residential or business property in France would be to sell the assets and leave the country. To combat that, an exit tax could be put in place.[64] In any case, such a tax avoidance strategy would imply selling the property (residence or

---

62. The general principle could be to apply the tax to the global wealth of all people residing in France and all owners of wealth part of which is situated in France (residents and businesses), who would be obliged to declare their wealth (under penalty of punitive sanctions). Agreements could be worked out to avoid double taxation if it can be proven that the owner in question pays a wealth tax equal to or greater than the French tax in some other country (with the understanding that what we want to avoid is the current situation where transborder wealth is not taxed at all).

63. Such a reform could be done without reducing tax revenues, given that the real estate tax currently yields about 40 billion euros in France (nearly 2 percent of GDP), while the ISF yielded about 5 billion euros (less than 0.3 percent of GDP) before it was transformed into the IFI in 2018–2019. Given the concentration of wealth, the top centile (which holds about 20–25 percent of total wealth) would yield revenues of at least 10–15 billion euros. This reform could also be made to yield greater revenues if coupled with an increase in the progressivity of the inheritance tax, in order to finance a universal capital endowment of the type I described earlier (Table 17.1).

64. The justification for an exit tax is that there is no natural right to enrich oneself by taking advantage of a country's legal and educational systems, and so on, and then extracting the wealth without returning part of it to the community. The exit tax system established in 2008, although much less rigorous than the one currently under debate in the United States (because it dealt solely with latent capital gains and not with total wealth and allowed for numerous exemptions) was almost totally rescinded in 2018–2019 as revenues from the wealth tax were cut by 80 percent.

business), which would decrease the corresponding price and lead to purchase by people remaining in the country (presumably much larger in number, including millions of highly competent individuals). Indeed, the possible decrease in asset prices would be an excellent thing, at least up to a point. In France and elsewhere, skyrocketing real estate prices (especially in large cities) have been driven in part by French and foreign buyers acquiring property they have no use for, which could usefully be purchased by less wealthy individuals. The important point is that, even without agreement with other countries, a country like France could easily impose new transparency rules on firms (and other "moral persons") owning property on French soil.[65]

On Writing Fiscal Justice into the Constitution

Finally, it is important to add that developing new forms of fiscal progressivity in order to move from private ownership to social and temporary ownership may require constitutional changes. This is not new. In 1913, the US Constitution had to be amended to allow the creation of a federal income tax and, later, a federal inheritance tax. The development of co-management and the inclusion of unions in corporate governance structures led to a new social and collective definition of property being written into the German constitutions of 1919 and 1949.[66] Similarly, to institute the power sharing in corporations and progressive wealth and income taxes described above, it may be necessary to amend existing constitutions in some countries.

Broadly speaking, the constitutions and declarations of rights that emerged in the late eighteenth century or the following century were steeped in the proprietarian ideology of the era. Existing property rights enjoyed veritable constitutional protection, which could not be challenged for any reason, no matter what the politics of the government in power. It was also in this climate that the United Kingdom and France chose to compensate slaveowners when slavery was abolished in 1833 and 1848. In the mind of the ruling class at the time, it was simply unthinkable to deprive anyone of property without just compensation. By contrast, no one considered it useful to compensate the slaves for the wrongs they had suffered.[67] Respect for property owners continues to permeate

---

65. Although it would obviously be preferable to move toward wealth transparency in an international social-federalist framework, as we will see in a moment.

66. See Chap. 11 for more on this.

67. See Chap. 6.

any number of constitutions around the world today. These will need to be amended before circulation of property and universal capital endowments can become a reality. It would also be a good idea to constitutionally enshrine an explicit principle of fiscal justice based on progressive taxation so that it will be impossible for the rich to pay proportionately less in taxes than the poor (and possible for them to pay more, if legislators so decide; no constitutional judge should be allowed to obstruct the will of the majority in this regard).[68]

In the same spirit, the constitution (or other fundamental law) should require the government to publish accurate annual estimates of the amounts of tax actually paid by different classes of income and wealth so that citizens can participate in informed debates on tax issues and their representatives can have reliable figures on which to base adjustments to the parameters of the tax system. This is especially important because the lack of sufficiently detailed information is one of the major factors preventing citizens from mobilizing and monitoring government action on these issues. This is true not only in capitalist democracies (where the lack of fiscal transparency is manifest, for example, in Europe, the United States, and India) but also in other political systems, such as Russia and communist China, where official rhetoric about combating corruption stands in stark contrast to the paucity of published fiscal data.[69]

Recall, moreover, that the US Supreme Court and other constitutional tribunals that have the last word on constitutional issues in the various Western countries have often shown themselves to be extremely conservative on social and economic issues. Wherever the constitution leaves a crack through which they can inject their partisan views, justices are quick to pass their opinions off as law. Hence it is essential for the constitution to define fiscal justice and the principle of progressivity as precisely as possible while leaving it up to elected legislative bodies to determine how much progressivity there should be, allowing no room for judges to insert themselves into the process. Any number of episodes in constitutional history from the nine-

---

68. Here is possible wording: "The law sets the conditions of ownership and seeks to encourage the diffusion of property if need be through a system of progressive taxation of wealth coupled with capital endowments. In general, the tax should be apportioned among all citizens in proportion to their ability to pay. If one expresses the amount of tax actually paid as a proportion of property owned or income received by each citizen, that proportion may not be smaller for wealthier citizens than for poorer ones. It may be higher, under terms to be set by law."

69. See Chaps. 12 and 13.

teenth century to the present show the need to be cautious and wary of the power of judges in economic and social matters. In 1895, the US Supreme Court chose to interpret the ambiguous terms of the constitution in a clearly conservative manner when they decided that a federal income tax would be unconstitutional (initiating a lengthy process that led to the Sixteenth Amendment in 1913). The following year, the same judges held in the sinister *Plessy v. Ferguson* case that it was perfectly legal for the southern states to practice racial segregation.[70]

During the 1930s, the Supreme Court once again distinguished itself by striking down New Deal social and fiscal legislation on the grounds that certain new regulations unconstitutionally infringed on freedom of enterprise and private contract.[71] Reelected in November 1936 with 61 percent of the vote and furious at having to delay implementation of his program, President Franklin D. Roosevelt announced in early 1937 that he intended to submit a bill that would allow him to appoint additional justices to the Supreme Court to end the stalemate.[72] Ultimately, under pressure from the political branches, the court approved a key minimum wage law that it had previously struck down, ending the crisis.[73]

---

70. In *Plessy* (1896), the Supreme Court by a seven-to-one vote found in favor of Ferguson, a Louisiana judge, against Plessy, the plaintiff, a person of mixed race (specifically, an "octoroon," that is, a person whose ancestors were seven-eighths European and one-eighth African). Plessy had challenged an 1890 Louisiana law banning any person with black blood from entering a train car reserved for whites. This decision had the force of law and served as the legal foundation of the segregationist order in the United States until *Brown v. Board of Education* in 1954 and the civil rights laws of 1964–1965.

71. Note, however, that the Supreme Court could not block the steeply progressive tax that Roosevelt put in place, notably his 1935 "wealth tax" setting a 75 percent rate on top incomes. Since the Sixteenth Amendment of 1913 and the strong push for progressivity in the late 1910s, it was established that the government was free to set tax rates.

72. Since the US Constitution says nothing about the number of Supreme Court justices, it was only by statute and tradition that that number was set at nine, nominated for life, with no age limit (like the Pope or the Supreme Leader in Iran). The Judicial Procedures Reform Bill of 1937 (commonly referred to as the "court-packing plan") allowed Roosevelt to appoint up to six new justices (for each justice over the age of 70) and thus to change the majority in his favor.

73. This key 1937 decision is generally considered to mark the beginning of a new era in the history of the Supreme Court, which became more amenable to government intervention in the economy. Note, however, that the Democratic majority in the

Since the 1970s, thanks to justices appointed by Republican presidents, the Supreme Court has taken an increasingly conservative turn, striking down all legislation aimed at limiting the influence of private money in politics and campaign financing, all in the name of "free speech" as interpreted by the justices.[74] If the Democrats should decide in the future to legislate in this area, they will need to begin by amending the constitution (which is difficult, but it has been done many times in the past and should be kept in mind as a possible option when needed), or else they must change the composition of the Supreme Court, which is easier but generally viewed with suspicion.[75]

Examples of abuse of judicial power are unfortunately not limited to the US Supreme Court. The Kirchhof affair in Germany is a particularly egregious case in point. A tax lawyer clearly angry about the tax system, Paul Kirchhof was presented as the person who would be named Angela Merkel's finance minister if her party won the 2005 elections. He proposed limiting the tax rate on top earners to 25 percent. In politics, everyone is of course entitled to an opinion, but German voters were not impressed by Kirchhof's ideas: his flat tax proposal significantly reduced the Christian Democratic Union's margin of vic-

---

Congress refused to approve Roosevelt's "court-packing plan," preventing the president from appointing new justices. The Democrats did this both because of constitutional conservatism and because the Supreme Court changed its attitude in the face of pressure.

74. Specifically, the *Buckley* decision of 1976 struck down the principle of a ceiling on total campaign contributions while the *Citizens United* decision of 2010 struck down contribution limits on corporations and the McCutcheon decision of 2014 abolished all limits on individual gifts. See J. Cagé, *The Price of Democracy* (Harvard University Press, 2020). See also T. Kuhner, *Capitalism v. Democracy: Money in Politics and the Free Market Constitution* (Stanford University Press, 2014); J. Attanasio, *Politics and Capital. Auctioning the American Dream* (Oxford University Press, 2018).

75. As a general rule, intellectuals in the United States who are close to the Democrats have become fairly conservative on constitutional issues. In regard to the Supreme Court, many think that the best one can do is to restore the previous equilibrium by allowing each president to appoint the justices of his choosing (an equilibrium disrupted in 2016 when the Republican Senate refused to consider President Barack Obama's appointment of the centrist Merrick Garland in order to allow Trump to appoint the next justice). See, for example, S. Levitsky and D. Ziblatt, *How Democracies Die* (Penguin, 2018), pp. 118–119, which delivers a very harsh judgment of FDR's "court-packing plan." Yet there was nothing particularly virtuous or rational about the status quo prior to 2016. Depending on the health of elderly judges and the dates of presidential elections, the composition of the Court can change quickly and block the political process for decades.

tory so that Merkel was eventually forced to form a coalition with the Social Democratic Party and jettison her would-be adviser. But the interesting point is that in 1995, when Kirchhof acted as a judge on the German constitutional court, he was able to condemn any tax above 50 percent as unconstitutional. This caused a scandal, and the decision was eventually overturned by other judges in 1999, who confirmed in 2006 that it was not within the power of judges to set quantitative limits on taxes.

In France, a former president of the Constitutional Council who served in several ministerial posts under conservative governments recently explained that the decision he was most proud of was a 2012 judgment declaring that a marginal tax rate of 75 percent on income above 1 million euros was unconstitutional. The decision was justified, he argued, because under the French constitution a tax is a "contribution" and cannot be "confiscatory."[76] But nowhere does the constitution mention any specific figure, so this judgment rested on a purely personal interpretation by the judge.[77] Like any citizen, the former president of the Constitutional Council is obviously entitled to regard tax rates of 70–90 percent, which were assessed for decades on top incomes and inheritances in many countries in the twentieth century (including the United States and United Kingdom), as having failed to yield the desired results or as poor policy.[78] He is free to publish his arguments in the press, deliver them in speeches, share them with his friends, or even write a book. But to use his position as a constitutional judge to enforce his opinion without the slightest argument to support it represents a clear abuse of power.

To round out this discussion, let me add that constitutional courts are invaluable but fragile institutions. It is important to limit the ability of elected governments to instrumentalize them for their own purposes. Yet precisely because these institutions are so invaluable and fragile, it is also important to prevent judges to whom such eminent functions are entrusted from instrumentalizing them for *their* own purposes. It is therefore crucial to be clear about what belongs to the juridical realm and what to the political. In my view, the wisest course would be to write into the constitution a minimal principle of

---

76. See interview with J.-L. Debré on France Inter, February 16, 2019.

77. In this instance, there was an additional problem: the François Hollande government did not really want to enact this last-minute campaign promise by candidate Hollande and specifically refused to apply it to all incomes as a permanent new income tax bracket. Ultimately, the measure was applied in 2013–2014 as an exceptional tax on firms paying salaries above 1 million euros.

78. See Figs. 10.11–10.12.

fiscal justice based on nonregressivity (that is, the proportionate burden of the wealth or income tax on the wealthiest segment of the population should not be lower than the proportionate burden on the poorest segment) and requiring the government to publish adequate information on how the tax is apportioned so that citizens can judge whether the principle of nonregressivity has been respected. It is essential to leave it to elected parliaments to set the desirable degree of progressivity after public deliberation and on the basis of historical and personal experience; judges should not be allowed to intervene.

Basic Income and Just Wage: The Role of the Progressive Income Tax

I have thus far concentrated on the question of diffusion of wealth. As important as this is, it is far from the only goal of inequality reduction. Under the tax system shown in Table 17.1, the progressive property tax (combining both the annual tax and the inheritance tax) would yield annual revenues equivalent to 5 percent of national income, compared with the 45 percent of national income generated by the progressive income tax. Of course, this does not mean that the wealth tax is only one-ninth as important as the income tax. The wealth component of my plan, which consists of the progressive property tax plus the universal capital endowment, will have a long-term structural effect on the distribution of wealth and economic power, which far outweighs its purely fiscal significance. Nevertheless, the progressive income tax remains, in my view, the principal source of financing of the welfare state and of public expenses in general (education, health, pensions, etc.). To simplify matters, I have included under the head of income tax not just the income tax in the strict sense but also social security and other payroll and self-employment taxes and compulsory social contributions that are based on labor income (and in some instances on capital income).

These social taxes are in fact a form of income tax, in the sense that their amount depends on income, in some cases with rates that vary with income. The key difference is that the revenues from social taxes usually flow not to the state treasury but to special funds created to finance health insurance, pensions, unemployment insurance, and so on. It is essential, I believe, that such special funds continue as the repository for social taxes. In view of the very high level of total taxation (set here at 50 percent of national income, but which could be even higher if justified by need), it is important to ensure that citizens have a better idea of how their money is being used and in particular of the social purposes to which it is being put. Having separate funds for different types of expenditure might be one way of achieving that goal. In general, we need the greatest possible transparency as to the source and destination of all tax monies.

In practice, we find great diversity in sources of tax revenues from country to country. In Western Europe, where revenues have stabilized at 40–50 percent of national income in the period 1990–2020, we find that the income tax (including the corporate income tax) brings in 10–15 percent of national income[79] while social contributions amount to 15–20 percent of national income; indirect taxes (such as the value-added tax, or VAT, and other consumption taxes) yield 10–15 percent of national income.[80] Broadly speaking, indirect taxes (especially customs duties) were dominant until the nineteenth century in all countries but were gradually replaced by income taxes and social contributions as the main sources of revenue. In my view, there is no real justification for indirect taxes (except when necessary to correct an externality,[81] as in the case of the carbon tax, about which I will say more later); they should therefore be replaced by taxes on income or wealth. Indirect taxes such as the VAT do not allow taxes to be apportioned as a function of income or wealth, which is a major limitation in terms of both economic and democratic transparency.[82]

---

79. I am including the corporate tax in the progressive income tax system because it is better to analyze the two taxes together. Ideally, the corporate tax could be a sort of deduction from the income tax to be paid by stockholders on their dividends. In practice, owing to the lack of international cooperation and transparency regarding the ultimate ownership of firms, some taxpayers escape paying any taxes on their capital income so that it is crucial to maintain a direct tax on corporations. I will say more later about this issue.

80. See Chaps. 10–11 (and especially Figs. 10.15–10.15 and 11.9) for a more detailed analysis of the various types of taxes and expenditures. In some countries, such as Denmark, social contributions are formally integrated into the income tax so that the income tax alone yields about 35 percent of national income. See European Commission, *Taxation Trends in the EU,* 2018 ed., pp. 76–77, Table DK.1.

81. An externality occurs when the consumption of a good or service by an individual imposes undesirable costs on other individuals, typically by way of pollution or greenhouse gas emission.

82. With the VAT and other indirect taxes, it is of course possible to tax some goods at a lower rate than others, but this is a cruder way to target specific social groups than a direct tax on income or wealth. The other argument in favor of the VAT has to do with the ability to tax imports while exempting exports, but there is no real reason for this, and in any case it is more a sign of lack of international fiscal coordination (particularly where intra-European tax competition is concerned). I will say more later about the possible use of an import tax to compensate for the lack of international cooperation. Finally, note that the VAT in practice exempts many

Detailed analysis of the best way to organize public expenditure and the many components of the social state (universal health insurance, unified pension system, etc.) would take us far beyond the scope of this book. I will say more later about allocating spending on education, which plays a central role in generating and perpetuating inequality. Here, I will focus on the role of the basic income as an element of the social state and the just society. The fact that a basic (or minimum guaranteed) income exists in many countries and in particular in most Western European countries is an excellent thing. Basic income systems can and should be improved specifically by making them more automatic and universal, especially for the homeless, many of whom face great difficulty in obtaining access to the basic income, housing, and, more generally, the help they need to find work and secure a place for themselves in society. It is also essential to extend the basic income to people earning very low wages or receiving activity bonuses (that is, welfare-to-work supplements); the basic stipend should be automatically added to their wages without requiring them to apply for it (this can be linked to the progressive income tax, which is already withheld on paychecks).

Consider, for example, the relatively ambitious basic income shown in Table 17.1. We set the minimum basic income for individuals with no other resources at 60 percent of average after-tax income; this amount would decline as other income increased. It would apply to about 30 percent of the population for a total cost of about 5 percent of national income.[83] Once again, these figures are given for illustrative purposes only; any decision would come only after wide deliberation, and it is not the purpose of this book to say what the exact outcome of that debate should be.[84]

---

goods and services (such as financial services and investment goods) for unclear distributive reasons. A VAT that truly taxed all value added would be equivalent to a proportional tax on all income (profits and total wages) and could be seen as the first component of an income tax system. See Saez and Zucman, *The Triumph of Injustice* and the discussion of the "national income tax."

83. The average amount paid would be on the order of 30 percent of average after-tax income, or about 16.5 percent of average national income per adult (given an average income tax of 45 percent, counting social contributions and carbon taxes), for a total cost of 5 percent of national income if that amount is paid out to 30 percent of the population. See the online appendix.

84. For a more detailed description of such a system in the French case, including automatic inclusion of the basic income on pay stubs, see for example P. A. Muet, *Un impôt juste, c'est possible!* (Seuil, 2018). In the United States, an ambitious proposal to increase the Earned Income Tax Credit (EITC) (which is in effect a boost to low wages) was

The point I want to emphasize here is that even after the basic income is established, much more needs to be done to achieve social justice. In the example shown in Table 17.1, public spending on the social state represents about 40 percent of national income (covering health, education, pensions, unemployment insurance, family benefits, etc.), compared with just 5 percent for the basic income and 5 percent of the capital endowment. These orders of magnitude are important. They express the fact that a just society must be based on universal access to fundamental goods, foremost among which are health, education, employment, the wage relation, and deferred wages for the elderly and unemployed. The goal should be to transform the entire distribution of income and wealth and, beyond that, the distribution of power and opportunities; it goes far beyond just setting a floor on income. The ambition must be to create a society based on just remuneration of labor—in other words, a just wage. The basic income can contribute to that goal by raising the income of individuals who are otherwise poorly paid. More than that, however, justice also requires a thorough reconsideration of a whole range of mutually complementary institutional arrangements.

One of those institutions is the educational system. If every individual is to have a chance of finding decently remunerated employment, we must put an end to the hypocritical practice of investing more in elitist educational programs and institutions than in institutions that cater to the disadvantaged. The labor code and, more generally, the entire legal system need to be overhauled. New systems of wage bargaining, a higher minimum wage, a fairer wage scale, and sharing of voting rights within firms between workers and shareholders can all contribute to the establishment of a just wage, a more equal distribution of economic power, and a deeper involvement of workers in shaping the strategy of their employers.

The other important institution I want to discuss is the fiscal system itself. In addition to the progressive property tax and the universal capital endowment,

recently put forward by L. Kenworthy, *Social Democratic Capitalism* (Oxford University Press, 2019), p. 210, Fig. 7.15. One important difference is that the EITC would continue to be paid separately. In general, the advantage of automatic payment is that it links the basic income idea to a vision of the just society based on the wage relation and the right to work and unionize. By contrast, a system based on separate payment of the basic income (as proposed, for example, by Van Parijs and Vanderborght, *Basic Income,* who envisage a payment to each adult, independent of wages) risks weakening that link and might be instrumentalized to favor hyper-flexibilization and the fragmentation of labor. This could lead to an artificial inflation of the tax level, with the danger of decreasing resources available for the social state.

which encourages worker participation, the progressive income tax can help to achieve a just wage by reducing the income gap to a level consistent with a just society. History shows that marginal rates on the order of 70–90 percent on the highest incomes made it possible to eliminate pointless high salaries, much to the great benefit of workers lower down in the distribution, while at the same time increasing overall economic and social efficiency.[85] Indeed, all signs are that a tax schedule like the one shown in Table 17.1 would compress the pay scale and increase the pay of people at the bottom and in the middle of the distribution.[86] Note, moreover, that the proposed schedule rises quickly to fairly high levels, with an effective overall rate on the order of 40 percent (including social contributions) on incomes twice the national average. Such high rates are necessary to pay for an ambitious universal social state and especially for health care and pensions. Note, however, that in the absence of such public systems, workers would have to pay large sums to private pension funds and health insurance companies, which in practice can prove to be more costly than public equivalents.[87]

To sum up, one should avoid looking at the basic income as a sort of miraculous solution that would make all these other institutions unnecessary. In the past, the idea of a basic income was sometimes instrumentalized as a form of "payment in full" of all social obligations and invoked to justify cuts to other social programs.[88] Hence it is important to think of the basic income as one component of a more ambitious package, which should include progressive taxes on wealth and income, a universal capital endowment, and an ambitious social state.

On Progressive Taxation of Carbon Emissions

I turn now to the carbon tax. As I said earlier, along with rising inequality, global warming is the greatest challenge the planet faces today. There are several reasons to believe that these two challenges are intimately related and can be re-

---

85. See Chap. 11.

86. Obviously, I do not mean to imply that the purely illustrative figures given in Table 17.1 completely settle the question of just inequality. How much the pay scale needs to be compressed for the benefit of the disadvantaged remains an open question; the only way to make progress is to engage in realistic experiments.

87. In the United States, if one counts the cost of private insurance as though it were tax, the schedule of payments becomes highly regressive to the detriment of the lower and middle classes. See Saez and Zucman, *The Triumph of Injustice,* p. 213.

88. This was the spirit in which Milton Friedman proposed a basic income and negative income tax in his book with R. D. Friedman, *Free to Choose* (Harcourt, 1980).

solved only if dealt with simultaneously. First, carbon emissions are strongly concentrated among a small group of people, primarily individuals with high incomes and large fortunes living in the wealthiest countries in the world (especially in the United States).[89] Second, the magnitude of the lifestyle changes required to cope with the climate crisis is so great that it is hard to imagine how to make those changes socially and politically acceptable without establishing stringent and verifiable norms of justice. In other words, it is hard to see why the lower and middle classes in the rich countries would be willing to make a major effort to curtail emissions if they feel that the upper class is free to go on living and emitting greenhouse gases as before.

The inequality reduction measures I discussed earlier, including a sharp increase in the progressivity of taxes on high incomes and large fortunes, are therefore a necessary condition for combating climate change. They are not a sufficient condition, however. Among the other tools that have been widely discussed is a tax on carbon emissions. Several conditions have to be met, however, for such a solution to become viable. First, the carbon tax must not be seen as the only approach to dealing with the problem. Often, the most effective way to reduce emissions is to establish norms; prohibit certain practices; and agree on strict standards for automobile emissions, heating equipment, building insulation, and so on. In many cases these are more effective choices than just placing a high tax on carbon.

Second, no carbon tax will be fully accepted and effective unless all of the revenue it generates is used to compensate lower- and middle-class households affected by the tax and to pay for the transition to renewable sources of energy. The most natural way to do this would be to integrate the carbon tax into the progressive income tax, as I have done in Table 17.1. With each increase in the carbon tax, one has to calculate the average impact on people at different income levels as a function of the structure of average expenditures; one can then automatically adjust the income tax schedule and basic income transfer system to neutralize the effect. That way, one would preserve the price signal (because consuming items with high carbon content would cost more than consuming items low in carbon, thus giving consumers incentives to change their behavior) but without diminishing the purchasing power of people of modest means.[90]

---

89. See Fig. 13.7.
90. In some cases, the calculation of compensatory transfers will need to consider not only income but also type and place of residence, existence of public transportation, and so on.

By contrast, the method used in France in 2017–2018 consists in increasing carbon taxes on people of modest means to pay for tax cuts for the rich, leading to the so-called Yellow Vests uprising and the breakdown of the whole French carbon tax system. This is the method to avoid at all costs.[91]

Finally, it is legitimate to ask whether it would be a good idea to implement a progressive tax on carbon emissions. To date, carbon taxes have been basically proportional. All emissions are taxed at the same rate, whether the person or persons responsible emit five to ten tons of carbon (CO_2 equivalent) per year, which is roughly the world average, or 100–150 tons, which is the amount emitted by the top 1 percent of individual emitters globally. The problem with such a system is that if the heaviest emitters have the means, they can avoid making any effort to reduce their emissions, which is not necessarily the best way to establish a norm of environmental justice acceptable to the majority. Reducing overall levels of wealth and income inequality through progressive taxation can diminish these disparities and make them more acceptable, but by itself that might still not be enough. One proposed solution is to issue every individual a "carbon card" authorizing an annual quota of emissions (of, say, five to ten tons); each person would then be entitled to sell all or part of this quota. The problem is that anyone with modest resources or low emissions would then have a financial interest in allowing the wealthy and heavier polluters to emit more, which once again would mean that those with sufficient financial resources would be able to emit as much carbon as they pleased. What is more, experience with businesses purchasing the right to pollute on the open market suggests that if that market were extended to private individuals, it would likely prove to be extremely volatile and easy to manipulate, giving rise to waves of speculation and allowing some to reap enormous profits at the expense of others; meanwhile, the price signal emanating from such a market would be a particularly noisy one.

A better solution might be a true progressive tax on carbon emissions at the level of individual consumers. For example, the first five tons of individual emissions might be taxed little if at all, the next ten tons somewhat more, and so on up to some maximum level beyond which all emissions would be prohibited, with violations subject to fines (such as a confiscatory tax on income and/or wealth).[92] Like the "carbon card," this solution assumes that one can

---

91. See Chap. 14.

92. This carbon tax schedule is intended for illustrative purposes only and may be taken as a starting point, given that the average emission level worldwide is around

measure emissions at the individual level. This raises complex issues, which could nevertheless be overcome (for example, by using credit card information) if the issue were deemed important enough for the future of the planet.[93] Carbon content is already measured for certain types of consumption, such as electricity (it is reflected in electric bills). Initially, it might be possible to approximate a progressive carbon tax by setting higher tax rates on goods and services associated with high carbon emissions, such as jet fuel or, better yet, business class airline tickets. What is certain is that the development of a sustainable climate policy will require new norms of environmental and fiscal justice that the majority can accept, which is definitely not the case today.[94]

On Constructing a Norm of Educational Justice

I turn next to the question of educational justice. Emancipation through education and diffusion of knowledge must be at the heart of any project to build a just society and participatory socialism. History shows that economic development and human progress depend on education and not on the sacralization of inequality and property.[95] In previous chapters we saw how the expansion

---

five to six tons per person. It should be rapidly increased, however, if one wants to meet the goal of limiting global warming to 1.5–2 degrees (which according to estimates will require reducing carbon emissions to one to two tons per person by the end of the century).

93. In the past, every new tax has been accused of being impractical, impossibly complex, and inquisitorial. This was true, for instance, of the income tax in the nineteenth century and beyond. That said, the idea of using credit card data does raise serious privacy issues. In my view, however, it is strange not to consider the possibility of developing procedures for making use of such information in a controlled way, just as we have learned to trust private banks not to use the same information for nefarious purposes.

94. Another question is whether the progressive carbon tax should apply only to individual consumption (which might seem logical given the need to make consumers behave responsibly, especially in the rich countries) or whether one should also look into the possible of a progressive tax on individual production (based on individual income—wages and profits—generated by the production of goods and services responsible for the emission of carbon), which might be more effective in some cases. The two types of taxes (on consumption and production) are in principle equivalent when the tax is proportional. This is no longer the case when the tax is progressive.

95. See Chaps. 11 and 12. On the central role of achieving equality through education and knowledge in a Durkheimian (rather than Marxist) perspective, see B. Karsenti and C. Lemieux, *Socialisme et sociologie* (EHESS, 2017), pp. 43–48.

of education and the development of higher education coincided with a complete reversal of political cleavages. In the period 1950–1980, the Democratic Party, the Labour Party, and various socialist and social-democratic parties realized their best scores among voters with the least education. This cleavage gradually reversed, and by the period 1990–2020, the same parties were achieving their best results among voters with the most education. In sum, the political forces that constituted workers' parties in the years after World War II gradually turned into parties of the highly educated in the late twentieth and early twenty-first centuries. The most natural explanation is that less educated voters felt that these parties had abandoned them by shifting their attention and priorities to the winners of the educational system and to some extent of globalization. This political-ideological transformation is crucially important for our study. It is especially important for understanding the collapse of the postwar left-right system and the rise of inequality since the 1980s.[96]

I have already discussed at some length the very significant inequality of access to higher education in the United States, where the likelihood of attending college is linked to the parents' standing in the income distribution and where the system is highly stratified, with a wide gap separating the best universities from the rest.[97] If the Democratic Party wants to win back the voters it has lost, it will no doubt need to offer tangible proof that it is more concerned with the children of the lower and middle classes and somewhat less focused on the children of parents who are themselves graduates of the most elitist schools and universities. I also noted that educational inequality and hypocritical talk about meritocracy is common also in countries where the educational system is mainly public and supposedly egalitarian, such as France, even if the mechanisms of discrimination are different.[98]

Before delving further into this point, I want to call attention to Fig. 17.1, which shows the current distribution of educational investment in France. If one looks at the entire cohort of young people turning 20 in 2018, one can estimate (using available data and trends) that each of them will have benefited on average from about 120,000 euros in educational investment (from preschool to university), which corresponds to fifteen years of schooling at an average cost of approximately 8,000 euros per year. But this average conceals enormous disparities within the group related primarily to the age when schooling ends and to

---

96. See Chaps. 14–16.
97. See Fig. I.8 and Chap. 15.
98. See Chap. 14.

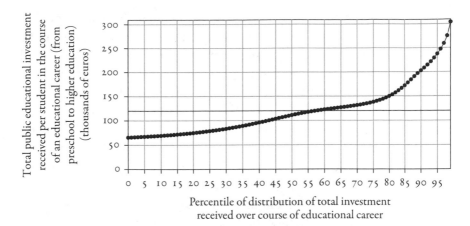

FIG. 17.1. Inequality of educational investment in France, 2018

Interpretation: The total public educational investment per student over the course of an educational career (preschool to university) for the generation of students turning 20 in 2018 averages out to around 120,000 euros (or about 8,000 euros per year over fifteen years). Within this generation, the 10 percent of students receiving the smallest public investment received 65,000–70,000 euros, while the 10 percent receiving the most received 200,000–300,000 euros. *Note:* The average cost per track per year of schooling in 2015–2018 works out to 5,000–6,000 euros in preschool and primary school, 8,000–10,000 euros in secondary school, 9,000–10,000 euros in university, and 15,000–16,000 euros in preparatory classes for the grandes écoles. *Sources and series:* piketty.pse.ens.fr/ideology.

course selection in high school and above all in the higher education system.[99] Within this cohort, the 10 percent of students in whom public investment was smallest received 65,000–70,000 euros each, while the 10 percent in whom most was invested received 200,000–300,000 euros each. The first group

---

99. Variations in preschool attendance are also significant. Preschool is available to children aged 3 to 6 but is not compulsory; in some years and some places it has been available as early as age 2. In any case, its role in creating disparities is far less than the factors mentioned in the text. The estimates given here are based on household surveys that allow us to estimate the distribution of educational choices in each age cohort. The method is to assign a constant cost per year depending on the type of education (primary, middle school, *lycée*, etc.). All details on the construction of the data set are available online. See also S. Zuber, *L'inégalité de la dépense publique d'éducation en France: 1900–2000* (EHESS, working paper, 2003), and C. Bonneau, *The Concentration of Educational Investment in the US (1970–2018), with a Comparison to France* (EHESS and PSE, working paper, 2019).

consists of people who left school at age 16 (the minimum legal age) after just ten years of schooling for an average cost of 6,000–7,000 euros per year. By contrast, the second group consists of students who took advanced degrees and in some cases remained in school until age 25 for a total of twenty years or more of education. Apart from the length of study, the other distinctive feature of this group is that its members followed highly selective tracks, usually passing through the preparatory classes for the *grandes écoles,* where students receive much more intense instruction than in the nonselective university tracks.[100]

Ultimately, these disparities are quite substantial: the inequality of public expenditure per student is 150,000 euros if one compares students in the top decile to those in the bottom decile and more than 200,000 euros if one compares students in the top centile to those in the bottom decile—the equivalent of the average wealth per adult in France today. It is as if some children receive an additional inheritance compared with others, and inheritances are already very unequally distributed.[101] Furthermore, although the students who stay in school for the shortest time are not systematically those from disadvantaged families and students who stay in school longest are not always the most advantaged, there is of course a significant positive correlation between these two dimensions so that in many cases the effect of public educational investment combines with the effect of private inheritance.[102] Finally, note that the assumptions we made to calculate these estimates probably lead to seriously understating the actual size of these spending disparities. Specifically, the official estimates of the cost of selective and nonselective tracks that we use here likely strongly understate the actual gap.[103]

---

100. According to official data, the cost per student in the preparatory classes is 15,000–16,000 euros per year, compared with 9,000–10,000 euros in the universities. Note, moreover, that real investment per student in higher education decreased by about 10 percent between 2010 and 2018 because budgets did not increase as rapidly as the number of students. See Ministère de l'éducation nationale, *Repères et références statistiques 2018* (2019), p. 325, section 10.5. See also the online appendix, Fig. S14.11e.

101. Recall that the 50 percent of individuals inheriting the least receive virtually nothing (barely 10,000–20,000 euros on average), while the 10 percent inheriting the most receive hundreds of thousands of euros and in some cases millions or even tens of millions of euros.

102. Available data show that the link between parental income and access to higher education is less extreme in France than in the United States but still high. See the online appendix.

103. Official estimates (15,000–16,000 euros per year for preparatory classes and 9,000–10,000 euros for university classes) include the cost of university research

Let me now ask what principles might be invoked to define a just distribution of the educational investment. Once again, as with the question of the just wealth and income taxes, the goal is obviously not to provide a closed solution, which I am incapable of doing, but simply to propose some possible avenues for collective deliberation. First, private educational investment clearly needs to be considered, which would widen the educational spending gap even more. In a country like France, where the educational system is primarily public, the effect of this would be limited. But in the United States it would be hugely important because investment per student there can attain extremely high levels for those who attend the richest and most expensive private universities, whose resources greatly surpass those of public universities and community colleges.[104]

How should one think about a just distribution of public educational investment in a country like France? A relatively natural norm would be that every child should have the right to the same educational funding, which could be used for either schooling or other training. In other words, a person who quit school at age 16 or 18, who would thus have consumed only 70,000–100,000 euros during her public schooling (which is the case for 40 percent of each age cohort) could then draw on educational capital worth 100,000 to 150,000 euros before reaching the level of the best funded 10 percent of her cohort (Fig. 17.1).[105] With this capital she could acquire additional training at age 25 or 35 or at any

---

laboratories, which do not necessarily benefit students, at least in the early years of university. In the preparatory classes, teachers are not engaged in research and concentrate on the objective of training students, which seriously biases the comparison. If one were to subtract research expenses and focus on university students in the first two years, the cost per year of study would be less than 5,000 euros. See the online appendix.

104. In fact, the concentration of total educational expenditure (public and private) is significantly higher in the United States than in France and has risen sharply in recent years. Note that the available data do not allow us to measure these inequalities perfectly at the primary, secondary, or tertiary level (in the United States, primary and secondary education is largely financed by local taxes). See Bonneau, *The Concentration of Educational Investment in the US*.

105. Another solution might be to charge high tuition fees to those students fortunate enough to continue their higher education (and who are on average socially advantaged), as New Labour did in the United Kingdom (see Chap. 15). The problem is that this presents a hardship to students of modest background, who may be discouraged from pursuing their studies or find themselves indebted for a long period of time, while students from wealthier backgrounds enjoy financial

point in her life.[106] Indeed, one could also think of allowing such individuals, under certain conditions, to use part of this sum as financial capital, which could be added to the universal capital endowment. Nevertheless, the priority should be to use these funds to improve educational opportunities for everyone, especially young people from disadvantaged classes.[107] Of course, many people would probably not take advantage of the opportunity to go back to school, so more should be invested in primary and secondary education in order to foster emancipation through education during the normal years of schooling.

The truth is that there is a great deal of hypocrisy in this area. In France and many other countries, extra funding is supposedly earmarked for socially disadvantaged neighborhoods and schools. In fact, as we saw earlier, it is the socially advantaged schools that benefit from the most experienced, best trained, and highest paid teachers, and this clearly counts for more than the meager extra funds provided to the novice and contract teachers who work in the disadvantaged schools.[108] If there were any real increase in the resources allocated to the least advantaged primary and secondary schools, this would show up in Fig. 17.1 as an increase in educational investment at the lower end of the distribution, signaling that educational spending had become more egalitarian and more just.

Renouncing Educational Hypocrisy, Promoting Transparency

If the goal is really to develop acceptable norms of educational justice, then there is no choice but to demand greater transparency in the allocation of educational resources. In most countries today, the procedures for apportioning

---

support from their parents. It seems preferable to require the latter to pay more for everyone's children and not just their own.

106. One might also use part of the educational capital as an allotment during years of study, even before age 25 (the age at which basic income becomes available in France), and not simply for free access to classes.

107. If spending on the bottom 90 percent of students in France today were raised to the level of spending on the top 10 percent (currently 200,000 euros a year), the additional cost would be on the order of 2.5–3 percent of national income (compared with a total current educational budget of 5.5–6 percent of national income). This cost would be significant but not insurmountable and justified in view of the stakes and the dangerous stagnation of educational investment in the wealthy countries since the 1980s. See Fig. 10.15.

108. See Chap. 14 and the research by A. Benhenda. Disadvantaged schools have fewer students per class, but this merely compensates for the effect of teacher pay, which goes in the opposite direction.

educational spending are quite opaque, and it is not easy for citizens or communities to understand them. We find ourselves with average teacher pay greater in socially advantaged schools; public educational investment is four times higher for certain groups (who also happen to be among the most favored) than for others in the same cohort. Yet no one has ever made a conscious decision that things should be this way, and the results are never examined or debated or challenged. I am not saying that educational justice is easy to define, and this book is certainly not going to end all debate. But if there is to be a real debate, data of the type I am providing here needs to be made public; indeed, there should be a law (or constitutional obligation) that the facts about educational investment should be available to everyone. Only then can goals be set and progress verified year after to see how close we come to achieving them.

Two goals strike me as reasonable: first, average teacher pay should no longer be an increasing function of the percentage of better off students in the schools, and second, the amounts invested in the least advantaged primary and secondary schools should be substantially increased to make the overall distribution of educational investment by age cohort more equal (see Fig. 17.1). These changes, which would be significant, need to be publicly verifiable. They should noticeably increase the likelihood that students from disadvantaged backgrounds attend university. All studies show that early intervention, particularly in primary and middle school, is the best way to correct scholastic inequality between students of different social backgrounds.

That said, the allocation of additional resources to less advantaged schools needs to be complemented by admissions procedures at *lycées* and universities that take the student's social origins into account. This can be done in two ways: social origins can be considered at the individual level (for example, by assigning points according to parental income or adopting social quotas by track, which is probably preferable), or the neighborhood in which the student resides or the school is located can be used as a criterion (for instance, the best students from each middle school or *lycée* in designated districts could be admitted automatically to specific programs). Again, it is not up to me to give answers to such delicate questions. Choices like these will require complex social and political compromises, which can come only after sophisticated experiments have been carried out and there has been broad debate with full citizen involvement. Any such choices will need to be reviewed constantly, improved, and adapted as the situation evolves. It is important to stress, however, that coming up with a norm of justice acceptable to all or, more modestly, capable of inspiring a minimum degree of collective confidence in the system is an extremely delicate and fragile process. Great transparency is essential, and transparency is often foreign to the habits of political officials and school administrators.

Some countries, such as India, have more experience than others in applying quotas and "reservations" to university admissions for specific social categories. In India, quotas were first applied in the 1950s to groups that had been discriminated against in the past; in 1990 they were extended to all socially disadvantaged classes, which played a major role in reshaping the contours of political-ideological conflict in the country.[109] While these experiences are instructive, they obviously cannot be directly copied in different context. Many countries in Europe have recently begun to take family background into account in admissions procedures, unfortunately with very little transparency. In France, the algorithms used for admissions to *lycées* (Affelnet) and higher education (first Admission Post-Bac and then, since 2018, Parcoursup) remain essentially state secrets.[110] Furthermore, the way family background and parental income are taken into account establish sharp social discontinuities, which make it more difficult to reach any social consensus about the procedures.[111] In the United States, the court-ordered ban on the use of racial criteria in admissions procedures is coupled with a similar ban on the use of parental income (which is much more debatable); therefore, social quotas usually rely on neighborhood.[112] Unfortunately, this criterion cannot achieve the desired level of social diversity because the beneficiaries are often the most advantaged residents of the least advantaged neighborhoods. Hence as a general rule it is better to rely on individual characteristics such as parental income. In the United Kingdom, there is a proposal to allow students who score above a certain level on exams to draw

---

109. See Chaps. 8 and 16.

110. In particular, the quotas of scholarship students who must be accepted into different programs (especially preparatory classes) are not made public.

111. Specifically, scholarship students (roughly the 15–20 percent of students with lowest parental income) receive extra points in Affelnet (or benefit from social quotas in Parcoursup), which increases social diversity to their advantage but is unfair to groups with just slightly higher parental income. A system that adjusted for parental income in a more continuous way would clearly be preferable. See S. T. Ly, E. Maurin, and A. Riegert, *La mixité sociale et scolaire dans les lycées d'Ile-de-France* (Institut des Politiques Publiques, Working Paper No. 4, June 2014).

112. See, for example, the study of Chicago public schools by G. Ellison and P. Pathak, *The Efficiency of Race-Neutral Alternatives to Race-Based Affirmative Action: Evidence from Chicago's Exam Schools* (National Bureau of Economic Research, NBER Working Paper No. 22589, 2016).

lots so as to democratize access to the most elitist institutions, in effect applying social quotas. Such randomization has the advantage of discouraging parents from overinvesting financially and emotionally in seeking ways for their children to achieve ever higher test scores, such as paying for extra coaching at earlier and earlier ages. This of course excludes parents who lack the necessary means to pay for extra help and very likely would not know where to find it if they did have the means.[113] A good compromise might be to take grades into account to a limited extent (above a certain threshold) while retaining a high level of social mixing as a priority goal. There is little doubt that these kinds of debates, which in many ways have only just begun, will play a central role in decades to come. Their politicization is still in the early stages. Ultimately, it could once again transform the educational cleavage structure.[114]

To conclude, let me mention the specific problem posed by the coexistence of public and private schools, not only at the tertiary level but also at the primary and secondary levels. In practice, private schools generally benefit from direct or indirect public financing because they enjoy special legal and fiscal status. They participate in the provision of an essential public service: disseminating knowledge to the young. Hence they should be subject to the same regulations as public schools with respect to both available resources and admissions procedures. Otherwise, the effort to construct acceptable norms of justice in the public sector will be undermined by flight to the private sector. In France, private primary and middle schools and *lycées* receive substantial public funding, which is combined with additional resources provided by parents; they also enjoy the right to select students from whatever social background they choose.[115] It is hard to see how these advantages can be made compatible with the principles of educational justice. In the United States, private universities refuse to make their admissions procedures and algorithms public and insist on being taken at their word when they claim that preferential admissions for the children of graduates and important donors are used sparingly.[116] Once again, this does not facilitate the task of elaborating a norm of justice acceptable to all.

---

113. See L. E. Major and S. Machin, *Social Mobility: And Its Enemies* (Pelican Books, 2018).
114. Let us hope that things evolve in a more peaceful way than Michael Young envisioned in *The Rise of Meritocracy* (1958). See Chap. 14.
115. See Chap. 14.
116. See Chaps. 11 and 15.

In recent decades, the dizzying increase in the capital endowments of the wealthiest private universities, especially in the United States, owing to the high returns their portfolios have yielded on international markets, has also posed specific problems.[117] To prevent these endowments from growing without limit, one proposal is to raise the portion of the endowment that must be spent annually from the current 4–5 percent (depending on the university) to 10 or 15 percent. The problem is that the wealthiest universities already have trouble figuring out how to spend their money while public colleges and universities open to the disadvantaged cruelly lack resources.[118] Under such conditions it would be logical to impose a progressive tax on university endowments to finance an endowment fund for the poorest universities. There is no reason why the schedule of this tax should be the same as that applied to the wealth of private individuals because the socioeconomic context is different. While it is not up to me to say what it should be, I do think that the question is worth pondering. Indeed, it is very hard to imagine any scenario leading to a just educational policy in the United States if one allows the disparities between elitist and poor universities to grow without limit. The same question could also be raised about foundations and other nonprofit entities in other sectors such as culture, health, and the media. In each case the answer should depend on how one defines the general interest.[119]

Just Democracy: Democratic Equality Vouchers

All the historical trajectories we have looked at in this book show how intimately the structure of inequality is related to the nature of the political regime. Whether we were looking at premodern trifunctional societies or nineteenth-century proprietarian societies or slave societies or colonial societies, it was the way political power was organized that allowed a certain type of inequality

---

117. On this point, see Chap. 11, and Piketty, *Capital in the Twenty-First Century,* chap. 12, table 12.2.

118. To get an idea of the problem, recall that the thirty most elitist US universities admit more students from the wealthiest 1 percent than from the poorest 60 percent of the income distribution. See Chap. 15.

119. In the case of foundations serving the interests of families or private individuals, it is obvious that they should be taxed as private property. The boundary line is not always easy to draw, however, and that is why we need precise rules concerning the governance of foundations (which should not be controlled solely by their generous donor) to determine what foundations deserve special tax treatment.

regime to persist. People sometimes think that the political institutions of Western society achieved a kind of unsurpassable perfection in the parliamentary democracy of the mid-twentieth century. In fact, one can certainly improve on the parliamentary democratic model, which is increasingly contested.

Among the most obvious limitations of the parliamentary model today is its inability to stem the tide of rising inequality. In this book I have tried to show how today's difficulties need to be seen in the context of a long and complex political and ideological history—the history of inequality regimes. Our present problems cannot be solved without major changes to existing political rules. For example, I noted earlier that to establish social and temporary ownership through corporate power sharing and progressive taxation of wealth, constitutional and legal changes may be needed. This was also true in the past when similar questions arose: for example, the German Constitution of 1949 had to be written in such a way as to allow co-management and social ownership of corporations, and the US Constitution had to be amended in 1913 to authorize federal income and inheritance taxes, which were subsequently made progressive. Other changes of political rules played equally important roles in reducing inequality in other countries. In the United Kingdom, the House of Lords had to be stripped of its veto in the constitutional crisis of 1910–1911 in order for progressive taxation to see the light of day. In France, the social and fiscal reforms of 1945 and 1981 would have been much harder to achieve if the Senate had retained the veto power it enjoyed under the Third Republic—a power that the Socialists and Communists fought hard to eliminate in 1945–1946. It would be a mistake to think that things will be different in the future: transformation of the structure of inequality will continue to go hand in hand with transformation of the political regime. To shrink from changing the rules because it is too complicated is to ignore the lessons of history and forgo any possibility of real change. In Chapter 16 I discussed the EU's unanimity rule on fiscal matters and the need to rebuild Europe on a social-federalist foundation. I will say more in a moment about the need to change the rules and treaties that govern social and economic relations between states.

Another aspect of the political regime is also in need of urgent attention: the financing of political campaigns and of political life more generally. In theory, universal suffrage is based on a simple principle: one woman (or man), one vote. In practice, financial and economic interests can exert an outsized influence on the political process, either directly by financing parties and campaigns or indirectly through the media, think tanks, or universities. Earlier, I discussed the case of nonprofit media organizations, which could become the standard for producing news, affording newspaper and other media companies much greater independence from their financiers (including major shareholders, owing to the ceiling on voting rights within the company).[120] Direct financing of political campaigns and parties can obviously influence the priorities of political parties and complicate the adoption of measures to combat inequality, owing for instance to the radical hostility of many wealthy donors to more steeply progressive taxes.

The question of political financing has never really been considered in a comprehensive way. To be sure, many countries have passed laws limiting the influence of private money in politics. Some countries have engaged in timid efforts of public financing, such as Germany in the 1950s, the United States and Italy in the 1970s and 1980s, and France in the 1990s. But it is striking to see how fragmented and incomplete those efforts have been and how little they have built on one another. In other areas of lawmaking, governments are quick to copy one another (as in the case of progressive taxation, for better and for worse), but when it comes to regulating the influence of money in politics, each country seems to act almost completely independently of the others. Recent work by Julia Cagé has shown, however, that meticulous examination of this complicated history can be highly instructive. In particular, analysis of the various measures that have been tried so far suggests that "democratic equality vouchers" offer an especially promising avenue for exploration.[121]

In a nutshell, the idea would be to provide every citizen with an annual voucher worth, say, 5 euros, which could be assigned to the political party or movement of his or her choosing. The choice would be made online, for instance, when validating one's income or wealth declaration. Only movements supported by some minimal percentage of the population (which might be set at, say, 1 percent) would be eligible. If an individual chooses not to support any party (or if support for the chosen party falls below the threshold), the value of his or her voucher would be allocated in proportion to the choices made by

---

120. See Cagé, *Saving the Media*. In addition to supporting new participatory citizen-controlled media, the public should take control of (or at least strongly regulate) digital platforms in quasi-monopolistic situations and should impose very strict rules to combat sponsored content and unlimited extension of advertising (which today pollutes even the facades of historic monuments). Egalitarian democratic deliberation should be promoted.

121. See Cagé, *The Price of Democracy*. Full disclosure: Julia Cagé is my partner, which does not prevent her from writing excellent books, nor does it prevent me from reading those books in a critical spirit.

other citizens.[122] This last point is important because the absence of a rule of this type led to the collapse of the public financing experiment in the United States, where many citizens chose not to participate in public financing of political parties of any kind. But democracy is not an option: if some people do not wish to participate, that should not reduce the level of public financing (which in any case is not enormous). Apart from the democratic equality vouchers, political contributions by firms and other "moral persons" would be totally prohibited (as is already the case in many European countries, such as France since 1995), and there would be a strict ceiling on private individual donations (which Julia Cagé proposes to limit to 200 euros per year). This new political financing regime would include very strict requirements for parties and movements that want to sponsor candidates; they would be required not only to publish their accounts but also to be totally transparent about their internal statutes and rules of governance, which at present are often extremely opaque.

Toward a Participatory and Egalitarian Democracy

The central goal of democratic equality vouchers is to promote participatory and egalitarian democracy. Currently, the prevalence of private financing significantly biases the political process. This is particularly true of the United States where campaign finance laws (always inadequate) have been set aside by recent decisions of the Supreme Court. But it is also true in emerging democracies such as India and Brazil as well as in Europe, where current laws are equally inadequate and in some cases totally scandalous. Take France, for example: political contributions by private individuals are permitted up to 7,500 euros per year per taxpayer, two-thirds of which may be deducting from one's income tax (yielding a 5,000 euro deduction for a 7,500 euro contribution). It will come as no surprise that the contributors who come close to the ceiling are mainly quite wealthy, from the top centile of the income distribution. In other words, the political preferences of the rich are directly and explicitly subsidized by the rest of the population. The sums in question are far from negligible: total income-tax deductions for political contributions amount to 60–70 million euros per year, roughly equivalent to the total official public financing

---

122. To encourage the emergence of new movements, one might also imagine citizens making two choices: one to apply if the chosen movement makes it above the 1 percent threshold, the other in case it does not.

of French parties (which is proportionate to votes received and seats won in the most recent legislative elections).[123] Concretely, the current French system earmarks 2–3 euros per year per citizen for official funding of parties, plus up to 5,000 euros a year to subsidize the preferences of each rich donor. Democratic equality vouchers would make it possible to totally eliminate tax deductions for political contributions; the increase in tax revenues could then be distributed in an egalitarian fashion. Compared with the current system, which is based on the results of the most recent legislative elections, this proposal would also encourage more responsive citizen participation and more rapid renewal of political parties and movements.

As Cagé points out, the logic of democratic equality vouchers could also be applied to issues other than political financing. Indeed, vouchers could replace the existing system of tax deductions for charitable contributions, which in reality is just another way of subsidizing the cultural and philanthropic preferences of the rich. One could start with the sums currently lost to tax deductions and benefits of various kinds and reallocate those amounts in the form of vouchers distributed to each taxpayer. What organizations and foundations in which sectors would be eligible to receive these vouchers? Candidates might include health, culture, the fight against poverty, education, the media, and so on. All these suggestions are worthy of further debate. A similar procedure might also figure in thinking about the thorny issue of financing religious activities.[124]

---

123. See Cagé, *The Price of Democracy*. In general, it is striking to see how each country has cobbled together an inconsistent set of rules for dealing with political contributions without seeking to learn from others. For example, France prohibited gifts by "moral persons" but came up with an improbable system for directly subsidizing the political preferences of the wealthy (other countries also allow tax deductions for political contributions but generally less extreme). By contrast, after World War II, Germany pioneered an innovative system for public financing of parties and foundations attached to the parties and devoted to producing political ideas and programs. But Germany also failed to prohibit contributions by moral persons so that all large German firms subsidize all the parties; this may not be without influence on German government positions on exports and trade surpluses.

124. Currently, countries like Italy have a system in which taxpayers can indicate which religion they would like a portion of their taxes to go to (currently 0.8 percent), while in other countries, such as Germany, the tax authorities collect a religion tax (taxpayers who declare affiliation with a religious group pay a tax supplement). In contrast to the Italian system, this raises their tax bill. Note that Islam is excluded in both cases (and in Italy, Muslims pay de facto to subsidize other religions). Officially, the

The question of how much money can be justly allocated this way is also central, and I do not propose to resolve it here. If the sums involved represented a significant fraction of total tax receipts, this would be a highly elaborate form of direct democracy, which would allow citizens to decide themselves how a large portion of the public budget should be spent. This is a promising avenue for promoting greater citizen participation in a democratic process that often seems unresponsive to the desires of ordinary people.[125] In practice, the system of parliamentary deliberation is nevertheless indispensable for deciding how to allocate the vast majority of public funds. Budget decisions call for extensive public deliberation with an opportunity for all sides to be heard and with oversight by media and ordinary citizens. The scope of direct democracy should be expanded through participatory budgeting, egalitarian vouchers, and referenda.[126] But direct democracy is unlikely to replace the deliberative setting afforded by parliamentary democracy. The spirit of the democratic equality voucher is rather to make parliamentary democracy more dynamic and participatory by encouraging all citizens, regardless of their social background or

---

reason for this is that the government has not identified a proper Muslim organization to receive public funds. See F. Messner, ed., *Public Funding of Religions in Europe* (Ashgate, 2015). See also Cagé, *The Price of Democracy*, pp. 77–78. In France, the system is particularly hypocritical: religions receive no official public financing other than for religious edifices built prior to 1905 (most of which are Catholic churches) and existing private schools and *lycées* (the vast majority of which are Catholic). Note, moreover, that the special regime for financing religion in Alsace and Moselle also excludes Islam, just like the rest of the system.

125. The current system of tax deductions for political and charitable gifts amounts to granting the rich greater say in defining the public good. In this respect it resembles the censitary voting system. The transition to an egalitarian voucher would represent a decisive improvement. Taxpaying citizens who do not wish to choose a philanthropic cause could choose to have their voucher allocated in proportion to the wishes of those who do choose, or in accordance with the average allocation of public funds established by parliament.

126. As noted earlier, however, in the case of Brexit and other complex and crucial issues such as debt cancellation, referenda are useful only if precise alternatives are formulated and presented to the voters. This calls for extensive deliberation in an appropriate setting. In practice, the illusion of direct spontaneous democracy without a parliament or intermediary bodies can easily lead to a usurpation of power more extreme than the power imbalance one is seeking to remedy. Hence rules governing the financing of referendum campaigns are essential, failing which the vote may be captured by lobbies and financial interests. All these issues can be dealt with but must be carefully thought through.

financial means, to participate regularly in the renewal of political movements and parties. They can thus shape new ideas and platforms, which can then become the subject of deliberations and decisions by elected assemblies.[127]

Just Borders: Rethinking Social Federalism on a Global Scale

We come now to what is undoubtedly the most delicate question in defining the just society: the question of just borders. We are so accustomed to the principles by which the world is currently organized that they seem impossible to supersede, but in reality they stem from a very specific type of political-ideological regime. On the one hand, goods, services, and capital are supposed to flow freely across borders; to reject this principle is tantamount to seceding from the civilized world. On the other hand, political choices made within a country's borders, especially in regard to fiscal, social, and legal systems, are matters of strict national sovereignty; no other country is supposed to have a say in them. The problem is that these two principles lead directly to contradictions that have only grown worse in recent decades; these contradictions threaten to blow up the global system as it currently exists. The solution is to organize the system differently: existing trade agreements should be replaced with much more ambitious treaties that seek to promote equitable and sustainable development, which will require setting verifiable common goals in regard to matters such as just taxation and carbon emissions. If necessary, appropriate democratic deliberation procedures can be developed for us in transnational assemblies. I call this new type of international accord a "treaty for codevelopment." Codevelopment treaties may include measures to facilitate trade, but liberalization of commercial and financial flows should no longer constitute the heart of the global system. Trade and finance would then become what they always should have been: means in the service of higher ends.

One of the most obvious contradictions of the current system is that the free circulation of goods and capital is organized in such a way that it significantly

---

127. Cagé's proposal also includes the creation of social quotas (based on the Indian model) to ensure better representation of people of different social backgrounds in parliamentary assemblies. See Cagé, *The Price of Democracy*. Greater social diversity in representative bodies could also be achieved by drawing lots, which would avoid the possible social stigma associated with quotas. But this would mean giving up our collective ability to choose the people we believe best qualified to represent us (including within a given social group), which would be rather nihilistic if applied on a large scale.

limits the ability of states to choose their fiscal and social policies. In other words, current international rules do not establish the neutral framework they purport to create but rather compel countries to adopt certain policies and directly restrict national sovereignty. More specifically, we saw earlier that the agreements of the 1980s that liberalized capital flows included no mechanism for fiscal cooperation or automatic transmission of information about cross-border asset flows and the identity of asset owners.[128] In this realm Europe led the world by adopting rules that de facto prevented governments from combating strategies of tax and regulatory avoidance involving offshore structures (or at the very least forced states to abrogate treaties if they wished to impose adequate sanctions).[129] The choice of this specific legal regime to some extent reflects the conscious will of certain actors to promote fiscal competition among European states (deemed to be spendthrifts). It was also a consequence of a certain improvisation around decisions whose consequences had not been fully anticipated in the 1980s, specifically having to do with the growth of tax havens and offshore finance. In short, these agreements were signed in a different era before inequality, the excesses of financial capitalism, and the dangers of identitarian and nationalist retreat were as worrisome as they have become today.

Furthermore, the fiction of strictly national sovereignty over social and fiscal choices has been demolished by the fact that representations of justice are increasingly transnational. Why do wealthy countries aid poor ones (notwithstanding the fact that the aid supplied is insufficient and often ill adapted to

---

128. See Chaps. 11 and 13.

129. For example, the requirement I described earlier for owners of residences or businesses located in France to declare their ownership might be challenged on the grounds that they would impinge on the free circulation of capital. It is nevertheless urgent that all entities that own assets (under any legal regime whatsoever) be subject to very strict rules of transparency. It should be almost impossible to register a corporation in a territory or jurisdiction where it does virtually no actual business. Currently, the rules governing "conflict of laws" (the situation that arises when two or more jurisdictions apply to the same entity) are very favorable to companies that have the means to circumvent the law in the sense that countries often allow firms to organize their business through entities over which they have no jurisdiction. In a number of cases, the Court of Justice of the European Union has enforced a very strict reading of the capital mobility rules (some of which are imprecisely codified in the Maastricht Treaty), finding, for example, that Germany had to suspend use of the "real seat theory" under which it did not recognize an entity based in the Netherlands as a "moral person." See K. Pistor, *The Code of Capital* (Princeton University Press, 2019).

its purpose)? It is not solely for self-interested reasons, such as stanching the flow of immigrants. It is also because residents of the wealthy countries (or at least part of them) believe that it is unjust for people born in the poor countries to have opportunities so much more limited than their own. They want, to a degree at least, to correct this unjust inequality and are willing to sacrifice to that end, provided that the cost is not too high. Exactly how much they are willing to spend depends on complex and changing perceptions, which are shaped by what limited information they possess about the volume of aid and the success or failure of various strategies of development. Today, the norm is the following: a country should devote 1 percent of its GDP to developmental assistance. Although this is not an extraordinarily generous amount, it is nevertheless substantial compared with other forms of international transfer.[130]

Furthermore, perceptions regarding transnational and global justice play an increasing role in debates about the environment, the Anthropocene, biodiversity, and climate change. Of course, efforts to limit global warming have been notoriously insufficient. But the very fact that certain countries and regions of the world are reducing their emissions without waiting for the rest of the world to follow would be hard to explain in a world where it was every man for himself or every country for itself. Nevertheless, there is a great deal of hypocrisy in these debates and much inconsistency. In December 2015, 196 countries met in Paris and agreed on a theoretical goal of limiting global warming to less than 1.5 degrees above preindustrial levels, which would require leaving in the ground a great deal of hydrocarbon, such as that extracted from the tar sands of Alberta, which Canada wants to resume exploiting. That did not prevent the European Union from signing a new trade agreement with Canada in 2016—the Comprehensive Economic and Trade Agreement, or CETA, which includes all sorts of binding decisions regarding the liberalization of trade and investment flows but none concerning environmental or fiscal issues. It would have been possible,

---

130. Developmental aid is about 1 percent of gross national income in Sweden, 0.7 percent in the United Kingdom, and 0.4 percent in Germany and France. The official objective set by the Organisation for Economic Co-operation and Development is 0.7 percent, but the Swedish figure is often taken as the implicit new goal. These amounts are greater than net transfers within the European Union (roughly 0.2–0.3 percent of gross national income), attacks on which played a nonnegligible role in the Brexit debates. See Chaps. 12 and 15. This suggests that such flows are seen differently depending on the level of development of the receiving country and are perhaps more readily accepted when seen as aiding countries perceived to be especially poor.

however, to add carbon emission targets or specify minimum common rates of corporate taxation, together with verification mechanisms and sanctions to ensure enforcement, as was done for trade and financial issues.[131]

Of course, the most conspicuous contradiction between the way globalization is organized today and ideas of transnational justice has to do with the free circulation of persons. Under the dominant paradigm, civilized states are required to allow free circulation of goods, services, and capital but are perfectly free to block the free movement of people as they see fit. Hence this becomes in a sense the only issue of legitimate political confrontation. The European Union is defined by having achieved free circulation within its borders while maintaining much more restrictive policies with respect to individuals arriving from Africa or the Middle East, including those fleeing poverty and war. Since the refugee crisis of 2015, most European leaders have supported the idea that the migrant influx must be stopped, no matter what the cost, even if it means allowing tens of thousands of people to drown in the Mediterranean to discourage anyone who might be tempted to follow.[132] Part of the European public opposes this policy, but another part evinces great hostility to non-European migrants and supports one or another of the nativist political movements that have cropped up in Europe since the 1980s–1990s to exploit identity issues. This has greatly changed political cleavage structures. As we saw earlier, however, the change began well before the immigration issue became central. Waning support for policies that would redistribute wealth and income and reduce inequality was just as important as hostility to immigrants in bringing about this change.[133]

In sum, ideas of justice are important at the transnational as well as the national level in regard to developmental aid, the environment, and free circulation of persons, but those ideas are often confused and contradictory. The important point is that they are not set in stone: they are historically and politically constructed.

---

131. The very name "Comprehensive Economic and Trade Agreement" signifies that this is not a standard trade agreement but an accord that includes measures aimed at "comprehensive" transformation of the economy, which in practice means additional measures of "investor protection" (which allow investors to avoid ordinary courts of law and rely on private arbitrators to settle their disputes with governments). Clearly, there are different conceptions of how treaties should be understood.

132. The International Organization for Migration officially counts 19,000 migrants as having drowned in the Mediterranean between 2014 and 2018 (see their website at www.iom.int).

133. See Chaps. 14–15.

Toward a Transnational Justice

With these preliminaries in mind, how should transnational justice be defined? It is easiest to begin by discussing countries at approximately the same level of development, such as the countries of Europe. In the previous chapter, we saw how social federalism might work at the European level.[134] The general principle was to delegate to a transnational assembly (in this instance the European Assembly) responsibility for decisions concerning global public goods, such as protecting the environment and promoting research, and for global fiscal justice, including the possibility of imposing common taxes on income and property, large firms, and carbon emissions (Table 17.2). This transnational assembly could be composed of members of the national parliaments of member states or of transnational deputies expressly elected to serve in this capacity, or of a mixture of the two. In the European case I stressed the importance of developing a European parliamentary sovereignty that would rest primarily on the sovereignty of national parliaments so as to involve national deputies in the political process and prevent them from shifting blame for unpopular policies to the federal level, which could doom the whole project. But clearly there are many ways to organize a transnational assembly, and it is reasonable to experiment with different solutions in different contexts.

We also saw that the question of transfer payments was highly sensitive in the European context, even between countries with virtually identical average incomes, such as Germany and France. Establishing trust will take time, and meanwhile it makes sense to impose strict limits on transfers for as long as necessary. The hope is that the importance of joint projects and shared goals, especially in the areas of environmental protection, basic research, justice, and inequality reduction, will ultimately overshadow petty bookkeeping concerns. In general, there is no essential reason why there should be more solidarity between Bavarians and Lower Saxons or between Greater Parisians and Bretons than between all four and Piedmontese or Catalans. None of these solidarities exist spontaneously: they are historically and politically constructed and come into being when people see that the advantages of belonging to the same community outweigh the advantages of maintaining borders.[135]

---

134. See Chap. 16.
135. On the construction of common images as the basis of nation-states linked to the diffusion of printing, see the classic work by B. Anderson, *Imagined Communities. Reflection on the Origins and Spread of Modern Nationalism* (Verso, 1983; new

TABLE 17.2

A new organization of globalization: Transnational democracy

Transnational Assembly			
In charge of global public goods (climate, research, etc.) and global fiscal justice (common taxes on the largest fortunes and highest incomes, largest firms, carbon taxes)			

National Assembly Country A	National Assembly Country B	National Assembly Country C	National Assembly Country D ...

Interpretation: Under the proposed organization, the treaties regulating globalization (circulation of goods, capital, and people) will henceforth provide for the states and regional unions concerned to create a transnational assembly in charge of global public goods (climate, research, etc.) and global fiscal justice (common taxes on the largest fortunes, highest incomes, largest firms, and carbon taxes). *Note:* Countries A, B, C, and D may be states like France, Germany, Italy, Spain, and so on, in which case the transnational assembly would be the European Assembly, or they could be regional unions like the European Union, the African Union, and so on, in which case the transnational assembly would be the Euro-African Assembly. The transnational assembly may consist of deputies of national assemblies and/or transnational deputies specially elected for the purpose, as the case may be.

This model of transnational democracy on a European scale could also be extended more broadly. Owing to bonds of proximity stemming from more intense human and economic exchanges, the most logical next step would be to foster collaboration between regional entities: for example, between the European Union and the African Union,[136] between the European Union and the United States, and so on. When decisions can be taken directly within the framework of an intergovernmental treaty, there is no reason to delegate them

---

ed., 2006). Despite the success of the ideology of the national state, more or less decentralized imperial or federal polities have actually never ceased to play a central role. See J. Burbank and F. Cooper, *Empires in World History* (Princeton University Press, 2010); "Un monde d'empires," in P. Boucheron and N. Delalande, *Pour une histoire-monde* (Presses Universitaires de France, 2013), pp. 37–48. See also Chap. 7 on the work of F. Cooper on federalist debates in the French empire and Africa in 1945–1960 and Chap. 11 on H. Arendt's analysis of imperial and federal ideologies. See also U. Beck and E. Grande, *Das kosmopolitische Europa* (Suhrkamp, 2004).

136. In 2002 the African Union (AU) replaced the Organization for African Unity. During the AU summit meeting in Addis Ababa in 2018, the principles of a trade union and possible common taxes were approved along with a protocol on free circulation of persons within the AU.

to a transnational assembly. But the fact is there are many decisions that stand in need of constant revision and updating and should be subject to open public deliberation in a parliamentary setting where all points of view can be heard. Legislators need to hear the diversity of opinions within each member state. This would totally change the nature of the debate compared with the present procedure under which decisions are taken in closed-door meetings of heads of state, where discussion is defined by the clash of national interests (or what the heads of state take their national interests to be). For instance, a Euro-African Assembly might be responsible for deciding how to tax European multinationals investing in Africa (or, someday, African companies operating in Europe), how to combat global warming with compensatory measures, or how to regulate the flow of migrants.

As for transfers, it is important to set limits on their size at the outset without precluding modifications to those limits in the future. Compared with present-day developmental aid, much of which goes to paying Western consultants, the general principle might be that transfers should go directly to the treasuries of the states concerned once certain conditions are met, including respect for individual rights and fair voting procedures (which should be spelled out in detail). Circumvention of state institutions in Africa (and, more generally, in poor countries) by both governmental and nongovernmental organizations has been a factor slowing the process of state formation in recent decades. So has the loss of revenue due to the very rapid elimination of tariffs by the rich countries, which have not generally assisted the poor countries in developing more just taxes to replace them—namely, taxes on profits, income, and wealth.[137] If developmental aid money were paid directly to African governments, those governments would have significantly greater resources to pay for better schools and health services. No one can say in advance where such transnational democratic deliberations and procedures would lead, but it is not out of the question that a norm of educational equality (according to which all children, whether born in Europe or Africa, would be entitled to equal investment in their education) might gradually take hold, along with ultimately an equal capital endowment for everyone as well.[138]

---

137. See Fig. 13.12.

138. This norm of transnational justice should take price differences into account (that is, the universal capital endowment should be expressed in terms of purchasing power parity). Nevertheless, such a norm at the Euro-African or global level would clearly result in a significant decrease in the capital endowment for

Hypothetically, transnational assemblies could decide to approve rules to move toward free circulation of people. On this point, it is worth noting that there are some important restrictions on free circulation even within the European Union. In practice, citizens of member states have the right to travel and work in other members states without special authorization, which is a significant right, especially when compared with the problems that citizens of other countries (and their prospective employers) face in obtaining work visas. Nevertheless, if they do not find employment, their residency in another member state is generally limited to three months. Furthermore, they must wait up to five years before becoming eligible for social assistance or permanent resident status.[139] In the abstract, there is no reason why European treaties could not be amended to eliminate the waiting period for social assistance. But in that case, there would have to be agreement on mutualizing the corresponding social costs. This example shows why it is important to treat fundamental rights (such as free circulation of people) together with fiscal and budgetary questions. Unless simultaneous progress is made on both fronts, the result will be unbalanced and fragile.[140]

University tuition fees are another case in point. In 2019, the French government decided that only students from the European Union would continue paying the current fees, which are fairly modest (170 euros per year for the *licence,* 240 euros for the *master*). Non-European students would be charged much higher amounts (2,800 euros and 3,800 euros, respectively). The government's order does allow for exceptions but on the express condition

---

young adults in the rich countries (which would be cut roughly in half). Such a norm would be much more satisfactory than the international and intergenerational reparations discussed in the case of relations between France and Haiti (see Chap. 6). But if there were no such norm and reparations would have a similar effect, it would be difficult to oppose them.

139. See D. Chalmers, G. Davies, and G. Monti, *European Union Law: Text and Materials,* 3rd ed. (Cambridge University Press, 2014), pp. 475–491.

140. The development of free circulation in Britain in the eighteenth and nineteenth centuries, which Karl Polanyi analyzed, illustrates this danger. For Polanyi, the limited mobility of the poorest English workers prior to the late eighteenth century was linked to local financing of benefits available under the so-called Poor Laws. Polanyi, who has no intention of idealizing this authoritarian and stingy system, shows how the constitution of a unified national labor market in the nineteenth century coincided with a social disembedding of economic forces and aggravation of inequality.

that they apply to no more than 10 percent of all students. In other words, in the vast majority of cases, students from Mali or Sudan will have to pay ten to twenty times as much as students from Luxembourg or Norway, even if the parents of the latter earn ten to twenty times as much as the parents of the former.[141] Quite understandably, many French students and academics have a hard time understanding the logic of this new standard—one more brainchild of the current government.

The case is interesting because it shows once again the need to link the question of free circulation to that of mutualized financing of public services and therefore common taxes. In this case, the principle that all European students should be allowed to study in the country of their choosing and pay the same fees as nationals is an excellent thing. But the principle would be make more sense if there were common financing, which could come from a federal tax levied at the European level on the highest earners, with progressive rates and a schedule that would be subject to debate and approval by the European Assembly. Creating rights without worrying about their financing is not a good idea, and the problem becomes even more difficult when common taxes are excluded and fiscal competition is intensified. Under these conditions it becomes more difficult to pay for higher education and for public education in general. Furthermore, if common financing existed, at least among those European states willing to agree to it, it would be possible to find a solution for non-European students as well. Specifically, if Germany and France financed their universities with a common progressive tax based on parental income, it would make sense to propose a similar arrangement for Malian students. Germany, France, and Mali could sign a codevelopment treaty under which Malian students would pay the same tuition as German and French students, provided that the wealthiest Malian parents pay the same progressive tax into a common fund for university financing.[142] This would be one possible standard of justice. Open public democratic deliberation seems to me the logical way to get there.

---

141. European tuition rates also apply to citizens of states associated with the European Union, such as Norway and Switzerland.

142. Because Malian incomes are low (even after adjusting the tax schedule to reflect purchasing power parity), it is likely that the Malian contribution to the common fund would be quite low and no doubt significantly lower than developmental funds paid to Mali.

Between Cooperation and Retreat: The Evolution of the Transnational Inequality Regime

What I have just described is a cooperative and ideal (not to say idyllic) scenario that would lead via concentric circles to a vast transnational democracy, ultimately resulting in just common taxes, a universal right to education and a capital endowment, free circulation of people, and de facto virtual abolition of borders.[143] I am aware that other scenarios are possible. As we saw in Chapter 16, there is no assurance that EU member states (or any subset of them) will be able to agree anytime soon on a democratic procedure for levying common taxes. Meanwhile, the Indian Union with its 1.3 billion people has adopted a progressive income tax on all its citizens together with common rules that give the disadvantaged classes access to universities. The Indian model has other problems, however. Still, it shows that democratic federalism can take forms that people in France, Switzerland, or Luxembourg might never imagine. Establishing mutual confidence and norms of transnational justice is a delicate, highly fragile exercise, and no one can predict how cooperative arrangements might evolve.

Between the ideal path to global federalism and the path of generalized nationalist and identitarian retreat, many trajectories are of course possible, with multiple switch points. To make progress toward a more just globalization, two principles should be kept in mind. First, although it is clear that many of the rules and treaties that currently govern international trade and finance must be profoundly reformed, it is important to propose a new international legal framework before dismantling the old one. As we saw in the discussion of European institutional reforms in Chapter 16, political leaders may be tempted to renounce existing treaties without specifying what new ones they would like to put in their place. This is what happened with Brexit. British Conservatives chose to ask voters to decide by referendum whether or not they wished to exit the European Union but did not indicate how they planned to organize their future relations with the European Union in case of exit. Without returning to autarky (which no one wants), there are many ways of regulating these

---

143. To be clear, under the scenario described here, most decisions would continue to be taken and administered by national, regional, or local assemblies, which would also approve most financing. In many cases it is better to organize deliberation at this level (for example, on curricula in different languages, local infrastructure and transportation, health systems, etc.), within the logic of the decentralized participatory socialism I am advocating. Only global public goods and taxing of transnational economic actors are to be regulated directly at the transnational level.

relations; the postreferendum debate has shown how difficult it is to agree on any of them.[144]

Second, while it is essential to propose a new framework for cooperation before abandoning the old one, it is impossible to wait for the entire world to agree before moving ahead. It is therefore crucial to think of solutions that will allow a few countries to move toward social federalism by signing codevelopment treaties among themselves while remaining open to others who might eventually wish to join them. This is true not only at the European level but at the international level more generally. For example, if one or more countries abrogate one of the treaties that currently mandate the free flow of capital, they must first create a new arrangement that would still allow for international investment and cross-border ownership; then they must invite others to join them, but only on condition that any country joining the agreement abide by the rules for transmitting information about asset ownership. This is necessary to allow proper assessment of taxes based on each person's ability to contribute (as measured by wealth and income).

Similarly, sanctions imposed on noncooperating states must be reversible; it should be made clear that the goal is to establish a cooperative, egalitarian, and inclusive system and not to heighten international tensions. Ideally, all states, in Europe and elsewhere, would end harmful competition and establish new forms of cooperation. Profits earned by large multinational corporations should be apportioned among states in a transparent manner, with minimal tax rates compatible with the general level of taxation and financing consistent with the social state. In practice, if agreement on apportionment cannot be reached, any group of countries (or even a single country) could act on its own, imposing its share of the global tax on a company in proportion to that company's sales of goods and services on its territory.[145] Some may denounce this

---

144. Among the solutions considered was the possibility that the United Kingdom would continue to abide by the same trade rules that applied before Brexit despite having relinquished the right to participate in the elaboration of those rules. Whatever solution is finally adopted, it is likely that relations between the British Isles and the continent will continue to be the subject of debate for decades to come, depending on what new forms of fiscal, social, and environment union EU member states establish (or not) and on their ability to impose new rules of codevelopment linked to free circulation of goods and capital.

145. See Chap. 16 and Saez and Zucman, *The Triumph of Injustice*. In other words, if a company earns $100 billion in profits throughout the world and 10 percent of its sales occur in a given country, and that country levies a 30 percent tax on corpo-

system as a return to protectionism, but in reality it is something quite different: corporate profits are the target, not trade, which simply serves as a verifiable index for apportioning profits (in the absence of adequate cooperation). Once adequate cooperation is achieved, the transitional system can be replaced by a better one.

Corporate taxes are especially important because the current race to the bottom, which could end in exempting corporate profits from all taxation, is undoubtedly the biggest risk currently facing the global fiscal system. Ultimately, if nothing is done to stop it, the very possibility of a progressive income tax will be in jeopardy.[146] The same logic can be applied to other taxes. Earlier I discussed the progressive property tax. Companies that refuse to cooperate by supplying information about their stockholders may have to pay the forgone property tax revenues, again in proportion to their sales of goods and services in a given country. The same goes for the carbon tax. In the absence of an adequate coordinated policy for reduction of emissions, it will be imperative to impose a carbon tax based on sales of goods and services in each country. Once again, it is important to be clear that the desired cooperative solution is different (for instance, it could take the form of coordinated progressive taxation of individual emissions) and to indicate a route for reaching that goal.

To recapitulate: The current ideology of globalization, which first developed in the 1980s, is in crisis and entering a transitional phase. The frustrations

---

rate profits, then that company would have to pay $3 billion to the country in question. A company's global profits can be estimated from various sources, and each country can impose sanctions on companies that fail to provide required information. Recall that this is how taxable profits are allocated among the several states of the United States.

146. In a perfectly cooperative and transparent system, the tax on corporate profits would play only a limited role: it would simply amount to a prepayment of the income tax due by the stockholder receiving dividends and other income from the company. But in a noncooperative and nontransparent environment, the corporate tax plays a much more important role because this prepayment is often the only tax that the ultimate owners of the company will pay unless the individuals to whom the profits are ultimately distributed can be identified. Furthermore, it is easy to disguise any kind of income as corporate profits. Income from consulting or author royalties can be sheltered in a corporate structure with the active assistance of financial advisers, who take such strategies for granted, or by payment of taxes in another country. That is why it is essential to develop a strategy to end the race to the bottom, which will end in avoidance of all taxes by those with the means to pay for such tax avoidance strategies.

created by rising inequality have little by little made the lower and middle classes of the rich countries wary of international integration and unlimited economic liberalism. The resulting tensions have contributed to the emergence of nationalist and identitarian movements, which could unleash unpredictable challenges to the current trade regime. Nationalist ideology could (and probably will) intensify competition between states, leading to further fiscal and social dumping at the expense of rival states while encouraging authoritarian and anti-immigrant policies at home so as to unite the native-born population against its supposed foreign enemies. This has already begun to happen not only in Europe and the United States but also in India and Brazil and in some ways in China (in its attitude toward dissidents). In view of the impending collapse of both liberal and nationalist ideologies, the only way to overcome these contradictions is to move toward a true participatory and internationalist socialism based on social-federalist political structures and a new cooperative organization of the world economy. Given the magnitude of the challenges, I have tried to outline solutions that could gradually make progress toward that goal possible. These proposals are not intended to answer every question. Their only purpose is to show that human societies have yet to exhaust their capacity to imagine new ideological and institutional solutions. As the histories of the various inequality regimes we have studied in this book show, the political-ideological repertoire is vast. Change comes when the short-term logic of events intersects with the long-term evolution of ideas. Every ideology has its weaknesses, but no human society can live without an ideology to make sense of its inequalities. The future will be no different, but from now on the scale will be transnational.

Conclusion

In this book I have tried to offer an economic, social, intellectual, and political history of inequality regimes; that is, a history of the systems by which inequality is justified and structured, from premodern trifunctional and slave societies to modern postcolonial and hypercapitalist ones. Obviously, such a project is never-ending. No book can exhaust so vast a subject. All my conclusions are tentative and fragile by their very nature. They are based on research that needs to be supplemented and extended in the future. I hope nevertheless that this book will have helped readers clarify their own ideas and their own ideologies of social equality and inequality and will stimulate further reflection on these issues.

History as a Struggle of Ideologies and Quest for Justice

"The history of all hitherto existing society is the history of class struggles," wrote Karl Marx and Friedrich Engels in *The Communist Manifesto* (1848). Their assertion remains pertinent, but now that this book is done, I am tempted to reformulate it as follows: The history of all hitherto existing societies is the history of the struggle of ideologies and the quest for justice. In other words, ideas and ideologies count in history. Social position, as important as it is, is not enough to forge a theory of the just society, a theory of property, a theory of borders, a theory of taxes, of education, wages, or democracy. Without precise answers to these complex questions, without a clear strategy of political experimentation and social learning, struggle does not know where to turn politically. Once power is seized, this lacuna may well be filled by political-ideological constructs more oppressive than those that were overthrown.

With the history of the twentieth century and of the communist disaster in mind, it is imperative that we carefully scrutinize today's inequality regimes and the way they are justified. Above all, we need to understand what institutional arrangements and what types of socioeconomic organization can truly contribute to human and social emancipation. The history of inequality cannot be reduced to an eternal clash between oppressors of the people and proud defenders. On both sides one finds sophisticated intellectual and institutional constructs. To be sure, on the side of the dominant groups, these constructs are not always devoid of hypocrisy and reflect a determination to remain in power, but they still need to be studied closely. Unlike the class struggle, the struggle of ideologies involves shared knowledge and experiences, respect for others, deliberation, and democracy. No one will ever possess the absolute truth about just ownership, just borders, just democracy, just taxes and education. The history of human societies can be seen as a quest for justice. Progress is possible only through detailed comparison of personal and historical experiences and the widest possible deliberation.

Nevertheless, the struggle of ideologies and the quest for justice also entails the expression of clearly defined positions and clearly designated antagonists. Based on the experiences analyzed in this book, I am convinced that capitalism and private property can be superseded and that a just society can be established on the basis of participatory socialism and social federalism. The first step is to establish a regime of social and temporary ownership. This will require power sharing between workers and shareholders and a ceiling on the number of votes that can be cast by any one shareholder. It will also require a steeply progressive tax on property, a universal capital endowment, and permanent circulation of wealth. In addition, it implies a progressive income tax and collective regulation of carbon emissions, the proceeds from which will go to pay for social insurance and a basic income, the ecological transition, and true educational equality. Finally, the global economy will need to be reorganized by means of codevelopment treaties incorporating quantified objectives of social, fiscal, and environmental justice; liberalization of trade and financial flows must be conditioned on progress toward meeting those primary goals. This redefinition of the global legal framework will require abandonment of some existing treaties, most notably those concerning the free circulation of capital that came into effect in the 1980s–1990s because these stand in the way of meeting the above-mentioned goals. Those treaties will need to be replaced by new rules based on the principles of financial transparency, fiscal cooperation, and transnational democracy.

Some of these conclusions may seem radical. In reality, they belong to a historical movement toward democratic socialism, which since the late nineteenth century has been working toward profound transformations of the legal, social, and fiscal system. The significant reduction of inequality that took place in the mid-twentieth century was made possible by the construction of a social state based on relative educational equality and a number of radical innovations, such as co-management in the Germanic and Nordic countries and progressive taxation in the United States and United Kingdom. The conservative revolution of the 1980s and the fall of communism interrupted this movement; the world entered a new era of self-regulated markets and quasi-sacralization of property. The inability of the social-democratic coalition to move beyond the confines of the nation-state and renew its program in an era of globalized trade and expanded higher education contributed to the collapse of the left-right political system that made the postwar reduction of inequality possible. However, in the face of challenges raised by the historic resumption of inequality, the rejection of globalization, and the development of new forms of identitarian retreat, awareness of the limits of deregulated capitalism has grown rapidly since the financial crisis of 2008. People have once again begun thinking about a new, more equitable, more sustainable economic model. My discussion here of participatory socialism and social federalism draw largely on developments taking place in various parts of the world; my contribution here is simply to place them in a broader historical perspective.

The history of the inequality regimes studied in this book shows that such political-ideological transformations should not be seen as deterministic. Multiple trajectories are always possible. The balance of power at any moment depends on the interaction of the short-term logic of events with long-term intellectual evolutions from which come a wide range of ideas that can be drawn on in moments of crisis. Unfortunately, there is a very real danger that countries will try to avoid fundamental change by intensifying the competition of all against all and engaging in a new round of fiscal and social dumping. This could in turn intensify nationalist and identitarian conflict, which is already conspicuous in Europe, the United States, India, Brazil, and China.

On the Limits of "De-Westernizing" Our Gaze

In this book I have tried to decenter our way of looking at the history of inequality regimes. The case of India turns out to be particularly instructive. The Indian Union is an example of very large-scale democratic federalism. More than that, it shows how the state can use legal tools to overcome the heavy inegalitarian legacy of an ancient society of castes made more rigid by the encounter with British colonial power. The institutional tools that India developed to deal with this legacy took the form of quotas and "reservations" of places in universities, public employment, and elective office: places were reserved for individuals born into disadvantaged social classes that had suffered historically from discrimination. This system has not resolved all of India's problems—far from it. But such experiences are highly instructive for the rest of the world and in particular for Western democracies, which are also dealing with enormous educational inequalities (which have long been neglected) and are just beginning to deal with multiconfessionalism (which India has known for ten centuries). More generally, I have tried to show that, to understand the world today, it is indispensable to study the long history of inequality regimes, and especially the way European proprietarian and colonial powers affected the development of non-European trifunctional societies. The traces of that lengthy history remain quite visible in the structure of contemporary inequality. Beyond that, the study of the sophisticated inegalitarian ideologies of the past helps place today's ideologies in perspective. One sees that they are not always wiser than the ideologies that preceded them and that they, too, will someday be replaced.

Despite my efforts to decenter our gaze, I have to say that this book remains unbalanced—somewhat less so than my previous book but still quite unbalanced on the whole. The French Revolution comes up repeatedly, and the experiences of Europe and the United States are constantly cited, much more so than their demographic weight warrants. Jack Goody, in his book *The Theft of History,* rightly denounced the often-irresistible temptation to write history from a Western-centric point of view, which afflicts even well-intentioned social scientists. Writers attribute to Europe and America inventions they did not invent or even cultural practices such as courtly love, the love of liberty, filial affection, the nuclear family, humanism, and democracy.[1] I have tried to avoid this bias in this book, but I am not sure I succeeded. The reason is simple: my gaze is profoundly influenced by my cultural roots, the limits of my knowledge, and above all by the serious weakness of my linguistic competence. This book is the work of an author who reads fluently only in French and English and who is familiar with only a limited range of primary sources. Yet this study ranges widely—perhaps too widely—and I beg the pardon of specialists in other fields for the approximations and condensations they will find here. I hope that this work will soon be complemented and superseded by many others, which will add to our understanding of specific inequality regimes, especially those in the many geographical and cultural regions poorly covered by this work.

No doubt my gaze has also been shaped by my personal history, perhaps even more than I imagine. I could describe the diversity of the social milieus and political ideas to which I was exposed by my family background. My two grandmothers suffered from the patriarchal model imposed by their generation. One was unhappy in her bourgeois life and died prematurely in Paris in

---

1. See J. Goody, *The Theft of History* (Cambridge University Press, 2006).

1987. The other became a servant on a farm at age 13 during World War II and died in 2018 in Indre-et-Loire. From one of my great-grandmothers, who was born in 1897 and died in 2001, I heard stories of France before 1914, when the country was preparing its revenge against Germany. Born in 1971, I obtained from my parents the freedom I needed to become an adult. As a student in 1989, I listened to the collapse of the communist dictatorships on the radio. In 1991 I listened to reports of the Gulf War. When I look at how my vision of history and economics has evolved since I was 18, I think that it was the study of history—the sources I discovered and the books I read—that led me to change my views significantly (I was initially more liberal and less socialist than I am now). In particular, writing *Top Incomes in France in the Twentieth Century: Inequality and Redistribution, 1901–1998* made me realize in 2001 how much violence accompanied the reduction of inequality in the twentieth century. The crisis of 2008 led me to take a greater interest in the fragilities of global capitalism and the history of capital and its accumulation, subjects at the heart of *Capital in the Twenty-First Century* (2013). The present book is based on new sources—most prominently, colonial histories and postelection surveys—which led me to develop a new political-ideological approach to inequality regimes. It is possible that this reconstruction is too rational; I may neglect the hidden effects of my early and more recent experiences in shaping this or that argument. Nevertheless, I have tried to make the reader aware of at least the conscious part of my progress by citing the historical sources, books, and other readings that led me to the positions I take here, insofar as I am aware of them.

On the Civic and Political Role of the Social Sciences

Social scientists are very lucky. Society pays them to write books, explore sources, synthesize what can be learned from archives and surveys, and then try to pay back the people who make their work possible—namely, the rest of society. Now and then researchers in the social sciences waste too much time in sterile disciplinary quarrels and status disputes. Nevertheless, the social sciences play an indispensable role in public debate and democratic dialogue. In this book I have tried to show how the sources and methods of the various social science could be used to analyze the history of inequality regimes in their social, economic, political, and intellectual dimensions.

I am convinced that some of today's democratic disarray stems from the fact that, insofar as the civic and political sphere is concerned, economics has cut itself free from the other social sciences. This "autonomization" of economics is partly a result of the technical nature and increasing complexity of the economic sphere. But it is also the result of a recurrent temptation on the part of professional economists, whether in the university or the marketplace, to claim a monopoly of expertise and analytic capacity they do not possess. In reality, it is only by combining economic, historical, sociological, cultural, and political approaches that progress in our understanding of socioeconomic phenomena becomes possible. This is true, of course, for the study of inequalities between social classes and their transformations throughout history, but the lesson seems to me far more general. This book draws on the work of many social scientists in many disciplines, without whom it would not exist.[2] I have also tried to show how literature and film can also shed light on our subject in a way that complements the light shed by the social sciences.

Another consequence of the excessive autonomization of economics is that historians, sociologists, political scientists, and philosophers too often abandon the study of economic questions to economists. But political economy and economic history involve all the social sciences, as I have tried to show in this book. All social scientists should try to include socioeconomic trends in their analysis and gather quantitative and historical data whenever useful and should rely on other methods and sources when necessary. The neglect of quantitative and statistical sources by many social scientists is unfortunate, particularly since critical examination of the sources and the conditions under which they are socially, historically, and politically constructed is necessary to make proper use of them. This neglect has contributed not only to the autonomization of economics but also to its impoverishment. I hope that this book will help to remedy that.

Beyond the realm of research, the autonomization of economic knowledge has also been bad for the civic and political sphere because it encourages fatalism and fosters feelings of helplessness. In particular, journalists and citizens all too often bow to the expertise of economists, limited though it is, and hesitate to express opinions about wages and profits, taxes and debts, trade and capital. But if the people are to be sovereign—as democracy says they should

---

2. Among the researchers whose recent and not-so-recent work I have relied on most heavily, I would like to mention Mathieu Arnoux, Rafe Blaufarb, Erik Bengtsson, Denis Cogneau, Fredrick Cooper, Nicolas Barreyre, Julia Cagé, Noam Maggor, Katrina Pistor, Sanjay Subrahmanyan, Serge Gruzinski, Susan Bayly, Ken Pomeranz, Hannah Arendt, Karl Polanyi, Or Rosenboim, Barbara Wooton, Christophe Jaffrelot, etc. Dozens of other authors are cited in the footnotes to each chapter.

be—these subjects are not optional. Their complexity is such that it is unjusti-fiable to abandon them to a small caste of experts. The contrary is true. Pre-cisely because they are so complex, only broad collective deliberation, based on reason and on the past history and experience of every citizen, can lead to progress toward resolving these issues. Ultimately, this book has only one goal: to enable citizens to reclaim possession of economic and historical knowledge. Whether or not the reader agrees with my specific conclusions basically does not matter because my purpose is to begin debate, not to end it. If this book has been able to awaken the reader's interest in new questions and enlighten her with knowledge she did not previously possess, my goal will have been fully achieved.

Glossary

Here is a brief list of terms that may be unfamiliar to the reader. These are marked with an asterisk at the point of first occurrence in the text.

CENSITARY: A censitary regime (from the French *censitaire*) was a regime in which the right to vote was subject to a property qualification, generally met by paying above a certain amount of property tax. For instance, during the Restoration in France (1815–1830), the right to vote was reserved to men over the age of 30 who paid at least 300 francs in direct taxes (which in practice granted eligibility to vote to about 100,000 people or roughly 1 percent of adult males). The precise requirement varied over time.

GINI COEFFICIENT: A statistical measure of distribution which was developed by the Italian statistician Corrado Gini in 1912. It is used as a gauge of economic inequality, measuring income distribution among a population. The coefficient ranges from zero to one, with zero representing perfect equality and one representing perfect inequality.

GREAT DEMARCATION: A term introduced by the historian Rafe Blaufarb to describe a shift in the property ownership regime that occurred during the French Revolution, which resulted in a strict separation between regalian functions (henceforth the monopoly of the centralized state) and property rights (henceforth to be granted solely to private individuals), whereas trifunctional society was based on an inextricable imbrication of both.

IDENTITARIAN (Fr. *identitaire*): An identitarian ideology is an ideology structured around identification with a specific social group, often based on an ethnic, racial, or religious identity.

INEQUALITY REGIME: A set of discourses and institutional arrangements intended to justify and structure the economic, social, and political inequalities of a given society.

LIVRE TOURNOIS: Monetary unit of account used in France during the Middle Ages and early modern period.

OWNERSHIP SOCIETY (sometimes called proprietarian society): A social order based on a quasi-religious defense of property rights as the sine qua non of social and political stability. Ownership societies flourished in Europe and the United States in the nineteenth and early twentieth centuries.

PATRIMONIAL MIDDLE CLASS: That portion of the wealth distribution extending from the fiftieth to the ninetieth percentile. In other words, the "middle 40 percent" of the wealth distribution standing between the bottom 50 percent and the top 10 percent.

PREMODERN: As used in this book, "premodern" means prior to the eighteenth century.

PROPRIETARIAN: See Ownership society, also called proprietarian society. Proprietarian ideology is the ideology of ownership society, based on the sacralization of property rights.

REGALIAN RIGHTS OR POWERS: The powers of security, justice, and legitimate use of violence.

SOCIETY OF ORDERS: A type of society based on an equilibrium between intellectual and warrior elites and on specific forms of ownership and power relations. See also Trifunctional society.

SUCCESSORAL: Pertaining to inheritance.

TERNARY SOCIETY: See Trifunctional society.

TRAJECTORIES AND SWITCH POINTS: The French text refers to *trajectoires et bifurcations* to describe the paths taken by different societies in their historical evolutions. Here, *bifurcations* has been translated as "switch points" to refer to points in time where a crucial turn was taken.

TRIFUNCTIONAL SOCIETY: A trifunctional society is one whose structure comprises three functional groups: clergy, nobility, and workers (the third estate). The ternary or trifunctional pattern can be found in nearly all premodern societies throughout the world, including China and Japan.

Contents in Detail

Tables and Illustrations

Index